America's Top-Rated Cities

In-Depth Statistics & Comparative Rankings
of the Best Big Cities in America

T0394840

2025
Thirty-second Edition

America's
Top-Rated Cities
In-Depth Statistics & Comparative Rankings
of the Best Big Cities in America

Volume 2: Western Region

Grey House Publishing

Cover images: Portland, Oregon

PUBLISHER: Leslie Mackenzie
EDITORIAL DIRECTOR: Stuart Paterson
SENIOR EDITOR: David Garoogian

RESEARCHER & WRITER: Jael Bridgemahon; Laura Mars
MARKETING DIRECTOR: Jessica Moody

Grey House Publishing, Inc.
4919 Route 22
Amenia, NY 12501
518.789.8700 • Fax 845.373.6390
www.greyhouse.com
books@greyhouse.com

While every effort has been made to ensure the reliability of the information presented in this publication, Grey House Publishing neither guarantees the accuracy of the data contained herein nor assumes any responsibility for errors, omissions or discrepancies. Grey House accepts no payment for listing; inclusion in the publication of any organization, agency, institution, publication, service or individual does not imply endorsement of the editors or publisher.

Errors brought to the attention of the publisher and verified to the satisfaction of the publisher will be corrected in future editions.

Thirty-second Edition
Printed in the U.S.A.

Publisher's Cataloging-in-Publication Data
(Prepared by The Donohue Group, Inc.)

America's top-rated cities. Vol. 2, Western region : in-depth statistics & comparative rankings of the best big cities in america. — 1992-

  v. : ill. ; cm.
  Annual, 1995-
  Irregular, 1992-1993
  ISSN: 1082-7102

1. Cities and towns—Ratings—Western States—Statistics—Periodicals. 2. Cities and towns—Western States—Statistics—Periodicals. 3. Social indicators—Western States—Periodicals. 4. Quality of life—Western States—Statistics—Periodicals. 5. Western States—Social conditions—Statistics—Periodicals. I. Title: America's top rated cities. II. Title: Western region

HT123.5.S6 A44
307.76/0973/05 95644648

4-Volume Set   ISBN: 979-8-89179-096-4
Volume 1   ISBN: 979-8-89179-098-8
Volume 2   **ISBN: 979-8-89179-099-5**
Volume 3   ISBN: 979-8-89179-100-8
Volume 4   ISBN: 979-8-89179-101-5

Boulder, Colorado

Colorado Springs, Colorado

Denver, Colorado

Eugene, Oregon

Fort Collins, Colorado

Honolulu, Hawaii

Las Vegas, Nevada

Los Angeles, California

Phoenix, Arizona

Provo, Utah

Portland, Oregon

Reno, Nevada

Sacramento, California

Salem, Oregon

Salt Lake City, Utah

San Diego, California

Tucson, Arizona

Appendixes

Introduction

This thirty-second edition of *America's Top-Rated Cities* is a concise, statistical, 4-volume work identifying America's top-rated cities with estimated populations of 100,000 or more. It profiles 97 cities that have received high marks for business and living based on our unique weighting system.

Each volume covers a different region of the country—Southern, Western, Central, Eastern—and includes a detailed Table of Contents, City Chapters, Appendices, and Maps. Each city chapter incorporates information from hundreds of resources to create the following major sections:

- **Background**—lively narrative of significant, up-to-date news for both businesses and residents. These combine historical facts with current developments, "known-for" annual events, and climate data.
- **Rankings**—fun-to-read, bulleted survey results from over 100 books, magazines, and online articles, ranging from general (Great Places to Live), to specific (Friendliest Cities), and everything in between.
- **Statistical Tables**—88 tables and detailed topics that offer an unparalleled view of each city's Business and Living Environments. They are carefully organized with data that is easy to read and understand.
- **Appendices**—five in all, appear at the end of each volume. These range from listings of Metropolitan Statistical Areas to Comparative Statistics for all 97 cities.

This new edition of *America's Top-Rated Cities* includes cities that not only surveyed well, but ranked highest using the following criteria: population growth, crime, household income, poverty, housing affordability, educational attainment, and unemployment. Part of the criteria, in most cases, is that it be the "primary" city in a given metropolitan area. For example, if the metro area is Raleigh-Cary, North Carolina, we would consider Raleigh, not Cary. This allows for a more equitable core city comparison. In general, the core city of a metro area is defined as having substantial influence on neighboring cities. A final consideration is location—we strive to include as many states in the country as possible.

You'll find that we have included several American cities despite having lower rankings in some categories. New York, Los Angeles, and Miami remain world-class cities despite challenges faced by many large urban centers. We also decided to include all major cities with historic or cultural significance. For example, Detroit, Michigan, the birthplace of the American automotive industry.

New to this edition are:
Volume 1: Midland, TX
Volume 2: Salem, OR
Volume 3: Green Bay, WI; St. Paul, MN

Praise for previous editions:

> *"... [ATRC] has...proven its worth to a wide audience...from businesspeople and corporations planning to launch, relocate, or expand their operations to market researchers, real estate professionals, urban planners, job-seekers, students...interested in...reliable, attractively presented statistical information about larger U.S. cities."*
> —ARBA

> *"... For individuals or businesses looking to relocate, this resource conveniently reports rankings from more than 300 sources for the top 100 U.S. cities. Recommended..."*
> —Choice

> *"... While patrons are becoming increasingly comfortable locating statistical data online, there is still something to be said for the ease associated with such a compendium of otherwise scattered data. A well-organized and appropriate update..."*
> —Library Journal

BACKGROUND
Each city begins with an informative Background that combines history with current events. These narratives often reflect changes that have occurred during the past year, and touch on the city's environment, politics, employment, cultural offerings, and climate, and include interesting trivia. For example: Tampa, Florida was known as the Cigar Capital of the World in the early 1900s; Wilmington, North Carolina was the site of one of the first rebellions in the United States'

revolt against British rule; and the first mail-order business, Montgomery Ward, was established in Chicago in 1872. Current events include: the most devastating fires recorded in the city of Los Angeles destroyed entire neighborhoods, including Pacific Palisades in January 2025; MARTA (Metropolitan Atlanta Rapid Transit Authority) unveiled its first state-of-the-art CQ400 railcar in early 2025; and Jaialdi, a large Basque festival held once every five years, is being held in Boise City in July 2025.

RANKINGS

This section has rankings from over 100 articles and reports. For easy reference, these Rankings are categorized into 16 topics including Business/Finance, Dating/Romance, and Health/Fitness.

The Rankings are presented in an easy-to-read, bulleted format and include results from both annual surveys and one-shot studies. **Fastest Job Growth** . . . **Best Drivers** . . . **Most Well-Read** . . . **Most Wired** . . . **Healthiest for Women** . . . **Best for Minority Entrepreneurs** . . . **Safest** . . . **Best to Retire** . . . **Most Polite** . . . **Best for Moviemakers** . . . **Most Frugal** . . . **Best for Bikes** . . . **Most Cultured** . . . **Least Stressful** . . . **Best for Families** . . . **Most Romantic** . . . **Most Charitable** . . . **Best for Telecommuters** . . . **Best for Singles** . . . **Nerdiest** . . . **Fittest** . . . **Best for Dogs** . . . **Most Tattooed** . . . **Best for Veterans** . . . **Best for Wheelchair Users**, and more.

Sources for these Rankings include both well-known magazines and other organizations, including *The Advocate*, *Condé Nast Traveler*, *Forbes*, *Kiplinger*, and *National Geographic*, as well as American Lung Association, Asthma & Allergy Foundation of America, National Civic League, People for the Ethical Treatment of Animals, and *Site Selection*.

Rankings cover a variety of geographic areas; see Appendix B for full geographic definitions.

STATISTICAL TABLES

Each city chapter includes 88 tables and detailed topics—45 in Business and 43 in Living. Over 90% of statistical data has been updated. This edition also includes new data on the economy from the U.S. Bureau of Economic Analysis and mortality rates from accidental poisonings and exposure to noxious substances.

Business Environment includes hard facts and figures on 8 major categories, including Demographics, Income, Economy, Employment, and Taxes. *Living Environment* includes 11 major categories, such as Cost of Living, Housing, Health, Education, Safety, and Climate.

To compile the Statistical Tables, editors have again turned to a wide range of sources, some well known, such as the Bureau of Labor Statistics, Centers for Disease Control and Prevention, Federal Bureau of Investigation, U.S. Census Bureau, and U.S. Environmental Protection Agency, plus others like The Council for Community and Economic Research, Federal Housing Finance Agency, and Texas A&M Transportation Institute.

APPENDIXES: Data for all cities appear in all volumes.
- **Appendix A**—*Comparative Statistics*
- **Appendix B**—*Metropolitan Area Definitions*
- **Appendix C**—*Government Type and County*
- **Appendix D**—*Chambers of Commerce and Economic Development Organizations*
- **Appendix E**—*State Departments of Labor and Employment*

Material provided by public and private agencies and organizations was supplemented by original research, numerous library sources and Internet sites. *America's Top-Rated Cities* is designed for a wide range of readers: private individuals considering relocating a residence or business; professionals considering expanding their businesses or changing careers; corporations considering relocating, opening up additional offices or creating new divisions; government agencies; general and market researchers; real estate consultants; human resource personnel; urban planners; investors; and urban government students.

Customers who purchase the four-volume set receive free online access to *America's Top-Rated Cities* allowing them to download city reports and sort and rank these cities by 50-plus data points.

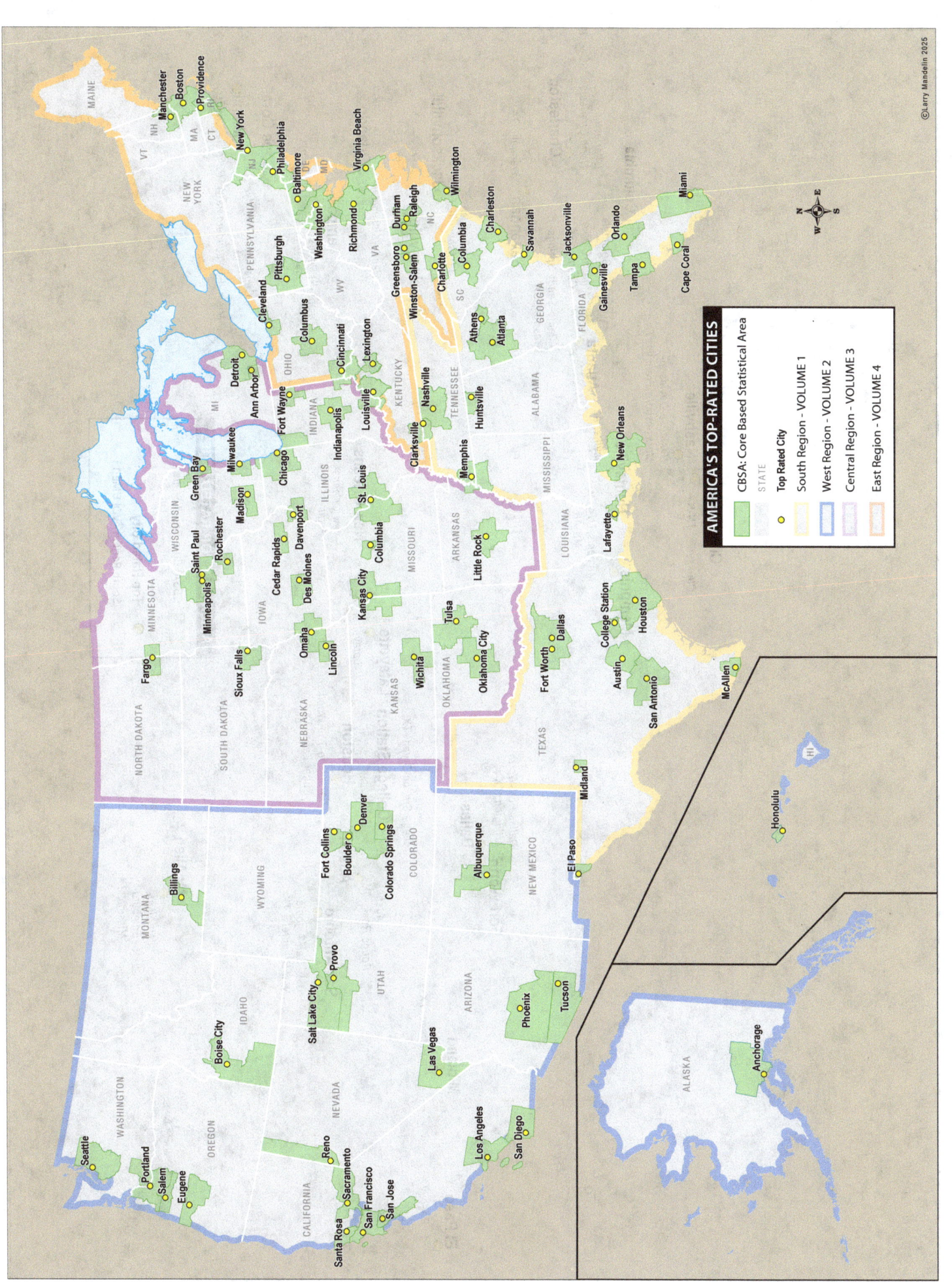

AMERICA'S TOP-RATED CITIES

- CBSA: Core Based Statistical Area
- STATE
- Top Rated City
- South Region - VOLUME 1
- West Region - VOLUME 2
- Central Region - VOLUME 3
- East Region - VOLUME 4

©Larry Mandelin 2025

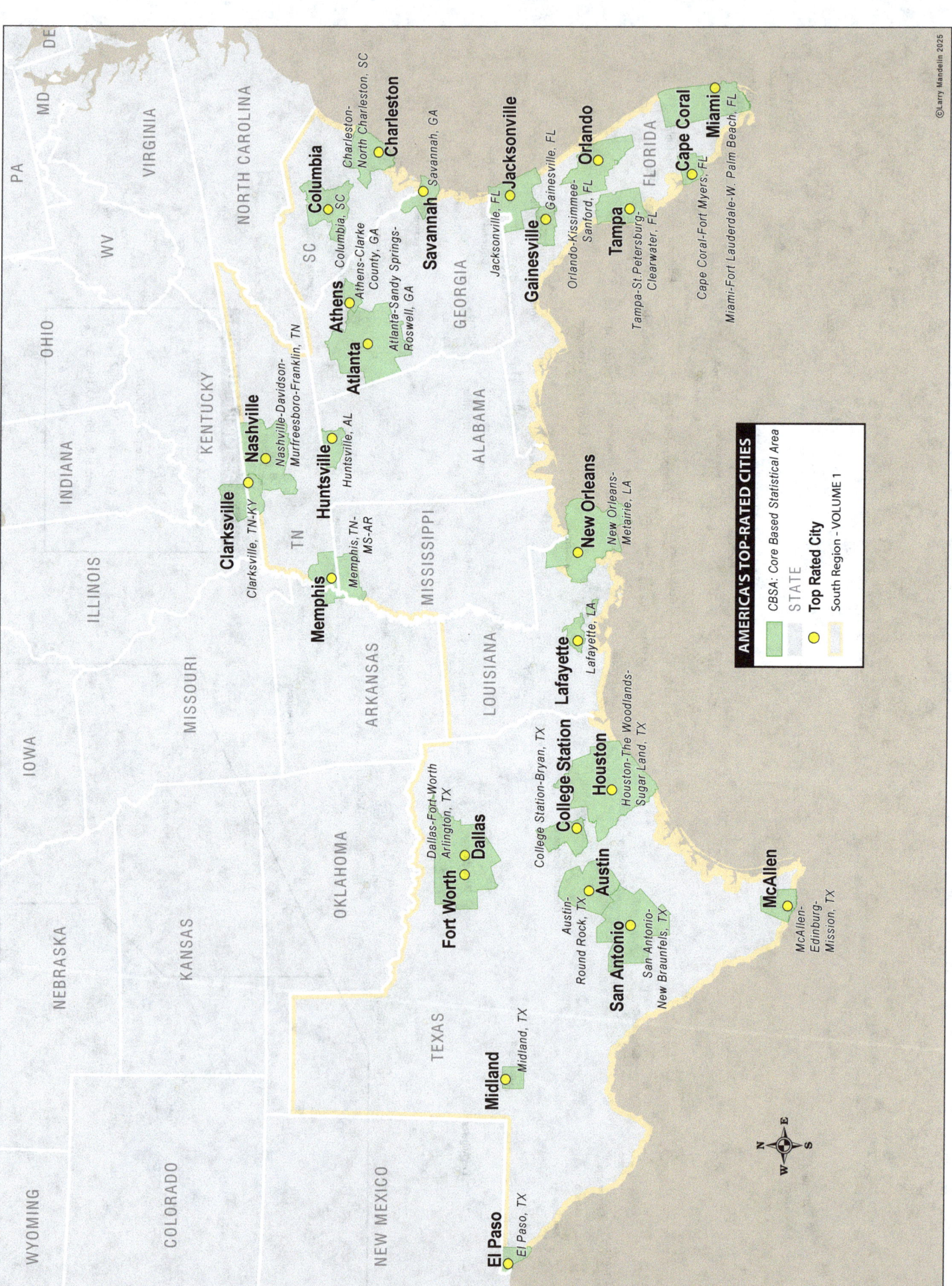

AMERICA'S TOP-RATED CITIES

CBSA: Core Based Statistical Area
STATE
Top Rated City
South Region – VOLUME 1

©Larry Mandelin 2025

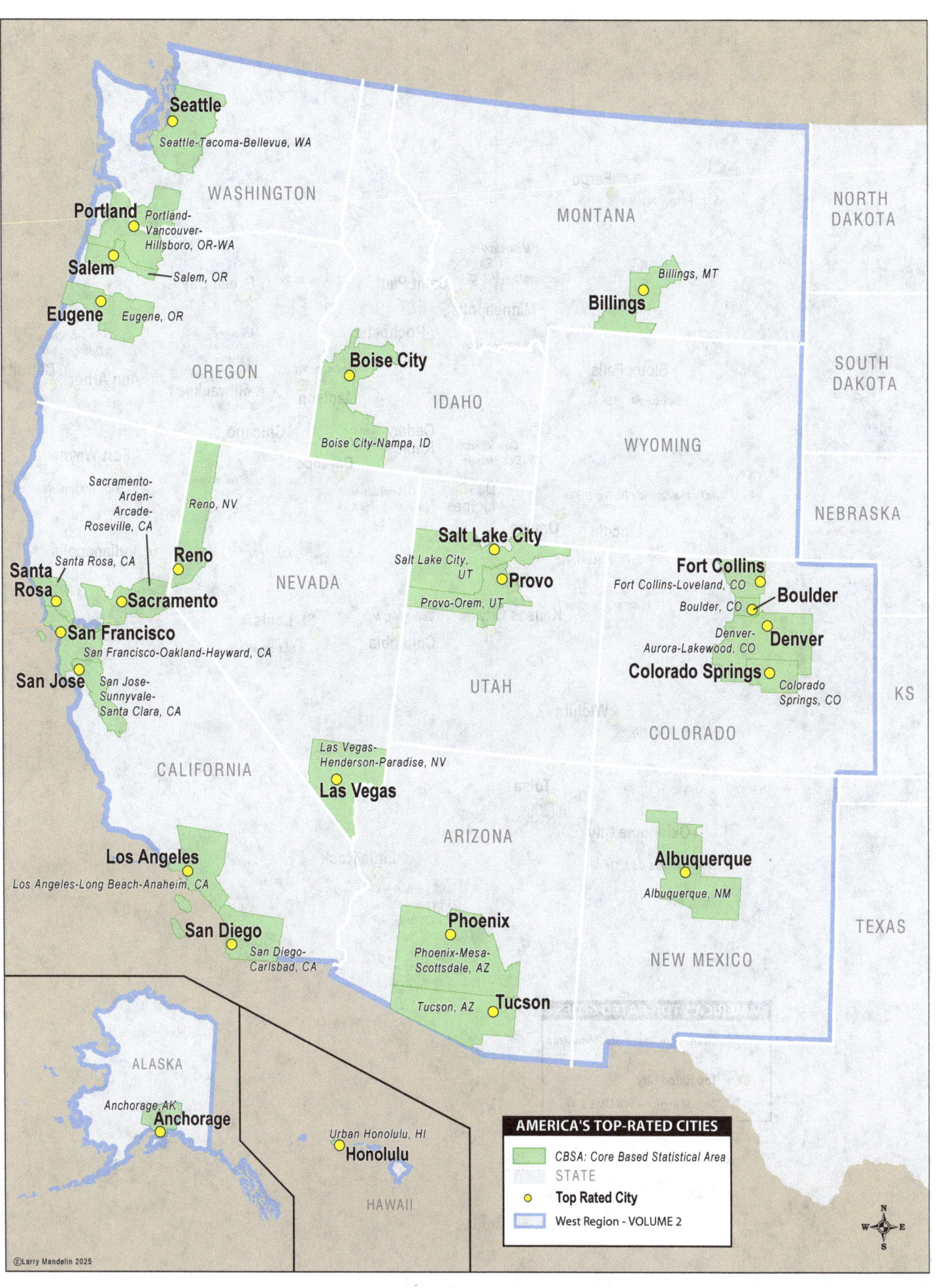

Seattle
Seattle-Tacoma-Bellevue, WA

WASHINGTON

MONTANA

NORTH DAKOTA

Portland
Portland-Vancouver-Hillsboro, OR-WA

Salem
Salem, OR

Eugene
Eugene, OR

OREGON

Billings
Billings, MT

Boise City
Boise City-Nampa, ID

IDAHO

WYOMING

SOUTH DAKOTA

NEBRASKA

Sacramento-Arden-Arcade-Roseville, CA

Reno, NV

Santa Rosa
Santa Rosa, CA

Reno

Sacramento

San Francisco
San Francisco-Oakland-Hayward, CA

San Jose
San Jose-Sunnyvale-Santa Clara, CA

NEVADA

Salt Lake City
Salt Lake City, UT

Provo
Provo-Orem, UT

UTAH

Fort Collins
Fort Collins-Loveland, CO

Boulder
Boulder, CO

Denver
Denver-Aurora-Lakewood, CO

Colorado Springs
Colorado Springs, CO

COLORADO

KS

Las Vegas-Henderson-Paradise, NV

Las Vegas

CALIFORNIA

Los Angeles
Los Angeles-Long Beach-Anaheim, CA

San Diego
San Diego-Carlsbad, CA

ARIZONA

Phoenix
Phoenix-Mesa-Scottsdale, AZ

Tucson, AZ Tucson

Albuquerque
Albuquerque, NM

NEW MEXICO

TEXAS

ALASKA

Anchorage, AK
Anchorage

Urban Honolulu, HI
Honolulu

HAWAII

AMERICA'S TOP-RATED CITIES

CBSA: Core Based Statistical Area
STATE
Top Rated City
West Region - VOLUME 2

N
W E
S

©Larry Mandelin 2025

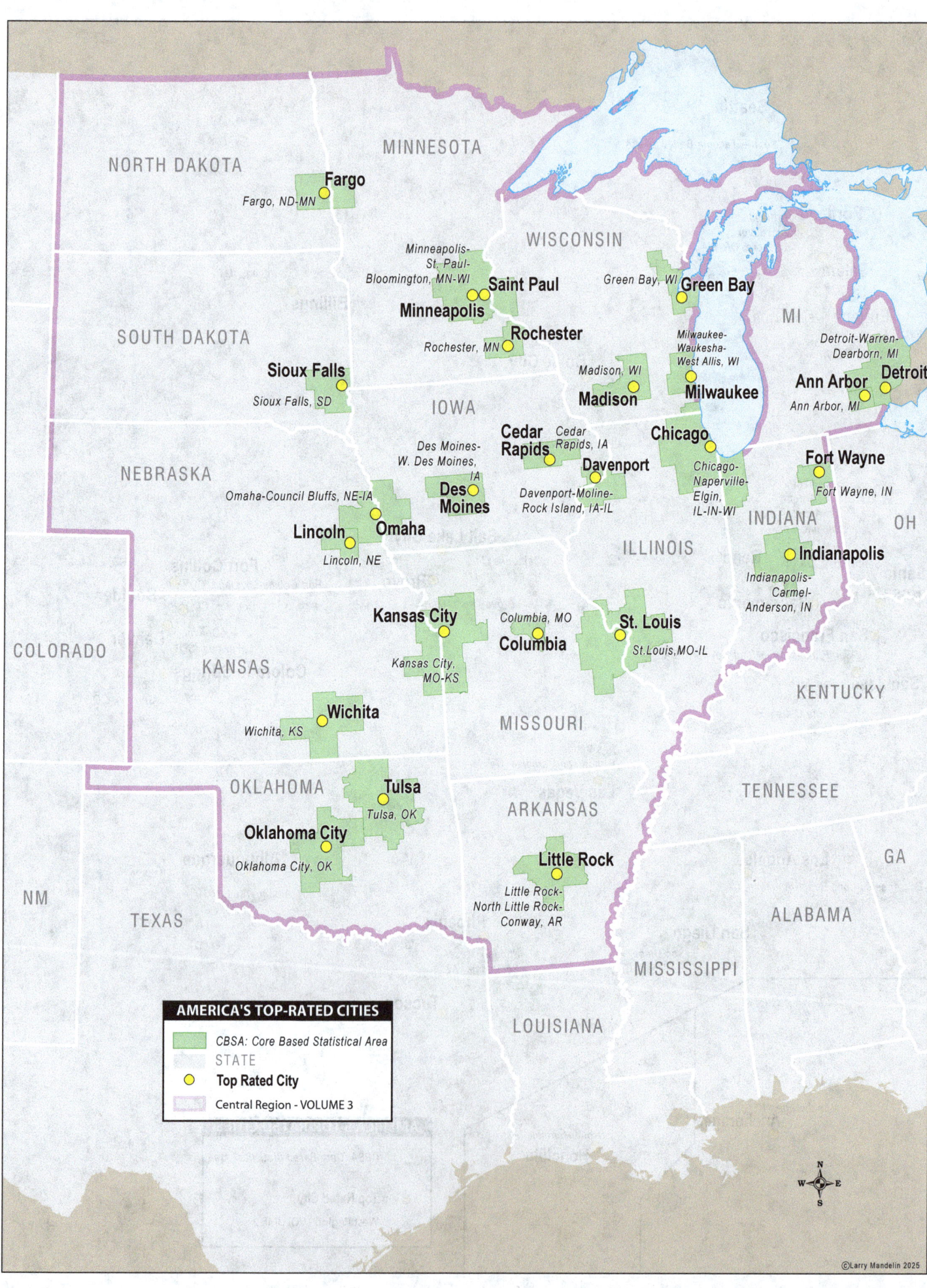

AMERICA'S TOP-RATED CITIES

CBSA: Core Based Statistical Area
STATE
Top Rated City
Central Region - VOLUME 3

NORTH DAKOTA

MINNESOTA

WISCONSIN

MI

Fargo
Fargo, ND-MN

Minneapolis-
St. Paul-
Bloomington, MN-WI
Saint Paul
Minneapolis

Green Bay, WI
Green Bay

Detroit-Warren-
Dearborn, MI

Rochester
Rochester, MN

Milwaukee-
Waukesha-
West Allis, WI

Ann Arbor
Ann Arbor, MI
Detroit

SOUTH DAKOTA

Sioux Falls
Sioux Falls, SD

IOWA

Madison, WI
Madison

Milwaukee

NEBRASKA

Des Moines-
W. Des Moines,
IA

Cedar
Rapids
*Cedar
Rapids, IA*
Davenport

Chicago

Fort Wayne
Fort Wayne, IN

Omaha-Council Bluffs, NE-IA

Des
Moines

Davenport-Moline-
Rock Island, IA-IL

Chicago-
Naperville-
Elgin,
IL-IN-WI

INDIANA

OH

Lincoln
Omaha
Lincoln, NE

ILLINOIS

Indianapolis

COLORADO

KANSAS

Kansas City
Columbia, MO
Columbia
St. Louis
St.Louis,MO-IL

Indianapolis-
Carmel-
Anderson, IN

KENTUCKY

*Kansas City,
MO-KS*

MISSOURI

Wichita
Wichita, KS

NM

OKLAHOMA
Tulsa
Tulsa, OK

ARKANSAS

TENNESSEE

GA

Oklahoma City
Oklahoma City, OK

Little Rock

ALABAMA

TEXAS

Little Rock-
North Little Rock-
Conway, AR

MISSISSIPPI

LOUISIANA

N
W   E
S

©Larry Mandelin 2025

AMERICA'S TOP-RATED CITIES

- CBSA: Core Based Statistical Area
- STATE
- ● Top Rated City
- East Region - VOLUME 4

MAINE

VT · NH

VERMONT

NEW YORK

MA

CT · RI

Manchester
Manchester-Nashua, NH

Boston-Cambridge-Newton, MA-NH

Boston

Providence
Providence-Warwick, RI-MA

MICHIGAN

New York
New York-Newark-Jersey City, NY-NJ-PA

PENNSYLVANIA

Cleveland, OH

Cleveland

Pittsburgh
Pittsburgh, PA

Philadelphia
Philadelphia-Camden-Wilmington, PA-NJ-DE-MD

NJ

OHIO

Columbus
Columbus, OH

Baltimore-Columbia-Towson, MD

Baltimore

DE

MD

INDIANA

IL

Cincinnati, OH-KY-IN

Washington
Washington-Arlington-Alexandria, DC-VA-MD-WV

WV

Cincinnati

Louisville/Jefferson County, KY-IN

Richmond

VA

Virginia Beach-Norfolk-Newport News, VA-NC

Lexington
Lexington-Fayette, KY

Richmond, VA

Louisville

KENTUCKY

Virginia Beach

Greensboro
Durham
Durham-Chapel Hill, NC

Winston-Salem
Winston-Salem, NC

Raleigh
Raleigh, NC

Greensboro-High Point, NC

TENNESSEE

NC

Wilmington, NC

Charlotte
Charlotte-Concord-Gastonia, NC-SC

Wilmington

S.CAROLINA

MS   ALABAMA   GEORGIA

N
W · E
S

©Larry Mandelin 2025

Albuquerque, New Mexico

Background

Pueblo Indians originally inhabited what is now the Albuquerque metropolitan area. In the sixteenth century, Spaniards began arriving from Mexico in search of riches, but it was not until 1706 that they founded the settlement, naming it after the viceroy of New Spain, San Francisco de Alburquerque, a duke whose permission was needed to set up the town. Eventually, the city's name would lose a consonant and become Albuquerque. The city earned the sobriquet "Duke City" because of its namesake.

In the early nineteenth century, Mexico secured independence from Spanish rule and allowed Americans to enter the province of New Mexico to trade. During the Mexican War of the 1840s, Americans under the command of General Stephen Kearny captured the town, and New Mexico became part of the United States in the Treaty of Guadalupe Hidalgo, ending the war.

During the Civil War, Confederates held the town briefly before surrendering it to a besieging Union army. After the war, the railroad arrived in 1880, bringing with it people and business. In 1891 the town received a city charter. Albuquerque became an important site for tuberculosis sanatoriums during the next few decades because of the healing nature of the dry desert air.

World War II had a great impact on Albuquerque, as Kirtland Air Force Base located in the city became an important site for the manufacture of the atomic bomb. Sandia National Laboratories was founded in the city after the war and was important in defense-related research during the Cold War.

The defense industry is of prime significance to Albuquerque. Institutions in the city that were once dedicated to defense research are now involved in applying such technology to the private sector, making the city a perfect place for high-tech concerns. In addition to Sandia, the city hosts a branch of the Air Force Research Laboratories and the Los Alamos National Laboratory. Biotech and semiconductor industries also have had a positive impact on the city's economy.

Albuquerque and New Mexico have many programs to assist business. The state has property taxes that are among the lowest in the nation. The city consistently ranks high in business and engineering careers, and generally among best places to live. Additionally, traditional jobs, such as ranching, still have a large presence in the city.

Albuquerque is also a critical transportation center for the American Southwest, with two major interstates that intersect there. Its airport, Albuquerque International Sunport, is served by both major commercial and commuter carriers. The city is home to state-of-the-art manufacturing and shipping facilities and Mesa del Sol, a mixed-used development site connected to the airport by light-rail and a commuter rail line that also serves the region. The New Mexico Rail Runner Express system as well as the Rapid Ride bus service serves Albuquerque's residents. The city also gets high points for its walkability. According to 2024 figures, the city's Park Management Division maintains and manages more than 290 park sites. The total amount of parkland is 42.9 square miles, or about 23% of the city's total area—one of the highest percentages among large cities in the U.S.

The city recently broke ground on the Tortugas Arroyo Improvements Project, designed to protect the Rio Grande River from industrial waste.

There are various venues for higher education located in Albuquerque, the most significant of which is the University of New Mexico.

Popular festive events scheduled throughout the year include the annual International Albuquerque International Balloon Fiesta and the annual Gathering of Nations Powwow, an international event that is North America's biggest powwow, featuring over 3,000 indigenous Native American dancers and singers representing more than 500 tribes. The city was also the setting for television shows *Breaking Bad*, *Get Shorty*, and *Succession*.

Albuquerque enjoys a dry, arid climate, with plenty of sunshine, low humidity, and scant rainfall. More than three-fourths of the daylight hours have sunshine, summer and winter. As in all desert climates, temperatures can fluctuate widely between day and night, all year round. Precipitation is meager during the winter, more abundant in summer with afternoon and evening thunderstorms.

Rankings

General Rankings

- To help military veterans find the best places in which to settle down, *WalletHub* compared the 100 largest U.S. cities across 19 key indicators of livability, affordability and veteran-friendliness. They range from the share of military skill-related jobs to veteran income growth to the availability of VA health facilities. Albuquerque ranked #56. *Wallethub.com, "Best & Worst Places for Veterans to Live (2025)," November 7, 2024*

Business/Finance Rankings

- The Albuquerque metro area appeared on the Milken Institute "2025 Best Performing Cities" list. Rank: #72 out of 200 large metro areas (based on performance category). Criteria: job growth; wage growth; high-tech growth and impact; community resilience; housing affordability; household broadband access. *Milken Institute, "Best-Performing Cities 2025," January 14, 2025*

Culture/Performing Arts Rankings

- Albuquerque was selected as one of the 25 best cities for moviemakers in North America. Great film cities are places where filmmaking dreams can come true, that offer more creative space, lower costs, and great outdoor locations. NYC & LA were intentionally excluded. Criteria: film industry presence and culture; tax incentives; affordability; and proximity of festivals and schools. The city was ranked #1. *MovieMaker Magazine, "Best Places to Live and Work as a Moviemaker, 2025," January 29, 2025*

Education Rankings

- Personal finance website *WalletHub* analyzed the 150 largest U.S. metropolitan statistical areas to determine where the most educated Americans are putting their degrees to work. Criteria: education levels; percentage of workers with degrees; education quality and attainment gap; public school quality rankings; quality and enrollment of each metro area's universities. Albuquerque was ranked #60 (#1 = most educated city). *WalletHub.com, "Most & Least Educated Cities in America, 2025" July 2, 2024*

Environmental Rankings

- Albuquerque was highlighted as one of the 25 most ozone-polluted metro areas in the U.S. during 2021 through 2023. The area ranked #22. *American Lung Association, "State of the Air 2025," April 23, 2025*

Health/Fitness Rankings

- For each of the 100 largest cities in the United States, the American Fitness Index®, compiled in partnership between the American College of Sports Medicine and the Elevance Health Foundation, evaluated community infrastructure and more than 30 health behaviors including preventive health, levels of chronic disease conditions, food insecurity, pedestrian safety, air quality, and community/environment resources that support physical activity. Albuquerque ranked #25 for "community fitness." *americanfitnessindex.org, "2024 ACSM American Fitness Index Summary Report," July 23, 2024*

- Albuquerque was identified as a "2025 Allergy Capital." The area ranked #79 out of the nation's 100 largest metropolitan areas. Three groups of factors were used to identify the most challenging cities for people with allergies: annual tree, grass, and weed pollen scores; over the counter allergy medicine use; number of board-certified allergy specialists. *Asthma and Allergy Foundation of America, "2025 Allergy Capitals: The Most Challenging Places to Live with Allergies," March 18, 2025*

- Albuquerque was identified as a "2024 Asthma Capital." The area ranked #54 out of the nation's 100 largest metropolitan areas. Criteria: estimated asthma prevalence; asthma-related mortality; and ER visits due to asthma. Risk factors analyzed but not factored in the rankings: annual air quality including pollution and ozone levels; public smoking laws; indoor air quality; access to asthma specialists; rescue and controller medication use; uninsured rate; pollen allergy; poverty rate. *Asthma and Allergy Foundation of America, "Asthma Capitals 2024: The Most Challenging Places to Live With Asthma," September 10, 2024*

Real Estate Rankings

- *WalletHub* compared the most populated U.S. cities to determine which had the best markets for real estate agents. Albuquerque ranked #135 where demand was high and pay was the best. Criteria: sales per agent; annual median wage for real-estate agents; monthly average starting salary for real estate agents; real estate job density and competition; unemployment rate; home turnover rate; housing-market health index; and other relevant metrics. *WalletHub.com, "2021 Best Places to Be a Real Estate Agent," May 12, 2021*

- Albuquerque was ranked #131 out of 176 metro areas in terms of cost of housing in 2024 by the National Association of Home Builders (#1 = most affordable). Criteria: the portion of an average family's income necessary to pay the mortgage on a median-priced home. *National Association of Home Builders®, NAHB-Wells Fargo Cost of Housing Index, 4th Quarter 2024*

Safety Rankings

- To identify the most dangerous cities in America, *24/7 Wall St.* focused on violent crime categories—murder, non-negligent manslaughter, rape, robbery, and aggravated assault—as reported for every 100,000 residents using data from the FBI's 2020 annual Uniform Crime Report. For cities with populations over 25,000, Albuquerque was ranked #28. *247wallst.com, "America's Most Dangerous Cities" November 12, 2021*

- Allstate ranked the 100 most populous cities in America in terms of driver safety. Albuquerque ranked #100. Criteria based on anonymized driving behavior data from Allstate's mobile app powered by Arity: high speed driving (over 80 mph), phone handling, and hard braking. The report helps increase the importance of safety and awareness behind the wheel. *Allstate, "16th Allstate America's Best Drivers Report®" July 11, 2024*

- Albuquerque was identified as one of the most dangerous cities in America by NeighborhoodScout. The city ranked #30 out of 100 (#1 = most dangerous). Criteria: number of violent crimes per 1,000 residents. The editors evaluated cities with 25,000 or more residents. *NeighborhoodScout.com, "2023 Top 100 Most Dangerous Cities in the U.S.," January 12, 2023*

Sports/Recreation Rankings

- Albuquerque was chosen as a bicycle friendly community by the League of American Bicyclists. A "Bicycle Friendly Community" welcomes cyclists by providing safe and supportive accommodation for cycling and encouraging people to bike for transportation and recreation. There are four award levels: Platinum; Gold; Silver; and Bronze. The community achieved an award level of Silver. *League of American Bicyclists, "2024 Awards-New & Renewing Bicycle Friendly Communities List," January 28, 2025*

Women/Minorities Rankings

- Personal finance website *WalletHub* compared more than 180 U.S. cities across two key dimensions, "Hispanic Business-Friendliness" and "Hispanic Purchasing Power," to arrive at the most favorable conditions for Hispanic entrepreneurs. Albuquerque was ranked #13 out of 182. Criteria includes: share of Hispanic-Owned Businesses; average growth of Hispanic Business revenues; Small Business-Friendliness score; affordability; and number of Hispanics with at least a bachelor's degree. *WalletHub.com, "Best Cities for Hispanic Entrepreneurs," September 4, 2024*

Miscellaneous Rankings

- Albuquerque was selected as a 2024 Digital Cities Survey winner. The city ranked #10 in the large city (500,000 or more population) category. The survey examined and assessed how city governments are utilizing new technology and modernized applications to provide residents an array of contactless services and conveniences. Survey questions focused on ten initiatives: cybersecurity; citizen experience; disaster recovery; business intelligence; IT personnel retention; data governance; business automation; AI/machine learning; application modernization; and IT collaboration. *Center for Digital Government, "2024 Digital Cities Survey," November 5, 2024*

- *WalletHub* compared 148 of the most populated U.S. cities to determine their operating efficiency. A "Quality of Services" score was constructed for each city and then measured against the total budget per capita to reveal which were managed the best. Albuquerque ranked #37. Criteria: financial stability; economy; education; safety; health; infrastructure and pollution. *WalletHub.com, "2025's Best- & Worst-Run Cities in America," June 18, 2024*

Business Environment

DEMOGRAPHICS

Population Growth

Area	1990 Census	2000 Census	2010 Census	2020 Census	2023 Estimate[2]	Population Growth 1990-2023 (%)
City	388,375	448,607	545,852	564,559	562,488	44.8
MSA[1]	599,416	729,649	887,077	916,528	918,567	53.2
U.S.	248,709,873	281,421,906	308,745,538	331,449,281	332,387,540	33.6

Note: (1) Figures cover the Albuquerque, NM Metropolitan Statistical Area; (2) 2019-2023 5-year ACS population estimate
Source: U.S. Census Bureau, 1990 Census, 2000 Census, 2010 Census, 2020 Census, 2019-2023 American Community Survey 5-Year Estimates

Race

Area	White Alone[2] (%)	Black Alone[2] (%)	Asian Alone[2] (%)	AIAN[3] Alone[2] (%)	NHOPI[4] Alone[2] (%)	Other Race Alone[2] (%)	Two or More Races (%)
City	55.3	3.3	3.3	5.0	0.1	11.1	21.9
MSA[1]	55.2	2.7	2.5	6.2	0.1	10.9	22.3
U.S.	63.4	12.4	5.8	0.9	0.2	6.6	10.7

Note: (1) Figures cover the Albuquerque, NM Metropolitan Statistical Area; (2) Alone is defined as not being in combination with one or more other races; (3) American Indian and Alaska Native; (4) Native Hawaiian and Other Pacific Islander
Source: U.S. Census Bureau, 2019-2023 American Community Survey 5-Year Estimates

Hispanic or Latino Origin

Area	Total (%)	Mexican (%)	Puerto Rican (%)	Cuban (%)	Other (%)
City	47.9	28.9	0.7	0.5	17.9
MSA[1]	48.3	28.5	0.7	0.4	18.6
U.S.	19.0	11.3	1.8	0.7	5.2

Note: Persons of Hispanic or Latino origin can be of any race; (1) Figures cover the Albuquerque, NM Metropolitan Statistical Area
Source: U.S. Census Bureau, 2019-2023 American Community Survey 5-Year Estimates

Age

Area	Under Age 5	Age 5–19	Age 20–34	Age 35–44	Age 45–54	Age 55–64	Age 65–74	Age 75–84	Age 85+	Median Age
City	5.1	18.0	21.5	13.9	11.7	12.5	10.4	4.7	2.1	38.7
MSA[1]	5.0	18.5	20.0	13.4	11.8	12.9	11.1	5.1	2.0	39.6
U.S.	5.7	19.1	20.2	13.1	12.3	12.8	10.0	4.9	1.9	38.7

Note: (1) Figures cover the Albuquerque, NM Metropolitan Statistical Area
Source: U.S. Census Bureau, 2019-2023 American Community Survey 5-Year Estimates

Disability by Age

Area	All Ages	Under 18 Years Old	18 to 64 Years Old	65 Years and Over
City	15.2	4.8	13.2	35.2
MSA[1]	16.1	4.7	14.1	36.3
U.S.	13.0	4.7	10.7	32.9

Note: Figures show percent of the civilian noninstitutionalized population that reported having a disability. Disability status is determined from six types of difficulty: vision, hearing, cognitive, ambulatory, self-care, and independent living. For children under 5 years old, hearing and vision difficulty are used to determine disability status. For children between the ages of 5 and 14, disability status is determined from hearing, vision, cognitive, ambulatory, and self-care difficulties. For people aged 15 years and older, they are considered to have a disability if they have difficulty with any one of the six difficulty types; Note: (1) Figures cover the Albuquerque, NM Metropolitan Statistical Area
Source: U.S. Census Bureau, 2019-2023 American Community Survey 5-Year Estimates

Ancestry

Area	German	Irish	English	American	Italian	Polish	French[2]	European	Scottish
City	9.8	7.9	9.1	3.1	3.4	1.4	1.8	1.6	1.5
MSA[1]	9.7	7.6	8.9	3.7	3.3	1.4	1.8	1.6	1.7
U.S.	12.6	9.4	9.1	5.5	4.9	2.6	2.0	1.6	1.6

Note: Figures are the percentage of the total population reporting a particular ancestry. The nine most commonly reported ancestries in the U.S. are shown. Figures include multiple ancestries (e.g. if a person reported being Irish and Italian, they were included in both columns); (1) Figures cover the Albuquerque, NM Metropolitan Statistical Area; (2) Excludes Basque
Source: U.S. Census Bureau, 2019-2023 American Community Survey 5-Year Estimates

Foreign-born Population

Area	Any Foreign Country	Asia	Mexico	Europe	Caribbean	Central America[2]	South America	Africa	Canada
				Percent of Population Born in					
City	10.4	2.7	5.0	1.0	0.4	0.2	0.5	0.4	0.1
MSA[1]	9.2	2.0	4.9	0.8	0.3	0.2	0.4	0.4	0.1
U.S.	13.9	4.3	3.3	1.4	1.4	1.2	1.2	0.8	0.2

Note: (1) Figures cover the Albuquerque, NM Metropolitan Statistical Area; (2) Excludes Mexico.
Source: U.S. Census Bureau, 2019-2023 American Community Survey 5-Year Estimates

Household Size

Area	One	Two	Three	Four	Five	Six	Seven or More	Average Household Size
			Persons in Household (%)					
City	37.3	32.4	13.7	9.8	4.6	1.4	0.8	2.29
MSA[1]	33.0	33.6	14.6	10.8	5.0	1.9	1.2	2.44
U.S.	28.5	33.8	15.4	12.7	5.9	2.3	1.4	2.54

Note: (1) Figures cover the Albuquerque, NM Metropolitan Statistical Area
Source: U.S. Census Bureau, 2019-2023 American Community Survey 5-Year Estimates

Household Relationships

Area	House-holder	Opposite-sex Spouse	Same-sex Spouse	Opposite-sex Unmarried Partner	Same-sex Unmarried Partner	Child[2]	Grand-child	Other Relatives	Non-relatives
City	42.1	15.1	0.3	3.4	0.3	27.0	2.5	4.6	3.2
MSA[1]	40.1	16.3	0.3	3.1	0.3	27.7	3.1	4.6	2.9
U.S.	38.3	17.5	0.2	2.5	0.2	28.3	2.4	4.8	3.4

Note: Figures are percent of the total population; (1) Figures cover the Albuquerque, NM Metropolitan Statistical Area; (2) Includes biological, adopted, and stepchildren of the householder
Source: U.S. Census Bureau, 2020 Census

Gender

Area	Males	Females	Males per 100 Females
City	275,413	287,075	95.9
MSA[1]	452,929	465,638	97.3
U.S.	164,545,087	167,842,453	98.0

Note: (1) Figures cover the Albuquerque, NM Metropolitan Statistical Area
Source: U.S. Census Bureau, 2019-2023 American Community Survey 5-Year Estimates

Marital Status

Area	Never Married	Now Married[2]	Separated	Widowed	Divorced
City	38.6	39.4	1.5	5.5	15.1
MSA[1]	36.1	43.1	1.4	5.4	13.9
U.S.	34.1	47.9	1.7	5.6	10.7

Note: Figures are percentages and cover the population 15 years of age and older; (1) Figures cover the Albuquerque, NM Metropolitan Statistical Area; (2) Excludes separated
Source: U.S. Census Bureau, 2019-2023 American Community Survey 5-Year Estimates

Religious Groups by Family

Area	Catholic	Baptist	Methodist	LDS[2]	Pentecostal	Lutheran	Islam	Adventist	Other
MSA[1]	32.6	3.2	0.9	2.7	1.7	0.4	0.7	1.5	10.8
U.S.	18.7	7.3	3.0	2.0	1.8	1.7	1.3	1.3	11.6

Note: Figures are the number of adherents as a percentage of the total population and cover the eight largest religious groups in the U.S; (1) Figures cover the Albuquerque, NM Metropolitan Statistical Area; (2) Church of Jesus Christ of Latter-day Saints
Sources: 2020 U.S. Religion Census, Association of Statisticians of American Religious Bodies; The Association of Religion Data Archives (ARDA)

Religious Groups by Tradition

Area	Catholic	Evangelical Protestant	Mainline Protestant	Black Protestant	Islam	Judaism	Hinduism	Orthodox	Buddhism
MSA[1]	32.6	13.4	2.2	0.5	0.7	0.2	0.2	0.1	0.6
U.S.	18.7	16.5	5.2	2.3	1.3	0.6	0.4	0.4	0.3

Note: Figures are the number of adherents as a percentage of the total population; (1) Figures cover the Albuquerque, NM Metropolitan Statistical Area
Sources: 2020 U.S. Religion Census, Association of Statisticians of American Religious Bodies; The Association of Religion Data Archives (ARDA)

ECONOMY

Real Gross Domestic Product (GDP)

Area	2017	2018	2019	2020	2021	2022	2023	Rank[3]
MSA[1]	41.9	42.7	43.9	43.3	45.7	47.4	48.6	70
U.S.[2]	17,619.1	18,160.7	18,642.5	18,238.9	19,387.6	19,896.6	20,436.3	–

Note: Figures are in billions of chained 2017 dollars; (1) Figures cover the Albuquerque, NM Metropolitan Statistical Area; (2) Figures cover real GDP within metropolitan areas; (3) Rank is based on 2023 data and ranges from 1 to 384
Source: U.S. Bureau of Economic Analysis

Economic Growth

Area	2014	2015	2016	2017	2018	2019	2020	2021	2022	2023
MSA[1]	2.0	1.2	1.7	0.4	1.9	2.9	-1.3	5.4	3.9	2.4
U.S.[2]	2.6	3.2	2.0	2.7	3.1	2.7	-2.2	6.3	2.6	2.7

Note: Figures are real gross domestic product growth rates and represent percent change from preceding period; (1) Figures cover the Albuquerque, NM Metropolitan Statistical Area; (2) Figures are the average growth rates within metropolitan areas
Source: U.S. Bureau of Economic Analysis

Metropolitan Area Exports

Area	2018	2019	2020	2021	2022	2023	Rank[2]
MSA[1]	771.5	1,629.7	1,265.3	2,215.0	939.7	789.4	195
U.S.	1,664,056.1	1,645,173.7	1,431,406.6	1,753,941.4	2,062,937.4	2,019,160.5	–

Note: Figures are in millions of dollars; (1) Figures cover the Albuquerque, NM Metropolitan Statistical Area; (2) Rank is based on 2023 data and ranges from 1 to 386
Source: U.S. Department of Commerce, International Trade Administration, Office of Trade and Economic Analysis, Industry and Analysis, Exports by Metropolitan Area, data extracted April 2, 2025

Building Permits

Area	Single-Family			Multi-Family			Total		
	2023	2024	Pct. Chg.	2023	2024	Pct. Chg.	2023	2024	Pct. Chg.
City	587	525	-10.6	512	574	12.1	1,099	1,099	0.0
MSA[1]	2,057	2,064	0.3	777	812	4.5	2,834	2,876	1.5
U.S.	920,000	981,900	6.7	591,100	496,100	-16.1	1,511,100	1,478,000	-2.2

Note: (1) Figures cover the Albuquerque, NM Metropolitan Statistical Area; Figures represent new, privately-owned housing units authorized (unadjusted data)
Source: U.S. Census Bureau, Building Permits Survey (BPS), 2023, 2024

Bankruptcy Filings

Area	Business Filings			Nonbusiness Filings		
	2023	2024	% Chg.	2023	2024	% Chg.
Bernalillo County	24	33	37.5	373	454	21.7
U.S.	18,926	23,107	22.1	434,064	494,201	13.9

Note: Business filings include Chapter 7, Chapter 9, Chapter 11, Chapter 12, Chapter 13, Chapter 15, and Section 304; Nonbusiness filings include Chapter 7, Chapter 11, and Chapter 13
Source: Administrative Office of the U.S. Courts, Business and Nonbusiness Bankruptcy, County Cases Commenced by Chapter of the Bankruptcy Code, During the 12-Month Period Ending December 31, 2023 and Business and Nonbusiness Bankruptcy, County Cases Commenced by Chapter of the Bankruptcy Code, During the 12-Month Period Ending December 31, 2024

Housing Vacancy Rates

Area	Gross Vacancy Rate[3] (%)			Year-Round Vacancy Rate[4] (%)			Rental Vacancy Rate[5] (%)			Homeowner Vacancy Rate[6] (%)		
	2022	2023	2024	2022	2023	2024	2022	2023	2024	2022	2023	2024
MSA[1]	5.3	5.6	6.4	5.1	5.4	6.1	5.5	6.1	6.7	1.0	0.7	1.6
U.S.[2]	9.1	9.0	9.1	7.5	7.5	7.6	5.7	6.5	6.8	0.8	0.8	1.0

Note: (1) Figures cover the Albuquerque, NM Metropolitan Statistical Area; (2) Figures cover the 75 largest Metropolitan Statistical Areas; (3) The percentage of the total housing inventory that is vacant; (4) The percentage of the housing inventory (excluding seasonal units) that is year-round vacant; (5) The percentage of rental inventory that is vacant for rent; (6) The percentage of homeowner inventory that is vacant for sale
Source: U.S. Census Bureau, Housing Vacancies and Homeownership Annual Statistics: 2022, 2023, 2024

INCOME

Income

Area	Per Capita ($)	Median Household ($)	Average Household ($)
City	39,117	65,604	88,262
MSA[1]	38,300	67,995	91,376
U.S.	43,289	78,538	110,491

Note: (1) Figures cover the Albuquerque, NM Metropolitan Statistical Area
Source: U.S. Census Bureau, 2019-2023 American Community Survey 5-Year Estimates

Household Income Distribution

Area	Percent of Households Earning							
	Under $15,000	$15,000 -$24,999	$25,000 -$34,999	$35,000 -$49,999	$50,000 -$74,999	$75,000 -$99,999	$100,000 -$149,999	$150,000 and up
City	10.9	8.5	7.9	11.5	17.5	12.6	16.0	15.2
MSA[1]	10.3	7.9	7.6	11.2	17.5	12.8	16.6	16.0
U.S.	8.5	6.6	6.8	10.4	15.7	12.7	17.4	21.9

Note: (1) Figures cover the Albuquerque, NM Metropolitan Statistical Area
Source: U.S. Census Bureau, 2019-2023 American Community Survey 5-Year Estimates

Poverty Rate

Area	All Ages	Under 18 Years Old	18 to 64 Years Old	65 Years and Over
City	16.0	20.8	15.3	12.6
MSA[1]	15.1	19.6	14.5	12.0
U.S.	12.4	16.3	11.6	10.4

Note: Figures are percentage of people whose income during the past 12 months was below the poverty level;
(1) Figures cover the Albuquerque, NM Metropolitan Statistical Area
Source: U.S. Census Bureau, 2019-2023 American Community Survey 5-Year Estimates

EMPLOYMENT

Labor Force and Employment

Area	Civilian Labor Force			Workers Employed		
	Dec. 2023	Dec. 2024	% Chg.	Dec. 2023	Dec. 2024	% Chg.
City	295,286	297,348	0.7	286,112	286,738	0.2
MSA[1]	459,168	462,519	0.7	444,472	445,570	0.2
U.S.	166,661,000	167,746,000	0.7	160,754,000	161,294,000	0.3

Note: Data is not seasonally adjusted and covers workers 16 years of age and older; (1) Figures cover the Albuquerque, NM Metropolitan Statistical Area
Source: Bureau of Labor Statistics, Local Area Unemployment Statistics

Unemployment Rate

Area	2024											
	Jan.	Feb.	Mar.	Apr.	May	Jun.	Jul.	Aug.	Sep.	Oct.	Nov.	Dec.
City	3.5	3.4	3.1	3.1	3.5	4.4	4.9	4.3	3.8	3.9	3.9	3.6
MSA[1]	3.6	3.5	3.2	3.3	3.6	4.6	5.1	4.4	3.9	4.0	4.1	3.7
U.S.	4.1	4.2	3.9	3.5	3.7	4.3	4.5	4.4	3.9	3.9	4.0	3.8

Note: Data is not seasonally adjusted and covers workers 16 years of age and older; (1) Figures cover the Albuquerque, NM Metropolitan Statistical Area
Source: Bureau of Labor Statistics, Local Area Unemployment Statistics

Average Wages

Occupation	$/Hr.	Occupation	$/Hr.
Accountants and Auditors	40.90	Maintenance and Repair Workers	23.82
Automotive Mechanics	25.69	Marketing Managers	62.50
Bookkeepers	23.51	Network and Computer Systems Admin.	44.51
Carpenters	26.42	Nurses, Licensed Practical	26.25
Cashiers	14.93	Nurses, Registered	45.99
Computer Programmers	43.80	Nursing Assistants	18.59
Computer Systems Analysts	46.83	Office Clerks, General	18.52
Computer User Support Specialists	24.18	Physical Therapists	48.32
Construction Laborers	20.58	Physicians	146.53
Cooks, Restaurant	16.62	Plumbers, Pipefitters and Steamfitters	30.61
Customer Service Representatives	20.23	Police and Sheriff's Patrol Officers	33.46
Dentists	92.52	Postal Service Mail Carriers	28.74
Electricians	28.48	Real Estate Sales Agents	40.95
Engineers, Electrical	71.65	Retail Salespersons	16.73
Fast Food and Counter Workers	14.78	Sales Representatives, Technical/Scientific	41.73
Financial Managers	67.06	Secretaries, Exc. Legal/Medical/Executive	21.86
First-Line Supervisors of Office Workers	31.40	Security Guards	21.72
General and Operations Managers	59.24	Surgeons	219.96
Hairdressers/Cosmetologists	18.37	Teacher Assistants, Exc. Postsecondary[1]	15.58
Home Health and Personal Care Aides	14.44	Teachers, Secondary School, Exc. Sp. Ed.[1]	32.70
Janitors and Cleaners	16.27	Telemarketers	33.59
Landscaping/Groundskeeping Workers	18.15	Truck Drivers, Heavy/Tractor-Trailer	25.68
Lawyers	67.75	Truck Drivers, Light/Delivery Services	20.59
Maids and Housekeeping Cleaners	15.65	Waiters and Waitresses	18.83

Note: Wage data covers the Albuquerque, NM Metropolitan Statistical Area; (1) Hourly wages were calculated from annual wage data based on a 40 hour work week
Source: Bureau of Labor Statistics, Metro Area Occupational Employment & Wage Estimates, May 2024

Employment by Industry

Sector	MSA[1]		U.S.
	Number of Employees	Percent of Total	Percent of Total
Construction, Mining, and Logging	28,300	6.6	5.5
Financial Activities	19,600	4.6	5.8
Government	84,700	19.8	14.9
Information	5,400	1.3	1.9
Leisure and Hospitality	44,400	10.4	10.4
Manufacturing	17,300	4.0	8.0
Other Services	13,400	3.1	3.7
Private Education and Health Services	74,100	17.3	16.9
Professional and Business Services	68,400	16.0	14.2
Retail Trade	44,100	10.3	10.0
Transportation, Warehousing, and Utilities	16,700	3.9	4.8
Wholesale Trade	11,600	2.7	3.9

Note: Figures are non-farm employment as of December 2024. Figures are not seasonally adjusted and include workers 16 years of age and older; (1) Figures cover the Albuquerque, NM Metropolitan Statistical Area
Source: Bureau of Labor Statistics, Current Employment Statistics, Employment, Hours, and Earnings

Employment by Occupation

Occupation Classification	City (%)	MSA[1] (%)	U.S. (%)
Management, Business, Science, and Arts	46.6	44.4	42.0
Natural Resources, Construction, and Maintenance	7.0	8.3	8.6
Production, Transportation, and Material Moving	8.5	9.3	13.0
Sales and Office	20.0	20.2	19.9
Service	17.9	17.8	16.5

Note: Figures cover employed civilians 16 years of age and older; (1) Figures cover the Albuquerque, NM Metropolitan Statistical Area
Source: U.S. Census Bureau, 2019-2023 American Community Survey 5-Year Estimates

Occupations with Greatest Projected Employment Growth: 2022 – 2032

Occupation[1]	2022 Employment	2032 Projected Employment	Numeric Employment Change	Percent Employment Change
Home Health and Personal Care Aides	36,890	50,200	13,310	36.1
Fast Food and Counter Workers	24,460	28,830	4,370	17.9
Cooks, Restaurant	9,040	12,930	3,890	43.0
Registered Nurses	19,020	21,940	2,920	15.4
Stockers and Order Fillers	15,760	18,220	2,460	15.6
General and Operations Managers	16,750	19,130	2,380	14.2
Medical Assistants	6,920	9,130	2,210	31.9
Construction Laborers	14,730	16,810	2,080	14.1
Retail Salespersons	23,030	25,110	2,080	9.0
Waiters and Waitresses	12,390	14,350	1,960	15.8

Note: Projections cover New Mexico; (1) Sorted by numeric employment change
Source: www.projectionscentral.org, State Occupational Projections, 2022–2032 Long-Term Projections

Fastest-Growing Occupations: 2022 – 2032

Occupation[1]	2022 Employment	2032 Projected Employment	Numeric Employment Change	Percent Employment Change
Nurse Practitioners	1,590	2,620	1,030	64.8
Solar Photovoltaic Installers	290	430	140	48.3
Physical Therapist Assistants	890	1,310	420	47.2
Tour and Travel Guides	500	730	230	46.0
Information Security Analysts (SOC 2018)	1,620	2,360	740	45.7
Physician Assistants	570	830	260	45.6
Fitness Trainers and Aerobics Instructors	1,480	2,140	660	44.6
Cooks, Restaurant	9,040	12,930	3,890	43.0
Gaming Dealers	280	400	120	42.9
Data Scientists	380	540	160	42.1

Note: Projections cover New Mexico; (1) Sorted by percent employment change and excludes occupations with numeric employment change less than 50
Source: www.projectionscentral.org, State Occupational Projections, 2022–2032 Long-Term Projections

CITY FINANCES

City Government Finances

Component	2022 ($000)	2022 ($ per capita)
Total Revenues	1,229,038	2,185
Total Expenditures	1,178,846	2,096
Debt Outstanding	1,355,549	2,410

Source: U.S. Census Bureau, State & Local Government Finances 2022

City Government Revenue by Source

Source	2022 ($000)	2022 ($ per capita)	2022 (%)
General Revenue			
From Federal Government	156,937	279	12.8
From State Government	37,280	66	3.0
From Local Governments	3,340	6	0.3
Taxes			
Property	169,508	301	13.8
Sales and Gross Receipts	315,391	561	25.7
Personal Income	0	0	0.0
Corporate Income	0	0	0.0
Motor Vehicle License	0	0	0.0
Other Taxes	13,984	25	1.1
Current Charges	287,147	510	23.4
Liquor Store	0	0	0.0
Utility	153,442	273	12.5

Source: U.S. Census Bureau, State & Local Government Finances 2022

City Government Expenditures by Function

Function	2022 ($000)	2022 ($ per capita)	2022 (%)
General Direct Expenditures			
Air Transportation	61,606	109	5.2
Corrections	0	0	0.0
Education	0	0	0.0
Employment Security Administration	0	0	0.0
Financial Administration	27,468	48	2.3
Fire Protection	82,100	145	7.0
General Public Buildings	16,767	29	1.4
Governmental Administration, Other	27,076	48	2.3
Health	34,515	61	2.9
Highways	83,178	147	7.1
Hospitals	0	0	0.0
Housing and Community Development	51,455	91	4.4
Interest on General Debt	37,788	67	3.2
Judicial and Legal	8,280	14	0.7
Libraries	14,947	26	1.3
Parking	3,740	6	0.3
Parks and Recreation	113,042	200	9.6
Police Protection	197,029	350	16.7
Public Welfare	82,090	145	7.0
Sewerage	64,641	114	5.5
Solid Waste Management	82,837	147	7.0
Veterans' Services	0	0	0.0
Liquor Store	0	0	0.0
Utility	187,723	333	15.9

Source: U.S. Census Bureau, State & Local Government Finances 2022

TAXES

State Corporate Income Tax Rates

State	Tax Rate (%)	Income Brackets ($)	Num. of Brackets	Financial Institution Tax Rate (%)[a]	Federal Income Tax Ded.
New Mexico	4.8 - 5.9	500,000	2	4.8 - 5.9	No

Note: Tax rates for tax year 2024; (a) Rates listed are the corporate income tax rate applied to financial institutions or excise taxes based on income. Some states have other taxes based upon the value of deposits or shares.
Source: Federation of Tax Administrators, State Corporate Income Tax Rates, January 1, 2025

State Individual Income Tax Rates

State	Tax Rate (%)	Income Brackets ($)	Personal Exemptions ($)			Standard Ded. ($)	
			Single	Married	Depend.	Single	Married
New Mexico	1.7 - 5.9	10,000 - 210,000 (r)	(d)	(d)	(d)	14,600	29,200 (d)

Note: Tax rates for tax year 2024; Local- and county-level taxes are not included; Federal income tax is not deductible on state income tax returns; (d) These states use the personal exemption/standard deduction amounts provided in the federal Internal Revenue Code. Montana personal exemption subject to repeal under Section 15-30-2114; (r) The income brackets reported for New Mexico are for single individuals. For married couples filing jointly, the same tax rates apply to income brackets ranging from $10,000 to $315,000.
Source: Federation of Tax Administrators, State Individual Income Tax Rates, January 1, 2025

Various State Sales and Excise Tax Rates

State	State Sales Tax (%)	Gasoline[1] ($/gal.)	Cigarette[2] ($/pack)	Spirits[3] ($/gal.)	Wine[4] ($/gal.)	Beer[5] ($/gal.)	Recreational Marijuana (%)
New Mexico	4.88	0.19	2.00	6.06	1.70	0.41	(q)

Note: All tax rates as of January 1, 2025; (1) The American Petroleum Institute has developed a methodology for determining the average tax rate on a gallon of fuel. Rates may include any of the following: excise taxes, environmental fees, storage tank fees, other fees or taxes, general sales tax, and local taxes; (2) The federal excise tax of $1.0066 per pack and local taxes are not included; (3) Rates are those applicable to off-premise sales of 40% alcohol by volume (a.b.v.) distilled spirits in 750ml containers. Local excise taxes are excluded; (4) Rates are those applicable to off-premise sales of 11% a.b.v. non-carbonated wine in 750ml containers; (5) Rates are those applicable to off-premise sales of 4.7% a.b.v. beer in 12 ounce containers; (q) 12% excise tax (retail price)
Source: Tax Foundation, 2025 Facts & Figures: How Does Your State Compare?

State Tax Competitiveness Index

State	Overall Rank	Corporate Tax Rank	Individual Income Tax Rank	Sales Tax Rank	Property Tax Rank	Unemployment Insurance Tax Rank
New Mexico	31	22	37	41	2	16

Note: The Tax Foundation's State Tax Competitiveness Index enables policymakers, taxpayers, and business leaders to gauge how their states' tax systems compare. A rank of 1 is best, 50 is worst. Rankings do not average to the total. States without a tax rank equally as 1. DC's scores and rankings do not affect other states. The report shows tax systems as of July 1, 2024 (the beginning of Fiscal Year 2025).
Source: Tax Foundation, State Tax Competitiveness Index 2025

TRANSPORTATION

Means of Transportation to Work

Area	Car/Truck/Van		Public Transportation			Bicycle	Walked	Other Means	Worked at Home
	Drove Alone	Car-pooled	Bus	Subway	Railroad				
City	73.2	8.8	1.2	0.0	0.1	0.9	1.9	1.2	12.8
MSA[1]	73.5	9.1	0.8	0.0	0.1	0.6	1.6	1.3	12.9
U.S.	70.2	8.5	1.7	1.3	0.4	0.4	2.4	1.6	13.5

Note: Figures are percentages and cover workers 16 years of age and older; (1) Figures cover the Albuquerque, NM Metropolitan Statistical Area
Source: U.S. Census Bureau, 2019-2023 American Community Survey 5-Year Estimates

Travel Time to Work

Area	Less Than 10 Minutes	10 to 19 Minutes	20 to 29 Minutes	30 to 44 Minutes	45 to 59 Minutes	60 to 89 Minutes	90 Minutes or More
City	11.7	36.0	27.6	17.3	3.0	2.5	1.9
MSA[1]	11.5	31.1	25.0	20.6	5.8	3.8	2.3
U.S.	12.6	28.6	21.2	20.8	8.1	6.0	2.8

Note: Note: Figures are percentages and include workers 16 years old and over; (1) Figures cover the Albuquerque, NM Metropolitan Statistical Area
Source: U.S. Census Bureau, 2019-2023 American Community Survey 5-Year Estimates

Key Congestion Measures

Measure	2000	2010	2015	2020	2022
Annual Hours of Delay, Total (000)	15,165	16,874	19,390	10,229	19,417
Annual Hours of Delay, Per Auto Commuter	39	37	43	22	44
Annual Congestion Cost, Per Auto Commuter ($)	693	980	1,055	577	1,065

Note: Figures cover the Albuquerque NM urban area
Source: Texas A&M Transportation Institute, 2023 Urban Mobility Report

Freeway Travel Time Index

Measure	1985	1990	1995	2000	2005	2010	2015	2020	2022
Urban Area Index[1]	1.07	1.07	1.11	1.14	1.14	1.15	1.16	1.06	1.16
Urban Area Rank[1,2]	48	74	66	62	73	65	57	75	50

Note: Freeway Travel Time Index—the ratio of travel time in the peak period to the travel time at free-flow conditions. For example, a value of 1.30 indicates a 20-minute free-flow trip takes 26 minutes in the peak (20 minutes x 1.30 = 26 minutes); (1) Covers the Albuquerque NM urban area; (2) Rank is based on 101 larger urban areas (#1 = highest travel time index)
Source: Texas A&M Transportation Institute, 2023 Urban Mobility Report

Public Transportation

Agency Name / Mode of Transportation	Vehicles Operated in Maximum Service[1]	Annual Unlinked Passenger Trips[2] (in thous.)	Annual Passenger Miles[3] (in thous.)
ABQ Ride			
Bus (directly operated)	86	4,588.9	14,290.8
Bus Rapid Transit (directly operated)	13	2,067.8	7,382.1
Demand Response (directly operated)	54	184.2	1,689.1

Note: (1) Number of revenue vehicles operated by the given mode and type of service to meet the annual maximum service requirement. This is the revenue vehicle count during the peak season of the year; on the week and day that maximum service is provided. Vehicles operated in maximum service (VOMS) exclude atypical days and one-time special events; (2) Number of passengers who boarded public transportation vehicles. Passengers are counted each time they board a vehicle no matter how many vehicles they use to travel from their origin to their destination. (3) Sum of the distances ridden by all passengers during the entire fiscal year.
Source: Federal Transit Administration, National Transit Database, 2023

Air Transportation

Airport Name and Code / Type of Service	Passenger Airlines[1]	Passenger Enplanements	Freight Carriers[2]	Freight (lbs)
Albuquerque International (ABQ)				
Domestic service (U.S. carriers only)	20	2,690,201	13	43,688,724
International service (U.S. carriers only)	0	0	0	0

Note: (1) Includes all U.S.-based major, minor and commuter airlines that carried at least one passenger during the year; (2) Includes all U.S.-based airlines and freight carriers that transported at least one pound of freight during the year.
Source: Bureau of Transportation Statistics, The Intermodal Transportation Database, Air Carriers: T-100 Domestic Market (U.S. carriers only), 2024; Bureau of Transportation Statistics, The Intermodal Transportation Database, Air Carriers: T-100 International Market (U.S. carriers only), 2024

BUSINESSES

Major Business Headquarters

Company Name	Industry	Rankings Fortune[1]	Forbes[2]
No companies listed	-	-	-

Note: (1) Companies that produce a 10-K are ranked 1 to 500 based on 2023 revenue; (2) All private companies with at least $2 billion in annual revenue through the end of their most current fiscal year are ranked 1 to 275; companies listed are headquartered in the city; dashes indicate no ranking
Source: Fortune, "Fortune 500," 2024; Forbes, "America's Largest Private Companies," 2024

Fastest-Growing Businesses

According to *Inc.*, Albuquerque is home to one of America's 500 fastest-growing private companies: **City Mobile Group** (#225). Criteria: must be an independent, privately-held, for-profit, U.S. corporation, proprietorship or partnership as of December 31, 2023; revenues must be at least $100,000 in 2020 and $2 million in 2023; must have four-year operating/sales history. *Inc., "America's 500 Fastest-Growing Private Companies," 2024*

Living Environment

COST OF LIVING

Cost of Living Index

Composite Index	Groceries	Housing	Utilities	Trans-portation	Health Care	Misc. Goods/ Services
94.9	97.4	89.1	87.3	85.9	102.0	101.8

Note: The Cost of Living Index measures regional differences in the cost of consumer goods and services, excluding taxes and non-consumer expenditures, for professional and managerial households in the top income quintile. It is based on more than 50,000 prices covering almost 60 different items for which prices are collected three times a year by chambers of commerce, economic development organizations or university applied economic centers in each participating urban area. The numbers shown should be read as a percentage above or below the national average of 100. For example, a value of 115.4 in the groceries column indicates that grocery prices are 15.4% higher than the national average. Small differences in the index numbers should not be interpreted as significant; Figures cover the Albuquerque NM urban area.
Source: The Council for Community and Economic Research, Cost of Living Index, 2024

Grocery Prices

Area[1]	T-Bone Steak ($/pound)	Frying Chicken ($/pound)	Whole Milk ($/half gal.)	Eggs ($/dozen)	Orange Juice ($/64 oz.)	Coffee ($/11.5 oz.)
City[2]	14.86	1.51	4.61	3.01	4.27	5.45
Avg.	15.42	1.55	4.69	3.25	4.41	5.46
Min.	14.50	1.16	4.43	2.75	4.00	4.85
Max.	17.56	2.89	5.49	4.78	5.54	7.89

*Note: (1) Values for the local area are compared with the average, minimum and maximum values for all 276 areas in the Cost of Living Index; (2) Figures cover the Albuquerque NM urban area; **T-Bone Steak** (price per pound); **Frying Chicken** (price per pound, whole fryer); **Whole Milk** (half gallon carton); **Eggs** (price per dozen, Grade A, large); **Orange Juice** (64 oz. Tropicana or Florida Natural); **Coffee** (11.5 oz. can, vacuum-packed, Maxwell House, Hills Bros, or Folgers).*
Source: The Council for Community and Economic Research, Cost of Living Index, 2024

Housing and Utility Costs

Area[1]	New Home Price ($)	Apartment Rent ($/month)	All Electric ($/month)	Part Electric ($/month)	Other Energy ($/month)	Telephone ($/month)
City[2]	424,687	1,574	-	115.74	50.09	192.92
Avg.	515,975	1,550	210.99	123.07	82.07	194.99
Min.	265,375	692	104.33	53.68	36.26	179.42
Max.	2,775,821	5,719	529.02	397.28	361.63	223.33

*Note: (1) Values for the local area are compared with the average, minimum and maximum values for all 276 areas in the Cost of Living Index; (2) Figures cover the Albuquerque NM urban area; **New Home Price** (2,400 sf living area, 8,000 sf lot, in urban area with full utilities); **Apartment Rent** (950 sf 2 bedroom/1.5 or 2 bath, unfurnished, excluding all utilities except water); **All Electric** (average monthly cost for an all-electric home); **Part Electric** (average monthly cost for a part-electric home); **Other Energy** (average monthly cost for natural gas, fuel oil, coal, wood, and any other forms of energy except electricity); **Telephone** (price includes the base monthly rate plus taxes and fees for three lines of mobile phone service).*
Source: The Council for Community and Economic Research, Cost of Living Index, 2024

Health Care, Transportation, and Other Costs

Area[1]	Doctor ($/visit)	Dentist ($/visit)	Optometrist ($/visit)	Gasoline ($/gallon)	Beauty Salon ($/visit)	Men's Shirt ($)
City[2]	133.41	115.32	145.00	3.10	47.25	37.35
Avg.	143.77	117.51	129.23	3.32	48.57	38.14
Min.	36.74	58.67	67.33	2.80	24.00	13.41
Max.	270.44	216.82	307.33	5.28	94.00	63.89

*Note: (1) Values for the local area are compared with the average, minimum and maximum values for all 276 areas in the Cost of Living Index; (2) Figures cover the Albuquerque NM urban area; **Doctor** (general practitioners routine exam of an established patient); **Dentist** (adult teeth cleaning and periodic oral examination); **Optometrist** (full vision eye exam for established adult patient); **Gasoline** (one gallon regular unleaded, national brand, including all taxes, cash price at self-service pump if available); **Beauty Salon** (woman's shampoo, trim, and blow-dry); **Men's Shirt** (cotton/polyester dress shirt, pinpoint weave, long sleeves).*
Source: The Council for Community and Economic Research, Cost of Living Index, 2024

HOUSING

Homeownership Rate

Area	2017 (%)	2018 (%)	2019 (%)	2020 (%)	2021 (%)	2022 (%)	2023 (%)	2024 (%)
MSA[1]	67.0	67.9	70.0	69.5	66.5	67.3	69.1	71.8
U.S.	63.9	64.4	64.6	66.6	65.5	65.8	65.9	65.6

Note: (1) Figures cover the Albuquerque, NM Metropolitan Statistical Area
Source: U.S. Census Bureau, Housing Vacancies and Homeownership Annual Statistics: 2017-2024

House Price Index (HPI)

Area	National Ranking[2]	Quarterly Change (%)	One-Year Change (%)	Five-Year Change (%)	Since 1991Q1 (%)
MSA[1]	152	0.28	4.68	60.38	291.99
U.S.[3]	–	1.43	4.51	57.13	327.82

Note: The HPI is a weighted repeat sales index. It measures average price changes in repeat sales or refinancings on the same properties. This information is obtained by reviewing repeat mortgage transactions on single-family properties whose mortgages have been purchased or securitized by Fannie Mae or Freddie Mac since January 1975; (1) Figures cover the Albuquerque, NM Metropolitan Statistical Area; (2) Rankings are based on annual percentage change for all metro areas containing at least 15,000 transactions over the last 10 years and ranges from 1 to 241; (3) figures based on a weighted average of Census Division estimates using a seasonally adjusted, purchase-only index; all figures are for the period ending December 31, 2024
Source: Federal Housing Finance Agency, Change in FHFA Metropolitan Area House Price Indexes, All Transactions Index, 2024Q4

Home Value

Area	Under $100,000	$100,000 -$199,999	$200,000 -$299,999	$300,000 -$399,999	$400,000 -$499,999	$500,000 -$999,999	$1,000,000 or more	Median ($)
City	6.9	18.8	34.6	19.9	10.2	8.7	0.9	266,700
MSA[1]	9.6	19.3	31.5	17.9	9.9	10.1	1.6	263,500
U.S.	12.1	17.8	19.5	14.4	10.5	19.1	6.5	303,400

Note: Figures are percentages except for median and cover owner-occupied housing units; (1) Figures cover the Albuquerque, NM Metropolitan Statistical Area
Source: U.S. Census Bureau, 2019-2023 American Community Survey 5-Year Estimates

Year Housing Structure Built

Area	2020 or Later	2010 -2019	2000 -2009	1990 -1999	1980 -1989	1970 -1979	1960 -1969	1950 -1959	1940 -1949	Before 1940	Median Year
City	0.7	6.9	16.2	14.2	14.1	19.2	9.5	12.3	3.9	3.0	1982
MSA[1]	0.9	7.5	17.4	16.2	15.7	17.7	8.6	9.5	3.3	3.2	1985
U.S.	1.2	8.9	13.6	12.8	13.0	14.4	10.0	9.7	4.5	11.9	1980

Note: Figures are percentages except for Median Year; Note: (1) Figures cover the Albuquerque, NM Metropolitan Statistical Area
Source: U.S. Census Bureau, 2019-2023 American Community Survey 5-Year Estimates

Gross Monthly Rent

Area	Under $500	$500 -$999	$1,000 -$1,499	$1,500 -$1,999	$2,000 -$2,499	$2,500 -$2,999	$3,000 and up	Median ($)
City	5.3	37.7	35.1	16.1	3.9	0.8	1.1	1,085
MSA[1]	5.5	36.2	35.3	16.7	4.3	0.9	1.1	1,102
U.S.	6.5	22.3	29.5	20.2	10.8	4.8	5.9	1,348

Note: Figures are percentages except for median; Gross rent is the contract rent plus the estimated average monthly cost of utilities (electricity, gas, and water and sewer) and fuels (oil, coal, kerosene, wood, etc.) if these are paid by the renter (or paid for the renter by someone else); (1) Figures cover the Albuquerque, NM Metropolitan Statistical Area
Source: U.S. Census Bureau, 2019-2023 American Community Survey 5-Year Estimates

HEALTH

Health Risk Factors

Category	MSA[1] (%)	U.S. (%)
Adults aged 18–64 who have any kind of health care coverage	88.9	90.8
Adults who reported being in good or better health	78.3	81.8
Adults who have been told they have high blood cholesterol	36.1	36.9
Adults who have been told they have high blood pressure	35.1	34.0
Adults who are current smokers	12.0	12.1
Adults who currently use e-cigarettes	9.1	7.7
Adults who currently use chewing tobacco, snuff, or snus	3.5	3.2
Adults who are heavy drinkers[2]	4.9	6.1
Adults who are binge drinkers[3]	12.0	15.2
Adults who are overweight (BMI 25.0 - 29.9)	33.9	34.4
Adults who are obese (BMI 30.0 - 99.8)	33.1	34.3
Adults who participated in any physical activities in the past month	79.8	75.8

Note: All figures are crude prevalence; (1) Figures cover the Albuquerque, NM Metropolitan Statistical Area; (2) Heavy drinkers are classified as adult men having more than 14 drinks per week and adult women having more than 7 drinks per week; (3) Binge drinkers are classified as males having five or more drinks on one occasion or females having four or more drinks on one occasion
Source: Centers for Disease Control and Prevention, Behaviorial Risk Factor Surveillance System, SMART: Selected Metropolitan Area Risk Trends, 2023

Acute and Chronic Health Conditions

Category	MSA[1] (%)	U.S. (%)
Adults who have ever been told they had a heart attack	4.8	4.2
Adults who have ever been told they have angina or coronary heart disease	n/a	4.0
Adults who have ever been told they had a stroke	3.7	3.3
Adults who have ever been told they have asthma	14.8	15.7
Adults who have ever been told they have arthritis	27.4	26.3
Adults who have ever been told they have diabetes[2]	13.0	11.5
Adults who have ever been told they had skin cancer	5.8	5.6
Adults who have ever been told they had any other types of cancer	9.3	8.4
Adults who have ever been told they have COPD	3.6	6.4
Adults who have ever been told they have kidney disease	4.0	3.7
Adults who have ever been told they have a form of depression	26.6	22.0

Note: All figures are crude prevalence; (1) Figures cover the Albuquerque, NM Metropolitan Statistical Area; (2) Figures do not include pregnancy-related, borderline, or pre-diabetes
Source: Centers for Disease Control and Prevention, Behavioral Risk Factor Surveillance System, SMART: Selected Metropolitan Area Risk Trends, 2023

Health Screening and Vaccination Rates

Category	MSA[1] (%)	U.S. (%)
Adults who have ever been tested for HIV	38.9	37.5
Adults who have had their blood cholesterol checked within the last five years	88.1	87.0
Adults aged 65+ who have had flu shot within the past year	69.4	63.4
Adults aged 65+ who have ever had a pneumonia vaccination	69.7	71.9

Note: All figures are crude prevalence; (1) Figures cover the Albuquerque, NM Metropolitan Statistical Area.
Source: Centers for Disease Control and Prevention, Behavioral Risk Factor Surveillance System, SMART: Selected Metropolitan Area Risk Trends, 2023

Disability Status

Category	MSA[1] (%)	U.S. (%)
Adults who reported being deaf	7.8	7.4
Are you blind or have serious difficulty seeing, even when wearing glasses?	7.0	4.9
Do you have difficulty doing errands alone?	8.1	7.8
Do you have difficulty dressing or bathing?	3.1	3.6
Do you have serious difficulty concentrating/remembering/making decisions?	14.4	13.7
Do you have serious difficulty walking or climbing stairs?	12.2	13.2

Note: All figures are crude prevalence; (1) Figures cover the Albuquerque, NM Metropolitan Statistical Area.
Source: Centers for Disease Control and Prevention, Behavioral Risk Factor Surveillance System, SMART: Selected Metropolitan Area Risk Trends, 2023

Mortality Rates for the Top 10 Causes of Death in the U.S.

ICD-10[a] Sub-Chapter	ICD-10[a] Code	Crude Mortality Rate[2] per 100,000 population	
		County[3]	U.S.
Malignant neoplasms	C00-C97	169.1	182.7
Ischaemic heart diseases	I20-I25	126.4	109.6
Provisional assignment of new diseases of uncertain etiology[1]	U00-U49	70.6	65.3
Other forms of heart disease	I30-I51	47.8	65.1
Other degenerative diseases of the nervous system	G30-G31	53.4	52.4
Other external causes of accidental injury	W00-X59	89.5	52.3
Cerebrovascular diseases	I60-I69	53.3	49.1
Chronic lower respiratory diseases	J40-J47	47.4	43.5
Hypertensive diseases	I10-I15	19.0	38.9
Organic, including symptomatic, mental disorders	F01-F09	28.9	33.9

Note: (a) ICD-10 = International Classification of Diseases 10th Revision; (1) Includes COVID-19, adverse effects to COVID-19 vaccines, SARS, and vaping-related disorders; (2) Crude mortality rates are a three-year average covering 2021-2023; (3) Figures cover Bernalillo County.
Source: Centers for Disease Control and Prevention, National Center for Health Statistics. National Vital Statistics System, Mortality 2018-2023 on CDC WONDER Online Database

Mortality Rates for Selected Causes of Death

Cause of Death	ICD-10[a] Code	Crude Mortality Rate[1] per 100,000 population	
		County[2]	U.S.
Accidental poisoning and exposure to noxious substances	X40-X49	64.3	30.5
Alzheimer disease	G30	40.8	35.4
Assault	X85-Y09	18.3	7.3
COVID-19	U07.1	70.6	65.3
Diabetes mellitus	E10-E14	30.8	30.0
Diseases of the liver	K70-K76	42.5	20.8
Human immunodeficiency virus (HIV) disease	B20-B24	1.1	1.5
Influenza and pneumonia	J09-J18	13.2	13.4
Intentional self-harm	X60-X84	23.8	14.7
Malnutrition	E40-E46	18.3	6.0
Obesity and other hyperalimentation	E65-E68	5.5	3.1
Renal failure	N17-N19	11.0	16.4
Transport accidents	V01-V99	20.2	14.4

Note: (a) ICD-10 = International Classification of Diseases 10th Revision; (1) Crude mortality rates are a three-year average covering 2021-2023; (2) Figures cover Bernalillo County; Data are suppressed when the data meet the criteria for confidentiality constraints; Crude mortality rates are flagged as unreliable when the rate would be calculated with a numerator of 20 or less.
Source: Centers for Disease Control and Prevention, National Center for Health Statistics. National Vital Statistics System, Mortality 2018-2023 on CDC WONDER Online Database

Health Insurance Coverage

Area	With Health Insurance	With Private Health Insurance	With Public Health Insurance	Without Health Insurance	Population Under Age 19 Without Health Insurance
City	91.7	60.1	45.1	8.3	5.0
MSA[1]	91.9	59.2	47.2	8.1	5.0
U.S.	91.4	67.3	36.3	8.6	5.4

Note: Figures are percentages that cover the civilian noninstitutionalized population; (1) Figures cover the Albuquerque, NM Metropolitan Statistical Area
Source: U.S. Census Bureau, 2019-2023 American Community Survey 5-Year Estimates

Number of Medical Professionals

Area	MDs[3]	DOs[3,4]	Dentists	Podiatrists	Chiropractors	Optometrists
County[1] (number)	3,386	206	587	63	167	119
County[1] (rate[2])	503.5	30.6	87.4	9.4	24.9	17.7
U.S. (rate[2])	302.5	29.2	74.6	6.4	29.5	18.0

Note: Data as of 2023 unless noted; (1) Data covers Bernalillo County; (2) Number of medical professionals per 100,000 population; (3) Data as of 2022 and includes all active, non-federal physicians; (4) Doctor of Osteopathic Medicine
Source: U.S. Department of Health and Human Services, Health Resources and Services Administration, Bureau of Health Professions, Area Resource File (ARF) 2023-2024

EDUCATION

Public School District Statistics

District Name	Schls	Pupils	Pupil/ Teacher Ratio	Minority Pupils[1] (%)	Total Rev. per Pupil ($)	Total Exp. per Pupil ($)
Albuquerque Public Schools	174	76,756	13.3	80.4	15,785	15,508
Mission Achievement and Success	2	2,255	16.5	94.5	12,824	12,889

Note: Table includes school districts with 2,000 or more students; (1) Percentage of students that are not non-Hispanic white.
Source: U.S. Department of Education, National Center for Education Statistics, Common Core of Data, Local Education Agency (School District) Universe Survey: School Year 2023-2024; U.S. Department of Education, National Center for Education Statistics, Common Core of Data, School District Finance Survey (F-33): School Year 2021–22

Best High Schools

According to *U.S. News,* Albuquerque is home to two of the top 500 high schools in the U.S.: **Albuquerque Institute of Math and Science** (#20); **Cottonwood Classical Prep** (#180). Nearly 25,000 public, magnet and charter schools were ranked based on their performance on state assessments and how well they prepare students for college. *U.S. News & World Report, "Best High Schools 2024"*

Highest Level of Education

Area	Less than H.S.	H.S. Diploma	Some College, No Deg.	Associate Degree	Bachelor's Degree	Master's Degree	Prof. School Degree	Doctorate Degree
City	9.1	21.6	21.2	9.5	20.9	12.0	2.8	2.9
MSA[1]	9.7	23.6	22.0	9.7	19.2	11.0	2.4	2.5
U.S.	10.6	26.2	19.4	8.8	21.3	9.8	2.3	1.6

Note: Figures cover persons age 25 and over; (1) Figures cover the Albuquerque, NM Metropolitan Statistical Area
Source: U.S. Census Bureau, 2019-2023 American Community Survey 5-Year Estimates

Educational Attainment by Race

Area	High School Graduate or Higher (%)					Bachelor's Degree or Higher (%)				
	Total	White	Black	Asian	Hisp.[2]	Total	White	Black	Asian	Hisp.[2]
City	90.9	94.6	94.0	88.3	84.4	38.7	45.2	38.8	51.0	25.4
MSA[1]	90.3	94.2	93.1	88.8	84.0	35.0	41.5	38.7	52.7	22.6
U.S.	89.4	92.9	88.1	88.0	72.5	35.0	37.7	24.7	57.0	19.9

Note: Figures shown cover persons 25 years old and over; (1) Figures cover the Albuquerque, NM Metropolitan Statistical Area; (2) People of Hispanic origin can be of any race
Source: U.S. Census Bureau, 2019-2023 American Community Survey 5-Year Estimates

School Enrollment by Grade and Control

Area	Preschool (%)		Kindergarten (%)		Grades 1 - 4 (%)		Grades 5 - 8 (%)		Grades 9 - 12 (%)	
	Public	Private	Public	Private	Public	Private	Public	Private	Public	Private
City	51.7	48.3	85.1	14.9	87.2	12.8	89.7	10.3	91.4	8.6
MSA[1]	60.4	39.6	84.3	15.7	86.3	13.7	88.4	11.6	90.3	9.7
U.S.	58.7	41.3	85.2	14.8	87.2	12.8	87.9	12.1	89.0	11.0

Note: Figures shown cover persons 3 years old and over; (1) Figures cover the Albuquerque, NM Metropolitan Statistical Area
Source: U.S. Census Bureau, 2019-2023 American Community Survey 5-Year Estimates

Higher Education

Four-Year Colleges			Two-Year Colleges			Medical Schools[1]	Law Schools[2]	Voc/ Tech[3]
Public	Private Non-profit	Private For-profit	Public	Private Non-profit	Private For-profit			
1	0	1	3	0	2	1	1	5

Note: Figures cover institutions located within the Albuquerque, NM Metropolitan Statistical Area and include main campuses only; (1) includes schools accredited by the Liaison Committee on Medical Education and the American Osteopathic Association's Commission on Osteopathic College Accreditation; (2) includes ABA-accredited schools, schools with provisional ABA accreditation, and state accredited schools; (3) includes all schools with programs that are less than 2 years.
Source: National Center for Education Statistics, Integrated Postsecondary Education System (IPEDS), 2023-24; Wikipedia, List of Medical Schools in the United States, accessed May 2, 2025; Wikipedia, List of Law Schools in the United States, accessed May 2, 2025

According to *U.S. News & World Report,* the Albuquerque, NM metro area is home to one of the top medical schools for primary care in the U.S.: **University of New Mexico** (Tier 1). *U.S. News* placed medical and osteopathic schools into tiers based on their research productivity, faculty and admissions data. Each school's tier was derived from its overall score, calculated by summing the weighted normalized values generated across several factors of academic quality, outlined below. There are four tiers, with tier 1 medical schools as the highest-performing and tier 4 as the lowest-performing. Only tier 1 and 2 schools are shown. Because of the tier presentation, *U.S. News* calculated overall scores based on their percentile performance among all rated schools instead of dividing against the rescaled score of the No. 1-performing schools. Tier 1 included schools with overall scores of 85 to 99. The cutoffs for tiers 2 through 4 were schools scoring 50 to 84, 15 to 49 and 1 to 14, respectively. The rankings are based on a weighted average of the following measures of quality: graduates practicing in primary care specialties; graduates entering primary care residencies; median MCAT total score; median undergraduate GPA; acceptance rate; and faculty resources. *U.S. News & World Report, "America's Best Graduate Schools, Medical, 2025"*

EMPLOYERS

Major Employers

Company Name	Industry
Albuquerque Public Schools	Education
Amazon	Online retail
Bernalilo County	Local government
Blue Cross Blue Shield	Call center/insurance
Central New Mexico Community College	Vocational schools
City of Albuquerque	Municipal government
City of Albuquerque Police Department	Municipal police
Jack Henry & Associates	Computers
Laguna Development Corporation	Grocery stores, independent
Mediplex of Massachusetts	Nursing home, exc skilled & intermediate care facility
Sandia Corporation	Noncommercial research organizations
Speridian Technologies	IT services
The Boeing Company	Aircraft
U.S. Fish and Wildlife Service	Fish & wildlife conservation agency, government
United States Department of Energy	Energy development & conservation agency, govt
United States Department of the Air Force	Testing laboratories
University of New Mexico	University
University of New Mexico Hospital	General medical & surgical hospitals
USAF	U.S. military
Veterans Health Administration	Administration of veterans' affiars
Veterans Hospital	General medical & surgical hospitals

Note: Companies shown are located within the Albuquerque, NM Metropolitan Statistical Area.
Source: Chambers of Commerce; State Departments of Labor; Wikipedia

PUBLIC SAFETY

Crime Rate

Area	Total Crime Rate	Violent Crime Rate				Property Crime Rate		
		Murder	Rape	Robbery	Aggrav. Assault	Burglary	Larceny -Theft	Motor Vehicle Theft
City	6,021.7	19.3	54.2	175.5	1,068.0	671.8	3,003.1	1,029.9
U.S.	2,290.9	5.7	38.0	66.5	264.1	250.7	1,347.2	318.7

Note: Figures are crimes per 100,000 population.
Source: FBI, Table 8, Offenses Known to Law Enforcement, by State by City, 2023

Hate Crimes

Area	Number of Quarters Reported	Number of Incidents per Bias Motivation					
		Race/Ethnicity/ Ancestry	Religion	Sexual Orientation	Disability	Gender	Gender Identity
City	4	2	0	1	0	0	0
U.S.	4	5,900	2,699	2,077	187	92	492

Source: Federal Bureau of Investigation, Hate Crime Statistics 2023

Identity Theft Consumer Reports

Area	Reports	Reports per 100,000 Population	Rank[2]
MSA[1]	1,563	170	219
U.S.	1,135,291	339	-

Note: (1) Figures cover the Albuquerque, NM Metropolitan Statistical Area; (2) Rank ranges from 1 to 401
where 1 indicates greatest number of identity theft reports per 100,000 population
Source: Federal Trade Commission, Consumer Sentinel Network Data Book 2024

Fraud and Other Consumer Reports

Area	Reports	Reports per 100,000 Population	Rank[2]
MSA[1]	10,534	1,147	146
U.S.	5,360,641	1,601	-

Note: (1) Figures cover the Albuquerque, NM Metropolitan Statistical Area; (2) Rank ranges from 1 to 401
where 1 indicates greatest number of fraud and other consumer reports per 100,000 population
Source: Federal Trade Commission, Consumer Sentinel Network Data Book 2024

POLITICS

2024 Presidential Election Results

Area	Trump (Rep.)	Harris (Dem.)	Stein (Green)	Kennedy (Ind.)	Oliver (Lib.)	Other
Bernalillo County	38.2	59.2	0.7	1.0	0.5	0.5
U.S.	49.7	48.2	0.6	0.5	0.4	0.6

Note: Results are percentages and may not add to 100% due to rounding
Source: Dave Leip's Atlas of U.S. Presidential Elections

SPORTS

Professional Sports Teams

Team Name	League	Year Established

No teams are located in the metro area
Source: Wikipedia, Major Professional Sports Teams of the United States and Canada, May 1, 2025

CLIMATE

Average and Extreme Temperatures

Temperature	Jan	Feb	Mar	Apr	May	Jun	Jul	Aug	Sep	Oct	Nov	Dec	Yr.
Extreme High (°F)	69	76	85	89	98	105	105	101	100	91	77	72	105
Average High (°F)	47	53	61	71	80	90	92	89	83	72	57	48	70
Average Temp. (°F)	35	40	47	56	65	75	79	76	70	58	45	36	57
Average Low (°F)	23	27	33	41	50	59	65	63	56	44	31	24	43
Extreme Low (°F)	-17	-5	8	19	28	40	52	50	37	21	-7	-7	-17

Note: Figures cover the years 1948-1992
Source: National Climatic Data Center, International Station Meteorological Climate Summary, 9/96

Average Precipitation/Snowfall/Humidity

Precip./Humidity	Jan	Feb	Mar	Apr	May	Jun	Jul	Aug	Sep	Oct	Nov	Dec	Yr.
Avg. Precip. (in.)	0.4	0.4	0.5	0.4	0.5	0.5	1.4	1.5	0.9	0.9	0.4	0.5	8.5
Avg. Snowfall (in.)	3	2	2	1	Tr	0	0	0	Tr	Tr	1	3	11
Avg. Rel. Hum. 5am (%)	68	64	55	48	48	45	60	65	61	60	63	68	59
Avg. Rel. Hum. 5pm (%)	41	33	25	20	19	18	27	30	29	29	35	43	29

Note: Figures cover the years 1948-1992; Tr = Trace amounts (<0.05 in. of rain; <0.5 in. of snow)
Source: National Climatic Data Center, International Station Meteorological Climate Summary, 9/96

Weather Conditions

Temperature			Daytime Sky			Precipitation		
10°F & below	32°F & below	90°F & above	Clear	Partly cloudy	Cloudy	0.01 inch or more precip.	0.1 inch or more snow/ice	Thunder-storms
4	114	65	140	160	65	60	9	38

Note: Figures are average number of days per year and cover the years 1948-1992
Source: National Climatic Data Center, International Station Meteorological Climate Summary, 9/96

HAZARDOUS WASTE

Superfund Sites

The Albuquerque, NM metro area is home to four sites on the EPA's Superfund National Priorities List (NPL) or Superfund Alternative Approach (SAA) list: **AT&SF (Albuquerque)** (Final NPL); **Carlisle Village Cleaners** (Proposed NPL); **Fruit Avenue Plume** (Final NPL); **South Valley** (Final NPL). The Superfund alternative approach uses the same investigation and cleanup process and standards that are used for sites listed on the National Priorities List. The SAA is an alternative to listing a site on the NPL; it is not an alternative to Superfund or the Superfund process. There are a total of 1,445 Superfund sites with a status of proposed or final on both lists in the United States. *U.S. Environmental Protection Agency, National Priorities List, May 1, 2025; U.S. Environmental Protection Agency, Superfund Alternative Approach Sites, May 1, 2025*

AIR QUALITY

Air Quality Trends: Ozone

	1990	1995	2000	2005	2010	2015	2020	2021	2022	2023
MSA[1]	0.072	0.070	0.072	0.073	0.066	0.066	0.071	0.071	0.071	0.067
U.S.	0.087	0.089	0.081	0.080	0.072	0.068	0.066	0.067	0.067	0.070

Note: (1) Data covers the Albuquerque, NM Metropolitan Statistical Area. The values shown are the composite ozone concentration averages among trend sites based on the highest fourth daily maximum 8-hour concentration in parts per million. These trends are based on sites having an adequate record of monitoring data during the trend period. Data from exceptional events are included.
Source: U.S. Environmental Protection Agency, Air Quality Monitoring Information, "Air Quality Trends by City, 1990-2023"

Air Quality Index

Area	Percent of Days when Air Quality was...[2]					AQI Statistics[2]	
	Good	Moderate	Unhealthy for Sensitive Groups	Unhealthy	Very Unhealthy	Maximum	Median
MSA[1]	26.6	72.3	0.8	0.0	0.3	207	60

Note: (1) Data covers the Albuquerque, NM Metropolitan Statistical Area; (2) Based on 365 days with AQI data in 2023. Air Quality Index (AQI) is an index for reporting daily air quality. EPA calculates the AQI for five major air pollutants regulated by the Clean Air Act: ground-level ozone, particle pollution (aka particulate matter), carbon monoxide, sulfur dioxide, and nitrogen dioxide. The AQI runs from 0 to 500. The higher the AQI value, the greater the level of air pollution and the greater the health concern. There are six AQI categories: "Good" AQI is between 0 and 50. Air quality is considered satisfactory; "Moderate" AQI is between 51 and 100. Air quality is acceptable; "Unhealthy for Sensitive Groups" When AQI values are between 101 and 150, members of sensitive groups may experience health effects; "Unhealthy" When AQI values are between 151 and 200 everyone may begin to experience health effects; "Very Unhealthy" AQI values between 201 and 300 trigger a health alert; "Hazardous" AQI values over 300 trigger warnings of emergency conditions (not shown).
Source: U.S. Environmental Protection Agency, Air Quality Index Report, 2023

Air Quality Index Pollutants

Area	Percent of Days when AQI Pollutant was...[2]					
	Carbon Monoxide	Nitrogen Dioxide	Ozone	Sulfur Dioxide	Particulate Matter 2.5	Particulate Matter 10
MSA[1]	0.0	0.3	53.2	(3)	23.8	22.7

Note: (1) Data covers the Albuquerque, NM Metropolitan Statistical Area; (2) Based on 365 days with AQI data in 2023. The Air Quality Index (AQI) is an index for reporting daily air quality. EPA calculates the AQI for five major air pollutants regulated by the Clean Air Act: ground-level ozone, particle pollution (also known as particulate matter), carbon monoxide, sulfur dioxide, and nitrogen dioxide. The AQI runs from 0 to 500. The higher the AQI value, the greater the level of air pollution and the greater the health concern; (3) Sulfur dioxide is no longer included in this table because SO_2 concentrations tend to be very localized and not necessarily representative of broad geographical areas like counties and CBSAs.
Source: U.S. Environmental Protection Agency, Air Quality Index Report, 2023

Maximum Air Pollutant Concentrations: Particulate Matter, Ozone, CO and Lead

	Particulate Matter 10 (ug/m^3)	Particulate Matter 2.5 Wtd AM (ug/m^3)	Particulate Matter 2.5 24-Hr (ug/m^3)	Ozone (ppm)	Carbon Monoxide (ppm)	Lead (ug/m^3)
MSA[1] Level	182	7.5	23	0.069	2	n/a
NAAQS[2]	150	15	35	0.075	9	0.15
Met NAAQS[2]	No	Yes	Yes	Yes	Yes	n/a

Note: (1) Data covers the Albuquerque, NM Metropolitan Statistical Area; Data from exceptional events are included; (2) National Ambient Air Quality Standards; ppm = parts per million; ug/m^3 = micrograms per cubic meter; n/a not available.
Concentrations: Particulate Matter 10 (coarse particulate)—highest second maximum 24-hour concentration; Particulate Matter 2.5 Wtd AM (fine particulate)—highest weighted annual mean concentration; Particulate Matter 2.5 24-Hour (fine particulate)—highest 98th percentile 24-hour concentration; Ozone—highest fourth daily maximum 8-hour concentration; Carbon Monoxide—highest second maximum non-overlapping 8-hour concentration; Lead—maximum running 3-month average
Source: U.S. Environmental Protection Agency, Air Quality Monitoring Information, "Air Quality Statistics by City, 2023"

Maximum Air Pollutant Concentrations: Nitrogen Dioxide and Sulfur Dioxide

	Nitrogen Dioxide AM (ppb)	Nitrogen Dioxide 1-Hr (ppb)	Sulfur Dioxide AM (ppb)	Sulfur Dioxide 1-Hr (ppb)	Sulfur Dioxide 24-Hr (ppb)
MSA[1] Level	8	43	n/a	n/a	n/a
NAAQS[2]	53	100	30	75	140
Met NAAQS[2]	Yes	Yes	n/a	n/a	n/a

Note: (1) Data covers the Albuquerque, NM Metropolitan Statistical Area; Data from exceptional events are included; (2) National Ambient Air Quality Standards; ppm = parts per million; ug/m^3 = micrograms per cubic meter; n/a not available.
Concentrations: Nitrogen Dioxide AM—highest arithmetic mean concentration; Nitrogen Dioxide 1-Hr—highest 98th percentile 1-hour daily maximum concentration; Sulfur Dioxide AM—highest annual mean concentration; Sulfur Dioxide 1-Hr—highest 99th percentile 1-hour daily maximum concentration; Sulfur Dioxide 24-Hr—highest second maximum 24-hour concentration
Source: U.S. Environmental Protection Agency, Air Quality Monitoring Information, "Air Quality Statistics by City, 2023"

Anchorage, Alaska

Background

Anchorage, in south central Alaska, is the state's largest city and a center for its communication, transportation, health care, and finance industries. Originally powered by the railroads and the fishing industry, Anchorage's economy has more recently been closely tied to petroleum production, which accounts for more than 20 percent of the nation's oil reserves.

This modern city lies in a spectacular natural setting, with the Chugach Mountain Range across its eastern skyline and the waters of the Cook Inlet to the west. The city boasts all the advantages of a dynamic urban center, while its residents enjoy a natural environment that teems with bear, moose, caribou, fox, eagles, wolves, Dall sheep, orcas, and beluga whales.

The city was incorporated in 1920 and grew slowly for several decades. During World War II, when airfields and roads were constructed to aid in the war effort, the population expanded dramatically; by 1946, Anchorage was home to more than 40,000 people.

In 1964, the region was hit by the strongest earthquake ever to strike North America. There was extensive damage and some loss of life, but the city was quickly rebuilt; in fact, reconstruction was so prompt, efficient, and successful that many look back on the period with considerable civic pride. Earthquakes are not uncommon to the region, and a moderate 5.7 event occurred in Anchorage in January 2009.

In 1951, Anchorage International Airport, now Ted Stevens International Airport (ANC), was completed, and the city became vital to the emerging air transport industry as new routes were created. Ted Stevens International Airport flies nearly 600 transcontinental cargo flights each week and is the busiest cargo airport in the country. Elmendorf Air Force Base at the northeast end of town, and Anchorage's pioneering development of bush aviation, which serves the entire interior of Alaska, further testify to the importance of air travel to the city's development. Also located at the airport are Fort Richardson Army Post and Kulis Air National Guard Base that together employ 8,500.

Oil in Alaska was first discovered in 1957, and 17 oil companies subsequently set up headquarters in Anchorage, giving the city a tremendous economic boost. In 1968, when the large North Slope field was discovered, Anchorage was again a major beneficiary. With the completion of the Trans-Alaskan Pipeline System in 1977, Anchorage entered its contemporary period of sustained population growth and dynamic economic development.

Tourism accounts for 1 in 9 jobs in Anchorage. More than $30 million is collected in local hotel and car rental taxes alone, and visitors spend hundreds of millions in Anchorage annually. Anchorage is also known as a tax-friendly city, with no sales or personal income tax.

The city's cultural amenities include the Anchorage Museum at Rasmuson Center and the Alaska Aviation Heritage Museum, which chronicles the story of Alaska's early and pioneering air transport system. Near the city is the Potter Section House Railway Museum, which pays homage to the state's vital rail industry. The city also boasts the Alaska Center for the Performing Arts and the Alaska Botanical Garden. Delaney Park, also known as the Park Strip, is a venerable and valued recreational resource in the city's business district, and its ongoing improvement looks toward a year-round "Central Park" for Anchorage. The Alaska State Fair has been recognized as one of the Top 100 Events in North America.

The city is an educational center with two universities and many technical, vocational, and private schools. A campus of the University of Alaska has been in Anchorage since 1954, and the city is also home to Alaska Pacific University. The city is part of the statewide homeschool program AKChoice K-12 Learning, offering the opportunity to combine home schooling with in school learning.

The natural environment of Anchorage is spectacular, and at nearby Portage Glacier, one can watch the glacier "calving," as huge blocks of ice crash into the lake below. Anchorage is also located at one end of the famous annual Iditarod Trail Sled Dog Race.

Because of its long summer days and relatively mild temperatures, Anchorage is called "The City of Lights and Flowers," and open grassy expanses are adorned throughout the summer season with lights and flowers. Summer also brings out a friendly competition among the city's residents, who plant colorful flowers along streets, in parks, private gardens, window boxes, and lobbies.

The weather in Anchorage, contrary to what many believe, is not savagely cold. It is tempered by the city's location on the coast and by the Alaska Mountain Range, which acts as a barrier to very cold air from the north. Snow season lasts from October to May. Summers can bring fog and rain.

Rankings

General Rankings

- To help military veterans find the best places in which to settle down, *WalletHub* compared the 100 largest U.S. cities across 19 key indicators of livability, affordability and veteran-friendliness. They range from the share of military skill-related jobs to veteran income growth to the availability of VA health facilities. Anchorage ranked #45. *Wallethub.com, "Best & Worst Places for Veterans to Live (2025)," November 7, 2024*

- *Insider* listed 23 places in the U.S. that travel industry trends reveal would be popular destinations in 2023. This year the list trends towards cultural and historical happenings, sports events, wellness experiences and invigorating outdoor escapes. According to the website insider.com Anchorage is a place to visit in 2023. *Insider, "23 of the Best Places You Should Travel to in the U.S. in 2023," December 17, 2022*

- Anchorage was selected as one of the happiest places to live in America by *Outside Magazine*. Criteria centered on overall well being; effect of climate change; inclusivity; affordability; outdoor access; and other demographic and population figures. Local experts shared highlights from hands-on experience in each location. *Outside Magazine, "The 15 Happiest Places to Live in the U.S.," September 18, 2023*

- In their annual survey, Livability.com looked at data for more than 2,000 mid-sized U.S. cities to assign a "Livability Score" for each. The top 100 scoring cities make up Livability's "Top 100 Best Places to Live in the U.S." in 2025. Anchorage was placed among the top 100 of the customizable list. Criteria: housing and economy; cost of living; environment; education; health care options; transportation; safety; and community amenities. *Livability.com, "Top 100 Best Places to Live in the U.S. in 2025" April 15, 2025*

Business/Finance Rankings

- The Anchorage metro area appeared on the Milken Institute "2025 Best Performing Cities" list. Rank: #49 out of 200 large metro areas (based on performance category). Criteria: job growth; wage growth; high-tech growth and impact; community resilience; housing affordability; household broadband access. *Milken Institute, "Best-Performing Cities 2025," January 14, 2025*

Education Rankings

- Personal finance website *WalletHub* analyzed the 150 largest U.S. metropolitan statistical areas to determine where the most educated Americans are putting their degrees to work. Criteria: education levels; percentage of workers with degrees; education quality and attainment gap; public school quality rankings; quality and enrollment of each metro area's universities. Anchorage was ranked #68 (#1 = most educated city). *WalletHub.com, "Most & Least Educated Cities in America, 2025" July 2, 2024*

Environmental Rankings

- Anchorage was highlighted as one of the top 25 cleanest metro areas for year-round particle pollution (Annual PM 2.5) in the U.S. during 2021 through 2023. The area ranked #6. *American Lung Association, "State of the Air 2025," April 23, 2025*

Health/Fitness Rankings

- For each of the 100 largest cities in the United States, the American Fitness Index®, compiled in partnership between the American College of Sports Medicine and the Elevance Health Foundation, evaluated community infrastructure and more than 30 health behaviors including preventive health, levels of chronic disease conditions, food insecurity, pedestrian safety, air quality, and community/environment resources that support physical activity. Anchorage ranked #39 for "community fitness." *americanfitnessindex.org, "2024 ACSM American Fitness Index Summary Report," July 23, 2024*

Real Estate Rankings

- *WalletHub* compared the most populated U.S. cities to determine which had the best markets for real estate agents. Anchorage ranked #140 where demand was high and pay was the best. Criteria: sales per agent; annual median wage for real-estate agents; monthly average starting salary for real estate agents; real estate job density and competition; unemployment rate; home turnover rate; housing-market health index; and other relevant metrics. *WalletHub.com, "2021 Best Places to Be a Real Estate Agent," May 12, 2021*

- The Anchorage metro area was identified as one of the 20 best housing markets in the U.S. in 2024. The area ranked #17 out of 226 markets. Criteria: year-over-year change of median sales price of existing single-family homes between the 4th quarter of 2023 and the 4th quarter of 2024. *National Association of Realtors®, Median Sales Price of Existing Single-Family Homes for Metropolitan Areas, 4th Quarter 2024*

Safety Rankings

- To identify the most dangerous cities in America, *24/7 Wall St.* focused on violent crime categories—murder, non-negligent manslaughter, rape, robbery, and aggravated assault—as reported for every 100,000 residents using data from the FBI's 2020 annual Uniform Crime Report. For cities with populations over 25,000, Anchorage was ranked #38. *247wallst.com, "America's Most Dangerous Cities" November 12, 2021*

- Anchorage was identified as one of the most dangerous cities in America by NeighborhoodScout. The city ranked #59 out of 100 (#1 = most dangerous). Criteria: number of violent crimes per 1,000 residents. The editors evaluated cities with 25,000 or more residents. *NeighborhoodScout.com, "2023 Top 100 Most Dangerous Cities in the U.S.," January 12, 2023*

Women/Minorities Rankings

- Personal finance website *WalletHub* compared more than 180 U.S. cities across two key dimensions, "Hispanic Business-Friendliness" and "Hispanic Purchasing Power," to arrive at the most favorable conditions for Hispanic entrepreneurs. Anchorage was ranked #84 out of 182. Criteria includes: share of Hispanic-Owned Businesses; average growth of Hispanic Business revenues; Small Business-Friendliness score; affordability; and number of Hispanics with at least a bachelor's degree. *WalletHub.com, "Best Cities for Hispanic Entrepreneurs," September 4, 2024*

Miscellaneous Rankings

- *WalletHub* compared 148 of the most populated U.S. cities to determine their operating efficiency. A "Quality of Services" score was constructed for each city and then measured against the total budget per capita to reveal which were managed the best. Anchorage ranked #75. Criteria: financial stability; economy; education; safety; health; infrastructure and pollution. *WalletHub.com, "2025's Best- & Worst-Run Cities in America," June 18, 2024*

Business Environment

DEMOGRAPHICS

Population Growth

Area	1990 Census	2000 Census	2010 Census	2020 Census	2023 Estimate[2]	Population Growth 1990-2023 (%)
City	226,338	260,283	291,826	291,247	289,069	27.7
MSA[1]	266,021	319,605	380,821	398,328	399,746	50.3
U.S.	248,709,873	281,421,906	308,745,538	331,449,281	332,387,540	33.6

Note: (1) Figures cover the Anchorage, AK Metropolitan Statistical Area; (2) 2019-2023 5-year ACS population estimate
Source: U.S. Census Bureau, 1990 Census, 2000 Census, 2010 Census, 2020 Census, 2019-2023 American Community Survey 5-Year Estimates

Race

Area	White Alone[2] (%)	Black Alone[2] (%)	Asian Alone[2] (%)	AIAN[3] Alone[2] (%)	NHOPI[4] Alone[2] (%)	Other Race Alone[2] (%)	Two or More Races (%)
City	58.3	5.3	9.8	7.3	3.1	3.1	13.1
MSA[1]	63.8	4.2	7.6	6.9	2.4	2.7	12.5
U.S.	63.4	12.4	5.8	0.9	0.2	6.6	10.7

Note: (1) Figures cover the Anchorage, AK Metropolitan Statistical Area; (2) Alone is defined as not being in combination with one or more other races; (3) American Indian and Alaska Native; (4) Native Hawaiian and Other Pacific Islander
Source: U.S. Census Bureau, 2019-2023 American Community Survey 5-Year Estimates

Hispanic or Latino Origin

Area	Total (%)	Mexican (%)	Puerto Rican (%)	Cuban (%)	Other (%)
City	9.3	4.2	1.4	0.5	3.1
MSA[1]	8.2	3.8	1.2	0.4	2.8
U.S.	19.0	11.3	1.8	0.7	5.2

Note: Persons of Hispanic or Latino origin can be of any race; (1) Figures cover the Anchorage, AK Metropolitan Statistical Area
Source: U.S. Census Bureau, 2019-2023 American Community Survey 5-Year Estimates

Age

Area	Under Age 5	Age 5–19	Age 20–34	Age 35–44	Age 45–54	Age 55–64	Age 65–74	Age 75–84	Age 85+	Median Age
City	6.5	19.6	24.0	14.2	11.6	11.6	8.2	3.4	0.9	34.9
MSA[1]	6.5	20.2	22.8	14.2	11.7	11.9	8.5	3.3	0.9	35.4
U.S.	5.7	19.1	20.2	13.1	12.3	12.8	10.0	4.9	1.9	38.7

Note: (1) Figures cover the Anchorage, AK Metropolitan Statistical Area
Source: U.S. Census Bureau, 2019-2023 American Community Survey 5-Year Estimates

Disability by Age

Area	All Ages	Under 18 Years Old	18 to 64 Years Old	65 Years and Over
City	12.2	4.9	10.7	33.7
MSA[1]	12.6	4.8	11.3	34.0
U.S.	13.0	4.7	10.7	32.9

Note: Figures show percent of the civilian noninstitutionalized population that reported having a disability. Disability status is determined from six types of difficulty: vision, hearing, cognitive, ambulatory, self-care, and independent living. For children under 5 years old, hearing and vision difficulty are used to determine disability status. For children between the ages of 5 and 14, disability status is determined from hearing, vision, cognitive, ambulatory, and self-care difficulties. For people aged 15 years and older, they are considered to have a disability if they have difficulty with any one of the six difficulty types; Note: (1) Figures cover the Anchorage, AK Metropolitan Statistical Area
Source: U.S. Census Bureau, 2019-2023 American Community Survey 5-Year Estimates

Ancestry

Area	German	Irish	English	American	Italian	Polish	French[2]	European	Scottish
City	13.5	9.0	9.9	3.6	3.1	1.9	1.9	2.1	1.8
MSA[1]	14.5	9.7	10.1	4.2	2.9	1.9	1.9	2.1	1.9
U.S.	12.6	9.4	9.1	5.5	4.9	2.6	2.0	1.6	1.6

Note: Figures are the percentage of the total population reporting a particular ancestry. The nine most commonly reported ancestries in the U.S. are shown. Figures include multiple ancestries (e.g. if a person reported being Irish and Italian, they were included in both columns); (1) Figures cover the Anchorage, AK Metropolitan Statistical Area; (2) Excludes Basque
Source: U.S. Census Bureau, 2019-2023 American Community Survey 5-Year Estimates

Foreign-born Population

Area	Any Foreign Country	Asia	Mexico	Europe	Caribbean	Central America[2]	South America	Africa	Canada
				Percent of Population Born in					
City	10.9	6.0	0.6	1.2	0.5	0.2	0.6	0.5	0.4
MSA[1]	8.7	4.6	0.5	1.2	0.4	0.2	0.5	0.4	0.3
U.S.	13.9	4.3	3.3	1.4	1.4	1.2	1.2	0.8	0.2

Note: (1) Figures cover the Anchorage, AK Metropolitan Statistical Area; (2) Excludes Mexico.
Source: U.S. Census Bureau, 2019-2023 American Community Survey 5-Year Estimates

Household Size

Area	One	Two	Three	Four	Five	Six	Seven or More	Average Household Size
	Persons in Household (%)							
City	28.5	33.7	14.8	13.5	5.4	2.3	1.8	2.61
MSA[1]	27.2	33.9	14.5	13.6	6.1	2.7	2.1	2.64
U.S.	28.5	33.8	15.4	12.7	5.9	2.3	1.4	2.54

Note: (1) Figures cover the Anchorage, AK Metropolitan Statistical Area
Source: U.S. Census Bureau, 2019-2023 American Community Survey 5-Year Estimates

Household Relationships

Area	House-holder	Opposite-sex Spouse	Same-sex Spouse	Opposite-sex Unmarried Partner	Same-sex Unmarried Partner	Child[2]	Grand-child	Other Relatives	Non-relatives
City	37.5	17.0	0.2	3.0	0.2	28.3	1.9	4.6	4.2
MSA[1]	37.1	17.6	0.2	2.9	0.1	29.1	1.9	4.2	4.0
U.S.	38.3	17.5	0.2	2.5	0.2	28.3	2.4	4.8	3.4

Note: Figures are percent of the total population; (1) Figures cover the Anchorage, AK Metropolitan Statistical Area; (2) Includes biological, adopted, and stepchildren of the householder
Source: U.S. Census Bureau, 2020 Census

Gender

Area	Males	Females	Males per 100 Females
City	147,620	141,449	104.4
MSA[1]	205,511	194,235	105.8
U.S.	164,545,087	167,842,453	98.0

Note: (1) Figures cover the Anchorage, AK Metropolitan Statistical Area
Source: U.S. Census Bureau, 2019-2023 American Community Survey 5-Year Estimates

Marital Status

Area	Never Married	Now Married[2]	Separated	Widowed	Divorced
City	34.6	47.7	1.9	3.5	12.2
MSA[1]	33.3	49.3	1.8	3.7	11.9
U.S.	34.1	47.9	1.7	5.6	10.7

Note: Figures are percentages and cover the population 15 years of age and older; (1) Figures cover the Anchorage, AK Metropolitan Statistical Area; (2) Excludes separated
Source: U.S. Census Bureau, 2019-2023 American Community Survey 5-Year Estimates

Religious Groups by Family

Area	Catholic	Baptist	Methodist	LDS[2]	Pentecostal	Lutheran	Islam	Adventist	Other
MSA[1]	4.9	3.4	1.0	5.1	1.7	1.5	0.1	1.7	16.3
U.S.	18.7	7.3	3.0	2.0	1.8	1.7	1.3	1.3	11.6

Note: Figures are the number of adherents as a percentage of the total population and cover the eight largest religious groups in the U.S; (1) Figures cover the Anchorage, AK Metropolitan Statistical Area; (2) Church of Jesus Christ of Latter-day Saints
Sources: 2020 U.S. Religion Census, Association of Statisticians of American Religious Bodies; The Association of Religion Data Archives (ARDA)

Religious Groups by Tradition

Area	Catholic	Evangelical Protestant	Mainline Protestant	Black Protestant	Islam	Judaism	Hinduism	Orthodox	Buddhism
MSA[1]	4.9	19.2	2.4	0.9	0.1	0.1	0.1	0.5	1.3
U.S.	18.7	16.5	5.2	2.3	1.3	0.6	0.4	0.4	0.3

Note: Figures are the number of adherents as a percentage of the total population; (1) Figures cover the Anchorage, AK Metropolitan Statistical Area
Sources: 2020 U.S. Religion Census, Association of Statisticians of American Religious Bodies; The Association of Religion Data Archives (ARDA)

ECONOMY

Real Gross Domestic Product (GDP)

Area	2017	2018	2019	2020	2021	2022	2023	Rank[3]
MSA[1]	25.8	26.0	26.0	25.3	25.9	26.3	27.3	116
U.S.[2]	17,619.1	18,160.7	18,642.5	18,238.9	19,387.6	19,896.6	20,436.3	–

Note: Figures are in billions of chained 2017 dollars; (1) Figures cover the Anchorage, AK Metropolitan Statistical Area; (2) Figures cover real GDP within metropolitan areas; (3) Rank is based on 2023 data and ranges from 1 to 384
Source: U.S. Bureau of Economic Analysis

Economic Growth

Area	2014	2015	2016	2017	2018	2019	2020	2021	2022	2023
MSA[1]	0.3	4.3	1.2	-1.5	0.7	-0.3	-2.6	2.6	1.4	3.7
U.S.[2]	2.6	3.2	2.0	2.7	3.1	2.7	-2.2	6.3	2.6	2.7

Note: Figures are real gross domestic product growth rates and represent percent change from preceding period; (1) Figures cover the Anchorage, AK Metropolitan Statistical Area; (2) Figures are the average growth rates within metropolitan areas
Source: U.S. Bureau of Economic Analysis

Metropolitan Area Exports

Area	2018	2019	2020	2021	2022	2023	Rank[2]
MSA[1]	1,510.8	1,348.0	990.9	n/a	n/a	n/a	n/a
U.S.	1,664,056.1	1,645,173.7	1,431,406.6	1,753,941.4	2,062,937.4	2,019,160.5	–

Note: Figures are in millions of dollars; (1) Figures cover the Anchorage, AK Metropolitan Statistical Area; (2) Rank is based on 2023 data and ranges from 1 to 386
Source: U.S. Department of Commerce, International Trade Administration, Office of Trade and Economic Analysis, Industry and Analysis, Exports by Metropolitan Area, data extracted April 2, 2025

Building Permits

Area	Single-Family			Multi-Family			Total		
	2023	2024	Pct. Chg.	2023	2024	Pct. Chg.	2023	2024	Pct. Chg.
City	271	161	-40.6	28	180	542.9	299	341	14.0
MSA[1]	338	198	-41.4	119	228	91.6	457	426	-6.8
U.S.	920,000	981,900	6.7	591,100	496,100	-16.1	1,511,100	1,478,000	-2.2

Note: (1) Figures cover the Anchorage, AK Metropolitan Statistical Area; Figures represent new, privately-owned housing units authorized (unadjusted data)
Source: U.S. Census Bureau, Building Permits Survey (BPS), 2023, 2024

Bankruptcy Filings

Area	Business Filings			Nonbusiness Filings		
	2023	2024	% Chg.	2023	2024	% Chg.
Anchorage Borough	9	7	-22.2	113	90	-20.4
U.S.	18,926	23,107	22.1	434,064	494,201	13.9

Note: Business filings include Chapter 7, Chapter 9, Chapter 11, Chapter 12, Chapter 13, Chapter 15, and Section 304; Nonbusiness filings include Chapter 7, Chapter 11, and Chapter 13
Source: Administrative Office of the U.S. Courts, Business and Nonbusiness Bankruptcy, County Cases Commenced by Chapter of the Bankruptcy Code, During the 12-Month Period Ending December 31, 2023 and Business and Nonbusiness Bankruptcy, County Cases Commenced by Chapter of the Bankruptcy Code, During the 12-Month Period Ending December 31, 2024

Housing Vacancy Rates

Area	Gross Vacancy Rate[3] (%)			Year-Round Vacancy Rate[4] (%)			Rental Vacancy Rate[5] (%)			Homeowner Vacancy Rate[6] (%)		
	2022	2023	2024	2022	2023	2024	2022	2023	2024	2022	2023	2024
MSA[1]	n/a	n/a	n/a	n/a	n/a	n/a	n/a	n/a	n/a	n/a	n/a	n/a
U.S.[2]	9.1	9.0	9.1	7.5	7.5	7.6	5.7	6.5	6.8	0.8	0.8	1.0

Note: (1) Figures cover the Anchorage, AK Metropolitan Statistical Area; (2) Figures cover the 75 largest Metropolitan Statistical Areas; (3) The percentage of the total housing inventory that is vacant; (4) The percentage of the housing inventory (excluding seasonal units) that is year-round vacant; (5) The percentage of rental inventory that is vacant for rent; (6) The percentage of homeowner inventory that is vacant for sale; n/a not available
Source: U.S. Census Bureau, Housing Vacancies and Homeownership Annual Statistics: 2022, 2023, 2024

INCOME

Income

Area	Per Capita ($)	Median Household ($)	Average Household ($)
City	49,338	98,152	127,598
MSA[1]	47,015	95,918	123,232
U.S.	43,289	78,538	110,491

Note: (1) Figures cover the Anchorage, AK Metropolitan Statistical Area
Source: U.S. Census Bureau, 2019-2023 American Community Survey 5-Year Estimates

Household Income Distribution

Area	Percent of Households Earning							
	Under $15,000	$15,000 -$24,999	$25,000 -$34,999	$35,000 -$49,999	$50,000 -$74,999	$75,000 -$99,999	$100,000 -$149,999	$150,000 and up
City	5.2	4.6	4.4	8.3	14.6	13.7	19.5	29.7
MSA[1]	5.4	4.9	4.7	8.5	14.6	13.8	19.8	28.2
U.S.	8.5	6.6	6.8	10.4	15.7	12.7	17.4	21.9

Note: (1) Figures cover the Anchorage, AK Metropolitan Statistical Area
Source: U.S. Census Bureau, 2019-2023 American Community Survey 5-Year Estimates

Poverty Rate

Area	All Ages	Under 18 Years Old	18 to 64 Years Old	65 Years and Over
City	9.3	11.3	8.8	7.8
MSA[1]	9.6	11.6	9.1	7.9
U.S.	12.4	16.3	11.6	10.4

Note: Figures are percentage of people whose income during the past 12 months was below the poverty level;
(1) Figures cover the Anchorage, AK Metropolitan Statistical Area
Source: U.S. Census Bureau, 2019-2023 American Community Survey 5-Year Estimates

EMPLOYMENT

Labor Force and Employment

Area	Civilian Labor Force			Workers Employed		
	Dec. 2023	Dec. 2024	% Chg.	Dec. 2023	Dec. 2024	% Chg.
City	153,020	155,068	1.3	147,538	149,604	1.4
MSA[1]	203,512	206,186	1.3	195,498	198,110	1.3
U.S.	166,661,000	167,746,000	0.7	160,754,000	161,294,000	0.3

Note: Data is not seasonally adjusted and covers workers 16 years of age and older; (1) Figures cover the Anchorage, AK Metropolitan Statistical Area
Source: Bureau of Labor Statistics, Local Area Unemployment Statistics

Unemployment Rate

Area	2024											
	Jan.	Feb.	Mar.	Apr.	May	Jun.	Jul.	Aug.	Sep.	Oct.	Nov.	Dec.
City	4.0	4.2	3.8	3.7	3.6	4.2	3.8	3.5	3.5	3.6	3.8	3.5
MSA[1]	4.4	4.6	4.2	4.0	3.9	4.5	4.1	3.7	3.7	3.9	4.2	3.9
U.S.	4.1	4.2	3.9	3.5	3.7	4.3	4.5	4.4	3.9	3.9	4.0	3.8

Note: Data is not seasonally adjusted and covers workers 16 years of age and older; (1) Figures cover the Anchorage, AK Metropolitan Statistical Area
Source: Bureau of Labor Statistics, Local Area Unemployment Statistics

Average Wages

Occupation	$/Hr.	Occupation	$/Hr.
Accountants and Auditors	42.24	Maintenance and Repair Workers	27.18
Automotive Mechanics	31.29	Marketing Managers	60.07
Bookkeepers	26.96	Network and Computer Systems Admin.	45.18
Carpenters	36.09	Nurses, Licensed Practical	37.16
Cashiers	17.64	Nurses, Registered	54.49
Computer Programmers	44.68	Nursing Assistants	22.44
Computer Systems Analysts	45.88	Office Clerks, General	25.42
Computer User Support Specialists	30.11	Physical Therapists	54.28
Construction Laborers	30.31	Physicians	n/a
Cooks, Restaurant	19.67	Plumbers, Pipefitters and Steamfitters	40.27
Customer Service Representatives	22.30	Police and Sheriff's Patrol Officers	52.82
Dentists	96.63	Postal Service Mail Carriers	27.61
Electricians	38.60	Real Estate Sales Agents	43.45
Engineers, Electrical	57.20	Retail Salespersons	19.57
Fast Food and Counter Workers	16.07	Sales Representatives, Technical/Scientific	40.10
Financial Managers	66.10	Secretaries, Exc. Legal/Medical/Executive	21.78
First-Line Supervisors of Office Workers	34.12	Security Guards	26.71
General and Operations Managers	67.82	Surgeons	n/a
Hairdressers/Cosmetologists	n/a	Teacher Assistants, Exc. Postsecondary[1]	16.43
Home Health and Personal Care Aides	18.20	Teachers, Secondary School, Exc. Sp. Ed.[1]	39.21
Janitors and Cleaners	19.57	Telemarketers	n/a
Landscaping/Groundskeeping Workers	21.86	Truck Drivers, Heavy/Tractor-Trailer	31.27
Lawyers	65.58	Truck Drivers, Light/Delivery Services	29.20
Maids and Housekeeping Cleaners	18.49	Waiters and Waitresses	20.08

Note: Wage data covers the Anchorage, AK Metropolitan Statistical Area; (1) Hourly wages were calculated from annual wage data based on a 40 hour work week
Source: Bureau of Labor Statistics, Metro Area Occupational Employment & Wage Estimates, May 2024

Employment by Industry

| Sector | MSA[1] | | U.S. |
	Number of Employees	Percent of Total	Percent of Total
Construction	11,300	6.2	5.1
Financial Activities	7,300	4.0	5.8
Government	35,000	19.3	14.9
Information	3,100	1.7	1.9
Leisure and Hospitality	19,800	10.9	10.4
Manufacturing	2,300	1.3	8.0
Mining and Logging	2,000	1.1	0.4
Other Services	6,800	3.7	3.7
Private Education and Health Services	34,600	19.1	16.9
Professional and Business Services	19,900	11.0	14.2
Retail Trade	19,700	10.9	10.0
Transportation, Warehousing, and Utilities	14,500	8.0	4.8
Wholesale Trade	5,100	2.8	3.9

Note: Figures are non-farm employment as of December 2024. Figures are not seasonally adjusted and include workers 16 years of age and older; (1) Figures cover the Anchorage, AK Metropolitan Statistical Area
Source: Bureau of Labor Statistics, Current Employment Statistics, Employment, Hours, and Earnings

Employment by Occupation

Occupation Classification	City (%)	MSA[1] (%)	U.S. (%)
Management, Business, Science, and Arts	42.7	41.1	42.0
Natural Resources, Construction, and Maintenance	8.3	10.4	8.6
Production, Transportation, and Material Moving	11.3	11.3	13.0
Sales and Office	20.4	20.0	19.9
Service	17.2	17.2	16.5

Note: Figures cover employed civilians 16 years of age and older; (1) Figures cover the Anchorage, AK Metropolitan Statistical Area
Source: U.S. Census Bureau, 2019-2023 American Community Survey 5-Year Estimates

Occupations with Greatest Projected Employment Growth: 2022 – 2032

Occupation[1]	2022 Employment	2032 Projected Employment	Numeric Employment Change	Percent Employment Change
Meat, Poultry, and Fish Cutters and Trimmers	5,220	5,960	740	14.2
Home Health and Personal Care Aides	4,550	5,260	710	15.6
Registered Nurses	6,130	6,800	670	10.9
Operating Engineers and Other Construction Equipment Operators	2,780	3,230	450	16.2
Fast Food and Counter Workers	7,570	8,010	440	5.8
Office and Administrative Support Workers, All Other	5,790	6,230	440	7.6
Service Unit Operators, Oil, Gas, and Mining	1,180	1,580	400	33.9
Janitors and Cleaners, Except Maids and Housekeeping Cleaners	5,330	5,680	350	6.6
Maids and Housekeeping Cleaners	3,030	3,380	350	11.6
Maintenance and Repair Workers, General	4,040	4,390	350	8.7

Note: Projections cover Alaska; (1) Sorted by numeric employment change
Source: www.projectionscentral.org, State Occupational Projections, 2022–2032 Long-Term Projections

Fastest-Growing Occupations: 2022 – 2032

Occupation[1]	2022 Employment	2032 Projected Employment	Numeric Employment Change	Percent Employment Change
Derrick Operators, Oil and Gas	120	180	60	50.0
Roustabouts, Oil and Gas	280	390	110	39.3
Service Unit Operators, Oil, Gas, and Mining	1,180	1,580	400	33.9
Petroleum Engineers	390	490	100	25.6
Tour and Travel Guides	1,170	1,450	280	23.9
Surveyors	340	420	80	23.5
First-Line Supervisors of Construction Trades and Extraction Workers	810	990	180	22.2
Fitness Trainers and Aerobics Instructors	660	800	140	21.2
Shuttle Drivers and Chauffeurs	330	390	60	18.2
Welders, Cutters, Solderers, and Brazers	720	850	130	18.1

Note: Projections cover Alaska; (1) Sorted by percent employment change and excludes occupations with numeric employment change less than 50
Source: www.projectionscentral.org, State Occupational Projections, 2022–2032 Long-Term Projections

CITY FINANCES

City Government Finances

Component	2022 ($000)	2022 ($ per capita)
Total Revenues	1,666,374	5,804
Total Expenditures	1,905,878	6,638
Debt Outstanding	1,247,711	4,346

Source: U.S. Census Bureau, State & Local Government Finances 2022

City Government Revenue by Source

Source	2022 ($000)	2022 ($ per capita)	2022 (%)
General Revenue			
From Federal Government	116,968	407	7.0
From State Government	495,962	1,728	29.8
From Local Governments	0	0	0.0
Taxes			
Property	612,858	2,135	36.8
Sales and Gross Receipts	88,880	310	5.3
Personal Income	0	0	0.0
Corporate Income	0	0	0.0
Motor Vehicle License	17,737	62	1.1
Other Taxes	9,269	32	0.6
Current Charges	148,909	519	8.9
Liquor Store	0	0	0.0
Utility	70,839	247	4.3

Source: U.S. Census Bureau, State & Local Government Finances 2022

City Government Expenditures by Function

Function	2022 ($000)	2022 ($ per capita)	2022 (%)
General Direct Expenditures			
Air Transportation	8,715	30	0.5
Corrections	0	0	0.0
Education	742,909	2,587	39.0
Employment Security Administration	0	0	0.0
Financial Administration	21,869	76	1.1
Fire Protection	124,501	433	6.5
General Public Buildings	0	0	0.0
Governmental Administration, Other	16,469	57	0.9
Health	122,777	427	6.4
Highways	92,580	322	4.9
Hospitals	0	0	0.0
Housing and Community Development	47,655	166	2.5
Interest on General Debt	33,842	117	1.8
Judicial and Legal	7,801	27	0.4
Libraries	8,738	30	0.5
Parking	4,939	17	0.3
Parks and Recreation	46,092	160	2.4
Police Protection	147,981	515	7.8
Public Welfare	2,863	10	0.2
Sewerage	40,771	142	2.1
Solid Waste Management	76,316	265	4.0
Veterans' Services	0	0	0.0
Liquor Store	0	0	0.0
Utility	82,721	288	4.3

Source: U.S. Census Bureau, State & Local Government Finances 2022

TAXES

State Corporate Income Tax Rates

State	Tax Rate (%)	Income Brackets ($)	Num. of Brackets	Financial Institution Tax Rate (%)[a]	Federal Income Tax Ded.
Alaska	0 - 9.4	10,000 - 90,000	10	0 - 9.4	No

Note: Tax rates for tax year 2024; (a) Rates listed are the corporate income tax rate applied to financial institutions or excise taxes based on income. Some states have other taxes based upon the value of deposits or shares.
Source: Federation of Tax Administrators, State Corporate Income Tax Rates, January 1, 2025

State Individual Income Tax Rates

State	Tax Rate (%)	Income Brackets ($)	Personal Exemptions ($)			Standard Ded. ($)	
			Single	Married	Depend.	Single	Married
Alaska							– No state income tax –

Note: Tax rates for tax year 2024; Local- and county-level taxes are not included
Source: Federation of Tax Administrators, State Individual Income Tax Rates, January 1, 2025

Various State Sales and Excise Tax Rates

State	State Sales Tax (%)	Gasoline[1] ($/gal.)	Cigarette[2] ($/pack)	Spirits[3] ($/gal.)	Wine[4] ($/gal.)	Beer[5] ($/gal.)	Recreational Marijuana (%)
Alaska	None	0.09	2.00	12.80	2.50	1.07	(a)

Note: All tax rates as of January 1, 2025; (1) The American Petroleum Institute has developed a methodology for determining the average tax rate on a gallon of fuel. Rates may include any of the following: excise taxes, environmental fees, storage tank fees, other fees or taxes, general sales tax, and local taxes; (2) The federal excise tax of $1.0066 per pack and local taxes are not included; (3) Rates are those applicable to off-premise sales of 40% alcohol by volume (a.b.v.) distilled spirits in 750ml containers. Local excise taxes are excluded; (4) Rates are those applicable to off-premise sales of 11% a.b.v. non-carbonated wine in 750ml containers; (5) Rates are those applicable to off-premise sales of 4.7% a.b.v. beer in 12 ounce containers; (a) $50/oz. mature flowers; $25/oz. immature flowers; $15/oz. trim, $1 per clone
Source: Tax Foundation, 2025 Facts & Figures: How Does Your State Compare?

State Tax Competitiveness Index

State	Overall Rank	Corporate Tax Rank	Individual Income Tax Rank	Sales Tax Rank	Property Tax Rank	Unemployment Insurance Tax Rank
Alaska	3	34	1	5	30	45

Note: The Tax Foundation's State Tax Competitiveness Index enables policymakers, taxpayers, and business leaders to gauge how their states' tax systems compare. A rank of 1 is best, 50 is worst. Rankings do not average to the total. States without a tax rank equally as 1. DC's scores and rankings do not affect other states. The report shows tax systems as of July 1, 2024 (the beginning of Fiscal Year 2025).
Source: Tax Foundation, State Tax Competitiveness Index 2025

TRANSPORTATION

Means of Transportation to Work

Area	Car/Truck/Van		Public Transportation			Bicycle	Walked	Other Means	Worked at Home
	Drove Alone	Car-pooled	Bus	Subway	Railroad				
City	71.0	12.4	1.3	0.0	0.0	0.6	2.6	2.5	9.6
MSA[1]	71.3	11.7	1.1	0.0	0.0	0.5	2.4	3.1	9.8
U.S.	70.2	8.5	1.7	1.3	0.4	0.4	2.4	1.6	13.5

Note: Figures are percentages and cover workers 16 years of age and older; (1) Figures cover the Anchorage, AK Metropolitan Statistical Area
Source: U.S. Census Bureau, 2019-2023 American Community Survey 5-Year Estimates

Travel Time to Work

Area	Less Than 10 Minutes	10 to 19 Minutes	20 to 29 Minutes	30 to 44 Minutes	45 to 59 Minutes	60 to 89 Minutes	90 Minutes or More
City	15.6	44.8	23.3	11.1	2.3	1.4	1.5
MSA[1]	14.7	40.5	21.8	11.4	5.1	4.0	2.6
U.S.	12.6	28.6	21.2	20.8	8.1	6.0	2.8

Note: Note: Figures are percentages and include workers 16 years old and over; (1) Figures cover the Anchorage, AK Metropolitan Statistical Area
Source: U.S. Census Bureau, 2019-2023 American Community Survey 5-Year Estimates

Key Congestion Measures

Measure	2000	2010	2015	2020	2022
Annual Hours of Delay, Total (000)	3,973	5,279	6,397	3,080	5,675
Annual Hours of Delay, Per Auto Commuter	32	37	41	18	35
Annual Congestion Cost, Per Auto Commuter ($)	1,025	1,089	1,216	629	1,151

Note: Figures cover the Anchorage AK urban area
Source: Texas A&M Transportation Institute, 2023 Urban Mobility Report

Freeway Travel Time Index

Measure	1985	1990	1995	2000	2005	2010	2015	2020	2022
Urban Area Index[1]	1.03	1.07	1.10	1.14	1.16	1.16	1.18	1.07	1.14
Urban Area Rank[1,2]	89	74	72	62	57	54	41	57	64

Note: Freeway Travel Time Index—the ratio of travel time in the peak period to the travel time at free-flow conditions. For example, a value of 1.30 indicates a 20-minute free-flow trip takes 26 minutes in the peak (20 minutes x 1.30 = 26 minutes); (1) Covers the Anchorage AK urban area; (2) Rank is based on 101 larger urban areas (#1 = highest travel time index)
Source: Texas A&M Transportation Institute, 2023 Urban Mobility Report

Public Transportation

Agency Name / Mode of Transportation	Vehicles Operated in Maximum Service[1]	Annual Unlinked Passenger Trips[2] (in thous.)	Annual Passenger Miles[3] (in thous.)
Municipality of Anchorage, dba Public Transportation			
Bus (directly operated)	47	2,745.0	10,797.6
Demand Response (purchased transportation)	40	153.7	998.6
Vanpool (purchased transportation)	94	219.1	8,795.2

Note: (1) Number of revenue vehicles operated by the given mode and type of service to meet the annual maximum service requirement. This is the revenue vehicle count during the peak season of the year; on the week and day that maximum service is provided. Vehicles operated in maximum service (VOMS) exclude atypical days and one-time special events; (2) Number of passengers who boarded public transportation vehicles. Passengers are counted each time they board a vehicle no matter how many vehicles they use to travel from their origin to their destination. (3) Sum of the distances ridden by all passengers during the entire fiscal year.
Source: Federal Transit Administration, National Transit Database, 2023

Air Transportation

Airport Name and Code / Type of Service	Passenger Airlines[1]	Passenger Enplanements	Freight Carriers[2]	Freight (lbs)
Anchorage International (ANC)				
Domestic service (U.S. carriers only)	25	2,699,874	30	3,020,160,699
International service (U.S. carriers only)	3	715	12	511,545,942

Note: (1) Includes all U.S.-based major, minor and commuter airlines that carried at least one passenger during the year; (2) Includes all U.S.-based airlines and freight carriers that transported at least one pound of freight during the year.
Source: Bureau of Transportation Statistics, The Intermodal Transportation Database, Air Carriers: T-100 Domestic Market (U.S. carriers only), 2024; Bureau of Transportation Statistics, The Intermodal Transportation Database, Air Carriers: T-100 International Market (U.S. carriers only), 2024

BUSINESSES

Major Business Headquarters

Company Name	Industry	Rankings	
		Fortune[1]	Forbes[2]
No companies listed	-	-	-

Note: (1) Companies that produce a 10-K are ranked 1 to 500 based on 2023 revenue; (2) All private companies with at least $2 billion in annual revenue through the end of their most current fiscal year are ranked 1 to 275; companies listed are headquartered in the city; dashes indicate no ranking
Source: Fortune, "Fortune 500," 2024; Forbes, "America's Largest Private Companies," 2024

Living Environment

COST OF LIVING

Cost of Living Index

Composite Index	Groceries	Housing	Utilities	Trans-portation	Health Care	Misc. Goods/ Services
122.8	126.5	133.1	112.4	113.6	147.1	114.1

Note: The Cost of Living Index measures regional differences in the cost of consumer goods and services, excluding taxes and non-consumer expenditures, for professional and managerial households in the top income quintile. It is based on more than 50,000 prices covering almost 60 different items for which prices are collected three times a year by chambers of commerce, economic development organizations or university applied economic centers in each participating urban area. The numbers shown should be read as a percentage above or below the national average of 100. For example, a value of 115.4 in the groceries column indicates that grocery prices are 15.4% higher than the national average. Small differences in the index numbers should not be interpreted as significant; Figures cover the Anchorage AK urban area.
Source: The Council for Community and Economic Research, Cost of Living Index, 2024

Grocery Prices

Area[1]	T-Bone Steak ($/pound)	Frying Chicken ($/pound)	Whole Milk ($/half gal.)	Eggs ($/dozen)	Orange Juice ($/64 oz.)	Coffee ($/11.5 oz.)
City[2]	17.56	2.89	5.34	4.09	5.40	7.86
Avg.	15.42	1.55	4.69	3.25	4.41	5.46
Min.	14.50	1.16	4.43	2.75	4.00	4.85
Max.	17.56	2.89	5.49	4.78	5.54	7.89

Note: (1) Values for the local area are compared with the average, minimum and maximum values for all 276 areas in the Cost of Living Index; (2) Figures cover the Anchorage AK urban area; **T-Bone Steak** (price per pound); **Frying Chicken** (price per pound, whole fryer); **Whole Milk** (half gallon carton); **Eggs** (price per dozen, Grade A, large); **Orange Juice** (64 oz. Tropicana or Florida Natural); **Coffee** (11.5 oz. can, vacuum-packed, Maxwell House, Hills Bros, or Folgers).
Source: The Council for Community and Economic Research, Cost of Living Index, 2024

Housing and Utility Costs

Area[1]	New Home Price ($)	Apartment Rent ($/month)	All Electric ($/month)	Part Electric ($/month)	Other Energy ($/month)	Telephone ($/month)
City[2]	758,772	1,670	-	108.68	138.69	193.41
Avg.	515,975	1,550	210.99	123.07	82.07	194.99
Min.	265,375	692	104.33	53.68	36.26	179.42
Max.	2,775,821	5,719	529.02	397.28	361.63	223.33

Note: (1) Values for the local area are compared with the average, minimum and maximum values for all 276 areas in the Cost of Living Index; (2) Figures cover the Anchorage AK urban area; **New Home Price** (2,400 sf living area, 8,000 sf lot, in urban area with full utilities); **Apartment Rent** (950 sf 2 bedroom/1.5 or 2 bath, unfurnished, excluding all utilities except water); **All Electric** (average monthly cost for an all-electric home); **Part Electric** (average monthly cost for a part-electric home); **Other Energy** (average monthly cost for natural gas, fuel oil, coal, wood, and any other forms of energy except electricity); **Telephone** (price includes the base monthly rate plus taxes and fees for three lines of mobile phone service).
Source: The Council for Community and Economic Research, Cost of Living Index, 2024

Health Care, Transportation, and Other Costs

Area[1]	Doctor ($/visit)	Dentist ($/visit)	Optometrist ($/visit)	Gasoline ($/gallon)	Beauty Salon ($/visit)	Men's Shirt ($)
City[2]	243.83	173.17	265.00	3.68	50.00	45.44
Avg.	143.77	117.51	129.23	3.32	48.57	38.14
Min.	36.74	58.67	67.33	2.80	24.00	13.41
Max.	270.44	216.82	307.33	5.28	94.00	63.89

Note: (1) Values for the local area are compared with the average, minimum and maximum values for all 276 areas in the Cost of Living Index; (2) Figures cover the Anchorage AK urban area; **Doctor** (general practitioners routine exam of an established patient); **Dentist** (adult teeth cleaning and periodic oral examination); **Optometrist** (full vision eye exam for established adult patient); **Gasoline** (one gallon regular unleaded, national brand, including all taxes, cash price at self-service pump if available); **Beauty Salon** (woman's shampoo, trim, and blow-dry); **Men's Shirt** (cotton/polyester dress shirt, pinpoint weave, long sleeves).
Source: The Council for Community and Economic Research, Cost of Living Index, 2024

HOUSING

Homeownership Rate

Area	2017 (%)	2018 (%)	2019 (%)	2020 (%)	2021 (%)	2022 (%)	2023 (%)	2024 (%)
MSA[1]	n/a	n/a	n/a	n/a	n/a	n/a	n/a	n/a
U.S.	63.9	64.4	64.6	66.6	65.5	65.8	65.9	65.6

Note: (1) Figures cover the Anchorage, AK Metropolitan Statistical Area; n/a not available
Source: U.S. Census Bureau, Housing Vacancies and Homeownership Annual Statistics: 2017-2024

House Price Index (HPI)

Area	National Ranking[2]	Quarterly Change (%)	One-Year Change (%)	Five-Year Change (%)	Since 1991Q1 (%)
MSA[1]	120	-2.19	5.44	38.20	272.70
U.S.[3]	–	1.43	4.51	57.13	327.82

Note: The HPI is a weighted repeat sales index. It measures average price changes in repeat sales or refinancings on the same properties. This information is obtained by reviewing repeat mortgage transactions on single-family properties whose mortgages have been purchased or securitized by Fannie Mae or Freddie Mac since January 1975; (1) Figures cover the Anchorage, AK Metropolitan Statistical Area; (2) Rankings are based on annual percentage change for all metro areas containing at least 15,000 transactions over the last 10 years and ranges from 1 to 241; (3) figures based on a weighted average of Census Division estimates using a seasonally adjusted, purchase-only index; all figures are for the period ending December 31, 2024
Source: Federal Housing Finance Agency, Change in FHFA Metropolitan Area House Price Indexes, All Transactions Index, 2024Q4

Home Value

Area	Under $100,000	$100,000 -$199,999	$200,000 -$299,999	$300,000 -$399,999	$400,000 -$499,999	$500,000 -$999,999	$1,000,000 or more	Median ($)
City	5.3	7.4	17.7	25.8	19.8	21.8	2.2	375,900
MSA[1]	5.4	8.2	21.3	25.5	18.1	19.7	1.8	358,900
U.S.	12.1	17.8	19.5	14.4	10.5	19.1	6.5	303,400

Note: Figures are percentages except for median and cover owner-occupied housing units; (1) Figures cover the Anchorage, AK Metropolitan Statistical Area
Source: U.S. Census Bureau, 2019-2023 American Community Survey 5-Year Estimates

Year Housing Structure Built

Area	2020 or Later	2010 -2019	2000 -2009	1990 -1999	1980 -1989	1970 -1979	1960 -1969	1950 -1959	1940 -1949	Before 1940	Median Year
City	0.2	6.6	12.1	11.6	24.8	27.5	9.7	5.8	0.9	0.8	1982
MSA[1]	0.5	9.5	16.8	12.5	23.9	22.9	7.8	4.6	0.8	0.7	1986
U.S.	1.2	8.9	13.6	12.8	13.0	14.4	10.0	9.7	4.5	11.9	1980

Note: Figures are percentages except for Median Year; Note: (1) Figures cover the Anchorage, AK Metropolitan Statistical Area
Source: U.S. Census Bureau, 2019-2023 American Community Survey 5-Year Estimates

Gross Monthly Rent

Area	Under $500	$500 -$999	$1,000 -$1,499	$1,500 -$1,999	$2,000 -$2,499	$2,500 -$2,999	$3,000 and up	Median ($)
City	3.5	14.0	35.7	25.6	12.6	5.5	3.0	1,453
MSA[1]	3.9	15.2	36.0	25.1	12.2	4.8	2.7	1,422
U.S.	6.5	22.3	29.5	20.2	10.8	4.8	5.9	1,348

Note: Figures are percentages except for median; Gross rent is the contract rent plus the estimated average monthly cost of utilities (electricity, gas, and water and sewer) and fuels (oil, coal, kerosene, wood, etc.) if these are paid by the renter (or paid for the renter by someone else); (1) Figures cover the Anchorage, AK Metropolitan Statistical Area
Source: U.S. Census Bureau, 2019-2023 American Community Survey 5-Year Estimates

HEALTH

Health Risk Factors

Category	MSA[1] (%)	U.S. (%)
Adults aged 18–64 who have any kind of health care coverage	92.1	90.8
Adults who reported being in good or better health	81.1	81.8
Adults who have been told they have high blood cholesterol	33.9	36.9
Adults who have been told they have high blood pressure	32.5	34.0
Adults who are current smokers	13.2	12.1
Adults who currently use e-cigarettes	7.4	7.7
Adults who currently use chewing tobacco, snuff, or snus	4.8	3.2
Adults who are heavy drinkers[2]	8.1	6.1
Adults who are binge drinkers[3]	16.6	15.2
Adults who are overweight (BMI 25.0 - 29.9)	32.4	34.4
Adults who are obese (BMI 30.0 - 99.8)	35.8	34.3
Adults who participated in any physical activities in the past month	79.8	75.8

Note: All figures are crude prevalence; (1) Figures cover the Anchorage, AK Metropolitan Statistical Area; (2) Heavy drinkers are classified as adult men having more than 14 drinks per week and adult women having more than 7 drinks per week; (3) Binge drinkers are classified as males having five or more drinks on one occasion or females having four or more drinks on one occasion
Source: Centers for Disease Control and Prevention, Behaviorial Risk Factor Surveillance System, SMART: Selected Metropolitan Area Risk Trends, 2023

Acute and Chronic Health Conditions

Category	MSA[1] (%)	U.S. (%)
Adults who have ever been told they had a heart attack	3.7	4.2
Adults who have ever been told they have angina or coronary heart disease	3.6	4.0
Adults who have ever been told they had a stroke	3.3	3.3
Adults who have ever been told they have asthma	17.6	15.7
Adults who have ever been told they have arthritis	25.7	26.3
Adults who have ever been told they have diabetes[2]	8.9	11.5
Adults who have ever been told they had skin cancer	3.4	5.6
Adults who have ever been told they had any other types of cancer	7.5	8.4
Adults who have ever been told they have COPD	5.6	6.4
Adults who have ever been told they have kidney disease	2.1	3.7
Adults who have ever been told they have a form of depression	21.8	22.0

Note: All figures are crude prevalence; (1) Figures cover the Anchorage, AK Metropolitan Statistical Area; (2) Figures do not include pregnancy-related, borderline, or pre-diabetes
Source: Centers for Disease Control and Prevention, Behaviorial Risk Factor Surveillance System, SMART: Selected Metropolitan Area Risk Trends, 2023

Health Screening and Vaccination Rates

Category	MSA[1] (%)	U.S. (%)
Adults who have ever been tested for HIV	45.2	37.5
Adults who have had their blood cholesterol checked within the last five years	84.3	87.0
Adults aged 65+ who have had flu shot within the past year	51.2	63.4
Adults aged 65+ who have ever had a pneumonia vaccination	65.8	71.9

Note: All figures are crude prevalence; (1) Figures cover the Anchorage, AK Metropolitan Statistical Area.
Source: Centers for Disease Control and Prevention, Behaviorial Risk Factor Surveillance System, SMART: Selected Metropolitan Area Risk Trends, 2023

Disability Status

Category	MSA[1] (%)	U.S. (%)
Adults who reported being deaf	8.3	7.4
Are you blind or have serious difficulty seeing, even when wearing glasses?	2.9	4.9
Do you have difficulty doing errands alone?	7.7	7.8
Do you have difficulty dressing or bathing?	3.2	3.6
Do you have serious difficulty concentrating/remembering/making decisions?	13.4	13.7
Do you have serious difficulty walking or climbing stairs?	12.2	13.2

Note: All figures are crude prevalence; (1) Figures cover the Anchorage, AK Metropolitan Statistical Area.
Source: Centers for Disease Control and Prevention, Behaviorial Risk Factor Surveillance System, SMART: Selected Metropolitan Area Risk Trends, 2023

Mortality Rates for the Top 10 Causes of Death in the U.S.

ICD-10[a] Sub-Chapter	ICD-10[a] Code	Crude Mortality Rate[2] per 100,000 population	
		County[3]	U.S.
Malignant neoplasms	C00-C97	140.6	182.7
Ischaemic heart diseases	I20-I25	62.6	109.6
Provisional assignment of new diseases of uncertain etiology[1]	U00-U49	46.8	65.3
Other forms of heart disease	I30-I51	48.9	65.1
Other degenerative diseases of the nervous system	G30-G31	33.3	52.4
Other external causes of accidental injury	W00-X59	73.4	52.3
Cerebrovascular diseases	I60-I69	31.1	49.1
Chronic lower respiratory diseases	J40-J47	25.2	43.5
Hypertensive diseases	I10-I15	21.2	38.9
Organic, including symptomatic, mental disorders	F01-F09	31.8	33.9

Note: (a) ICD-10 = International Classification of Diseases 10th Revision; (1) Includes COVID-19, adverse effects to COVID-19 vaccines, SARS, and vaping-related disorders; (2) Crude mortality rates are a three-year average covering 2021-2023; (3) Figures cover Anchorage Borough.
Source: Centers for Disease Control and Prevention, National Center for Health Statistics. National Vital Statistics System, Mortality 2018-2023 on CDC WONDER Online Database

Mortality Rates for Selected Causes of Death

Cause of Death	ICD-10[a] Code	Crude Mortality Rate[1] per 100,000 population	
		County[2]	U.S.
Accidental poisoning and exposure to noxious substances	X40-X49	53.9	30.5
Alzheimer disease	G30	28.2	35.4
Assault	X85-Y09	7.7	7.3
COVID-19	U07.1	46.8	65.3
Diabetes mellitus	E10-E14	24.1	30.0
Diseases of the liver	K70-K76	32.3	20.8
Human immunodeficiency virus (HIV) disease	B20-B24	Suppressed	1.5
Influenza and pneumonia	J09-J18	7.8	13.4
Intentional self-harm	X60-X84	21.5	14.7
Malnutrition	E40-E46	3.6	6.0
Obesity and other hyperalimentation	E65-E68	3.9	3.1
Renal failure	N17-N19	14.3	16.4
Transport accidents	V01-V99	12.4	14.4

Note: (a) ICD-10 = International Classification of Diseases 10th Revision; (1) Crude mortality rates are a three-year average covering 2021-2023; (2) Figures cover Anchorage Borough; Data are suppressed when the data meet the criteria for confidentiality constraints; Crude mortality rates are flagged as unreliable when the rate would be calculated with a numerator of 20 or less.
Source: Centers for Disease Control and Prevention, National Center for Health Statistics. National Vital Statistics System, Mortality 2018-2023 on CDC WONDER Online Database

Health Insurance Coverage

Area	With Health Insurance	With Private Health Insurance	With Public Health Insurance	Without Health Insurance	Population Under Age 19 Without Health Insurance
City	90.0	70.0	34.0	10.0	7.4
MSA[1]	89.4	68.4	35.1	10.6	8.2
U.S.	91.4	67.3	36.3	8.6	5.4

Note: Figures are percentages that cover the civilian noninstitutionalized population; (1) Figures cover the Anchorage, AK Metropolitan Statistical Area
Source: U.S. Census Bureau, 2019-2023 American Community Survey 5-Year Estimates

Number of Medical Professionals

Area	MDs[3]	DOs[3,4]	Dentists	Podiatrists	Chiropractors	Optometrists
Borough[1] (number)	1,104	159	386	17	188	90
Borough[1] (rate[2])	384.5	55.4	134.9	5.9	65.7	31.5
U.S. (rate[2])	302.5	29.2	74.6	6.4	29.5	18.0

Note: Data as of 2023 unless noted; (1) Data covers Anchorage Borough; (2) Number of medical professionals per 100,000 population; (3) Data as of 2022 and includes all active, non-federal physicians; (4) Doctor of Osteopathic Medicine
Source: U.S. Department of Health and Human Services, Health Resources and Services Administration, Bureau of Health Professions, Area Resource File (ARF) 2023-2024

EDUCATION

Public School District Statistics

District Name	Schls	Pupils	Pupil/ Teacher Ratio	Minority Pupils[1] (%)	Total Rev. per Pupil ($)	Total Exp. per Pupil ($)
Anchorage School District	95	43,363	18.0	60.3	18,710	18,698

Note: Table includes school districts with 2,000 or more students; (1) Percentage of students that are not non-Hispanic white.
Source: U.S. Department of Education, National Center for Education Statistics, Common Core of Data, Local Education Agency (School District) Universe Survey: School Year 2023-2024; U.S. Department of Education, National Center for Education Statistics, Common Core of Data, School District Finance Survey (F-33): School Year 2021–22

Highest Level of Education

Area	Less than H.S.	H.S. Diploma	Some College, No Deg.	Associate Degree	Bachelor's Degree	Master's Degree	Prof. School Degree	Doctorate Degree
City	6.0	24.5	23.2	8.6	23.4	9.9	2.7	1.7
MSA[1]	5.9	27.1	23.6	9.4	21.3	9.0	2.3	1.4
U.S.	10.6	26.2	19.4	8.8	21.3	9.8	2.3	1.6

Note: Figures cover persons age 25 and over; (1) Figures cover the Anchorage, AK Metropolitan Statistical Area
Source: U.S. Census Bureau, 2019-2023 American Community Survey 5-Year Estimates

Educational Attainment by Race

Area	High School Graduate or Higher (%)					Bachelor's Degree or Higher (%)				
	Total	White	Black	Asian	Hisp.[2]	Total	White	Black	Asian	Hisp.[2]
City	94.0	96.7	91.7	86.6	86.6	37.7	45.2	23.6	30.5	23.8
MSA[1]	94.1	96.2	91.7	86.6	87.7	34.0	38.9	23.5	29.7	23.9
U.S.	89.4	92.9	88.1	88.0	72.5	35.0	37.7	24.7	57.0	19.9

Note: Figures shown cover persons 25 years old and over; (1) Figures cover the Anchorage, AK Metropolitan Statistical Area; (2) People of Hispanic origin can be of any race
Source: U.S. Census Bureau, 2019-2023 American Community Survey 5-Year Estimates

School Enrollment by Grade and Control

Area	Preschool (%)		Kindergarten (%)		Grades 1 - 4 (%)		Grades 5 - 8 (%)		Grades 9 - 12 (%)	
	Public	Private	Public	Private	Public	Private	Public	Private	Public	Private
City	53.5	46.5	89.2	10.8	84.1	15.9	87.8	12.2	91.8	8.2
MSA[1]	51.9	48.1	87.7	12.3	83.6	16.4	86.9	13.1	89.7	10.3
U.S.	58.7	41.3	85.2	14.8	87.2	12.8	87.9	12.1	89.0	11.0

Note: Figures shown cover persons 3 years old and over; (1) Figures cover the Anchorage, AK Metropolitan Statistical Area
Source: U.S. Census Bureau, 2019-2023 American Community Survey 5-Year Estimates

Higher Education

Four-Year Colleges			Two-Year Colleges			Medical Schools[1]	Law Schools[2]	Voc/ Tech[3]
Public	Private Non-profit	Private For-profit	Public	Private Non-profit	Private For-profit			
1	2	1	0	0	1	0	0	0

Note: Figures cover institutions located within the Anchorage, AK Metropolitan Statistical Area and include main campuses only; (1) includes schools accredited by the Liaison Committee on Medical Education and the American Osteopathic Association's Commission on Osteopathic College Accreditation; (2) includes ABA-accredited schools, schools with provisional ABA accreditation, and state accredited schools; (3) includes all schools with programs that are less than 2 years.
Source: National Center for Education Statistics, Integrated Postsecondary Education System (IPEDS), 2023-24; Wikipedia, List of Medical Schools in the United States, accessed May 2, 2025; Wikipedia, List of Law Schools in the United States, accessed May 2, 2025

EMPLOYERS

Major Employers

Company Name	Industry
ASRC Energy Services	Oil & gas field services
AT&T	Telephone communication, except radio
BP Transportation (Alaska)	Crude petroleum production
Bureau of Land Management	Information bureau
Carrs/Safeway	Grocery stores
Federal Aviation Administration	Aircraft regulating agencies
Federal Express Corporation	Air cargo carrier, scheduled
Fred Meyer	Retail
Galen Hospital Alaska	General medical & surgical hospitals
Indian Health Service	General medical & surgical hospitals
Municipality of Anchorage	Mayors' office
Nabors Alaska Drilling	Drilling oil & gas wells
Providence Health Services	Healthcare
U.S. Fish and Wildlife Service	Fish & wildlife conservation agency, government
United States Department of the Air Force	U.S. military
USPHS AK Native Medical Center	General medical & surgical hospitals
Wal-Mart Stores	Retail

Note: Companies shown are located within the Anchorage, AK Metropolitan Statistical Area.
Source: Chambers of Commerce; State Departments of Labor; Wikipedia

PUBLIC SAFETY

Crime Rate

Area	Total Crime Rate	Violent Crime Rate				Property Crime Rate		
		Murder	Rape	Robbery	Aggrav. Assault	Burglary	Larceny -Theft	Motor Vehicle Theft
City	3,953.3	7.7	150.2	161.7	742.0	334.0	2,132.4	425.2
U.S.	2,290.9	5.7	38.0	66.5	264.1	250.7	1,347.2	318.7

Note: Figures are crimes per 100,000 population.
Source: FBI, Table 8, Offenses Known to Law Enforcement, by State by City, 2023

Hate Crimes

Area	Number of Quarters Reported	Number of Incidents per Bias Motivation					
		Race/Ethnicity/ Ancestry	Religion	Sexual Orientation	Disability	Gender	Gender Identity
City	4	1	2	0	0	0	1
U.S.	4	5,900	2,699	2,077	187	92	492

Source: Federal Bureau of Investigation, Hate Crime Statistics 2023

Identity Theft Consumer Reports

Area	Reports	Reports per 100,000 Population	Rank[2]
MSA[1]	464	116	340
U.S.	1,135,291	339	-

Note: (1) Figures cover the Anchorage, AK Metropolitan Statistical Area; (2) Rank ranges from 1 to 401 where 1 indicates greatest number of identity theft reports per 100,000 population
Source: Federal Trade Commission, Consumer Sentinel Network Data Book 2024

Fraud and Other Consumer Reports

Area	Reports	Reports per 100,000 Population	Rank[2]
MSA[1]	4,138	1,035	190
U.S.	5,360,641	1,601	-

Note: (1) Figures cover the Anchorage, AK Metropolitan Statistical Area; (2) Rank ranges from 1 to 401 where 1 indicates greatest number of fraud and other consumer reports per 100,000 population
Source: Federal Trade Commission, Consumer Sentinel Network Data Book 2024

POLITICS

2024 Presidential Election Results

Area	Trump (Rep.)	Harris (Dem.)	Stein (Green)	Kennedy (Ind.)	Oliver (Lib.)	Other
Alaska	54.5	41.4	0.7	1.7	0.9	0.8
U.S.	49.7	48.2	0.6	0.5	0.4	0.6

Note: Results are percentages and may not add to 100% due to rounding
Source: Dave Leip's Atlas of U.S. Presidential Elections

SPORTS

Professional Sports Teams

Team Name	League	Year Established

No teams are located in the metro area
Source: Wikipedia, Major Professional Sports Teams of the United States and Canada, May 1, 2025

CLIMATE

Average and Extreme Temperatures

Temperature	Jan	Feb	Mar	Apr	May	Jun	Jul	Aug	Sep	Oct	Nov	Dec	Yr.
Extreme High (°F)	50	48	51	65	77	85	82	82	73	61	53	48	85
Average High (°F)	22	25	33	43	55	62	65	63	55	41	28	22	43
Average Temp. (°F)	15	18	25	36	47	55	59	57	48	35	22	16	36
Average Low (°F)	8	11	17	28	39	47	51	49	41	28	15	10	29
Extreme Low (°F)	-34	-26	-24	-4	17	33	36	31	19	-5	-21	-30	-34

Note: Figures cover the years 1953-1995
Source: National Climatic Data Center, International Station Meteorological Climate Summary, 9/96

Average Precipitation/Snowfall/Humidity

Precip./Humidity	Jan	Feb	Mar	Apr	May	Jun	Jul	Aug	Sep	Oct	Nov	Dec	Yr.
Avg. Precip. (in.)	0.8	0.8	0.7	0.6	0.7	1.0	1.9	2.4	2.7	1.9	1.1	1.1	15.7
Avg. Snowfall (in.)	10	12	10	5	Tr	0	0	0	Tr	8	12	15	71
Avg. Rel. Hum. 6am (%)	74	74	72	75	73	74	80	84	84	78	78	78	77
Avg. Rel. Hum. 3pm (%)	73	67	57	54	50	55	62	64	64	67	74	76	64

Note: Figures cover the years 1953-1995; Tr = Trace amounts (<0.05 in. of rain; <0.5 in. of snow)
Source: National Climatic Data Center, International Station Meteorological Climate Summary, 9/96

Weather Conditions

Temperature			Daytime Sky			Precipitation		
0°F & below	32°F & below	65°F & above	Clear	Partly cloudy	Cloudy	0.01 inch or more precip.	0.1 inch or more snow/ice	Thunder-storms
32	194	41	50	115	200	113	49	2

Note: Figures are average number of days per year and cover the years 1953-1995
Source: National Climatic Data Center, International Station Meteorological Climate Summary, 9/96

HAZARDOUS WASTE **Superfund Sites**

The Anchorage, AK metro area is home to three sites on the EPA's Superfund National Priorities List (NPL) or Superfund Alternative Approach (SAA) list: **Alaska Railroad Anchorage Yard** (SAA); **Elmendorf Air Force Base** (Final NPL); **Fort Richardson (USARMY)** (Final NPL). The Superfund alternative approach uses the same investigation and cleanup process and standards that are used for sites listed on the National Priorities List. The SAA is an alternative to listing a site on the NPL; it is not an alternative to Superfund or the Superfund process. There are a total of 1,445 Superfund sites with a status of proposed or final on both lists in the United States. *U.S. Environmental Protection Agency, National Priorities List, May 1, 2025; U.S. Environmental Protection Agency, Superfund Alternative Approach Sites, May 1, 2025*

AIR QUALITY **Air Quality Trends: Ozone**

	1990	1995	2000	2005	2010	2015	2020	2021	2022	2023
MSA[1]	n/a	n/a	n/a	n/a	n/a	n/a	n/a	n/a	n/a	n/a
U.S.	0.087	0.089	0.081	0.080	0.072	0.068	0.066	0.067	0.067	0.070

Note: (1) Data covers the Anchorage, AK Metropolitan Statistical Area; n/a not available. The values shown are the composite ozone concentration averages among trend sites based on the highest fourth daily maximum 8-hour concentration in parts per million. These trends are based on sites having an adequate record of monitoring data during the trend period. Data from exceptional events are included.
Source: U.S. Environmental Protection Agency, Air Quality Monitoring Information, "Air Quality Trends by City, 1990-2023"

Air Quality Index

Area	Percent of Days when Air Quality was...[2]					AQI Statistics[2]	
	Good	Moderate	Unhealthy for Sensitive Groups	Unhealthy	Very Unhealthy	Maximum	Median
MSA[1]	81.1	18.6	0.3	0.0	0.0	102	25

Note: (1) Data covers the Anchorage, AK Metropolitan Statistical Area; (2) Based on 365 days with AQI data in 2023. Air Quality Index (AQI) is an index for reporting daily air quality. EPA calculates the AQI for five major air pollutants regulated by the Clean Air Act: ground-level ozone, particle pollution (aka particulate matter), carbon monoxide, sulfur dioxide, and nitrogen dioxide. The AQI runs from 0 to 500. The higher the AQI value, the greater the level of air pollution and the greater the health concern. There are six AQI categories: "Good" AQI is between 0 and 50. Air quality is considered satisfactory; "Moderate" AQI is between 51 and 100. Air quality is acceptable; "Unhealthy for Sensitive Groups" When AQI values are between 101 and 150, members of sensitive groups may experience health effects; "Unhealthy" When AQI values are between 151 and 200 everyone may begin to experience health effects; "Very Unhealthy" AQI values between 201 and 300 trigger a health alert; "Hazardous" AQI values over 300 trigger warnings of emergency conditions (not shown).
Source: U.S. Environmental Protection Agency, Air Quality Index Report, 2023

Air Quality Index Pollutants

Area	Percent of Days when AQI Pollutant was...[2]					
	Carbon Monoxide	Nitrogen Dioxide	Ozone	Sulfur Dioxide	Particulate Matter 2.5	Particulate Matter 10
MSA[1]	0.8	0.0	0.0	(3)	70.1	29.0

Note: (1) Data covers the Anchorage, AK Metropolitan Statistical Area; (2) Based on 365 days with AQI data in 2023. The Air Quality Index (AQI) is an index for reporting daily air quality. EPA calculates the AQI for five major air pollutants regulated by the Clean Air Act: ground-level ozone, particle pollution (also known as particulate matter), carbon monoxide, sulfur dioxide, and nitrogen dioxide. The AQI runs from 0 to 500. The higher the AQI value, the greater the level of air pollution and the greater the health concern; (3) Sulfur dioxide is no longer included in this table because SO_2 concentrations tend to be very localized and not necessarily representative of broad geographical areas like counties and CBSAs.
Source: U.S. Environmental Protection Agency, Air Quality Index Report, 2023

Maximum Air Pollutant Concentrations: Particulate Matter, Ozone, CO and Lead

	Particulate Matter 10 (ug/m³)	Particulate Matter 2.5 Wtd AM (ug/m³)	Particulate Matter 2.5 24-Hr (ug/m³)	Ozone (ppm)	Carbon Monoxide (ppm)	Lead (ug/m³)
MSA[1] Level	130	4.2	18	n/a	2	n/a
NAAQS[2]	150	15	35	0.075	9	0.15
Met NAAQS[2]	Yes	Yes	Yes	n/a	Yes	n/a

Note: (1) Data covers the Anchorage, AK Metropolitan Statistical Area; Data from exceptional events are included; (2) National Ambient Air Quality Standards; ppm = parts per million; ug/m³ = micrograms per cubic meter; n/a not available.
Concentrations: Particulate Matter 10 (coarse particulate)—highest second maximum 24-hour concentration; Particulate Matter 2.5 Wtd AM (fine particulate)—highest weighted annual mean concentration; Particulate Matter 2.5 24-Hour (fine particulate)—highest 98th percentile 24-hour concentration; Ozone—highest fourth daily maximum 8-hour concentration; Carbon Monoxide—highest second maximum non-overlapping 8-hour concentration; Lead—maximum running 3-month average
Source: U.S. Environmental Protection Agency, Air Quality Monitoring Information, "Air Quality Statistics by City, 2023"

Maximum Air Pollutant Concentrations: Nitrogen Dioxide and Sulfur Dioxide

	Nitrogen Dioxide AM (ppb)	Nitrogen Dioxide 1-Hr (ppb)	Sulfur Dioxide AM (ppb)	Sulfur Dioxide 1-Hr (ppb)	Sulfur Dioxide 24-Hr (ppb)
MSA[1] Level	n/a	n/a	n/a	n/a	n/a
NAAQS[2]	53	100	30	75	140
Met NAAQS[2]	n/a	n/a	n/a	n/a	n/a

Note: (1) Data covers the Anchorage, AK Metropolitan Statistical Area; Data from exceptional events are included; (2) National Ambient Air Quality Standards; ppm = parts per million; ug/m^3 = micrograms per cubic meter; n/a not available.

Concentrations: Nitrogen Dioxide AM—highest arithmetic mean concentration; Nitrogen Dioxide 1-Hr—highest 98th percentile 1-hour daily maximum concentration; Sulfur Dioxide AM—highest annual mean concentration; Sulfur Dioxide 1-Hr—highest 99th percentile 1-hour daily maximum concentration; Sulfur Dioxide 24-Hr—highest second maximum 24-hour concentration

Source: U.S. Environmental Protection Agency, Air Quality Monitoring Information, "Air Quality Statistics by City, 2023"

Billings, Montana

Background

Established in 1882 in Montana Territory, Billings is the largest city in the state. Located in the Yellowstone Valley, it was once home to prehistoric hunters and the Crow Indians. In 1806, William Clark (of the Lewis and Clark expedition) visited the area and inscribed his name on a pillar in 1806. Shortly after the city's establishment, it prospered as a rail hub by the Northern Pacific Railroad, which came to be known as Clark's Fork Bottom. Billings' location on the Yellowstone River made it a natural central point for traveling steamboats.

Shortly following Billings' settlement, entrepreneur Herman Clark arrived and announced ambitious plans to house 20,000 residents, build nearly a dozen sawmills, roads, and most importantly a massive railroad system. Clark's dream became a reality when the city added a transcontinental railroad in 1883 and had a growing population of 1,500 by 1888. In 1909, the Great Northern Railway laid tracks through Billings and Congress passed the Enlarged Homestead act, allowing settlers to lay claims to 320 acres of farmlands. This encouraged more growth, and settlers from around the world arrived in Billings.

Throughout the early half of the 20th century, Billings established itself as an industrial metropolis in Yellowstone Valley. By 1910, the population had peaked above 10,000 and the city included banks, hotels, shopping districts and government buildings. The discovery of oil and natural gas in the area helped Billings to propel itself into the post-war era of the 1940s and 50s. Due to its oil boom, the city secured a dominant role in the energy industry throughout the 1970s and onward. In the 1970s and 80s, while the rest of the country was experiencing a severe economic recession, Billings constructed the first high rise buildings in Montana and welcomed a handful of development companies to construct local shopping districts and residential areas.

Even in the 1990s, Billings continued to grow by expanding its I-90 corridor, welcoming large hotel chains and Fortune 500 corporations. This trend continued into the 21st century, as companies like GE and Wells Fargo joined Billings' downtown business district, and Skypoint became the city's highest elevated building and observation point. The rapid pace of construction coupled with low tax rates placed Billings at the top of a number of best cities lists. Today, Billings maintains high levels of employment, construction, and investments in the local community, and it continues to grow faster than any other city in Montana.

There is no lack of local flavor and attractions in Billings. The Western Romance Company offers wagons, horses, and equipment for visitors who wish to explore like the cowboys did. For kids and families, Billings offers multiple nearby water parks like Big Splash, the Amusement Park Drive-In, and local sports teams like the Billings Mustangs baseball team. Cultural attractions are abundant in the Downtown Historic District, with local theaters and museums, notably the Yellowstone Art Museum and the Billings Symphony Orchestra. Billings also boasts stunning geography, nestled between the Yellowstone Valley and the Yellowstone River.

Downtown Billings has a cold semi-arid climate with dry, hot summers, and cold, dry winters. However, areas outside of downtown can have a hot-summer continental climate, due to the urban heat island effect. The snowfall averages about 60 inches a year, but because of warm chinook winds that pass through the region during the winter, snow does not usually accumulate heavily or remain on the ground for long.

Rankings

General Rankings

- In their annual survey, Livability.com looked at data for more than 2,000 mid-sized U.S. cities to assign a "Livability Score"for each. The top 100 scoring cities make up Livability's "Top 100 Best Places to Live in the U.S." in 2025. Billings was placed among the top 100 of the customizable list. Criteria: housing and economy; cost of living; environment; education; health care options; transportation; safety; and community amenities. *Livability.com, "Top 100 Best Places to Live in the U.S. in 2025" April 15, 2025*

Business/Finance Rankings

- The Billings metro area appeared on the Milken Institute "2025 Best Performing Cities" list. Rank: #27 out of 203 small metro areas (based on performance category). Criteria: job growth; wage growth; high-tech growth and impact; community resilience; housing affordability; household broadband access. *Milken Institute, "Best-Performing Cities 2025," January 14, 2025*

Environmental Rankings

- *Niche* compiled a list of the nation's snowiest cities, based on the National Oceanic and Atmospheric Administration's 30-year average snowfall data. Among cities with a population of at least 50,000, Billings ranked #22. *Niche.com, Top 25 Snowiest Cities in America, December 10, 2018*

Real Estate Rankings

- *WalletHub* compared the most populated U.S. cities to determine which had the best markets for real estate agents. Billings ranked #14 where demand was high and pay was the best. Criteria: sales per agent; annual median wage for real-estate agents; monthly average starting salary for real estate agents; real estate job density and competition; unemployment rate; home turnover rate; housing-market health index; and other relevant metrics. *WalletHub.com, "2021 Best Places to Be a Real Estate Agent," May 12, 2021*

Safety Rankings

- Billings was identified as one of the most dangerous cities in America by NeighborhoodScout. The city ranked #79 out of 100 (#1 = most dangerous). Criteria: number of violent crimes per 1,000 residents. The editors evaluated cities with 25,000 or more residents. *NeighborhoodScout.com, "2023 Top 100 Most Dangerous Cities in the U.S.," January 12, 2023*

Women/Minorities Rankings

- Personal finance website *WalletHub* compared more than 180 U.S. cities across two key dimensions, "Hispanic Business-Friendliness" and "Hispanic Purchasing Power," to arrive at the most favorable conditions for Hispanic entrepreneurs. Billings was ranked #50 out of 182. Criteria includes: share of Hispanic-Owned Businesses; average growth of Hispanic Business revenues; Small Business-Friendliness score; affordability; and number of Hispanics with at least a bachelor's degree. *WalletHub.com, "Best Cities for Hispanic Entrepreneurs," September 4, 2024*

Miscellaneous Rankings

- *WalletHub* compared 148 of the most populated U.S. cities to determine their operating efficiency. A "Quality of Services" score was constructed for each city and then measured against the total budget per capita to reveal which were managed the best. Billings ranked #16. Criteria: financial stability; economy; education; safety; health; infrastructure and pollution. *WalletHub.com, "2025's Best- & Worst-Run Cities in America," June 18, 2024*

Business Environment

DEMOGRAPHICS

Population Growth

Area	1990 Census	2000 Census	2010 Census	2020 Census	2023 Estimate[2]	Population Growth 1990-2023 (%)
City	81,812	89,847	104,170	117,116	118,321	44.6
MSA[1]	121,499	138,904	158,050	184,167	187,269	54.1
U.S.	248,709,873	281,421,906	308,745,538	331,449,281	332,387,540	33.6

Note: (1) Figures cover the Billings, MT Metropolitan Statistical Area; (2) 2019-2023 5-year ACS population estimate
Source: U.S. Census Bureau, 1990 Census, 2000 Census, 2010 Census, 2020 Census, 2019-2023 American Community Survey 5-Year Estimates

Race

Area	White Alone[2] (%)	Black Alone[2] (%)	Asian Alone[2] (%)	AIAN[3] Alone[2] (%)	NHOPI[4] Alone[2] (%)	Other Race Alone[2] (%)	Two or More Races (%)
City	86.3	1.0	0.9	4.4	0.1	1.4	6.1
MSA[1]	87.5	0.8	0.8	3.6	0.0	1.6	5.7
U.S.	63.4	12.4	5.8	0.9	0.2	6.6	10.7

Note: (1) Figures cover the Billings, MT Metropolitan Statistical Area; (2) Alone is defined as not being in combination with one or more other races; (3) American Indian and Alaska Native; (4) Native Hawaiian and Other Pacific Islander
Source: U.S. Census Bureau, 2019-2023 American Community Survey 5-Year Estimates

Hispanic or Latino Origin

Area	Total (%)	Mexican (%)	Puerto Rican (%)	Cuban (%)	Other (%)
City	7.2	5.0	0.3	0.2	1.8
MSA[1]	6.1	4.4	0.2	0.1	1.3
U.S.	19.0	11.3	1.8	0.7	5.2

Note: Persons of Hispanic or Latino origin can be of any race; (1) Figures cover the Billings, MT Metropolitan Statistical Area
Source: U.S. Census Bureau, 2019-2023 American Community Survey 5-Year Estimates

Age

Area	Percent of Population									Median Age
	Under Age 5	Age 5–19	Age 20–34	Age 35–44	Age 45–54	Age 55–64	Age 65–74	Age 75–84	Age 85+	
City	5.9	18.9	21.1	14.0	10.2	11.6	10.3	5.4	2.6	38.1
MSA[1]	5.5	19.3	18.9	13.2	11.4	12.9	11.3	5.2	2.2	39.7
U.S.	5.7	19.1	20.2	13.1	12.3	12.8	10.0	4.9	1.9	38.7

Note: (1) Figures cover the Billings, MT Metropolitan Statistical Area
Source: U.S. Census Bureau, 2019-2023 American Community Survey 5-Year Estimates

Disability by Age

Area	All Ages	Under 18 Years Old	18 to 64 Years Old	65 Years and Over
City	14.5	4.4	11.8	36.3
MSA[1]	14.3	4.4	11.6	35.1
U.S.	13.0	4.7	10.7	32.9

Note: Figures show percent of the civilian noninstitutionalized population that reported having a disability. Disability status is determined from six types of difficulty: vision, hearing, cognitive, ambulatory, self-care, and independent living. For children under 5 years old, hearing and vision difficulty are used to determine disability status. For children between the ages of 5 and 14, disability status is determined from hearing, vision, cognitive, ambulatory, and self-care difficulties. For people aged 15 years and older, they are considered to have a disability if they have difficulty with any one of the six difficulty types; Note: (1) Figures cover the Billings, MT Metropolitan Statistical Area
Source: U.S. Census Bureau, 2019-2023 American Community Survey 5-Year Estimates

Ancestry

Area	German	Irish	English	American	Italian	Polish	French[2]	European	Scottish
City	27.7	13.2	13.3	3.7	3.1	1.7	2.6	2.0	2.8
MSA[1]	29.0	13.1	12.6	4.2	3.2	1.5	2.6	2.1	2.6
U.S.	12.6	9.4	9.1	5.5	4.9	2.6	2.0	1.6	1.6

Note: Figures are the percentage of the total population reporting a particular ancestry. The nine most commonly reported ancestries in the U.S. are shown. Figures include multiple ancestries (e.g. if a person reported being Irish and Italian, they were included in both columns); (1) Figures cover the Billings, MT Metropolitan Statistical Area; (2) Excludes Basque
Source: U.S. Census Bureau, 2019-2023 American Community Survey 5-Year Estimates

Foreign-born Population

Area	Any Foreign Country	Asia	Mexico	Europe	Caribbean	Central America[2]	South America	Africa	Canada
City	2.0	0.7	0.2	0.6	0.0	0.0	0.1	0.0	0.3
MSA[1]	1.8	0.5	0.2	0.5	0.0	0.0	0.1	0.1	0.2
U.S.	13.9	4.3	3.3	1.4	1.4	1.2	1.2	0.8	0.2

Note: (1) Figures cover the Billings, MT Metropolitan Statistical Area; (2) Excludes Mexico.
Source: U.S. Census Bureau, 2019-2023 American Community Survey 5-Year Estimates

Household Size

Area	Persons in Household (%)							Average Household Size
	One	Two	Three	Four	Five	Six	Seven or More	
City	34.0	35.0	13.2	10.8	4.7	1.2	1.1	2.29
MSA[1]	31.0	36.9	13.2	11.3	4.8	1.5	1.3	2.36
U.S.	28.5	33.8	15.4	12.7	5.9	2.3	1.4	2.54

Note: (1) Figures cover the Billings, MT Metropolitan Statistical Area
Source: U.S. Census Bureau, 2019-2023 American Community Survey 5-Year Estimates

Household Relationships

Area	House-holder	Opposite-sex Spouse	Same-sex Spouse	Opposite-sex Unmarried Partner	Same-sex Unmarried Partner	Child[2]	Grand-child	Other Relatives	Non-relatives
City	42.2	17.7	0.2	3.1	0.1	26.0	1.7	2.5	3.5
MSA[1]	41.3	19.5	0.1	2.8	0.1	26.5	1.8	2.5	3.1
U.S.	38.3	17.5	0.2	2.5	0.2	28.3	2.4	4.8	3.4

Note: Figures are percent of the total population; (1) Figures cover the Billings, MT Metropolitan Statistical Area; (2) Includes biological, adopted, and stepchildren of the householder
Source: U.S. Census Bureau, 2020 Census

Gender

Area	Males	Females	Males per 100 Females
City	58,615	59,706	98.2
MSA[1]	92,957	94,312	98.6
U.S.	164,545,087	167,842,453	98.0

Note: (1) Figures cover the Billings, MT Metropolitan Statistical Area
Source: U.S. Census Bureau, 2019-2023 American Community Survey 5-Year Estimates

Marital Status

Area	Never Married	Now Married[2]	Separated	Widowed	Divorced
City	31.9	47.2	1.0	5.6	14.3
MSA[1]	28.7	51.5	1.0	5.5	13.3
U.S.	34.1	47.9	1.7	5.6	10.7

Note: Figures are percentages and cover the population 15 years of age and older; (1) Figures cover the Billings, MT Metropolitan Statistical Area; (2) Excludes separated
Source: U.S. Census Bureau, 2019-2023 American Community Survey 5-Year Estimates

Religious Groups by Family

Area	Catholic	Baptist	Methodist	LDS[2]	Pentecostal	Lutheran	Islam	Adventist	Other
MSA[1]	7.4	1.9	1.1	5.2	3.6	4.9	n/a	1.2	7.8
U.S.	18.7	7.3	3.0	2.0	1.8	1.7	1.3	1.3	11.6

Note: Figures are the number of adherents as a percentage of the total population and cover the eight largest religious groups in the U.S; (1) Figures cover the Billings, MT Metropolitan Statistical Area; (2) Church of Jesus Christ of Latter-day Saints
Sources: 2020 U.S. Religion Census, Association of Statisticians of American Religious Bodies; The Association of Religion Data Archives (ARDA)

Religious Groups by Tradition

Area	Catholic	Evangelical Protestant	Mainline Protestant	Black Protestant	Islam	Judaism	Hinduism	Orthodox	Buddhism
MSA[1]	7.4	13.9	5.2	0.1	n/a	n/a	n/a	0.1	n/a
U.S.	18.7	16.5	5.2	2.3	1.3	0.6	0.4	0.4	0.3

Note: Figures are the number of adherents as a percentage of the total population; (1) Figures cover the Billings, MT Metropolitan Statistical Area
Sources: 2020 U.S. Religion Census, Association of Statisticians of American Religious Bodies; The Association of Religion Data Archives (ARDA)

ECONOMY

Real Gross Domestic Product (GDP)

Area	2017	2018	2019	2020	2021	2022	2023	Rank[3]
MSA[1]	10.2	10.3	10.0	9.8	10.5	10.5	10.9	215
U.S.[2]	17,619.1	18,160.7	18,642.5	18,238.9	19,387.6	19,896.6	20,436.3	–

Note: Figures are in billions of chained 2017 dollars; (1) Figures cover the Billings, MT Metropolitan Statistical Area; (2) Figures cover real GDP within metropolitan areas; (3) Rank is based on 2023 data and ranges from 1 to 384
Source: U.S. Bureau of Economic Analysis

Economic Growth

Area	2014	2015	2016	2017	2018	2019	2020	2021	2022	2023
MSA[1]	5.4	4.6	-5.8	7.2	0.6	-2.4	-2.3	7.3	0.1	3.5
U.S.[2]	2.6	3.2	2.0	2.7	3.1	2.7	-2.2	6.3	2.6	2.7

Note: Figures are real gross domestic product growth rates and represent percent change from preceding period; (1) Figures cover the Billings, MT Metropolitan Statistical Area; (2) Figures are the average growth rates within metropolitan areas
Source: U.S. Bureau of Economic Analysis

Metropolitan Area Exports

Area	2018	2019	2020	2021	2022	2023	Rank[2]
MSA[1]	114.3	141.9	116.0	173.8	156.0	119.2	349
U.S.	1,664,056.1	1,645,173.7	1,431,406.6	1,753,941.4	2,062,937.4	2,019,160.5	–

Note: Figures are in millions of dollars; (1) Figures cover the Billings, MT Metropolitan Statistical Area; (2) Rank is based on 2023 data and ranges from 1 to 386
Source: U.S. Department of Commerce, International Trade Administration, Office of Trade and Economic Analysis, Industry and Analysis, Exports by Metropolitan Area, data extracted April 2, 2025

Building Permits

Area	Single-Family			Multi-Family			Total		
	2023	2024	Pct. Chg.	2023	2024	Pct. Chg.	2023	2024	Pct. Chg.
City	259	327	26.3	0	328	–	259	655	152.9
MSA[1]	343	896	161.2	6	629	10,383.3	349	1,525	337.0
U.S.	920,000	981,900	6.7	591,100	496,100	-16.1	1,511,100	1,478,000	-2.2

Note: (1) Figures cover the Billings, MT Metropolitan Statistical Area; Figures represent new, privately-owned housing units authorized (unadjusted data)
Source: U.S. Census Bureau, Building Permits Survey (BPS), 2023, 2024

Bankruptcy Filings

Area	Business Filings			Nonbusiness Filings		
	2023	2024	% Chg.	2023	2024	% Chg.
Yellowstone County	5	9	80.0	111	153	37.8
U.S.	18,926	23,107	22.1	434,064	494,201	13.9

Note: Business filings include Chapter 7, Chapter 9, Chapter 11, Chapter 12, Chapter 13, Chapter 15, and Section 304; Nonbusiness filings include Chapter 7, Chapter 11, and Chapter 13
Source: Administrative Office of the U.S. Courts, Business and Nonbusiness Bankruptcy, County Cases Commenced by Chapter of the Bankruptcy Code, During the 12-Month Period Ending December 31, 2023 and Business and Nonbusiness Bankruptcy, County Cases Commenced by Chapter of the Bankruptcy Code, During the 12-Month Period Ending December 31, 2024

Housing Vacancy Rates

Area	Gross Vacancy Rate[3] (%)			Year-Round Vacancy Rate[4] (%)			Rental Vacancy Rate[5] (%)			Homeowner Vacancy Rate[6] (%)		
	2022	2023	2024	2022	2023	2024	2022	2023	2024	2022	2023	2024
MSA[1]	n/a	n/a	n/a	n/a	n/a	n/a	n/a	n/a	n/a	n/a	n/a	n/a
U.S.[2]	9.1	9.0	9.1	7.5	7.5	7.6	5.7	6.5	6.8	0.8	0.8	1.0

Note: (1) Figures cover the Billings, MT Metropolitan Statistical Area; (2) Figures cover the 75 largest Metropolitan Statistical Areas; (3) The percentage of the total housing inventory that is vacant; (4) The percentage of the housing inventory (excluding seasonal units) that is year-round vacant; (5) The percentage of rental inventory that is vacant for rent; (6) The percentage of homeowner inventory that is vacant for sale; n/a not available
Source: U.S. Census Bureau, Housing Vacancies and Homeownership Annual Statistics: 2022, 2023, 2024

INCOME

Income

Area	Per Capita ($)	Median Household ($)	Average Household ($)
City	42,639	71,855	98,655
MSA[1]	43,176	74,599	102,275
U.S.	43,289	78,538	110,491

Note: (1) Figures cover the Billings, MT Metropolitan Statistical Area
Source: U.S. Census Bureau, 2019-2023 American Community Survey 5-Year Estimates

Household Income Distribution

Area	Percent of Households Earning							
	Under $15,000	$15,000 -$24,999	$25,000 -$34,999	$35,000 -$49,999	$50,000 -$74,999	$75,000 -$99,999	$100,000 -$149,999	$150,000 and up
City	7.2	7.0	7.4	12.6	18.1	13.0	17.9	16.9
MSA[1]	6.6	6.8	7.6	11.5	17.6	13.4	18.1	18.2
U.S.	8.5	6.6	6.8	10.4	15.7	12.7	17.4	21.9

Note: (1) Figures cover the Billings, MT Metropolitan Statistical Area
Source: U.S. Census Bureau, 2019-2023 American Community Survey 5-Year Estimates

Poverty Rate

Area	All Ages	Under 18 Years Old	18 to 64 Years Old	65 Years and Over
City	10.6	13.0	10.2	8.9
MSA[1]	10.0	12.0	9.9	8.2
U.S.	12.4	16.3	11.6	10.4

Note: Figures are percentage of people whose income during the past 12 months was below the poverty level;
(1) Figures cover the Billings, MT Metropolitan Statistical Area
Source: U.S. Census Bureau, 2019-2023 American Community Survey 5-Year Estimates

EMPLOYMENT

Labor Force and Employment

Area	Civilian Labor Force			Workers Employed		
	Dec. 2023	Dec. 2024	% Chg.	Dec. 2023	Dec. 2024	% Chg.
City	59,483	58,785	-1.2	57,662	57,121	-0.9
MSA[1]	99,307	98,165	-1.2	96,370	95,349	-1.1
U.S.	166,661,000	167,746,000	0.7	160,754,000	161,294,000	0.3

Note: Data is not seasonally adjusted and covers workers 16 years of age and older; (1) Figures cover the
Billings, MT Metropolitan Statistical Area
Source: Bureau of Labor Statistics, Local Area Unemployment Statistics

Unemployment Rate

Area	2024											
	Jan.	Feb.	Mar.	Apr.	May	Jun.	Jul.	Aug.	Sep.	Oct.	Nov.	Dec.
City	3.5	3.3	3.0	2.6	2.6	3.2	3.1	3.0	2.5	2.5	2.6	2.8
MSA[1]	3.3	3.3	2.9	2.6	2.5	3.1	3.0	2.9	2.4	2.3	2.4	2.9
U.S.	4.1	4.2	3.9	3.5	3.7	4.3	4.5	4.4	3.9	3.9	4.0	3.8

Note: Data is not seasonally adjusted and covers workers 16 years of age and older; (1) Figures cover the
Billings, MT Metropolitan Statistical Area
Source: Bureau of Labor Statistics, Local Area Unemployment Statistics

Average Wages

Occupation	$/Hr.	Occupation	$/Hr.
Accountants and Auditors	39.29	Maintenance and Repair Workers	22.86
Automotive Mechanics	28.20	Marketing Managers	66.97
Bookkeepers	22.49	Network and Computer Systems Admin.	39.58
Carpenters	27.02	Nurses, Licensed Practical	26.99
Cashiers	14.91	Nurses, Registered	43.06
Computer Programmers	48.63	Nursing Assistants	20.43
Computer Systems Analysts	46.01	Office Clerks, General	21.25
Computer User Support Specialists	26.60	Physical Therapists	46.45
Construction Laborers	24.46	Physicians	n/a
Cooks, Restaurant	18.09	Plumbers, Pipefitters and Steamfitters	37.35
Customer Service Representatives	21.17	Police and Sheriff's Patrol Officers	35.12
Dentists	118.06	Postal Service Mail Carriers	28.52
Electricians	34.75	Real Estate Sales Agents	37.77
Engineers, Electrical	51.14	Retail Salespersons	17.80
Fast Food and Counter Workers	14.42	Sales Representatives, Technical/Scientific	49.31
Financial Managers	73.01	Secretaries, Exc. Legal/Medical/Executive	21.21
First-Line Supervisors of Office Workers	31.75	Security Guards	19.51
General and Operations Managers	52.57	Surgeons	n/a
Hairdressers/Cosmetologists	21.23	Teacher Assistants, Exc. Postsecondary[1]	15.66
Home Health and Personal Care Aides	16.16	Teachers, Secondary School, Exc. Sp. Ed.[1]	31.64
Janitors and Cleaners	18.70	Telemarketers	n/a
Landscaping/Groundskeeping Workers	19.81	Truck Drivers, Heavy/Tractor-Trailer	29.65
Lawyers	52.20	Truck Drivers, Light/Delivery Services	24.41
Maids and Housekeeping Cleaners	17.08	Waiters and Waitresses	14.05

Note: Wage data covers the Billings, MT Metropolitan Statistical Area; (1) Hourly wages were calculated from
annual wage data based on a 40 hour work week
Source: Bureau of Labor Statistics, Metro Area Occupational Employment & Wage Estimates, May 2024

Employment by Industry

Sector	MSA[1]		U.S.
	Number of Employees	Percent of Total	Percent of Total
Construction, Mining, and Logging	7,700	8.0	5.5
Financial Activities	5,200	5.4	5.8
Government	10,700	11.1	14.9
Information	900	0.9	1.9
Leisure and Hospitality	14,100	14.6	10.4
Manufacturing	4,200	4.3	8.0
Other Services	4,100	4.2	3.7
Private Education and Health Services	17,400	18.0	16.9
Professional and Business Services	9,500	9.8	14.2
Retail Trade	12,200	12.6	10.0
Transportation, Warehousing, and Utilities	4,800	5.0	4.8
Wholesale Trade	5,800	6.0	3.9

Note: Figures are non-farm employment as of December 2024. Figures are not seasonally adjusted and include workers 16 years of age and older; (1) Figures cover the Billings, MT Metropolitan Statistical Area
Source: Bureau of Labor Statistics, Current Employment Statistics, Employment, Hours, and Earnings

Employment by Occupation

Occupation Classification	City (%)	MSA[1] (%)	U.S. (%)
Management, Business, Science, and Arts	41.6	39.0	42.0
Natural Resources, Construction, and Maintenance	9.5	11.4	8.6
Production, Transportation, and Material Moving	9.2	11.0	13.0
Sales and Office	22.4	21.0	19.9
Service	17.2	17.7	16.5

Note: Figures cover employed civilians 16 years of age and older; (1) Figures cover the Billings, MT Metropolitan Statistical Area
Source: U.S. Census Bureau, 2019-2023 American Community Survey 5-Year Estimates

Occupations with Greatest Projected Employment Growth: 2022 – 2032

Occupation[1]	2022 Employment	2032 Projected Employment	Numeric Employment Change	Percent Employment Change
Home Health and Personal Care Aides	8,850	11,790	2,940	33.2
Cooks, Restaurant	6,500	8,680	2,180	33.5
Fast Food and Counter Workers	15,780	17,710	1,930	12.2
Registered Nurses	10,360	11,890	1,530	14.8
Stockers and Order Fillers	8,400	9,900	1,500	17.9
General and Operations Managers	9,800	11,170	1,370	14.0
Construction Laborers	5,730	7,080	1,350	23.6
First-Line Supervisors of Construction Trades and Extraction Workers	5,700	6,960	1,260	22.1
Carpenters	5,830	7,050	1,220	20.9
Retail Salespersons	15,440	16,630	1,190	7.7

Note: Projections cover Montana; (1) Sorted by numeric employment change
Source: www.projectionscentral.org, State Occupational Projections, 2022–2032 Long-Term Projections

Fastest-Growing Occupations: 2022 – 2032

Occupation[1]	2022 Employment	2032 Projected Employment	Numeric Employment Change	Percent Employment Change
Nurse Practitioners	880	1,330	450	51.1
Data Scientists	100	150	50	50.0
Medical and Health Services Managers	2,210	3,100	890	40.3
Personal Care and Service Workers, All Other	150	210	60	40.0
Physical Therapist Assistants	300	420	120	40.0
Physician Assistants	740	1,030	290	39.2
Mechanical Door Repairers	130	180	50	38.5
Software Developers	2,190	3,000	810	37.0
Veterinary Assistants and Laboratory Animal Caretakers	570	770	200	35.1
Cooks, Restaurant	6,500	8,680	2,180	33.5

Note: Projections cover Montana; (1) Sorted by percent employment change and excludes occupations with numeric employment change less than 50
Source: www.projectionscentral.org, State Occupational Projections, 2022–2032 Long-Term Projections

CITY FINANCES

City Government Finances

Component	2022 ($000)	2022 ($ per capita)
Total Revenues	239,802	2,185
Total Expenditures	194,820	1,775
Debt Outstanding	200,750	1,829

Source: U.S. Census Bureau, State & Local Government Finances 2022

City Government Revenue by Source

Source	2022 ($000)	2022 ($ per capita)	2022 (%)
General Revenue			
From Federal Government	18,778	171	7.8
From State Government	24,881	227	10.4
From Local Governments	0	0	0.0
Taxes			
Property	52,406	478	21.9
Sales and Gross Receipts	0	0	0.0
Personal Income	0	0	0.0
Corporate Income	0	0	0.0
Motor Vehicle License	2,687	24	1.1
Other Taxes	5,938	54	2.5
Current Charges	72,047	657	30.0
Liquor Store	0	0	0.0
Utility	32,139	293	13.4

Source: U.S. Census Bureau, State & Local Government Finances 2022

City Government Expenditures by Function

Function	2022 ($000)	2022 ($ per capita)	2022 (%)
General Direct Expenditures			
Air Transportation	24,825	226	12.7
Corrections	0	0	0.0
Education	0	0	0.0
Employment Security Administration	0	0	0.0
Financial Administration	1,626	14	0.8
Fire Protection	23,592	215	12.1
General Public Buildings	0	0	0.0
Governmental Administration, Other	3,541	32	1.8
Health	926	8	0.5
Highways	16,808	153	8.6
Hospitals	0	0	0.0
Housing and Community Development	1,623	14	0.8
Interest on General Debt	3,458	31	1.8
Judicial and Legal	3,394	30	1.7
Libraries	3,806	34	2.0
Parking	1,911	17	1.0
Parks and Recreation	8,632	78	4.4
Police Protection	27,261	248	14.0
Public Welfare	0	0	0.0
Sewerage	23,859	217	12.2
Solid Waste Management	15,363	140	7.9
Veterans' Services	0	0	0.0
Liquor Store	0	0	0.0
Utility	31,278	285	16.1

Source: U.S. Census Bureau, State & Local Government Finances 2022

TAXES

State Corporate Income Tax Rates

State	Tax Rate (%)	Income Brackets ($)	Num. of Brackets	Financial Institution Tax Rate (%)[a]	Federal Income Tax Ded.
Montana	6.75 (m)	Flat rate	1	6.75 (m)	No

Note: Tax rates for tax year 2024; (a) Rates listed are the corporate income tax rate applied to financial institutions or excise taxes based on income. Some states have other taxes based upon the value of deposits or shares; (m) Montana levies a 7% tax on taxpayers using water's edge combination. The minimum tax per corporation is $50; the $50 minimum applies to each corporation included on a combined tax return. Taxpayers with gross sales in Montana of $100,000 or less may pay an alternative tax of 0.5% on such sales, instead of the net income tax.
Source: Federation of Tax Administrators, State Corporate Income Tax Rates, January 1, 2025

State Individual Income Tax Rates

State	Tax Rate (%)	Income Brackets ($)	Personal Exemptions ($)			Standard Ded. ($)	
			Single	Married	Depend.	Single	Married
Montana (a)	4.7 - 5.9	20,500 - 41,000	(d)	(d)	(d)	5,090	10,180 (aa) (aa)

Note: Tax rates for tax year 2024; Local- and county-level taxes are not included; The deduction for federal SALT deductions is limited to $5,000 for individuals and $10,000 for joint returns in Missouri and Montana, and to $7,800 for all filers in Oregon; (a) 16 states have statutory provision for automatically adjusting to the rate of inflation the dollar values of the income tax brackets, standard deductions, and/or personal exemptions. Oregon does not index the income brackets for $125,000 and over See: INFL and SPEC above; (d) These states use the personal exemption/standard deduction amounts provided in the federal Internal Revenue Code. Montana personal exemption subject to repeal under Section 15-30-2114; (aa) Standard deduction amounts reported are maximums, Maryland standard deduction is 15% of AGI with an increased deduction above $17,000 - S/$34,333 - MFJ in 2023; Montana, 20% of AGI.
Source: Federation of Tax Administrators, State Individual Income Tax Rates, January 1, 2025

Various State Sales and Excise Tax Rates

State	State Sales Tax (%)	Gasoline[1] ($/gal.)	Cigarette[2] ($/pack)	Spirits[3] ($/gal.)	Wine[4] ($/gal.)	Beer[5] ($/gal.)	Recreational Marijuana (%)
Montana	None	0.34	1.70	10.55	1.06	0.14	(n)

Note: All tax rates as of January 1, 2025; (1) The American Petroleum Institute has developed a methodology for determining the average tax rate on a gallon of fuel. Rates may include any of the following: excise taxes, environmental fees, storage tank fees, other fees or taxes, general sales tax, and local taxes; (2) The federal excise tax of $1.0066 per pack and local taxes are not included; (3) Rates are those applicable to off-premise sales of 40% alcohol by volume (a.b.v.) distilled spirits in 750ml containers. Local excise taxes are excluded; (4) Rates are those applicable to off-premise sales of 11% a.b.v. non-carbonated wine in 750ml containers; (5) Rates are those applicable to off-premise sales of 4.7% a.b.v. beer in 12 ounce containers; (n) 20% excise tax (retail price)
Source: Tax Foundation, 2025 Facts & Figures: How Does Your State Compare?

State Tax Competitiveness Index

State	Overall Rank	Corporate Tax Rank	Individual Income Tax Rank	Sales Tax Rank	Property Tax Rank	Unemployment Insurance Tax Rank
Montana	5	19	10	3	18	21

Note: The Tax Foundation's State Tax Competitiveness Index enables policymakers, taxpayers, and business leaders to gauge how their states' tax systems compare. A rank of 1 is best, 50 is worst. Rankings do not average to the total. States without a tax rank equally as 1. DC's scores and rankings do not affect other states. The report shows tax systems as of July 1, 2024 (the beginning of Fiscal Year 2025).
Source: Tax Foundation, State Tax Competitiveness Index 2025

TRANSPORTATION

Means of Transportation to Work

Area	Car/Truck/Van		Public Transportation			Bicycle	Walked	Other Means	Worked at Home
	Drove Alone	Car-pooled	Bus	Subway	Railroad				
City	78.5	9.1	1.0	0.0	0.0	0.7	2.0	1.0	7.6
MSA[1]	76.5	10.5	1.0	0.0	0.0	0.5	2.3	1.0	8.2
U.S.	70.2	8.5	1.7	1.3	0.4	0.4	2.4	1.6	13.5

Note: Figures are percentages and cover workers 16 years of age and older; (1) Figures cover the Billings, MT Metropolitan Statistical Area
Source: U.S. Census Bureau, 2019-2023 American Community Survey 5-Year Estimates

Travel Time to Work

Area	Less Than 10 Minutes	10 to 19 Minutes	20 to 29 Minutes	30 to 44 Minutes	45 to 59 Minutes	60 to 89 Minutes	90 Minutes or More
City	19.3	51.9	18.3	6.8	1.2	1.2	1.2
MSA[1]	18.7	42.7	20.8	11.0	2.7	2.1	2.0
U.S.	12.6	28.6	21.2	20.8	8.1	6.0	2.8

Note: Note: Figures are percentages and include workers 16 years old and over; (1) Figures cover the Billings, MT Metropolitan Statistical Area
Source: U.S. Census Bureau, 2019-2023 American Community Survey 5-Year Estimates

Key Congestion Measures

Measure	2000	2010	2015	2020	2022
Annual Hours of Delay, Total (000)	n/a	n/a	2,065	1,151	2,269
Annual Hours of Delay, Per Auto Commuter	n/a	n/a	16	9	18
Annual Congestion Cost, Per Auto Commuter ($)	n/a	n/a	369	221	420

Note: n/a not available
Source: Texas A&M Transportation Institute, 2023 Urban Mobility Report

Freeway Travel Time Index

Measure	1985	1990	1995	2000	2005	2010	2015	2020	2022
Urban Area Index[1]	n/a	n/a	n/a	n/a	n/a	n/a	1.08	1.06	1.09
Urban Area Rank[1,2]	n/a	n/a	n/a	n/a	n/a	n/a	n/a	n/a	n/a

Note: Freeway Travel Time Index—the ratio of travel time in the peak period to the travel time at free-flow conditions. For example, a value of 1.30 indicates a 20-minute free-flow trip takes 26 minutes in the peak (20 minutes x 1.30 = 26 minutes); (1) Covers the Billings MT urban area; (2) Rank is based on 101 larger urban areas (#1 = highest travel time index); n/a not available
Source: Texas A&M Transportation Institute, 2023 Urban Mobility Report

Public Transportation

Agency Name / Mode of Transportation	Vehicles Operated in Maximum Service[1]	Annual Unlinked Passenger Trips[2] (in thous.)	Annual Passenger Miles[3] (in thous.)
Billings Metropolitan Transit (Billings MET Transit)			
Bus (directly operated)	16	325.6	1,527.0
Demand Response (directly operated)	13	42.0	246.9

Note: (1) Number of revenue vehicles operated by the given mode and type of service to meet the annual maximum service requirement. This is the revenue vehicle count during the peak season of the year; on the week and day that maximum service is provided. Vehicles operated in maximum service (VOMS) exclude atypical days and one-time special events; (2) Number of passengers who boarded public transportation vehicles. Passengers are counted each time they board a vehicle no matter how many vehicles they use to travel from their origin to their destination. (3) Sum of the distances ridden by all passengers during the entire fiscal year.
Source: Federal Transit Administration, National Transit Database, 2023

Air Transportation

Airport Name and Code / Type of Service	Passenger Airlines[1]	Passenger Enplanements	Freight Carriers[2]	Freight (lbs)
Logan International (BIL)				
Domestic service (U.S. carriers only)	15	475,319	6	27,840,554
International service (U.S. carriers only)	0	0	0	0

Note: (1) Includes all U.S.-based major, minor and commuter airlines that carried at least one passenger during the year; (2) Includes all U.S.-based airlines and freight carriers that transported at least one pound of freight during the year.
Source: Bureau of Transportation Statistics, The Intermodal Transportation Database, Air Carriers: T-100 Domestic Market (U.S. carriers only), 2024; Bureau of Transportation Statistics, The Intermodal Transportation Database, Air Carriers: T-100 International Market (U.S. carriers only), 2024

BUSINESSES

Major Business Headquarters

Company Name	Industry	Rankings	
		Fortune[1]	Forbes[2]
No companies listed	-	-	-

Note: (1) Companies that produce a 10-K are ranked 1 to 500 based on 2023 revenue; (2) All private companies with at least $2 billion in annual revenue through the end of their most current fiscal year are ranked 1 to 275; companies listed are headquartered in the city; dashes indicate no ranking
Source: Fortune, "Fortune 500," 2024; Forbes, "America's Largest Private Companies," 2024

Living Environment

COST OF LIVING

Cost of Living Index

Composite Index	Groceries	Housing	Utilities	Trans-portation	Health Care	Misc. Goods/ Services
99.8	103.5	95.3	82.7	120.0	114.8	98.9

Note: The Cost of Living Index measures regional differences in the cost of consumer goods and services, excluding taxes and non-consumer expenditures, for professional and managerial households in the top income quintile. It is based on more than 50,000 prices covering almost 60 different items for which prices are collected three times a year by chambers of commerce, economic development organizations or university applied economic centers in each participating urban area. The numbers shown should be read as a percentage above or below the national average of 100. For example, a value of 115.4 in the groceries column indicates that grocery prices are 15.4% higher than the national average. Small differences in the index numbers should not be interpreted as significant; Figures cover the Billings MT urban area.
Source: The Council for Community and Economic Research, Cost of Living Index, 2024

Grocery Prices

Area[1]	T-Bone Steak ($/pound)	Frying Chicken ($/pound)	Whole Milk ($/half gal.)	Eggs ($/dozen)	Orange Juice ($/64 oz.)	Coffee ($/11.5 oz.)
City[2]	15.52	1.47	4.72	3.46	4.19	6.92
Avg.	15.42	1.55	4.69	3.25	4.41	5.46
Min.	14.50	1.16	4.43	2.75	4.00	4.85
Max.	17.56	2.89	5.49	4.78	5.54	7.89

*Note: (1) Values for the local area are compared with the average, minimum and maximum values for all 276 areas in the Cost of Living Index; (2) Figures cover the Billings MT urban area; **T-Bone Steak** (price per pound); **Frying Chicken** (price per pound, whole fryer); **Whole Milk** (half gallon carton); **Eggs** (price per dozen, Grade A, large); **Orange Juice** (64 oz. Tropicana or Florida Natural); **Coffee** (11.5 oz. can, vacuum-packed, Maxwell House, Hills Bros, or Folgers).*
Source: The Council for Community and Economic Research, Cost of Living Index, 2024

Housing and Utility Costs

Area[1]	New Home Price ($)	Apartment Rent ($/month)	All Electric ($/month)	Part Electric ($/month)	Other Energy ($/month)	Telephone ($/month)
City[2]	517,409	1,317	-	94.77	60.66	185.25
Avg.	515,975	1,550	210.99	123.07	82.07	194.99
Min.	265,375	692	104.33	53.68	36.26	179.42
Max.	2,775,821	5,719	529.02	397.28	361.63	223.33

*Note: (1) Values for the local area are compared with the average, minimum and maximum values for all 276 areas in the Cost of Living Index; (2) Figures cover the Billings MT urban area; **New Home Price** (2,400 sf living area, 8,000 sf lot, in urban area with full utilities); **Apartment Rent** (950 sf 2 bedroom/1.5 or 2 bath, unfurnished, excluding all utilities except water); **All Electric** (average monthly cost for an all-electric home); **Part Electric** (average monthly cost for a part-electric home); **Other Energy** (average monthly cost for natural gas, fuel oil, coal, wood, and any other forms of energy except electricity); **Telephone** (price includes the base monthly rate plus taxes and fees for three lines of mobile phone service).*
Source: The Council for Community and Economic Research, Cost of Living Index, 2024

Health Care, Transportation, and Other Costs

Area[1]	Doctor ($/visit)	Dentist ($/visit)	Optometrist ($/visit)	Gasoline ($/gallon)	Beauty Salon ($/visit)	Men's Shirt ($)
City[2]	215.23	110.57	164.07	3.33	38.78	36.85
Avg.	143.77	117.51	129.23	3.32	48.57	38.14
Min.	36.74	58.67	67.33	2.80	24.00	13.41
Max.	270.44	216.82	307.33	5.28	94.00	63.89

*Note: (1) Values for the local area are compared with the average, minimum and maximum values for all 276 areas in the Cost of Living Index; (2) Figures cover the Billings MT urban area; **Doctor** (general practitioners routine exam of an established patient); **Dentist** (adult teeth cleaning and periodic oral examination); **Optometrist** (full vision eye exam for established adult patient); **Gasoline** (one gallon regular unleaded, national brand, including all taxes, cash price at self-service pump if available); **Beauty Salon** (woman's shampoo, trim, and blow-dry); **Men's Shirt** (cotton/polyester dress shirt, pinpoint weave, long sleeves).*
Source: The Council for Community and Economic Research, Cost of Living Index, 2024

HOUSING

Homeownership Rate

Area	2017 (%)	2018 (%)	2019 (%)	2020 (%)	2021 (%)	2022 (%)	2023 (%)	2024 (%)
MSA[1]	n/a	n/a	n/a	n/a	n/a	n/a	n/a	n/a
U.S.	63.9	64.4	64.6	66.6	65.5	65.8	65.9	65.6

Note: (1) Figures cover the Billings, MT Metropolitan Statistical Area; n/a not available
Source: U.S. Census Bureau, Housing Vacancies and Homeownership Annual Statistics: 2017-2024

House Price Index (HPI)

Area	National Ranking[2]	Quarterly Change (%)	One-Year Change (%)	Five-Year Change (%)	Since 1991Q1 (%)
MSA[1]	211	-0.95	2.58	54.45	434.47
U.S.[3]	–	1.43	4.51	57.13	327.82

Note: The HPI is a weighted repeat sales index. It measures average price changes in repeat sales or refinancings on the same properties. This information is obtained by reviewing repeat mortgage transactions on single-family properties whose mortgages have been purchased or securitized by Fannie Mae or Freddie Mac since January 1975; (1) Figures cover the Billings, MT Metropolitan Statistical Area; (2) Rankings are based on annual percentage change for all metro areas containing at least 15,000 transactions over the last 10 years and ranges from 1 to 241; (3) figures based on a weighted average of Census Division estimates using a seasonally adjusted, purchase-only index; all figures are for the period ending December 31, 2024
Source: Federal Housing Finance Agency, Change in FHFA Metropolitan Area House Price Indexes, All Transactions Index, 2024Q4

Home Value

Area	Under $100,000	$100,000 -$199,999	$200,000 -$299,999	$300,000 -$399,999	$400,000 -$499,999	$500,000 -$999,999	$1,000,000 or more	Median ($)
City	6.6	10.2	30.1	25.7	15.5	10.6	1.3	311,800
MSA[1]	8.9	10.1	25.9	22.6	14.8	15.5	2.2	322,700
U.S.	12.1	17.8	19.5	14.4	10.5	19.1	6.5	303,400

Note: Figures are percentages except for median and cover owner-occupied housing units; (1) Figures cover the Billings, MT Metropolitan Statistical Area
Source: U.S. Census Bureau, 2019-2023 American Community Survey 5-Year Estimates

Year Housing Structure Built

Area	2020 or Later	2010 -2019	2000 -2009	1990 -1999	1980 -1989	1970 -1979	1960 -1969	1950 -1959	1940 -1949	Before 1940	Median Year
City	2.3	12.7	10.6	11.9	11.3	16.3	9.0	13.1	5.5	7.4	1979
MSA[1]	2.1	12.3	12.8	12.9	11.6	16.7	7.7	10.1	4.8	9.1	1981
U.S.	1.2	8.9	13.6	12.8	13.0	14.4	10.0	9.7	4.5	11.9	1980

Note: Figures are percentages except for Median Year; Note: (1) Figures cover the Billings, MT Metropolitan Statistical Area
Source: U.S. Census Bureau, 2019-2023 American Community Survey 5-Year Estimates

Gross Monthly Rent

Area	Under $500	$500 -$999	$1,000 -$1,499	$1,500 -$1,999	$2,000 -$2,499	$2,500 -$2,999	$3,000 and up	Median ($)
City	7.9	34.2	37.7	14.4	3.3	0.7	1.7	1,097
MSA[1]	8.5	35.8	36.1	14.7	2.8	0.7	1.4	1,072
U.S.	6.5	22.3	29.5	20.2	10.8	4.8	5.9	1,348

Note: Figures are percentages except for median; Gross rent is the contract rent plus the estimated average monthly cost of utilities (electricity, gas, and water and sewer) and fuels (oil, coal, kerosene, wood, etc.) if these are paid by the renter (or paid for the renter by someone else); (1) Figures cover the Billings, MT Metropolitan Statistical Area
Source: U.S. Census Bureau, 2019-2023 American Community Survey 5-Year Estimates

HEALTH

Health Risk Factors

Category	MSA[1] (%)	U.S. (%)
Adults aged 18–64 who have any kind of health care coverage	92.9	90.8
Adults who reported being in good or better health	81.6	81.8
Adults who have been told they have high blood cholesterol	32.3	36.9
Adults who have been told they have high blood pressure	34.6	34.0
Adults who are current smokers	14.4	12.1
Adults who currently use e-cigarettes	8.9	7.7
Adults who currently use chewing tobacco, snuff, or snus	6.0	3.2
Adults who are heavy drinkers[2]	7.0	6.1
Adults who are binge drinkers[3]	19.0	15.2
Adults who are overweight (BMI 25.0 - 29.9)	37.0	34.4
Adults who are obese (BMI 30.0 - 99.8)	33.4	34.3
Adults who participated in any physical activities in the past month	80.1	75.8

Note: All figures are crude prevalence; (1) Figures cover the Billings, MT Metropolitan Statistical Area; (2) Heavy drinkers are classified as adult men having more than 14 drinks per week and adult women having more than 7 drinks per week; (3) Binge drinkers are classified as males having five or more drinks on one occasion or females having four or more drinks on one occasion
Source: Centers for Disease Control and Prevention, Behaviorial Risk Factor Surveillance System, SMART: Selected Metropolitan Area Risk Trends, 2023

Acute and Chronic Health Conditions

Category	MSA[1] (%)	U.S. (%)
Adults who have ever been told they had a heart attack	3.6	4.2
Adults who have ever been told they have angina or coronary heart disease	3.7	4.0
Adults who have ever been told they had a stroke	4.0	3.3
Adults who have ever been told they have asthma	13.8	15.7
Adults who have ever been told they have arthritis	28.2	26.3
Adults who have ever been told they have diabetes[2]	10.1	11.5
Adults who have ever been told they had skin cancer	7.8	5.6
Adults who have ever been told they had any other types of cancer	11.0	8.4
Adults who have ever been told they have COPD	6.2	6.4
Adults who have ever been told they have kidney disease	3.3	3.7
Adults who have ever been told they have a form of depression	28.7	22.0

Note: All figures are crude prevalence; (1) Figures cover the Billings, MT Metropolitan Statistical Area; (2) Figures do not include pregnancy-related, borderline, or pre-diabetes
Source: Centers for Disease Control and Prevention, Behaviorial Risk Factor Surveillance System, SMART: Selected Metropolitan Area Risk Trends, 2023

Health Screening and Vaccination Rates

Category	MSA[1] (%)	U.S. (%)
Adults who have ever been tested for HIV	41.7	37.5
Adults who have had their blood cholesterol checked within the last five years	85.7	87.0
Adults aged 65+ who have had flu shot within the past year	57.8	63.4
Adults aged 65+ who have ever had a pneumonia vaccination	75.2	71.9

Note: All figures are crude prevalence; (1) Figures cover the Billings, MT Metropolitan Statistical Area.
Source: Centers for Disease Control and Prevention, Behaviorial Risk Factor Surveillance System, SMART: Selected Metropolitan Area Risk Trends, 2023

Disability Status

Category	MSA[1] (%)	U.S. (%)
Adults who reported being deaf	10.5	7.4
Are you blind or have serious difficulty seeing, even when wearing glasses?	3.4	4.9
Do you have difficulty doing errands alone?	9.2	7.8
Do you have difficulty dressing or bathing?	3.5	3.6
Do you have serious difficulty concentrating/remembering/making decisions?	17.7	13.7
Do you have serious difficulty walking or climbing stairs?	13.1	13.2

Note: All figures are crude prevalence; (1) Figures cover the Billings, MT Metropolitan Statistical Area.
Source: Centers for Disease Control and Prevention, Behaviorial Risk Factor Surveillance System, SMART: Selected Metropolitan Area Risk Trends, 2023

Mortality Rates for the Top 10 Causes of Death in the U.S.

ICD-10[a] Sub-Chapter	ICD-10[a] Code	Crude Mortality Rate[2] per 100,000 population	
		County[3]	U.S.
Malignant neoplasms	C00-C97	196.3	182.7
Ischaemic heart diseases	I20-I25	130.0	109.6
Provisional assignment of new diseases of uncertain etiology[1]	U00-U49	69.9	65.3
Other forms of heart disease	I30-I51	67.0	65.1
Other degenerative diseases of the nervous system	G30-G31	35.1	52.4
Other external causes of accidental injury	W00-X59	55.1	52.3
Cerebrovascular diseases	I60-I69	35.6	49.1
Chronic lower respiratory diseases	J40-J47	57.3	43.5
Hypertensive diseases	I10-I15	29.5	38.9
Organic, including symptomatic, mental disorders	F01-F09	55.5	33.9

Note: (a) ICD-10 = International Classification of Diseases 10th Revision; (1) Includes COVID-19, adverse effects to COVID-19 vaccines, SARS, and vaping-related disorders; (2) Crude mortality rates are a three-year average covering 2021-2023; (3) Figures cover Yellowstone County.
Source: Centers for Disease Control and Prevention, National Center for Health Statistics. National Vital Statistics System, Mortality 2018-2023 on CDC WONDER Online Database

Mortality Rates for Selected Causes of Death

Cause of Death	ICD-10[a] Code	Crude Mortality Rate[1] per 100,000 population	
		County[2]	U.S.
Accidental poisoning and exposure to noxious substances	X40-X49	23.8	30.5
Alzheimer disease	G30	30.7	35.4
Assault	X85-Y09	6.5	7.3
COVID-19	U07.1	69.9	65.3
Diabetes mellitus	E10-E14	24.6	30.0
Diseases of the liver	K70-K76	30.7	20.8
Human immunodeficiency virus (HIV) disease	B20-B24	Suppressed	1.5
Influenza and pneumonia	J09-J18	8.3	13.4
Intentional self-harm	X60-X84	26.6	14.7
Malnutrition	E40-E46	25.6	6.0
Obesity and other hyperalimentation	E65-E68	Unreliable	3.1
Renal failure	N17-N19	12.2	16.4
Transport accidents	V01-V99	19.7	14.4

Note: (a) ICD-10 = International Classification of Diseases 10th Revision; (1) Crude mortality rates are a three-year average covering 2021-2023; (2) Figures cover Yellowstone County; Data are suppressed when the data meet the criteria for confidentiality constraints; Crude mortality rates are flagged as unreliable when the rate would be calculated with a numerator of 20 or less.
Source: Centers for Disease Control and Prevention, National Center for Health Statistics. National Vital Statistics System, Mortality 2018-2023 on CDC WONDER Online Database

Health Insurance Coverage

Area	With Health Insurance	With Private Health Insurance	With Public Health Insurance	Without Health Insurance	Population Under Age 19 Without Health Insurance
City	93.1	67.1	39.9	6.9	4.8
MSA[1]	93.2	68.2	39.6	6.8	5.2
U.S.	91.4	67.3	36.3	8.6	5.4

Note: Figures are percentages that cover the civilian noninstitutionalized population; (1) Figures cover the Billings, MT Metropolitan Statistical Area
Source: U.S. Census Bureau, 2019-2023 American Community Survey 5-Year Estimates

Number of Medical Professionals

Area	MDs[3]	DOs[3,4]	Dentists	Podiatrists	Chiropractors	Optometrists
County[1] (number)	644	68	173	16	66	46
County[1] (rate[2])	379.2	40.0	101.3	9.4	38.6	26.9
U.S. (rate[2])	302.5	29.2	74.6	6.4	29.5	18.0

Note: Data as of 2023 unless noted; (1) Data covers Yellowstone County; (2) Number of medical professionals per 100,000 population; (3) Data as of 2022 and includes all active, non-federal physicians; (4) Doctor of Osteopathic Medicine
Source: U.S. Department of Health and Human Services, Health Resources and Services Administration, Bureau of Health Professions, Area Resource File (ARF) 2023-2024

Best Hospitals

According to *U.S. News,* the Billings, MT metro area is home to one of the best hospitals in the U.S.: **Billings Clinic** (1 adult specialty). The hospital listed was nationally ranked in at least one of 15 adult or 11 pediatric specialties. The number of specialties shown cover the parent hospital. Only 160 U.S. hospitals performed well enough to be nationally ranked in one or more specialties. Twenty hospitals in the U.S. made the Honor Roll. The Best Hospitals Honor Roll takes both the national rankings and the procedure and condition ratings into account. Hospitals received points if they were nationally ranked in one of the 15 adult specialties—the higher they ranked, the more points they got—and how many ratings of "high performing" they earned in the 20 procedures and conditions. *U.S. News On-line, "America's Best Hospitals 2024-25"*

EDUCATION

Public School District Statistics

District Name	Schls	Pupils	Pupil/ Teacher Ratio	Minority Pupils[1] (%)	Total Rev. per Pupil ($)	Total Exp. per Pupil ($)
Billings Elementary	28	11,089	15.7	29.0	14,261	13,071
Billings High School	6	5,481	17.4	25.0	13,079	12,352

Note: Table includes school districts with 2,000 or more students; (1) Percentage of students that are not non-Hispanic white.
Source: U.S. Department of Education, National Center for Education Statistics, Common Core of Data, Local Education Agency (School District) Universe Survey: School Year 2023-2024; U.S. Department of Education, National Center for Education Statistics, Common Core of Data, School District Finance Survey (F-33): School Year 2021–22

Highest Level of Education

Area	Less than H.S.	H.S. Diploma	Some College, No Deg.	Associate Degree	Bachelor's Degree	Master's Degree	Prof. School Degree	Doctorate Degree
City	4.5	27.6	22.5	8.3	25.0	7.7	2.6	1.7
MSA[1]	4.8	30.1	22.7	9.0	22.8	7.0	2.2	1.5
U.S.	10.6	26.2	19.4	8.8	21.3	9.8	2.3	1.6

Note: Figures cover persons age 25 and over; (1) Figures cover the Billings, MT Metropolitan Statistical Area
Source: U.S. Census Bureau, 2019-2023 American Community Survey 5-Year Estimates

Educational Attainment by Race

Area	High School Graduate or Higher (%)					Bachelor's Degree or Higher (%)				
	Total	White	Black	Asian	Hisp.[2]	Total	White	Black	Asian	Hisp.[2]
City	95.5	96.2	98.6	89.9	85.1	37.0	38.3	35.8	56.4	14.6
MSA[1]	95.2	95.8	99.0	87.5	84.4	33.5	34.3	31.1	47.3	15.7
U.S.	89.4	92.9	88.1	88.0	72.5	35.0	37.7	24.7	57.0	19.9

Note: Figures shown cover persons 25 years old and over; (1) Figures cover the Billings, MT Metropolitan Statistical Area; (2) People of Hispanic origin can be of any race
Source: U.S. Census Bureau, 2019-2023 American Community Survey 5-Year Estimates

School Enrollment by Grade and Control

Area	Preschool (%)		Kindergarten (%)		Grades 1 - 4 (%)		Grades 5 - 8 (%)		Grades 9 - 12 (%)	
	Public	Private	Public	Private	Public	Private	Public	Private	Public	Private
City	39.2	60.8	80.1	19.9	84.7	15.3	84.3	15.7	86.1	13.9
MSA[1]	41.5	58.5	84.1	15.9	87.0	13.0	87.1	12.9	88.2	11.8
U.S.	58.7	41.3	85.2	14.8	87.2	12.8	87.9	12.1	89.0	11.0

Note: Figures shown cover persons 3 years old and over; (1) Figures cover the Billings, MT Metropolitan Statistical Area
Source: U.S. Census Bureau, 2019-2023 American Community Survey 5-Year Estimates

Higher Education

Four-Year Colleges			Two-Year Colleges			Medical Schools[1]	Law Schools[2]	Voc/ Tech[3]
Public	Private Non-profit	Private For-profit	Public	Private Non-profit	Private For-profit			
1	2	0	0	0	0	0	0	1

Note: Figures cover institutions located within the Billings, MT Metropolitan Statistical Area and include main campuses only; (1) includes schools accredited by the Liaison Committee on Medical Education and the American Osteopathic Association's Commission on Osteopathic College Accreditation; (2) includes ABA-accredited schools, schools with provisional ABA accreditation, and state accredited schools; (3) includes all schools with programs that are less than 2 years.
Source: National Center for Education Statistics, Integrated Postsecondary Education System (IPEDS), 2023-24; Wikipedia, List of Medical Schools in the United States, accessed May 2, 2025; Wikipedia, List of Law Schools in the United States, accessed May 2, 2025

EMPLOYERS

Major Employers

Company Name	Industry
Albertsons Companies	Supermarkets
Billings Clinic Health System	Healthcare
Charter Communications	Cable services
CHS Inc. (Cenex)	Agricultural cooperatives
Costco	Miscellaneous general merchandise stores
ExxonMobil	Energy, oil and gas
First Interstate Bank	Community banks
McDonalds	Accommodation & food services
Phillips 66 Company	Energy, oil and gas
Rocky Mountain College	Colleges & universities
ROI Solutions	Call center
SCL Health Medical Group	Healthcare
St. John's Lutheran Home	Senior living and healthcare
St. Vincent Healthcare	Healthcare
Sysco Food Services	Marketer and distributor of foodservice products
Target	Department stores, discount
Town Pump	Convenience stores
United Parcel Service	Shipping/delivery service
Wal-Mart Stores	Department stores, discount
Wells Fargo	National commercial banks

Note: Companies shown are located within the Billings, MT Metropolitan Statistical Area.
Source: Chambers of Commerce; State Departments of Labor; Wikipedia

PUBLIC SAFETY

Crime Rate

Area	Total Crime Rate	Violent Crime Rate				Property Crime Rate		
		Murder	Rape	Robbery	Aggrav. Assault	Burglary	Larceny -Theft	Motor Vehicle Theft
City	4,487.3	7.4	83.2	123.6	674.0	346.1	2,723.2	529.8
U.S.	2,290.9	5.7	38.0	66.5	264.1	250.7	1,347.2	318.7

Note: Figures are crimes per 100,000 population.
Source: FBI, Table 8, Offenses Known to Law Enforcement, by State by City, 2023

Hate Crimes

Area	Number of Quarters Reported	Number of Incidents per Bias Motivation					
		Race/Ethnicity/ Ancestry	Religion	Sexual Orientation	Disability	Gender	Gender Identity
City	4	0	0	0	0	0	0
U.S.	4	5,900	2,699	2,077	187	92	492

Source: Federal Bureau of Investigation, Hate Crime Statistics 2023

Identity Theft Consumer Reports

Area	Reports	Reports per 100,000 Population	Rank[2]
MSA[1]	279	149	269
U.S.	1,135,291	339	-

Note: (1) Figures cover the Billings, MT Metropolitan Statistical Area; (2) Rank ranges from 1 to 401 where 1 indicates greatest number of identity theft reports per 100,000 population
Source: Federal Trade Commission, Consumer Sentinel Network Data Book 2024

Fraud and Other Consumer Reports

Area	Reports	Reports per 100,000 Population	Rank[2]
MSA[1]	1,608	859	291
U.S.	5,360,641	1,601	-

Note: (1) Figures cover the Billings, MT Metropolitan Statistical Area; (2) Rank ranges from 1 to 401 where 1 indicates greatest number of fraud and other consumer reports per 100,000 population
Source: Federal Trade Commission, Consumer Sentinel Network Data Book 2024

POLITICS

2024 Presidential Election Results

Area	Trump (Rep.)	Harris (Dem.)	Stein (Green)	Kennedy (Ind.)	Oliver (Lib.)	Other
Yellowstone County	62.0	34.9	0.4	1.9	0.8	0.0
U.S.	49.7	48.2	0.6	0.5	0.4	0.6

Note: Results are percentages and may not add to 100% due to rounding
Source: Dave Leip's Atlas of U.S. Presidential Elections

SPORTS

Professional Sports Teams

Team Name	League	Year Established
No teams are located in the metro area		

Source: Wikipedia, Major Professional Sports Teams of the United States and Canada, May 1, 2025

CLIMATE

Average and Extreme Temperatures

Temperature	Jan	Feb	Mar	Apr	May	Jun	Jul	Aug	Sep	Oct	Nov	Dec	Yr.
Extreme High (°F)	68	72	79	90	95	105	105	105	103	90	77	69	105
Average High (°F)	32	38	45	57	67	77	86	85	72	61	45	36	59
Average Temp. (°F)	23	29	35	46	56	65	72	71	60	49	36	27	47
Average Low (°F)	14	19	25	34	44	52	58	57	47	37	26	18	36
Extreme Low (°F)	-28	-28	-19	9	14	32	41	35	22	-7	-22	-32	-32

Note: Figures cover the years 1948-1995
Source: National Climatic Data Center, International Station Meteorological Climate Summary, 9/96

Average Precipitation/Snowfall/Humidity

Precip./Humidity	Jan	Feb	Mar	Apr	May	Jun	Jul	Aug	Sep	Oct	Nov	Dec	Yr.
Avg. Precip. (in.)	0.8	0.6	1.1	1.8	2.4	2.1	1.1	0.9	1.3	1.1	0.8	0.7	14.6
Avg. Snowfall (in.)	10	7	10	9	2	Tr	0	Tr	1	4	7	9	59
Avg. Rel. Hum. 5am (%)	64	66	69	68	71	72	64	61	64	63	65	64	66
Avg. Rel. Hum. 5pm (%)	56	53	48	42	42	41	32	30	37	42	53	56	44

Note: Figures cover the years 1948-1995; Tr = Trace amounts (<0.05 in. of rain; <0.5 in. of snow)
Source: National Climatic Data Center, International Station Meteorological Climate Summary, 9/96

Weather Conditions

Temperature			Daytime Sky			Precipitation		
5°F & below	32°F & below	90°F & above	Clear	Partly cloudy	Cloudy	0.01 inch or more precip.	0.1 inch or more snow/ice	Thunder-storms
25	149	29	75	163	127	97	41	27

Note: Figures are average number of days per year and cover the years 1948-1995
Source: National Climatic Data Center, International Station Meteorological Climate Summary, 9/96

HAZARDOUS WASTE

Superfund Sites

The Billings, MT metro area is home to three sites on the EPA's Superfund National Priorities List (NPL) or Superfund Alternative Approach (SAA) list: **Billings Pce** (Final NPL); **Lockwood Solvent Ground Water Plume** (Final NPL); **Mouat Industries** (Final NPL). The Superfund alternative approach uses the same investigation and cleanup process and standards that are used for sites listed on the National Priorities List. The SAA is an alternative to listing a site on the NPL; it is not an alternative to Superfund or the Superfund process. There are a total of 1,445 Superfund sites with a status of proposed or final on both lists in the United States. *U.S. Environmental Protection Agency, National Priorities List, May 1, 2025; U.S. Environmental Protection Agency, Superfund Alternative Approach Sites, May 1, 2025*

AIR QUALITY

Air Quality Trends: Ozone

	1990	1995	2000	2005	2010	2015	2020	2021	2022	2023
MSA[1]	n/a	n/a	n/a	n/a	n/a	n/a	n/a	n/a	n/a	n/a
U.S.	0.087	0.089	0.081	0.080	0.072	0.068	0.066	0.067	0.067	0.070

Note: (1) Data covers the Billings, MT Metropolitan Statistical Area; n/a not available. The values shown are the composite ozone concentration averages among trend sites based on the highest fourth daily maximum 8-hour concentration in parts per million. These trends are based on sites having an adequate record of monitoring data during the trend period. Data from exceptional events are included.
Source: U.S. Environmental Protection Agency, Air Quality Monitoring Information, "Air Quality Trends by City, 1990-2023"

Air Quality Index

Area	Percent of Days when Air Quality was...[2]					AQI Statistics[2]	
	Good	Moderate	Unhealthy for Sensitive Groups	Unhealthy	Very Unhealthy	Maximum	Median
MSA[1]	85.7	13.2	0.8	0.3	0.0	191	29

Note: (1) Data covers the Billings, MT Metropolitan Statistical Area; (2) Based on 357 days with AQI data in 2023. Air Quality Index (AQI) is an index for reporting daily air quality. EPA calculates the AQI for five major air pollutants regulated by the Clean Air Act: ground-level ozone, particle pollution (aka particulate matter), carbon monoxide, sulfur dioxide, and nitrogen dioxide. The AQI runs from 0 to 500. The higher the AQI value, the greater the level of air pollution and the greater the health concern. There are six AQI categories: "Good" AQI is between 0 and 50. Air quality is considered satisfactory; "Moderate" AQI is between 51 and 100. Air quality is acceptable; "Unhealthy for Sensitive Groups" When AQI values are between 101 and 150, members of sensitive groups may experience health effects; "Unhealthy" When AQI values are between 151 and 200 everyone may begin to experience health effects; "Very Unhealthy" AQI values between 201 and 300 trigger a health alert; "Hazardous" AQI values over 300 trigger warnings of emergency conditions (not shown).
Source: U.S. Environmental Protection Agency, Air Quality Index Report, 2023

Air Quality Index Pollutants

Area	Percent of Days when AQI Pollutant was...[2]					
	Carbon Monoxide	Nitrogen Dioxide	Ozone	Sulfur Dioxide	Particulate Matter 2.5	Particulate Matter 10
MSA[1]	0.0	0.0	0.0	(3)	100.0	0.0

Note: (1) Data covers the Billings, MT Metropolitan Statistical Area; (2) Based on 357 days with AQI data in 2023. The Air Quality Index (AQI) is an index for reporting daily air quality. EPA calculates the AQI for five major air pollutants regulated by the Clean Air Act: ground-level ozone, particle pollution (also known as particulate matter), carbon monoxide, sulfur dioxide, and nitrogen dioxide. The AQI runs from 0 to 500. The higher the AQI value, the greater the level of air pollution and the greater the health concern; (3) Sulfur dioxide is no longer included in this table because SO_2 concentrations tend to be very localized and not necessarily representative of broad geographical areas like counties and CBSAs.
Source: U.S. Environmental Protection Agency, Air Quality Index Report, 2023

Maximum Air Pollutant Concentrations: Particulate Matter, Ozone, CO and Lead

	Particulate Matter 10 (ug/m^3)	Particulate Matter 2.5 Wtd AM (ug/m^3)	Particulate Matter 2.5 24-Hr (ug/m^3)	Ozone (ppm)	Carbon Monoxide (ppm)	Lead (ug/m^3)
MSA[1] Level	n/a	6.7	29	n/a	n/a	n/a
NAAQS[2]	150	15	35	0.075	9	0.15
Met NAAQS[2]	n/a	Yes	Yes	n/a	n/a	n/a

Note: (1) Data covers the Billings, MT Metropolitan Statistical Area; Data from exceptional events are included; (2) National Ambient Air Quality Standards; ppm = parts per million; ug/m^3 = micrograms per cubic meter; n/a not available.
Concentrations: Particulate Matter 10 (coarse particulate)—highest second maximum 24-hour concentration; Particulate Matter 2.5 Wtd AM (fine particulate)—highest weighted annual mean concentration; Particulate Matter 2.5 24-Hour (fine particulate)—highest 98th percentile 24-hour concentration; Ozone—highest fourth daily maximum 8-hour concentration; Carbon Monoxide—highest second maximum non-overlapping 8-hour concentration; Lead—maximum running 3-month average
Source: U.S. Environmental Protection Agency, Air Quality Monitoring Information, "Air Quality Statistics by City, 2023"

Maximum Air Pollutant Concentrations: Nitrogen Dioxide and Sulfur Dioxide

	Nitrogen Dioxide AM (ppb)	Nitrogen Dioxide 1-Hr (ppb)	Sulfur Dioxide AM (ppb)	Sulfur Dioxide 1-Hr (ppb)	Sulfur Dioxide 24-Hr (ppb)
MSA[1] Level	n/a	n/a	n/a	19	n/a
NAAQS[2]	53	100	30	75	140
Met NAAQS[2]	n/a	n/a	n/a	Yes	n/a

Note: (1) Data covers the Billings, MT Metropolitan Statistical Area; Data from exceptional events are included; (2) National Ambient Air Quality Standards; ppm = parts per million; ug/m^3 = micrograms per cubic meter; n/a not available.
Concentrations: Nitrogen Dioxide AM—highest arithmetic mean concentration; Nitrogen Dioxide 1-Hr—highest 98th percentile 1-hour daily maximum concentration; Sulfur Dioxide AM—highest annual mean concentration; Sulfur Dioxide 1-Hr—highest 99th percentile 1-hour daily maximum concentration; Sulfur Dioxide 24-Hr—highest second maximum 24-hour concentration
Source: U.S. Environmental Protection Agency, Air Quality Monitoring Information, "Air Quality Statistics by City, 2023"

Boise City, Idaho

Background

Boise (boy-see) is the capital and largest city in Idaho, lying along the Boise River adjacent to the foothills of the Rocky Mountains. The city is located southwest of the western slopes of the Rockies and is the site of a great system of natural warm water springs.

Boise's spectacular natural location is its most popular, and obvious, attraction. This, coupled with its dynamic economic growth in recent decades, makes Boise an altogether remarkable city. The splendor of its surroundings, together with an average 18-minute drive to work, has allowed the city to combine pleasure and production in an enviable mix.

French-Canadian trappers were familiar with Boise and its environs by 1811, and the name of the city is an Anglicization of the French Les Bois—the trees. The first substantial European settlement dates to 1863 when, in the spring of that year, I.M. Coston built from pegged driftwood a great house that served as a hub for the activities of prospectors, traders, and Native Americans. In the same year, the U.S. Army built Fort Boise, and considerable deposits of gold and silver were discovered in the area. The U.S. Assay Office in Boise, in 1870-71 alone, is said to have valuated more than $75 million in precious metals.

The area is rich in gold rush lore, and there is still talk of buried treasure from that era; an eastbound stagecoach from Boise was said to have been waylaid by a robber, six miles above the city on the south side of the river who, though wounded in the attack, managed to drag off a strongbox filled with $50,000 in gold. The robber died of his wounds and was discovered the next day, but the loot was never found.

The Boise area was subsequently developed for farming, as crops of grains, vegetables, and fruits replaced the mines as its source of wealth. It became the territorial capital of Idaho in 1864 and the state capital in 1890. Education was served with the opening of a university in 1932, which became Boise State University in 1974 and now enrolls about 20,000 students.

The city's natural setting offers a great range of outdoor activities that are pursued energetically by locals and visitors alike. Its rivers, mountains, deserts, and lakes offer world-class skiing, hiking, camping, kayaking, river rafting, hunting, and fishing. Bike paths run throughout the city and into Boise's large outdoor trail network, the Boise River Greenbelt. Recreational wilderness exists extensively just outside the city's limits. The Word Center for Birds of Prey is located on the city's southern frontier and is the site of the Peregrine Falcon's rehabilitation and release into the wild.

Many large regional, national, and international companies are headquartered in Boise, including major call centers for DIRECTV and T-Mobile. Top employers include St. Luke's Health Systems and Micron Technology.

The city produces high- and low-tech products and everything in between, including software, computer components, steel and sheet metal products, mobile homes, lumber products, farm machinery, packed meats, and processed foods. Increasingly an advanced technological center, Boise continues to serve as a trading center for the greater agricultural region.

By virtue of its history and geographical character, the city can be considered a presence on the Pacific Rim. In a more tangible vein, Boise, with nine airlines operating at its airport, is conveniently tied to the wider world.

Boise's Basque community is the largest in the United States and the third largest in the world outside Argentina and the Basque Country in Spain and France. A large Basque festival known as Jaialdi is held once every five years, with the next scheduled for July 2025.

The city is protected by the mountains to the north, largely unbothered by the extreme blizzards that affect eastern Idaho and parts of neighboring states. Boise, and this section of western Idaho generally, is affected by climatic influences from the Pacific Ocean and exhibits an unusually mild climate for this latitude. Summers can be hot, but nights are almost always cool, and sunshine generally prevails.

Rankings

General Rankings

- To help military veterans find the best places in which to settle down, *WalletHub* compared the 100 largest U.S. cities across 19 key indicators of livability, affordability and veteran-friendliness. They range from the share of military skill-related jobs to veteran income growth to the availability of VA health facilities. Boise City ranked #21. *Wallethub.com, "Best & Worst Places for Veterans to Live (2025)," November 7, 2024*

- *US News & World Report* conducted a survey of more than 3,500 people and analyzed the 150 largest metropolitan areas to determine what matters most when selecting the next place to live. Boise City ranked #2 out of the top 25 as having the best combination of desirable factors. Criteria: cost of living; quality of life and education; climate; job market; desirability; and other factors. *realestate.usnews.com, "Best Places to Live in the U.S. in 2024-2025," May 21, 2024*

- Boise City was selected as one of the best places in the world that are a "celebration of travel's power to transform us and our connections with one another" by *National Geographic Travel* editors. These cultural-rich spots are steeped in tradition, community, and history as reported on by its global community of experts. The list reflects 25 of the most extraordinary travel adventures for 2025. *NationalGeographic.com, "Best of the World, The 25 Best Places in the World to Travel to in 2025," October 22, 2024*

- Boise City was selected as one of the best places to live in the United States by *Money* magazine. The city placed among the top 50. This year's list focused on cities built around community spirit, thoughtful policy and civic engagement. Instead of relying on a predetermined dataset, the cities and towns were grouped according to their strengths and chosen due their affordability, good schools and strong job markets. *Money, "The 50 Best Places to Live in the U.S., 2024" April 8, 2024*

Business/Finance Rankings

- The Boise City metro area appeared on the Milken Institute "2025 Best Performing Cities" list. Rank: #10 out of 200 large metro areas (based on performance category). Criteria: job growth; wage growth; high-tech growth and impact; community resilience; housing affordability; household broadband access. *Milken Institute, "Best-Performing Cities 2025," January 14, 2025*

Education Rankings

- Personal finance website *WalletHub* analyzed the 150 largest U.S. metropolitan statistical areas to determine where the most educated Americans are putting their degrees to work. Criteria: education levels; percentage of workers with degrees; education quality and attainment gap; public school quality rankings; quality and enrollment of each metro area's universities. Boise City was ranked #50 (#1 = most educated city). *WalletHub.com, "Most & Least Educated Cities in America, 2025" July 2, 2024*

Health/Fitness Rankings

- For each of the 100 largest cities in the United States, the American Fitness Index®, compiled in partnership between the American College of Sports Medicine and the Elevance Health Foundation, evaluated community infrastructure and more than 30 health behaviors including preventive health, levels of chronic disease conditions, food insecurity, pedestrian safety, air quality, and community/environment resources that support physical activity. Boise City ranked #27 for "community fitness." *americanfitnessindex.org, "2024 ACSM American Fitness Index Summary Report," July 23, 2024*

- Boise City was identified as a "2025 Allergy Capital." The area ranked #95 out of the nation's 100 largest metropolitan areas. Three groups of factors were used to identify the most challenging cities for people with allergies: annual tree, grass, and weed pollen scores; over the counter allergy medicine use; number of board-certified allergy specialists. *Asthma and Allergy Foundation of America, "2025 Allergy Capitals: The Most Challenging Places to Live with Allergies," March 18, 2025*

- Boise City was identified as a "2024 Asthma Capital." The area ranked #90 out of the nation's 100 largest metropolitan areas. Criteria: estimated asthma prevalence; asthma-related mortality; and ER visits due to asthma. Risk factors analyzed but not factored in the rankings: annual air quality including pollution and ozone levels; public smoking laws; indoor air quality; access to asthma specialists; rescue and controller medication use; uninsured rate; pollen allergy; poverty rate. *Asthma and Allergy Foundation of America, "Asthma Capitals 2024: The Most Challenging Places to Live With Asthma," September 10, 2024*

Real Estate Rankings

- *WalletHub* compared the most populated U.S. cities to determine which had the best markets for real estate agents. Boise City ranked #107 where demand was high and pay was the best. Criteria: sales per agent; annual median wage for real-estate agents; monthly average starting salary for real estate agents; real estate job density and competition; unemployment rate; home turnover rate; housing-market health index; and other relevant metrics. *WalletHub.com, "2021 Best Places to Be a Real Estate Agent," May 12, 2021*

- The Boise City metro area was identified as one of the top 16 housing markets to invest in for 2025 by *Forbes*. Criteria: stable local economies with good population growth and increase in jobs providing good support for home prices and rents. *Forbes.com, "Best Local Markets For Real Estate Investing In 2025," November 6, 2024*

- The Boise City metro area was identified as one of the 20 worst housing markets in the U.S. in 2024. The area ranked #214 out of 226 markets. Criteria: year-over-year change of median sales price of existing single-family homes between the 4th quarter of 2023 and the 4th quarter of 2024. *National Association of Realtors®, Median Sales Price of Existing Single-Family Homes for Metropolitan Areas, 4th Quarter 2024*

- Boise City was ranked #145 out of 176 metro areas in terms of cost of housing in 2024 by the National Association of Home Builders (#1 = most affordable). Criteria: the portion of an average family's income necessary to pay the mortgage on a median-priced home. *National Association of Home Builders®, NAHB-Wells Fargo Cost of Housing Index, 4th Quarter 2024*

Sports/Recreation Rankings

- Boise City was chosen as a bicycle friendly community by the League of American Bicyclists. A "Bicycle Friendly Community" welcomes cyclists by providing safe and supportive accommodation for cycling and encouraging people to bike for transportation and recreation. There are four award levels: Platinum; Gold; Silver; and Bronze. The community achieved an award level of Gold. *League of American Bicyclists, "2024 Awards-New & Renewing Bicycle Friendly Communities List," January 28, 2025*

Women/Minorities Rankings

- Personal finance website *WalletHub* compared more than 180 U.S. cities across two key dimensions, "Hispanic Business-Friendliness" and "Hispanic Purchasing Power," to arrive at the most favorable conditions for Hispanic entrepreneurs. Boise City was ranked #36 out of 182. Criteria includes: share of Hispanic-Owned Businesses; average growth of Hispanic Business revenues; Small Business-Friendliness score; affordability; and number of Hispanics with at least a bachelor's degree. *WalletHub.com, "Best Cities for Hispanic Entrepreneurs," September 4, 2024*

Miscellaneous Rankings

- *WalletHub* compared 148 of the most populated U.S. cities to determine their operating efficiency. A "Quality of Services" score was constructed for each city and then measured against the total budget per capita to reveal which were managed the best. Boise City ranked #3. Criteria: financial stability; economy; education; safety; health; infrastructure and pollution. *WalletHub.com, "2025's Best- & Worst-Run Cities in America," June 18, 2024*

Business Environment

DEMOGRAPHICS

Population Growth

Area	1990 Census	2000 Census	2010 Census	2020 Census	2023 Estimate[2]	Population Growth 1990-2023 (%)
City	144,317	185,787	205,671	235,684	235,701	63.3
MSA[1]	319,596	464,840	616,561	764,718	790,640	147.4
U.S.	248,709,873	281,421,906	308,745,538	331,449,281	332,387,540	33.6

Note: (1) Figures cover the Boise City, ID Metropolitan Statistical Area; (2) 2019-2023 5-year ACS population estimate
Source: U.S. Census Bureau, 1990 Census, 2000 Census, 2010 Census, 2020 Census, 2019-2023 American Community Survey 5-Year Estimates

Race

Area	White Alone[2] (%)	Black Alone[2] (%)	Asian Alone[2] (%)	AIAN[3] Alone[2] (%)	NHOPI[4] Alone[2] (%)	Other Race Alone[2] (%)	Two or More Races (%)
City	83.6	1.4	3.3	0.7	0.3	3.0	7.6
MSA[1]	81.5	1.0	1.9	0.8	0.2	5.6	9.0
U.S.	63.4	12.4	5.8	0.9	0.2	6.6	10.7

Note: (1) Figures cover the Boise City, ID Metropolitan Statistical Area; (2) Alone is defined as not being in combination with one or more other races; (3) American Indian and Alaska Native; (4) Native Hawaiian and Other Pacific Islander
Source: U.S. Census Bureau, 2019-2023 American Community Survey 5-Year Estimates

Hispanic or Latino Origin

Area	Total (%)	Mexican (%)	Puerto Rican (%)	Cuban (%)	Other (%)
City	9.5	7.0	0.4	0.1	2.1
MSA[1]	14.7	11.8	0.4	0.1	2.4
U.S.	19.0	11.3	1.8	0.7	5.2

Note: Persons of Hispanic or Latino origin can be of any race; (1) Figures cover the Boise City, ID Metropolitan Statistical Area
Source: U.S. Census Bureau, 2019-2023 American Community Survey 5-Year Estimates

Age

Area	Percent of Population									Median Age
	Under Age 5	Age 5–19	Age 20–34	Age 35–44	Age 45–54	Age 55–64	Age 65–74	Age 75–84	Age 85+	
City	4.4	17.8	23.2	14.2	12.6	12.5	9.2	4.6	1.6	38.2
MSA[1]	5.7	20.8	19.9	13.9	12.2	11.8	9.6	4.6	1.4	37.4
U.S.	5.7	19.1	20.2	13.1	12.3	12.8	10.0	4.9	1.9	38.7

Note: (1) Figures cover the Boise City, ID Metropolitan Statistical Area
Source: U.S. Census Bureau, 2019-2023 American Community Survey 5-Year Estimates

Disability by Age

Area	All Ages	Under 18 Years Old	18 to 64 Years Old	65 Years and Over
City	12.1	5.3	10.2	29.4
MSA[1]	12.7	4.9	11.0	31.0
U.S.	13.0	4.7	10.7	32.9

Note: Figures show percent of the civilian noninstitutionalized population that reported having a disability. Disability status is determined from six types of difficulty: vision, hearing, cognitive, ambulatory, self-care, and independent living. For children under 5 years old, hearing and vision difficulty are used to determine disability status. For children between the ages of 5 and 14, disability status is determined from hearing, vision, cognitive, ambulatory, and self-care difficulties. For people aged 15 years and older, they are considered to have a disability if they have difficulty with any one of the six difficulty types; Note: (1) Figures cover the Boise City, ID Metropolitan Statistical Area
Source: U.S. Census Bureau, 2019-2023 American Community Survey 5-Year Estimates

Ancestry

Area	German	Irish	English	American	Italian	Polish	French[2]	European	Scottish
City	18.2	11.5	17.8	3.9	4.2	1.7	2.4	3.7	3.1
MSA[1]	17.0	10.2	18.2	4.8	3.5	1.4	2.4	3.1	3.1
U.S.	12.6	9.4	9.1	5.5	4.9	2.6	2.0	1.6	1.6

Note: Figures are the percentage of the total population reporting a particular ancestry. The nine most commonly reported ancestries in the U.S. are shown. Figures include multiple ancestries (e.g. if a person reported being Irish and Italian, they were included in both columns); (1) Figures cover the Boise City, ID Metropolitan Statistical Area; (2) Excludes Basque
Source: U.S. Census Bureau, 2019-2023 American Community Survey 5-Year Estimates

Foreign-born Population

Area	Any Foreign Country	Asia	Mexico	Europe	Caribbean	Central America[2]	South America	Africa	Canada
City	7.2	3.0	1.3	1.3	0.1	0.1	0.3	0.6	0.5
MSA[1]	6.6	1.5	2.6	1.1	0.0	0.3	0.3	0.3	0.3
U.S.	13.9	4.3	3.3	1.4	1.4	1.2	1.2	0.8	0.2

Note: (1) Figures cover the Boise City, ID Metropolitan Statistical Area; (2) Excludes Mexico.
Source: U.S. Census Bureau, 2019-2023 American Community Survey 5-Year Estimates

Household Size

Area	Persons in Household (%) One	Two	Three	Four	Five	Six	Seven or More	Average Household Size
City	30.1	37.7	15.0	10.9	4.2	1.5	0.7	2.30
MSA[1]	23.2	36.6	15.4	13.4	6.5	3.3	1.7	2.62
U.S.	28.5	33.8	15.4	12.7	5.9	2.3	1.4	2.54

Note: (1) Figures cover the Boise City, ID Metropolitan Statistical Area
Source: U.S. Census Bureau, 2019-2023 American Community Survey 5-Year Estimates

Household Relationships

Area	House-holder	Opposite-sex Spouse	Same-sex Spouse	Opposite-sex Unmarried Partner	Same-sex Unmarried Partner	Child[2]	Grand-child	Other Relatives	Non-relatives
City	41.4	17.8	0.2	3.2	0.2	24.7	1.3	2.9	5.4
MSA[1]	36.6	19.5	0.2	2.5	0.1	29.7	1.9	3.5	3.8
U.S.	38.3	17.5	0.2	2.5	0.2	28.3	2.4	4.8	3.4

Note: Figures are percent of the total population; (1) Figures cover the Boise City, ID Metropolitan Statistical Area; (2) Includes biological, adopted, and stepchildren of the householder
Source: U.S. Census Bureau, 2020 Census

Gender

Area	Males	Females	Males per 100 Females
City	118,294	117,407	100.8
MSA[1]	397,370	393,270	101.0
U.S.	164,545,087	167,842,453	98.0

Note: (1) Figures cover the Boise City, ID Metropolitan Statistical Area
Source: U.S. Census Bureau, 2019-2023 American Community Survey 5-Year Estimates

Marital Status

Area	Never Married	Now Married[2]	Separated	Widowed	Divorced
City	35.2	46.8	1.0	4.3	12.7
MSA[1]	28.9	54.0	1.0	4.4	11.8
U.S.	34.1	47.9	1.7	5.6	10.7

Note: Figures are percentages and cover the population 15 years of age and older; (1) Figures cover the Boise City, ID Metropolitan Statistical Area; (2) Excludes separated
Source: U.S. Census Bureau, 2019-2023 American Community Survey 5-Year Estimates

Religious Groups by Family

Area	Catholic	Baptist	Methodist	LDS[2]	Pentecostal	Lutheran	Islam	Adventist	Other
MSA[1]	13.0	0.8	2.5	15.0	1.6	0.8	0.3	1.7	10.0
U.S.	18.7	7.3	3.0	2.0	1.8	1.7	1.3	1.3	11.6

Note: Figures are the number of adherents as a percentage of the total population and cover the eight largest religious groups in the U.S; (1) Figures cover the Boise City, ID Metropolitan Statistical Area; (2) Church of Jesus Christ of Latter-day Saints
Sources: 2020 U.S. Religion Census, Association of Statisticians of American Religious Bodies; The Association of Religion Data Archives (ARDA)

Religious Groups by Tradition

Area	Catholic	Evangelical Protestant	Mainline Protestant	Black Protestant	Islam	Judaism	Hinduism	Orthodox	Buddhism
MSA[1]	13.0	11.9	3.9	<0.1	0.3	0.1	0.2	0.1	0.1
U.S.	18.7	16.5	5.2	2.3	1.3	0.6	0.4	0.4	0.3

Note: Figures are the number of adherents as a percentage of the total population; (1) Figures cover the Boise City, ID Metropolitan Statistical Area
Sources: 2020 U.S. Religion Census, Association of Statisticians of American Religious Bodies; The Association of Religion Data Archives (ARDA)

ECONOMY

Real Gross Domestic Product (GDP)

Area	2017	2018	2019	2020	2021	2022	2023	Rank[3]
MSA[1]	32.3	34.8	36.4	37.0	40.4	43.4	44.6	76
U.S.[2]	17,619.1	18,160.7	18,642.5	18,238.9	19,387.6	19,896.6	20,436.3	–

Note: Figures are in billions of chained 2017 dollars; (1) Figures cover the Boise City, ID Metropolitan Statistical Area; (2) Figures cover real GDP within metropolitan areas; (3) Rank is based on 2023 data and ranges from 1 to 384
Source: U.S. Bureau of Economic Analysis

Economic Growth

Area	2014	2015	2016	2017	2018	2019	2020	2021	2022	2023
MSA[1]	4.5	1.6	4.2	5.5	7.8	4.7	1.6	9.1	7.5	2.9
U.S.[2]	2.6	3.2	2.0	2.7	3.1	2.7	-2.2	6.3	2.6	2.7

Note: Figures are real gross domestic product growth rates and represent percent change from preceding period; (1) Figures cover the Boise City, ID Metropolitan Statistical Area; (2) Figures are the average growth rates within metropolitan areas
Source: U.S. Bureau of Economic Analysis

Metropolitan Area Exports

Area	2018	2019	2020	2021	2022	2023	Rank[2]
MSA[1]	2,771.7	2,062.8	1,632.9	1,937.1	2,156.7	1,922.6	121
U.S.	1,664,056.1	1,645,173.7	1,431,406.6	1,753,941.4	2,062,937.4	2,019,160.5	–

Note: Figures are in millions of dollars; (1) Figures cover the Boise City, ID Metropolitan Statistical Area; (2) Rank is based on 2023 data and ranges from 1 to 386
Source: U.S. Department of Commerce, International Trade Administration, Office of Trade and Economic Analysis, Industry and Analysis, Exports by Metropolitan Area, data extracted April 2, 2025

Building Permits

Area	Single-Family			Multi-Family			Total		
	2023	2024	Pct. Chg.	2023	2024	Pct. Chg.	2023	2024	Pct. Chg.
City	447	468	4.7	1,450	273	-81.2	1,897	741	-60.9
MSA[1]	6,508	8,252	26.8	3,383	811	-76.0	9,891	9,063	-8.4
U.S.	920,000	981,900	6.7	591,100	496,100	-16.1	1,511,100	1,478,000	-2.2

Note: (1) Figures cover the Boise City, ID Metropolitan Statistical Area; Figures represent new, privately-owned housing units authorized (unadjusted data)
Source: U.S. Census Bureau, Building Permits Survey (BPS), 2023, 2024

Bankruptcy Filings

Area	Business Filings			Nonbusiness Filings		
	2023	2024	% Chg.	2023	2024	% Chg.
Ada County	18	26	44.4	350	466	33.1
U.S.	18,926	23,107	22.1	434,064	494,201	13.9

Note: Business filings include Chapter 7, Chapter 9, Chapter 11, Chapter 12, Chapter 13, Chapter 15, and Section 304; Nonbusiness filings include Chapter 7, Chapter 11, and Chapter 13
Source: Administrative Office of the U.S. Courts, Business and Nonbusiness Bankruptcy, County Cases Commenced by Chapter of the Bankruptcy Code, During the 12-Month Period Ending December 31, 2023 and Business and Nonbusiness Bankruptcy, County Cases Commenced by Chapter of the Bankruptcy Code, During the 12-Month Period Ending December 31, 2024

Housing Vacancy Rates

Area	Gross Vacancy Rate[3] (%)			Year-Round Vacancy Rate[4] (%)			Rental Vacancy Rate[5] (%)			Homeowner Vacancy Rate[6] (%)		
	2022	2023	2024	2022	2023	2024	2022	2023	2024	2022	2023	2024
MSA[1]	n/a	n/a	n/a	n/a	n/a	n/a	n/a	n/a	n/a	n/a	n/a	n/a
U.S.[2]	9.1	9.0	9.1	7.5	7.5	7.6	5.7	6.5	6.8	0.8	0.8	1.0

Note: (1) Figures cover the Boise City, ID Metropolitan Statistical Area; (2) Figures cover the 75 largest Metropolitan Statistical Areas; (3) The percentage of the total housing inventory that is vacant; (4) The percentage of the housing inventory (excluding seasonal units) that is year-round vacant; (5) The percentage of rental inventory that is vacant for rent; (6) The percentage of homeowner inventory that is vacant for sale; n/a not available
Source: U.S. Census Bureau, Housing Vacancies and Homeownership Annual Statistics: 2022, 2023, 2024

INCOME

Income

Area	Per Capita ($)	Median Household ($)	Average Household ($)
City	48,274	81,308	112,482
MSA[1]	41,793	82,694	110,044
U.S.	43,289	78,538	110,491

Note: (1) Figures cover the Boise City, ID Metropolitan Statistical Area
Source: U.S. Census Bureau, 2019-2023 American Community Survey 5-Year Estimates

Household Income Distribution

Area	Percent of Households Earning							
	Under $15,000	$15,000 -$24,999	$25,000 -$34,999	$35,000 -$49,999	$50,000 -$74,999	$75,000 -$99,999	$100,000 -$149,999	$150,000 and up
City	5.7	6.0	6.3	11.2	16.6	15.1	17.4	21.6
MSA[1]	5.3	5.3	5.6	10.5	18.4	15.3	19.7	19.8
U.S.	8.5	6.6	6.8	10.4	15.7	12.7	17.4	21.9

Note: (1) Figures cover the Boise City, ID Metropolitan Statistical Area
Source: U.S. Census Bureau, 2019-2023 American Community Survey 5-Year Estimates

Poverty Rate

Area	All Ages	Under 18 Years Old	18 to 64 Years Old	65 Years and Over
City	10.6	12.7	10.8	7.3
MSA[1]	9.1	10.7	8.9	7.7
U.S.	12.4	16.3	11.6	10.4

Note: Figures are percentage of people whose income during the past 12 months was below the poverty level;
(1) Figures cover the Boise City, ID Metropolitan Statistical Area
Source: U.S. Census Bureau, 2019-2023 American Community Survey 5-Year Estimates

EMPLOYMENT

Labor Force and Employment

Area	Civilian Labor Force			Workers Employed		
	Dec. 2023	Dec. 2024	% Chg.	Dec. 2023	Dec. 2024	% Chg.
City	146,113	151,831	3.9	142,029	147,110	3.6
MSA[1]	432,273	448,781	3.8	418,731	433,330	3.5
U.S.	166,661,000	167,746,000	0.7	160,754,000	161,294,000	0.3

Note: Data is not seasonally adjusted and covers workers 16 years of age and older; (1) Figures cover the Boise City, ID Metropolitan Statistical Area
Source: Bureau of Labor Statistics, Local Area Unemployment Statistics

Unemployment Rate

Area	2024											
	Jan.	Feb.	Mar.	Apr.	May	Jun.	Jul.	Aug.	Sep.	Oct.	Nov.	Dec.
City	3.3	3.4	3.3	2.9	3.0	3.3	3.5	3.3	3.1	3.1	3.3	3.1
MSA[1]	3.8	3.9	3.7	3.2	3.3	3.6	3.8	3.7	3.3	3.4	3.6	3.4
U.S.	4.1	4.2	3.9	3.5	3.7	4.3	4.5	4.4	3.9	3.9	4.0	3.8

Note: Data is not seasonally adjusted and covers workers 16 years of age and older; (1) Figures cover the Boise City, ID Metropolitan Statistical Area
Source: Bureau of Labor Statistics, Local Area Unemployment Statistics

Average Wages

Occupation	$/Hr.	Occupation	$/Hr.
Accountants and Auditors	35.88	Maintenance and Repair Workers	24.14
Automotive Mechanics	24.94	Marketing Managers	62.17
Bookkeepers	23.92	Network and Computer Systems Admin.	49.66
Carpenters	24.55	Nurses, Licensed Practical	30.70
Cashiers	15.24	Nurses, Registered	44.68
Computer Programmers	43.27	Nursing Assistants	18.92
Computer Systems Analysts	44.48	Office Clerks, General	21.13
Computer User Support Specialists	26.79	Physical Therapists	46.02
Construction Laborers	22.50	Physicians	150.09
Cooks, Restaurant	16.50	Plumbers, Pipefitters and Steamfitters	28.71
Customer Service Representatives	21.14	Police and Sheriff's Patrol Officers	36.96
Dentists	85.60	Postal Service Mail Carriers	28.72
Electricians	29.13	Real Estate Sales Agents	n/a
Engineers, Electrical	65.01	Retail Salespersons	18.06
Fast Food and Counter Workers	13.54	Sales Representatives, Technical/Scientific	59.59
Financial Managers	68.45	Secretaries, Exc. Legal/Medical/Executive	20.77
First-Line Supervisors of Office Workers	30.86	Security Guards	20.32
General and Operations Managers	47.05	Surgeons	n/a
Hairdressers/Cosmetologists	15.23	Teacher Assistants, Exc. Postsecondary[1]	15.78
Home Health and Personal Care Aides	16.17	Teachers, Secondary School, Exc. Sp. Ed.[1]	32.07
Janitors and Cleaners	16.90	Telemarketers	18.37
Landscaping/Groundskeeping Workers	20.23	Truck Drivers, Heavy/Tractor-Trailer	27.48
Lawyers	67.91	Truck Drivers, Light/Delivery Services	27.08
Maids and Housekeeping Cleaners	16.90	Waiters and Waitresses	16.87

Note: Wage data covers the Boise City, ID Metropolitan Statistical Area; (1) Hourly wages were calculated from annual wage data based on a 40 hour work week
Source: Bureau of Labor Statistics, Metro Area Occupational Employment & Wage Estimates, May 2024

Employment by Industry

Sector	MSA[1]		U.S.
	Number of Employees	Percent of Total	Percent of Total
Construction, Mining, and Logging	37,800	9.1	5.5
Financial Activities	23,900	5.8	5.8
Government	55,100	13.3	14.9
Information	4,700	1.1	1.9
Leisure and Hospitality	41,200	10.0	10.4
Manufacturing	31,400	7.6	8.0
Other Services	14,600	3.5	3.7
Private Education and Health Services	63,800	15.4	16.9
Professional and Business Services	60,500	14.6	14.2
Retail Trade	41,500	10.0	10.0
Transportation, Warehousing, and Utilities	19,200	4.6	4.8
Wholesale Trade	19,600	4.7	3.9

Note: Figures are non-farm employment as of December 2024. Figures are not seasonally adjusted and include workers 16 years of age and older; (1) Figures cover the Boise City, ID Metropolitan Statistical Area
Source: Bureau of Labor Statistics, Current Employment Statistics, Employment, Hours, and Earnings

Employment by Occupation

Occupation Classification	City (%)	MSA[1] (%)	U.S. (%)
Management, Business, Science, and Arts	48.7	42.5	42.0
Natural Resources, Construction, and Maintenance	7.6	10.8	8.6
Production, Transportation, and Material Moving	8.8	10.9	13.0
Sales and Office	19.6	20.5	19.9
Service	15.3	15.3	16.5

Note: Figures cover employed civilians 16 years of age and older; (1) Figures cover the Boise City, ID Metropolitan Statistical Area
Source: U.S. Census Bureau, 2019-2023 American Community Survey 5-Year Estimates

Occupations with Greatest Projected Employment Growth: 2022 – 2032

Occupation[1]	2022 Employment	2032 Projected Employment	Numeric Employment Change	Percent Employment Change
Retail Salespersons	62,660	69,110	6,450	10.3
Home Health and Personal Care Aides	17,960	23,500	5,540	30.8
Carpenters	13,980	18,190	4,210	30.1
Construction Laborers	12,910	16,330	3,420	26.5
Registered Nurses	15,480	18,580	3,100	20.0
General and Operations Managers	16,100	18,790	2,690	16.7
Cooks, Restaurant	8,030	10,660	2,630	32.8
Laborers and Freight, Stock, and Material Movers, Hand	12,080	14,160	2,080	17.2
Fast Food and Counter Workers	16,630	18,680	2,050	12.3
Light Truck or Delivery Services Drivers	8,050	10,100	2,050	25.5

Note: Projections cover Idaho; (1) Sorted by numeric employment change
Source: www.projectionscentral.org, State Occupational Projections, 2022–2032 Long-Term Projections

Fastest-Growing Occupations: 2022 – 2032

Occupation[1]	2022 Employment	2032 Projected Employment	Numeric Employment Change	Percent Employment Change
Training and Development Managers	160	260	100	62.5
Nurse Practitioners	900	1,440	540	60.0
Instructional Coordinators	890	1,340	450	50.6
Medical and Health Services Managers	2,460	3,580	1,120	45.5
Occupational Therapy Assistants	200	290	90	45.0
Information Security Analysts (SOC 2018)	470	670	200	42.6
Physician Assistants	920	1,310	390	42.4
Computer and Information Research Scientists (SOC 2018)	190	270	80	42.1
Physical Therapist Assistants	540	760	220	40.7
Speech-Language Pathologists	790	1,100	310	39.2

Note: Projections cover Idaho; (1) Sorted by percent employment change and excludes occupations with numeric employment change less than 50
Source: www.projectionscentral.org, State Occupational Projections, 2022–2032 Long-Term Projections

CITY FINANCES

City Government Finances

Component	2022 ($000)	2022 ($ per capita)
Total Revenues	460,167	2,003
Total Expenditures	443,405	1,930
Debt Outstanding	118,845	517

Source: U.S. Census Bureau, State & Local Government Finances 2022

City Government Revenue by Source

Source	2022 ($000)	2022 ($ per capita)	2022 (%)
General Revenue			
From Federal Government	30,000	131	6.5
From State Government	53,831	234	11.7
From Local Governments	0	0	0.0
Taxes			
Property	155,006	675	33.7
Sales and Gross Receipts	8,653	38	1.9
Personal Income	0	0	0.0
Corporate Income	0	0	0.0
Motor Vehicle License	0	0	0.0
Other Taxes	9,966	43	2.2
Current Charges	190,579	829	41.4
Liquor Store	0	0	0.0
Utility	0	0	0.0

Source: U.S. Census Bureau, State & Local Government Finances 2022

City Government Expenditures by Function

Function	2022 ($000)	2022 ($ per capita)	2022 (%)
General Direct Expenditures			
Air Transportation	42,751	186	9.6
Corrections	0	0	0.0
Education	0	0	0.0
Employment Security Administration	0	0	0.0
Financial Administration	9,987	43	2.3
Fire Protection	60,424	263	13.6
General Public Buildings	5,679	24	1.3
Governmental Administration, Other	16,954	73	3.8
Health	2,765	12	0.6
Highways	0	0	0.0
Hospitals	0	0	0.0
Housing and Community Development	31,913	138	7.2
Interest on General Debt	2,530	11	0.6
Judicial and Legal	7,693	33	1.7
Libraries	15,232	66	3.4
Parking	50	< 1	< 0.1
Parks and Recreation	46,011	200	10.4
Police Protection	59,255	257	13.4
Public Welfare	0	0	0.0
Sewerage	38,799	168	8.8
Solid Waste Management	68,699	299	15.5
Veterans' Services	0	0	0.0
Liquor Store	0	0	0.0
Utility	2,023	8	0.5

Source: U.S. Census Bureau, State & Local Government Finances 2022

TAXES

State Corporate Income Tax Rates

State	Tax Rate (%)	Income Brackets ($)	Num. of Brackets	Financial Institution Tax Rate (%)[a]	Federal Income Tax Ded.
Idaho	5.8 (f)	Flat rate	1	5.8 (f)	No

Note: Tax rates for tax year 2024; (a) Rates listed are the corporate income tax rate applied to financial institutions or excise taxes based on income. Some states have other taxes based upon the value of deposits or shares; (f) Idaho's minimum tax on a corporation is $20. The $10 Permanent Building Fund Tax must be paid by each corporation in a unitary group filing a combined return. Taxpayers with gross sales in Idaho under $100,000, and with no property or payroll in Idaho, may elect to pay 1% on such sales (instead of the tax on net income).
Source: Federation of Tax Administrators, State Corporate Income Tax Rates, January 1, 2025

State Individual Income Tax Rates

State	Tax Rate (%)	Income Brackets ($)	Personal Exemptions ($) Single	Married	Depend.	Standard Ded. ($) Single	Married
Idaho	5.8	Flat rate	(d)	(d)	(d)	14,600	29,200 (d)

Note: Tax rates for tax year 2024; Local- and county-level taxes are not included; Federal income tax is not deductible on state income tax returns; (d) These states use the personal exemption/standard deduction amounts provided in the federal Internal Revenue Code. Montana personal exemption subject to repeal under Section 15-30-2114.
Source: Federation of Tax Administrators, State Individual Income Tax Rates, January 1, 2025

Various State Sales and Excise Tax Rates

State	State Sales Tax (%)	Gasoline[1] ($/gal.)	Cigarette[2] ($/pack)	Spirits[3] ($/gal.)	Wine[4] ($/gal.)	Beer[5] ($/gal.)	Recreational Marijuana (%)
Idaho	6	0.33	0.57	12.94	0.45	0.15	Not legal

Note: All tax rates as of January 1, 2025; (1) The American Petroleum Institute has developed a methodology for determining the average tax rate on a gallon of fuel. Rates may include any of the following: excise taxes, environmental fees, storage tank fees, other fees or taxes, general sales tax, and local taxes; (2) The federal excise tax of $1.0066 per pack and local taxes are not included; (3) Rates are those applicable to off-premise sales of 40% alcohol by volume (a.b.v.) distilled spirits in 750ml containers. Local excise taxes are excluded; (4) Rates are those applicable to off-premise sales of 11% a.b.v. non-carbonated wine in 750ml containers; (5) Rates are those applicable to off-premise sales of 4.7% a.b.v. beer in 12 ounce containers.
Source: Tax Foundation, 2025 Facts & Figures: How Does Your State Compare?

State Tax Competitiveness Index

State	Overall Rank	Corporate Tax Rank	Individual Income Tax Rank	Sales Tax Rank	Property Tax Rank	Unemployment Insurance Tax Rank
Idaho	11	21	11	9	3	35

Note: The Tax Foundation's State Tax Competitiveness Index enables policymakers, taxpayers, and business leaders to gauge how their states' tax systems compare. A rank of 1 is best, 50 is worst. Rankings do not average to the total. States without a tax rank equally as 1. DC's scores and rankings do not affect other states. The report shows tax systems as of July 1, 2024 (the beginning of Fiscal Year 2025).
Source: Tax Foundation, State Tax Competitiveness Index 2025

TRANSPORTATION

Means of Transportation to Work

Area	Car/Truck/Van Drove Alone	Car-pooled	Public Transportation Bus	Subway	Railroad	Bicycle	Walked	Other Means	Worked at Home
City	68.6	7.6	0.5	0.0	0.0	2.3	3.4	1.6	15.8
MSA[1]	71.7	8.3	0.3	0.0	0.0	1.1	2.2	1.4	15.1
U.S.	70.2	8.5	1.7	1.3	0.4	0.4	2.4	1.6	13.5

Note: Figures are percentages and cover workers 16 years of age and older; (1) Figures cover the Boise City, ID Metropolitan Statistical Area
Source: U.S. Census Bureau, 2019-2023 American Community Survey 5-Year Estimates

Travel Time to Work

Area	Less Than 10 Minutes	10 to 19 Minutes	20 to 29 Minutes	30 to 44 Minutes	45 to 59 Minutes	60 to 89 Minutes	90 Minutes or More
City	14.3	44.2	25.5	11.5	1.7	1.6	1.2
MSA[1]	13.4	31.8	25.2	19.9	5.8	2.3	1.5
U.S.	12.6	28.6	21.2	20.8	8.1	6.0	2.8

Note: Note: Figures are percentages and include workers 16 years old and over; (1) Figures cover the Boise City, ID Metropolitan Statistical Area
Source: U.S. Census Bureau, 2019-2023 American Community Survey 5-Year Estimates

Key Congestion Measures

Measure	2000	2010	2015	2020	2022
Annual Hours of Delay, Total (000)	5,019	9,599	10,855	5,102	10,214
Annual Hours of Delay, Per Auto Commuter	28	35	43	18	36
Annual Congestion Cost, Per Auto Commuter ($)	504	774	805	381	729

Note: Figures cover the Boise ID urban area
Source: Texas A&M Transportation Institute, 2023 Urban Mobility Report

Freeway Travel Time Index

Measure	1985	1990	1995	2000	2005	2010	2015	2020	2022
Urban Area Index[1]	1.01	1.04	1.06	1.11	1.15	1.15	1.15	1.05	1.15
Urban Area Rank[1,2]	100	94	93	79	68	65	67	85	54

Note: Freeway Travel Time Index—the ratio of travel time in the peak period to the travel time at free-flow conditions. For example, a value of 1.30 indicates a 20-minute free-flow trip takes 26 minutes in the peak (20 minutes x 1.30 = 26 minutes); (1) Covers the Boise ID urban area; (2) Rank is based on 101 larger urban areas (#1 = highest travel time index)
Source: Texas A&M Transportation Institute, 2023 Urban Mobility Report

Public Transportation

Agency Name / Mode of Transportation	Vehicles Operated in Maximum Service[1]	Annual Unlinked Passenger Trips[2] (in thous.)	Annual Passenger Miles[3] (in thous.)
Ada County Highway District, dba ACHD Commuteride			
Vanpool (directly operated)	92	130.7	5,076.9
Boise State University			
Bus (directly operated)	9	151.7	n/a

Note: (1) Number of revenue vehicles operated by the given mode and type of service to meet the annual maximum service requirement. This is the revenue vehicle count during the peak season of the year; on the week and day that maximum service is provided. Vehicles operated in maximum service (VOMS) exclude atypical days and one-time special events; (2) Number of passengers who boarded public transportation vehicles. Passengers are counted each time they board a vehicle no matter how many vehicles they use to travel from their origin to their destination. (3) Sum of the distances ridden by all passengers during the entire fiscal year. Source: Federal Transit Administration, National Transit Database, 2023

Air Transportation

Airport Name and Code / Type of Service	Passenger Airlines[1]	Passenger Enplanements	Freight Carriers[2]	Freight (lbs)
Boise Air Terminal-Gowen Field (BOI)				
Domestic service (U.S. carriers only)	18	2,474,747	12	44,604,157
International service (U.S. carriers only)	0	0	0	0

Note: (1) Includes all U.S.-based major, minor and commuter airlines that carried at least one passenger during the year; (2) Includes all U.S.-based airlines and freight carriers that transported at least one pound of freight during the year. Source: Bureau of Transportation Statistics, The Intermodal Transportation Database, Air Carriers: T-100 Domestic Market (U.S. carriers only), 2024; Bureau of Transportation Statistics, The Intermodal Transportation Database, Air Carriers: T-100 International Market (U.S. carriers only), 2024

BUSINESSES

Major Business Headquarters

Company Name	Industry	Rankings Fortune[1]	Rankings Forbes[2]
Albertsons	Food & drug stores	53	-
JR Simplot	Food, drink & tobacco	-	47
Micron Technology	Semiconductors and other electronic components	264	-
WinCo Foods	Retailing	-	53

Note: (1) Companies that produce a 10-K are ranked 1 to 500 based on 2023 revenue; (2) All private companies with at least $2 billion in annual revenue through the end of their most current fiscal year are ranked 1 to 275; companies listed are headquartered in the city; dashes indicate no ranking Source: Fortune, "Fortune 500," 2024; Forbes, "America's Largest Private Companies," 2024

Fastest-Growing Businesses

According to *Inc.*, Boise City is home to two of America's 500 fastest-growing private companies: **Fromley** (#250); **Strike Tax Advisory** (#297). Criteria: must be an independent, privately-held, for-profit, U.S. corporation, proprietorship or partnership as of December 31, 2023; revenues must be at least $100,000 in 2020 and $2 million in 2023; must have four-year operating/sales history. *Inc., "America's 500 Fastest-Growing Private Companies," 2024*

According to Deloitte, Boise City is home to one of North America's 500 fastest-growing high-technology companies: **Tackle** (#470). Companies are ranked by percentage growth in revenue over a four-year period. Criteria for inclusion: company must be headquartered within North America; must own proprietary intellectual property or technology that is sold to customers in products that contributes to a significant portion of the company's operating revenue; must have been in business for a minumum of four years with 2020 operating revenues of at least $50,000 USD/CD and 2023 operating revenues of at least $5 million USD/CD. *Deloitte, 2024 Technology Fast 500™*

Living Environment

COST OF LIVING

Cost of Living Index

Composite Index	Groceries	Housing	Utilities	Trans- portation	Health Care	Misc. Goods/ Services
102.1	103.7	101.0	77.8	109.9	98.2	106.6

Note: The Cost of Living Index measures regional differences in the cost of consumer goods and services, excluding taxes and non-consumer expenditures, for professional and managerial households in the top income quintile. It is based on more than 50,000 prices covering almost 60 different items for which prices are collected three times a year by chambers of commerce, economic development organizations or university applied economic centers in each participating urban area. The numbers shown should be read as a percentage above or below the national average of 100. For example, a value of 115.4 in the groceries column indicates that grocery prices are 15.4% higher than the national average. Small differences in the index numbers should not be interpreted as significant; Figures cover the Boise ID urban area.
Source: The Council for Community and Economic Research, Cost of Living Index, 2024

Grocery Prices

Area[1]	T-Bone Steak ($/pound)	Frying Chicken ($/pound)	Whole Milk ($/half gal.)	Eggs ($/dozen)	Orange Juice ($/64 oz.)	Coffee ($/11.5 oz.)
City[2]	15.52	1.52	4.75	3.63	4.45	6.38
Avg.	15.42	1.55	4.69	3.25	4.41	5.46
Min.	14.50	1.16	4.43	2.75	4.00	4.85
Max.	17.56	2.89	5.49	4.78	5.54	7.89

*Note: (1) Values for the local area are compared with the average, minimum and maximum values for all 276 areas in the Cost of Living Index; (2) Figures cover the Boise ID urban area; **T-Bone Steak** (price per pound); **Frying Chicken** (price per pound, whole fryer); **Whole Milk** (half gallon carton); **Eggs** (price per dozen, Grade A, large); **Orange Juice** (64 oz. Tropicana or Florida Natural); **Coffee** (11.5 oz. can, vacuum-packed, Maxwell House, Hills Bros, or Folgers).*
Source: The Council for Community and Economic Research, Cost of Living Index, 2024

Housing and Utility Costs

Area[1]	New Home Price ($)	Apartment Rent ($/month)	All Electric ($/month)	Part Electric ($/month)	Other Energy ($/month)	Telephone ($/month)
City[2]	514,076	1,611	-	83.70	59.41	179.42
Avg.	515,975	1,550	210.99	123.07	82.07	194.99
Min.	265,375	692	104.33	53.68	36.26	179.42
Max.	2,775,821	5,719	529.02	397.28	361.63	223.33

*Note: (1) Values for the local area are compared with the average, minimum and maximum values for all 276 areas in the Cost of Living Index; (2) Figures cover the Boise ID urban area; **New Home Price** (2,400 sf living area, 8,000 sf lot, in urban area with full utilities); **Apartment Rent** (950 sf 2 bedroom/1.5 or 2 bath, unfurnished, excluding all utilities except water); **All Electric** (average monthly cost for an all-electric home); **Part Electric** (average monthly cost for a part-electric home); **Other Energy** (average monthly cost for natural gas, fuel oil, coal, wood, and any other forms of energy except electricity); **Telephone** (price includes the base monthly rate plus taxes and fees for three lines of mobile phone service).*
Source: The Council for Community and Economic Research, Cost of Living Index, 2024

Health Care, Transportation, and Other Costs

Area[1]	Doctor ($/visit)	Dentist ($/visit)	Optometrist ($/visit)	Gasoline ($/gallon)	Beauty Salon ($/visit)	Men's Shirt ($)
City[2]	169.88	102.77	145.10	3.61	52.55	48.06
Avg.	143.77	117.51	129.23	3.32	48.57	38.14
Min.	36.74	58.67	67.33	2.80	24.00	13.41
Max.	270.44	216.82	307.33	5.28	94.00	63.89

*Note: (1) Values for the local area are compared with the average, minimum and maximum values for all 276 areas in the Cost of Living Index; (2) Figures cover the Boise ID urban area; **Doctor** (general practitioners routine exam of an established patient); **Dentist** (adult teeth cleaning and periodic oral examination); **Optometrist** (full vision eye exam for established adult patient); **Gasoline** (one gallon regular unleaded, national brand, including all taxes, cash price at self-service pump if available); **Beauty Salon** (woman's shampoo, trim, and blow-dry); **Men's Shirt** (cotton/polyester dress shirt, pinpoint weave, long sleeves).*
Source: The Council for Community and Economic Research, Cost of Living Index, 2024

HOUSING

Homeownership Rate

Area	2017 (%)	2018 (%)	2019 (%)	2020 (%)	2021 (%)	2022 (%)	2023 (%)	2024 (%)
MSA[1]	n/a	n/a	n/a	n/a	n/a	n/a	n/a	n/a
U.S.	63.9	64.4	64.6	66.6	65.5	65.8	65.9	65.6

Note: (1) Figures cover the Boise City, ID Metropolitan Statistical Area; n/a not available
Source: U.S. Census Bureau, Housing Vacancies and Homeownership Annual Statistics: 2017-2024

House Price Index (HPI)

Area	National Ranking[2]	Quarterly Change (%)	One-Year Change (%)	Five-Year Change (%)	Since 1991Q1 (%)
MSA[1]	156	0.77	4.58	63.16	546.52
U.S.[3]	–	1.43	4.51	57.13	327.82

Note: The HPI is a weighted repeat sales index. It measures average price changes in repeat sales or refinancings on the same properties. This information is obtained by reviewing repeat mortgage transactions on single-family properties whose mortgages have been purchased or securitized by Fannie Mae or Freddie Mac since January 1975; (1) Figures cover the Boise City, ID Metropolitan Statistical Area; (2) Rankings are based on annual percentage change for all metro areas containing at least 15,000 transactions over the last 10 years and ranges from 1 to 241; (3) figures based on a weighted average of Census Division estimates using a seasonally adjusted, purchase-only index; all figures are for the period ending December 31, 2024
Source: Federal Housing Finance Agency, Change in FHFA Metropolitan Area House Price Indexes, All Transactions Index, 2024Q4

Home Value

Area	Under $100,000	$100,000 -$199,999	$200,000 -$299,999	$300,000 -$399,999	$400,000 -$499,999	$500,000 -$999,999	$1,000,000 or more	Median ($)
City	4.2	3.9	12.0	18.2	21.0	33.8	6.9	456,000
MSA[1]	5.0	4.9	13.8	19.8	19.1	31.9	5.6	434,400
U.S.	12.1	17.8	19.5	14.4	10.5	19.1	6.5	303,400

Note: Figures are percentages except for median and cover owner-occupied housing units; (1) Figures cover the Boise City, ID Metropolitan Statistical Area
Source: U.S. Census Bureau, 2019-2023 American Community Survey 5-Year Estimates

Year Housing Structure Built

Area	2020 or Later	2010 -2019	2000 -2009	1990 -1999	1980 -1989	1970 -1979	1960 -1969	1950 -1959	1940 -1949	Before 1940	Median Year
City	1.3	10.8	11.4	19.6	14.4	17.8	7.8	7.2	3.7	6.3	1985
MSA[1]	3.5	17.3	22.2	17.7	8.9	13.4	4.7	4.2	2.8	5.2	1996
U.S.	1.2	8.9	13.6	12.8	13.0	14.4	10.0	9.7	4.5	11.9	1980

Note: Figures are percentages except for Median Year; Note: (1) Figures cover the Boise City, ID Metropolitan Statistical Area
Source: U.S. Census Bureau, 2019-2023 American Community Survey 5-Year Estimates

Gross Monthly Rent

Area	Under $500	$500 -$999	$1,000 -$1,499	$1,500 -$1,999	$2,000 -$2,499	$2,500 -$2,999	$3,000 and up	Median ($)
City	4.1	15.0	41.7	26.5	9.3	1.9	1.6	1,359
MSA[1]	4.7	16.9	37.0	26.4	10.2	2.7	2.2	1,383
U.S.	6.5	22.3	29.5	20.2	10.8	4.8	5.9	1,348

Note: Figures are percentages except for median; Gross rent is the contract rent plus the estimated average monthly cost of utilities (electricity, gas, and water and sewer) and fuels (oil, coal, kerosene, wood, etc.) if these are paid by the renter (or paid for the renter by someone else); (1) Figures cover the Boise City, ID Metropolitan Statistical Area
Source: U.S. Census Bureau, 2019-2023 American Community Survey 5-Year Estimates

HEALTH

Health Risk Factors

Category	MSA[1] (%)	U.S. (%)
Adults aged 18–64 who have any kind of health care coverage	89.1	90.8
Adults who reported being in good or better health	84.3	81.8
Adults who have been told they have high blood cholesterol	35.5	36.9
Adults who have been told they have high blood pressure	31.9	34.0
Adults who are current smokers	10.9	12.1
Adults who currently use e-cigarettes	10.0	7.7
Adults who currently use chewing tobacco, snuff, or snus	3.8	3.2
Adults who are heavy drinkers[2]	5.9	6.1
Adults who are binge drinkers[3]	16.6	15.2
Adults who are overweight (BMI 25.0 - 29.9)	35.1	34.4
Adults who are obese (BMI 30.0 - 99.8)	30.4	34.3
Adults who participated in any physical activities in the past month	80.1	75.8

Note: All figures are crude prevalence; (1) Figures cover the Boise City, ID Metropolitan Statistical Area; (2) Heavy drinkers are classified as adult men having more than 14 drinks per week and adult women having more than 7 drinks per week; (3) Binge drinkers are classified as males having five or more drinks on one occasion or females having four or more drinks on one occasion
Source: Centers for Disease Control and Prevention, Behaviorial Risk Factor Surveillance System, SMART: Selected Metropolitan Area Risk Trends, 2023

Acute and Chronic Health Conditions

Category	MSA[1] (%)	U.S. (%)
Adults who have ever been told they had a heart attack	3.7	4.2
Adults who have ever been told they have angina or coronary heart disease	3.2	4.0
Adults who have ever been told they had a stroke	2.9	3.3
Adults who have ever been told they have asthma	14.6	15.7
Adults who have ever been told they have arthritis	27.5	26.3
Adults who have ever been told they have diabetes[2]	10.6	11.5
Adults who have ever been told they had skin cancer	6.4	5.6
Adults who have ever been told they had any other types of cancer	8.9	8.4
Adults who have ever been told they have COPD	6.1	6.4
Adults who have ever been told they have kidney disease	4.0	3.7
Adults who have ever been told they have a form of depression	25.4	22.0

Note: All figures are crude prevalence; (1) Figures cover the Boise City, ID Metropolitan Statistical Area; (2) Figures do not include pregnancy-related, borderline, or pre-diabetes
Source: Centers for Disease Control and Prevention, Behaviorial Risk Factor Surveillance System, SMART: Selected Metropolitan Area Risk Trends, 2023

Health Screening and Vaccination Rates

Category	MSA[1] (%)	U.S. (%)
Adults who have ever been tested for HIV	37.2	37.5
Adults who have had their blood cholesterol checked within the last five years	85.2	87.0
Adults aged 65+ who have had flu shot within the past year	59.9	63.4
Adults aged 65+ who have ever had a pneumonia vaccination	77.8	71.9

Note: All figures are crude prevalence; (1) Figures cover the Boise City, ID Metropolitan Statistical Area.
Source: Centers for Disease Control and Prevention, Behaviorial Risk Factor Surveillance System, SMART: Selected Metropolitan Area Risk Trends, 2023

Disability Status

Category	MSA[1] (%)	U.S. (%)
Adults who reported being deaf	10.7	7.4
Are you blind or have serious difficulty seeing, even when wearing glasses?	5.3	4.9
Do you have difficulty doing errands alone?	9.2	7.8
Do you have difficulty dressing or bathing?	4.0	3.6
Do you have serious difficulty concentrating/remembering/making decisions?	16.6	13.7
Do you have serious difficulty walking or climbing stairs?	12.6	13.2

Note: All figures are crude prevalence; (1) Figures cover the Boise City, ID Metropolitan Statistical Area.
Source: Centers for Disease Control and Prevention, Behaviorial Risk Factor Surveillance System, SMART: Selected Metropolitan Area Risk Trends, 2023

Mortality Rates for the Top 10 Causes of Death in the U.S.

ICD-10[a] Sub-Chapter	ICD-10[a] Code	Crude Mortality Rate[2] per 100,000 population	
		County[3]	U.S.
Malignant neoplasms	C00-C97	153.3	182.7
Ischaemic heart diseases	I20-I25	66.8	109.6
Provisional assignment of new diseases of uncertain etiology[1]	U00-U49	41.3	65.3
Other forms of heart disease	I30-I51	43.8	65.1
Other degenerative diseases of the nervous system	G30-G31	60.2	52.4
Other external causes of accidental injury	W00-X59	41.5	52.3
Cerebrovascular diseases	I60-I69	35.3	49.1
Chronic lower respiratory diseases	J40-J47	34.1	43.5
Hypertensive diseases	I10-I15	36.8	38.9
Organic, including symptomatic, mental disorders	F01-F09	29.6	33.9

Note: (a) ICD-10 = International Classification of Diseases 10th Revision; (1) Includes COVID-19, adverse effects to COVID-19 vaccines, SARS, and vaping-related disorders; (2) Crude mortality rates are a three-year average covering 2021-2023; (3) Figures cover Ada County.
Source: Centers for Disease Control and Prevention, National Center for Health Statistics. National Vital Statistics System, Mortality 2018-2023 on CDC WONDER Online Database

Mortality Rates for Selected Causes of Death

Cause of Death	ICD-10[a] Code	Crude Mortality Rate[1] per 100,000 population	
		County[2]	U.S.
Accidental poisoning and exposure to noxious substances	X40-X49	18.3	30.5
Alzheimer disease	G30	48.9	35.4
Assault	X85-Y09	Unreliable	7.3
COVID-19	U07.1	41.3	65.3
Diabetes mellitus	E10-E14	18.0	30.0
Diseases of the liver	K70-K76	19.0	20.8
Human immunodeficiency virus (HIV) disease	B20-B24	Suppressed	1.5
Influenza and pneumonia	J09-J18	6.0	13.4
Intentional self-harm	X60-X84	21.6	14.7
Malnutrition	E40-E46	7.3	6.0
Obesity and other hyperalimentation	E65-E68	1.7	3.1
Renal failure	N17-N19	4.6	16.4
Transport accidents	V01-V99	10.0	14.4

Note: (a) ICD-10 = International Classification of Diseases 10th Revision; (1) Crude mortality rates are a three-year average covering 2021-2023; (2) Figures cover Ada County; Data are suppressed when the data meet the criteria for confidentiality constraints; Crude mortality rates are flagged as unreliable when the rate would be calculated with a numerator of 20 or less.
Source: Centers for Disease Control and Prevention, National Center for Health Statistics. National Vital Statistics System, Mortality 2018-2023 on CDC WONDER Online Database

Health Insurance Coverage

Area	With Health Insurance	With Private Health Insurance	With Public Health Insurance	Without Health Insurance	Population Under Age 19 Without Health Insurance
City	92.3	74.4	29.4	7.7	4.9
MSA[1]	91.4	72.1	31.8	8.6	6.2
U.S.	91.4	67.3	36.3	8.6	5.4

Note: Figures are percentages that cover the civilian noninstitutionalized population; (1) Figures cover the Boise City, ID Metropolitan Statistical Area
Source: U.S. Census Bureau, 2019-2023 American Community Survey 5-Year Estimates

Number of Medical Professionals

Area	MDs[3]	DOs[3,4]	Dentists	Podiatrists	Chiropractors	Optometrists
County[1] (number)	1,485	208	439	24	288	121
County[1] (rate[2])	286.2	40.1	83.7	4.6	54.9	23.1
U.S. (rate[2])	302.5	29.2	74.6	6.4	29.5	18.0

Note: Data as of 2023 unless noted; (1) Data covers Ada County; (2) Number of medical professionals per 100,000 population; (3) Data as of 2022 and includes all active, non-federal physicians; (4) Doctor of Osteopathic Medicine
Source: U.S. Department of Health and Human Services, Health Resources and Services Administration, Bureau of Health Professions, Area Resource File (ARF) 2023-2024

EDUCATION

Public School District Statistics

District Name	Schls	Pupils	Pupil/ Teacher Ratio	Minority Pupils[1] (%)	Total Rev. per Pupil ($)	Total Exp. per Pupil ($)
Boise Independent District	52	22,425	15.8	30.0	15,183	13,620

Note: Table includes school districts with 2,000 or more students; (1) Percentage of students that are not non-Hispanic white.
Source: U.S. Department of Education, National Center for Education Statistics, Common Core of Data, Local Education Agency (School District) Universe Survey: School Year 2023-2024; U.S. Department of Education, National Center for Education Statistics, Common Core of Data, School District Finance Survey (F-33): School Year 2021–22

Best High Schools

According to *U.S. News,* Boise City is home to one of the top 500 high schools in the U.S.: **Sage International School of Boise** (#468). Nearly 25,000 public, magnet and charter schools were ranked based on their performance on state assessments and how well they prepare students for college. *U.S. News & World Report, "Best High Schools 2024"*

Highest Level of Education

Area	Less than H.S.	H.S. Diploma	Some College, No Deg.	Associate Degree	Bachelor's Degree	Master's Degree	Prof. School Degree	Doctorate Degree
City	5.2	19.3	21.5	7.3	29.2	12.0	3.1	2.2
MSA[1]	7.5	23.3	24.0	8.6	24.3	8.8	2.1	1.4
U.S.	10.6	26.2	19.4	8.8	21.3	9.8	2.3	1.6

Note: Figures cover persons age 25 and over; (1) Figures cover the Boise City, ID Metropolitan Statistical Area
Source: U.S. Census Bureau, 2019-2023 American Community Survey 5-Year Estimates

Educational Attainment by Race

Area	High School Graduate or Higher (%)					Bachelor's Degree or Higher (%)				
	Total	White	Black	Asian	Hisp.[2]	Total	White	Black	Asian	Hisp.[2]
City	94.8	96.2	73.7	89.9	80.6	46.6	47.4	24.4	60.1	30.3
MSA[1]	92.5	94.9	80.7	90.9	72.9	36.6	38.2	24.7	55.8	19.1
U.S.	89.4	92.9	88.1	88.0	72.5	35.0	37.7	24.7	57.0	19.9

Note: Figures shown cover persons 25 years old and over; (1) Figures cover the Boise City, ID Metropolitan Statistical Area; (2) People of Hispanic origin can be of any race
Source: U.S. Census Bureau, 2019-2023 American Community Survey 5-Year Estimates

School Enrollment by Grade and Control

Area	Preschool (%)		Kindergarten (%)		Grades 1 - 4 (%)		Grades 5 - 8 (%)		Grades 9 - 12 (%)	
	Public	Private	Public	Private	Public	Private	Public	Private	Public	Private
City	34.8	65.2	80.0	20.0	85.7	14.3	89.3	10.7	86.4	13.6
MSA[1]	40.0	60.0	86.5	13.5	85.6	14.4	88.0	12.0	88.4	11.6
U.S.	58.7	41.3	85.2	14.8	87.2	12.8	87.9	12.1	89.0	11.0

Note: Figures shown cover persons 3 years old and over; (1) Figures cover the Boise City, ID Metropolitan Statistical Area
Source: U.S. Census Bureau, 2019-2023 American Community Survey 5-Year Estimates

Higher Education

Four-Year Colleges			Two-Year Colleges			Medical Schools[1]	Law Schools[2]	Voc/ Tech[3]
Public	Private Non-profit	Private For-profit	Public	Private Non-profit	Private For-profit			
1	3	2	1	0	1	1	1	8

Note: Figures cover institutions located within the Boise City, ID Metropolitan Statistical Area and include main campuses only; (1) includes schools accredited by the Liaison Committee on Medical Education and the American Osteopathic Association's Commission on Osteopathic College Accreditation; (2) includes ABA-accredited schools, schools with provisional ABA accreditation, and state accredited schools; (3) includes all schools with programs that are less than 2 years.
Source: National Center for Education Statistics, Integrated Postsecondary Education System (IPEDS), 2023-24; Wikipedia, List of Medical Schools in the United States, accessed May 2, 2025; Wikipedia, List of Law Schools in the United States, accessed May 2, 2025

EMPLOYERS

Major Employers

Company Name	Industry
Ada County	Administration, local government
Albertsons Companies	Retail grocery
Boise City ISD #1	Education, local government
Boise State University	Education, state government
City of Boise	Municipal government
DirectTV Customer Service	Administrative & waste service
Hewlett-Packard Co.	Manufacturing
Idaho Power Co	Utilities
J R Simplot Co	Manufacturing
McDonalds	Accommodation & food services
Meridian JSD #2	Education, local government
Micron Technology	Manufacturing
Nampa School District #13	Education, local government
St. Alphonsus Regional Medical Center	Healthcare
St. Lukes Health Systems	Healthcare
State of Idaho Department of Health	State government
State of Idaho Dept of Corrections	State government
U.S. Postal Service	Transportation & warehousing
U.S. Veterans Administration	Federal government, health care
WDS Global	Administrative & waste service

Note: Companies shown are located within the Boise City, ID Metropolitan Statistical Area.
Source: Chambers of Commerce; State Departments of Labor; Wikipedia

PUBLIC SAFETY

Crime Rate

Area	Total Crime Rate	Violent Crime Rate				Property Crime Rate		
		Murder	Rape	Robbery	Aggrav. Assault	Burglary	Larceny -Theft	Motor Vehicle Theft
City	1,512.1	2.1	67.9	21.9	177.7	131.7	971.9	138.8
U.S.	2,290.9	5.7	38.0	66.5	264.1	250.7	1,347.2	318.7

Note: Figures are crimes per 100,000 population.
Source: FBI, Table 8, Offenses Known to Law Enforcement, by State by City, 2023

Hate Crimes

Area	Number of Quarters Reported	Number of Incidents per Bias Motivation					
		Race/Ethnicity/ Ancestry	Religion	Sexual Orientation	Disability	Gender	Gender Identity
City[1]	4	7	1	3	0	0	0
U.S.	4	5,900	2,699	2,077	187	92	492

Note: (1) Figures include at least one incident reported with more than one bias motivation.
Source: Federal Bureau of Investigation, Hate Crime Statistics 2023

Identity Theft Consumer Reports

Area	Reports	Reports per 100,000 Population	Rank[2]
MSA[1]	1,173	148	274
U.S.	1,135,291	339	-

Note: (1) Figures cover the Boise City, ID Metropolitan Statistical Area; (2) Rank ranges from 1 to 401 where 1 indicates greatest number of identity theft reports per 100,000 population
Source: Federal Trade Commission, Consumer Sentinel Network Data Book 2024

Fraud and Other Consumer Reports

Area	Reports	Reports per 100,000 Population	Rank[2]
MSA[1]	7,571	958	237
U.S.	5,360,641	1,601	-

Note: (1) Figures cover the Boise City, ID Metropolitan Statistical Area; (2) Rank ranges from 1 to 401 where 1 indicates greatest number of fraud and other consumer reports per 100,000 population
Source: Federal Trade Commission, Consumer Sentinel Network Data Book 2024

POLITICS

2024 Presidential Election Results

Area	Trump (Rep.)	Harris (Dem.)	Stein (Green)	Kennedy (Ind.)	Oliver (Lib.)	Other
Ada County	53.8	43.4	0.4	1.3	0.6	0.5
U.S.	49.7	48.2	0.6	0.5	0.4	0.6

Note: Results are percentages and may not add to 100% due to rounding
Source: Dave Leip's Atlas of U.S. Presidential Elections

SPORTS

Professional Sports Teams

Team Name	League	Year Established

No teams are located in the metro area
Source: Wikipedia, Major Professional Sports Teams of the United States and Canada, May 1, 2025

CLIMATE

Average and Extreme Temperatures

Temperature	Jan	Feb	Mar	Apr	May	Jun	Jul	Aug	Sep	Oct	Nov	Dec	Yr.
Extreme High (°F)	63	70	81	92	98	105	111	110	101	94	74	65	111
Average High (°F)	36	44	53	62	71	80	90	88	78	65	48	38	63
Average Temp. (°F)	29	36	42	49	58	66	74	73	63	52	40	31	51
Average Low (°F)	22	27	31	37	44	52	58	57	48	39	30	23	39
Extreme Low (°F)	-17	-15	6	19	22	31	35	34	23	11	-3	-25	-25

Note: Figures cover the years 1948-1995
Source: National Climatic Data Center, International Station Meteorological Climate Summary, 9/96

Average Precipitation/Snowfall/Humidity

Precip./Humidity	Jan	Feb	Mar	Apr	May	Jun	Jul	Aug	Sep	Oct	Nov	Dec	Yr.
Avg. Precip. (in.)	1.4	1.1	1.2	1.2	1.2	0.9	0.3	0.3	0.6	0.7	1.4	1.4	11.8
Avg. Snowfall (in.)	7	4	2	1	Tr	Tr	0	0	0	Tr	2	6	22
Avg. Rel. Hum. 7am (%)	81	80	75	69	65	59	48	50	58	67	77	81	68
Avg. Rel. Hum. 4pm (%)	68	58	45	35	34	29	22	23	28	36	55	67	42

Note: Figures cover the years 1948-1995; Tr = Trace amounts (<0.05 in. of rain; <0.5 in. of snow)
Source: National Climatic Data Center, International Station Meteorological Climate Summary, 9/96

Weather Conditions

Temperature			Daytime Sky			Precipitation		
5°F & below	32°F & below	90°F & above	Clear	Partly cloudy	Cloudy	0.01 inch or more precip.	0.1 inch or more snow/ice	Thunder-storms
6	124	45	106	133	126	91	22	14

Note: Figures are average number of days per year and cover the years 1948-1995
Source: National Climatic Data Center, International Station Meteorological Climate Summary, 9/96

HAZARDOUS WASTE

Superfund Sites

The Boise City, ID metro area has no sites on the EPA's Superfund Final National Priorities List (NPL) or Superfund Alternative Approach (SAA) list. The Superfund alternative approach uses the same investigation and cleanup process and standards that are used for sites listed on the National Priorities List. The SAA is an alternative to listing a site on the NPL; it is not an alternative to Superfund or the Superfund process. There are a total of 1,445 Superfund sites with a status of proposed or final on both lists in the United States. *U.S. Environmental Protection Agency, National Priorities List, May 1, 2025; U.S. Environmental Protection Agency, Superfund Alternative Approach Sites, May 1, 2025*

AIR QUALITY

Air Quality Trends: Ozone

	1990	1995	2000	2005	2010	2015	2020	2021	2022	2023
MSA[1]	n/a	n/a	n/a	n/a	n/a	n/a	n/a	n/a	n/a	n/a
U.S.	0.087	0.089	0.081	0.080	0.072	0.068	0.066	0.067	0.067	0.070

Note: (1) Data covers the Boise City, ID Metropolitan Statistical Area; n/a not available. The values shown are the composite ozone concentration averages among trend sites based on the highest fourth daily maximum 8-hour concentration in parts per million. These trends are based on sites having an adequate record of monitoring data during the trend period. Data from exceptional events are included.
Source: U.S. Environmental Protection Agency, Air Quality Monitoring Information, "Air Quality Trends by City, 1990-2023"

Air Quality Index

Area	Percent of Days when Air Quality was...[2]					AQI Statistics[2]	
	Good	Moderate	Unhealthy for Sensitive Groups	Unhealthy	Very Unhealthy	Maximum	Median
MSA[1]	49.3	49.9	0.8	0.0	0.0	120	51

Note: (1) Data covers the Boise City, ID Metropolitan Statistical Area; (2) Based on 365 days with AQI data in 2023. Air Quality Index (AQI) is an index for reporting daily air quality. EPA calculates the AQI for five major air pollutants regulated by the Clean Air Act: ground-level ozone, particle pollution (aka particulate matter), carbon monoxide, sulfur dioxide, and nitrogen dioxide. The AQI runs from 0 to 500. The higher the AQI value, the greater the level of air pollution and the greater the health concern. There are six AQI categories: "Good" AQI is between 0 and 50. Air quality is considered satisfactory; "Moderate" AQI is between 51 and 100. Air quality is acceptable; "Unhealthy for Sensitive Groups" When AQI values are between 101 and 150, members of sensitive groups may experience health effects; "Unhealthy" When AQI values are between 151 and 200 everyone may begin to experience health effects; "Very Unhealthy" AQI values between 201 and 300 trigger a health alert; "Hazardous" AQI values over 300 trigger warnings of emergency conditions (not shown).
Source: U.S. Environmental Protection Agency, Air Quality Index Report, 2023

Air Quality Index Pollutants

Area	Percent of Days when AQI Pollutant was...[2]					
	Carbon Monoxide	Nitrogen Dioxide	Ozone	Sulfur Dioxide	Particulate Matter 2.5	Particulate Matter 10
MSA[1]	0.0	0.3	44.9	(3)	54.0	0.8

Note: (1) Data covers the Boise City, ID Metropolitan Statistical Area; (2) Based on 365 days with AQI data in 2023. The Air Quality Index (AQI) is an index for reporting daily air quality. EPA calculates the AQI for five major air pollutants regulated by the Clean Air Act: ground-level ozone, particle pollution (also known as particulate matter), carbon monoxide, sulfur dioxide, and nitrogen dioxide. The AQI runs from 0 to 500. The higher the AQI value, the greater the level of air pollution and the greater the health concern; (3) Sulfur dioxide is no longer included in this table because SO_2 concentrations tend to be very localized and not necessarily representative of broad geographical areas like counties and CBSAs.
Source: U.S. Environmental Protection Agency, Air Quality Index Report, 2023

Maximum Air Pollutant Concentrations: Particulate Matter, Ozone, CO and Lead

	Particulate Matter 10 (ug/m³)	Particulate Matter 2.5 Wtd AM (ug/m³)	Particulate Matter 2.5 24-Hr (ug/m³)	Ozone (ppm)	Carbon Monoxide (ppm)	Lead (ug/m³)
MSA[1] Level	84	n/a	n/a	0.066	1	n/a
NAAQS[2]	150	15	35	0.075	9	0.15
Met NAAQS[2]	Yes	n/a	n/a	Yes	Yes	n/a

Note: (1) Data covers the Boise City, ID Metropolitan Statistical Area; Data from exceptional events are included; (2) National Ambient Air Quality Standards; ppm = parts per million; ug/m³ = micrograms per cubic meter; n/a not available.
Concentrations: Particulate Matter 10 (coarse particulate)—highest second maximum 24-hour concentration; Particulate Matter 2.5 Wtd AM (fine particulate)—highest weighted annual mean concentration; Particulate Matter 2.5 24-Hour (fine particulate)—highest 98th percentile 24-hour concentration; Ozone—highest fourth daily maximum 8-hour concentration; Carbon Monoxide—highest second maximum non-overlapping 8-hour concentration; Lead—maximum running 3-month average
Source: U.S. Environmental Protection Agency, Air Quality Monitoring Information, "Air Quality Statistics by City, 2023"

Maximum Air Pollutant Concentrations: Nitrogen Dioxide and Sulfur Dioxide

	Nitrogen Dioxide AM (ppb)	Nitrogen Dioxide 1-Hr (ppb)	Sulfur Dioxide AM (ppb)	Sulfur Dioxide 1-Hr (ppb)	Sulfur Dioxide 24-Hr (ppb)
MSA[1] Level	8	38	n/a	3	n/a
NAAQS[2]	53	100	30	75	140
Met NAAQS[2]	Yes	Yes	n/a	Yes	n/a

Note: (1) Data covers the Boise City, ID Metropolitan Statistical Area; Data from exceptional events are included; (2) National Ambient Air Quality Standards; ppm = parts per million; ug/m³ = micrograms per cubic meter; n/a not available.
Concentrations: Nitrogen Dioxide AM—highest arithmetic mean concentration; Nitrogen Dioxide 1-Hr—highest 98th percentile 1-hour daily maximum concentration; Sulfur Dioxide AM—highest annual mean concentration; Sulfur Dioxide 1-Hr—highest 99th percentile 1-hour daily maximum concentration; Sulfur Dioxide 24-Hr—highest second maximum 24-hour concentration
Source: U.S. Environmental Protection Agency, Air Quality Monitoring Information, "Air Quality Statistics by City, 2023"

Boulder, Colorado

Background

Boulder, the eighth largest city in Colorado, lies at the foot of the Rocky Mountains in Boulder County. Tourism is a major industry in Boulder, which offers spectacular views from its elevation of 5,430 feet and many outdoor recreation opportunities in over 31,000 acres of open space.

Boulder Valley originally was home to the Southern Arapahoe tribe. The first white settlement was established by gold miners in 1858 near the entrance to Boulder Canyon at Red Rocks. In 1859, the Boulder City Town Company was formed. The town's first schoolhouse was built in 1860, and in 1874 the University of Colorado opened.

Boulder was incorporated as a town in 1871 and as a city in 1882. By 1890, the railroad provided service from Boulder to Golden, Denver, and the western mining camps. In 1905, amidst a weakening economy, Boulder began promoting tourism to boost its finances. The city raised money to construct a first-class hotel, which was completed in 1908 and named Hotel Boulderado.

Although tourism remained strong until the late 1930s, it had begun to decline by World War II. The U.S. Navy's Japanese language school, housed at the city's University of Colorado, proved to be an impressive introduction to the area and students, professionals, and veterans attending the university on the GI Bill, returned to Boulder. Consequently, Boulder's population grew from 12,958 in 1940 to 20,000 in 1950. To accommodate this huge increase, new public buildings, highways, residential areas, and shopping centers developed, spurring further economic expansion.

Many major tech companies have operations in Boulder, as does NOAA, the National Oceanic and Atmospheric Administration.

Boulder is home to the University of Colorado, which houses a robust research park. Cultural venues in the city include the Boulder Dushanbe Teahouse, a gift to the city from its sister city of Dushanbe in Tajikistan, and the Pearl Street Mall, an open-air walkway that was the city's original downtown and is rich with restaurants, cafes, bookstores, and street entertainers. Boulder offers many scenic opportunities for outdoor activities, with parks, recreation areas, and hiking trails. The city boasts hundreds of miles of bike trails, lanes, and paths as a part of their renowned network of citywide bikeways. Boulder has been recognized by the League of American Bicyclists as a leading bicyclist-friendly city.

Keeping with Boulder's tradition of outdoor recreation, BOLDERBoulder, a popular race for over 50,000 runners, joggers, walkers, and wheelers, happens each Memorial Day, with over 100,000 spectators.

Annual attractions include the Creek Festival in May, Art Fair in July, Fall Festival, and Lights of December Parade. The annual Boulder International Film Festival (BIFF) is held in February and has created a name for itself in the international film community.

Like the rest of Colorado, Boulder enjoys a cool, dry highland continental climate. In winter, the mountains to the west shield the city from the coldest temperatures. Humidity is generally low. Winter storms moving east from the Pacific drop most of their moisture on the mountains to the west, while summer precipitation comes from scattered thunderstorms.

Rankings

General Rankings

- *US News & World Report* conducted a survey of more than 3,500 people and analyzed the 150 largest metropolitan areas to determine what matters most when selecting the next place to live. Boulder ranked #10 out of the top 25 as having the best combination of desirable factors. Criteria: cost of living; quality of life and education; climate; job market; desirability; and other factors. *realestate.usnews.com, "Best Places to Live in the U.S. in 2024-2025," May 21, 2024*

Business/Finance Rankings

- According to *Business Insider*, the Boulder metro area is a prime place to run a startup or move an existing business to. The area ranked #4. More than 300 metro areas were analyzed for factors that were of top concern to new business owners. Data was based on the 2019 U.S. Census Bureau American Community Survey, statistics from the CDC, and University of Chicago analysis. Criteria: business formations; percentage of vaccinated population; percentage of households with internet subscriptions; median household income; and share of work that can be done from home. *BusinessInsider.com, "The 20 Best Cities for Starting a Business in 2022 Include Denver, Raleigh, and Olympia," June 7, 2022*

- The Boulder metro area appeared on the Milken Institute "2025 Best Performing Cities" list. Rank: #41 out of 200 large metro areas (based on performance category). Criteria: job growth; wage growth; high-tech growth and impact; community resilience; housing affordability; household broadband access. *Milken Institute, "Best-Performing Cities 2025," January 14, 2025*

Environmental Rankings

- *Niche* compiled a list of the nation's snowiest cities, based on the National Oceanic and Atmospheric Administration's 30-year average snowfall data. Among cities with a population of at least 50,000, Boulder ranked #6. *Niche.com, Top 25 Snowiest Cities in America, December 10, 2018*

Health/Fitness Rankings

- The Sharecare Community Well-Being Index evaluates 10 individual and social health factors in order to measure what matters to Americans in the communities in which they live. The Boulder metro area ranked #10 in the top 10 across all 10 domains. Criteria: access to healthcare, food, and community resources; housing and transportation; economic security; feeling of purpose; and physical, financial, social, and community well-being. *Sharecare.com, "Community Well-Being Index: 2020 Metro Area & County Rankings Report," August 30, 2021*

Real Estate Rankings

- The Boulder metro area was identified as one of the 20 worst housing markets in the U.S. in 2024. The area ranked #210 out of 226 markets. Criteria: year-over-year change of median sales price of existing single-family homes between the 4th quarter of 2023 and the 4th quarter of 2024. *National Association of Realtors®, Median Sales Price of Existing Single-Family Homes for Metropolitan Areas, 4th Quarter 2024*

- The Boulder metro area was identified as one of the 20 least affordable housing markets in the U.S. in 2024. The area ranked #217 out of 226 markets. Criteria: qualification for a mortgage loan with a 10 percent down payment on a typical home. *National Association of Realtors®, Qualifying Income Based on Sales Price of Existing Single-Family Homes for Metropolitan Areas, February 6, 2025*

- Boulder was ranked #165 out of 176 metro areas in terms of cost of housing in 2024 by the National Association of Home Builders (#1 = most affordable). Criteria: the portion of an average family's income necessary to pay the mortgage on a median-priced home. *National Association of Home Builders®, NAHB-Wells Fargo Cost of Housing Index, 4th Quarter 2024*

Women/Minorities Rankings

- *Travel + Leisure* listed the best cities in and around the U.S. for a memorable and fun girls' trip, even on a budget. Whether it is for a special occasion, to make new memories or just to get away, Boulder is sure to have something for all the ladies in your tribe. *Travel + Leisure, "25 Affordable Girls Weekend Getaways That Won't Break the Bank," January 30, 2025*

Business Environment

DEMOGRAPHICS

Population Growth

Area	1990 Census	2000 Census	2010 Census	2020 Census	2023 Estimate[2]	Population Growth 1990-2023 (%)
City	87,737	94,673	97,385	108,250	106,274	21.1
MSA[1]	208,898	269,758	294,567	330,758	328,317	57.2
U.S.	248,709,873	281,421,906	308,745,538	331,449,281	332,387,540	33.6

Note: (1) Figures cover the Boulder, CO Metropolitan Statistical Area; (2) 2019-2023 5-year ACS population estimate
Source: U.S. Census Bureau, 1990 Census, 2000 Census, 2010 Census, 2020 Census, 2019-2023 American Community Survey 5-Year Estimates

Race

Area	White Alone[2] (%)	Black Alone[2] (%)	Asian Alone[2] (%)	AIAN[3] Alone[2] (%)	NHOPI[4] Alone[2] (%)	Other Race Alone[2] (%)	Two or More Races (%)
City	81.8	1.1	5.8	0.3	0.1	1.8	9.2
MSA[1]	80.7	0.8	4.7	0.3	0.1	2.9	10.6
U.S.	63.4	12.4	5.8	0.9	0.2	6.6	10.7

Note: (1) Figures cover the Boulder, CO Metropolitan Statistical Area; (2) Alone is defined as not being in combination with one or more other races; (3) American Indian and Alaska Native; (4) Native Hawaiian and Other Pacific Islander
Source: U.S. Census Bureau, 2019-2023 American Community Survey 5-Year Estimates

Hispanic or Latino Origin

Area	Total (%)	Mexican (%)	Puerto Rican (%)	Cuban (%)	Other (%)
City	11.2	6.6	0.3	0.5	3.8
MSA[1]	14.6	9.8	0.5	0.3	3.9
U.S.	19.0	11.3	1.8	0.7	5.2

Note: Persons of Hispanic or Latino origin can be of any race; (1) Figures cover the Boulder, CO Metropolitan Statistical Area
Source: U.S. Census Bureau, 2019-2023 American Community Survey 5-Year Estimates

Age

Area	Percent of Population									Median Age
	Under Age 5	Age 5–19	Age 20–34	Age 35–44	Age 45–54	Age 55–64	Age 65–74	Age 75–84	Age 85+	
City	2.0	20.2	36.8	10.3	10.0	8.4	7.4	3.2	1.8	28.8
MSA[1]	4.0	19.1	23.8	12.6	12.6	12.2	9.8	4.2	1.8	37.5
U.S.	5.7	19.1	20.2	13.1	12.3	12.8	10.0	4.9	1.9	38.7

Note: (1) Figures cover the Boulder, CO Metropolitan Statistical Area
Source: U.S. Census Bureau, 2019-2023 American Community Survey 5-Year Estimates

Disability by Age

Area	All Ages	Under 18 Years Old	18 to 64 Years Old	65 Years and Over
City	7.5	2.9	6.1	20.9
MSA[1]	8.8	2.9	6.9	23.8
U.S.	13.0	4.7	10.7	32.9

Note: Figures show percent of the civilian noninstitutionalized population that reported having a disability. Disability status is determined from six types of difficulty: vision, hearing, cognitive, ambulatory, self-care, and independent living. For children under 5 years old, hearing and vision difficulty are used to determine disability status. For children between the ages of 5 and 14, disability status is determined from hearing, vision, cognitive, ambulatory, and self-care difficulties. For people aged 15 years and older, they are considered to have a disability if they have difficulty with any one of the six difficulty types; Note: (1) Figures cover the Boulder, CO Metropolitan Statistical Area
Source: U.S. Census Bureau, 2019-2023 American Community Survey 5-Year Estimates

Ancestry

Area	German	Irish	English	American	Italian	Polish	French[2]	European	Scottish
City	16.0	11.3	11.4	2.6	5.2	3.4	2.4	4.2	3.2
MSA[1]	18.0	12.1	14.5	3.0	5.1	3.0	2.8	3.2	2.9
U.S.	12.6	9.4	9.1	5.5	4.9	2.6	2.0	1.6	1.6

Note: Figures are the percentage of the total population reporting a particular ancestry. The nine most commonly reported ancestries in the U.S. are shown. Figures include multiple ancestries (e.g. if a person reported being Irish and Italian, they were included in both columns); (1) Figures cover the Boulder, CO Metropolitan Statistical Area; (2) Excludes Basque
Source: U.S. Census Bureau, 2019-2023 American Community Survey 5-Year Estimates

Foreign-born Population

Area	Any Foreign Country	Percent of Population Born in							
		Asia	Mexico	Europe	Caribbean	Central America[2]	South America	Africa	Canada
City	10.2	4.2	1.0	3.0	0.2	0.4	0.6	0.3	0.6
MSA[1]	10.0	3.4	2.0	2.5	0.1	0.4	0.7	0.3	0.5
U.S.	13.9	4.3	3.3	1.4	1.4	1.2	1.2	0.8	0.2

Note: (1) Figures cover the Boulder, CO Metropolitan Statistical Area; (2) Excludes Mexico.
Source: U.S. Census Bureau, 2019-2023 American Community Survey 5-Year Estimates

Household Size

Area	Persons in Household (%)							Average Household Size
	One	Two	Three	Four	Five	Six	Seven or More	
City	34.9	36.6	13.9	10.9	2.5	0.6	0.7	2.16
MSA[1]	29.8	37.0	14.5	12.6	4.2	1.3	0.6	2.33
U.S.	28.5	33.8	15.4	12.7	5.9	2.3	1.4	2.54

Note: (1) Figures cover the Boulder, CO Metropolitan Statistical Area
Source: U.S. Census Bureau, 2019-2023 American Community Survey 5-Year Estimates

Household Relationships

Area	House-holder	Opposite-sex Spouse	Same-sex Spouse	Opposite-sex Unmarried Partner	Same-sex Unmarried Partner	Child[2]	Grand-child	Other Relatives	Non-relatives
City	40.2	13.0	0.3	3.1	0.2	16.4	0.3	1.6	12.3
MSA[1]	40.1	18.0	0.3	2.8	0.2	23.8	1.0	2.6	6.8
U.S.	38.3	17.5	0.2	2.5	0.2	28.3	2.4	4.8	3.4

Note: Figures are percent of the total population; (1) Figures cover the Boulder, CO Metropolitan Statistical Area; (2) Includes biological, adopted, and stepchildren of the householder
Source: U.S. Census Bureau, 2020 Census

Gender

Area	Males	Females	Males per 100 Females
City	55,022	51,252	107.4
MSA[1]	165,677	162,640	101.9
U.S.	164,545,087	167,842,453	98.0

Note: (1) Figures cover the Boulder, CO Metropolitan Statistical Area
Source: U.S. Census Bureau, 2019-2023 American Community Survey 5-Year Estimates

Marital Status

Area	Never Married	Now Married[2]	Separated	Widowed	Divorced
City	57.8	30.4	0.5	2.2	9.0
MSA[1]	39.2	45.4	0.7	3.7	11.1
U.S.	34.1	47.9	1.7	5.6	10.7

Note: Figures are percentages and cover the population 15 years of age and older; (1) Figures cover the Boulder, CO Metropolitan Statistical Area; (2) Excludes separated
Source: U.S. Census Bureau, 2019-2023 American Community Survey 5-Year Estimates

Religious Groups by Family

Area	Catholic	Baptist	Methodist	LDS[2]	Pentecostal	Lutheran	Islam	Adventist	Other
MSA[1]	16.0	0.3	0.7	0.7	0.5	1.7	0.4	0.9	15.2
U.S.	18.7	7.3	3.0	2.0	1.8	1.7	1.3	1.3	11.6

Note: Figures are the number of adherents as a percentage of the total population and cover the eight largest religious groups in the U.S; (1) Figures cover the Boulder, CO Metropolitan Statistical Area; (2) Church of Jesus Christ of Latter-day Saints
Sources: 2020 U.S. Religion Census, Association of Statisticians of American Religious Bodies; The Association of Religion Data Archives (ARDA)

Religious Groups by Tradition

Area	Catholic	Evangelical Protestant	Mainline Protestant	Black Protestant	Islam	Judaism	Hinduism	Orthodox	Buddhism
MSA[1]	16.0	12.7	3.4	n/a	0.4	0.7	0.5	0.2	1.0
U.S.	18.7	16.5	5.2	2.3	1.3	0.6	0.4	0.4	0.3

Note: Figures are the number of adherents as a percentage of the total population; (1) Figures cover the Boulder, CO Metropolitan Statistical Area
Sources: 2020 U.S. Religion Census, Association of Statisticians of American Religious Bodies; The Association of Religion Data Archives (ARDA)

ECONOMY

Real Gross Domestic Product (GDP)

Area	2017	2018	2019	2020	2021	2022	2023	Rank[3]
MSA[1]	26.3	27.2	29.7	29.1	31.3	31.9	32.9	100
U.S.[2]	17,619.1	18,160.7	18,642.5	18,238.9	19,387.6	19,896.6	20,436.3	–

Note: Figures are in billions of chained 2017 dollars; (1) Figures cover the Boulder, CO Metropolitan Statistical Area; (2) Figures cover real GDP within metropolitan areas; (3) Rank is based on 2023 data and ranges from 1 to 384
Source: U.S. Bureau of Economic Analysis

Economic Growth

Area	2014	2015	2016	2017	2018	2019	2020	2021	2022	2023
MSA[1]	3.3	3.9	3.5	4.9	3.7	9.0	-1.9	7.5	1.9	3.4
U.S.[2]	2.6	3.2	2.0	2.7	3.1	2.7	-2.2	6.3	2.6	2.7

Note: Figures are real gross domestic product growth rates and represent percent change from preceding period; (1) Figures cover the Boulder, CO Metropolitan Statistical Area; (2) Figures are the average growth rates within metropolitan areas
Source: U.S. Bureau of Economic Analysis

Metropolitan Area Exports

Area	2018	2019	2020	2021	2022	2023	Rank[2]
MSA[1]	1,044.1	1,014.9	1,110.4	1,078.0	1,201.9	1,213.1	153
U.S.	1,664,056.1	1,645,173.7	1,431,406.6	1,753,941.4	2,062,937.4	2,019,160.5	–

Note: Figures are in millions of dollars; (1) Figures cover the Boulder, CO Metropolitan Statistical Area; (2) Rank is based on 2023 data and ranges from 1 to 386
Source: U.S. Department of Commerce, International Trade Administration, Office of Trade and Economic Analysis, Industry and Analysis, Exports by Metropolitan Area, data extracted April 2, 2025

Building Permits

Area	Single-Family			Multi-Family			Total		
	2023	2024	Pct. Chg.	2023	2024	Pct. Chg.	2023	2024	Pct. Chg.
City	30	35	16.7	225	371	64.9	255	406	59.2
MSA[1]	791	441	-44.2	851	1,239	45.6	1,642	1,680	2.3
U.S.	920,000	981,900	6.7	591,100	496,100	-16.1	1,511,100	1,478,000	-2.2

Note: (1) Figures cover the Boulder, CO Metropolitan Statistical Area; Figures represent new, privately-owned housing units authorized (unadjusted data)
Source: U.S. Census Bureau, Building Permits Survey (BPS), 2023, 2024

Bankruptcy Filings

Area	Business Filings			Nonbusiness Filings		
	2023	2024	% Chg.	2023	2024	% Chg.
Boulder County	25	35	40.0	228	247	8.3
U.S.	18,926	23,107	22.1	434,064	494,201	13.9

Note: Business filings include Chapter 7, Chapter 9, Chapter 11, Chapter 12, Chapter 13, Chapter 15, and Section 304; Nonbusiness filings include Chapter 7, Chapter 11, and Chapter 13
Source: Administrative Office of the U.S. Courts, Business and Nonbusiness Bankruptcy, County Cases Commenced by Chapter of the Bankruptcy Code, During the 12-Month Period Ending December 31, 2023 and Business and Nonbusiness Bankruptcy, County Cases Commenced by Chapter of the Bankruptcy Code, During the 12-Month Period Ending December 31, 2024

Housing Vacancy Rates

Area	Gross Vacancy Rate[3] (%)			Year-Round Vacancy Rate[4] (%)			Rental Vacancy Rate[5] (%)			Homeowner Vacancy Rate[6] (%)		
	2022	2023	2024	2022	2023	2024	2022	2023	2024	2022	2023	2024
MSA[1]	n/a	n/a	n/a	n/a	n/a	n/a	n/a	n/a	n/a	n/a	n/a	n/a
U.S.[2]	9.1	9.0	9.1	7.5	7.5	7.6	5.7	6.5	6.8	0.8	0.8	1.0

Note: (1) Figures cover the Boulder, CO Metropolitan Statistical Area; (2) Figures cover the 75 largest Metropolitan Statistical Areas; (3) The percentage of the total housing inventory that is vacant; (4) The percentage of the housing inventory (excluding seasonal units) that is year-round vacant; (5) The percentage of rental inventory that is vacant for rent; (6) The percentage of homeowner inventory that is vacant for sale; n/a not available
Source: U.S. Census Bureau, Housing Vacancies and Homeownership Annual Statistics: 2022, 2023, 2024

INCOME

Income

Area	Per Capita ($)	Median Household ($)	Average Household ($)
City	59,450	85,364	140,662
MSA[1]	60,272	102,772	144,869
U.S.	43,289	78,538	110,491

Note: (1) Figures cover the Boulder, CO Metropolitan Statistical Area
Source: U.S. Census Bureau, 2019-2023 American Community Survey 5-Year Estimates

Household Income Distribution

Area	Percent of Households Earning							
	Under $15,000	$15,000 -$24,999	$25,000 -$34,999	$35,000 -$49,999	$50,000 -$74,999	$75,000 -$99,999	$100,000 -$149,999	$150,000 and up
City	12.4	6.7	7.3	7.7	11.5	9.5	14.0	30.9
MSA[1]	7.5	5.3	5.2	7.4	12.4	11.1	17.3	33.9
U.S.	8.5	6.6	6.8	10.4	15.7	12.7	17.4	21.9

Note: (1) Figures cover the Boulder, CO Metropolitan Statistical Area
Source: U.S. Census Bureau, 2019-2023 American Community Survey 5-Year Estimates

Poverty Rate

Area	All Ages	Under 18 Years Old	18 to 64 Years Old	65 Years and Over
City	21.8	9.7	26.8	6.2
MSA[1]	11.4	7.5	13.7	7.1
U.S.	12.4	16.3	13.7	10.4

Note: Figures are percentage of people whose income during the past 12 months was below the poverty level;
(1) Figures cover the Boulder, CO Metropolitan Statistical Area
Source: U.S. Census Bureau, 2019-2023 American Community Survey 5-Year Estimates

EMPLOYMENT

Labor Force and Employment

Area	Civilian Labor Force			Workers Employed		
	Dec. 2023	Dec. 2024	% Chg.	Dec. 2023	Dec. 2024	% Chg.
City	68,299	68,728	0.6	66,297	66,171	-0.2
MSA[1]	204,348	205,677	0.7	197,756	197,382	-0.2
U.S.	166,661,000	167,746,000	0.7	160,754,000	161,294,000	0.3

Note: Data is not seasonally adjusted and covers workers 16 years of age and older; (1) Figures cover the
Boulder, CO Metropolitan Statistical Area
Source: Bureau of Labor Statistics, Local Area Unemployment Statistics

Unemployment Rate

Area	2024											
	Jan.	Feb.	Mar.	Apr.	May	Jun.	Jul.	Aug.	Sep.	Oct.	Nov.	Dec.
City	3.3	3.5	3.4	3.2	4.0	4.5	4.5	4.5	4.1	4.1	4.4	3.7
MSA[1]	3.6	3.7	3.4	3.3	3.7	4.2	4.4	4.3	4.0	4.1	4.3	4.0
U.S.	4.1	4.2	3.9	3.5	3.7	4.3	4.5	4.4	3.9	3.9	4.0	3.8

Note: Data is not seasonally adjusted and covers workers 16 years of age and older; (1) Figures cover the
Boulder, CO Metropolitan Statistical Area
Source: Bureau of Labor Statistics, Local Area Unemployment Statistics

Average Wages

Occupation	$/Hr.	Occupation	$/Hr.
Accountants and Auditors	46.39	Maintenance and Repair Workers	28.09
Automotive Mechanics	28.81	Marketing Managers	89.78
Bookkeepers	26.63	Network and Computer Systems Admin.	53.52
Carpenters	29.94	Nurses, Licensed Practical	32.93
Cashiers	17.71	Nurses, Registered	47.77
Computer Programmers	71.62	Nursing Assistants	22.19
Computer Systems Analysts	67.66	Office Clerks, General	27.23
Computer User Support Specialists	36.17	Physical Therapists	47.73
Construction Laborers	22.30	Physicians	157.65
Cooks, Restaurant	20.42	Plumbers, Pipefitters and Steamfitters	33.25
Customer Service Representatives	22.82	Police and Sheriff's Patrol Officers	43.85
Dentists	85.12	Postal Service Mail Carriers	29.62
Electricians	31.85	Real Estate Sales Agents	37.36
Engineers, Electrical	63.49	Retail Salespersons	20.20
Fast Food and Counter Workers	17.78	Sales Representatives, Technical/Scientific	68.73
Financial Managers	93.87	Secretaries, Exc. Legal/Medical/Executive	23.54
First-Line Supervisors of Office Workers	36.12	Security Guards	25.69
General and Operations Managers	81.98	Surgeons	n/a
Hairdressers/Cosmetologists	25.46	Teacher Assistants, Exc. Postsecondary[1]	19.34
Home Health and Personal Care Aides	19.56	Teachers, Secondary School, Exc. Sp. Ed.[1]	37.59
Janitors and Cleaners	19.68	Telemarketers	n/a
Landscaping/Groundskeeping Workers	23.16	Truck Drivers, Heavy/Tractor-Trailer	28.09
Lawyers	120.91	Truck Drivers, Light/Delivery Services	24.74
Maids and Housekeeping Cleaners	18.76	Waiters and Waitresses	22.52

Note: Data in this table was taken from the May 2023 Metro Area Occupational Employment & Wage Estimates due to data quality concerns for the state of Colorado and substate areas. On November 20, 2024, the Quarterly Census of Employment and Wages (QCEW) suspended publication of industry and substate data for Colorado due to these concerns. As of May 1, 2025, the quality concerns with Colorado data have been sufficiently addressed to resume QCEW publication, however, because of the processing time required, the May 2024 Metro Area Occupational Employment & Wage Estimates data release does not include data for Colorado and its substate areas; n/a not available; (1) Hourly wages were calculated from annual wage data based on a 40 hour work week
Source: Bureau of Labor Statistics, Metro Area Occupational Employment & Wage Estimates, May 2023

Employment by Industry

Sector	MSA[1]		U.S.
	Number of Employees	Percent of Total	Percent of Total
Construction, Mining, and Logging	5,600	2.7	5.5
Financial Activities	6,800	3.3	5.8
Government	41,000	19.7	14.9
Information	8,300	4.0	1.9
Leisure and Hospitality	20,000	9.6	10.4
Manufacturing	20,700	10.0	8.0
Other Services	9,000	4.3	3.7
Private Education and Health Services	27,500	13.2	16.9
Professional and Business Services	41,800	20.1	14.2
Retail Trade	17,100	8.2	10.0
Transportation, Warehousing, and Utilities	2,300	1.1	4.8
Wholesale Trade	7,600	3.7	3.9

Note: Figures are non-farm employment as of December 2024. Figures are not seasonally adjusted and include workers 16 years of age and older; (1) Figures cover the Boulder, CO Metropolitan Statistical Area
Source: Bureau of Labor Statistics, Current Employment Statistics, Employment, Hours, and Earnings

Employment by Occupation

Occupation Classification	City (%)	MSA[1] (%)	U.S. (%)
Management, Business, Science, and Arts	59.7	57.4	42.0
Natural Resources, Construction, and Maintenance	2.8	4.9	8.6
Production, Transportation, and Material Moving	5.2	7.3	13.0
Sales and Office	15.5	16.7	19.9
Service	16.8	13.7	16.5

Note: Figures cover employed civilians 16 years of age and older; (1) Figures cover the Boulder, CO Metropolitan Statistical Area
Source: U.S. Census Bureau, 2019-2023 American Community Survey 5-Year Estimates

Occupations with Greatest Projected Employment Growth: 2022 – 2032

Occupation[1]	2022 Employment	2032 Projected Employment	Numeric Employment Change	Percent Employment Change
Software Developers	43,390	60,490	17,100	39.4
Cooks, Restaurant	34,160	44,800	10,640	31.1
Home Health and Personal Care Aides	38,300	48,710	10,410	27.2
Registered Nurses	53,720	63,290	9,570	17.8
Market Research Analysts and Marketing Specialists	35,930	44,390	8,460	23.5
Fast Food and Counter Workers	77,680	86,000	8,320	10.7
Business Operations Specialists, All Other	61,930	69,980	8,050	13.0
Stockers and Order Fillers	51,900	59,630	7,730	14.9
Sales Representatives of Services, Except Advertising, Insurance, Financial Services, and Travel	41,910	49,490	7,580	18.1
General and Operations Managers	56,730	64,050	7,320	12.9

Note: Projections cover Colorado; (1) Sorted by numeric employment change
Source: www.projectionscentral.org, State Occupational Projections, 2022–2032 Long-Term Projections

Fastest-Growing Occupations: 2022 – 2032

Occupation[1]	2022 Employment	2032 Projected Employment	Numeric Employment Change	Percent Employment Change
Flight Attendants	5,300	8,440	3,140	59.2
Nurse Practitioners	3,700	5,780	2,080	56.2
Epidemiologists	620	940	320	51.6
Information Security Analysts (SOC 2018)	6,110	9,220	3,110	50.9
Solar Photovoltaic Installers	580	870	290	50.0
Statisticians	1,560	2,290	730	46.8
Airline Pilots, Copilots, and Flight Engineers	5,040	7,380	2,340	46.4
Data Scientists	4,150	6,030	1,880	45.3
Veterinary Assistants and Laboratory Animal Caretakers	2,570	3,640	1,070	41.6
Medical and Health Services Managers	7,310	10,220	2,910	39.8

Note: Projections cover Colorado; (1) Sorted by percent employment change and excludes occupations with numeric employment change less than 50
Source: www.projectionscentral.org, State Occupational Projections, 2022–2032 Long-Term Projections

CITY FINANCES

City Government Finances

Component	2022 ($000)	2022 ($ per capita)
Total Revenues	317,338	2,948
Total Expenditures	265,269	2,464
Debt Outstanding	208,814	1,940

Source: U.S. Census Bureau, State & Local Government Finances 2022

City Government Revenue by Source

Source	2022 ($000)	2022 ($ per capita)	2022 (%)
General Revenue			
From Federal Government	1,313	12	0.4
From State Government	7,812	73	2.5
From Local Governments	841	8	0.3
Taxes			
Property	52,592	489	16.6
Sales and Gross Receipts	109,464	1,017	34.5
Personal Income	0	0	0.0
Corporate Income	0	0	0.0
Motor Vehicle License	0	0	0.0
Other Taxes	23,983	223	7.6
Current Charges	70,860	658	22.3
Liquor Store	0	0	0.0
Utility	35,825	333	11.3

Source: U.S. Census Bureau, State & Local Government Finances 2022

City Government Expenditures by Function

Function	2022 ($000)	2022 ($ per capita)	2022 (%)
General Direct Expenditures			
Air Transportation	1,010	9	0.4
Corrections	0	0	0.0
Education	0	0	0.0
Employment Security Administration	0	0	0.0
Financial Administration	0	0	0.0
Fire Protection	0	0	0.0
General Public Buildings	0	0	0.0
Governmental Administration, Other	30,973	287	11.7
Health	0	0	0.0
Highways	0	0	0.0
Hospitals	0	0	0.0
Housing and Community Development	25,375	235	9.6
Interest on General Debt	5,292	49	2.0
Judicial and Legal	0	0	0.0
Libraries	1,407	13	0.5
Parking	487	4	0.2
Parks and Recreation	32,395	300	12.2
Police Protection	61,945	575	23.4
Public Welfare	0	0	0.0
Sewerage	28,637	266	10.8
Solid Waste Management	0	0	0.0
Veterans' Services	0	0	0.0
Liquor Store	0	0	0.0
Utility	31,465	292	11.9

Source: U.S. Census Bureau, State & Local Government Finances 2022

TAXES

State Corporate Income Tax Rates

State	Tax Rate (%)	Income Brackets ($)	Num. of Brackets	Financial Institution Tax Rate (%)[a]	Federal Income Tax Ded.
Colorado	4.4	Flat rate	1	4.4	No

Note: Tax rates for tax year 2024; (a) Rates listed are the corporate income tax rate applied to financial institutions or excise taxes based on income. Some states have other taxes based upon the value of deposits or shares.
Source: Federation of Tax Administrators, State Corporate Income Tax Rates, January 1, 2025

State Individual Income Tax Rates

State	Tax Rate (%)	Income Brackets ($)	Personal Exemptions ($) Single	Married	Depend.	Standard Ded. ($) Single	Married
Colorado	4.4	Flat rate	(d)	(d)	(d)	14,600	29,200 (d)

Note: Tax rates for tax year 2024; Local- and county-level taxes are not included; (d) These states use the personal exemption/standard deduction amounts provided in the federal Internal Revenue Code. Montana personal exemption subject to repeal under Section 15-30-2114.
Source: Federation of Tax Administrators, State Individual Income Tax Rates, January 1, 2025

Various State Sales and Excise Tax Rates

State	State Sales Tax (%)	Gasoline[1] ($/gal.)	Cigarette[2] ($/pack)	Spirits[3] ($/gal.)	Wine[4] ($/gal.)	Beer[5] ($/gal.)	Recreational Marijuana (%)
Colorado	2.9	0.28	2.24	2.28	0.32	0.08	(d)

Note: All tax rates as of January 1, 2025; (1) The American Petroleum Institute has developed a methodology for determining the average tax rate on a gallon of fuel. Rates may include any of the following: excise taxes, environmental fees, storage tank fees, other fees or taxes, general sales tax, and local taxes; (2) The federal excise tax of $1.0066 per pack and local taxes are not included; (3) Rates are those applicable to off-premise sales of 40% alcohol by volume (a.b.v.) distilled spirits in 750ml containers. Local excise taxes are excluded; (4) Rates are those applicable to off-premise sales of 11% a.b.v. non-carbonated wine in 750ml containers; (5) Rates are those applicable to off-premise sales of 4.7% a.b.v. beer in 12 ounce containers; (d) 15% excise tax (levied on wholesale at average market rate); 15% excise tax (retail price)
Source: Tax Foundation, 2025 Facts & Figures: How Does Your State Compare?

State Tax Competitiveness Index

State	Overall Rank	Corporate Tax Rank	Individual Income Tax Rank	Sales Tax Rank	Property Tax Rank	Unemployment Insurance Tax Rank
Colorado	32	10	18	37	36	39

Note: The Tax Foundation's State Tax Competitiveness Index enables policymakers, taxpayers, and business leaders to gauge how their states' tax systems compare. A rank of 1 is best, 50 is worst. Rankings do not average to the total. States without a tax rank equally as 1. DC's scores and rankings do not affect other states. The report shows tax systems as of July 1, 2024 (the beginning of Fiscal Year 2025).
Source: Tax Foundation, State Tax Competitiveness Index 2025

TRANSPORTATION

Means of Transportation to Work

Area	Car/Truck/Van		Public Transportation			Bicycle	Walked	Other Means	Worked at Home
	Drove Alone	Car-pooled	Bus	Subway	Railroad				
City	41.9	3.6	5.8	0.0	0.0	7.6	8.6	0.9	31.6
MSA[1]	55.6	5.7	3.1	0.0	0.0	3.0	3.8	0.9	27.9
U.S.	70.2	8.5	1.7	1.3	0.4	0.4	2.4	1.6	13.5

Note: Figures are percentages and cover workers 16 years of age and older; (1) Figures cover the Boulder, CO Metropolitan Statistical Area
Source: U.S. Census Bureau, 2019-2023 American Community Survey 5-Year Estimates

Travel Time to Work

Area	Less Than 10 Minutes	10 to 19 Minutes	20 to 29 Minutes	30 to 44 Minutes	45 to 59 Minutes	60 to 89 Minutes	90 Minutes or More
City	20.2	44.2	16.9	9.4	5.0	2.9	1.3
MSA[1]	15.0	34.3	20.7	17.0	6.9	4.4	1.6
U.S.	12.6	28.6	21.2	20.8	8.1	6.0	2.8

Note: Note: Figures are percentages and include workers 16 years old and over; (1) Figures cover the Boulder, CO Metropolitan Statistical Area
Source: U.S. Census Bureau, 2019-2023 American Community Survey 5-Year Estimates

Key Congestion Measures

Measure	2000	2010	2015	2020	2022
Annual Hours of Delay, Total (000)	2,194	3,362	4,092	2,312	4,057
Annual Hours of Delay, Per Auto Commuter	30	37	43	23	43
Annual Congestion Cost, Per Auto Commuter ($)	603	738	832	487	856

Note: Figures cover the Boulder CO urban area
Source: Texas A&M Transportation Institute, 2023 Urban Mobility Report

Freeway Travel Time Index

Measure	1985	1990	1995	2000	2005	2010	2015	2020	2022
Urban Area Index[1]	1.04	1.08	1.13	1.17	1.20	1.21	1.21	1.08	1.21
Urban Area Rank[1,2]	81	62	47	36	36	33	36	44	33

Note: Freeway Travel Time Index—the ratio of travel time in the peak period to the travel time at free-flow conditions. For example, a value of 1.30 indicates a 20-minute free-flow trip takes 26 minutes in the peak (20 minutes x 1.30 = 26 minutes); (1) Covers the Boulder CO urban area; (2) Rank is based on 101 larger urban areas (#1 = highest travel time index)
Source: Texas A&M Transportation Institute, 2023 Urban Mobility Report

Public Transportation

Agency Name / Mode of Transportation	Vehicles Operated in Maximum Service[1]	Annual Unlinked Passenger Trips[2] (in thous.)	Annual Passenger Miles[3] (in thous.)
Community Transit Network			
Bus (directly operated)	299	26,750.8	128,826.8
Bus (purchased transportation)	218	15,687.7	58,730.0
Commuter Rail (directly operated)	8	1,152.6	11,016.4
Commuter Rail (purchased transportation)	36	7,425.7	95,605.2
Demand Response (purchased transportation)	310	776.8	7,857.3
Light Rail (directly operated)	97	12,740.4	80,870.8

Note: (1) Number of revenue vehicles operated by the given mode and type of service to meet the annual maximum service requirement. This is the revenue vehicle count during the peak season of the year; on the week and day that maximum service is provided. Vehicles operated in maximum service (VOMS) exclude atypical days and one-time special events; (2) Number of passengers who boarded public transportation vehicles. Passengers are counted each time they board a vehicle no matter how many vehicles they use to travel from their origin to their destination. (3) Sum of the distances ridden by all passengers during the entire fiscal year.
Source: Federal Transit Administration, National Transit Database, 2023

Air Transportation

Airport Name and Code / Type of Service	Passenger Airlines[1]	Passenger Enplanements	Freight Carriers[2]	Freight (lbs)
Denver International (40 miles) (DEN)				
Domestic service (U.S. carriers only)	30	37,751,107	13	268,238,885
International service (U.S. carriers only)	8	1,461,931	3	8,628,050

Note: (1) Includes all U.S.-based major, minor and commuter airlines that carried at least one passenger during the year; (2) Includes all U.S.-based airlines and freight carriers that transported at least one pound of freight during the year.
Source: Bureau of Transportation Statistics, The Intermodal Transportation Database, Air Carriers: T-100 Domestic Market (U.S. carriers only), 2024; Bureau of Transportation Statistics, The Intermodal Transportation Database, Air Carriers: T-100 International Market (U.S. carriers only), 2024

BUSINESSES

Major Business Headquarters

Company Name	Industry	Rankings	
		Fortune[1]	Forbes[2]
No companies listed	-	-	-

Note: (1) Companies that produce a 10-K are ranked 1 to 500 based on 2023 revenue; (2) All private companies with at least $2 billion in annual revenue through the end of their most current fiscal year are ranked 1 to 275; companies listed are headquartered in the city; dashes indicate no ranking
Source: Fortune, "Fortune 500," 2024; Forbes, "America's Largest Private Companies," 2024

Living Environment

COST OF LIVING

Cost of Living Index

Composite Index	Groceries	Housing	Utilities	Trans-portation	Health Care	Misc. Goods/ Services
n/a	n/a	n/a	n/a	n/a	n/a	n/a

Note: The Cost of Living Index measures regional differences in the cost of consumer goods and services, excluding taxes and non-consumer expenditures, for professional and managerial households in the top income quintile. It is based on more than 50,000 prices covering almost 60 different items for which prices are collected three times a year by chambers of commerce, economic development organizations or university applied economic centers in each participating urban area. The numbers shown should be read as a percentage above or below the national average of 100. For example, a value of 115.4 in the groceries column indicates that grocery prices are 15.4% higher than the national average. Small differences in the index numbers should not be interpreted as significant; n/a not available.
Source: The Council for Community and Economic Research, Cost of Living Index, 2024

Grocery Prices

Area[1]	T-Bone Steak ($/pound)	Frying Chicken ($/pound)	Whole Milk ($/half gal.)	Eggs ($/dozen)	Orange Juice ($/64 oz.)	Coffee ($/11.5 oz.)
City[2]	n/a	n/a	n/a	n/a	n/a	n/a
Avg.	15.42	1.55	4.69	3.25	4.41	5.46
Min.	14.50	1.16	4.43	2.75	4.00	4.85
Max.	17.56	2.89	5.49	4.78	5.54	7.89

*Note: (1) Values for the local area are compared with the average, minimum and maximum values for all 276 areas in the Cost of Living Index; (2) Figures cover the Boulder CO urban area; n/a not available; **T-Bone Steak** (price per pound); **Frying Chicken** (price per pound, whole fryer); **Whole Milk** (half gallon carton); **Eggs** (price per dozen, Grade A, large); **Orange Juice** (64 oz. Tropicana or Florida Natural); **Coffee** (11.5 oz. can, vacuum-packed, Maxwell House, Hills Bros, or Folgers).*
Source: The Council for Community and Economic Research, Cost of Living Index, 2024

Housing and Utility Costs

Area[1]	New Home Price ($)	Apartment Rent ($/month)	All Electric ($/month)	Part Electric ($/month)	Other Energy ($/month)	Telephone ($/month)
City[2]	n/a	n/a	n/a	n/a	n/a	n/a
Avg.	515,975	1,550	210.99	123.07	82.07	194.99
Min.	265,375	692	104.33	53.68	36.26	179.42
Max.	2,775,821	5,719	529.02	397.28	361.63	223.33

*Note: (1) Values for the local area are compared with the average, minimum and maximum values for all 276 areas in the Cost of Living Index; (2) Figures cover the Boulder CO urban area; n/a not available; **New Home Price** (2,400 sf living area, 8,000 sf lot, in urban area with full utilities); **Apartment Rent** (950 sf 2 bedroom/1.5 or 2 bath, unfurnished, excluding all utilities except water); **All Electric** (average monthly cost for an all-electric home); **Part Electric** (average monthly cost for a part-electric home); **Other Energy** (average monthly cost for natural gas, fuel oil, coal, wood, and any other forms of energy except electricity); **Telephone** (price includes the base monthly rate plus taxes and fees for three lines of mobile phone service).*
Source: The Council for Community and Economic Research, Cost of Living Index, 2024

Health Care, Transportation, and Other Costs

Area[1]	Doctor ($/visit)	Dentist ($/visit)	Optometrist ($/visit)	Gasoline ($/gallon)	Beauty Salon ($/visit)	Men's Shirt ($)
City[2]	n/a	n/a	n/a	n/a	n/a	n/a
Avg.	143.77	117.51	129.23	3.32	48.57	38.14
Min.	36.74	58.67	67.33	2.80	24.00	13.41
Max.	270.44	216.82	307.33	5.28	94.00	63.89

*Note: (1) Values for the local area are compared with the average, minimum and maximum values for all 276 areas in the Cost of Living Index; (2) Figures cover the Boulder CO urban area; n/a not available; **Doctor** (general practitioners routine exam of an established patient); **Dentist** (adult teeth cleaning and periodic oral examination); **Optometrist** (full vision eye exam for established adult patient); **Gasoline** (one gallon regular unleaded, national brand, including all taxes, cash price at self-service pump if available); **Beauty Salon** (woman's shampoo, trim, and blow-dry); **Men's Shirt** (cotton/polyester dress shirt, pinpoint weave, long sleeves).*
Source: The Council for Community and Economic Research, Cost of Living Index, 2024

HOUSING

Homeownership Rate

Area	2017 (%)	2018 (%)	2019 (%)	2020 (%)	2021 (%)	2022 (%)	2023 (%)	2024 (%)
MSA[1]	n/a	n/a	n/a	n/a	n/a	n/a	n/a	n/a
U.S.	63.9	64.4	64.6	66.6	65.5	65.8	65.9	65.6

Note: (1) Figures cover the Boulder, CO Metropolitan Statistical Area; n/a not available
Source: U.S. Census Bureau, Housing Vacancies and Homeownership Annual Statistics: 2017-2024

House Price Index (HPI)

Area	National Ranking[2]	Quarterly Change (%)	One-Year Change (%)	Five-Year Change (%)	Since 1991Q1 (%)
MSA[1]	218	0.54	2.49	40.60	618.40
U.S.[3]	–	1.43	4.51	57.13	327.82

Note: The HPI is a weighted repeat sales index. It measures average price changes in repeat sales or refinancings on the same properties. This information is obtained by reviewing repeat mortgage transactions on single-family properties whose mortgages have been purchased or securitized by Fannie Mae or Freddie Mac since January 1975; (1) Figures cover the Boulder, CO Metropolitan Statistical Area; (2) Rankings are based on annual percentage change for all metro areas containing at least 15,000 transactions over the last 10 years and ranges from 1 to 241; (3) figures based on a weighted average of Census Division estimates using a seasonally adjusted, purchase-only index; all figures are for the period ending December 31, 2024
Source: Federal Housing Finance Agency, Change in FHFA Metropolitan Area House Price Indexes, All Transactions Index, 2024Q4

Home Value

Area	Under $100,000	$100,000 -$199,999	$200,000 -$299,999	$300,000 -$399,999	$400,000 -$499,999	$500,000 -$999,999	$1,000,000 or more	Median ($)
City	4.3	2.6	2.6	3.9	4.0	33.9	48.6	982,600
MSA[1]	3.9	1.2	2.5	6.2	10.6	49.6	25.9	713,900
U.S.	12.1	17.8	19.5	14.4	10.5	19.1	6.5	303,400

Note: Figures are percentages except for median and cover owner-occupied housing units; (1) Figures cover the Boulder, CO Metropolitan Statistical Area
Source: U.S. Census Bureau, 2019-2023 American Community Survey 5-Year Estimates

Year Housing Structure Built

Area	2020 or Later	2010 -2019	2000 -2009	1990 -1999	1980 -1989	1970 -1979	1960 -1969	1950 -1959	1940 -1949	Before 1940	Median Year
City	0.5	8.5	8.8	12.4	15.5	19.8	16.2	9.0	1.5	7.7	1978
MSA[1]	1.5	11.2	12.5	18.7	14.7	19.1	9.9	5.0	1.4	6.2	1986
U.S.	1.2	8.9	13.6	12.8	13.0	14.4	10.0	9.7	4.5	11.9	1980

Note: Figures are percentages except for Median Year; Note: (1) Figures cover the Boulder, CO Metropolitan Statistical Area
Source: U.S. Census Bureau, 2019-2023 American Community Survey 5-Year Estimates

Gross Monthly Rent

Area	Under $500	$500 -$999	$1,000 -$1,499	$1,500 -$1,999	$2,000 -$2,499	$2,500 -$2,999	$3,000 and up	Median ($)
City	2.9	4.3	17.5	29.8	18.2	10.7	16.5	1,924
MSA[1]	3.0	4.7	17.7	31.3	20.8	10.0	12.5	1,893
U.S.	6.5	22.3	29.5	20.2	10.8	4.8	5.9	1,348

Note: Figures are percentages except for median; Gross rent is the contract rent plus the estimated average monthly cost of utilities (electricity, gas, and water and sewer) and fuels (oil, coal, kerosene, wood, etc.) if these are paid by the renter (or paid for the renter by someone else); (1) Figures cover the Boulder, CO Metropolitan Statistical Area
Source: U.S. Census Bureau, 2019-2023 American Community Survey 5-Year Estimates

HEALTH

Health Risk Factors

Category	MSA[1] (%)	U.S. (%)
Adults aged 18–64 who have any kind of health care coverage	n/a	90.8
Adults who reported being in good or better health	n/a	81.8
Adults who have been told they have high blood cholesterol	n/a	36.9
Adults who have been told they have high blood pressure	n/a	34.0
Adults who are current smokers	n/a	12.1
Adults who currently use e-cigarettes	n/a	7.7
Adults who currently use chewing tobacco, snuff, or snus	n/a	3.2
Adults who are heavy drinkers[2]	n/a	6.1
Adults who are binge drinkers[3]	n/a	15.2
Adults who are overweight (BMI 25.0 - 29.9)	n/a	34.4
Adults who are obese (BMI 30.0 - 99.8)	n/a	34.3
Adults who participated in any physical activities in the past month	n/a	75.8

Note: All figures are crude prevalence; (1) Figures for the Boulder, CO Metropolitan Statistical Area were not available.
(2) Heavy drinkers are classified as adult men having more than 14 drinks per week and adult women having more than 7 drinks per week; (3) Binge drinkers are classified as males having five or more drinks on one occasion or females having four or more drinks on one occasion
Source: Centers for Disease Control and Prevention, Behaviorial Risk Factor Surveillance System, SMART: Selected Metropolitan Area Risk Trends, 2023

Acute and Chronic Health Conditions

Category	MSA[1] (%)	U.S. (%)
Adults who have ever been told they had a heart attack	n/a	4.2
Adults who have ever been told they have angina or coronary heart disease	n/a	4.0
Adults who have ever been told they had a stroke	n/a	3.3
Adults who have ever been told they have asthma	n/a	15.7
Adults who have ever been told they have arthritis	n/a	26.3
Adults who have ever been told they have diabetes[2]	n/a	11.5
Adults who have ever been told they had skin cancer	n/a	5.6
Adults who have ever been told they had any other types of cancer	n/a	8.4
Adults who have ever been told they have COPD	n/a	6.4
Adults who have ever been told they have kidney disease	n/a	3.7
Adults who have ever been told they have a form of depression	n/a	22.0

Note: All figures are crude prevalence; (1) Figures for the Boulder, CO Metropolitan Statistical Area were not available.
(2) Figures do not include pregnancy-related, borderline, or pre-diabetes
Source: Centers for Disease Control and Prevention, Behaviorial Risk Factor Surveillance System, SMART: Selected Metropolitan Area Risk Trends, 2023

Health Screening and Vaccination Rates

Category	MSA[1] (%)	U.S. (%)
Adults who have ever been tested for HIV	n/a	37.5
Adults who have had their blood cholesterol checked within the last five years	n/a	87.0
Adults aged 65+ who have had flu shot within the past year	n/a	63.4
Adults aged 65+ who have ever had a pneumonia vaccination	n/a	71.9

Note: All figures are crude prevalence; (1) Figures for the Boulder, CO Metropolitan Statistical Area were not available.
Source: Centers for Disease Control and Prevention, Behaviorial Risk Factor Surveillance System, SMART: Selected Metropolitan Area Risk Trends, 2023

Disability Status

Category	MSA[1] (%)	U.S. (%)
Adults who reported being deaf	n/a	7.4
Are you blind or have serious difficulty seeing, even when wearing glasses?	n/a	4.9
Do you have difficulty doing errands alone?	n/a	7.8
Do you have difficulty dressing or bathing?	n/a	3.6
Do you have serious difficulty concentrating/remembering/making decisions?	n/a	13.7
Do you have serious difficulty walking or climbing stairs?	n/a	13.2

Note: All figures are crude prevalence; (1) Figures for the Boulder, CO Metropolitan Statistical Area were not available.
Source: Centers for Disease Control and Prevention, Behaviorial Risk Factor Surveillance System, SMART: Selected Metropolitan Area Risk Trends, 2023

Mortality Rates for the Top 10 Causes of Death in the U.S.

ICD-10[a] Sub-Chapter	ICD-10[a] Code	Crude Mortality Rate[2] per 100,000 population	
		County[3]	U.S.
Malignant neoplasms	C00-C97	126.8	182.7
Ischaemic heart diseases	I20-I25	51.4	109.6
Provisional assignment of new diseases of uncertain etiology[1]	U00-U49	25.2	65.3
Other forms of heart disease	I30-I51	37.2	65.1
Other degenerative diseases of the nervous system	G30-G31	44.5	52.4
Other external causes of accidental injury	W00-X59	38.1	52.3
Cerebrovascular diseases	I60-I69	40.5	49.1
Chronic lower respiratory diseases	J40-J47	26.7	43.5
Hypertensive diseases	I10-I15	32.3	38.9
Organic, including symptomatic, mental disorders	F01-F09	33.1	33.9

Note: (a) ICD-10 = International Classification of Diseases 10th Revision; (1) Includes COVID-19, adverse effects to COVID-19 vaccines, SARS, and vaping-related disorders; (2) Crude mortality rates are a three-year average covering 2021-2023; (3) Figures cover Boulder County.
Source: Centers for Disease Control and Prevention, National Center for Health Statistics. National Vital Statistics System, Mortality 2018-2023 on CDC WONDER Online Database

Mortality Rates for Selected Causes of Death

Cause of Death	ICD-10[a] Code	Crude Mortality Rate[1] per 100,000 population	
		County[2]	U.S.
Accidental poisoning and exposure to noxious substances	X40-X49	14.1	30.5
Alzheimer disease	G30	28.1	35.4
Assault	X85-Y09	4.3	7.3
COVID-19	U07.1	25.2	65.3
Diabetes mellitus	E10-E14	10.9	30.0
Diseases of the liver	K70-K76	17.0	20.8
Human immunodeficiency virus (HIV) disease	B20-B24	Suppressed	1.5
Influenza and pneumonia	J09-J18	4.3	13.4
Intentional self-harm	X60-X84	20.8	14.7
Malnutrition	E40-E46	4.9	6.0
Obesity and other hyperalimentation	E65-E68	Unreliable	3.1
Renal failure	N17-N19	5.1	16.4
Transport accidents	V01-V99	11.3	14.4

Note: (a) ICD-10 = International Classification of Diseases 10th Revision; (1) Crude mortality rates are a three-year average covering 2021-2023; (2) Figures cover Boulder County; Data are suppressed when the data meet the criteria for confidentiality constraints; Crude mortality rates are flagged as unreliable when the rate would be calculated with a numerator of 20 or less.
Source: Centers for Disease Control and Prevention, National Center for Health Statistics. National Vital Statistics System, Mortality 2018-2023 on CDC WONDER Online Database

Health Insurance Coverage

Area	With Health Insurance	With Private Health Insurance	With Public Health Insurance	Without Health Insurance	Population Under Age 19 Without Health Insurance
City	96.5	83.8	21.0	3.5	1.0
MSA[1]	95.6	79.6	26.6	4.4	2.0
U.S.	91.4	67.3	36.3	8.6	5.4

Note: Figures are percentages that cover the civilian noninstitutionalized population; (1) Figures cover the Boulder, CO Metropolitan Statistical Area
Source: U.S. Census Bureau, 2019-2023 American Community Survey 5-Year Estimates

Number of Medical Professionals

Area	MDs[3]	DOs[3,4]	Dentists	Podiatrists	Chiropractors	Optometrists
County[1] (number)	1,197	112	382	21	276	98
County[1] (rate[2])	365.5	34.2	116.9	6.4	84.4	30.0
U.S. (rate[2])	302.5	29.2	74.6	6.4	29.5	18.0

Note: Data as of 2023 unless noted; (1) Data covers Boulder County; (2) Number of medical professionals per 100,000 population; (3) Data as of 2022 and includes all active, non-federal physicians; (4) Doctor of Osteopathic Medicine
Source: U.S. Department of Health and Human Services, Health Resources and Services Administration, Bureau of Health Professions, Area Resource File (ARF) 2023-2024

EDUCATION

Public School District Statistics

District Name	Schls	Pupils	Pupil/ Teacher Ratio	Minority Pupils[1] (%)	Total Rev. per Pupil ($)	Total Exp. per Pupil ($)
Boulder Valley SD No. Re2	56	28,357	17.2	34.4	18,438	17,381

Note: Table includes school districts with 2,000 or more students; (1) Percentage of students that are not non-Hispanic white.
Source: U.S. Department of Education, National Center for Education Statistics, Common Core of Data, Local Education Agency (School District) Universe Survey: School Year 2023-2024; U.S. Department of Education, National Center for Education Statistics, Common Core of Data, School District Finance Survey (F-33): School Year 2021–22

Best High Schools

According to *U.S. News,* Boulder is home to one of the top 500 high schools in the U.S.: **Fairview High School** (#425). Nearly 25,000 public, magnet and charter schools were ranked based on their performance on state assessments and how well they prepare students for college. *U.S. News & World Report, "Best High Schools 2024"*

Highest Level of Education

Area	Less than H.S.	H.S. Diploma	Some College, No Deg.	Associate Degree	Bachelor's Degree	Master's Degree	Prof. School Degree	Doctorate Degree
City	3.1	6.4	10.2	3.5	36.9	25.7	5.1	9.1
MSA[1]	4.5	11.0	14.5	6.1	34.5	20.0	3.8	5.6
U.S.	10.6	26.2	19.4	8.8	21.3	9.8	2.3	1.6

Note: Figures cover persons age 25 and over; (1) Figures cover the Boulder, CO Metropolitan Statistical Area
Source: U.S. Census Bureau, 2019-2023 American Community Survey 5-Year Estimates

Educational Attainment by Race

Area	High School Graduate or Higher (%)					Bachelor's Degree or Higher (%)				
	Total	White	Black	Asian	Hisp.[2]	Total	White	Black	Asian	Hisp.[2]
City	96.9	98.3	95.0	95.1	78.4	76.8	79.1	43.7	79.9	48.6
MSA[1]	95.5	97.6	93.4	92.4	76.4	63.9	67.0	40.6	70.1	30.8
U.S.	89.4	92.9	88.1	88.0	72.5	35.0	37.7	24.7	57.0	19.9

Note: Figures shown cover persons 25 years old and over; (1) Figures cover the Boulder, CO Metropolitan Statistical Area; (2) People of Hispanic origin can be of any race
Source: U.S. Census Bureau, 2019-2023 American Community Survey 5-Year Estimates

School Enrollment by Grade and Control

Area	Preschool (%)		Kindergarten (%)		Grades 1 - 4 (%)		Grades 5 - 8 (%)		Grades 9 - 12 (%)	
	Public	Private	Public	Private	Public	Private	Public	Private	Public	Private
City	43.0	57.0	93.0	7.0	86.9	13.1	92.7	7.3	90.7	9.3
MSA[1]	48.1	51.9	87.6	12.4	88.7	11.3	91.5	8.5	93.0	7.0
U.S.	58.7	41.3	85.2	14.8	87.2	12.8	87.9	12.1	89.0	11.0

Note: Figures shown cover persons 3 years old and over; (1) Figures cover the Boulder, CO Metropolitan Statistical Area
Source: U.S. Census Bureau, 2019-2023 American Community Survey 5-Year Estimates

Higher Education

Four-Year Colleges			Two-Year Colleges			Medical Schools[1]	Law Schools[2]	Voc/ Tech[3]
Public	Private Non-profit	Private For-profit	Public	Private Non-profit	Private For-profit			
1	2	0	0	0	1	0	1	1

Note: Figures cover institutions located within the Boulder, CO Metropolitan Statistical Area and include main campuses only; (1) includes schools accredited by the Liaison Committee on Medical Education and the American Osteopathic Association's Commission on Osteopathic College Accreditation; (2) includes ABA-accredited schools, schools with provisional ABA accreditation, and state accredited schools; (3) includes all schools with programs that are less than 2 years.
Source: National Center for Education Statistics, Integrated Postsecondary Education System (IPEDS), 2023-24; Wikipedia, List of Medical Schools in the United States, accessed May 2, 2025; Wikipedia, List of Law Schools in the United States, accessed May 2, 2025

According to *U.S. News & World Report*, the Boulder, CO metro area is home to one of the top 200 national universities in the U.S.: **University of Colorado Boulder** (#98 tie). The indicators used to capture academic quality fall into a number of categories: assessment by administrators at peer institutions; retention of students; faculty resources; student selectivity; financial resources; alumni giving; high school counselor ratings of colleges; and graduation rate. *U.S. News & World Report, "America's Best Colleges 2025"*

According to *U.S. News & World Report*, the Boulder, CO metro area is home to one of the top 100 law schools in the U.S.: **University of Colorado—Boulder** (#46 tie). The rankings are based on a weighted average of 12 measures of quality: peer assessment score; assessment score by lawyers/judges; median LSAT scores; median undergrad GPA; acceptance rate; employment rates for graduates; placement success; bar passage rate; faculty resources; expenditures per student; student/faculty ratio; and library resources. *U.S. News & World Report, "America's Best Graduate Schools, Law, 2025"*

EMPLOYERS

Major Employers

Company Name	Industry
Agilent Technologies	Instruments to measure electricity
America's Note Network	Mortgage bankers & loan correspondents
Ball Aerospace & Technologies Corp.	Search & navigation equipment
Ball Corporation	Space research & technology
Corden Pharma Colorado	Pharmaceutical preparations
County of Boulder	County government
Crispin Porter Bogusky	Business services at non-commercial site
Health Carechain	Medical field-related associations
IBM	Magnetic storage devices, computer
Lockheed Martin Corporation	Search & navigation equipment
Micro Motion	Liquid meters
National Oceanic and Atmospheric Admin	Environmental protection agency, government
Natl Inst of Standards & Technology	Commercial physical research
Qualcomm Incorporated	Integrated circuits, semiconductor networks
Staffing Solutions Southwest	Temporary help services
The Regents of the University of Colorado	Noncommercial research organizations
Tyco Healthcare Group	Medical instruments & equipment, blood & bone work
University Corp for Atmospheric Research	Noncommercial research organizations
University of Colorado	Colleges & universities
Wall Street On Demand	Financial services

Note: Companies shown are located within the Boulder, CO Metropolitan Statistical Area.
Source: Chambers of Commerce; State Departments of Labor; Wikipedia

PUBLIC SAFETY

Crime Rate

Area	Total Crime Rate	Violent Crime Rate				Property Crime Rate		
		Murder	Rape	Robbery	Aggrav. Assault	Burglary	Larceny -Theft	Motor Vehicle Theft
City	3,414.5	2.9	38.4	36.5	279.2	457.6	2,276.7	323.3
U.S.	2,290.9	5.7	38.0	66.5	264.1	250.7	1,347.2	318.7

Note: Figures are crimes per 100,000 population.
Source: FBI, Table 8, Offenses Known to Law Enforcement, by State by City, 2023

Hate Crimes

Area	Number of Quarters Reported	Number of Incidents per Bias Motivation					
		Race/Ethnicity/ Ancestry	Religion	Sexual Orientation	Disability	Gender	Gender Identity
City	4	3	3	0	0	0	2
U.S.	4	5,900	2,699	2,077	187	92	492

Source: Federal Bureau of Investigation, Hate Crime Statistics 2023

Identity Theft Consumer Reports

Area	Reports	Reports per 100,000 Population	Rank[2]
MSA[1]	677	206	147
U.S.	1,135,291	339	-

Note: (1) Figures cover the Boulder, CO Metropolitan Statistical Area; (2) Rank ranges from 1 to 401 where 1 indicates greatest number of identity theft reports per 100,000 population
Source: Federal Trade Commission, Consumer Sentinel Network Data Book 2024

Fraud and Other Consumer Reports

Area	Reports	Reports per 100,000 Population	Rank[2]
MSA[1]	4,462	1,359	83
U.S.	5,360,641	1,601	-

Note: (1) Figures cover the Boulder, CO Metropolitan Statistical Area; (2) Rank ranges from 1 to 401 where 1 indicates greatest number of fraud and other consumer reports per 100,000 population
Source: Federal Trade Commission, Consumer Sentinel Network Data Book 2024

POLITICS

2024 Presidential Election Results

Area	Trump (Rep.)	Harris (Dem.)	Stein (Green)	Kennedy (Ind.)	Oliver (Lib.)	Other
Boulder County	20.8	76.5	0.8	0.9	0.6	0.4
U.S.	49.7	48.2	0.6	0.5	0.4	0.6

Note: Results are percentages and may not add to 100% due to rounding
Source: Dave Leip's Atlas of U.S. Presidential Elections

SPORTS

Professional Sports Teams

Team Name	League	Year Established

No teams are located in the metro area
Source: Wikipedia, Major Professional Sports Teams of the United States and Canada, May 1, 2025

CLIMATE

Average and Extreme Temperatures

Temperature	Jan	Feb	Mar	Apr	May	Jun	Jul	Aug	Sep	Oct	Nov	Dec	Yr.
Extreme High (°F)	73	76	84	90	93	102	103	100	97	89	79	75	103
Average High (°F)	43	47	52	62	71	81	88	86	77	67	52	45	64
Average Temp. (°F)	30	34	39	48	58	67	73	72	63	52	39	32	51
Average Low (°F)	16	20	25	34	44	53	59	57	48	37	25	18	37
Extreme Low (°F)	-25	-25	-10	-2	22	30	43	41	17	3	-8	-25	-25

Note: Figures cover the years 1948-1992
Source: National Climatic Data Center, International Station Meteorological Climate Summary, 9/96

Average Precipitation/Snowfall/Humidity

Precip./Humidity	Jan	Feb	Mar	Apr	May	Jun	Jul	Aug	Sep	Oct	Nov	Dec	Yr.
Avg. Precip. (in.)	0.6	0.6	1.3	1.7	2.5	1.7	1.9	1.5	1.1	1.0	0.9	0.6	15.5
Avg. Snowfall (in.)	9	7	14	9	2	Tr	0	0	2	4	9	8	63
Avg. Rel. Hum. 5am (%)	62	65	67	66	70	68	67	68	66	63	66	63	66
Avg. Rel. Hum. 5pm (%)	49	44	40	35	38	34	34	34	32	34	47	50	39

Note: Figures cover the years 1948-1992; Tr = Trace amounts (<0.05 in. of rain; <0.5 in. of snow)
Source: National Climatic Data Center, International Station Meteorological Climate Summary, 9/96

Weather Conditions

Temperature			Daytime Sky			Precipitation		
10°F & below	32°F & below	90°F & above	Clear	Partly cloudy	Cloudy	0.01 inch or more precip.	0.1 inch or more snow/ice	Thunder-storms
24	155	33	99	177	89	90	38	39

Note: Figures are average number of days per year and cover the years 1948-1992
Source: National Climatic Data Center, International Station Meteorological Climate Summary, 9/96

HAZARDOUS WASTE

Superfund Sites

The Boulder, CO metro area is home to two sites on the EPA's Superfund National Priorities List (NPL) or Superfund Alternative Approach (SAA) list: **Captain Jack Mill** (Final NPL); **Marshall Landfill** (Final NPL). The Superfund alternative approach uses the same investigation and cleanup process and standards that are used for sites listed on the National Priorities List. The SAA is an alternative to listing a site on the NPL; it is not an alternative to Superfund or the Superfund process. There are a total of 1,445 Superfund sites with a status of proposed or final on both lists in the United States. *U.S. Environmental Protection Agency, National Priorities List, May 1, 2025; U.S. Environmental Protection Agency, Superfund Alternative Approach Sites, May 1, 2025*

AIR QUALITY

Air Quality Trends: Ozone

	1990	1995	2000	2005	2010	2015	2020	2021	2022	2023
MSA[1]	n/a	n/a	n/a	n/a	n/a	n/a	n/a	n/a	n/a	n/a
U.S.	0.087	0.089	0.081	0.080	0.072	0.068	0.066	0.067	0.067	0.070

Note: (1) Data covers the Boulder, CO Metropolitan Statistical Area; n/a not available. The values shown are the composite ozone concentration averages among trend sites based on the highest fourth daily maximum 8-hour concentration in parts per million. These trends are based on sites having an adequate record of monitoring data during the trend period. Data from exceptional events are included.
Source: U.S. Environmental Protection Agency, Air Quality Monitoring Information, "Air Quality Trends by City, 1990-2023"

Air Quality Index

Area	Percent of Days when Air Quality was...[2]					AQI Statistics[2]	
	Good	Moderate	Unhealthy for Sensitive Groups	Unhealthy	Very Unhealthy	Maximum	Median
MSA[1]	52.6	45.8	1.1	0.5	0.0	181	50

Note: (1) Data covers the Boulder, CO Metropolitan Statistical Area; (2) Based on 365 days with AQI data in 2023. Air Quality Index (AQI) is an index for reporting daily air quality. EPA calculates the AQI for five major air pollutants regulated by the Clean Air Act: ground-level ozone, particle pollution (aka particulate matter), carbon monoxide, sulfur dioxide, and nitrogen dioxide. The AQI runs from 0 to 500. The higher the AQI value, the greater the level of air pollution and the greater the health concern. There are six AQI categories: "Good" AQI is between 0 and 50. Air quality is considered satisfactory; "Moderate" AQI is between 51 and 100. Air quality is acceptable; "Unhealthy for Sensitive Groups" When AQI values are between 101 and 150, members of sensitive groups may experience health effects; "Unhealthy" When AQI values are between 151 and 200 everyone may begin to experience health effects; "Very Unhealthy" AQI values between 201 and 300 trigger a health alert; "Hazardous" AQI values over 300 trigger warnings of emergency conditions (not shown).
Source: U.S. Environmental Protection Agency, Air Quality Index Report, 2023

Air Quality Index Pollutants

Area	Percent of Days when AQI Pollutant was...[2]					
	Carbon Monoxide	Nitrogen Dioxide	Ozone	Sulfur Dioxide	Particulate Matter 2.5	Particulate Matter 10
MSA[1]	0.0	0.0	74.5	(3)	25.5	0.0

Note: (1) Data covers the Boulder, CO Metropolitan Statistical Area; (2) Based on 365 days with AQI data in 2023. The Air Quality Index (AQI) is an index for reporting daily air quality. EPA calculates the AQI for five major air pollutants regulated by the Clean Air Act: ground-level ozone, particle pollution (also known as particulate matter), carbon monoxide, sulfur dioxide, and nitrogen dioxide. The AQI runs from 0 to 500. The higher the AQI value, the greater the level of air pollution and the greater the health concern; (3) Sulfur dioxide is no longer included in this table because SO_2 concentrations tend to be very localized and not necessarily representative of broad geographical areas like counties and CBSAs.
Source: U.S. Environmental Protection Agency, Air Quality Index Report, 2023

Maximum Air Pollutant Concentrations: Particulate Matter, Ozone, CO and Lead

	Particulate Matter 10 (ug/m^3)	Particulate Matter 2.5 Wtd AM (ug/m^3)	Particulate Matter 2.5 24-Hr (ug/m^3)	Ozone (ppm)	Carbon Monoxide (ppm)	Lead (ug/m^3)
MSA[1] Level	39	6.8	19	0.071	n/a	n/a
NAAQS[2]	150	15	35	0.075	9	0.15
Met NAAQS[2]	Yes	Yes	Yes	Yes	n/a	n/a

Note: (1) Data covers the Boulder, CO Metropolitan Statistical Area; Data from exceptional events are included; (2) National Ambient Air Quality Standards; ppm = parts per million; ug/m^3 = micrograms per cubic meter; n/a not available.
Concentrations: Particulate Matter 10 (coarse particulate)—highest second maximum 24-hour concentration; Particulate Matter 2.5 Wtd AM (fine particulate)—highest weighted annual mean concentration; Particulate Matter 2.5 24-Hour (fine particulate)—highest 98th percentile 24-hour concentration; Ozone—highest fourth daily maximum 8-hour concentration; Carbon Monoxide—highest second maximum non-overlapping 8-hour concentration; Lead—maximum running 3-month average
Source: U.S. Environmental Protection Agency, Air Quality Monitoring Information, "Air Quality Statistics by City, 2023"

Maximum Air Pollutant Concentrations: Nitrogen Dioxide and Sulfur Dioxide

	Nitrogen Dioxide AM (ppb)	Nitrogen Dioxide 1-Hr (ppb)	Sulfur Dioxide AM (ppb)	Sulfur Dioxide 1-Hr (ppb)	Sulfur Dioxide 24-Hr (ppb)
MSA[1] Level	n/a	n/a	n/a	n/a	n/a
NAAQS[2]	53	100	30	75	140
Met NAAQS[2]	n/a	n/a	n/a	n/a	n/a

Note: (1) Data covers the Boulder, CO Metropolitan Statistical Area; Data from exceptional events are included; (2) National Ambient Air Quality Standards; ppm = parts per million; ug/m^3 = micrograms per cubic meter; n/a not available.
Concentrations: Nitrogen Dioxide AM—highest arithmetic mean concentration; Nitrogen Dioxide 1-Hr—highest 98th percentile 1-hour daily maximum concentration; Sulfur Dioxide AM—highest annual mean concentration; Sulfur Dioxide 1-Hr—highest 99th percentile 1-hour daily maximum concentration; Sulfur Dioxide 24-Hr—highest second maximum 24-hour concentration
Source: U.S. Environmental Protection Agency, Air Quality Monitoring Information, "Air Quality Statistics by City, 2023"

Colorado Springs, Colorado

Background

Colorado Springs is the seat of El Paso County in central Colorado and sits at the foot of Pike's Peak, the highest summit of the Southern Front Range of the Rock Mountains in North America. A dynamic and growing city, its economy is based on health care, high-tech manufacturing, tourism, and sports, with strong employment links to nearby military installations. With its economy and gorgeous surroundings, it is no wonder that Colorado Springs ranks as one of the fastest-growing cities in the country.

In 1806, Lieutenant Zebulon Pike visited the site and the mountain that now bears his name, but settlement did not begin in earnest until gold was discovered in 1859 and miners flooded into the area.

In 1871, General William Jackson Palmer, a railroad tycoon, purchased the site for $10,000 and began promoting the area as a health and recreation resort. Pike's Peak was already well known as a scenic landmark, and very soon the Garden of the Gods, Seven Falls, Cheyenne Mountain, and Manitou Springs were widely known for their spectacular natural beauty. Perhaps the highest testimonial came from Katherine Lee Bates, who, after a trip to Pike's Peak in 1893, wrote "America the Beautiful."

The planned community of Colorado Springs was incorporated in 1876. As a resort, it was wildly successful, hosting the likes of Oscar Wilde and John D. Rockefeller. It became a special favorite of English visitors, one of whom made the claim that there were two "civilized" places between the Atlantic and the Pacific—Chicago and Colorado Springs.

The English were so enamored of the place, in fact, that it came to be called "Little London," as English visitors settled in the area, introducing golf, cricket, polo, and fox hunting. Since there were no local foxes, an artificial scent was spread out for the hounds, or sometimes a coyote was substituted. Several sumptuous hotels were built during this period, as was an elegantly appointed opera house.

In 1891, gold was again discovered, and the city's population tripled to 35,000 in the following decade. Sufficient gold deposits allowed a lucky few to amass considerable fortunes and build huge houses north of the city. However, not all the newly minted millionaires were inclined toward conspicuous display; Winfield Scott Stratton, "Midas of the Rockies," bruised emerging aesthetic sensibilities by constructing a crude wooden frame house near the business district.

After the 1890s rush ended, Colorado Springs resumed a more measured pace of growth. World War II caused considerable development as Fort Carson and the Peterson Air Force Base were established, followed by the North American Aerospace Defense Command (NORAD) and the U.S. Air Force Academy in the 1950s. Today NORAD is primarily concerned with the tracking of Intercontinental Ballistic Missiles (ICBM) and celebrated its 64th anniversary in 2022. The city's military connection has contributed in large part to the economic base of the area, and its highly educated and technically skilled workforce. In late 2008, Fort Carson became the home station of the 4th Infantry Division, nearly doubling the population of the base.

Colorado Springs is the site of the headquarters of the United States Olympics Committee, which maintains an important Olympic training center there. The U.S. Olympic and Paralympic Museum opened in 2020.

The city is also home to the World Figure Skating Museum and Hall of Fame, the Pro Rodeo Hall of Fame, and Museum of the American Cowboy. The state-of-the-art Pikes Peak Summit Center opened in 2021, and includes a visitor center, utilities facility, and high-altitude research laboratory.

The city hosts several institutions of higher learning, including Colorado College (1874), the U.S. Air Force Academy (1954), a campus of the University of Colorado (1965), and Nazarene Bible College (1967). Cultural amenities include the Fine Arts Center and Theatreworks at the University of Colorado.

Although recreational marijuana has been legal for more than a decade, the city just approved recreational cannabis shop to open early in 2025.

Colorado Springs has a cooler, dry-winter semi-arid climate. Its location just east of the Rocky Mountains sees the rapid warming influence from chinook winds during winter but also drastic day-to-day variability in weather conditions. The city has abundant sunshine year-round, averaging 243 sunny days per year, and receives approximately 16 inches of annual precipitation. Colorado Springs is also one of the most active lightning strike areas in the United States, which led Nikola Tesla to build his lab in Colorado Springs to study electricity.

Rankings

General Rankings

- To help military veterans find the best places in which to settle down, *WalletHub* compared the 100 largest U.S. cities across 19 key indicators of livability, affordability and veteran-friendliness. They range from the share of military skill-related jobs to veteran income growth to the availability of VA health facilities. Colorado Springs ranked #13. *Wallethub.com, "Best & Worst Places for Veterans to Live (2025)," November 7, 2024*

- *US News & World Report* conducted a survey of more than 3,500 people and analyzed the 150 largest metropolitan areas to determine what matters most when selecting the next place to live. Colorado Springs ranked #3 out of the top 25 as having the best combination of desirable factors. Criteria: cost of living; quality of life and education; climate; job market; desirability; and other factors. *realestate.usnews.com, "Best Places to Live in the U.S. in 2024-2025," May 21, 2024*

- In their annual survey, Livability.com looked at data for more than 2,000 mid-sized U.S. cities to assign a "Livability Score"for each. The top 100 scoring cities make up Livability's "Top 100 Best Places to Live in the U.S." in 2025. Colorado Springs was placed among the top 100 of the customizable list. Criteria: housing and economy; cost of living; environment; education; health care options; transportation; safety; and community amenities. *Livability.com, "Top 100 Best Places to Live in the U.S. in 2025" April 15, 2025*

Business/Finance Rankings

- The Colorado Springs metro area appeared on the Milken Institute "2025 Best Performing Cities" list. Rank: #5 out of 200 large metro areas (based on performance category). Criteria: job growth; wage growth; high-tech growth and impact; community resilience; housing affordability; household broadband access. *Milken Institute, "Best-Performing Cities 2025," January 14, 2025*

Education Rankings

- Personal finance website *WalletHub* analyzed the 150 largest U.S. metropolitan statistical areas to determine where the most educated Americans are putting their degrees to work. Criteria: education levels; percentage of workers with degrees; education quality and attainment gap; public school quality rankings; quality and enrollment of each metro area's universities. Colorado Springs was ranked #16 (#1 = most educated city). *WalletHub.com, "Most & Least Educated Cities in America, 2025" July 2, 2024*

Environmental Rankings

- Colorado Springs was highlighted as one of the 25 most ozone-polluted metro areas in the U.S. during 2021 through 2023. The area ranked #23. *American Lung Association, "State of the Air 2025," April 23, 2025*

- Colorado Springs was highlighted as one of the top 25 cleanest metro areas for year-round particle pollution (Annual PM 2.5) in the U.S. during 2021 through 2023. The area ranked #9. *American Lung Association, "State of the Air 2025," April 23, 2025*

Health/Fitness Rankings

- For each of the 100 largest cities in the United States, the American Fitness Index®, compiled in partnership between the American College of Sports Medicine and the Elevance Health Foundation, evaluated community infrastructure and more than 30 health behaviors including preventive health, levels of chronic disease conditions, food insecurity, pedestrian safety, air quality, and community/environment resources that support physical activity. Colorado Springs ranked #34 for "community fitness." *americanfitnessindex.org, "2024 ACSM American Fitness Index Summary Report," July 23, 2024*

- Colorado Springs was identified as a "2025 Allergy Capital." The area ranked #84 out of the nation's 100 largest metropolitan areas. Three groups of factors were used to identify the most challenging cities for people with allergies: annual tree, grass, and weed pollen scores; over the counter allergy medicine use; number of board-certified allergy specialists. *Asthma and Allergy Foundation of America, "2025 Allergy Capitals: The Most Challenging Places to Live with Allergies," March 18, 2025*

- Colorado Springs was identified as a "2024 Asthma Capital." The area ranked #95 out of the nation's 100 largest metropolitan areas. Criteria: estimated asthma prevalence; asthma-related mortality; and ER visits due to asthma. Risk factors analyzed but not factored in the rankings: annual air quality including pollution and ozone levels; public smoking laws; indoor air quality; access to asthma specialists; rescue and controller medication use; uninsured rate; pollen allergy; poverty rate. *Asthma and Allergy Foundation of America, "Asthma Capitals 2024: The Most Challenging Places to Live With Asthma," September 10, 2024*

Pet Rankings

- Colorado Springs was selected by *Sniffspot.com* as one of the most dog-friendly cities in the U.S., ranking #15 out of 50. Criteria: dog parks; hiking; sniffspots; public parks; dog-friendly businesses; housing; dog waste cleanliness; leash laws; dog services; and overall cost. *Sniffspot.com, "The Top 50 Most Dog-Friendly Cities in the U.S.," September 30, 2024*

Real Estate Rankings

- *WalletHub* compared the most populated U.S. cities to determine which had the best markets for real estate agents. Colorado Springs ranked #38 where demand was high and pay was the best. Criteria: sales per agent; annual median wage for real-estate agents; monthly average starting salary for real estate agents; real estate job density and competition; unemployment rate; home turnover rate; housing-market health index; and other relevant metrics. *WalletHub.com, "2021 Best Places to Be a Real Estate Agent," May 12, 2021*

- The Colorado Springs metro area appeared on Realtor.com's list of hot housing markets to watch in 2025. The area ranked #1. Criteria: forecasted home price and sales growth; overall economy; population trends. *Realtor.com®, "Top 10 Housing Markets Positioned for Growth in 2025," December 10, 2024*

- The Colorado Springs metro area was identified as one of the 20 worst housing markets in the U.S. in 2024. The area ranked #209 out of 226 markets. Criteria: year-over-year change of median sales price of existing single-family homes between the 4th quarter of 2023 and the 4th quarter of 2024. *National Association of Realtors®, Median Sales Price of Existing Single-Family Homes for Metropolitan Areas, 4th Quarter 2024*

- Colorado Springs was ranked #131 out of 176 metro areas in terms of cost of housing in 2024 by the National Association of Home Builders (#1 = most affordable). Criteria: the portion of an average family's income necessary to pay the mortgage on a median-priced home. *National Association of Home Builders®, NAHB-Wells Fargo Cost of Housing Index, 4th Quarter 2024*

Safety Rankings

- Allstate ranked the 100 most populous cities in America in terms of driver safety. Colorado Springs ranked #60. Criteria based on anonymized driving behavior data from Allstate's mobile app powered by Arity: high speed driving (over 80 mph), phone handling, and hard braking. The report helps increase the importance of safety and awareness behind the wheel. *Allstate, "16th Allstate America's Best Drivers Report®" July 11, 2024*

Women/Minorities Rankings

- Personal finance website *WalletHub* compared more than 180 U.S. cities across two key dimensions, "Hispanic Business-Friendliness" and "Hispanic Purchasing Power," to arrive at the most favorable conditions for Hispanic entrepreneurs. Colorado Springs was ranked #68 out of 182. Criteria includes: share of Hispanic-Owned Businesses; average growth of Hispanic Business revenues; Small Business-Friendliness score; affordability; and number of Hispanics with at least a bachelor's degree. *WalletHub.com, "Best Cities for Hispanic Entrepreneurs," September 4, 2024*

Miscellaneous Rankings

- *WalletHub* compared 148 of the most populated U.S. cities to determine their operating efficiency. A "Quality of Services" score was constructed for each city and then measured against the total budget per capita to reveal which were managed the best. Colorado Springs ranked #46. Criteria: financial stability; economy; education; safety; health; infrastructure and pollution. *WalletHub.com, "2025's Best- & Worst-Run Cities in America," June 18, 2024*

Business Environment

DEMOGRAPHICS

Population Growth

Area	1990 Census	2000 Census	2010 Census	2020 Census	2023 Estimate[2]	Population Growth 1990-2023 (%)
City	283,798	360,890	416,427	478,961	483,099	70.2
MSA[1]	409,482	537,484	645,613	755,105	760,782	85.8
U.S.	248,709,873	281,421,906	308,745,538	331,449,281	332,387,540	33.6

Note: (1) Figures cover the Colorado Springs, CO Metropolitan Statistical Area; (2) 2019-2023 5-year ACS population estimate
Source: U.S. Census Bureau, 1990 Census, 2000 Census, 2010 Census, 2020 Census, 2019-2023 American Community Survey 5-Year Estimates

Race

Area	White Alone[2] (%)	Black Alone[2] (%)	Asian Alone[2] (%)	AIAN[3] Alone[2] (%)	NHOPI[4] Alone[2] (%)	Other Race Alone[2] (%)	Two or More Races (%)
City	72.3	5.8	3.0	1.0	0.2	4.9	12.8
MSA[1]	73.1	5.8	2.8	0.9	0.3	4.3	12.8
U.S.	63.4	12.4	5.8	0.9	0.2	6.6	10.7

Note: (1) Figures cover the Colorado Springs, CO Metropolitan Statistical Area; (2) Alone is defined as not being in combination with one or more other races; (3) American Indian and Alaska Native; (4) Native Hawaiian and Other Pacific Islander
Source: U.S. Census Bureau, 2019-2023 American Community Survey 5-Year Estimates

Hispanic or Latino Origin

Area	Total (%)	Mexican (%)	Puerto Rican (%)	Cuban (%)	Other (%)
City	18.7	12.0	1.2	0.2	5.3
MSA[1]	18.0	10.8	1.5	0.3	5.3
U.S.	19.0	11.3	1.8	0.7	5.2

Note: Persons of Hispanic or Latino origin can be of any race; (1) Figures cover the Colorado Springs, CO Metropolitan Statistical Area
Source: U.S. Census Bureau, 2019-2023 American Community Survey 5-Year Estimates

Age

Area	Percent of Population									Median Age
	Under Age 5	Age 5–19	Age 20–34	Age 35–44	Age 45–54	Age 55–64	Age 65–74	Age 75–84	Age 85+	
City	5.9	18.5	24.7	13.7	11.2	11.2	8.7	4.3	1.7	35.6
MSA[1]	6.1	19.7	23.6	13.5	11.3	11.7	8.7	3.9	1.4	35.4
U.S.	5.7	19.1	20.2	13.1	12.3	12.8	10.0	4.9	1.9	38.7

Note: (1) Figures cover the Colorado Springs, CO Metropolitan Statistical Area
Source: U.S. Census Bureau, 2019-2023 American Community Survey 5-Year Estimates

Disability by Age

Area	All Ages	Under 18 Years Old	18 to 64 Years Old	65 Years and Over
City	13.2	5.7	11.9	30.1
MSA[1]	12.5	5.4	11.3	29.7
U.S.	13.0	4.7	10.7	32.9

Note: Figures show percent of the civilian noninstitutionalized population that reported having a disability. Disability status is determined from six types of difficulty: vision, hearing, cognitive, ambulatory, self-care, and independent living. For children under 5 years old, hearing and vision difficulty are used to determine disability status. For children between the ages of 5 and 14, disability status is determined from hearing, vision, cognitive, ambulatory, and self-care difficulties. For people aged 15 years and older, they are considered to have a disability if they have difficulty with any one of the six difficulty types; Note: (1) Figures cover the Colorado Springs, CO Metropolitan Statistical Area
Source: U.S. Census Bureau, 2019-2023 American Community Survey 5-Year Estimates

Ancestry

Area	German	Irish	English	American	Italian	Polish	French[2]	European	Scottish
City	17.8	11.4	12.8	4.2	4.7	2.6	2.4	2.9	2.6
MSA[1]	17.6	11.0	12.3	4.5	4.5	2.4	2.3	3.0	2.7
U.S.	12.6	9.4	9.1	5.5	4.9	2.6	2.0	1.6	1.6

Note: Figures are the percentage of the total population reporting a particular ancestry. The nine most commonly reported ancestries in the U.S. are shown. Figures include multiple ancestries (e.g. if a person reported being Irish and Italian, they were included in both columns); (1) Figures cover the Colorado Springs, CO Metropolitan Statistical Area; (2) Excludes Basque
Source: U.S. Census Bureau, 2019-2023 American Community Survey 5-Year Estimates

Foreign-born Population

Area	Any Foreign Country	Asia	Mexico	Europe	Caribbean	Central America[2]	South America	Africa	Canada
						Percent of Population Born in			
City	7.4	2.0	1.7	1.5	0.2	0.6	0.4	0.5	0.3
MSA[1]	6.7	1.8	1.5	1.4	0.3	0.5	0.4	0.4	0.3
U.S.	13.9	4.3	3.3	1.4	1.4	1.2	1.2	0.8	0.2

Note: (1) Figures cover the Colorado Springs, CO Metropolitan Statistical Area; (2) Excludes Mexico.
Source: U.S. Census Bureau, 2019-2023 American Community Survey 5-Year Estimates

Household Size

Area	Persons in Household (%)							Average Household Size
	One	Two	Three	Four	Five	Six	Seven or More	
City	28.2	36.1	15.4	11.8	5.3	2.2	1.0	2.39
MSA[1]	24.8	36.1	16.2	13.0	6.1	2.4	1.4	2.51
U.S.	28.5	33.8	15.4	12.7	5.9	2.3	1.4	2.54

Note: (1) Figures cover the Colorado Springs, CO Metropolitan Statistical Area
Source: U.S. Census Bureau, 2019-2023 American Community Survey 5-Year Estimates

Household Relationships

Area	House-holder	Opposite-sex Spouse	Same-sex Spouse	Opposite-sex Unmarried Partner	Same-sex Unmarried Partner	Child[2]	Grand-child	Other Relatives	Non-relatives
City	39.7	18.3	0.3	2.6	0.2	27.5	1.9	3.6	4.3
MSA[1]	37.5	19.3	0.2	2.2	0.1	28.5	2.0	3.6	3.8
U.S.	38.3	17.5	0.2	2.5	0.2	28.3	2.4	4.8	3.4

Note: Figures are percent of the total population; (1) Figures cover the Colorado Springs, CO Metropolitan Statistical Area; (2) Includes biological, adopted, and stepchildren of the householder
Source: U.S. Census Bureau, 2020 Census

Gender

Area	Males	Females	Males per 100 Females
City	241,781	241,318	100.2
MSA[1]	386,799	373,983	103.4
U.S.	164,545,087	167,842,453	98.0

Note: (1) Figures cover the Colorado Springs, CO Metropolitan Statistical Area
Source: U.S. Census Bureau, 2019-2023 American Community Survey 5-Year Estimates

Marital Status

Area	Never Married	Now Married[2]	Separated	Widowed	Divorced
City	30.7	50.8	1.5	4.5	12.5
MSA[1]	29.4	53.8	1.3	4.1	11.5
U.S.	34.1	47.9	1.7	5.6	10.7

Note: Figures are percentages and cover the population 15 years of age and older; (1) Figures cover the Colorado Springs, CO Metropolitan Statistical Area; (2) Excludes separated
Source: U.S. Census Bureau, 2019-2023 American Community Survey 5-Year Estimates

Religious Groups by Family

Area	Catholic	Baptist	Methodist	LDS[2]	Pentecostal	Lutheran	Islam	Adventist	Other
MSA[1]	16.4	2.6	1.3	3.0	1.0	1.2	0.1	1.0	16.2
U.S.	18.7	7.3	3.0	2.0	1.8	1.7	1.3	1.3	11.6

Note: Figures are the number of adherents as a percentage of the total population and cover the eight largest religious groups in the U.S; (1) Figures cover the Colorado Springs, CO Metropolitan Statistical Area; (2) Church of Jesus Christ of Latter-day Saints
Sources: 2020 U.S. Religion Census, Association of Statisticians of American Religious Bodies; The Association of Religion Data Archives (ARDA)

Religious Groups by Tradition

Area	Catholic	Evangelical Protestant	Mainline Protestant	Black Protestant	Islam	Judaism	Hinduism	Orthodox	Buddhism
MSA[1]	16.4	18.3	2.9	0.9	0.1	<0.1	<0.1	0.1	0.3
U.S.	18.7	16.5	5.2	2.3	1.3	0.6	0.4	0.4	0.3

Note: Figures are the number of adherents as a percentage of the total population; (1) Figures cover the Colorado Springs, CO Metropolitan Statistical Area
Sources: 2020 U.S. Religion Census, Association of Statisticians of American Religious Bodies; The Association of Religion Data Archives (ARDA)

ECONOMY

Real Gross Domestic Product (GDP)

Area	2017	2018	2019	2020	2021	2022	2023	Rank[3]
MSA[1]	35.1	36.2	37.7	38.8	41.1	41.8	43.6	79
U.S.[2]	17,619.1	18,160.7	18,642.5	18,238.9	19,387.6	19,896.6	20,436.3	–

Note: Figures are in billions of chained 2017 dollars; (1) Figures cover the Colorado Springs, CO Metropolitan Statistical Area; (2) Figures cover real GDP within metropolitan areas; (3) Rank is based on 2023 data and ranges from 1 to 384
Source: U.S. Bureau of Economic Analysis

Economic Growth

Area	2014	2015	2016	2017	2018	2019	2020	2021	2022	2023
MSA[1]	0.9	1.1	2.0	4.2	3.3	4.2	2.9	5.8	1.7	4.4
U.S.[2]	2.6	3.2	2.0	2.7	3.1	2.7	-2.2	6.3	2.6	2.7

Note: Figures are real gross domestic product growth rates and represent percent change from preceding period; (1) Figures cover the Colorado Springs, CO Metropolitan Statistical Area; (2) Figures are the average growth rates within metropolitan areas
Source: U.S. Bureau of Economic Analysis

Metropolitan Area Exports

Area	2018	2019	2020	2021	2022	2023	Rank[2]
MSA[1]	850.6	864.2	979.2	866.9	1,209.5	1,425.7	137
U.S.	1,664,056.1	1,645,173.7	1,431,406.6	1,753,941.4	2,062,937.4	2,019,160.5	–

Note: Figures are in millions of dollars; (1) Figures cover the Colorado Springs, CO Metropolitan Statistical Area; (2) Rank is based on 2023 data and ranges from 1 to 386
Source: U.S. Department of Commerce, International Trade Administration, Office of Trade and Economic Analysis, Industry and Analysis, Exports by Metropolitan Area, data extracted April 2, 2025

Building Permits

Area	Single-Family			Multi-Family			Total		
	2023	2024	Pct. Chg.	2023	2024	Pct. Chg.	2023	2024	Pct. Chg.
City	n/a	n/a	n/a	n/a	n/a	n/a	n/a	n/a	n/a
MSA[1]	2,670	2,878	7.8	2,607	1,116	-57.2	5,277	3,994	-24.3
U.S.	920,000	981,900	6.7	591,100	496,100	-16.1	1,511,100	1,478,000	-2.2

Note: (1) Figures cover the Colorado Springs, CO Metropolitan Statistical Area; Figures represent new, privately-owned housing units authorized (unadjusted data)
Source: U.S. Census Bureau, Building Permits Survey (BPS), 2023, 2024

Bankruptcy Filings

Area	Business Filings			Nonbusiness Filings		
	2023	2024	% Chg.	2023	2024	% Chg.
El Paso County	23	50	117.4	784	973	24.1
U.S.	18,926	23,107	22.1	434,064	494,201	13.9

Note: Business filings include Chapter 7, Chapter 9, Chapter 11, Chapter 12, Chapter 13, Chapter 15, and Section 304; Nonbusiness filings include Chapter 7, Chapter 11, and Chapter 13
Source: Administrative Office of the U.S. Courts, Business and Nonbusiness Bankruptcy, County Cases Commenced by Chapter of the Bankruptcy Code, During the 12-Month Period Ending December 31, 2023 and Business and Nonbusiness Bankruptcy, County Cases Commenced by Chapter of the Bankruptcy Code, During the 12-Month Period Ending December 31, 2024

Housing Vacancy Rates

Area	Gross Vacancy Rate[3] (%)			Year-Round Vacancy Rate[4] (%)			Rental Vacancy Rate[5] (%)			Homeowner Vacancy Rate[6] (%)		
	2022	2023	2024	2022	2023	2024	2022	2023	2024	2022	2023	2024
MSA[1]	n/a	n/a	n/a	n/a	n/a	n/a	n/a	n/a	n/a	n/a	n/a	n/a
U.S.[2]	9.1	9.0	9.1	7.5	7.5	7.6	5.7	6.5	6.8	0.8	0.8	1.0

Note: (1) Figures cover the Colorado Springs, CO Metropolitan Statistical Area; (2) Figures cover the 75 largest Metropolitan Statistical Areas; (3) The percentage of the total housing inventory that is vacant; (4) The percentage of the housing inventory (excluding seasonal units) that is year-round vacant; (5) The percentage of rental inventory that is vacant for rent; (6) The percentage of homeowner inventory that is vacant for sale; n/a not available
Source: U.S. Census Bureau, Housing Vacancies and Homeownership Annual Statistics: 2022, 2023, 2024

INCOME

Income

Area	Per Capita ($)	Median Household ($)	Average Household ($)
City	44,893	83,198	108,459
MSA[1]	44,315	87,180	112,662
U.S.	43,289	78,538	110,491

Note: (1) Figures cover the Colorado Springs, CO Metropolitan Statistical Area
Source: U.S. Census Bureau, 2019-2023 American Community Survey 5-Year Estimates

Household Income Distribution

Area	Percent of Households Earning							
	Under $15,000	$15,000 -$24,999	$25,000 -$34,999	$35,000 -$49,999	$50,000 -$74,999	$75,000 -$99,999	$100,000 -$149,999	$150,000 and up
City	6.2	5.3	5.8	10.4	17.7	13.6	19.8	21.3
MSA[1]	5.7	4.8	5.6	9.8	16.9	13.7	20.3	23.3
U.S.	8.5	6.6	6.8	10.4	15.7	12.7	17.4	21.9

Note: (1) Figures cover the Colorado Springs, CO Metropolitan Statistical Area
Source: U.S. Census Bureau, 2019-2023 American Community Survey 5-Year Estimates

Poverty Rate

Area	All Ages	Under 18 Years Old	18 to 64 Years Old	65 Years and Over
City	9.3	10.8	9.2	7.7
MSA[1]	8.5	10.2	8.2	6.9
U.S.	12.4	16.3	11.6	10.4

Note: Figures are percentage of people whose income during the past 12 months was below the poverty level;
(1) Figures cover the Colorado Springs, CO Metropolitan Statistical Area
Source: U.S. Census Bureau, 2019-2023 American Community Survey 5-Year Estimates

EMPLOYMENT

Labor Force and Employment

Area	Civilian Labor Force			Workers Employed		
	Dec. 2023	Dec. 2024	% Chg.	Dec. 2023	Dec. 2024	% Chg.
City	254,636	258,951	1.7	245,377	247,188	0.7
MSA[1]	380,947	387,217	1.6	366,679	369,336	0.7
U.S.	166,661,000	167,746,000	0.7	160,754,000	161,294,000	0.3

Note: Data is not seasonally adjusted and covers workers 16 years of age and older; (1) Figures cover the Colorado Springs, CO Metropolitan Statistical Area
Source: Bureau of Labor Statistics, Local Area Unemployment Statistics

Unemployment Rate

Area	2024											
	Jan.	Feb.	Mar.	Apr.	May	Jun.	Jul.	Aug.	Sep.	Oct.	Nov.	Dec.
City	4.1	4.2	3.8	3.7	3.9	4.4	4.7	4.6	4.3	4.4	4.7	4.5
MSA[1]	4.2	4.3	3.9	3.8	4.0	4.5	4.8	4.8	4.4	4.5	4.8	4.6
U.S.	4.1	4.2	3.9	3.5	3.7	4.3	4.5	4.4	3.9	3.9	4.0	3.8

Note: Data is not seasonally adjusted and covers workers 16 years of age and older; (1) Figures cover the Colorado Springs, CO Metropolitan Statistical Area
Source: Bureau of Labor Statistics, Local Area Unemployment Statistics

Average Wages

Occupation	$/Hr.	Occupation	$/Hr.
Accountants and Auditors	41.44	Maintenance and Repair Workers	23.63
Automotive Mechanics	26.83	Marketing Managers	81.56
Bookkeepers	23.32	Network and Computer Systems Admin.	49.17
Carpenters	26.46	Nurses, Licensed Practical	30.52
Cashiers	16.36	Nurses, Registered	41.57
Computer Programmers	53.50	Nursing Assistants	20.55
Computer Systems Analysts	54.60	Office Clerks, General	25.08
Computer User Support Specialists	30.73	Physical Therapists	47.11
Construction Laborers	21.28	Physicians	145.41
Cooks, Restaurant	19.05	Plumbers, Pipefitters and Steamfitters	29.44
Customer Service Representatives	20.87	Police and Sheriff's Patrol Officers	40.85
Dentists	88.76	Postal Service Mail Carriers	27.18
Electricians	28.83	Real Estate Sales Agents	33.25
Engineers, Electrical	56.23	Retail Salespersons	18.80
Fast Food and Counter Workers	15.91	Sales Representatives, Technical/Scientific	53.78
Financial Managers	84.63	Secretaries, Exc. Legal/Medical/Executive	21.04
First-Line Supervisors of Office Workers	32.60	Security Guards	19.20
General and Operations Managers	70.11	Surgeons	n/a
Hairdressers/Cosmetologists	22.98	Teacher Assistants, Exc. Postsecondary[1]	16.56
Home Health and Personal Care Aides	17.68	Teachers, Secondary School, Exc. Sp. Ed.[1]	28.08
Janitors and Cleaners	17.57	Telemarketers	25.27
Landscaping/Groundskeeping Workers	20.66	Truck Drivers, Heavy/Tractor-Trailer	26.24
Lawyers	69.39	Truck Drivers, Light/Delivery Services	21.53
Maids and Housekeeping Cleaners	16.92	Waiters and Waitresses	21.16

Note: Data in this table was taken from the May 2023 Metro Area Occupational Employment & Wage Estimates due to data quality concerns for the state of Colorado and substate areas. On November 20, 2024, the Quarterly Census of Employment and Wages (QCEW) suspended publication of industry and substate data for Colorado due to these concerns. As of May 1, 2025, the quality concerns with Colorado data have been sufficiently addressed to resume QCEW publication, however, because of the processing time required, the May 2024 Metro Area Occupational Employment & Wage Estimates data release does not include data for Colorado and its substate areas; n/a not available; (1) Hourly wages were calculated from annual wage data based on a 40 hour work week
Source: Bureau of Labor Statistics, Metro Area Occupational Employment & Wage Estimates, May 2023

Employment by Industry

Sector	MSA[1]		U.S.
	Number of Employees	Percent of Total	Percent of Total
Construction, Mining, and Logging	18,000	5.4	5.5
Financial Activities	19,500	5.8	5.8
Government	60,000	17.9	14.9
Information	5,000	1.5	1.9
Leisure and Hospitality	41,500	12.4	10.4
Manufacturing	12,100	3.6	8.0
Other Services	23,600	7.0	3.7
Private Education and Health Services	48,900	14.6	16.9
Professional and Business Services	53,600	16.0	14.2
Retail Trade	34,100	10.2	10.0
Transportation, Warehousing, and Utilities	12,800	3.8	4.8
Wholesale Trade	6,700	2.0	3.9

Note: Figures are non-farm employment as of December 2024. Figures are not seasonally adjusted and include workers 16 years of age and older; (1) Figures cover the Colorado Springs, CO Metropolitan Statistical Area
Source: Bureau of Labor Statistics, Current Employment Statistics, Employment, Hours, and Earnings

Employment by Occupation

Occupation Classification	City (%)	MSA[1] (%)	U.S. (%)
Management, Business, Science, and Arts	47.0	46.6	42.0
Natural Resources, Construction, and Maintenance	7.3	8.1	8.6
Production, Transportation, and Material Moving	8.9	9.3	13.0
Sales and Office	20.3	19.9	19.9
Service	16.5	16.1	16.5

Note: Figures cover employed civilians 16 years of age and older; (1) Figures cover the Colorado Springs, CO Metropolitan Statistical Area
Source: U.S. Census Bureau, 2019-2023 American Community Survey 5-Year Estimates

Occupations with Greatest Projected Employment Growth: 2022 – 2032

Occupation[1]	2022 Employment	2032 Projected Employment	Numeric Employment Change	Percent Employment Change
Software Developers	43,390	60,490	17,100	39.4
Cooks, Restaurant	34,160	44,800	10,640	31.1
Home Health and Personal Care Aides	38,300	48,710	10,410	27.2
Registered Nurses	53,720	63,290	9,570	17.8
Market Research Analysts and Marketing Specialists	35,930	44,390	8,460	23.5
Fast Food and Counter Workers	77,680	86,000	8,320	10.7
Business Operations Specialists, All Other	61,930	69,980	8,050	13.0
Stockers and Order Fillers	51,900	59,630	7,730	14.9
Sales Representatives of Services, Except Advertising, Insurance, Financial Services, and Travel	41,910	49,490	7,580	18.1
General and Operations Managers	56,730	64,050	7,320	12.9

Note: Projections cover Colorado; (1) Sorted by numeric employment change
Source: www.projectionscentral.org, State Occupational Projections, 2022–2032 Long-Term Projections

Fastest-Growing Occupations: 2022 – 2032

Occupation[1]	2022 Employment	2032 Projected Employment	Numeric Employment Change	Percent Employment Change
Flight Attendants	5,300	8,440	3,140	59.2
Nurse Practitioners	3,700	5,780	2,080	56.2
Epidemiologists	620	940	320	51.6
Information Security Analysts (SOC 2018)	6,110	9,220	3,110	50.9
Solar Photovoltaic Installers	580	870	290	50.0
Statisticians	1,560	2,290	730	46.8
Airline Pilots, Copilots, and Flight Engineers	5,040	7,380	2,340	46.4
Data Scientists	4,150	6,030	1,880	45.3
Veterinary Assistants and Laboratory Animal Caretakers	2,570	3,640	1,070	41.6
Medical and Health Services Managers	7,310	10,220	2,910	39.8

Note: Projections cover Colorado; (1) Sorted by percent employment change and excludes occupations with numeric employment change less than 50
Source: www.projectionscentral.org, State Occupational Projections, 2022–2032 Long-Term Projections

CITY FINANCES

City Government Finances

Component	2022 ($000)	2022 ($ per capita)
Total Revenues	1,909,216	3,960
Total Expenditures	1,668,187	3,460
Debt Outstanding	2,594,628	5,382

Source: U.S. Census Bureau, State & Local Government Finances 2022

City Government Revenue by Source

Source	2022 ($000)	2022 ($ per capita)	2022 (%)
General Revenue			
From Federal Government	98,137	204	5.1
From State Government	7,288	15	0.4
From Local Governments	1,606	3	0.1
Taxes			
Property	61,342	127	3.2
Sales and Gross Receipts	393,752	817	20.6
Personal Income	0	0	0.0
Corporate Income	0	0	0.0
Motor Vehicle License	0	0	0.0
Other Taxes	3,483	7	0.2
Current Charges	141,073	293	7.4
Liquor Store	0	0	0.0
Utility	992,198	2,058	52.0

Source: U.S. Census Bureau, State & Local Government Finances 2022

City Government Expenditures by Function

Function	2022 ($000)	2022 ($ per capita)	2022 (%)
General Direct Expenditures			
Air Transportation	38,039	78	2.3
Corrections	0	0	0.0
Education	0	0	0.0
Employment Security Administration	0	0	0.0
Financial Administration	50,177	104	3.0
Fire Protection	64,140	133	3.8
General Public Buildings	0	0	0.0
Governmental Administration, Other	33,873	70	2.0
Health	0	0	0.0
Highways	145,239	301	8.7
Hospitals	0	0	0.0
Housing and Community Development	75,661	156	4.5
Interest on General Debt	21,552	44	1.3
Judicial and Legal	11,491	23	0.7
Libraries	0	0	0.0
Parking	4,815	10	0.3
Parks and Recreation	32,290	67	1.9
Police Protection	128,771	267	7.7
Public Welfare	0	0	0.0
Sewerage	47,513	98	2.8
Solid Waste Management	0	0	0.0
Veterans' Services	0	0	0.0
Liquor Store	0	0	0.0
Utility	906,447	1,880	54.3

Source: U.S. Census Bureau, State & Local Government Finances 2022

TAXES

State Corporate Income Tax Rates

State	Tax Rate (%)	Income Brackets ($)	Num. of Brackets	Financial Institution Tax Rate (%)[a]	Federal Income Tax Ded.
Colorado	4.4	Flat rate	1	4.4	No

Note: Tax rates for tax year 2024; (a) Rates listed are the corporate income tax rate applied to financial institutions or excise taxes based on income. Some states have other taxes based upon the value of deposits or shares.
Source: Federation of Tax Administrators, State Corporate Income Tax Rates, January 1, 2025

State Individual Income Tax Rates

State	Tax Rate (%)	Income Brackets ($)	Personal Exemptions ($) Single	Personal Exemptions ($) Married	Personal Exemptions ($) Depend.	Standard Ded. ($) Single	Standard Ded. ($) Married
Colorado	4.4	Flat rate	(d)	(d)	(d)	14,600	29,200 (d)

Note: Tax rates for tax year 2024; Local- and county-level taxes are not included; (d) These states use the personal exemption/standard deduction amounts provided in the federal Internal Revenue Code. Montana personal exemption subject to repeal under Section 15-30-2114.
Source: Federation of Tax Administrators, State Individual Income Tax Rates, January 1, 2025

Various State Sales and Excise Tax Rates

State	State Sales Tax (%)	Gasoline[1] ($/gal.)	Cigarette[2] ($/pack)	Spirits[3] ($/gal.)	Wine[4] ($/gal.)	Beer[5] ($/gal.)	Recreational Marijuana (%)
Colorado	2.9	0.28	2.24	2.28	0.32	0.08	(d)

Note: All tax rates as of January 1, 2025; (1) The American Petroleum Institute has developed a methodology for determining the average tax rate on a gallon of fuel. Rates may include any of the following: excise taxes, environmental fees, storage tank fees, other fees or taxes, general sales tax, and local taxes; (2) The federal excise tax of $1.0066 per pack and local taxes are not included; (3) Rates are those applicable to off-premise sales of 40% alcohol by volume (a.b.v.) distilled spirits in 750ml containers. Local excise taxes are excluded; (4) Rates are those applicable to off-premise sales of 11% a.b.v. non-carbonated wine in 750ml containers; (5) Rates are those applicable to off-premise sales of 4.7% a.b.v. beer in 12 ounce containers; (d) 15% excise tax (levied on wholesale at average market rate); 15% excise tax (retail price)
Source: Tax Foundation, 2025 Facts & Figures: How Does Your State Compare?

State Tax Competitiveness Index

State	Overall Rank	Corporate Tax Rank	Individual Income Tax Rank	Sales Tax Rank	Property Tax Rank	Unemployment Insurance Tax Rank
Colorado	32	10	18	37	36	39

Note: The Tax Foundation's State Tax Competitiveness Index enables policymakers, taxpayers, and business leaders to gauge how their states' tax systems compare. A rank of 1 is best, 50 is worst. Rankings do not average to the total. States without a tax rank equally as 1. DC's scores and rankings do not affect other states. The report shows tax systems as of July 1, 2024 (the beginning of Fiscal Year 2025).
Source: Tax Foundation, State Tax Competitiveness Index 2025

TRANSPORTATION

Means of Transportation to Work

Area	Car/Truck/Van		Public Transportation			Bicycle	Walked	Other Means	Worked at Home
	Drove Alone	Car-pooled	Bus	Subway	Railroad				
City	71.1	9.0	0.4	0.0	0.0	0.5	1.8	1.1	16.1
MSA[1]	70.5	9.0	0.3	0.0	0.0	0.4	3.3	1.1	15.4
U.S.	70.2	8.5	1.7	1.3	0.4	0.4	2.4	1.6	13.5

Note: Figures are percentages and cover workers 16 years of age and older; (1) Figures cover the Colorado Springs, CO Metropolitan Statistical Area
Source: U.S. Census Bureau, 2019-2023 American Community Survey 5-Year Estimates

Travel Time to Work

Area	Less Than 10 Minutes	10 to 19 Minutes	20 to 29 Minutes	30 to 44 Minutes	45 to 59 Minutes	60 to 89 Minutes	90 Minutes or More
City	11.6	35.7	27.6	16.9	3.0	3.0	2.1
MSA[1]	12.1	32.3	26.6	19.0	4.3	3.5	2.2
U.S.	12.6	28.6	21.2	20.8	8.1	6.0	2.8

Note: Note: Figures are percentages and include workers 16 years old and over; (1) Figures cover the Colorado Springs, CO Metropolitan Statistical Area
Source: U.S. Census Bureau, 2019-2023 American Community Survey 5-Year Estimates

Key Congestion Measures

Measure	2000	2010	2015	2020	2022
Annual Hours of Delay, Total (000)	11,169	15,234	17,103	12,116	21,162
Annual Hours of Delay, Per Auto Commuter	34	36	40	29	53
Annual Congestion Cost, Per Auto Commuter ($)	787	853	887	651	1,101

Note: Figures cover the Colorado Springs CO urban area
Source: Texas A&M Transportation Institute, 2023 Urban Mobility Report

Freeway Travel Time Index

Measure	1985	1990	1995	2000	2005	2010	2015	2020	2022
Urban Area Index[1]	1.04	1.09	1.12	1.15	1.16	1.15	1.15	1.08	1.17
Urban Area Rank[1,2]	81	56	57	53	57	65	67	44	44

Note: Freeway Travel Time Index—the ratio of travel time in the peak period to the travel time at free-flow conditions. For example, a value of 1.30 indicates a 20-minute free-flow trip takes 26 minutes in the peak (20 minutes x 1.30 = 26 minutes); (1) Covers the Colorado Springs CO urban area; (2) Rank is based on 101 larger urban areas (#1 = highest travel time index)
Source: Texas A&M Transportation Institute, 2023 Urban Mobility Report

Public Transportation

Agency Name / Mode of Transportation	Vehicles Operated in Maximum Service[1]	Annual Unlinked Passenger Trips[2] (in thous.)	Annual Passenger Miles[3] (in thous.)
Colorado Springs Transit System			
Bus (purchased transportation)	58	2,865.6	9,783.1
Demand Response (purchased transportation)	34	116.9	956.1
Demand Response - Taxi	3	0.6	3.2
Vanpool (directly operated)	6	7.8	476.4

Note: (1) Number of revenue vehicles operated by the given mode and type of service to meet the annual maximum service requirement. This is the revenue vehicle count during the peak season of the year; on the week and day that maximum service is provided. Vehicles operated in maximum service (VOMS) exclude atypical days and one-time special events; (2) Number of passengers who boarded public transportation vehicles. Passengers are counted each time they board a vehicle no matter how many vehicles they use to travel from their origin to their destination. (3) Sum of the distances ridden by all passengers during the entire fiscal year.
Source: Federal Transit Administration, National Transit Database, 2023

Air Transportation

Airport Name and Code / Type of Service	Passenger Airlines[1]	Passenger Enplanements	Freight Carriers[2]	Freight (lbs)
City of Colorado Springs Municipal (COS)				
Domestic service (U.S. carriers only)	20	1,244,078	4	8,230,125
International service (U.S. carriers only)	0	0	0	0

Note: (1) Includes all U.S.-based major, minor and commuter airlines that carried at least one passenger during the year; (2) Includes all U.S.-based airlines and freight carriers that transported at least one pound of freight during the year.
Source: Bureau of Transportation Statistics, The Intermodal Transportation Database, Air Carriers: T-100 Domestic Market (U.S. carriers only), 2024; Bureau of Transportation Statistics, The Intermodal Transportation Database, Air Carriers: T-100 International Market (U.S. carriers only), 2024

BUSINESSES

Major Business Headquarters

Company Name	Industry	Rankings	
		Fortune[1]	Forbes[2]
No companies listed	-	-	-

Note: (1) Companies that produce a 10-K are ranked 1 to 500 based on 2023 revenue; (2) All private companies with at least $2 billion in annual revenue through the end of their most current fiscal year are ranked 1 to 275; companies listed are headquartered in the city; dashes indicate no ranking
Source: Fortune, "Fortune 500," 2024; Forbes, "America's Largest Private Companies," 2024

Fastest-Growing Businesses

According to Deloitte, Colorado Springs is home to two of North America's 500 fastest-growing high-technology companies: **Caliola Engineering** (#102); **Quantum Metric** (#472). Companies are ranked by percentage growth in revenue over a four-year period. Criteria for inclusion: company must be headquartered within North America; must own proprietary intellectual property or technology that is sold to customers in products that contributes to a significant portion of the company's operating revenue; must have been in business for a minumum of four years with 2020 operating revenues of at least $50,000 USD/CD and 2023 operating revenues of at least $5 million USD/CD. *Deloitte, 2024 Technology Fast 500*[TM]

Living Environment

COST OF LIVING

Cost of Living Index

Composite Index	Groceries	Housing	Utilities	Trans-portation	Health Care	Misc. Goods/ Services
101.9	101.9	110.2	75.7	95.1	95.5	104.0

Note: The Cost of Living Index measures regional differences in the cost of consumer goods and services, excluding taxes and non-consumer expenditures, for professional and managerial households in the top income quintile. It is based on more than 50,000 prices covering almost 60 different items for which prices are collected three times a year by chambers of commerce, economic development organizations or university applied economic centers in each participating urban area. The numbers shown should be read as a percentage above or below the national average of 100. For example, a value of 115.4 in the groceries column indicates that grocery prices are 15.4% higher than the national average. Small differences in the index numbers should not be interpreted as significant; Figures cover the Colorado Springs CO urban area.
Source: The Council for Community and Economic Research, Cost of Living Index, 2024

Grocery Prices

Area[1]	T-Bone Steak ($/pound)	Frying Chicken ($/pound)	Whole Milk ($/half gal.)	Eggs ($/dozen)	Orange Juice ($/64 oz.)	Coffee ($/11.5 oz.)
City[2]	15.53	1.46	4.60	2.91	4.42	6.03
Avg.	15.42	1.55	4.69	3.25	4.41	5.46
Min.	14.50	1.16	4.43	2.75	4.00	4.85
Max.	17.56	2.89	5.49	4.78	5.54	7.89

*Note: (1) Values for the local area are compared with the average, minimum and maximum values for all 276 areas in the Cost of Living Index; (2) Figures cover the Colorado Springs CO urban area; **T-Bone Steak** (price per pound); **Frying Chicken** (price per pound, whole fryer); **Whole Milk** (half gallon carton); **Eggs** (price per dozen, Grade A, large); **Orange Juice** (64 oz. Tropicana or Florida Natural); **Coffee** (11.5 oz. can, vacuum-packed, Maxwell House, Hills Bros, or Folgers).*
Source: The Council for Community and Economic Research, Cost of Living Index, 2024

Housing and Utility Costs

Area[1]	New Home Price ($)	Apartment Rent ($/month)	All Electric ($/month)	Part Electric ($/month)	Other Energy ($/month)	Telephone ($/month)
City[2]	557,240	1,828	-	86.01	42.49	192.15
Avg.	515,975	1,550	210.99	123.07	82.07	194.99
Min.	265,375	692	104.33	53.68	36.26	179.42
Max.	2,775,821	5,719	529.02	397.28	361.63	223.33

*Note: (1) Values for the local area are compared with the average, minimum and maximum values for all 276 areas in the Cost of Living Index; (2) Figures cover the Colorado Springs CO urban area; **New Home Price** (2,400 sf living area, 8,000 sf lot, in urban area with full utilities); **Apartment Rent** (950 sf 2 bedroom/1.5 or 2 bath, unfurnished, excluding all utilities except water); **All Electric** (average monthly cost for an all-electric home); **Part Electric** (average monthly cost for a part-electric home); **Other Energy** (average monthly cost for natural gas, fuel oil, coal, wood, and any other forms of energy except electricity); **Telephone** (price includes the base monthly rate plus taxes and fees for three lines of mobile phone service).*
Source: The Council for Community and Economic Research, Cost of Living Index, 2024

Health Care, Transportation, and Other Costs

Area[1]	Doctor ($/visit)	Dentist ($/visit)	Optometrist ($/visit)	Gasoline ($/gallon)	Beauty Salon ($/visit)	Men's Shirt ($)
City[2]	134.99	106.17	132.00	3.04	50.14	30.58
Avg.	143.77	117.51	129.23	3.32	48.57	38.14
Min.	36.74	58.67	67.33	2.80	24.00	13.41
Max.	270.44	216.82	307.33	5.28	94.00	63.89

*Note: (1) Values for the local area are compared with the average, minimum and maximum values for all 276 areas in the Cost of Living Index; (2) Figures cover the Colorado Springs CO urban area; **Doctor** (general practitioners routine exam of an established patient); **Dentist** (adult teeth cleaning and periodic oral examination); **Optometrist** (full vision eye exam for established adult patient); **Gasoline** (one gallon regular unleaded, national brand, including all taxes, cash price at self-service pump if available); **Beauty Salon** (woman's shampoo, trim, and blow-dry); **Men's Shirt** (cotton/polyester dress shirt, pinpoint weave, long sleeves).*
Source: The Council for Community and Economic Research, Cost of Living Index, 2024

HOUSING

Homeownership Rate

Area	2017 (%)	2018 (%)	2019 (%)	2020 (%)	2021 (%)	2022 (%)	2023 (%)	2024 (%)
MSA[1]	n/a	n/a	n/a	n/a	n/a	n/a	n/a	n/a
U.S.	63.9	64.4	64.6	66.6	65.5	65.8	65.9	65.6

Note: (1) Figures cover the Colorado Springs, CO Metropolitan Statistical Area; n/a not available
Source: U.S. Census Bureau, Housing Vacancies and Homeownership Annual Statistics: 2017-2024

House Price Index (HPI)

Area	National Ranking[2]	Quarterly Change (%)	One-Year Change (%)	Five-Year Change (%)	Since 1991Q1 (%)
MSA[1]	196	-0.38	3.24	49.58	453.42
U.S.[3]	–	1.43	4.51	57.13	327.82

Note: The HPI is a weighted repeat sales index. It measures average price changes in repeat sales or refinancings on the same properties. This information is obtained by reviewing repeat mortgage transactions on single-family properties whose mortgages have been purchased or securitized by Fannie Mae or Freddie Mac since January 1975; (1) Figures cover the Colorado Springs, CO Metropolitan Statistical Area; (2) Rankings are based on annual percentage change for all metro areas containing at least 15,000 transactions over the last 10 years and ranges from 1 to 241; (3) figures based on a weighted average of Census Division estimates using a seasonally adjusted, purchase-only index; all figures are for the period ending December 31, 2024
Source: Federal Housing Finance Agency, Change in FHFA Metropolitan Area House Price Indexes, All Transactions Index, 2024Q4

Home Value

Area	Under $100,000	$100,000 -$199,999	$200,000 -$299,999	$300,000 -$399,999	$400,000 -$499,999	$500,000 -$999,999	$1,000,000 or more	Median ($)
City	4.1	3.5	14.0	23.8	22.3	29.5	2.8	420,700
MSA[1]	4.0	3.9	13.2	22.2	21.5	31.2	4.1	431,600
U.S.	12.1	17.8	19.5	14.4	10.5	19.1	6.5	303,400

Note: Figures are percentages except for median and cover owner-occupied housing units; (1) Figures cover the Colorado Springs, CO Metropolitan Statistical Area
Source: U.S. Census Bureau, 2019-2023 American Community Survey 5-Year Estimates

Year Housing Structure Built

Area	2020 or Later	2010 -2019	2000 -2009	1990 -1999	1980 -1989	1970 -1979	1960 -1969	1950 -1959	1940 -1949	Before 1940	Median Year
City	1.9	11.6	14.9	14.2	17.5	16.8	9.3	7.0	1.7	5.3	1986
MSA[1]	1.9	12.9	17.5	15.2	16.4	15.8	8.0	5.9	1.4	4.9	1988
U.S.	1.2	8.9	13.6	12.8	13.0	14.4	10.0	9.7	4.5	11.9	1980

Note: Figures are percentages except for Median Year; Note: (1) Figures cover the Colorado Springs, CO Metropolitan Statistical Area
Source: U.S. Census Bureau, 2019-2023 American Community Survey 5-Year Estimates

Gross Monthly Rent

Area	Under $500	$500 -$999	$1,000 -$1,499	$1,500 -$1,999	$2,000 -$2,499	$2,500 -$2,999	$3,000 and up	Median ($)
City	2.7	10.7	32.8	30.0	15.9	4.3	3.6	1,562
MSA[1]	2.7	10.6	30.1	29.6	18.6	5.0	3.4	1,611
U.S.	6.5	22.3	29.5	20.2	10.8	4.8	5.9	1,348

Note: Figures are percentages except for median; Gross rent is the contract rent plus the estimated average monthly cost of utilities (electricity, gas, and water and sewer) and fuels (oil, coal, kerosene, wood, etc.) if these are paid by the renter (or paid for the renter by someone else); (1) Figures cover the Colorado Springs, CO Metropolitan Statistical Area
Source: U.S. Census Bureau, 2019-2023 American Community Survey 5-Year Estimates

HEALTH

Health Risk Factors

Category	MSA[1] (%)	U.S. (%)
Adults aged 18–64 who have any kind of health care coverage	93.0	90.8
Adults who reported being in good or better health	82.5	81.8
Adults who have been told they have high blood cholesterol	35.8	36.9
Adults who have been told they have high blood pressure	28.6	34.0
Adults who are current smokers	8.9	12.1
Adults who currently use e-cigarettes	8.9	7.7
Adults who currently use chewing tobacco, snuff, or snus	3.3	3.2
Adults who are heavy drinkers[2]	5.9	6.1
Adults who are binge drinkers[3]	15.2	15.2
Adults who are overweight (BMI 25.0 - 29.9)	33.4	34.4
Adults who are obese (BMI 30.0 - 99.8)	26.6	34.3
Adults who participated in any physical activities in the past month	80.1	75.8

Note: All figures are crude prevalence; (1) Figures cover the Colorado Springs, CO Metropolitan Statistical Area; (2) Heavy drinkers are classified as adult men having more than 14 drinks per week and adult women having more than 7 drinks per week; (3) Binge drinkers are classified as males having five or more drinks on one occasion or females having four or more drinks on one occasion
Source: Centers for Disease Control and Prevention, Behavioral Risk Factor Surveillance System, SMART: Selected Metropolitan Area Risk Trends, 2023

Acute and Chronic Health Conditions

Category	MSA[1] (%)	U.S. (%)
Adults who have ever been told they had a heart attack	2.7	4.2
Adults who have ever been told they have angina or coronary heart disease	2.7	4.0
Adults who have ever been told they had a stroke	4.3	3.3
Adults who have ever been told they have asthma	17.5	15.7
Adults who have ever been told they have arthritis	23.9	26.3
Adults who have ever been told they have diabetes[2]	10.2	11.5
Adults who have ever been told they had skin cancer	6.7	5.6
Adults who have ever been told they had any other types of cancer	8.1	8.4
Adults who have ever been told they have COPD	5.1	6.4
Adults who have ever been told they have kidney disease	3.7	3.7
Adults who have ever been told they have a form of depression	23.8	22.0

Note: All figures are crude prevalence; (1) Figures cover the Colorado Springs, CO Metropolitan Statistical Area; (2) Figures do not include pregnancy-related, borderline, or pre-diabetes
Source: Centers for Disease Control and Prevention, Behaviorial Risk Factor Surveillance System, SMART: Selected Metropolitan Area Risk Trends, 2023

Health Screening and Vaccination Rates

Category	MSA[1] (%)	U.S. (%)
Adults who have ever been tested for HIV	40.7	37.5
Adults who have had their blood cholesterol checked within the last five years	86.8	87.0
Adults aged 65+ who have had flu shot within the past year	60.3	63.4
Adults aged 65+ who have ever had a pneumonia vaccination	68.1	71.9

Note: All figures are crude prevalence; (1) Figures cover the Colorado Springs, CO Metropolitan Statistical Area.
Source: Centers for Disease Control and Prevention, Behaviorial Risk Factor Surveillance System, SMART: Selected Metropolitan Area Risk Trends, 2023

Disability Status

Category	MSA[1] (%)	U.S. (%)
Adults who reported being deaf	8.0	7.4
Are you blind or have serious difficulty seeing, even when wearing glasses?	2.6	4.9
Do you have difficulty doing errands alone?	7.0	7.8
Do you have difficulty dressing or bathing?	3.7	3.6
Do you have serious difficulty concentrating/remembering/making decisions?	16.6	13.7
Do you have serious difficulty walking or climbing stairs?	12.9	13.2

Note: All figures are crude prevalence; (1) Figures cover the Colorado Springs, CO Metropolitan Statistical Area.
Source: Centers for Disease Control and Prevention, Behaviorial Risk Factor Surveillance System, SMART: Selected Metropolitan Area Risk Trends, 2023

Mortality Rates for the Top 10 Causes of Death in the U.S.

ICD-10[a] Sub-Chapter	ICD-10[a] Code	Crude Mortality Rate[2] per 100,000 population	
		County[3]	U.S.
Malignant neoplasms	C00-C97	140.0	182.7
Ischaemic heart diseases	I20-I25	64.9	109.6
Provisional assignment of new diseases of uncertain etiology[1]	U00-U49	54.1	65.3
Other forms of heart disease	I30-I51	43.5	65.1
Other degenerative diseases of the nervous system	G30-G31	50.4	52.4
Other external causes of accidental injury	W00-X59	73.1	52.3
Cerebrovascular diseases	I60-I69	39.3	49.1
Chronic lower respiratory diseases	J40-J47	42.4	43.5
Hypertensive diseases	I10-I15	27.0	38.9
Organic, including symptomatic, mental disorders	F01-F09	26.9	33.9

Note: (a) ICD-10 = International Classification of Diseases 10th Revision; (1) Includes COVID-19, adverse effects to COVID-19 vaccines, SARS, and vaping-related disorders; (2) Crude mortality rates are a three-year average covering 2021-2023; (3) Figures cover El Paso County.
Source: Centers for Disease Control and Prevention, National Center for Health Statistics. National Vital Statistics System, Mortality 2018-2023 on CDC WONDER Online Database

Mortality Rates for Selected Causes of Death

Cause of Death	ICD-10[a] Code	Crude Mortality Rate[1] per 100,000 population	
		County[2]	U.S.
Accidental poisoning and exposure to noxious substances	X40-X49	50.5	30.5
Alzheimer disease	G30	30.0	35.4
Assault	X85-Y09	9.1	7.3
COVID-19	U07.1	54.1	65.3
Diabetes mellitus	E10-E14	22.9	30.0
Diseases of the liver	K70-K76	24.4	20.8
Human immunodeficiency virus (HIV) disease	B20-B24	1.1	1.5
Influenza and pneumonia	J09-J18	5.1	13.4
Intentional self-harm	X60-X84	29.2	14.7
Malnutrition	E40-E46	7.2	6.0
Obesity and other hyperalimentation	E65-E68	4.5	3.1
Renal failure	N17-N19	8.6	16.4
Transport accidents	V01-V99	17.9	14.4

Note: (a) ICD-10 = International Classification of Diseases 10th Revision; (1) Crude mortality rates are a three-year average covering 2021-2023; (2) Figures cover El Paso County; Data are suppressed when the data meet the criteria for confidentiality constraints; Crude mortality rates are flagged as unreliable when the rate would be calculated with a numerator of 20 or less.
Source: Centers for Disease Control and Prevention, National Center for Health Statistics. National Vital Statistics System, Mortality 2018-2023 on CDC WONDER Online Database

Health Insurance Coverage

Area	With Health Insurance	With Private Health Insurance	With Public Health Insurance	Without Health Insurance	Population Under Age 19 Without Health Insurance
City	92.3	69.8	36.4	7.7	4.7
MSA[1]	92.9	71.5	35.9	7.1	4.6
U.S.	91.4	67.3	36.3	8.6	5.4

Note: Figures are percentages that cover the civilian noninstitutionalized population; (1) Figures cover the Colorado Springs, CO Metropolitan Statistical Area
Source: U.S. Census Bureau, 2019-2023 American Community Survey 5-Year Estimates

Number of Medical Professionals

Area	MDs[3]	DOs[3,4]	Dentists	Podiatrists	Chiropractors	Optometrists
County[1] (number)	1,585	281	797	40	355	191
County[1] (rate[2])	214.0	37.9	107.1	5.4	47.7	25.7
U.S. (rate[2])	302.5	29.2	74.6	6.4	29.5	18.0

Note: Data as of 2023 unless noted; (1) Data covers El Paso County; (2) Number of medical professionals per 100,000 population; (3) Data as of 2022 and includes all active, non-federal physicians; (4) Doctor of Osteopathic Medicine
Source: U.S. Department of Health and Human Services, Health Resources and Services Administration, Bureau of Health Professions, Area Resource File (ARF) 2023-2024

EDUCATION

Public School District Statistics

District Name	Schls	Pupils	Pupil/ Teacher Ratio	Minority Pupils[1] (%)	Total Rev. per Pupil ($)	Total Exp. per Pupil ($)
Academy School District No. 20	39	25,674	15.7	33.2	13,301	12,372
Cheyenne Mountain SD No. 12	9	3,763	15.0	29.7	15,113	13,272
Colorado Springs SD No. 11	58	22,740	15.6	53.9	17,298	15,578
Harrison School District No. 2	28	12,024	15.5	76.5	14,971	17,595
School District No. 3	18	9,377	15.6	57.7	13,117	13,481

Note: Table includes school districts with 2,000 or more students; (1) Percentage of students that are not non-Hispanic white.
Source: U.S. Department of Education, National Center for Education Statistics, Common Core of Data, Local Education Agency (School District) Universe Survey: School Year 2023-2024; U.S. Department of Education, National Center for Education Statistics, Common Core of Data, School District Finance Survey (F-33): School Year 2021–22

Best High Schools

According to *U.S. News*, Colorado Springs is home to two of the top 500 high schools in the U.S.: **The Vanguard School** (#197); **The Classical Academy High School** (#465). Nearly 25,000 public, magnet and charter schools were ranked based on their performance on state assessments and how well they prepare students for college. *U.S. News & World Report, "Best High Schools 2024"*

Highest Level of Education

Area	Less than H.S.	H.S. Diploma	Some College, No Deg.	Associate Degree	Bachelor's Degree	Master's Degree	Prof. School Degree	Doctorate Degree
City	5.4	19.2	23.0	10.6	25.2	12.8	2.1	1.9
MSA[1]	4.9	19.7	23.4	11.0	24.9	12.6	1.8	1.7
U.S.	10.6	26.2	19.4	8.8	21.3	9.8	2.3	1.6

Note: Figures cover persons age 25 and over; (1) Figures cover the Colorado Springs, CO Metropolitan Statistical Area
Source: U.S. Census Bureau, 2019-2023 American Community Survey 5-Year Estimates

Educational Attainment by Race

Area	High School Graduate or Higher (%)					Bachelor's Degree or Higher (%)				
	Total	White	Black	Asian	Hisp.[2]	Total	White	Black	Asian	Hisp.[2]
City	94.6	96.4	94.1	89.0	84.6	41.9	45.3	32.1	43.8	21.6
MSA[1]	95.1	96.6	95.2	90.1	86.4	41.0	43.8	32.5	44.9	23.2
U.S.	89.4	92.9	88.1	88.0	72.5	35.0	37.7	24.7	57.0	19.9

Note: Figures shown cover persons 25 years old and over; (1) Figures cover the Colorado Springs, CO Metropolitan Statistical Area; (2) People of Hispanic origin can be of any race
Source: U.S. Census Bureau, 2019-2023 American Community Survey 5-Year Estimates

School Enrollment by Grade and Control

Area	Preschool (%)		Kindergarten (%)		Grades 1 - 4 (%)		Grades 5 - 8 (%)		Grades 9 - 12 (%)	
	Public	Private	Public	Private	Public	Private	Public	Private	Public	Private
City	64.6	35.4	88.0	12.0	87.3	12.7	88.4	11.6	90.7	9.3
MSA[1]	66.9	33.1	86.3	13.7	87.4	12.6	88.5	11.5	89.8	10.2
U.S.	58.7	41.3	85.2	14.8	87.2	12.8	87.9	12.1	89.0	11.0

Note: Figures shown cover persons 3 years old and over; (1) Figures cover the Colorado Springs, CO Metropolitan Statistical Area
Source: U.S. Census Bureau, 2019-2023 American Community Survey 5-Year Estimates

Higher Education

Four-Year Colleges			Two-Year Colleges			Medical Schools[1]	Law Schools[2]	Voc/ Tech[3]
Public	Private Non-profit	Private For-profit	Public	Private Non-profit	Private For-profit			
3	2	1	0	0	4	0	0	4

Note: Figures cover institutions located within the Colorado Springs, CO Metropolitan Statistical Area and include main campuses only; (1) includes schools accredited by the Liaison Committee on Medical Education and the American Osteopathic Association's Commission on Osteopathic College Accreditation; (2) includes ABA-accredited schools, schools with provisional ABA accreditation, and state accredited schools; (3) includes all schools with programs that are less than 2 years.
Source: National Center for Education Statistics, Integrated Postsecondary Education System (IPEDS), 2023-24; Wikipedia, List of Medical Schools in the United States, accessed May 2, 2025; Wikipedia, List of Law Schools in the United States, accessed May 2, 2025

According to *U.S. News & World Report,* the Colorado Springs, CO metro area is home to two of the top 100 liberal arts colleges in the U.S.: **United States Air Force Academy** (#8 tie); **Colorado College** (#29 tie). The indicators used to capture academic quality fall into a number of categories: assessment by administrators at peer institutions; retention of students; faculty resources; student selectivity; financial resources; alumni giving; high school counselor ratings of colleges; and graduation rate. *U.S. News & World Report, "America's Best Colleges 2025"*

EMPLOYERS

Major Employers

Company Name	Industry
Children's Hospital Colorado	Healthcare
Colorado State University	Education
Community Hospital Assn	Healthcare
Denver International Airport	Airports
Exempla St Joseph Hospital	Healthcare
Great-West Funds Inc	Financial services
Great-West Life & Annuity Ins	Insurance
Level 3 Communications Inc	Communications
Lockheed Martin Corp	Technology
Lockheed Martin Space Systems	Defense systems & equipment
Memorial Hospital North	Healthcare
Penrose Hospital	Healthcare
Peterson AFB	U.S. military
Poudre Valley Hospital	Healthcare
Schriever Air Force Base	U.S. military
Terumo	Healthcare
University of Boulder	Education
University of Colorado Health	Healthcare
University of Colorado-Boulder	Education
University of Northern Colorado	Education

Note: Companies shown are located within the Colorado Springs, CO Metropolitan Statistical Area.
Source: Chambers of Commerce; State Departments of Labor; Wikipedia

Best Companies to Work For

Altia, headquartered in Colorado Springs, is among the "Best Places to Work in IT." To qualify, companies had to have a minimum of 100 total employees and five IT employees. The best places to work were selected based on DEI (diversity, equity, and inclusion) practices; IT turnover, promotions, and growth; IT retention and engagement programs; remote/hybrid working; benefits and perks (such as elder care and child care, flextime, and reimbursement for college tuition); and training and career development opportunities. *Computerworld, "Best Places to Work in IT," 2025*

PUBLIC SAFETY

Crime Rate

Area	Total Crime Rate	Violent Crime Rate				Property Crime Rate		
		Murder	Rape	Robbery	Aggrav. Assault	Burglary	Larceny -Theft	Motor Vehicle Theft
City	4,386.7	4.9	104.2	76.4	506.5	521.6	2,354.6	818.4
U.S.	2,290.9	5.7	38.0	66.5	264.1	250.7	1,347.2	318.7

Note: Figures are crimes per 100,000 population.
Source: FBI, Table 8, Offenses Known to Law Enforcement, by State by City, 2023

Hate Crimes

Area	Number of Quarters Reported	Number of Incidents per Bias Motivation					
		Race/Ethnicity/ Ancestry	Religion	Sexual Orientation	Disability	Gender	Gender Identity
City	4	9	4	2	2	0	0
U.S.	4	5,900	2,699	2,077	187	92	492

Source: Federal Bureau of Investigation, Hate Crime Statistics 2023

Identity Theft Consumer Reports

Area	Reports	Reports per 100,000 Population	Rank[2]
MSA[1]	1,692	222	129
U.S.	1,135,291	339	-

Note: (1) Figures cover the Colorado Springs, CO Metropolitan Statistical Area; (2) Rank ranges from 1 to 401 where 1 indicates greatest number of identity theft reports per 100,000 population
Source: Federal Trade Commission, Consumer Sentinel Network Data Book 2024

Fraud and Other Consumer Reports

Area	Reports	Reports per 100,000 Population	Rank[2]
MSA[1]	10,275	1,351	85
U.S.	5,360,641	1,601	-

Note: (1) Figures cover the Colorado Springs, CO Metropolitan Statistical Area; (2) Rank ranges from 1 to 401 where 1 indicates greatest number of fraud and other consumer reports per 100,000 population
Source: Federal Trade Commission, Consumer Sentinel Network Data Book 2024

POLITICS

2024 Presidential Election Results

Area	Trump (Rep.)	Harris (Dem.)	Stein (Green)	Kennedy (Ind.)	Oliver (Lib.)	Other
El Paso County	53.5	43.7	0.5	1.1	0.8	0.4
U.S.	49.7	48.2	0.6	0.5	0.4	0.6

Note: Results are percentages and may not add to 100% due to rounding
Source: Dave Leip's Atlas of U.S. Presidential Elections

SPORTS

Professional Sports Teams

Team Name	League	Year Established

No teams are located in the metro area
Source: Wikipedia, Major Professional Sports Teams of the United States and Canada, May 1, 2025

CLIMATE

Average and Extreme Temperatures

Temperature	Jan	Feb	Mar	Apr	May	Jun	Jul	Aug	Sep	Oct	Nov	Dec	Yr.
Extreme High (°F)	71	72	78	87	93	99	98	97	94	86	78	75	99
Average High (°F)	41	44	51	61	68	79	85	81	75	63	49	41	62
Average Temp. (°F)	29	32	39	48	55	66	71	69	61	50	37	30	49
Average Low (°F)	17	20	26	34	42	52	57	55	48	36	24	17	36
Extreme Low (°F)	-20	-19	-3	8	22	36	48	39	22	7	-5	-24	-24

Note: Figures cover the years 1948-1993
Source: National Climatic Data Center, International Station Meteorological Climate Summary, 9/96

Average Precipitation/Snowfall/Humidity

Precip./Humidity	Jan	Feb	Mar	Apr	May	Jun	Jul	Aug	Sep	Oct	Nov	Dec	Yr.
Avg. Precip. (in.)	0.3	0.4	1.3	1.3	2.6	2.1	2.6	3.4	1.0	0.9	0.6	0.5	17.0
Avg. Snowfall (in.)	6	6	10	5	2	0	0	0	Tr	3	7	8	48
Avg. Rel. Hum. 5am (%)	57	60	62	62	69	67	66	71	66	59	60	59	63
Avg. Rel. Hum. 5pm (%)	48	43	39	34	39	36	36	43	36	36	45	52	41

Note: Figures cover the years 1948-1993; Tr = Trace amounts (<0.05 in. of rain; <0.5 in. of snow)
Source: National Climatic Data Center, International Station Meteorological Climate Summary, 9/96

Weather Conditions

Temperature			Daytime Sky			Precipitation		
10°F & below	32°F & below	90°F & above	Clear	Partly cloudy	Cloudy	0.01 inch or more precip.	0.1 inch or more snow/ice	Thunder-storms
21	161	18	108	157	100	98	33	49

Note: Figures are average number of days per year and cover the years 1948-1993
Source: National Climatic Data Center, International Station Meteorological Climate Summary, 9/96

HAZARDOUS WASTE

Superfund Sites

The Colorado Springs, CO metro area has no sites on the EPA's Superfund Final National Priorities List (NPL) or Superfund Alternative Approach (SAA) list. The Superfund alternative approach uses the same investigation and cleanup process and standards that are used for sites listed on the National Priorities List. The SAA is an alternative to listing a site on the NPL; it is not an alternative to Superfund or the Superfund process. There are a total of 1,445 Superfund sites with a status of proposed or final on both lists in the United States. *U.S. Environmental Protection Agency, National Priorities List, May 1, 2025; U.S. Environmental Protection Agency, Superfund Alternative Approach Sites, May 1, 2025*

AIR QUALITY

Air Quality Trends: Ozone

	1990	1995	2000	2005	2010	2015	2020	2021	2022	2023
MSA[1]	n/a	n/a	n/a	n/a	n/a	n/a	n/a	n/a	n/a	n/a
U.S.	0.087	0.089	0.081	0.080	0.072	0.068	0.066	0.067	0.067	0.070

Note: (1) Data covers the Colorado Springs, CO Metropolitan Statistical Area; n/a not available. The values shown are the composite ozone concentration averages among trend sites based on the highest fourth daily maximum 8-hour concentration in parts per million. These trends are based on sites having an adequate record of monitoring data during the trend period. Data from exceptional events are included.
Source: U.S. Environmental Protection Agency, Air Quality Monitoring Information, "Air Quality Trends by City, 1990-2023"

Air Quality Index

Area	Percent of Days when Air Quality was...[2]					AQI Statistics[2]	
	Good	Moderate	Unhealthy for Sensitive Groups	Unhealthy	Very Unhealthy	Maximum	Median
MSA[1]	65.8	33.7	0.3	0.3	0.0	154	47

Note: (1) Data covers the Colorado Springs, CO Metropolitan Statistical Area; (2) Based on 365 days with AQI data in 2023. Air Quality Index (AQI) is an index for reporting daily air quality. EPA calculates the AQI for five major air pollutants regulated by the Clean Air Act: ground-level ozone, particle pollution (aka particulate matter), carbon monoxide, sulfur dioxide, and nitrogen dioxide. The AQI runs from 0 to 500. The higher the AQI value, the greater the level of air pollution and the greater the health concern. There are six AQI categories: "Good" AQI is between 0 and 50. Air quality is considered satisfactory; "Moderate" AQI is between 51 and 100. Air quality is acceptable; "Unhealthy for Sensitive Groups" When AQI values are between 101 and 150, members of sensitive groups may experience health effects; "Unhealthy" When AQI values are between 151 and 200 everyone may begin to experience health effects; "Very Unhealthy" AQI values between 201 and 300 trigger a health alert; "Hazardous" AQI values over 300 trigger warnings of emergency conditions (not shown).
Source: U.S. Environmental Protection Agency, Air Quality Index Report, 2023

Air Quality Index Pollutants

Area	Percent of Days when AQI Pollutant was...[2]					
	Carbon Monoxide	Nitrogen Dioxide	Ozone	Sulfur Dioxide	Particulate Matter 2.5	Particulate Matter 10
MSA[1]	0.0	0.0	91.5	(3)	8.5	0.0

Note: (1) Data covers the Colorado Springs, CO Metropolitan Statistical Area; (2) Based on 365 days with AQI data in 2023. The Air Quality Index (AQI) is an index for reporting daily air quality. EPA calculates the AQI for five major air pollutants regulated by the Clean Air Act: ground-level ozone, particle pollution (also known as particulate matter), carbon monoxide, sulfur dioxide, and nitrogen dioxide. The AQI runs from 0 to 500. The higher the AQI value, the greater the level of air pollution and the greater the health concern; (3) Sulfur dioxide is no longer included in this table because SO_2 concentrations tend to be very localized and not necessarily representative of broad geographical areas like counties and CBSAs.
Source: U.S. Environmental Protection Agency, Air Quality Index Report, 2023

Maximum Air Pollutant Concentrations: Particulate Matter, Ozone, CO and Lead

	Particulate Matter 10 (ug/m^3)	Particulate Matter 2.5 Wtd AM (ug/m^3)	Particulate Matter 2.5 24-Hr (ug/m^3)	Ozone (ppm)	Carbon Monoxide (ppm)	Lead (ug/m^3)
MSA[1] Level	32	5.4	13	0.069	1	n/a
NAAQS[2]	150	15	35	0.075	9	0.15
Met NAAQS[2]	Yes	Yes	Yes	Yes	Yes	n/a

Note: (1) Data covers the Colorado Springs, CO Metropolitan Statistical Area; Data from exceptional events are included; (2) National Ambient Air Quality Standards; ppm = parts per million; ug/m^3 = micrograms per cubic meter; n/a not available.
Concentrations: Particulate Matter 10 (coarse particulate)—highest second maximum 24-hour concentration; Particulate Matter 2.5 Wtd AM (fine particulate)—highest weighted annual mean concentration; Particulate Matter 2.5 24-Hour (fine particulate)—highest 98th percentile 24-hour concentration; Ozone—highest fourth daily maximum 8-hour concentration; Carbon Monoxide—highest second maximum non-overlapping 8-hour concentration; Lead—maximum running 3-month average
Source: U.S. Environmental Protection Agency, Air Quality Monitoring Information, "Air Quality Statistics by City, 2023"

Maximum Air Pollutant Concentrations: Nitrogen Dioxide and Sulfur Dioxide

	Nitrogen Dioxide AM (ppb)	Nitrogen Dioxide 1-Hr (ppb)	Sulfur Dioxide AM (ppb)	Sulfur Dioxide 1-Hr (ppb)	Sulfur Dioxide 24-Hr (ppb)
MSA[1] Level	n/a	n/a	n/a	5	n/a
NAAQS[2]	53	100	30	75	140
Met NAAQS[2]	n/a	n/a	n/a	Yes	n/a

Note: (1) Data covers the Colorado Springs, CO Metropolitan Statistical Area; Data from exceptional events are included; (2) National Ambient Air Quality Standards; ppm = parts per million; ug/m^3 = micrograms per cubic meter; n/a not available.
Concentrations: Nitrogen Dioxide AM—highest arithmetic mean concentration; Nitrogen Dioxide 1-Hr—highest 98th percentile 1-hour daily maximum concentration; Sulfur Dioxide AM—highest annual mean concentration; Sulfur Dioxide 1-Hr—highest 99th percentile 1-hour daily maximum concentration; Sulfur Dioxide 24-Hr—highest second maximum 24-hour concentration
Source: U.S. Environmental Protection Agency, Air Quality Monitoring Information, "Air Quality Statistics by City, 2023"

Denver, Colorado

Background

The 14,000-foot Rocky Mountains are visible from almost anywhere in the state capital of Denver, whose downtown sits just 12 miles east of the foothills. As breathtaking as the views are, the city's early settlers were attracted to the city not for the vistas, but for the gold.

In 1858, there were rumors that gold had been discovered in Denver's Cherry Creek. By 1867, the city's gold and silver established Denver on its way to the sparkling, dramatic skyline, and steel towers of the modern city it is today—a manufacturing, distribution, and transportation center that serves not only the western regions of the United States, but the entire nation. "The Mile High City" is also home to many companies that are engaged in alternative fuel research and development.

Denver hosted the Democratic National Convention in both 1908 and 2008, and the international G7 (now G8) summit in 1997. These events bolstered Denver's international reputation both on a political and socioeconomic level.

The Colorado Convention Center—2,200,000 square feet—is a magnet for regional and national conferences and shows and is enhanced by the 5,000-seat Bellco Theatre and light rail train station. The renovated historic Denver Union Station operates as a mixed-use retail and multi-modal transportation hub. Another architecturally interesting building is the Jeppesen Terminal at Denver's airport, the largest international hub in the United States. The unique roof is made of heat- and light-reflecting tension fabric. The airport is huge, with 53 square miles and 6 million square feet of public space and 93 gates.

The city is also home to a lively cultural, recreational, and educational scene, including concerts at the Boettcher Concert Hall and seasonal drives through the Denver Mountain Park Circle Drive. Awesome skiing and hiking in the Rockies is just 90 minutes away. Other area attractions include the Denver Museum of Nature and Science, Colorado History Museum, Denver Art Museum, and Museum Residencies condominiums.

The city's multibillion-dollar public transportation expansion plan, FasTracks, continues in metropolitan Denver. New bus service, and several light rail and commuter rail lines have been completed, as has a $200 million renovation to Denver Union Station. Total completion of the project is anticipated in 2050.

The city also has its share of offbeat, distinctive places, including the hip Capitol Hill district, which offers small music venues and intimate bars that appeal to University of Denver students. Sports fans enjoy the Colorado Avalanche hockey team, Denver Nuggets basketball team, Colorado Rockies baseball team, and Denver Broncos football team. In 2019, the Denver Bandits became part of the Women's National Football League and the first professional women's football team in the state. Denver was awarded a National Women's Soccer team in 2025.

In 2005, Denver became the first major city in the U.S. to legalize the private possession of marijuana. In 2012, Colorado Amendment 64 was signed into law by Governor John Hickenlooper, in 2014 Colorado became the first state to allow the sale of marijuana for recreational use, and in 2019, Denver became the first U.S. city to decriminalize psilocybin mushrooms.

The Denver Zoo is open year-round and houses nearly 4,000 animals representing 700 species, including the okapi, red-bellied lemur, Amur leopard, black rhino, and Siberian tiger. The zoo continues work on its master modernization plan of habitats, having completed Predator Ridge, home to 14 African species of mammals, birds and reptiles, and an indoor tropical rain forest. In a plan to transform the zoo into a conservation center, a 570-acre facility —The Lembke Family Preserve— is under construction.

The University of Denver, Community College of Denver, Metropolitan State College, and the University of Colorado at Denver are only a few of the many excellent educational opportunities available in the city.

Denver's invigorating climate matches much of the central Rocky Mountain region, without the frigidly cold mornings of the higher elevations during winter, or the hot afternoons of summer at lower altitudes. Extreme cold and heat are generally short-lived. Low relative humidity, light precipitation, and abundant sunshine characterize Denver's weather. Spring is the cloudiest, wettest, and windiest season, while autumn is the most pleasant.

Rankings

General Rankings

- To help military veterans find the best places in which to settle down, *WalletHub* compared the 100 largest U.S. cities across 19 key indicators of livability, affordability and veteran-friendliness. They range from the share of military skill-related jobs to veteran income growth to the availability of VA health facilities. Denver ranked #27. *Wallethub.com, "Best & Worst Places for Veterans to Live (2025)," November 7, 2024*

Business/Finance Rankings

- According to *Business Insider*, the Denver metro area is a prime place to run a startup or move an existing business to. The area ranked #11. More than 300 metro areas were analyzed for factors that were of top concern to new business owners. Data was based on the 2019 U.S. Census Bureau American Community Survey, statistics from the CDC, and University of Chicago analysis. Criteria: business formations; percentage of vaccinated population; percentage of households with internet subscriptions; median household income; and share of work that can be done from home. *BusinessInsider.com, "The 20 Best Cities for Starting a Business in 2022 Include Denver, Raleigh, and Olympia," June 7, 2022*

- Payscale.com ranked the 32 largest metro areas in terms of wage growth. The Denver metro area ranked #22. Criteria: quarterly changes in private industry employee and education professional wage growth from the previous year. *PayScale, "Wage Trends by Metro Area-4th Quarter," February 4, 2025*

- The Denver metro area appeared on the Milken Institute "2025 Best Performing Cities" list. Rank: #29 out of 200 large metro areas (based on performance category). Criteria: job growth; wage growth; high-tech growth and impact; community resilience; housing affordability; household broadband access. *Milken Institute, "Best-Performing Cities 2025," January 14, 2025*

Education Rankings

- Personal finance website *WalletHub* analyzed the 150 largest U.S. metropolitan statistical areas to determine where the most educated Americans are putting their degrees to work. Criteria: education levels; percentage of workers with degrees; education quality and attainment gap; public school quality rankings; quality and enrollment of each metro area's universities. Denver was ranked #11 (#1 = most educated city). *WalletHub.com, "Most & Least Educated Cities in America, 2025" July 2, 2024*

Environmental Rankings

- *Niche* compiled a list of the nation's snowiest cities, based on the National Oceanic and Atmospheric Administration's 30-year average snowfall data. Among cities with a population of at least 50,000, Denver ranked #25. *Niche.com, Top 25 Snowiest Cities in America, December 10, 2018*

- The U.S. Environmental Protection Agency (EPA) released its list of U.S. metropolitan areas with the most ENERGY STAR certified buildings in 2023. The Denver metro area was ranked #7 out of 25. *U.S. Environmental Protection Agency, "2024 Energy Star Top Cities," May 22, 2024*

- Denver was highlighted as one of the 25 most ozone-polluted metro areas in the U.S. during 2021 through 2023. The area ranked #6. *American Lung Association, "State of the Air 2025," April 23, 2025*

Health/Fitness Rankings

- For each of the 100 largest cities in the United States, the American Fitness Index®, compiled in partnership between the American College of Sports Medicine and the Elevance Health Foundation, evaluated community infrastructure and more than 30 health behaviors including preventive health, levels of chronic disease conditions, food insecurity, pedestrian safety, air quality, and community/environment resources that support physical activity. Denver ranked #7 for "community fitness." *americanfitnessindex.org, "2024 ACSM American Fitness Index Summary Report," July 23, 2024*

- The Denver metro area was identified as one of the worst cities for bed bugs in America by pest control company Orkin. The area ranked #15 out of 50 based on the number of bed bug treatments Orkin performed from December 2022 to November 2023. *Orkin, "Chicago Joins Paris In Global Bed Bug Spotlight Ranking As The Worst City On Orkin's U.S. Bed Bug Cities List," January 22, 2024*

- Denver was identified as a "2025 Allergy Capital." The area ranked #91 out of the nation's 100 largest metropolitan areas. Three groups of factors were used to identify the most challenging cities for people with allergies: annual tree, grass, and weed pollen scores; over the counter allergy medicine use; number of board-certified allergy specialists. *Asthma and Allergy Foundation of America, "2025 Allergy Capitals: The Most Challenging Places to Live with Allergies," March 18, 2025*

- Denver was identified as a "2024 Asthma Capital." The area ranked #85 out of the nation's 100 largest metropolitan areas. Criteria: estimated asthma prevalence; asthma-related mortality; and ER visits due to asthma. Risk factors analyzed but not factored in the rankings: annual air quality including pollution and ozone levels; public smoking laws; indoor air quality; access to asthma specialists; rescue and controller medication use; uninsured rate; pollen allergy; poverty rate. *Asthma and Allergy Foundation of America, "Asthma Capitals 2024: The Most Challenging Places to Live With Asthma," September 10, 2024*

Pet Rankings

- Denver appeared on *The Dogington Post* site as one of the top cities for dog lovers, ranking #1 out of 15. The real estate marketplace, Zillow®, and Rover, the largest pet sitter and dog walker network, introduced a new list of "Top Emerging Dog-Friendly Cities" for 2021. Criteria: number of new dog accounts on the Rover platform; and rentals and listings that mention features that attract dog owners (fenced-in yards, dog houses, dog door or proximity to a dog park). *Dogingtonpost.com, "15 Cities Emerging as Dog-Friendliest in 2021," May 11, 2021*

- Denver was selected by *Sniffspot.com* as one of the most dog-friendly cities in the U.S., ranking #23 out of 50. Criteria: dog parks; hiking; sniffspots; public parks; dog-friendly businesses; housing; dog waste cleanliness; leash laws; dog services; and overall cost. *Sniffspot.com, "The Top 50 Most Dog-Friendly Cities in the U.S.," September 30, 2024*

Real Estate Rankings

- *WalletHub* compared the most populated U.S. cities to determine which had the best markets for real estate agents. Denver ranked #5 where demand was high and pay was the best. Criteria: sales per agent; annual median wage for real-estate agents; monthly average starting salary for real estate agents; real estate job density and competition; unemployment rate; home turnover rate; housing-market health index; and other relevant metrics. *WalletHub.com, "2021 Best Places to Be a Real Estate Agent," May 12, 2021*

- The Denver metro area was identified as one of the 20 worst housing markets in the U.S. in 2024. The area ranked #223 out of 226 markets. Criteria: year-over-year change of median sales price of existing single-family homes between the 4th quarter of 2023 and the 4th quarter of 2024. *National Association of Realtors®, Median Sales Price of Existing Single-Family Homes for Metropolitan Areas, 4th Quarter 2024*

- Denver was ranked #150 out of 176 metro areas in terms of cost of housing in 2024 by the National Association of Home Builders (#1 = most affordable). Criteria: the portion of an average family's income necessary to pay the mortgage on a median-priced home. *National Association of Home Builders®, NAHB-Wells Fargo Cost of Housing Index, 4th Quarter 2024*

Safety Rankings

- Allstate ranked the 100 most populous cities in America in terms of driver safety. Denver ranked #84. Criteria based on anonymized driving behavior data from Allstate's mobile app powered by Arity: high speed driving (over 80 mph), phone handling, and hard braking. The report helps increase the importance of safety and awareness behind the wheel. *Allstate, "16th Allstate America's Best Drivers Report®" July 11, 2024*

- Denver was identified as one of the most dangerous cities in America by NeighborhoodScout. The city ranked #85 out of 100 (#1 = most dangerous). Criteria: number of violent crimes per 1,000 residents. The editors evaluated cities with 25,000 or more residents. *NeighborhoodScout.com, "2023 Top 100 Most Dangerous Cities in the U.S.," January 12, 2023*

- The National Insurance Crime Bureau ranked the largest metro areas in the U.S. in terms of per capita rates of vehicle theft. The Denver metro area ranked #8 out of the top 10 (#1 = highest rate). Criteria: number of vehicle theft offenses per 100,000 inhabitants in 2023. *National Insurance Crime Bureau, "Vehicle Thefts Surge Nationwide in 2023," April 9, 2024*

Women/Minorities Rankings

- Denver was listed as one of the most LGBTQ-friendly cities in America by *The Advocate*, as compiled by the real estate data site *Clever*. The city ranked #5 out of 15. Criteria, among many: Pride events; gay bars; LGBTQ-affirming healthcare options; state and local laws; number of PFLAG chapters; LGBTQ+ population. *The Advocate, "These Are the 15 Most LGBTQ-Friendly Cities in the U.S." November 1, 2023*

- Personal finance website *WalletHub* compared more than 180 U.S. cities across two key dimensions, "Hispanic Business-Friendliness" and "Hispanic Purchasing Power," to arrive at the most favorable conditions for Hispanic entrepreneurs. Denver was ranked #30 out of 182. Criteria includes: share of Hispanic-Owned Businesses; average growth of Hispanic Business revenues; Small Business-Friendliness score; affordability; and number of Hispanics with at least a bachelor's degree. *WalletHub.com, "Best Cities for Hispanic Entrepreneurs," September 4, 2024*

Miscellaneous Rankings

- Denver was selected as a 2024 Digital Cities Survey winner. The city ranked #5 in the large city (500,000 or more population) category. The survey examined and assessed how city governments are utilizing new technology and modernized applications to provide residents an array of contactless services and conveniences. Survey questions focused on ten initiatives: cybersecurity; citizen experience; disaster recovery; business intelligence; IT personnel retention; data governance; business automation; AI/machine learning; application modernization; and IT collaboration. *Center for Digital Government, "2024 Digital Cities Survey," November 5, 2024*

- *WalletHub* compared 148 of the most populated U.S. cities to determine their operating efficiency. A "Quality of Services" score was constructed for each city and then measured against the total budget per capita to reveal which were managed the best. Denver ranked #141. Criteria: financial stability; economy; education; safety; health; infrastructure and pollution. *WalletHub.com, "2025's Best- & Worst-Run Cities in America," June 18, 2024*

Business Environment

DEMOGRAPHICS

Population Growth

Area	1990 Census	2000 Census	2010 Census	2020 Census	2023 Estimate[2]	Population Growth 1990-2023 (%)
City	467,153	554,636	600,158	715,522	713,734	52.8
MSA[1]	1,666,935	2,179,296	2,543,482	2,963,821	2,977,085	78.6
U.S.	248,709,873	281,421,906	308,745,538	331,449,281	332,387,540	33.6

Note: (1) Figures cover the Denver-Aurora-Centennial, CO Metropolitan Statistical Area; (2) 2019-2023 5-year ACS population estimate
Source: U.S. Census Bureau, 1990 Census, 2000 Census, 2010 Census, 2020 Census, 2019-2023 American Community Survey 5-Year Estimates

Race

Area	White Alone[2] (%)	Black Alone[2] (%)	Asian Alone[2] (%)	AIAN[3] Alone[2] (%)	NHOPI[4] Alone[2] (%)	Other Race Alone[2] (%)	Two or More Races (%)
City	62.9	8.8	3.6	0.9	0.1	8.2	15.5
MSA[1]	69.1	5.6	4.3	0.9	0.2	6.4	13.6
U.S.	63.4	12.4	5.8	0.9	0.2	6.6	10.7

Note: (1) Figures cover the Denver-Aurora-Centennial, CO Metropolitan Statistical Area; (2) Alone is defined as not being in combination with one or more other races; (3) American Indian and Alaska Native; (4) Native Hawaiian and Other Pacific Islander
Source: U.S. Census Bureau, 2019-2023 American Community Survey 5-Year Estimates

Hispanic or Latino Origin

Area	Total (%)	Mexican (%)	Puerto Rican (%)	Cuban (%)	Other (%)
City	27.9	20.9	0.7	0.3	6.1
MSA[1]	23.6	17.5	0.7	0.2	5.3
U.S.	19.0	11.3	1.8	0.7	5.2

Note: Persons of Hispanic or Latino origin can be of any race; (1) Figures cover the Denver-Aurora-Centennial, CO Metropolitan Statistical Area
Source: U.S. Census Bureau, 2019-2023 American Community Survey 5-Year Estimates

Age

Area	Percent of Population									Median Age
	Under Age 5	Age 5–19	Age 20–34	Age 35–44	Age 45–54	Age 55–64	Age 65–74	Age 75–84	Age 85+	
City	5.5	14.8	29.4	16.9	11.7	9.5	7.6	3.3	1.4	35.2
MSA[1]	5.5	18.2	22.7	15.4	12.8	11.6	8.6	3.8	1.4	37.2
U.S.	5.7	19.1	20.2	13.1	12.3	12.8	10.0	4.9	1.9	38.7

Note: (1) Figures cover the Denver-Aurora-Centennial, CO Metropolitan Statistical Area
Source: U.S. Census Bureau, 2019-2023 American Community Survey 5-Year Estimates

Disability by Age

Area	All Ages	Under 18 Years Old	18 to 64 Years Old	65 Years and Over
City	10.1	3.3	8.3	30.7
MSA[1]	10.2	3.7	8.4	29.1
U.S.	13.0	4.7	10.7	32.9

Note: Figures show percent of the civilian noninstitutionalized population that reported having a disability. Disability status is determined from six types of difficulty: vision, hearing, cognitive, ambulatory, self-care, and independent living. For children under 5 years old, hearing and vision difficulty are used to determine disability status. For children between the ages of 5 and 14, disability status is determined from hearing, vision, cognitive, ambulatory, and self-care difficulties. For people aged 15 years and older, they are considered to have a disability if they have difficulty with any one of the six difficulty types; Note: (1) Figures cover the Denver-Aurora-Centennial, CO Metropolitan Statistical Area
Source: U.S. Census Bureau, 2019-2023 American Community Survey 5-Year Estimates

Ancestry

Area	German	Irish	English	American	Italian	Polish	French[2]	European	Scottish
City	14.0	10.9	10.4	3.0	5.5	2.8	2.1	2.5	2.0
MSA[1]	16.9	11.0	11.7	3.3	5.2	2.5	2.2	2.6	2.2
U.S.	12.6	9.4	9.1	5.5	4.9	2.6	2.0	1.6	1.6

Note: Figures are the percentage of the total population reporting a particular ancestry. The nine most commonly reported ancestries in the U.S. are shown. Figures include multiple ancestries (e.g. if a person reported being Irish and Italian, they were included in both columns); (1) Figures cover the Denver-Aurora-Centennial, CO Metropolitan Statistical Area; (2) Excludes Basque
Source: U.S. Census Bureau, 2019-2023 American Community Survey 5-Year Estimates

Foreign-born Population

Area	Percent of Population Born in								
	Any Foreign Country	Asia	Mexico	Europe	Caribbean	Central America[2]	South America	Africa	Canada
City	13.8	2.7	5.8	1.5	0.3	0.5	1.2	1.5	0.3
MSA[1]	12.1	3.1	4.5	1.4	0.2	0.5	0.8	1.2	0.3
U.S.	13.9	4.3	3.3	1.4	1.4	1.2	1.2	0.8	0.2

Note: (1) Figures cover the Denver-Aurora-Centennial, CO Metropolitan Statistical Area; (2) Excludes Mexico.
Source: U.S. Census Bureau, 2019-2023 American Community Survey 5-Year Estimates

Household Size

Area	Persons in Household (%)							Average Household Size
	One	Two	Three	Four	Five	Six	Seven or More	
City	40.0	33.5	11.4	9.0	3.7	1.5	1.0	2.12
MSA[1]	29.2	34.9	14.8	12.7	5.0	2.2	1.2	2.45
U.S.	28.5	33.8	15.4	12.7	5.9	2.3	1.4	2.54

Note: (1) Figures cover the Denver-Aurora-Centennial, CO Metropolitan Statistical Area
Source: U.S. Census Bureau, 2019-2023 American Community Survey 5-Year Estimates

Household Relationships

Area	House-holder	Opposite-sex Spouse	Same-sex Spouse	Opposite-sex Unmarried Partner	Same-sex Unmarried Partner	Child[2]	Grand-child	Other Relatives	Non-relatives
City	44.4	14.0	0.5	4.1	0.4	22.3	1.9	4.4	5.9
MSA[1]	39.4	17.9	0.3	2.9	0.2	27.4	1.9	4.4	4.3
U.S.	38.3	17.5	0.2	2.5	0.2	28.3	2.4	4.8	3.4

Note: Figures are percent of the total population; (1) Figures cover the Denver-Aurora-Centennial, CO Metropolitan Statistical Area; (2) Includes biological, adopted, and stepchildren of the householder
Source: U.S. Census Bureau, 2020 Census

Gender

Area	Males	Females	Males per 100 Females
City	359,969	353,765	101.8
MSA[1]	1,499,649	1,477,436	101.5
U.S.	164,545,087	167,842,453	98.0

Note: (1) Figures cover the Denver-Aurora-Centennial, CO Metropolitan Statistical Area
Source: U.S. Census Bureau, 2019-2023 American Community Survey 5-Year Estimates

Marital Status

Area	Never Married	Now Married[2]	Separated	Widowed	Divorced
City	44.4	39.3	1.3	3.4	11.5
MSA[1]	34.5	49.4	1.3	3.7	11.0
U.S.	34.1	47.9	1.7	5.6	10.7

Note: Figures are percentages and cover the population 15 years of age and older; (1) Figures cover the Denver-Aurora-Centennial, CO Metropolitan Statistical Area; (2) Excludes separated
Source: U.S. Census Bureau, 2019-2023 American Community Survey 5-Year Estimates

Religious Groups by Family

Area	Catholic	Baptist	Methodist	LDS[2]	Pentecostal	Lutheran	Islam	Adventist	Other
MSA[1]	16.1	1.5	1.0	2.1	0.6	1.4	0.3	1.1	10.4
U.S.	18.7	7.3	3.0	2.0	1.8	1.7	1.3	1.3	11.6

Note: Figures are the number of adherents as a percentage of the total population and cover the eight largest religious groups in the U.S; (1) Figures cover the Denver-Aurora-Centennial, CO Metropolitan Statistical Area; (2) Church of Jesus Christ of Latter-day Saints
Sources: 2020 U.S. Religion Census, Association of Statisticians of American Religious Bodies; The Association of Religion Data Archives (ARDA)

Religious Groups by Tradition

Area	Catholic	Evangelical Protestant	Mainline Protestant	Black Protestant	Islam	Judaism	Hinduism	Orthodox	Buddhism
MSA[1]	16.1	9.6	2.8	0.6	0.3	0.4	0.5	0.4	0.5
U.S.	18.7	16.5	5.2	2.3	1.3	0.6	0.4	0.4	0.3

Note: Figures are the number of adherents as a percentage of the total population; (1) Figures cover the Denver-Aurora-Centennial, CO Metropolitan Statistical Area
Sources: 2020 U.S. Religion Census, Association of Statisticians of American Religious Bodies; The Association of Religion Data Archives (ARDA)

ECONOMY

Real Gross Domestic Product (GDP)

Area	2017	2018	2019	2020	2021	2022	2023	Rank[3]
MSA[1]	202.2	211.2	222.5	222.8	239.1	250.3	259.0	18
U.S.[2]	17,619.1	18,160.7	18,642.5	18,238.9	19,387.6	19,896.6	20,436.3	–

Note: Figures are in billions of chained 2017 dollars; (1) Figures cover the Denver-Aurora-Centennial, CO Metropolitan Statistical Area; (2) Figures cover real GDP within metropolitan areas; (3) Rank is based on 2023 data and ranges from 1 to 384
Source: U.S. Bureau of Economic Analysis

Economic Growth

Area	2014	2015	2016	2017	2018	2019	2020	2021	2022	2023
MSA[1]	4.5	5.3	2.2	3.8	4.4	5.3	0.1	7.3	4.7	3.5
U.S.[2]	2.6	3.2	2.0	2.7	3.1	2.7	-2.2	6.3	2.6	2.7

Note: Figures are real gross domestic product growth rates and represent percent change from preceding period; (1) Figures cover the Denver-Aurora-Centennial, CO Metropolitan Statistical Area; (2) Figures are the average growth rates within metropolitan areas
Source: U.S. Bureau of Economic Analysis

Metropolitan Area Exports

Area	2018	2019	2020	2021	2022	2023	Rank[2]
MSA[1]	4,544.3	4,555.6	4,604.4	4,670.8	5,761.7	5,724.2	59
U.S.	1,664,056.1	1,645,173.7	1,431,406.6	1,753,941.4	2,062,937.4	2,019,160.5	–

Note: Figures are in millions of dollars; (1) Figures cover the Denver-Aurora-Centennial, CO Metropolitan Statistical Area; (2) Rank is based on 2023 data and ranges from 1 to 386
Source: U.S. Department of Commerce, International Trade Administration, Office of Trade and Economic Analysis, Industry and Analysis, Exports by Metropolitan Area, data extracted April 2, 2025

Building Permits

Area	Single-Family			Multi-Family			Total		
	2023	2024	Pct. Chg.	2023	2024	Pct. Chg.	2023	2024	Pct. Chg.
City	1,174	872	-25.7	4,551	3,122	-31.4	5,725	3,994	-30.2
MSA[1]	9,012	9,012	0.0	11,638	6,558	-43.7	20,650	15,570	-24.6
U.S.	920,000	981,900	6.7	591,100	496,100	-16.1	1,511,100	1,478,000	-2.2

Note: (1) Figures cover the Denver-Aurora-Centennial, CO Metropolitan Statistical Area; Figures represent new, privately-owned housing units authorized (unadjusted data)
Source: U.S. Census Bureau, Building Permits Survey (BPS), 2023, 2024

Bankruptcy Filings

Area	Business Filings			Nonbusiness Filings		
	2023	2024	% Chg.	2023	2024	% Chg.
Denver County	61	79	29.5	669	854	27.7
U.S.	18,926	23,107	22.1	434,064	494,201	13.9

Note: Business filings include Chapter 7, Chapter 9, Chapter 11, Chapter 12, Chapter 13, Chapter 15, and Section 304; Nonbusiness filings include Chapter 7, Chapter 11, and Chapter 13
Source: Administrative Office of the U.S. Courts, Business and Nonbusiness Bankruptcy, County Cases Commenced by Chapter of the Bankruptcy Code, During the 12-Month Period Ending December 31, 2023 and Business and Nonbusiness Bankruptcy, County Cases Commenced by Chapter of the Bankruptcy Code, During the 12-Month Period Ending December 31, 2024

Housing Vacancy Rates

Area	Gross Vacancy Rate[3] (%)			Year-Round Vacancy Rate[4] (%)			Rental Vacancy Rate[5] (%)			Homeowner Vacancy Rate[6] (%)		
	2022	2023	2024	2022	2023	2024	2022	2023	2024	2022	2023	2024
MSA[1]	5.8	6.0	4.9	5.2	5.5	4.4	5.1	5.3	4.7	0.3	0.7	0.7
U.S.[2]	9.1	9.0	9.1	7.5	7.5	7.6	5.7	6.5	6.8	0.8	0.8	1.0

Note: (1) Figures cover the Denver-Aurora-Centennial, CO Metropolitan Statistical Area; (2) Figures cover the 75 largest Metropolitan Statistical Areas; (3) The percentage of the total housing inventory that is vacant; (4) The percentage of the housing inventory (excluding seasonal units) that is year-round vacant; (5) The percentage of rental inventory that is vacant for rent; (6) The percentage of homeowner inventory that is vacant for sale
Source: U.S. Census Bureau, Housing Vacancies and Homeownership Annual Statistics: 2022, 2023, 2024

INCOME

Income

Area	Per Capita ($)	Median Household ($)	Average Household ($)
City	61,202	91,681	131,349
MSA[1]	55,529	102,339	135,703
U.S.	43,289	78,538	110,491

Note: (1) Figures cover the Denver-Aurora-Centennial, CO Metropolitan Statistical Area
Source: U.S. Census Bureau, 2019-2023 American Community Survey 5-Year Estimates

Household Income Distribution

Area	Percent of Households Earning							
	Under $15,000	$15,000 -$24,999	$25,000 -$34,999	$35,000 -$49,999	$50,000 -$74,999	$75,000 -$99,999	$100,000 -$149,999	$150,000 and up
City	7.8	5.2	5.1	8.6	14.4	12.6	17.9	28.4
MSA[1]	5.7	4.1	4.5	7.9	14.0	12.8	19.7	31.4
U.S.	8.5	6.6	6.8	10.4	15.7	12.7	17.4	21.9

Note: (1) Figures cover the Denver-Aurora-Centennial, CO Metropolitan Statistical Area
Source: U.S. Census Bureau, 2019-2023 American Community Survey 5-Year Estimates

Poverty Rate

Area	All Ages	Under 18 Years Old	18 to 64 Years Old	65 Years and Over
City	11.2	14.9	10.2	11.5
MSA[1]	8.2	10.3	7.6	7.6
U.S.	12.4	16.3	11.6	10.4

Note: Figures are percentage of people whose income during the past 12 months was below the poverty level;
(1) Figures cover the Denver-Aurora-Centennial, CO Metropolitan Statistical Area
Source: U.S. Census Bureau, 2019-2023 American Community Survey 5-Year Estimates

EMPLOYMENT

Labor Force and Employment

Area	Civilian Labor Force			Workers Employed		
	Dec. 2023	Dec. 2024	% Chg.	Dec. 2023	Dec. 2024	% Chg.
City	439,297	444,521	1.2	421,359	422,120	0.2
MSA[1]	1,731,722	1,751,255	1.1	1,667,215	1,670,077	0.2
U.S.	166,661,000	167,746,000	0.7	160,754,000	161,294,000	0.3

Note: Data is not seasonally adjusted and covers workers 16 years of age and older; (1) Figures cover the
Denver-Aurora-Centennial, CO Metropolitan Statistical Area
Source: Bureau of Labor Statistics, Local Area Unemployment Statistics

Unemployment Rate

Area	2024											
	Jan.	Feb.	Mar.	Apr.	May	Jun.	Jul.	Aug.	Sep.	Oct.	Nov.	Dec.
City	4.5	4.5	4.0	4.1	4.1	4.5	4.9	4.9	4.6	4.8	5.0	5.0
MSA[1]	4.1	4.2	3.8	3.8	3.9	4.4	4.6	4.7	4.3	4.5	4.7	4.6
U.S.	4.1	4.2	3.9	3.5	3.7	4.3	4.5	4.4	3.9	3.9	4.0	3.8

Note: Data is not seasonally adjusted and covers workers 16 years of age and older; (1) Figures cover the
Denver-Aurora-Centennial, CO Metropolitan Statistical Area
Source: Bureau of Labor Statistics, Local Area Unemployment Statistics

Average Wages

Occupation	$/Hr.	Occupation	$/Hr.
Accountants and Auditors	46.80	Maintenance and Repair Workers	26.82
Automotive Mechanics	28.10	Marketing Managers	89.00
Bookkeepers	26.85	Network and Computer Systems Admin.	51.25
Carpenters	27.44	Nurses, Licensed Practical	31.94
Cashiers	17.46	Nurses, Registered	44.80
Computer Programmers	54.01	Nursing Assistants	21.50
Computer Systems Analysts	56.16	Office Clerks, General	27.01
Computer User Support Specialists	36.27	Physical Therapists	47.63
Construction Laborers	22.62	Physicians	148.66
Cooks, Restaurant	20.14	Plumbers, Pipefitters and Steamfitters	32.33
Customer Service Representatives	22.82	Police and Sheriff's Patrol Officers	44.76
Dentists	64.29	Postal Service Mail Carriers	29.38
Electricians	30.65	Real Estate Sales Agents	n/a
Engineers, Electrical	55.39	Retail Salespersons	20.04
Fast Food and Counter Workers	16.95	Sales Representatives, Technical/Scientific	57.52
Financial Managers	93.78	Secretaries, Exc. Legal/Medical/Executive	23.31
First-Line Supervisors of Office Workers	36.61	Security Guards	22.24
General and Operations Managers	79.34	Surgeons	n/a
Hairdressers/Cosmetologists	23.38	Teacher Assistants, Exc. Postsecondary[1]	18.20
Home Health and Personal Care Aides	18.27	Teachers, Secondary School, Exc. Sp. Ed.[1]	34.07
Janitors and Cleaners	18.56	Telemarketers	24.12
Landscaping/Groundskeeping Workers	21.35	Truck Drivers, Heavy/Tractor-Trailer	29.22
Lawyers	95.55	Truck Drivers, Light/Delivery Services	24.04
Maids and Housekeeping Cleaners	18.17	Waiters and Waitresses	18.83

Note: Data in this table was taken from the May 2023 Metro Area Occupational Employment & Wage Estimates due to data quality concerns for the state of Colorado and substate areas. On November 20, 2024, the Quarterly Census of Employment and Wages (QCEW) suspended publication of industry and substate data for Colorado due to these concerns. As of May 1, 2025, the quality concerns with Colorado data have been sufficiently addressed to resume QCEW publication, however, because of the processing time required, the May 2024 Metro Area Occupational Employment & Wage Estimates data release does not include data for Colorado and its substate areas; n/a not available; (1) Hourly wages were calculated from annual wage data based on a 40 hour work week
Source: Bureau of Labor Statistics, Metro Area Occupational Employment & Wage Estimates, May 2023

Employment by Industry

Sector	MSA[1]		U.S.
	Number of Employees	Percent of Total	Percent of Total
Construction, Mining, and Logging	112,900	6.9	5.5
Financial Activities	116,400	7.1	5.8
Government	225,100	13.7	14.9
Information	49,200	3.0	1.9
Leisure and Hospitality	170,700	10.4	10.4
Manufacturing	66,700	4.0	8.0
Other Services	68,700	4.2	3.7
Private Education and Health Services	213,100	12.9	16.9
Professional and Business Services	320,100	19.4	14.2
Retail Trade	140,800	8.5	10.0
Transportation, Warehousing, and Utilities	86,700	5.3	4.8
Wholesale Trade	77,600	4.7	3.9

Note: Figures are non-farm employment as of December 2024. Figures are not seasonally adjusted and include workers 16 years of age and older; (1) Figures cover the Denver-Aurora-Centennial, CO Metropolitan Statistical Area
Source: Bureau of Labor Statistics, Current Employment Statistics, Employment, Hours, and Earnings

Employment by Occupation

Occupation Classification	City (%)	MSA[1] (%)	U.S. (%)
Management, Business, Science, and Arts	55.1	49.7	42.0
Natural Resources, Construction, and Maintenance	6.2	7.6	8.6
Production, Transportation, and Material Moving	7.6	9.2	13.0
Sales and Office	17.8	19.5	19.9
Service	13.3	14.1	16.5

Note: Figures cover employed civilians 16 years of age and older; (1) Figures cover the Denver-Aurora-Centennial, CO Metropolitan Statistical Area
Source: U.S. Census Bureau, 2019-2023 American Community Survey 5-Year Estimates

Occupations with Greatest Projected Employment Growth: 2022 – 2032

Occupation[1]	2022 Employment	2032 Projected Employment	Numeric Employment Change	Percent Employment Change
Software Developers	43,390	60,490	17,100	39.4
Cooks, Restaurant	34,160	44,800	10,640	31.1
Home Health and Personal Care Aides	38,300	48,710	10,410	27.2
Registered Nurses	53,720	63,290	9,570	17.8
Market Research Analysts and Marketing Specialists	35,930	44,390	8,460	23.5
Fast Food and Counter Workers	77,680	86,000	8,320	10.7
Business Operations Specialists, All Other	61,930	69,980	8,050	13.0
Stockers and Order Fillers	51,900	59,630	7,730	14.9
Sales Representatives of Services, Except Advertising, Insurance, Financial Services, and Travel	41,910	49,490	7,580	18.1
General and Operations Managers	56,730	64,050	7,320	12.9

Note: Projections cover Colorado; (1) Sorted by numeric employment change
Source: www.projectionscentral.org, State Occupational Projections, 2022–2032 Long-Term Projections

Fastest-Growing Occupations: 2022 – 2032

Occupation[1]	2022 Employment	2032 Projected Employment	Numeric Employment Change	Percent Employment Change
Flight Attendants	5,300	8,440	3,140	59.2
Nurse Practitioners	3,700	5,780	2,080	56.2
Epidemiologists	620	940	320	51.6
Information Security Analysts (SOC 2018)	6,110	9,220	3,110	50.9
Solar Photovoltaic Installers	580	870	290	50.0
Statisticians	1,560	2,290	730	46.8
Airline Pilots, Copilots, and Flight Engineers	5,040	7,380	2,340	46.4
Data Scientists	4,150	6,030	1,880	45.3
Veterinary Assistants and Laboratory Animal Caretakers	2,570	3,640	1,070	41.6
Medical and Health Services Managers	7,310	10,220	2,910	39.8

Note: Projections cover Colorado; (1) Sorted by percent employment change and excludes occupations with numeric employment change less than 50
Source: www.projectionscentral.org, State Occupational Projections, 2022–2032 Long-Term Projections

CITY FINANCES

City Government Finances

Component	2022 ($000)	2022 ($ per capita)
Total Revenues	5,054,025	6,871
Total Expenditures	5,411,465	7,357
Debt Outstanding	8,676,262	11,796

Source: U.S. Census Bureau, State & Local Government Finances 2022

City Government Revenue by Source

Source	2022 ($000)	2022 ($ per capita)	2022 (%)
General Revenue			
From Federal Government	518,005	704	10.2
From State Government	241,442	328	4.8
From Local Governments	35,316	48	0.7
Taxes			
Property	539,872	734	10.7
Sales and Gross Receipts	1,217,451	1,655	24.1
Personal Income	0	0	0.0
Corporate Income	0	0	0.0
Motor Vehicle License	34,318	47	0.7
Other Taxes	127,112	173	2.5
Current Charges	1,599,345	2,174	31.6
Liquor Store	0	0	0.0
Utility	335,994	457	6.6

Source: U.S. Census Bureau, State & Local Government Finances 2022

City Government Expenditures by Function

Function	2022 ($000)	2022 ($ per capita)	2022 (%)
General Direct Expenditures			
Air Transportation	1,405,436	1,910	26.0
Corrections	160,229	217	3.0
Education	0	0	0.0
Employment Security Administration	0	0	0.0
Financial Administration	164,334	223	3.0
Fire Protection	124,557	169	2.3
General Public Buildings	243,520	331	4.5
Governmental Administration, Other	133,954	182	2.5
Health	112,201	152	2.1
Highways	188,569	256	3.5
Hospitals	29,229	39	0.5
Housing and Community Development	309,438	420	5.7
Interest on General Debt	309,569	420	5.7
Judicial and Legal	100,585	136	1.9
Libraries	68,876	93	1.3
Parking	9,092	12	0.2
Parks and Recreation	339,980	462	6.3
Police Protection	262,038	356	4.8
Public Welfare	153,774	209	2.8
Sewerage	154,935	210	2.9
Solid Waste Management	14,041	19	0.3
Veterans' Services	0	0	0.0
Liquor Store	0	0	0.0
Utility	561,348	763	10.4

Source: U.S. Census Bureau, State & Local Government Finances 2022

TAXES

State Corporate Income Tax Rates

State	Tax Rate (%)	Income Brackets ($)	Num. of Brackets	Financial Institution Tax Rate (%)[a]	Federal Income Tax Ded.
Colorado	4.4	Flat rate	1	4.4	No

Note: Tax rates for tax year 2024; (a) Rates listed are the corporate income tax rate applied to financial institutions or excise taxes based on income. Some states have other taxes based upon the value of deposits or shares.
Source: Federation of Tax Administrators, State Corporate Income Tax Rates, January 1, 2025

State Individual Income Tax Rates

State	Tax Rate (%)	Income Brackets ($)	Personal Exemptions ($) Single	Married	Depend.	Standard Ded. ($) Single	Married
Colorado	4.4	Flat rate	(d)	(d)	(d)	14,600	29,200 (d)

Note: Tax rates for tax year 2024; Local- and county-level taxes are not included; (d) These states use the personal exemption/standard deduction amounts provided in the federal Internal Revenue Code. Montana personal exemption subject to repeal under Section 15-30-2114.
Source: Federation of Tax Administrators, State Individual Income Tax Rates, January 1, 2025

Various State Sales and Excise Tax Rates

State	State Sales Tax (%)	Gasoline[1] ($/gal.)	Cigarette[2] ($/pack)	Spirits[3] ($/gal.)	Wine[4] ($/gal.)	Beer[5] ($/gal.)	Recreational Marijuana (%)
Colorado	2.9	0.28	2.24	2.28	0.32	0.08	(d)

Note: All tax rates as of January 1, 2025; (1) The American Petroleum Institute has developed a methodology for determining the average tax rate on a gallon of fuel. Rates may include any of the following: excise taxes, environmental fees, storage tank fees, other fees or taxes, general sales tax, and local taxes; (2) The federal excise tax of $1.0066 per pack and local taxes are not included; (3) Rates are those applicable to off-premise sales of 40% alcohol by volume (a.b.v.) distilled spirits in 750ml containers. Local excise taxes are excluded; (4) Rates are those applicable to off-premise sales of 11% a.b.v. non-carbonated wine in 750ml containers; (5) Rates are those applicable to off-premise sales of 4.7% a.b.v. beer in 12 ounce containers; (d) 15% excise tax (levied on wholesale at average market rate); 15% excise tax (retail price)
Source: Tax Foundation, 2025 Facts & Figures: How Does Your State Compare?

State Tax Competitiveness Index

State	Overall Rank	Corporate Tax Rank	Individual Income Tax Rank	Sales Tax Rank	Property Tax Rank	Unemployment Insurance Tax Rank
Colorado	32	10	18	37	36	39

Note: The Tax Foundation's State Tax Competitiveness Index enables policymakers, taxpayers, and business leaders to gauge how their states' tax systems compare. A rank of 1 is best, 50 is worst. Rankings do not average to the total. States without a tax rank equally as 1. DC's scores and rankings do not affect other states. The report shows tax systems as of July 1, 2024 (the beginning of Fiscal Year 2025).
Source: Tax Foundation, State Tax Competitiveness Index 2025

TRANSPORTATION

Means of Transportation to Work

Area	Car/Truck/Van		Public Transportation			Bicycle	Walked	Other Means	Worked at Home
	Drove Alone	Car-pooled	Bus	Subway	Railroad				
City	57.7	6.5	2.8	0.3	0.1	1.6	3.9	2.7	24.4
MSA[1]	65.0	7.3	1.6	0.1	0.1	0.7	2.0	2.0	21.2
U.S.	70.2	8.5	1.7	1.3	0.4	0.4	2.4	1.6	13.5

Note: Figures are percentages and cover workers 16 years of age and older; (1) Figures cover the Denver-Aurora-Centennial, CO Metropolitan Statistical Area
Source: U.S. Census Bureau, 2019-2023 American Community Survey 5-Year Estimates

Travel Time to Work

Area	Less Than 10 Minutes	10 to 19 Minutes	20 to 29 Minutes	30 to 44 Minutes	45 to 59 Minutes	60 to 89 Minutes	90 Minutes or More
City	8.6	28.3	25.3	25.9	6.5	3.9	1.5
MSA[1]	8.8	25.1	23.7	26.4	9.0	5.1	1.9
U.S.	12.6	28.6	21.2	20.8	8.1	6.0	2.8

Note: Note: Figures are percentages and include workers 16 years old and over; (1) Figures cover the Denver-Aurora-Centennial, CO Metropolitan Statistical Area
Source: U.S. Census Bureau, 2019-2023 American Community Survey 5-Year Estimates

Key Congestion Measures

Measure	2000	2010	2015	2020	2022
Annual Hours of Delay, Total (000)	58,062	87,604	103,318	46,181	110,908
Annual Hours of Delay, Per Auto Commuter	44	50	58	26	66
Annual Congestion Cost, Per Auto Commuter ($)	1,010	1,211	1,319	609	1,454

Note: Figures cover the Denver-Aurora CO urban area
Source: Texas A&M Transportation Institute, 2023 Urban Mobility Report

Freeway Travel Time Index

Measure	1985	1990	1995	2000	2005	2010	2015	2020	2022
Urban Area Index[1]	1.13	1.14	1.19	1.27	1.32	1.29	1.31	1.09	1.28
Urban Area Rank[1,2]	19	26	23	10	8	13	15	40	15

Note: Freeway Travel Time Index—the ratio of travel time in the peak period to the travel time at free-flow conditions. For example, a value of 1.30 indicates a 20-minute free-flow trip takes 26 minutes in the peak (20 minutes x 1.30 = 26 minutes); (1) Covers the Denver-Aurora CO urban area; (2) Rank is based on 101 larger urban areas (#1 = highest travel time index)
Source: Texas A&M Transportation Institute, 2023 Urban Mobility Report

Public Transportation

Agency Name / Mode of Transportation	Vehicles Operated in Maximum Service[1]	Annual Unlinked Passenger Trips[2] (in thous.)	Annual Passenger Miles[3] (in thous.)
Denver Regional Transportation District (RTD)			
Bus (directly operated)	299	26,750.8	128,826.8
Bus (purchased transportation)	218	15,687.7	58,730.0
Commuter Rail (directly operated)	8	1,152.6	11,016.4
Commuter Rail (purchased transportation)	36	7,425.7	95,605.2
Demand Response (purchased transportation)	310	776.8	7,857.3
Light Rail (directly operated)	97	12,740.4	80,870.8

Note: (1) Number of revenue vehicles operated by the given mode and type of service to meet the annual maximum service requirement. This is the revenue vehicle count during the peak season of the year; on the week and day that maximum service is provided. Vehicles operated in maximum service (VOMS) exclude atypical days and one-time special events; (2) Number of passengers who boarded public transportation vehicles. Passengers are counted each time they board a vehicle no matter how many vehicles they use to travel from their origin to their destination. (3) Sum of the distances ridden by all passengers during the entire fiscal year.
Source: Federal Transit Administration, National Transit Database, 2023

Air Transportation

Airport Name and Code / Type of Service	Passenger Airlines[1]	Passenger Enplanements	Freight Carriers[2]	Freight (lbs)
Denver International (DEN)				
Domestic service (U.S. carriers only)	30	37,751,107	13	268,238,885
International service (U.S. carriers only)	8	1,461,931	3	8,628,050

Note: (1) Includes all U.S.-based major, minor and commuter airlines that carried at least one passenger during the year; (2) Includes all U.S.-based airlines and freight carriers that transported at least one pound of freight during the year.
Source: Bureau of Transportation Statistics, The Intermodal Transportation Database, Air Carriers: T-100 Domestic Market (U.S. carriers only), 2024; Bureau of Transportation Statistics, The Intermodal Transportation Database, Air Carriers: T-100 International Market (U.S. carriers only), 2024

BUSINESSES

Major Business Headquarters

Company Name	Industry	Rankings	
		Fortune[1]	Forbes[2]
DaVita	Health care: medical facilities	341	-
Leprino Foods	Food, drink & tobacco	-	170
Newmont	Mining, crude-oil production	349	-
Ovintiv	Mining, crude-oil production	373	-
VF	Apparel	355	-

Note: (1) Companies that produce a 10-K are ranked 1 to 500 based on 2023 revenue; (2) All private companies with at least $2 billion in annual revenue through the end of their most current fiscal year are ranked 1 to 275; companies listed are headquartered in the city; dashes indicate no ranking
Source: Fortune, "Fortune 500," 2024; Forbes, "America's Largest Private Companies," 2024

Fastest-Growing Businesses

According to *Inc.*, Denver is home to seven of America's 500 fastest-growing private companies: **The Luxe Room** (#54); **Maestro Media** (#167); **Pneuma Media** (#170); **Simple Homes** (#193); **Western Veterinary Partners** (#208); **Blazy Susan** (#382); **Pie Insurance** (#441). Criteria: must be an independent, privately-held, for-profit, U.S. corporation, proprietorship or partnership as of December 31, 2023; revenues must be at least $100,000 in 2020 and $2 million in 2023; must have four-year operating/sales history. *Inc., "America's 500 Fastest-Growing Private Companies," 2024*

According to Deloitte, Denver is home to two of North America's 500 fastest-growing high-technology companies: **Pie Insurance** (#117); **Aytu BioPharma** (#380). Companies are ranked by percentage growth in revenue over a four-year period. Criteria for inclusion: company must be headquartered within North America; must own proprietary intellectual property or technology that is sold to customers in products that contributes to a significant portion of the company's operating revenue; must have been in business for a minumum of four years with 2020 operating revenues of at least $50,000 USD/CD and 2023 operating revenues of at least $5 million USD/CD. *Deloitte, 2024 Technology Fast 500*™

Living Environment

COST OF LIVING

Cost of Living Index

Composite Index	Groceries	Housing	Utilities	Trans-portation	Health Care	Misc. Goods/ Services
108.6	101.3	123.4	89.3	94.7	109.6	107.7

Note: The Cost of Living Index measures regional differences in the cost of consumer goods and services, excluding taxes and non-consumer expenditures, for professional and managerial households in the top income quintile. It is based on more than 50,000 prices covering almost 60 different items for which prices are collected three times a year by chambers of commerce, economic development organizations or university applied economic centers in each participating urban area. The numbers shown should be read as a percentage above or below the national average of 100. For example, a value of 115.4 in the groceries column indicates that grocery prices are 15.4% higher than the national average. Small differences in the index numbers should not be interpreted as significant; Figures cover the Denver CO urban area.
Source: The Council for Community and Economic Research, Cost of Living Index, 2024

Grocery Prices

Area[1]	T-Bone Steak ($/pound)	Frying Chicken ($/pound)	Whole Milk ($/half gal.)	Eggs ($/dozen)	Orange Juice ($/64 oz.)	Coffee ($/11.5 oz.)
City[2]	15.52	1.45	4.62	2.98	4.42	6.16
Avg.	15.42	1.55	4.69	3.25	4.41	5.46
Min.	14.50	1.16	4.43	2.75	4.00	4.85
Max.	17.56	2.89	5.49	4.78	5.54	7.89

*Note: (1) Values for the local area are compared with the average, minimum and maximum values for all 276 areas in the Cost of Living Index; (2) Figures cover the Denver CO urban area; **T-Bone Steak** (price per pound); **Frying Chicken** (price per pound, whole fryer); **Whole Milk** (half gallon carton); **Eggs** (price per dozen, Grade A, large); **Orange Juice** (64 oz. Tropicana or Florida Natural); **Coffee** (11.5 oz. can, vacuum-packed, Maxwell House, Hills Bros, or Folgers).*
Source: The Council for Community and Economic Research, Cost of Living Index, 2024

Housing and Utility Costs

Area[1]	New Home Price ($)	Apartment Rent ($/month)	All Electric ($/month)	Part Electric ($/month)	Other Energy ($/month)	Telephone ($/month)
City[2]	650,555	1,899	-	93.55	76.25	197.22
Avg.	515,975	1,550	210.99	123.07	82.07	194.99
Min.	265,375	692	104.33	53.68	36.26	179.42
Max.	2,775,821	5,719	529.02	397.28	361.63	223.33

*Note: (1) Values for the local area are compared with the average, minimum and maximum values for all 276 areas in the Cost of Living Index; (2) Figures cover the Denver CO urban area; **New Home Price** (2,400 sf living area, 8,000 sf lot, in urban area with full utilities); **Apartment Rent** (950 sf 2 bedroom/1.5 or 2 bath, unfurnished, excluding all utilities except water); **All Electric** (average monthly cost for an all-electric home); **Part Electric** (average monthly cost for a part-electric home); **Other Energy** (average monthly cost for natural gas, fuel oil, coal, wood, and any other forms of energy except electricity); **Telephone** (price includes the base monthly rate plus taxes and fees for three lines of mobile phone service).*
Source: The Council for Community and Economic Research, Cost of Living Index, 2024

Health Care, Transportation, and Other Costs

Area[1]	Doctor ($/visit)	Dentist ($/visit)	Optometrist ($/visit)	Gasoline ($/gallon)	Beauty Salon ($/visit)	Men's Shirt ($)
City[2]	134.18	140.57	122.31	3.05	50.44	22.71
Avg.	143.77	117.51	129.23	3.32	48.57	38.14
Min.	36.74	58.67	67.33	2.80	24.00	13.41
Max.	270.44	216.82	307.33	5.28	94.00	63.89

*Note: (1) Values for the local area are compared with the average, minimum and maximum values for all 276 areas in the Cost of Living Index; (2) Figures cover the Denver CO urban area; **Doctor** (general practitioners routine exam of an established patient); **Dentist** (adult teeth cleaning and periodic oral examination); **Optometrist** (full vision eye exam for established adult patient); **Gasoline** (one gallon regular unleaded, national brand, including all taxes, cash price at self-service pump if available); **Beauty Salon** (woman's shampoo, trim, and blow-dry); **Men's Shirt** (cotton/polyester dress shirt, pinpoint weave, long sleeves).*
Source: The Council for Community and Economic Research, Cost of Living Index, 2024

HOUSING

Homeownership Rate

Area	2017 (%)	2018 (%)	2019 (%)	2020 (%)	2021 (%)	2022 (%)	2023 (%)	2024 (%)
MSA[1]	59.3	60.1	63.5	62.9	62.8	64.6	65.9	61.6
U.S.	63.9	64.4	64.6	66.6	65.5	65.8	65.9	65.6

Note: (1) Figures cover the Denver-Aurora-Centennial, CO Metropolitan Statistical Area
Source: U.S. Census Bureau, Housing Vacancies and Homeownership Annual Statistics: 2017-2024

House Price Index (HPI)

Area	National Ranking[2]	Quarterly Change (%)	One-Year Change (%)	Five-Year Change (%)	Since 1991Q1 (%)
MSA[1]	193	0.30	3.30	43.23	580.34
U.S.[3]	–	1.43	4.51	57.13	327.82

Note: The HPI is a weighted repeat sales index. It measures average price changes in repeat sales or refinancings on the same properties. This information is obtained by reviewing repeat mortgage transactions on single-family properties whose mortgages have been purchased or securitized by Fannie Mae or Freddie Mac since January 1975; (1) Figures cover the Denver-Aurora-Lakewood, CO Metropolitan Statistical Area; (2) Rankings are based on annual percentage change for all metro areas containing at least 15,000 transactions over the last 10 years and ranges from 1 to 241; (3) figures based on a weighted average of Census Division estimates using a seasonally adjusted, purchase-only index; all figures are for the period ending December 31, 2024
Source: Federal Housing Finance Agency, Change in FHFA Metropolitan Area House Price Indexes, All Transactions Index, 2024Q4

Home Value

Area	Under $100,000	$100,000 -$199,999	$200,000 -$299,999	$300,000 -$399,999	$400,000 -$499,999	$500,000 -$999,999	$1,000,000 or more	Median ($)
City	2.3	2.1	6.6	11.4	17.3	44.6	15.7	586,700
MSA[1]	3.2	1.7	5.1	11.3	18.6	49.8	10.3	570,300
U.S.	12.1	17.8	19.5	14.4	10.5	19.1	6.5	303,400

Note: Figures are percentages except for median and cover owner-occupied housing units; (1) Figures cover the Denver-Aurora-Centennial, CO Metropolitan Statistical Area
Source: U.S. Census Bureau, 2019-2023 American Community Survey 5-Year Estimates

Year Housing Structure Built

Area	2020 or Later	2010 -2019	2000 -2009	1990 -1999	1980 -1989	1970 -1979	1960 -1969	1950 -1959	1940 -1949	Before 1940	Median Year
City	2.3	15.5	10.9	6.6	7.4	12.0	9.9	13.0	5.2	17.2	1974
MSA[1]	1.9	13.0	15.6	13.8	13.5	16.4	8.7	8.4	2.4	6.3	1986
U.S.	1.2	8.9	13.6	12.8	13.0	14.4	10.0	9.7	4.5	11.9	1980

Note: Figures are percentages except for Median Year; Note: (1) Figures cover the Denver-Aurora-Centennial, CO Metropolitan Statistical Area
Source: U.S. Census Bureau, 2019-2023 American Community Survey 5-Year Estimates

Gross Monthly Rent

Area	Under $500	$500 -$999	$1,000 -$1,499	$1,500 -$1,999	$2,000 -$2,499	$2,500 -$2,999	$3,000 and up	Median ($)
City	5.7	6.3	22.4	28.8	19.9	9.0	7.9	1,770
MSA[1]	3.6	5.3	21.2	32.6	21.1	9.5	6.7	1,805
U.S.	6.5	22.3	29.5	20.2	10.8	4.8	5.9	1,348

Note: Figures are percentages except for median; Gross rent is the contract rent plus the estimated average monthly cost of utilities (electricity, gas, and water and sewer) and fuels (oil, coal, kerosene, wood, etc.) if these are paid by the renter (or paid for the renter by someone else); (1) Figures cover the Denver-Aurora-Centennial, CO Metropolitan Statistical Area
Source: U.S. Census Bureau, 2019-2023 American Community Survey 5-Year Estimates

HEALTH

Health Risk Factors

Category	MSA[1] (%)	U.S. (%)
Adults aged 18–64 who have any kind of health care coverage	87.6	90.8
Adults who reported being in good or better health	86.1	81.8
Adults who have been told they have high blood cholesterol	32.0	36.9
Adults who have been told they have high blood pressure	26.6	34.0
Adults who are current smokers	10.0	12.1
Adults who currently use e-cigarettes	8.3	7.7
Adults who currently use chewing tobacco, snuff, or snus	3.1	3.2
Adults who are heavy drinkers[2]	7.6	6.1
Adults who are binge drinkers[3]	20.0	15.2
Adults who are overweight (BMI 25.0 - 29.9)	35.5	34.4
Adults who are obese (BMI 30.0 - 99.8)	24.0	34.3
Adults who participated in any physical activities in the past month	84.0	75.8

Note: All figures are crude prevalence; (1) Figures cover the Denver-Aurora-Lakewood, CO Metropolitan Statistical Area; (2) Heavy drinkers are classified as adult men having more than 14 drinks per week and adult women having more than 7 drinks per week; (3) Binge drinkers are classified as males having five or more drinks on one occasion or females having four or more drinks on one occasion
Source: Centers for Disease Control and Prevention, Behaviorial Risk Factor Surveillance System, SMART: Selected Metropolitan Area Risk Trends, 2023

Acute and Chronic Health Conditions

Category	MSA[1] (%)	U.S. (%)
Adults who have ever been told they had a heart attack	2.4	4.2
Adults who have ever been told they have angina or coronary heart disease	3.1	4.0
Adults who have ever been told they had a stroke	2.0	3.3
Adults who have ever been told they have asthma	16.6	15.7
Adults who have ever been told they have arthritis	21.4	26.3
Adults who have ever been told they have diabetes[2]	7.6	11.5
Adults who have ever been told they had skin cancer	6.0	5.6
Adults who have ever been told they had any other types of cancer	7.5	8.4
Adults who have ever been told they have COPD	4.0	6.4
Adults who have ever been told they have kidney disease	3.4	3.7
Adults who have ever been told they have a form of depression	20.5	22.0

Note: All figures are crude prevalence; (1) Figures cover the Denver-Aurora-Lakewood, CO Metropolitan Statistical Area; (2) Figures do not include pregnancy-related, borderline, or pre-diabetes
Source: Centers for Disease Control and Prevention, Behaviorial Risk Factor Surveillance System, SMART: Selected Metropolitan Area Risk Trends, 2023

Health Screening and Vaccination Rates

Category	MSA[1] (%)	U.S. (%)
Adults who have ever been tested for HIV	42.6	37.5
Adults who have had their blood cholesterol checked within the last five years	86.8	87.0
Adults aged 65+ who have had flu shot within the past year	74.6	63.4
Adults aged 65+ who have ever had a pneumonia vaccination	82.5	71.9

Note: All figures are crude prevalence; (1) Figures cover the Denver-Aurora-Lakewood, CO Metropolitan Statistical Area.
Source: Centers for Disease Control and Prevention, Behaviorial Risk Factor Surveillance System, SMART: Selected Metropolitan Area Risk Trends, 2023

Disability Status

Category	MSA[1] (%)	U.S. (%)
Adults who reported being deaf	5.7	7.4
Are you blind or have serious difficulty seeing, even when wearing glasses?	4.6	4.9
Do you have difficulty doing errands alone?	6.0	7.8
Do you have difficulty dressing or bathing?	2.4	3.6
Do you have serious difficulty concentrating/remembering/making decisions?	12.1	13.7
Do you have serious difficulty walking or climbing stairs?	8.8	13.2

Note: All figures are crude prevalence; (1) Figures cover the Denver-Aurora-Lakewood, CO Metropolitan Statistical Area.
Source: Centers for Disease Control and Prevention, Behaviorial Risk Factor Surveillance System, SMART: Selected Metropolitan Area Risk Trends, 2023

Mortality Rates for the Top 10 Causes of Death in the U.S.

ICD-10[a] Sub-Chapter	ICD-10[a] Code	Crude Mortality Rate[2] per 100,000 population	
		County[3]	U.S.
Malignant neoplasms	C00-C97	122.0	182.7
Ischaemic heart diseases	I20-I25	61.1	109.6
Provisional assignment of new diseases of uncertain etiology[1]	U00-U49	33.0	65.3
Other forms of heart disease	I30-I51	34.0	65.1
Other degenerative diseases of the nervous system	G30-G31	39.2	52.4
Other external causes of accidental injury	W00-X59	68.4	52.3
Cerebrovascular diseases	I60-I69	30.5	49.1
Chronic lower respiratory diseases	J40-J47	33.8	43.5
Hypertensive diseases	I10-I15	24.8	38.9
Organic, including symptomatic, mental disorders	F01-F09	25.1	33.9

Note: (a) ICD-10 = International Classification of Diseases 10th Revision; (1) Includes COVID-19, adverse effects to COVID-19 vaccines, SARS, and vaping-related disorders; (2) Crude mortality rates are a three-year average covering 2021-2023; (3) Figures cover Denver County.
Source: Centers for Disease Control and Prevention, National Center for Health Statistics. National Vital Statistics System, Mortality 2018-2023 on CDC WONDER Online Database

Mortality Rates for Selected Causes of Death

Cause of Death	ICD-10[a] Code	Crude Mortality Rate[1] per 100,000 population	
		County[2]	U.S.
Accidental poisoning and exposure to noxious substances	X40-X49	42.7	30.5
Alzheimer disease	G30	23.0	35.4
Assault	X85-Y09	10.9	7.3
COVID-19	U07.1	33.0	65.3
Diabetes mellitus	E10-E14	22.5	30.0
Diseases of the liver	K70-K76	29.1	20.8
Human immunodeficiency virus (HIV) disease	B20-B24	1.7	1.5
Influenza and pneumonia	J09-J18	5.7	13.4
Intentional self-harm	X60-X84	21.7	14.7
Malnutrition	E40-E46	7.0	6.0
Obesity and other hyperalimentation	E65-E68	4.2	3.1
Renal failure	N17-N19	9.1	16.4
Transport accidents	V01-V99	13.3	14.4

Note: (a) ICD-10 = International Classification of Diseases 10th Revision; (1) Crude mortality rates are a three-year average covering 2021-2023; (2) Figures cover Denver County; Data are suppressed when the data meet the criteria for confidentiality constraints; Crude mortality rates are flagged as unreliable when the rate would be calculated with a numerator of 20 or less.
Source: Centers for Disease Control and Prevention, National Center for Health Statistics. National Vital Statistics System, Mortality 2018-2023 on CDC WONDER Online Database

Health Insurance Coverage

Area	With Health Insurance	With Private Health Insurance	With Public Health Insurance	Without Health Insurance	Population Under Age 19 Without Health Insurance
City	91.2	68.3	30.8	8.8	5.3
MSA[1]	92.2	72.2	29.4	7.8	5.0
U.S.	91.4	67.3	36.3	8.6	5.4

Note: Figures are percentages that cover the civilian noninstitutionalized population; (1) Figures cover the Denver-Aurora-Centennial, CO Metropolitan Statistical Area
Source: U.S. Census Bureau, 2019-2023 American Community Survey 5-Year Estimates

Number of Medical Professionals

Area	MDs[3]	DOs[3,4]	Dentists	Podiatrists	Chiropractors	Optometrists
County[1] (number)	4,351	259	608	49	291	124
County[1] (rate[2])	610.0	36.3	84.8	6.8	40.6	17.3
U.S. (rate[2])	302.5	29.2	74.6	6.4	29.5	18.0

Note: Data as of 2023 unless noted; (1) Data covers Denver County; (2) Number of medical professionals per 100,000 population; (3) Data as of 2022 and includes all active, non-federal physicians; (4) Doctor of Osteopathic Medicine
Source: U.S. Department of Health and Human Services, Health Resources and Services Administration, Bureau of Health Professions, Area Resource File (ARF) 2023-2024

Best Hospitals

According to *U.S. News,* the Denver-Aurora-Centennial, CO metro area is home to four of the best hospitals in the U.S.: **Craig Hospital** (1 adult specialty); **National Jewish Health, Denver-University of Colorado Hospital** (1 adult specialty); **UCHealth University of Colorado Hospital** (4 adult specialties); **University of Colorado Cancer Center-UCHealth University of Colorado Hospital** (4 adult specialties). The hospitals listed were nationally ranked in at least one of 15 adult or 11 pediatric specialties. The number of specialties shown cover the parent hospital. Only 160 U.S. hospitals performed well enough to be nationally ranked in one or more specialties. Twenty hospitals in the U.S. made the Honor Roll. The Best Hospitals Honor Roll takes both the national rankings and the procedure and condition ratings into account. Hospitals received points if they were nationally ranked in one of the 15 adult specialties—the higher they ranked, the more points they got—and how many ratings of "high performing" they earned in the 20 procedures and conditions. *U.S. News Online, "America's Best Hospitals 2024-25"*

According to *U.S. News,* the Denver-Aurora-Centennial, CO metro area is home to one of the best children's hospitals in the U.S.: **Children's Hospital Colorado** (Honor Roll/11 pediatric specialties). The hospital listed was highly ranked in at least one of 11 pediatric specialties. One hundred five children's hospitals in the U.S. were nationally ranked in at least one specialty. Hospitals received points for being ranked in a specialty, and the 10 hospitals with the most points across the 11 specialties make up the Honor Roll. *U.S. News Online, "America's Best Children's Hospitals 2024-25"*

EDUCATION

Public School District Statistics

District Name	Schls	Pupils	Pupil/ Teacher Ratio	Minority Pupils[1] (%)	Total Rev. per Pupil ($)	Total Exp. per Pupil ($)
Mapleton School District No. 1	20	7,016	17.7	86.4	15,686	16,096
School District No. 1	197	88,258	14.8	74.8	19,838	19,296
State Charter School Institute	44	19,593	16.8	49.9	13,946	12,972

Note: Table includes school districts with 2,000 or more students; (1) Percentage of students that are not non-Hispanic white.
Source: U.S. Department of Education, National Center for Education Statistics, Common Core of Data, Local Education Agency (School District) Universe Survey: School Year 2023-2024; U.S. Department of Education, National Center for Education Statistics, Common Core of Data, School District Finance Survey (F-33): School Year 2021–22

Best High Schools

According to *U.S. News,* Denver is home to two of the top 500 high schools in the U.S.: **D'Evelyn Junior/Senior High School** (#59); **Denver School of the Arts** (#266). Nearly 25,000 public, magnet and charter schools were ranked based on their performance on state assessments and how well they prepare students for college. *U.S. News & World Report, "Best High Schools 2024"*

Highest Level of Education

Area	Less than H.S.	H.S. Diploma	Some College, No Deg.	Associate Degree	Bachelor's Degree	Master's Degree	Prof. School Degree	Doctorate Degree
City	8.6	14.8	15.7	5.3	33.8	15.0	4.7	2.2
MSA[1]	7.7	18.4	18.2	7.3	30.3	13.3	2.9	1.9
U.S.	10.6	26.2	19.4	8.8	21.3	9.8	2.3	1.6

Note: Figures cover persons age 25 and over; (1) Figures cover the Denver-Aurora-Centennial, CO Metropolitan Statistical Area
Source: U.S. Census Bureau, 2019-2023 American Community Survey 5-Year Estimates

Educational Attainment by Race

Area	High School Graduate or Higher (%)					Bachelor's Degree or Higher (%)				
	Total	White	Black	Asian	Hisp.[2]	Total	White	Black	Asian	Hisp.[2]
City	91.4	96.4	91.5	87.1	72.5	55.6	66.7	31.4	58.1	23.3
MSA[1]	92.3	96.0	90.8	86.3	75.5	48.4	54.4	30.3	55.4	21.7
U.S.	89.4	92.9	88.1	88.0	72.5	35.0	37.7	24.7	57.0	19.9

Note: Figures shown cover persons 25 years old and over; (1) Figures cover the Denver-Aurora-Centennial, CO Metropolitan Statistical Area; (2) People of Hispanic origin can be of any race
Source: U.S. Census Bureau, 2019-2023 American Community Survey 5-Year Estimates

School Enrollment by Grade and Control

Area	Preschool (%)		Kindergarten (%)		Grades 1 - 4 (%)		Grades 5 - 8 (%)		Grades 9 - 12 (%)	
	Public	Private	Public	Private	Public	Private	Public	Private	Public	Private
City	56.0	44.0	85.1	14.9	89.4	10.6	88.2	11.8	92.7	7.3
MSA[1]	58.5	41.5	86.4	13.6	89.3	10.7	89.9	10.1	91.6	8.4
U.S.	58.7	41.3	85.2	14.8	87.2	12.8	87.9	12.1	89.0	11.0

Note: Figures shown cover persons 3 years old and over; (1) Figures cover the Denver-Aurora-Centennial, CO Metropolitan Statistical Area
Source: U.S. Census Bureau, 2019-2023 American Community Survey 5-Year Estimates

Higher Education

Four-Year Colleges			Two-Year Colleges			Medical Schools[1]	Law Schools[2]	Voc/ Tech[3]
Public	Private Non-profit	Private For-profit	Public	Private Non-profit	Private For-profit			
8	6	8	2	0	6	2	1	13

Note: Figures cover institutions located within the Denver-Aurora-Centennial, CO Metropolitan Statistical Area and include main campuses only; (1) includes schools accredited by the Liaison Committee on Medical Education and the American Osteopathic Association's Commission on Osteopathic College Accreditation; (2) includes ABA-accredited schools, schools with provisional ABA accreditation, and state accredited schools; (3) includes all schools with programs that are less than 2 years.
Source: National Center for Education Statistics, Integrated Postsecondary Education System (IPEDS), 2023-24; Wikipedia, List of Medical Schools in the United States, accessed May 2, 2025; Wikipedia, List of Law Schools in the United States, accessed May 2, 2025

According to *U.S. News & World Report,* the Denver-Aurora-Centennial, CO metro area is home to two of the top 200 national universities in the U.S.: **Colorado School of Mines** (#76 tie); **University of Denver** (#121 tie). The indicators used to capture academic quality fall into a number of categories: assessment by administrators at peer institutions; retention of students; faculty resources; student selectivity; financial resources; alumni giving; high school counselor ratings of colleges; and graduation rate. *U.S. News & World Report, "America's Best Colleges 2025"*

According to *U.S. News & World Report,* the Denver-Aurora-Centennial, CO metro area is home to one of the top 100 law schools in the U.S.: **University of Denver (Sturm)** (#88 tie). The rankings are based on a weighted average of 12 measures of quality: peer assessment score; assessment score by lawyers/judges; median LSAT scores; median undergrad GPA; acceptance rate; employment rates for graduates; placement success; bar passage rate; faculty resources; expenditures per student; student/faculty ratio; and library resources. *U.S. News & World Report, "America's Best Graduate Schools, Law, 2025"*

According to *U.S. News & World Report,* the Denver-Aurora-Centennial, CO metro area is home to one of the top medical schools for research in the U.S.: **University of Colorado** (Tier 2). *U.S. News* placed medical and osteopathic schools into tiers based on their research productivity, faculty and admissions data. Each school's tier was derived from its overall score, calculated by summing the weighted normalized values generated across several factors of academic quality, outlined below. There are four tiers, with tier 1 medical schools as the highest-performing and tier 4 as the lowest-performing. Only tier 1 and 2 schools are shown. Because of the tier presentation, *U.S. News* calculated overall scores based on their percentile performance among all rated schools instead of dividing against the rescaled score of the No. 1-performing schools. Tier 1 included schools with overall scores of 85 to 99. The cutoffs for tiers 2 through 4 were schools scoring 50 to 84, 15 to 49 and 1 to 14, respectively. The rankings are based on a weighted average of the following measures of quality: total research activity; average research activity per faculty member; total NIH research grants at the medical school and its affiliated hospitals; average NIH research grants per faculty; median MCAT total score; median undergraduate GPA; acceptance rate; and faculty resources. *U.S. News & World Report, "America's Best Graduate Schools, Medical, 2025"*

EMPLOYERS

Major Employers

Company Name	Industry
Centura Health	Healthcare
Century Link	Telecommunications
Charles Schwab	Financial services
Children's Hospital Colorado	Healthcare
City of Denver	Local government
DaVita	Healthcare
Denver International Airport	Aviation
HealthONE Corporation	Healthcare
Ing Security	Financial services
JBS	Pork processing & packaging
Kaiser Permanente	Healthcare
Lockheed Martin	Aviation/aerospace
SCL Health Systems	Healthcare
TTEC	Technology
United Airlines	Aviation
University of Colorado Health	Healthcare, research
Wells Fargo	Financial services

Note: Companies shown are located within the Denver-Aurora-Centennial, CO Metropolitan Statistical Area.
Source: Chambers of Commerce; State Departments of Labor; Wikipedia

Best Companies to Work For

PCL Construction, headquartered in Denver, is among "The 100 Best Companies to Work For." To pick the best companies, *Fortune* partnered with the Great Place to Work Institute. Using their proprietary Trust Index^{TM} survey, the core of what creates great a workplace is measured—key behaviors that drive trust in management, connection with colleagues, and loyalty to the company. To be eligible for the *Fortune* 100 Best Companies to Work For list, employers must have 1,000 or more employees in the U.S. and cannot be a government agency. *Fortune, "The 100 Best Companies to Work For," 2025*

Colorado Housing and Finance Authority, headquartered in Denver, is among "Fortune's Best Workplaces for Parents." To pick the best companies, *Fortune* partnered with the Great Place to Work Institute. To be considered for the list, companies must be Great Place To Work-Certified and have at least 50 responses from parents in the US. The survey enables employees to share confidential quantitative and qualitative feedback about their organization's culture by responding to 60 statements on a 5-point scale and answering two open-ended questions. Collectively, these statements describe a great employee experience, defined by high levels of trust, respect, credibility, fairness, pride, and camaraderie. In addition, companies provide organizational data like size, location, industry, demographics, roles, and levels; and provide information about parental leave, adoption, flexible schedule, childcare and dependent health care benefits. *Fortune, "Best Workplaces for Parents," 2024*

Colorado Housing and Finance Authority, headquartered in Denver, is among "Fortune's Best Workplaces for Women." To pick the best companies, *Fortune* partnered with the Great Place to Work Institute. To be considered for the list, companies must be Great Place To Work-Certified.

Companies must also employ at least 50 women, at least 20% of their non-executive managers must be female, and at least one executive must be female. To determine the Best Workplaces for Women, Great Place To Work measured the differences in women's survey responses to those of their peers and assesses the impact of demographics and roles on the quality and consistency of women's experiences. Great Place To Work also analyzed the gender balance of each workplace, how it compared to each company's industry, and patterns in representation as women rise from front-line positions to the board of directors. *Fortune, "Best Workplaces for Women," 2024*

Cubby Beds; DaVita, headquartered in Denver, are among "Best Workplaces in Health Care." To determine the Best Workplaces in Health Care list, Great Place To Work analyzed the survey responses of over 185,000 employees from Great Place To Work-Certified companies in the health care industry. Survey data analysis and company-provided datapoints are then factored into a combined score to compare and rank the companies that create the most consistently positive experience for all employees in this industry. *Fortune, "Best Workplaces in Health Care," 2024*

AIMCO; Healthpeak; Northwood Investors, headquartered in Denver, are among "Best Workplaces in Real Estate." To determine the Best Workplaces in Real Estate list, Great Place To Work analyzed the survey responses of over 29,000 employees from Great Place To Work-Certified companies in the real estate industry. Survey data analysis and company-provided datapoints are then factored into a combined score to compare and rank the companies that create the most consistently positive experience for all employees in this industry. *Fortune, "Best Workplaces in Real Estate," 2024*

PUBLIC SAFETY

Crime Rate

Area	Total Crime Rate	Violent Crime Rate				Property Crime Rate		
		Murder	Rape	Robbery	Aggrav. Assault	Burglary	Larceny -Theft	Motor Vehicle Theft
City	6,772.3	11.9	93.2	175.8	740.8	716.9	3,284.7	1,749.0
U.S.	2,290.9	5.7	38.0	66.5	264.1	250.7	1,347.2	318.7

Note: Figures are crimes per 100,000 population.
Source: FBI, Table 8, Offenses Known to Law Enforcement, by State by City, 2023

Hate Crimes

Area	Number of Quarters Reported	Number of Incidents per Bias Motivation					
		Race/Ethnicity/ Ancestry	Religion	Sexual Orientation	Disability	Gender	Gender Identity
City[1]	4	49	14	39	0	0	7
U.S.	4	5,900	2,699	2,077	187	92	492

Note: (1) Figures include at least one incident reported with more than one bias motivation.
Source: Federal Bureau of Investigation, Hate Crime Statistics 2023

Identity Theft Consumer Reports

Area	Reports	Reports per 100,000 Population	Rank[2]
MSA[1]	7,056	237	112
U.S.	1,135,291	339	-

Note: (1) Figures cover the Denver-Aurora-Centennial, CO Metropolitan Statistical Area; (2) Rank ranges from 1 to 401 where 1 indicates greatest number of identity theft reports per 100,000 population
Source: Federal Trade Commission, Consumer Sentinel Network Data Book 2024

Fraud and Other Consumer Reports

Area	Reports	Reports per 100,000 Population	Rank[2]
MSA[1]	39,443	1,325	91
U.S.	5,360,641	1,601	-

Note: (1) Figures cover the Denver-Aurora-Centennial, CO Metropolitan Statistical Area; (2) Rank ranges from 1 to 401 where 1 indicates greatest number of fraud and other consumer reports per 100,000 population
Source: Federal Trade Commission, Consumer Sentinel Network Data Book 2024

POLITICS

2024 Presidential Election Results

Area	Trump (Rep.)	Harris (Dem.)	Stein (Green)	Kennedy (Ind.)	Oliver (Lib.)	Other
Denver County	20.6	76.6	0.9	0.8	0.6	0.5
U.S.	49.7	48.2	0.6	0.5	0.4	0.6

Note: Results are percentages and may not add to 100% due to rounding
Source: Dave Leip's Atlas of U.S. Presidential Elections

SPORTS

Professional Sports Teams

Team Name	League	Year Established
Colorado Avalanche	National Hockey League (NHL)	1995
Colorado Rapids	Major League Soccer (MLS)	1996
Colorado Rockies	Major League Baseball (MLB)	1993
Denver Broncos	National Football League (NFL)	1960
Denver Nuggets	National Basketball Association (NBA)	1967

Note: Includes teams located in the Denver-Aurora-Centennial, CO Metropolitan Statistical Area.
Source: Wikipedia, Major Professional Sports Teams of the United States and Canada, May 1, 2025

CLIMATE

Average and Extreme Temperatures

Temperature	Jan	Feb	Mar	Apr	May	Jun	Jul	Aug	Sep	Oct	Nov	Dec	Yr.
Extreme High (°F)	73	76	84	90	93	102	103	100	97	89	79	75	103
Average High (°F)	43	47	52	62	71	81	88	86	77	67	52	45	64
Average Temp. (°F)	30	34	39	48	58	67	73	72	63	52	39	32	51
Average Low (°F)	16	20	25	34	44	53	59	57	48	37	25	18	37
Extreme Low (°F)	-25	-25	-10	-2	22	30	43	41	17	3	-8	-25	-25

Note: Figures cover the years 1948-1992
Source: National Climatic Data Center, International Station Meteorological Climate Summary, 9/96

Average Precipitation/Snowfall/Humidity

Precip./Humidity	Jan	Feb	Mar	Apr	May	Jun	Jul	Aug	Sep	Oct	Nov	Dec	Yr.
Avg. Precip. (in.)	0.6	0.6	1.3	1.7	2.5	1.7	1.9	1.5	1.1	1.0	0.9	0.6	15.5
Avg. Snowfall (in.)	9	7	14	9	2	Tr	0	0	2	4	9	8	63
Avg. Rel. Hum. 5am (%)	62	65	67	66	70	68	67	68	66	63	66	63	66
Avg. Rel. Hum. 5pm (%)	49	44	40	35	38	34	34	34	32	34	47	50	39

Note: Figures cover the years 1948-1992; Tr = Trace amounts (<0.05 in. of rain; <0.5 in. of snow)
Source: National Climatic Data Center, International Station Meteorological Climate Summary, 9/96

Weather Conditions

Temperature			Daytime Sky			Precipitation		
10°F & below	32°F & below	90°F & above	Clear	Partly cloudy	Cloudy	0.01 inch or more precip.	0.1 inch or more snow/ice	Thunder-storms
24	155	33	99	177	89	90	38	39

Note: Figures are average number of days per year and cover the years 1948-1992
Source: National Climatic Data Center, International Station Meteorological Climate Summary, 9/96

HAZARDOUS WASTE

Superfund Sites

The Denver-Aurora-Centennial, CO metro area is home to nine sites on the EPA's Superfund National Priorities List (NPL) or Superfund Alternative Approach (SAA) list: **Air Force Plant PJKS** (Final NPL); **Broderick Wood Products** (Final NPL); **Central City, Clear Creek** (Final NPL); **Chemical Sales Co.** (Final NPL); **Denver Radium Site** (Final NPL); **Lowry Landfill** (Final NPL); **Rocky Flats Plant (USDOE)** (Final NPL); **Rocky Mountain Arsenal (USARMY)** (Final NPL); **Vasquez Boulevard and I-70** (Final NPL). The Superfund alternative approach uses the same investigation and cleanup process and standards that are used for sites listed on the National Priorities List. The SAA is an alternative to listing a site on the NPL; it is not an alternative to Superfund or the Superfund process. There are a total of 1,445 Superfund sites with a status of proposed or final on both lists in the United States. *U.S. Environmental Protection Agency, National Priorities List, May 1, 2025; U.S. Environmental Protection Agency, Superfund Alternative Approach Sites, May 1, 2025*

AIR QUALITY

Air Quality Trends: Ozone

	1990	1995	2000	2005	2010	2015	2020	2021	2022	2023
MSA[1]	0.076	0.070	0.069	0.077	0.069	0.072	0.081	0.082	0.074	0.073
U.S.	0.087	0.089	0.081	0.080	0.072	0.068	0.066	0.067	0.067	0.070

Note: (1) Data covers the Denver-Aurora-Centennial, CO Metropolitan Statistical Area. The values shown are the composite ozone concentration averages among trend sites based on the highest fourth daily maximum 8-hour concentration in parts per million. These trends are based on sites having an adequate record of monitoring data during the trend period. Data from exceptional events are included.
Source: U.S. Environmental Protection Agency, Air Quality Monitoring Information, "Air Quality Trends by City, 1990-2023"

Air Quality Index

Area	Percent of Days when Air Quality was...[2]					AQI Statistics[2]	
	Good	Moderate	Unhealthy for Sensitive Groups	Unhealthy	Very Unhealthy	Maximum	Median
MSA[1]	19.7	72.3	7.4	0.5	0.0	179	64

Note: (1) Data covers the Denver-Aurora-Centennial, CO Metropolitan Statistical Area; (2) Based on 365 days with AQI data in 2023. Air Quality Index (AQI) is an index for reporting daily air quality. EPA calculates the AQI for five major air pollutants regulated by the Clean Air Act: ground-level ozone, particle pollution (aka particulate matter), carbon monoxide, sulfur dioxide, and nitrogen dioxide. The AQI runs from 0 to 500. The higher the AQI value, the greater the level of air pollution and the greater the health concern. There are six AQI categories: "Good" AQI is between 0 and 50. Air quality is considered satisfactory; "Moderate" AQI is between 51 and 100. Air quality is acceptable; "Unhealthy for Sensitive Groups" When AQI values are between 101 and 150, members of sensitive groups may experience health effects; "Unhealthy" When AQI values are between 151 and 200 everyone may begin to experience health effects; "Very Unhealthy" AQI values between 201 and 300 trigger a health alert; "Hazardous" AQI values over 300 trigger warnings of emergency conditions (not shown).
Source: U.S. Environmental Protection Agency, Air Quality Index Report, 2023

Air Quality Index Pollutants

Area	Percent of Days when AQI Pollutant was...[2]					
	Carbon Monoxide	Nitrogen Dioxide	Ozone	Sulfur Dioxide	Particulate Matter 2.5	Particulate Matter 10
MSA[1]	0.0	5.5	66.6	(3)	23.3	4.7

Note: (1) Data covers the Denver-Aurora-Centennial, CO Metropolitan Statistical Area; (2) Based on 365 days with AQI data in 2023. The Air Quality Index (AQI) is an index for reporting daily air quality. EPA calculates the AQI for five major air pollutants regulated by the Clean Air Act: ground-level ozone, particle pollution (also known as particulate matter), carbon monoxide, sulfur dioxide, and nitrogen dioxide. The AQI runs from 0 to 500. The higher the AQI value, the greater the level of air pollution and the greater the health concern; (3) Sulfur dioxide is no longer included in this table because SO_2 concentrations tend to be very localized and not necessarily representative of broad geographical areas like counties and CBSAs.
Source: U.S. Environmental Protection Agency, Air Quality Index Report, 2023

Maximum Air Pollutant Concentrations: Particulate Matter, Ozone, CO and Lead

	Particulate Matter 10 (ug/m³)	Particulate Matter 2.5 Wtd AM (ug/m³)	Particulate Matter 2.5 24-Hr (ug/m³)	Ozone (ppm)	Carbon Monoxide (ppm)	Lead (ug/m³)
MSA[1] Level	89	8.7	24	0.077	2	n/a
NAAQS[2]	150	15	35	0.075	9	0.15
Met NAAQS[2]	Yes	Yes	Yes	No	Yes	n/a

Note: (1) Data covers the Denver-Aurora-Centennial, CO Metropolitan Statistical Area; Data from exceptional events are included; (2) National Ambient Air Quality Standards; ppm = parts per million;
ug/m³ = micrograms per cubic meter; n/a not available.
Concentrations: Particulate Matter 10 (coarse particulate)—highest second maximum 24-hour concentration; Particulate Matter 2.5 Wtd AM (fine particulate)—highest weighted annual mean concentration; Particulate Matter 2.5 24-Hour (fine particulate)—highest 98th percentile 24-hour concentration; Ozone—highest fourth daily maximum 8-hour concentration; Carbon Monoxide—highest second maximum non-overlapping 8-hour concentration; Lead—maximum running 3-month average
Source: U.S. Environmental Protection Agency, Air Quality Monitoring Information, "Air Quality Statistics by City, 2023"

Maximum Air Pollutant Concentrations: Nitrogen Dioxide and Sulfur Dioxide

	Nitrogen Dioxide AM (ppb)	Nitrogen Dioxide 1-Hr (ppb)	Sulfur Dioxide AM (ppb)	Sulfur Dioxide 1-Hr (ppb)	Sulfur Dioxide 24-Hr (ppb)
MSA[1] Level	24	65	n/a	6	n/a
NAAQS[2]	53	100	30	75	140
Met NAAQS[2]	Yes	Yes	n/a	Yes	n/a

Note: (1) Data covers the Denver-Aurora-Centennial, CO Metropolitan Statistical Area; Data from exceptional events are included; (2) National Ambient Air Quality Standards; ppm = parts per million;
ug/m³ = micrograms per cubic meter; n/a not available.
Concentrations: Nitrogen Dioxide AM—highest arithmetic mean concentration; Nitrogen Dioxide 1-Hr—highest 98th percentile 1-hour daily maximum concentration; Sulfur Dioxide AM—highest annual mean concentration; Sulfur Dioxide 1-Hr—highest 99th percentile 1-hour daily maximum concentration; Sulfur Dioxide 24-Hr—highest second maximum 24-hour concentration
Source: U.S. Environmental Protection Agency, Air Quality Monitoring Information, "Air Quality Statistics by City, 2023"

Eugene, Oregon

Background

Eugene F. Skinner, the city's namesake, and his family settled in the lush Willamette Valley in 1846. In 1853, the town became the seat of the newly created Lane County. The city was incorporated in 1862, and in 1876 the University of Oregon was established.

Eugene is Oregon's third-largest city and was a major processing and shipping center for lumber until the decline of the timber industry in the 1980s. Eugene's economy struggled until the late 1990s, when recovery was in full swing.

The city now enjoys a diverse economic base, with 10,000 businesses in and around Eugene. Government, education, and health care remain the largest providers of jobs. The city's major employers include the state's two major universities—University of Oregon in Eugene and Oregon State University in Corvallis. The local economy is also considerably bolstered by many small and medium-sized businesses. Many of the leading companies in the natural and organic foods movement found their start in Eugene, including The Organically Grown Company, Nancy's Yogurt, Yogi Tea, and Emerald Valley Kitchen.

Eugene Airport, also known as Mahlon Sweet Field, is owned and operated by the City of Eugene, and is the fifth-largest airport in the Pacific Northwest. In addition to commercial flights, it also has an expanded air cargo facility to serve the growing demands of the region. Recent airport improvements include a new 6,000-foot runway and several rehabilitated taxiways, allowing two aircraft to land or take off at the same time.

The Eugene/Springfield area boasts more than 100 organizations and facilities providing performing, literary, ethnic, and visual arts activities. The state-of-the-art Hult Center is home to resident ballet, symphony, opera, and musical theater companies and also attracts top performers from around the world. There are seven area museums and over a dozen galleries featuring local, national, and international artists' work. The Science Factory Children's Museum & Planetarium is the second-largest facility of its kind in the Northwest, seating 125 under a 40-foot dome. The University of Oregon's natural history museum has been recently renovated.

Other fairs, festivals, and special events occur throughout the year, including the Lane County Fair, the Oregon Country Fair, Art and the Vineyard, the Asian Celebration, and the internationally acclaimed Oregon Bach Festival. The Lane County Ice Arena hosts world-class skaters, three Olympic Track and Field Trials, the Olympic Scientific Congress, the World Veterans' Championships, and the International Music Educator's Society.

Located in the famed South Willamette Valley wine country, Eugene is home to nine wineries and within easy reach of dozens more; there are more than 200 wineries in the Willamette Valley. The cool climate is particularly congenial to the early-ripening Pinot Noir grape, but Chardonnay and Pinot Gris are also grown here.

In addition to the University of Oregon, several colleges are located in Eugene, such as Eugene Bible College, Northwest Christian College, and Lane Community College. The city offers a wide ethnic variety of restaurants and plenty of shops, cinemas, and nightclubs.

Friendly people, scenery/terrain, and outdoor recreation as among the top reasons for Eugene's popularity. To the east of the city, the Cascade Range lures skiers to the area. Eugene is one of the few municipalities in the U.S. that does not fluoridate its water supply.

The Coast Range, west of the city, acts as a barrier to coastal fog, but active storms cross with little hindrance. To the east, the Cascade Range blocks all but the strongest continental air masses. Fire hazards occur during dry, hot summer weather. Winters days are often sunny and cool, while winter nights can be frosty. Temperatures are largely controlled by maritime air from the Pacific Ocean, so that long periods of extremely hot or cold weather are rare.

Rankings

General Rankings

- Eugene was selected as one of the best places to live in the United States by *Money* magazine. The city placed among the top 50. This year's list focused on cities built around community spirit, thoughtful policy and civic engagement. Instead of relying on a predetermined dataset, the cities and towns were grouped according to their strengths and chosen due their affordability, good schools and strong job markets. *Money, "The 50 Best Places to Live in the U.S., 2024" April 8, 2024*

- In their annual survey, Livability.com looked at data for more than 2,000 mid-sized U.S. cities to assign a "Livability Score"for each. The top 100 scoring cities make up Livability's "Top 100 Best Places to Live in the U.S." in 2025. Eugene was placed among the top 100 of the customizable list. Criteria: housing and economy; cost of living; environment; education; health care options; transportation; safety; and community amenities. *Livability.com, "Top 100 Best Places to Live in the U.S. in 2025" April 15, 2025*

Business/Finance Rankings

- The Eugene metro area appeared on the Milken Institute "2025 Best Performing Cities" list. Rank: #129 out of 200 large metro areas (based on performance category). Criteria: job growth; wage growth; high-tech growth and impact; community resilience; housing affordability; household broadband access. *Milken Institute, "Best-Performing Cities 2025," January 14, 2025*

Education Rankings

- Personal finance website *WalletHub* analyzed the 150 largest U.S. metropolitan statistical areas to determine where the most educated Americans are putting their degrees to work. Criteria: education levels; percentage of workers with degrees; education quality and attainment gap; public school quality rankings; quality and enrollment of each metro area's universities. Eugene was ranked #37 (#1 = most educated city). *WalletHub.com, "Most & Least Educated Cities in America, 2025" July 2, 2024*

Environmental Rankings

- Eugene was highlighted as one of the 25 metro areas most polluted by year-round particle pollution (Annual PM 2.5) in the U.S. during 2021 through 2023. The area ranked #4. *American Lung Association, "State of the Air 2025," April 23, 2025*

- Eugene was highlighted as one of the 25 metro areas most polluted by short-term particle pollution (24-hour PM 2.5) in the U.S. during 2021 through 2023. The area ranked #3. *American Lung Association, "State of the Air 2025," April 23, 2025*

Pet Rankings

- Eugene was selected by *Sniffspot.com* as one of the most dog-friendly cities in the U.S., ranking #13 out of 50. Criteria: dog parks; hiking; sniffspots; public parks; dog-friendly businesses; housing; dog waste cleanliness; leash laws; dog services; and overall cost. *Sniffspot.com, "The Top 50 Most Dog-Friendly Cities in the U.S.," September 30, 2024*

Real Estate Rankings

- Eugene was ranked #162 out of 176 metro areas in terms of cost of housing in 2024 by the National Association of Home Builders (#1 = most affordable). Criteria: the portion of an average family's income necessary to pay the mortgage on a median-priced home. *National Association of Home Builders®, NAHB-Wells Fargo Cost of Housing Index, 4th Quarter 2024*

Seniors/Retirement Rankings

- Eugene was identified as #16 of 20 most captivating places to retire in the U.S. by *Topretirements.com*. After consulting its visitor logs, the list primarily reflects the 20 cities that members are most interested in for retirement, based on which reviews were visited the most. *Topretirements.com, "20 Most Captivating Places to Retire for 2022," January 12, 2022*

Sports/Recreation Rankings

- Eugene was chosen as a bicycle friendly community by the League of American Bicyclists. A "Bicycle Friendly Community" welcomes cyclists by providing safe and supportive accommodation for cycling and encouraging people to bike for transportation and recreation. There are four award levels: Platinum; Gold; Silver; and Bronze. The community achieved an award level of Gold. *League of American Bicyclists, "2024 Awards-New & Renewing Bicycle Friendly Communities List," January 28, 2025*

Miscellaneous Rankings

- *MoveHub* ranked 446 hipster cities across 20 countries, using its new and improved alternative Hipster Index and Eugene came out as #12 among the top 50. Criteria: population over 150,000; number of vintage boutiques; density of tattoo parlors; vegan places to eat; coffee shops; and density of vinyl record stores. *MoveHub.com, "The Hipster Index: Brighton Pips Portland to Global Top Spot," July 28, 2021*

- *WalletHub* compared 148 of the most populated U.S. cities to determine their operating efficiency. A "Quality of Services" score was constructed for each city and then measured against the total budget per capita to reveal which were managed the best. Eugene ranked #55. Criteria: financial stability; economy; education; safety; health; infrastructure and pollution. *WalletHub.com, "2025's Best- & Worst-Run Cities in America," June 18, 2024*

Business Environment

DEMOGRAPHICS

Population Growth

Area	1990 Census	2000 Census	2010 Census	2020 Census	2023 Estimate[2]	Population Growth 1990-2023 (%)
City	118,073	137,893	156,185	176,654	177,520	50.3
MSA[1]	282,912	322,959	351,715	382,971	382,628	35.2
U.S.	248,709,873	281,421,906	308,745,538	331,449,281	332,387,540	33.6

Note: (1) Figures cover the Eugene-Springfield, OR Metropolitan Statistical Area; (2) 2019-2023 5-year ACS population estimate
Source: U.S. Census Bureau, 1990 Census, 2000 Census, 2010 Census, 2020 Census, 2019-2023 American Community Survey 5-Year Estimates

Race

Area	White Alone[2] (%)	Black Alone[2] (%)	Asian Alone[2] (%)	AIAN[3] Alone[2] (%)	NHOPI[4] Alone[2] (%)	Other Race Alone[2] (%)	Two or More Races (%)
City	78.9	1.8	3.9	0.8	0.4	3.8	10.5
MSA[1]	82.0	1.2	2.6	1.0	0.2	3.6	9.5
U.S.	63.4	12.4	5.8	0.9	0.2	6.6	10.7

Note: (1) Figures cover the Eugene-Springfield, OR Metropolitan Statistical Area; (2) Alone is defined as not being in combination with one or more other races; (3) American Indian and Alaska Native; (4) Native Hawaiian and Other Pacific Islander
Source: U.S. Census Bureau, 2019-2023 American Community Survey 5-Year Estimates

Hispanic or Latino Origin

Area	Total (%)	Mexican (%)	Puerto Rican (%)	Cuban (%)	Other (%)
City	11.4	8.0	0.4	0.2	2.8
MSA[1]	10.2	7.3	0.4	0.2	2.3
U.S.	19.0	11.3	1.8	0.7	5.2

Note: Persons of Hispanic or Latino origin can be of any race; (1) Figures cover the Eugene-Springfield, OR Metropolitan Statistical Area
Source: U.S. Census Bureau, 2019-2023 American Community Survey 5-Year Estimates

Age

Area	Percent of Population									Median Age
	Under Age 5	Age 5–19	Age 20–34	Age 35–44	Age 45–54	Age 55–64	Age 65–74	Age 75–84	Age 85+	
City	3.9	17.1	28.5	12.4	10.4	10.1	10.4	5.2	2.1	35.4
MSA[1]	4.4	16.8	22.2	12.5	11.2	12.5	12.5	5.8	2.2	40.2
U.S.	5.7	19.1	20.2	13.1	12.3	12.8	10.0	4.9	1.9	38.7

Note: (1) Figures cover the Eugene-Springfield, OR Metropolitan Statistical Area
Source: U.S. Census Bureau, 2019-2023 American Community Survey 5-Year Estimates

Disability by Age

Area	All Ages	Under 18 Years Old	18 to 64 Years Old	65 Years and Over
City	15.1	4.8	13.2	31.7
MSA[1]	17.1	6.2	15.0	33.4
U.S.	13.0	4.7	10.7	32.9

Note: Figures show percent of the civilian noninstitutionalized population that reported having a disability. Disability status is determined from six types of difficulty: vision, hearing, cognitive, ambulatory, self-care, and independent living. For children under 5 years old, hearing and vision difficulty are used to determine disability status. For children between the ages of 5 and 14, disability status is determined from hearing, vision, cognitive, ambulatory, and self-care difficulties. For people aged 15 years and older, they are considered to have a disability if they have difficulty with any one of the six difficulty types; Note: (1) Figures cover the Eugene-Springfield, OR Metropolitan Statistical Area
Source: U.S. Census Bureau, 2019-2023 American Community Survey 5-Year Estimates

Ancestry

Area	German	Irish	English	American	Italian	Polish	French[2]	European	Scottish
City	18.4	12.9	14.5	3.1	5.2	1.9	3.1	3.8	3.9
MSA[1]	18.3	13.1	14.6	3.9	4.4	1.6	3.3	3.4	3.3
U.S.	12.6	9.4	9.1	5.5	4.9	2.6	2.0	1.6	1.6

Note: Figures are the percentage of the total population reporting a particular ancestry. The nine most commonly reported ancestries in the U.S. are shown. Figures include multiple ancestries (e.g. if a person reported being Irish and Italian, they were included in both columns); (1) Figures cover the Eugene-Springfield, OR Metropolitan Statistical Area; (2) Excludes Basque
Source: U.S. Census Bureau, 2019-2023 American Community Survey 5-Year Estimates

Foreign-born Population

Area	Any Foreign Country	Asia	Mexico	Europe	Caribbean	Central America[2]	South America	Africa	Canada
City	6.8	2.7	1.5	1.2	0.1	0.4	0.2	0.4	0.3
MSA[1]	5.4	1.7	1.6	0.8	0.1	0.2	0.1	0.3	0.4
U.S.	13.9	4.3	3.3	1.4	1.4	1.2	1.2	0.8	0.2

Note: (1) Figures cover the Eugene-Springfield, OR Metropolitan Statistical Area; (2) Excludes Mexico.
Source: U.S. Census Bureau, 2019-2023 American Community Survey 5-Year Estimates

Household Size

Area	Persons in Household (%)							Average Household Size
	One	Two	Three	Four	Five	Six	Seven or More	
City	34.3	35.7	13.6	10.6	4.0	1.2	0.5	2.23
MSA[1]	29.5	38.4	14.1	10.8	4.8	1.5	0.9	2.34
U.S.	28.5	33.8	15.4	12.7	5.9	2.3	1.4	2.54

Note: (1) Figures cover the Eugene-Springfield, OR Metropolitan Statistical Area
Source: U.S. Census Bureau, 2019-2023 American Community Survey 5-Year Estimates

Household Relationships

Area	House-holder	Opposite-sex Spouse	Same-sex Spouse	Opposite-sex Unmarried Partner	Same-sex Unmarried Partner	Child[2]	Grand-child	Other Relatives	Non-relatives
City	41.6	14.7	0.3	3.8	0.3	20.7	1.1	2.7	8.3
MSA[1]	40.9	17.0	0.3	3.7	0.2	22.7	1.8	3.5	6.6
U.S.	38.3	17.5	0.2	2.5	0.2	28.3	2.4	4.8	3.4

Note: Figures are percent of the total population; (1) Figures cover the Eugene-Springfield, OR Metropolitan Statistical Area; (2) Includes biological, adopted, and stepchildren of the householder
Source: U.S. Census Bureau, 2020 Census

Gender

Area	Males	Females	Males per 100 Females
City	87,095	90,425	96.3
MSA[1]	189,067	193,561	97.7
U.S.	164,545,087	167,842,453	98.0

Note: (1) Figures cover the Eugene-Springfield, OR Metropolitan Statistical Area
Source: U.S. Census Bureau, 2019-2023 American Community Survey 5-Year Estimates

Marital Status

Area	Never Married	Now Married[2]	Separated	Widowed	Divorced
City	44.6	37.5	1.3	4.2	12.4
MSA[1]	35.8	44.3	1.3	5.4	13.2
U.S.	34.1	47.9	1.7	5.6	10.7

Note: Figures are percentages and cover the population 15 years of age and older; (1) Figures cover the Eugene-Springfield, OR Metropolitan Statistical Area; (2) Excludes separated
Source: U.S. Census Bureau, 2019-2023 American Community Survey 5-Year Estimates

Religious Groups by Family

Area	Catholic	Baptist	Methodist	LDS[2]	Pentecostal	Lutheran	Islam	Adventist	Other
MSA[1]	5.6	0.7	0.5	2.8	2.5	0.8	<0.1	2.0	9.0
U.S.	18.7	7.3	3.0	2.0	1.8	1.7	1.3	1.3	11.6

Note: Figures are the number of adherents as a percentage of the total population and cover the eight largest religious groups in the U.S; (1) Figures cover the Eugene-Springfield, OR Metropolitan Statistical Area; (2) Church of Jesus Christ of Latter-day Saints
Sources: 2020 U.S. Religion Census, Association of Statisticians of American Religious Bodies; The Association of Religion Data Archives (ARDA)

Religious Groups by Tradition

Area	Catholic	Evangelical Protestant	Mainline Protestant	Black Protestant	Islam	Judaism	Hinduism	Orthodox	Buddhism
MSA[1]	5.6	10.3	2.3	0.1	<0.1	0.4	0.3	0.1	0.5
U.S.	18.7	16.5	5.2	2.3	1.3	0.6	0.4	0.4	0.3

Note: Figures are the number of adherents as a percentage of the total population; (1) Figures cover the Eugene-Springfield, OR Metropolitan Statistical Area
Sources: 2020 U.S. Religion Census, Association of Statisticians of American Religious Bodies; The Association of Religion Data Archives (ARDA)

ECONOMY

Real Gross Domestic Product (GDP)

Area	2017	2018	2019	2020	2021	2022	2023	Rank[3]
MSA[1]	15.9	16.3	16.4	16.3	17.4	17.7	18.1	157
U.S.[2]	17,619.1	18,160.7	18,642.5	18,238.9	19,387.6	19,896.6	20,436.3	–

Note: Figures are in billions of chained 2017 dollars; (1) Figures cover the Eugene-Springfield, OR Metropolitan Statistical Area; (2) Figures cover real GDP within metropolitan areas; (3) Rank is based on 2023 data and ranges from 1 to 384
Source: U.S. Bureau of Economic Analysis

Economic Growth

Area	2014	2015	2016	2017	2018	2019	2020	2021	2022	2023
MSA[1]	1.5	5.0	3.0	3.8	2.7	0.4	-0.7	7.0	1.9	2.3
U.S.[2]	2.6	3.2	2.0	2.7	3.1	2.7	-2.2	6.3	2.6	2.7

Note: Figures are real gross domestic product growth rates and represent percent change from preceding period; (1) Figures cover the Eugene-Springfield, OR Metropolitan Statistical Area; (2) Figures are the average growth rates within metropolitan areas
Source: U.S. Bureau of Economic Analysis

Metropolitan Area Exports

Area	2018	2019	2020	2021	2022	2023	Rank[2]
MSA[1]	400.1	360.0	340.6	426.7	434.9	415.2	241
U.S.	1,664,056.1	1,645,173.7	1,431,406.6	1,753,941.4	2,062,937.4	2,019,160.5	–

Note: Figures are in millions of dollars; (1) Figures cover the Eugene-Springfield, OR Metropolitan Statistical Area; (2) Rank is based on 2023 data and ranges from 1 to 386
Source: U.S. Department of Commerce, International Trade Administration, Office of Trade and Economic Analysis, Industry and Analysis, Exports by Metropolitan Area, data extracted April 2, 2025

Building Permits

Area	Single-Family			Multi-Family			Total		
	2023	2024	Pct. Chg.	2023	2024	Pct. Chg.	2023	2024	Pct. Chg.
City	171	309	80.7	422	693	64.2	593	1,002	69.0
MSA[1]	732	799	9.2	507	1,015	100.2	1,239	1,814	46.4
U.S.	920,000	981,900	6.7	591,100	496,100	-16.1	1,511,100	1,478,000	-2.2

Note: (1) Figures cover the Eugene-Springfield, OR Metropolitan Statistical Area; Figures represent new, privately-owned housing units authorized (unadjusted data)
Source: U.S. Census Bureau, Building Permits Survey (BPS), 2023, 2024

Bankruptcy Filings

Area	Business Filings			Nonbusiness Filings		
	2023	2024	% Chg.	2023	2024	% Chg.
Lane County	12	18	50.0	535	707	32.1
U.S.	18,926	23,107	22.1	434,064	494,201	13.9

Note: Business filings include Chapter 7, Chapter 9, Chapter 11, Chapter 12, Chapter 13, Chapter 15, and Section 304; Nonbusiness filings include Chapter 7, Chapter 11, and Chapter 13
Source: Administrative Office of the U.S. Courts, Business and Nonbusiness Bankruptcy, County Cases Commenced by Chapter of the Bankruptcy Code, During the 12-Month Period Ending December 31, 2023 and Business and Nonbusiness Bankruptcy, County Cases Commenced by Chapter of the Bankruptcy Code, During the 12-Month Period Ending December 31, 2024

Housing Vacancy Rates

Area	Gross Vacancy Rate[3] (%)			Year-Round Vacancy Rate[4] (%)			Rental Vacancy Rate[5] (%)			Homeowner Vacancy Rate[6] (%)		
	2022	2023	2024	2022	2023	2024	2022	2023	2024	2022	2023	2024
MSA[1]	n/a	n/a	n/a	n/a	n/a	n/a	n/a	n/a	n/a	n/a	n/a	n/a
U.S.[2]	9.1	9.0	9.1	7.5	7.5	7.6	5.7	6.5	6.8	0.8	0.8	1.0

Note: (1) Figures cover the Eugene-Springfield, OR Metropolitan Statistical Area; (2) Figures cover the 75 largest Metropolitan Statistical Areas; (3) The percentage of the total housing inventory that is vacant; (4) The percentage of the housing inventory (excluding seasonal units) that is year-round vacant; (5) The percentage of rental inventory that is vacant for rent; (6) The percentage of homeowner inventory that is vacant for sale; n/a not available
Source: U.S. Census Bureau, Housing Vacancies and Homeownership Annual Statistics: 2022, 2023, 2024

INCOME

Income

Area	Per Capita ($)	Median Household ($)	Average Household ($)
City	41,035	63,836	94,063
MSA[1]	38,563	69,311	91,348
U.S.	43,289	78,538	110,491

Note: (1) Figures cover the Eugene-Springfield, OR Metropolitan Statistical Area
Source: U.S. Census Bureau, 2019-2023 American Community Survey 5-Year Estimates

Household Income Distribution

| Area | Percent of Households Earning | | | | | | | |
	Under $15,000	$15,000 -$24,999	$25,000 -$34,999	$35,000 -$49,999	$50,000 -$74,999	$75,000 -$99,999	$100,000 -$149,999	$150,000 and up
City	11.3	7.8	7.6	13.2	15.5	12.5	15.8	16.3
MSA[1]	10.0	7.3	7.5	12.5	16.2	14.2	17.8	14.6
U.S.	8.5	6.6	6.8	10.4	15.7	12.7	17.4	21.9

Note: (1) Figures cover the Eugene-Springfield, OR Metropolitan Statistical Area
Source: U.S. Census Bureau, 2019-2023 American Community Survey 5-Year Estimates

Poverty Rate

Area	All Ages	Under 18 Years Old	18 to 64 Years Old	65 Years and Over
City	18.2	15.1	21.4	9.4
MSA[1]	15.3	14.3	17.4	9.7
U.S.	12.4	16.3	11.6	10.4

Note: Figures are percentage of people whose income during the past 12 months was below the poverty level;
(1) Figures cover the Eugene-Springfield, OR Metropolitan Statistical Area
Source: U.S. Census Bureau, 2019-2023 American Community Survey 5-Year Estimates

EMPLOYMENT

Labor Force and Employment

| Area | Civilian Labor Force | | | Workers Employed | | |
	Dec. 2023	Dec. 2024	% Chg.	Dec. 2023	Dec. 2024	% Chg.
City	86,438	87,547	1.3	82,952	83,877	1.1
MSA[1]	184,890	187,239	1.3	177,117	179,091	1.1
U.S.	166,661,000	167,746,000	0.7	160,754,000	161,294,000	0.3

Note: Data is not seasonally adjusted and covers workers 16 years of age and older; (1) Figures cover the
Eugene-Springfield, OR Metropolitan Statistical Area
Source: Bureau of Labor Statistics, Local Area Unemployment Statistics

Unemployment Rate

| Area | 2024 | | | | | | | | | | | |
	Jan.	Feb.	Mar.	Apr.	May	Jun.	Jul.	Aug.	Sep.	Oct.	Nov.	Dec.
City	4.6	4.5	4.2	3.6	3.6	4.1	4.5	4.4	4.0	3.9	3.8	4.2
MSA[1]	4.9	4.7	4.4	3.8	3.8	4.2	4.7	4.6	4.1	4.1	4.1	4.4
U.S.	4.1	4.2	3.9	3.5	3.7	4.3	4.5	4.4	3.9	3.9	4.0	3.8

Note: Data is not seasonally adjusted and covers workers 16 years of age and older; (1) Figures cover the
Eugene-Springfield, OR Metropolitan Statistical Area
Source: Bureau of Labor Statistics, Local Area Unemployment Statistics

Average Wages

Occupation	$/Hr.	Occupation	$/Hr.
Accountants and Auditors	40.17	Maintenance and Repair Workers	24.77
Automotive Mechanics	26.31	Marketing Managers	64.41
Bookkeepers	23.97	Network and Computer Systems Admin.	45.54
Carpenters	29.35	Nurses, Licensed Practical	35.15
Cashiers	16.41	Nurses, Registered	54.25
Computer Programmers	44.82	Nursing Assistants	23.01
Computer Systems Analysts	51.80	Office Clerks, General	22.54
Computer User Support Specialists	30.29	Physical Therapists	47.48
Construction Laborers	24.26	Physicians	165.85
Cooks, Restaurant	18.28	Plumbers, Pipefitters and Steamfitters	40.25
Customer Service Representatives	21.66	Police and Sheriff's Patrol Officers	42.81
Dentists	107.76	Postal Service Mail Carriers	27.06
Electricians	40.45	Real Estate Sales Agents	26.12
Engineers, Electrical	54.89	Retail Salespersons	18.58
Fast Food and Counter Workers	16.00	Sales Representatives, Technical/Scientific	52.14
Financial Managers	72.01	Secretaries, Exc. Legal/Medical/Executive	23.51
First-Line Supervisors of Office Workers	33.88	Security Guards	19.91
General and Operations Managers	52.88	Surgeons	186.25
Hairdressers/Cosmetologists	21.53	Teacher Assistants, Exc. Postsecondary[1]	18.52
Home Health and Personal Care Aides	19.39	Teachers, Secondary School, Exc. Sp. Ed.[1]	38.08
Janitors and Cleaners	18.09	Telemarketers	n/a
Landscaping/Groundskeeping Workers	19.74	Truck Drivers, Heavy/Tractor-Trailer	28.02
Lawyers	68.79	Truck Drivers, Light/Delivery Services	23.03
Maids and Housekeeping Cleaners	17.08	Waiters and Waitresses	18.82

Note: Wage data covers the Eugene-Springfield, OR Metropolitan Statistical Area; (1) Hourly wages were
calculated from annual wage data based on a 40 hour work week
Source: Bureau of Labor Statistics, Metro Area Occupational Employment & Wage Estimates, May 2024

Employment by Industry

Sector	MSA[1]		U.S.
	Number of Employees	Percent of Total	Percent of Total
Construction	7,400	4.4	5.1
Financial Activities	8,700	5.2	5.8
Government	33,000	19.8	14.9
Information	2,000	1.2	1.9
Leisure and Hospitality	16,800	10.1	10.4
Manufacturing	14,100	8.5	8.0
Mining and Logging	1,000	0.6	0.4
Other Services	5,100	3.1	3.7
Private Education and Health Services	31,000	18.6	16.9
Professional and Business Services	18,100	10.9	14.2
Retail Trade	19,400	11.7	10.0
Transportation, Warehousing, and Utilities	3,900	2.3	4.8
Wholesale Trade	5,900	3.5	3.9

Note: Figures are non-farm employment as of December 2024. Figures are not seasonally adjusted and include workers 16 years of age and older; (1) Figures cover the Eugene-Springfield, OR Metropolitan Statistical Area
Source: Bureau of Labor Statistics, Current Employment Statistics, Employment, Hours, and Earnings

Employment by Occupation

Occupation Classification	City (%)	MSA[1] (%)	U.S. (%)
Management, Business, Science, and Arts	45.0	39.1	42.0
Natural Resources, Construction, and Maintenance	5.5	8.8	8.6
Production, Transportation, and Material Moving	10.9	12.4	13.0
Sales and Office	20.0	20.7	19.9
Service	18.6	18.9	16.5

Note: Figures cover employed civilians 16 years of age and older; (1) Figures cover the Eugene-Springfield, OR Metropolitan Statistical Area
Source: U.S. Census Bureau, 2019-2023 American Community Survey 5-Year Estimates

Occupations with Greatest Projected Employment Growth: 2022 – 2032

Occupation[1]	2022 Employment	2032 Projected Employment	Numeric Employment Change	Percent Employment Change
Home Health and Personal Care Aides	36,900	46,170	9,270	25.1
Fast Food and Counter Workers	61,880	70,300	8,420	13.6
Software Developers	20,630	26,850	6,220	30.2
General and Operations Managers	44,700	50,550	5,850	13.1
Cooks, Restaurant	20,480	25,960	5,480	26.8
Stockers and Order Fillers	44,430	49,500	5,070	11.4
Registered Nurses	42,720	47,680	4,960	11.6
Laborers and Freight, Stock, and Material Movers, Hand	25,990	29,120	3,130	12.0
Personal Care and Service Workers, All Other	21,590	24,720	3,130	14.5
Construction Laborers	18,310	21,420	3,110	17.0

Note: Projections cover Oregon; (1) Sorted by numeric employment change
Source: www.projectionscentral.org, State Occupational Projections, 2022–2032 Long-Term Projections

Fastest-Growing Occupations: 2022 – 2032

Occupation[1]	2022 Employment	2032 Projected Employment	Numeric Employment Change	Percent Employment Change
Nurse Practitioners	2,240	3,420	1,180	52.7
Physical Therapist Assistants	840	1,160	320	38.1
Data Scientists	1,420	1,960	540	38.0
Curators	190	260	70	36.8
Information Security Analysts (SOC 2018)	1,390	1,900	510	36.7
Physician Assistants	1,420	1,930	510	35.9
Medical and Health Services Managers	5,080	6,880	1,800	35.4
Wind Turbine Service Technicians	290	390	100	34.5
Solar Photovoltaic Installers	350	470	120	34.3
Statisticians	570	760	190	33.3

Note: Projections cover Oregon; (1) Sorted by percent employment change and excludes occupations with numeric employment change less than 50
Source: www.projectionscentral.org, State Occupational Projections, 2022–2032 Long-Term Projections

CITY FINANCES

City Government Finances

Component	2022 ($000)	2022 ($ per capita)
Total Revenues	720,038	4,156
Total Expenditures	719,521	4,153
Debt Outstanding	336,845	1,944

Source: U.S. Census Bureau, State & Local Government Finances 2022

City Government Revenue by Source

Source	2022 ($000)	2022 ($ per capita)	2022 (%)
General Revenue			
From Federal Government	38,350	221	5.3
From State Government	27,268	157	3.8
From Local Governments	21,426	124	3.0
Taxes			
Property	143,091	826	19.9
Sales and Gross Receipts	20,132	116	2.8
Personal Income	0	0	0.0
Corporate Income	0	0	0.0
Motor Vehicle License	0	0	0.0
Other Taxes	30,922	178	4.3
Current Charges	118,149	682	16.4
Liquor Store	0	0	0.0
Utility	299,863	1,731	41.6

Source: U.S. Census Bureau, State & Local Government Finances 2022

City Government Expenditures by Function

Function	2022 ($000)	2022 ($ per capita)	2022 (%)
General Direct Expenditures			
Air Transportation	24,865	143	3.5
Corrections	0	0	0.0
Education	0	0	0.0
Employment Security Administration	0	0	0.0
Financial Administration	5,355	30	0.7
Fire Protection	49,471	285	6.9
General Public Buildings	54,092	312	7.5
Governmental Administration, Other	16,916	97	2.4
Health	0	0	0.0
Highways	8,003	46	1.1
Hospitals	0	0	0.0
Housing and Community Development	26,874	155	3.7
Interest on General Debt	1,373	7	0.2
Judicial and Legal	6,945	40	1.0
Libraries	14,322	82	2.0
Parking	5,120	29	0.7
Parks and Recreation	40,299	232	5.6
Police Protection	67,134	387	9.3
Public Welfare	0	0	0.0
Sewerage	42,617	246	5.9
Solid Waste Management	2,682	15	0.4
Veterans' Services	0	0	0.0
Liquor Store	0	0	0.0
Utility	325,543	1,879	45.2

Source: U.S. Census Bureau, State & Local Government Finances 2022

TAXES

State Corporate Income Tax Rates

State	Tax Rate (%)	Income Brackets ($)	Num. of Brackets	Financial Institution Tax Rate (%)[a]	Federal Income Tax Ded.
Oregon	6.6 - 7.6 (s)	1 million	2	6.6 - 7.6 (s)	No

Note: Tax rates for tax year 2024; (a) Rates listed are the corporate income tax rate applied to financial institutions or excise taxes based on income. Some states have other taxes based upon the value of deposits or shares; (s) Oregon's minimum tax for C corporations depends on the Oregon sales of the filing group. The minimum tax ranges from $150 for corporations with sales under $500,000, up to $100,000 for companies with sales of $100 million or above. Oregon also imposes Corporate Activity Tax [CAT] of $250 plus 0.57% of activity in excess of $1 million.
Source: Federation of Tax Administrators, State Corporate Income Tax Rates, January 1, 2025

State Individual Income Tax Rates

State	Tax Rate (%)	Income Brackets ($)	Personal Exemptions ($)			Standard Ded. ($)	
			Single	Married	Depend.	Single	Married
Oregon (a)	4.75 - 9.9	4,050 -125,000 (b)	236	472	236 (c)	2,745	5,495

Note: Tax rates for tax year 2024; Local- and county-level taxes are not included; The deduction for federal SALT deductions is limited to $5,000 for individuals and $10,000 for joint returns in Missouri and Montana, and to $7,800 for all filers in Oregon; (a) 16 states have statutory provision for automatically adjusting to the rate of inflation the dollar values of the income tax brackets, standard deductions, and/or personal exemptions. Oregon does not index the income brackets for $125,000 and over See: INFL and SPEC above; (b) For joint returns, taxes are twice the tax on half the couple's income. California brackets violate this formula at the two highest tax brackets in 2024; (c) The personal exemption takes the form of a tax credit instead of a deduction
Source: Federation of Tax Administrators, State Individual Income Tax Rates, January 1, 2025

Various State Sales and Excise Tax Rates

State	State Sales Tax (%)	Gasoline[1] ($/gal.)	Cigarette[2] ($/pack)	Spirits[3] ($/gal.)	Wine[4] ($/gal.)	Beer[5] ($/gal.)	Recreational Marijuana (%)
Oregon	None	0.40	3.33	22.86	0.67	0.08	(t)

Note: All tax rates as of January 1, 2025; (1) The American Petroleum Institute has developed a methodology for determining the average tax rate on a gallon of fuel. Rates may include any of the following: excise taxes, environmental fees, storage tank fees, other fees or taxes, general sales tax, and local taxes; (2) The federal excise tax of $1.0066 per pack and local taxes are not included; (3) Rates are those applicable to off-premise sales of 40% alcohol by volume (a.b.v.) distilled spirits in 750ml containers. Local excise taxes are excluded; (4) Rates are those applicable to off-premise sales of 11% a.b.v. non-carbonated wine in 750ml containers; (5) Rates are those applicable to off-premise sales of 4.7% a.b.v. beer in 12 ounce containers; (t) 17% excise tax (retail price)
Source: Tax Foundation, 2025 Facts & Figures: How Does Your State Compare?

State Tax Competitiveness Index

State	Overall Rank	Corporate Tax Rank	Individual Income Tax Rank	Sales Tax Rank	Property Tax Rank	Unemployment Insurance Tax Rank
Oregon	30	49	40	4	31	41

Note: The Tax Foundation's State Tax Competitiveness Index enables policymakers, taxpayers, and business leaders to gauge how their states' tax systems compare. A rank of 1 is best, 50 is worst. Rankings do not average to the total. States without a tax rank equally as 1. DC's scores and rankings do not affect other states. The report shows tax systems as of July 1, 2024 (the beginning of Fiscal Year 2025).
Source: Tax Foundation, State Tax Competitiveness Index 2025

TRANSPORTATION

Means of Transportation to Work

Area	Car/Truck/Van		Public Transportation			Bicycle	Walked	Other Means	Worked at Home
	Drove Alone	Car-pooled	Bus	Subway	Railroad				
City	63.0	7.9	2.6	0.0	0.0	4.7	5.3	1.1	15.3
MSA[1]	67.4	8.9	1.9	0.0	0.0	2.8	4.1	1.1	13.9
U.S.	70.2	8.5	1.7	1.3	0.4	2.8	2.4	1.6	13.5

Note: Figures are percentages and cover workers 16 years of age and older; (1) Figures cover the Eugene-Springfield, OR Metropolitan Statistical Area
Source: U.S. Census Bureau, 2019-2023 American Community Survey 5-Year Estimates

Travel Time to Work

Area	Less Than 10 Minutes	10 to 19 Minutes	20 to 29 Minutes	30 to 44 Minutes	45 to 59 Minutes	60 to 89 Minutes	90 Minutes or More
City	16.3	50.9	19.5	7.2	2.2	2.1	1.9
MSA[1]	16.0	43.1	21.9	11.6	3.0	2.6	1.8
U.S.	12.6	28.6	21.2	20.8	8.1	6.0	2.8

Note: Note: Figures are percentages and include workers 16 years old and over; (1) Figures cover the Eugene-Springfield, OR Metropolitan Statistical Area
Source: U.S. Census Bureau, 2019-2023 American Community Survey 5-Year Estimates

Key Congestion Measures

Measure	2000	2010	2015	2020	2022
Annual Hours of Delay, Total (000)	4,041	5,246	6,281	3,172	7,326
Annual Hours of Delay, Per Auto Commuter	30	33	39	19	44
Annual Congestion Cost, Per Auto Commuter ($)	691	718	794	415	945

Note: Figures cover the Eugene OR urban area
Source: Texas A&M Transportation Institute, 2023 Urban Mobility Report

Freeway Travel Time Index

Measure	1985	1990	1995	2000	2005	2010	2015	2020	2022
Urban Area Index[1]	1.05	1.10	1.13	1.16	1.17	1.17	1.17	1.07	1.14
Urban Area Rank[1,2]	64	47	47	43	49	41	46	57	64

Note: Freeway Travel Time Index—the ratio of travel time in the peak period to the travel time at free-flow conditions. For example, a value of 1.30 indicates a 20-minute free-flow trip takes 26 minutes in the peak (20 minutes x 1.30 = 26 minutes); (1) Covers the Eugene OR urban area; (2) Rank is based on 101 larger urban areas (#1 = highest travel time index)
Source: Texas A&M Transportation Institute, 2023 Urban Mobility Report

Public Transportation

Agency Name / Mode of Transportation	Vehicles Operated in Maximum Service[1]	Annual Unlinked Passenger Trips[2] (in thous.)	Annual Passenger Miles[3] (in thous.)
Lane Transit District (LTD)			
Bus (directly operated)	57	3,405.7	12,630.1
Bus (purchased transportation)	2	13.1	324.2
Bus Rapid Transit (directly operated)	13	2,554.3	6,305.0
Demand Response (purchased transportation)	21	95.2	622.6
Demand Response - Taxi	34	233.5	2,407.9
Vanpool (purchased transportation)	5	9.9	490.1

Note: (1) Number of revenue vehicles operated by the given mode and type of service to meet the annual maximum service requirement. This is the revenue vehicle count during the peak season of the year; on the week and day that maximum service is provided. Vehicles operated in maximum service (VOMS) exclude atypical days and one-time special events; (2) Number of passengers who boarded public transportation vehicles. Passengers are counted each time they board a vehicle no matter how many vehicles they use to travel from their origin to their destination. (3) Sum of the distances ridden by all passengers during the entire fiscal year.
Source: Federal Transit Administration, National Transit Database, 2023

Air Transportation

Airport Name and Code / Type of Service	Passenger Airlines[1]	Passenger Enplanements	Freight Carriers[2]	Freight (lbs)
Mahlon Sweet Field (EUG)				
Domestic service (U.S. carriers only)	20	824,632	7	1,005,264
International service (U.S. carriers only)	0	0	0	0

Note: (1) Includes all U.S.-based major, minor and commuter airlines that carried at least one passenger during the year; (2) Includes all U.S.-based airlines and freight carriers that transported at least one pound of freight during the year.
Source: Bureau of Transportation Statistics, The Intermodal Transportation Database, Air Carriers: T-100 Domestic Market (U.S. carriers only), 2024; Bureau of Transportation Statistics, The Intermodal Transportation Database, Air Carriers: T-100 International Market (U.S. carriers only), 2024

BUSINESSES

Major Business Headquarters

Company Name	Industry	Rankings Fortune[1]	Forbes[2]
No companies listed	-	-	-

Note: (1) Companies that produce a 10-K are ranked 1 to 500 based on 2023 revenue; (2) All private companies with at least $2 billion in annual revenue through the end of their most current fiscal year are ranked 1 to 275; companies listed are headquartered in the city; dashes indicate no ranking
Source: Fortune, "Fortune 500," 2024; Forbes, "America's Largest Private Companies," 2024

Living Environment

COST OF LIVING

Cost of Living Index

Composite Index	Groceries	Housing	Utilities	Trans-portation	Health Care	Misc. Goods/ Services
107.3	105.2	120.6	92.5	110.3	108.2	100.0

Note: The Cost of Living Index measures regional differences in the cost of consumer goods and services, excluding taxes and non-consumer expenditures, for professional and managerial households in the top income quintile. It is based on more than 50,000 prices covering almost 60 different items for which prices are collected three times a year by chambers of commerce, economic development organizations or university applied economic centers in each participating urban area. The numbers shown should be read as a percentage above or below the national average of 100. For example, a value of 115.4 in the groceries column indicates that grocery prices are 15.4% higher than the national average. Small differences in the index numbers should not be interpreted as significant; Figures cover the Eugene OR urban area.
Source: The Council for Community and Economic Research, Cost of Living Index, 2024

Grocery Prices

Area[1]	T-Bone Steak ($/pound)	Frying Chicken ($/pound)	Whole Milk ($/half gal.)	Eggs ($/dozen)	Orange Juice ($/64 oz.)	Coffee ($/11.5 oz.)
City[2]	15.53	1.92	4.92	3.47	4.49	6.40
Avg.	15.42	1.55	4.69	3.25	4.41	5.46
Min.	14.50	1.16	4.43	2.75	4.00	4.85
Max.	17.56	2.89	5.49	4.78	5.54	7.89

Note: (1) Values for the local area are compared with the average, minimum and maximum values for all 276 areas in the Cost of Living Index; (2) Figures cover the Eugene OR urban area; **T-Bone Steak** (price per pound); **Frying Chicken** (price per pound, whole fryer); **Whole Milk** (half gallon carton); **Eggs** (price per dozen, Grade A, large); **Orange Juice** (64 oz. Tropicana or Florida Natural); **Coffee** (11.5 oz. can, vacuum-packed, Maxwell House, Hills Bros, or Folgers).
Source: The Council for Community and Economic Research, Cost of Living Index, 2024

Housing and Utility Costs

Area[1]	New Home Price ($)	Apartment Rent ($/month)	All Electric ($/month)	Part Electric ($/month)	Other Energy ($/month)	Telephone ($/month)
City[2]	666,539	1,654	-	89.38	96.37	187.81
Avg.	515,975	1,550	210.99	123.07	82.07	194.99
Min.	265,375	692	104.33	53.68	36.26	179.42
Max.	2,775,821	5,719	529.02	397.28	361.63	223.33

Note: (1) Values for the local area are compared with the average, minimum and maximum values for all 276 areas in the Cost of Living Index; (2) Figures cover the Eugene OR urban area; **New Home Price** (2,400 sf living area, 8,000 sf lot, in urban area with full utilities); **Apartment Rent** (950 sf 2 bedroom/1.5 or 2 bath, unfurnished, excluding all utilities except water); **All Electric** (average monthly cost for an all-electric home); **Part Electric** (average monthly cost for a part-electric home); **Other Energy** (average monthly cost for natural gas, fuel oil, coal, wood, and any other forms of energy except electricity); **Telephone** (price includes the base monthly rate plus taxes and fees for three lines of mobile phone service).
Source: The Council for Community and Economic Research, Cost of Living Index, 2024

Health Care, Transportation, and Other Costs

Area[1]	Doctor ($/visit)	Dentist ($/visit)	Optometrist ($/visit)	Gasoline ($/gallon)	Beauty Salon ($/visit)	Men's Shirt ($)
City[2]	196.75	117.67	126.00	3.83	40.19	36.32
Avg.	143.77	117.51	129.23	3.32	48.57	38.14
Min.	36.74	58.67	67.33	2.80	24.00	13.41
Max.	270.44	216.82	307.33	5.28	94.00	63.89

Note: (1) Values for the local area are compared with the average, minimum and maximum values for all 276 areas in the Cost of Living Index; (2) Figures cover the Eugene OR urban area; **Doctor** (general practitioners routine exam of an established patient); **Dentist** (adult teeth cleaning and periodic oral examination); **Optometrist** (full vision eye exam for established adult patient); **Gasoline** (one gallon regular unleaded, national brand, including all taxes, cash price at self-service pump if available); **Beauty Salon** (woman's shampoo, trim, and blow-dry); **Men's Shirt** (cotton/polyester dress shirt, pinpoint weave, long sleeves).
Source: The Council for Community and Economic Research, Cost of Living Index, 2024

HOUSING

Homeownership Rate

Area	2017 (%)	2018 (%)	2019 (%)	2020 (%)	2021 (%)	2022 (%)	2023 (%)	2024 (%)
MSA[1]	n/a	n/a	n/a	n/a	n/a	n/a	n/a	n/a
U.S.	63.9	64.4	64.6	66.6	65.5	65.8	65.9	65.6

Note: (1) Figures cover the Eugene-Springfield, OR Metropolitan Statistical Area; n/a not available
Source: U.S. Census Bureau, Housing Vacancies and Homeownership Annual Statistics: 2017-2024

House Price Index (HPI)

Area	National Ranking[2]	Quarterly Change (%)	One-Year Change (%)	Five-Year Change (%)	Since 1991Q1 (%)
MSA[1]	220	-1.37	2.45	48.27	459.38
U.S.[3]	–	1.43	4.51	57.13	327.82

Note: The HPI is a weighted repeat sales index. It measures average price changes in repeat sales or refinancings on the same properties. This information is obtained by reviewing repeat mortgage transactions on single-family properties whose mortgages have been purchased or securitized by Fannie Mae or Freddie Mac since January 1975; (1) Figures cover the Eugene, OR Metropolitan Statistical Area; (2) Rankings are based on annual percentage change for all metro areas containing at least 15,000 transactions over the last 10 years and ranges from 1 to 241; (3) figures based on a weighted average of Census Division estimates using a seasonally adjusted, purchase-only index; all figures are for the period ending December 31, 2024
Source: Federal Housing Finance Agency, Change in FHFA Metropolitan Area House Price Indexes, All Transactions Index, 2024Q4

Home Value

Area	Under $100,000	$100,000 -$199,999	$200,000 -$299,999	$300,000 -$399,999	$400,000 -$499,999	$500,000 -$999,999	$1,000,000 or more	Median ($)
City	6.5	3.0	11.6	20.1	24.6	31.0	3.0	435,400
MSA[1]	7.7	4.1	16.6	22.5	19.7	25.8	3.5	395,800
U.S.	12.1	17.8	19.5	14.4	10.5	19.1	6.5	303,400

Note: Figures are percentages except for median and cover owner-occupied housing units; (1) Figures cover the Eugene-Springfield, OR Metropolitan Statistical Area
Source: U.S. Census Bureau, 2019-2023 American Community Survey 5-Year Estimates

Year Housing Structure Built

Area	2020 or Later	2010 -2019	2000 -2009	1990 -1999	1980 -1989	1970 -1979	1960 -1969	1950 -1959	1940 -1949	Before 1940	Median Year
City	0.7	10.2	13.3	15.0	9.2	19.9	11.7	8.5	5.5	6.0	1979
MSA[1]	0.8	7.5	12.2	14.5	9.1	21.0	13.2	8.5	6.7	6.4	1977
U.S.	1.2	8.9	13.6	12.8	13.0	14.4	10.0	9.7	4.5	11.9	1980

Note: Figures are percentages except for Median Year; Note: (1) Figures cover the Eugene-Springfield, OR Metropolitan Statistical Area
Source: U.S. Census Bureau, 2019-2023 American Community Survey 5-Year Estimates

Gross Monthly Rent

Area	Under $500	$500 -$999	$1,000 -$1,499	$1,500 -$1,999	$2,000 -$2,499	$2,500 -$2,999	$3,000 and up	Median ($)
City	4.5	22.0	34.3	25.4	8.7	2.5	2.6	1,347
MSA[1]	5.4	23.6	36.5	23.0	7.6	1.9	1.9	1,287
U.S.	6.5	22.3	29.5	20.2	10.8	4.8	5.9	1,348

Note: Figures are percentages except for median; Gross rent is the contract rent plus the estimated average monthly cost of utilities (electricity, gas, and water and sewer) and fuels (oil, coal, kerosene, wood, etc.) if these are paid by the renter (or paid for the renter by someone else); (1) Figures cover the Eugene-Springfield, OR Metropolitan Statistical Area
Source: U.S. Census Bureau, 2019-2023 American Community Survey 5-Year Estimates

HEALTH

Health Risk Factors

Category	MSA[1] (%)	U.S. (%)
Adults aged 18–64 who have any kind of health care coverage	n/a	90.8
Adults who reported being in good or better health	n/a	81.8
Adults who have been told they have high blood cholesterol	n/a	36.9
Adults who have been told they have high blood pressure	n/a	34.0
Adults who are current smokers	n/a	12.1
Adults who currently use e-cigarettes	n/a	7.7
Adults who currently use chewing tobacco, snuff, or snus	n/a	3.2
Adults who are heavy drinkers[2]	n/a	6.1
Adults who are binge drinkers[3]	n/a	15.2
Adults who are overweight (BMI 25.0 - 29.9)	n/a	34.4
Adults who are obese (BMI 30.0 - 99.8)	n/a	34.3
Adults who participated in any physical activities in the past month	n/a	75.8

Note: All figures are crude prevalence; (1) Figures for the Eugene-Springfield, OR Metropolitan Statistical Area were not available.
(2) Heavy drinkers are classified as adult men having more than 14 drinks per week and adult women having more than 7 drinks per week; (3) Binge drinkers are classified as males having five or more drinks on one occasion or females having four or more drinks on one occasion
Source: Centers for Disease Control and Prevention, Behaviorial Risk Factor Surveillance System, SMART: Selected Metropolitan Area Risk Trends, 2023

Acute and Chronic Health Conditions

Category	MSA[1] (%)	U.S. (%)
Adults who have ever been told they had a heart attack	n/a	4.2
Adults who have ever been told they have angina or coronary heart disease	n/a	4.0
Adults who have ever been told they had a stroke	n/a	3.3
Adults who have ever been told they have asthma	n/a	15.7
Adults who have ever been told they have arthritis	n/a	26.3
Adults who have ever been told they have diabetes[2]	n/a	11.5
Adults who have ever been told they had skin cancer	n/a	5.6
Adults who have ever been told they had any other types of cancer	n/a	8.4
Adults who have ever been told they have COPD	n/a	6.4
Adults who have ever been told they have kidney disease	n/a	3.7
Adults who have ever been told they have a form of depression	n/a	22.0

Note: All figures are crude prevalence; (1) Figures for the Eugene-Springfield, OR Metropolitan Statistical Area were not available.
(2) Figures do not include pregnancy-related, borderline, or pre-diabetes
Source: Centers for Disease Control and Prevention, Behaviorial Risk Factor Surveillance System, SMART: Selected Metropolitan Area Risk Trends, 2023

Health Screening and Vaccination Rates

Category	MSA[1] (%)	U.S. (%)
Adults who have ever been tested for HIV	n/a	37.5
Adults who have had their blood cholesterol checked within the last five years	n/a	87.0
Adults aged 65+ who have had flu shot within the past year	n/a	63.4
Adults aged 65+ who have ever had a pneumonia vaccination	n/a	71.9

Note: All figures are crude prevalence; (1) Figures for the Eugene-Springfield, OR Metropolitan Statistical Area were not available.
Source: Centers for Disease Control and Prevention, Behaviorial Risk Factor Surveillance System, SMART: Selected Metropolitan Area Risk Trends, 2023

Disability Status

Category	MSA[1] (%)	U.S. (%)
Adults who reported being deaf	n/a	7.4
Are you blind or have serious difficulty seeing, even when wearing glasses?	n/a	4.9
Do you have difficulty doing errands alone?	n/a	7.8
Do you have difficulty dressing or bathing?	n/a	3.6
Do you have serious difficulty concentrating/remembering/making decisions?	n/a	13.7
Do you have serious difficulty walking or climbing stairs?	n/a	13.2

Note: All figures are crude prevalence; (1) Figures for the Eugene-Springfield, OR Metropolitan Statistical Area were not available.
Source: Centers for Disease Control and Prevention, Behaviorial Risk Factor Surveillance System, SMART: Selected Metropolitan Area Risk Trends, 2023

Mortality Rates for the Top 10 Causes of Death in the U.S.

ICD-10[a] Sub-Chapter	ICD-10[a] Code	Crude Mortality Rate[2] per 100,000 population	
		County[3]	U.S.
Malignant neoplasms	C00-C97	230.1	182.7
Ischaemic heart diseases	I20-I25	93.3	109.6
Provisional assignment of new diseases of uncertain etiology[1]	U00-U49	38.5	65.3
Other forms of heart disease	I30-I51	74.8	65.1
Other degenerative diseases of the nervous system	G30-G31	103.4	52.4
Other external causes of accidental injury	W00-X59	81.2	52.3
Cerebrovascular diseases	I60-I69	60.3	49.1
Chronic lower respiratory diseases	J40-J47	56.6	43.5
Hypertensive diseases	I10-I15	46.1	38.9
Organic, including symptomatic, mental disorders	F01-F09	39.4	33.9

Note: (a) ICD-10 = International Classification of Diseases 10th Revision; (1) Includes COVID-19, adverse effects to COVID-19 vaccines, SARS, and vaping-related disorders; (2) Crude mortality rates are a three-year average covering 2021-2023; (3) Figures cover Lane County.
Source: Centers for Disease Control and Prevention, National Center for Health Statistics. National Vital Statistics System, Mortality 2018-2023 on CDC WONDER Online Database

Mortality Rates for Selected Causes of Death

Cause of Death	ICD-10[a] Code	Crude Mortality Rate[1] per 100,000 population County[2]	U.S.
Accidental poisoning and exposure to noxious substances	X40-X49	43.3	30.5
Alzheimer disease	G30	79.8	35.4
Assault	X85-Y09	3.0	7.3
COVID-19	U07.1	38.5	65.3
Diabetes mellitus	E10-E14	31.3	30.0
Diseases of the liver	K70-K76	33.0	20.8
Human immunodeficiency virus (HIV) disease	B20-B24	Suppressed	1.5
Influenza and pneumonia	J09-J18	6.5	13.4
Intentional self-harm	X60-X84	25.6	14.7
Malnutrition	E40-E46	18.9	6.0
Obesity and other hyperalimentation	E65-E68	5.1	3.1
Renal failure	N17-N19	9.3	16.4
Transport accidents	V01-V99	15.7	14.4

Note: (a) ICD-10 = International Classification of Diseases 10th Revision; (1) Crude mortality rates are a three-year average covering 2021-2023; (2) Figures cover Lane County; Data are suppressed when the data meet the criteria for confidentiality constraints; Crude mortality rates are flagged as unreliable when the rate would be calculated with a numerator of 20 or less.
Source: Centers for Disease Control and Prevention, National Center for Health Statistics. National Vital Statistics System, Mortality 2018-2023 on CDC WONDER Online Database

Health Insurance Coverage

Area	With Health Insurance	With Private Health Insurance	With Public Health Insurance	Without Health Insurance	Population Under Age 19 Without Health Insurance
City	94.5	68.2	39.0	5.5	2.3
MSA[1]	94.1	63.9	44.5	5.9	2.9
U.S.	91.4	67.3	36.3	8.6	5.4

Note: Figures are percentages that cover the civilian noninstitutionalized population; (1) Figures cover the Eugene-Springfield, OR Metropolitan Statistical Area
Source: U.S. Census Bureau, 2019-2023 American Community Survey 5-Year Estimates

Number of Medical Professionals

Area	MDs[3]	DOs[3,4]	Dentists	Podiatrists	Chiropractors	Optometrists
County[1] (number)	958	63	288	20	112	66
County[1] (rate[2])	250.6	16.5	75.6	5.2	29.4	17.3
U.S. (rate[2])	302.5	29.2	74.6	6.4	29.5	18.0

Note: Data as of 2023 unless noted; (1) Data covers Lane County; (2) Number of medical professionals per 100,000 population; (3) Data as of 2022 and includes all active, non-federal physicians; (4) Doctor of Osteopathic Medicine
Source: U.S. Department of Health and Human Services, Health Resources and Services Administration, Bureau of Health Professions, Area Resource File (ARF) 2023-2024

EDUCATION

Public School District Statistics

District Name	Schls	Pupils	Pupil/ Teacher Ratio	Minority Pupils[1] (%)	Total Rev. per Pupil ($)	Total Exp. per Pupil ($)
Bethel SD 52	11	5,003	17.0	42.1	17,284	18,213
Eugene SD 4J	36	16,283	17.9	34.6	18,568	22,924

Note: Table includes school districts with 2,000 or more students; (1) Percentage of students that are not non-Hispanic white.
Source: U.S. Department of Education, National Center for Education Statistics, Common Core of Data, Local Education Agency (School District) Universe Survey: School Year 2023-2024; U.S. Department of Education, National Center for Education Statistics, Common Core of Data, School District Finance Survey (F-33): School Year 2021–22

Highest Level of Education

Area	Less than H.S.	H.S. Diploma	Some College, No Deg.	Associate Degree	Bachelor's Degree	Master's Degree	Prof. School Degree	Doctorate Degree
City	5.2	17.4	24.3	8.8	23.7	13.5	3.6	3.5
MSA[1]	6.9	22.8	27.0	9.9	19.7	9.4	2.3	2.1
U.S.	10.6	26.2	19.4	8.8	21.3	9.8	2.3	1.6

Note: Figures cover persons age 25 and over; (1) Figures cover the Eugene-Springfield, OR Metropolitan Statistical Area
Source: U.S. Census Bureau, 2019-2023 American Community Survey 5-Year Estimates

Educational Attainment by Race

Area	High School Graduate or Higher (%)					Bachelor's Degree or Higher (%)				
	Total	White	Black	Asian	Hisp.[2]	Total	White	Black	Asian	Hisp.[2]
City	94.8	95.7	98.0	92.9	86.2	44.2	44.8	37.2	59.1	33.3
MSA[1]	93.1	94.1	96.1	90.4	81.3	33.4	33.6	33.2	53.7	25.3
U.S.	89.4	92.9	88.1	88.0	72.5	35.0	37.7	24.7	57.0	19.9

Note: Figures shown cover persons 25 years old and over; (1) Figures cover the Eugene-Springfield, OR Metropolitan Statistical Area; (2) People of Hispanic origin can be of any race
Source: U.S. Census Bureau, 2019-2023 American Community Survey 5-Year Estimates

School Enrollment by Grade and Control

Area	Preschool (%)		Kindergarten (%)		Grades 1 - 4 (%)		Grades 5 - 8 (%)		Grades 9 - 12 (%)	
	Public	Private	Public	Private	Public	Private	Public	Private	Public	Private
City	52.8	47.2	85.1	14.9	88.6	11.4	89.0	11.0	93.6	6.4
MSA[1]	54.2	45.8	84.1	15.9	87.0	13.0	89.6	10.4	91.4	8.6
U.S.	58.7	41.3	85.2	14.8	87.2	12.8	87.9	12.1	89.0	11.0

Note: Figures shown cover persons 3 years old and over; (1) Figures cover the Eugene-Springfield, OR Metropolitan Statistical Area
Source: U.S. Census Bureau, 2019-2023 American Community Survey 5-Year Estimates

Higher Education

Four-Year Colleges			Two-Year Colleges			Medical Schools[1]	Law Schools[2]	Voc/ Tech[3]
Public	Private Non-profit	Private For-profit	Public	Private Non-profit	Private For-profit			
1	2	0	1	0	1	0	1	0

Note: Figures cover institutions located within the Eugene-Springfield, OR Metropolitan Statistical Area and include main campuses only; (1) includes schools accredited by the Liaison Committee on Medical Education and the American Osteopathic Association's Commission on Osteopathic College Accreditation; (2) includes ABA-accredited schools, schools with provisional ABA accreditation, and state accredited schools; (3) includes all schools with programs that are less than 2 years.
Source: National Center for Education Statistics, Integrated Postsecondary Education System (IPEDS), 2023-24; Wikipedia, List of Medical Schools in the United States, accessed May 2, 2025; Wikipedia, List of Law Schools in the United States, accessed May 2, 2025

According to *U.S. News & World Report,* the Eugene-Springfield, OR metro area is home to one of the top 200 national universities in the U.S.: **University of Oregon** (#109 tie). The indicators used to capture academic quality fall into a number of categories: assessment by administrators at peer institutions; retention of students; faculty resources; student selectivity; financial resources; alumni giving; high school counselor ratings of colleges; and graduation rate. *U.S. News & World Report, "America's Best Colleges 2025"*

According to *U.S. News & World Report,* the Eugene-Springfield, OR metro area is home to one of the top 100 law schools in the U.S.: **University of Oregon** (#94 tie). The rankings are based on a weighted average of 12 measures of quality: peer assessment score; assessment score by lawyers/judges; median LSAT scores; median undergrad GPA; acceptance rate; employment rates for graduates; placement success; bar passage rate; faculty resources; expenditures per student; student/faculty ratio; and library resources. *U.S. News & World Report, "America's Best Graduate Schools, Law, 2025"*

EMPLOYERS

Major Employers

Company Name	Industry
Abby's	Pizzeria, chain
Arclin USA	Plastics materials & resins
Bi-Mart Corporation	Miscellaneous general merchandise stores
County of Lane	County government
Datalogic Adc	Magnetic ink & optical scanning devices
Datalogic Scanning	Calculating & accounting equipment
Farwest Steel Corporation	Fabricated structural metal
Lane Community College	Community college
Lane County School District #52	Public combined elementary & secondary school
Lane County School District 4J	Public elementary & secondary schools
Market of Choice	Supermarkets, independent
McKenzie-Williamette Medical Services	General medical & surgical hospitals
Navistar RV	Motor homes
Oregon University System	University
Pacificsource Health Plans	Accident & health insurance
Papé Material Handling	Industrial machinery & equipment
Peacehealth	Medical laboratories
Pinnacle Healthcare	Skilled nursing facility
S Butler-Rosboro Corporation	Glow lamp bulbs
Springfield School District 19	Public elementary & secondary schools

Note: Companies shown are located within the Eugene-Springfield, OR Metropolitan Statistical Area.
Source: Chambers of Commerce; State Departments of Labor; Wikipedia

PUBLIC SAFETY

Crime Rate

Area	Total Crime Rate	Violent Crime Rate				Property Crime Rate		
		Murder	Rape	Robbery	Aggrav. Assault	Burglary	Larceny -Theft	Motor Vehicle Theft
City	3,545.1	3.4	56.7	77.4	210.4	497.8	2,306.5	392.8
U.S.	2,290.9	5.7	38.0	66.5	264.1	250.7	1,347.2	318.7

Note: Figures are crimes per 100,000 population.
Source: FBI, Table 8, Offenses Known to Law Enforcement, by State by City, 2023

Hate Crimes

Area	Number of Quarters Reported	Number of Incidents per Bias Motivation					
		Race/Ethnicity/ Ancestry	Religion	Sexual Orientation	Disability	Gender	Gender Identity
City[1]	4	13	0	3	0	0	2
U.S.	4	5,900	2,699	2,077	187	92	492

Note: (1) Figures include at least one incident reported with more than one bias motivation.
Source: Federal Bureau of Investigation, Hate Crime Statistics 2023

Identity Theft Consumer Reports

Area	Reports	Reports per 100,000 Population	Rank[2]
MSA[1]	605	158	243
U.S.	1,135,291	339	-

Note: (1) Figures cover the Eugene-Springfield, OR Metropolitan Statistical Area; (2) Rank ranges from 1 to
401 where 1 indicates greatest number of identity theft reports per 100,000 population
Source: Federal Trade Commission, Consumer Sentinel Network Data Book 2024

Fraud and Other Consumer Reports

Area	Reports	Reports per 100,000 Population	Rank[2]
MSA[1]	4,165	1,089	166
U.S.	5,360,641	1,601	-

Note: (1) Figures cover the Eugene-Springfield, OR Metropolitan Statistical Area; (2) Rank ranges from 1 to
401 where 1 indicates greatest number of fraud and other consumer reports per 100,000 population
Source: Federal Trade Commission, Consumer Sentinel Network Data Book 2024

POLITICS

2024 Presidential Election Results

Area	Trump (Rep.)	Harris (Dem.)	Stein (Green)	Kennedy (Ind.)	Oliver (Lib.)	Other
Lane County	36.6	59.5	0.9	1.5	0.4	1.1
U.S.	49.7	48.2	0.6	0.5	0.4	0.6

Note: Results are percentages and may not add to 100% due to rounding
Source: Dave Leip's Atlas of U.S. Presidential Elections

SPORTS

Professional Sports Teams

Team Name	League	Year Established

No teams are located in the metro area

Source: Wikipedia, Major Professional Sports Teams of the United States and Canada, May 1, 2025

CLIMATE

Average and Extreme Temperatures

Temperature	Jan	Feb	Mar	Apr	May	Jun	Jul	Aug	Sep	Oct	Nov	Dec	Yr.
Extreme High (°F)	67	69	77	86	93	102	105	108	103	94	76	68	108
Average High (°F)	46	51	55	61	67	74	82	82	76	64	53	47	63
Average Temp. (°F)	40	44	46	50	55	61	67	67	62	53	46	41	53
Average Low (°F)	33	35	37	39	43	48	51	51	48	42	38	35	42
Extreme Low (°F)	-4	-3	20	27	28	32	39	38	32	19	12	-12	-12

Note: Figures cover the years 1948-1992
Source: National Climatic Data Center, International Station Meteorological Climate Summary, 9/96

Average Precipitation/Snowfall/Humidity

Precip./Humidity	Jan	Feb	Mar	Apr	May	Jun	Jul	Aug	Sep	Oct	Nov	Dec	Yr.
Avg. Precip. (in.)	7.8	5.6	5.3	3.0	2.2	1.4	0.4	0.8	1.4	3.6	7.6	8.2	47.3
Avg. Snowfall (in.)	4	1	1	Tr	Tr	0	0	0	0	Tr	Tr	1	7
Avg. Rel. Hum. 7am (%)	91	92	91	88	84	81	78	82	88	93	93	92	88
Avg. Rel. Hum. 4pm (%)	79	73	64	57	54	49	38	39	44	61	79	84	60

Note: Figures cover the years 1948-1992; Tr = Trace amounts (<0.05 in. of rain; <0.5 in. of snow)
Source: National Climatic Data Center, International Station Meteorological Climate Summary, 9/96

Weather Conditions

Temperature			Daytime Sky			Precipitation		
32°F & below	45°F & below	90°F & above	Clear	Partly cloudy	Cloudy	0.01 inch or more precip.	0.1 inch or more snow/ice	Thunder-storms
54	233	15	75	115	175	136	4	3

Note: Figures are average number of days per year and cover the years 1948-1992
Source: National Climatic Data Center, International Station Meteorological Climate Summary, 9/96

HAZARDOUS WASTE

Superfund Sites

The Eugene-Springfield, OR metro area is home to two sites on the EPA's Superfund National Priorities List (NPL) or Superfund Alternative Approach (SAA) list: **Black Butte Mine** (Final NPL); **J. H. Baxter** (Proposed NPL). The Superfund alternative approach uses the same investigation and cleanup process and standards that are used for sites listed on the National Priorities List. The SAA is an alternative to listing a site on the NPL; it is not an alternative to Superfund or the Superfund process. There are a total of 1,445 Superfund sites with a status of proposed or final on both lists in the United States. *U.S. Environmental Protection Agency, National Priorities List, May 1, 2025; U.S. Environmental Protection Agency, Superfund Alternative Approach Sites, May 1, 2025*

AIR QUALITY

Air Quality Trends: Ozone

	1990	1995	2000	2005	2010	2015	2020	2021	2022	2023
MSA[1]	0.068	0.062	0.056	0.068	0.058	0.070	0.054	0.061	0.058	0.060
U.S.	0.087	0.089	0.081	0.080	0.072	0.066	0.066	0.067	0.067	0.070

Note: (1) Data covers the Eugene-Springfield, OR Metropolitan Statistical Area. The values shown are the composite ozone concentration averages among trend sites based on the highest fourth daily maximum 8-hour concentration in parts per million. These trends are based on sites having an adequate record of monitoring data during the trend period. Data from exceptional events are included.
Source: U.S. Environmental Protection Agency, Air Quality Monitoring Information, "Air Quality Trends by City, 1990-2023"

Air Quality Index

Area	Percent of Days when Air Quality was...[2]					AQI Statistics[2]	
	Good	Moderate	Unhealthy for Sensitive Groups	Unhealthy	Very Unhealthy	Maximum	Median
MSA[1]	52.1	43.6	2.5	1.6	0.3	211	49

Note: (1) Data covers the Eugene-Springfield, OR Metropolitan Statistical Area; (2) Based on 365 days with AQI data in 2023. Air Quality Index (AQI) is an index for reporting daily air quality. EPA calculates the AQI for five major air pollutants regulated by the Clean Air Act: ground-level ozone, particle pollution (aka particulate matter), carbon monoxide, sulfur dioxide, and nitrogen dioxide. The AQI runs from 0 to 500. The higher the AQI value, the greater the level of air pollution and the greater the health concern. There are six AQI categories: "Good" AQI is between 0 and 50. Air quality is considered satisfactory; "Moderate" AQI is between 51 and 100. Air quality is acceptable; "Unhealthy for Sensitive Groups" When AQI values are between 101 and 150, members of sensitive groups may experience health effects; "Unhealthy" When AQI values are between 151 and 200 everyone may begin to experience health effects; "Very Unhealthy" AQI values between 201 and 300 trigger a health alert; "Hazardous" AQI values over 300 trigger warnings of emergency conditions (not shown).
Source: U.S. Environmental Protection Agency, Air Quality Index Report, 2023

Air Quality Index Pollutants

Area	Percent of Days when AQI Pollutant was...[2]					
	Carbon Monoxide	Nitrogen Dioxide	Ozone	Sulfur Dioxide	Particulate Matter 2.5	Particulate Matter 10
MSA[1]	0.0	0.0	21.4	(3)	78.6	0.0

Note: (1) Data covers the Eugene-Springfield, OR Metropolitan Statistical Area; (2) Based on 365 days with AQI data in 2023. The Air Quality Index (AQI) is an index for reporting daily air quality. EPA calculates the AQI for five major air pollutants regulated by the Clean Air Act: ground-level ozone, particle pollution (also known as particulate matter), carbon monoxide, sulfur dioxide, and nitrogen dioxide. The AQI runs from 0 to 500. The higher the AQI value, the greater the level of air pollution and the greater the health concern; (3) Sulfur dioxide is no longer included in this table because SO_2 concentrations tend to be very localized and not necessarily representative of broad geographical areas like counties and CBSAs.
Source: U.S. Environmental Protection Agency, Air Quality Index Report, 2023

Maximum Air Pollutant Concentrations: Particulate Matter, Ozone, CO and Lead

	Particulate Matter 10 (ug/m^3)	Particulate Matter 2.5 Wtd AM (ug/m^3)	Particulate Matter 2.5 24-Hr (ug/m^3)	Ozone (ppm)	Carbon Monoxide (ppm)	Lead (ug/m^3)
MSA[1] Level	118	10.1	46	0.06	n/a	n/a
NAAQS[2]	150	15	35	0.075	9	0.15
Met NAAQS[2]	Yes	Yes	No	Yes	n/a	n/a

Note: (1) Data covers the Eugene-Springfield, OR Metropolitan Statistical Area; Data from exceptional events are included; (2) National Ambient Air Quality Standards; ppm = parts per million; ug/m^3 = micrograms per cubic meter; n/a not available.
Concentrations: Particulate Matter 10 (coarse particulate)—highest second maximum 24-hour concentration; Particulate Matter 2.5 Wtd AM (fine particulate)—highest weighted annual mean concentration; Particulate Matter 2.5 24-Hour (fine particulate)—highest 98th percentile 24-hour concentration; Ozone—highest fourth daily maximum 8-hour concentration; Carbon Monoxide—highest second maximum non-overlapping 8-hour concentration; Lead—maximum running 3-month average
Source: U.S. Environmental Protection Agency, Air Quality Monitoring Information, "Air Quality Statistics by City, 2023"

Maximum Air Pollutant Concentrations: Nitrogen Dioxide and Sulfur Dioxide

	Nitrogen Dioxide AM (ppb)	Nitrogen Dioxide 1-Hr (ppb)	Sulfur Dioxide AM (ppb)	Sulfur Dioxide 1-Hr (ppb)	Sulfur Dioxide 24-Hr (ppb)
MSA[1] Level	n/a	n/a	n/a	n/a	n/a
NAAQS[2]	53	100	30	75	140
Met NAAQS[2]	n/a	n/a	n/a	n/a	n/a

Note: (1) Data covers the Eugene-Springfield, OR Metropolitan Statistical Area; Data from exceptional events are included; (2) National Ambient Air Quality Standards; ppm = parts per million; ug/m^3 = micrograms per cubic meter; n/a not available.
Concentrations: Nitrogen Dioxide AM—highest arithmetic mean concentration; Nitrogen Dioxide 1-Hr—highest 98th percentile 1-hour daily maximum concentration; Sulfur Dioxide AM—highest annual mean concentration; Sulfur Dioxide 1-Hr—highest 99th percentile 1-hour daily maximum concentration; Sulfur Dioxide 24-Hr—highest second maximum 24-hour concentration
Source: U.S. Environmental Protection Agency, Air Quality Monitoring Information, "Air Quality Statistics by City, 2023"

Fort Collins, Colorado

Background

At 4,985 feet, Fort Collins lies high in the eastern base of the Rocky Mountains' front range along the Cache la Poudre River about one hour from Denver. Although not quite as large as Denver, Fort Collins, home to Colorado State University and its own symphony orchestra, offers virtually everything its citizens need with a spectacular landscape, strong economy, and world-class outdoor adventure opportunities.

Fort Collins owes its name to Colonel William Collins of the Civil War era, who was sent with a regiment of Union soldiers to guard farmers and ranchers scattered throughout the valley, and to provide security for the Overland Stage trail. Originally called Camp Collins, it remained a military reservation until 1866 and was incorporated in 1879.

The early economy of the town depended first on lumber, and then on the raising of livestock and produce, with alfalfa, grain, and sugar beets as the chief crops. Sugar refineries, dairies, and meatpacking plants bolstered the wealth of the town, as did the products of mining and quarrying. Fort Collins is still the commercial center for a rich agricultural region that produces hay, barley, and sugar beets.

Colorado State University, the land-grant University of Colorado, was established in Fort Collins in 1879, and offers innumerable cultural, economic, and educational benefits to residents. More than 32,900 students are enrolled at CSU, which is the largest employer in the city. CSU offers a world-class range of undergraduate and graduate programs, and is an internationally recognized center for forestry, agricultural science, veterinary medicine, and civil engineering.

Fort Collins' businesses produce motion-picture film, combustion engines, prefabricated metal buildings, arc welders and rods, cement products, dental hygiene appliances, and miscellaneous plastics.

The Fort Collins public school system operates within the Poudre School District, is one of the area's largest employers. The city's public library system, Poudre River Public Libraries, operates three branches.

Gateway Natural Area, 15 miles from Fort Collins, offers several recreation opportunities, including a quarter-mile nature trail and a designated boat launch. Lakes are easily accessible for all water sports, and the Cache La Poudre River offers some of the best trout fishing in Colorado. For hunters, the area is a paradise, with ample supplies of antelope, black bear, deer, elk, mountain lion, and small game.

Fort Collins also offers a great range of cultural amenities. The city's Lincoln Center presents year-round performances by a variety of artists. Old Town, a historic downtown shopping district, hosts several large festivals each year. Fort Collins Symphony, the Larimer Chorale, Open Stage Theatre, and the Canyon Concert Ballet call Fort Collins their home. The city also cultivates the visual arts, with "Art in Public Places" sponsored by the city, and provides exhibits at the Lincoln Center, Fort Collins Museum, and private galleries.

Transportation in and around the city is convenient. The municipality operates its own bus service, and interstate bus service is available. Residents are served by three nearby airports—Fort Collins/Loveland Airport, Cheyenne Municipal Airport, and Denver International Airport, one of the nation's busiest airports.

Fort Collins features four distinct seasons and, though high in the foothills, is buffered from both summer and winter temperature extremes. A typical day in Fort Collins is warm and dry with mild nights. The town enjoys on average more than 300 sunny days per year, and an annual snowfall of 51 inches, with far less rainfall. Summers are comfortable, while winters are cold.

Rankings

Business/Finance Rankings

- The Fort Collins metro area appeared on the Milken Institute "2025 Best Performing Cities" list. Rank: #21 out of 200 large metro areas (based on performance category). Criteria: job growth; wage growth; high-tech growth and impact; community resilience; housing affordability; household broadband access. *Milken Institute, "Best-Performing Cities 2025," January 14, 2025*

Children/Family Rankings

- Fort Collins was selected as one of the best cities for newlyweds by *Rent.com*. The city ranked #13 of 15. Criteria: cost of living; availability of affordable rental inventory; annual household income; entertainment, culture and restaurant options; percentage of married couples; concentration of millennials; and safety. *Rent.com, "The 15 Best Cities for Newlyweds," September 2, 2021*

Environmental Rankings

- The U.S. Environmental Protection Agency (EPA) released its list of mid-size U.S. metropolitan areas with the most ENERGY STAR certified buildings in 2023. The Fort Collins metro area was ranked #8 out of 10. *U.S. Environmental Protection Agency, "2024 Energy Star Top Cities," May 22, 2024*

- Fort Collins was highlighted as one of the 25 most ozone-polluted metro areas in the U.S. during 2021 through 2023. The area ranked #13. *American Lung Association, "State of the Air 2025," April 23, 2025*

Real Estate Rankings

- Fort Collins was ranked #152 out of 176 metro areas in terms of cost of housing in 2024 by the National Association of Home Builders (#1 = most affordable). Criteria: the portion of an average family's income necessary to pay the mortgage on a median-priced home. *National Association of Home Builders®, NAHB-Wells Fargo Cost of Housing Index, 4th Quarter 2024*

Miscellaneous Rankings

- *MoveHub* ranked 446 hipster cities across 20 countries, using its new and improved alternative Hipster Index and Fort Collins came out as #48 among the top 50. Criteria: population over 150,000; number of vintage boutiques; density of tattoo parlors; vegan places to eat; coffee shops; and density of vinyl record stores. *MoveHub.com, "The Hipster Index: Brighton Pips Portland to Global Top Spot," July 28, 2021*

Business Environment

DEMOGRAPHICS

Population Growth

Area	1990 Census	2000 Census	2010 Census	2020 Census	2023 Estimate[2]	Population Growth 1990-2023 (%)
City	89,555	118,652	143,986	169,810	169,705	89.5
MSA[1]	186,136	251,494	299,630	359,066	363,561	95.3
U.S.	248,709,873	281,421,906	308,745,538	331,449,281	332,387,540	33.6

Note: (1) Figures cover the Fort Collins-Loveland, CO Metropolitan Statistical Area; (2) 2019-2023 5-year ACS population estimate
Source: U.S. Census Bureau, 1990 Census, 2000 Census, 2010 Census, 2020 Census, 2019-2023 American Community Survey 5-Year Estimates

Race

Area	White Alone[2] (%)	Black Alone[2] (%)	Asian Alone[2] (%)	AIAN[3] Alone[2] (%)	NHOPI[4] Alone[2] (%)	Other Race Alone[2] (%)	Two or More Races (%)
City	81.7	1.4	3.3	0.8	0.1	2.2	10.5
MSA[1]	84.1	1.0	2.1	0.6	0.1	2.6	9.5
U.S.	63.4	12.4	5.8	0.9	0.2	6.6	10.7

Note: (1) Figures cover the Fort Collins-Loveland, CO Metropolitan Statistical Area; (2) Alone is defined as not being in combination with one or more other races; (3) American Indian and Alaska Native; (4) Native Hawaiian and Other Pacific Islander
Source: U.S. Census Bureau, 2019-2023 American Community Survey 5-Year Estimates

Hispanic or Latino Origin

Area	Total (%)	Mexican (%)	Puerto Rican (%)	Cuban (%)	Other (%)
City	12.3	8.2	0.7	0.2	3.3
MSA[1]	12.7	9.0	0.5	0.2	3.0
U.S.	19.0	11.3	1.8	0.7	5.2

Note: Persons of Hispanic or Latino origin can be of any race; (1) Figures cover the Fort Collins-Loveland, CO Metropolitan Statistical Area
Source: U.S. Census Bureau, 2019-2023 American Community Survey 5-Year Estimates

Age

Area	Percent of Population									Median Age
	Under Age 5	Age 5–19	Age 20–34	Age 35–44	Age 45–54	Age 55–64	Age 65–74	Age 75–84	Age 85+	
City	3.9	18.9	33.6	12.6	9.4	9.4	7.3	3.3	1.6	30.6
MSA[1]	4.5	18.2	24.9	12.9	11.0	11.7	10.5	4.5	1.8	36.6
U.S.	5.7	19.1	20.2	13.1	12.8	10.0	4.9	1.9		38.7

Note: (1) Figures cover the Fort Collins-Loveland, CO Metropolitan Statistical Area
Source: U.S. Census Bureau, 2019-2023 American Community Survey 5-Year Estimates

Disability by Age

Area	All Ages	Under 18 Years Old	18 to 64 Years Old	65 Years and Over
City	8.9	3.0	7.7	24.0
MSA[1]	10.3	3.3	8.2	26.6
U.S.	13.0	4.7	10.7	32.9

Note: Figures show percent of the civilian noninstitutionalized population that reported having a disability. Disability status is determined from six types of difficulty: vision, hearing, cognitive, ambulatory, self-care, and independent living. For children under 5 years old, hearing and vision difficulty are used to determine disability status. For children between the ages of 5 and 14, disability status is determined from hearing, vision, cognitive, ambulatory, and self-care difficulties. For people aged 15 years and older, they are considered to have a disability if they have difficulty with any one of the six difficulty types; Note: (1) Figures cover the Fort Collins-Loveland, CO Metropolitan Statistical Area
Source: U.S. Census Bureau, 2019-2023 American Community Survey 5-Year Estimates

Ancestry

Area	German	Irish	English	American	Italian	Polish	French[2]	European	Scottish
City	23.1	12.3	14.9	3.2	5.6	3.4	3.1	3.6	3.5
MSA[1]	24.4	12.6	16.0	4.2	5.1	2.9	3.2	3.5	3.5
U.S.	12.6	9.4	9.1	5.5	4.9	2.6	2.0	1.6	1.6

Note: Figures are the percentage of the total population reporting a particular ancestry. The nine most commonly reported ancestries in the U.S. are shown. Figures include multiple ancestries (e.g. if a person reported being Irish and Italian, they were included in both columns); (1) Figures cover the Fort Collins-Loveland, CO Metropolitan Statistical Area; (2) Excludes Basque
Source: U.S. Census Bureau, 2019-2023 American Community Survey 5-Year Estimates

Foreign-born Population

Area	Any Foreign Country	Percent of Population Born in							
		Asia	Mexico	Europe	Caribbean	Central America[2]	South America	Africa	Canada
City	6.6	2.5	1.2	1.3	0.1	0.3	0.6	0.3	0.2
MSA[1]	5.4	1.6	1.4	1.1	0.1	0.3	0.4	0.2	0.2
U.S.	13.9	4.3	3.3	1.4	1.4	1.2	1.2	0.8	0.2

Note: (1) Figures cover the Fort Collins-Loveland, CO Metropolitan Statistical Area; (2) Excludes Mexico.
Source: U.S. Census Bureau, 2019-2023 American Community Survey 5-Year Estimates

Household Size

Area	Persons in Household (%)							Average Household Size
	One	Two	Three	Four	Five	Six	Seven or More	
City	26.6	37.8	17.6	12.5	4.1	1.0	0.4	2.27
MSA[1]	25.5	39.2	16.4	12.1	4.5	1.4	0.9	2.33
U.S.	28.5	33.8	15.4	12.7	5.9	2.3	1.4	2.54

Note: (1) Figures cover the Fort Collins-Loveland, CO Metropolitan Statistical Area
Source: U.S. Census Bureau, 2019-2023 American Community Survey 5-Year Estimates

Household Relationships

Area	House-holder	Opposite-sex Spouse	Same-sex Spouse	Opposite-sex Unmarried Partner	Same-sex Unmarried Partner	Child[2]	Grand-child	Other Relatives	Non-relatives
City	39.9	16.0	0.2	3.3	0.2	22.1	0.9	2.4	9.0
MSA[1]	40.2	19.4	0.2	2.8	0.2	24.0	1.2	2.7	6.0
U.S.	38.3	17.5	0.2	2.5	0.2	28.3	2.4	4.8	3.4

Note: Figures are percent of the total population; (1) Figures cover the Fort Collins-Loveland, CO Metropolitan Statistical Area; (2) Includes biological, adopted, and stepchildren of the householder
Source: U.S. Census Bureau, 2020 Census

Gender

Area	Males	Females	Males per 100 Females
City	84,686	85,019	99.6
MSA[1]	181,725	181,836	99.9
U.S.	164,545,087	167,842,453	98.0

Note: (1) Figures cover the Fort Collins-Loveland, CO Metropolitan Statistical Area
Source: U.S. Census Bureau, 2019-2023 American Community Survey 5-Year Estimates

Marital Status

Area	Never Married	Now Married[2]	Separated	Widowed	Divorced
City	46.5	41.1	0.7	3.0	8.8
MSA[1]	35.3	50.3	0.8	3.9	9.7
U.S.	34.1	47.9	1.7	5.6	10.7

Note: Figures are percentages and cover the population 15 years of age and older; (1) Figures cover the Fort Collins-Loveland, CO Metropolitan Statistical Area; (2) Excludes separated
Source: U.S. Census Bureau, 2019-2023 American Community Survey 5-Year Estimates

Religious Groups by Family

Area	Catholic	Baptist	Methodist	LDS[2]	Pentecostal	Lutheran	Islam	Adventist	Other
MSA[1]	9.9	1.2	1.3	4.0	2.7	2.5	<0.1	1.2	12.1
U.S.	18.7	7.3	3.0	2.0	1.8	1.7	1.3	1.3	11.6

Note: Figures are the number of adherents as a percentage of the total population and cover the eight largest religious groups in the U.S; (1) Figures cover the Fort Collins-Loveland, CO Metropolitan Statistical Area; (2) Church of Jesus Christ of Latter-day Saints
Sources: 2020 U.S. Religion Census, Association of Statisticians of American Religious Bodies; The Association of Religion Data Archives (ARDA)

Religious Groups by Tradition

Area	Catholic	Evangelical Protestant	Mainline Protestant	Black Protestant	Islam	Judaism	Hinduism	Orthodox	Buddhism
MSA[1]	9.9	15.6	3.3	0.4	<0.1	n/a	0.1	0.1	0.1
U.S.	18.7	16.5	5.2	2.3	1.3	0.6	0.4	0.4	0.3

Note: Figures are the number of adherents as a percentage of the total population; (1) Figures cover the Fort Collins-Loveland, CO Metropolitan Statistical Area
Sources: 2020 U.S. Religion Census, Association of Statisticians of American Religious Bodies; The Association of Religion Data Archives (ARDA)

ECONOMY

Real Gross Domestic Product (GDP)

Area	2017	2018	2019	2020	2021	2022	2023	Rank[3]
MSA[1]	18.6	19.5	20.3	20.2	21.3	21.7	22.0	139
U.S.[2]	17,619.1	18,160.7	18,642.5	18,238.9	19,387.6	19,896.6	20,436.3	–

Note: Figures are in billions of chained 2017 dollars; (1) Figures cover the Fort Collins-Loveland, CO Metropolitan Statistical Area; (2) Figures cover real GDP within metropolitan areas; (3) Rank is based on 2023 data and ranges from 1 to 384
Source: U.S. Bureau of Economic Analysis

Economic Growth

Area	2014	2015	2016	2017	2018	2019	2020	2021	2022	2023
MSA[1]	5.3	4.6	4.0	7.7	4.8	4.4	-0.9	5.8	1.9	1.3
U.S.[2]	2.6	3.2	2.0	2.7	3.1	2.7	-2.2	6.3	2.6	2.7

Note: Figures are real gross domestic product growth rates and represent percent change from preceding period; (1) Figures cover the Fort Collins-Loveland, CO Metropolitan Statistical Area; (2) Figures are the average growth rates within metropolitan areas
Source: U.S. Bureau of Economic Analysis

Metropolitan Area Exports

Area	2018	2019	2020	2021	2022	2023	Rank[2]
MSA[1]	1,021.8	1,060.0	1,092.5	1,132.5	1,178.8	1,180.5	157
U.S.	1,664,056.1	1,645,173.7	1,431,406.6	1,753,941.4	2,062,937.4	2,019,160.5	–

Note: Figures are in millions of dollars; (1) Figures cover the Fort Collins-Loveland, CO Metropolitan Statistical Area; (2) Rank is based on 2023 data and ranges from 1 to 386
Source: U.S. Department of Commerce, International Trade Administration, Office of Trade and Economic Analysis, Industry and Analysis, Exports by Metropolitan Area, data extracted April 2, 2025

Building Permits

Area	Single-Family			Multi-Family			Total		
	2023	2024	Pct. Chg.	2023	2024	Pct. Chg.	2023	2024	Pct. Chg.
City	372	371	-0.3	631	314	-50.2	1,003	685	-31.7
MSA[1]	1,289	1,370	6.3	1,397	416	-70.2	2,686	1,786	-33.5
U.S.	920,000	981,900	6.7	591,100	496,100	-16.1	1,511,100	1,478,000	-2.2

Note: (1) Figures cover the Fort Collins-Loveland, CO Metropolitan Statistical Area; Figures represent new, privately-owned housing units authorized (unadjusted data)
Source: U.S. Census Bureau, Building Permits Survey (BPS), 2023, 2024

Bankruptcy Filings

Area	Business Filings			Nonbusiness Filings		
	2023	2024	% Chg.	2023	2024	% Chg.
Larimer County	21	28	33.3	347	417	20.2
U.S.	18,926	23,107	22.1	434,064	494,201	13.9

Note: Business filings include Chapter 7, Chapter 9, Chapter 11, Chapter 12, Chapter 13, Chapter 15, and Section 304; Nonbusiness filings include Chapter 7, Chapter 11, and Chapter 13
Source: Administrative Office of the U.S. Courts, Business and Nonbusiness Bankruptcy, County Cases Commenced by Chapter of the Bankruptcy Code, During the 12-Month Period Ending December 31, 2023 and Business and Nonbusiness Bankruptcy, County Cases Commenced by Chapter of the Bankruptcy Code, During the 12-Month Period Ending December 31, 2024

Housing Vacancy Rates

Area	Gross Vacancy Rate[3] (%)			Year-Round Vacancy Rate[4] (%)			Rental Vacancy Rate[5] (%)			Homeowner Vacancy Rate[6] (%)		
	2022	2023	2024	2022	2023	2024	2022	2023	2024	2022	2023	2024
MSA[1]	n/a	n/a	n/a	n/a	n/a	n/a	n/a	n/a	n/a	n/a	n/a	n/a
U.S.[2]	9.1	9.0	9.1	7.5	7.5	7.6	5.7	6.5	6.8	0.8	0.8	1.0

Note: (1) Figures cover the Fort Collins-Loveland, CO Metropolitan Statistical Area; (2) Figures cover the 75 largest Metropolitan Statistical Areas; (3) The percentage of the total housing inventory that is vacant; (4) The percentage of the housing inventory (excluding seasonal units) that is year-round vacant; (5) The percentage of rental inventory that is vacant for rent; (6) The percentage of homeowner inventory that is vacant for sale; n/a not available
Source: U.S. Census Bureau, Housing Vacancies and Homeownership Annual Statistics: 2022, 2023, 2024

INCOME

Income

Area	Per Capita ($)	Median Household ($)	Average Household ($)
City	46,341	83,598	110,629
MSA[1]	49,323	91,364	118,812
U.S.	43,289	78,538	110,491

Note: (1) Figures cover the Fort Collins-Loveland, CO Metropolitan Statistical Area
Source: U.S. Census Bureau, 2019-2023 American Community Survey 5-Year Estimates

Household Income Distribution

Area	Percent of Households Earning							
	Under $15,000	$15,000 -$24,999	$25,000 -$34,999	$35,000 -$49,999	$50,000 -$74,999	$75,000 -$99,999	$100,000 -$149,999	$150,000 and up
City	9.5	5.7	5.5	10.0	14.9	12.5	18.4	23.5
MSA[1]	7.2	5.1	5.3	8.9	14.9	13.5	19.9	25.2
U.S.	8.5	6.6	6.8	10.4	15.7	12.7	17.4	21.9

Note: (1) Figures cover the Fort Collins-Loveland, CO Metropolitan Statistical Area
Source: U.S. Census Bureau, 2019-2023 American Community Survey 5-Year Estimates

Poverty Rate

Area	All Ages	Under 18 Years Old	18 to 64 Years Old	65 Years and Over
City	16.0	9.2	19.1	8.0
MSA[1]	11.1	8.5	12.9	7.1
U.S.	12.4	16.3	11.6	10.4

Note: Figures are percentage of people whose income during the past 12 months was below the poverty level;
(1) Figures cover the Fort Collins-Loveland, CO Metropolitan Statistical Area
Source: U.S. Census Bureau, 2019-2023 American Community Survey 5-Year Estimates

EMPLOYMENT

Labor Force and Employment

Area	Civilian Labor Force			Workers Employed		
	Dec. 2023	Dec. 2024	% Chg.	Dec. 2023	Dec. 2024	% Chg.
City	104,877	106,076	1.1	101,643	102,156	0.5
MSA[1]	216,529	219,305	1.3	209,634	210,691	0.5
U.S.	166,661,000	167,746,000	0.7	160,754,000	161,294,000	0.3

Note: Data is not seasonally adjusted and covers workers 16 years of age and older; (1) Figures cover the Fort Collins-Loveland, CO Metropolitan Statistical Area
Source: Bureau of Labor Statistics, Local Area Unemployment Statistics

Unemployment Rate

Area	2024											
	Jan.	Feb.	Mar.	Apr.	May	Jun.	Jul.	Aug.	Sep.	Oct.	Nov.	Dec.
City	3.5	3.6	3.3	3.1	3.5	3.9	4.1	4.1	3.8	3.7	4.1	3.7
MSA[1]	3.6	3.8	3.4	3.3	3.5	3.9	4.1	4.2	3.8	3.9	4.2	3.9
U.S.	4.1	4.2	3.9	3.5	3.7	4.3	4.5	4.4	3.9	3.9	4.0	3.8

Note: Data is not seasonally adjusted and covers workers 16 years of age and older; (1) Figures cover the Fort Collins-Loveland, CO Metropolitan Statistical Area
Source: Bureau of Labor Statistics, Local Area Unemployment Statistics

Average Wages

Occupation	$/Hr.	Occupation	$/Hr.
Accountants and Auditors	43.11	Maintenance and Repair Workers	24.61
Automotive Mechanics	27.93	Marketing Managers	88.03
Bookkeepers	24.64	Network and Computer Systems Admin.	47.68
Carpenters	26.93	Nurses, Licensed Practical	30.10
Cashiers	16.61	Nurses, Registered	43.16
Computer Programmers	54.48	Nursing Assistants	20.38
Computer Systems Analysts	53.23	Office Clerks, General	25.12
Computer User Support Specialists	32.68	Physical Therapists	44.64
Construction Laborers	21.53	Physicians	119.01
Cooks, Restaurant	18.75	Plumbers, Pipefitters and Steamfitters	30.07
Customer Service Representatives	20.21	Police and Sheriff's Patrol Officers	44.59
Dentists	100.41	Postal Service Mail Carriers	28.36
Electricians	29.77	Real Estate Sales Agents	32.17
Engineers, Electrical	55.88	Retail Salespersons	18.87
Fast Food and Counter Workers	16.21	Sales Representatives, Technical/Scientific	52.65
Financial Managers	90.82	Secretaries, Exc. Legal/Medical/Executive	21.68
First-Line Supervisors of Office Workers	32.90	Security Guards	19.32
General and Operations Managers	67.45	Surgeons	n/a
Hairdressers/Cosmetologists	28.72	Teacher Assistants, Exc. Postsecondary[1]	17.53
Home Health and Personal Care Aides	18.19	Teachers, Secondary School, Exc. Sp. Ed.[1]	31.75
Janitors and Cleaners	18.27	Telemarketers	n/a
Landscaping/Groundskeeping Workers	20.58	Truck Drivers, Heavy/Tractor-Trailer	26.38
Lawyers	104.22	Truck Drivers, Light/Delivery Services	22.67
Maids and Housekeeping Cleaners	17.22	Waiters and Waitresses	21.70

Note: Data in this table was taken from the May 2023 Metro Area Occupational Employment & Wage Estimates due to data quality concerns for the state of Colorado and substate areas. On November 20, 2024, the Quarterly Census of Employment and Wages (QCEW) suspended publication of industry and substate data for Colorado due to these concerns. As of May 1, 2025, the quality concerns with Colorado data have been sufficiently addressed to resume QCEW publication, however, because of the processing time required, the May 2024 Metro Area Occupational Employment & Wage Estimates data release does not include data for Colorado and its substate areas; n/a not available; (1) Hourly wages were calculated from annual wage data based on a 40 hour work week
Source: Bureau of Labor Statistics, Metro Area Occupational Employment & Wage Estimates, May 2023

Employment by Industry

Sector	MSA[1]		U.S.
	Number of Employees	Percent of Total	Percent of Total
Construction, Mining, and Logging	11,200	6.0	5.5
Financial Activities	7,100	3.8	5.8
Government	49,200	26.3	14.9
Information	2,400	1.3	1.9
Leisure and Hospitality	22,600	12.1	10.4
Manufacturing	14,900	8.0	8.0
Other Services	6,800	3.6	3.7
Private Education and Health Services	21,200	11.3	16.9
Professional and Business Services	21,700	11.6	14.2
Retail Trade	19,600	10.5	10.0
Transportation, Warehousing, and Utilities	4,600	2.5	4.8
Wholesale Trade	5,900	3.2	3.9

Note: Figures are non-farm employment as of December 2024. Figures are not seasonally adjusted and include workers 16 years of age and older; (1) Figures cover the Fort Collins-Loveland, CO Metropolitan Statistical Area
Source: Bureau of Labor Statistics, Current Employment Statistics, Employment, Hours, and Earnings

Employment by Occupation

Occupation Classification	City (%)	MSA[1] (%)	U.S. (%)
Management, Business, Science, and Arts	51.9	48.6	42.0
Natural Resources, Construction, and Maintenance	5.9	8.1	8.6
Production, Transportation, and Material Moving	7.6	9.1	13.0
Sales and Office	18.1	19.4	19.9
Service	16.5	14.8	16.5

Note: Figures cover employed civilians 16 years of age and older; (1) Figures cover the Fort Collins-Loveland, CO Metropolitan Statistical Area
Source: U.S. Census Bureau, 2019-2023 American Community Survey 5-Year Estimates

Occupations with Greatest Projected Employment Growth: 2022 – 2032

Occupation[1]	2022 Employment	2032 Projected Employment	Numeric Employment Change	Percent Employment Change
Software Developers	43,390	60,490	17,100	39.4
Cooks, Restaurant	34,160	44,800	10,640	31.1
Home Health and Personal Care Aides	38,300	48,710	10,410	27.2
Registered Nurses	53,720	63,290	9,570	17.8
Market Research Analysts and Marketing Specialists	35,930	44,390	8,460	23.5
Fast Food and Counter Workers	77,680	86,000	8,320	10.7
Business Operations Specialists, All Other	61,930	69,980	8,050	13.0
Stockers and Order Fillers	51,900	59,630	7,730	14.9
Sales Representatives of Services, Except Advertising, Insurance, Financial Services, and Travel	41,910	49,490	7,580	18.1
General and Operations Managers	56,730	64,050	7,320	12.9

Note: Projections cover Colorado; (1) Sorted by numeric employment change
Source: www.projectionscentral.org, State Occupational Projections, 2022–2032 Long-Term Projections

Fastest-Growing Occupations: 2022 – 2032

Occupation[1]	2022 Employment	2032 Projected Employment	Numeric Employment Change	Percent Employment Change
Flight Attendants	5,300	8,440	3,140	59.2
Nurse Practitioners	3,700	5,780	2,080	56.2
Epidemiologists	620	940	320	51.6
Information Security Analysts (SOC 2018)	6,110	9,220	3,110	50.9
Solar Photovoltaic Installers	580	870	290	50.0
Statisticians	1,560	2,290	730	46.8
Airline Pilots, Copilots, and Flight Engineers	5,040	7,380	2,340	46.4
Data Scientists	4,150	6,030	1,880	45.3
Veterinary Assistants and Laboratory Animal Caretakers	2,570	3,640	1,070	41.6
Medical and Health Services Managers	7,310	10,220	2,910	39.8

Note: Projections cover Colorado; (1) Sorted by percent employment change and excludes occupations with numeric employment change less than 50
Source: www.projectionscentral.org, State Occupational Projections, 2022–2032 Long-Term Projections

CITY FINANCES

City Government Finances

Component	2022 ($000)	2022 ($ per capita)
Total Revenues	575,021	3,418
Total Expenditures	716,679	4,260
Debt Outstanding	224,205	1,333

Source: U.S. Census Bureau, State & Local Government Finances 2022

City Government Revenue by Source

Source	2022 ($000)	2022 ($ per capita)	2022 (%)
General Revenue			
From Federal Government	40,775	242	7.1
From State Government	5,542	33	1.0
From Local Governments	32,130	191	5.6
Taxes			
Property	49,137	292	8.5
Sales and Gross Receipts	164,279	976	28.6
Personal Income	0	0	0.0
Corporate Income	0	0	0.0
Motor Vehicle License	0	0	0.0
Other Taxes	2,571	15	0.4
Current Charges	79,757	474	13.9
Liquor Store	0	0	0.0
Utility	190,761	1,134	33.2

Source: U.S. Census Bureau, State & Local Government Finances 2022

City Government Expenditures by Function

Function	2022 ($000)	2022 ($ per capita)	2022 (%)
General Direct Expenditures			
Air Transportation	0	0	0.0
Corrections	0	0	0.0
Education	0	0	0.0
Employment Security Administration	0	0	0.0
Financial Administration	4,969	29	0.7
Fire Protection	30,988	184	4.3
General Public Buildings	62,455	371	8.7
Governmental Administration, Other	28,170	167	3.9
Health	0	0	0.0
Highways	35,260	209	4.9
Hospitals	0	0	0.0
Housing and Community Development	26,575	158	3.7
Interest on General Debt	2,154	12	0.3
Judicial and Legal	0	0	0.0
Libraries	0	0	0.0
Parking	3,092	18	0.4
Parks and Recreation	36,228	215	5.1
Police Protection	47,737	283	6.7
Public Welfare	15,676	93	2.2
Sewerage	79,522	472	11.1
Solid Waste Management	0	0	0.0
Veterans' Services	0	0	0.0
Liquor Store	0	0	0.0
Utility	284,498	1,691	39.7

Source: U.S. Census Bureau, State & Local Government Finances 2022

TAXES

State Corporate Income Tax Rates

State	Tax Rate (%)	Income Brackets ($)	Num. of Brackets	Financial Institution Tax Rate (%)[a]	Federal Income Tax Ded.
Colorado	4.4	Flat rate	1	4.4	No

Note: Tax rates for tax year 2024; (a) Rates listed are the corporate income tax rate applied to financial institutions or excise taxes based on income. Some states have other taxes based upon the value of deposits or shares.
Source: Federation of Tax Administrators, State Corporate Income Tax Rates, January 1, 2025

State Individual Income Tax Rates

State	Tax Rate (%)	Income Brackets ($)	Personal Exemptions ($) Single	Married	Depend.	Standard Ded. ($) Single	Married
Colorado	4.4	Flat rate	(d)	(d)	(d)	14,600	29,200 (d)

Note: Tax rates for tax year 2024; Local- and county-level taxes are not included; (d) These states use the personal exemption/standard deduction amounts provided in the federal Internal Revenue Code. Montana personal exemption subject to repeal under Section 15-30-2114.
Source: Federation of Tax Administrators, State Individual Income Tax Rates, January 1, 2025

Various State Sales and Excise Tax Rates

State	State Sales Tax (%)	Gasoline[1] ($/gal.)	Cigarette[2] ($/pack)	Spirits[3] ($/gal.)	Wine[4] ($/gal.)	Beer[5] ($/gal.)	Recreational Marijuana (%)
Colorado	2.9	0.28	2.24	2.28	0.32	0.08	(d)

Note: All tax rates as of January 1, 2025; (1) The American Petroleum Institute has developed a methodology for determining the average tax rate on a gallon of fuel. Rates may include any of the following: excise taxes, environmental fees, storage tank fees, other fees or taxes, general sales tax, and local taxes; (2) The federal excise tax of $1.0066 per pack and local taxes are not included; (3) Rates are those applicable to off-premise sales of 40% alcohol by volume (a.b.v.) distilled spirits in 750ml containers. Local excise taxes are excluded; (4) Rates are those applicable to off-premise sales of 11% a.b.v. non-carbonated wine in 750ml containers; (5) Rates are those applicable to off-premise sales of 4.7% a.b.v. beer in 12 ounce containers; (d) 15% excise tax (levied on wholesale at average market rate); 15% excise tax (retail price)
Source: Tax Foundation, 2025 Facts & Figures: How Does Your State Compare?

State Tax Competitiveness Index

State	Overall Rank	Corporate Tax Rank	Individual Income Tax Rank	Sales Tax Rank	Property Tax Rank	Unemployment Insurance Tax Rank
Colorado	32	10	18	37	36	39

Note: The Tax Foundation's State Tax Competitiveness Index enables policymakers, taxpayers, and business leaders to gauge how their states' tax systems compare. A rank of 1 is best, 50 is worst. Rankings do not average to the total. States without a tax rank equally as 1. DC's scores and rankings do not affect other states. The report shows tax systems as of July 1, 2024 (the beginning of Fiscal Year 2025).
Source: Tax Foundation, State Tax Competitiveness Index 2025

TRANSPORTATION

Means of Transportation to Work

Area	Car/Truck/Van		Public Transportation			Bicycle	Walked	Other Means	Worked at Home
	Drove Alone	Car-pooled	Bus	Subway	Railroad				
City	63.3	5.6	1.4	0.0	0.0	4.2	4.2	1.0	20.2
MSA[1]	68.4	5.6	0.9	0.0	0.0	2.4	2.8	1.1	18.9
U.S.	70.2	8.5	1.7	1.3	0.4	0.4	2.4	1.6	13.5

Note: Figures are percentages and cover workers 16 years of age and older; (1) Figures cover the Fort Collins-Loveland, CO Metropolitan Statistical Area
Source: U.S. Census Bureau, 2019-2023 American Community Survey 5-Year Estimates

Travel Time to Work

Area	Less Than 10 Minutes	10 to 19 Minutes	20 to 29 Minutes	30 to 44 Minutes	45 to 59 Minutes	60 to 89 Minutes	90 Minutes or More
City	15.6	45.7	19.3	10.1	4.6	3.3	1.4
MSA[1]	13.9	36.1	21.5	15.8	6.0	4.6	2.1
U.S.	12.6	28.6	21.2	20.8	8.1	6.0	2.8

Note: Note: Figures are percentages and include workers 16 years old and over; (1) Figures cover the Fort Collins-Loveland, CO Metropolitan Statistical Area
Source: U.S. Census Bureau, 2019-2023 American Community Survey 5-Year Estimates

Key Congestion Measures

Measure	2000	2010	2015	2020	2022
Annual Hours of Delay, Total (000)	n/a	n/a	5,902	3,465	7,223
Annual Hours of Delay, Per Auto Commuter	n/a	n/a	21	12	25
Annual Congestion Cost, Per Auto Commuter ($)	n/a	n/a	471	286	569

Note: n/a not available
Source: Texas A&M Transportation Institute, 2023 Urban Mobility Report

Freeway Travel Time Index

Measure	1985	1990	1995	2000	2005	2010	2015	2020	2022
Urban Area Index[1]	n/a	n/a	n/a	n/a	n/a	n/a	1.10	1.07	1.12
Urban Area Rank[1,2]	n/a	n/a	n/a	n/a	n/a	n/a	n/a	n/a	n/a

Note: Freeway Travel Time Index—the ratio of travel time in the peak period to the travel time at free-flow conditions. For example, a value of 1.30 indicates a 20-minute free-flow trip takes 26 minutes in the peak (20 minutes x 1.30 = 26 minutes); (1) Covers the Fort Collins CO urban area; (2) Rank is based on 101 larger urban areas (#1 = highest travel time index); n/a not available
Source: Texas A&M Transportation Institute, 2023 Urban Mobility Report

Public Transportation

Agency Name / Mode of Transportation	Vehicles Operated in Maximum Service[1]	Annual Unlinked Passenger Trips[2] (in thous.)	Annual Passenger Miles[3] (in thous.)
Transfort			
Bus (directly operated)	26	1,587.1	5,948.3
Bus (purchased transportation)	2	13.7	41.6
Bus Rapid Transit (directly operated)	6	451.1	1,274.6
Demand Response (purchased transportation)	2	4.7	47.3
Demand Response - Taxi	10	28.0	146.0

Note: (1) Number of revenue vehicles operated by the given mode and type of service to meet the annual maximum service requirement. This is the revenue vehicle count during the peak season of the year; on the week and day that maximum service is provided. Vehicles operated in maximum service (VOMS) exclude atypical days and one-time special events; (2) Number of passengers who boarded public transportation vehicles. Passengers are counted each time they board a vehicle no matter how many vehicles they use to travel from their origin to their destination. (3) Sum of the distances ridden by all passengers during the entire fiscal year.
Source: Federal Transit Administration, National Transit Database, 2023

Air Transportation

Airport Name and Code / Type of Service	Passenger Airlines[1]	Passenger Enplanements	Freight Carriers[2]	Freight (lbs)
Denver International (60 miles) (DEN)				
Domestic service (U.S. carriers only)	30	37,751,107	13	268,238,885
International service (U.S. carriers only)	8	1,461,931	3	8,628,050

Note: (1) Includes all U.S.-based major, minor and commuter airlines that carried at least one passenger during the year; (2) Includes all U.S.-based airlines and freight carriers that transported at least one pound of freight during the year.
Source: Bureau of Transportation Statistics, The Intermodal Transportation Database, Air Carriers: T-100 Domestic Market (U.S. carriers only), 2024; Bureau of Transportation Statistics, The Intermodal Transportation Database, Air Carriers: T-100 International Market (U.S. carriers only), 2024

BUSINESSES

Major Business Headquarters

Company Name	Industry	Rankings	
		Fortune[1]	Forbes[2]
No companies listed	-	-	-

Note: (1) Companies that produce a 10-K are ranked 1 to 500 based on 2023 revenue; (2) All private companies with at least $2 billion in annual revenue through the end of their most current fiscal year are ranked 1 to 275; companies listed are headquartered in the city; dashes indicate no ranking
Source: Fortune, "Fortune 500," 2024; Forbes, "America's Largest Private Companies," 2024

Living Environment

COST OF LIVING

Cost of Living Index

Composite Index	Groceries	Housing	Utilities	Trans-portation	Health Care	Misc. Goods/ Services
n/a	n/a	n/a	n/a	n/a	n/a	n/a

Note: The Cost of Living Index measures regional differences in the cost of consumer goods and services, excluding taxes and non-consumer expenditures, for professional and managerial households in the top income quintile. It is based on more than 50,000 prices covering almost 60 different items for which prices are collected three times a year by chambers of commerce, economic development organizations or university applied economic centers in each participating urban area. The numbers shown should be read as a percentage above or below the national average of 100. For example, a value of 115.4 in the groceries column indicates that grocery prices are 15.4% higher than the national average. Small differences in the index numbers should not be interpreted as significant; n/a not available.
Source: The Council for Community and Economic Research, Cost of Living Index, 2024

Grocery Prices

Area[1]	T-Bone Steak ($/pound)	Frying Chicken ($/pound)	Whole Milk ($/half gal.)	Eggs ($/dozen)	Orange Juice ($/64 oz.)	Coffee ($/11.5 oz.)
City[2]	n/a	n/a	n/a	n/a	n/a	n/a
Avg.	15.42	1.55	4.69	3.25	4.41	5.46
Min.	14.50	1.16	4.43	2.75	4.00	4.85
Max.	17.56	2.89	5.49	4.78	5.54	7.89

*Note: (1) Values for the local area are compared with the average, minimum and maximum values for all 276 areas in the Cost of Living Index; (2) Figures cover the Fort Collins CO urban area; n/a not available; **T-Bone Steak** (price per pound); **Frying Chicken** (price per pound, whole fryer); **Whole Milk** (half gallon carton); **Eggs** (price per dozen, Grade A, large); **Orange Juice** (64 oz. Tropicana or Florida Natural); **Coffee** (11.5 oz. can, vacuum-packed, Maxwell House, Hills Bros, or Folgers).*
Source: The Council for Community and Economic Research, Cost of Living Index, 2024

Housing and Utility Costs

Area[1]	New Home Price ($)	Apartment Rent ($/month)	All Electric ($/month)	Part Electric ($/month)	Other Energy ($/month)	Telephone ($/month)
City[2]	n/a	n/a	n/a	n/a	n/a	n/a
Avg.	515,975	1,550	210.99	123.07	82.07	194.99
Min.	265,375	692	104.33	53.68	36.26	179.42
Max.	2,775,821	5,719	529.02	397.28	361.63	223.33

*Note: (1) Values for the local area are compared with the average, minimum and maximum values for all 276 areas in the Cost of Living Index; (2) Figures cover the Fort Collins CO urban area; n/a not available; **New Home Price** (2,400 sf living area, 8,000 sf lot, in urban area with full utilities); **Apartment Rent** (950 sf 2 bedroom/1.5 or 2 bath, unfurnished, excluding all utilities except water); **All Electric** (average monthly cost for an all-electric home); **Part Electric** (average monthly cost for a part-electric home); **Other Energy** (average monthly cost for natural gas, fuel oil, coal, wood, and any other forms of energy except electricity); **Telephone** (price includes the base monthly rate plus taxes and fees for three lines of mobile phone service).*
Source: The Council for Community and Economic Research, Cost of Living Index, 2024

Health Care, Transportation, and Other Costs

Area[1]	Doctor ($/visit)	Dentist ($/visit)	Optometrist ($/visit)	Gasoline ($/gallon)	Beauty Salon ($/visit)	Men's Shirt ($)
City[2]	n/a	n/a	n/a	n/a	n/a	n/a
Avg.	143.77	117.51	129.23	3.32	48.57	38.14
Min.	36.74	58.67	67.33	2.80	24.00	13.41
Max.	270.44	216.82	307.33	5.28	94.00	63.89

*Note: (1) Values for the local area are compared with the average, minimum and maximum values for all 276 areas in the Cost of Living Index; (2) Figures cover the Fort Collins CO urban area; n/a not available; **Doctor** (general practitioners routine exam of an established patient); **Dentist** (adult teeth cleaning and periodic oral examination); **Optometrist** (full vision eye exam for established adult patient); **Gasoline** (one gallon regular unleaded, national brand, including all taxes, cash price at self-service pump if available); **Beauty Salon** (woman's shampoo, trim, and blow-dry); **Men's Shirt** (cotton/polyester dress shirt, pinpoint weave, long sleeves).*
Source: The Council for Community and Economic Research, Cost of Living Index, 2024

HOUSING

Homeownership Rate

Area	2017 (%)	2018 (%)	2019 (%)	2020 (%)	2021 (%)	2022 (%)	2023 (%)	2024 (%)
MSA[1]	n/a	n/a	n/a	n/a	n/a	n/a	n/a	n/a
U.S.	63.9	64.4	64.6	66.6	65.5	65.8	65.9	65.6

Note: (1) Figures cover the Fort Collins-Loveland, CO Metropolitan Statistical Area; n/a not available
Source: U.S. Census Bureau, Housing Vacancies and Homeownership Annual Statistics: 2017-2024

House Price Index (HPI)

Area	National Ranking[2]	Quarterly Change (%)	One-Year Change (%)	Five-Year Change (%)	Since 1991Q1 (%)
MSA[1]	215	-0.72	2.52	44.72	544.83
U.S.[3]	–	1.43	4.51	57.13	327.82

Note: The HPI is a weighted repeat sales index. It measures average price changes in repeat sales or refinancings on the same properties. This information is obtained by reviewing repeat mortgage transactions on single-family properties whose mortgages have been purchased or securitized by Fannie Mae or Freddie Mac since January 1975; (1) Figures cover the Fort Collins, CO Metropolitan Statistical Area; (2) Rankings are based on annual percentage change for all metro areas containing at least 15,000 transactions over the last 10 years and ranges from 1 to 241; (3) figures based on a weighted average of Census Division estimates using a seasonally adjusted, purchase-only index; all figures are for the period ending December 31, 2024
Source: Federal Housing Finance Agency, Change in FHFA Metropolitan Area House Price Indexes, All Transactions Index, 2024Q4

Home Value

Area	Under $100,000	$100,000 -$199,999	$200,000 -$299,999	$300,000 -$399,999	$400,000 -$499,999	$500,000 -$999,999	$1,000,000 or more	Median ($)
City	3.7	1.7	4.2	9.6	22.7	52.5	5.6	548,400
MSA[1]	4.8	1.6	4.6	11.8	22.6	47.6	6.9	532,200
U.S.	12.1	17.8	19.5	14.4	10.5	19.1	6.5	303,400

Note: Figures are percentages except for median and cover owner-occupied housing units; (1) Figures cover the Fort Collins-Loveland, CO Metropolitan Statistical Area
Source: U.S. Census Bureau, 2019-2023 American Community Survey 5-Year Estimates

Year Housing Structure Built

Area	2020 or Later	2010 -2019	2000 -2009	1990 -1999	1980 -1989	1970 -1979	1960 -1969	1950 -1959	1940 -1949	Before 1940	Median Year
City	1.5	15.0	18.9	19.0	14.5	15.7	6.5	3.0	1.3	4.5	1992
MSA[1]	2.2	16.8	18.4	17.5	12.3	16.7	5.8	3.2	1.8	5.3	1993
U.S.	1.2	8.9	13.6	12.8	13.0	14.4	10.0	9.7	4.5	11.9	1980

Note: Figures are percentages except for Median Year; Note: (1) Figures cover the Fort Collins-Loveland, CO Metropolitan Statistical Area
Source: U.S. Census Bureau, 2019-2023 American Community Survey 5-Year Estimates

Gross Monthly Rent

Area	Under $500	$500 -$999	$1,000 -$1,499	$1,500 -$1,999	$2,000 -$2,499	$2,500 -$2,999	$3,000 and up	Median ($)
City	2.5	10.8	26.1	33.0	19.7	6.0	1.9	1,661
MSA[1]	2.6	10.0	25.7	33.1	18.9	6.6	3.1	1,677
U.S.	6.5	22.3	29.5	20.2	10.8	4.8	5.9	1,348

Note: Figures are percentages except for median; Gross rent is the contract rent plus the estimated average monthly cost of utilities (electricity, gas, and water and sewer) and fuels (oil, coal, kerosene, wood, etc.) if these are paid by the renter (or paid for the renter by someone else); (1) Figures cover the Fort Collins-Loveland, CO Metropolitan Statistical Area
Source: U.S. Census Bureau, 2019-2023 American Community Survey 5-Year Estimates

HEALTH

Health Risk Factors

Category	MSA[1] (%)	U.S. (%)
Adults aged 18–64 who have any kind of health care coverage	n/a	90.8
Adults who reported being in good or better health	n/a	81.8
Adults who have been told they have high blood cholesterol	n/a	36.9
Adults who have been told they have high blood pressure	n/a	34.0
Adults who are current smokers	n/a	12.1
Adults who currently use e-cigarettes	n/a	7.7
Adults who currently use chewing tobacco, snuff, or snus	n/a	3.2
Adults who are heavy drinkers[2]	n/a	6.1
Adults who are binge drinkers[3]	n/a	15.2
Adults who are overweight (BMI 25.0 - 29.9)	n/a	34.4
Adults who are obese (BMI 30.0 - 99.8)	n/a	34.3
Adults who participated in any physical activities in the past month	n/a	75.8

Note: All figures are crude prevalence; (1) Figures for the Fort Collins-Loveland, CO Metropolitan Statistical Area were not available.
(2) Heavy drinkers are classified as adult men having more than 14 drinks per week and adult women having more than 7 drinks per week; (3) Binge drinkers are classified as males having five or more drinks on one occasion or females having four or more drinks on one occasion
Source: Centers for Disease Control and Prevention, Behaviorial Risk Factor Surveillance System, SMART: Selected Metropolitan Area Risk Trends, 2023

Acute and Chronic Health Conditions

Category	MSA[1] (%)	U.S. (%)
Adults who have ever been told they had a heart attack	n/a	4.2
Adults who have ever been told they have angina or coronary heart disease	n/a	4.0
Adults who have ever been told they had a stroke	n/a	3.3
Adults who have ever been told they have asthma	n/a	15.7
Adults who have ever been told they have arthritis	n/a	26.3
Adults who have ever been told they have diabetes[2]	n/a	11.5
Adults who have ever been told they had skin cancer	n/a	5.6
Adults who have ever been told they had any other types of cancer	n/a	8.4
Adults who have ever been told they have COPD	n/a	6.4
Adults who have ever been told they have kidney disease	n/a	3.7
Adults who have ever been told they have a form of depression	n/a	22.0

Note: All figures are crude prevalence; (1) Figures for the Fort Collins-Loveland, CO Metropolitan Statistical Area were not available.
(2) Figures do not include pregnancy-related, borderline, or pre-diabetes
Source: Centers for Disease Control and Prevention, Behaviorial Risk Factor Surveillance System, SMART: Selected Metropolitan Area Risk Trends, 2023

Health Screening and Vaccination Rates

Category	MSA[1] (%)	U.S. (%)
Adults who have ever been tested for HIV	n/a	37.5
Adults who have had their blood cholesterol checked within the last five years	n/a	87.0
Adults aged 65+ who have had flu shot within the past year	n/a	63.4
Adults aged 65+ who have ever had a pneumonia vaccination	n/a	71.9

Note: All figures are crude prevalence; (1) Figures for the Fort Collins-Loveland, CO Metropolitan Statistical Area were not available.
Source: Centers for Disease Control and Prevention, Behaviorial Risk Factor Surveillance System, SMART: Selected Metropolitan Area Risk Trends, 2023

Disability Status

Category	MSA[1] (%)	U.S. (%)
Adults who reported being deaf	n/a	7.4
Are you blind or have serious difficulty seeing, even when wearing glasses?	n/a	4.9
Do you have difficulty doing errands alone?	n/a	7.8
Do you have difficulty dressing or bathing?	n/a	3.6
Do you have serious difficulty concentrating/remembering/making decisions?	n/a	13.7
Do you have serious difficulty walking or climbing stairs?	n/a	13.2

Note: All figures are crude prevalence; (1) Figures for the Fort Collins-Loveland, CO Metropolitan Statistical Area were not available.
Source: Centers for Disease Control and Prevention, Behaviorial Risk Factor Surveillance System, SMART: Selected Metropolitan Area Risk Trends, 2023

Mortality Rates for the Top 10 Causes of Death in the U.S.

ICD-10[a] Sub-Chapter	ICD-10[a] Code	Crude Mortality Rate[2] per 100,000 population	
		County[3]	U.S.
Malignant neoplasms	C00-C97	143.6	182.7
Ischaemic heart diseases	I20-I25	58.9	109.6
Provisional assignment of new diseases of uncertain etiology[1]	U00-U49	35.6	65.3
Other forms of heart disease	I30-I51	50.4	65.1
Other degenerative diseases of the nervous system	G30-G31	53.6	52.4
Other external causes of accidental injury	W00-X59	39.6	52.3
Cerebrovascular diseases	I60-I69	42.9	49.1
Chronic lower respiratory diseases	J40-J47	34.3	43.5
Hypertensive diseases	I10-I15	27.2	38.9
Organic, including symptomatic, mental disorders	F01-F09	34.5	33.9

Note: (a) ICD-10 = International Classification of Diseases 10th Revision; (1) Includes COVID-19, adverse effects to COVID-19 vaccines, SARS, and vaping-related disorders; (2) Crude mortality rates are a three-year average covering 2021-2023; (3) Figures cover Larimer County.
Source: Centers for Disease Control and Prevention, National Center for Health Statistics. National Vital Statistics System, Mortality 2018-2023 on CDC WONDER Online Database

Mortality Rates for Selected Causes of Death

Cause of Death	ICD-10[a] Code	Crude Mortality Rate[1] per 100,000 population	
		County[2]	U.S.
Accidental poisoning and exposure to noxious substances	X40-X49	17.3	30.5
Alzheimer disease	G30	41.3	35.4
Assault	X85-Y09	1.9	7.3
COVID-19	U07.1	35.6	65.3
Diabetes mellitus	E10-E14	20.0	30.0
Diseases of the liver	K70-K76	18.7	20.8
Human immunodeficiency virus (HIV) disease	B20-B24	Suppressed	1.5
Influenza and pneumonia	J09-J18	5.5	13.4
Intentional self-harm	X60-X84	19.5	14.7
Malnutrition	E40-E46	Unreliable	6.0
Obesity and other hyperalimentation	E65-E68	Unreliable	3.1
Renal failure	N17-N19	7.3	16.4
Transport accidents	V01-V99	11.5	14.4

Note: (a) ICD-10 = International Classification of Diseases 10th Revision; (1) Crude mortality rates are a three-year average covering 2021-2023; (2) Figures cover Larimer County; Data are suppressed when the data meet the criteria for confidentiality constraints; Crude mortality rates are flagged as unreliable when the rate would be calculated with a numerator of 20 or less.
Source: Centers for Disease Control and Prevention, National Center for Health Statistics. National Vital Statistics System, Mortality 2018-2023 on CDC WONDER Online Database

Health Insurance Coverage

Area	With Health Insurance	With Private Health Insurance	With Public Health Insurance	Without Health Insurance	Population Under Age 19 Without Health Insurance
City	94.4	78.3	25.0	5.6	4.8
MSA[1]	94.3	74.9	31.0	5.7	3.8
U.S.	91.4	67.3	36.3	8.6	5.4

Note: Figures are percentages that cover the civilian noninstitutionalized population; (1) Figures cover the Fort Collins-Loveland, CO Metropolitan Statistical Area
Source: U.S. Census Bureau, 2019-2023 American Community Survey 5-Year Estimates

Number of Medical Professionals

Area	MDs[3]	DOs[3,4]	Dentists	Podiatrists	Chiropractors	Optometrists
County[1] (number)	924	144	316	24	213	79
County[1] (rate[2])	251.9	39.3	85.2	6.5	57.4	21.3
U.S. (rate[2])	302.5	29.2	74.6	6.4	29.5	18.0

Note: Data as of 2023 unless noted; (1) Data covers Larimer County; (2) Number of medical professionals per 100,000 population; (3) Data as of 2022 and includes all active, non-federal physicians; (4) Doctor of Osteopathic Medicine
Source: U.S. Department of Health and Human Services, Health Resources and Services Administration, Bureau of Health Professions, Area Resource File (ARF) 2023-2024

EDUCATION

Public School District Statistics

District Name	Schls	Pupils	Pupil/ Teacher Ratio	Minority Pupils[1] (%)	Total Rev. per Pupil ($)	Total Exp. per Pupil ($)
Poudre School District R-1	52	29,772	15.8	29.5	15,135	17,617

Note: Table includes school districts with 2,000 or more students; (1) Percentage of students that are not non-Hispanic white.
Source: U.S. Department of Education, National Center for Education Statistics, Common Core of Data, Local Education Agency (School District) Universe Survey: School Year 2023-2024; U.S. Department of Education, National Center for Education Statistics, Common Core of Data, School District Finance Survey (F-33): School Year 2021–22

Best High Schools

According to *U.S. News,* Fort Collins is home to one of the top 500 high schools in the U.S.: **Liberty Common Charter School** (#145). Nearly 25,000 public, magnet and charter schools were ranked based on their performance on state assessments and how well they prepare students for college. *U.S. News & World Report, "Best High Schools 2024"*

Highest Level of Education

Area	Less than H.S.	H.S. Diploma	Some College, No Deg.	Associate Degree	Bachelor's Degree	Master's Degree	Prof. School Degree	Doctorate Degree
City	2.4	13.5	16.1	8.2	34.3	18.9	2.8	3.9
MSA[1]	3.4	16.8	19.3	8.8	31.0	14.9	2.7	3.1
U.S.	10.6	26.2	19.4	8.8	21.3	9.8	2.3	1.6

Note: Figures cover persons age 25 and over; (1) Figures cover the Fort Collins-Loveland, CO Metropolitan Statistical Area
Source: U.S. Census Bureau, 2019-2023 American Community Survey 5-Year Estimates

Educational Attainment by Race

Area	High School Graduate or Higher (%)					Bachelor's Degree or Higher (%)				
	Total	White	Black	Asian	Hisp.[2]	Total	White	Black	Asian	Hisp.[2]
City	97.6	98.4	87.7	95.1	91.1	59.9	62.0	34.6	76.2	37.0
MSA[1]	96.6	97.7	91.5	95.6	85.2	51.7	53.4	37.7	69.3	29.5
U.S.	89.4	92.9	88.1	88.0	72.5	35.0	37.7	24.7	57.0	19.9

Note: Figures shown cover persons 25 years old and over; (1) Figures cover the Fort Collins-Loveland, CO Metropolitan Statistical Area; (2) People of Hispanic origin can be of any race
Source: U.S. Census Bureau, 2019-2023 American Community Survey 5-Year Estimates

School Enrollment by Grade and Control

Area	Preschool (%)		Kindergarten (%)		Grades 1 - 4 (%)		Grades 5 - 8 (%)		Grades 9 - 12 (%)	
	Public	Private	Public	Private	Public	Private	Public	Private	Public	Private
City	48.1	51.9	87.7	12.3	89.2	10.8	92.4	7.6	94.5	5.5
MSA[1]	52.8	47.2	85.7	14.3	85.4	14.6	86.7	13.3	88.2	11.8
U.S.	58.7	41.3	85.2	14.8	87.2	12.8	87.9	12.1	89.0	11.0

Note: Figures shown cover persons 3 years old and over; (1) Figures cover the Fort Collins-Loveland, CO Metropolitan Statistical Area
Source: U.S. Census Bureau, 2019-2023 American Community Survey 5-Year Estimates

Higher Education

Four-Year Colleges			Two-Year Colleges			Medical Schools[1]	Law Schools[2]	Voc/ Tech[3]
Public	Private Non-profit	Private For-profit	Public	Private Non-profit	Private For-profit			
1	0	0	0	0	1	0	0	2

Note: Figures cover institutions located within the Fort Collins-Loveland, CO Metropolitan Statistical Area and include main campuses only; (1) includes schools accredited by the Liaison Committee on Medical Education and the American Osteopathic Association's Commission on Osteopathic College Accreditation; (2) includes ABA-accredited schools, schools with provisional ABA accreditation, and state accredited schools; (3) includes all schools with programs that are less than 2 years.
Source: National Center for Education Statistics, Integrated Postsecondary Education System (IPEDS), 2023-24; Wikipedia, List of Medical Schools in the United States, accessed May 2, 2025; Wikipedia, List of Law Schools in the United States, accessed May 2, 2025

According to *U.S. News & World Report,* the Fort Collins-Loveland, CO metro area is home to one of the top 200 national universities in the U.S.: **Colorado State University** (#148 tie). The indicators used to capture academic quality fall into a number of categories: assessment by administrators at peer institutions; retention of students; faculty resources; student selectivity; financial resources; alumni giving; high school counselor ratings of colleges; and graduation rate. *U.S. News & World Report, "America's Best Colleges 2025"*

EMPLOYERS

Major Employers

Company Name	Industry
Advanced Energy Industries	Energy
Boyd Group Services	Financial services
Broadcom	Manufacturing
City of Fort Collins	Local government
Colorado State University	Higher education
Larimer County	Local government
Poudre School District	Education
Rimrock	Electric utilities
University of Colorado Health	Healthcare system
Woodward	Aerospace, energy

Note: Companies shown are located within the Fort Collins-Loveland, CO Metropolitan Statistical Area.
Source: Chambers of Commerce; State Departments of Labor; Wikipedia

PUBLIC SAFETY

Crime Rate

| Area | Total Crime Rate | Violent Crime Rate | | | | Property Crime Rate | | |
		Murder	Rape	Robbery	Aggrav. Assault	Burglary	Larceny -Theft	Motor Vehicle Theft
City	2,736.2	0.6	29.0	36.7	229.7	273.6	1,958.1	208.4
U.S.	2,290.9	5.7	38.0	66.5	264.1	250.7	1,347.2	318.7

Note: Figures are crimes per 100,000 population.
Source: FBI, Table 8, Offenses Known to Law Enforcement, by State by City, 2023

Hate Crimes

| Area | Number of Quarters Reported | Number of Incidents per Bias Motivation | | | | | |
		Race/Ethnicity/ Ancestry	Religion	Sexual Orientation	Disability	Gender	Gender Identity
City[1]	4	8	0	4	0	0	1
U.S.	4	5,900	2,699	2,077	187	92	492

Note: (1) Figures include at least one incident reported with more than one bias motivation.
Source: Federal Bureau of Investigation, Hate Crime Statistics 2023

Identity Theft Consumer Reports

Area	Reports	Reports per 100,000 Population	Rank[2]
MSA[1]	588	162	237
U.S.	1,135,291	339	-

Note: (1) Figures cover the Fort Collins-Loveland, CO Metropolitan Statistical Area; (2) Rank ranges from 1 to 401 where 1 indicates greatest number of identity theft reports per 100,000 population
Source: Federal Trade Commission, Consumer Sentinel Network Data Book 2024

Fraud and Other Consumer Reports

Area	Reports	Reports per 100,000 Population	Rank[2]
MSA[1]	5,396	1,484	63
U.S.	5,360,641	1,601	-

Note: (1) Figures cover the Fort Collins-Loveland, CO Metropolitan Statistical Area; (2) Rank ranges from 1 to 401 where 1 indicates greatest number of fraud and other consumer reports per 100,000 population
Source: Federal Trade Commission, Consumer Sentinel Network Data Book 2024

POLITICS

2024 Presidential Election Results

Area	Trump (Rep.)	Harris (Dem.)	Stein (Green)	Kennedy (Ind.)	Oliver (Lib.)	Other
Larimer County	39.7	57.3	0.5	1.2	0.8	0.5
U.S.	49.7	48.2	0.6	0.5	0.4	0.6

Note: Results are percentages and may not add to 100% due to rounding
Source: Dave Leip's Atlas of U.S. Presidential Elections

SPORTS

Professional Sports Teams

Team Name	League	Year Established

No teams are located in the metro area
Source: Wikipedia, Major Professional Sports Teams of the United States and Canada, May 1, 2025

CLIMATE

Average and Extreme Temperatures

Temperature	Jan	Feb	Mar	Apr	May	Jun	Jul	Aug	Sep	Oct	Nov	Dec	Yr.
Extreme High (°F)	73	76	84	90	93	102	103	100	97	89	79	75	103
Average High (°F)	43	47	52	62	71	81	88	86	77	67	52	45	64
Average Temp. (°F)	30	34	39	48	58	67	73	72	63	52	39	32	51
Average Low (°F)	16	20	25	34	44	53	59	57	48	37	25	18	37
Extreme Low (°F)	-25	-25	-10	-2	22	30	43	41	17	3	-8	-25	-25

Note: Figures cover the years 1948-1992
Source: National Climatic Data Center, International Station Meteorological Climate Summary, 9/96

Average Precipitation/Snowfall/Humidity

Precip./Humidity	Jan	Feb	Mar	Apr	May	Jun	Jul	Aug	Sep	Oct	Nov	Dec	Yr.
Avg. Precip. (in.)	0.6	0.6	1.3	1.7	2.5	1.7	1.9	1.5	1.1	1.0	0.9	0.6	15.5
Avg. Snowfall (in.)	9	7	14	9	2	Tr	0	0	2	4	9	8	63
Avg. Rel. Hum. 5am (%)	62	65	67	66	70	68	67	68	66	63	66	63	66
Avg. Rel. Hum. 5pm (%)	49	44	40	35	38	34	34	34	32	34	47	50	39

Note: Figures cover the years 1948-1992; Tr = Trace amounts (<0.05 in. of rain; <0.5 in. of snow)
Source: National Climatic Data Center, International Station Meteorological Climate Summary, 9/96

Weather Conditions

Temperature			Daytime Sky			Precipitation		
10°F & below	32°F & below	90°F & above	Clear	Partly cloudy	Cloudy	0.01 inch or more precip.	0.1 inch or more snow/ice	Thunder-storms
24	155	33	99	177	89	90	38	39

Note: Figures are average number of days per year and cover the years 1948-1992
Source: National Climatic Data Center, International Station Meteorological Climate Summary, 9/96

HAZARDOUS WASTE

Superfund Sites

The Fort Collins-Loveland, CO metro area has no sites on the EPA's Superfund Final National Priorities List (NPL) or Superfund Alternative Approach (SAA) list. The Superfund alternative approach uses the same investigation and cleanup process and standards that are used for sites listed on the National Priorities List. The SAA is an alternative to listing a site on the NPL; it is not an alternative to Superfund or the Superfund process. There are a total of 1,445 Superfund sites with a status of proposed or final on both lists in the United States. *U.S. Environmental Protection Agency, National Priorities List, May 1, 2025; U.S. Environmental Protection Agency, Superfund Alternative Approach Sites, May 1, 2025*

AIR QUALITY

Air Quality Trends: Ozone

	1990	1995	2000	2005	2010	2015	2020	2021	2022	2023
MSA[1]	0.066	0.072	0.074	0.075	0.072	0.070	0.070	0.077	0.070	0.067
U.S.	0.087	0.089	0.081	0.080	0.072	0.068	0.066	0.067	0.067	0.070

Note: (1) Data covers the Fort Collins-Loveland, CO Metropolitan Statistical Area. The values shown are the composite ozone concentration averages among trend sites based on the highest fourth daily maximum 8-hour concentration in parts per million. These trends are based on sites having an adequate record of monitoring data during the trend period. Data from exceptional events are included.
Source: U.S. Environmental Protection Agency, Air Quality Monitoring Information, "Air Quality Trends by City, 1990-2023"

Air Quality Index

Area	Percent of Days when Air Quality was...[2]					AQI Statistics[2]	
	Good	Moderate	Unhealthy for Sensitive Groups	Unhealthy	Very Unhealthy	Maximum	Median
MSA[1]	47.9	50.7	1.1	0.3	0.0	156	51

Note: (1) Data covers the Fort Collins-Loveland, CO Metropolitan Statistical Area; (2) Based on 365 days with AQI data in 2023. Air Quality Index (AQI) is an index for reporting daily air quality. EPA calculates the AQI for five major air pollutants regulated by the Clean Air Act: ground-level ozone, particle pollution (aka particulate matter), carbon monoxide, sulfur dioxide, and nitrogen dioxide. The AQI runs from 0 to 500. The higher the AQI value, the greater the level of air pollution and the greater the health concern. There are six AQI categories: "Good" AQI is between 0 and 50. Air quality is considered satisfactory; "Moderate" AQI is between 51 and 100. Air quality is acceptable; "Unhealthy for Sensitive Groups" When AQI values are between 101 and 150, members of sensitive groups may experience health effects; "Unhealthy" When AQI values are between 151 and 200 everyone may begin to experience health effects; "Very Unhealthy" AQI values between 201 and 300 trigger a health alert; "Hazardous" AQI values over 300 trigger warnings of emergency conditions (not shown).
Source: U.S. Environmental Protection Agency, Air Quality Index Report, 2023

Air Quality Index Pollutants

Area	Percent of Days when AQI Pollutant was...[2]					
	Carbon Monoxide	Nitrogen Dioxide	Ozone	Sulfur Dioxide	Particulate Matter 2.5	Particulate Matter 10
MSA[1]	0.0	0.0	83.3	(3)	16.7	0.0

Note: (1) Data covers the Fort Collins-Loveland, CO Metropolitan Statistical Area; (2) Based on 365 days with AQI data in 2023. The Air Quality Index (AQI) is an index for reporting daily air quality. EPA calculates the AQI for five major air pollutants regulated by the Clean Air Act: ground-level ozone, particle pollution (also known as particulate matter), carbon monoxide, sulfur dioxide, and nitrogen dioxide. The AQI runs from 0 to 500. The higher the AQI value, the greater the level of air pollution and the greater the health concern; (3) Sulfur dioxide is no longer included in this table because SO_2 concentrations tend to be very localized and not necessarily representative of broad geographical areas like counties and CBSAs.
Source: U.S. Environmental Protection Agency, Air Quality Index Report, 2023

Maximum Air Pollutant Concentrations: Particulate Matter, Ozone, CO and Lead

	Particulate Matter 10 (ug/m^3)	Particulate Matter 2.5 Wtd AM (ug/m^3)	Particulate Matter 2.5 24-Hr (ug/m^3)	Ozone (ppm)	Carbon Monoxide (ppm)	Lead (ug/m^3)
MSA[1] Level	n/a	n/a	n/a	0.071	1	n/a
NAAQS[2]	150	15	35	0.075	9	0.15
Met NAAQS[2]	n/a	n/a	n/a	Yes	Yes	n/a

Note: (1) Data covers the Fort Collins-Loveland, CO Metropolitan Statistical Area; Data from exceptional events are included; (2) National Ambient Air Quality Standards; ppm = parts per million; ug/m^3 = micrograms per cubic meter; n/a not available.
Concentrations: Particulate Matter 10 (coarse particulate)—highest second maximum 24-hour concentration; Particulate Matter 2.5 Wtd AM (fine particulate)—highest weighted annual mean concentration; Particulate Matter 2.5 24-Hour (fine particulate)—highest 98th percentile 24-hour concentration; Ozone—highest fourth daily maximum 8-hour concentration; Carbon Monoxide—highest second maximum non-overlapping 8-hour concentration; Lead—maximum running 3-month average
Source: U.S. Environmental Protection Agency, Air Quality Monitoring Information, "Air Quality Statistics by City, 2023"

Maximum Air Pollutant Concentrations: Nitrogen Dioxide and Sulfur Dioxide

	Nitrogen Dioxide AM (ppb)	Nitrogen Dioxide 1-Hr (ppb)	Sulfur Dioxide AM (ppb)	Sulfur Dioxide 1-Hr (ppb)	Sulfur Dioxide 24-Hr (ppb)
MSA[1] Level	n/a	n/a	n/a	n/a	n/a
NAAQS[2]	53	100	30	75	140
Met NAAQS[2]	n/a	n/a	n/a	n/a	n/a

Note: (1) Data covers the Fort Collins-Loveland, CO Metropolitan Statistical Area; Data from exceptional events are included; (2) National Ambient Air Quality Standards; ppm = parts per million; ug/m^3 = micrograms per cubic meter; n/a not available.
Concentrations: Nitrogen Dioxide AM—highest arithmetic mean concentration; Nitrogen Dioxide 1-Hr—highest 98th percentile 1-hour daily maximum concentration; Sulfur Dioxide AM—highest annual mean concentration; Sulfur Dioxide 1-Hr—highest 99th percentile 1-hour daily maximum concentration; Sulfur Dioxide 24-Hr—highest second maximum 24-hour concentration
Source: U.S. Environmental Protection Agency, Air Quality Monitoring Information, "Air Quality Statistics by City, 2023"

Honolulu, Hawaii

Background

Honolulu, whose name means "sheltered harbor," is the capital of Hawaii and the seat of Honolulu County. The city sits in one of the most famously attractive areas of the world, on the island of Oahu, home to the extinct volcano Diamond Head, Waikiki Beach, and two mountain ranges, the Koolau and the Waianae. Honolulu is the economic hub of Hawaii and a major seaport. Tourism has continued to increase in recent years, after a drop during the pandemic.

Traditionally home to fishing and horticultural tribal groups, the Hawaiian Islands were politically united under the reign of King Kamehameha I, who first moved his triumphant court to Waikiki and subsequently to a site in what is now downtown Honolulu (1804). It was during his time that the port became a center for the sandalwood trade, thus establishing the region as an international presence even before the political interventions of non-Hawaiians.

European activity dates from 1794, when the English sea captain William Brown entered Honolulu, dubbing it Fair Harbor. Two decades later, the first missionaries arrived. American Congregationalists were followed by French Catholics and, later, Mormons and Anglicans. By the end of the nineteenth century, non-Hawaiians owned most of the land. In 1898 Hawaii was annexed by the U.S.

As is true for many strategically located cities, the events of World War II had a profound effect on Honolulu. The Japanese attack on December 7, 1941, forever etched the name of Pearl Harbor into the national memory. During the war, existing military bases were expanded, and new bases built, providing considerable economic stimuli. The Vietnam War also had a dramatic effect on Honolulu and by the end of the twentieth century, military families accounted for 10 percent of the population.

Today, the U.S. military employs more than 45,000 throughout the state. Fruit, primarily pineapple, processing and light manufacturing are also important to the economy. Aquaculture, which includes cultivated species of shellfish, finfish, and algae, has grown in recent years, as has biotechnology.

Tourism is the private-sector mainstay of Honolulu's economy, with nearly a million tourists and $10 billion to the local economy annually. Honolulu is a required stop for any holiday ship cruising these waters, and it is also the center for the inter-island air services that ferry tourists to various resort locations. In 2020, the Hawaii Tourism Authority launched a strategic plan to support tourism through 2025.

The center of Honolulu's downtown district is dominated by the Iolani Palace, once home to Hawaii's original royal family. Nearby are the State Capitol Building and the State Supreme Court Building, known as Ali'iolani Hall. The Aloha Tower Development Corporation has modernized the mixed-use space in and around the Aloha Tower Complex along the city's piers.

Honolulu has grown along the southern coast of Oahu with a mix of residential zones, with single-family dwellings and relatively small multi-unit buildings, making this major metropolitan area feel like cozy neighborhoods. In fact, Honolulu is governed in part through a Neighborhood Board System, which insures maximal local input with regard to planning decisions and city services.

Cultural amenities include the Bishop Museum, the Honolulu Academy of Arts, and the Contemporary Museum, which together offer world-class collections in Polynesian art and artifacts, Japanese, Chinese, and Korean art, and modern art from the world over. Honolulu also hosts a symphony orchestra, the oldest U.S. symphony orchestra west of the Rocky Mountains, which performs at the Neal S. Blaisdell Center. Honolulu is also the official home of the Pokémon World Championship.

Barack Obama, the United States' 44th president, was born in Honolulu, the first president from Hawaii. As a result, the city garnered a fair amount of attention during the 2008 presidential election.

Honolulu's weather is subtropical, with temperatures moderated by the surrounding ocean and the trade winds. There are only slight variations in temperature from summer to winter. Rain is moderate, though heavier in summer, sometimes in the form of quick showers while the sun is shining—known locally as "liquid sunshine."

Rankings

General Rankings

- To help military veterans find the best places in which to settle down, *WalletHub* compared the 100 largest U.S. cities across 19 key indicators of livability, affordability and veteran-friendliness. They range from the share of military skill-related jobs to veteran income growth to the availability of VA health facilities. Honolulu ranked #85. *Wallethub.com, "Best & Worst Places for Veterans to Live (2025)," November 7, 2024*

- The human resources consulting firm Mercer ranked 241 major cities worldwide in terms of overall quality of life. Honolulu ranked #39. Criteria: political and personal safety, social, and economic factors; medical and health considerations; schools and education; public services and transportation; recreation; connectivity; housing and infrastructure; and climate. *Mercer, "Mercer 2024 Quality of Living Survey," December 2024*

- Honolulu appeared on *Travel + Leisure's* list of "The 15 Best Cities in the United States." The city was ranked #4. Criteria: walkability; sights/landmarks; culture; food; friendliness; shopping; and overall value. *Travel + Leisure, "The World's Best Awards 2024" July 9, 2024*

Business/Finance Rankings

- For its annual survey of the "Most Expensive U.S. Cities to Live In," Kiplinger applied Cost of Living Index statistics developed by the Council for Community and Economic Research to U.S. Census Bureau population and median household income data for 265 urban areas. Honolulu ranked #2 among the most expensive in the country. *Kiplinger.com, "The 10 Most Expensive Cities to Live in the U.S.," February 3, 2025*

- The Honolulu metro area appeared on the Milken Institute "2025 Best Performing Cities" list. Rank: #141 out of 200 large metro areas (based on performance category). Criteria: job growth; wage growth; high-tech growth and impact; community resilience; housing affordability; household broadband access. *Milken Institute, "Best-Performing Cities 2025," January 14, 2025*

- Mercer Human Resources Consulting ranked 226 cities worldwide in terms of cost-of-living. Honolulu ranked #12 (the lower the ranking, the higher the cost-of-living). The survey measured the comparative cost of over 200 items (such as housing, food, clothing, domestic supplies, transportation, and recreation/entertainment) in each location. *Mercer, "2024 Cost of Living City Ranking," June 17, 2024*

Education Rankings

- Personal finance website *WalletHub* analyzed the 150 largest U.S. metropolitan statistical areas to determine where the most educated Americans are putting their degrees to work. Criteria: education levels; percentage of workers with degrees; education quality and attainment gap; public school quality rankings; quality and enrollment of each metro area's universities. Honolulu was ranked #28 (#1 = most educated city). *WalletHub.com, "Most & Least Educated Cities in America, 2025" July 2, 2024*

Environmental Rankings

- Honolulu was highlighted as one of the cleanest metro areas for ozone air pollution in the U.S. during 2021 through 2023. The list represents cities with no monitored ozone air pollution in unhealthful ranges. *American Lung Association, "State of the Air 2025," April 23, 2025*

- Honolulu was highlighted as one of the top 25 cleanest metro areas for year-round particle pollution (Annual PM 2.5) in the U.S. during 2021 through 2023. The area ranked #1. *American Lung Association, "State of the Air 2025," April 23, 2025*

Health/Fitness Rankings

- For each of the 100 largest cities in the United States, the American Fitness Index®, compiled in partnership between the American College of Sports Medicine and the Elevance Health Foundation, evaluated community infrastructure and more than 30 health behaviors including preventive health, levels of chronic disease conditions, food insecurity, pedestrian safety, air quality, and community/environment resources that support physical activity. Honolulu ranked #15 for "community fitness." *americanfitnessindex.org, "2024 ACSM American Fitness Index Summary Report," July 23, 2024*

- The Sharecare Community Well-Being Index evaluates 10 individual and social health factors in order to measure what matters to Americans in the communities in which they live. The Honolulu metro area ranked #6 in the top 10 across all 10 domains. Criteria: access to healthcare, food, and community resources; housing and transportation; economic security; feeling of purpose; and physical, financial, social, and community well-being. *Sharecare.com, "Community Well-Being Index: 2020 Metro Area & County Rankings Report," August 30, 2021*

Real Estate Rankings

- *WalletHub* compared the most populated U.S. cities to determine which had the best markets for real estate agents. Honolulu ranked #41 where demand was high and pay was the best. Criteria: sales per agent; annual median wage for real-estate agents; monthly average starting salary for real estate agents; real estate job density and competition; unemployment rate; home turnover rate; housing-market health index; and other relevant metrics. *WalletHub.com, "2021 Best Places to Be a Real Estate Agent," May 12, 2021*

- Honolulu was ranked #1 in the top 20 out of the 100 largest metro areas in terms of house price appreciation in 2024 (#1 = highest rate). *Federal Housing Finance Agency, "House Price Index, 4th Quarter 2024," February 25, 2025*

- The Honolulu metro area was identified as one of the 20 least affordable housing markets in the U.S. in 2024. The area ranked #223 out of 226 markets. Criteria: qualification for a mortgage loan with a 10 percent down payment on a typical home. *National Association of Realtors®, Qualifying Income Based on Sales Price of Existing Single-Family Homes for Metropolitan Areas, February 6, 2025*

- Honolulu was ranked #175 out of 176 metro areas in terms of cost of housing in 2024 by the National Association of Home Builders (#1 = most affordable). Criteria: the portion of an average family's income necessary to pay the mortgage on a median-priced home. *National Association of Home Builders®, NAHB-Wells Fargo Cost of Housing Index, 4th Quarter 2024*

Safety Rankings

- Allstate ranked the 100 most populous cities in America in terms of driver safety. Honolulu ranked #1. Criteria based on anonymized driving behavior data from Allstate's mobile app powered by Arity: high speed driving (over 80 mph), phone handling, and hard braking. The report helps increase the importance of safety and awareness behind the wheel. *Allstate, "16th Allstate America's Best Drivers Report®" July 11, 2024*

Sports/Recreation Rankings

- Honolulu was chosen as a bicycle friendly community by the League of American Bicyclists. A "Bicycle Friendly Community" welcomes cyclists by providing safe and supportive accommodation for cycling and encouraging people to bike for transportation and recreation. There are four award levels: Platinum; Gold; Silver; and Bronze. The community achieved an award level of Silver. *League of American Bicyclists, "2024 Awards-New & Renewing Bicycle Friendly Communities List," January 28, 2025*

Women/Minorities Rankings

- Personal finance website *WalletHub* compared more than 180 U.S. cities across two key dimensions, "Hispanic Business-Friendliness" and "Hispanic Purchasing Power," to arrive at the most favorable conditions for Hispanic entrepreneurs. Honolulu was ranked #160 out of 182. Criteria includes: share of Hispanic-Owned Businesses; average growth of Hispanic Business revenues; Small Business-Friendliness score; affordability; and number of Hispanics with at least a bachelor's degree. *WalletHub.com, "Best Cities for Hispanic Entrepreneurs," September 4, 2024*

Miscellaneous Rankings

- *MoveHub* ranked 446 hipster cities across 20 countries, using its new and improved alternative Hipster Index and Honolulu came out as #45 among the top 50. Criteria: population over 150,000; number of vintage boutiques; density of tattoo parlors; vegan places to eat; coffee shops; and density of vinyl record stores. *MoveHub.com, "The Hipster Index: Brighton Pips Portland to Global Top Spot," July 28, 2021*

- The financial planning site *SmartAsset* has compiled its annual study on the best places for Halloween in the U.S. for 2022. 146 cities were compared to determine that Honolulu ranked #28 out of 35 for still being able to enjoy the festivities despite COVID-19. Metrics included: safety, family-friendliness, percentage of children in the population, concentration of candy and costume shops, weather and COVID infection rates. *SmartAsset.com, "2022 Edition-Best Places to Celebrate Halloween," October 19, 2022*

Business Environment

DEMOGRAPHICS

Population Growth

Area	1990 Census	2000 Census	2010 Census	2020 Census	2023 Estimate[2]	Population Growth 1990-2023 (%)
City	376,465	371,657	337,256	350,964	346,323	-8.0
MSA[1]	836,231	876,156	953,207	1,016,508	1,003,666	20.0
U.S.	248,709,873	281,421,906	308,745,538	331,449,281	332,387,540	33.6

Note: (1) Figures cover the Urban Honolulu, HI Metropolitan Statistical Area; (2) 2019-2023 5-year ACS population estimate
Source: U.S. Census Bureau, 1990 Census, 2000 Census, 2010 Census, 2020 Census, 2019-2023 American Community Survey 5-Year Estimates

Race

Area	White Alone[2] (%)	Black Alone[2] (%)	Asian Alone[2] (%)	AIAN[3] Alone[2] (%)	NHOPI[4] Alone[2] (%)	Other Race Alone[2] (%)	Two or More Races (%)
City	17.0	1.8	52.9	0.2	8.5	1.2	18.4
MSA[1]	18.8	2.4	42.6	0.2	9.9	1.6	24.4
U.S.	63.4	12.4	5.8	0.9	0.2	6.6	10.7

Note: (1) Figures cover the Urban Honolulu, HI Metropolitan Statistical Area; (2) Alone is defined as not being in combination with one or more other races; (3) American Indian and Alaska Native; (4) Native Hawaiian and Other Pacific Islander
Source: U.S. Census Bureau, 2019-2023 American Community Survey 5-Year Estimates

Hispanic or Latino Origin

Area	Total (%)	Mexican (%)	Puerto Rican (%)	Cuban (%)	Other (%)
City	6.6	2.3	1.8	0.1	2.4
MSA[1]	9.3	3.1	3.1	0.2	3.0
U.S.	19.0	11.3	1.8	0.7	5.2

Note: Persons of Hispanic or Latino origin can be of any race; (1) Figures cover the Urban Honolulu, HI Metropolitan Statistical Area
Source: U.S. Census Bureau, 2019-2023 American Community Survey 5-Year Estimates

Age

Area	Percent of Population									Median Age
	Under Age 5	Age 5–19	Age 20–34	Age 35–44	Age 45–54	Age 55–64	Age 65–74	Age 75–84	Age 85+	
City	4.5	13.9	20.6	13.8	12.8	12.7	11.5	6.5	3.6	42.9
MSA[1]	5.8	17.0	21.0	13.3	11.8	12.0	10.3	5.8	3.0	39.4
U.S.	5.7	19.1	20.2	13.1	12.3	12.8	10.0	4.9	1.9	38.7

Note: (1) Figures cover the Urban Honolulu, HI Metropolitan Statistical Area
Source: U.S. Census Bureau, 2019-2023 American Community Survey 5-Year Estimates

Disability by Age

Area	All Ages	Under 18 Years Old	18 to 64 Years Old	65 Years and Over
City	12.5	3.9	7.9	32.1
MSA[1]	12.2	3.6	8.5	32.8
U.S.	13.0	4.7	10.7	32.9

Note: Figures show percent of the civilian noninstitutionalized population that reported having a disability. Disability status is determined from six types of difficulty: vision, hearing, cognitive, ambulatory, self-care, and independent living. For children under 5 years old, hearing and vision difficulty are used to determine disability status. For children between the ages of 5 and 14, disability status is determined from hearing, vision, cognitive, ambulatory, and self-care difficulties. For people aged 15 years and older, they are considered to have a disability if they have difficulty with any one of the six difficulty types; Note: (1) Figures cover the Urban Honolulu, HI Metropolitan Statistical Area
Source: U.S. Census Bureau, 2019-2023 American Community Survey 5-Year Estimates

Ancestry

Area	German	Irish	English	American	Italian	Polish	French[2]	European	Scottish
City	4.5	3.4	3.6	1.4	1.3	0.9	1.0	0.5	0.7
MSA[1]	5.2	4.0	4.1	1.3	1.8	0.8	1.0	0.6	0.7
U.S.	12.6	9.4	9.1	5.5	4.9	2.6	2.0	1.6	1.6

Note: Figures are the percentage of the total population reporting a particular ancestry. The nine most commonly reported ancestries in the U.S. are shown. Figures include multiple ancestries (e.g. if a person reported being Irish and Italian, they were included in both columns); (1) Figures cover the Urban Honolulu, HI Metropolitan Statistical Area; (2) Excludes Basque
Source: U.S. Census Bureau, 2019-2023 American Community Survey 5-Year Estimates

Foreign-born Population

| Area | Percent of Population Born in | | | | | | | | |
	Any Foreign Country	Asia	Mexico	Europe	Caribbean	Central America[2]	South America	Africa	Canada
City	27.8	22.9	0.2	1.0	0.1	0.1	0.3	0.2	0.2
MSA[1]	19.6	15.7	0.2	0.7	0.1	0.1	0.2	0.1	0.3
U.S.	13.9	4.3	3.3	1.4	1.4	1.2	1.2	0.8	0.2

Note: (1) Figures cover the Urban Honolulu, HI Metropolitan Statistical Area; (2) Excludes Mexico.
Source: U.S. Census Bureau, 2019-2023 American Community Survey 5-Year Estimates

Household Size

| Area | Persons in Household (%) | | | | | | | Average Household Size |
	One	Two	Three	Four	Five	Six	Seven or More	
City	35.0	31.1	14.6	9.7	4.5	2.1	3.0	2.47
MSA[1]	24.9	30.8	16.7	13.1	6.8	3.5	4.1	2.88
U.S.	28.5	33.8	15.4	12.7	5.9	2.3	1.4	2.54

Note: (1) Figures cover the Urban Honolulu, HI Metropolitan Statistical Area
Source: U.S. Census Bureau, 2019-2023 American Community Survey 5-Year Estimates

Household Relationships

Area	House-holder	Opposite-sex Spouse	Same-sex Spouse	Opposite-sex Unmarried Partner	Same-sex Unmarried Partner	Child[2]	Grand-child	Other Relatives	Non-relatives
City	39.1	15.0	0.3	2.4	0.2	22.2	3.1	9.1	5.6
MSA[1]	33.1	16.3	0.2	1.9	0.1	26.2	4.5	9.2	4.9
U.S.	38.3	17.5	0.2	2.5	0.2	28.3	2.4	4.8	3.4

Note: Figures are percent of the total population; (1) Figures cover the Urban Honolulu, HI Metropolitan Statistical Area; (2) Includes biological, adopted, and stepchildren of the householder
Source: U.S. Census Bureau, 2020 Census

Gender

Area	Males	Females	Males per 100 Females
City	173,028	173,295	99.8
MSA[1]	507,355	496,311	102.2
U.S.	164,545,087	167,842,453	98.0

Note: (1) Figures cover the Urban Honolulu, HI Metropolitan Statistical Area
Source: U.S. Census Bureau, 2019-2023 American Community Survey 5-Year Estimates

Marital Status

Area	Never Married	Now Married[2]	Separated	Widowed	Divorced
City	38.0	44.0	1.2	6.6	10.1
MSA[1]	34.6	49.5	1.1	6.0	8.7
U.S.	34.1	47.9	1.7	5.6	10.7

Note: Figures are percentages and cover the population 15 years of age and older; (1) Figures cover the Urban Honolulu, HI Metropolitan Statistical Area; (2) Excludes separated
Source: U.S. Census Bureau, 2019-2023 American Community Survey 5-Year Estimates

Religious Groups by Family

Area	Catholic	Baptist	Methodist	LDS[2]	Pentecostal	Lutheran	Islam	Adventist	Other
MSA[1]	18.0	1.4	0.5	4.1	2.6	0.2	<0.1	1.9	9.8
U.S.	18.7	7.3	3.0	2.0	1.8	1.7	1.3	1.3	11.6

Note: Figures are the number of adherents as a percentage of the total population and cover the eight largest religious groups in the U.S; (1) Figures cover the Urban Honolulu, HI Metropolitan Statistical Area; (2) Church of Jesus Christ of Latter-day Saints
Sources: 2020 U.S. Religion Census, Association of Statisticians of American Religious Bodies; The Association of Religion Data Archives (ARDA)

Religious Groups by Tradition

Area	Catholic	Evangelical Protestant	Mainline Protestant	Black Protestant	Islam	Judaism	Hinduism	Orthodox	Buddhism
MSA[1]	18.0	8.1	2.3	0.2	<0.1	0.1	0.2	<0.1	4.0
U.S.	18.7	16.5	5.2	2.3	1.3	0.6	0.4	0.4	0.3

Note: Figures are the number of adherents as a percentage of the total population; (1) Figures cover the Urban Honolulu, HI Metropolitan Statistical Area
Sources: 2020 U.S. Religion Census, Association of Statisticians of American Religious Bodies; The Association of Religion Data Archives (ARDA)

ECONOMY

Real Gross Domestic Product (GDP)

Area	2017	2018	2019	2020	2021	2022	2023	Rank[3]
MSA[1]	65.8	66.0	65.6	60.1	62.8	64.5	66.0	55
U.S.[2]	17,619.1	18,160.7	18,642.5	18,238.9	19,387.6	19,896.6	20,436.3	—

Note: Figures are in billions of chained 2017 dollars; (1) Figures cover the Urban Honolulu, HI Metropolitan Statistical Area; (2) Figures cover real GDP within metropolitan areas; (3) Rank is based on 2023 data and ranges from 1 to 384
Source: U.S. Bureau of Economic Analysis

Economic Growth

Area	2014	2015	2016	2017	2018	2019	2020	2021	2022	2023
MSA[1]	0.9	2.7	1.9	2.1	0.4	-0.6	-8.5	4.5	2.6	2.4
U.S.[2]	2.6	3.2	2.0	2.7	3.1	2.7	-2.2	6.3	2.6	2.7

Note: Figures are real gross domestic product growth rates and represent percent change from preceding period; (1) Figures cover the Urban Honolulu, HI Metropolitan Statistical Area; (2) Figures are the average growth rates within metropolitan areas
Source: U.S. Bureau of Economic Analysis

Metropolitan Area Exports

Area	2018	2019	2020	2021	2022	2023	Rank[2]
MSA[1]	438.9	308.6	169.0	164.3	258.8	450.6	234
U.S.	1,664,056.1	1,645,173.7	1,431,406.6	1,753,941.4	2,062,937.4	2,019,160.5	—

Note: Figures are in millions of dollars; (1) Figures cover the Urban Honolulu, HI Metropolitan Statistical Area; (2) Rank is based on 2023 data and ranges from 1 to 386
Source: U.S. Department of Commerce, International Trade Administration, Office of Trade and Economic Analysis, Industry and Analysis, Exports by Metropolitan Area, data extracted April 2, 2025

Building Permits

Area	Single-Family			Multi-Family			Total		
	2023	2024	Pct. Chg.	2023	2024	Pct. Chg.	2023	2024	Pct. Chg.
City	n/a	n/a	n/a	n/a	n/a	n/a	n/a	n/a	n/a
MSA[1]	657	706	7.5	1,194	932	-21.9	1,851	1,638	-11.5
U.S.	920,000	981,900	6.7	591,100	496,100	-16.1	1,511,100	1,478,000	-2.2

Note: (1) Figures cover the Urban Honolulu, HI Metropolitan Statistical Area; Figures represent new, privately-owned housing units authorized (unadjusted data)
Source: U.S. Census Bureau, Building Permits Survey (BPS), 2023, 2024

Bankruptcy Filings

Area	Business Filings			Nonbusiness Filings		
	2023	2024	% Chg.	2023	2024	% Chg.
Honolulu County	36	38	5.6	757	840	11.0
U.S.	18,926	23,107	22.1	434,064	494,201	13.9

Note: Business filings include Chapter 7, Chapter 9, Chapter 11, Chapter 12, Chapter 13, Chapter 15, and Section 304; Nonbusiness filings include Chapter 7, Chapter 11, and Chapter 13
Source: Administrative Office of the U.S. Courts, Business and Nonbusiness Bankruptcy, County Cases Commenced by Chapter of the Bankruptcy Code, During the 12-Month Period Ending December 31, 2023 and Business and Nonbusiness Bankruptcy, County Cases Commenced by Chapter of the Bankruptcy Code, During the 12-Month Period Ending December 31, 2024

Housing Vacancy Rates

Area	Gross Vacancy Rate[3] (%)			Year-Round Vacancy Rate[4] (%)			Rental Vacancy Rate[5] (%)			Homeowner Vacancy Rate[6] (%)		
	2022	2023	2024	2022	2023	2024	2022	2023	2024	2022	2023	2024
MSA[1]	10.6	11.5	11.9	10.0	10.7	11.1	5.7	6.8	6.2	0.6	0.5	0.9
U.S.[2]	9.1	9.0	9.1	7.5	7.5	7.6	5.7	6.5	6.8	0.8	0.8	1.0

Note: (1) Figures cover the Urban Honolulu, HI Metropolitan Statistical Area; (2) Figures cover the 75 largest Metropolitan Statistical Areas; (3) The percentage of the total housing inventory that is vacant; (4) The percentage of the housing inventory (excluding seasonal units) that is year-round vacant; (5) The percentage of rental inventory that is vacant for rent; (6) The percentage of homeowner inventory that is vacant for sale
Source: U.S. Census Bureau, Housing Vacancies and Homeownership Annual Statistics: 2022, 2023, 2024

INCOME

Income

Area	Per Capita ($)	Median Household ($)	Average Household ($)
City	48,465	85,428	120,718
MSA[1]	46,361	104,264	133,753
U.S.	43,289	78,538	110,491

Note: (1) Figures cover the Urban Honolulu, HI Metropolitan Statistical Area
Source: U.S. Census Bureau, 2019-2023 American Community Survey 5-Year Estimates

Household Income Distribution

Area	Percent of Households Earning							
	Under $15,000	$15,000 -$24,999	$25,000 -$34,999	$35,000 -$49,999	$50,000 -$74,999	$75,000 -$99,999	$100,000 -$149,999	$150,000 and up
City	8.8	5.7	5.1	9.4	15.2	12.7	17.4	25.7
MSA[1]	6.3	4.2	4.2	7.9	12.9	12.6	20.4	31.6
U.S.	8.5	6.6	6.8	10.4	15.7	12.7	17.4	21.9

Note: (1) Figures cover the Urban Honolulu, HI Metropolitan Statistical Area
Source: U.S. Census Bureau, 2019-2023 American Community Survey 5-Year Estimates

Poverty Rate

Area	All Ages	Under 18 Years Old	18 to 64 Years Old	65 Years and Over
City	11.9	15.0	11.1	11.7
MSA[1]	9.1	11.4	8.5	8.7
U.S.	12.4	16.3	11.6	10.4

Note: Figures are percentage of people whose income during the past 12 months was below the poverty level;
(1) Figures cover the Urban Honolulu, HI Metropolitan Statistical Area
Source: U.S. Census Bureau, 2019-2023 American Community Survey 5-Year Estimates

EMPLOYMENT

Labor Force and Employment

Area	Civilian Labor Force			Workers Employed		
	Dec. 2023	Dec. 2024	% Chg.	Dec. 2023	Dec. 2024	% Chg.
City	458,516	467,102	1.9	447,781	454,669	1.5
MSA[1]	458,516	467,102	1.9	447,781	454,669	1.5
U.S.	166,661,000	167,746,000	0.7	160,754,000	161,294,000	0.3

Note: Data is not seasonally adjusted and covers workers 16 years of age and older; (1) Figures cover the
Urban Honolulu, HI Metropolitan Statistical Area
Source: Bureau of Labor Statistics, Local Area Unemployment Statistics

Unemployment Rate

Area	2024											
	Jan.	Feb.	Mar.	Apr.	May	Jun.	Jul.	Aug.	Sep.	Oct.	Nov.	Dec.
City	2.5	2.5	2.4	2.4	2.3	3.2	3.0	3.1	3.1	2.9	3.0	2.7
MSA[1]	2.5	2.5	2.4	2.4	2.3	3.2	3.0	3.1	3.1	2.9	3.0	2.7
U.S.	4.1	4.2	3.9	3.5	4.3	4.5	4.4	3.9	3.9	3.9	4.0	3.8

Note: Data is not seasonally adjusted and covers workers 16 years of age and older; (1) Figures cover the
Urban Honolulu, HI Metropolitan Statistical Area
Source: Bureau of Labor Statistics, Local Area Unemployment Statistics

Average Wages

Occupation	$/Hr.	Occupation	$/Hr.
Accountants and Auditors	36.77	Maintenance and Repair Workers	27.07
Automotive Mechanics	27.01	Marketing Managers	63.78
Bookkeepers	23.29	Network and Computer Systems Admin.	48.37
Carpenters	42.67	Nurses, Licensed Practical	32.75
Cashiers	17.05	Nurses, Registered	60.17
Computer Programmers	50.07	Nursing Assistants	21.81
Computer Systems Analysts	44.25	Office Clerks, General	21.33
Computer User Support Specialists	28.29	Physical Therapists	48.19
Construction Laborers	33.27	Physicians	152.85
Cooks, Restaurant	21.30	Plumbers, Pipefitters and Steamfitters	40.69
Customer Service Representatives	21.38	Police and Sheriff's Patrol Officers	45.53
Dentists	65.12	Postal Service Mail Carriers	27.98
Electricians	42.47	Real Estate Sales Agents	33.03
Engineers, Electrical	50.66	Retail Salespersons	19.06
Fast Food and Counter Workers	16.01	Sales Representatives, Technical/Scientific	58.17
Financial Managers	67.37	Secretaries, Exc. Legal/Medical/Executive	25.07
First-Line Supervisors of Office Workers	32.34	Security Guards	20.40
General and Operations Managers	60.89	Surgeons	n/a
Hairdressers/Cosmetologists	24.25	Teacher Assistants, Exc. Postsecondary[1]	17.06
Home Health and Personal Care Aides	17.39	Teachers, Secondary School, Exc. Sp. Ed.[1]	30.19
Janitors and Cleaners	18.20	Telemarketers	n/a
Landscaping/Groundskeeping Workers	20.46	Truck Drivers, Heavy/Tractor-Trailer	27.42
Lawyers	58.87	Truck Drivers, Light/Delivery Services	23.32
Maids and Housekeeping Cleaners	25.07	Waiters and Waitresses	25.96

Note: Wage data covers the Urban Honolulu, HI Metropolitan Statistical Area; (1) Hourly wages were
calculated from annual wage data based on a 40 hour work week
Source: Bureau of Labor Statistics, Metro Area Occupational Employment & Wage Estimates, May 2024

Employment by Industry

Sector	MSA[1] Number of Employees	Percent of Total	U.S. Percent of Total
Construction, Mining, and Logging	28,200	6.0	5.5
Financial Activities	21,300	4.5	5.8
Government	99,400	21.0	14.9
Information	7,100	1.5	1.9
Leisure and Hospitality	74,900	15.8	10.4
Manufacturing	9,800	2.1	8.0
Other Services	20,800	4.4	3.7
Private Education and Health Services	70,400	14.9	16.9
Professional and Business Services	57,500	12.1	14.2
Retail Trade	44,200	9.3	10.0
Transportation, Warehousing, and Utilities	26,000	5.5	4.8
Wholesale Trade	13,800	2.9	3.9

Note: Figures are non-farm employment as of December 2024. Figures are not seasonally adjusted and include workers 16 years of age and older; (1) Figures cover the Urban Honolulu, HI Metropolitan Statistical Area
Source: Bureau of Labor Statistics, Current Employment Statistics, Employment, Hours, and Earnings

Employment by Occupation

Occupation Classification	City (%)	MSA[1] (%)	U.S. (%)
Management, Business, Science, and Arts	42.6	40.9	42.0
Natural Resources, Construction, and Maintenance	5.5	8.2	8.6
Production, Transportation, and Material Moving	8.4	9.0	13.0
Sales and Office	21.7	21.7	19.9
Service	21.9	20.2	16.5

Note: Figures cover employed civilians 16 years of age and older; (1) Figures cover the Urban Honolulu, HI Metropolitan Statistical Area
Source: U.S. Census Bureau, 2019-2023 American Community Survey 5-Year Estimates

Occupations with Greatest Projected Employment Growth: –

Projections not available at time of publication.

Fastest-Growing Occupations: –

Projections not available at time of publication.

CITY FINANCES

City Government Finances

Component	2022 ($000)	2022 ($ per capita)
Total Revenues	3,908,058	4,055
Total Expenditures	3,470,963	3,601
Debt Outstanding	7,298,369	7,572

Source: U.S. Census Bureau, State & Local Government Finances 2022

City Government Revenue by Source

Source	2022 ($000)	2022 ($ per capita)	2022 (%)
General Revenue			
From Federal Government	360,828	374	9.2
From State Government	157,747	164	4.0
From Local Governments	24,647	26	0.6
Taxes			
Property	1,357,907	1,409	34.7
Sales and Gross Receipts	540,763	561	13.8
Personal Income	0	0	0.0
Corporate Income	0	0	0.0
Motor Vehicle License	213,538	222	5.5
Other Taxes	30,300	31	0.8
Current Charges	658,397	683	16.8
Liquor Store	0	0	0.0
Utility	283,148	294	7.2

Source: U.S. Census Bureau, State & Local Government Finances 2022

City Government Expenditures by Function

Function	2022 ($000)	2022 ($ per capita)	2022 (%)
General Direct Expenditures			
Air Transportation	0	0	0.0
Corrections	0	0	0.0
Education	0	0	0.0
Employment Security Administration	0	0	0.0
Financial Administration	45,147	46	1.3
Fire Protection	144,323	149	4.2
General Public Buildings	33,856	35	1.0
Governmental Administration, Other	232,028	240	6.7
Health	40,124	41	1.2
Highways	82,238	85	2.4
Hospitals	0	0	0.0
Housing and Community Development	118,128	122	3.4
Interest on General Debt	240,625	249	6.9
Judicial and Legal	31,249	32	0.9
Libraries	0	0	0.0
Parking	2,416	2	0.1
Parks and Recreation	158,661	164	4.6
Police Protection	302,960	314	8.7
Public Welfare	14,676	15	0.4
Sewerage	412,789	428	11.9
Solid Waste Management	187,924	195	5.4
Veterans' Services	0	0	0.0
Liquor Store	0	0	0.0
Utility	1,100,688	1,142	31.7

Source: U.S. Census Bureau, State & Local Government Finances 2022

TAXES

State Corporate Income Tax Rates

State	Tax Rate (%)	Income Brackets ($)	Num. of Brackets	Financial Institution Tax Rate (%)[a]	Federal Income Tax Ded.
Hawaii	4.4 - 6.4 (e)	25,000 - 100,001	3	7.92 (e)	No

Note: Tax rates for tax year 2024; (a) Rates listed are the corporate income tax rate applied to financial institutions or excise taxes based on income. Some states have other taxes based upon the value of deposits or shares; (e) Hawaii taxes capital gains at 4%. Financial institutions pay a franchise tax of 7.92% of taxable income (in lieu of the corporate income tax and general excise taxes).
Source: Federation of Tax Administrators, State Corporate Income Tax Rates, January 1, 2025

State Individual Income Tax Rates

State	Tax Rate (%)	Income Brackets ($)	Personal Exemptions ($) Single	Married	Depend.	Standard Ded. ($) Single	Married
Hawaii	1.4 - 11.0	2,400 - 200,000 (b)	1,144	2,288	1,144	2,200	4,400

Note: Tax rates for tax year 2024; Local- and county-level taxes are not included; Federal income tax is not deductible on state income tax returns; (b) For joint returns, taxes are twice the tax on half the couple's income. California brackets violate this formula at the two highest tax brackets in 2024.
Source: Federation of Tax Administrators, State Individual Income Tax Rates, January 1, 2025

Various State Sales and Excise Tax Rates

State	State Sales Tax (%)	Gasoline[1] ($/gal.)	Cigarette[2] ($/pack)	Spirits[3] ($/gal.)	Wine[4] ($/gal.)	Beer[5] ($/gal.)	Recreational Marijuana (%)
Hawaii	4	0.19	3.20	5.98	1.38	0.93	Not legal

Note: All tax rates as of January 1, 2025; (1) The American Petroleum Institute has developed a methodology for determining the average tax rate on a gallon of fuel. Rates may include any of the following: excise taxes, environmental fees, storage tank fees, other fees or taxes, general sales tax, and local taxes; (2) The federal excise tax of $1.0066 per pack and local taxes are not included; (3) Rates are those applicable to off-premise sales of 40% alcohol by volume (a.b.v.) distilled spirits in 750ml containers. Local excise taxes are excluded; (4) Rates are those applicable to off-premise sales of 11% a.b.v. non-carbonated wine in 750ml containers; (5) Rates are those applicable to off-premise sales of 4.7% a.b.v. beer in 12 ounce containers.
Source: Tax Foundation, 2025 Facts & Figures: How Does Your State Compare?

State Tax Competitiveness Index

State	Overall Rank	Corporate Tax Rank	Individual Income Tax Rank	Sales Tax Rank	Property Tax Rank	Unemployment Insurance Tax Rank
Hawaii	42	25	46	28	24	49

Note: The Tax Foundation's State Tax Competitiveness Index enables policymakers, taxpayers, and business leaders to gauge how their states' tax systems compare. A rank of 1 is best, 50 is worst. Rankings do not average to the total. States without a tax rank equally as 1. DC's scores and rankings do not affect other states. The report shows tax systems as of July 1, 2024 (the beginning of Fiscal Year 2025).
Source: Tax Foundation, State Tax Competitiveness Index 2025

TRANSPORTATION

Means of Transportation to Work

Area	Car/Truck/Van		Public Transportation			Bicycle	Walked	Other Means	Worked at Home
	Drove Alone	Car-pooled	Bus	Subway	Railroad				
City	55.7	14.2	7.9	0.0	0.0	1.8	7.7	3.7	8.9
MSA[1]	64.0	13.7	5.2	0.0	0.0	1.0	5.0	2.6	8.4
U.S.	70.2	8.5	1.7	1.3	0.4	0.4	2.4	1.6	13.5

Note: Figures are percentages and cover workers 16 years of age and older; (1) Figures cover the Urban Honolulu, HI Metropolitan Statistical Area
Source: U.S. Census Bureau, 2019-2023 American Community Survey 5-Year Estimates

Travel Time to Work

Area	Less Than 10 Minutes	10 to 19 Minutes	20 to 29 Minutes	30 to 44 Minutes	45 to 59 Minutes	60 to 89 Minutes	90 Minutes or More
City	9.0	39.2	22.3	20.5	4.5	3.4	1.2
MSA[1]	9.9	27.1	20.0	25.2	9.1	6.5	2.1
U.S.	12.6	28.6	21.2	20.8	8.1	6.0	2.8

Note: Note: Figures are percentages and include workers 16 years old and over; (1) Figures cover the Urban Honolulu, HI Metropolitan Statistical Area
Source: U.S. Census Bureau, 2019-2023 American Community Survey 5-Year Estimates

Key Congestion Measures

Measure	2000	2010	2015	2020	2022
Annual Hours of Delay, Total (000)	18,787	27,593	32,628	13,365	37,456
Annual Hours of Delay, Per Auto Commuter	44	55	60	24	67
Annual Congestion Cost, Per Auto Commuter ($)	1,144	1,332	1,456	628	1,741

Note: Figures cover the Honolulu HI urban area
Source: Texas A&M Transportation Institute, 2023 Urban Mobility Report

Freeway Travel Time Index

Measure	1985	1990	1995	2000	2005	2010	2015	2020	2022
Urban Area Index[1]	1.18	1.23	1.28	1.32	1.37	1.38	1.40	1.11	1.41
Urban Area Rank[1,2]	8	4	4	4	3	3	4	20	3

Note: Freeway Travel Time Index—the ratio of travel time in the peak period to the travel time at free-flow conditions. For example, a value of 1.30 indicates a 20-minute free-flow trip takes 26 minutes in the peak (20 minutes x 1.30 = 26 minutes); (1) Covers the Honolulu HI urban area; (2) Rank is based on 101 larger urban areas (#1 = highest travel time index)
Source: Texas A&M Transportation Institute, 2023 Urban Mobility Report

Public Transportation

Agency Name / Mode of Transportation	Vehicles Operated in Maximum Service[1]	Annual Unlinked Passenger Trips[2] (in thous.)	Annual Passenger Miles[3] (in thous.)
City and County of Honolulu Dept. of Transportation Services (DTS)			
Bus (purchased transportation)	382	38,992.5	182,046.1
Demand Response (purchased transportation)	193	1,042.6	10,626.7
Demand Response - Taxi	93	73.5	612.5
Heavy Rail (purchased transportation)	20	8.9	42.4

Note: (1) Number of revenue vehicles operated by the given mode and type of service to meet the annual maximum service requirement. This is the revenue vehicle count during the peak season of the year; on the week and day that maximum service is provided. Vehicles operated in maximum service (VOMS) exclude atypical days and one-time special events; (2) Number of passengers who boarded public transportation vehicles. Passengers are counted each time they board a vehicle no matter how many vehicles they use to travel from their origin to their destination. (3) Sum of the distances ridden by all passengers during the entire fiscal year.
Source: Federal Transit Administration, National Transit Database, 2023

Air Transportation

Airport Name and Code / Type of Service	Passenger Airlines[1]	Passenger Enplanements	Freight Carriers[2]	Freight (lbs)
Honolulu International (HNL)				
Domestic service (U.S. carriers only)	12	8,708,478	16	452,845,162
International service (U.S. carriers only)	6	538,043	11	114,439,324

Note: (1) Includes all U.S.-based major, minor and commuter airlines that carried at least one passenger during the year; (2) Includes all U.S.-based airlines and freight carriers that transported at least one pound of freight during the year.
Source: Bureau of Transportation Statistics, The Intermodal Transportation Database, Air Carriers: T-100 Domestic Market (U.S. carriers only), 2024; Bureau of Transportation Statistics, The Intermodal Transportation Database, Air Carriers: T-100 International Market (U.S. carriers only), 2024

BUSINESSES

Major Business Headquarters

Company Name	Industry	Rankings	
		Fortune[1]	Forbes[2]
No companies listed	-	-	-

Note: (1) Companies that produce a 10-K are ranked 1 to 500 based on 2023 revenue; (2) All private companies with at least $2 billion in annual revenue through the end of their most current fiscal year are ranked 1 to 275; companies listed are headquartered in the city; dashes indicate no ranking
Source: Fortune, "Fortune 500," 2024; Forbes, "America's Largest Private Companies," 2024

Fastest-Growing Businesses

According to *Inc.*, Honolulu is home to one of America's 500 fastest-growing private companies: **Malama Solar** (#483). Criteria: must be an independent, privately-held, for-profit, U.S. corporation, proprietorship or partnership as of December 31, 2023; revenues must be at least $100,000 in 2020 and $2 million in 2023; must have four-year operating/sales history. *Inc., "America's 500 Fastest-Growing Private Companies," 2024*

Living Environment

COST OF LIVING

Cost of Living Index

Composite Index	Groceries	Housing	Utilities	Trans- portation	Health Care	Misc. Goods/ Services
186.8	130.4	310.0	197.6	133.6	120.8	130.4

Note: The Cost of Living Index measures regional differences in the cost of consumer goods and services, excluding taxes and non-consumer expenditures, for professional and managerial households in the top income quintile. It is based on more than 50,000 prices covering almost 60 different items for which prices are collected three times a year by chambers of commerce, economic development organizations or university applied economic centers in each participating urban area. The numbers shown should be read as a percentage above or below the national average of 100. For example, a value of 115.4 in the groceries column indicates that grocery prices are 15.4% higher than the national average. Small differences in the index numbers should not be interpreted as significant; Figures cover the Honolulu HI urban area.
Source: The Council for Community and Economic Research, Cost of Living Index, 2024

Grocery Prices

Area[1]	T-Bone Steak ($/pound)	Frying Chicken ($/pound)	Whole Milk ($/half gal.)	Eggs ($/dozen)	Orange Juice ($/64 oz.)	Coffee ($/11.5 oz.)
City[2]	16.57	2.86	5.49	3.98	5.19	7.89
Avg.	15.42	1.55	4.69	3.25	4.41	5.46
Min.	14.50	1.16	4.43	2.75	4.00	4.85
Max.	17.56	2.89	5.49	4.78	5.54	7.89

Note: (1) Values for the local area are compared with the average, minimum and maximum values for all 276 areas in the Cost of Living Index; (2) Figures cover the Honolulu HI urban area; T-Bone Steak (price per pound); Frying Chicken (price per pound, whole fryer); Whole Milk (half gallon carton); Eggs (price per dozen, Grade A, large); Orange Juice (64 oz. Tropicana or Florida Natural); Coffee (11.5 oz. can, vacuum-packed, Maxwell House, Hills Bros, or Folgers).
Source: The Council for Community and Economic Research, Cost of Living Index, 2024

Housing and Utility Costs

Area[1]	New Home Price ($)	Apartment Rent ($/month)	All Electric ($/month)	Part Electric ($/month)	Other Energy ($/month)	Telephone ($/month)
City[2]	1,681,170	4,424	529.02	-	-	187.39
Avg.	515,975	1,550	210.99	123.07	82.07	194.99
Min.	265,375	692	104.33	53.68	36.26	179.42
Max.	2,775,821	5,719	529.02	397.28	361.63	223.33

Note: (1) Values for the local area are compared with the average, minimum and maximum values for all 276 areas in the Cost of Living Index; (2) Figures cover the Honolulu HI urban area; New Home Price (2,400 sf living area, 8,000 sf lot, in urban area with full utilities); Apartment Rent (950 sf 2 bedroom/1.5 or 2 bath, unfurnished, excluding all utilities except water); All Electric (average monthly cost for an all-electric home); Part Electric (average monthly cost for a part-electric home); Other Energy (average monthly cost for natural gas, fuel oil, coal, wood, and any other forms of energy except electricity); Telephone (price includes the base monthly rate plus taxes and fees for three lines of mobile phone service).
Source: The Council for Community and Economic Research, Cost of Living Index, 2024

Health Care, Transportation, and Other Costs

Area[1]	Doctor ($/visit)	Dentist ($/visit)	Optometrist ($/visit)	Gasoline ($/gallon)	Beauty Salon ($/visit)	Men's Shirt ($)
City[2]	201.94	127.00	258.67	4.58	75.33	58.48
Avg.	143.77	117.51	129.23	3.32	48.57	38.14
Min.	36.74	58.67	67.33	2.80	24.00	13.41
Max.	270.44	216.82	307.33	5.28	94.00	63.89

Note: (1) Values for the local area are compared with the average, minimum and maximum values for all 276 areas in the Cost of Living Index; (2) Figures cover the Honolulu HI urban area; Doctor (general practitioners routine exam of an established patient); Dentist (adult teeth cleaning and periodic oral examination); Optometrist (full vision eye exam for established adult patient); Gasoline (one gallon regular unleaded, national brand, including all taxes, cash price at self-service pump if available); Beauty Salon (woman's shampoo, trim, and blow-dry); Men's Shirt (cotton/polyester dress shirt, pinpoint weave, long sleeves).
Source: The Council for Community and Economic Research, Cost of Living Index, 2024

HOUSING

Homeownership Rate

Area	2017 (%)	2018 (%)	2019 (%)	2020 (%)	2021 (%)	2022 (%)	2023 (%)	2024 (%)
MSA[1]	53.8	57.7	59.0	56.9	55.9	57.7	60.4	58.5
U.S.	63.9	64.4	64.6	66.6	65.5	65.8	65.9	65.6

Note: (1) Figures cover the Urban Honolulu, HI Metropolitan Statistical Area
Source: U.S. Census Bureau, Housing Vacancies and Homeownership Annual Statistics: 2017-2024

House Price Index (HPI)

Area	National Ranking[2]	Quarterly Change (%)	One-Year Change (%)	Five-Year Change (%)	Since 1991Q1 (%)
MSA[1]	183	-0.33	3.85	35.89	242.48
U.S.[3]	–	1.43	4.51	57.13	327.82

Note: The HPI is a weighted repeat sales index. It measures average price changes in repeat sales or refinancings on the same properties. This information is obtained by reviewing repeat mortgage transactions on single-family properties whose mortgages have been purchased or securitized by Fannie Mae or Freddie Mac since January 1975; (1) Figures cover the Urban Honolulu, HI Metropolitan Statistical Area; (2) Rankings are based on annual percentage change for all metro areas containing at least 15,000 transactions over the last 10 years and ranges from 1 to 241; (3) figures based on a weighted average of Census Division estimates using a seasonally adjusted, purchase-only index; all figures are for the period ending December 31, 2024
Source: Federal Housing Finance Agency, Change in FHFA Metropolitan Area House Price Indexes, All Transactions Index, 2024Q4

Home Value

Area	Under $100,000	$100,000 -$199,999	$200,000 -$299,999	$300,000 -$399,999	$400,000 -$499,999	$500,000 -$999,999	$1,000,000 or more	Median ($)
City	2.1	1.6	3.1	8.6	10.6	35.0	39.0	834,100
MSA[1]	2.2	1.5	2.2	5.1	7.6	43.9	37.6	873,000
U.S.	12.1	17.8	19.5	14.4	10.5	19.1	6.5	303,400

Note: Figures are percentages except for median and cover owner-occupied housing units; (1) Figures cover the Urban Honolulu, HI Metropolitan Statistical Area
Source: U.S. Census Bureau, 2019-2023 American Community Survey 5-Year Estimates

Year Housing Structure Built

Area	2020 or Later	2010 -2019	2000 -2009	1990 -1999	1980 -1989	1970 -1979	1960 -1969	1950 -1959	1940 -1949	Before 1940	Median Year
City	0.5	7.5	6.7	7.8	10.5	25.9	19.6	11.6	5.1	4.8	1973
MSA[1]	0.6	7.7	9.6	11.4	12.8	23.9	17.3	10.0	3.8	3.0	1977
U.S.	1.2	8.9	13.6	12.8	13.0	14.4	10.0	9.7	4.5	11.9	1980

Note: Figures are percentages except for Median Year; Note: (1) Figures cover the Urban Honolulu, HI Metropolitan Statistical Area
Source: U.S. Census Bureau, 2019-2023 American Community Survey 5-Year Estimates

Gross Monthly Rent

Area	Under $500	$500 -$999	$1,000 -$1,499	$1,500 -$1,999	$2,000 -$2,499	$2,500 -$2,999	$3,000 and up	Median ($)
City	5.7	7.6	21.8	26.2	16.6	7.5	14.5	1,783
MSA[1]	4.7	6.3	16.7	20.6	15.8	11.3	24.6	2,054
U.S.	6.5	22.3	29.5	20.2	10.8	4.8	5.9	1,348

Note: Figures are percentages except for median; Gross rent is the contract rent plus the estimated average monthly cost of utilities (electricity, gas, and water and sewer) and fuels (oil, coal, kerosene, wood, etc.) if these are paid by the renter (or paid for the renter by someone else); (1) Figures cover the Urban Honolulu, HI Metropolitan Statistical Area
Source: U.S. Census Bureau, 2019-2023 American Community Survey 5-Year Estimates

HEALTH

Health Risk Factors

Category	MSA[1] (%)	U.S. (%)
Adults aged 18–64 who have any kind of health care coverage	n/a	90.8
Adults who reported being in good or better health	n/a	81.8
Adults who have been told they have high blood cholesterol	n/a	36.9
Adults who have been told they have high blood pressure	n/a	34.0
Adults who are current smokers	n/a	12.1
Adults who currently use e-cigarettes	n/a	7.7
Adults who currently use chewing tobacco, snuff, or snus	n/a	3.2
Adults who are heavy drinkers[2]	n/a	6.1
Adults who are binge drinkers[3]	n/a	15.2
Adults who are overweight (BMI 25.0 - 29.9)	n/a	34.4
Adults who are obese (BMI 30.0 - 99.8)	n/a	34.3
Adults who participated in any physical activities in the past month	n/a	75.8

Note: All figures are crude prevalence; (1) Figures for the Urban Honolulu, HI Metropolitan Statistical Area were not available.
(2) Heavy drinkers are classified as adult men having more than 14 drinks per week and adult women having more than 7 drinks per week; (3) Binge drinkers are classified as males having five or more drinks on one occasion or females having four or more drinks on one occasion
Source: Centers for Disease Control and Prevention, Behaviorial Risk Factor Surveillance System, SMART: Selected Metropolitan Area Risk Trends, 2023

Acute and Chronic Health Conditions

Category	MSA[1] (%)	U.S. (%)
Adults who have ever been told they had a heart attack	n/a	4.2
Adults who have ever been told they have angina or coronary heart disease	n/a	4.0
Adults who have ever been told they had a stroke	n/a	3.3
Adults who have ever been told they have asthma	n/a	15.7
Adults who have ever been told they have arthritis	n/a	26.3
Adults who have ever been told they have diabetes[2]	n/a	11.5
Adults who have ever been told they had skin cancer	n/a	5.6
Adults who have ever been told they had any other types of cancer	n/a	8.4
Adults who have ever been told they have COPD	n/a	6.4
Adults who have ever been told they have kidney disease	n/a	3.7
Adults who have ever been told they have a form of depression	n/a	22.0

Note: All figures are crude prevalence; (1) Figures for the Urban Honolulu, HI Metropolitan Statistical Area were not available.
(2) Figures do not include pregnancy-related, borderline, or pre-diabetes
Source: Centers for Disease Control and Prevention, Behaviorial Risk Factor Surveillance System, SMART: Selected Metropolitan Area Risk Trends, 2023

Health Screening and Vaccination Rates

Category	MSA[1] (%)	U.S. (%)
Adults who have ever been tested for HIV	n/a	37.5
Adults who have had their blood cholesterol checked within the last five years	n/a	87.0
Adults aged 65+ who have had flu shot within the past year	n/a	63.4
Adults aged 65+ who have ever had a pneumonia vaccination	n/a	71.9

Note: All figures are crude prevalence; (1) Figures for the Urban Honolulu, HI Metropolitan Statistical Area were not available.
Source: Centers for Disease Control and Prevention, Behaviorial Risk Factor Surveillance System, SMART: Selected Metropolitan Area Risk Trends, 2023

Disability Status

Category	MSA[1] (%)	U.S. (%)
Adults who reported being deaf	n/a	7.4
Are you blind or have serious difficulty seeing, even when wearing glasses?	n/a	4.9
Do you have difficulty doing errands alone?	n/a	7.8
Do you have difficulty dressing or bathing?	n/a	3.6
Do you have serious difficulty concentrating/remembering/making decisions?	n/a	13.7
Do you have serious difficulty walking or climbing stairs?	n/a	13.2

Note: All figures are crude prevalence; (1) Figures for the Urban Honolulu; HI Metropolitan Statistical Area were not available.
Source: Centers for Disease Control and Prevention, Behaviorial Risk Factor Surveillance System, SMART: Selected Metropolitan Area Risk Trends, 2023

Mortality Rates for the Top 10 Causes of Death in the U.S.

ICD-10[a] Sub-Chapter	ICD-10[a] Code	Crude Mortality Rate[2] per 100,000 population	
		County[3]	U.S.
Malignant neoplasms	C00-C97	170.7	182.7
Ischaemic heart diseases	I20-I25	96.0	109.6
Provisional assignment of new diseases of uncertain etiology[1]	U00-U49	31.1	65.3
Other forms of heart disease	I30-I51	59.1	65.1
Other degenerative diseases of the nervous system	G30-G31	50.9	52.4
Other external causes of accidental injury	W00-X59	39.6	52.3
Cerebrovascular diseases	I60-I69	61.6	49.1
Chronic lower respiratory diseases	J40-J47	22.8	43.5
Hypertensive diseases	I10-I15	35.5	38.9
Organic, including symptomatic, mental disorders	F01-F09	60.6	33.9

Note: (a) ICD-10 = International Classification of Diseases 10th Revision; (1) Includes COVID-19, adverse effects to COVID-19 vaccines, SARS, and vaping-related disorders; (2) Crude mortality rates are a three-year average covering 2021-2023; (3) Figures cover Honolulu County.
Source: Centers for Disease Control and Prevention, National Center for Health Statistics. National Vital Statistics System, Mortality 2018-2023 on CDC WONDER Online Database

Mortality Rates for Selected Causes of Death

Cause of Death	ICD-10[a] Code	Crude Mortality Rate[1] per 100,000 population	
		County[2]	U.S.
Accidental poisoning and exposure to noxious substances	X40-X49	17.9	30.5
Alzheimer disease	G30	42.3	35.4
Assault	X85-Y09	2.8	7.3
COVID-19	U07.1	31.0	65.3
Diabetes mellitus	E10-E14	23.5	30.0
Diseases of the liver	K70-K76	12.6	20.8
Human immunodeficiency virus (HIV) disease	B20-B24	0.9	1.5
Influenza and pneumonia	J09-J18	18.8	13.4
Intentional self-harm	X60-X84	13.1	14.7
Malnutrition	E40-E46	1.6	6.0
Obesity and other hyperalimentation	E65-E68	1.5	3.1
Renal failure	N17-N19	19.7	16.4
Transport accidents	V01-V99	6.1	14.4

Note: (a) ICD-10 = International Classification of Diseases 10th Revision; (1) Crude mortality rates are a three-year average covering 2021-2023; (2) Figures cover Honolulu County; Data are suppressed when the data meet the criteria for confidentiality constraints; Crude mortality rates are flagged as unreliable when the rate would be calculated with a numerator of 20 or less.
Source: Centers for Disease Control and Prevention, National Center for Health Statistics. National Vital Statistics System, Mortality 2018-2023 on CDC WONDER Online Database

Health Insurance Coverage

Area	With Health Insurance	With Private Health Insurance	With Public Health Insurance	Without Health Insurance	Population Under Age 19 Without Health Insurance
City	96.2	75.5	38.3	3.8	2.4
MSA[1]	96.6	78.2	36.3	3.4	2.6
U.S.	91.4	67.3	36.3	8.6	5.4

Note: Figures are percentages that cover the civilian noninstitutionalized population; (1) Figures cover the Urban Honolulu, HI Metropolitan Statistical Area
Source: U.S. Census Bureau, 2019-2023 American Community Survey 5-Year Estimates

Number of Medical Professionals

Area	MDs[3]	DOs[3,4]	Dentists	Podiatrists	Chiropractors	Optometrists
County[1] (number)	3,556	237	1,028	39	224	255
County[1] (rate[2])	357.2	23.8	103.9	3.9	22.6	25.8
U.S. (rate[2])	302.5	29.2	74.6	6.4	29.5	18.0

Note: Data as of 2023 unless noted; (1) Data covers Honolulu County; (2) Number of medical professionals per 100,000 population; (3) Data as of 2022 and includes all active, non-federal physicians; (4) Doctor of Osteopathic Medicine
Source: U.S. Department of Health and Human Services, Health Resources and Services Administration, Bureau of Health Professions, Area Resource File (ARF) 2023-2024

Best Hospitals

According to *U.S. News*, the Urban Honolulu, HI metro area is home to one of the best hospitals in the U.S.: **Queen's Medical Center** (2 adult specialties). The hospital listed was nationally ranked in at least one of 15 adult or 11 pediatric specialties. The number of specialties shown cover the parent hospital. Only 160 U.S. hospitals performed well enough to be nationally ranked in one or more specialties. Twenty hospitals in the U.S. made the Honor Roll. The Best Hospitals Honor Roll takes both the national rankings and the procedure and condition ratings into account. Hospitals received points if they were nationally ranked in one of the 15 adult specialties—the higher they ranked, the more points they got—and how many ratings of "high performing" they earned in the 20 procedures and conditions. *U.S. News Online, "America's Best Hospitals 2024-25"*

EDUCATION

Public School District Statistics

District Name	Schls	Pupils	Pupil/ Teacher Ratio	Minority Pupils[1] (%)	Total Rev. per Pupil ($)	Total Exp. per Pupil ($)
Hawaii Department of Education	296	169,308	14.0	88.9	20,584	19,381

Note: Table includes school districts with 2,000 or more students; (1) Percentage of students that are not non-Hispanic white.
Source: U.S. Department of Education, National Center for Education Statistics, Common Core of Data, Local Education Agency (School District) Universe Survey: School Year 2023-2024; U.S. Department of Education, National Center for Education Statistics, Common Core of Data, School District Finance Survey (F-33): School Year 2021–22

Highest Level of Education

Area	Less than H.S.	H.S. Diploma	Some College, No Deg.	Associate Degree	Bachelor's Degree	Master's Degree	Prof. School Degree	Doctorate Degree
City	9.1	22.8	17.2	10.1	25.2	9.9	3.4	2.2
MSA[1]	7.1	25.2	19.0	11.0	23.7	9.4	2.8	1.8
U.S.	10.6	26.2	19.4	8.8	21.3	9.8	2.3	1.6

Note: Figures cover persons age 25 and over; (1) Figures cover the Urban Honolulu, HI Metropolitan Statistical Area
Source: U.S. Census Bureau, 2019-2023 American Community Survey 5-Year Estimates

Educational Attainment by Race

Area	High School Graduate or Higher (%)					Bachelor's Degree or Higher (%)				
	Total	White	Black	Asian	Hisp.[2]	Total	White	Black	Asian	Hisp.[2]
City	90.9	97.6	91.5	88.1	93.6	40.8	54.6	32.5	40.7	30.5
MSA[1]	92.9	97.2	95.8	90.6	94.5	37.7	51.2	32.8	39.2	29.2
U.S.	89.4	92.9	88.1	88.0	72.5	35.0	37.7	24.7	57.0	19.9

Note: Figures shown cover persons 25 years old and over; (1) Figures cover the Urban Honolulu, HI Metropolitan Statistical Area; (2) People of Hispanic origin can be of any race
Source: U.S. Census Bureau, 2019-2023 American Community Survey 5-Year Estimates

School Enrollment by Grade and Control

Area	Preschool (%)		Kindergarten (%)		Grades 1 - 4 (%)		Grades 5 - 8 (%)		Grades 9 - 12 (%)	
	Public	Private	Public	Private	Public	Private	Public	Private	Public	Private
City	36.4	63.6	74.0	26.0	79.9	20.1	76.4	23.6	69.1	30.9
MSA[1]	34.7	65.3	79.0	21.0	79.9	20.1	78.2	21.8	74.9	25.1
U.S.	58.7	41.3	85.2	14.8	87.2	12.8	87.9	12.1	89.0	11.0

Note: Figures shown cover persons 3 years old and over; (1) Figures cover the Urban Honolulu, HI Metropolitan Statistical Area
Source: U.S. Census Bureau, 2019-2023 American Community Survey 5-Year Estimates

Higher Education

Four-Year Colleges			Two-Year Colleges			Medical Schools[1]	Law Schools[2]	Voc/ Tech[3]
Public	Private Non-profit	Private For-profit	Public	Private Non-profit	Private For-profit			
2	4	2	4	1	2	0	0	2

Note: Figures cover institutions located within the Urban Honolulu, HI Metropolitan Statistical Area and include main campuses only; (1) includes schools accredited by the Liaison Committee on Medical Education and the American Osteopathic Association's Commission on Osteopathic College Accreditation; (2) includes ABA-accredited schools, schools with provisional ABA accreditation, and state accredited schools; (3) includes all schools with programs that are less than 2 years.
Source: National Center for Education Statistics, Integrated Postsecondary Education System (IPEDS), 2023-24; Wikipedia, List of Medical Schools in the United States, accessed May 2, 2025; Wikipedia, List of Law Schools in the United States, accessed May 2, 2025

According to *U.S. News & World Report,* the Urban Honolulu, HI metro area is home to one of the top 200 national universities in the U.S.: **University of Hawaii at Manoa** (#171 tie). The indicators used to capture academic quality fall into a number of categories: assessment by administrators at peer institutions; retention of students; faculty resources; student selectivity; financial resources; alumni giving; high school counselor ratings of colleges; and graduation rate. *U.S. News & World Report, "America's Best Colleges 2025"*

According to *U.S. News & World Report,* the Urban Honolulu, HI metro area is home to one of the top 100 law schools in the U.S.: **University of Hawaii—Manoa (Richardson)** (#99 tie). The rankings are based on a weighted average of 12 measures of quality: peer assessment score; assessment score by lawyers/judges; median LSAT scores; median undergrad GPA; acceptance rate; employment rates for graduates; placement success; bar passage rate; faculty resources; expenditures per student; student/faculty ratio; and library resources. *U.S. News & World Report, "America's Best Graduate Schools, Law, 2025"*

According to *U.S. News & World Report,* the Urban Honolulu, HI metro area is home to one of the top medical schools for research in the U.S.: **University of Hawaii—Manoa (Burns)** (Tier 2). *U.S. News* placed medical and osteopathic schools into tiers based on their research productivity, faculty and admissions data. Each school's tier was derived from its overall score, calculated by summing the weighted normalized values generated across several factors of academic quality, outlined below. There are four tiers, with tier 1 medical schools as the highest-performing and tier 4 as the lowest-performing. Only tier 1 and 2 schools are shown. Because of the tier presentation, *U.S. News* calculated overall scores based on their percentile performance among all rated schools instead of dividing against the rescaled score of the No. 1-performing schools. Tier 1 included schools with overall scores of 85 to 99. The cutoffs for tiers 2 through 4 were schools scoring 50 to 84, 15 to 49 and 1 to 14, respectively. The rankings are based on a weighted average of the following measures of quality:

total research activity; average research activity per faculty member; total NIH research grants at the medical school and its affiliated hospitals; average NIH research grants per faculty; median MCAT total score; median undergraduate GPA; acceptance rate; and faculty resources. *U.S. News & World Report, "America's Best Graduate Schools, Medical, 2025"*

According to *U.S. News & World Report,* the Urban Honolulu, HI metro area is home to one of the top medical schools for primary care in the U.S.: **University of Hawaii—Manoa (Burns)** (Tier 1). *U.S. News* placed medical and osteopathic schools into tiers based on their research productivity, faculty and admissions data. Each school's tier was derived from its overall score, calculated by summing the weighted normalized values generated across several factors of academic quality, outlined below. There are four tiers, with tier 1 medical schools as the highest-performing and tier 4 as the lowest-performing. Only tier 1 and 2 schools are shown. Because of the tier presentation, *U.S. News* calculated overall scores based on their percentile performance among all rated schools instead of dividing against the rescaled score of the No. 1-performing schools. Tier 1 included schools with overall scores of 85 to 99. The cutoffs for tiers 2 through 4 were schools scoring 50 to 84, 15 to 49 and 1 to 14, respectively. The rankings are based on a weighted average of the following measures of quality: graduates practicing in primary care specialties; graduates entering primary care residencies; median MCAT total score; median undergraduate GPA; acceptance rate; and faculty resources. *U.S. News & World Report, "America's Best Graduate Schools, Medical, 2025"*

EMPLOYERS

Major Employers

Company Name	Industry
Altres Industrial	Employment agencies
City and County of Honolulu	Civil service/commission government
First Hawaiian Bank	State commercial banks
Hawaii Dept of Health	Administration of public health programs
Hawaii Dept of Transportation	Administration of transportation
Hawaii Mediacal Services Assoc	Hospital & medical services plans
Hawaii Pacific Health	General medical & surgical hospitals
Hawaiian Telecom	Local & long distance telephone
Hilton-Hawaiian Vlg Waikiki	Hotels & motels
Kapiolani Medical Ctr	General medical & surgical hospitals
KYO YA Hotels and Resorts	Hotels & motels
Mormon Church	Misc denominational church
OAHU transit Services	Bus line operations
Outrigger Hotels & Resorts	Hotels & motels
St. Francis Healthcare Sys of Hawaii	Skilled nursing facility
State of Hawaii	State government
The Boeing Company	Airplanes, fixed or rotary wing
The Queens Medical Center	General medical & surgical hospitals
Trustess of the Estate of Bernice Bishop	Private elementary/secondary schools
University of Hawaii System	Colleges & universities

Note: Companies shown are located within the Urban Honolulu, HI Metropolitan Statistical Area.
Source: Chambers of Commerce; State Departments of Labor; Wikipedia

PUBLIC SAFETY

Crime Rate

Area	Total Crime Rate	Violent Crime Rate				Property Crime Rate		
		Murder	Rape	Robbery	Aggrav. Assault	Burglary	Larceny -Theft	Motor Vehicle Theft
City	2,128.6	0.6	28.0	51.7	105.8	193.1	1,377.3	372.0
U.S.	2,290.9	5.7	38.0	66.5	264.1	250.7	1,347.2	318.7

Note: Figures are crimes per 100,000 population; n/a not available.
Source: FBI, Table 8, Offenses Known to Law Enforcement, by State by City, 2023

Hate Crimes

Area	Number of Quarters Reported	Number of Incidents per Bias Motivation					
		Race/Ethnicity/ Ancestry	Religion	Sexual Orientation	Disability	Gender	Gender Identity
City	4	13	3	1	1	0	0
U.S.	4	5,900	2,699	2,077	187	92	492

Source: Federal Bureau of Investigation, Hate Crime Statistics 2023

Identity Theft Consumer Reports

Area	Reports	Reports per 100,000 Population	Rank[2]
MSA[1]	1,433	143	293
U.S.	1,135,291	339	-

Note: (1) Figures cover the Urban Honolulu, HI Metropolitan Statistical Area; (2) Rank ranges from 1 to 401 where 1 indicates greatest number of identity theft reports per 100,000 population
Source: Federal Trade Commission, Consumer Sentinel Network Data Book 2024

Fraud and Other Consumer Reports

Area	Reports	Reports per 100,000 Population	Rank[2]
MSA[1]	9,823	979	225
U.S.	5,360,641	1,601	-

Note: (1) Figures cover the Urban Honolulu, HI Metropolitan Statistical Area; (2) Rank ranges from 1 to 401 where 1 indicates greatest number of fraud and other consumer reports per 100,000 population
Source: Federal Trade Commission, Consumer Sentinel Network Data Book 2024

POLITICS

2024 Presidential Election Results

Area	Trump (Rep.)	Harris (Dem.)	Stein (Green)	Kennedy (Ind.)	Oliver (Lib.)	Other
Honolulu County	38.3	59.9	0.7	0.0	0.5	0.5
U.S.	49.7	48.2	0.6	0.5	0.4	0.6

Note: Results are percentages and may not add to 100% due to rounding
Source: Dave Leip's Atlas of U.S. Presidential Elections

SPORTS

Professional Sports Teams

Team Name	League	Year Established

No teams are located in the metro area
Source: Wikipedia, Major Professional Sports Teams of the United States and Canada, May 1, 2025

CLIMATE

Average and Extreme Temperatures

Temperature	Jan	Feb	Mar	Apr	May	Jun	Jul	Aug	Sep	Oct	Nov	Dec	Yr.
Extreme High (°F)	87	88	89	89	93	92	92	93	94	94	93	89	94
Average High (°F)	80	80	81	82	84	86	87	88	88	86	84	81	84
Average Temp. (°F)	73	73	74	76	77	79	80	81	81	79	77	74	77
Average Low (°F)	66	66	67	69	70	72	73	74	73	72	70	67	70
Extreme Low (°F)	52	53	55	56	60	65	66	67	66	64	57	54	52

Note: Figures cover the years 1949-1990
Source: National Climatic Data Center, International Station Meteorological Climate Summary, 9/96

Average Precipitation/Snowfall/Humidity

Precip./Humidity	Jan	Feb	Mar	Apr	May	Jun	Jul	Aug	Sep	Oct	Nov	Dec	Yr.
Avg. Precip. (in.)	3.7	2.5	2.8	1.4	1.0	0.4	0.5	0.6	0.7	2.0	2.8	3.7	22.4
Avg. Snowfall (in.)	0	0	0	0	0	0	0	0	0	0	0	0	0
Avg. Rel. Hum. 5am (%)	82	80	78	77	76	75	75	75	76	78	79	80	78
Avg. Rel. Hum. 5pm (%)	66	64	62	61	60	58	58	58	60	63	66	66	62

Note: Figures cover the years 1949-1990; Tr = Trace amounts (<0.05 in. of rain; <0.5 in. of snow)
Source: National Climatic Data Center, International Station Meteorological Climate Summary, 9/96

Weather Conditions

Temperature			Daytime Sky			Precipitation		
32°F & below	45°F & below	90°F & above	Clear	Partly cloudy	Cloudy	0.01 inch or more precip.	0.1 inch or more snow/ice	Thunder-storms
0	0	23	25	286	54	98	0	7

Note: Figures are average number of days per year and cover the years 1949-1990
Source: National Climatic Data Center, International Station Meteorological Climate Summary, 9/96

HAZARDOUS WASTE

Superfund Sites

The Urban Honolulu, HI metro area is home to three sites on the EPA's Superfund National Priorities List (NPL) or Superfund Alternative Approach (SAA) list: **Del Monte Corp. (Oahu Plantation)** (Final NPL); **Naval Computer and Telecommunications Area Master Station Eastern Pacific** (Final NPL); **Pearl Harbor Naval Complex** (Final NPL). The Superfund alternative approach uses the same investigation and cleanup process and standards that are used for sites listed on the National Priorities List. The SAA is an alternative to listing a site on the NPL; it is not an alternative to Superfund or the Superfund process. There are a total of 1,445 Superfund sites with a status of proposed or final on both lists in the United States. *U.S. Environmental Protection Agency, National Priorities List, May 1, 2025; U.S. Environmental Protection Agency, Superfund Alternative Approach Sites, May 1, 2025*

AIR QUALITY

Air Quality Trends: Ozone

	1990	1995	2000	2005	2010	2015	2020	2021	2022	2023
MSA[1]	0.034	0.049	0.044	0.042	0.046	0.048	0.044	0.045	0.044	0.046
U.S.	0.087	0.089	0.081	0.080	0.072	0.068	0.066	0.067	0.067	0.070

Note: (1) Data covers the Urban Honolulu, HI Metropolitan Statistical Area. The values shown are the composite ozone concentration averages among trend sites based on the highest fourth daily maximum 8-hour concentration in parts per million. These trends are based on sites having an adequate record of monitoring data during the trend period. Data from exceptional events are included.
Source: U.S. Environmental Protection Agency, Air Quality Monitoring Information, "Air Quality Trends by City, 1990-2023"

Air Quality Index

Area	Percent of Days when Air Quality was...[2]					AQI Statistics[2]	
	Good	Moderate	Unhealthy for Sensitive Groups	Unhealthy	Very Unhealthy	Maximum	Median
MSA[1]	92.3	7.4	0.3	0.0	0.0	117	31

Note: (1) Data covers the Urban Honolulu, HI Metropolitan Statistical Area; (2) Based on 365 days with AQI data in 2023. Air Quality Index (AQI) is an index for reporting daily air quality. EPA calculates the AQI for five major air pollutants regulated by the Clean Air Act: ground-level ozone, particle pollution (aka particulate matter), carbon monoxide, sulfur dioxide, and nitrogen dioxide. The AQI runs from 0 to 500. The higher the AQI value, the greater the level of air pollution and the greater the health concern. There are six AQI categories: "Good" AQI is between 0 and 50. Air quality is considered satisfactory; "Moderate" AQI is between 51 and 100. Air quality is acceptable; "Unhealthy for Sensitive Groups" When AQI values are between 101 and 150, members of sensitive groups may experience health effects; "Unhealthy" When AQI values are between 151 and 200 everyone may begin to experience health effects; "Very Unhealthy" AQI values between 201 and 300 trigger a health alert; "Hazardous" AQI values over 300 trigger warnings of emergency conditions (not shown).
Source: U.S. Environmental Protection Agency, Air Quality Index Report, 2023

Air Quality Index Pollutants

Area	Percent of Days when AQI Pollutant was...[2]					
	Carbon Monoxide	Nitrogen Dioxide	Ozone	Sulfur Dioxide	Particulate Matter 2.5	Particulate Matter 10
MSA[1]	0.0	0.0	47.7	(3)	51.2	1.1

Note: (1) Data covers the Urban Honolulu, HI Metropolitan Statistical Area; (2) Based on 365 days with AQI data in 2023. The Air Quality Index (AQI) is an index for reporting daily air quality. EPA calculates the AQI for five major air pollutants regulated by the Clean Air Act: ground-level ozone, particle pollution (also known as particulate matter), carbon monoxide, sulfur dioxide, and nitrogen dioxide. The AQI runs from 0 to 500. The higher the AQI value, the greater the level of air pollution and the greater the health concern; (3) Sulfur dioxide is no longer included in this table because SO_2 concentrations tend to be very localized and not necessarily representative of broad geographical areas like counties and CBSAs.
Source: U.S. Environmental Protection Agency, Air Quality Index Report, 2023

Maximum Air Pollutant Concentrations: Particulate Matter, Ozone, CO and Lead

	Particulate Matter 10 (ug/m³)	Particulate Matter 2.5 Wtd AM (ug/m³)	Particulate Matter 2.5 24-Hr (ug/m³)	Ozone (ppm)	Carbon Monoxide (ppm)	Lead (ug/m³)
MSA[1] Level	46	4.1	10	0.046	0	n/a
NAAQS[2]	150	15	35	0.075	9	0.15
Met NAAQS[2]	Yes	Yes	Yes	Yes	Yes	n/a

Note: (1) Data covers the Urban Honolulu, HI Metropolitan Statistical Area; Data from exceptional events are included; (2) National Ambient Air Quality Standards; ppm = parts per million; ug/m³ = micrograms per cubic meter; n/a not available.
Concentrations: Particulate Matter 10 (coarse particulate)—highest second maximum 24-hour concentration; Particulate Matter 2.5 Wtd AM (fine particulate)—highest weighted annual mean concentration; Particulate Matter 2.5 24-Hour (fine particulate)—highest 98th percentile 24-hour concentration; Ozone—highest fourth daily maximum 8-hour concentration; Carbon Monoxide—highest second maximum non-overlapping 8-hour concentration; Lead—maximum running 3-month average
Source: U.S. Environmental Protection Agency, Air Quality Monitoring Information, "Air Quality Statistics by City, 2023"

Maximum Air Pollutant Concentrations: Nitrogen Dioxide and Sulfur Dioxide

	Nitrogen Dioxide AM (ppb)	Nitrogen Dioxide 1-Hr (ppb)	Sulfur Dioxide AM (ppb)	Sulfur Dioxide 1-Hr (ppb)	Sulfur Dioxide 24-Hr (ppb)
MSA[1] Level	3	23	n/a	60	n/a
NAAQS[2]	53	100	30	75	140
Met NAAQS[2]	Yes	Yes	n/a	Yes	n/a

Note: (1) Data covers the Urban Honolulu, HI Metropolitan Statistical Area; Data from exceptional events are included; (2) National Ambient Air Quality Standards; ppm = parts per million; ug/m^3 = micrograms per cubic meter; n/a not available.

Concentrations: Nitrogen Dioxide AM—highest arithmetic mean concentration; Nitrogen Dioxide 1-Hr—highest 98th percentile 1-hour daily maximum concentration; Sulfur Dioxide AM—highest annual mean concentration; Sulfur Dioxide 1-Hr—highest 99th percentile 1-hour daily maximum concentration; Sulfur Dioxide 24-Hr—highest second maximum 24-hour concentration

Source: U.S. Environmental Protection Agency, Air Quality Monitoring Information, "Air Quality Statistics by City, 2023"

Las Vegas, Nevada

Background

Las Vegas is a desert town 225 miles northeast of Los Angeles. Legalized gambling, combined with spectacular, neon-lit entertainment, lures over 40 million visitors to the city every year.

Before celebrities and tourists flocked to Las Vegas, it was a temporary stopping place for a diverse group of people. In the early 1880s, Las Vegas was a watering hole for those on the trail to California. Areas of the Las Vegas Valley contained artesian wells that supported extensive green meadows, or *vega* in Spanish, hence the name Las Vegas. In 1855 the area was settled by Mormon missionaries, who stayed only two years. In the late 1800s ranching was a primary industry.

In the beginning of the twentieth century, the seeds of the present Las Vegas began to sprout. The arrival of the Union Pacific Railroad came with businesses, saloons, and gambling houses sprinkled along it tracks and the city was formally founded on May 15, 1905.

During the Great Depression, men working on the nearby Hoover Dam spent much of their earnings in the city's establishments, and gambling was quickly legalized. Hydroelectric power from the Hoover Dam lit the city in neon, and hotels began to compete for the brightest stars and the plushest surroundings. Las Vegas was an overnight success, attracting many people with get-rich-quick dreams.

In the recent past, seniors are the fastest-growing segment of the Las Vegas population, taking advantage of the dry climate, reasonably priced housing, low property taxes, no sales tax, and plenty of entertainment. Nevada continues to lead the nation in growth of its senior citizen population, with many programs to ensure their comfort and welfare, including quality economic, legal, and medical plans.

The city is home to several museums, including the Neon Museum (with many of the historical signs from Las Vegas's mid-20th century heyday), The Mob Museum, the Las Vegas Natural History Museum, the DISCOVERY Children's Museum, the Nevada State Museum and the Old Las Vegas Mormon Fort State Historic Park. The city is also home to an extensive Downtown Arts District, which hosts numerous galleries and events including the annual Las Vegas Film Festival.

The Las Vegas Valley is home to three major professional sports teams: Vegas Golden Knights (NHL); Las Vegas Raiders (NFL); and Las Vegas Aces (WNBA). The Oakland Athletics of Major League Baseball (MLB) are moving to Las Vegas for the 2028 season.

One of the more serious problems facing the fast-growing city is its diminishing water supply. It's estimated that Las Vegas gets up to 90 percent of its water from Lake Mead, whose levels are falling, not only due to usage (219 gallons daily person, more than most U.S. cities), but also due to climate change. The city employs reuse and recycle programs and encourages conservation by homeowners and businesses through desert landscaping.

The city made national headlines in October 2017 when a gunman opened fire on a crowd of concert goers on Las Vegas Boulevard, killing 58 people and injuring 800. This mass shooting, and others in recent years, contributed to the ongoing national debate on gun control.

Las Vegas is located near the center of a broad desert valley, which is nearly surrounded by mountains ranging from 2,000 to 10,000 feet. Four seasons are well defined. Summers have desert conditions with extreme high temperatures, but nights are relatively cool due to the closeness of the mountains. For about two weeks almost every summer, warm, moist air causes higher-than-average humidity and scattered, severe thunderstorms. Winters are generally mild and pleasant with clear skies prevailing. Strong winds, associated with major storms, usually reach the valley from the southwest or through the pass from the northwest. Winds over 50 miles per hour are infrequent but troublesome because of the dust and sand they stir up.

Rankings

General Rankings

- To help military veterans find the best places in which to settle down, *WalletHub* compared the 100 largest U.S. cities across 19 key indicators of livability, affordability and veteran-friendliness. They range from the share of military skill-related jobs to veteran income growth to the availability of VA health facilities. Las Vegas ranked #30. *Wallethub.com, "Best & Worst Places for Veterans to Live (2025)," November 7, 2024*

- *Insider* listed 23 places in the U.S. that travel industry trends reveal would be popular destinations in 2023. This year the list trends towards cultural and historical happenings, sports events, wellness experiences and invigorating outdoor escapes. According to the website insider.com Las Vegas is a place to visit in 2023. *Insider, "23 of the Best Places You Should Travel to in the U.S. in 2023," December 17, 2022*

Business/Finance Rankings

- The Las Vegas metro area appeared on the Milken Institute "2025 Best Performing Cities" list. Rank: #34 out of 200 large metro areas (based on performance category). Criteria: job growth; wage growth; high-tech growth and impact; community resilience; housing affordability; household broadband access. *Milken Institute, "Best-Performing Cities 2025," January 14, 2025*

Education Rankings

- Personal finance website *WalletHub* analyzed the 150 largest U.S. metropolitan statistical areas to determine where the most educated Americans are putting their degrees to work. Criteria: education levels; percentage of workers with degrees; education quality and attainment gap; public school quality rankings; quality and enrollment of each metro area's universities. Las Vegas was ranked #128 (#1 = most educated city). *WalletHub.com, "Most & Least Educated Cities in America, 2025" July 2, 2024*

Environmental Rankings

- Las Vegas was highlighted as one of the 25 most ozone-polluted metro areas in the U.S. during 2021 through 2023. The area ranked #12. *American Lung Association, "State of the Air 2025," April 23, 2025*

Food/Drink Rankings

- WalletHub compared the 100 largest U.S. cities across 17 key indicators of vegan- and vegetarian-friendliness. Las Vegas was ranked #14. Cities were selected based on metrics such as the cost of groceries for vegetarians, the share of restaurants serving meatless options and the number of salad shops per capita. *WalletHub.com, "Best Cities for Vegans & Vegetarians (2025)," September 24, 2024*

Health/Fitness Rankings

- For each of the 100 largest cities in the United States, the American Fitness Index®, compiled in partnership between the American College of Sports Medicine and the Elevance Health Foundation, evaluated community infrastructure and more than 30 health behaviors including preventive health, levels of chronic disease conditions, food insecurity, pedestrian safety, air quality, and community/environment resources that support physical activity. Las Vegas ranked #90 for "community fitness." *americanfitnessindex.org, "2024 ACSM American Fitness Index Summary Report," July 23, 2024*

- The Las Vegas metro area was identified as one of the worst cities for bed bugs in America by pest control company Orkin. The area ranked #35 out of 50 based on the number of bed bug treatments Orkin performed from December 2022 to November 2023. *Orkin, "Chicago Joins Paris In Global Bed Bug Spotlight Ranking As The Worst City On Orkin's U.S. Bed Bug Cities List," January 22, 2024*

- Las Vegas was identified as a "2025 Allergy Capital." The area ranked #38 out of the nation's 100 largest metropolitan areas. Three groups of factors were used to identify the most challenging cities for people with allergies: annual tree, grass, and weed pollen scores; over the counter allergy medicine use; number of board-certified allergy specialists. *Asthma and Allergy Foundation of America, "2025 Allergy Capitals: The Most Challenging Places to Live with Allergies," March 18, 2025*

- Las Vegas was identified as a "2024 Asthma Capital." The area ranked #38 out of the nation's 100 largest metropolitan areas. Criteria: estimated asthma prevalence; asthma-related mortality; and ER visits due to asthma. Risk factors analyzed but not factored in the rankings: annual air quality including pollution and ozone levels; public smoking laws; indoor air quality; access to asthma specialists; rescue and controller medication use; uninsured rate; pollen allergy; poverty rate. *Asthma and Allergy Foundation of America, "Asthma Capitals 2024: The Most Challenging Places to Live With Asthma," September 10, 2024*

Pet Rankings

- Las Vegas was selected by *Sniffspot.com* as one of the most dog-friendly cities in the U.S., ranking #25 out of 50. Criteria: dog parks; hiking; sniffspots; public parks; dog-friendly businesses; housing; dog waste cleanliness; leash laws; dog services; and overall cost. *Sniffspot.com, "The Top 50 Most Dog-Friendly Cities in the U.S.," September 30, 2024*

Real Estate Rankings

- *WalletHub* compared the most populated U.S. cities to determine which had the best markets for real estate agents. Las Vegas ranked #87 where demand was high and pay was the best. Criteria: sales per agent; annual median wage for real-estate agents; monthly average starting salary for real estate agents; real estate job density and competition; unemployment rate; home turnover rate; housing-market health index; and other relevant metrics. *WalletHub.com, "2021 Best Places to Be a Real Estate Agent," May 12, 2021*

- According to Penske Truck Rental, the Las Vegas metro area was named the #5 moving destination in 2023, based on one-way consumer truck rental reservations made through Penske's website, rental locations, and reservations call center. *gopenske.com, "Penske Truck Rental's 2023 Top Moving Destinations," May 7, 2024*

- The Las Vegas metro area was identified as one of the top 16 housing markets to invest in for 2025 by *Forbes*. Criteria: stable local economies with good population growth and increase in jobs providing good support for home prices and rents. *Forbes.com, "Best Local Markets For Real Estate Investing In 2025," November 6, 2024*

- Las Vegas was ranked #12 in the top 20 out of the 100 largest metro areas in terms of house price appreciation in 2024 (#1 = highest rate). *Federal Housing Finance Agency, "House Price Index, 4th Quarter 2024," February 25, 2025*

- Las Vegas was ranked #162 out of 176 metro areas in terms of cost of housing in 2024 by the National Association of Home Builders (#1 = most affordable). Criteria: the portion of an average family's income necessary to pay the mortgage on a median-priced home. *National Association of Home Builders®, NAHB-Wells Fargo Cost of Housing Index, 4th Quarter 2024*

Safety Rankings

- Allstate ranked the 100 most populous cities in America in terms of driver safety. Las Vegas ranked #52. Criteria based on anonymized driving behavior data from Allstate's mobile app powered by Arity: high speed driving (over 80 mph), phone handling, and hard braking. The report helps increase the importance of safety and awareness behind the wheel. *Allstate, "16th Allstate America's Best Drivers Report®" July 11, 2024*

Women/Minorities Rankings

- *Travel + Leisure* listed the best cities in and around the U.S. for a memorable and fun girls' trip, even on a budget. Whether it is for a special occasion, to make new memories or just to get away, Las Vegas is sure to have something for all the ladies in your tribe. *Travel + Leisure, "25 Affordable Girls Weekend Getaways That Won't Break the Bank," January 30, 2025*

- Las Vegas was listed as one of the most LGBTQ-friendly cities in America by *The Advocate*, as compiled by the real estate data site *Clever*. The city ranked #3 out of 15. Criteria, among many: Pride events; gay bars; LGBTQ-affirming healthcare options; state and local laws; number of PFLAG chapters; LGBTQ+ population. *The Advocate, "These Are the 15 Most LGBTQ-Friendly Cities in the U.S." November 1, 2023*

- Personal finance website *WalletHub* compared more than 180 U.S. cities across two key dimensions, "Hispanic Business-Friendliness" and "Hispanic Purchasing Power," to arrive at the most favorable conditions for Hispanic entrepreneurs. Las Vegas was ranked #95 out of 182. Criteria includes: share of Hispanic-Owned Businesses; average growth of Hispanic Business revenues; Small Business-Friendliness score; affordability; and number of Hispanics with at least a bachelor's degree. *WalletHub.com, "Best Cities for Hispanic Entrepreneurs," September 4, 2024*

Miscellaneous Rankings

- *MoveHub* ranked 446 hipster cities across 20 countries, using its new and improved alternative Hipster Index and Las Vegas came out as #19 among the top 50. Criteria: population over 150,000; number of vintage boutiques; density of tattoo parlors; vegan places to eat; coffee shops; and density of vinyl record stores. *MoveHub.com, "The Hipster Index: Brighton Pips Portland to Global Top Spot," July 28, 2021*

- The financial planning site *SmartAsset* has compiled its annual study on the best places for Halloween in the U.S. for 2022. 146 cities were compared to determine that Las Vegas ranked #6 out of 35 for still being able to enjoy the festivities despite COVID-19. Metrics included: safety, family-friendliness, percentage of children in the population, concentration of candy and costume shops, weather and COVID infection rates. *SmartAsset.com, "2022 Edition-Best Places to Celebrate Halloween," October 19, 2022*

- *WalletHub* compared 148 of the most populated U.S. cities to determine their operating efficiency. A "Quality of Services" score was constructed for each city and then measured against the total budget per capita to reveal which were managed the best. Las Vegas ranked #47. Criteria: financial stability; economy; education; safety; health; infrastructure and pollution. *WalletHub.com, "2025's Best- & Worst-Run Cities in America," June 18, 2024*

Business Environment

DEMOGRAPHICS

Population Growth

Area	1990 Census	2000 Census	2010 Census	2020 Census	2023 Estimate[2]	Population Growth 1990-2023 (%)
City	261,374	478,434	583,756	641,903	650,873	149.0
MSA[1]	741,459	1,375,765	1,951,269	2,265,461	2,293,764	209.4
U.S.	248,709,873	281,421,906	308,745,538	331,449,281	332,387,540	33.6

Note: (1) Figures cover the Las Vegas-Henderson-North Las Vegas, NV Metropolitan Statistical Area;
(2) 2019-2023 5-year ACS population estimate
Source: U.S. Census Bureau, 1990 Census, 2000 Census, 2010 Census, 2020 Census, 2019-2023 American Community Survey 5-Year Estimates

Race

Area	White Alone[2] (%)	Black Alone[2] (%)	Asian Alone[2] (%)	AIAN[3] Alone[2] (%)	NHOPI[4] Alone[2] (%)	Other Race Alone[2] (%)	Two or More Races (%)
City	49.2	11.9	6.9	1.1	0.8	13.9	16.2
MSA[1]	47.1	12.1	10.5	1.1	0.8	12.9	15.5
U.S.	63.4	12.4	5.8	0.9	0.2	6.6	10.7

Note: (1) Figures cover the Las Vegas-Henderson-North Las Vegas, NV Metropolitan Statistical Area;
(2) Alone is defined as not being in combination with one or more other races; (3) American Indian and Alaska Native; (4) Native Hawaiian and Other Pacific Islander
Source: U.S. Census Bureau, 2019-2023 American Community Survey 5-Year Estimates

Hispanic or Latino Origin

Area	Total (%)	Mexican (%)	Puerto Rican (%)	Cuban (%)	Other (%)
City	34.1	24.7	1.2	1.6	6.6
MSA[1]	31.4	22.7	1.1	1.5	6.1
U.S.	19.0	11.3	1.8	0.7	5.2

Note: Persons of Hispanic or Latino origin can be of any race; (1) Figures cover the Las Vegas-Henderson-North Las Vegas, NV Metropolitan Statistical Area
Source: U.S. Census Bureau, 2019-2023 American Community Survey 5-Year Estimates

Age

Area	Percent of Population									Median Age
	Under Age 5	Age 5–19	Age 20–34	Age 35–44	Age 45–54	Age 55–64	Age 65–74	Age 75–84	Age 85+	
City	5.8	19.1	20.4	13.7	13.0	12.4	9.3	4.8	1.5	38.5
MSA[1]	5.8	19.0	20.5	14.1	13.0	12.1	9.5	4.7	1.3	38.3
U.S.	5.7	19.1	20.2	13.1	12.3	12.8	10.0	4.9	1.9	38.7

Note: (1) Figures cover the Las Vegas-Henderson-North Las Vegas, NV Metropolitan Statistical Area
Source: U.S. Census Bureau, 2019-2023 American Community Survey 5-Year Estimates

Disability by Age

Area	All Ages	Under 18 Years Old	18 to 64 Years Old	65 Years and Over
City	13.3	4.5	11.3	34.2
MSA[1]	13.0	4.4	10.7	34.3
U.S.	13.0	4.7	10.7	32.9

Note: Figures show percent of the civilian noninstitutionalized population that reported having a disability. Disability status is determined from six types of difficulty: vision, hearing, cognitive, ambulatory, self-care, and independent living. For children under 5 years old, hearing and vision difficulty are used to determine disability status. For children between the ages of 5 and 14, disability status is determined from hearing, vision, cognitive, ambulatory, and self-care difficulties. For people aged 15 years and older, they are considered to have a disability if they have difficulty with any one of the six difficulty types; Note: (1) Figures cover the Las Vegas-Henderson-North Las Vegas, NV Metropolitan Statistical Area
Source: U.S. Census Bureau, 2019-2023 American Community Survey 5-Year Estimates

Ancestry

Area	German	Irish	English	American	Italian	Polish	French[2]	European	Scottish
City	8.0	7.2	7.2	2.9	4.9	1.8	1.5	1.6	1.3
MSA[1]	7.9	6.8	7.0	2.9	4.7	1.7	1.4	1.3	1.2
U.S.	12.6	9.4	9.1	5.5	4.9	2.6	2.0	1.6	1.6

Note: Figures are the percentage of the total population reporting a particular ancestry. The nine most commonly reported ancestries in the U.S. are shown. Figures include multiple ancestries (e.g. if a person reported being Irish and Italian, they were included in both columns); (1) Figures cover the Las Vegas-Henderson-North Las Vegas, NV Metropolitan Statistical Area; (2) Excludes Basque
Source: U.S. Census Bureau, 2019-2023 American Community Survey 5-Year Estimates

Foreign-born Population

Area	Percent of Population Born in								
	Any Foreign Country	Asia	Mexico	Europe	Caribbean	Central America[2]	South America	Africa	Canada
City	20.9	5.3	8.5	1.6	1.3	2.2	1.0	0.4	0.4
MSA[1]	21.7	7.4	7.3	1.6	1.3	1.8	0.9	0.9	0.4
U.S.	13.9	4.3	3.3	1.4	1.4	1.2	1.2	0.8	0.2

Note: (1) Figures cover the Las Vegas-Henderson-North Las Vegas, NV Metropolitan Statistical Area;
(2) Excludes Mexico.
Source: U.S. Census Bureau, 2019-2023 American Community Survey 5-Year Estimates

Household Size

Area	Persons in Household (%)							Average Household Size
	One	Two	Three	Four	Five	Six	Seven or More	
City	30.3	31.2	15.8	11.9	6.3	2.7	1.9	2.63
MSA[1]	28.0	32.7	15.8	12.3	6.8	2.8	1.8	2.68
U.S.	28.5	33.8	15.4	12.7	5.9	2.3	1.4	2.54

Note: (1) Figures cover the Las Vegas-Henderson-North Las Vegas, NV Metropolitan Statistical Area
Source: U.S. Census Bureau, 2019-2023 American Community Survey 5-Year Estimates

Household Relationships

Area	House-holder	Opposite-sex Spouse	Same-sex Spouse	Opposite-sex Unmarried Partner	Same-sex Unmarried Partner	Child[2]	Grand-child	Other Relatives	Non-relatives
City	37.5	15.2	0.3	2.9	0.2	29.3	2.7	6.7	4.3
MSA[1]	37.3	15.5	0.3	3.0	0.2	28.7	2.6	7.0	4.4
U.S.	38.3	17.5	0.2	2.5	0.2	28.3	2.4	4.8	3.4

Note: Figures are percent of the total population; (1) Figures cover the Las Vegas-Henderson-North Las Vegas, NV Metropolitan Statistical Area; (2) Includes biological, adopted, and stepchildren of the householder
Source: U.S. Census Bureau, 2020 Census

Gender

Area	Males	Females	Males per 100 Females
City	325,629	325,244	100.1
MSA[1]	1,148,112	1,145,652	100.2
U.S.	164,545,087	167,842,453	98.0

Note: (1) Figures cover the Las Vegas-Henderson-North Las Vegas, NV Metropolitan Statistical Area
Source: U.S. Census Bureau, 2019-2023 American Community Survey 5-Year Estimates

Marital Status

Area	Never Married	Now Married[2]	Separated	Widowed	Divorced
City	36.4	42.8	1.8	5.3	13.5
MSA[1]	35.6	44.3	2.0	5.1	13.1
U.S.	34.1	47.9	1.7	5.6	10.7

Note: Figures are percentages and cover the population 15 years of age and older; (1) Figures cover the Las Vegas-Henderson-North Las Vegas, NV Metropolitan Statistical Area; (2) Excludes separated
Source: U.S. Census Bureau, 2019-2023 American Community Survey 5-Year Estimates

Religious Groups by Family

Area	Catholic	Baptist	Methodist	LDS[2]	Pentecostal	Lutheran	Islam	Adventist	Other
MSA[1]	26.2	1.9	0.3	5.8	1.5	0.6	0.3	1.3	5.5
U.S.	18.7	7.3	3.0	2.0	1.8	1.7	1.3	1.3	11.6

Note: Figures are the number of adherents as a percentage of the total population and cover the eight largest religious groups in the U.S; (1) Figures cover the Las Vegas-Henderson-North Las Vegas, NV Metropolitan Statistical Area; (2) Church of Jesus Christ of Latter-day Saints
Sources: 2020 U.S. Religion Census, Association of Statisticians of American Religious Bodies; The Association of Religion Data Archives (ARDA)

Religious Groups by Tradition

Area	Catholic	Evangelical Protestant	Mainline Protestant	Black Protestant	Islam	Judaism	Hinduism	Orthodox	Buddhism
MSA[1]	26.2	6.6	1.0	0.5	0.3	0.3	0.2	0.6	0.7
U.S.	18.7	16.5	5.2	2.3	1.3	0.6	0.4	0.4	0.3

Note: Figures are the number of adherents as a percentage of the total population; (1) Figures cover the Las Vegas-Henderson-North Las Vegas, NV Metropolitan Statistical Area
Sources: 2020 U.S. Religion Census, Association of Statisticians of American Religious Bodies; The Association of Religion Data Archives (ARDA)

ECONOMY

Real Gross Domestic Product (GDP)

Area	2017	2018	2019	2020	2021	2022	2023	Rank[3]
MSA[1]	116.3	122.7	128.2	117.3	130.1	138.5	142.8	35
U.S.[2]	17,619.1	18,160.7	18,642.5	18,238.9	19,387.6	19,896.6	20,436.3	–

Note: Figures are in billions of chained 2017 dollars; (1) Figures cover the Las Vegas-Henderson-North Las Vegas, NV Metropolitan Statistical Area; (2) Figures cover real GDP within metropolitan areas; (3) Rank is based on 2023 data and ranges from 1 to 384
Source: U.S. Bureau of Economic Analysis

Economic Growth

Area	2014	2015	2016	2017	2018	2019	2020	2021	2022	2023
MSA[1]	1.5	4.4	3.2	3.6	5.5	4.5	-8.5	10.9	6.4	3.2
U.S.[2]	2.6	3.2	2.0	2.7	3.1	2.7	-2.2	6.3	2.6	2.7

Note: Figures are real gross domestic product growth rates and represent percent change from preceding period; (1) Figures cover the Las Vegas-Henderson-North Las Vegas, NV Metropolitan Statistical Area; (2) Figures are the average growth rates within metropolitan areas
Source: U.S. Bureau of Economic Analysis

Metropolitan Area Exports

Area	2018	2019	2020	2021	2022	2023	Rank[2]
MSA[1]	2,240.6	2,430.8	1,705.9	1,866.2	2,116.3	2,762.3	91
U.S.	1,664,056.1	1,645,173.7	1,431,406.6	1,753,941.4	2,062,937.4	2,019,160.5	–

Note: Figures are in millions of dollars; (1) Figures cover the Las Vegas-Henderson-North Las Vegas, NV Metropolitan Statistical Area; (2) Rank is based on 2023 data and ranges from 1 to 386
Source: U.S. Department of Commerce, International Trade Administration, Office of Trade and Economic Analysis, Industry and Analysis, Exports by Metropolitan Area, data extracted April 2, 2025

Building Permits

Area	Single-Family			Multi-Family			Total		
	2023	2024	Pct. Chg.	2023	2024	Pct. Chg.	2023	2024	Pct. Chg.
City	2,590	2,655	2.5	1,026	935	-8.9	3,616	3,590	-0.7
MSA[1]	10,087	12,277	21.7	2,986	2,477	-17.0	13,073	14,754	12.9
U.S.	920,000	981,900	6.7	591,100	496,100	-16.1	1,511,100	1,478,000	-2.2

Note: (1) Figures cover the Las Vegas-Henderson-North Las Vegas, NV Metropolitan Statistical Area; Figures represent new, privately-owned housing units authorized (unadjusted data)
Source: U.S. Census Bureau, Building Permits Survey (BPS), 2023, 2024

Bankruptcy Filings

Area	Business Filings			Nonbusiness Filings		
	2023	2024	% Chg.	2023	2024	% Chg.
Clark County	194	178	-8.2	5,622	6,690	19.0
U.S.	18,926	23,107	22.1	434,064	494,201	13.9

Note: Business filings include Chapter 7, Chapter 9, Chapter 11, Chapter 12, Chapter 13, Chapter 15, and Section 304; Nonbusiness filings include Chapter 7, Chapter 11, and Chapter 13
Source: Administrative Office of the U.S. Courts, Business and Nonbusiness Bankruptcy, County Cases Commenced by Chapter of the Bankruptcy Code, During the 12-Month Period Ending December 31, 2023 and Business and Nonbusiness Bankruptcy, County Cases Commenced by Chapter of the Bankruptcy Code, During the 12-Month Period Ending December 31, 2024

Housing Vacancy Rates

Area	Gross Vacancy Rate[3] (%)			Year-Round Vacancy Rate[4] (%)			Rental Vacancy Rate[5] (%)			Homeowner Vacancy Rate[6] (%)		
	2022	2023	2024	2022	2023	2024	2022	2023	2024	2022	2023	2024
MSA[1]	9.2	9.6	9.7	8.3	8.8	9.3	5.7	7.2	8.3	0.9	1.1	1.1
U.S.[2]	9.1	9.0	9.1	7.5	7.5	7.6	5.7	6.5	6.8	0.8	0.8	1.0

Note: (1) Figures cover the Las Vegas-Henderson-North Las Vegas, NV Metropolitan Statistical Area; (2) Figures cover the 75 largest Metropolitan Statistical Areas; (3) The percentage of the total housing inventory that is vacant; (4) The percentage of the housing inventory (excluding seasonal units) that is year-round vacant; (5) The percentage of rental inventory that is vacant for rent; (6) The percentage of homeowner inventory that is vacant for sale
Source: U.S. Census Bureau, Housing Vacancies and Homeownership Annual Statistics: 2022, 2023, 2024

INCOME

Income

Area	Per Capita ($)	Median Household ($)	Average Household ($)
City	38,421	70,723	98,664
MSA[1]	38,654	73,845	101,010
U.S.	43,289	78,538	110,491

Note: (1) Figures cover the Las Vegas-Henderson-North Las Vegas, NV Metropolitan Statistical Area
Source: U.S. Census Bureau, 2019-2023 American Community Survey 5-Year Estimates

Household Income Distribution

Area	Percent of Households Earning							
	Under $15,000	$15,000 -$24,999	$25,000 -$34,999	$35,000 -$49,999	$50,000 -$74,999	$75,000 -$99,999	$100,000 -$149,999	$150,000 and up
City	10.0	6.7	7.5	11.4	17.3	12.9	16.8	17.4
MSA[1]	8.6	6.4	7.2	11.3	17.2	13.6	17.4	18.2
U.S.	8.5	6.6	6.8	10.4	15.7	12.7	17.4	21.9

Note: (1) Figures cover the Las Vegas-Henderson-North Las Vegas, NV Metropolitan Statistical Area
Source: U.S. Census Bureau, 2019-2023 American Community Survey 5-Year Estimates

Poverty Rate

Area	All Ages	Under 18 Years Old	18 to 64 Years Old	65 Years and Over
City	14.2	18.8	13.2	11.7
MSA[1]	13.2	18.1	12.1	10.6
U.S.	12.4	16.3	11.6	10.4

Note: Figures are percentage of people whose income during the past 12 months was below the poverty level;
(1) Figures cover the Las Vegas-Henderson-North Las Vegas, NV Metropolitan Statistical Area
Source: U.S. Census Bureau, 2019-2023 American Community Survey 5-Year Estimates

EMPLOYMENT

Labor Force and Employment

Area	Civilian Labor Force			Workers Employed		
	Dec. 2023	Dec. 2024	% Chg.	Dec. 2023	Dec. 2024	% Chg.
City	330,736	337,672	2.1	312,658	317,296	1.5
MSA[1]	1,199,294	1,224,775	2.1	1,135,389	1,152,230	1.5
U.S.	166,661,000	167,746,000	0.7	160,754,000	161,294,000	0.3

Note: Data is not seasonally adjusted and covers workers 16 years of age and older; (1) Figures cover the Las Vegas-Henderson-North Las Vegas, NV Metropolitan Statistical Area
Source: Bureau of Labor Statistics, Local Area Unemployment Statistics

Unemployment Rate

Area	2024											
	Jan.	Feb.	Mar.	Apr.	May	Jun.	Jul.	Aug.	Sep.	Oct.	Nov.	Dec.
City	5.7	5.8	5.7	5.5	5.6	6.2	6.5	6.3	5.9	6.0	6.1	6.0
MSA[1]	5.6	5.6	5.5	5.4	5.5	6.1	6.4	6.2	5.8	5.9	6.0	5.9
U.S.	4.1	4.2	3.9	3.5	3.7	4.3	4.5	4.4	3.9	3.9	4.0	3.8

Note: Data is not seasonally adjusted and covers workers 16 years of age and older; (1) Figures cover the Las Vegas-Henderson-North Las Vegas, NV Metropolitan Statistical Area
Source: Bureau of Labor Statistics, Local Area Unemployment Statistics

Average Wages

Occupation	$/Hr.	Occupation	$/Hr.
Accountants and Auditors	39.57	Maintenance and Repair Workers	26.40
Automotive Mechanics	25.88	Marketing Managers	59.85
Bookkeepers	24.90	Network and Computer Systems Admin.	49.09
Carpenters	32.87	Nurses, Licensed Practical	34.18
Cashiers	14.94	Nurses, Registered	49.23
Computer Programmers	44.52	Nursing Assistants	21.32
Computer Systems Analysts	47.58	Office Clerks, General	21.50
Computer User Support Specialists	27.07	Physical Therapists	55.52
Construction Laborers	24.69	Physicians	108.49
Cooks, Restaurant	19.59	Plumbers, Pipefitters and Steamfitters	31.52
Customer Service Representatives	19.65	Police and Sheriff's Patrol Officers	41.22
Dentists	69.07	Postal Service Mail Carriers	28.67
Electricians	34.73	Real Estate Sales Agents	32.12
Engineers, Electrical	51.25	Retail Salespersons	17.32
Fast Food and Counter Workers	14.78	Sales Representatives, Technical/Scientific	51.43
Financial Managers	68.81	Secretaries, Exc. Legal/Medical/Executive	22.21
First-Line Supervisors of Office Workers	30.93	Security Guards	19.00
General and Operations Managers	60.08	Surgeons	n/a
Hairdressers/Cosmetologists	16.64	Teacher Assistants, Exc. Postsecondary[1]	15.55
Home Health and Personal Care Aides	14.71	Teachers, Secondary School, Exc. Sp. Ed.[1]	31.27
Janitors and Cleaners	18.25	Telemarketers	16.68
Landscaping/Groundskeeping Workers	19.84	Truck Drivers, Heavy/Tractor-Trailer	28.15
Lawyers	n/a	Truck Drivers, Light/Delivery Services	22.31
Maids and Housekeeping Cleaners	20.07	Waiters and Waitresses	15.55

Note: Wage data covers the Las Vegas-Henderson-North Las Vegas, NV Metropolitan Statistical Area; (1) Hourly wages were calculated from annual wage data based on a 40 hour work week
Source: Bureau of Labor Statistics, Metro Area Occupational Employment & Wage Estimates, May 2024

Employment by Industry

Sector	MSA[1]		U.S.
	Number of Employees	Percent of Total	Percent of Total
Construction	79,200	6.8	5.1
Financial Activities	62,100	5.3	5.8
Government	124,400	10.7	14.9
Information	15,100	1.3	1.9
Leisure and Hospitality	300,600	25.8	10.4
Manufacturing	30,100	2.6	8.0
Mining and Logging	500	<0.1	0.4
Other Services	35,100	3.0	3.7
Private Education and Health Services	132,200	11.4	16.9
Professional and Business Services	166,200	14.3	14.2
Retail Trade	113,900	9.8	10.0
Transportation, Warehousing, and Utilities	78,400	6.7	4.8
Wholesale Trade	26,500	2.3	3.9

Note: Figures are non-farm employment as of December 2024. Figures are not seasonally adjusted and include workers 16 years of age and older; (1) Figures cover the Las Vegas-Henderson-North Las Vegas, NV Metropolitan Statistical Area
Source: Bureau of Labor Statistics, Current Employment Statistics, Employment, Hours, and Earnings

Employment by Occupation

Occupation Classification	City (%)	MSA[1] (%)	U.S. (%)
Management, Business, Science, and Arts	33.8	33.0	42.0
Natural Resources, Construction, and Maintenance	8.9	8.3	8.6
Production, Transportation, and Material Moving	11.2	11.9	13.0
Sales and Office	22.0	22.0	19.9
Service	24.1	24.9	16.5

Note: Figures cover employed civilians 16 years of age and older; (1) Figures cover the Las Vegas-Henderson-North Las Vegas, NV Metropolitan Statistical Area
Source: U.S. Census Bureau, 2019-2023 American Community Survey 5-Year Estimates

Occupations with Greatest Projected Employment Growth: 2022 – 2032

Occupation[1]	2022 Employment	2032 Projected Employment	Numeric Employment Change	Percent Employment Change
Laborers and Freight, Stock, and Material Movers, Hand	42,160	58,010	15,850	37.6
Taxi Drivers	22,490	31,920	9,430	41.9
Cooks, Restaurant	21,100	27,730	6,630	31.4
General and Operations Managers	42,740	48,840	6,100	14.3
Home Health and Personal Care Aides	16,000	21,330	5,330	33.3
Stockers and Order Fillers	22,320	27,550	5,230	23.4
Janitors and Cleaners, Except Maids and Housekeeping Cleaners	31,300	36,250	4,950	15.8
Heavy and Tractor-Trailer Truck Drivers	17,650	22,350	4,700	26.6
Fast Food and Counter Workers	40,690	45,260	4,570	11.2
Registered Nurses	24,290	28,810	4,520	18.6

Note: Projections cover Nevada; (1) Sorted by numeric employment change
Source: www.projectionscentral.org, State Occupational Projections, 2022–2032 Long-Term Projections

Fastest-Growing Occupations: 2022 – 2032

Occupation[1]	2022 Employment	2032 Projected Employment	Numeric Employment Change	Percent Employment Change
Farmworkers and Laborers, Crop, Nursery, and Greenhouse	2,760	5,210	2,450	88.8
Farm Equipment Mechanics and Service Technicians	120	210	90	75.0
Farmers, Ranchers, and Other Agricultural Managers	2,370	3,870	1,500	63.3
Bus Drivers, Transit and Intercity (SOC 2018)	1,720	2,770	1,050	61.0
Orthotists and Prosthetists	140	220	80	57.1
Solar Photovoltaic Installers	140	220	80	57.1
Nurse Practitioners	1,840	2,780	940	51.1
Helpers—Extraction Workers	660	990	330	50.0
Occupational Health and Safety Technicians (SOC 2018)	320	470	150	46.9
Shuttle Drivers and Chauffeurs	2,630	3,840	1,210	46.0

Note: Projections cover Nevada; (1) Sorted by percent employment change and excludes occupations with numeric employment change less than 50
Source: www.projectionscentral.org, State Occupational Projections, 2022–2032 Long-Term Projections

CITY FINANCES

City Government Finances

Component	2022 ($000)	2022 ($ per capita)
Total Revenues	1,242,151	1,875
Total Expenditures	1,042,301	1,574
Debt Outstanding	532,070	803

Source: U.S. Census Bureau, State & Local Government Finances 2022

City Government Revenue by Source

Source	2022 ($000)	2022 ($ per capita)	2022 (%)
General Revenue			
From Federal Government	40,730	61	3.3
From State Government	494,163	746	39.8
From Local Governments	91,980	139	7.4
Taxes			
Property	165,462	250	13.3
Sales and Gross Receipts	65,666	99	5.3
Personal Income	0	0	0.0
Corporate Income	0	0	0.0
Motor Vehicle License	0	0	0.0
Other Taxes	62,281	94	5.0
Current Charges	181,589	274	14.6
Liquor Store	0	0	0.0
Utility	0	0	0.0

Source: U.S. Census Bureau, State & Local Government Finances 2022

City Government Expenditures by Function

Function	2022 ($000)	2022 ($ per capita)	2022 (%)
General Direct Expenditures			
Air Transportation	0	0	0.0
Corrections	60,076	90	5.8
Education	0	0	0.0
Employment Security Administration	0	0	0.0
Financial Administration	10,813	16	1.0
Fire Protection	161,629	244	15.5
General Public Buildings	9,916	15	1.0
Governmental Administration, Other	32,858	49	3.2
Health	17,084	25	1.6
Highways	163,474	246	15.7
Hospitals	0	0	0.0
Housing and Community Development	42,592	64	4.1
Interest on General Debt	28,171	42	2.7
Judicial and Legal	34,985	52	3.4
Libraries	0	0	0.0
Parking	12,606	19	1.2
Parks and Recreation	77,813	117	7.5
Police Protection	18,037	27	1.7
Public Welfare	0	0	0.0
Sewerage	116,866	176	11.2
Solid Waste Management	7,720	11	0.7
Veterans' Services	0	0	0.0
Liquor Store	0	0	0.0
Utility	0	0	0.0

Source: U.S. Census Bureau, State & Local Government Finances 2022

TAXES

State Corporate Income Tax Rates

State	Tax Rate (%)	Income Brackets ($)	Num. of Brackets	Financial Institution Tax Rate (%)[a]	Federal Income Tax Ded.
Nevada	None	–	–	–	–

Note: Tax rates for tax year 2024; (a) Rates listed are the corporate income tax rate applied to financial institutions or excise taxes based on income. Some states have other taxes based upon the value of deposits or shares.
Source: Federation of Tax Administrators, State Corporate Income Tax Rates, January 1, 2025

State Individual Income Tax Rates

State	Tax Rate (%)	Income Brackets ($)	Personal Exemptions ($)			Standard Ded. ($)	
			Single	Married	Depend.	Single	Married
Nevada				– No state income tax –			

Note: Tax rates for tax year 2024; Local- and county-level taxes are not included
Source: Federation of Tax Administrators, State Individual Income Tax Rates, January 1, 2025

Various State Sales and Excise Tax Rates

State	State Sales Tax (%)	Gasoline[1] ($/gal.)	Cigarette[2] ($/pack)	Spirits[3] ($/gal.)	Wine[4] ($/gal.)	Beer[5] ($/gal.)	Recreational Marijuana (%)
Nevada	6.85	0.24	1.80	3.60	0.70	0.16	(o)

Note: All tax rates as of January 1, 2025; (1) The American Petroleum Institute has developed a methodology for determining the average tax rate on a gallon of fuel. Rates may include any of the following: excise taxes, environmental fees, storage tank fees, other fees or taxes, general sales tax, and local taxes; (2) The federal excise tax of $1.0066 per pack and local taxes are not included; (3) Rates are those applicable to off-premise sales of 40% alcohol by volume (a.b.v.) distilled spirits in 750ml containers. Local excise taxes are excluded; (4) Rates are those applicable to off-premise sales of 11% a.b.v. non-carbonated wine in 750ml containers; (5) Rates are those applicable to off-premise sales of 4.7% a.b.v. beer in 12 ounce containers; (o) 15% excise tax (fair market value at wholesale); 10% excise tax (retail price)
Source: Tax Foundation, 2025 Facts & Figures: How Does Your State Compare?

State Tax Competitiveness Index

State	Overall Rank	Corporate Tax Rank	Individual Income Tax Rank	Sales Tax Rank	Property Tax Rank	Unemployment Insurance Tax Rank
Nevada	17	39	7	40	7	46

Note: The Tax Foundation's State Tax Competitiveness Index enables policymakers, taxpayers, and business leaders to gauge how their states' tax systems compare. A rank of 1 is best, 50 is worst. Rankings do not average to the total. States without a tax rank equally as 1. DC's scores and rankings do not affect other states. The report shows tax systems as of July 1, 2024 (the beginning of Fiscal Year 2025).
Source: Tax Foundation, State Tax Competitiveness Index 2025

TRANSPORTATION

Means of Transportation to Work

Area	Car/Truck/Van		Public Transportation			Bicycle	Walked	Other Means	Worked at Home
	Drove Alone	Car-pooled	Bus	Subway	Railroad				
City	72.6	10.0	2.4	0.0	0.0	0.3	1.3	2.9	10.5
MSA[1]	72.6	10.3	2.3	0.0	0.0	0.2	1.2	2.6	10.7
U.S.	70.2	8.5	1.7	1.3	0.4	0.4	2.4	1.6	13.5

Note: Figures are percentages and cover workers 16 years of age and older; (1) Figures cover the Las Vegas-Henderson-North Las Vegas, NV Metropolitan Statistical Area
Source: U.S. Census Bureau, 2019-2023 American Community Survey 5-Year Estimates

Travel Time to Work

Area	Less Than 10 Minutes	10 to 19 Minutes	20 to 29 Minutes	30 to 44 Minutes	45 to 59 Minutes	60 to 89 Minutes	90 Minutes or More
City	7.3	24.0	30.9	27.3	6.0	2.6	1.9
MSA[1]	7.9	27.2	29.2	25.9	5.3	2.6	2.0
U.S.	12.6	28.6	21.2	20.8	8.1	6.0	2.8

Note: Note: Figures are percentages and include workers 16 years old and over; (1) Figures cover the Las Vegas-Henderson-North Las Vegas, NV Metropolitan Statistical Area
Source: U.S. Census Bureau, 2019-2023 American Community Survey 5-Year Estimates

Key Congestion Measures

Measure	2000	2010	2015	2020	2022
Annual Hours of Delay, Total (000)	31,658	48,936	56,055	21,702	60,080
Annual Hours of Delay, Per Auto Commuter	41	44	49	18	50
Annual Congestion Cost, Per Auto Commuter ($)	792	974	1,031	406	1,103

Note: Figures cover the Las Vegas-Henderson NV urban area
Source: Texas A&M Transportation Institute, 2023 Urban Mobility Report

Freeway Travel Time Index

Measure	1985	1990	1995	2000	2005	2010	2015	2020	2022
Urban Area Index[1]	1.10	1.16	1.21	1.24	1.27	1.25	1.24	1.07	1.22
Urban Area Rank[1,2]	27	19	16	18	18	21	26	57	28

Note: Freeway Travel Time Index—the ratio of travel time in the peak period to the travel time at free-flow conditions. For example, a value of 1.30 indicates a 20-minute free-flow trip takes 26 minutes in the peak (20 minutes x 1.30 = 26 minutes); (1) Covers the Las Vegas-Henderson NV urban area; (2) Rank is based on 101 larger urban areas (#1 = highest travel time index)
Source: Texas A&M Transportation Institute, 2023 Urban Mobility Report

Public Transportation

Agency Name / Mode of Transportation	Vehicles Operated in Maximum Service[1]	Annual Unlinked Passenger Trips[2] (in thous.)	Annual Passenger Miles[3] (in thous.)
Regional Transportation Commission of Southern Nevada (RTC)			
Bus (purchased transportation)	280	49,591.0	183,473.4
Demand Response (purchased transportation)	331	1,438.8	15,484.8

Note: (1) Number of revenue vehicles operated by the given mode and type of service to meet the annual maximum service requirement. This is the revenue vehicle count during the peak season of the year; on the week and day that maximum service is provided. Vehicles operated in maximum service (VOMS) exclude atypical days and one-time special events; (2) Number of passengers who boarded public transportation vehicles. Passengers are counted each time they board a vehicle no matter how many vehicles they use to travel from their origin to their destination. (3) Sum of the distances ridden by all passengers during the entire fiscal year.
Source: Federal Transit Administration, National Transit Database, 2023

Air Transportation

Airport Name and Code / Type of Service	Passenger Airlines[1]	Passenger Enplanements	Freight Carriers[2]	Freight (lbs)
McCarran International (LAS)				
Domestic service (U.S. carriers only)	31	26,383,142	12	94,545,286
International service (U.S. carriers only)	8	17,046	2	148,003

Note: (1) Includes all U.S.-based major, minor and commuter airlines that carried at least one passenger during the year; (2) Includes all U.S.-based airlines and freight carriers that transported at least one pound of freight during the year.
Source: Bureau of Transportation Statistics, The Intermodal Transportation Database, Air Carriers: T-100 Domestic Market (U.S. carriers only), 2024; Bureau of Transportation Statistics, The Intermodal Transportation Database, Air Carriers: T-100 International Market (U.S. carriers only), 2024

BUSINESSES

Major Business Headquarters

Company Name	Industry	Rankings	
		Fortune[1]	Forbes[2]
BradyPLUS	Materials	-	128
Las Vegas Sands	Hotels, casinos, resorts	387	-
MGM Resorts International	Hotels, casinos, resorts	251	-

Note: (1) Companies that produce a 10-K are ranked 1 to 500 based on 2023 revenue; (2) All private companies with at least $2 billion in annual revenue through the end of their most current fiscal year are ranked 1 to 275; companies listed are headquartered in the city; dashes indicate no ranking
Source: Fortune, "Fortune 500," 2024; Forbes, "America's Largest Private Companies," 2024

Fastest-Growing Businesses

According to *Inc.*, Las Vegas is home to one of America's 500 fastest-growing private companies: **Codingscape** (#310). Criteria: must be an independent, privately-held, for-profit, U.S. corporation, proprietorship or partnership as of December 31, 2023; revenues must be at least $100,000 in 2020 and $2 million in 2023; must have four-year operating/sales history. *Inc., "America's 500 Fastest-Growing Private Companies," 2024*

Living Environment

COST OF LIVING

Cost of Living Index

Composite Index	Groceries	Housing	Utilities	Trans- portation	Health Care	Misc. Goods/ Services
98.5	103.7	104.6	113.8	115.0	85.2	85.1

Note: The Cost of Living Index measures regional differences in the cost of consumer goods and services, excluding taxes and non-consumer expenditures, for professional and managerial households in the top income quintile. It is based on more than 50,000 prices covering almost 60 different items for which prices are collected three times a year by chambers of commerce, economic development organizations or university applied economic centers in each participating urban area. The numbers shown should be read as a percentage above or below the national average of 100. For example, a value of 115.4 in the groceries column indicates that grocery prices are 15.4% higher than the national average. Small differences in the index numbers should not be interpreted as significant; Figures cover the Las Vegas NV urban area.
Source: The Council for Community and Economic Research, Cost of Living Index, 2024

Grocery Prices

Area[1]	T-Bone Steak ($/pound)	Frying Chicken ($/pound)	Whole Milk ($/half gal.)	Eggs ($/dozen)	Orange Juice ($/64 oz.)	Coffee ($/11.5 oz.)
City[2]	15.54	1.74	4.78	3.08	4.43	6.31
Avg.	15.42	1.55	4.69	3.25	4.41	5.46
Min.	14.50	1.16	4.43	2.75	4.00	4.85
Max.	17.56	2.89	5.49	4.78	5.54	7.89

*Note: (1) Values for the local area are compared with the average, minimum and maximum values for all 276 areas in the Cost of Living Index; (2) Figures cover the Las Vegas NV urban area; **T-Bone Steak** (price per pound); **Frying Chicken** (price per pound, whole fryer); **Whole Milk** (half gallon carton); **Eggs** (price per dozen, Grade A, large); **Orange Juice** (64 oz. Tropicana or Florida Natural); **Coffee** (11.5 oz. can, vacuum-packed, Maxwell House, Hills Bros, or Folgers).*
Source: The Council for Community and Economic Research, Cost of Living Index, 2024

Housing and Utility Costs

Area[1]	New Home Price ($)	Apartment Rent ($/month)	All Electric ($/month)	Part Electric ($/month)	Other Energy ($/month)	Telephone ($/month)
City[2]	554,723	1,576	-	160.52	94.44	188.64
Avg.	515,975	1,550	210.99	123.07	82.07	194.99
Min.	265,375	692	104.33	53.68	36.26	179.42
Max.	2,775,821	5,719	529.02	397.28	361.63	223.33

*Note: (1) Values for the local area are compared with the average, minimum and maximum values for all 276 areas in the Cost of Living Index; (2) Figures cover the Las Vegas NV urban area; **New Home Price** (2,400 sf living area, 8,000 sf lot, in urban area with full utilities); **Apartment Rent** (950 sf 2 bedroom/1.5 or 2 bath, unfurnished, excluding all utilities except water); **All Electric** (average monthly cost for an all-electric home); **Part Electric** (average monthly cost for a part-electric home); **Other Energy** (average monthly cost for natural gas, fuel oil, coal, wood, and any other forms of energy except electricity); **Telephone** (price includes the base monthly rate plus taxes and fees for three lines of mobile phone service).*
Source: The Council for Community and Economic Research, Cost of Living Index, 2024

Health Care, Transportation, and Other Costs

Area[1]	Doctor ($/visit)	Dentist ($/visit)	Optometrist ($/visit)	Gasoline ($/gallon)	Beauty Salon ($/visit)	Men's Shirt ($)
City[2]	110.44	99.25	100.78	4.13	48.86	25.05
Avg.	143.77	117.51	129.23	3.32	48.57	38.14
Min.	36.74	58.67	67.33	2.80	24.00	13.41
Max.	270.44	216.82	307.33	5.28	94.00	63.89

*Note: (1) Values for the local area are compared with the average, minimum and maximum values for all 276 areas in the Cost of Living Index; (2) Figures cover the Las Vegas NV urban area; **Doctor** (general practitioners routine exam of an established patient); **Dentist** (adult teeth cleaning and periodic oral examination); **Optometrist** (full vision eye exam for established adult patient); **Gasoline** (one gallon regular unleaded, national brand, including all taxes, cash price at self-service pump if available); **Beauty Salon** (woman's shampoo, trim, and blow-dry); **Men's Shirt** (cotton/polyester dress shirt, pinpoint weave, long sleeves).*
Source: The Council for Community and Economic Research, Cost of Living Index, 2024

HOUSING

Homeownership Rate

Area	2017 (%)	2018 (%)	2019 (%)	2020 (%)	2021 (%)	2022 (%)	2023 (%)	2024 (%)
MSA[1]	54.4	58.1	56.0	57.3	57.7	58.7	58.9	58.5
U.S.	63.9	64.4	64.6	66.6	65.5	65.8	65.9	65.6

Note: (1) Figures cover the Las Vegas-Henderson-North Las Vegas, NV Metropolitan Statistical Area
Source: U.S. Census Bureau, Housing Vacancies and Homeownership Annual Statistics: 2017-2024

House Price Index (HPI)

Area	National Ranking[2]	Quarterly Change (%)	One-Year Change (%)	Five-Year Change (%)	Since 1991Q1 (%)
MSA[1]	44	1.27	7.43	58.90	295.91
U.S.[3]	–	1.43	4.51	57.13	327.82

Note: The HPI is a weighted repeat sales index. It measures average price changes in repeat sales or refinancings on the same properties. This information is obtained by reviewing repeat mortgage transactions on single-family properties whose mortgages have been purchased or securitized by Fannie Mae or Freddie Mac since January 1975; (1) Figures cover the Las Vegas-Henderson-Paradise, NV Metropolitan Statistical Area; (2) Rankings are based on annual percentage change for all metro areas containing at least 15,000 transactions over the last 10 years and ranges from 1 to 241; (3) figures based on a weighted average of Census Division estimates using a seasonally adjusted, purchase-only index; all figures are for the period ending December 31, 2024
Source: Federal Housing Finance Agency, Change in FHFA Metropolitan Area House Price Indexes, All Transactions Index, 2024Q4

Home Value

Area	Under $100,000	$100,000 -$199,999	$200,000 -$299,999	$300,000 -$399,999	$400,000 -$499,999	$500,000 -$999,999	$1,000,000 or more	Median ($)
City	3.9	4.5	17.2	25.6	19.7	24.9	4.2	395,300
MSA[1]	4.7	4.8	15.2	25.2	21.6	24.5	4.1	400,800
U.S.	12.1	17.8	19.5	14.4	10.5	19.1	6.5	303,400

Note: Figures are percentages except for median and cover owner-occupied housing units; (1) Figures cover the Las Vegas-Henderson-North Las Vegas, NV Metropolitan Statistical Area
Source: U.S. Census Bureau, 2019-2023 American Community Survey 5-Year Estimates

Year Housing Structure Built

Area	2020 or Later	2010 -2019	2000 -2009	1990 -1999	1980 -1989	1970 -1979	1960 -1969	1950 -1959	1940 -1949	Before 1940	Median Year
City	1.4	8.8	21.4	29.3	16.3	10.2	7.0	4.1	1.0	0.5	1994
MSA[1]	1.9	12.3	28.8	25.5	13.7	10.1	4.7	2.0	0.6	0.4	1997
U.S.	1.2	8.9	13.6	12.8	13.0	14.4	10.0	9.7	4.5	11.9	1980

Note: Figures are percentages except for Median Year; Note: (1) Figures cover the Las Vegas-Henderson-North Las Vegas, NV Metropolitan Statistical Area
Source: U.S. Census Bureau, 2019-2023 American Community Survey 5-Year Estimates

Gross Monthly Rent

Area	Under $500	$500 -$999	$1,000 -$1,499	$1,500 -$1,999	$2,000 -$2,499	$2,500 -$2,999	$3,000 and up	Median ($)
City	3.1	14.4	35.9	29.4	11.7	3.5	1.9	1,456
MSA[1]	1.8	12.2	34.8	31.6	13.6	3.7	2.2	1,518
U.S.	6.5	22.3	29.5	20.2	10.8	4.4	5.9	1,348

Note: Figures are percentages except for median; Gross rent is the contract rent plus the estimated average monthly cost of utilities (electricity, gas, and water and sewer) and fuels (oil, coal, kerosene, wood, etc.) if these are paid by the renter (or paid for the renter by someone else); (1) Figures cover the Las Vegas-Henderson-North Las Vegas, NV Metropolitan Statistical Area
Source: U.S. Census Bureau, 2019-2023 American Community Survey 5-Year Estimates

HEALTH

Health Risk Factors

Category	MSA[1] (%)	U.S. (%)
Adults aged 18–64 who have any kind of health care coverage	n/a	90.8
Adults who reported being in good or better health	n/a	81.8
Adults who have been told they have high blood cholesterol	n/a	36.9
Adults who have been told they have high blood pressure	n/a	34.0
Adults who are current smokers	n/a	12.1
Adults who currently use e-cigarettes	n/a	7.7
Adults who currently use chewing tobacco, snuff, or snus	n/a	3.2
Adults who are heavy drinkers[2]	n/a	6.1
Adults who are binge drinkers[3]	n/a	15.2
Adults who are overweight (BMI 25.0 - 29.9)	n/a	34.4
Adults who are obese (BMI 30.0 - 99.8)	n/a	34.3
Adults who participated in any physical activities in the past month	n/a	75.8

Note: All figures are crude prevalence; (1) Figures for the Las Vegas-Henderson-North Las Vegas, NV Metropolitan Statistical Area were not available.
(2) Heavy drinkers are classified as adult men having more than 14 drinks per week and adult women having more than 7 drinks per week; (3) Binge drinkers are classified as males having five or more drinks on one occasion or females having four or more drinks on one occasion
Source: Centers for Disease Control and Prevention, Behaviorial Risk Factor Surveillance System, SMART: Selected Metropolitan Area Risk Trends, 2023

Acute and Chronic Health Conditions

Category	MSA[1] (%)	U.S. (%)
Adults who have ever been told they had a heart attack	n/a	4.2
Adults who have ever been told they have angina or coronary heart disease	n/a	4.0
Adults who have ever been told they had a stroke	n/a	3.3
Adults who have ever been told they have asthma	n/a	15.7
Adults who have ever been told they have arthritis	n/a	26.3
Adults who have ever been told they have diabetes[2]	n/a	11.5
Adults who have ever been told they had skin cancer	n/a	5.6
Adults who have ever been told they had any other types of cancer	n/a	8.4
Adults who have ever been told they have COPD	n/a	6.4
Adults who have ever been told they have kidney disease	n/a	3.7
Adults who have ever been told they have a form of depression	n/a	22.0

Note: All figures are crude prevalence; (1) Figures for the Las Vegas-Henderson-North Las Vegas, NV Metropolitan Statistical Area were not available.
(2) Figures do not include pregnancy-related, borderline, or pre-diabetes
Source: Centers for Disease Control and Prevention, Behaviorial Risk Factor Surveillance System, SMART: Selected Metropolitan Area Risk Trends, 2023

Health Screening and Vaccination Rates

Category	MSA[1] (%)	U.S. (%)
Adults who have ever been tested for HIV	n/a	37.5
Adults who have had their blood cholesterol checked within the last five years	n/a	87.0
Adults aged 65+ who have had flu shot within the past year	n/a	63.4
Adults aged 65+ who have ever had a pneumonia vaccination	n/a	71.9

Note: All figures are crude prevalence; (1) Figures for the Las Vegas-Henderson-North Las Vegas, NV Metropolitan Statistical Area were not available.
Source: Centers for Disease Control and Prevention, Behaviorial Risk Factor Surveillance System, SMART: Selected Metropolitan Area Risk Trends, 2023

Disability Status

Category	MSA[1] (%)	U.S. (%)
Adults who reported being deaf	n/a	7.4
Are you blind or have serious difficulty seeing, even when wearing glasses?	n/a	4.9
Do you have difficulty doing errands alone?	n/a	7.8
Do you have difficulty dressing or bathing?	n/a	3.6
Do you have serious difficulty concentrating/remembering/making decisions?	n/a	13.7
Do you have serious difficulty walking or climbing stairs?	n/a	13.2

Note: All figures are crude prevalence; (1) Figures for the Las Vegas-Henderson-North Las Vegas, NV Metropolitan Statistical Area were not available.
Source: Centers for Disease Control and Prevention, Behaviorial Risk Factor Surveillance System, SMART: Selected Metropolitan Area Risk Trends, 2023

Mortality Rates for the Top 10 Causes of Death in the U.S.

ICD-10[a] Sub-Chapter	ICD-10[a] Code	Crude Mortality Rate[2] per 100,000 population	
		County[3]	U.S.
Malignant neoplasms	C00-C97	162.7	182.7
Ischaemic heart diseases	I20-I25	106.6	109.6
Provisional assignment of new diseases of uncertain etiology[1]	U00-U49	84.4	65.3
Other forms of heart disease	I30-I51	63.5	65.1
Other degenerative diseases of the nervous system	G30-G31	50.0	52.4
Other external causes of accidental injury	W00-X59	50.2	52.3
Cerebrovascular diseases	I60-I69	40.3	49.1
Chronic lower respiratory diseases	J40-J47	42.0	43.5
Hypertensive diseases	I10-I15	60.0	38.9
Organic, including symptomatic, mental disorders	F01-F09	14.8	33.9

Note: (a) ICD-10 = International Classification of Diseases 10th Revision; (1) Includes COVID-19, adverse effects to COVID-19 vaccines, SARS, and vaping-related disorders; (2) Crude mortality rates are a three-year average covering 2021-2023; (3) Figures cover Clark County.
Source: Centers for Disease Control and Prevention, National Center for Health Statistics. National Vital Statistics System, Mortality 2018-2023 on CDC WONDER Online Database

Mortality Rates for Selected Causes of Death

Cause of Death	ICD-10[a] Code	Crude Mortality Rate[1] per 100,000 population	
		County[2]	U.S.
Accidental poisoning and exposure to noxious substances	X40-X49	30.3	30.5
Alzheimer disease	G30	28.1	35.4
Assault	X85-Y09	8.7	7.3
COVID-19	U07.1	84.4	65.3
Diabetes mellitus	E10-E14	26.7	30.0
Diseases of the liver	K70-K76	21.4	20.8
Human immunodeficiency virus (HIV) disease	B20-B24	1.7	1.5
Influenza and pneumonia	J09-J18	17.3	13.4
Intentional self-harm	X60-X84	19.1	14.7
Malnutrition	E40-E46	5.2	6.0
Obesity and other hyperalimentation	E65-E68	2.8	3.1
Renal failure	N17-N19	7.8	16.4
Transport accidents	V01-V99	13.2	14.4

Note: (a) ICD-10 = International Classification of Diseases 10th Revision; (1) Crude mortality rates are a three-year average covering 2021-2023; (2) Figures cover Clark County; Data are suppressed when the data meet the criteria for confidentiality constraints; Crude mortality rates are flagged as unreliable when the rate would be calculated with a numerator of 20 or less.
Source: Centers for Disease Control and Prevention, National Center for Health Statistics. National Vital Statistics System, Mortality 2018-2023 on CDC WONDER Online Database

Health Insurance Coverage

Area	With Health Insurance	With Private Health Insurance	With Public Health Insurance	Without Health Insurance	Population Under Age 19 Without Health Insurance
City	86.8	60.3	36.5	13.2	8.8
MSA[1]	87.9	62.5	35.9	12.1	8.3
U.S.	91.4	67.3	36.3	8.6	5.4

Note: Figures are percentages that cover the civilian noninstitutionalized population; (1) Figures cover the Las Vegas-Henderson-North Las Vegas, NV Metropolitan Statistical Area
Source: U.S. Census Bureau, 2019-2023 American Community Survey 5-Year Estimates

Number of Medical Professionals

Area	MDs[3]	DOs[3,4]	Dentists	Podiatrists	Chiropractors	Optometrists
County[1] (number)	4,375	981	1,614	110	492	345
County[1] (rate[2])	188.3	42.2	69.1	4.7	21.1	14.8
U.S. (rate[2])	302.5	29.2	74.6	6.4	29.5	18.0

Note: Data as of 2023 unless noted; (1) Data covers Clark County; (2) Number of medical professionals per 100,000 population; (3) Data as of 2022 and includes all active, non-federal physicians; (4) Doctor of Osteopathic Medicine
Source: U.S. Department of Health and Human Services, Health Resources and Services Administration, Bureau of Health Professions, Area Resource File (ARF) 2023-2024

EDUCATION

Public School District Statistics

District Name	Schls	Pupils	Pupil/ Teacher Ratio	Minority Pupils[1] (%)	Total Rev. per Pupil ($)	Total Exp. per Pupil ($)
Clark County School District	384	304,565	20.7	80.0	14,482	13,359

Note: Table includes school districts with 2,000 or more students; (1) Percentage of students that are not non-Hispanic white.
Source: U.S. Department of Education, National Center for Education Statistics, Common Core of Data, Local Education Agency (School District) Universe Survey: School Year 2023-2024; U.S. Department of Education, National Center for Education Statistics, Common Core of Data, School District Finance Survey (F-33): School Year 2021–22

Best High Schools

According to *U.S. News,* Las Vegas is home to one of the top 500 high schools in the U.S.: **Advanced Technologies Academy** (#88). Nearly 25,000 public, magnet and charter schools were ranked based on their performance on state assessments and how well they prepare students for college. *U.S. News & World Report, "Best High Schools 2024"*

Highest Level of Education

Area	Less than H.S.	H.S. Diploma	Some College, No Deg.	Associate Degree	Bachelor's Degree	Master's Degree	Prof. School Degree	Doctorate Degree
City	14.2	26.7	23.7	8.1	17.3	6.9	2.1	1.0
MSA[1]	13.2	27.6	23.4	8.5	18.0	6.6	1.7	1.0
U.S.	10.6	26.2	19.4	8.8	21.3	9.8	2.3	1.6

Note: Figures cover persons age 25 and over; (1) Figures cover the Las Vegas-Henderson-North Las Vegas, NV Metropolitan Statistical Area
Source: U.S. Census Bureau, 2019-2023 American Community Survey 5-Year Estimates

Educational Attainment by Race

Area	High School Graduate or Higher (%)					Bachelor's Degree or Higher (%)				
	Total	White	Black	Asian	Hisp.[2]	Total	White	Black	Asian	Hisp.[2]
City	85.8	91.7	88.5	91.7	66.8	27.3	32.2	19.5	44.8	12.5
MSA[1]	86.8	91.8	90.6	90.6	69.6	27.3	31.1	21.2	42.9	12.7
U.S.	89.4	92.9	88.1	88.0	72.5	35.0	37.7	24.7	57.0	19.9

Note: Figures shown cover persons 25 years old and over; (1) Figures cover the Las Vegas-Henderson-North Las Vegas, NV Metropolitan Statistical Area; (2) People of Hispanic origin can be of any race
Source: U.S. Census Bureau, 2019-2023 American Community Survey 5-Year Estimates

School Enrollment by Grade and Control

Area	Preschool (%)		Kindergarten (%)		Grades 1 - 4 (%)		Grades 5 - 8 (%)		Grades 9 - 12 (%)	
	Public	Private	Public	Private	Public	Private	Public	Private	Public	Private
City	68.6	31.4	91.1	8.9	87.6	12.4	89.3	10.7	91.2	8.8
MSA[1]	64.0	36.0	87.1	12.9	88.8	11.2	90.1	9.9	91.8	8.2
U.S.	58.7	41.3	85.2	14.8	87.2	12.8	87.9	12.1	89.0	11.0

Note: Figures shown cover persons 3 years old and over; (1) Figures cover the Las Vegas-Henderson-North Las Vegas, NV Metropolitan Statistical Area
Source: U.S. Census Bureau, 2019-2023 American Community Survey 5-Year Estimates

Higher Education

Four-Year Colleges			Two-Year Colleges			Medical Schools[1]	Law Schools[2]	Voc/ Tech[3]
Public	Private Non-profit	Private For-profit	Public	Private Non-profit	Private For-profit			
3	3	6	0	0	5	2	1	11

Note: Figures cover institutions located within the Las Vegas-Henderson-North Las Vegas, NV Metropolitan Statistical Area and include main campuses only; (1) includes schools accredited by the Liaison Committee on Medical Education and the American Osteopathic Association's Commission on Osteopathic College Accreditation; (2) includes ABA-accredited schools, schools with provisional ABA accreditation, and state accredited schools; (3) includes all schools with programs that are less than 2 years.
Source: National Center for Education Statistics, Integrated Postsecondary Education System (IPEDS), 2023-24; Wikipedia, List of Medical Schools in the United States, accessed May 2, 2025; Wikipedia, List of Law Schools in the United States, accessed May 2, 2025

According to *U.S. News & World Report,* the Las Vegas-Henderson-North Las Vegas, NV metro area is home to one of the top 100 law schools in the U.S.: **University of Nevada—Las Vegas (Boyd)** (#79 tie). The rankings are based on a weighted average of 12 measures of quality: peer assessment score; assessment score by lawyers/judges; median LSAT scores; median undergrad GPA; acceptance rate; employment rates for graduates; placement success; bar passage rate; faculty resources; expenditures per student; student/faculty ratio; and library resources. *U.S. News & World Report, "America's Best Graduate Schools, Law, 2025"*

EMPLOYERS

Major Employers

Company Name	Industry
Allegiant	Airline
Amazon.com	Online retail
Boyd Gaming	Gaming
Caesars Entertainment	Gaming
City of Las Vegas	Local government
Clark County School District	Education
Flamingo	Gaming
Fontainebleau	Gaming
IGT	Gaming
Las Vegas Metropolitan Police	Law enforcement
MGM Grand	Gaming
Mountainview Hospital	Healthcare
Nellis Air Force Base	Military
Palms Casino & Resort	Gaming
Sahara	Gaming
State of Nevada	State government
Station Casinos	Gaming
University Medical Center	Healthcare
University of Nevada Las Vegas	Higher education
Wynn Resorts	Hospitality

Note: Companies shown are located within the Las Vegas-Henderson-North Las Vegas, NV Metropolitan Statistical Area.
Source: Chambers of Commerce; State Departments of Labor; Wikipedia

PUBLIC SAFETY

Crime Rate

Area	Total Crime Rate	Violent Crime Rate				Property Crime Rate		
		Murder	Rape	Robbery	Aggrav. Assault	Burglary	Larceny -Theft	Motor Vehicle Theft
City	3,551.8	8.0	49.8	77.6	334.6	524.7	1,681.3	875.9
U.S.	2,290.9	5.7	38.0	66.5	264.1	250.7	1,347.2	318.7

Note: Figures are crimes per 100,000 population.
Source: FBI, Table 8, Offenses Known to Law Enforcement, by State by City, 2023

Hate Crimes

Area	Number of Quarters Reported	Number of Incidents per Bias Motivation					
		Race/Ethnicity/ Ancestry	Religion	Sexual Orientation	Disability	Gender	Gender Identity
City	4	21	14	12	2	0	2
U.S.	4	5,900	2,699	2,077	187	92	492

Source: Federal Bureau of Investigation, Hate Crime Statistics 2023

Identity Theft Consumer Reports

Area	Reports	Reports per 100,000 Population	Rank[2]
MSA[1]	13,075	570	4
U.S.	1,135,291	339	-

Note: (1) Figures cover the Las Vegas-Henderson-North Las Vegas, NV Metropolitan Statistical Area; (2) Rank ranges from 1 to 401 where 1 indicates greatest number of identity theft reports per 100,000 population
Source: Federal Trade Commission, Consumer Sentinel Network Data Book 2024

Fraud and Other Consumer Reports

Area	Reports	Reports per 100,000 Population	Rank[2]
MSA[1]	48,682	2,122	8
U.S.	5,360,641	1,601	-

Note: (1) Figures cover the Las Vegas-Henderson-North Las Vegas, NV Metropolitan Statistical Area; (2) Rank ranges from 1 to 401 where 1 indicates greatest number of fraud and other consumer reports per 100,000 population
Source: Federal Trade Commission, Consumer Sentinel Network Data Book 2024

POLITICS

2024 Presidential Election Results

Area	Trump (Rep.)	Harris (Dem.)	Stein (Green)	Kennedy (Ind.)	Oliver (Lib.)	Other
Clark County	47.8	50.4	0.0	0.0	0.4	1.4
U.S.	49.7	48.2	0.6	0.5	0.4	0.6

Note: Results are percentages and may not add to 100% due to rounding
Source: Dave Leip's Atlas of U.S. Presidential Elections

SPORTS

Professional Sports Teams

Team Name	League	Year Established
Las Vegas Raiders	National Football League (NFL)	2020
Vegas Golden Nights	National Hockey League (NHL)	2017

Note: Includes teams located in the Las Vegas-Henderson-North Las Vegas, NV Metropolitan Statistical Area.
Source: Wikipedia, Major Professional Sports Teams of the United States and Canada, May 1, 2025

CLIMATE

Average and Extreme Temperatures

Temperature	Jan	Feb	Mar	Apr	May	Jun	Jul	Aug	Sep	Oct	Nov	Dec	Yr.
Extreme High (°F)	77	87	91	99	109	115	116	116	113	103	87	77	116
Average High (°F)	56	62	69	78	88	99	104	102	94	81	66	57	80
Average Temp. (°F)	45	50	56	65	74	84	90	88	80	68	54	46	67
Average Low (°F)	33	38	43	51	60	69	76	74	66	54	41	34	53
Extreme Low (°F)	8	16	23	31	40	49	60	56	43	26	21	11	8

Note: Figures cover the years 1948-1990
Source: National Climatic Data Center, International Station Meteorological Climate Summary, 9/96

Average Precipitation/Snowfall/Humidity

Precip./Humidity	Jan	Feb	Mar	Apr	May	Jun	Jul	Aug	Sep	Oct	Nov	Dec	Yr.
Avg. Precip. (in.)	0.5	0.4	0.4	0.2	0.2	0.1	0.4	0.5	0.3	0.2	0.4	0.3	4.0
Avg. Snowfall (in.)	1	Tr	Tr	Tr	0	0	0	0	0	0	Tr	Tr	1
Avg. Rel. Hum. 7am (%)	59	52	41	31	26	20	26	31	30	36	47	56	38
Avg. Rel. Hum. 4pm (%)	32	25	20	15	13	10	14	16	16	18	26	31	20

Note: Figures cover the years 1948-1990; Tr = Trace amounts (<0.05 in. of rain; <0.5 in. of snow)
Source: National Climatic Data Center, International Station Meteorological Climate Summary, 9/96

Weather Conditions

Temperature			Daytime Sky			Precipitation		
10°F & below	32°F & below	90°F & above	Clear	Partly cloudy	Cloudy	0.01 inch or more precip.	0.1 inch or more snow/ice	Thunder-storms
< 1	37	134	185	132	48	27	2	13

Note: Figures are average number of days per year and cover the years 1948-1990
Source: National Climatic Data Center, International Station Meteorological Climate Summary, 9/96

HAZARDOUS WASTE

Superfund Sites

The Las Vegas-Henderson-North Las Vegas, NV metro area has no sites on the EPA's Superfund Final National Priorities List (NPL) or Superfund Alternative Approach (SAA) list. The Superfund alternative approach uses the same investigation and cleanup process and standards that are used for sites listed on the National Priorities List. The SAA is an alternative to listing a site on the NPL; it is not an alternative to Superfund or the Superfund process. There are a total of 1,445 Superfund sites with a status of proposed or final on both lists in the United States. *U.S. Environmental Protection Agency, National Priorities List, May 1, 2025; U.S. Environmental Protection Agency, Superfund Alternative Approach Sites, May 1, 2025*

AIR QUALITY

Air Quality Trends: Ozone

	1990	1995	2000	2005	2010	2015	2020	2021	2022	2023
MSA[1]	n/a	n/a	n/a	n/a	n/a	n/a	n/a	n/a	n/a	n/a
U.S.	0.087	0.089	0.081	0.080	0.072	0.068	0.066	0.067	0.067	0.070

Note: (1) Data covers the Las Vegas-Henderson-North Las Vegas, NV Metropolitan Statistical Area; n/a not available. The values shown are the composite ozone concentration averages among trend sites based on the highest fourth daily maximum 8-hour concentration in parts per million. These trends are based on sites having an adequate record of monitoring data during the trend period. Data from exceptional events are included.
Source: U.S. Environmental Protection Agency, Air Quality Monitoring Information, "Air Quality Trends by City, 1990-2023"

Air Quality Index

Area	Percent of Days when Air Quality was...[2]					AQI Statistics[2]	
	Good	Moderate	Unhealthy for Sensitive Groups	Unhealthy	Very Unhealthy	Maximum	Median
MSA[1]	29.0	63.8	6.8	0.3	0.0	197	61

Note: (1) Data covers the Las Vegas-Henderson-North Las Vegas, NV Metropolitan Statistical Area; (2) Based on 365 days with AQI data in 2023. Air Quality Index (AQI) is an index for reporting daily air quality. EPA calculates the AQI for five major air pollutants regulated by the Clean Air Act: ground-level ozone, particle pollution (aka particulate matter), carbon monoxide, sulfur dioxide, and nitrogen dioxide. The AQI runs from 0 to 500. The higher the AQI value, the greater the level of air pollution and the greater the health concern. There are six AQI categories: "Good" AQI is between 0 and 50. Air quality is considered satisfactory; "Moderate" AQI is between 51 and 100. Air quality is acceptable; "Unhealthy for Sensitive Groups" When AQI values are between 101 and 150, members of sensitive groups may experience health effects; "Unhealthy" When AQI values are between 151 and 200 everyone may begin to experience health effects; "Very Unhealthy" AQI values between 201 and 300 trigger a health alert; "Hazardous" AQI values over 300 trigger warnings of emergency conditions (not shown).
Source: U.S. Environmental Protection Agency, Air Quality Index Report, 2023

Air Quality Index Pollutants

Area	Percent of Days when AQI Pollutant was...[2]					
	Carbon Monoxide	Nitrogen Dioxide	Ozone	Sulfur Dioxide	Particulate Matter 2.5	Particulate Matter 10
MSA[1]	0.0	0.3	67.7	(3)	27.7	4.4

Note: (1) Data covers the Las Vegas-Henderson-North Las Vegas, NV Metropolitan Statistical Area; (2) Based on 365 days with AQI data in 2023. The Air Quality Index (AQI) is an index for reporting daily air quality. EPA calculates the AQI for five major air pollutants regulated by the Clean Air Act: ground-level ozone, particle pollution (also known as particulate matter), carbon monoxide, sulfur dioxide, and nitrogen dioxide. The AQI runs from 0 to 500. The higher the AQI value, the greater the level of air pollution and the greater the health concern; (3) Sulfur dioxide is no longer included in this table because SO_2 concentrations tend to be very localized and not necessarily representative of broad geographical areas like counties and CBSAs.
Source: U.S. Environmental Protection Agency, Air Quality Index Report, 2023

Maximum Air Pollutant Concentrations: Particulate Matter, Ozone, CO and Lead

	Particulate Matter 10 (ug/m^3)	Particulate Matter 2.5 Wtd AM (ug/m^3)	Particulate Matter 2.5 24-Hr (ug/m^3)	Ozone (ppm)	Carbon Monoxide (ppm)	Lead (ug/m^3)
MSA[1] Level	209	8.2	27	0.074	2	n/a
NAAQS[2]	150	15	35	0.075	9	0.15
Met NAAQS[2]	No	Yes	Yes	Yes	Yes	n/a

Note: (1) Data covers the Las Vegas-Henderson-North Las Vegas, NV Metropolitan Statistical Area; Data from exceptional events are included; (2) National Ambient Air Quality Standards; ppm = parts per million; ug/m^3 = micrograms per cubic meter; n/a not available.
Concentrations: Particulate Matter 10 (coarse particulate)—highest second maximum 24-hour concentration; Particulate Matter 2.5 Wtd AM (fine particulate)—highest weighted annual mean concentration; Particulate Matter 2.5 24-Hour (fine particulate)—highest 98th percentile 24-hour concentration; Ozone—highest fourth daily maximum 8-hour concentration; Carbon Monoxide—highest second maximum non-overlapping 8-hour concentration; Lead—maximum running 3-month average
Source: U.S. Environmental Protection Agency, Air Quality Monitoring Information, "Air Quality Statistics by City, 2023"

Maximum Air Pollutant Concentrations: Nitrogen Dioxide and Sulfur Dioxide

	Nitrogen Dioxide AM (ppb)	Nitrogen Dioxide 1-Hr (ppb)	Sulfur Dioxide AM (ppb)	Sulfur Dioxide 1-Hr (ppb)	Sulfur Dioxide 24-Hr (ppb)
MSA[1] Level	20	52	n/a	5	n/a
NAAQS[2]	53	100	30	75	140
Met NAAQS[2]	Yes	Yes	n/a	Yes	n/a

Note: (1) Data covers the Las Vegas-Henderson-North Las Vegas, NV Metropolitan Statistical Area; Data from exceptional events are included; (2) National Ambient Air Quality Standards; ppm = parts per million; ug/m^3 = micrograms per cubic meter; n/a not available.
Concentrations: Nitrogen Dioxide AM—highest arithmetic mean concentration; Nitrogen Dioxide 1-Hr—highest 98th percentile 1-hour daily maximum concentration; Sulfur Dioxide AM—highest annual mean concentration; Sulfur Dioxide 1-Hr—highest 99th percentile 1-hour daily maximum concentration; Sulfur Dioxide 24-Hr—highest second maximum 24-hour concentration
Source: U.S. Environmental Protection Agency, Air Quality Monitoring Information, "Air Quality Statistics by City, 2023"

Los Angeles, California

Background

Los Angeles is immense, lying in a basin in Southern California adjacent to the Pacific Ocean. The city acquired its many communities such as Hollywood, Glendale, Burbank, and Alhambra when those cities wanted to share in the water piped into Los Angeles from the Owens River and had to join the Los Angeles municipal system to do so. Los Angeles is now one of the largest U.S. cities in both acreage and population, and one of the most racially diverse.

The city's communities are connected through a complex system of freeways which gives Los Angeles its reputation as a congested, car-oriented culture. What was founded in 1781 as a sleepy pueblo of 44 people is now a city leading the nation in commerce, transportation, finance, and, especially, entertainment—with most of all motion pictures made in the United States still produced in the Los Angeles area. Its top non-government employers are Kaiser Permanente, University of California, Northrop Grumman Corp., Cedars-Sinai Medical Centers, and Allied Universal.

There are 841 museums and art galleries in Los Angeles. The Getty Center and Museum, an architectural masterpiece designed by Richard Meier built on a commanding hill, is a dramatic venue for visual arts and other events. The Los Angeles Opera, under the direction of Placido Domingo, offers a lively season of operas as well as recitals by such luminaries as Cecilia Bartoli and Renee Fleming. The Los Angeles Philharmonic performs in the Walt Disney Concert Hall, designed by Frank Gehry, famed architect of the Guggenheim Museum at Bilbao. The city's iconic music venue, The Hollywood Bowl, celebrated its 103rd anniversary in 2025.

In 2022, Karen Bass became the city's first female mayor, making Los Angeles the largest U.S. city to be led by a woman.

Los Angeles has hosted the Olympic and Paralympic Games twice and will again in 2028, making it the third city after London and Paris to host the Olympic Games three times. Major league baseball's Los Angeles Dodgers won the World Series in 2020, ending a 32-year drought, and again in 2024. In 2022, the Los Angeles Rams won Super Bowl LVI at their new SoFi Stadium in neighboring Inglewood and it is one of 11 U.S. cities to host the 2026 FIFA World Cup.

The climate of Los Angeles is normally pleasant and mild throughout the year, with unusual differences in temperature, humidity, cloudiness, fog, rain, and sunshine over short distances in the metro area. Low clouds are common at night and in the morning along the coast during spring and summer. Near the foothills, clouds form later in the day and clear a short time later. Annual percentages of fog and cloudiness are greatest near the ocean. Sunshine totals are highest on the inland side of the city. Inland and up foothill slopes, both high and low temperatures become more extreme and the relative humidity, which is frequently high near the coast, drops. Most rain falls November through March, while the summers are very dry. Destructive flash floods occasionally develop in and below some mountain canyons. Snow is often visible on the nearby mountains in the winter but is extremely rare in the coastal basin. Thunderstorms are infrequent.

High concentrations of air pollution affect the Los Angeles coastal basin and adjacent areas. In fall and winter, the Santa Ana winds pick up considerable amounts of dust and can blow strongly in the northern and eastern sections of the city and in outlying areas in the north and east, increasing the threat of wildfires in the region. In January 2025, the most devastating fires recorded in the city destroyed entire neighborhoods, including Pacific Palisades.

Rankings

General Rankings

- To help military veterans find the best places in which to settle down, *WalletHub* compared the 100 largest U.S. cities across 19 key indicators of livability, affordability and veteran-friendliness. They range from the share of military skill-related jobs to veteran income growth to the availability of VA health facilities. Los Angeles ranked #79. *Wallethub.com, "Best & Worst Places for Veterans to Live (2025)," November 7, 2024*

- *Insider* listed 23 places in the U.S. that travel industry trends reveal would be popular destinations in 2023. This year the list trends towards cultural and historical happenings, sports events, wellness experiences and invigorating outdoor escapes. According to the website insider.com Los Angeles is a place to visit in 2023. *Insider, "23 of the Best Places You Should Travel to in the U.S. in 2023," December 17, 2022*

- Los Angeles was selected as one of the best places in the world that are a "celebration of travel's power to transform us and our connections with one another" by *National Geographic Travel* editors. These cultural-rich spots are steeped in tradition, community, and history as reported on by its global community of experts. The list reflects 25 of the most extraordinary travel adventures for 2025. *NationalGeographic.com, "Best of the World, The 25 Best Places in the World to Travel to in 2025," October 22, 2024*

- The human resources consulting firm Mercer ranked 241 major cities worldwide in terms of overall quality of life. Los Angeles ranked #44. Criteria: political and personal safety, social, and economic factors; medical and health considerations; schools and education; public services and transportation; recreation; connectivity; housing and infrastructure; and climate. *Mercer, "Mercer 2024 Quality of Living Survey," December 2024*

Business/Finance Rankings

- According to *Business Insider*, the Los Angeles metro area is a prime place to run a startup or move an existing business to. The area ranked #9. More than 300 metro areas were analyzed for factors that were of top concern to new business owners. Data was based on the 2019 U.S. Census Bureau American Community Survey, statistics from the CDC, and University of Chicago analysis. Criteria: business formations; percentage of vaccinated population; percentage of households with internet subscriptions; median household income; and share of work that can be done from home. *BusinessInsider.com, "The 20 Best Cities for Starting a Business in 2022 Include Denver, Raleigh, and Olympia," June 7, 2022*

- Payscale.com ranked the 32 largest metro areas in terms of wage growth. The Los Angeles metro area ranked #3. Criteria: quarterly changes in private industry employee and education professional wage growth from the previous year. *PayScale, "Wage Trends by Metro Area-4th Quarter," February 4, 2025*

- For its annual survey of the "Most Expensive U.S. Cities to Live In," Kiplinger applied Cost of Living Index statistics developed by the Council for Community and Economic Research to U.S. Census Bureau population and median household income data for 265 urban areas. Los Angeles ranked #8 among the most expensive in the country. *Kiplinger.com, "The 10 Most Expensive Cities to Live in the U.S.," February 3, 2025*

- The Los Angeles metro area appeared on the Milken Institute "2025 Best Performing Cities" list. Rank: #151 out of 200 large metro areas (based on performance category). Criteria: job growth; wage growth; high-tech growth and impact; community resilience; housing affordability; household broadband access. *Milken Institute, "Best-Performing Cities 2025," January 14, 2025*

- Mercer Human Resources Consulting ranked 226 cities worldwide in terms of cost-of-living. Los Angeles ranked #10 (the lower the ranking, the higher the cost-of-living). The survey measured the comparative cost of over 200 items (such as housing, food, clothing, domestic supplies, transportation, and recreation/entertainment) in each location. *Mercer, "2024 Cost of Living City Ranking," June 17, 2024*

Education Rankings

- Personal finance website *WalletHub* analyzed the 150 largest U.S. metropolitan statistical areas to determine where the most educated Americans are putting their degrees to work. Criteria: education levels; percentage of workers with degrees; education quality and attainment gap; public school quality rankings; quality and enrollment of each metro area's universities. Los Angeles was ranked #87 (#1 = most educated city). *WalletHub.com, "Most & Least Educated Cities in America, 2025" July 2, 2024*

Environmental Rankings

- The U.S. Environmental Protection Agency (EPA) released its list of U.S. metropolitan areas with the most ENERGY STAR certified buildings in 2023. The Los Angeles metro area was ranked #1 out of 25. *U.S. Environmental Protection Agency, "2024 Energy Star Top Cities," May 22, 2024*

- Los Angeles was highlighted as one of the 25 most ozone-polluted metro areas in the U.S. during 2021 through 2023. The area ranked #1. *American Lung Association, "State of the Air 2025," April 23, 2025*

- Los Angeles was highlighted as one of the 25 metro areas most polluted by year-round particle pollution (Annual PM 2.5) in the U.S. during 2021 through 2023. The area ranked #5. *American Lung Association, "State of the Air 2025," April 23, 2025*

- Los Angeles was highlighted as one of the 25 metro areas most polluted by short-term particle pollution (24-hour PM 2.5) in the U.S. during 2021 through 2023. The area ranked #7. *American Lung Association, "State of the Air 2025," April 23, 2025*

Food/Drink Rankings

- Los Angeles was identified as one of the cities in America ordering the most vegan food options by GrubHub.com. The city ranked #1 out of 5. Criteria: percentage of vegan, vegetarian and plant-based food orders compared to the overall number of orders. *GrubHub.com, "State of the Plate Report 2021: Top Cities for Vegans," June 20, 2021*

- WalletHub compared the 100 largest U.S. cities across 17 key indicators of vegan- and vegetarian-friendliness. Los Angeles was ranked #1. Cities were selected based on metrics such as the cost of groceries for vegetarians, the share of restaurants serving meatless options and the number of salad shops per capita. *WalletHub.com, "Best Cities for Vegans & Vegetarians (2025)," September 24, 2024*

Health/Fitness Rankings

- For each of the 100 largest cities in the United States, the American Fitness Index®, compiled in partnership between the American College of Sports Medicine and the Elevance Health Foundation, evaluated community infrastructure and more than 30 health behaviors including preventive health, levels of chronic disease conditions, food insecurity, pedestrian safety, air quality, and community/environment resources that support physical activity. Los Angeles ranked #54 for "community fitness." *americanfitnessindex.org, "2024 ACSM American Fitness Index Summary Report," July 23, 2024*

- The Los Angeles metro area was identified as one of the worst cities for bed bugs in America by pest control company Orkin. The area ranked #5 out of 50 based on the number of bed bug treatments Orkin performed from December 2022 to November 2023. *Orkin, "Chicago Joins Paris In Global Bed Bug Spotlight Ranking As The Worst City On Orkin's U.S. Bed Bug Cities List," January 22, 2024*

- Los Angeles was identified as a "2025 Allergy Capital." The area ranked #51 out of the nation's 100 largest metropolitan areas. Three groups of factors were used to identify the most challenging cities for people with allergies: annual tree, grass, and weed pollen scores; over the counter allergy medicine use; number of board-certified allergy specialists. *Asthma and Allergy Foundation of America, "2025 Allergy Capitals: The Most Challenging Places to Live with Allergies," March 18, 2025*

- Los Angeles was identified as a "2024 Asthma Capital." The area ranked #49 out of the nation's 100 largest metropolitan areas. Criteria: estimated asthma prevalence; asthma-related mortality; and ER visits due to asthma. Risk factors analyzed but not factored in the rankings: annual air quality including pollution and ozone levels; public smoking laws; indoor air quality; access to asthma specialists; rescue and controller medication use; uninsured rate; pollen allergy; poverty rate. *Asthma and Allergy Foundation of America, "Asthma Capitals 2024: The Most Challenging Places to Live With Asthma," September 10, 2024*

Pet Rankings

- Los Angeles was selected by *Sniffspot.com* as one of the most dog-friendly cities in the U.S., ranking #39 out of 50. Criteria: dog parks; hiking; sniffspots; public parks; dog-friendly businesses; housing; dog waste cleanliness; leash laws; dog services; and overall cost. *Sniffspot.com, "The Top 50 Most Dog-Friendly Cities in the U.S.," September 30, 2024*

Real Estate Rankings

- *WalletHub* compared the most populated U.S. cities to determine which had the best markets for real estate agents. Los Angeles ranked #40 where demand was high and pay was the best. Criteria: sales per agent; annual median wage for real-estate agents; monthly average starting salary for real estate agents; real estate job density and competition; unemployment rate; home turnover rate; housing-market health index; and other relevant metrics. *WalletHub.com, "2021 Best Places to Be a Real Estate Agent," May 12, 2021*

- The Los Angeles metro area was identified as one of the 20 least affordable housing markets in the U.S. in 2024. The area ranked #220 out of 226 markets. Criteria: qualification for a mortgage loan with a 10 percent down payment on a typical home. *National Association of Realtors®, Qualifying Income Based on Sales Price of Existing Single-Family Homes for Metropolitan Areas, February 6, 2025*

- The nation's largest metro areas were analyzed in terms of the percentage of households entering some stage of foreclosure in 2024. The Los Angeles metro area ranked #4 out of 5 (#1 = highest foreclosure rate). *ATTOM Data Solutions, "2024 Year-End U.S. Foreclosure Market Report™," January 15, 2025*

Safety Rankings

- Allstate ranked the 100 most populous cities in America in terms of driver safety. Los Angeles ranked #74. Criteria based on anonymized driving behavior data from Allstate's mobile app powered by Arity: high speed driving (over 80 mph), phone handling, and hard braking. The report helps increase the importance of safety and awareness behind the wheel. *Allstate, "16th Allstate America's Best Drivers Report®" July 11, 2024*

- The National Insurance Crime Bureau ranked the largest metro areas in the U.S. in terms of per capita rates of vehicle theft. The Los Angeles metro area ranked #1 out of the top 10 (#1 = highest rate). Criteria: number of vehicle theft offenses per 100,000 inhabitants in 2023. *National Insurance Crime Bureau, "Vehicle Thefts Surge Nationwide in 2023," April 9, 2024*

Transportation Rankings

- Los Angeles was identified as one of the most congested metro areas in the U.S. The area ranked #1 out of 10. Criteria: yearly delay per auto commuter in hours. *Texas A&M Transportation Institute, "2023 Urban Mobility Report," June 2024*

- According to the INRIX "2024 Global Traffic Scorecard," Los Angeles was identified as one of the most congested metro areas in the U.S. The area ranked #3 out of 10 in the country and among the top 25 most congested in the world. Criteria: average annual time spent in traffic and average cost of congestion per motorist. *Inrix.com, "Employees & Consumers Returned to Downtowns, Traffic Delays & Costs Grew," January 6, 2025*

Women/Minorities Rankings

- Los Angeles was listed as one of the most LGBTQ-friendly cities in America by *The Advocate*, as compiled by the real estate data site *Clever*. The city ranked #6 out of 15. Criteria, among many: Pride events; gay bars; LGBTQ-affirming healthcare options; state and local laws; number of PFLAG chapters; LGBTQ+ population. *The Advocate, "These Are the 15 Most LGBTQ-Friendly Cities in the U.S." November 1, 2023*

- Personal finance website *WalletHub* compared more than 180 U.S. cities across two key dimensions, "Hispanic Business-Friendliness" and "Hispanic Purchasing Power," to arrive at the most favorable conditions for Hispanic entrepreneurs. Los Angeles was ranked #131 out of 182. Criteria includes: share of Hispanic-Owned Businesses; average growth of Hispanic Business revenues; Small Business-Friendliness score; affordability; and number of Hispanics with at least a bachelor's degree. *WalletHub.com, "Best Cities for Hispanic Entrepreneurs," September 4, 2024*

Miscellaneous Rankings

- Los Angeles was selected as a 2024 Digital Cities Survey winner. The city ranked #2 in the large city (500,000 or more population) category. The survey examined and assessed how city governments are utilizing new technology and modernized applications to provide residents an array of contactless services and conveniences. Survey questions focused on ten initiatives: cybersecurity; citizen experience; disaster recovery; business intelligence; IT personnel retention; data governance; business automation; AI/machine learning; application modernization; and IT collaboration. *Center for Digital Government, "2024 Digital Cities Survey," November 5, 2024*

- *WalletHub* compared 148 of the most populated U.S. cities to determine their operating efficiency. A "Quality of Services" score was constructed for each city and then measured against the total budget per capita to reveal which were managed the best. Los Angeles ranked #139. Criteria: financial stability; economy; education; safety; health; infrastructure and pollution. *WalletHub.com, "2025's Best- & Worst-Run Cities in America," June 18, 2024*

Business Environment

DEMOGRAPHICS

Population Growth

Area	1990 Census	2000 Census	2010 Census	2020 Census	2023 Estimate[2]	Population Growth 1990-2023 (%)
City	3,487,671	3,694,820	3,792,621	3,898,747	3,857,897	10.6
MSA[1]	11,273,720	12,365,627	12,828,837	13,200,998	13,012,469	15.4
U.S.	248,709,873	281,421,906	308,745,538	331,449,281	332,387,540	33.6

Note: (1) Figures cover the Los Angeles-Long Beach-Anaheim, CA Metropolitan Statistical Area; (2) 2019-2023 5-year ACS population estimate
Source: U.S. Census Bureau, 1990 Census, 2000 Census, 2010 Census, 2020 Census, 2019-2023 American Community Survey 5-Year Estimates

Race

Area	White Alone[2] (%)	Black Alone[2] (%)	Asian Alone[2] (%)	AIAN[3] Alone[2] (%)	NHOPI[4] Alone[2] (%)	Other Race Alone[2] (%)	Two or More Races (%)
City	37.3	8.5	12.0	1.2	0.1	25.1	15.7
MSA[1]	38.1	6.3	16.7	1.1	0.2	21.2	16.2
U.S.	63.4	12.4	5.8	0.9	0.2	6.6	10.7

Note: (1) Figures cover the Los Angeles-Long Beach-Anaheim, CA Metropolitan Statistical Area; (2) Alone is defined as not being in combination with one or more other races; (3) American Indian and Alaska Native; (4) Native Hawaiian and Other Pacific Islander
Source: U.S. Census Bureau, 2019-2023 American Community Survey 5-Year Estimates

Hispanic or Latino Origin

Area	Total (%)	Mexican (%)	Puerto Rican (%)	Cuban (%)	Other (%)
City	47.2	30.0	0.5	0.4	16.3
MSA[1]	44.8	33.8	0.5	0.4	10.2
U.S.	19.0	11.3	1.8	0.7	5.2

Note: Persons of Hispanic or Latino origin can be of any race; (1) Figures cover the Los Angeles-Long Beach-Anaheim, CA Metropolitan Statistical Area
Source: U.S. Census Bureau, 2019-2023 American Community Survey 5-Year Estimates

Age

Area	Under Age 5	Age 5–19	Age 20–34	Age 35–44	Age 45–54	Age 55–64	Age 65–74	Age 75–84	Age 85+	Median Age
City	5.2	16.8	24.8	14.8	13.0	11.6	8.1	3.8	1.9	36.9
MSA[1]	5.3	18.2	21.9	13.8	13.3	12.6	8.7	4.3	2.0	38.2
U.S.	5.7	19.1	20.2	13.1	12.3	12.8	10.0	4.9	1.9	38.7

Note: (1) Figures cover the Los Angeles-Long Beach-Anaheim, CA Metropolitan Statistical Area
Source: U.S. Census Bureau, 2019-2023 American Community Survey 5-Year Estimates

Disability by Age

Area	All Ages	Under 18 Years Old	18 to 64 Years Old	65 Years and Over
City	11.1	3.5	8.3	36.3
MSA[1]	10.5	3.5	7.7	32.8
U.S.	13.0	4.7	10.7	32.9

Note: Figures show percent of the civilian noninstitutionalized population that reported having a disability. Disability status is determined from six types of difficulty: vision, hearing, cognitive, ambulatory, self-care, and independent living. For children under 5 years old, hearing and vision difficulty are used to determine disability status. For children between the ages of 5 and 14, disability status is determined from hearing, vision, cognitive, ambulatory, and self-care difficulties. For people aged 15 years and older, they are considered to have a disability if they have difficulty with any one of the six difficulty types; Note: (1) Figures cover the Los Angeles-Long Beach-Anaheim, CA Metropolitan Statistical Area
Source: U.S. Census Bureau, 2019-2023 American Community Survey 5-Year Estimates

Ancestry

Area	German	Irish	English	American	Italian	Polish	French[2]	European	Scottish
City	3.9	3.7	3.5	3.8	2.7	1.3	1.1	1.3	0.7
MSA[1]	5.1	4.3	4.5	3.5	2.8	1.1	1.1	1.2	0.8
U.S.	12.6	9.4	9.1	5.5	4.9	2.6	2.0	1.6	1.6

Note: Figures are the percentage of the total population reporting a particular ancestry. The nine most commonly reported ancestries in the U.S. are shown. Figures include multiple ancestries (e.g. if a person reported being Irish and Italian, they were included in both columns); (1) Figures cover the Los Angeles-Long Beach-Anaheim, CA Metropolitan Statistical Area; (2) Excludes Basque
Source: U.S. Census Bureau, 2019-2023 American Community Survey 5-Year Estimates

Foreign-born Population

Area	Percent of Population Born in								
	Any Foreign Country	Asia	Mexico	Europe	Caribbean	Central America[2]	South America	Africa	Canada
City	35.8	11.2	11.2	2.4	0.3	8.3	1.2	0.7	0.4
MSA[1]	32.5	13.0	11.1	1.7	0.3	4.3	1.0	0.6	0.3
U.S.	13.9	4.3	3.3	1.4	1.4	1.2	1.2	0.8	0.2

Note: (1) Figures cover the Los Angeles-Long Beach-Anaheim, CA Metropolitan Statistical Area; (2) Excludes Mexico.
Source: U.S. Census Bureau, 2019-2023 American Community Survey 5-Year Estimates

Household Size

Area	Persons in Household (%)							Average Household Size
	One	Two	Three	Four	Five	Six	Seven or More	
City	31.5	28.9	15.5	12.5	6.4	2.6	2.5	2.64
MSA[1]	25.1	29.0	17.0	15.1	7.7	3.2	2.8	2.86
U.S.	28.5	33.8	15.4	12.7	5.9	2.3	1.4	2.54

Note: (1) Figures cover the Los Angeles-Long Beach-Anaheim, CA Metropolitan Statistical Area
Source: U.S. Census Bureau, 2019-2023 American Community Survey 5-Year Estimates

Household Relationships

Area	House-holder	Opposite-sex Spouse	Same-sex Spouse	Opposite-sex Unmarried Partner	Same-sex Unmarried Partner	Child[2]	Grand-child	Other Relatives	Non-relatives
City	36.2	13.1	0.3	2.8	0.3	26.5	2.8	9.0	6.3
MSA[1]	34.0	15.2	0.2	2.3	0.2	29.0	3.0	9.1	5.1
U.S.	38.3	17.5	0.2	2.5	0.2	28.3	2.4	4.8	3.4

Note: Figures are percent of the total population; (1) Figures cover the Los Angeles-Long Beach-Anaheim, CA Metropolitan Statistical Area; (2) Includes biological, adopted, and stepchildren of the householder
Source: U.S. Census Bureau, 2020 Census

Gender

Area	Males	Females	Males per 100 Females
City	1,921,735	1,936,162	99.3
MSA[1]	6,447,486	6,564,983	98.2
U.S.	164,545,087	167,842,453	98.0

Note: (1) Figures cover the Los Angeles-Long Beach-Anaheim, CA Metropolitan Statistical Area
Source: U.S. Census Bureau, 2019-2023 American Community Survey 5-Year Estimates

Marital Status

Area	Never Married	Now Married[2]	Separated	Widowed	Divorced
City	46.5	38.6	2.3	4.5	8.0
MSA[1]	40.7	44.3	2.0	4.7	8.3
U.S.	34.1	47.9	1.7	5.6	10.7

Note: Figures are percentages and cover the population 15 years of age and older; (1) Figures cover the Los Angeles-Long Beach-Anaheim, CA Metropolitan Statistical Area; (2) Excludes separated
Source: U.S. Census Bureau, 2019-2023 American Community Survey 5-Year Estimates

Religious Groups by Family

Area	Catholic	Baptist	Methodist	LDS[2]	Pentecostal	Lutheran	Islam	Adventist	Other
MSA[1]	31.1	2.6	0.8	1.5	2.4	0.4	1.4	1.5	9.1
U.S.	18.7	7.3	3.0	2.0	1.8	1.7	1.3	1.3	11.6

Note: Figures are the number of adherents as a percentage of the total population and cover the eight largest religious groups in the U.S; (1) Figures cover the Los Angeles-Long Beach-Anaheim, CA Metropolitan Statistical Area; (2) Church of Jesus Christ of Latter-day Saints
Sources: 2020 U.S. Religion Census, Association of Statisticians of American Religious Bodies; The Association of Religion Data Archives (ARDA)

Religious Groups by Tradition

Area	Catholic	Evangelical Protestant	Mainline Protestant	Black Protestant	Islam	Judaism	Hinduism	Orthodox	Buddhism
MSA[1]	31.1	9.3	1.5	1.7	1.4	0.8	0.4	0.9	0.9
U.S.	18.7	16.5	5.2	2.3	1.3	0.6	0.4	0.4	0.3

Note: Figures are the number of adherents as a percentage of the total population; (1) Figures cover the Los Angeles-Long Beach-Anaheim, CA Metropolitan Statistical Area
Sources: 2020 U.S. Religion Census, Association of Statisticians of American Religious Bodies; The Association of Religion Data Archives (ARDA)

ECONOMY

Real Gross Domestic Product (GDP)

Area[1]	2017	2018	2019	2020	2021	2022	2023	Rank[3]
MSA[1]	965.3	991.3	1,026.5	982.0	1,041.7	1,065.3	1,075.1	2
U.S.[2]	17,619.1	18,160.7	18,642.5	18,238.9	19,387.6	19,896.6	20,436.3	–

Note: Figures are in billions of chained 2017 dollars; (1) Figures cover the Los Angeles-Long Beach-Anaheim, CA Metropolitan Statistical Area; (2) Figures cover real GDP within metropolitan areas; (3) Rank is based on 2023 data and ranges from 1 to 384
Source: U.S. Bureau of Economic Analysis

Economic Growth

Area	2014	2015	2016	2017	2018	2019	2020	2021	2022	2023
MSA[1]	2.7	4.3	1.8	3.7	2.7	3.6	-4.3	6.1	2.3	0.9
U.S.[2]	2.6	3.2	2.0	2.7	3.1	2.7	-2.2	6.3	2.6	2.7

Note: Figures are real gross domestic product growth rates and represent percent change from preceding period; (1) Figures cover the Los Angeles-Long Beach-Anaheim, CA Metropolitan Statistical Area; (2) Figures are the average growth rates within metropolitan areas
Source: U.S. Bureau of Economic Analysis

Metropolitan Area Exports

Area	2018	2019	2020	2021	2022	2023	Rank[2]
MSA[1]	64,814.6	61,041.1	50,185.4	58,588.4	60,979.7	59,561.6	4
U.S.	1,664,056.1	1,645,173.7	1,431,406.6	1,753,941.4	2,062,937.4	2,019,160.5	–

Note: Figures are in millions of dollars; (1) Figures cover the Los Angeles-Long Beach-Anaheim, CA Metropolitan Statistical Area; (2) Rank is based on 2023 data and ranges from 1 to 386
Source: U.S. Department of Commerce, International Trade Administration, Office of Trade and Economic Analysis, Industry and Analysis, Exports by Metropolitan Area, data extracted April 2, 2025

Building Permits

Area	Single-Family			Multi-Family			Total		
	2023	2024	Pct. Chg.	2023	2024	Pct. Chg.	2023	2024	Pct. Chg.
City	2,918	3,041	4.2	10,236	7,447	-27.2	13,154	10,488	-20.3
MSA[1]	12,035	11,777	-2.1	18,732	15,004	-19.9	30,767	26,781	-13.0
U.S.	920,000	981,900	6.7	591,100	496,100	-16.1	1,511,100	1,478,000	-2.2

Note: (1) Figures cover the Los Angeles-Long Beach-Anaheim, CA Metropolitan Statistical Area; Figures represent new, privately-owned housing units authorized (unadjusted data)
Source: U.S. Census Bureau, Building Permits Survey (BPS), 2023, 2024

Bankruptcy Filings

Area	Business Filings			Nonbusiness Filings		
	2023	2024	% Chg.	2023	2024	% Chg.
Los Angeles County	815	977	19.9	10,059	12,169	21.0
U.S.	18,926	23,107	22.1	434,064	494,201	13.9

Note: Business filings include Chapter 7, Chapter 9, Chapter 11, Chapter 12, Chapter 13, Chapter 15, and Section 304; Nonbusiness filings include Chapter 7, Chapter 11, and Chapter 13
Source: Administrative Office of the U.S. Courts, Business and Nonbusiness Bankruptcy, County Cases Commenced by Chapter of the Bankruptcy Code, During the 12-Month Period Ending December 31, 2023 and Business and Nonbusiness Bankruptcy, County Cases Commenced by Chapter of the Bankruptcy Code, During the 12-Month Period Ending December 31, 2024

Housing Vacancy Rates

Area	Gross Vacancy Rate[3] (%)			Year-Round Vacancy Rate[4] (%)			Rental Vacancy Rate[5] (%)			Homeowner Vacancy Rate[6] (%)		
	2022	2023	2024	2022	2023	2024	2022	2023	2024	2022	2023	2024
MSA[1]	5.9	5.8	6.2	5.5	5.7	6.1	4.1	4.0	4.8	0.5	0.6	0.7
U.S.[2]	9.1	9.0	9.1	7.5	7.5	7.6	5.7	6.5	6.8	0.8	0.8	1.0

Note: (1) Figures cover the Los Angeles-Long Beach-Anaheim, CA Metropolitan Statistical Area; (2) Figures cover the 75 largest Metropolitan Statistical Areas; (3) The percentage of the total housing inventory that is vacant; (4) The percentage of the housing inventory (excluding seasonal units) that is year-round vacant; (5) The percentage of rental inventory that is vacant for rent; (6) The percentage of homeowner inventory that is vacant for sale
Source: U.S. Census Bureau, Housing Vacancies and Homeownership Annual Statistics: 2022, 2023, 2024

INCOME

Income

Area	Per Capita ($)	Median Household ($)	Average Household ($)
City	46,270	80,366	122,610
MSA[1]	46,385	93,525	132,022
U.S.	43,289	78,538	110,491

Note: (1) Figures cover the Los Angeles-Long Beach-Anaheim, CA Metropolitan Statistical Area
Source: U.S. Census Bureau, 2019-2023 American Community Survey 5-Year Estimates

Household Income Distribution

Area	Percent of Households Earning							
	Under $15,000	$15,000 -$24,999	$25,000 -$34,999	$35,000 -$49,999	$50,000 -$74,999	$75,000 -$99,999	$100,000 -$149,999	$150,000 and up
City	10.8	6.7	6.5	9.4	14.0	11.5	16.0	25.1
MSA[1]	8.3	5.4	5.6	8.5	13.4	11.7	17.9	29.3
U.S.	8.5	6.6	6.8	10.4	15.7	12.7	17.4	21.9

Note: (1) Figures cover the Los Angeles-Long Beach-Anaheim, CA Metropolitan Statistical Area
Source: U.S. Census Bureau, 2019-2023 American Community Survey 5-Year Estimates

Poverty Rate

Area	All Ages	Under 18 Years Old	18 to 64 Years Old	65 Years and Over
City	16.5	22.1	14.8	16.9
MSA[1]	12.6	16.0	11.4	13.1
U.S.	12.4	16.3	11.6	10.4

Note: Figures are percentage of people whose income during the past 12 months was below the poverty level;
(1) Figures cover the Los Angeles-Long Beach-Anaheim, CA Metropolitan Statistical Area
Source: U.S. Census Bureau, 2019-2023 American Community Survey 5-Year Estimates

EMPLOYMENT

Labor Force and Employment

Area	Civilian Labor Force			Workers Employed		
	Dec. 2023	Dec. 2024	% Chg.	Dec. 2023	Dec. 2024	% Chg.
City	2,074,549	2,094,633	1.0	1,964,638	1,972,226	0.4
MD[1]	5,037,643	5,091,130	1.1	4,782,176	4,800,645	0.4
U.S.	166,661,000	167,746,000	0.7	160,754,000	161,294,000	0.3

Note: Data is not seasonally adjusted and covers workers 16 years of age and older; (1) Figures cover the Los Angeles-Long Beach-Glendale, CA Metropolitan Division
Source: Bureau of Labor Statistics, Local Area Unemployment Statistics

Unemployment Rate

Area	2024											
	Jan.	Feb.	Mar.	Apr.	May	Jun.	Jul.	Aug.	Sep.	Oct.	Nov.	Dec.
City	5.8	5.5	5.4	5.1	5.5	6.2	6.8	6.8	6.1	6.1	6.1	5.8
MD[1]	5.6	5.3	5.3	5.0	5.4	6.1	6.7	6.7	6.0	6.0	6.0	5.7
U.S.	4.1	4.2	3.9	3.5	3.7	4.3	4.5	4.4	3.9	3.9	4.0	3.8

Note: Data is not seasonally adjusted and covers workers 16 years of age and older; (1) Figures cover the Los Angeles-Long Beach-Glendale, CA Metropolitan Division
Source: Bureau of Labor Statistics, Local Area Unemployment Statistics

Average Wages

Occupation	$/Hr.	Occupation	$/Hr.
Accountants and Auditors	48.45	Maintenance and Repair Workers	27.74
Automotive Mechanics	30.20	Marketing Managers	87.09
Bookkeepers	28.58	Network and Computer Systems Admin.	53.71
Carpenters	36.97	Nurses, Licensed Practical	37.14
Cashiers	18.47	Nurses, Registered	66.35
Computer Programmers	50.36	Nursing Assistants	23.03
Computer Systems Analysts	59.72	Office Clerks, General	23.99
Computer User Support Specialists	35.73	Physical Therapists	56.57
Construction Laborers	31.23	Physicians	82.19
Cooks, Restaurant	21.28	Plumbers, Pipefitters and Steamfitters	37.49
Customer Service Representatives	25.04	Police and Sheriff's Patrol Officers	52.17
Dentists	83.74	Postal Service Mail Carriers	29.11
Electricians	39.39	Real Estate Sales Agents	36.15
Engineers, Electrical	65.77	Retail Salespersons	20.52
Fast Food and Counter Workers	18.75	Sales Representatives, Technical/Scientific	56.19
Financial Managers	96.29	Secretaries, Exc. Legal/Medical/Executive	26.51
First-Line Supervisors of Office Workers	37.23	Security Guards	21.76
General and Operations Managers	81.25	Surgeons	181.61
Hairdressers/Cosmetologists	27.74	Teacher Assistants, Exc. Postsecondary[1]	21.70
Home Health and Personal Care Aides	17.43	Teachers, Secondary School, Exc. Sp. Ed.[1]	49.74
Janitors and Cleaners	19.78	Telemarketers	19.37
Landscaping/Groundskeeping Workers	21.42	Truck Drivers, Heavy/Tractor-Trailer	28.59
Lawyers	130.10	Truck Drivers, Light/Delivery Services	24.21
Maids and Housekeeping Cleaners	21.39	Waiters and Waitresses	20.65

Note: Wage data covers the Los Angeles-Long Beach-Anaheim, CA Metropolitan Statistical Area; (1) Hourly wages were calculated from annual wage data based on a 40 hour work week
Source: Bureau of Labor Statistics, Metro Area Occupational Employment & Wage Estimates, May 2024

Employment by Industry

Sector	MD[1]		U.S.
	Number of Employees	Percent of Total	Percent of Total
Construction	147,900	3.2	5.1
Financial Activities	208,300	4.5	5.8
Government	601,700	12.9	14.9
Information	191,000	4.1	1.9
Leisure and Hospitality	538,700	11.6	10.4
Manufacturing	304,900	6.5	8.0
Mining and Logging	1,600	<0.1	0.4
Other Services	157,900	3.4	3.7
Private Education and Health Services	995,200	21.4	16.9
Professional and Business Services	669,200	14.4	14.2
Retail Trade	416,200	8.9	10.0
Transportation, Warehousing, and Utilities	229,500	4.9	4.8
Wholesale Trade	195,600	4.2	3.9

Note: Figures are non-farm employment as of December 2024. Figures are not seasonally adjusted and include workers 16 years of age and older; (1) Figures cover the Los Angeles-Long Beach-Glendale, CA Metropolitan Division
Source: Bureau of Labor Statistics, Current Employment Statistics, Employment, Hours, and Earnings

Employment by Occupation

Occupation Classification	City (%)	MSA[1] (%)	U.S. (%)
Management, Business, Science, and Arts	43.2	42.6	42.0
Natural Resources, Construction, and Maintenance	7.6	7.2	8.6
Production, Transportation, and Material Moving	11.3	12.2	13.0
Sales and Office	18.8	20.4	19.9
Service	19.2	17.6	16.5

Note: Figures cover employed civilians 16 years of age and older; (1) Figures cover the Los Angeles-Long Beach-Anaheim, CA Metropolitan Statistical Area
Source: U.S. Census Bureau, 2019-2023 American Community Survey 5-Year Estimates

Occupations with Greatest Projected Employment Growth: 2022 – 2032

Occupation[1]	2022 Employment	2032 Projected Employment	Numeric Employment Change	Percent Employment Change
Home Health and Personal Care Aides	796,900	1,060,200	263,300	33.0
Software Developers	313,700	388,000	74,300	23.7
Registered Nurses	333,700	376,900	43,200	12.9
Cooks, Restaurant	142,100	184,000	41,900	29.5
Laborers and Freight, Stock, and Material Movers, Hand	399,500	437,300	37,800	9.5
Janitors and Cleaners, Except Maids and Housekeeping Cleaners	262,900	300,200	37,300	14.2
Fast Food and Counter Workers	419,100	455,200	36,100	8.6
Stockers and Order Fillers	289,900	322,900	33,000	11.4
Medical Assistants	108,000	135,700	27,700	25.6
Landscaping and Groundskeeping Workers	135,200	162,100	26,900	19.9

Note: Projections cover California; (1) Sorted by numeric employment change
Source: www.projectionscentral.org, State Occupational Projections, 2022–2032 Long-Term Projections

Fastest-Growing Occupations: 2022 – 2032

Occupation[1]	2022 Employment	2032 Projected Employment	Numeric Employment Change	Percent Employment Change
Nurse Practitioners	21,500	34,100	12,600	58.6
Physical Therapist Assistants	7,900	11,200	3,300	41.8
Solar Photovoltaic Installers	7,900	11,200	3,300	41.8
Physician Assistants	13,000	18,200	5,200	40.0
Medical and Health Services Managers	58,300	81,400	23,100	39.6
Statisticians	2,800	3,900	1,100	39.3
Taxi Drivers	48,100	66,800	18,700	38.9
Occupational Therapy Assistants	2,700	3,600	900	33.3
Home Health and Personal Care Aides	796,900	1,060,200	263,300	33.0
Data Scientists	33,900	45,000	11,100	32.7

Note: Projections cover California; (1) Sorted by percent employment change and excludes occupations with numeric employment change less than 50
Source: www.projectionscentral.org, State Occupational Projections, 2022–2032 Long-Term Projections

CITY FINANCES

City Government Finances

Component	2022 ($000)	2022 ($ per capita)
Total Revenues	19,870,225	5,005
Total Expenditures	19,369,904	4,879
Debt Outstanding	37,323,309	9,401

Source: U.S. Census Bureau, State & Local Government Finances 2022

City Government Revenue by Source

Source	2022 ($000)	2022 ($ per capita)	2022 (%)
General Revenue			
From Federal Government	1,466,485	369	7.4
From State Government	465,915	117	2.3
From Local Governments	481,499	121	2.4
Taxes			
Property	2,642,578	666	13.3
Sales and Gross Receipts	2,169,222	546	10.9
Personal Income	0	0	0.0
Corporate Income	0	0	0.0
Motor Vehicle License	0	0	0.0
Other Taxes	1,273,189	321	6.4
Current Charges	4,951,864	1,247	24.9
Liquor Store	0	0	0.0
Utility	5,946,142	1,498	29.9

Source: U.S. Census Bureau, State & Local Government Finances 2022

City Government Expenditures by Function

Function	2022 ($000)	2022 ($ per capita)	2022 (%)
General Direct Expenditures			
Air Transportation	1,747,982	440	9.0
Corrections	0	0	0.0
Education	0	0	0.0
Employment Security Administration	0	0	0.0
Financial Administration	204,448	51	1.1
Fire Protection	647,780	163	3.3
General Public Buildings	54,815	13	0.3
Governmental Administration, Other	610,153	153	3.2
Health	451,948	113	2.3
Highways	976,935	246	5.0
Hospitals	0	0	0.0
Housing and Community Development	708,976	178	3.7
Interest on General Debt	511,189	128	2.6
Judicial and Legal	159,843	40	0.8
Libraries	239,684	60	1.2
Parking	45,311	11	0.2
Parks and Recreation	696,361	175	3.6
Police Protection	2,599,040	654	13.4
Public Welfare	1,073	< 1	< 0.1
Sewerage	1,170,614	294	6.0
Solid Waste Management	510,089	128	2.6
Veterans' Services	0	0	0.0
Liquor Store	0	0	0.0
Utility	6,478,075	1,631	33.4

Source: U.S. Census Bureau, State & Local Government Finances 2022

TAXES

State Corporate Income Tax Rates

State	Tax Rate (%)	Income Brackets ($)	Num. of Brackets	Financial Institution Tax Rate (%)[a]	Federal Income Tax Ded.
California	8.84 (b)	Flat rate	1	10.84 (b)	No

Note: Tax rates for tax year 2024; (a) Rates listed are the corporate income tax rate applied to financial institutions or excise taxes based on income. Some states have other taxes based upon the value of deposits or shares; (b) Minimum tax is $800 in California, $250 in District of Columbia, $50 in Arizona and North Dakota (banks), $400 ($100 banks) in Rhode Island, $200 per location in South Dakota (banks), $100 in Utah, in Vermont, simplified entity business tax for residents only at $250, otherwise minimum tax ($100 - $100,000) is based upon gross receipts.
Source: Federation of Tax Administrators, State Corporate Income Tax Rates, January 1, 2025

State Individual Income Tax Rates

State	Tax Rate (%)	Income Brackets ($)	Personal Exemptions ($)			Standard Ded. ($)	
			Single	Married	Depend.	Single	Married
California (a)	1.0 - 13.3 (g)	10,099 - 677,276 (b)	134	268	367 (c)	5,202	10,404 (a)

Note: Tax rates for tax year 2024; Local- and county-level taxes are not included; Federal income tax is not deductible on state income tax returns; (a) 16 states have statutory provision for automatically adjusting to the rate of inflation the dollar values of the income tax brackets, standard deductions, and/or personal exemptions. Oregon does not index the income brackets for $125,000 and over See: INFL and SPEC above; (b) For joint returns, taxes are twice the tax on half the couple's income. California brackets violate this formula at the two highest tax brackets in 2024; (c) The personal exemption takes the form of a tax credit instead of a deduction; (g) California imposes an additional 1% tax on taxable income over $1 million, making the maximum rate 13.3% over $1 million in 2023. Unreleased projections indicate 14.4% in 2024.
Source: Federation of Tax Administrators, State Individual Income Tax Rates, January 1, 2025

Various State Sales and Excise Tax Rates

State	State Sales Tax (%)	Gasoline[1] ($/gal.)	Cigarette[2] ($/pack)	Spirits[3] ($/gal.)	Wine[4] ($/gal.)	Beer[5] ($/gal.)	Recreational Marijuana (%)
California	7.25	0.70	2.87	3.30	0.20	0.20	(c)

Note: All tax rates as of January 1, 2025; (1) The American Petroleum Institute has developed a methodology for determining the average tax rate on a gallon of fuel. Rates may include any of the following: excise taxes, environmental fees, storage tank fees, other fees or taxes, general sales tax, and local taxes; (2) The federal excise tax of $1.0066 per pack and local taxes are not included; (3) Rates are those applicable to off-premise sales of 40% alcohol by volume (a.b.v.) distilled spirits in 750ml containers. Local excise taxes are excluded; (4) Rates are those applicable to off-premise sales of 11% a.b.v. non-carbonated wine in 750ml containers; (5) Rates are those applicable to off-premise sales of 4.7% a.b.v. beer in 12 ounce containers; (c) 15% excise tax (retail gross receipts)
Source: Tax Foundation, 2025 Facts & Figures: How Does Your State Compare?

State Tax Competitiveness Index

State	Overall Rank	Corporate Tax Rank	Individual Income Tax Rank	Sales Tax Rank	Property Tax Rank	Unemployment Insurance Tax Rank
California	48	41	49	46	23	25

Note: The Tax Foundation's State Tax Competitiveness Index enables policymakers, taxpayers, and business leaders to gauge how their states' tax systems compare. A rank of 1 is best, 50 is worst. Rankings do not average to the total. States without a tax rank equally as 1. DC's scores and rankings do not affect other states. The report shows tax systems as of July 1, 2024 (the beginning of Fiscal Year 2025).
Source: Tax Foundation, State Tax Competitiveness Index 2025

TRANSPORTATION

Means of Transportation to Work

Area	Car/Truck/Van		Public Transportation			Bicycle	Walked	Other Means	Worked at Home
	Drove Alone	Car-pooled	Bus	Subway	Railroad				
City	61.4	8.8	5.7	0.6	0.1	0.7	3.1	2.3	17.3
MSA[1]	67.1	9.2	2.9	0.3	0.1	0.6	2.3	1.9	15.5
U.S.	70.2	8.5	1.7	1.3	0.4	0.4	2.4	1.6	13.5

Note: Figures are percentages and cover workers 16 years of age and older; (1) Figures cover the Los Angeles-Long Beach-Anaheim, CA Metropolitan Statistical Area
Source: U.S. Census Bureau, 2019-2023 American Community Survey 5-Year Estimates

Travel Time to Work

Area	Less Than 10 Minutes	10 to 19 Minutes	20 to 29 Minutes	30 to 44 Minutes	45 to 59 Minutes	60 to 89 Minutes	90 Minutes or More
City	6.3	22.2	19.9	28.5	10.4	9.4	3.3
MSA[1]	7.3	25.0	20.8	25.4	9.7	8.5	3.3
U.S.	12.6	28.6	21.2	20.8	8.1	6.0	2.8

Note: Note: Figures are percentages and include workers 16 years old and over; (1) Figures cover the Los Angeles-Long Beach-Anaheim, CA Metropolitan Statistical Area
Source: U.S. Census Bureau, 2019-2023 American Community Survey 5-Year Estimates

Key Congestion Measures

Measure	2000	2010	2015	2020	2022
Annual Hours of Delay, Total (000)	673,878	812,204	924,196	365,543	905,556
Annual Hours of Delay, Per Auto Commuter	84	97	113	46	122
Annual Congestion Cost, Per Auto Commuter ($)	2,902	2,780	3,005	1,277	3,214

Note: Figures cover the Los Angeles-Long Beach-Anaheim CA urban area
Source: Texas A&M Transportation Institute, 2023 Urban Mobility Report

Freeway Travel Time Index

Measure	1985	1990	1995	2000	2005	2010	2015	2020	2022
Urban Area Index[1]	1.31	1.34	1.38	1.41	1.45	1.45	1.49	1.16	1.50
Urban Area Rank[1,2]	1	1	1	1	1	1	1	2	1

Note: Freeway Travel Time Index—the ratio of travel time in the peak period to the travel time at free-flow conditions. For example, a value of 1.30 indicates a 20-minute free-flow trip takes 26 minutes in the peak (20 minutes x 1.30 = 26 minutes); (1) Covers the Los Angeles-Long Beach-Anaheim CA urban area; (2) Rank is based on 101 larger urban areas (#1 = highest travel time index)
Source: Texas A&M Transportation Institute, 2023 Urban Mobility Report

Public Transportation

Agency Name / Mode of Transportation	Vehicles Operated in Maximum Service[1]	Annual Unlinked Passenger Trips[2] (in thous.)	Annual Passenger Miles[3] (in thous.)
Los Angeles Co. Metro Transportation Authority (LACMTA)			
Bus (directly operated)	1,453	196,666.7	676,814.2
Bus (purchased transportation)	108	9,573.7	40,581.3
Bus Rapid Transit (directly operated)	24	4,371.9	26,699.5
Demand Response (directly operated)	67	696.1	2,670.4
Heavy Rail (directly operated)	52	26,854.9	133,671.1
Light Rail (directly operated)	166	36,588.0	240,434.8
Vanpool (purchased transportation)	781	1,551.1	69,855.5
City of Los Angeles Department of Transportation (LADOT)			
Bus (purchased transportation)	180	14,344.2	24,548.2
Commuter Bus (purchased transportation)	94	873.2	14,334.3
Demand Response (purchased transportation)	87	180.8	614.4
Demand Response - Taxi	9	84.5	215.0

Note: (1) Number of revenue vehicles operated by the given mode and type of service to meet the annual maximum service requirement. This is the revenue vehicle count during the peak season of the year; on the week and day that maximum service is provided. Vehicles operated in maximum service (VOMS) exclude atypical days and one-time special events; (2) Number of passengers who boarded public transportation vehicles. Passengers are counted each time they board a vehicle no matter how many vehicles they use to travel from their origin to their destination. (3) Sum of the distances ridden by all passengers during the entire fiscal year.
Source: Federal Transit Administration, National Transit Database, 2023

Air Transportation

Airport Name and Code / Type of Service	Passenger Airlines[1]	Passenger Enplanements	Freight Carriers[2]	Freight (lbs)
Los Angeles International (LAX)				
Domestic service (U.S. carriers only)	33	26,239,010	22	830,680,479
International service (U.S. carriers only)	14	2,968,916	13	197,669,049

Note: (1) Includes all U.S.-based major, minor and commuter airlines that carried at least one passenger during the year; (2) Includes all U.S.-based airlines and freight carriers that transported at least one pound of freight during the year.
Source: Bureau of Transportation Statistics, The Intermodal Transportation Database, Air Carriers: T-100 Domestic Market (U.S. carriers only), 2024; Bureau of Transportation Statistics, The Intermodal Transportation Database, Air Carriers: T-100 International Market (U.S. carriers only), 2024

BUSINESSES

Major Business Headquarters

Company Name	Industry	Rankings	
		Fortune[1]	Forbes[2]
Capital Group Companies	Diversified financials	-	66
Farmers Insurance Exchange	Insurance: property and casualty (mutual)	273	-
Gibson, Dunn & Crutcher	Services	-	200
JM Eagle	Materials	-	247
Quinn Emanuel Urquhart & Sullivan	Services	-	263
The Wonderful Company	Multicompany	-	104

Note: (1) Companies that produce a 10-K are ranked 1 to 500 based on 2023 revenue; (2) All private companies with at least $2 billion in annual revenue through the end of their most current fiscal year are ranked 1 to 275; companies listed are headquartered in the city; dashes indicate no ranking
Source: Fortune, "Fortune 500," 2024; Forbes, "America's Largest Private Companies," 2024

Fastest-Growing Businesses

According to *Inc.*, Los Angeles is home to 10 of America's 500 fastest-growing private companies: **Gamefam** (#40); **Religion of Sports** (#64); **The Plug Drink** (#147); **Praxis Labs** (#150); **Boulevard** (#163); **Little Sleepies** (#333); **Bloom Nutrition** (#357); **Laughland Sciences** (#358); **MVP Builders** (#371); **Aloware** (#460). Criteria: must be an independent, privately-held, for-profit, U.S. corporation, proprietorship or partnership as of December 31, 2023; revenues must be at least $100,000 in

2020 and $2 million in 2023; must have four-year operating/sales history. *Inc., "America's 500 Fastest-Growing Private Companies," 2024*

According to *Initiative for a Competitive Inner City (ICIC)*, Los Angeles is home to three of America's 100 fastest-growing "inner city" companies: **Sea Pac Engineering** (#33); **O2EPCM dba O2 Engineering, Projects & Construction Management** (#84); **City Design Studio** (#96). To be eligible for the IC100, companies have to be independently operated, privately held, for-profit businesses with revenues of at least $50,000 in 2019 and $500,000 in 2023, and headquartered in an under-resourced community. Recognizing that concentrated poverty exists within metropolitan areas outside of big cities (and that poverty overall is suburbanizing), ICIC defines under-resourced communities as large low-income, high-poverty areas located in the urban and suburban parts of all but the smallest metropolitan areas. Companies were ranked overall by revenue growth over the five-year period between 2019 and 2023. *Initiative for a Competitive Inner City (ICIC), "Inner City 100 Companies," 2024*

According to Deloitte, Los Angeles is home to seven of North America's 500 fastest-growing high-technology companies: **Gamefam** (#30); **Boulevard** (#62); **Xos** (#81); **Akido Labs** (#105); **Sunbit** (#161); **FloQast** (#282); **HAAWK** (#411). Companies are ranked by percentage growth in revenue over a four-year period. Criteria for inclusion: company must be headquartered within North America; must own proprietary intellectual property or technology that is sold to customers in products that contributes to a significant portion of the company's operating revenue; must have been in business for a minumum of four years with 2020 operating revenues of at least $50,000 USD/CD and 2023 operating revenues of at least $5 million USD/CD. *Deloitte, 2024 Technology Fast 500*[TM]

Living Environment

COST OF LIVING

Cost of Living Index

Composite Index	Groceries	Housing	Utilities	Trans-portation	Health Care	Misc. Goods/ Services
149.4	109.3	232.5	107.2	136.1	101.1	118.9

Note: The Cost of Living Index measures regional differences in the cost of consumer goods and services, excluding taxes and non-consumer expenditures, for professional and managerial households in the top income quintile. It is based on more than 50,000 prices covering almost 60 different items for which prices are collected three times a year by chambers of commerce, economic development organizations or university applied economic centers in each participating urban area. The numbers shown should be read as a percentage above or below the national average of 100. For example, a value of 115.4 in the groceries column indicates that grocery prices are 15.4% higher than the national average. Small differences in the index numbers should not be interpreted as significant; Figures cover the Los Angeles-Long Beach CA urban area.
Source: The Council for Community and Economic Research, Cost of Living Index, 2024

Grocery Prices

Area[1]	T-Bone Steak ($/pound)	Frying Chicken ($/pound)	Whole Milk ($/half gal.)	Eggs ($/dozen)	Orange Juice ($/64 oz.)	Coffee ($/11.5 oz.)
City[2]	15.55	2.45	5.00	3.14	4.55	6.68
Avg.	15.42	1.55	4.69	3.25	4.41	5.46
Min.	14.50	1.16	4.43	2.75	4.00	4.85
Max.	17.56	2.89	5.49	4.78	5.54	7.89

*Note: (1) Values for the local area are compared with the average, minimum and maximum values for all 276 areas in the Cost of Living Index; (2) Figures cover the Los Angeles-Long Beach CA urban area; **T-Bone Steak** (price per pound); **Frying Chicken** (price per pound, whole fryer); **Whole Milk** (half gallon carton); **Eggs** (price per dozen, Grade A, large); **Orange Juice** (64 oz. Tropicana or Florida Natural); **Coffee** (11.5 oz. can, vacuum-packed, Maxwell House, Hills Bros, or Folgers).*
Source: The Council for Community and Economic Research, Cost of Living Index, 2024

Housing and Utility Costs

Area[1]	New Home Price ($)	Apartment Rent ($/month)	All Electric ($/month)	Part Electric ($/month)	Other Energy ($/month)	Telephone ($/month)
City[2]	1,311,286	2,988	-	163.45	65.93	194.86
Avg.	515,975	1,550	210.99	123.07	82.07	194.99
Min.	265,375	692	104.33	53.68	36.26	179.42
Max.	2,775,821	5,719	529.02	397.28	361.63	223.33

*Note: (1) Values for the local area are compared with the average, minimum and maximum values for all 276 areas in the Cost of Living Index; (2) Figures cover the Los Angeles-Long Beach CA urban area; **New Home Price** (2,400 sf living area, 8,000 sf lot, in urban area with full utilities); **Apartment Rent** (950 sf 2 bedroom/1.5 or 2 bath, unfurnished, excluding all utilities except water); **All Electric** (average monthly cost for an all-electric home); **Part Electric** (average monthly cost for a part-electric home); **Other Energy** (average monthly cost for natural gas, fuel oil, coal, wood, and any other forms of energy except electricity); **Telephone** (price includes the base monthly rate plus taxes and fees for three lines of mobile phone service).*
Source: The Council for Community and Economic Research, Cost of Living Index, 2024

Health Care, Transportation, and Other Costs

Area[1]	Doctor ($/visit)	Dentist ($/visit)	Optometrist ($/visit)	Gasoline ($/gallon)	Beauty Salon ($/visit)	Men's Shirt ($)
City[2]	130.00	133.17	127.53	4.85	94.00	38.64
Avg.	143.77	117.51	129.23	3.32	48.57	38.14
Min.	36.74	58.67	67.33	2.80	24.00	13.41
Max.	270.44	216.82	307.33	5.28	94.00	63.89

*Note: (1) Values for the local area are compared with the average, minimum and maximum values for all 276 areas in the Cost of Living Index; (2) Figures cover the Los Angeles-Long Beach CA urban area; **Doctor** (general practitioners routine exam of an established patient); **Dentist** (adult teeth cleaning and periodic oral examination); **Optometrist** (full vision eye exam for established adult patient); **Gasoline** (one gallon regular unleaded, national brand, including all taxes, cash price at self-service pump if available); **Beauty Salon** (woman's shampoo, trim, and blow-dry); **Men's Shirt** (cotton/polyester dress shirt, pinpoint weave, long sleeves).*
Source: The Council for Community and Economic Research, Cost of Living Index, 2024

HOUSING

Homeownership Rate

Area	2017 (%)	2018 (%)	2019 (%)	2020 (%)	2021 (%)	2022 (%)	2023 (%)	2024 (%)
MSA[1]	49.1	49.5	48.2	48.5	47.9	48.3	48.0	48.3
U.S.	63.9	64.4	64.6	66.6	65.5	65.8	65.9	65.6

Note: (1) Figures cover the Los Angeles-Long Beach-Anaheim, CA Metropolitan Statistical Area
Source: U.S. Census Bureau, Housing Vacancies and Homeownership Annual Statistics: 2017-2024

House Price Index (HPI)

Area	National Ranking[2]	Quarterly Change (%)	One-Year Change (%)	Five-Year Change (%)	Since 1991Q1 (%)
MD[1]	114	0.65	5.59	48.41	341.40
U.S.[3]	–	1.43	4.51	57.13	327.82

Note: The HPI is a weighted repeat sales index. It measures average price changes in repeat sales or refinancings on the same properties. This information is obtained by reviewing repeat mortgage transactions on single-family properties whose mortgages have been purchased or securitized by Fannie Mae or Freddie Mac since January 1975; (1) Figures cover the Los Angeles-Long Beach-Glendale, CA Metropolitan Division; (2) Rankings are based on annual percentage change for all metro areas containing at least 15,000 transactions over the last 10 years and ranges from 1 to 241; (3) figures based on a weighted average of Census Division estimates using a seasonally adjusted, purchase-only index; all figures are for the period ending December 31, 2024
Source: Federal Housing Finance Agency, Change in FHFA Metropolitan Area House Price Indexes, All Transactions Index, 2024Q4

Home Value

Area	Under $100,000	$100,000 -$199,999	$200,000 -$299,999	$300,000 -$399,999	$400,000 -$499,999	$500,000 -$999,999	$1,000,000 or more	Median ($)
City	2.5	1.2	1.2	2.5	5.7	47.7	39.2	879,500
MSA[1]	3.2	1.7	1.8	3.2	6.3	50.5	33.3	825,300
U.S.	12.1	17.8	19.5	14.4	10.5	19.1	6.5	303,400

Note: Figures are percentages except for median and cover owner-occupied housing units; (1) Figures cover the Los Angeles-Long Beach-Anaheim, CA Metropolitan Statistical Area
Source: U.S. Census Bureau, 2019-2023 American Community Survey 5-Year Estimates

Year Housing Structure Built

Area	2020 or Later	2010 -2019	2000 -2009	1990 -1999	1980 -1989	1970 -1979	1960 -1969	1950 -1959	1940 -1949	Before 1940	Median Year
City	0.8	6.1	5.6	5.7	10.8	13.4	13.2	16.2	9.1	19.2	1964
MSA[1]	0.6	5.3	6.3	7.4	12.6	15.9	15.0	17.6	7.8	11.5	1969
U.S.	1.2	8.9	13.6	12.8	13.0	14.4	10.0	9.7	4.5	11.9	1980

Note: Figures are percentages except for Median Year; Note: (1) Figures cover the Los Angeles-Long Beach-Anaheim, CA Metropolitan Statistical Area
Source: U.S. Census Bureau, 2019-2023 American Community Survey 5-Year Estimates

Gross Monthly Rent

Area	Under $500	$500 -$999	$1,000 -$1,499	$1,500 -$1,999	$2,000 -$2,499	$2,500 -$2,999	$3,000 and up	Median ($)
City	4.6	7.2	20.1	23.9	18.3	10.6	15.3	1,879
MSA[1]	3.5	5.8	16.8	24.5	21.1	12.0	16.3	1,987
U.S.	6.5	22.3	29.5	20.2	10.8	4.8	5.9	1,348

Note: Figures are percentages except for median; Gross rent is the contract rent plus the estimated average monthly cost of utilities (electricity, gas, and water and sewer) and fuels (oil, coal, kerosene, wood, etc.) if these are paid by the renter (or paid for the renter by someone else); (1) Figures cover the Los Angeles-Long Beach-Anaheim, CA Metropolitan Statistical Area
Source: U.S. Census Bureau, 2019-2023 American Community Survey 5-Year Estimates

HEALTH

Health Risk Factors

Category	MSA[1] (%)	U.S. (%)
Adults aged 18–64 who have any kind of health care coverage	90.3	90.8
Adults who reported being in good or better health	77.5	81.8
Adults who have been told they have high blood cholesterol	39.6	36.9
Adults who have been told they have high blood pressure	30.4	34.0
Adults who are current smokers	8.2	12.1
Adults who currently use e-cigarettes	5.7	7.7
Adults who currently use chewing tobacco, snuff, or snus	1.3	3.2
Adults who are heavy drinkers[2]	3.9	6.1
Adults who are binge drinkers[3]	13.6	15.2
Adults who are overweight (BMI 25.0 - 29.9)	38.4	34.4
Adults who are obese (BMI 30.0 - 99.8)	24.4	34.3
Adults who participated in any physical activities in the past month	75.8	75.8

Note: All figures are crude prevalence; (1) Figures cover the Los Angeles-Long Beach-Anaheim, CA Metropolitan Statistical Area; (2) Heavy drinkers are classified as adult men having more than 14 drinks per week and adult women having more than 7 drinks per week; (3) Binge drinkers are classified as males having five or more drinks on one occasion or females having four or more drinks on one occasion
Source: Centers for Disease Control and Prevention, Behaviorial Risk Factor Surveillance System, SMART: Selected Metropolitan Area Risk Trends, 2023

Acute and Chronic Health Conditions

Category	MSA[1] (%)	U.S. (%)
Adults who have ever been told they had a heart attack	3.5	4.2
Adults who have ever been told they have angina or coronary heart disease	3.4	4.0
Adults who have ever been told they had a stroke	3.0	3.3
Adults who have ever been told they have asthma	14.0	15.7
Adults who have ever been told they have arthritis	19.0	26.3
Adults who have ever been told they have diabetes[2]	13.8	11.5
Adults who have ever been told they had skin cancer	3.1	5.6
Adults who have ever been told they had any other types of cancer	6.4	8.4
Adults who have ever been told they have COPD	3.6	6.4
Adults who have ever been told they have kidney disease	3.4	3.7
Adults who have ever been told they have a form of depression	15.6	22.0

Note: All figures are crude prevalence; (1) Figures cover the Los Angeles-Long Beach-Anaheim, CA Metropolitan Statistical Area; (2) Figures do not include pregnancy-related, borderline, or pre-diabetes
Source: Centers for Disease Control and Prevention, Behaviorial Risk Factor Surveillance System, SMART: Selected Metropolitan Area Risk Trends, 2023

Health Screening and Vaccination Rates

Category	MSA[1] (%)	U.S. (%)
Adults who have ever been tested for HIV	39.1	37.5
Adults who have had their blood cholesterol checked within the last five years	87.4	87.0
Adults aged 65+ who have had flu shot within the past year	67.4	63.4
Adults aged 65+ who have ever had a pneumonia vaccination	71.5	71.9

Note: All figures are crude prevalence; (1) Figures cover the Los Angeles-Long Beach-Anaheim, CA Metropolitan Statistical Area.
Source: Centers for Disease Control and Prevention, Behaviorial Risk Factor Surveillance System, SMART: Selected Metropolitan Area Risk Trends, 2023

Disability Status

Category	MSA[1] (%)	U.S. (%)
Adults who reported being deaf	5.6	7.4
Are you blind or have serious difficulty seeing, even when wearing glasses?	6.1	4.9
Do you have difficulty doing errands alone?	7.0	7.8
Do you have difficulty dressing or bathing?	4.5	3.6
Do you have serious difficulty concentrating/remembering/making decisions?	13.4	13.7
Do you have serious difficulty walking or climbing stairs?	12.8	13.2

Note: All figures are crude prevalence; (1) Figures cover the Los Angeles-Long Beach-Anaheim, CA Metropolitan Statistical Area.
Source: Centers for Disease Control and Prevention, Behaviorial Risk Factor Surveillance System, SMART: Selected Metropolitan Area Risk Trends, 2023

Mortality Rates for the Top 10 Causes of Death in the U.S.

ICD-10[a] Sub-Chapter	ICD-10[a] Code	Crude Mortality Rate[2] per 100,000 population	
		County[3]	U.S.
Malignant neoplasms	C00-C97	147.4	182.7
Ischaemic heart diseases	I20-I25	113.8	109.6
Provisional assignment of new diseases of uncertain etiology[1]	U00-U49	68.3	65.3
Other forms of heart disease	I30-I51	39.7	65.1
Other degenerative diseases of the nervous system	G30-G31	52.3	52.4
Other external causes of accidental injury	W00-X59	32.5	52.3
Cerebrovascular diseases	I60-I69	40.4	49.1
Chronic lower respiratory diseases	J40-J47	26.8	43.5
Hypertensive diseases	I10-I15	38.9	38.9
Organic, including symptomatic, mental disorders	F01-F09	13.2	33.9

Note: (a) ICD-10 = International Classification of Diseases 10th Revision; (1) Includes COVID-19, adverse effects to COVID-19 vaccines, SARS, and vaping-related disorders; (2) Crude mortality rates are a three-year average covering 2021-2023; (3) Figures cover Los Angeles County.
Source: Centers for Disease Control and Prevention, National Center for Health Statistics. National Vital Statistics System, Mortality 2018-2023 on CDC WONDER Online Database

Mortality Rates for Selected Causes of Death

Cause of Death	ICD-10[a] Code	Crude Mortality Rate[1] per 100,000 population	
		County[2]	U.S.
Accidental poisoning and exposure to noxious substances	X40-X49	24.1	30.5
Alzheimer disease	G30	47.6	35.4
Assault	X85-Y09	7.3	7.3
COVID-19	U07.1	68.3	65.3
Diabetes mellitus	E10-E14	36.2	30.0
Diseases of the liver	K70-K76	20.0	20.8
Human immunodeficiency virus (HIV) disease	B20-B24	1.9	1.5
Influenza and pneumonia	J09-J18	18.3	13.4
Intentional self-harm	X60-X84	8.8	14.7
Malnutrition	E40-E46	1.7	6.0
Obesity and other hyperalimentation	E65-E68	3.0	3.1
Renal failure	N17-N19	16.4	16.4
Transport accidents	V01-V99	11.8	14.4

Note: (a) ICD-10 = International Classification of Diseases 10th Revision; (1) Crude mortality rates are a three-year average covering 2021-2023; (2) Figures cover Los Angeles County; Data are suppressed when the data meet the criteria for confidentiality constraints; Crude mortality rates are flagged as unreliable when the rate would be calculated with a numerator of 20 or less.
Source: Centers for Disease Control and Prevention, National Center for Health Statistics. National Vital Statistics System, Mortality 2018-2023 on CDC WONDER Online Database

Health Insurance Coverage

Area	With Health Insurance	With Private Health Insurance	With Public Health Insurance	Without Health Insurance	Population Under Age 19 Without Health Insurance
City	90.0	55.2	41.9	10.0	3.6
MSA[1]	91.8	60.8	38.8	8.2	3.5
U.S.	91.4	67.3	36.3	8.6	5.4

Note: Figures are percentages that cover the civilian noninstitutionalized population; (1) Figures cover the Los Angeles-Long Beach-Anaheim, CA Metropolitan Statistical Area
Source: U.S. Census Bureau, 2019-2023 American Community Survey 5-Year Estimates

Number of Medical Professionals

Area	MDs[3]	DOs[3,4]	Dentists	Podiatrists	Chiropractors	Optometrists
County[1] (number)	32,697	1,712	9,607	668	3,105	2,008
County[1] (rate[2])	336.3	17.6	99.4	6.9	32.1	20.8
U.S. (rate[2])	302.5	29.2	74.6	6.4	29.5	18.0

Note: Data as of 2023 unless noted; (1) Data covers Los Angeles County; (2) Number of medical professionals per 100,000 population; (3) Data as of 2022 and includes all active, non-federal physicians; (4) Doctor of Osteopathic Medicine
Source: U.S. Department of Health and Human Services, Health Resources and Services Administration, Bureau of Health Professions, Area Resource File (ARF) 2023-2024

Best Hospitals

According to *U.S. News,* the Los Angeles-Long Beach-Anaheim, CA metro area is home to 22 of the best hospitals in the U.S.: **California Rehabilitation Institute** (1 adult specialty); **Cedars-Sinai Medical Center** (Honor Roll/11 adult specialties); **City of Hope Comprehensive Cancer Center** (2 adult specialties); **Hoag Memorial Hospital Presbyterian** (1 adult specialty); **Hoag Orthopedic Institute** (1 adult specialty); **Huntington Health Medical Center-Pasadena** (1 adult specialty); **Kaiser Permanente Anaheim and Irvine Medical Centers** (1 adult specialty); **Kaiser Permanente Los Angeles Medical Center** (1 adult specialty); **Keck Medical Center of USC** (8 adult specialties); **MemorialCare Long Beach Medical Center** (1 adult specialty); **Providence Mission Hospital-Mission Viejo and Laguna Beach** (1 adult specialty); **Providence Saint John's Health Center** (1 adult specialty); **Providence St. Jude Medical Center** (1 adult specialty); **Rancho Los Amigos National Rehabilitation Center** (1 adult specialty); **Resnick Neuropsychiatric Hospital at UCLA** (1 adult specialty); **Santa Monica-UCLA Medical Center and Orthopedic Hospital** (1 adult specialty); **Stein and Doheny Eye Institutes, UCLA Medical Center** (14 adult specialties and 8 pediatric specialties); **Torrance Memorial Medical Center** (2 adult specialties); **UCLA Medical Center** (Honor Roll/14 adult specialties and 8 pediatric specialties); **USC Arcadia Hospital** (8 adult specialties); **USC Norris Cancer Hospital-Keck Medical Center of USC** (1 adult specialty); **USC Roski Eye Institute** (8 adult specialties). The hospitals listed were nationally ranked in at least one of 15 adult or 11 pediatric specialties. The number of specialties shown cover the parent hospital. Only 160 U.S. hospitals performed well enough to be nationally ranked in one or more specialties. Twenty hospitals in the U.S. made the Honor Roll. The Best Hospitals Honor Roll takes both the national rankings and the procedure and condition ratings into account. Hospitals received points if they were nationally ranked in one of the 15 adult specialties—the higher they ranked, the more points they got—and how many ratings of "high performing" they earned in the 20 procedures and conditions.
U.S. News Online, "America's Best Hospitals 2024-25"

According to *U.S. News,* the Los Angeles-Long Beach-Anaheim, CA metro area is home to three of the best children's hospitals in the U.S.: **CHOC Children's Hospital** (8 pediatric specialties); **Children's Hospital Los Angeles** (Honor Roll/11 pediatric specialties); **UCLA Mattel Children's Hospital** (8 pediatric specialties). The hospitals listed were highly ranked in at least one of 11 pediatric specialties. One hundred five children's hospitals in the U.S. were nationally ranked in at least one specialty. Hospitals received points for being ranked in a specialty, and the 10 hospitals with the most points across the 11 specialties make up the Honor Roll. *U.S. News Online, "America's Best Children's Hospitals 2024-25"*

EDUCATION

Public School District Statistics

District Name	Schls	Pupils	Pupil/ Teacher Ratio	Minority Pupils[1] (%)	Total Rev. per Pupil ($)	Total Exp. per Pupil ($)
Los Angeles Unified	785	419,929	19.3	90.0	28,702	25,877

Note: Table includes school districts with 2,000 or more students; (1) Percentage of students that are not non-Hispanic white.
Source: U.S. Department of Education, National Center for Education Statistics, Common Core of Data, Local Education Agency (School District) Universe Survey: School Year 2023-2024; U.S. Department of Education, National Center for Education Statistics, Common Core of Data, School District Finance Survey (F-33): School Year 2021–22

Best High Schools

According to *U.S. News,* Los Angeles is home to five of the top 500 high schools in the U.S.: **Science Academy Stem Magnet** (#12); **Harbor Teacher Preparation Academy** (#47); **Girls Academic Leadership Academy Dr. Michelle King School STEM** (#160); **Downtown Business High School** (#272); **Los Angeles Center for Enriched Studies** (#331). Nearly 25,000 public, magnet and charter schools were ranked based on their performance on state assessments and how well they prepare students for college. *U.S. News & World Report, "Best High Schools 2024"*

Highest Level of Education

Area	Less than H.S.	H.S. Diploma	Some College, No Deg.	Associate Degree	Bachelor's Degree	Master's Degree	Prof. School Degree	Doctorate Degree
City	20.7	18.5	16.6	6.3	24.5	8.7	3.1	1.6
MSA[1]	17.8	19.5	18.1	7.1	23.9	9.2	2.8	1.6
U.S.	10.6	26.2	19.4	8.8	21.3	9.8	2.3	1.6

Note: Figures cover persons age 25 and over; (1) Figures cover the Los Angeles-Long Beach-Anaheim, CA Metropolitan Statistical Area
Source: U.S. Census Bureau, 2019-2023 American Community Survey 5-Year Estimates

Educational Attainment by Race

Area	High School Graduate or Higher (%)					Bachelor's Degree or Higher (%)				
	Total	White	Black	Asian	Hisp.[2]	Total	White	Black	Asian	Hisp.[2]
City	79.3	89.6	90.1	91.1	59.4	37.8	51.6	31.9	57.6	15.1
MSA[1]	82.2	90.4	91.1	89.2	65.7	37.4	46.4	31.8	55.5	16.2
U.S.	89.4	92.9	88.1	88.0	72.5	35.0	37.7	24.7	57.0	19.9

Note: Figures shown cover persons 25 years old and over; (1) Figures cover the Los Angeles-Long Beach-Anaheim, CA Metropolitan Statistical Area; (2) People of Hispanic origin can be of any race
Source: U.S. Census Bureau, 2019-2023 American Community Survey 5-Year Estimates

School Enrollment by Grade and Control

Area	Preschool (%)		Kindergarten (%)		Grades 1 - 4 (%)		Grades 5 - 8 (%)		Grades 9 - 12 (%)	
	Public	Private	Public	Private	Public	Private	Public	Private	Public	Private
City	55.2	44.8	85.7	14.3	87.7	12.3	87.5	12.5	88.0	12.0
MSA[1]	54.7	45.3	86.6	13.4	89.1	10.9	89.9	10.1	90.6	9.4
U.S.	58.7	41.3	85.2	14.8	87.2	12.8	87.9	12.1	89.0	11.0

Note: Figures shown cover persons 3 years old and over; (1) Figures cover the Los Angeles-Long Beach-Anaheim, CA Metropolitan Statistical Area
Source: U.S. Census Bureau, 2019-2023 American Community Survey 5-Year Estimates

Higher Education

Four-Year Colleges			Two-Year Colleges			Medical Schools[1]	Law Schools[2]	Voc/ Tech[3]
Public	Private Non-profit	Private For-profit	Public	Private Non-profit	Private For-profit			
15	73	36	27	1	30	6	22	68

Note: Figures cover institutions located within the Los Angeles-Long Beach-Anaheim, CA Metropolitan Statistical Area and include main campuses only; (1) includes schools accredited by the Liaison Committee on Medical Education and the American Osteopathic Association's Commission on Osteopathic College Accreditation; (2) includes ABA-accredited schools, schools with provisional ABA accreditation, and state accredited schools; (3) includes all schools with programs that are less than 2 years.
Source: National Center for Education Statistics, Integrated Postsecondary Education System (IPEDS), 2023-24; Wikipedia, List of Medical Schools in the United States, accessed May 2, 2025; Wikipedia, List of Law Schools in the United States, accessed May 2, 2025

According to *U.S. News & World Report,* the Los Angeles-Long Beach-Anaheim, CA metro area is home to 10 of the top 200 national universities in the U.S.: **California Institute of Technology** (#6 tie); **University of California—Los Angeles** (#15 tie); **University of Southern California** (#27 tie); **University of California—Irvine** (#33 tie); **Pepperdine University** (#80 tie); **Loyola Marymount University** (#91 tie); **California State University—Long Beach** (#109 tie); **Chapman University** (#121 tie); **California State University—Fullerton** (#136 tie); **University of La Verne** (#196 tie). The indicators used to capture academic quality fall into a number of categories: assessment by administrators at peer institutions; retention of students; faculty resources; student selectivity; financial resources; alumni giving; high school counselor ratings of colleges; and graduation rate. *U.S. News & World Report, "America's Best Colleges 2025"*

According to *U.S. News & World Report,* the Los Angeles-Long Beach-Anaheim, CA metro area is home to eight of the top 100 liberal arts colleges in the U.S.: **Pomona College** (#5 tie); **Claremont McKenna College** (#8 tie); **Harvey Mudd College** (#12 tie); **Occidental College** (#34 tie); **Pitzer College** (#36 tie); **Scripps College** (#44); **Soka University of America** (#45 tie); **Whittier College** (#95 tie). The indicators used to capture academic quality fall into a number of categories: assessment by administrators at peer institutions; retention of students; faculty resources; student selectivity; financial resources; alumni giving; high school counselor ratings of colleges; and graduation rate. *U.S. News & World Report, "America's Best Colleges 2025"*

According to *U.S. News & World Report,* the Los Angeles-Long Beach-Anaheim, CA metro area is home to five of the top 100 law schools in the U.S.: **University of California—Los Angeles 1** (#12); **University of Southern California (Gould)** (#26 tie); **University of California—Irvine 1** (#38 tie); **Pepperdine University (Caruso)** (#55 tie); **Loyola Marymount University** (#71 tie). The rankings are based on a weighted average of 12 measures of quality: peer assessment score; assessment score by lawyers/judges; median LSAT scores; median undergrad GPA; acceptance rate; employment rates for graduates; placement success; bar passage rate; faculty resources; expenditures per student; student/faculty ratio; and library resources. *U.S. News & World Report, "America's Best Graduate Schools, Law, 2025"*

According to *U.S. News & World Report,* the Los Angeles-Long Beach-Anaheim, CA metro area is home to two of the top medical schools for research in the U.S.: **University of California—Los Angeles (Geffen)** (Tier 1); **University of California—Irvine** (Tier 2). *U.S. News* placed medical and osteopathic schools into tiers based on their research productivity, faculty and admissions data. Each school's tier was derived from its overall score, calculated by summing the weighted normalized values generated across several factors of academic quality, outlined below. There are four tiers, with tier 1 medical schools as the highest-performing and tier 4 as the lowest-performing. Only tier 1 and 2 schools are shown. Because of the tier presentation, *U.S. News* calculated overall scores based on their percentile performance among all rated schools instead of dividing against the rescaled score of the No. 1-performing schools. Tier 1 included schools with overall scores of 85 to 99. The cutoffs for tiers 2 through 4 were schools scoring 50 to 84, 15 to 49 and 1 to 14, respectively. The rankings are based on a weighted average of the following measures of quality: total research activity; average research activity per faculty member; total NIH research grants at the medical school and its affiliated hospitals; average NIH research grants per faculty; median MCAT total score; median undergraduate GPA; acceptance rate; and faculty resources. *U.S. News & World Report, "America's Best Graduate Schools, Medical, 2025"*

According to *U.S. News & World Report,* the Los Angeles-Long Beach-Anaheim, CA metro area is home to two of the top medical schools for primary care in the U.S.: **Western University of Health Sciences** (Tier 1); **University of California—Los Angeles (Geffen)** (Tier 2). *U.S. News* placed medical and osteopathic schools into tiers based on their research productivity, faculty and admissions data. Each school's tier was derived from its overall score, calculated by summing the weighted normalized values generated across several factors of academic quality, outlined below. There are four tiers, with tier 1 medical schools as the highest-performing and tier 4 as the lowest-performing. Only tier 1 and 2 schools are shown. Because of the tier presentation, *U.S. News* calculated overall scores based on their percentile performance among all rated schools instead of dividing against the rescaled score of the No. 1-performing schools. Tier 1 included schools with overall scores of 85 to

99. The cutoffs for tiers 2 through 4 were schools scoring 50 to 84, 15 to 49 and 1 to 14, respectively. The rankings are based on a weighted average of the following measures of quality: graduates practicing in primary care specialties; graduates entering primary care residencies; median MCAT total score; median undergraduate GPA; acceptance rate; and faculty resources. *U.S. News & World Report, "America's Best Graduate Schools, Medical, 2025"*

According to *U.S. News & World Report,* the Los Angeles-Long Beach-Anaheim, CA metro area is home to four of the top 75 business schools in the U.S.: **University of California—Los Angeles (Anderson)** (#18 tie); **University of Southern California (Marshall)** (#24 tie); **University of California—Irvine (Merage)** (#43 tie); **Chapman University (Argyros)** (#66 tie). The rankings are based on a weighted average of the following nine measures: quality assessment; peer assessment; recruiter assessment; placement success; mean starting salary and bonus; student selectivity; mean GMAT and GRE scores; mean undergraduate GPA; and acceptance rate. *U.S. News & World Report, "America's Best Graduate Schools, Business, 2025"*

EMPLOYERS

Major Employers

Company Name	Industry
Allied Universal	Security & janitorial services
Amazon.com	Online retail
Boeing	Aerospace manufacturing
Cedars-Sinai Medical Center	Healthcare, private
City of Los Angeles	Local government
County of Los Angeles	Local government
Kaiser Permanente	Healthcare, private
Los Angeles Community College District	Colleges & universities
Los Angeles County Metro Transportation	Transportation, public
Los Angeles Unified School District	Education, public K-12
NBC/Universal	Amusement
Northrop Grumman Corp.	Aerospace manufacturing
Providence Health & Services	Healthcare, private
Ralph's/Food 4 Less (Kroger's)	Grocery
State of California (non-education)	State government
Target Corp.	General retail
University of California, Los Angeles	Colleges & universities
University of Southern California	Colleges & universities
UPS (United Parcel Service)	Transportation couriers
Walt Disney Co.	Amusement

Note: Companies shown are located within the Los Angeles-Long Beach-Anaheim, CA Metropolitan Statistical Area.
Source: Chambers of Commerce; State Departments of Labor; Wikipedia

Best Companies to Work For

The Wonderful Company, headquartered in Los Angeles, is among "The 100 Best Companies to Work For." To pick the best companies, *Fortune* partnered with the Great Place to Work Institute. Using their proprietary Trust Index™ survey, the core of what creates great a workplace is measured—key behaviors that drive trust in management, connection with colleagues, and loyalty to the company. To be eligible for the *Fortune* 100 Best Companies to Work For list, employers must have 1,000 or more employees in the U.S. and cannot be a government agency. *Fortune, "The 100 Best Companies to Work For," 2025*

FloQast, headquartered in Los Angeles, is among "Fortune's Best Workplaces for Parents." To pick the best companies, *Fortune* partnered with the Great Place to Work Institute. To be considered for the list, companies must be Great Place To Work-Certified and have at least 50 responses from parents in the US. The survey enables employees to share confidential quantitative and qualitative feedback about their organization's culture by responding to 60 statements on a 5-point scale and answering two open-ended questions. Collectively, these statements describe a great employee experience, defined by high levels of trust, respect, credibility, fairness, pride, and camaraderie. In addition, companies provide organizational data like size, location, industry, demographics, roles, and levels; and provide information about parental leave, adoption, flexible schedule, childcare and dependent health care benefits. *Fortune, "Best Workplaces for Parents," 2024*

Cedars Sinai; Keck Medicine of USC, headquartered in Los Angeles, are among the "Best Places to Work in IT." To qualify, companies had to have a minimum of 100 total employees and five IT employees. The best places to work were selected based on DEI (diversity, equity, and inclusion) practices; IT turnover, promotions, and growth; IT retention and engagement programs; remote/hybrid working; benefits and perks (such as elder care and child care, flextime, and reimbursement for college tuition); and training and career development opportunities. *Computerworld, "Best Places to Work in IT," 2025*

PUBLIC SAFETY

Crime Rate

Area	Total Crime Rate	Violent Crime Rate				Property Crime Rate		
		Murder	Rape	Robbery	Aggrav. Assault	Burglary	Larceny -Theft	Motor Vehicle Theft
City	3,666.8	8.6	51.4	230.1	530.0	406.4	1,764.3	676.0
U.S.	2,290.9	5.7	38.0	66.5	264.1	250.7	1,347.2	318.7

Note: Figures are crimes per 100,000 population.
Source: FBI, Table 8, Offenses Known to Law Enforcement, by State by City, 2023

Hate Crimes

Area	Number of Quarters Reported	Number of Incidents per Bias Motivation					
		Race/Ethnicity/ Ancestry	Religion	Sexual Orientation	Disability	Gender	Gender Identity
City[1]	4	201	89	105	2	0	12
U.S.	4	5,900	2,699	2,077	187	92	492

Note: (1) Figures include at least one incident reported with more than one bias motivation.
Source: Federal Bureau of Investigation, Hate Crime Statistics 2023

Identity Theft Consumer Reports

Area	Reports	Reports per 100,000 Population	Rank[2]
MSA[1]	71,624	550	6
U.S.	1,135,291	339	-

Note: (1) Figures cover the Los Angeles-Long Beach-Anaheim, CA Metropolitan Statistical Area; (2) Rank ranges from 1 to 401 where 1 indicates greatest number of identity theft reports per 100,000 population
Source: Federal Trade Commission, Consumer Sentinel Network Data Book 2024

Fraud and Other Consumer Reports

Area	Reports	Reports per 100,000 Population	Rank[2]
MSA[1]	191,725	1,473	64
U.S.	5,360,641	1,601	-

Note: (1) Figures cover the Los Angeles-Long Beach-Anaheim, CA Metropolitan Statistical Area; (2) Rank ranges from 1 to 401 where 1 indicates greatest number of fraud and other consumer reports per 100,000 population
Source: Federal Trade Commission, Consumer Sentinel Network Data Book 2024

POLITICS

2024 Presidential Election Results

Area	Trump (Rep.)	Harris (Dem.)	Stein (Green)	Kennedy (Ind.)	Oliver (Lib.)	Other
Los Angeles County	31.9	64.8	1.1	1.2	0.3	0.6
U.S.	49.7	48.2	0.6	0.5	0.4	0.6

Note: Results are percentages and may not add to 100% due to rounding
Source: Dave Leip's Atlas of U.S. Presidential Elections

SPORTS

Professional Sports Teams

Team Name	League	Year Established
Anaheim Ducks	National Hockey League (NHL)	1993
C.D. Chivas USA	Major League Soccer (MLS)	2004
LA Galaxy	Major League Soccer (MLS)	1996
Los Angeles Angels	Major League Baseball (MLB)	1961
Los Angeles Chargers	National Football League (NFL)	2017
Los Angeles Clippers	National Basketball Association (NBA)	1984
Los Angeles Dodgers	Major League Baseball (MLB)	1958
Los Angeles FC	Major League Soccer (MLS)	2018
Los Angeles Kings	National Hockey League (NHL)	1967
Los Angeles Lakers	National Basketball Association (NBA)	1960
Los Angeles Rams	National Football League (NFL)	2016

Note: Includes teams located in the Los Angeles-Long Beach-Anaheim, CA Metropolitan Statistical Area.
Source: Wikipedia, Major Professional Sports Teams of the United States and Canada, May 1, 2025

CLIMATE

Average and Extreme Temperatures

Temperature	Jan	Feb	Mar	Apr	May	Jun	Jul	Aug	Sep	Oct	Nov	Dec	Yr.
Extreme High (°F)	88	92	95	102	97	104	97	98	110	106	101	94	110
Average High (°F)	65	66	65	67	69	72	75	76	76	74	71	66	70
Average Temp. (°F)	56	57	58	60	63	66	69	70	70	67	62	57	63
Average Low (°F)	47	49	50	53	56	59	63	64	63	59	52	48	55
Extreme Low (°F)	27	34	37	43	45	48	52	51	47	43	38	32	27

Note: Figures cover the years 1947-1990
Source: National Climatic Data Center, International Station Meteorological Climate Summary, 9/96

Average Precipitation/Snowfall/Humidity

Precip./Humidity	Jan	Feb	Mar	Apr	May	Jun	Jul	Aug	Sep	Oct	Nov	Dec	Yr.
Avg. Precip. (in.)	2.6	2.3	1.8	0.8	0.1	Tr	Tr	0.1	0.2	0.3	1.5	1.5	11.3
Avg. Snowfall (in.)	Tr	0	0	0	0	0	0	0	0	0	0	0	Tr
Avg. Rel. Hum. 7am (%)	69	72	76	76	77	80	80	81	80	76	69	67	75
Avg. Rel. Hum. 4pm (%)	60	62	64	64	66	67	67	68	67	66	61	60	64

Note: Figures cover the years 1947-1990; Tr = Trace amounts (<0.05 in. of rain; <0.5 in. of snow)
Source: National Climatic Data Center, International Station Meteorological Climate Summary, 9/96

Weather Conditions

Temperature			Daytime Sky			Precipitation		
10°F & below	32°F & below	90°F & above	Clear	Partly cloudy	Cloudy	0.01 inch or more precip.	0.1 inch or more snow/ice	Thunder-storms
0	< 1	5	131	125	109	34	0	1

Note: Figures are average number of days per year and cover the years 1947-1990
Source: National Climatic Data Center, International Station Meteorological Climate Summary, 9/96

HAZARDOUS WASTE

Superfund Sites

The Los Angeles-Long Beach-Glendale, CA metro division is home to 18 sites on the EPA's Superfund National Priorities List (NPL) or Superfund Alternative Approach (SAA) list: **Cooper Drum Co.** (Final NPL); **Del Amo** (Final NPL); **Exide Technologies - Vernon** (Proposed NPL); **Jervis B. Webb Co.** (Final NPL); **Jet Propulsion Laboratory (NASA)** (Final NPL); **Montrose Chemical Corp.** (Final NPL); **Omega Chemical Corporation** (Final NPL); **Operating Industries, Inc., Landfill** (Final NPL); **Pemaco Maywood** (Final NPL); **San Fernando Valley (Area 1)** (Final NPL); **San Fernando Valley (Area 2)** (Final NPL); **San Fernando Valley (Area 4)** (Final NPL); **San Gabriel Valley (Area 1)** (Final NPL); **San Gabriel Valley (Area 2)** (Final NPL); **San Gabriel Valley (Area 3)** (Final NPL); **San Gabriel Valley (Area 4)** (Final NPL); **Southern Avenue Industrial Area** (Final NPL); **Waste Disposal, Inc.** (Final NPL). The Superfund alternative approach uses the same investigation and cleanup process and standards that are used for sites listed on the National Priorities List. The SAA is an alternative to listing a site on the NPL; it is not an alternative to Superfund or the Superfund process. There are a total of 1,445 Superfund sites with a status of proposed or final on both lists in the United States. *U.S. Environmental Protection Agency, National Priorities List, May 1, 2025; U.S. Environmental Protection Agency, Superfund Alternative Approach Sites, May 1, 2025*

AIR QUALITY

Air Quality Trends: Ozone

	1990	1995	2000	2005	2010	2015	2020	2021	2022	2023
MSA[1]	0.128	0.109	0.090	0.086	0.074	0.082	0.096	0.076	0.077	0.081
U.S.	0.087	0.089	0.081	0.080	0.072	0.068	0.066	0.067	0.067	0.070

Note: (1) Data covers the Los Angeles-Long Beach-Anaheim, CA Metropolitan Statistical Area. The values shown are the composite ozone concentration averages among trend sites based on the highest fourth daily maximum 8-hour concentration in parts per million. These trends are based on sites having an adequate record of monitoring data during the trend period. Data from exceptional events are included.
Source: U.S. Environmental Protection Agency, Air Quality Monitoring Information, "Air Quality Trends by City, 1990-2023"

Air Quality Index

Area	Percent of Days when Air Quality was...[2]					AQI Statistics[2]	
	Good	Moderate	Unhealthy for Sensitive Groups	Unhealthy	Very Unhealthy	Maximum	Median
MSA[1]	11.2	64.9	14.2	8.8	0.8	210	67

Note: (1) Data covers the Los Angeles-Long Beach-Anaheim, CA Metropolitan Statistical Area; (2) Based on 365 days with AQI data in 2023. Air Quality Index (AQI) is an index for reporting daily air quality. EPA calculates the AQI for five major air pollutants regulated by the Clean Air Act: ground-level ozone, particle pollution (aka particulate matter), carbon monoxide, sulfur dioxide, and nitrogen dioxide. The AQI runs from 0 to 500. The higher the AQI value, the greater the level of air pollution and the greater the health concern. There are six AQI categories: "Good" AQI is between 0 and 50. Air quality is considered satisfactory; "Moderate" AQI is between 51 and 100. Air quality is acceptable; "Unhealthy for Sensitive Groups" When AQI values are between 101 and 150, members of sensitive groups may experience health effects; "Unhealthy" When AQI values are between 151 and 200 everyone may begin to experience health effects; "Very Unhealthy" AQI values between 201 and 300 trigger a health alert; "Hazardous" AQI values over 300 trigger warnings of emergency conditions (not shown).
Source: U.S. Environmental Protection Agency, Air Quality Index Report, 2023

Air Quality Index Pollutants

Area	Percent of Days when AQI Pollutant was...[2]					
	Carbon Monoxide	Nitrogen Dioxide	Ozone	Sulfur Dioxide	Particulate Matter 2.5	Particulate Matter 10
MSA[1]	0.0	1.4	41.1	(3)	55.6	1.9

Note: (1) Data covers the Los Angeles-Long Beach-Anaheim, CA Metropolitan Statistical Area; (2) Based on 365 days with AQI data in 2023. The Air Quality Index (AQI) is an index for reporting daily air quality. EPA calculates the AQI for five major air pollutants regulated by the Clean Air Act: ground-level ozone, particle pollution (also known as particulate matter), carbon monoxide, sulfur dioxide, and nitrogen dioxide. The AQI runs from 0 to 500. The higher the AQI value, the greater the level of air pollution and the greater the health concern; (3) Sulfur dioxide is no longer included in this table because SO_2 concentrations tend to be very localized and not necessarily representative of broad geographical areas like counties and CBSAs.
Source: U.S. Environmental Protection Agency, Air Quality Index Report, 2023

Maximum Air Pollutant Concentrations: Particulate Matter, Ozone, CO and Lead

	Particulate Matter 10 (ug/m^3)	Particulate Matter 2.5 Wtd AM (ug/m^3)	Particulate Matter 2.5 24-Hr (ug/m^3)	Ozone (ppm)	Carbon Monoxide (ppm)	Lead (ug/m^3)
MSA[1] Level	124	11.1	28	0.103	3	0.02
NAAQS[2]	150	15	35	0.075	9	0.15
Met NAAQS[2]	Yes	Yes	Yes	No	Yes	Yes

Note: (1) Data covers the Los Angeles-Long Beach-Anaheim, CA Metropolitan Statistical Area; Data from exceptional events are included; (2) National Ambient Air Quality Standards; ppm = parts per million; ug/m^3 = micrograms per cubic meter; n/a not available.
Concentrations: Particulate Matter 10 (coarse particulate)—highest second maximum 24-hour concentration; Particulate Matter 2.5 Wtd AM (fine particulate)—highest weighted annual mean concentration; Particulate Matter 2.5 24-Hour (fine particulate)—highest 98th percentile 24-hour concentration; Ozone—highest fourth daily maximum 8-hour concentration; Carbon Monoxide—highest second maximum non-overlapping 8-hour concentration; Lead—maximum running 3-month average
Source: U.S. Environmental Protection Agency, Air Quality Monitoring Information, "Air Quality Statistics by City, 2023"

Maximum Air Pollutant Concentrations: Nitrogen Dioxide and Sulfur Dioxide

	Nitrogen Dioxide AM (ppb)	Nitrogen Dioxide 1-Hr (ppb)	Sulfur Dioxide AM (ppb)	Sulfur Dioxide 1-Hr (ppb)	Sulfur Dioxide 24-Hr (ppb)
MSA[1] Level	21	61	n/a	8	n/a
NAAQS[2]	53	100	30	75	140
Met NAAQS[2]	Yes	Yes	n/a	Yes	n/a

Note: (1) Data covers the Los Angeles-Long Beach-Anaheim, CA Metropolitan Statistical Area; Data from exceptional events are included; (2) National Ambient Air Quality Standards; ppm = parts per million; ug/m^3 = micrograms per cubic meter; n/a not available.
Concentrations: Nitrogen Dioxide AM—highest arithmetic mean concentration; Nitrogen Dioxide 1-Hr—highest 98th percentile 1-hour daily maximum concentration; Sulfur Dioxide AM—highest annual mean concentration; Sulfur Dioxide 1-Hr—highest 99th percentile 1-hour daily maximum concentration; Sulfur Dioxide 24-Hr—highest second maximum 24-hour concentration
Source: U.S. Environmental Protection Agency, Air Quality Monitoring Information, "Air Quality Statistics by City, 2023"

Phoenix, Arizona

Background

Phoenix, the arid "Valley of the Sun," and the capital of Arizona, was named by the English soldier and prospector, "Lord Darell" Duppa for the mythical bird of ancient Greek/Phoenician lore. According to the legend, the Phoenix was a beautiful bird that destroyed itself with its own flames. When nothing remained but embers, it would rise again from the ashes, more awesome and beautiful than before. Like the romantic tale, Duppa hoped that his city of Phoenix would rise again from the mysteriously abandoned Hohokam village which occupied the Phoenix area for 2,000 years.

Many might agree that Phoenix fulfilled Duppa's wish. Within 15 years after its second founding in 1867, Phoenix had grown to be an important supply point for the mining districts of north-central Arizona, as well as an important trading site for farmers, cattlemen, and prospectors. Around this time, Phoenix entered its Wild West phase, complete with stagecoaches, saloons, gambling houses, soldiers, cowboys, miners, and the pungent air of outlawry. Two public hangings near the end of the 1800s set a dramatic example and helped turn the tide.

Today, Phoenix is just as exciting as ever, but more law-abiding, and many continue to be attracted to Phoenix's natural beauty. Despite occasional sprawling suburbs and shopping malls, the sophisticated blend of Spanish, Native American, and cowboy culture is obvious in the city's architecture, arts, and crafts. Downtown Phoenix underwent a major renaissance in the 1990s with the completion of a history museum, expanded art museum, new central library, Arizona Science Center, and a renovated concert hall. Today it also features the 20,000-square-foot Musical Instrument Museum with musical instruments from around the world. More than 300 arts and entertainment venues are in the Phoenix region, as well as five professional sports teams. Phoenix Concept 2000 split the city into 15 urban villages, each with its own building height and density permits, further shaping the city's free-market development culture.

Phoenix is the country's fifth-largest city, with more than one million people, while the Phoenix metro area population has grown to nearly five million. This increase in population continues to make Phoenix an attractive location for companies that are expanding in the fields of electronics and communications. Renewable energy, biomedicine, advanced business services, manufacturing and distribution, aerospace and aviation, and emerging technologies from start-ups are key industries in the region, as are insurance, healthcare, and technology.

Phoenix is home to several professional sports franchises. The Phoenix Suns of the NBA and the Phoenix Mercury of the WNBA both play at the Footprint Center. The Mercury have won the WNBA championships three times: in 2007, 2009, and 2014. The Arizona Diamondbacks of Major League Baseball play their home games in Chase Field and defeated the New York Yankees in 2001 to claim the World Series title. The Arizona Cardinals is the oldest continuously run professional football franchise in the nation, though they originated in Chicago. They play at University of Phoenix Stadium in Glendale, 20 miles from Phoenix, which hosted Super Bowl in 2008, 2015, and 2023.

In 1981, Phoenix resident Sandra Day O'Connor broke the gender barrier on the U.S. Supreme Court when she was sworn in as the first female justice.

Temperatures in Phoenix are mild in winter and very hot in summer. The low humidity makes the summer heat more bearable than one might expect. Rainfall is slight and comes in two seasons: winter rain comes on winds from the Pacific, ending by April; summer rain with severe thunderstorms comes from the southeast.

Rankings

General Rankings

- To help military veterans find the best places in which to settle down, *WalletHub* compared the 100 largest U.S. cities across 19 key indicators of livability, affordability and veteran-friendliness. They range from the share of military skill-related jobs to veteran income growth to the availability of VA health facilities. Phoenix ranked #75. *Wallethub.com, "Best & Worst Places for Veterans to Live (2025)," November 7, 2024*

- *Insider* listed 23 places in the U.S. that travel industry trends reveal would be popular destinations in 2023. This year the list trends towards cultural and historical happenings, sports events, wellness experiences and invigorating outdoor escapes. According to the website insider.com Phoenix is a place to visit in 2023. *Insider, "23 of the Best Places You Should Travel to in the U.S. in 2023," December 17, 2022*

Business/Finance Rankings

- Payscale.com ranked the 32 largest metro areas in terms of wage growth. The Phoenix metro area ranked #8. Criteria: quarterly changes in private industry employee and education professional wage growth from the previous year. *PayScale, "Wage Trends by Metro Area-4th Quarter," February 4, 2025*

- The Phoenix metro area appeared on the Milken Institute "2025 Best Performing Cities" list. Rank: #23 out of 200 large metro areas (based on performance category). Criteria: job growth; wage growth; high-tech growth and impact; community resilience; housing affordability; household broadband access. *Milken Institute, "Best-Performing Cities 2025," January 14, 2025*

Education Rankings

- Personal finance website *WalletHub* analyzed the 150 largest U.S. metropolitan statistical areas to determine where the most educated Americans are putting their degrees to work. Criteria: education levels; percentage of workers with degrees; education quality and attainment gap; public school quality rankings; quality and enrollment of each metro area's universities. Phoenix was ranked #74 (#1 = most educated city). *WalletHub.com, "Most & Least Educated Cities in America, 2025" July 2, 2024*

Environmental Rankings

- Sperling's *BestPlaces* assessed the 50 largest metropolitan areas of the United States for the likelihood of dangerously extreme weather events or earthquakes. In general the Southeast and South-Central regions have the highest risk of weather extremes and earthquakes, while the Pacific Northwest enjoys the lowest risk. Of the most risky metropolitan areas, the Phoenix metro area was ranked #9. *Bestplaces.net, "Avoid Natural Disasters: BestPlaces Reveals The Top 10 Safest Places to Live," October 25, 2017*

- The U.S. Environmental Protection Agency (EPA) released its list of U.S. metropolitan areas with the most ENERGY STAR certified buildings in 2023. The Phoenix metro area was ranked #17 out of 25. *U.S. Environmental Protection Agency, "2024 Energy Star Top Cities," May 22, 2024*

- Phoenix was highlighted as one of the 25 most ozone-polluted metro areas in the U.S. during 2021 through 2023. The area ranked #4. *American Lung Association, "State of the Air 2025," April 23, 2025*

- Phoenix was highlighted as one of the 25 metro areas most polluted by year-round particle pollution (Annual PM 2.5) in the U.S. during 2021 through 2023. The area ranked #20. *American Lung Association, "State of the Air 2025," April 23, 2025*

Food/Drink Rankings

- WalletHub compared the 100 largest U.S. cities across 17 key indicators of vegan- and vegetarian-friendliness. Phoenix was ranked #9. Cities were selected based on metrics such as the cost of groceries for vegetarians, the share of restaurants serving meatless options and the number of salad shops per capita. *WalletHub.com, "Best Cities for Vegans & Vegetarians (2025)," September 24, 2024*

Health/Fitness Rankings

- For each of the 100 largest cities in the United States, the American Fitness Index®, compiled in partnership between the American College of Sports Medicine and the Elevance Health Foundation, evaluated community infrastructure and more than 30 health behaviors including preventive health, levels of chronic disease conditions, food insecurity, pedestrian safety, air quality, and community/environment resources that support physical activity. Phoenix ranked #74 for "community fitness." *americanfitnessindex.org, "2024 ACSM American Fitness Index Summary Report," July 23, 2024*

- Phoenix was identified as a "2025 Allergy Capital." The area ranked #71 out of the nation's 100 largest metropolitan areas. Three groups of factors were used to identify the most challenging cities for people with allergies: annual tree, grass, and weed pollen scores; over the counter allergy medicine use; number of board-certified allergy specialists. *Asthma and Allergy Foundation of America, "2025 Allergy Capitals: The Most Challenging Places to Live with Allergies," March 18, 2025*

- Phoenix was identified as a "2024 Asthma Capital." The area ranked #21 out of the nation's 100 largest metropolitan areas. Criteria: estimated asthma prevalence; asthma-related mortality; and ER visits due to asthma. Risk factors analyzed but not factored in the rankings: annual air quality including pollution and ozone levels; public smoking laws; indoor air quality; access to asthma specialists; rescue and controller medication use; uninsured rate; pollen allergy; poverty rate. *Asthma and Allergy Foundation of America, "Asthma Capitals 2024: The Most Challenging Places to Live With Asthma," September 10, 2024*

Real Estate Rankings

- *WalletHub* compared the most populated U.S. cities to determine which had the best markets for real estate agents. Phoenix ranked #45 where demand was high and pay was the best. Criteria: sales per agent; annual median wage for real-estate agents; monthly average starting salary for real estate agents; real estate job density and competition; unemployment rate; home turnover rate; housing-market health index; and other relevant metrics. *WalletHub.com, "2021 Best Places to Be a Real Estate Agent," May 12, 2021*

- The Phoenix metro area appeared on Realtor.com's list of hot housing markets to watch in 2025. The area ranked #8. Criteria: forecasted home price and sales growth; overall economy; population trends. *Realtor.com®, "Top 10 Housing Markets Positioned for Growth in 2025," December 10, 2024*

- Phoenix was ranked #136 out of 176 metro areas in terms of cost of housing in 2024 by the National Association of Home Builders (#1 = most affordable). Criteria: the portion of an average family's income necessary to pay the mortgage on a median-priced home. *National Association of Home Builders®, NAHB-Wells Fargo Cost of Housing Index, 4th Quarter 2024*

Safety Rankings

- Allstate ranked the 100 most populous cities in America in terms of driver safety. Phoenix ranked #88. Criteria based on anonymized driving behavior data from Allstate's mobile app powered by Arity: high speed driving (over 80 mph), phone handling, and hard braking. The report helps increase the importance of safety and awareness behind the wheel. *Allstate, "16th Allstate America's Best Drivers Report®" July 11, 2024*

Sports/Recreation Rankings

- Phoenix was chosen as a bicycle friendly community by the League of American Bicyclists. A "Bicycle Friendly Community" welcomes cyclists by providing safe and supportive accommodation for cycling and encouraging people to bike for transportation and recreation. There are four award levels: Platinum; Gold; Silver; and Bronze. The community achieved an award level of Bronze. *League of American Bicyclists, "2024 Awards-New & Renewing Bicycle Friendly Communities List," January 28, 2025*

Women/Minorities Rankings

- Personal finance website *WalletHub* compared more than 180 U.S. cities across two key dimensions, "Hispanic Business-Friendliness" and "Hispanic Purchasing Power," to arrive at the most favorable conditions for Hispanic entrepreneurs. Phoenix was ranked #113 out of 182. Criteria includes: share of Hispanic-Owned Businesses; average growth of Hispanic Business revenues; Small Business-Friendliness score; affordability; and number of Hispanics with at least a bachelor's degree. *WalletHub.com, "Best Cities for Hispanic Entrepreneurs," September 4, 2024*

Miscellaneous Rankings

- Phoenix was selected as a 2024 Digital Cities Survey winner. The city ranked #7 in the large city (500,000 or more population) category. The survey examined and assessed how city governments are utilizing new technology and modernized applications to provide residents an array of contactless services and conveniences. Survey questions focused on ten initiatives: cybersecurity; citizen experience; disaster recovery; business intelligence; IT personnel retention; data governance; business automation; AI/machine learning; application modernization; and IT collaboration. *Center for Digital Government, "2024 Digital Cities Survey," November 5, 2024*

- The financial planning site *SmartAsset* has compiled its annual study on the best places for Halloween in the U.S. for 2022. 146 cities were compared to determine that Phoenix ranked #27 out of 35 for still being able to enjoy the festivities despite COVID-19. Metrics included: safety, family-friendliness, percentage of children in the population, concentration of candy and costume shops, weather and COVID infection rates. *SmartAsset.com, "2022 Edition-Best Places to Celebrate Halloween," October 19, 2022*

- *WalletHub* compared 148 of the most populated U.S. cities to determine their operating efficiency. A "Quality of Services" score was constructed for each city and then measured against the total budget per capita to reveal which were managed the best. Phoenix ranked #33. Criteria: financial stability; economy; education; safety; health; infrastructure and pollution. *WalletHub.com, "2025's Best- & Worst-Run Cities in America," June 18, 2024*

Business Environment

DEMOGRAPHICS

Population Growth

Area	1990 Census	2000 Census	2010 Census	2020 Census	2023 Estimate[2]	Population Growth 1990-2023 (%)
City	989,873	1,321,045	1,445,632	1,608,139	1,624,832	64.1
MSA[1]	2,238,480	3,251,876	4,192,887	4,845,832	4,941,206	120.7
U.S.	248,709,873	281,421,906	308,745,538	331,449,281	332,387,540	33.6

Note: (1) Figures cover the Phoenix-Mesa-Chandler, AZ Metropolitan Statistical Area; (2) 2019-2023 5-year ACS population estimate
Source: U.S. Census Bureau, 1990 Census, 2000 Census, 2010 Census, 2020 Census, 2019-2023 American Community Survey 5-Year Estimates

Race

Area	White Alone[2] (%)	Black Alone[2] (%)	Asian Alone[2] (%)	AIAN[3] Alone[2] (%)	NHOPI[4] Alone[2] (%)	Other Race Alone[2] (%)	Two or More Races (%)
City	53.7	7.8	3.9	2.3	0.2	11.4	20.8
MSA[1]	63.2	5.7	4.1	2.2	0.2	8.4	16.1
U.S.	63.4	12.4	5.8	0.9	0.2	6.6	10.7

Note: (1) Figures cover the Phoenix-Mesa-Chandler, AZ Metropolitan Statistical Area; (2) Alone is defined as not being in combination with one or more other races; (3) American Indian and Alaska Native; (4) Native Hawaiian and Other Pacific Islander
Source: U.S. Census Bureau, 2019-2023 American Community Survey 5-Year Estimates

Hispanic or Latino Origin

Area	Total (%)	Mexican (%)	Puerto Rican (%)	Cuban (%)	Other (%)
City	41.8	36.7	0.7	0.4	4.0
MSA[1]	30.8	26.2	0.7	0.3	3.6
U.S.	19.0	11.3	1.8	0.7	5.2

Note: Persons of Hispanic or Latino origin can be of any race; (1) Figures cover the Phoenix-Mesa-Chandler, AZ Metropolitan Statistical Area
Source: U.S. Census Bureau, 2019-2023 American Community Survey 5-Year Estimates

Age

Area	Percent of Population									Median Age
	Under Age 5	Age 5–19	Age 20–34	Age 35–44	Age 45–54	Age 55–64	Age 65–74	Age 75–84	Age 85+	
City	6.1	20.7	23.4	14.1	12.5	11.2	7.4	3.2	1.2	34.8
MSA[1]	5.7	19.6	20.9	13.3	12.3	11.8	9.5	5.2	1.8	37.7
U.S.	5.7	19.1	20.2	13.1	12.8	11.8	10.0	4.9	1.9	38.7

Note: (1) Figures cover the Phoenix-Mesa-Chandler, AZ Metropolitan Statistical Area
Source: U.S. Census Bureau, 2019-2023 American Community Survey 5-Year Estimates

Disability by Age

Area	All Ages	Under 18 Years Old	18 to 64 Years Old	65 Years and Over
City	11.5	4.6	10.2	32.5
MSA[1]	12.3	4.9	10.1	31.1
U.S.	13.0	4.7	10.7	32.9

Note: Figures show percent of the civilian noninstitutionalized population that reported having a disability. Disability status is determined from six types of difficulty: vision, hearing, cognitive, ambulatory, self-care, and independent living. For children under 5 years old, hearing and vision difficulty are used to determine disability status. For children between the ages of 5 and 14, disability status is determined from hearing, vision, cognitive, ambulatory, and self-care difficulties. For people aged 15 years and older, they are considered to have a disability if they have difficulty with any one of the six difficulty types; Note: (1) Figures cover the Phoenix-Mesa-Chandler, AZ Metropolitan Statistical Area
Source: U.S. Census Bureau, 2019-2023 American Community Survey 5-Year Estimates

Ancestry

Area	German	Irish	English	American	Italian	Polish	French[2]	European	Scottish
City	9.6	7.4	6.8	2.7	3.9	1.8	1.4	1.5	1.3
MSA[1]	12.6	8.7	9.5	4.2	4.5	2.2	1.8	1.8	1.6
U.S.	12.6	9.4	9.1	5.5	4.9	2.6	2.0	1.6	1.6

Note: Figures are the percentage of the total population reporting a particular ancestry. The nine most commonly reported ancestries in the U.S. are shown. Figures include multiple ancestries (e.g. if a person reported being Irish and Italian, they were included in both columns); (1) Figures cover the Phoenix-Mesa-Chandler, AZ Metropolitan Statistical Area; (2) Excludes Basque
Source: U.S. Census Bureau, 2019-2023 American Community Survey 5-Year Estimates

Foreign-born Population

Area	Any Foreign Country	Asia	Mexico	Europe	Caribbean	Central America[2]	South America	Africa	Canada
						Percent of Population Born in			
City	19.0	3.1	11.3	1.3	0.4	0.9	0.4	1.1	0.3
MSA[1]	13.9	3.3	6.6	1.3	0.3	0.6	0.4	0.7	0.6
U.S.	13.9	4.3	3.3	1.4	1.4	1.2	1.2	0.8	0.2

Note: (1) Figures cover the Phoenix-Mesa-Chandler, AZ Metropolitan Statistical Area; (2) Excludes Mexico.
Source: U.S. Census Bureau, 2019-2023 American Community Survey 5-Year Estimates

Household Size

Area	One	Two	Three	Four	Five	Six	Seven or More	Average Household Size
				Persons in Household (%)				
City	28.3	30.6	15.2	12.8	7.3	3.3	2.5	2.66
MSA[1]	26.0	34.8	14.8	12.6	6.7	3.0	2.1	2.62
U.S.	28.5	33.8	15.4	12.7	5.9	2.3	1.4	2.54

Note: (1) Figures cover the Phoenix-Mesa-Chandler, AZ Metropolitan Statistical Area
Source: U.S. Census Bureau, 2019-2023 American Community Survey 5-Year Estimates

Household Relationships

Area	House-holder	Opposite-sex Spouse	Same-sex Spouse	Opposite-sex Unmarried Partner	Same-sex Unmarried Partner	Child[2]	Grand-child	Other Relatives	Non-relatives
City	36.3	14.4	0.3	3.1	0.3	30.2	2.9	6.6	4.2
MSA[1]	36.9	17.2	0.2	2.8	0.2	29.0	2.5	5.4	3.7
U.S.	38.3	17.5	0.2	2.5	0.2	28.3	2.4	4.8	3.4

Note: Figures are percent of the total population; (1) Figures cover the Phoenix-Mesa-Chandler, AZ Metropolitan Statistical Area; (2) Includes biological, adopted, and stepchildren of the householder
Source: U.S. Census Bureau, 2020 Census

Gender

Area	Males	Females	Males per 100 Females
City	815,308	809,524	100.7
MSA[1]	2,466,995	2,474,211	99.7
U.S.	164,545,087	167,842,453	98.0

Note: (1) Figures cover the Phoenix-Mesa-Chandler, AZ Metropolitan Statistical Area
Source: U.S. Census Bureau, 2019-2023 American Community Survey 5-Year Estimates

Marital Status

Area	Never Married	Now Married[2]	Separated	Widowed	Divorced
City	40.2	42.0	1.9	4.0	11.9
MSA[1]	34.3	47.9	1.4	4.9	11.5
U.S.	34.1	47.9	1.7	5.6	10.7

Note: Figures are percentages and cover the population 15 years of age and older; (1) Figures cover the Phoenix-Mesa-Chandler, AZ Metropolitan Statistical Area; (2) Excludes separated
Source: U.S. Census Bureau, 2019-2023 American Community Survey 5-Year Estimates

Religious Groups by Family

Area	Catholic	Baptist	Methodist	LDS[2]	Pentecostal	Lutheran	Islam	Adventist	Other
MSA[1]	22.9	1.7	0.6	6.2	1.5	1.0	1.9	1.5	9.3
U.S.	18.7	7.3	3.0	2.0	1.8	1.7	1.3	1.3	11.6

Note: Figures are the number of adherents as a percentage of the total population and cover the eight largest religious groups in the U.S; (1) Figures cover the Phoenix-Mesa-Chandler, AZ Metropolitan Statistical Area; (2) Church of Jesus Christ of Latter-day Saints
Sources: 2020 U.S. Religion Census, Association of Statisticians of American Religious Bodies; The Association of Religion Data Archives (ARDA)

Religious Groups by Tradition

Area	Catholic	Evangelical Protestant	Mainline Protestant	Black Protestant	Islam	Judaism	Hinduism	Orthodox	Buddhism
MSA[1]	22.9	11.0	1.6	0.3	1.9	0.3	0.5	0.4	0.2
U.S.	18.7	16.5	5.2	2.3	1.3	0.6	0.4	0.4	0.3

Note: Figures are the number of adherents as a percentage of the total population; (1) Figures cover the Phoenix-Mesa-Chandler, AZ Metropolitan Statistical Area
Sources: 2020 U.S. Religion Census, Association of Statisticians of American Religious Bodies; The Association of Religion Data Archives (ARDA)

ECONOMY

Real Gross Domestic Product (GDP)

Area	2017	2018	2019	2020	2021	2022	2023	Rank[3]
MSA[1]	246.1	257.4	269.4	274.6	299.1	313.6	322.8	14
U.S.[2]	17,619.1	18,160.7	18,642.5	18,238.9	19,387.6	19,896.6	20,436.3	–

Note: Figures are in billions of chained 2017 dollars; (1) Figures cover the Phoenix-Mesa-Chandler, AZ Metropolitan Statistical Area; (2) Figures cover real GDP within metropolitan areas; (3) Rank is based on 2023 data and ranges from 1 to 384
Source: U.S. Bureau of Economic Analysis

Economic Growth

Area	2014	2015	2016	2017	2018	2019	2020	2021	2022	2023
MSA[1]	1.6	3.1	3.6	4.6	4.6	4.7	1.9	8.9	4.8	2.9
U.S.[2]	2.6	3.2	2.0	2.7	3.1	2.7	-2.2	6.3	2.6	2.7

Note: Figures are real gross domestic product growth rates and represent percent change from preceding period; (1) Figures cover the Phoenix-Mesa-Chandler, AZ Metropolitan Statistical Area; (2) Figures are the average growth rates within metropolitan areas
Source: U.S. Bureau of Economic Analysis

Metropolitan Area Exports

Area	2018	2019	2020	2021	2022	2023	Rank[2]
MSA[1]	13,614.9	15,136.6	11,073.9	14,165.1	16,658.8	17,553.6	26
U.S.	1,664,056.1	1,645,173.7	1,431,406.6	1,753,941.4	2,062,937.4	2,019,160.5	–

Note: Figures are in millions of dollars; (1) Figures cover the Phoenix-Mesa-Chandler, AZ Metropolitan Statistical Area; (2) Rank is based on 2023 data and ranges from 1 to 386
Source: U.S. Department of Commerce, International Trade Administration, Office of Trade and Economic Analysis, Industry and Analysis, Exports by Metropolitan Area, data extracted April 2, 2025

Building Permits

Area	Single-Family			Multi-Family			Total		
	2023	2024	Pct. Chg.	2023	2024	Pct. Chg.	2023	2024	Pct. Chg.
City	4,200	4,062	-3.3	10,268	4,935	-51.9	14,468	8,997	-37.8
MSA[1]	24,708	30,277	22.5	20,908	15,607	-25.4	45,616	45,884	0.6
U.S.	920,000	981,900	6.7	591,100	496,100	-16.1	1,511,100	1,478,000	-2.2

Note: (1) Figures cover the Phoenix-Mesa-Chandler, AZ Metropolitan Statistical Area; Figures represent new, privately-owned housing units authorized (unadjusted data)
Source: U.S. Census Bureau, Building Permits Survey (BPS), 2023, 2024

Bankruptcy Filings

Area	Business Filings			Nonbusiness Filings		
	2023	2024	% Chg.	2023	2024	% Chg.
Maricopa County	252	355	40.9	6,085	7,026	15.5
U.S.	18,926	23,107	22.1	434,064	494,201	13.9

Note: Business filings include Chapter 7, Chapter 9, Chapter 11, Chapter 12, Chapter 13, Chapter 15, and Section 304; Nonbusiness filings include Chapter 7, Chapter 11, and Chapter 13
Source: Administrative Office of the U.S. Courts, Business and Nonbusiness Bankruptcy, County Cases Commenced by Chapter of the Bankruptcy Code, During the 12-Month Period Ending December 31, 2023 and Business and Nonbusiness Bankruptcy, County Cases Commenced by Chapter of the Bankruptcy Code, During the 12-Month Period Ending December 31, 2024

Housing Vacancy Rates

Area	Gross Vacancy Rate[3] (%)			Year-Round Vacancy Rate[4] (%)			Rental Vacancy Rate[5] (%)			Homeowner Vacancy Rate[6] (%)		
	2022	2023	2024	2022	2023	2024	2022	2023	2024	2022	2023	2024
MSA[1]	10.9	11.0	12.6	6.7	7.2	7.9	6.4	8.0	7.9	0.9	0.7	1.0
U.S.[2]	9.1	9.0	9.1	7.5	7.5	7.6	5.7	6.5	6.8	0.8	0.8	1.0

Note: (1) Figures cover the Phoenix-Mesa-Chandler, AZ Metropolitan Statistical Area; (2) Figures cover the 75 largest Metropolitan Statistical Areas; (3) The percentage of the total housing inventory that is vacant; (4) The percentage of the housing inventory (excluding seasonal units) that is year-round vacant; (5) The percentage of rental inventory that is vacant for rent; (6) The percentage of homeowner inventory that is vacant for sale
Source: U.S. Census Bureau, Housing Vacancies and Homeownership Annual Statistics: 2022, 2023, 2024

INCOME

Income

Area	Per Capita ($)	Median Household ($)	Average Household ($)
City	40,309	77,041	106,845
MSA[1]	43,395	84,703	113,623
U.S.	43,289	78,538	110,491

Note: (1) Figures cover the Phoenix-Mesa-Chandler, AZ Metropolitan Statistical Area
Source: U.S. Census Bureau, 2019-2023 American Community Survey 5-Year Estimates

Household Income Distribution

Area	Percent of Households Earning							
	Under $15,000	$15,000 -$24,999	$25,000 -$34,999	$35,000 -$49,999	$50,000 -$74,999	$75,000 -$99,999	$100,000 -$149,999	$150,000 and up
City	7.7	5.6	6.7	11.5	17.3	13.7	17.4	20.1
MSA[1]	6.6	5.0	5.9	10.1	16.6	13.9	19.3	22.5
U.S.	8.5	6.6	6.8	10.4	15.7	12.7	17.4	21.9

Note: (1) Figures cover the Phoenix-Mesa-Chandler, AZ Metropolitan Statistical Area
Source: U.S. Census Bureau, 2019-2023 American Community Survey 5-Year Estimates

Poverty Rate

Area	All Ages	Under 18 Years Old	18 to 64 Years Old	65 Years and Over
City	14.3	20.3	12.5	11.7
MSA[1]	11.2	15.1	10.3	9.2
U.S.	12.4	16.3	11.6	10.4

Note: Figures are percentage of people whose income during the past 12 months was below the poverty level;
(1) Figures cover the Phoenix-Mesa-Chandler, AZ Metropolitan Statistical Area
Source: U.S. Census Bureau, 2019-2023 American Community Survey 5-Year Estimates

EMPLOYMENT

Labor Force and Employment

Area	Civilian Labor Force			Workers Employed		
	Dec. 2023	Dec. 2024	% Chg.	Dec. 2023	Dec. 2024	% Chg.
City	913,817	927,572	1.5	887,451	898,365	1.2
MSA[1]	2,660,126	2,699,326	1.5	2,583,768	2,614,930	1.2
U.S.	166,661,000	167,746,000	0.7	160,754,000	161,294,000	0.3

Note: Data is not seasonally adjusted and covers workers 16 years of age and older; (1) Figures cover the
Phoenix-Mesa-Chandler, AZ Metropolitan Statistical Area
Source: Bureau of Labor Statistics, Local Area Unemployment Statistics

Unemployment Rate

Area	2024											
	Jan.	Feb.	Mar.	Apr.	May	Jun.	Jul.	Aug.	Sep.	Oct.	Nov.	Dec.
City	3.0	3.0	2.7	2.5	2.9	3.5	3.8	3.7	3.4	3.4	3.4	3.1
MSA[1]	3.0	3.0	2.7	2.6	3.0	3.5	3.8	3.6	3.4	3.4	3.3	3.1
U.S.	4.1	4.2	3.9	3.5	3.7	4.3	4.5	4.4	3.9	3.9	4.0	3.8

Note: Data is not seasonally adjusted and covers workers 16 years of age and older; (1) Figures cover the
Phoenix-Mesa-Chandler, AZ Metropolitan Statistical Area
Source: Bureau of Labor Statistics, Local Area Unemployment Statistics

Average Wages

Occupation	$/Hr.	Occupation	$/Hr.
Accountants and Auditors	42.29	Maintenance and Repair Workers	25.41
Automotive Mechanics	28.52	Marketing Managers	74.34
Bookkeepers	25.59	Network and Computer Systems Admin.	46.72
Carpenters	28.74	Nurses, Licensed Practical	35.33
Cashiers	16.53	Nurses, Registered	46.26
Computer Programmers	40.51	Nursing Assistants	21.03
Computer Systems Analysts	51.41	Office Clerks, General	24.26
Computer User Support Specialists	32.43	Physical Therapists	50.72
Construction Laborers	23.17	Physicians	101.37
Cooks, Restaurant	19.56	Plumbers, Pipefitters and Steamfitters	33.45
Customer Service Representatives	22.50	Police and Sheriff's Patrol Officers	42.24
Dentists	98.52	Postal Service Mail Carriers	29.45
Electricians	29.58	Real Estate Sales Agents	33.31
Engineers, Electrical	59.00	Retail Salespersons	18.61
Fast Food and Counter Workers	16.50	Sales Representatives, Technical/Scientific	47.67
Financial Managers	75.51	Secretaries, Exc. Legal/Medical/Executive	23.90
First-Line Supervisors of Office Workers	33.09	Security Guards	20.06
General and Operations Managers	59.06	Surgeons	201.58
Hairdressers/Cosmetologists	19.33	Teacher Assistants, Exc. Postsecondary[1]	17.41
Home Health and Personal Care Aides	17.28	Teachers, Secondary School, Exc. Sp. Ed.[1]	33.10
Janitors and Cleaners	18.02	Telemarketers	25.15
Landscaping/Groundskeeping Workers	19.42	Truck Drivers, Heavy/Tractor-Trailer	27.04
Lawyers	81.05	Truck Drivers, Light/Delivery Services	25.25
Maids and Housekeeping Cleaners	17.66	Waiters and Waitresses	23.73

Note: Wage data covers the Phoenix-Mesa-Chandler, AZ Metropolitan Statistical Area; (1) Hourly wages were
calculated from annual wage data based on a 40 hour work week
Source: Bureau of Labor Statistics, Metro Area Occupational Employment & Wage Estimates, May 2024

Employment by Industry

Sector	MSA[1]		U.S.
	Number of Employees	Percent of Total	Percent of Total
Construction	178,100	7.2	5.1
Financial Activities	211,000	8.5	5.8
Government	261,100	10.5	14.9
Information	39,700	1.6	1.9
Leisure and Hospitality	265,200	10.7	10.4
Manufacturing	149,900	6.0	8.0
Mining and Logging	3,700	0.1	0.4
Other Services	79,200	3.2	3.7
Private Education and Health Services	420,600	16.9	16.9
Professional and Business Services	388,000	15.6	14.2
Retail Trade	255,900	10.3	10.0
Transportation, Warehousing, and Utilities	130,800	5.3	4.8
Wholesale Trade	102,400	4.1	3.9

Note: Figures are non-farm employment as of December 2024. Figures are not seasonally adjusted and include workers 16 years of age and older; (1) Figures cover the Phoenix-Mesa-Chandler, AZ Metropolitan Statistical Area
Source: Bureau of Labor Statistics, Current Employment Statistics, Employment, Hours, and Earnings

Employment by Occupation

Occupation Classification	City (%)	MSA[1] (%)	U.S. (%)
Management, Business, Science, and Arts	39.0	41.8	42.0
Natural Resources, Construction, and Maintenance	9.5	8.5	8.6
Production, Transportation, and Material Moving	12.4	11.1	13.0
Sales and Office	22.1	22.9	19.9
Service	16.9	15.8	16.5

Note: Figures cover employed civilians 16 years of age and older; (1) Figures cover the Phoenix-Mesa-Chandler, AZ Metropolitan Statistical Area
Source: U.S. Census Bureau, 2019-2023 American Community Survey 5-Year Estimates

Occupations with Greatest Projected Employment Growth: 2022 – 2032

Occupation[1]	2022 Employment	2032 Projected Employment	Numeric Employment Change	Percent Employment Change
Home Health and Personal Care Aides	68,550	96,120	27,570	40.2
Laborers and Freight, Stock, and Material Movers, Hand	72,140	89,140	17,000	23.6
General and Operations Managers	96,240	111,360	15,120	15.7
Software Developers	39,420	53,530	14,110	35.8
Stockers and Order Fillers	60,920	74,660	13,740	22.6
Registered Nurses	59,110	72,050	12,940	21.9
Fast Food and Counter Workers	85,580	98,010	12,430	14.5
Retail Salespersons	85,240	96,850	11,610	13.6
Heavy and Tractor-Trailer Truck Drivers	43,020	53,850	10,830	25.2
Cooks, Restaurant	28,890	38,830	9,940	34.4

Note: Projections cover Arizona; (1) Sorted by numeric employment change
Source: www.projectionscentral.org, State Occupational Projections, 2022–2032 Long-Term Projections

Fastest-Growing Occupations: 2022 – 2032

Occupation[1]	2022 Employment	2032 Projected Employment	Numeric Employment Change	Percent Employment Change
Nurse Practitioners	6,540	11,200	4,660	71.3
Physician Assistants	3,440	5,180	1,740	50.6
Medical and Health Services Managers	9,580	14,390	4,810	50.2
Data Scientists	2,960	4,380	1,420	48.0
Physical Therapist Assistants	1,480	2,180	700	47.3
Occupational Therapy Assistants	1,140	1,670	530	46.5
Statisticians	1,010	1,460	450	44.6
Solar Photovoltaic Installers	750	1,070	320	42.7
Home Health and Personal Care Aides	68,550	96,120	27,570	40.2
Information Security Analysts (SOC 2018)	3,660	5,110	1,450	39.6

Note: Projections cover Arizona; (1) Sorted by percent employment change and excludes occupations with numeric employment change less than 50
Source: www.projectionscentral.org, State Occupational Projections, 2022–2032 Long-Term Projections

CITY FINANCES

City Government Finances

Component	2022 ($000)	2022 ($ per capita)
Total Revenues	4,742,268	2,776
Total Expenditures	4,083,135	2,390
Debt Outstanding	8,161,345	4,778

Source: U.S. Census Bureau, State & Local Government Finances 2022

City Government Revenue by Source

Source	2022 ($000)	2022 ($ per capita)	2022 (%)
General Revenue			
From Federal Government	562,144	329	11.9
From State Government	817,687	479	17.2
From Local Governments	41,855	25	0.9
Taxes			
Property	289,349	169	6.1
Sales and Gross Receipts	1,214,026	711	25.6
Personal Income	0	0	0.0
Corporate Income	0	0	0.0
Motor Vehicle License	0	0	0.0
Other Taxes	156,543	92	3.3
Current Charges	947,443	555	20.0
Liquor Store	0	0	0.0
Utility	514,132	301	10.8

Source: U.S. Census Bureau, State & Local Government Finances 2022

City Government Expenditures by Function

Function	2022 ($000)	2022 ($ per capita)	2022 (%)
General Direct Expenditures			
Air Transportation	610,572	357	15.0
Corrections	0	0	0.0
Education	34,055	19	0.8
Employment Security Administration	0	0	0.0
Financial Administration	52,873	31	1.3
Fire Protection	361,015	211	8.8
General Public Buildings	11,562	6	0.3
Governmental Administration, Other	46,805	27	1.1
Health	2,327	1	0.1
Highways	142,657	83	3.5
Hospitals	0	0	0.0
Housing and Community Development	276,998	162	6.8
Interest on General Debt	278,919	163	6.8
Judicial and Legal	52,240	30	1.3
Libraries	38,112	22	0.9
Parking	1,765	1	0.0
Parks and Recreation	126,841	74	3.1
Police Protection	547,806	320	13.4
Public Welfare	18,964	11	0.5
Sewerage	93,497	54	2.3
Solid Waste Management	129,317	75	3.2
Veterans' Services	0	0	0.0
Liquor Store	0	0	0.0
Utility	1,067,181	624	26.1

Source: U.S. Census Bureau, State & Local Government Finances 2022

TAXES

State Corporate Income Tax Rates

State	Tax Rate (%)	Income Brackets ($)	Num. of Brackets	Financial Institution Tax Rate (%)[a]	Federal Income Tax Ded.
Arizona	4.9 (b)	Flat rate	1	4.9 (b)	No

Note: Tax rates for tax year 2024; (a) Rates listed are the corporate income tax rate applied to financial institutions or excise taxes based on income. Some states have other taxes based upon the value of deposits or shares; (b) Minimum tax is $800 in California, $250 in District of Columbia, $50 in Arizona and North Dakota (banks), $400 ($100 banks) in Rhode Island, $200 per location in South Dakota (banks), $100 in Utah, in Vermont, simplified entity business tax for residents only at $250, otherwise minimum tax ($100 - $100,000) is based upon gross receipts.
Source: Federation of Tax Administrators, State Corporate Income Tax Rates, January 1, 2025

State Individual Income Tax Rates

State	Tax Rate (%)	Income Brackets ($)	Personal Exemptions ($)			Standard Ded. ($)	
			Single	Married	Depend.	Single	Married
Arizona	2.5	Flat rate	–	–	100 (c)	14,600	29,200

Note: Tax rates for tax year 2024; Local- and county-level taxes are not included; Federal income tax is not deductible on state income tax returns; (c) The personal exemption takes the form of a tax credit instead of a deduction
Source: Federation of Tax Administrators, State Individual Income Tax Rates, January 1, 2025

Various State Sales and Excise Tax Rates

State	State Sales Tax (%)	Gasoline[1] ($/gal.)	Cigarette[2] ($/pack)	Spirits[3] ($/gal.)	Wine[4] ($/gal.)	Beer[5] ($/gal.)	Recreational Marijuana (%)
Arizona	5.6	0.19	2.00	3.00	0.84	0.16	(b)

Note: All tax rates as of January 1, 2025; (1) The American Petroleum Institute has developed a methodology for determining the average tax rate on a gallon of fuel. Rates may include any of the following: excise taxes, environmental fees, storage tank fees, other fees or taxes, general sales tax, and local taxes; (2) The federal excise tax of $1.0066 per pack and local taxes are not included; (3) Rates are those applicable to off-premise sales of 40% alcohol by volume (a.b.v.) distilled spirits in 750ml containers. Local excise taxes are excluded; (4) Rates are those applicable to off-premise sales of 11% a.b.v. non-carbonated wine in 750ml containers; (5) Rates are those applicable to off-premise sales of 4.7% a.b.v. beer in 12 ounce containers; (b) 16% excise tax (retail price)
Source: Tax Foundation, 2025 Facts & Figures: How Does Your State Compare?

State Tax Competitiveness Index

State	Overall Rank	Corporate Tax Rank	Individual Income Tax Rank	Sales Tax Rank	Property Tax Rank	Unemployment Insurance Tax Rank
Arizona	15	13	8	45	13	2

Note: The Tax Foundation's State Tax Competitiveness Index enables policymakers, taxpayers, and business leaders to gauge how their states' tax systems compare. A rank of 1 is best, 50 is worst. Rankings do not average to the total. States without a tax rank equally as 1. DC's scores and rankings do not affect other states. The report shows tax systems as of July 1, 2024 (the beginning of Fiscal Year 2025).
Source: Tax Foundation, State Tax Competitiveness Index 2025

TRANSPORTATION

Means of Transportation to Work

Area	Car/Truck/Van		Public Transportation			Bicycle	Walked	Other Means	Worked at Home
	Drove Alone	Car-pooled	Bus	Subway	Railroad				
City	66.1	10.9	1.8	0.0	0.0	0.4	1.6	2.2	16.9
MSA[1]	66.9	9.7	1.0	0.0	0.0	0.5	1.4	2.0	18.5
U.S.	70.2	8.5	1.7	0.0	0.4	0.4	2.4	1.6	13.5

Note: Figures are percentages and cover workers 16 years of age and older; (1) Figures cover the Phoenix-Mesa-Chandler, AZ Metropolitan Statistical Area
Source: U.S. Census Bureau, 2019-2023 American Community Survey 5-Year Estimates

Travel Time to Work

Area	Less Than 10 Minutes	10 to 19 Minutes	20 to 29 Minutes	30 to 44 Minutes	45 to 59 Minutes	60 to 89 Minutes	90 Minutes or More
City	9.0	26.7	26.8	24.6	7.1	4.2	1.6
MSA[1]	10.2	26.0	24.3	23.7	8.7	5.3	1.8
U.S.	12.6	28.6	21.2	20.8	8.1	6.0	2.8

Note: Note: Figures are percentages and include workers 16 years old and over; (1) Figures cover the Phoenix-Mesa-Chandler, AZ Metropolitan Statistical Area
Source: U.S. Census Bureau, 2019-2023 American Community Survey 5-Year Estimates

Key Congestion Measures

Measure	2000	2010	2015	2020	2022
Annual Hours of Delay, Total (000)	86,505	133,493	156,520	68,645	178,541
Annual Hours of Delay, Per Auto Commuter	45	50	59	25	69
Annual Congestion Cost, Per Auto Commuter ($)	927	1,137	1,232	547	1,441

Note: Figures cover the Phoenix-Mesa AZ urban area
Source: Texas A&M Transportation Institute, 2023 Urban Mobility Report

Freeway Travel Time Index

Measure	1985	1990	1995	2000	2005	2010	2015	2020	2022
Urban Area Index[1]	1.20	1.21	1.22	1.25	1.28	1.28	1.27	1.08	1.22
Urban Area Rank[1,2]	5	7	13	16	14	16	20	44	28

Note: Freeway Travel Time Index—the ratio of travel time in the peak period to the travel time at free-flow conditions. For example, a value of 1.30 indicates a 20-minute free-flow trip takes 26 minutes in the peak (20 minutes x 1.30 = 26 minutes); (1) Covers the Phoenix-Mesa AZ urban area; (2) Rank is based on 101 larger urban areas (#1 = highest travel time index)
Source: Texas A&M Transportation Institute, 2023 Urban Mobility Report

Public Transportation

Agency Name / Mode of Transportation	Vehicles Operated in Maximum Service[1]	Annual Unlinked Passenger Trips[2] (in thous.)	Annual Passenger Miles[3] (in thous.)
City of Phoenix Public Transit Dept. (Valley Metro)			
Bus (purchased transportation)	439	19,227.6	73,463.8
Demand Response (purchased transportation)	110	296.7	3,035.4

Note: (1) Number of revenue vehicles operated by the given mode and type of service to meet the annual maximum service requirement. This is the revenue vehicle count during the peak season of the year; on the week and day that maximum service is provided. Vehicles operated in maximum service (VOMS) exclude atypical days and one-time special events; (2) Number of passengers who boarded public transportation vehicles. Passengers are counted each time they board a vehicle no matter how many vehicles they use to travel from their origin to their destination. (3) Sum of the distances ridden by all passengers during the entire fiscal year.
Source: Federal Transit Administration, National Transit Database, 2023

Air Transportation

Airport Name and Code / Type of Service	Passenger Airlines[1]	Passenger Enplanements	Freight Carriers[2]	Freight (lbs)
Phoenix Sky Harbor International (PHX)				
Domestic service (U.S. carriers only)	36	24,145,821	18	302,779,049
International service (U.S. carriers only)	8	777,479	4	1,047,945

Note: (1) Includes all U.S.-based major, minor and commuter airlines that carried at least one passenger during the year; (2) Includes all U.S.-based airlines and freight carriers that transported at least one pound of freight during the year.
Source: Bureau of Transportation Statistics, The Intermodal Transportation Database, Air Carriers: T-100 Domestic Market (U.S. carriers only), 2024; Bureau of Transportation Statistics, The Intermodal Transportation Database, Air Carriers: T-100 International Market (U.S. carriers only), 2024

BUSINESSES

Major Business Headquarters

Company Name	Industry	Rankings Fortune[1]	Rankings Forbes[2]
Avnet	Wholesalers: electronics and office equipment	157	-
Freeport-McMoRan	Mining, crude-oil production	178	-
Knight-Swift Transportation Hldgs.	Trucking, truck leasing	495	-
Petsmart	Specialty	-	52
Republic Services	Waste management	276	-
Shamrock Foods	Food, drink & tobacco	-	103

Note: (1) Companies that produce a 10-K are ranked 1 to 500 based on 2023 revenue; (2) All private companies with at least $2 billion in annual revenue through the end of their most current fiscal year are ranked 1 to 275; companies listed are headquartered in the city; dashes indicate no ranking
Source: Fortune, "Fortune 500," 2024; Forbes, "America's Largest Private Companies," 2024

Fastest-Growing Businesses

According to *Inc.*, Phoenix is home to three of America's 500 fastest-growing private companies: **Verde Clean** (#219); **Directed IRA** (#391); **The Call Gurus** (#481). Criteria: must be an independent, privately-held, for-profit, U.S. corporation, proprietorship or partnership as of December 31, 2023; revenues must be at least $100,000 in 2020 and $2 million in 2023; must have four-year operating/sales history. *Inc., "America's 500 Fastest-Growing Private Companies," 2024*

According to Deloitte, Phoenix is home to two of North America's 500 fastest-growing high-technology companies: **Virtuous Software** (#219); **qBotica** (#344). Companies are ranked by percentage growth in revenue over a four-year period. Criteria for inclusion: company must be headquartered within North America; must own proprietary intellectual property or technology that is sold to customers in products that contributes to a significant portion of the company's operating revenue; must have been in business for a minumum of four years with 2020 operating revenues of at least $50,000 USD/CD and 2023 operating revenues of at least $5 million USD/CD. *Deloitte, 2024 Technology Fast 500*™

Living Environment

COST OF LIVING

Cost of Living Index

Composite Index	Groceries	Housing	Utilities	Trans-portation	Health Care	Misc. Goods/ Services
106.3	102.8	115.6	106.6	105.4	91.6	102.2

Note: The Cost of Living Index measures regional differences in the cost of consumer goods and services, excluding taxes and non-consumer expenditures, for professional and managerial households in the top income quintile. It is based on more than 50,000 prices covering almost 60 different items for which prices are collected three times a year by chambers of commerce, economic development organizations or university applied economic centers in each participating urban area. The numbers shown should be read as a percentage above or below the national average of 100. For example, a value of 115.4 in the groceries column indicates that grocery prices are 15.4% higher than the national average. Small differences in the index numbers should not be interpreted as significant; Figures cover the Phoenix AZ urban area.
Source: The Council for Community and Economic Research, Cost of Living Index, 2024

Grocery Prices

Area[1]	T-Bone Steak ($/pound)	Frying Chicken ($/pound)	Whole Milk ($/half gal.)	Eggs ($/dozen)	Orange Juice ($/64 oz.)	Coffee ($/11.5 oz.)
City[2]	15.53	1.77	4.76	2.95	4.40	6.24
Avg.	15.42	1.55	4.69	3.25	4.41	5.46
Min.	14.50	1.16	4.43	2.75	4.00	4.85
Max.	17.56	2.89	5.49	4.78	5.54	7.89

*Note: (1) Values for the local area are compared with the average, minimum and maximum values for all 276 areas in the Cost of Living Index; (2) Figures cover the Phoenix AZ urban area; **T-Bone Steak** (price per pound); **Frying Chicken** (price per pound, whole fryer); **Whole Milk** (half gallon carton); **Eggs** (price per dozen, Grade A, large); **Orange Juice** (64 oz. Tropicana or Florida Natural); **Coffee** (11.5 oz. can, vacuum-packed, Maxwell House, Hills Bros, or Folgers).*
Source: The Council for Community and Economic Research, Cost of Living Index, 2024

Housing and Utility Costs

Area[1]	New Home Price ($)	Apartment Rent ($/month)	All Electric ($/month)	Part Electric ($/month)	Other Energy ($/month)	Telephone ($/month)
City[2]	609,926	1,792	232.03	-	-	187.62
Avg.	515,975	1,550	210.99	123.07	82.07	194.99
Min.	265,375	692	104.33	53.68	36.26	179.42
Max.	2,775,821	5,719	529.02	397.28	361.63	223.33

*Note: (1) Values for the local area are compared with the average, minimum and maximum values for all 276 areas in the Cost of Living Index; (2) Figures cover the Phoenix AZ urban area; **New Home Price** (2,400 sf living area, 8,000 sf lot, in urban area with full utilities); **Apartment Rent** (950 sf 2 bedroom/1.5 or 2 bath, unfurnished, excluding all utilities except water); **All Electric** (average monthly cost for an all-electric home); **Part Electric** (average monthly cost for a part-electric home); **Other Energy** (average monthly cost for natural gas, fuel oil, coal, wood, and any other forms of energy except electricity); **Telephone** (price includes the base monthly rate plus taxes and fees for three lines of mobile phone service).*
Source: The Council for Community and Economic Research, Cost of Living Index, 2024

Health Care, Transportation, and Other Costs

Area[1]	Doctor ($/visit)	Dentist ($/visit)	Optometrist ($/visit)	Gasoline ($/gallon)	Beauty Salon ($/visit)	Men's Shirt ($)
City[2]	99.00	127.08	103.50	3.64	55.36	22.95
Avg.	143.77	117.51	129.23	3.32	48.57	38.14
Min.	36.74	58.67	67.33	2.80	24.00	13.41
Max.	270.44	216.82	307.33	5.28	94.00	63.89

*Note: (1) Values for the local area are compared with the average, minimum and maximum values for all 276 areas in the Cost of Living Index; (2) Figures cover the Phoenix AZ urban area; **Doctor** (general practitioners routine exam of an established patient); **Dentist** (adult teeth cleaning and periodic oral examination); **Optometrist** (full vision eye exam for established adult patient); **Gasoline** (one gallon regular unleaded, national brand, including all taxes, cash price at self-service pump if available); **Beauty Salon** (woman's shampoo, trim, and blow-dry); **Men's Shirt** (cotton/polyester dress shirt, pinpoint weave, long sleeves).*
Source: The Council for Community and Economic Research, Cost of Living Index, 2024

HOUSING

Homeownership Rate

Area	2017 (%)	2018 (%)	2019 (%)	2020 (%)	2021 (%)	2022 (%)	2023 (%)	2024 (%)
MSA[1]	64.0	65.3	65.9	67.9	65.2	68.0	69.7	69.4
U.S.	63.9	64.4	64.6	66.6	65.5	65.8	65.9	65.6

Note: (1) Figures cover the Phoenix-Mesa-Chandler, AZ Metropolitan Statistical Area
Source: U.S. Census Bureau, Housing Vacancies and Homeownership Annual Statistics: 2017-2024

House Price Index (HPI)

Area	National Ranking[2]	Quarterly Change (%)	One-Year Change (%)	Five-Year Change (%)	Since 1991Q1 (%)
MSA[1]	200	0.13	3.14	69.09	488.41
U.S.[3]	–	1.43	4.51	57.13	327.82

Note: The HPI is a weighted repeat sales index. It measures average price changes in repeat sales or refinancings on the same properties. This information is obtained by reviewing repeat mortgage transactions on single-family properties whose mortgages have been purchased or securitized by Fannie Mae or Freddie Mac since January 1975; (1) Figures cover the Phoenix-Mesa-Scottsdale, AZ Metropolitan Statistical Area; (2) Rankings are based on annual percentage change for all metro areas containing at least 15,000 transactions over the last 10 years and ranges from 1 to 241; (3) figures based on a weighted average of Census Division estimates using a seasonally adjusted, purchase-only index; all figures are for the period ending December 31, 2024
Source: Federal Housing Finance Agency, Change in FHFA Metropolitan Area House Price Indexes, All Transactions Index, 2024Q4

Home Value

Area	Under $100,000	$100,000 -$199,999	$200,000 -$299,999	$300,000 -$399,999	$400,000 -$499,999	$500,000 -$999,999	$1,000,000 or more	Median ($)
City	5.7	6.6	20.5	21.1	16.0	24.9	5.2	381,900
MSA[1]	6.7	5.9	16.8	20.3	17.5	26.9	5.9	401,400
U.S.	12.1	17.8	19.5	14.4	10.5	19.1	6.5	303,400

Note: Figures are percentages except for median and cover owner-occupied housing units; (1) Figures cover the Phoenix-Mesa-Chandler, AZ Metropolitan Statistical Area
Source: U.S. Census Bureau, 2019-2023 American Community Survey 5-Year Estimates

Year Housing Structure Built

Area	2020 or Later	2010 -2019	2000 -2009	1990 -1999	1980 -1989	1970 -1979	1960 -1969	1950 -1959	1940 -1949	Before 1940	Median Year
City	1.1	8.6	16.4	14.3	17.3	18.9	9.5	9.6	2.4	1.9	1984
MSA[1]	1.9	12.2	23.7	17.9	16.2	14.9	6.3	4.8	1.1	0.9	1993
U.S.	1.2	8.9	13.6	12.8	13.0	14.4	10.0	9.7	4.5	11.9	1980

Note: Figures are percentages except for Median Year; Note: (1) Figures cover the Phoenix-Mesa-Chandler, AZ Metropolitan Statistical Area
Source: U.S. Census Bureau, 2019-2023 American Community Survey 5-Year Estimates

Gross Monthly Rent

Area	Under $500	$500 -$999	$1,000 -$1,499	$1,500 -$1,999	$2,000 -$2,499	$2,500 -$2,999	$3,000 and up	Median ($)
City	3.5	13.5	36.2	29.1	12.0	3.7	2.0	1,458
MSA[1]	2.7	10.8	31.5	30.9	15.3	5.2	3.5	1,581
U.S.	6.5	22.3	29.5	20.2	10.8	4.8	5.9	1,348

Note: Figures are percentages except for median; Gross rent is the contract rent plus the estimated average monthly cost of utilities (electricity, gas, and water and sewer) and fuels (oil, coal, kerosene, wood, etc.) if these are paid by the renter (or paid for the renter by someone else); (1) Figures cover the Phoenix-Mesa-Chandler, AZ Metropolitan Statistical Area
Source: U.S. Census Bureau, 2019-2023 American Community Survey 5-Year Estimates

HEALTH

Health Risk Factors

Category	MSA[1] (%)	U.S. (%)
Adults aged 18–64 who have any kind of health care coverage	86.2	90.8
Adults who reported being in good or better health	82.0	81.8
Adults who have been told they have high blood cholesterol	38.5	36.9
Adults who have been told they have high blood pressure	31.7	34.0
Adults who are current smokers	9.5	12.1
Adults who currently use e-cigarettes	6.5	7.7
Adults who currently use chewing tobacco, snuff, or snus	2.4	3.2
Adults who are heavy drinkers[2]	5.6	6.1
Adults who are binge drinkers[3]	14.9	15.2
Adults who are overweight (BMI 25.0 - 29.9)	34.3	34.4
Adults who are obese (BMI 30.0 - 99.8)	31.7	34.3
Adults who participated in any physical activities in the past month	79.6	75.8

Note: All figures are crude prevalence; (1) Figures cover the Phoenix-Mesa-Scottsdale, AZ Metropolitan Statistical Area; (2) Heavy drinkers are classified as adult men having more than 14 drinks per week and adult women having more than 7 drinks per week; (3) Binge drinkers are classified as males having five or more drinks on one occasion or females having four or more drinks on one occasion
Source: Centers for Disease Control and Prevention, Behaviorial Risk Factor Surveillance System, SMART: Selected Metropolitan Area Risk Trends, 2023

Acute and Chronic Health Conditions

Category	MSA[1] (%)	U.S. (%)
Adults who have ever been told they had a heart attack	3.9	4.2
Adults who have ever been told they have angina or coronary heart disease	3.3	4.0
Adults who have ever been told they had a stroke	2.9	3.3
Adults who have ever been told they have asthma	15.4	15.7
Adults who have ever been told they have arthritis	23.8	26.3
Adults who have ever been told they have diabetes[2]	11.0	11.5
Adults who have ever been told they had skin cancer	7.5	5.6
Adults who have ever been told they had any other types of cancer	8.7	8.4
Adults who have ever been told they have COPD	5.2	6.4
Adults who have ever been told they have kidney disease	4.4	3.7
Adults who have ever been told they have a form of depression	17.6	22.0

Note: All figures are crude prevalence; (1) Figures cover the Phoenix-Mesa-Scottsdale, AZ Metropolitan Statistical Area; (2) Figures do not include pregnancy-related, borderline, or pre-diabetes
Source: Centers for Disease Control and Prevention, Behaviorial Risk Factor Surveillance System, SMART: Selected Metropolitan Area Risk Trends, 2023

Health Screening and Vaccination Rates

Category	MSA[1] (%)	U.S. (%)
Adults who have ever been tested for HIV	34.7	37.5
Adults who have had their blood cholesterol checked within the last five years	87.7	87.0
Adults aged 65+ who have had flu shot within the past year	61.8	63.4
Adults aged 65+ who have ever had a pneumonia vaccination	73.3	71.9

Note: All figures are crude prevalence; (1) Figures cover the Phoenix-Mesa-Scottsdale, AZ Metropolitan Statistical Area.
Source: Centers for Disease Control and Prevention, Behaviorial Risk Factor Surveillance System, SMART: Selected Metropolitan Area Risk Trends, 2023

Disability Status

Category	MSA[1] (%)	U.S. (%)
Adults who reported being deaf	7.3	7.4
Are you blind or have serious difficulty seeing, even when wearing glasses?	5.0	4.9
Do you have difficulty doing errands alone?	6.8	7.8
Do you have difficulty dressing or bathing?	2.9	3.6
Do you have serious difficulty concentrating/remembering/making decisions?	12.8	13.7
Do you have serious difficulty walking or climbing stairs?	12.5	13.2

Note: All figures are crude prevalence; (1) Figures cover the Phoenix-Mesa-Scottsdale, AZ Metropolitan Statistical Area.
Source: Centers for Disease Control and Prevention, Behaviorial Risk Factor Surveillance System, SMART: Selected Metropolitan Area Risk Trends, 2023

Mortality Rates for the Top 10 Causes of Death in the U.S.

ICD-10[a] Sub-Chapter	ICD-10[a] Code	Crude Mortality Rate[2] per 100,000 population	
		County[3]	U.S.
Malignant neoplasms	C00-C97	155.2	182.7
Ischaemic heart diseases	I20-I25	98.4	109.6
Provisional assignment of new diseases of uncertain etiology[1]	U00-U49	71.4	65.3
Other forms of heart disease	I30-I51	41.2	65.1
Other degenerative diseases of the nervous system	G30-G31	70.1	52.4
Other external causes of accidental injury	W00-X59	58.5	52.3
Cerebrovascular diseases	I60-I69	39.9	49.1
Chronic lower respiratory diseases	J40-J47	39.1	43.5
Hypertensive diseases	I10-I15	44.8	38.9
Organic, including symptomatic, mental disorders	F01-F09	14.0	33.9

Note: (a) ICD-10 = International Classification of Diseases 10th Revision; (1) Includes COVID-19, adverse effects to COVID-19 vaccines, SARS, and vaping-related disorders; (2) Crude mortality rates are a three-year average covering 2021-2023; (3) Figures cover Maricopa County.
Source: Centers for Disease Control and Prevention, National Center for Health Statistics. National Vital Statistics System, Mortality 2018-2023 on CDC WONDER Online Database

Mortality Rates for Selected Causes of Death

Cause of Death	ICD-10[a] Code	Crude Mortality Rate[1] per 100,000 population	
		County[2]	U.S.
Accidental poisoning and exposure to noxious substances	X40-X49	34.7	30.5
Alzheimer disease	G30	35.7	35.4
Assault	X85-Y09	7.7	7.3
COVID-19	U07.1	71.4	65.3
Diabetes mellitus	E10-E14	29.7	30.0
Diseases of the liver	K70-K76	19.8	20.8
Human immunodeficiency virus (HIV) disease	B20-B24	1.3	1.5
Influenza and pneumonia	J09-J18	10.7	13.4
Intentional self-harm	X60-X84	17.1	14.7
Malnutrition	E40-E46	6.2	6.0
Obesity and other hyperalimentation	E65-E68	3.2	3.1
Renal failure	N17-N19	8.0	16.4
Transport accidents	V01-V99	16.5	14.4

Note: (a) ICD-10 = International Classification of Diseases 10th Revision; (1) Crude mortality rates are a three-year average covering 2021-2023; (2) Figures cover Maricopa County; Data are suppressed when the data meet the criteria for confidentiality constraints; Crude mortality rates are flagged as unreliable when the rate would be calculated with a numerator of 20 or less.
Source: Centers for Disease Control and Prevention, National Center for Health Statistics. National Vital Statistics System, Mortality 2018-2023 on CDC WONDER Online Database

Health Insurance Coverage

Area	With Health Insurance	With Private Health Insurance	With Public Health Insurance	Without Health Insurance	Population Under Age 19 Without Health Insurance
City	85.5	58.6	34.6	14.5	9.8
MSA[1]	89.3	66.2	34.1	10.7	8.6
U.S.	91.4	67.3	36.3	8.6	5.4

Note: Figures are percentages that cover the civilian noninstitutionalized population; (1) Figures cover the Phoenix-Mesa-Chandler, AZ Metropolitan Statistical Area
Source: U.S. Census Bureau, 2019-2023 American Community Survey 5-Year Estimates

Number of Medical Professionals

Area	MDs[3]	DOs[3,4]	Dentists	Podiatrists	Chiropractors	Optometrists
County[1] (number)	11,751	1,721	3,382	338	1,573	804
County[1] (rate[2])	258.2	37.8	73.7	7.4	34.3	17.5
U.S. (rate[2])	302.5	29.2	74.6	6.4	29.5	18.0

Note: Data as of 2023 unless noted; (1) Data covers Maricopa County; (2) Number of medical professionals per 100,000 population; (3) Data as of 2022 and includes all active, non-federal physicians; (4) Doctor of Osteopathic Medicine
Source: U.S. Department of Health and Human Services, Health Resources and Services Administration, Bureau of Health Professions, Area Resource File (ARF) 2023-2024

Best Hospitals

According to *U.S. News,* the Phoenix-Mesa-Chandler, AZ metro area is home to four of the best hospitals in the U.S.: **Banner Rehabilitation Hospital** (1 adult specialty); **Banner-University Medical Center Phoenix** (1 adult specialty); **Barrow Neurological Institute** (1 adult specialty); **Mayo Clinic-Arizona** (Honor Roll/10 adult specialties). The hospitals listed were nationally ranked in at least one of 15 adult or 11 pediatric specialties. The number of specialties shown cover the parent hospital. Only 160 U.S. hospitals performed well enough to be nationally ranked in one or more specialties. Twenty hospitals in the U.S. made the Honor Roll. The Best Hospitals Honor Roll takes both the national rankings and the procedure and condition ratings into account. Hospitals received points if they were nationally ranked in one of the 15 adult specialties—the higher they ranked, the more points they got—and how many ratings of "high performing" they earned in the 20 procedures and conditions. *U.S. News Online, "America's Best Hospitals 2024-25"*

According to *U.S. News,* the Phoenix-Mesa-Chandler, AZ metro area is home to one of the best children's hospitals in the U.S.: **Phoenix Children's Hospital** (8 pediatric specialties). The hospital listed was highly ranked in at least one of 11 pediatric specialties. One hundred five children's hospitals in the U.S. were nationally ranked in at least one specialty. Hospitals received points for being ranked in a specialty, and the 10 hospitals with the most points across the 11 specialties make up the Honor Roll. *U.S. News Online, "America's Best Children's Hospitals 2024-25"*

EDUCATION

Public School District Statistics

District Name	Schls	Pupils	Pupil/ Teacher Ratio	Minority Pupils[1] (%)	Total Rev. per Pupil ($)	Total Exp. per Pupil ($)
Alhambra Elementary District	18	9,854	17.2	95.6	14,709	13,717
Balsz Elementary District	6	2,092	16.0	95.5	13,111	14,734
Cartwright Elementary District	23	13,720	19.9	97.7	15,359	16,285
Creighton Elementary District	11	4,900	16.8	94.5	14,661	13,562
Deer Valley Unified District	41	32,837	17.0	38.6	11,886	11,201
Fowler Elementary District	8	3,511	19.8	95.8	10,595	11,620
Isaac Elementary District	13	4,826	15.9	98.5	12,056	15,054
Madison Elementary District	9	5,874	21.1	56.4	15,151	13,461
Osborn Elementary District	7	2,425	18.8	89.0	17,439	13,425
Paradise Valley Unified District	45	27,034	15.5	48.7	14,433	14,378
Pendergast Elementary District	13	8,251	19.9	91.0	12,368	12,408
Phoenix Elementary District	17	5,034	14.6	93.2	17,650	16,830
Phoenix Union High SD	20	26,753	19.0	96.3	17,636	14,520
Portable Practical Ed. Prep.	2	5,547	n/a	63.0	10,437	9,664
Roosevelt Elementary District	20	7,274	16.4	97.3	20,704	17,489

Note: Table includes school districts with 2,000 or more students; (1) Percentage of students that are not non-Hispanic white.
Source: U.S. Department of Education, National Center for Education Statistics, Common Core of Data, Local Education Agency (School District) Universe Survey: School Year 2023-2024; U.S. Department of Education, National Center for Education Statistics, Common Core of Data, School District Finance Survey (F-33): School Year 2021–22

Best High Schools

According to *U.S. News,* Phoenix is home to two of the top 500 high schools in the U.S.: **BASIS Ahwatukee** (#34); **BASIS Phoenix** (#45). Nearly 25,000 public, magnet and charter schools were ranked based on their performance on state assessments and how well they prepare students for college. *U.S. News & World Report, "Best High Schools 2024"*

Highest Level of Education

Area	Less than H.S.	H.S. Diploma	Some College, No Deg.	Associate Degree	Bachelor's Degree	Master's Degree	Prof. School Degree	Doctorate Degree
City	15.6	23.1	21.1	7.9	19.9	8.9	2.3	1.3
MSA[1]	10.5	22.7	23.0	9.2	21.6	9.4	2.1	1.4
U.S.	10.6	26.2	19.4	8.8	21.3	9.8	2.3	1.6

Note: Figures cover persons age 25 and over; (1) Figures cover the Phoenix-Mesa-Chandler, AZ Metropolitan Statistical Area
Source: U.S. Census Bureau, 2019-2023 American Community Survey 5-Year Estimates

Educational Attainment by Race

Area	High School Graduate or Higher (%)					Bachelor's Degree or Higher (%)				
	Total	White	Black	Asian	Hisp.[2]	Total	White	Black	Asian	Hisp.[2]
City	84.4	91.2	89.2	89.2	66.9	32.3	38.9	27.3	62.6	13.6
MSA[1]	89.5	93.7	91.6	90.3	73.5	34.6	38.2	29.8	60.9	16.4
U.S.	89.4	92.9	88.1	88.0	72.5	35.0	37.7	24.7	57.0	19.9

Note: Figures shown cover persons 25 years old and over; (1) Figures cover the Phoenix-Mesa-Chandler, AZ Metropolitan Statistical Area; (2) People of Hispanic origin can be of any race
Source: U.S. Census Bureau, 2019-2023 American Community Survey 5-Year Estimates

School Enrollment by Grade and Control

Area	Preschool (%)		Kindergarten (%)		Grades 1 - 4 (%)		Grades 5 - 8 (%)		Grades 9 - 12 (%)	
	Public	Private	Public	Private	Public	Private	Public	Private	Public	Private
City	62.6	37.4	86.7	13.3	88.9	11.1	91.5	8.5	92.2	7.8
MSA[1]	60.3	39.7	85.5	14.5	88.1	11.9	90.4	9.6	91.9	8.1
U.S.	58.7	41.3	85.2	14.8	87.2	12.8	87.9	12.1	89.0	11.0

Note: Figures shown cover persons 3 years old and over; (1) Figures cover the Phoenix-Mesa-Chandler, AZ Metropolitan Statistical Area
Source: U.S. Census Bureau, 2019-2023 American Community Survey 5-Year Estimates

Higher Education

Four-Year Colleges			Two-Year Colleges			Medical Schools[1]	Law Schools[2]	Voc/ Tech[3]
Public	Private Non-profit	Private For-profit	Public	Private Non-profit	Private For-profit			
6	8	15	8	0	13	3	1	25

Note: Figures cover institutions located within the Phoenix-Mesa-Chandler, AZ Metropolitan Statistical Area and include main campuses only; (1) includes schools accredited by the Liaison Committee on Medical Education and the American Osteopathic Association's Commission on Osteopathic College Accreditation; (2) includes ABA-accredited schools, schools with provisional ABA accreditation, and state accredited schools; (3) includes all schools with programs that are less than 2 years.
Source: National Center for Education Statistics, Integrated Postsecondary Education System (IPEDS), 2023-24; Wikipedia, List of Medical Schools in the United States, accessed May 2, 2025; Wikipedia, List of Law Schools in the United States, accessed May 2, 2025

According to *U.S. News & World Report*, the Phoenix-Mesa-Chandler, AZ metro area is home to one of the top 200 national universities in the U.S.: **Arizona State University** (#121 tie). The indicators used to capture academic quality fall into a number of categories: assessment by administrators at peer institutions; retention of students; faculty resources; student selectivity; financial resources; alumni giving; high school counselor ratings of colleges; and graduation rate. *U.S. News & World Report, "America's Best Colleges 2025"*

According to *U.S. News & World Report*, the Phoenix-Mesa-Chandler, AZ metro area is home to one of the top 100 law schools in the U.S.: **Arizona State University (O'Connor)** (#45). The rankings are based on a weighted average of 12 measures of quality: peer assessment score; assessment score by lawyers/judges; median LSAT scores; median undergrad GPA; acceptance rate; employment rates for graduates; placement success; bar passage rate; faculty resources; expenditures per student; student/faculty ratio; and library resources. *U.S. News & World Report, "America's Best Graduate Schools, Law, 2025"*

According to *U.S. News & World Report*, the Phoenix-Mesa-Chandler, AZ metro area is home to one of the top 75 business schools in the U.S.: **Arizona State University (W.P. Carey)** (#35 tie). The rankings are based on a weighted average of the following nine measures: quality assessment; peer assessment; recruiter assessment; placement success; mean starting salary and bonus; student selectivity; mean GMAT and GRE scores; mean undergraduate GPA; and acceptance rate. *U.S. News & World Report, "America's Best Graduate Schools, Business, 2025"*

EMPLOYERS

Major Employers

Company Name	Industry
Amazon.com	Online retail
Arizona Dept of Transportation	Public transportation
Arizona State University	Higher education
Banner Health	Healthcare
City of Mesa	Local government
City of Phoenix	Local government
Fry's Food Stores of Arizona Inc.	Grocery
Grand Canyon Education	Colleges & universities
Kroger	Grocery
Maricopa County	Local government
State of Arizona	State government
University of Arizona	Higher education
Veterans Health Administration	General medical & surgical hospitals
Wal-Mart Stores	Retail
Wells Fargo	Financial services

Note: Companies shown are located within the Phoenix-Mesa-Chandler, AZ Metropolitan Statistical Area.
Source: Chambers of Commerce; State Departments of Labor; Wikipedia

Best Companies to Work For

Avnet; Banner Health, headquartered in Phoenix, are among the "Best Places to Work in IT." To qualify, companies had to have a minimum of 100 total employees and five IT employees. The best places to work were selected based on DEI (diversity, equity, and inclusion) practices; IT turnover, promotions, and growth; IT retention and engagement programs; remote/hybrid working; benefits and perks (such as elder care and child care, flextime, and reimbursement for college tuition); and training and career development opportunities. *Computerworld, "Best Places to Work in IT," 2025*

PUBLIC SAFETY

Crime Rate

Area	Total Crime Rate	Violent Crime Rate				Property Crime Rate		
		Murder	Rape	Robbery	Aggrav. Assault	Burglary	Larceny -Theft	Motor Vehicle Theft
City	3,268.6	11.5	65.6	168.8	538.9	342.6	1,577.4	563.9
U.S.	2,290.9	5.7	38.0	66.5	264.1	250.7	1,347.2	318.7

Note: Figures are crimes per 100,000 population.
Source: FBI, Table 8, Offenses Known to Law Enforcement, by State by City, 2023

Hate Crimes

Area	Number of Quarters Reported	Number of Incidents per Bias Motivation					
		Race/Ethnicity/ Ancestry	Religion	Sexual Orientation	Disability	Gender	Gender Identity
City[1]	4	80	12	18	0	11	4
U.S.	4	5,900	2,699	2,077	187	92	492

Note: (1) Figures include at least one incident reported with more than one bias motivation.
Source: Federal Bureau of Investigation, Hate Crime Statistics 2023

Identity Theft Consumer Reports

Area	Reports	Reports per 100,000 Population	Rank[2]
MSA[1]	16,677	338	45
U.S.	1,135,291	339	-

Note: (1) Figures cover the Phoenix-Mesa-Chandler, AZ Metropolitan Statistical Area; (2) Rank ranges from 1 to 401 where 1 indicates greatest number of identity theft reports per 100,000 population
Source: Federal Trade Commission, Consumer Sentinel Network Data Book 2024

Fraud and Other Consumer Reports

Area	Reports	Reports per 100,000 Population	Rank[2]
MSA[1]	76,729	1,553	50
U.S.	5,360,641	1,601	-

Note: (1) Figures cover the Phoenix-Mesa-Chandler, AZ Metropolitan Statistical Area; (2) Rank ranges from 1 to 401 where 1 indicates greatest number of fraud and other consumer reports per 100,000 population
Source: Federal Trade Commission, Consumer Sentinel Network Data Book 2024

POLITICS

2024 Presidential Election Results

Area	Trump (Rep.)	Harris (Dem.)	Stein (Green)	Kennedy (Ind.)	Oliver (Lib.)	Other
Maricopa County	51.0	47.5	0.6	0.0	0.5	0.4
U.S.	49.7	48.2	0.6	0.5	0.4	0.6

Note: Results are percentages and may not add to 100% due to rounding
Source: Dave Leip's Atlas of U.S. Presidential Elections

SPORTS

Professional Sports Teams

Team Name	League	Year Established
Arizona Cardinals	National Football League (NFL)	1988
Arizona Diamondbacks	Major League Baseball (MLB)	1998
Phoenix Suns	National Basketball Association (NBA)	1968

Note: Includes teams located in the Phoenix-Mesa-Chandler, AZ Metropolitan Statistical Area.
Source: Wikipedia, Major Professional Sports Teams of the United States and Canada, May 1, 2025

CLIMATE

Average and Extreme Temperatures

Temperature	Jan	Feb	Mar	Apr	May	Jun	Jul	Aug	Sep	Oct	Nov	Dec	Yr.
Extreme High (°F)	88	92	100	105	113	122	118	116	118	107	93	88	122
Average High (°F)	66	70	75	84	93	103	105	103	99	88	75	67	86
Average Temp. (°F)	53	57	62	70	78	88	93	91	85	74	62	54	72
Average Low (°F)	40	44	48	55	63	72	80	78	72	60	48	41	59
Extreme Low (°F)	17	22	25	37	40	51	66	61	47	34	27	22	17

Note: Figures cover the years 1948-1990
Source: National Climatic Data Center, International Station Meteorological Climate Summary, 9/96

Average Precipitation/Snowfall/Humidity

Precip./Humidity	Jan	Feb	Mar	Apr	May	Jun	Jul	Aug	Sep	Oct	Nov	Dec	Yr.
Avg. Precip. (in.)	0.7	0.6	0.8	0.3	0.1	0.1	0.8	1.0	0.7	0.6	0.6	0.9	7.3
Avg. Snowfall (in.)	Tr	Tr	0	0	0	0	0	0	0	0	0	Tr	Tr
Avg. Rel. Hum. 5am (%)	68	63	56	45	37	33	47	53	50	53	59	66	53
Avg. Rel. Hum. 5pm (%)	34	28	24	17	14	12	21	24	23	24	28	34	24

Note: Figures cover the years 1948-1990; Tr = Trace amounts (<0.05 in. of rain; <0.5 in. of snow)
Source: National Climatic Data Center, International Station Meteorological Climate Summary, 9/96

Weather Conditions

Temperature			Daytime Sky			Precipitation		
10°F & below	32°F & below	90°F & above	Clear	Partly cloudy	Cloudy	0.01 inch or more precip.	0.1 inch or more snow/ice	Thunder-storms
0	10	167	186	125	54	37	< 1	23

Note: Figures are average number of days per year and cover the years 1948-1990
Source: National Climatic Data Center, International Station Meteorological Climate Summary, 9/96

HAZARDOUS WASTE

Superfund Sites

The Phoenix-Mesa-Chandler, AZ metro area is home to six sites on the EPA's Superfund National Priorities List (NPL) or Superfund Alternative Approach (SAA) list: **Cyprus Tohono Mine** (SAA); **Hassayampa Landfill** (Final NPL); **Indian Bend Wash Area** (Final NPL); **Motorola, Inc. (52nd Street Plant)** (Final NPL); **Phoenix-Goodyear Airport Area** (Final NPL); **Williams Air Force Base** (Final NPL). The Superfund alternative approach uses the same investigation and cleanup process and standards that are used for sites listed on the National Priorities List. The SAA is an alternative to listing a site on the NPL; it is not an alternative to Superfund or the Superfund process. There are a total of 1,445 Superfund sites with a status of proposed or final on both lists in the United States.
U.S. Environmental Protection Agency, National Priorities List, May 1, 2025; U.S. Environmental Protection Agency, Superfund Alternative Approach Sites, May 1, 2025

AIR QUALITY

Air Quality Trends: Ozone

	1990	1995	2000	2005	2010	2015	2020	2021	2022	2023
MSA[1]	0.080	0.086	0.082	0.077	0.075	0.072	0.079	0.079	0.074	0.077
U.S.	0.087	0.089	0.081	0.080	0.072	0.068	0.066	0.067	0.067	0.070

Note: (1) Data covers the Phoenix-Mesa-Chandler, AZ Metropolitan Statistical Area. The values shown are the composite ozone concentration averages among trend sites based on the highest fourth daily maximum 8-hour concentration in parts per million. These trends are based on sites having an adequate record of monitoring data during the trend period. Data from exceptional events are included.
Source: U.S. Environmental Protection Agency, Air Quality Monitoring Information, "Air Quality Trends by City, 1990-2023"

Air Quality Index

Area	Percent of Days when Air Quality was...[2]					AQI Statistics[2]	
	Good	Moderate	Unhealthy for Sensitive Groups	Unhealthy	Very Unhealthy	Maximum	Median
MSA[1]	8.5	67.9	20.3	2.7	0.3	709	78

Note: (1) Data covers the Phoenix-Mesa-Chandler, AZ Metropolitan Statistical Area; (2) Based on 365 days with AQI data in 2023. Air Quality Index (AQI) is an index for reporting daily air quality. EPA calculates the AQI for five major air pollutants regulated by the Clean Air Act: ground-level ozone, particle pollution (aka particulate matter), carbon monoxide, sulfur dioxide, and nitrogen dioxide. The AQI runs from 0 to 500. The higher the AQI value, the greater the level of air pollution and the greater the health concern. There are six AQI categories: "Good" AQI is between 0 and 50. Air quality is considered satisfactory; "Moderate" AQI is between 51 and 100. Air quality is acceptable; "Unhealthy for Sensitive Groups" When AQI values are between 101 and 150, members of sensitive groups may experience health effects; "Unhealthy" When AQI values are between 151 and 200 everyone may begin to experience health effects; "Very Unhealthy" AQI values between 201 and 300 trigger a health alert; "Hazardous" AQI values over 300 trigger warnings of emergency conditions (not shown).
Source: U.S. Environmental Protection Agency, Air Quality Index Report, 2023

Air Quality Index Pollutants

Area	Percent of Days when AQI Pollutant was...[2]					
	Carbon Monoxide	Nitrogen Dioxide	Ozone	Sulfur Dioxide	Particulate Matter 2.5	Particulate Matter 10
MSA[1]	0.0	0.0	41.9	(3)	24.1	34.0

Note: (1) Data covers the Phoenix-Mesa-Chandler, AZ Metropolitan Statistical Area; (2) Based on 365 days with AQI data in 2023. The Air Quality Index (AQI) is an index for reporting daily air quality. EPA calculates the AQI for five major air pollutants regulated by the Clean Air Act: ground-level ozone, particle pollution (also known as particulate matter), carbon monoxide, sulfur dioxide, and nitrogen dioxide. The AQI runs from 0 to 500. The higher the AQI value, the greater the level of air pollution and the greater the health concern; (3) Sulfur dioxide is no longer included in this table because SO_2 concentrations tend to be very localized and not necessarily representative of broad geographical areas like counties and CBSAs.
Source: U.S. Environmental Protection Agency, Air Quality Index Report, 2023

Maximum Air Pollutant Concentrations: Particulate Matter, Ozone, CO and Lead

	Particulate Matter 10 (ug/m^3)	Particulate Matter 2.5 Wtd AM (ug/m^3)	Particulate Matter 2.5 24-Hr (ug/m^3)	Ozone (ppm)	Carbon Monoxide (ppm)	Lead (ug/m^3)
MSA[1] Level	387	9.8	32	0.083	2	n/a
NAAQS[2]	150	15	35	0.075	9	0.15
Met NAAQS[2]	No	Yes	Yes	No	Yes	n/a

Note: (1) Data covers the Phoenix-Mesa-Chandler, AZ Metropolitan Statistical Area; Data from exceptional events are included; (2) National Ambient Air Quality Standards; ppm = parts per million; ug/m^3 = micrograms per cubic meter; n/a not available.
Concentrations: Particulate Matter 10 (coarse particulate)—highest second maximum 24-hour concentration; Particulate Matter 2.5 Wtd AM (fine particulate)—highest weighted annual mean concentration; Particulate Matter 2.5 24-Hour (fine particulate)—highest 98th percentile 24-hour concentration; Ozone—highest fourth daily maximum 8-hour concentration; Carbon Monoxide—highest second maximum non-overlapping 8-hour concentration; Lead—maximum running 3-month average
Source: U.S. Environmental Protection Agency, Air Quality Monitoring Information, "Air Quality Statistics by City, 2023"

Maximum Air Pollutant Concentrations: Nitrogen Dioxide and Sulfur Dioxide

	Nitrogen Dioxide AM (ppb)	Nitrogen Dioxide 1-Hr (ppb)	Sulfur Dioxide AM (ppb)	Sulfur Dioxide 1-Hr (ppb)	Sulfur Dioxide 24-Hr (ppb)
MSA[1] Level	24	58	n/a	4	n/a
NAAQS[2]	53	100	30	75	140
Met NAAQS[2]	Yes	Yes	n/a	Yes	n/a

Note: (1) Data covers the Phoenix-Mesa-Chandler, AZ Metropolitan Statistical Area; Data from exceptional events are included; (2) National Ambient Air Quality Standards; ppm = parts per million; ug/m^3 = micrograms per cubic meter; n/a not available.
Concentrations: Nitrogen Dioxide AM—highest arithmetic mean concentration; Nitrogen Dioxide 1-Hr—highest 98th percentile 1-hour daily maximum concentration; Sulfur Dioxide AM—highest annual mean concentration; Sulfur Dioxide 1-Hr—highest 99th percentile 1-hour daily maximum concentration; Sulfur Dioxide 24-Hr—highest second maximum 24-hour concentration
Source: U.S. Environmental Protection Agency, Air Quality Monitoring Information, "Air Quality Statistics by City, 2023"

Portland, Oregon

Background

Portland sits on the Willamette River in northwestern Oregon near the border with Washington state. It is the kind of city that inspires civic pride and the desire to preserve, offering magnificent views of the Cascade Mountains, a mild climate, and an attractive combination of historical brick structures and contemporary architecture.

Nature is the undisputed queen of Portland and embodied in Portlandia, the city's statue of an earth mother kneeling among her animal children. The number of activities, such as fishing, skiing, and hunting, as well as the number of outdoor zoological gardens, attest to the mindset of the typical Portlander.

Portland is a major industrial and commercial center that boasts clean air and water within its city limits, as many of the factories use the electricity generated by mountain rivers controlling the soot and smoke. Manufacturing specializing in high-tech electronics and specialty metal fabrication is leading industry in the city, and major employers include Intel, NIKE, Precision Castparts and Columbia Sportswear. Health services and the highly-rated University of Portland also make a significant impact in the city.

The city is a major cultural center, with art museums such as the Portland Art Museum and the Oregon Museum of Science and Industry, and educational institutions including Reed College and the University of Portland.

Portland area's metro region includes 24 cities and parts of three counties. Established in the late 1970s, it is the nation's first and only elected regional government. It attempts to control growth by using its authority over land use, transportation, and the environment. This experiment in urban planning is designed to protect farms, forests, and open space. Portland today has a downtown area that caters to pedestrians and includes a heavily used city park. Visible from the air is a clear line against sprawl—with cities on one side and open spaces on the other. Portland is Oregon's biggest city, and a role model for twenty-first century urban development. The city's well-organized mass-transit system makes living there more enjoyable, and Portland Streetcar continues to add track, streetcars, and additional improvements.

In 2000, the Portland Art Museum completed its "Program for the Millennium," a multi-stage expansion program that brought total exhibition space to 240,000 square feet. In 2005, restoration of the North Building, a former Masonic Temple, was completed. While preserving the historical integrity, the restoration provides space for the Portland Art Museum's Center for Modern and Contemporary Art.

The Portland metropolitan area has a significant LGBTQ+ population. The city held its first pride festival in 1975 on the Portland State University campus.

Portland has been cited as the least religious city in the United States with over 42 percent of residents identifying as religiously "unaffiliated" in 2020, according to the nonpartisan and nonprofit Public Religion Research Institute's American Values Atlas.

Many films have been shot in Portland, from independents to big-budget productions. The city has been featured in various television programs, most notably the comedy series *Portlandia*, which ran 2011 to 2018. Shot on location in Portland, it lovingly satirized the city as a hub of liberal politics, organic food, alternative lifestyles, and anti-establishment attitudes.

Portland has a warm-summer Mediterranean climate, with cool and rainy winters, and warm and dry summers. This climate is characterized by overcast, wet, and changing weather conditions in fall, winter, and spring, as Portland lies in the direct path of the stormy westerly flow, and warm, dry summers when the North Pacific High reaches its northernmost point in mid-summer. Fall and early winter bring the most frequent fog. Destructive storms are infrequent, with thunderstorms occurring once a month through the spring and summer.

Rankings

General Rankings

- To help military veterans find the best places in which to settle down, *WalletHub* compared the 100 largest U.S. cities across 19 key indicators of livability, affordability and veteran-friendliness. They range from the share of military skill-related jobs to veteran income growth to the availability of VA health facilities. Portland ranked #77. *Wallethub.com, "Best & Worst Places for Veterans to Live (2025)," November 7, 2024*

- *Insider* listed 23 places in the U.S. that travel industry trends reveal would be popular destinations in 2023. This year the list trends towards cultural and historical happenings, sports events, wellness experiences and invigorating outdoor escapes. According to the website insider.com Portland is a place to visit in 2023. *Insider, "23 of the Best Places You Should Travel to in the U.S. in 2023," December 17, 2022*

- The human resources consulting firm Mercer ranked 241 major cities worldwide in terms of overall quality of life. Portland ranked #48. Criteria: political and personal safety; social, and economic factors; medical and health considerations; schools and education; public services and transportation; recreation; connectivity; housing and infrastructure; and climate. *Mercer, "Mercer 2024 Quality of Living Survey," December 2024*

Business/Finance Rankings

- Payscale.com ranked the 32 largest metro areas in terms of wage growth. The Portland metro area ranked #18. Criteria: quarterly changes in private industry employee and education professional wage growth from the previous year. *PayScale, "Wage Trends by Metro Area-4th Quarter," February 4, 2025*

- The Portland metro area appeared on the Milken Institute "2025 Best Performing Cities" list. Rank: #105 out of 200 large metro areas (based on performance category). Criteria: job growth; wage growth; high-tech growth and impact; community resilience; housing affordability; household broadband access. *Milken Institute, "Best-Performing Cities 2025," January 14, 2025*

- Mercer Human Resources Consulting ranked 226 cities worldwide in terms of cost-of-living. Portland ranked #65 (the lower the ranking, the higher the cost-of-living). The survey measured the comparative cost of over 200 items (such as housing, food, clothing, domestic supplies, transportation, and recreation/entertainment) in each location. *Mercer, "2024 Cost of Living City Ranking," June 17, 2024*

Culture/Performing Arts Rankings

- Portland was selected as one of the 25 best cities for moviemakers in North America. Great film cities are places where filmmaking dreams can come true, that offer more creative space, lower costs, and great outdoor locations. NYC & LA were intentionally excluded. Criteria: film industry presence and culture; tax incentives; affordability; and proximity of festivals and schools. The city was ranked #14. *MovieMaker Magazine, "Best Places to Live and Work as a Moviemaker, 2025," January 29, 2025*

Education Rankings

- Personal finance website *WalletHub* analyzed the 150 largest U.S. metropolitan statistical areas to determine where the most educated Americans are putting their degrees to work. Criteria: education levels; percentage of workers with degrees; education quality and attainment gap; public school quality rankings; quality and enrollment of each metro area's universities. Portland was ranked #14 (#1 = most educated city). *WalletHub.com, "Most & Least Educated Cities in America, 2025" July 2, 2024*

Environmental Rankings

- Sperling's *BestPlaces* assessed the 50 largest metropolitan areas of the United States for the likelihood of dangerously extreme weather events or earthquakes. In general the Southeast and South-Central regions have the highest risk of weather extremes and earthquakes, while the Pacific Northwest enjoys the lowest risk. Of the least risky metropolitan areas, the Portland metro area was ranked #1. *Bestplaces.net, "Avoid Natural Disasters: BestPlaces Reveals The Top 10 Safest Places to Live," October 25, 2017*

- Portland was highlighted as one of the top 25 cleanest metro areas for year-round particle pollution (Annual PM 2.5) in the U.S. during 2021 through 2023. The area ranked #23. *American Lung Association, "State of the Air 2025," April 23, 2025*

Food/Drink Rankings

- Portland was identified as one of the cities in America ordering the most vegan food options by GrubHub.com. The city ranked #3 out of 5. Criteria: percentage of vegan, vegetarian and plant-based food orders compared to the overall number of orders. *GrubHub.com, "State of the Plate Report 2021: Top Cities for Vegans," June 20, 2021*

- WalletHub compared the 100 largest U.S. cities across 17 key indicators of vegan- and vegetarian-friendliness. Portland was ranked #3. Cities were selected based on metrics such as the cost of groceries for vegetarians, the share of restaurants serving meatless options and the number of salad shops per capita. *WalletHub.com, "Best Cities for Vegans & Vegetarians (2025)," September 24, 2024*

Health/Fitness Rankings

- For each of the 100 largest cities in the United States, the American Fitness Index®, compiled in partnership between the American College of Sports Medicine and the Elevance Health Foundation, evaluated community infrastructure and more than 30 health behaviors including preventive health, levels of chronic disease conditions, food insecurity, pedestrian safety, air quality, and community/environment resources that support physical activity. Portland ranked #12 for "community fitness." *americanfitnessindex.org, "2024 ACSM American Fitness Index Summary Report," July 23, 2024*

- Portland was identified as a "2025 Allergy Capital." The area ranked #52 out of the nation's 100 largest metropolitan areas. Three groups of factors were used to identify the most challenging cities for people with allergies: annual tree, grass, and weed pollen scores; over the counter allergy medicine use; number of board-certified allergy specialists. *Asthma and Allergy Foundation of America, "2025 Allergy Capitals: The Most Challenging Places to Live with Allergies," March 18, 2025*

- Portland was identified as a "2024 Asthma Capital." The area ranked #88 out of the nation's 100 largest metropolitan areas. Criteria: estimated asthma prevalence; asthma-related mortality; and ER visits due to asthma. Risk factors analyzed but not factored in the rankings: annual air quality including pollution and ozone levels; public smoking laws; indoor air quality; access to asthma specialists; rescue and controller medication use; uninsured rate; pollen allergy; poverty rate. *Asthma and Allergy Foundation of America, "Asthma Capitals 2024: The Most Challenging Places to Live With Asthma," September 10, 2024*

Pet Rankings

- Portland was selected by *Sniffspot.com* as one of the most dog-friendly cities in the U.S., ranking #4 out of 50. Criteria: dog parks; hiking; sniffspots; public parks; dog-friendly businesses; housing; dog waste cleanliness; leash laws; dog services; and overall cost. *Sniffspot.com, "The Top 50 Most Dog-Friendly Cities in the U.S.," September 30, 2024*

Real Estate Rankings

- *WalletHub* compared the most populated U.S. cities to determine which had the best markets for real estate agents. Portland ranked #16 where demand was high and pay was the best. Criteria: sales per agent; annual median wage for real-estate agents; monthly average starting salary for real estate agents; real estate job density and competition; unemployment rate; home turnover rate; housing-market health index; and other relevant metrics. *WalletHub.com, "2021 Best Places to Be a Real Estate Agent," May 12, 2021*

- Portland was ranked #159 out of 176 metro areas in terms of cost of housing in 2024 by the National Association of Home Builders (#1 = most affordable). Criteria: the portion of an average family's income necessary to pay the mortgage on a median-priced home. *National Association of Home Builders®, NAHB-Wells Fargo Cost of Housing Index, 4th Quarter 2024*

Safety Rankings

- Allstate ranked the 100 most populous cities in America in terms of driver safety. Portland ranked #4. Criteria based on anonymized driving behavior data from Allstate's mobile app powered by Arity: high speed driving (over 80 mph), phone handling, and hard braking. The report helps increase the importance of safety and awareness behind the wheel. *Allstate, "16th Allstate America's Best Drivers Report®" July 11, 2024*

Women/Minorities Rankings

- Portland was listed as one of the most LGBTQ-friendly cities in America by *The Advocate*, as compiled by the real estate data site *Clever*. The city ranked #4 out of 15. Criteria, among many: Pride events; gay bars; LGBTQ-affirming healthcare options; state and local laws; number of PFLAG chapters; LGBTQ+ population. *The Advocate, "These Are the 15 Most LGBTQ-Friendly Cities in the U.S." November 1, 2023*

- Personal finance website *WalletHub* compared more than 180 U.S. cities across two key dimensions, "Hispanic Business-Friendliness" and "Hispanic Purchasing Power," to arrive at the most favorable conditions for Hispanic entrepreneurs. Portland was ranked #125 out of 182. Criteria includes: share of Hispanic-Owned Businesses; average growth of Hispanic Business revenues; Small Business-Friendliness score; affordability; and number of Hispanics with at least a bachelor's degree. *WalletHub.com, "Best Cities for Hispanic Entrepreneurs," September 4, 2024*

Miscellaneous Rankings

- *MoveHub* ranked 446 hipster cities across 20 countries, using its new and improved alternative Hipster Index and Portland came out as #2 among the top 50. Criteria: population over 150,000; number of vintage boutiques; density of tattoo parlors; vegan places to eat; coffee shops; and density of vinyl record stores. *MoveHub.com, "The Hipster Index: Brighton Pips Portland to Global Top Spot," July 28, 2021*

- *WalletHub* compared 148 of the most populated U.S. cities to determine their operating efficiency. A "Quality of Services" score was constructed for each city and then measured against the total budget per capita to reveal which were managed the best. Portland ranked #81. Criteria: financial stability; economy; education; safety; health; infrastructure and pollution. *WalletHub.com, "2025's Best- & Worst-Run Cities in America," June 18, 2024*

Business Environment

DEMOGRAPHICS

Population Growth

Area	1990 Census	2000 Census	2010 Census	2020 Census	2023 Estimate[2]	Population Growth 1990-2023 (%)
City	485,833	529,121	583,776	652,503	642,715	32.3
MSA[1]	1,523,741	1,927,881	2,226,009	2,512,859	2,510,529	64.8
U.S.	248,709,873	281,421,906	308,745,538	331,449,281	332,387,540	33.6

Note: (1) Figures cover the Portland-Vancouver-Hillsboro, OR-WA Metropolitan Statistical Area;
(2) 2019-2023 5-year ACS population estimate
Source: U.S. Census Bureau, 1990 Census, 2000 Census, 2010 Census, 2020 Census, 2019-2023 American
Community Survey 5-Year Estimates

Race

Area	White Alone[2] (%)	Black Alone[2] (%)	Asian Alone[2] (%)	AIAN[3] Alone[2] (%)	NHOPI[4] Alone[2] (%)	Other Race Alone[2] (%)	Two or More Races (%)
City	70.1	5.8	8.1	0.8	0.5	3.3	11.3
MSA[1]	73.0	3.0	7.0	0.8	0.5	4.5	11.2
U.S.	63.4	12.4	5.8	0.9	0.2	6.6	10.7

Note: (1) Figures cover the Portland-Vancouver-Hillsboro, OR-WA Metropolitan Statistical Area; (2) Alone is
defined as not being in combination with one or more other races; (3) American Indian and Alaska Native;
(4) Native Hawaiian and Other Pacific Islander
Source: U.S. Census Bureau, 2019-2023 American Community Survey 5-Year Estimates

Hispanic or Latino Origin

Area	Total (%)	Mexican (%)	Puerto Rican (%)	Cuban (%)	Other (%)
City	11.3	7.6	0.5	0.4	2.8
MSA[1]	13.5	10.2	0.4	0.2	2.6
U.S.	19.0	11.3	1.8	0.7	5.2

Note: Persons of Hispanic or Latino origin can be of any race; (1) Figures cover the
Portland-Vancouver-Hillsboro, OR-WA Metropolitan Statistical Area
Source: U.S. Census Bureau, 2019-2023 American Community Survey 5-Year Estimates

Age

Area	Under Age 5	Age 5–19	Age 20–34	Age 35–44	Age 45–54	Age 55–64	Age 65–74	Age 75–84	Age 85+	Median Age
City	4.3	14.5	24.5	18.0	13.8	10.7	8.8	3.9	1.5	38.6
MSA[1]	5.1	17.7	20.9	15.2	13.2	12.0	9.8	4.4	1.7	39.1
U.S.	5.7	19.1	20.2	13.1	12.3	12.8	10.0	4.9	1.9	38.7

Note: (1) Figures cover the Portland-Vancouver-Hillsboro, OR-WA Metropolitan Statistical Area
Source: U.S. Census Bureau, 2019-2023 American Community Survey 5-Year Estimates

Disability by Age

Area	All Ages	Under 18 Years Old	18 to 64 Years Old	65 Years and Over
City	13.2	4.9	10.9	34.3
MSA[1]	12.9	4.5	10.8	32.6
U.S.	13.0	4.7	10.7	32.9

Note: Figures show percent of the civilian noninstitutionalized population that reported having a disability.
Disability status is determined from six types of difficulty: vision, hearing, cognitive, ambulatory, self-care, and
independent living. For children under 5 years old, hearing and vision difficulty are used to determine
disability status. For children between the ages of 5 and 14, disability status is determined from hearing, vision,
cognitive, ambulatory, and self-care difficulties. For people aged 15 years and older, they are considered to
have a disability if they have difficulty with any one of the six difficulty types; Note: (1) Figures cover the
Portland-Vancouver-Hillsboro, OR-WA Metropolitan Statistical Area
Source: U.S. Census Bureau, 2019-2023 American Community Survey 5-Year Estimates

Ancestry

Area	German	Irish	English	American	Italian	Polish	French[2]	European	Scottish
City	15.2	11.6	12.9	4.3	4.5	2.4	2.6	4.4	3.1
MSA[1]	16.0	10.5	12.8	4.4	3.5	1.7	2.4	3.8	2.8
U.S.	12.6	9.4	9.1	5.5	4.9	2.6	2.0	1.6	1.6

Note: Figures are the percentage of the total population reporting a particular ancestry. The nine most
commonly reported ancestries in the U.S. are shown. Figures include multiple ancestries (e.g. if a person
reported being Irish and Italian, they were included in both columns); (1) Figures cover the
Portland-Vancouver-Hillsboro, OR-WA Metropolitan Statistical Area; (2) Excludes Basque
Source: U.S. Census Bureau, 2019-2023 American Community Survey 5-Year Estimates

Foreign-born Population

Area	Any Foreign Country	Percent of Population Born in							
		Asia	Mexico	Europe	Caribbean	Central America[2]	South America	Africa	Canada
City	12.4	5.5	2.0	2.3	0.2	0.4	0.3	0.8	0.5
MSA[1]	12.5	5.0	3.0	2.3	0.2	0.5	0.4	0.6	0.4
U.S.	13.9	4.3	3.3	1.4	1.4	1.2	1.2	0.8	0.2

Note: (1) Figures cover the Portland-Vancouver-Hillsboro, OR-WA Metropolitan Statistical Area; (2) Excludes Mexico.
Source: U.S. Census Bureau, 2019-2023 American Community Survey 5-Year Estimates

Household Size

Area	Persons in Household (%)							Average Household Size
	One	Two	Three	Four	Five	Six	Seven or More	
City	36.4	34.8	13.8	9.9	3.2	1.1	0.7	2.18
MSA[1]	27.6	35.7	15.6	12.8	5.2	1.9	1.2	2.47
U.S.	28.5	33.8	15.4	12.7	5.9	2.3	1.4	2.54

Note: (1) Figures cover the Portland-Vancouver-Hillsboro, OR-WA Metropolitan Statistical Area
Source: U.S. Census Bureau, 2019-2023 American Community Survey 5-Year Estimates

Household Relationships

Area	House-holder	Opposite-sex Spouse	Same-sex Spouse	Opposite-sex Unmarried Partner	Same-sex Unmarried Partner	Child[2]	Grand-child	Other Relatives	Non-relatives
City	43.2	14.9	0.7	4.4	0.6	21.2	1.1	3.7	7.2
MSA[1]	39.0	18.1	0.4	3.2	0.3	26.7	1.6	4.2	4.9
U.S.	38.3	17.5	0.2	2.5	0.2	28.3	2.4	4.8	3.4

Note: Figures are percent of the total population; (1) Figures cover the Portland-Vancouver-Hillsboro, OR-WA Metropolitan Statistical Area; (2) Includes biological, adopted, and stepchildren of the householder
Source: U.S. Census Bureau, 2020 Census

Gender

Area	Males	Females	Males per 100 Females
City	319,454	323,261	98.8
MSA[1]	1,251,055	1,259,474	99.3
U.S.	164,545,087	167,842,453	98.0

Note: (1) Figures cover the Portland-Vancouver-Hillsboro, OR-WA Metropolitan Statistical Area
Source: U.S. Census Bureau, 2019-2023 American Community Survey 5-Year Estimates

Marital Status

Area	Never Married	Now Married[2]	Separated	Widowed	Divorced
City	42.9	39.8	1.3	3.5	12.6
MSA[1]	33.7	48.9	1.3	4.3	11.8
U.S.	34.1	47.9	1.7	5.6	10.7

Note: Figures are percentages and cover the population 15 years of age and older; (1) Figures cover the Portland-Vancouver-Hillsboro, OR-WA Metropolitan Statistical Area; (2) Excludes separated
Source: U.S. Census Bureau, 2019-2023 American Community Survey 5-Year Estimates

Religious Groups by Family

Area	Catholic	Baptist	Methodist	LDS[2]	Pentecostal	Lutheran	Islam	Adventist	Other
MSA[1]	11.8	0.8	0.6	3.3	1.4	1.1	0.2	2.0	14.4
U.S.	18.7	7.3	3.0	2.0	1.8	1.7	1.3	1.3	11.6

Note: Figures are the number of adherents as a percentage of the total population and cover the eight largest religious groups in the U.S; (1) Figures cover the Portland-Vancouver-Hillsboro, OR-WA Metropolitan Statistical Area; (2) Church of Jesus Christ of Latter-day Saints
Sources: 2020 U.S. Religion Census, Association of Statisticians of American Religious Bodies; The Association of Religion Data Archives (ARDA)

Religious Groups by Tradition

Area	Catholic	Evangelical Protestant	Mainline Protestant	Black Protestant	Islam	Judaism	Hinduism	Orthodox	Buddhism
MSA[1]	11.8	14.6	2.3	0.4	0.2	0.3	0.7	0.3	0.4
U.S.	18.7	16.5	5.2	2.3	1.3	0.6	0.4	0.4	0.3

Note: Figures are the number of adherents as a percentage of the total population; (1) Figures cover the Portland-Vancouver-Hillsboro, OR-WA Metropolitan Statistical Area
Sources: 2020 U.S. Religion Census, Association of Statisticians of American Religious Bodies; The Association of Religion Data Archives (ARDA)

ECONOMY

Real Gross Domestic Product (GDP)

Area	2017	2018	2019	2020	2021	2022	2023	Rank[3]
MSA[1]	155.8	162.7	166.7	164.9	174.8	178.8	182.0	25
U.S.[2]	17,619.1	18,160.7	18,642.5	18,238.9	19,387.6	19,896.6	20,436.3	—

Note: Figures are in billions of chained 2017 dollars; (1) Figures cover the Portland-Vancouver-Hillsboro, OR-WA Metropolitan Statistical Area; (2) Figures cover real GDP within metropolitan areas; (3) Rank is based on 2023 data and ranges from 1 to 384
Source: U.S. Bureau of Economic Analysis

Economic Growth

Area	2014	2015	2016	2017	2018	2019	2020	2021	2022	2023
MSA[1]	3.4	5.7	4.7	5.7	4.4	2.5	-1.1	6.0	2.3	1.8
U.S.[2]	2.6	3.2	2.0	2.7	3.1	2.7	-2.2	6.3	2.6	2.7

Note: Figures are real gross domestic product growth rates and represent percent change from preceding period; (1) Figures cover the Portland-Vancouver-Hillsboro, OR-WA Metropolitan Statistical Area; (2) Figures are the average growth rates within metropolitan areas
Source: U.S. Bureau of Economic Analysis

Metropolitan Area Exports

Area	2018	2019	2020	2021	2022	2023	Rank[2]
MSA[1]	21,442.9	23,761.9	27,824.7	33,787.5	34,368.0	26,973.2	18
U.S.	1,664,056.1	1,645,173.7	1,431,406.6	1,753,941.4	2,062,937.4	2,019,160.5	—

Note: Figures are in millions of dollars; (1) Figures cover the Portland-Vancouver-Hillsboro, OR-WA Metropolitan Statistical Area; (2) Rank is based on 2023 data and ranges from 1 to 386
Source: U.S. Department of Commerce, International Trade Administration, Office of Trade and Economic Analysis, Industry and Analysis, Exports by Metropolitan Area, data extracted April 2, 2025

Building Permits

Area	Single-Family			Multi-Family			Total		
	2023	2024	Pct. Chg.	2023	2024	Pct. Chg.	2023	2024	Pct. Chg.
City	877	815	-7.1	2,212	885	-60.0	3,089	1,700	-45.0
MSA[1]	6,326	6,345	0.3	5,056	3,108	-38.5	11,382	9,453	-16.9
U.S.	920,000	981,900	6.7	591,100	496,100	-16.1	1,511,100	1,478,000	-2.2

Note: (1) Figures cover the Portland-Vancouver-Hillsboro, OR-WA Metropolitan Statistical Area; Figures represent new, privately-owned housing units authorized (unadjusted data)
Source: U.S. Census Bureau, Building Permits Survey (BPS), 2023, 2024

Bankruptcy Filings

Area	Business Filings			Nonbusiness Filings		
	2023	2024	% Chg.	2023	2024	% Chg.
Multnomah County	35	61	74.3	938	1,078	14.9
U.S.	18,926	23,107	22.1	434,064	494,201	13.9

Note: Business filings include Chapter 7, Chapter 9, Chapter 11, Chapter 12, Chapter 13, Chapter 15, and Section 304; Nonbusiness filings include Chapter 7, Chapter 11, and Chapter 13
Source: Administrative Office of the U.S. Courts, Business and Nonbusiness Bankruptcy, County Cases Commenced by Chapter of the Bankruptcy Code, During the 12-Month Period Ending December 31, 2023 and Business and Nonbusiness Bankruptcy, County Cases Commenced by Chapter of the Bankruptcy Code, During the 12-Month Period Ending December 31, 2024

Housing Vacancy Rates

Area	Gross Vacancy Rate[3] (%)			Year-Round Vacancy Rate[4] (%)			Rental Vacancy Rate[5] (%)			Homeowner Vacancy Rate[6] (%)		
	2022	2023	2024	2022	2023	2024	2022	2023	2024	2022	2023	2024
MSA[1]	5.4	5.4	5.7	5.1	5.1	5.5	4.0	6.8	5.7	1.2	0.8	1.0
U.S.[2]	9.1	9.0	9.1	7.5	7.5	7.6	5.7	6.5	6.8	0.8	0.8	1.0

Note: (1) Figures cover the Portland-Vancouver-Hillsboro, OR-WA Metropolitan Statistical Area; (2) Figures cover the 75 largest Metropolitan Statistical Areas; (3) The percentage of the total housing inventory that is vacant; (4) The percentage of the housing inventory (excluding seasonal units) that is year-round vacant; (5) The percentage of rental inventory that is vacant for rent; (6) The percentage of homeowner inventory that is vacant for sale
Source: U.S. Census Bureau, Housing Vacancies and Homeownership Annual Statistics: 2022, 2023, 2024

INCOME

Income

Area	Per Capita ($)	Median Household ($)	Average Household ($)
City	55,312	88,792	122,267
MSA[1]	50,158	94,573	124,372
U.S.	43,289	78,538	110,491

Note: (1) Figures cover the Portland-Vancouver-Hillsboro, OR-WA Metropolitan Statistical Area
Source: U.S. Census Bureau, 2019-2023 American Community Survey 5-Year Estimates

Household Income Distribution

Area	Percent of Households Earning							
	Under $15,000	$15,000 -$24,999	$25,000 -$34,999	$35,000 -$49,999	$50,000 -$74,999	$75,000 -$99,999	$100,000 -$149,999	$150,000 and up
City	8.8	5.3	5.6	9.2	14.2	11.9	17.6	27.3
MSA[1]	6.4	4.7	5.1	8.8	14.6	13.1	19.7	27.6
U.S.	8.5	6.6	6.8	10.4	15.7	12.7	17.4	21.9

Note: (1) Figures cover the Portland-Vancouver-Hillsboro, OR-WA Metropolitan Statistical Area
Source: U.S. Census Bureau, 2019-2023 American Community Survey 5-Year Estimates

Poverty Rate

Area	All Ages	Under 18 Years Old	18 to 64 Years Old	65 Years and Over
City	12.8	14.5	12.5	11.8
MSA[1]	9.5	10.5	9.4	9.0
U.S.	12.4	16.3	11.6	10.4

Note: Figures are percentage of people whose income during the past 12 months was below the poverty level;
(1) Figures cover the Portland-Vancouver-Hillsboro, OR-WA Metropolitan Statistical Area
Source: U.S. Census Bureau, 2019-2023 American Community Survey 5-Year Estimates

EMPLOYMENT

Labor Force and Employment

Area	Civilian Labor Force			Workers Employed		
	Dec. 2023	Dec. 2024	% Chg.	Dec. 2023	Dec. 2024	% Chg.
City	386,871	388,825	0.5	372,067	372,849	0.2
MSA[1]	1,358,801	1,358,994	0.0	1,305,393	1,301,850	-0.3
U.S.	166,661,000	167,746,000	0.7	160,754,000	161,294,000	0.3

Note: Data is not seasonally adjusted and covers workers 16 years of age and older; (1) Figures cover the
Portland-Vancouver-Hillsboro, OR-WA Metropolitan Statistical Area
Source: Bureau of Labor Statistics, Local Area Unemployment Statistics

Unemployment Rate

Area	2024											
	Jan.	Feb.	Mar.	Apr.	May	Jun.	Jul.	Aug.	Sep.	Oct.	Nov.	Dec.
City	4.5	4.4	4.3	3.6	3.6	4.0	4.4	4.3	3.9	3.9	4.0	4.1
MSA[1]	4.4	4.5	4.2	3.6	3.7	3.9	4.4	4.3	3.9	3.9	4.0	4.2
U.S.	4.1	4.2	3.9	3.5	3.7	4.3	4.5	4.4	3.9	3.9	4.0	3.8

Note: Data is not seasonally adjusted and covers workers 16 years of age and older; (1) Figures cover the
Portland-Vancouver-Hillsboro, OR-WA Metropolitan Statistical Area
Source: Bureau of Labor Statistics, Local Area Unemployment Statistics

Average Wages

Occupation	$/Hr.	Occupation	$/Hr.
Accountants and Auditors	44.95	Maintenance and Repair Workers	28.31
Automotive Mechanics	29.63	Marketing Managers	81.04
Bookkeepers	26.60	Network and Computer Systems Admin.	50.92
Carpenters	35.28	Nurses, Licensed Practical	38.94
Cashiers	17.91	Nurses, Registered	59.41
Computer Programmers	57.44	Nursing Assistants	24.32
Computer Systems Analysts	60.32	Office Clerks, General	24.99
Computer User Support Specialists	31.89	Physical Therapists	51.26
Construction Laborers	27.95	Physicians	145.16
Cooks, Restaurant	20.13	Plumbers, Pipefitters and Steamfitters	46.10
Customer Service Representatives	23.78	Police and Sheriff's Patrol Officers	45.23
Dentists	94.71	Postal Service Mail Carriers	28.58
Electricians	46.08	Real Estate Sales Agents	33.65
Engineers, Electrical	57.53	Retail Salespersons	20.03
Fast Food and Counter Workers	17.61	Sales Representatives, Technical/Scientific	60.80
Financial Managers	86.12	Secretaries, Exc. Legal/Medical/Executive	26.92
First-Line Supervisors of Office Workers	36.29	Security Guards	23.38
General and Operations Managers	70.26	Surgeons	n/a
Hairdressers/Cosmetologists	25.82	Teacher Assistants, Exc. Postsecondary[1]	19.63
Home Health and Personal Care Aides	21.37	Teachers, Secondary School, Exc. Sp. Ed.[1]	42.02
Janitors and Cleaners	20.22	Telemarketers	19.64
Landscaping/Groundskeeping Workers	21.90	Truck Drivers, Heavy/Tractor-Trailer	31.98
Lawyers	76.99	Truck Drivers, Light/Delivery Services	24.55
Maids and Housekeeping Cleaners	19.20	Waiters and Waitresses	22.74

Note: Wage data covers the Portland-Vancouver-Hillsboro, OR-WA Metropolitan Statistical Area; (1) Hourly
wages were calculated from annual wage data based on a 40 hour work week
Source: Bureau of Labor Statistics, Metro Area Occupational Employment & Wage Estimates, May 2024

Employment by Industry

| Sector | MSA[1] | | U.S. |
	Number of Employees	Percent of Total	Percent of Total
Construction	79,300	6.3	5.1
Financial Activities	72,700	5.8	5.8
Government	161,800	12.9	14.9
Information	26,500	2.1	1.9
Leisure and Hospitality	117,600	9.4	10.4
Manufacturing	119,900	9.6	8.0
Mining and Logging	1,100	0.1	0.4
Other Services	44,100	3.5	3.7
Private Education and Health Services	207,700	16.6	16.9
Professional and Business Services	194,200	15.5	14.2
Retail Trade	117,100	9.3	10.0
Transportation, Warehousing, and Utilities	53,400	4.3	4.8
Wholesale Trade	57,900	4.6	3.9

Note: Figures are non-farm employment as of December 2024. Figures are not seasonally adjusted and include workers 16 years of age and older; (1) Figures cover the Portland-Vancouver-Hillsboro, OR-WA Metropolitan Statistical Area
Source: Bureau of Labor Statistics, Current Employment Statistics, Employment, Hours, and Earnings

Employment by Occupation

Occupation Classification	City (%)	MSA[1] (%)	U.S. (%)
Management, Business, Science, and Arts	54.8	46.7	42.0
Natural Resources, Construction, and Maintenance	4.5	7.3	8.6
Production, Transportation, and Material Moving	9.5	11.9	13.0
Sales and Office	17.1	19.0	19.9
Service	14.2	15.1	16.5

Note: Figures cover employed civilians 16 years of age and older; (1) Figures cover the Portland-Vancouver-Hillsboro, OR-WA Metropolitan Statistical Area
Source: U.S. Census Bureau, 2019-2023 American Community Survey 5-Year Estimates

Occupations with Greatest Projected Employment Growth: 2022 – 2032

Occupation[1]	2022 Employment	2032 Projected Employment	Numeric Employment Change	Percent Employment Change
Home Health and Personal Care Aides	36,900	46,170	9,270	25.1
Fast Food and Counter Workers	61,880	70,300	8,420	13.6
Software Developers	20,630	26,850	6,220	30.2
General and Operations Managers	44,700	50,550	5,850	13.1
Cooks, Restaurant	20,480	25,960	5,480	26.8
Stockers and Order Fillers	44,430	49,500	5,070	11.4
Registered Nurses	42,720	47,680	4,960	11.6
Laborers and Freight, Stock, and Material Movers, Hand	25,990	29,120	3,130	12.0
Personal Care and Service Workers, All Other	21,590	24,720	3,130	14.5
Construction Laborers	18,310	21,420	3,110	17.0

Note: Projections cover Oregon; (1) Sorted by numeric employment change
Source: www.projectionscentral.org, State Occupational Projections, 2022–2032 Long-Term Projections

Fastest-Growing Occupations: 2022 – 2032

Occupation[1]	2022 Employment	2032 Projected Employment	Numeric Employment Change	Percent Employment Change
Nurse Practitioners	2,240	3,420	1,180	52.7
Physical Therapist Assistants	840	1,160	320	38.1
Data Scientists	1,420	1,960	540	38.0
Curators	190	260	70	36.8
Information Security Analysts (SOC 2018)	1,390	1,900	510	36.7
Physician Assistants	1,420	1,930	510	35.9
Medical and Health Services Managers	5,080	6,880	1,800	35.4
Wind Turbine Service Technicians	290	390	100	34.5
Solar Photovoltaic Installers	350	470	120	34.3
Statisticians	570	760	190	33.3

Note: Projections cover Oregon; (1) Sorted by percent employment change and excludes occupations with numeric employment change less than 50
Source: www.projectionscentral.org, State Occupational Projections, 2022–2032 Long-Term Projections

CITY FINANCES

City Government Finances

Component	2022 ($000)	2022 ($ per capita)
Total Revenues	2,617,414	3,985
Total Expenditures	2,123,194	3,233
Debt Outstanding	3,099,340	4,719

Source: U.S. Census Bureau, State & Local Government Finances 2022

City Government Revenue by Source

Source	2022 ($000)	2022 ($ per capita)	2022 (%)
General Revenue			
From Federal Government	177,932	271	6.8
From State Government	86,425	132	3.3
From Local Governments	124,244	189	4.7
Taxes			
Property	726,357	1,106	27.8
Sales and Gross Receipts	320,503	488	12.2
Personal Income	0	0	0.0
Corporate Income	0	0	0.0
Motor Vehicle License	0	0	0.0
Other Taxes	280,468	427	10.7
Current Charges	622,410	948	23.8
Liquor Store	0	0	0.0
Utility	229,635	350	8.8

Source: U.S. Census Bureau, State & Local Government Finances 2022

City Government Expenditures by Function

Function	2022 ($000)	2022 ($ per capita)	2022 (%)
General Direct Expenditures			
Air Transportation	0	0	0.0
Corrections	0	0	0.0
Education	0	0	0.0
Employment Security Administration	0	0	0.0
Financial Administration	87,973	134	4.1
Fire Protection	146,972	223	6.9
General Public Buildings	7,692	11	0.4
Governmental Administration, Other	61,405	93	2.9
Health	0	0	0.0
Highways	255,388	388	12.0
Hospitals	0	0	0.0
Housing and Community Development	223,622	340	10.5
Interest on General Debt	139,927	213	6.6
Judicial and Legal	16,575	25	0.8
Libraries	0	0	0.0
Parking	10,280	15	0.5
Parks and Recreation	155,622	237	7.3
Police Protection	214,482	326	10.1
Public Welfare	0	0	0.0
Sewerage	347,550	529	16.4
Solid Waste Management	6,195	9	0.3
Veterans' Services	0	0	0.0
Liquor Store	0	0	0.0
Utility	262,005	398	12.3

Source: U.S. Census Bureau, State & Local Government Finances 2022

TAXES

State Corporate Income Tax Rates

State	Tax Rate (%)	Income Brackets ($)	Num. of Brackets	Financial Institution Tax Rate (%)[a]	Federal Income Tax Ded.
Oregon	6.6 - 7.6 (s)	1 million	2	6.6 - 7.6 (s)	No

Note: Tax rates for tax year 2024; (a) Rates listed are the corporate income tax rate applied to financial institutions or excise taxes based on income. Some states have other taxes based upon the value of deposits or shares; (s) Oregon's minimum tax for C corporations depends on the Oregon sales of the filing group. The minimum tax ranges from $150 for corporations with sales under $500,000, up to $100,000 for companies with sales of $100 million or above. Oregon also imposes Corporate Activity Tax [CAT] of $250 plus 0.57% of activity in excess of $1 million.
Source: Federation of Tax Administrators, State Corporate Income Tax Rates, January 1, 2025

State Individual Income Tax Rates

State	Tax Rate (%)	Income Brackets ($)	Personal Exemptions ($)			Standard Ded. ($)	
			Single	Married	Depend.	Single	Married
Oregon (a)	4.75 - 9.9	4,050 -125,000 (b)	236	472	236 (c)	2,745	5,495

Note: Tax rates for tax year 2024; Local- and county-level taxes are not included; The deduction for federal SALT deductions is limited to $5,000 for individuals and $10,000 for joint returns in Missouri and Montana, and to $7,800 for all filers in Oregon; (a) 16 states have statutory provision for automatically adjusting to the rate of inflation the dollar values of the income tax brackets, standard deductions, and/or personal exemptions. Oregon does not index the income brackets for $125,000 and over See: INFL and SPEC above; (b) For joint returns, taxes are twice the tax on half the couple's income. California brackets violate this formula at the two highest tax brackets in 2024; (c) The personal exemption takes the form of a tax credit instead of a deduction
Source: Federation of Tax Administrators, State Individual Income Tax Rates, January 1, 2025

Various State Sales and Excise Tax Rates

State	State Sales Tax (%)	Gasoline[1] ($/gal.)	Cigarette[2] ($/pack)	Spirits[3] ($/gal.)	Wine[4] ($/gal.)	Beer[5] ($/gal.)	Recreational Marijuana (%)
Oregon	None	0.40	3.33	22.86	0.67	0.08	(t)

Note: All tax rates as of January 1, 2025; (1) The American Petroleum Institute has developed a methodology for determining the average tax rate on a gallon of fuel. Rates may include any of the following: excise taxes, environmental fees, storage tank fees, other fees or taxes, general sales tax, and local taxes; (2) The federal excise tax of $1.0066 per pack and local taxes are not included; (3) Rates are those applicable to off-premise sales of 40% alcohol by volume (a.b.v.) distilled spirits in 750ml containers. Local excise taxes are excluded; (4) Rates are those applicable to off-premise sales of 11% a.b.v. non-carbonated wine in 750ml containers; (5) Rates are those applicable to off-premise sales of 4.7% a.b.v. beer in 12 ounce containers; (t) 17% excise tax (retail price)
Source: Tax Foundation, 2025 Facts & Figures: How Does Your State Compare?

State Tax Competitiveness Index

State	Overall Rank	Corporate Tax Rank	Individual Income Tax Rank	Sales Tax Rank	Property Tax Rank	Unemployment Insurance Tax Rank
Oregon	30	49	40	4	31	41

Note: The Tax Foundation's State Tax Competitiveness Index enables policymakers, taxpayers, and business leaders to gauge how their states' tax systems compare. A rank of 1 is best, 50 is worst. Rankings do not average to the total. States without a tax rank equally as 1. DC's scores and rankings do not affect other states. The report shows tax systems as of July 1, 2024 (the beginning of Fiscal Year 2025).
Source: Tax Foundation, State Tax Competitiveness Index 2025

TRANSPORTATION

Means of Transportation to Work

Area	Car/Truck/Van		Public Transportation			Bicycle	Walked	Other Means	Worked at Home
	Drove Alone	Car-pooled	Bus	Subway	Railroad				
City	50.5	7.0	5.4	0.2	0.1	3.7	4.8	3.0	25.3
MSA[1]	62.7	7.7	2.6	0.2	0.1	1.4	3.1	2.0	20.4
U.S.	70.2	8.5	1.7	1.3	0.4	0.4	2.4	1.6	13.5

Note: Figures are percentages and cover workers 16 years of age and older; (1) Figures cover the Portland-Vancouver-Hillsboro, OR-WA Metropolitan Statistical Area
Source: U.S. Census Bureau, 2019-2023 American Community Survey 5-Year Estimates

Travel Time to Work

Area	Less Than 10 Minutes	10 to 19 Minutes	20 to 29 Minutes	30 to 44 Minutes	45 to 59 Minutes	60 to 89 Minutes	90 Minutes or More
City	9.3	29.9	27.1	22.5	6.1	3.7	1.5
MSA[1]	11.5	29.0	23.7	21.7	7.7	4.5	1.8
U.S.	12.6	28.6	21.2	20.8	8.1	6.0	2.8

Note: Note: Figures are percentages and include workers 16 years old and over; (1) Figures cover the Portland-Vancouver-Hillsboro, OR-WA Metropolitan Statistical Area
Source: U.S. Census Bureau, 2019-2023 American Community Survey 5-Year Estimates

Key Congestion Measures

Measure	2000	2010	2015	2020	2022
Annual Hours of Delay, Total (000)	37,832	57,165	71,704	36,065	76,232
Annual Hours of Delay, Per Auto Commuter	44	51	62	31	70
Annual Congestion Cost, Per Auto Commuter ($)	1,052	1,263	1,462	771	1,616

Note: Figures cover the Portland OR-WA urban area
Source: Texas A&M Transportation Institute, 2023 Urban Mobility Report

Freeway Travel Time Index

Measure	1985	1990	1995	2000	2005	2010	2015	2020	2022
Urban Area Index[1]	1.16	1.19	1.25	1.30	1.32	1.32	1.36	1.10	1.33
Urban Area Rank[1,2]	10	12	6	5	8	8	6	29	7

Note: Freeway Travel Time Index—the ratio of travel time in the peak period to the travel time at free-flow conditions. For example, a value of 1.30 indicates a 20-minute free-flow trip takes 26 minutes in the peak (20 minutes x 1.30 = 26 minutes); (1) Covers the Portland OR-WA urban area; (2) Rank is based on 101 larger urban areas (#1 = highest travel time index)
Source: Texas A&M Transportation Institute, 2023 Urban Mobility Report

Public Transportation

Agency Name / Mode of Transportation	Vehicles Operated in Maximum Service[1]	Annual Unlinked Passenger Trips[2] (in thous.)	Annual Passenger Miles[3] (in thous.)
Tri-County Metropolitan Transportation District of Oregon (Tri-Met)			
Bus (directly operated)	443	34,970.1	113,234.6
Demand Response (purchased transportation)	138	480.7	3,847.9
Demand Response - Taxi	28	56.2	562.7
Demand Response - Transportation Network Company	10	2.6	45.4
Hybrid Rail (purchased transportation)	4	117.5	912.2
Light Rail (directly operated)	94	21,815.5	112,827.7
Ride Connection, Inc.			
Bus (directly operated)	8	85.1	273.0
Demand Response (directly operated)	24	37.5	341.8
Demand Response - Taxi	27	41.6	279.8
City of Portland			
Aerial Tramway (purchased transportation)	2	1,091.4	698.5
Streetcar Rail (purchased transportation)	12	2,601.3	3,715.4

Note: (1) Number of revenue vehicles operated by the given mode and type of service to meet the annual maximum service requirement. This is the revenue vehicle count during the peak season of the year; on the week and day that maximum service is provided. Vehicles operated in maximum service (VOMS) exclude atypical days and one-time special events; (2) Number of passengers who boarded public transportation vehicles. Passengers are counted each time they board a vehicle no matter how many vehicles they use to travel from their origin to their destination. (3) Sum of the distances ridden by all passengers during the entire fiscal year.
Source: Federal Transit Administration, National Transit Database, 2023

Air Transportation

Airport Name and Code / Type of Service	Passenger Airlines[1]	Passenger Enplanements	Freight Carriers[2]	Freight (lbs)
Portland International (PDX)				
Domestic service (U.S. carriers only)	24	8,223,580	15	223,047,020
International service (U.S. carriers only)	7	138,121	4	12,619,586

Note: (1) Includes all U.S.-based major, minor and commuter airlines that carried at least one passenger during the year; (2) Includes all U.S.-based airlines and freight carriers that transported at least one pound of freight during the year.
Source: Bureau of Transportation Statistics, The Intermodal Transportation Database, Air Carriers: T-100 Domestic Market (U.S. carriers only), 2024; Bureau of Transportation Statistics, The Intermodal Transportation Database, Air Carriers: T-100 International Market (U.S. carriers only), 2024

BUSINESSES

Major Business Headquarters

Company Name	Industry	Rankings	
		Fortune[1]	Forbes[2]
Hoffman	Construction	-	113

Note: (1) Companies that produce a 10-K are ranked 1 to 500 based on 2023 revenue; (2) All private companies with at least $2 billion in annual revenue through the end of their most current fiscal year are ranked 1 to 275; companies listed are headquartered in the city; dashes indicate no ranking
Source: Fortune, "Fortune 500," 2024; Forbes, "America's Largest Private Companies," 2024

Fastest-Growing Businesses

According to *Inc.*, Portland is home to three of America's 500 fastest-growing private companies: **Brightside Windows** (#60); **Boulder Care** (#140); **Danielhouse Club** (#377). Criteria: must be an independent, privately-held, for-profit, U.S. corporation, proprietorship or partnership as of December 31, 2023; revenues must be at least $100,000 in 2020 and $2 million in 2023; must have four-year operating/sales history. *Inc., "America's 500 Fastest-Growing Private Companies," 2024*

According to *Initiative for a Competitive Inner City (ICIC)*, Portland is home to two of America's 100 fastest-growing "inner city" companies: **Above The Fray Design** (#23); **Pepper Foster Consulting** (#45). To be eligible for the IC100, companies have to be independently operated, privately held, for-profit businesses with revenues of at least $50,000 in 2019 and $500,000 in 2023, and headquartered in an under-resourced community. Recognizing that concentrated poverty exists within metropolitan areas outside of big cities (and that poverty overall is suburbanizing), ICIC defines under-resourced communities as large low-income, high-poverty areas located in the urban and suburban parts of all but the smallest metropolitan areas. Companies were ranked overall by revenue growth over the five-year period between 2019 and 2023. *Initiative for a Competitive Inner City (ICIC), "Inner City 100 Companies," 2024*

Living Environment

COST OF LIVING

Cost of Living Index

Composite Index	Groceries	Housing	Utilities	Trans-portation	Health Care	Misc. Goods/Services
116.6	107.2	146.0	86.6	127.4	110.5	101.9

Note: The Cost of Living Index measures regional differences in the cost of consumer goods and services, excluding taxes and non-consumer expenditures, for professional and managerial households in the top income quintile. It is based on more than 50,000 prices covering almost 60 different items for which prices are collected three times a year by chambers of commerce, economic development organizations or university applied economic centers in each participating urban area. The numbers shown should be read as a percentage above or below the national average of 100. For example, a value of 115.4 in the groceries column indicates that grocery prices are 15.4% higher than the national average. Small differences in the index numbers should not be interpreted as significant; Figures cover the Portland OR urban area.
Source: The Council for Community and Economic Research, Cost of Living Index, 2024

Grocery Prices

Area[1]	T-Bone Steak ($/pound)	Frying Chicken ($/pound)	Whole Milk ($/half gal.)	Eggs ($/dozen)	Orange Juice ($/64 oz.)	Coffee ($/11.5 oz.)
City[2]	15.52	1.89	4.93	3.57	4.49	6.85
Avg.	15.42	1.55	4.69	3.25	4.41	5.46
Min.	14.50	1.16	4.43	2.75	4.00	4.85
Max.	17.56	2.89	5.49	4.78	5.54	7.89

*Note: (1) Values for the local area are compared with the average, minimum and maximum values for all 276 areas in the Cost of Living Index; (2) Figures cover the Portland OR urban area; **T-Bone Steak** (price per pound); **Frying Chicken** (price per pound, whole fryer); **Whole Milk** (half gallon carton); **Eggs** (price per dozen, Grade A, large); **Orange Juice** (64 oz. Tropicana or Florida Natural); **Coffee** (11.5 oz. can, vacuum-packed, Maxwell House, Hills Bros, or Folgers).*
Source: The Council for Community and Economic Research, Cost of Living Index, 2024

Housing and Utility Costs

Area[1]	New Home Price ($)	Apartment Rent ($/month)	All Electric ($/month)	Part Electric ($/month)	Other Energy ($/month)	Telephone ($/month)
City[2]	723,737	2,574	-	70.81	96.37	186.81
Avg.	515,975	1,550	210.99	123.07	82.07	194.99
Min.	265,375	692	104.33	53.68	36.26	179.42
Max.	2,775,821	5,719	529.02	397.28	361.63	223.33

*Note: (1) Values for the local area are compared with the average, minimum and maximum values for all 276 areas in the Cost of Living Index; (2) Figures cover the Portland OR urban area; **New Home Price** (2,400 sf living area, 8,000 sf lot, in urban area with full utilities); **Apartment Rent** (950 sf 2 bedroom/1.5 or 2 bath, unfurnished, excluding all utilities except water); **All Electric** (average monthly cost for an all-electric home); **Part Electric** (average monthly cost for a part-electric home); **Other Energy** (average monthly cost for natural gas, fuel oil, coal, wood, and any other forms of energy except electricity); **Telephone** (price includes the base monthly rate plus taxes and fees for three lines of mobile phone service).*
Source: The Council for Community and Economic Research, Cost of Living Index, 2024

Health Care, Transportation, and Other Costs

Area[1]	Doctor ($/visit)	Dentist ($/visit)	Optometrist ($/visit)	Gasoline ($/gallon)	Beauty Salon ($/visit)	Men's Shirt ($)
City[2]	218.48	116.33	147.50	4.17	60.17	35.98
Avg.	143.77	117.51	129.23	3.32	48.57	38.14
Min.	36.74	58.67	67.33	2.80	24.00	13.41
Max.	270.44	216.82	307.33	5.28	94.00	63.89

*Note: (1) Values for the local area are compared with the average, minimum and maximum values for all 276 areas in the Cost of Living Index; (2) Figures cover the Portland OR urban area; **Doctor** (general practitioners routine exam of an established patient); **Dentist** (adult teeth cleaning and periodic oral examination); **Optometrist** (full vision eye exam for established adult patient); **Gasoline** (one gallon regular unleaded, national brand, including all taxes, cash price at self-service pump if available); **Beauty Salon** (woman's shampoo, trim, and blow-dry); **Men's Shirt** (cotton/polyester dress shirt, pinpoint weave, long sleeves).*
Source: The Council for Community and Economic Research, Cost of Living Index, 2024

HOUSING

Homeownership Rate

Area	2017 (%)	2018 (%)	2019 (%)	2020 (%)	2021 (%)	2022 (%)	2023 (%)	2024 (%)
MSA[1]	61.1	59.2	60.0	62.5	64.1	65.2	65.6	61.1
U.S.	63.9	64.4	64.6	66.6	65.5	65.8	65.9	65.6

Note: (1) Figures cover the Portland-Vancouver-Hillsboro, OR-WA Metropolitan Statistical Area
Source: U.S. Census Bureau, Housing Vacancies and Homeownership Annual Statistics: 2017-2024

House Price Index (HPI)

Area	National Ranking[2]	Quarterly Change (%)	One-Year Change (%)	Five-Year Change (%)	Since 1991Q1 (%)
MSA[1]	182	0.32	3.88	37.41	518.30
U.S.[3]	–	1.43	4.51	57.13	327.82

Note: The HPI is a weighted repeat sales index. It measures average price changes in repeat sales or refinancings on the same properties. This information is obtained by reviewing repeat mortgage transactions on single-family properties whose mortgages have been purchased or securitized by Fannie Mae or Freddie Mac since January 1975; (1) Figures cover the Portland-Vancouver-Hillsboro, OR-WA Metropolitan Statistical Area; (2) Rankings are based on annual percentage change for all metro areas containing at least 15,000 transactions over the last 10 years and ranges from 1 to 241; (3) figures based on a weighted average of Census Division estimates using a seasonally adjusted, purchase-only index; all figures are for the period ending December 31, 2024
Source: Federal Housing Finance Agency, Change in FHFA Metropolitan Area House Price Indexes, All Transactions Index, 2024Q4

Home Value

Area	Under $100,000	$100,000 -$199,999	$200,000 -$299,999	$300,000 -$399,999	$400,000 -$499,999	$500,000 -$999,999	$1,000,000 or more	Median ($)
City	2.5	1.5	4.8	11.9	21.2	50.0	8.1	557,600
MSA[1]	3.9	2.2	5.4	12.8	22.0	46.6	7.0	526,500
U.S.	12.1	17.8	19.5	14.4	10.5	19.1	6.5	303,400

Note: Figures are percentages except for median and cover owner-occupied housing units; (1) Figures cover the Portland-Vancouver-Hillsboro, OR-WA Metropolitan Statistical Area
Source: U.S. Census Bureau, 2019-2023 American Community Survey 5-Year Estimates

Year Housing Structure Built

Area	2020 or Later	2010 -2019	2000 -2009	1990 -1999	1980 -1989	1970 -1979	1960 -1969	1950 -1959	1940 -1949	Before 1940	Median Year
City	0.9	11.0	10.1	7.3	6.4	10.5	8.4	11.0	7.2	27.1	1966
MSA[1]	1.4	11.1	14.0	16.3	10.9	16.0	8.0	6.7	4.2	11.3	1983
U.S.	1.2	8.9	13.6	12.8	13.0	14.4	10.0	9.7	4.5	11.9	1980

Note: Figures are percentages except for Median Year; Note: (1) Figures cover the Portland-Vancouver-Hillsboro, OR-WA Metropolitan Statistical Area
Source: U.S. Census Bureau, 2019-2023 American Community Survey 5-Year Estimates

Gross Monthly Rent

Area	Under $500	$500 -$999	$1,000 -$1,499	$1,500 -$1,999	$2,000 -$2,499	$2,500 -$2,999	$3,000 and up	Median ($)
City	4.6	9.6	30.1	29.6	15.0	6.3	4.8	1,596
MSA[1]	3.4	7.7	28.4	33.9	16.2	6.3	4.1	1,654
U.S.	6.5	22.3	29.5	20.2	10.8	4.8	5.9	1,348

Note: Figures are percentages except for median; Gross rent is the contract rent plus the estimated average monthly cost of utilities (electricity, gas, and water and sewer) and fuels (oil, coal, kerosene, wood, etc.) if these are paid by the renter (or paid for the renter by someone else); (1) Figures cover the Portland-Vancouver-Hillsboro, OR-WA Metropolitan Statistical Area
Source: U.S. Census Bureau, 2019-2023 American Community Survey 5-Year Estimates

HEALTH

Health Risk Factors

Category	MSA[1] (%)	U.S. (%)
Adults aged 18–64 who have any kind of health care coverage	94.3	90.8
Adults who reported being in good or better health	81.8	81.8
Adults who have been told they have high blood cholesterol	33.7	36.9
Adults who have been told they have high blood pressure	30.7	34.0
Adults who are current smokers	10.0	12.1
Adults who currently use e-cigarettes	7.8	7.7
Adults who currently use chewing tobacco, snuff, or snus	2.4	3.2
Adults who are heavy drinkers[2]	6.3	6.1
Adults who are binge drinkers[3]	14.1	15.2
Adults who are overweight (BMI 25.0 - 29.9)	33.1	34.4
Adults who are obese (BMI 30.0 - 99.8)	32.1	34.3
Adults who participated in any physical activities in the past month	81.6	75.8

Note: All figures are crude prevalence; (1) Figures cover the Portland-Vancouver-Hillsboro, OR-WA Metropolitan Statistical Area; (2) Heavy drinkers are classified as adult men having more than 14 drinks per week and adult women having more than 7 drinks per week; (3) Binge drinkers are classified as males having five or more drinks on one occasion or females having four or more drinks on one occasion
Source: Centers for Disease Control and Prevention, Behaviorial Risk Factor Surveillance System, SMART: Selected Metropolitan Area Risk Trends, 2023

Acute and Chronic Health Conditions

Category	MSA[1] (%)	U.S. (%)
Adults who have ever been told they had a heart attack	3.5	4.2
Adults who have ever been told they have angina or coronary heart disease	3.3	4.0
Adults who have ever been told they had a stroke	2.7	3.3
Adults who have ever been told they have asthma	18.2	15.7
Adults who have ever been told they have arthritis	23.2	26.3
Adults who have ever been told they have diabetes[2]	9.7	11.5
Adults who have ever been told they had skin cancer	6.0	5.6
Adults who have ever been told they had any other types of cancer	8.6	8.4
Adults who have ever been told they have COPD	4.9	6.4
Adults who have ever been told they have kidney disease	3.5	3.7
Adults who have ever been told they have a form of depression	26.1	22.0

Note: All figures are crude prevalence; (1) Figures cover the Portland-Vancouver-Hillsboro, OR-WA Metropolitan Statistical Area; (2) Figures do not include pregnancy-related, borderline, or pre-diabetes
Source: Centers for Disease Control and Prevention, Behaviorial Risk Factor Surveillance System, SMART: Selected Metropolitan Area Risk Trends, 2023

Health Screening and Vaccination Rates

Category	MSA[1] (%)	U.S. (%)
Adults who have ever been tested for HIV	42.1	37.5
Adults who have had their blood cholesterol checked within the last five years	86.0	87.0
Adults aged 65+ who have had flu shot within the past year	69.8	63.4
Adults aged 65+ who have ever had a pneumonia vaccination	76.1	71.9

Note: All figures are crude prevalence; (1) Figures cover the Portland-Vancouver-Hillsboro, OR-WA Metropolitan Statistical Area.
Source: Centers for Disease Control and Prevention, Behaviorial Risk Factor Surveillance System, SMART: Selected Metropolitan Area Risk Trends, 2023

Disability Status

Category	MSA[1] (%)	U.S. (%)
Adults who reported being deaf	5.4	7.4
Are you blind or have serious difficulty seeing, even when wearing glasses?	3.3	4.9
Do you have difficulty doing errands alone?	7.6	7.8
Do you have difficulty dressing or bathing?	2.4	3.6
Do you have serious difficulty concentrating/remembering/making decisions?	13.7	13.7
Do you have serious difficulty walking or climbing stairs?	10.1	13.2

Note: All figures are crude prevalence; (1) Figures cover the Portland-Vancouver-Hillsboro, OR-WA Metropolitan Statistical Area.
Source: Centers for Disease Control and Prevention, Behaviorial Risk Factor Surveillance System, SMART: Selected Metropolitan Area Risk Trends, 2023

Mortality Rates for the Top 10 Causes of Death in the U.S.

ICD-10[a] Sub-Chapter	ICD-10[a] Code	Crude Mortality Rate[2] per 100,000 population	
		County[3]	U.S.
Malignant neoplasms	C00-C97	159.1	182.7
Ischaemic heart diseases	I20-I25	63.1	109.6
Provisional assignment of new diseases of uncertain etiology[1]	U00-U49	34.5	65.3
Other forms of heart disease	I30-I51	56.5	65.1
Other degenerative diseases of the nervous system	G30-G31	47.5	52.4
Other external causes of accidental injury	W00-X59	80.8	52.3
Cerebrovascular diseases	I60-I69	47.7	49.1
Chronic lower respiratory diseases	J40-J47	31.6	43.5
Hypertensive diseases	I10-I15	31.1	38.9
Organic, including symptomatic, mental disorders	F01-F09	34.5	33.9

Note: (a) ICD-10 = International Classification of Diseases 10th Revision; (1) Includes COVID-19, adverse effects to COVID-19 vaccines, SARS, and vaping-related disorders; (2) Crude mortality rates are a three-year average covering 2021-2023; (3) Figures cover Multnomah County.
Source: Centers for Disease Control and Prevention, National Center for Health Statistics. National Vital Statistics System, Mortality 2018-2023 on CDC WONDER Online Database

Mortality Rates for Selected Causes of Death

Cause of Death	ICD-10[a] Code	Crude Mortality Rate[1] per 100,000 population	
		County[2]	U.S.
Accidental poisoning and exposure to noxious substances	X40-X49	57.4	30.5
Alzheimer disease	G30	34.4	35.4
Assault	X85-Y09	9.8	7.3
COVID-19	U07.1	34.5	65.3
Diabetes mellitus	E10-E14	28.5	30.0
Diseases of the liver	K70-K76	21.4	20.8
Human immunodeficiency virus (HIV) disease	B20-B24	2.6	1.5
Influenza and pneumonia	J09-J18	5.3	13.4
Intentional self-harm	X60-X84	18.7	14.7
Malnutrition	E40-E46	5.6	6.0
Obesity and other hyperalimentation	E65-E68	3.9	3.1
Renal failure	N17-N19	8.0	16.4
Transport accidents	V01-V99	11.4	14.4

Note: (a) ICD-10 = International Classification of Diseases 10th Revision; (1) Crude mortality rates are a three-year average covering 2021-2023; (2) Figures cover Multnomah County; Data are suppressed when the data meet the criteria for confidentiality constraints; Crude mortality rates are flagged as unreliable when the rate would be calculated with a numerator of 20 or less.
Source: Centers for Disease Control and Prevention, National Center for Health Statistics. National Vital Statistics System, Mortality 2018-2023 on CDC WONDER Online Database

Health Insurance Coverage

Area	With Health Insurance	With Private Health Insurance	With Public Health Insurance	Without Health Insurance	Population Under Age 19 Without Health Insurance
City	94.5	71.5	33.1	5.5	2.1
MSA[1]	94.2	72.3	34.0	5.8	3.2
U.S.	91.4	67.3	36.3	8.6	5.4

Note: Figures are percentages that cover the civilian noninstitutionalized population; (1) Figures cover the Portland-Vancouver-Hillsboro, OR-WA Metropolitan Statistical Area
Source: U.S. Census Bureau, 2019-2023 American Community Survey 5-Year Estimates

Number of Medical Professionals

Area	MDs[3]	DOs[3,4]	Dentists	Podiatrists	Chiropractors	Optometrists
County[1] (number)	5,464	353	830	40	633	207
County[1] (rate[2])	687.2	44.4	105.1	5.1	80.2	26.2
U.S. (rate[2])	302.5	29.2	74.6	6.4	29.5	18.0

Note: Data as of 2023 unless noted; (1) Data covers Multnomah County; (2) Number of medical professionals per 100,000 population; (3) Data as of 2022 and includes all active, non-federal physicians; (4) Doctor of Osteopathic Medicine
Source: U.S. Department of Health and Human Services, Health Resources and Services Administration, Bureau of Health Professions, Area Resource File (ARF) 2023-2024

Best Hospitals

According to *U.S. News,* the Portland-Vancouver-Hillsboro, OR-WA metro area is home to four of the best hospitals in the U.S.: **Legacy Good Samaritan Medical Center** (1 adult specialty); **OHSU Casey Eye Institute** (5 adult specialties); **OHSU Hospital** (5 adult specialties); **OHSU Hospital-Knight Cancer Institute** (5 adult specialties). The hospitals listed were nationally ranked in at least one of 15 adult or 11 pediatric specialties. The number of specialties shown cover the parent hospital. Only 160 U.S. hospitals performed well enough to be nationally ranked in one or more specialties. Twenty hospitals in the U.S. made the Honor Roll. The Best Hospitals Honor Roll takes both the national rankings and the procedure and condition ratings into account. Hospitals received points if they were nationally ranked in one of the 15 adult specialties—the higher they ranked, the more points they got—and how many ratings of "high performing" they earned in the 20 procedures and conditions. *U.S. News Online, "America's Best Hospitals 2024-25"*

EDUCATION

Public School District Statistics

District Name	Schls	Pupils	Pupil/ Teacher Ratio	Minority Pupils[1] (%)	Total Rev. per Pupil ($)	Total Exp. per Pupil ($)
Centennial SD 28J	9	5,513	20.9	65.4	21,013	22,033
David Douglas SD 40	14	8,714	18.7	69.5	22,147	20,822
Parkrose SD 3	6	2,874	19.6	71.7	18,086	17,243
Portland SD 1J	86	44,039	16.3	46.0	22,865	26,919
Reynolds SD 7	20	9,668	15.9	73.1	19,340	17,756

Note: Table includes school districts with 2,000 or more students; (1) Percentage of students that are not non-Hispanic white.
Source: U.S. Department of Education, National Center for Education Statistics, Common Core of Data, Local Education Agency (School District) Universe Survey: School Year 2023-2024; U.S. Department of Education, National Center for Education Statistics, Common Core of Data, School District Finance Survey (F-33): School Year 2021–22

Best High Schools

According to *U.S. News,* Portland is home to one of the top 500 high schools in the U.S.: **Grant High School** (#322). Nearly 25,000 public, magnet and charter schools were ranked based on their performance on state assessments and how well they prepare students for college. *U.S. News & World Report, "Best High Schools 2024"*

Highest Level of Education

Area	Less than H.S.	H.S. Diploma	Some College, No Deg.	Associate Degree	Bachelor's Degree	Master's Degree	Prof. School Degree	Doctorate Degree
City	6.7	14.7	18.5	6.7	32.1	14.2	4.5	2.7
MSA[1]	7.2	19.8	22.1	8.8	26.0	11.1	2.8	2.1
U.S.	10.6	26.2	19.4	8.8	21.3	9.8	2.3	1.6

Note: Figures cover persons age 25 and over; (1) Figures cover the Portland-Vancouver-Hillsboro, OR-WA Metropolitan Statistical Area
Source: U.S. Census Bureau, 2019-2023 American Community Survey 5-Year Estimates

Educational Attainment by Race

Area	High School Graduate or Higher (%)					Bachelor's Degree or Higher (%)				
	Total	White	Black	Asian	Hisp.[2]	Total	White	Black	Asian	Hisp.[2]
City	93.3	96.2	88.6	81.7	80.0	53.5	58.1	29.8	47.3	35.7
MSA[1]	92.8	95.2	90.7	88.4	74.5	42.1	43.3	31.8	55.8	23.6
U.S.	89.4	92.9	88.1	88.0	72.5	35.0	37.7	24.7	57.0	19.9

Note: Figures shown cover persons 25 years old and over; (1) Figures cover the Portland-Vancouver-Hillsboro, OR-WA Metropolitan Statistical Area; (2) People of Hispanic origin can be of any race
Source: U.S. Census Bureau, 2019-2023 American Community Survey 5-Year Estimates

School Enrollment by Grade and Control

Area	Preschool (%)		Kindergarten (%)		Grades 1 - 4 (%)		Grades 5 - 8 (%)		Grades 9 - 12 (%)	
	Public	Private	Public	Private	Public	Private	Public	Private	Public	Private
City	36.8	63.2	84.3	15.7	87.0	13.0	86.9	13.1	85.7	14.3
MSA[1]	40.0	60.0	83.8	16.2	85.8	14.2	88.1	11.9	89.6	10.4
U.S.	58.7	41.3	85.2	14.8	87.2	12.8	87.9	12.1	89.0	11.0

Note: Figures shown cover persons 3 years old and over; (1) Figures cover the Portland-Vancouver-Hillsboro, OR-WA Metropolitan Statistical Area
Source: U.S. Census Bureau, 2019-2023 American Community Survey 5-Year Estimates

Higher Education

Four-Year Colleges			Two-Year Colleges			Medical Schools[1]	Law Schools[2]	Voc/ Tech[3]
Public	Private Non-profit	Private For-profit	Public	Private Non-profit	Private For-profit			
4	14	2	2	1	8	1	2	5

Note: Figures cover institutions located within the Portland-Vancouver-Hillsboro, OR-WA Metropolitan Statistical Area and include main campuses only; (1) includes schools accredited by the Liaison Committee on Medical Education and the American Osteopathic Association's Commission on Osteopathic College Accreditation; (2) includes ABA-accredited schools, schools with provisional ABA accreditation, and state accredited schools; (3) includes all schools with programs that are less than 2 years.
Source: National Center for Education Statistics, Integrated Postsecondary Education System (IPEDS), 2023-24; Wikipedia, List of Medical Schools in the United States, accessed May 2, 2025; Wikipedia, List of Law Schools in the United States, accessed May 2, 2025

According to *U.S. News & World Report,* the Portland-Vancouver-Hillsboro, OR-WA metro area is home to one of the top 100 liberal arts colleges in the U.S.: **Reed College** (#63 tie). The indicators used to capture academic quality fall into a number of categories: assessment by administrators at peer institutions; retention of students; faculty resources; student selectivity; financial resources; alumni giving; high school counselor ratings of colleges; and graduation rate. *U.S. News & World Report, "America's Best Colleges 2025"*

According to *U.S. News & World Report,* the Portland-Vancouver-Hillsboro, OR-WA metro area is home to one of the top 100 law schools in the U.S.: **Lewis & Clark College (Northwestern)** (#99 tie). The rankings are based on a weighted average of 12 measures of quality: peer assessment score; assessment score by lawyers/judges; median LSAT scores; median undergrad GPA; acceptance rate; employment rates for graduates; placement success; bar passage rate; faculty resources; expenditures per student; student/faculty ratio; and library resources. *U.S. News & World Report, "America's Best Graduate Schools, Law, 2025"*

EMPLOYERS

Major Employers

Company Name	Industry
Children's Creative Learning Center	Child day care services
Clackamas Community College	Community college
Coho Distributing	Liquor
Con-Way Enterprise Services	Accounting, auditing, & bookkeeping
Legacy Emanuel Hospital and Health Center	General medical & surgical hospitals
Nike	Rubber & plastics footwear
Oregon Health & Science University	Colleges & universities
PCC Structurals	Aircraft parts & equipment
Portland Adventist Medical Center	General medical & surgical hospitals
Portland Community College	Community college
Portland State University	Colleges & universities
Providence Health & Services - Oregon	Skilled nursing facility
School Dist 1 Multnomah County	Public elementary & secondary schools
Shilo Management Corp.	Hotels & motels
Southwest Washington Medical Center	General medical & surgical hospitals
Stancorp Mortgage Investors	Life insurance
SW Washington Hospital	General medical & surgical hospitals
Tektronix	Instruments to measure elasticity
The Evergreen Aviation and Space Museum	Museums & art galleries
Veterans Health Administration	Administration of veterans' affairs

Note: Companies shown are located within the Portland-Vancouver-Hillsboro, OR-WA Metropolitan Statistical Area.
Source: Chambers of Commerce; State Departments of Labor; Wikipedia

Best Companies to Work For

Boulder Care, headquartered in Portland, is among "Best Workplaces in Health Care." To determine the Best Workplaces in Health Care list, Great Place To Work analyzed the survey responses of over 185,000 employees from Great Place To Work-Certified companies in the health care industry. Survey data analysis and company-provided datapoints are then factored into a combined score to compare and rank the companies that create the most consistently positive experience for all employees in this industry. *Fortune, "Best Workplaces in Health Care," 2024*

Cambia Health Solutions; Portland State University, headquartered in Portland, are among the "Best Places to Work in IT." To qualify, companies had to have a minimum of 100 total employees and five IT employees. The best places to work were selected based on DEI (diversity, equity, and inclusion) practices; IT turnover, promotions, and growth; IT retention and engagement programs; remote/hybrid working; benefits and perks (such as elder care and child care, flextime, and reimbursement for college tuition); and training and career development opportunities. *Computerworld, "Best Places to Work in IT," 2025*

PUBLIC SAFETY

Crime Rate

Area	Total Crime Rate	Violent Crime Rate				Property Crime Rate		
		Murder	Rape	Robbery	Aggrav. Assault	Burglary	Larceny -Theft	Motor Vehicle Theft
City	6,575.8	11.8	51.1	193.1	459.2	792.8	3,756.6	1,311.2
U.S.	2,290.9	5.7	38.0	66.5	264.1	250.7	1,347.2	318.7

Note: Figures are crimes per 100,000 population.
Source: FBI, Table 8, Offenses Known to Law Enforcement, by State by City, 2023

Hate Crimes

Area	Number of Quarters Reported	Number of Incidents per Bias Motivation					
		Race/Ethnicity/ Ancestry	Religion	Sexual Orientation	Disability	Gender	Gender Identity
City[1]	4	43	11	18	3	0	2
U.S.	4	5,900	2,699	2,077	187	92	492

Note: (1) Figures include at least one incident reported with more than one bias motivation.
Source: Federal Bureau of Investigation, Hate Crime Statistics 2023

Identity Theft Consumer Reports

Area	Reports	Reports per 100,000 Population	Rank[2]
MSA[1]	4,548	181	195
U.S.	1,135,291	339	-

Note: (1) Figures cover the Portland-Vancouver-Hillsboro, OR-WA Metropolitan Statistical Area; (2) Rank ranges from 1 to 401 where 1 indicates greatest number of identity theft reports per 100,000 population
Source: Federal Trade Commission, Consumer Sentinel Network Data Book 2024

Fraud and Other Consumer Reports

Area	Reports	Reports per 100,000 Population	Rank[2]
MSA[1]	29,934	1,192	129
U.S.	5,360,641	1,601	-

Note: (1) Figures cover the Portland-Vancouver-Hillsboro, OR-WA Metropolitan Statistical Area; (2) Rank ranges from 1 to 401 where 1 indicates greatest number of fraud and other consumer reports per 100,000 population
Source: Federal Trade Commission, Consumer Sentinel Network Data Book 2024

POLITICS

2024 Presidential Election Results

Area	Trump (Rep.)	Harris (Dem.)	Stein (Green)	Kennedy (Ind.)	Oliver (Lib.)	Other
Multnomah County	17.1	78.7	1.5	1.0	0.3	1.4
U.S.	49.7	48.2	0.6	0.5	0.4	0.6

Note: Results are percentages and may not add to 100% due to rounding
Source: Dave Leip's Atlas of U.S. Presidential Elections

SPORTS

Professional Sports Teams

Team Name	League	Year Established
Portland Timbers	Major League Soccer (MLS)	2011
Portland Trail Blazers	National Basketball Association (NBA)	1970

Note: Includes teams located in the Portland-Vancouver-Hillsboro, OR-WA Metropolitan Statistical Area.
Source: Wikipedia, Major Professional Sports Teams of the United States and Canada, May 1, 2025

CLIMATE

Average and Extreme Temperatures

Temperature	Jan	Feb	Mar	Apr	May	Jun	Jul	Aug	Sep	Oct	Nov	Dec	Yr.
Extreme High (°F)	65	71	83	93	100	102	107	107	105	92	73	64	107
Average High (°F)	45	50	56	61	68	73	80	79	74	64	53	46	62
Average Temp. (°F)	39	43	48	52	58	63	68	68	63	55	46	41	54
Average Low (°F)	34	36	39	42	48	53	57	57	52	46	40	36	45
Extreme Low (°F)	-2	-3	19	29	29	39	43	44	34	26	13	6	-3

Note: Figures cover the years 1926-1992
Source: National Climatic Data Center, International Station Meteorological Climate Summary, 9/96

Average Precipitation/Snowfall/Humidity

Precip./Humidity	Jan	Feb	Mar	Apr	May	Jun	Jul	Aug	Sep	Oct	Nov	Dec	Yr.
Avg. Precip. (in.)	5.5	4.2	3.8	2.4	2.0	1.5	0.5	0.9	1.7	3.0	5.5	6.6	37.5
Avg. Snowfall (in.)	3	1	1	Tr	Tr	0	0	0	0	0	1	2	7
Avg. Rel. Hum. 7am (%)	85	86	86	84	80	78	77	81	87	90	88	87	84
Avg. Rel. Hum. 4pm (%)	75	67	60	55	53	50	45	45	49	61	74	79	59

Note: Figures cover the years 1926-1992; Tr = Trace amounts (<0.05 in. of rain; <0.5 in. of snow)
Source: National Climatic Data Center, International Station Meteorological Climate Summary, 9/96

Weather Conditions

Temperature			Daytime Sky			Precipitation		
5°F & below	32°F & below	90°F & above	Clear	Partly cloudy	Cloudy	0.01 inch or more precip.	0.1 inch or more snow/ice	Thunder-storms
< 1	37	11	67	116	182	152	4	7

Note: Figures are average number of days per year and cover the years 1926-1992
Source: National Climatic Data Center, International Station Meteorological Climate Summary, 9/96

HAZARDOUS WASTE

Superfund Sites

The Portland-Vancouver-Hillsboro, OR-WA metro area is home to seven sites on the EPA's Superfund National Priorities List (NPL) or Superfund Alternative Approach (SAA) list: **Boomsnub/Airco** (Final NPL); **Bradford Island** (Final NPL); **McCormick & Baxter Creosoting Co. (Portland Plant)** (Final NPL); **Northwest Pipe & Casing/Hall Process Company** (Final NPL); **Portland Harbor** (Final NPL); **Reynolds Metals Company** (Final NPL); **Taylor Lumber And Treating** (Final NPL). The Superfund alternative approach uses the same investigation and cleanup process and standards that are used for sites listed on the National Priorities List. The SAA is an alternative to listing a site on the NPL; it is not an alternative to Superfund or the Superfund process. There are a total of 1,445 Superfund sites with a status of proposed or final on both lists in the United States. *U.S. Environmental Protection Agency, National Priorities List, May 1, 2025; U.S. Environmental Protection Agency, Superfund Alternative Approach Sites, May 1, 2025*

AIR QUALITY

Air Quality Trends: Ozone

	1990	1995	2000	2005	2010	2015	2020	2021	2022	2023
MSA[1]	0.081	0.065	0.059	0.059	0.056	0.064	0.058	0.058	0.059	0.062
U.S.	0.087	0.089	0.081	0.080	0.072	0.068	0.066	0.067	0.067	0.070

Note: (1) Data covers the Portland-Vancouver-Hillsboro, OR-WA Metropolitan Statistical Area. The values shown are the composite ozone concentration averages among trend sites based on the highest fourth daily maximum 8-hour concentration in parts per million. These trends are based on sites having an adequate record of monitoring data during the trend period. Data from exceptional events are included.
Source: U.S. Environmental Protection Agency, Air Quality Monitoring Information, "Air Quality Trends by City, 1990-2023"

Air Quality Index

Area	Percent of Days when Air Quality was...[2]					AQI Statistics[2]	
	Good	Moderate	Unhealthy for Sensitive Groups	Unhealthy	Very Unhealthy	Maximum	Median
MSA[1]	60.0	38.4	1.1	0.5	0.0	153	43

Note: (1) Data covers the Portland-Vancouver-Hillsboro, OR-WA Metropolitan Statistical Area; (2) Based on 365 days with AQI data in 2023. Air Quality Index (AQI) is an index for reporting daily air quality. EPA calculates the AQI for five major air pollutants regulated by the Clean Air Act: ground-level ozone, particle pollution (aka particulate matter), carbon monoxide, sulfur dioxide, and nitrogen dioxide. The AQI runs from 0 to 500. The higher the AQI value, the greater the level of air pollution and the greater the health concern. There are six AQI categories: "Good" AQI is between 0 and 50. Air quality is considered satisfactory; "Moderate" AQI is between 51 and 100. Air quality is acceptable; "Unhealthy for Sensitive Groups" When AQI values are between 101 and 150, members of sensitive groups may experience health effects; "Unhealthy" When AQI values are between 151 and 200 everyone may begin to experience health effects; "Very Unhealthy" AQI values between 201 and 300 trigger a health alert; "Hazardous" AQI values over 300 trigger warnings of emergency conditions (not shown).
Source: U.S. Environmental Protection Agency, Air Quality Index Report, 2023

Air Quality Index Pollutants

Area	Percent of Days when AQI Pollutant was...[2]					
	Carbon Monoxide	Nitrogen Dioxide	Ozone	Sulfur Dioxide	Particulate Matter 2.5	Particulate Matter 10
MSA[1]	0.0	1.1	42.7	(3)	56.2	0.0

Note: (1) Data covers the Portland-Vancouver-Hillsboro, OR-WA Metropolitan Statistical Area; (2) Based on 365 days with AQI data in 2023. The Air Quality Index (AQI) is an index for reporting daily air quality. EPA calculates the AQI for five major air pollutants regulated by the Clean Air Act: ground-level ozone, particle pollution (also known as particulate matter), carbon monoxide, sulfur dioxide, and nitrogen dioxide. The AQI runs from 0 to 500. The higher the AQI value, the greater the level of air pollution and the greater the health concern; (3) Sulfur dioxide is no longer included in this table because SO_2 concentrations tend to be very localized and not necessarily representative of broad geographical areas like counties and CBSAs.
Source: U.S. Environmental Protection Agency, Air Quality Index Report, 2023

Maximum Air Pollutant Concentrations: Particulate Matter, Ozone, CO and Lead

	Particulate Matter 10 (ug/m^3)	Particulate Matter 2.5 Wtd AM (ug/m^3)	Particulate Matter 2.5 24-Hr (ug/m^3)	Ozone (ppm)	Carbon Monoxide (ppm)	Lead (ug/m^3)
MSA[1] Level	27	6.5	25	0.068	1	n/a
NAAQS[2]	150	15	35	0.075	9	0.15
Met NAAQS[2]	Yes	Yes	Yes	Yes	Yes	n/a

Note: (1) Data covers the Portland-Vancouver-Hillsboro, OR-WA Metropolitan Statistical Area; Data from exceptional events are included; (2) National Ambient Air Quality Standards; ppm = parts per million; ug/m^3 = micrograms per cubic meter; n/a not available.
Concentrations: Particulate Matter 10 (coarse particulate)—highest second maximum 24-hour concentration; Particulate Matter 2.5 Wtd AM (fine particulate)—highest weighted annual mean concentration; Particulate Matter 2.5 24-Hour (fine particulate)—highest 98th percentile 24-hour concentration; Ozone—highest fourth daily maximum 8-hour concentration; Carbon Monoxide—highest second maximum non-overlapping 8-hour concentration; Lead—maximum running 3-month average
Source: U.S. Environmental Protection Agency, Air Quality Monitoring Information, "Air Quality Statistics by City, 2023"

Maximum Air Pollutant Concentrations: Nitrogen Dioxide and Sulfur Dioxide

	Nitrogen Dioxide AM (ppb)	Nitrogen Dioxide 1-Hr (ppb)	Sulfur Dioxide AM (ppb)	Sulfur Dioxide 1-Hr (ppb)	Sulfur Dioxide 24-Hr (ppb)
MSA[1] Level	9	29	n/a	n/a	n/a
NAAQS[2]	53	100	30	75	140
Met NAAQS[2]	Yes	Yes	n/a	n/a	n/a

Note: (1) Data covers the Portland-Vancouver-Hillsboro, OR-WA Metropolitan Statistical Area; Data from exceptional events are included; (2) National Ambient Air Quality Standards; ppm = parts per million; ug/m^3 = micrograms per cubic meter; n/a not available.
Concentrations: Nitrogen Dioxide AM—highest arithmetic mean concentration; Nitrogen Dioxide 1-Hr—highest 98th percentile 1-hour daily maximum concentration; Sulfur Dioxide AM—highest annual mean concentration; Sulfur Dioxide 1-Hr—highest 99th percentile 1-hour daily maximum concentration; Sulfur Dioxide 24-Hr—highest second maximum 24-hour concentration
Source: U.S. Environmental Protection Agency, Air Quality Monitoring Information, "Air Quality Statistics by City, 2023"

Provo, Utah

Background

Provo is situated on the Provo River, 43 miles south of Salt Lake City, at a site that originally sat under the waters of Lake Bonneville. Today, Provo enjoys one of the country's highest employment rates, a growing high-tech economy, a low crime rate, and a magnificent natural environment. The seat of Utah County, it lies at the base of the steep Wasatch Mountains, with Provo Peak rising to a height of 11,054 feet just east of the city, making Provo convenient to Utah's famed ski areas and to the Uinta National Forest.

Spanish missionaries Francisco Silvestre Velez de Escalante and Francisco Atanasio Dominguez, exploring for a more direct route from present-day New Mexico to California, were likely the first Europeans to view the area. They did not establish a permanent mission but did note that the area could easily be irrigated and developed into an important agricultural settlement. Etienne Prevot, a Canadian trapper and explorer, likewise visited but did not settle, though he too remarked on the beauty and potential of the site. These early explorers also met, and conflicted with, the area's original inhabitants, the Ute Native American, who held an important fish festival on the river every spring.

Permanent European settlement of Provo is strongly linked to Mormon history. In 1849, John S. Higbee, with 30 families in a wagon train, left the larger Salt Lake City community to move north. As they arrived in the region, they confronted a group of Ute, with whom white settlers had already been in some conflict. A short-lived peace agreement gave way to further conflict and a series of battles, after which the Native Americans agreed to resettlement. Peace ensued, and Provo was subject to long periods of peaceful relations with the Native American tribe, unlike many other young Western towns.

Irrigation was central to Provo's success, and in the year of Higbee's arrival, two large canals were dug, taking water from the Provo River. Grain mills were constructed to serve the needs of nearby farmers, and important rail links were completed in the 1870s connecting Provo to Salt Lake City and to the Union Pacific System, giving impetus to the region's agricultural and mining industries.

Provo's growth took off, with an electric generating plant built in 1890, and an interurban commuter rail service between Provo and Salt Lake City in 1914. The town had become a major regional industrial center, with ironworks, flourmills, and brickyards. Today, the area has the second largest concentration of software technology companies in the country and the third concentration of high-tech companies. Also important to the economy of the region are biotech companies and top employers Adobe, Intermountain Health Care, Revere Health, Nestle Dairy, and NuSkin Enterprises.

Favorite son Dr. Harvey Fletcher, of Bell Laboratories, was the inventor of aids to the deaf and hearing-impaired, and an important early leader of the National Acoustic Association. Philo T. Farnsworth, raised in Provo, developed the fundamental concepts of television in 1924 at the age of 18. Provo is home to Farnsworth's alma mater, Brigham Young University (BYU), a private university operated by The Church of Jesus Christ of Latter-day Saints (LDS). Founded in 1875 it has earned national respect for everything from football and undergraduate liberal arts programs to its graduate programs in business and law. The Provo Tabernacle, destroyed by fire in 2010, was rebuilt as the Provo City Center Temple in 2016, making Provo the second city in the LDS Church to have two temples.

Provo hosts the annual America's Freedom Festival, a private, non-profit, non-political event, and one of the largest and longest (May to July) patriotic celebrations in the country. It's not without controversy, as it has prevented certain entities, namely Mormons and LGBTQ+ groups, from participating over the years. Festival Latinoamericano is an annual family-oriented Labor Day weekend event in downtown Provo that offers the community a taste of the region's Hispanic culture through ethnic food, vendors, and performances.

The climate of Provo is semi-arid continental. Summers are generally hot and dry. Winters are cold but not severe. Precipitation is generally light, with most of the rain falling in the spring.

Rankings

Business/Finance Rankings

- The Provo metro area appeared on the Milken Institute "2025 Best Performing Cities" list. Rank: #15 out of 200 large metro areas (based on performance category). Criteria: job growth; wage growth; high-tech growth and impact; community resilience; housing affordability; household broadband access. *Milken Institute, "Best-Performing Cities 2025," January 14, 2025*

Education Rankings

- Personal finance website *WalletHub* analyzed the 150 largest U.S. metropolitan statistical areas to determine where the most educated Americans are putting their degrees to work. Criteria: education levels; percentage of workers with degrees; education quality and attainment gap; public school quality rankings; quality and enrollment of each metro area's universities. Provo was ranked #12 (#1 = most educated city). *WalletHub.com, "Most & Least Educated Cities in America, 2025" July 2, 2024*

Environmental Rankings

- *Niche* compiled a list of the nation's snowiest cities, based on the National Oceanic and Atmospheric Administration's 30-year average snowfall data. Among cities with a population of at least 50,000, Provo ranked #20. *Niche.com, Top 25 Snowiest Cities in America, December 10, 2018*

- The U.S. Environmental Protection Agency (EPA) released its list of U.S. metropolitan areas with the most ENERGY STAR certified buildings in 2023. The Provo metro area was ranked #20 out of 25. *U.S. Environmental Protection Agency, "2024 Energy Star Top Cities," May 22, 2024*

- The U.S. Environmental Protection Agency (EPA) released its list of mid-size U.S. metropolitan areas with the most ENERGY STAR certified buildings in 2023. The Provo metro area was ranked #1 out of 10. *U.S. Environmental Protection Agency, "2024 Energy Star Top Cities," May 22, 2024*

Health/Fitness Rankings

- Provo was identified as a "2025 Allergy Capital." The area ranked #94 out of the nation's 100 largest metropolitan areas. Three groups of factors were used to identify the most challenging cities for people with allergies: annual tree, grass, and weed pollen scores; over the counter allergy medicine use; number of board-certified allergy specialists. *Asthma and Allergy Foundation of America, "2025 Allergy Capitals: The Most Challenging Places to Live with Allergies," March 18, 2025*

- Provo was identified as a "2024 Asthma Capital." The area ranked #99 out of the nation's 100 largest metropolitan areas. Criteria: estimated asthma prevalence; asthma-related mortality; and ER visits due to asthma. Risk factors analyzed but not factored in the rankings: annual air quality including pollution and ozone levels; public smoking laws; indoor air quality; access to asthma specialists; rescue and controller medication use; uninsured rate; pollen allergy; poverty rate. *Asthma and Allergy Foundation of America, "Asthma Capitals 2024: The Most Challenging Places to Live With Asthma," September 10, 2024*

Safety Rankings

- Allstate ranked the 100 most populous cities in America in terms of driver safety. Provo ranked #65. Criteria based on anonymized driving behavior data from Allstate's mobile app powered by Arity: high speed driving (over 80 mph), phone handling, and hard braking. The report helps increase the importance of safety and awareness behind the wheel. *Allstate, "16th Allstate America's Best Drivers Report®" July 11, 2024*

Seniors/Retirement Rankings

- *AARP the Magazine* selected Provo as one of the great places in the United States for seniors, as well as younger generations, that represent "a place to call home." For the list, the magazine recognized the change in criteria due to the pandemic, and looked for cities with easy access to exercise/outdoors, quality healthcare, sense of community, relatively affordable housing costs, job markets that accommodate working from home, and reliable internet access. *AARP The Magazine, "Best Places to Live and Retire Now," November 29, 2021*

Miscellaneous Rankings

- *WalletHub* compared 148 of the most populated U.S. cities to determine their operating efficiency. A "Quality of Services" score was constructed for each city and then measured against the total budget per capita to reveal which were managed the best. Provo ranked #7. Criteria: financial stability; economy; education; safety; health; infrastructure and pollution. *WalletHub.com, "2025's Best- & Worst-Run Cities in America," June 18, 2024*

Business Environment

DEMOGRAPHICS

Population Growth

Area	1990 Census	2000 Census	2010 Census	2020 Census	2023 Estimate[2]	Population Growth 1990-2023 (%)
City	87,148	105,166	112,488	115,162	114,303	31.2
MSA[1]	269,407	376,774	526,810	671,185	695,895	158.3
U.S.	248,709,873	281,421,906	308,745,538	331,449,281	332,387,540	33.6

Note: (1) Figures cover the Provo-Orem-Lehi, UT Metropolitan Statistical Area; (2) 2019-2023 5-year ACS population estimate
Source: U.S. Census Bureau, 1990 Census, 2000 Census, 2010 Census, 2020 Census, 2019-2023 American Community Survey 5-Year Estimates

Race

Area	White Alone[2] (%)	Black Alone[2] (%)	Asian Alone[2] (%)	AIAN[3] Alone[2] (%)	NHOPI[4] Alone[2] (%)	Other Race Alone[2] (%)	Two or More Races (%)
City	78.6	1.1	2.2	1.0	1.4	5.4	10.2
MSA[1]	83.9	0.7	1.4	0.6	0.8	4.0	8.6
U.S.	63.4	12.4	5.8	0.9	0.2	6.6	10.7

Note: (1) Figures cover the Provo-Orem-Lehi, UT Metropolitan Statistical Area; (2) Alone is defined as not being in combination with one or more other races; (3) American Indian and Alaska Native; (4) Native Hawaiian and Other Pacific Islander
Source: U.S. Census Bureau, 2019-2023 American Community Survey 5-Year Estimates

Hispanic or Latino Origin

Area	Total (%)	Mexican (%)	Puerto Rican (%)	Cuban (%)	Other (%)
City	18.9	11.4	0.7	0.2	6.6
MSA[1]	13.7	8.1	0.4	0.1	5.1
U.S.	19.0	11.3	1.8	0.7	5.2

Note: Persons of Hispanic or Latino origin can be of any race; (1) Figures cover the Provo-Orem-Lehi, UT Metropolitan Statistical Area
Source: U.S. Census Bureau, 2019-2023 American Community Survey 5-Year Estimates

Age

Area	Percent of Population									Median Age
	Under Age 5	Age 5–19	Age 20–34	Age 35–44	Age 45–54	Age 55–64	Age 65–74	Age 75–84	Age 85+	
City	5.8	20.1	48.3	8.2	5.7	5.3	3.7	1.9	0.9	23.7
MSA[1]	8.7	27.7	27.3	12.5	9.2	6.7	4.8	2.3	0.8	25.6
U.S.	5.7	19.1	20.2	13.1	12.8	10.0	4.9	1.9		38.7

Note: (1) Figures cover the Provo-Orem-Lehi, UT Metropolitan Statistical Area
Source: U.S. Census Bureau, 2019-2023 American Community Survey 5-Year Estimates

Disability by Age

Area	All Ages	Under 18 Years Old	18 to 64 Years Old	65 Years and Over
City	10.2	4.2	8.9	42.2
MSA[1]	8.7	3.9	8.3	31.3
U.S.	13.0	4.7	10.7	32.9

Note: Figures show percent of the civilian noninstitutionalized population that reported having a disability. Disability status is determined from six types of difficulty: vision, hearing, cognitive, ambulatory, self-care, and independent living. For children under 5 years old, hearing and vision difficulty are used to determine disability status. For children between the ages of 5 and 14, disability status is determined from hearing, vision, cognitive, ambulatory, and self-care difficulties. For people aged 15 years and older, they are considered to have a disability if they have difficulty with any one of the six difficulty types; Note: (1) Figures cover the Provo-Orem-Lehi, UT Metropolitan Statistical Area
Source: U.S. Census Bureau, 2019-2023 American Community Survey 5-Year Estimates

Ancestry

Area	German	Irish	English	American	Italian	Polish	French[2]	European	Scottish
City	10.4	4.9	28.2	2.2	2.2	0.7	1.3	4.0	3.6
MSA[1]	10.0	4.9	32.1	4.1	2.1	0.5	1.4	4.8	4.1
U.S.	12.6	9.4	9.1	5.5	4.9	2.6	2.0	1.6	1.6

Note: Figures are the percentage of the total population reporting a particular ancestry. The nine most commonly reported ancestries in the U.S. are shown. Figures include multiple ancestries (e.g. if a person reported being Irish and Italian, they were included in both columns); (1) Figures cover the Provo-Orem-Lehi, UT Metropolitan Statistical Area; (2) Excludes Basque
Source: U.S. Census Bureau, 2019-2023 American Community Survey 5-Year Estimates

Foreign-born Population

Area	Any Foreign Country	Asia	Mexico	Europe	Caribbean	Central America[2]	South America	Africa	Canada
						Percent of Population Born in			
City	12.2	1.6	3.8	0.7	0.4	1.0	3.3	0.5	0.4
MSA[1]	7.7	1.0	2.5	0.5	0.2	0.6	2.0	0.3	0.3
U.S.	13.9	4.3	3.3	1.4	1.4	1.2	1.2	0.8	0.2

Note: (1) Figures cover the Provo-Orem-Lehi, UT Metropolitan Statistical Area; (2) Excludes Mexico.
Source: U.S. Census Bureau, 2019-2023 American Community Survey 5-Year Estimates

Household Size

Area	Persons in Household (%)							Average Household Size
	One	Two	Three	Four	Five	Six	Seven or More	
City	14.0	36.9	17.7	14.4	7.6	6.5	3.0	2.98
MSA[1]	12.3	29.0	16.2	16.6	12.5	8.1	5.3	3.40
U.S.	28.5	33.8	15.4	12.7	5.9	2.3	1.4	2.54

Note: (1) Figures cover the Provo-Orem-Lehi, UT Metropolitan Statistical Area
Source: U.S. Census Bureau, 2019-2023 American Community Survey 5-Year Estimates

Household Relationships

Area	House-holder	Opposite-sex Spouse	Same-sex Spouse	Opposite-sex Unmarried Partner	Same-sex Unmarried Partner	Child[2]	Grand-child	Other Relatives	Non-relatives
City	29.6	15.9	0.1	0.6	0.0	25.7	1.6	4.0	12.7
MSA[1]	28.0	18.8	0.1	0.7	0.0	39.0	2.1	4.0	4.8
U.S.	38.3	17.5	0.2	2.5	0.2	28.3	2.4	4.8	3.4

Note: Figures are percent of the total population; (1) Figures cover the Provo-Orem-Lehi, UT Metropolitan Statistical Area; (2) Includes biological, adopted, and stepchildren of the householder
Source: U.S. Census Bureau, 2020 Census

Gender

Area	Males	Females	Males per 100 Females
City	56,107	58,196	96.4
MSA[1]	353,303	342,592	103.1
U.S.	164,545,087	167,842,453	98.0

Note: (1) Figures cover the Provo-Orem-Lehi, UT Metropolitan Statistical Area
Source: U.S. Census Bureau, 2019-2023 American Community Survey 5-Year Estimates

Marital Status

Area	Never Married	Now Married[2]	Separated	Widowed	Divorced
City	49.3	43.5	0.7	2.2	4.3
MSA[1]	33.4	57.7	0.8	2.6	5.5
U.S.	34.1	47.9	1.7	5.6	10.7

Note: Figures are percentages and cover the population 15 years of age and older; (1) Figures cover the Provo-Orem-Lehi, UT Metropolitan Statistical Area; (2) Excludes separated
Source: U.S. Census Bureau, 2019-2023 American Community Survey 5-Year Estimates

Religious Groups by Family

Area	Catholic	Baptist	Methodist	LDS[2]	Pentecostal	Lutheran	Islam	Adventist	Other
MSA[1]	4.9	0.1	<0.1	82.6	0.1	<0.1	0.3	0.3	0.4
U.S.	18.7	7.3	3.0	2.0	1.8	1.7	1.3	1.3	11.6

Note: Figures are the number of adherents as a percentage of the total population and cover the eight largest religious groups in the U.S; (1) Figures cover the Provo-Orem-Lehi, UT Metropolitan Statistical Area; (2) Church of Jesus Christ of Latter-day Saints
Sources: 2020 U.S. Religion Census, Association of Statisticians of American Religious Bodies; The Association of Religion Data Archives (ARDA)

Religious Groups by Tradition

Area	Catholic	Evangelical Protestant	Mainline Protestant	Black Protestant	Islam	Judaism	Hinduism	Orthodox	Buddhism
MSA[1]	4.9	0.4	<0.1	n/a	0.3	n/a	0.1	n/a	n/a
U.S.	18.7	16.5	5.2	2.3	1.3	0.6	0.4	0.4	0.3

Note: Figures are the number of adherents as a percentage of the total population; (1) Figures cover the Provo-Orem-Lehi, UT Metropolitan Statistical Area
Sources: 2020 U.S. Religion Census, Association of Statisticians of American Religious Bodies; The Association of Religion Data Archives (ARDA)

ECONOMY

Real Gross Domestic Product (GDP)

Area	2017	2018	2019	2020	2021	2022	2023	Rank[3]
MSA[1]	25.5	27.6	30.1	31.5	34.1	35.8	37.4	90
U.S.[2]	17,619.1	18,160.7	18,642.5	18,238.9	19,387.6	19,896.6	20,436.3	–

Note: Figures are in billions of chained 2017 dollars; (1) Figures cover the Provo-Orem-Lehi, UT Metropolitan Statistical Area; (2) Figures cover real GDP within metropolitan areas; (3) Rank is based on 2023 data and ranges from 1 to 384
Source: U.S. Bureau of Economic Analysis

Economic Growth

Area	2014	2015	2016	2017	2018	2019	2020	2021	2022	2023
MSA[1]	4.7	8.2	7.0	6.8	8.3	9.1	4.6	8.3	4.9	4.4
U.S.[2]	2.6	3.2	2.0	2.7	3.1	2.7	-2.2	6.3	2.6	2.7

Note: Figures are real gross domestic product growth rates and represent percent change from preceding period; (1) Figures cover the Provo-Orem-Lehi, UT Metropolitan Statistical Area; (2) Figures are the average growth rates within metropolitan areas
Source: U.S. Bureau of Economic Analysis

Metropolitan Area Exports

Area	2018	2019	2020	2021	2022	2023	Rank[2]
MSA[1]	1,788.1	1,783.7	1,888.5	2,053.8	1,318.4	1,416.7	140
U.S.	1,664,056.1	1,645,173.7	1,431,406.6	1,753,941.4	2,062,937.4	2,019,160.5	–

Note: Figures are in millions of dollars; (1) Figures cover the Provo-Orem-Lehi, UT Metropolitan Statistical Area; (2) Rank is based on 2023 data and ranges from 1 to 386
Source: U.S. Department of Commerce, International Trade Administration, Office of Trade and Economic Analysis, Industry and Analysis, Exports by Metropolitan Area, data extracted April 2, 2025

Building Permits

Area	Single-Family			Multi-Family			Total		
	2023	2024	Pct. Chg.	2023	2024	Pct. Chg.	2023	2024	Pct. Chg.
City	147	133	-9.5	80	153	91.3	227	286	26.0
MSA[1]	4,663	5,246	12.5	1,518	1,182	-22.1	6,181	6,428	4.0
U.S.	920,000	981,900	6.7	591,100	496,100	-16.1	1,511,100	1,478,000	-2.2

Note: (1) Figures cover the Provo-Orem-Lehi, UT Metropolitan Statistical Area; Figures represent new, privately-owned housing units authorized (unadjusted data)
Source: U.S. Census Bureau, Building Permits Survey (BPS), 2023, 2024

Bankruptcy Filings

Area	Business Filings			Nonbusiness Filings		
	2023	2024	% Chg.	2023	2024	% Chg.
Utah County	33	36	9.1	925	1,070	15.7
U.S.	18,926	23,107	22.1	434,064	494,201	13.9

Note: Business filings include Chapter 7, Chapter 9, Chapter 11, Chapter 12, Chapter 13, Chapter 15, and Section 304; Nonbusiness filings include Chapter 7, Chapter 11, and Chapter 13
Source: Administrative Office of the U.S. Courts, Business and Nonbusiness Bankruptcy, County Cases Commenced by Chapter of the Bankruptcy Code, During the 12-Month Period Ending December 31, 2023 and Business and Nonbusiness Bankruptcy, County Cases Commenced by Chapter of the Bankruptcy Code, During the 12-Month Period Ending December 31, 2024

Housing Vacancy Rates

Area	Gross Vacancy Rate[3] (%)			Year-Round Vacancy Rate[4] (%)			Rental Vacancy Rate[5] (%)			Homeowner Vacancy Rate[6] (%)		
	2022	2023	2024	2022	2023	2024	2022	2023	2024	2022	2023	2024
MSA[1]	n/a	n/a	n/a	n/a	n/a	n/a	n/a	n/a	n/a	n/a	n/a	n/a
U.S.[2]	9.1	9.0	9.1	7.5	7.5	7.6	5.7	6.5	6.8	0.8	0.8	1.0

Note: (1) Figures cover the Provo-Orem-Lehi, UT Metropolitan Statistical Area; (2) Figures cover the 75 largest Metropolitan Statistical Areas; (3) The percentage of the total housing inventory that is vacant; (4) The percentage of the housing inventory (excluding seasonal units) that is year-round vacant; (5) The percentage of rental inventory that is vacant for rent; (6) The percentage of homeowner inventory that is vacant for sale; n/a not available
Source: U.S. Census Bureau, Housing Vacancies and Homeownership Annual Statistics: 2022, 2023, 2024

INCOME

Income

Area	Per Capita ($)	Median Household ($)	Average Household ($)
City	26,755	62,800	86,072
MSA[1]	35,045	96,745	121,112
U.S.	43,289	78,538	110,491

Note: (1) Figures cover the Provo-Orem-Lehi, UT Metropolitan Statistical Area
Source: U.S. Census Bureau, 2019-2023 American Community Survey 5-Year Estimates

Household Income Distribution

Area	Percent of Households Earning							
	Under $15,000	$15,000 -$24,999	$25,000 -$34,999	$35,000 -$49,999	$50,000 -$74,999	$75,000 -$99,999	$100,000 -$149,999	$150,000 and up
City	9.4	8.2	9.2	13.5	17.7	13.6	14.5	13.8
MSA[1]	4.4	4.1	4.6	8.5	15.1	15.0	22.7	25.6
U.S.	8.5	6.6	6.8	10.4	15.7	12.7	17.4	21.9

Note: (1) Figures cover the Provo-Orem-Lehi, UT Metropolitan Statistical Area
Source: U.S. Census Bureau, 2019-2023 American Community Survey 5-Year Estimates

Poverty Rate

Area	All Ages	Under 18 Years Old	18 to 64 Years Old	65 Years and Over
City	22.3	12.8	26.3	9.4
MSA[1]	8.7	7.2	10.0	5.5
U.S.	12.4	16.3	11.6	10.4

Note: Figures are percentage of people whose income during the past 12 months was below the poverty level;
(1) Figures cover the Provo-Orem-Lehi, UT Metropolitan Statistical Area
Source: U.S. Census Bureau, 2019-2023 American Community Survey 5-Year Estimates

EMPLOYMENT

Labor Force and Employment

Area	Civilian Labor Force			Workers Employed		
	Dec. 2023	Dec. 2024	% Chg.	Dec. 2023	Dec. 2024	% Chg.
City	73,763	74,411	0.9	72,156	72,484	0.5
MSA[1]	363,569	366,874	0.9	354,453	356,068	0.5
U.S.	166,661,000	167,746,000	0.7	160,754,000	161,294,000	0.3

Note: Data is not seasonally adjusted and covers workers 16 years of age and older; (1) Figures cover the
Provo-Orem-Lehi, UT Metropolitan Statistical Area
Source: Bureau of Labor Statistics, Local Area Unemployment Statistics

Unemployment Rate

Area	2024											
	Jan.	Feb.	Mar.	Apr.	May	Jun.	Jul.	Aug.	Sep.	Oct.	Nov.	Dec.
City	2.6	2.6	2.4	2.4	3.2	3.8	3.2	3.4	2.9	2.6	2.8	2.6
MSA[1]	3.0	3.2	3.0	2.9	3.2	3.7	3.6	3.7	3.1	3.0	3.1	2.9
U.S.	4.1	4.2	3.9	3.5	3.7	4.3	4.5	4.4	3.9	3.9	4.0	3.8

Note: Data is not seasonally adjusted and covers workers 16 years of age and older; (1) Figures cover the
Provo-Orem-Lehi, UT Metropolitan Statistical Area
Source: Bureau of Labor Statistics, Local Area Unemployment Statistics

Average Wages

Occupation	$/Hr.	Occupation	$/Hr.
Accountants and Auditors	38.12	Maintenance and Repair Workers	24.23
Automotive Mechanics	23.63	Marketing Managers	70.63
Bookkeepers	23.58	Network and Computer Systems Admin.	46.73
Carpenters	25.60	Nurses, Licensed Practical	28.85
Cashiers	15.11	Nurses, Registered	40.74
Computer Programmers	43.63	Nursing Assistants	18.10
Computer Systems Analysts	48.54	Office Clerks, General	20.61
Computer User Support Specialists	28.65	Physical Therapists	47.91
Construction Laborers	22.38	Physicians	138.71
Cooks, Restaurant	17.58	Plumbers, Pipefitters and Steamfitters	27.75
Customer Service Representatives	19.85	Police and Sheriff's Patrol Officers	34.98
Dentists	66.32	Postal Service Mail Carriers	29.07
Electricians	29.16	Real Estate Sales Agents	24.11
Engineers, Electrical	60.54	Retail Salespersons	17.69
Fast Food and Counter Workers	13.85	Sales Representatives, Technical/Scientific	38.31
Financial Managers	75.16	Secretaries, Exc. Legal/Medical/Executive	20.88
First-Line Supervisors of Office Workers	33.39	Security Guards	20.05
General and Operations Managers	54.43	Surgeons	n/a
Hairdressers/Cosmetologists	18.78	Teacher Assistants, Exc. Postsecondary[1]	15.72
Home Health and Personal Care Aides	17.59	Teachers, Secondary School, Exc. Sp. Ed.[1]	32.55
Janitors and Cleaners	15.34	Telemarketers	19.36
Landscaping/Groundskeeping Workers	20.19	Truck Drivers, Heavy/Tractor-Trailer	27.39
Lawyers	70.82	Truck Drivers, Light/Delivery Services	21.30
Maids and Housekeeping Cleaners	16.07	Waiters and Waitresses	16.73

Note: Wage data covers the Provo-Orem-Lehi, UT Metropolitan Statistical Area; (1) Hourly wages were
calculated from annual wage data based on a 40 hour work week
Source: Bureau of Labor Statistics, Metro Area Occupational Employment & Wage Estimates, May 2024

Employment by Industry

Sector	MSA[1]		U.S.
	Number of Employees	Percent of Total	Percent of Total
Construction, Mining, and Logging	30,500	9.5	5.5
Financial Activities	12,700	4.0	5.8
Government	38,300	11.9	14.9
Information	12,600	3.9	1.9
Leisure and Hospitality	29,100	9.1	10.4
Manufacturing	25,000	7.8	8.0
Other Services	7,400	2.3	3.7
Private Education and Health Services	70,900	22.1	16.9
Professional and Business Services	46,100	14.4	14.2
Retail Trade	34,800	10.8	10.0
Transportation, Warehousing, and Utilities	6,300	2.0	4.8
Wholesale Trade	7,100	2.2	3.9

Note: Figures are non-farm employment as of December 2024. Figures are not seasonally adjusted and include workers 16 years of age and older; (1) Figures cover the Provo-Orem-Lehi, UT Metropolitan Statistical Area
Source: Bureau of Labor Statistics, Current Employment Statistics, Employment, Hours, and Earnings

Employment by Occupation

Occupation Classification	City (%)	MSA[1] (%)	U.S. (%)
Management, Business, Science, and Arts	44.1	45.5	42.0
Natural Resources, Construction, and Maintenance	5.9	7.9	8.6
Production, Transportation, and Material Moving	10.6	10.4	13.0
Sales and Office	21.2	21.5	19.9
Service	18.2	14.7	16.5

Note: Figures cover employed civilians 16 years of age and older; (1) Figures cover the Provo-Orem-Lehi, UT Metropolitan Statistical Area
Source: U.S. Census Bureau, 2019-2023 American Community Survey 5-Year Estimates

Occupations with Greatest Projected Employment Growth: 2022 – 2032

Occupation[1]	2022 Employment	2032 Projected Employment	Numeric Employment Change	Percent Employment Change
Fast Food and Counter Workers	50,740	67,110	16,370	32.3
General and Operations Managers	59,210	75,020	15,810	26.7
Software Developers	20,260	29,920	9,660	47.7
Construction Laborers	27,050	36,570	9,520	35.2
Cooks, Restaurant	12,890	20,160	7,270	56.4
Stockers and Order Fillers	27,150	33,880	6,730	24.8
Registered Nurses	25,300	31,710	6,410	25.3
Janitors and Cleaners, Except Maids and Housekeeping Cleaners	25,050	31,380	6,330	25.3
Landscaping and Groundskeeping Workers	14,560	19,690	5,130	35.2
Laborers and Freight, Stock, and Material Movers, Hand	25,010	29,990	4,980	19.9

Note: Projections cover Utah; (1) Sorted by numeric employment change
Source: www.projectionscentral.org, State Occupational Projections, 2022–2032 Long-Term Projections

Fastest-Growing Occupations: 2022 – 2032

Occupation[1]	2022 Employment	2032 Projected Employment	Numeric Employment Change	Percent Employment Change
Solar Photovoltaic Installers	390	660	270	69.2
Physical Therapist Assistants	650	1,090	440	67.7
Chiropractors	480	800	320	66.7
Occupational Therapy Assistants	300	500	200	66.7
Statisticians	470	760	290	61.7
Nurse Practitioners	3,680	5,900	2,220	60.3
Ophthalmic Medical Technicians	270	430	160	59.3
Data Scientists	3,100	4,900	1,800	58.1
Information Security Analysts (SOC 2018)	1,650	2,600	950	57.6
Orthotists and Prosthetists	660	1,040	380	57.6

Note: Projections cover Utah; (1) Sorted by percent employment change and excludes occupations with numeric employment change less than 50
Source: www.projectionscentral.org, State Occupational Projections, 2022–2032 Long-Term Projections

CITY FINANCES

City Government Finances

Component	2022 ($000)	2022 ($ per capita)
Total Revenues	203,940	1,754
Total Expenditures	274,867	2,364
Debt Outstanding	20,154	173

Source: U.S. Census Bureau, State & Local Government Finances 2022

City Government Revenue by Source

Source	2022 ($000)	2022 ($ per capita)	2022 (%)
General Revenue			
From Federal Government	2,627	23	1.3
From State Government	2,876	25	1.4
From Local Governments	3,969	34	1.9
Taxes			
Property	19,675	169	9.6
Sales and Gross Receipts	20,179	174	9.9
Personal Income	0	0	0.0
Corporate Income	0	0	0.0
Motor Vehicle License	0	0	0.0
Other Taxes	1,261	11	0.6
Current Charges	47,264	406	23.2
Liquor Store	0	0	0.0
Utility	89,068	766	43.7

Source: U.S. Census Bureau, State & Local Government Finances 2022

City Government Expenditures by Function

Function	2022 ($000)	2022 ($ per capita)	2022 (%)
General Direct Expenditures			
Air Transportation	24,510	210	8.9
Corrections	0	0	0.0
Education	0	0	0.0
Employment Security Administration	0	0	0.0
Financial Administration	2,221	19	0.8
Fire Protection	10,804	92	3.9
General Public Buildings	0	0	0.0
Governmental Administration, Other	5,041	43	1.8
Health	0	0	0.0
Highways	3,664	31	1.3
Hospitals	0	0	0.0
Housing and Community Development	4,862	41	1.8
Interest on General Debt	80	< 1	< 0.1
Judicial and Legal	2,887	24	1.1
Libraries	3,888	33	1.4
Parking	6	< 1	< 0.1
Parks and Recreation	17,251	148	6.3
Police Protection	18,071	155	6.6
Public Welfare	0	0	0.0
Sewerage	57,351	493	20.9
Solid Waste Management	0	0	0.0
Veterans' Services	0	0	0.0
Liquor Store	0	0	0.0
Utility	68,550	589	24.9

Source: U.S. Census Bureau, State & Local Government Finances 2022

TAXES

State Corporate Income Tax Rates

State	Tax Rate (%)	Income Brackets ($)	Num. of Brackets	Financial Institution Tax Rate (%)[a]	Federal Income Tax Ded.
Utah	4.65 (b)	Flat rate	–	4.65 (b)	No

Note: Tax rates for tax year 2024; (a) Rates listed are the corporate income tax rate applied to financial institutions or excise taxes based on income. Some states have other taxes based upon the value of deposits or shares; (b) Minimum tax is $800 in California, $250 in District of Columbia, $50 in Arizona and North Dakota (banks), $400 ($100 banks) in Rhode Island, $200 per location in South Dakota (banks), $100 in Utah, in Vermont, simplified entity business tax for residents only at $250, otherwise minimum tax ($100 - $100,000) is based upon gross receipts.
Source: Federation of Tax Administrators, State Corporate Income Tax Rates, January 1, 2025

State Individual Income Tax Rates

State	Tax Rate (%)	Income Brackets ($)	Personal Exemptions ($)			Standard Ded. ($)	
			Single	Married	Depend.	Single	Married
Utah	4.8	Flat rate	None	None	1,750	(w)	(w)

Note: Tax rates for tax year 2024; Local- and county-level taxes are not included; Federal income tax is not deductible on state income tax returns; (w) Utah provides a tax credit equal to 6% of the federal personal exemption amounts (and applicable standard deduction). The tax credit is reduced by $.013 for each dollar by which a claimant's state taxable income exceeds: $15,095 - S; $22,643 - HOH; $30,190 - MFJ in 2023.
Source: Federation of Tax Administrators, State Individual Income Tax Rates, January 1, 2025

Various State Sales and Excise Tax Rates

State	State Sales Tax (%)	Gasoline[1] ($/gal.)	Cigarette[2] ($/pack)	Spirits[3] ($/gal.)	Wine[4] ($/gal.)	Beer[5] ($/gal.)	Recreational Marijuana (%)
Utah	6.1	0.39	1.70	16.07	0.00	0.43	Not legal

Note: All tax rates as of January 1, 2025; (1) The American Petroleum Institute has developed a methodology for determining the average tax rate on a gallon of fuel. Rates may include any of the following: excise taxes, environmental fees, storage tank fees, other fees or taxes, general sales tax, and local taxes; (2) The federal excise tax of $1.0066 per pack and local taxes are not included; (3) Rates are those applicable to off-premise sales of 40% alcohol by volume (a.b.v.) distilled spirits in 750ml containers. Local excise taxes are excluded; (4) Rates are those applicable to off-premise sales of 11% a.b.v. non-carbonated wine in 750ml containers; (5) Rates are those applicable to off-premise sales of 4.7% a.b.v. beer in 12 ounce containers.
Source: Tax Foundation, 2025 Facts & Figures: How Does Your State Compare?

State Tax Competitiveness Index

State	Overall Rank	Corporate Tax Rank	Individual Income Tax Rank	Sales Tax Rank	Property Tax Rank	Unemployment Insurance Tax Rank
Utah	16	17	9	27	12	29

Note: The Tax Foundation's State Tax Competitiveness Index enables policymakers, taxpayers, and business leaders to gauge how their states' tax systems compare. A rank of 1 is best, 50 is worst. Rankings do not average to the total. States without a tax rank equally as 1. DC's scores and rankings do not affect other states. The report shows tax systems as of July 1, 2024 (the beginning of Fiscal Year 2025).
Source: Tax Foundation, State Tax Competitiveness Index 2025

TRANSPORTATION

Means of Transportation to Work

Area	Car/Truck/Van		Public Transportation			Bicycle	Walked	Other Means	Worked at Home
	Drove Alone	Car-pooled	Bus	Subway	Railroad				
City	57.4	10.4	4.3	0.1	0.9	1.4	10.3	1.1	14.2
MSA[1]	66.7	10.1	1.2	0.0	0.6	0.5	2.9	1.0	17.1
U.S.	70.2	8.5	1.7	1.3	0.4	0.4	2.4	1.6	13.5

Note: Figures are percentages and cover workers 16 years of age and older; (1) Figures cover the Provo-Orem-Lehi, UT Metropolitan Statistical Area
Source: U.S. Census Bureau, 2019-2023 American Community Survey 5-Year Estimates

Travel Time to Work

Area	Less Than 10 Minutes	10 to 19 Minutes	20 to 29 Minutes	30 to 44 Minutes	45 to 59 Minutes	60 to 89 Minutes	90 Minutes or More
City	20.5	44.9	16.6	10.2	4.4	2.3	1.1
MSA[1]	17.2	34.7	19.9	17.0	6.2	3.7	1.3
U.S.	12.6	28.6	21.2	20.8	8.1	6.0	2.8

Note: Note: Figures are percentages and include workers 16 years old and over; (1) Figures cover the Provo-Orem-Lehi, UT Metropolitan Statistical Area
Source: U.S. Census Bureau, 2019-2023 American Community Survey 5-Year Estimates

Key Congestion Measures

Measure	2000	2010	2015	2020	2022
Annual Hours of Delay, Total (000)	4,001	6,075	8,107	5,275	10,456
Annual Hours of Delay, Per Auto Commuter	18	21	23	15	30
Annual Congestion Cost, Per Auto Commuter ($)	348	424	521	345	649

Note: Figures cover the Provo-Orem UT urban area
Source: Texas A&M Transportation Institute, 2023 Urban Mobility Report

Freeway Travel Time Index

Measure	1985	1990	1995	2000	2005	2010	2015	2020	2022
Urban Area Index[1]	1.05	1.07	1.08	1.10	1.12	1.11	1.11	1.05	1.12
Urban Area Rank[1,2]	64	74	84	85	86	93	96	85	81

Note: Freeway Travel Time Index—the ratio of travel time in the peak period to the travel time at free-flow conditions. For example, a value of 1.30 indicates a 20-minute free-flow trip takes 26 minutes in the peak (20 minutes x 1.30 = 26 minutes); (1) Covers the Provo-Orem UT urban area; (2) Rank is based on 101 larger urban areas (#1 = highest travel time index)
Source: Texas A&M Transportation Institute, 2023 Urban Mobility Report

Public Transportation

Agency Name / Mode of Transportation	Vehicles Operated in Maximum Service[1]	Annual Unlinked Passenger Trips[2] (in thous.)	Annual Passenger Miles[3] (in thous.)
Utah Transit Authority (UT)			
Bus (directly operated)	302	17,797.2	69,048.6
Bus (purchased transportation)	7	98.0	578.6
Commuter Bus (directly operated)	38	592.6	9,082.3
Commuter Rail (directly operated)	40	3,736.6	107,783.0
Demand Response (directly operated)	52	212.7	2,050.2
Demand Response (purchased transportation)	89	545.9	3,288.6
Light Rail (directly operated)	74	11,043.7	48,914.3
Vanpool (directly operated)	442	1,033.1	38,627.4

Note: (1) Number of revenue vehicles operated by the given mode and type of service to meet the annual maximum service requirement. This is the revenue vehicle count during the peak season of the year; on the week and day that maximum service is provided. Vehicles operated in maximum service (VOMS) exclude atypical days and one-time special events; (2) Number of passengers who boarded public transportation vehicles. Passengers are counted each time they board a vehicle no matter how many vehicles they use to travel from their origin to their destination. (3) Sum of the distances ridden by all passengers during the entire fiscal year.
Source: Federal Transit Administration, National Transit Database, 2023

Air Transportation

Airport Name and Code / Type of Service	Passenger Airlines[1]	Passenger Enplanements	Freight Carriers[2]	Freight (lbs)
Salt Lake City International (50 miles) (SLC)				
Domestic service (U.S. carriers only)	29	12,883,266	15	153,520,130
International service (U.S. carriers only)	6	572,505	1	3,194,061

Note: (1) Includes all U.S.-based major, minor and commuter airlines that carried at least one passenger during the year; (2) Includes all U.S.-based airlines and freight carriers that transported at least one pound of freight during the year.
Source: Bureau of Transportation Statistics, The Intermodal Transportation Database, Air Carriers: T-100 Domestic Market (U.S. carriers only), 2024; Bureau of Transportation Statistics, The Intermodal Transportation Database, Air Carriers: T-100 International Market (U.S. carriers only), 2024

BUSINESSES

Major Business Headquarters

Company Name	Industry	Rankings	
		Fortune[1]	Forbes[2]
No companies listed	-	-	-

Note: (1) Companies that produce a 10-K are ranked 1 to 500 based on 2023 revenue; (2) All private companies with at least $2 billion in annual revenue through the end of their most current fiscal year are ranked 1 to 275; companies listed are headquartered in the city; dashes indicate no ranking
Source: Fortune, "Fortune 500," 2024; Forbes, "America's Largest Private Companies," 2024

Living Environment

COST OF LIVING

Cost of Living Index

Composite Index	Groceries	Housing	Utilities	Trans-portation	Health Care	Misc. Goods/Services
102.5	96.7	111.3	93.2	107.4	89.9	100.5

Note: The Cost of Living Index measures regional differences in the cost of consumer goods and services, excluding taxes and non-consumer expenditures, for professional and managerial households in the top income quintile. It is based on more than 50,000 prices covering almost 60 different items for which prices are collected three times a year by chambers of commerce, economic development organizations or university applied economic centers in each participating urban area. The numbers shown should be read as a percentage above or below the national average of 100. For example, a value of 115.4 in the groceries column indicates that grocery prices are 15.4% higher than the national average. Small differences in the index numbers should not be interpreted as significant; Figures cover the Provo-Orem UT urban area.
Source: The Council for Community and Economic Research, Cost of Living Index, 2024

Grocery Prices

Area[1]	T-Bone Steak ($/pound)	Frying Chicken ($/pound)	Whole Milk ($/half gal.)	Eggs ($/dozen)	Orange Juice ($/64 oz.)	Coffee ($/11.5 oz.)
City[2]	15.52	1.54	4.57	2.91	4.17	5.79
Avg.	15.42	1.55	4.69	3.25	4.41	5.46
Min.	14.50	1.16	4.43	2.75	4.00	4.85
Max.	17.56	2.89	5.49	4.78	5.54	7.89

*Note: (1) Values for the local area are compared with the average, minimum and maximum values for all 276 areas in the Cost of Living Index; (2) Figures cover the Provo-Orem UT urban area; **T-Bone Steak** (price per pound); **Frying Chicken** (price per pound, whole fryer); **Whole Milk** (half gallon carton); **Eggs** (price per dozen, Grade A, large); **Orange Juice** (64 oz. Tropicana or Florida Natural); **Coffee** (11.5 oz. can, vacuum-packed, Maxwell House, Hills Bros, or Folgers).*
Source: The Council for Community and Economic Research, Cost of Living Index, 2024

Housing and Utility Costs

Area[1]	New Home Price ($)	Apartment Rent ($/month)	All Electric ($/month)	Part Electric ($/month)	Other Energy ($/month)	Telephone ($/month)
City[2]	612,973	1,544	-	77.11	106.23	195.59
Avg.	515,975	1,550	210.99	123.07	82.07	194.99
Min.	265,375	692	104.33	53.68	36.26	179.42
Max.	2,775,821	5,719	529.02	397.28	361.63	223.33

*Note: (1) Values for the local area are compared with the average, minimum and maximum values for all 276 areas in the Cost of Living Index; (2) Figures cover the Provo-Orem UT urban area; **New Home Price** (2,400 sf living area, 8,000 sf lot, in urban area with full utilities); **Apartment Rent** (950 sf 2 bedroom/1.5 or 2 bath, unfurnished, excluding all utilities except water); **All Electric** (average monthly cost for an all-electric home); **Part Electric** (average monthly cost for a part-electric home); **Other Energy** (average monthly cost for natural gas, fuel oil, coal, wood, and any other forms of energy except electricity); **Telephone** (price includes the base monthly rate plus taxes and fees for three lines of mobile phone service).*
Source: The Council for Community and Economic Research, Cost of Living Index, 2024

Health Care, Transportation, and Other Costs

Area[1]	Doctor ($/visit)	Dentist ($/visit)	Optometrist ($/visit)	Gasoline ($/gallon)	Beauty Salon ($/visit)	Men's Shirt ($)
City[2]	113.66	105.45	127.59	3.41	51.34	49.04
Avg.	143.77	117.51	129.23	3.32	48.57	38.14
Min.	36.74	58.67	67.33	2.80	24.00	13.41
Max.	270.44	216.82	307.33	5.28	94.00	63.89

*Note: (1) Values for the local area are compared with the average, minimum and maximum values for all 276 areas in the Cost of Living Index; (2) Figures cover the Provo-Orem UT urban area; **Doctor** (general practitioners routine exam of an established patient); **Dentist** (adult teeth cleaning and periodic oral examination); **Optometrist** (full vision eye exam for established adult patient); **Gasoline** (one gallon regular unleaded, national brand, including all taxes, cash price at self-service pump if available); **Beauty Salon** (woman's shampoo, trim, and blow-dry); **Men's Shirt** (cotton/polyester dress shirt, pinpoint weave, long sleeves).*
Source: The Council for Community and Economic Research, Cost of Living Index, 2024

HOUSING

Homeownership Rate

Area	2017 (%)	2018 (%)	2019 (%)	2020 (%)	2021 (%)	2022 (%)	2023 (%)	2024 (%)
MSA[1]	n/a	n/a	n/a	n/a	n/a	n/a	n/a	n/a
U.S.	63.9	64.4	64.6	66.6	65.5	65.8	65.9	65.6

Note: (1) Figures cover the Provo-Orem-Lehi, UT Metropolitan Statistical Area; n/a not available
Source: U.S. Census Bureau, Housing Vacancies and Homeownership Annual Statistics: 2017-2024

House Price Index (HPI)

Area	National Ranking[2]	Quarterly Change (%)	One-Year Change (%)	Five-Year Change (%)	Since 1991Q1 (%)
MSA[1]	139	-1.41	4.94	59.50	545.94
U.S.[3]	–	1.43	4.51	57.13	327.82

Note: The HPI is a weighted repeat sales index. It measures average price changes in repeat sales or refinancings on the same properties. This information is obtained by reviewing repeat mortgage transactions on single-family properties whose mortgages have been purchased or securitized by Fannie Mae or Freddie Mac since January 1975; (1) Figures cover the Provo-Orem, UT Metropolitan Statistical Area; (2) Rankings are based on annual percentage change for all metro areas containing at least 15,000 transactions over the last 10 years and ranges from 1 to 241; (3) figures based on a weighted average of Census Division estimates using a seasonally adjusted, purchase-only index; all figures are for the period ending December 31, 2024
Source: Federal Housing Finance Agency, Change in FHFA Metropolitan Area House Price Indexes, All Transactions Index, 2024Q4

Home Value

Area	Under $100,000	$100,000 -$199,999	$200,000 -$299,999	$300,000 -$399,999	$400,000 -$499,999	$500,000 -$999,999	$1,000,000 or more	Median ($)
City	5.1	1.8	10.4	24.4	22.4	31.3	4.6	437,100
MSA[1]	3.5	1.6	7.4	18.5	22.0	41.2	6.0	487,200
U.S.	12.1	17.8	19.5	14.4	10.5	19.1	6.5	303,400

Note: Figures are percentages except for median and cover owner-occupied housing units; (1) Figures cover the Provo-Orem-Lehi, UT Metropolitan Statistical Area
Source: U.S. Census Bureau, 2019-2023 American Community Survey 5-Year Estimates

Year Housing Structure Built

Area	2020 or Later	2010 -2019	2000 -2009	1990 -1999	1980 -1989	1970 -1979	1960 -1969	1950 -1959	1940 -1949	Before 1940	Median Year
City	1.1	7.6	11.6	18.7	14.7	17.7	9.7	7.3	5.0	6.6	1982
MSA[1]	3.7	22.3	22.9	16.1	8.5	11.7	4.3	4.2	2.6	3.9	1999
U.S.	1.2	8.9	13.6	12.8	13.0	14.4	10.0	9.7	4.5	11.9	1980

Note: Figures are percentages except for Median Year; Note: (1) Figures cover the Provo-Orem-Lehi, UT Metropolitan Statistical Area
Source: U.S. Census Bureau, 2019-2023 American Community Survey 5-Year Estimates

Gross Monthly Rent

Area	Under $500	$500 -$999	$1,000 -$1,499	$1,500 -$1,999	$2,000 -$2,499	$2,500 -$2,999	$3,000 and up	Median ($)
City	5.6	28.6	40.3	16.6	6.4	1.9	0.5	1,152
MSA[1]	3.1	16.5	34.5	27.9	12.6	3.7	1.8	1,434
U.S.	6.5	22.3	29.5	20.2	10.8	4.8	5.9	1,348

Note: Figures are percentages except for median; Gross rent is the contract rent plus the estimated average monthly cost of utilities (electricity, gas, and water and sewer) and fuels (oil, coal, kerosene, wood, etc.) if these are paid by the renter (or paid for the renter by someone else); (1) Figures cover the Provo-Orem-Lehi, UT Metropolitan Statistical Area
Source: U.S. Census Bureau, 2019-2023 American Community Survey 5-Year Estimates

HEALTH

Health Risk Factors

Category	MSA[1] (%)	U.S. (%)
Adults aged 18–64 who have any kind of health care coverage	90.9	90.8
Adults who reported being in good or better health	87.7	81.8
Adults who have been told they have high blood cholesterol	28.8	36.9
Adults who have been told they have high blood pressure	24.1	34.0
Adults who are current smokers	4.2	12.1
Adults who currently use e-cigarettes	5.1	7.7
Adults who currently use chewing tobacco, snuff, or snus	1.6	3.2
Adults who are heavy drinkers[2]	2.2	6.1
Adults who are binge drinkers[3]	7.5	15.2
Adults who are overweight (BMI 25.0 - 29.9)	33.6	34.4
Adults who are obese (BMI 30.0 - 99.8)	29.0	34.3
Adults who participated in any physical activities in the past month	87.5	75.8

Note: All figures are crude prevalence; (1) Figures cover the Provo-Orem, UT Metropolitan Statistical Area; (2) Heavy drinkers are classified as adult men having more than 14 drinks per week and adult women having more than 7 drinks per week; (3) Binge drinkers are classified as males having five or more drinks on one occasion or females having four or more drinks on one occasion
Source: Centers for Disease Control and Prevention, Behaviorial Risk Factor Surveillance System, SMART: Selected Metropolitan Area Risk Trends, 2023

Acute and Chronic Health Conditions

Category	MSA[1] (%)	U.S. (%)
Adults who have ever been told they had a heart attack	2.9	4.2
Adults who have ever been told they have angina or coronary heart disease	2.5	4.0
Adults who have ever been told they had a stroke	1.7	3.3
Adults who have ever been told they have asthma	12.9	15.7
Adults who have ever been told they have arthritis	18.0	26.3
Adults who have ever been told they have diabetes[2]	6.6	11.5
Adults who have ever been told they had skin cancer	4.2	5.6
Adults who have ever been told they had any other types of cancer	7.5	8.4
Adults who have ever been told they have COPD	3.0	6.4
Adults who have ever been told they have kidney disease	2.7	3.7
Adults who have ever been told they have a form of depression	24.9	22.0

Note: All figures are crude prevalence; (1) Figures cover the Provo-Orem, UT Metropolitan Statistical Area; (2) Figures do not include pregnancy-related, borderline, or pre-diabetes
Source: Centers for Disease Control and Prevention, Behaviorial Risk Factor Surveillance System, SMART: Selected Metropolitan Area Risk Trends, 2023

Health Screening and Vaccination Rates

Category	MSA[1] (%)	U.S. (%)
Adults who have ever been tested for HIV	23.2	37.5
Adults who have had their blood cholesterol checked within the last five years	79.5	87.0
Adults aged 65+ who have had flu shot within the past year	51.0	63.4
Adults aged 65+ who have ever had a pneumonia vaccination	66.6	71.9

Note: All figures are crude prevalence; (1) Figures cover the Provo-Orem, UT Metropolitan Statistical Area.
Source: Centers for Disease Control and Prevention, Behaviorial Risk Factor Surveillance System, SMART: Selected Metropolitan Area Risk Trends, 2023

Disability Status

Category	MSA[1] (%)	U.S. (%)
Adults who reported being deaf	5.1	7.4
Are you blind or have serious difficulty seeing, even when wearing glasses?	4.2	4.9
Do you have difficulty doing errands alone?	5.9	7.8
Do you have difficulty dressing or bathing?	2.3	3.6
Do you have serious difficulty concentrating/remembering/making decisions?	13.7	13.7
Do you have serious difficulty walking or climbing stairs?	8.1	13.2

Note: All figures are crude prevalence; (1) Figures cover the Provo-Orem, UT Metropolitan Statistical Area.
Source: Centers for Disease Control and Prevention, Behaviorial Risk Factor Surveillance System, SMART: Selected Metropolitan Area Risk Trends, 2023

Mortality Rates for the Top 10 Causes of Death in the U.S.

ICD-10[a] Sub-Chapter	ICD-10[a] Code	Crude Mortality Rate[2] per 100,000 population	
		County[3]	U.S.
Malignant neoplasms	C00-C97	71.9	182.7
Ischaemic heart diseases	I20-I25	36.2	109.6
Provisional assignment of new diseases of uncertain etiology[1]	U00-U49	27.2	65.3
Other forms of heart disease	I30-I51	45.0	65.1
Other degenerative diseases of the nervous system	G30-G31	32.1	52.4
Other external causes of accidental injury	W00-X59	23.5	52.3
Cerebrovascular diseases	I60-I69	19.5	49.1
Chronic lower respiratory diseases	J40-J47	12.1	43.5
Hypertensive diseases	I10-I15	11.9	38.9
Organic, including symptomatic, mental disorders	F01-F09	18.6	33.9

Note: (a) ICD-10 = International Classification of Diseases 10th Revision; (1) Includes COVID-19, adverse effects to COVID-19 vaccines, SARS, and vaping-related disorders; (2) Crude mortality rates are a three-year average covering 2021-2023; (3) Figures cover Utah County.
Source: Centers for Disease Control and Prevention, National Center for Health Statistics. National Vital Statistics System, Mortality 2018-2023 on CDC WONDER Online Database

Mortality Rates for Selected Causes of Death

Cause of Death	ICD-10[a] Code	Crude Mortality Rate[1] per 100,000 population	
		County[2]	U.S.
Accidental poisoning and exposure to noxious substances	X40-X49	9.9	30.5
Alzheimer disease	G30	22.6	35.4
Assault	X85-Y09	0.9	7.3
COVID-19	U07.1	27.2	65.3
Diabetes mellitus	E10-E14	15.2	30.0
Diseases of the liver	K70-K76	6.9	20.8
Human immunodeficiency virus (HIV) disease	B20-B24	Suppressed	1.5
Influenza and pneumonia	J09-J18	5.7	13.4
Intentional self-harm	X60-X84	14.1	14.7
Malnutrition	E40-E46	7.2	6.0
Obesity and other hyperalimentation	E65-E68	2.1	3.1
Renal failure	N17-N19	8.8	16.4
Transport accidents	V01-V99	6.7	14.4

Note: (a) ICD-10 = International Classification of Diseases 10th Revision; (1) Crude mortality rates are a three-year average covering 2021-2023; (2) Figures cover Utah County; Data are suppressed when the data meet the criteria for confidentiality constraints; Crude mortality rates are flagged as unreliable when the rate would be calculated with a numerator of 20 or less.
Source: Centers for Disease Control and Prevention, National Center for Health Statistics. National Vital Statistics System, Mortality 2018-2023 on CDC WONDER Online Database

Health Insurance Coverage

Area	With Health Insurance	With Private Health Insurance	With Public Health Insurance	Without Health Insurance	Population Under Age 19 Without Health Insurance
City	90.6	78.6	17.5	9.4	9.8
MSA[1]	92.3	82.1	17.4	7.7	6.0
U.S.	91.4	67.3	36.3	8.6	5.4

Note: Figures are percentages that cover the civilian noninstitutionalized population; (1) Figures cover the Provo-Orem-Lehi, UT Metropolitan Statistical Area
Source: U.S. Census Bureau, 2019-2023 American Community Survey 5-Year Estimates

Number of Medical Professionals

Area	MDs[3]	DOs[3,4]	Dentists	Podiatrists	Chiropractors	Optometrists
County[1] (number)	814	171	434	34	192	82
County[1] (rate[2])	115.9	24.3	60.3	4.7	26.7	11.4
U.S. (rate[2])	302.5	29.2	74.6	6.4	29.5	18.0

Note: Data as of 2023 unless noted; (1) Data covers Utah County; (2) Number of medical professionals per 100,000 population; (3) Data as of 2022 and includes all active, non-federal physicians; (4) Doctor of Osteopathic Medicine
Source: U.S. Department of Health and Human Services, Health Resources and Services Administration, Bureau of Health Professions, Area Resource File (ARF) 2023-2024

EDUCATION

Public School District Statistics

District Name	Schls	Pupils	Pupil/ Teacher Ratio	Minority Pupils[1] (%)	Total Rev. per Pupil ($)	Total Exp. per Pupil ($)
Freedom Preparatory Academy	3	2,161	17.4	46.0	11,114	13,779
Provo District	22	13,887	19.5	43.8	12,327	13,633

Note: Table includes school districts with 2,000 or more students; (1) Percentage of students that are not non-Hispanic white.
Source: U.S. Department of Education, National Center for Education Statistics, Common Core of Data, Local Education Agency (School District) Universe Survey: School Year 2023-2024; U.S. Department of Education, National Center for Education Statistics, Common Core of Data, School District Finance Survey (F-33): School Year 2021–22

Highest Level of Education

Area	Less than H.S.	H.S. Diploma	Some College, No Deg.	Associate Degree	Bachelor's Degree	Master's Degree	Prof. School Degree	Doctorate Degree
City	7.5	14.4	24.4	8.7	31.1	9.5	1.7	2.6
MSA[1]	4.7	17.1	24.8	10.1	30.1	9.9	1.7	1.6
U.S.	10.6	26.2	19.4	8.8	21.3	9.8	2.3	1.6

Note: Figures cover persons age 25 and over; (1) Figures cover the Provo-Orem-Lehi, UT Metropolitan Statistical Area
Source: U.S. Census Bureau, 2019-2023 American Community Survey 5-Year Estimates

Educational Attainment by Race

Area	High School Graduate or Higher (%)					Bachelor's Degree or Higher (%)				
	Total	White	Black	Asian	Hisp.[2]	Total	White	Black	Asian	Hisp.[2]
City	92.5	95.3	99.6	84.9	75.2	45.0	49.0	29.9	52.7	20.8
MSA[1]	95.3	96.5	97.2	94.6	83.1	43.4	44.7	38.3	62.7	26.4
U.S.	89.4	92.9	88.1	88.0	72.5	35.0	37.7	24.7	57.0	19.9

Note: Figures shown cover persons 25 years old and over; (1) Figures cover the Provo-Orem-Lehi, UT Metropolitan Statistical Area; (2) People of Hispanic origin can be of any race
Source: U.S. Census Bureau, 2019-2023 American Community Survey 5-Year Estimates

School Enrollment by Grade and Control

Area	Preschool (%)		Kindergarten (%)		Grades 1 - 4 (%)		Grades 5 - 8 (%)		Grades 9 - 12 (%)	
	Public	Private	Public	Private	Public	Private	Public	Private	Public	Private
City	64.9	35.1	88.2	11.8	91.6	8.4	95.6	4.4	91.6	8.4
MSA[1]	55.5	44.5	87.9	12.1	90.3	9.7	92.6	7.4	94.0	6.0
U.S.	58.7	41.3	85.2	14.8	87.2	12.8	87.9	12.1	89.0	11.0

Note: Figures shown cover persons 3 years old and over; (1) Figures cover the Provo-Orem-Lehi, UT Metropolitan Statistical Area
Source: U.S. Census Bureau, 2019-2023 American Community Survey 5-Year Estimates

Higher Education

Four-Year Colleges			Two-Year Colleges			Medical Schools[1]	Law Schools[2]	Voc/ Tech[3]
Public	Private Non-profit	Private For-profit	Public	Private Non-profit	Private For-profit			
1	1	3	0	0	0	1	1	8

Note: Figures cover institutions located within the Provo-Orem-Lehi, UT Metropolitan Statistical Area and include main campuses only; (1) includes schools accredited by the Liaison Committee on Medical Education and the American Osteopathic Association's Commission on Osteopathic College Accreditation; (2) includes ABA-accredited schools, schools with provisional ABA accreditation, and state accredited schools; (3) includes all schools with programs that are less than 2 years.
Source: National Center for Education Statistics, Integrated Postsecondary Education System (IPEDS), 2023-24; Wikipedia, List of Medical Schools in the United States, accessed May 2, 2025; Wikipedia, List of Law Schools in the United States, accessed May 2, 2025

According to *U.S. News & World Report,* the Provo-Orem-Lehi, UT metro area is home to one of the top 200 national universities in the U.S.: **Brigham Young University** (#109 tie). The indicators used to capture academic quality fall into a number of categories: assessment by administrators at peer institutions; retention of students; faculty resources; student selectivity; financial resources; alumni giving; high school counselor ratings of colleges; and graduation rate. *U.S. News & World Report, "America's Best Colleges 2025"*

According to *U.S. News & World Report,* the Provo-Orem-Lehi, UT metro area is home to one of the top 100 law schools in the U.S.: **Brigham Young University (Clark)** (#28 tie). The rankings are based on a weighted average of 12 measures of quality: peer assessment score; assessment score by lawyers/judges; median LSAT scores; median undergrad GPA; acceptance rate; employment rates for graduates; placement success; bar passage rate; faculty resources; expenditures per student; student/faculty ratio; and library resources. *U.S. News & World Report, "America's Best Graduate Schools, Law, 2025"*

According to *U.S. News & World Report,* the Provo-Orem-Lehi, UT metro area is home to one of the top 75 business schools in the U.S.: **Brigham Young University (Marriott)** (#38 tie). The rankings are based on a weighted average of the following nine measures: quality assessment; peer assessment; recruiter assessment; placement success; mean starting salary and bonus; student selectivity; mean GMAT and GRE scores; mean undergraduate GPA; and acceptance rate. *U.S. News & World Report, "America's Best Graduate Schools, Business, 2025"*

EMPLOYERS

Major Employers

Company Name	Industry
About Time Technologies	Movements, clock or watch
Ancestry.com	Communication services
Aptive Environmental	Pest control
APX Group	Energy
Brigham Young University	Colleges & universities
City of Provo	Municipal government
Intermountain Health Care	General medical & surgical hospitals
Morinda Holdings	Bottled & canned soft drinks
Nu Skin Enterprises United States	Drugs, proprietaries, & sundries
Nu Skin International	Toilet preparations
Qualtrics	Experience management
RBM Services	Building cleaning service
TPUSA	Telemarketing services
Utah Community Credit Union	Credit unions
Utah Dept of Human Services	Mental hospital, except for the mentally retarded
Utah Valley University	Colleges & universities
Vivint Smart Home	Home consulting and installation
Wal-Mart Stores	Department stores, discount
Wasatch Summit	Management consulting services
Ziplocal	Directories, phone: publish only, not printed on site

Note: Companies shown are located within the Provo-Orem-Lehi, UT Metropolitan Statistical Area.
Source: Chambers of Commerce; State Departments of Labor; Wikipedia

PUBLIC SAFETY

Crime Rate

Area	Total Crime Rate	Violent Crime Rate				Property Crime Rate		
		Murder	Rape	Robbery	Aggrav. Assault	Burglary	Larceny -Theft	Motor Vehicle Theft
City	1,531.8	0.0	60.3	16.0	98.5	110.0	1,149.5	97.6
U.S.	2,290.9	5.7	38.0	66.5	264.1	250.7	1,347.2	318.7

Note: Figures are crimes per 100,000 population.
Source: FBI, Table 8, Offenses Known to Law Enforcement, by State by City, 2023

Hate Crimes

Area	Number of Quarters Reported	Number of Incidents per Bias Motivation					
		Race/Ethnicity/ Ancestry	Religion	Sexual Orientation	Disability	Gender	Gender Identity
City	4	0	0	0	0	0	0
U.S.	4	5,900	2,699	2,077	187	92	492

Source: Federal Bureau of Investigation, Hate Crime Statistics 2023

Identity Theft Consumer Reports

Area	Reports	Reports per 100,000 Population	Rank[2]
MSA[1]	1,042	150	266
U.S.	1,135,291	339	-

Note: (1) Figures cover the Provo-Orem-Lehi, UT Metropolitan Statistical Area; (2) Rank ranges from 1 to 401 where 1 indicates greatest number of identity theft reports per 100,000 population
Source: Federal Trade Commission, Consumer Sentinel Network Data Book 2024

Fraud and Other Consumer Reports

Area	Reports	Reports per 100,000 Population	Rank[2]
MSA[1]	5,697	819	314
U.S.	5,360,641	1,601	-

Note: (1) Figures cover the Provo-Orem-Lehi, UT Metropolitan Statistical Area; (2) Rank ranges from 1 to 401 where 1 indicates greatest number of fraud and other consumer reports per 100,000 population
Source: Federal Trade Commission, Consumer Sentinel Network Data Book 2024

POLITICS

2024 Presidential Election Results

Area	Trump (Rep.)	Harris (Dem.)	Stein (Green)	Kennedy (Ind.)	Oliver (Lib.)	Other
Utah County	66.7	27.8	0.5	0.0	1.4	3.6
U.S.	49.7	48.2	0.6	0.5	0.4	0.6

Note: Results are percentages and may not add to 100% due to rounding
Source: Dave Leip's Atlas of U.S. Presidential Elections

SPORTS

Professional Sports Teams

Team Name	League	Year Established

No teams are located in the metro area
Source: Wikipedia, Major Professional Sports Teams of the United States and Canada, May 1, 2025

CLIMATE

Average and Extreme Temperatures

Temperature	Jan	Feb	Mar	Apr	May	Jun	Jul	Aug	Sep	Oct	Nov	Dec	Yr.
Extreme High (°F)	62	69	78	85	93	104	107	104	100	89	75	67	107
Average High (°F)	37	43	52	62	72	83	93	90	80	66	50	38	64
Average Temp. (°F)	28	34	41	50	59	69	78	76	65	53	40	30	52
Average Low (°F)	19	24	31	38	46	54	62	61	51	40	30	22	40
Extreme Low (°F)	-22	-14	2	15	25	35	40	37	27	16	-14	-15	-22

Note: Figures cover the years 1948-1990
Source: National Climatic Data Center, International Station Meteorological Climate Summary, 9/96

Average Precipitation/Snowfall/Humidity

Precip./Humidity	Jan	Feb	Mar	Apr	May	Jun	Jul	Aug	Sep	Oct	Nov	Dec	Yr.
Avg. Precip. (in.)	1.3	1.2	1.8	2.0	1.7	0.9	0.8	0.9	1.1	1.3	1.3	1.4	15.6
Avg. Snowfall (in.)	13	10	11	6	1	Tr	0	0	Tr	2	6	13	63
Avg. Rel. Hum. 5am (%)	79	77	71	67	66	60	53	54	60	68	75	79	67
Avg. Rel. Hum. 5pm (%)	69	59	47	38	33	26	22	23	28	40	59	71	43

Note: Figures cover the years 1948-1990; Tr = Trace amounts (<0.05 in. of rain; <0.5 in. of snow)
Source: National Climatic Data Center, International Station Meteorological Climate Summary, 9/96

Weather Conditions

Temperature			Daytime Sky			Precipitation		
5°F & below	32°F & below	90°F & above	Clear	Partly cloudy	Cloudy	0.01 inch or more precip.	0.1 inch or more snow/ice	Thunder-storms
7	128	56	94	152	119	92	38	38

Note: Figures are average number of days per year and cover the years 1948-1990
Source: National Climatic Data Center, International Station Meteorological Climate Summary, 9/96

HAZARDOUS WASTE

Superfund Sites

The Provo-Orem-Lehi, UT metro area has no sites on the EPA's Superfund Final National Priorities List (NPL) or Superfund Alternative Approach (SAA) list. The Superfund alternative approach uses the same investigation and cleanup process and standards that are used for sites listed on the National Priorities List. The SAA is an alternative to listing a site on the NPL; it is not an alternative to Superfund or the Superfund process. There are a total of 1,445 Superfund sites with a status of proposed or final on both lists in the United States. *U.S. Environmental Protection Agency, National Priorities List, May 1, 2025; U.S. Environmental Protection Agency, Superfund Alternative Approach Sites, May 1, 2025*

AIR QUALITY

Air Quality Trends: Ozone

	1990	1995	2000	2005	2010	2015	2020	2021	2022	2023
MSA[1]	n/a	n/a	n/a	n/a	n/a	n/a	n/a	n/a	n/a	n/a
U.S.	0.087	0.089	0.081	0.080	0.072	0.068	0.066	0.067	0.067	0.070

Note: (1) Data covers the Provo-Orem-Lehi, UT Metropolitan Statistical Area; n/a not available. The values shown are the composite ozone concentration averages among trend sites based on the highest fourth daily maximum 8-hour concentration in parts per million. These trends are based on sites having an adequate record of monitoring data during the trend period. Data from exceptional events are included.
Source: U.S. Environmental Protection Agency, Air Quality Monitoring Information, "Air Quality Trends by City, 1990-2023"

Air Quality Index

Area	Percent of Days when Air Quality was...[2]					AQI Statistics[2]	
	Good	Moderate	Unhealthy for Sensitive Groups	Unhealthy	Very Unhealthy	Maximum	Median
MSA[1]	55.1	44.7	0.3	0.0	0.0	104	48

Note: (1) Data covers the Provo-Orem-Lehi, UT Metropolitan Statistical Area; (2) Based on 365 days with AQI data in 2023. Air Quality Index (AQI) is an index for reporting daily air quality. EPA calculates the AQI for five major air pollutants regulated by the Clean Air Act: ground-level ozone, particle pollution (aka particulate matter), carbon monoxide, sulfur dioxide, and nitrogen dioxide. The AQI runs from 0 to 500. The higher the AQI value, the greater the level of air pollution and the greater the health concern. There are six AQI categories: "Good" AQI is between 0 and 50. Air quality is considered satisfactory; "Moderate" AQI is between 51 and 100. Air quality is acceptable; "Unhealthy for Sensitive Groups" When AQI values are between 101 and 150, members of sensitive groups may experience health effects; "Unhealthy" When AQI values are between 151 and 200 everyone may begin to experience health effects; "Very Unhealthy" AQI values between 201 and 300 trigger a health alert; "Hazardous" AQI values over 300 trigger warnings of emergency conditions (not shown).
Source: U.S. Environmental Protection Agency, Air Quality Index Report, 2023

Air Quality Index Pollutants

Area	Percent of Days when AQI Pollutant was...[2]					
	Carbon Monoxide	Nitrogen Dioxide	Ozone	Sulfur Dioxide	Particulate Matter 2.5	Particulate Matter 10
MSA[1]	0.0	0.3	63.3	(3)	36.2	0.3

Note: (1) Data covers the Provo-Orem-Lehi, UT Metropolitan Statistical Area; (2) Based on 365 days with AQI data in 2023. The Air Quality Index (AQI) is an index for reporting daily air quality. EPA calculates the AQI for five major air pollutants regulated by the Clean Air Act: ground-level ozone, particle pollution (also known as particulate matter), carbon monoxide, sulfur dioxide, and nitrogen dioxide. The AQI runs from 0 to 500. The higher the AQI value, the greater the level of air pollution and the greater the health concern; (3) Sulfur dioxide is no longer included in this table because SO_2 concentrations tend to be very localized and not necessarily representative of broad geographical areas like counties and CBSAs.
Source: U.S. Environmental Protection Agency, Air Quality Index Report, 2023

Maximum Air Pollutant Concentrations: Particulate Matter, Ozone, CO and Lead

	Particulate Matter 10 (ug/m³)	Particulate Matter 2.5 Wtd AM (ug/m³)	Particulate Matter 2.5 24-Hr (ug/m³)	Ozone (ppm)	Carbon Monoxide (ppm)	Lead (ug/m³)
MSA[1] Level	76	6.8	21	0.066	1	n/a
NAAQS[2]	150	15	35	0.075	9	0.15
Met NAAQS[2]	Yes	Yes	Yes	Yes	Yes	n/a

Note: (1) Data covers the Provo-Orem-Lehi, UT Metropolitan Statistical Area; Data from exceptional events are included; (2) National Ambient Air Quality Standards; ppm = parts per million; ug/m³ = micrograms per cubic meter; n/a not available.
Concentrations: Particulate Matter 10 (coarse particulate)—highest second maximum 24-hour concentration; Particulate Matter 2.5 Wtd AM (fine particulate)—highest weighted annual mean concentration; Particulate Matter 2.5 24-Hour (fine particulate)—highest 98th percentile 24-hour concentration; Ozone—highest fourth daily maximum 8-hour concentration; Carbon Monoxide—highest second maximum non-overlapping 8-hour concentration; Lead—maximum running 3-month average
Source: U.S. Environmental Protection Agency, Air Quality Monitoring Information, "Air Quality Statistics by City, 2023"

Maximum Air Pollutant Concentrations: Nitrogen Dioxide and Sulfur Dioxide

	Nitrogen Dioxide AM (ppb)	Nitrogen Dioxide 1-Hr (ppb)	Sulfur Dioxide AM (ppb)	Sulfur Dioxide 1-Hr (ppb)	Sulfur Dioxide 24-Hr (ppb)
MSA[1] Level	8	39	n/a	n/a	n/a
NAAQS[2]	53	100	30	75	140
Met NAAQS[2]	Yes	Yes	n/a	n/a	n/a

Note: (1) Data covers the Provo-Orem-Lehi, UT Metropolitan Statistical Area; Data from exceptional events are included; (2) National Ambient Air Quality Standards; ppm = parts per million; ug/m³ = micrograms per cubic meter; n/a not available.
Concentrations: Nitrogen Dioxide AM—highest arithmetic mean concentration; Nitrogen Dioxide 1-Hr—highest 98th percentile 1-hour daily maximum concentration; Sulfur Dioxide AM—highest annual mean concentration; Sulfur Dioxide 1-Hr—highest 99th percentile 1-hour daily maximum concentration; Sulfur Dioxide 24-Hr—highest second maximum 24-hour concentration
Source: U.S. Environmental Protection Agency, Air Quality Monitoring Information, "Air Quality Statistics by City, 2023"

Reno, Nevada

Background

Reno sits in the northwest section of Nevada, along the state's border with California and 30 miles north of the capital Carson City. Native American Washoes and Paiutes roamed the area before white explorers led by the famed John C. Fremont arrived in the nineteenth century. Due to the Truckee River running through it, the area became a stopping point for those traveling to California during the 1849 gold rush. In 1859, prospectors discovered the Comstock Lode—a massive vein of gold and silver forty miles to the south of the Truckee.

Entrepreneur Charles Fuller built a hotel and a toll bridge across the river for prospectors desperate to reach the lode. Floods kept destroying Fuller's bridge, and he sold the land to Myron Lake in 1861, who constructed another bridge around which a settlement grew. Lake gave several dozen acres of land to the Central Pacific Railroad in exchange for half of the transcontinental railroad running through the area. Here, the town of Reno was founded in 1868 and named after Jesse Lee Reno, a Union officer killed during the Civil War. Reno became an important shipping point for the mines of the Comstock Lode.

By 1900, the lode was in decline and Reno had to look to other commercial ventures. One was the quick divorce—a six weeks' residency requirement was approved by the state legislature in 1931. In a continuing effort to jumpstart the state's economy during the Great Depression, Nevada legalized gambling in 1931. As the number of gambling houses increased in Reno, so did its population.

The Reno Arch, emblazoned with the city's nickname—Biggest Little City in the World—welcomes tourists to an array of glittering casinos and hotels. The tourist and gambling industries are still quite important to the area's commerce, but other commercial ventures have taken root in Reno's business-friendly environment—no corporate or personal income taxes, and no inventory or franchise taxes. Key industries throughout the Greater Reno-Sparks-Tahoe area include manufacturing; distribution/logistics/internet fulfillment; back office/business support; financial and intangible assets; clean energy; and aerospace/aviation/defense. Companies with distribution and fulfillment operations in the city include JC Penny and Chewy. Major employers include University of Nevada, Walmart, Renown Health, and Washoe Country School District.

The University of Nevada at Reno opened its Earthquake Engineering Laboratory in 2014, the largest seismic stimulation facility in the country and the second largest in the world. The city boasts significant renovated meeting space at both the Reno-Sparks Convention Center and Reno Events Center, a premier venue for concerts, community events, tradeshows, and sporting events. Reno is home to the National Bowling Stadium and the Reno-Sparks Livestock Events Center, which, this year, is undergoing a major renovation. The Reno Aces play ball under the flag of the MLB-affiliated Pacific Coast League. The city hosts ArtTown, in which music, visual arts, film, dance, theater and historical tours are highlighted every year in July, for one of the country's largest visual and performing arts festivals.

Skiing and snowboarding are popular winter sports and draw many tourists. There are 18 ski resorts within a 98-mile radius of the Reno-Tahoe International Airport. In 2018, the city changed its flag to a colorful mountain graphic. Other popular winter activities include snowshoeing, ice skating, and snowmobiling, with many bike paths for summertime fun.

Located on a semi-arid plateau to the east of the Sierra Nevada mountains, Reno offers short, hot summers and relatively mild winters. Temperatures can vary widely from day to night. More than half of the city's precipitation falls as a rain-snow mixture during winter. Located at the edge of the Sierra Nevada, snow can pile up but tends to melt within a few days. Reno sees relatively little rain.

Rankings

General Rankings

- To help military veterans find the best places in which to settle down, *WalletHub* compared the 100 largest U.S. cities across 19 key indicators of livability, affordability and veteran-friendliness. They range from the share of military skill-related jobs to veteran income growth to the availability of VA health facilities. Reno ranked #72. *Wallethub.com, "Best & Worst Places for Veterans to Live (2025)," November 7, 2024*

- Reno was selected as one of the happiest places to live in America by *Outside Magazine.* Criteria centered on overall well being; effect of climate change; inclusivity; affordability; outdoor access; and other demographic and population figures. Local experts shared highlights from hands-on experience in each location. *Outside Magazine, "The 15 Happiest Places to Live in the U.S.," September 18, 2023*

Business/Finance Rankings

- The Reno metro area appeared on the Milken Institute "2025 Best Performing Cities" list. Rank: #93 out of 200 large metro areas (based on performance category). Criteria: job growth; wage growth; high-tech growth and impact; community resilience; housing affordability; household broadband access. *Milken Institute, "Best-Performing Cities 2025," January 14, 2025*

Education Rankings

- Personal finance website *WalletHub* analyzed the 150 largest U.S. metropolitan statistical areas to determine where the most educated Americans are putting their degrees to work. Criteria: education levels; percentage of workers with degrees; education quality and attainment gap; public school quality rankings; quality and enrollment of each metro area's universities. Reno was ranked #77 (#1 = most educated city). *WalletHub.com, "Most & Least Educated Cities in America, 2025" July 2, 2024*

Environmental Rankings

- The U.S. Conference of Mayors and Walmart Stores sponsor the Mayors' Climate Protection Awards Program which recognize mayors for outstanding and innovative practices that address the climate crisis: increase energy efficiency in their cities, reduce carbon emissions and expand renewable energy. Reno received First Place Honors in the large city category. *U.S. Conference of Mayors, "2024 Mayors' Climate Protection Awards," June 20, 2024*

- Reno was highlighted as one of the 25 metro areas most polluted by short-term particle pollution (24-hour PM 2.5) in the U.S. during 2021 through 2023. The area ranked #6. *American Lung Association, "State of the Air 2025," April 23, 2025*

Health/Fitness Rankings

- For each of the 100 largest cities in the United States, the American Fitness Index®, compiled in partnership between the American College of Sports Medicine and the Elevance Health Foundation, evaluated community infrastructure and more than 30 health behaviors including preventive health, levels of chronic disease conditions, food insecurity, pedestrian safety, air quality, and community/environment resources that support physical activity. Reno ranked #57 for "community fitness." *americanfitnessindex.org, "2024 ACSM American Fitness Index Summary Report," July 23, 2024*

Real Estate Rankings

- *WalletHub* compared the most populated U.S. cities to determine which had the best markets for real estate agents. Reno ranked #12 where demand was high and pay was the best. Criteria: sales per agent; annual median wage for real-estate agents; monthly average starting salary for real estate agents; real estate job density and competition; unemployment rate; home turnover rate; housing-market health index; and other relevant metrics. *WalletHub.com, "2021 Best Places to Be a Real Estate Agent," May 12, 2021*

- The Reno metro area was identified as one of the 10 worst condo markets in the U.S. in 2024. The area ranked #60 out of 63 markets. Criteria: year-over-year change of median sales price of existing apartment condo-coop homes between the 4th quarter of 2023 and the 4th quarter of 2024. *National Association of Realtors®, Median Sales Price of Existing Apartment Condo-Coops Homes for Metropolitan Areas, 4th Quarter 2024*

- Reno was ranked #167 out of 176 metro areas in terms of cost of housing in 2024 by the National Association of Home Builders (#1 = most affordable). Criteria: the portion of an average family's income necessary to pay the mortgage on a median-priced home. *National Association of Home Builders®, NAHB-Wells Fargo Cost of Housing Index, 4th Quarter 2024*

Safety Rankings

- Allstate ranked the 100 most populous cities in America in terms of driver safety. Reno ranked #10. Criteria based on anonymized driving behavior data from Allstate's mobile app powered by Arity: high speed driving (over 80 mph), phone handling, and hard braking. The report helps increase the importance of safety and awareness behind the wheel. *Allstate, "16th Allstate America's Best Drivers Report®" July 11, 2024*

Women/Minorities Rankings

- Personal finance website *WalletHub* compared more than 180 U.S. cities across two key dimensions, "Hispanic Business-Friendliness" and "Hispanic Purchasing Power," to arrive at the most favorable conditions for Hispanic entrepreneurs. Reno was ranked #94 out of 182. Criteria includes: share of Hispanic-Owned Businesses; average growth of Hispanic Business revenues; Small Business-Friendliness score; affordability; and number of Hispanics with at least a bachelor's degree. *WalletHub.com, "Best Cities for Hispanic Entrepreneurs," September 4, 2024*

Miscellaneous Rankings

- *WalletHub* compared 148 of the most populated U.S. cities to determine their operating efficiency. A "Quality of Services" score was constructed for each city and then measured against the total budget per capita to reveal which were managed the best. Reno ranked #39. Criteria: financial stability; economy; education; safety; health; infrastructure and pollution. *WalletHub.com, "2025's Best- & Worst-Run Cities in America," June 18, 2024*

Business Environment

DEMOGRAPHICS

Population Growth

Area	1990 Census	2000 Census	2010 Census	2020 Census	2023 Estimate[2]	Population Growth 1990-2023 (%)
City	139,950	180,480	225,221	264,165	268,959	92.2
MSA[1]	257,193	342,885	425,417	490,596	556,539	116.4
U.S.	248,709,873	281,421,906	308,745,538	331,449,281	332,387,540	33.6

Note: (1) Figures cover the Reno, NV Metropolitan Statistical Area; (2) 2019-2023 5-year ACS population estimate
Source: U.S. Census Bureau, 1990 Census, 2000 Census, 2010 Census, 2020 Census, 2019-2023 American Community Survey 5-Year Estimates

Race

Area	White Alone[2] (%)	Black Alone[2] (%)	Asian Alone[2] (%)	AIAN[3] Alone[2] (%)	NHOPI[4] Alone[2] (%)	Other Race Alone[2] (%)	Two or More Races (%)
City	63.5	3.2	7.0	1.0	0.7	11.1	13.5
MSA[1]	66.9	2.3	5.1	1.4	0.6	10.0	13.7
U.S.	63.4	12.4	5.8	0.9	0.2	6.6	10.7

Note: (1) Figures cover the Reno, NV Metropolitan Statistical Area; (2) Alone is defined as not being in combination with one or more other races; (3) American Indian and Alaska Native; (4) Native Hawaiian and Other Pacific Islander
Source: U.S. Census Bureau, 2019-2023 American Community Survey 5-Year Estimates

Hispanic or Latino Origin

Area	Total (%)	Mexican (%)	Puerto Rican (%)	Cuban (%)	Other (%)
City	24.6	17.9	0.7	0.3	5.7
MSA[1]	24.7	18.9	0.6	0.3	5.0
U.S.	19.0	11.3	1.8	0.7	5.2

Note: Persons of Hispanic or Latino origin can be of any race; (1) Figures cover the Reno, NV Metropolitan Statistical Area
Source: U.S. Census Bureau, 2019-2023 American Community Survey 5-Year Estimates

Age

Area	Percent of Population									Median Age
	Under Age 5	Age 5–19	Age 20–34	Age 35–44	Age 45–54	Age 55–64	Age 65–74	Age 75–84	Age 85+	
City	5.3	17.2	23.9	13.8	11.0	12.3	10.1	4.6	1.6	37.3
MSA[1]	5.4	17.8	20.9	13.0	11.8	13.1	11.3	5.1	1.6	39.4
U.S.	5.7	19.1	20.2	13.1	12.3	12.8	10.0	4.9	1.9	38.7

Note: (1) Figures cover the Reno, NV Metropolitan Statistical Area
Source: U.S. Census Bureau, 2019-2023 American Community Survey 5-Year Estimates

Disability by Age

Area	All Ages	Under 18 Years Old	18 to 64 Years Old	65 Years and Over
City	12.1	4.0	9.8	31.2
MSA[1]	13.0	4.7	10.4	31.7
U.S.	13.0	4.7	10.7	32.9

Note: Figures show percent of the civilian noninstitutionalized population that reported having a disability. Disability status is determined from six types of difficulty: vision, hearing, cognitive, ambulatory, self-care, and independent living. For children under 5 years old, hearing and vision difficulty are used to determine disability status. For children between the ages of 5 and 14, disability status is determined from hearing, vision, cognitive, ambulatory, and self-care difficulties. For people aged 15 years and older, they are considered to have a disability if they have difficulty with any one of the six difficulty types; Note: (1) Figures cover the Reno, NV Metropolitan Statistical Area
Source: U.S. Census Bureau, 2019-2023 American Community Survey 5-Year Estimates

Ancestry

Area	German	Irish	English	American	Italian	Polish	French[2]	European	Scottish
City	12.3	11.0	11.1	4.4	5.9	1.6	2.2	2.6	2.0
MSA[1]	12.7	10.9	11.6	4.0	6.0	1.6	2.3	3.5	2.0
U.S.	12.6	9.4	9.1	5.5	4.9	2.6	2.0	1.6	1.6

Note: Figures are the percentage of the total population reporting a particular ancestry. The nine most commonly reported ancestries in the U.S. are shown. Figures include multiple ancestries (e.g. if a person reported being Irish and Italian, they were included in both columns); (1) Figures cover the Reno, NV Metropolitan Statistical Area; (2) Excludes Basque
Source: U.S. Census Bureau, 2019-2023 American Community Survey 5-Year Estimates

Foreign-born Population

Area	Any Foreign Country	____	____	Percent of Population Born in					
		Asia	Mexico	Europe	Caribbean	Central America[2]	South America	Africa	Canada
City	16.1	5.4	5.3	1.4	0.3	2.2	0.4	0.5	0.3
MSA[1]	13.4	3.6	5.5	1.1	0.2	1.6	0.4	0.3	0.3
U.S.	13.9	4.3	3.3	1.4	1.4	1.2	1.2	0.8	0.2

Note: (1) Figures cover the Reno, NV Metropolitan Statistical Area; (2) Excludes Mexico.
Source: U.S. Census Bureau, 2019-2023 American Community Survey 5-Year Estimates

Household Size

Area	Persons in Household (%)							Average Household Size
	One	Two	Three	Four	Five	Six	Seven or More	
City	31.9	34.1	14.9	12.1	4.5	1.3	1.2	2.35
MSA[1]	27.5	35.2	15.5	12.9	5.6	2.1	1.3	2.49
U.S.	28.5	33.8	15.4	12.7	5.9	2.3	1.4	2.54

Note: (1) Figures cover the Reno, NV Metropolitan Statistical Area
Source: U.S. Census Bureau, 2019-2023 American Community Survey 5-Year Estimates

Household Relationships

Area	House-holder	Opposite-sex Spouse	Same-sex Spouse	Opposite-sex Unmarried Partner	Same-sex Unmarried Partner	Child[2]	Grand-child	Other Relatives	Non-relatives
City	41.1	15.2	0.3	3.8	0.2	24.8	1.7	4.7	5.7
MSA[1]	39.5	17.2	0.2	3.4	0.2	26.1	2.1	5.0	4.9
U.S.	38.3	17.5	0.2	2.5	0.2	28.3	2.4	4.8	3.4

Note: Figures are percent of the total population; (1) Figures cover the Reno, NV Metropolitan Statistical Area; (2) Includes biological, adopted, and stepchildren of the householder
Source: U.S. Census Bureau, 2020 Census

Gender

Area	Males	Females	Males per 100 Females
City	136,341	132,618	102.8
MSA[1]	283,387	273,152	103.7
U.S.	164,545,087	167,842,453	98.0

Note: (1) Figures cover the Reno, NV Metropolitan Statistical Area
Source: U.S. Census Bureau, 2019-2023 American Community Survey 5-Year Estimates

Marital Status

Area	Never Married	Now Married[2]	Separated	Widowed	Divorced
City	37.7	41.7	1.5	4.9	14.2
MSA[1]	32.6	47.1	1.4	5.1	13.8
U.S.	34.1	47.9	1.7	5.6	10.7

Note: Figures are percentages and cover the population 15 years of age and older; (1) Figures cover the Reno, NV Metropolitan Statistical Area; (2) Excludes separated
Source: U.S. Census Bureau, 2019-2023 American Community Survey 5-Year Estimates

Religious Groups by Family

Area	Catholic	Baptist	Methodist	LDS[2]	Pentecostal	Lutheran	Islam	Adventist	Other
MSA[1]	24.4	1.4	0.5	4.0	0.9	0.5	0.3	1.4	5.3
U.S.	18.7	7.3	3.0	2.0	1.8	1.7	1.3	1.3	11.6

Note: Figures are the number of adherents as a percentage of the total population and cover the eight largest religious groups in the U.S; (1) Figures cover the Reno, NV Metropolitan Statistical Area; (2) Church of Jesus Christ of Latter-day Saints
Sources: 2020 U.S. Religion Census, Association of Statisticians of American Religious Bodies; The Association of Religion Data Archives (ARDA)

Religious Groups by Tradition

Area	Catholic	Evangelical Protestant	Mainline Protestant	Black Protestant	Islam	Judaism	Hinduism	Orthodox	Buddhism
MSA[1]	24.4	6.8	1.3	0.2	0.3	0.1	0.1	0.1	0.2
U.S.	18.7	16.5	5.2	2.3	1.3	0.6	0.4	0.4	0.3

Note: Figures are the number of adherents as a percentage of the total population; (1) Figures cover the Reno, NV Metropolitan Statistical Area
Sources: 2020 U.S. Religion Census, Association of Statisticians of American Religious Bodies; The Association of Religion Data Archives (ARDA)

ECONOMY

Real Gross Domestic Product (GDP)

Area	2017	2018	2019	2020	2021	2022	2023	Rank[3]
MSA[1]	29.4	28.8	29.9	30.1	33.2	33.6	34.1	96
U.S.[2]	17,619.1	18,160.7	18,642.5	18,238.9	19,387.6	19,896.6	20,436.3	–

Note: Figures are in billions of chained 2017 dollars; (1) Figures cover the Reno, NV Metropolitan Statistical Area; (2) Figures cover real GDP within metropolitan areas; (3) Rank is based on 2023 data and ranges from 1 to 384
Source: U.S. Bureau of Economic Analysis

Economic Growth

Area	2014	2015	2016	2017	2018	2019	2020	2021	2022	2023
MSA[1]	0.4	7.7	4.1	7.1	-2.0	3.9	0.8	10.2	1.4	1.4
U.S.[2]	2.6	3.2	2.0	2.7	3.1	2.7	-2.2	6.3	2.6	2.7

Note: Figures are real gross domestic product growth rates and represent percent change from preceding period; (1) Figures cover the Reno, NV Metropolitan Statistical Area; (2) Figures are the average growth rates within metropolitan areas
Source: U.S. Bureau of Economic Analysis

Metropolitan Area Exports

Area	2018	2019	2020	2021	2022	2023	Rank[2]
MSA[1]	2,631.7	2,598.3	4,553.3	4,503.0	3,864.0	3,434.1	78
U.S.	1,664,056.1	1,645,173.7	1,431,406.6	1,753,941.4	2,062,937.4	2,019,160.5	–

Note: Figures are in millions of dollars; (1) Figures cover the Reno, NV Metropolitan Statistical Area; (2) Rank is based on 2023 data and ranges from 1 to 386
Source: U.S. Department of Commerce, International Trade Administration, Office of Trade and Economic Analysis, Industry and Analysis, Exports by Metropolitan Area, data extracted April 2, 2025

Building Permits

Area	Single-Family			Multi-Family			Total		
	2023	2024	Pct. Chg.	2023	2024	Pct. Chg.	2023	2024	Pct. Chg.
City	1,059	1,087	2.6	2,176	1,636	-24.8	3,235	2,723	-15.8
MSA[1]	1,992	2,474	24.2	2,279	1,917	-15.9	4,271	4,391	2.8
U.S.	920,000	981,900	6.7	591,100	496,100	-16.1	1,511,100	1,478,000	-2.2

Note: (1) Figures cover the Reno, NV Metropolitan Statistical Area; Figures represent new, privately-owned housing units authorized (unadjusted data)
Source: U.S. Census Bureau, Building Permits Survey (BPS), 2023, 2024

Bankruptcy Filings

Area	Business Filings			Nonbusiness Filings		
	2023	2024	% Chg.	2023	2024	% Chg.
Washoe County	35	59	68.6	610	860	41.0
U.S.	18,926	23,107	22.1	434,064	494,201	13.9

Note: Business filings include Chapter 7, Chapter 9, Chapter 11, Chapter 12, Chapter 13, Chapter 15, and Section 304; Nonbusiness filings include Chapter 7, Chapter 11, and Chapter 13
Source: Administrative Office of the U.S. Courts, Business and Nonbusiness Bankruptcy, County Cases Commenced by Chapter of the Bankruptcy Code, During the 12-Month Period Ending December 31, 2023 and Business and Nonbusiness Bankruptcy, County Cases Commenced by Chapter of the Bankruptcy Code, During the 12-Month Period Ending December 31, 2024

Housing Vacancy Rates

Area	Gross Vacancy Rate[3] (%)			Year-Round Vacancy Rate[4] (%)			Rental Vacancy Rate[5] (%)			Homeowner Vacancy Rate[6] (%)		
	2022	2023	2024	2022	2023	2024	2022	2023	2024	2022	2023	2024
MSA[1]	n/a	n/a	n/a	n/a	n/a	n/a	n/a	n/a	n/a	n/a	n/a	n/a
U.S.[2]	9.1	9.0	9.1	7.5	7.5	7.6	5.7	6.5	6.8	0.8	0.8	1.0

Note: (1) Figures cover the Reno, NV Metropolitan Statistical Area; (2) Figures cover the 75 largest Metropolitan Statistical Areas; (3) The percentage of the total housing inventory that is vacant; (4) The percentage of the housing inventory (excluding seasonal units) that is year-round vacant; (5) The percentage of rental inventory that is vacant for rent; (6) The percentage of homeowner inventory that is vacant for sale; n/a not available
Source: U.S. Census Bureau, Housing Vacancies and Homeownership Annual Statistics: 2022, 2023, 2024

INCOME

Income

Area	Per Capita ($)	Median Household ($)	Average Household ($)
City	45,180	78,448	107,386
MSA[1]	45,849	84,684	114,037
U.S.	43,289	78,538	110,491

Note: (1) Figures cover the Reno, NV Metropolitan Statistical Area
Source: U.S. Census Bureau, 2019-2023 American Community Survey 5-Year Estimates

Household Income Distribution

Area	Percent of Households Earning							
	Under $15,000	$15,000 -$24,999	$25,000 -$34,999	$35,000 -$49,999	$50,000 -$74,999	$75,000 -$99,999	$100,000 -$149,999	$150,000 and up
City	7.9	6.4	6.9	10.2	16.6	13.2	18.7	19.9
MSA[1]	6.9	5.4	6.0	9.9	16.4	13.4	20.5	21.6
U.S.	8.5	6.6	6.8	10.4	15.7	12.7	17.4	21.9

Note: (1) Figures cover the Reno, NV Metropolitan Statistical Area
Source: U.S. Census Bureau, 2019-2023 American Community Survey 5-Year Estimates

Poverty Rate

Area	All Ages	Under 18 Years Old	18 to 64 Years Old	65 Years and Over
City	12.5	13.9	12.2	11.8
MSA[1]	10.7	12.1	10.3	10.3
U.S.	12.4	16.3	11.6	10.4

Note: Figures are percentage of people whose income during the past 12 months was below the poverty level;
(1) Figures cover the Reno, NV Metropolitan Statistical Area
Source: U.S. Census Bureau, 2019-2023 American Community Survey 5-Year Estimates

EMPLOYMENT

Labor Force and Employment

Area	Civilian Labor Force			Workers Employed		
	Dec. 2023	Dec. 2024	% Chg.	Dec. 2023	Dec. 2024	% Chg.
City	144,664	147,939	2.3	138,887	141,134	1.6
MSA[1]	291,520	298,309	2.3	279,599	284,384	1.7
U.S.	166,661,000	167,746,000	0.7	160,754,000	161,294,000	0.3

Note: Data is not seasonally adjusted and covers workers 16 years of age and older; (1) Figures cover the Reno, NV Metropolitan Statistical Area
Source: Bureau of Labor Statistics, Local Area Unemployment Statistics

Unemployment Rate

Area	2024											
	Jan.	Feb.	Mar.	Apr.	May	Jun.	Jul.	Aug.	Sep.	Oct.	Nov.	Dec.
City	4.5	4.6	4.6	4.4	4.6	4.9	5.1	4.9	4.4	4.6	4.5	4.6
MSA[1]	4.7	4.8	4.7	4.5	4.6	5.0	5.1	4.9	4.5	4.6	4.6	4.7
U.S.	4.1	4.2	3.9	3.5	3.7	4.3	4.5	4.4	3.9	3.9	4.0	3.8

Note: Data is not seasonally adjusted and covers workers 16 years of age and older; (1) Figures cover the Reno, NV Metropolitan Statistical Area
Source: Bureau of Labor Statistics, Local Area Unemployment Statistics

Average Wages

Occupation	$/Hr.	Occupation	$/Hr.
Accountants and Auditors	41.47	Maintenance and Repair Workers	25.86
Automotive Mechanics	27.04	Marketing Managers	73.52
Bookkeepers	25.86	Network and Computer Systems Admin.	48.59
Carpenters	32.80	Nurses, Licensed Practical	35.06
Cashiers	15.27	Nurses, Registered	49.60
Computer Programmers	49.79	Nursing Assistants	21.66
Computer Systems Analysts	47.77	Office Clerks, General	22.82
Computer User Support Specialists	28.19	Physical Therapists	51.17
Construction Laborers	27.64	Physicians	119.36
Cooks, Restaurant	18.27	Plumbers, Pipefitters and Steamfitters	34.61
Customer Service Representatives	20.68	Police and Sheriff's Patrol Officers	40.69
Dentists	74.31	Postal Service Mail Carriers	28.83
Electricians	32.97	Real Estate Sales Agents	27.04
Engineers, Electrical	57.15	Retail Salespersons	18.04
Fast Food and Counter Workers	15.29	Sales Representatives, Technical/Scientific	54.60
Financial Managers	67.77	Secretaries, Exc. Legal/Medical/Executive	23.35
First-Line Supervisors of Office Workers	32.24	Security Guards	20.48
General and Operations Managers	59.24	Surgeons	n/a
Hairdressers/Cosmetologists	23.92	Teacher Assistants, Exc. Postsecondary[1]	17.00
Home Health and Personal Care Aides	16.38	Teachers, Secondary School, Exc. Sp. Ed.[1]	36.97
Janitors and Cleaners	17.04	Telemarketers	16.27
Landscaping/Groundskeeping Workers	21.79	Truck Drivers, Heavy/Tractor-Trailer	31.35
Lawyers	96.52	Truck Drivers, Light/Delivery Services	24.02
Maids and Housekeeping Cleaners	18.19	Waiters and Waitresses	13.93

Note: Wage data covers the Reno, NV Metropolitan Statistical Area; (1) Hourly wages were calculated from annual wage data based on a 40 hour work week
Source: Bureau of Labor Statistics, Metro Area Occupational Employment & Wage Estimates, May 2024

Employment by Industry

Sector	MSA[1]		U.S.
	Number of Employees	Percent of Total	Percent of Total
Construction	24,400	8.5	5.1
Financial Activities	12,000	4.2	5.8
Government	36,400	12.8	14.9
Information	3,900	1.4	1.9
Leisure and Hospitality	40,400	14.2	10.4
Manufacturing	30,300	10.6	8.0
Mining and Logging	800	0.3	0.4
Other Services	7,700	2.7	3.7
Private Education and Health Services	33,100	11.6	16.9
Professional and Business Services	34,400	12.1	14.2
Retail Trade	26,900	9.4	10.0
Transportation, Warehousing, and Utilities	25,200	8.8	4.8
Wholesale Trade	9,900	3.5	3.9

Note: Figures are non-farm employment as of December 2024. Figures are not seasonally adjusted and include workers 16 years of age and older; (1) Figures cover the Reno, NV Metropolitan Statistical Area
Source: Bureau of Labor Statistics, Current Employment Statistics, Employment, Hours, and Earnings

Employment by Occupation

Occupation Classification	City (%)	MSA[1] (%)	U.S. (%)
Management, Business, Science, and Arts	38.0	36.6	42.0
Natural Resources, Construction, and Maintenance	8.3	9.5	8.6
Production, Transportation, and Material Moving	14.2	15.3	13.0
Sales and Office	20.8	20.9	19.9
Service	18.8	17.7	16.5

Note: Figures cover employed civilians 16 years of age and older; (1) Figures cover the Reno, NV Metropolitan Statistical Area
Source: U.S. Census Bureau, 2019-2023 American Community Survey 5-Year Estimates

Occupations with Greatest Projected Employment Growth: 2022 – 2032

Occupation[1]	2022 Employment	2032 Projected Employment	Numeric Employment Change	Percent Employment Change
Laborers and Freight, Stock, and Material Movers, Hand	42,160	58,010	15,850	37.6
Taxi Drivers	22,490	31,920	9,430	41.9
Cooks, Restaurant	21,100	27,730	6,630	31.4
General and Operations Managers	42,740	48,840	6,100	14.3
Home Health and Personal Care Aides	16,000	21,330	5,330	33.3
Stockers and Order Fillers	22,320	27,550	5,230	23.4
Janitors and Cleaners, Except Maids and Housekeeping Cleaners	31,300	36,250	4,950	15.8
Heavy and Tractor-Trailer Truck Drivers	17,650	22,350	4,700	26.6
Fast Food and Counter Workers	40,690	45,260	4,570	11.2
Registered Nurses	24,290	28,810	4,520	18.6

Note: Projections cover Nevada; (1) Sorted by numeric employment change
Source: www.projectionscentral.org, State Occupational Projections, 2022–2032 Long-Term Projections

Fastest-Growing Occupations: 2022 – 2032

Occupation[1]	2022 Employment	2032 Projected Employment	Numeric Employment Change	Percent Employment Change
Farmworkers and Laborers, Crop, Nursery, and Greenhouse	2,760	5,210	2,450	88.8
Farm Equipment Mechanics and Service Technicians	120	210	90	75.0
Farmers, Ranchers, and Other Agricultural Managers	2,370	3,870	1,500	63.3
Bus Drivers, Transit and Intercity (SOC 2018)	1,720	2,770	1,050	61.0
Orthotists and Prosthetists	140	220	80	57.1
Solar Photovoltaic Installers	140	220	80	57.1
Nurse Practitioners	1,840	2,780	940	51.1
Helpers—Extraction Workers	660	990	330	50.0
Occupational Health and Safety Technicians (SOC 2018)	320	470	150	46.9
Shuttle Drivers and Chauffeurs	2,630	3,840	1,210	46.0

Note: Projections cover Nevada; (1) Sorted by percent employment change and excludes occupations with numeric employment change less than 50
Source: www.projectionscentral.org, State Occupational Projections, 2022–2032 Long-Term Projections

CITY FINANCES

City Government Finances

Component	2022 ($000)	2022 ($ per capita)
Total Revenues	461,151	1,779
Total Expenditures	423,247	1,632
Debt Outstanding	461,200	1,779

Source: U.S. Census Bureau, State & Local Government Finances 2022

City Government Revenue by Source

Source	2022 ($000)	2022 ($ per capita)	2022 (%)
General Revenue			
From Federal Government	9,868	38	2.1
From State Government	126,218	487	27.4
From Local Governments	18,025	70	3.9
Taxes			
Property	92,467	357	20.1
Sales and Gross Receipts	48,192	186	10.5
Personal Income	0	0	0.0
Corporate Income	0	0	0.0
Motor Vehicle License	0	0	0.0
Other Taxes	43,289	167	9.4
Current Charges	96,077	371	20.8
Liquor Store	0	0	0.0
Utility	0	0	0.0

Source: U.S. Census Bureau, State & Local Government Finances 2022

City Government Expenditures by Function

Function	2022 ($000)	2022 ($ per capita)	2022 (%)
General Direct Expenditures			
Air Transportation	0	0	0.0
Corrections	0	0	0.0
Education	0	0	0.0
Employment Security Administration	0	0	0.0
Financial Administration	3,282	12	0.8
Fire Protection	63,093	243	14.9
General Public Buildings	0	0	0.0
Governmental Administration, Other	15,907	61	3.8
Health	0	0	0.0
Highways	39,689	153	9.4
Hospitals	0	0	0.0
Housing and Community Development	30,218	116	7.1
Interest on General Debt	16,168	62	3.8
Judicial and Legal	13,026	50	3.1
Libraries	0	0	0.0
Parking	509	2	0.1
Parks and Recreation	14,654	56	3.5
Police Protection	100,445	387	23.7
Public Welfare	0	0	0.0
Sewerage	89,473	345	21.1
Solid Waste Management	0	0	0.0
Veterans' Services	0	0	0.0
Liquor Store	0	0	0.0
Utility	0	0	0.0

Source: U.S. Census Bureau, State & Local Government Finances 2022

TAXES

State Corporate Income Tax Rates

State	Tax Rate (%)	Income Brackets ($)	Num. of Brackets	Financial Institution Tax Rate (%)[a]	Federal Income Tax Ded.
Nevada	None	–	–	–	–

Note: Tax rates for tax year 2024; (a) Rates listed are the corporate income tax rate applied to financial institutions or excise taxes based on income. Some states have other taxes based upon the value of deposits or shares.
Source: Federation of Tax Administrators, State Corporate Income Tax Rates, January 1, 2025

State Individual Income Tax Rates

State	Tax Rate (%)	Income Brackets ($)	Personal Exemptions ($) Single	Married	Depend.	Standard Ded. ($) Single	Married
Nevada			– No state income tax –				

Note: Tax rates for tax year 2024; Local- and county-level taxes are not included
Source: Federation of Tax Administrators, State Individual Income Tax Rates, January 1, 2025

Various State Sales and Excise Tax Rates

State	State Sales Tax (%)	Gasoline[1] ($/gal.)	Cigarette[2] ($/pack)	Spirits[3] ($/gal.)	Wine[4] ($/gal.)	Beer[5] ($/gal.)	Recreational Marijuana (%)
Nevada	6.85	0.24	1.80	3.60	0.70	0.16	(o)

Note: All tax rates as of January 1, 2025; (1) The American Petroleum Institute has developed a methodology for determining the average tax rate on a gallon of fuel. Rates may include any of the following: excise taxes, environmental fees, storage tank fees, other fees or taxes, general sales tax, and local taxes; (2) The federal excise tax of $1.0066 per pack and local taxes are not included; (3) Rates are those applicable to off-premise sales of 40% alcohol by volume (a.b.v.) distilled spirits in 750ml containers. Local excise taxes are excluded; (4) Rates are those applicable to off-premise sales of 11% a.b.v. non-carbonated wine in 750ml containers; (5) Rates are those applicable to off-premise sales of 4.7% a.b.v. beer in 12 ounce containers; (o) 15% excise tax (fair market value at wholesale); 10% excise tax (retail price)
Source: Tax Foundation, 2025 Facts & Figures: How Does Your State Compare?

State Tax Competitiveness Index

State	Overall Rank	Corporate Tax Rank	Individual Income Tax Rank	Sales Tax Rank	Property Tax Rank	Unemployment Insurance Tax Rank
Nevada	17	39	7	40	7	46

Note: The Tax Foundation's State Tax Competitiveness Index enables policymakers, taxpayers, and business leaders to gauge how their states' tax systems compare. A rank of 1 is best, 50 is worst. Rankings do not average to the total. States without a tax rank equally as 1. DC's scores and rankings do not affect other states. The report shows tax systems as of July 1, 2024 (the beginning of Fiscal Year 2025).
Source: Tax Foundation, State Tax Competitiveness Index 2025

TRANSPORTATION

Means of Transportation to Work

| Area | Car/Truck/Van | | Public Transportation | | | Bicycle | Walked | Other Means | Worked at Home |
	Drove Alone	Car-pooled	Bus	Subway	Railroad				
City	67.6	12.6	2.4	0.0	0.0	0.6	3.2	2.8	10.8
MSA[1]	70.2	12.5	1.8	0.0	0.0	0.4	2.2	2.1	10.8
U.S.	70.2	8.5	1.7	1.3	0.4	0.4	2.4	1.6	13.5

Note: Figures are percentages and cover workers 16 years of age and older; (1) Figures cover the Reno, NV Metropolitan Statistical Area
Source: U.S. Census Bureau, 2019-2023 American Community Survey 5-Year Estimates

Travel Time to Work

Area	Less Than 10 Minutes	10 to 19 Minutes	20 to 29 Minutes	30 to 44 Minutes	45 to 59 Minutes	60 to 89 Minutes	90 Minutes or More
City	15.1	39.7	23.5	13.2	4.9	2.4	1.2
MSA[1]	12.8	34.1	24.2	17.6	6.0	3.6	1.6
U.S.	12.6	28.6	21.2	20.8	8.1	6.0	2.8

Note: Note: Figures are percentages and include workers 16 years old and over; (1) Figures cover the Reno, NV Metropolitan Statistical Area
Source: U.S. Census Bureau, 2019-2023 American Community Survey 5-Year Estimates

Key Congestion Measures

Measure	2000	2010	2015	2020	2022
Annual Hours of Delay, Total (000)	n/a	n/a	10,688	4,936	15,030
Annual Hours of Delay, Per Auto Commuter	n/a	n/a	26	11	34
Annual Congestion Cost, Per Auto Commuter ($)	n/a	n/a	603	294	902

Note: n/a not available
Source: Texas A&M Transportation Institute, 2023 Urban Mobility Report

Freeway Travel Time Index

Measure	1985	1990	1995	2000	2005	2010	2015	2020	2022
Urban Area Index[1]	n/a	n/a	n/a	n/a	n/a	n/a	1.13	1.07	1.19
Urban Area Rank[1,2]	n/a	n/a	n/a	n/a	n/a	n/a	n/a	n/a	n/a

Note: Freeway Travel Time Index—the ratio of travel time in the peak period to the travel time at free-flow conditions. For example, a value of 1.30 indicates a 20-minute free-flow trip takes 26 minutes in the peak (20 minutes x 1.30 = 26 minutes); (1) Covers the Reno NV-CA urban area; (2) Rank is based on 101 larger urban areas (#1 = highest travel time index); n/a not available
Source: Texas A&M Transportation Institute, 2023 Urban Mobility Report

Public Transportation

Agency Name / Mode of Transportation	Vehicles Operated in Maximum Service[1]	Annual Unlinked Passenger Trips[2] (in thous.)	Annual Passenger Miles[3] (in thous.)
Regional Transportation Commission of Washoe County (RTC)			
Bus (purchased transportation)	51	4,847.0	15,547.0
Commuter Bus (purchased transportation)	3	18.8	433.7
Demand Response (purchased transportation)	41	164.6	1,127.2
Vanpool (purchased transportation)	350	722.8	24,731.6

Note: (1) Number of revenue vehicles operated by the given mode and type of service to meet the annual maximum service requirement. This is the revenue vehicle count during the peak season of the year; on the week and day that maximum service is provided. Vehicles operated in maximum service (VOMS) exclude atypical days and one-time special events; (2) Number of passengers who boarded public transportation vehicles. Passengers are counted each time they board a vehicle no matter how many vehicles they use to travel from their origin to their destination. (3) Sum of the distances ridden by all passengers during the entire fiscal year.
Source: Federal Transit Administration, National Transit Database, 2023

Air Transportation

Airport Name and Code / Type of Service	Passenger Airlines[1]	Passenger Enplanements	Freight Carriers[2]	Freight (lbs)
Reno-Tahoe International (RNO)				
Domestic service (U.S. carriers only)	25	2,342,128	10	65,479,861
International service (U.S. carriers only)	2	902	0	0

Note: (1) Includes all U.S.-based major, minor and commuter airlines that carried at least one passenger during the year; (2) Includes all U.S.-based airlines and freight carriers that transported at least one pound of freight during the year.
Source: Bureau of Transportation Statistics, The Intermodal Transportation Database, Air Carriers: T-100 Domestic Market (U.S. carriers only), 2024; Bureau of Transportation Statistics, The Intermodal Transportation Database, Air Carriers: T-100 International Market (U.S. carriers only), 2024

BUSINESSES

Major Business Headquarters

Company Name	Industry	Rankings	
		Fortune[1]	Forbes[2]
Caesars Entertainment	Hotels, casinos, resorts	353	-

Note: (1) Companies that produce a 10-K are ranked 1 to 500 based on 2023 revenue; (2) All private companies with at least $2 billion in annual revenue through the end of their most current fiscal year are ranked 1 to 275; companies listed are headquartered in the city; dashes indicate no ranking
Source: Fortune, "Fortune 500," 2024; Forbes, "America's Largest Private Companies," 2024

Fastest-Growing Businesses

According to Deloitte, Reno is home to one of North America's 500 fastest-growing high-technology companies: **SendCutSend** (#131). Companies are ranked by percentage growth in revenue over a four-year period. Criteria for inclusion: company must be headquartered within North America; must own proprietary intellectual property or technology that is sold to customers in products that contributes to a significant portion of the company's operating revenue; must have been in business for a minumum of four years with 2020 operating revenues of at least $50,000 USD/CD and 2023 operating revenues of at least $5 million USD/CD. *Deloitte, 2024 Technology Fast 500*[TM]

Living Environment

COST OF LIVING

Cost of Living Index

Composite Index	Groceries	Housing	Utilities	Trans-portation	Health Care	Misc. Goods/Services
104.0	102.9	110.9	93.4	123.5	88.5	98.6

Note: The Cost of Living Index measures regional differences in the cost of consumer goods and services, excluding taxes and non-consumer expenditures, for professional and managerial households in the top income quintile. It is based on more than 50,000 prices covering almost 60 different items for which prices are collected three times a year by chambers of commerce, economic development organizations or university applied economic centers in each participating urban area. The numbers shown should be read as a percentage above or below the national average of 100. For example, a value of 115.4 in the groceries column indicates that grocery prices are 15.4% higher than the national average. Small differences in the index numbers should not be interpreted as significant; Figures cover the Reno-Sparks NV urban area.
Source: The Council for Community and Economic Research, Cost of Living Index, 2024

Grocery Prices

Area[1]	T-Bone Steak ($/pound)	Frying Chicken ($/pound)	Whole Milk ($/half gal.)	Eggs ($/dozen)	Orange Juice ($/64 oz.)	Coffee ($/11.5 oz.)
City[2]	15.53	2.26	4.66	2.91	4.36	5.88
Avg.	15.42	1.55	4.69	3.25	4.41	5.46
Min.	14.50	1.16	4.43	2.75	4.00	4.85
Max.	17.56	2.89	5.49	4.78	5.54	7.89

Note: (1) Values for the local area are compared with the average, minimum and maximum values for all 276 areas in the Cost of Living Index; (2) Figures cover the Reno-Sparks NV urban area; T-Bone Steak (price per pound); Frying Chicken (price per pound, whole fryer); Whole Milk (half gallon carton); Eggs (price per dozen, Grade A, large); Orange Juice (64 oz. Tropicana or Florida Natural); Coffee (11.5 oz. can, vacuum-packed, Maxwell House, Hills Bros, or Folgers).
Source: The Council for Community and Economic Research, Cost of Living Index, 2024

Housing and Utility Costs

Area[1]	New Home Price ($)	Apartment Rent ($/month)	All Electric ($/month)	Part Electric ($/month)	Other Energy ($/month)	Telephone ($/month)
City[2]	596,654	1,646	-	129.17	59.21	188.64
Avg.	515,975	1,550	210.99	123.07	82.07	194.99
Min.	265,375	692	104.33	53.68	36.26	179.42
Max.	2,775,821	5,719	529.02	397.28	361.63	223.33

Note: (1) Values for the local area are compared with the average, minimum and maximum values for all 276 areas in the Cost of Living Index; (2) Figures cover the Reno-Sparks NV urban area; New Home Price (2,400 sf living area, 8,000 sf lot, in urban area with full utilities); Apartment Rent (950 sf 2 bedroom/1.5 or 2 bath, unfurnished, excluding all utilities except water); All Electric (average monthly cost for an all-electric home); Part Electric (average monthly cost for a part-electric home); Other Energy (average monthly cost for natural gas, fuel oil, coal, wood, and any other forms of energy except electricity); Telephone (price includes the base monthly rate plus taxes and fees for three lines of mobile phone service).
Source: The Council for Community and Economic Research, Cost of Living Index, 2024

Health Care, Transportation, and Other Costs

Area[1]	Doctor ($/visit)	Dentist ($/visit)	Optometrist ($/visit)	Gasoline ($/gallon)	Beauty Salon ($/visit)	Men's Shirt ($)
City[2]	115.00	105.00	118.17	4.35	49.17	27.27
Avg.	143.77	117.51	129.23	3.32	48.57	38.14
Min.	36.74	58.67	67.33	2.80	24.00	13.41
Max.	270.44	216.82	307.33	5.28	94.00	63.89

Note: (1) Values for the local area are compared with the average, minimum and maximum values for all 276 areas in the Cost of Living Index; (2) Figures cover the Reno-Sparks NV urban area; Doctor (general practitioners routine exam of an established patient); Dentist (adult teeth cleaning and periodic oral examination); Optometrist (full vision eye exam for established adult patient); Gasoline (one gallon regular unleaded, national brand, including all taxes, cash price at self-service pump if available); Beauty Salon (woman's shampoo, trim, and blow-dry); Men's Shirt (cotton/polyester dress shirt, pinpoint weave, long sleeves).
Source: The Council for Community and Economic Research, Cost of Living Index, 2024

HOUSING

Homeownership Rate

Area	2017 (%)	2018 (%)	2019 (%)	2020 (%)	2021 (%)	2022 (%)	2023 (%)	2024 (%)
MSA[1]	n/a	n/a	n/a	n/a	n/a	n/a	n/a	n/a
U.S.	63.9	64.4	64.6	66.6	65.5	65.8	65.9	65.6

Note: (1) Figures cover the Reno, NV Metropolitan Statistical Area; n/a not available
Source: U.S. Census Bureau, Housing Vacancies and Homeownership Annual Statistics: 2017-2024

House Price Index (HPI)

Area	National Ranking[2]	Quarterly Change (%)	One-Year Change (%)	Five-Year Change (%)	Since 1991Q1 (%)
MSA[1]	121	0.31	5.40	49.95	361.77
U.S.[3]	–	1.43	4.51	57.13	327.82

Note: The HPI is a weighted repeat sales index. It measures average price changes in repeat sales or refinancings on the same properties. This information is obtained by reviewing repeat mortgage transactions on single-family properties whose mortgages have been purchased or securitized by Fannie Mae or Freddie Mac since January 1975; (1) Figures cover the Reno, NV Metropolitan Statistical Area; (2) Rankings are based on annual percentage change for all metro areas containing at least 15,000 transactions over the last 10 years and ranges from 1 to 241; (3) figures based on a weighted average of Census Division estimates using a seasonally adjusted, purchase-only index; all figures are for the period ending December 31, 2024
Source: Federal Housing Finance Agency, Change in FHFA Metropolitan Area House Price Indexes, All Transactions Index, 2024Q4

Home Value

Area	Under $100,000	$100,000 -$199,999	$200,000 -$299,999	$300,000 -$399,999	$400,000 -$499,999	$500,000 -$999,999	$1,000,000 or more	Median ($)
City	6.1	3.0	6.9	14.9	19.3	42.7	7.1	498,600
MSA[1]	5.5	4.0	9.4	17.0	18.9	36.5	8.6	474,000
U.S.	12.1	17.8	19.5	14.4	10.5	19.1	6.5	303,400

Note: Figures are percentages except for median and cover owner-occupied housing units; (1) Figures cover the Reno, NV Metropolitan Statistical Area
Source: U.S. Census Bureau, 2019-2023 American Community Survey 5-Year Estimates

Year Housing Structure Built

Area	2020 or Later	2010 -2019	2000 -2009	1990 -1999	1980 -1989	1970 -1979	1960 -1969	1950 -1959	1940 -1949	Before 1940	Median Year
City	3.0	11.6	19.1	15.0	13.3	17.7	8.5	5.7	3.1	2.9	1989
MSA[1]	2.3	10.8	21.1	16.9	14.2	17.6	7.9	4.6	2.3	2.3	1991
U.S.	1.2	8.9	13.6	12.8	13.0	14.4	10.0	9.7	4.5	11.9	1980

Note: Figures are percentages except for Median Year; Note: (1) Figures cover the Reno, NV Metropolitan Statistical Area
Source: U.S. Census Bureau, 2019-2023 American Community Survey 5-Year Estimates

Gross Monthly Rent

Area	Under $500	$500 -$999	$1,000 -$1,499	$1,500 -$1,999	$2,000 -$2,499	$2,500 -$2,999	$3,000 and up	Median ($)
City	4.9	15.0	33.3	26.7	13.4	4.0	2.7	1,453
MSA[1]	4.2	14.7	31.6	27.3	14.8	4.0	3.4	1,491
U.S.	6.5	22.3	29.5	20.2	10.8	4.8	5.9	1,348

Note: Figures are percentages except for median; Gross rent is the contract rent plus the estimated average monthly cost of utilities (electricity, gas, and water and sewer) and fuels (oil, coal, kerosene, wood, etc.) if these are paid by the renter (or paid for the renter by someone else); (1) Figures cover the Reno, NV Metropolitan Statistical Area
Source: U.S. Census Bureau, 2019-2023 American Community Survey 5-Year Estimates

HEALTH

Health Risk Factors

Category	MSA[1] (%)	U.S. (%)
Adults aged 18–64 who have any kind of health care coverage	86.8	90.8
Adults who reported being in good or better health	76.3	81.8
Adults who have been told they have high blood cholesterol	37.1	36.9
Adults who have been told they have high blood pressure	28.2	34.0
Adults who are current smokers	9.1	12.1
Adults who currently use e-cigarettes	6.9	7.7
Adults who currently use chewing tobacco, snuff, or snus	4.5	3.2
Adults who are heavy drinkers[2]	8.0	6.1
Adults who are binge drinkers[3]	19.0	15.2
Adults who are overweight (BMI 25.0 - 29.9)	30.9	34.4
Adults who are obese (BMI 30.0 - 99.8)	33.6	34.3
Adults who participated in any physical activities in the past month	78.6	75.8

Note: All figures are crude prevalence; (1) Figures cover the Reno, NV Metropolitan Statistical Area; (2) Heavy drinkers are classified as adult men having more than 14 drinks per week and adult women having more than 7 drinks per week; (3) Binge drinkers are classified as males having five or more drinks on one occasion or females having four or more drinks on one occasion
Source: Centers for Disease Control and Prevention, Behaviorial Risk Factor Surveillance System, SMART: Selected Metropolitan Area Risk Trends, 2023

Acute and Chronic Health Conditions

Category	MSA[1] (%)	U.S. (%)
Adults who have ever been told they had a heart attack	2.7	4.2
Adults who have ever been told they have angina or coronary heart disease	3.9	4.0
Adults who have ever been told they had a stroke	2.5	3.3
Adults who have ever been told they have asthma	14.5	15.7
Adults who have ever been told they have arthritis	27.3	26.3
Adults who have ever been told they have diabetes[2]	8.1	11.5
Adults who have ever been told they had skin cancer	8.2	5.6
Adults who have ever been told they had any other types of cancer	10.7	8.4
Adults who have ever been told they have COPD	6.6	6.4
Adults who have ever been told they have kidney disease	3.3	3.7
Adults who have ever been told they have a form of depression	20.4	22.0

Note: All figures are crude prevalence; (1) Figures cover the Reno, NV Metropolitan Statistical Area; (2) Figures do not include pregnancy-related, borderline, or pre-diabetes
Source: Centers for Disease Control and Prevention, Behaviorial Risk Factor Surveillance System, SMART: Selected Metropolitan Area Risk Trends, 2023

Health Screening and Vaccination Rates

Category	MSA[1] (%)	U.S. (%)
Adults who have ever been tested for HIV	43.4	37.5
Adults who have had their blood cholesterol checked within the last five years	83.6	87.0
Adults aged 65+ who have had flu shot within the past year	65.4	63.4
Adults aged 65+ who have ever had a pneumonia vaccination	76.1	71.9

Note: All figures are crude prevalence; (1) Figures cover the Reno, NV Metropolitan Statistical Area.
Source: Centers for Disease Control and Prevention, Behaviorial Risk Factor Surveillance System, SMART: Selected Metropolitan Area Risk Trends, 2023

Disability Status

Category	MSA[1] (%)	U.S. (%)
Adults who reported being deaf	7.8	7.4
Are you blind or have serious difficulty seeing, even when wearing glasses?	6.1	4.9
Do you have difficulty doing errands alone?	9.6	7.8
Do you have difficulty dressing or bathing?	3.7	3.6
Do you have serious difficulty concentrating/remembering/making decisions?	17.1	13.7
Do you have serious difficulty walking or climbing stairs?	13.5	13.2

Note: All figures are crude prevalence; (1) Figures cover the Reno, NV Metropolitan Statistical Area.
Source: Centers for Disease Control and Prevention, Behaviorial Risk Factor Surveillance System, SMART: Selected Metropolitan Area Risk Trends, 2023

Mortality Rates for the Top 10 Causes of Death in the U.S.

ICD-10[a] Sub-Chapter	ICD-10[a] Code	Crude Mortality Rate[2] per 100,000 population	
		County[3]	U.S.
Malignant neoplasms	C00-C97	168.4	182.7
Ischaemic heart diseases	I20-I25	115.1	109.6
Provisional assignment of new diseases of uncertain etiology[1]	U00-U49	53.8	65.3
Other forms of heart disease	I30-I51	51.5	65.1
Other degenerative diseases of the nervous system	G30-G31	42.6	52.4
Other external causes of accidental injury	W00-X59	68.9	52.3
Cerebrovascular diseases	I60-I69	57.4	49.1
Chronic lower respiratory diseases	J40-J47	47.0	43.5
Hypertensive diseases	I10-I15	41.9	38.9
Organic, including symptomatic, mental disorders	F01-F09	20.6	33.9

Note: (a) ICD-10 = International Classification of Diseases 10th Revision; (1) Includes COVID-19, adverse effects to COVID-19 vaccines, SARS, and vaping-related disorders; (2) Crude mortality rates are a three-year average covering 2021-2023; (3) Figures cover Washoe County.
Source: Centers for Disease Control and Prevention, National Center for Health Statistics. National Vital Statistics System, Mortality 2018-2023 on CDC WONDER Online Database

Mortality Rates for Selected Causes of Death

Cause of Death	ICD-10[a] Code	Crude Mortality Rate[1] per 100,000 population	
		County[2]	U.S.
Accidental poisoning and exposure to noxious substances	X40-X49	40.5	30.5
Alzheimer disease	G30	15.3	35.4
Assault	X85-Y09	6.5	7.3
COVID-19	U07.1	53.8	65.3
Diabetes mellitus	E10-E14	25.5	30.0
Diseases of the liver	K70-K76	24.3	20.8
Human immunodeficiency virus (HIV) disease	B20-B24	1.3	1.5
Influenza and pneumonia	J09-J18	9.1	13.4
Intentional self-harm	X60-X84	24.1	14.7
Malnutrition	E40-E46	16.9	6.0
Obesity and other hyperalimentation	E65-E68	3.0	3.1
Renal failure	N17-N19	11.4	16.4
Transport accidents	V01-V99	13.7	14.4

Note: (a) ICD-10 = International Classification of Diseases 10th Revision; (1) Crude mortality rates are a three-year average covering 2021-2023; (2) Figures cover Washoe County; Data are suppressed when the data meet the criteria for confidentiality constraints; Crude mortality rates are flagged as unreliable when the rate would be calculated with a numerator of 20 or less.
Source: Centers for Disease Control and Prevention, National Center for Health Statistics. National Vital Statistics System, Mortality 2018-2023 on CDC WONDER Online Database

Health Insurance Coverage

Area	With Health Insurance	With Private Health Insurance	With Public Health Insurance	Without Health Insurance	Population Under Age 19 Without Health Insurance
City	89.5	67.9	31.5	10.5	7.0
MSA[1]	90.4	69.0	32.8	9.6	6.8
U.S.	91.4	67.3	36.3	8.6	5.4

Note: Figures are percentages that cover the civilian noninstitutionalized population; (1) Figures cover the Reno, NV Metropolitan Statistical Area
Source: U.S. Census Bureau, 2019-2023 American Community Survey 5-Year Estimates

Number of Medical Professionals

Area	MDs[3]	DOs[3,4]	Dentists	Podiatrists	Chiropractors	Optometrists
County[1] (number)	1,541	125	359	22	153	118
County[1] (rate[2])	310.2	25.2	72.1	4.4	30.7	23.7
U.S. (rate[2])	302.5	29.2	74.6	6.4	29.5	18.0

Note: Data as of 2023 unless noted; (1) Data covers Washoe County; (2) Number of medical professionals per 100,000 population; (3) Data as of 2022 and includes all active, non-federal physicians; (4) Doctor of Osteopathic Medicine
Source: U.S. Department of Health and Human Services, Health Resources and Services Administration, Bureau of Health Professions, Area Resource File (ARF) 2023-2024

EDUCATION

Public School District Statistics

District Name	Schls	Pupils	Pupil/ Teacher Ratio	Minority Pupils[1] (%)	Total Rev. per Pupil ($)	Total Exp. per Pupil ($)
Washoe County School District	117	63,777	19.4	59.2	13,452	14,973

Note: Table includes school districts with 2,000 or more students; (1) Percentage of students that are not non-Hispanic white.
Source: U.S. Department of Education, National Center for Education Statistics, Common Core of Data, Local Education Agency (School District) Universe Survey: School Year 2023-2024; U.S. Department of Education, National Center for Education Statistics, Common Core of Data, School District Finance Survey (F-33): School Year 2021–22

Highest Level of Education

Area	Less than H.S.	H.S. Diploma	Some College, No Deg.	Associate Degree	Bachelor's Degree	Master's Degree	Prof. School Degree	Doctorate Degree
City	10.7	22.8	22.6	8.3	21.4	9.4	2.8	2.2
MSA[1]	11.4	24.4	24.0	8.8	19.2	8.4	2.2	1.6
U.S.	10.6	26.2	19.4	8.8	21.3	9.8	2.3	1.6

Note: Figures cover persons age 25 and over; (1) Figures cover the Reno, NV Metropolitan Statistical Area
Source: U.S. Census Bureau, 2019-2023 American Community Survey 5-Year Estimates

Educational Attainment by Race

Area	High School Graduate or Higher (%)					Bachelor's Degree or Higher (%)				
	Total	White	Black	Asian	Hisp.[2]	Total	White	Black	Asian	Hisp.[2]
City	89.3	94.9	91.5	90.5	65.3	35.7	39.9	26.6	49.2	15.2
MSA[1]	88.6	93.5	90.2	90.5	65.8	31.4	34.6	21.8	45.8	14.4
U.S.	89.4	92.9	88.1	88.0	72.5	35.0	37.7	24.7	57.0	19.9

Note: Figures shown cover persons 25 years old and over; (1) Figures cover the Reno, NV Metropolitan Statistical Area; (2) People of Hispanic origin can be of any race
Source: U.S. Census Bureau, 2019-2023 American Community Survey 5-Year Estimates

School Enrollment by Grade and Control

Area	Preschool (%)		Kindergarten (%)		Grades 1 - 4 (%)		Grades 5 - 8 (%)		Grades 9 - 12 (%)	
	Public	Private	Public	Private	Public	Private	Public	Private	Public	Private
City	54.6	45.4	96.7	3.3	89.2	10.8	88.3	11.7	93.6	6.4
MSA[1]	51.8	48.2	90.8	9.2	90.9	9.1	89.7	10.3	92.1	7.9
U.S.	58.7	41.3	85.2	14.8	87.2	12.8	87.9	12.1	89.0	11.0

Note: Figures shown cover persons 3 years old and over; (1) Figures cover the Reno, NV Metropolitan Statistical Area
Source: U.S. Census Bureau, 2019-2023 American Community Survey 5-Year Estimates

Higher Education

Four-Year Colleges			Two-Year Colleges			Medical Schools[1]	Law Schools[2]	Voc/ Tech[3]
Public	Private Non-profit	Private For-profit	Public	Private Non-profit	Private For-profit			
2	0	0	0	0	2	1	0	4

Note: Figures cover institutions located within the Reno, NV Metropolitan Statistical Area and include main campuses only; (1) includes schools accredited by the Liaison Committee on Medical Education and the American Osteopathic Association's Commission on Osteopathic College Accreditation; (2) includes ABA-accredited schools, schools with provisional ABA accreditation, and state accredited schools; (3) includes all schools with programs that are less than 2 years.
Source: National Center for Education Statistics, Integrated Postsecondary Education System (IPEDS), 2023-24; Wikipedia, List of Medical Schools in the United States, accessed May 2, 2025; Wikipedia, List of Law Schools in the United States, accessed May 2, 2025

According to *U.S. News & World Report*, the Reno, NV metro area is home to one of the top medical schools for primary care in the U.S.: **University of Nevada—Reno** (Tier 2). *U.S. News* placed medical and osteopathic schools into tiers based on their research productivity, faculty and admissions data. Each school's tier was derived from its overall score, calculated by summing the weighted normalized values generated across several factors of academic quality, outlined below. There are four tiers, with tier 1 medical schools as the highest-performing and tier 4 as the lowest-performing. Only tier 1 and 2 schools are shown. Because of the tier presentation, *U.S. News* calculated overall scores based on their percentile performance among all rated schools instead of dividing against the rescaled score of the No. 1-performing schools. Tier 1 included schools with overall scores of 85 to 99. The cutoffs for tiers 2 through 4 were schools scoring 50 to 84, 15 to 49 and 1 to 14, respectively. The rankings are based on a weighted average of the following measures of quality: graduates practicing in primary care specialties; graduates entering primary care residencies; median MCAT total score; median undergraduate GPA; acceptance rate; and faculty resources. *U.S. News & World Report, "America's Best Graduate Schools, Medical, 2025"*

EMPLOYERS

Major Employers

Company Name	Industry
Atlantis Casino Resort	Casino hotels
Bellagio	Casino hotels
Circus Circus Casinos - Reno	Casino hotels
City of Reno	Municipal government
Desert Palace	Casino hotels
Eldorado Hotel & Casino	Casino hotels
Grand Sierra Resort & Casino	Casino hotels
Harrahs Reno	Casino hotels
IGT	All other miscellaneous manufacturing
Integrity Staffing Solutions	Temporary help services
Mandalay Corp	Casino hotels
Peppermill Hotel Casino - Reno	Casino hotels
Renown Regional Medical Center	General medical & surgical hospitals
Saint Marys	General medical & surgical hospitals
Sierra Nevada Healthcare System	General medical & surgical hospitals
Silver Legacy Resort Casino	Casino hotels
Sparks Nugget	Casino hotels
Truckee Meadows Community Coll	Junior colleges
United Parcel Service	Package delivery services
University of Nevada-Reno	Colleges & universities

Note: Companies shown are located within the Reno, NV Metropolitan Statistical Area.
Source: Chambers of Commerce; State Departments of Labor; Wikipedia

PUBLIC SAFETY

Crime Rate

Area	Total Crime Rate	Violent Crime Rate				Property Crime Rate		
		Murder	Rape	Robbery	Aggrav. Assault	Burglary	Larceny -Theft	Motor Vehicle Theft
City	3,234.8	6.8	102.2	111.6	375.1	381.9	1,838.8	418.3
U.S.	2,290.9	5.7	38.0	66.5	264.1	250.7	1,347.2	318.7

Note: Figures are crimes per 100,000 population.
Source: FBI, Table 8, Offenses Known to Law Enforcement, by State by City, 2023

Hate Crimes

Area	Number of Quarters Reported	Number of Incidents per Bias Motivation					
		Race/Ethnicity/ Ancestry	Religion	Sexual Orientation	Disability	Gender	Gender Identity
City	4	11	1	1	0	1	0
U.S.	4	5,900	2,699	2,077	187	92	492

Source: Federal Bureau of Investigation, Hate Crime Statistics 2023

Identity Theft Consumer Reports

Area	Reports	Reports per 100,000 Population	Rank[2]
MSA[1]	1,069	192	177
U.S.	1,135,291	339	-

Note: (1) Figures cover the Reno, NV Metropolitan Statistical Area; (2) Rank ranges from 1 to 401 where 1 indicates greatest number of identity theft reports per 100,000 population
Source: Federal Trade Commission, Consumer Sentinel Network Data Book 2024

Fraud and Other Consumer Reports

Area	Reports	Reports per 100,000 Population	Rank[2]
MSA[1]	6,697	1,203	126
U.S.	5,360,641	1,601	-

Note: (1) Figures cover the Reno, NV Metropolitan Statistical Area; (2) Rank ranges from 1 to 401 where 1 indicates greatest number of fraud and other consumer reports per 100,000 population
Source: Federal Trade Commission, Consumer Sentinel Network Data Book 2024

POLITICS

2024 Presidential Election Results

Area	Trump (Rep.)	Harris (Dem.)	Stein (Green)	Kennedy (Ind.)	Oliver (Lib.)	Other
Washoe County	48.3	49.3	0.0	0.0	0.5	1.8
U.S.	49.7	48.2	0.6	0.5	0.4	0.6

Note: Results are percentages and may not add to 100% due to rounding
Source: Dave Leip's Atlas of U.S. Presidential Elections

SPORTS

Professional Sports Teams

Team Name	League	Year Established

No teams are located in the metro area
Source: Wikipedia, Major Professional Sports Teams of the United States and Canada, May 1, 2025

CLIMATE

Average and Extreme Temperatures

Temperature	Jan	Feb	Mar	Apr	May	Jun	Jul	Aug	Sep	Oct	Nov	Dec	Yr.
Extreme High (°F)	70	75	83	89	96	103	104	105	101	91	77	70	105
Average High (°F)	45	51	56	64	73	82	91	89	81	70	55	46	67
Average Temp. (°F)	32	38	41	48	56	63	70	68	61	51	40	33	50
Average Low (°F)	19	23	26	31	38	44	49	47	40	32	25	20	33
Extreme Low (°F)	-16	-16	0	13	18	25	33	24	20	8	1	-16	-16

Note: Figures cover the years 1949-1992
Source: National Climatic Data Center, International Station Meteorological Climate Summary, 9/96

Average Precipitation/Snowfall/Humidity

Precip./Humidity	Jan	Feb	Mar	Apr	May	Jun	Jul	Aug	Sep	Oct	Nov	Dec	Yr.
Avg. Precip. (in.)	1.0	0.9	0.7	0.4	0.7	0.4	0.3	0.2	0.3	0.4	0.8	1.0	7.2
Avg. Snowfall (in.)	6	5	4	1	1	Tr	0	0	Tr	Tr	2	4	24
Avg. Rel. Hum. 7am (%)	79	77	71	61	55	51	49	55	64	72	78	80	66
Avg. Rel. Hum. 4pm (%)	51	41	34	27	26	22	19	19	22	27	41	51	32

Note: Figures cover the years 1949-1992; Tr = Trace amounts (<0.05 in. of rain; <0.5 in. of snow)
Source: National Climatic Data Center, International Station Meteorological Climate Summary, 9/96

Weather Conditions

Temperature			Daytime Sky			Precipitation		
10°F & below	32°F & below	90°F & above	Clear	Partly cloudy	Cloudy	0.01 inch or more precip.	0.1 inch or more snow/ice	Thunder-storms
14	178	50	143	139	83	50	17	14

Note: Figures are average number of days per year and cover the years 1949-1992
Source: National Climatic Data Center, International Station Meteorological Climate Summary, 9/96

HAZARDOUS WASTE

Superfund Sites

The Reno, NV metro area is home to two sites on the EPA's Superfund National Priorities List (NPL) or Superfund Alternative Approach (SAA) list: **Anaconda Copper Mine** (Proposed NPL); **Carson River Mercury Site** (Final NPL). The Superfund alternative approach uses the same investigation and cleanup process and standards that are used for sites listed on the National Priorities List. The SAA is an alternative to listing a site on the NPL; it is not an alternative to Superfund or the Superfund process. There are a total of 1,445 Superfund sites with a status of proposed or final on both lists in the United States. *U.S. Environmental Protection Agency, National Priorities List, May 1, 2025; U.S. Environmental Protection Agency, Superfund Alternative Approach Sites, May 1, 2025*

AIR QUALITY

Air Quality Trends: Ozone

	1990	1995	2000	2005	2010	2015	2020	2021	2022	2023
MSA[1]	0.074	0.069	0.067	0.069	0.068	0.071	0.073	0.078	0.064	0.065
U.S.	0.087	0.089	0.081	0.080	0.072	0.068	0.066	0.067	0.067	0.070

Note: (1) Data covers the Reno, NV Metropolitan Statistical Area. The values shown are the composite ozone concentration averages among trend sites based on the highest fourth daily maximum 8-hour concentration in parts per million. These trends are based on sites having an adequate record of monitoring data during the trend period. Data from exceptional events are included.
Source: U.S. Environmental Protection Agency, Air Quality Monitoring Information, "Air Quality Trends by City, 1990-2023"

Air Quality Index

Area	Percent of Days when Air Quality was...[2]					AQI Statistics[2]	
	Good	Moderate	Unhealthy for Sensitive Groups	Unhealthy	Very Unhealthy	Maximum	Median
MSA[1]	52.3	47.7	0.0	0.0	0.0	97	50

*Note: (1) Data covers the Reno, NV Metropolitan Statistical Area; (2) Based on 365 days with AQI data in 2023. Air Quality Index (AQI) is an index for reporting daily air quality. EPA calculates the AQI for five major air pollutants regulated by the Clean Air Act: ground-level ozone, particle pollution (aka particulate matter), carbon monoxide, sulfur dioxide, and nitrogen dioxide. The AQI runs from 0 to 500. The higher the AQI value, the greater the level of air pollution and the greater the health concern. There are six AQI categories: "Good" AQI is between 0 and 50. Air quality is considered satisfactory; "Moderate" AQI is between 51 and 100. Air quality is acceptable; "Unhealthy for Sensitive Groups" When AQI values are between 101 and 150, members of sensitive groups may experience health effects; "Unhealthy" When AQI values are between 151 and 200 everyone may begin to experience health effects; "Very Unhealthy" AQI values between 201 and 300 trigger a health alert; "Hazardous" AQI values over 300 trigger warnings of emergency conditions (not shown).
Source: U.S. Environmental Protection Agency, Air Quality Index Report, 2023*

Air Quality Index Pollutants

Area	Percent of Days when AQI Pollutant was...[2]					
	Carbon Monoxide	Nitrogen Dioxide	Ozone	Sulfur Dioxide	Particulate Matter 2.5	Particulate Matter 10
MSA[1]	0.0	1.1	67.9	(3)	30.7	0.3

*Note: (1) Data covers the Reno, NV Metropolitan Statistical Area; (2) Based on 365 days with AQI data in 2023. The Air Quality Index (AQI) is an index for reporting daily air quality. EPA calculates the AQI for five major air pollutants regulated by the Clean Air Act: ground-level ozone, particle pollution (also known as particulate matter), carbon monoxide, sulfur dioxide, and nitrogen dioxide. The AQI runs from 0 to 500. The higher the AQI value, the greater the level of air pollution and the greater the health concern; (3) Sulfur dioxide is no longer included in this table because SO_2 concentrations tend to be very localized and not necessarily representative of broad geographical areas like counties and CBSAs.
Source: U.S. Environmental Protection Agency, Air Quality Index Report, 2023*

Maximum Air Pollutant Concentrations: Particulate Matter, Ozone, CO and Lead

	Particulate Matter 10 (ug/m^3)	Particulate Matter 2.5 Wtd AM (ug/m^3)	Particulate Matter 2.5 24-Hr (ug/m^3)	Ozone (ppm)	Carbon Monoxide (ppm)	Lead (ug/m^3)
MSA[1] Level	63	7.2	18	0.067	2	n/a
NAAQS[2]	150	15	35	0.075	9	0.15
Met NAAQS[2]	Yes	Yes	Yes	Yes	Yes	n/a

*Note: (1) Data covers the Reno, NV Metropolitan Statistical Area; Data from exceptional events are included; (2) National Ambient Air Quality Standards; ppm = parts per million; ug/m^3 = micrograms per cubic meter; n/a not available.
Concentrations: Particulate Matter 10 (coarse particulate)—highest second maximum 24-hour concentration; Particulate Matter 2.5 Wtd AM (fine particulate)—highest weighted annual mean concentration; Particulate Matter 2.5 24-Hour (fine particulate)—highest 98th percentile 24-hour concentration; Ozone—highest fourth daily maximum 8-hour concentration; Carbon Monoxide—highest second maximum non-overlapping 8-hour concentration; Lead—maximum running 3-month average
Source: U.S. Environmental Protection Agency, Air Quality Monitoring Information, "Air Quality Statistics by City, 2023"*

Maximum Air Pollutant Concentrations: Nitrogen Dioxide and Sulfur Dioxide

	Nitrogen Dioxide AM (ppb)	Nitrogen Dioxide 1-Hr (ppb)	Sulfur Dioxide AM (ppb)	Sulfur Dioxide 1-Hr (ppb)	Sulfur Dioxide 24-Hr (ppb)
MSA[1] Level	11	49	n/a	3	n/a
NAAQS[2]	53	100	30	75	140
Met NAAQS[2]	Yes	Yes	n/a	Yes	n/a

*Note: (1) Data covers the Reno, NV Metropolitan Statistical Area; Data from exceptional events are included; (2) National Ambient Air Quality Standards; ppm = parts per million; ug/m^3 = micrograms per cubic meter; n/a not available.
Concentrations: Nitrogen Dioxide AM—highest arithmetic mean concentration; Nitrogen Dioxide 1-Hr—highest 98th percentile 1-hour daily maximum concentration; Sulfur Dioxide AM—highest annual mean concentration; Sulfur Dioxide 1-Hr—highest 99th percentile 1-hour daily maximum concentration; Sulfur Dioxide 24-Hr—highest second maximum 24-hour concentration
Source: U.S. Environmental Protection Agency, Air Quality Monitoring Information, "Air Quality Statistics by City, 2023"*

Sacramento, California

Background

Sacramento is the capital of California, the seat of Sacramento County, and the sixth-largest city in the state. It was named after the Sacramento River which was named after the Catholic sacrament of the Holy Eucharist. It lies at the juncture of the Sacramento and American rivers.

A Swiss soldier, Captain John Augustus Sutter, settled Sacramento in 1839, when he received permission from the Mexican government to establish a new colony which became known as New Helvetia. The 50,000-acre land grant included a wide swath of the rich and fertile valley between the two rivers. Sutter's ranch, trading post, and agricultural projects were soon productive and profitable. When American troops occupied the area in 1846, Sutter was well-positioned to take advantage, and his trade soon extended well up the northern coast.

In 1848, one of Sutter's employees, a carpenter named James W. Marshall, discovered gold at what became known as "Sutter's Mill" in the settlement of Coloma. The discovery brought an onslaught of prospectors and the beginning of the California Gold Rush, overwhelming New Helvetia's resources and the havoc that followed destroyed the economic foundation of the town. The newcomers overran Sutter's land and claimed it as their own. Sutter ceded land along the Sacramento River to his son, who founded the town that became the city we know today.

Sacramento supported miners with housing, food, banking, transportation and equipment. One of Sacramento's most famous entrepreneurs is Levi Strauss who sold the ultimate mining pants known as "Levi's." Sacramento's economy was booming, but plagued by floods, fire, and a cholera epidemic. Today, flooding that is endemic to the area is controlled by a series of dams, which also supply a large amount of electricity to the area.

On April 3, 1860, the legendary Pony Express carried mail from Sacramento to St. Joseph, Missouri on horseback in record time. The ten-day journey of nearly 1,800 miles was unprofitable but caught the attention of the federal government and helped launch our current postal system.

In the years since, the city has grown rapidly, passing 400,000 in 2000 and 500,000 in 2020. As befitting a state capital, government is the largest employer, followed by the health industry, including UC Davis Health, Sutter Health, Intel, and Apple. Other notable companies in the area include Blue Diamond Growers, Raley's Corp., and SAFE Credit Union.

Sutter's Fort State Historical Monument features a restoration of John Sutter's original ranch and trading post, and a designated Old Sacramento Historical Area preserves many buildings from the gold rush period and thereafter. At the city's Crocker Art Museum, visitors can view an extensive collection of works by Michelangelo, Rembrandt, and Leonardo da Vinci. In October 2010, the Crocker completed a 100,000-ft. expansion that more than tripled its size.

The Wells Fargo Museum is a monument to the history of the Pony Express and the era of the gold rush. Housed in the original bank building that managed the Pony Express, its staff conducts tours dressed in period attire. The museum displays include tools, gold nuggets, documents, and other relevant artifacts.

The Woodland Opera House opened in 1896 in nearby Woodland, California. It closed in 1913, when motion pictures took hold of the public's interest and the building stayed dormant until 1971 when Yolo County Historic Society saved it from demolition. They gave it to the state in 1980 and it underwent a total renovation in 1982. Today it is a major entertainment venue and on the National Register of Historic Places.

Since 1985, Sacramento has hosted NBA basketball when the Kings relocated from Kansas City. The city fields a professional soccer team, the Sacramento Republic FC of the USL Championship League, and a minor league baseball team, the River Cats, the AAA affiliate of the San Francisco Giants. Golden 1 Center sports arena, with a capacity of 17,608, opened in 2016.

Sacramento has a hot-summer climate, characterized by hot, long, dry summers and cool winters with a fair amount of rainfall. The wet season is generally October through April, though there may be some light rainfall in June or September. Summer heat is sometimes moderated by a sea breeze known as the "delta breeze" which comes through the Sacramento-San Joaquin River Delta from the San Francisco Bay, and temperatures cool down sharply at night. The foggiest months are December and January. The area's dense tule fog (names for tule reeds that once covered the valley floor) occurs in winter and can lower visibility to less than 100 feet, sometimes lasting for several days or weeks at a time. Snowfall is rare in Sacramento, which is only 25 feet above sea level. In the downtown area, only three significant snow accumulations have occurred since 1900.

Rankings

General Rankings

- To help military veterans find the best places in which to settle down, *WalletHub* compared the 100 largest U.S. cities across 19 key indicators of livability, affordability and veteran-friendliness. They range from the share of military skill-related jobs to veteran income growth to the availability of VA health facilities. Sacramento ranked #68. *Wallethub.com, "Best & Worst Places for Veterans to Live (2025)," November 7, 2024*

- Sacramento was selected as one of the best places to live in the United States by *Money* magazine. The city placed among the top 50. This year's list focused on cities built around community spirit, thoughtful policy and civic engagement. Instead of relying on a predetermined dataset, the cities and towns were grouped according to their strengths and chosen due their affordability, good schools and strong job markets. *Money, "The 50 Best Places to Live in the U.S., 2024" April 8, 2024*

Business/Finance Rankings

- The Sacramento metro area appeared on the Milken Institute "2025 Best Performing Cities" list. Rank: #59 out of 200 large metro areas (based on performance category). Criteria: job growth; wage growth; high-tech growth and impact; community resilience; housing affordability; household broadband access. *Milken Institute, "Best-Performing Cities 2025," January 14, 2025*

Education Rankings

- Personal finance website *WalletHub* analyzed the 150 largest U.S. metropolitan statistical areas to determine where the most educated Americans are putting their degrees to work. Criteria: education levels; percentage of workers with degrees; education quality and attainment gap; public school quality rankings; quality and enrollment of each metro area's universities. Sacramento was ranked #49 (#1 = most educated city). *WalletHub.com, "Most & Least Educated Cities in America, 2025" July 2, 2024*

Environmental Rankings

- Sperling's *BestPlaces* assessed the 50 largest metropolitan areas of the United States for the likelihood of dangerously extreme weather events or earthquakes. In general the Southeast and South-Central regions have the highest risk of weather extremes and earthquakes, while the Pacific Northwest enjoys the lowest risk. Of the least risky metropolitan areas, the Sacramento metro area was ranked #3. *Bestplaces.net, "Avoid Natural Disasters: BestPlaces Reveals The Top 10 Safest Places to Live," October 25, 2017*

- The U.S. Environmental Protection Agency (EPA) released its list of U.S. metropolitan areas with the most ENERGY STAR certified buildings in 2023. The Sacramento metro area was ranked #19 out of 25. *U.S. Environmental Protection Agency, "2024 Energy Star Top Cities," May 22, 2024*

- Sacramento was highlighted as one of the 25 most ozone-polluted metro areas in the U.S. during 2021 through 2023. The area ranked #11. *American Lung Association, "State of the Air 2025," April 23, 2025*

- Sacramento was highlighted as one of the 25 metro areas most polluted by year-round particle pollution (Annual PM 2.5) in the U.S. during 2021 through 2023. The area ranked #14. *American Lung Association, "State of the Air 2025," April 23, 2025*

- Sacramento was highlighted as one of the 25 metro areas most polluted by short-term particle pollution (24-hour PM 2.5) in the U.S. during 2021 through 2023. The area ranked #10. *American Lung Association, "State of the Air 2025," April 23, 2025*

Food/Drink Rankings

- WalletHub compared the 100 largest U.S. cities across 17 key indicators of vegan- and vegetarian-friendliness. Sacramento was ranked #19. Cities were selected based on metrics such as the cost of groceries for vegetarians, the share of restaurants serving meatless options and the number of salad shops per capita. *WalletHub.com, "Best Cities for Vegans & Vegetarians (2025)," September 24, 2024*

Health/Fitness Rankings

- For each of the 100 largest cities in the United States, the American Fitness Index®, compiled in partnership between the American College of Sports Medicine and the Elevance Health Foundation, evaluated community infrastructure and more than 30 health behaviors including preventive health, levels of chronic disease conditions, food insecurity, pedestrian safety, air quality, and community/environment resources that support physical activity. Sacramento ranked #32 for "community fitness." *americanfitnessindex.org, "2024 ACSM American Fitness Index Summary Report," July 23, 2024*

- Sacramento was identified as a "2025 Allergy Capital." The area ranked #23 out of the nation's 100 largest metropolitan areas. Three groups of factors were used to identify the most challenging cities for people with allergies: annual tree, grass, and weed pollen scores; over the counter allergy medicine use; number of board-certified allergy specialists. *Asthma and Allergy Foundation of America, "2025 Allergy Capitals: The Most Challenging Places to Live with Allergies," March 18, 2025*

- Sacramento was identified as a "2024 Asthma Capital." The area ranked #22 out of the nation's 100 largest metropolitan areas. Criteria: estimated asthma prevalence; asthma-related mortality; and ER visits due to asthma. Risk factors analyzed but not factored in the rankings: annual air quality including pollution and ozone levels; public smoking laws; indoor air quality; access to asthma specialists; rescue and controller medication use; uninsured rate; pollen allergy; poverty rate. *Asthma and Allergy Foundation of America, "Asthma Capitals 2024: The Most Challenging Places to Live With Asthma," September 10, 2024*

Pet Rankings

- Sacramento was selected by *Sniffspot.com* as one of the most dog-friendly cities in the U.S., ranking #45 out of 50. Criteria: dog parks; hiking; sniffspots; public parks; dog-friendly businesses; housing; dog waste cleanliness; leash laws; dog services; and overall cost. *Sniffspot.com, "The Top 50 Most Dog-Friendly Cities in the U.S.," September 30, 2024*

Real Estate Rankings

- *WalletHub* compared the most populated U.S. cities to determine which had the best markets for real estate agents. Sacramento ranked #3 where demand was high and pay was the best. Criteria: sales per agent; annual median wage for real-estate agents; monthly average starting salary for real estate agents; real estate job density and competition; unemployment rate; home turnover rate; housing-market health index; and other relevant metrics. *WalletHub.com, "2021 Best Places to Be a Real Estate Agent," May 12, 2021*

- The Sacramento metro area was identified as one of the 10 worst condo markets in the U.S. in 2024. The area ranked #60 out of 63 markets. Criteria: year-over-year change of median sales price of existing apartment condo-coop homes between the 4th quarter of 2023 and the 4th quarter of 2024. *National Association of Realtors®, Median Sales Price of Existing Apartment Condo-Coops Homes for Metropolitan Areas, 4th Quarter 2024*

- Sacramento was ranked #145 out of 176 metro areas in terms of cost of housing in 2024 by the National Association of Home Builders (#1 = most affordable). Criteria: the portion of an average family's income necessary to pay the mortgage on a median-priced home. *National Association of Home Builders®, NAHB-Wells Fargo Cost of Housing Index, 4th Quarter 2024*

Safety Rankings

- Allstate ranked the 100 most populous cities in America in terms of driver safety. Sacramento ranked #66. Criteria based on anonymized driving behavior data from Allstate's mobile app powered by Arity: high speed driving (over 80 mph), phone handling, and hard braking. The report helps increase the importance of safety and awareness behind the wheel. *Allstate, "16th Allstate America's Best Drivers Report®" July 11, 2024*

Women/Minorities Rankings

- Sacramento was listed as one of the most LGBTQ-friendly cities in America by *The Advocate*, as compiled by the real estate data site *Clever*. The city ranked #8 out of 15. Criteria, among many: Pride events; gay bars; LGBTQ-affirming healthcare options; state and local laws; number of PFLAG chapters; LGBTQ+ population. *The Advocate, "These Are the 15 Most LGBTQ-Friendly Cities in the U.S." November 1, 2023*

- Personal finance website *WalletHub* compared more than 180 U.S. cities across two key dimensions, "Hispanic Business-Friendliness" and "Hispanic Purchasing Power," to arrive at the most favorable conditions for Hispanic entrepreneurs. Sacramento was ranked #118 out of 182. Criteria includes: share of Hispanic-Owned Businesses; average growth of Hispanic Business revenues; Small Business-Friendliness score; affordability; and number of Hispanics with at least a bachelor's degree. *WalletHub.com, "Best Cities for Hispanic Entrepreneurs," September 4, 2024*

Miscellaneous Rankings

- *MoveHub* ranked 446 hipster cities across 20 countries, using its new and improved alternative Hipster Index and Sacramento came out as #35 among the top 50. Criteria: population over 150,000; number of vintage boutiques; density of tattoo parlors; vegan places to eat; coffee shops; and density of vinyl record stores. *MoveHub.com, "The Hipster Index: Brighton Pips Portland to Global Top Spot," July 28, 2021*

- Sacramento was selected as a 2024 Digital Cities Survey winner. The city ranked #9 in the large city (500,000 or more population) category. The survey examined and assessed how city governments are utilizing new technology and modernized applications to provide residents an array of contactless services and conveniences. Survey questions focused on ten initiatives: cybersecurity; citizen experience; disaster recovery; business intelligence; IT personnel retention; data governance; business automation; AI/machine learning; application modernization; and IT collaboration. *Center for Digital Government, "2024 Digital Cities Survey," November 5, 2024*

- *WalletHub* compared 148 of the most populated U.S. cities to determine their operating efficiency. A "Quality of Services" score was constructed for each city and then measured against the total budget per capita to reveal which were managed the best. Sacramento ranked #136. Criteria: financial stability; economy; education; safety; health; infrastructure and pollution. *WalletHub.com, "2025's Best- & Worst-Run Cities in America," June 18, 2024*

Business Environment

DEMOGRAPHICS

Population Growth

Area	1990 Census	2000 Census	2010 Census	2020 Census	2023 Estimate[2]	Population Growth 1990-2023 (%)
City	368,923	407,018	466,488	524,943	524,802	42.3
MSA[1]	1,481,126	1,796,857	2,149,127	2,397,382	2,406,563	62.5
U.S.	248,709,873	281,421,906	308,745,538	331,449,281	332,387,540	33.6

Note: (1) Figures cover the Sacramento-Roseville-Folsom, CA Metropolitan Statistical Area; (2) 2019-2023 5-year ACS population estimate
Source: U.S. Census Bureau, 1990 Census, 2000 Census, 2010 Census, 2020 Census, 2019-2023 American Community Survey 5-Year Estimates

Race

Area	White Alone[2] (%)	Black Alone[2] (%)	Asian Alone[2] (%)	AIAN[3] Alone[2] (%)	NHOPI[4] Alone[2] (%)	Other Race Alone[2] (%)	Two or More Races (%)
City	36.8	12.4	19.7	1.0	1.7	13.4	15.0
MSA[1]	54.8	6.9	14.8	0.8	0.8	8.7	13.2
U.S.	63.4	12.4	5.8	0.9	0.2	6.6	10.7

Note: (1) Figures cover the Sacramento-Roseville-Folsom, CA Metropolitan Statistical Area; (2) Alone is defined as not being in combination with one or more other races; (3) American Indian and Alaska Native; (4) Native Hawaiian and Other Pacific Islander
Source: U.S. Census Bureau, 2019-2023 American Community Survey 5-Year Estimates

Hispanic or Latino Origin

Area	Total (%)	Mexican (%)	Puerto Rican (%)	Cuban (%)	Other (%)
City	29.5	24.1	0.9	0.1	4.4
MSA[1]	22.6	17.9	0.7	0.2	3.8
U.S.	19.0	11.3	1.8	0.7	5.2

Note: Persons of Hispanic or Latino origin can be of any race; (1) Figures cover the Sacramento-Roseville-Folsom, CA Metropolitan Statistical Area
Source: U.S. Census Bureau, 2019-2023 American Community Survey 5-Year Estimates

Age

Area	Under Age 5	Age 5–19	Age 20–34	Age 35–44	Age 45–54	Age 55–64	Age 65–74	Age 75–84	Age 85+	Median Age
City	5.9	18.4	24.4	14.7	11.6	11.0	8.5	3.8	1.7	35.7
MSA[1]	5.6	19.3	20.3	13.8	12.2	12.3	9.7	4.6	2.0	38.3
U.S.	5.7	19.1	20.2	13.1	12.3	12.8	10.0	4.9	1.9	38.7

Note: (1) Figures cover the Sacramento-Roseville-Folsom, CA Metropolitan Statistical Area
Source: U.S. Census Bureau, 2019-2023 American Community Survey 5-Year Estimates

Disability by Age

Area	All Ages	Under 18 Years Old	18 to 64 Years Old	65 Years and Over
City	12.4	4.0	10.1	35.8
MSA[1]	12.3	4.0	9.6	33.8
U.S.	13.0	4.7	10.7	32.9

Note: Figures show percent of the civilian noninstitutionalized population that reported having a disability. Disability status is determined from six types of difficulty: vision, hearing, cognitive, ambulatory, self-care, and independent living. For children under 5 years old, hearing and vision difficulty are used to determine disability status. For children between the ages of 5 and 14, disability status is determined from hearing, vision, cognitive, ambulatory, and self-care difficulties. For people aged 15 years and older, they are considered to have a disability if they have difficulty with any one of the six difficulty types; Note: (1) Figures cover the Sacramento-Roseville-Folsom, CA Metropolitan Statistical Area
Source: U.S. Census Bureau, 2019-2023 American Community Survey 5-Year Estimates

Ancestry

Area	German	Irish	English	American	Italian	Polish	French[2]	European	Scottish
City	6.5	5.8	6.0	2.3	3.4	1.0	1.4	1.4	1.0
MSA[1]	10.1	8.0	9.4	2.6	4.5	1.2	1.8	2.4	1.7
U.S.	12.6	9.4	9.1	5.5	4.9	2.6	2.0	1.6	1.6

Note: Figures are the percentage of the total population reporting a particular ancestry. The nine most commonly reported ancestries in the U.S. are shown. Figures include multiple ancestries (e.g. if a person reported being Irish and Italian, they were included in both columns); (1) Figures cover the Sacramento-Roseville-Folsom, CA Metropolitan Statistical Area; (2) Excludes Basque
Source: U.S. Census Bureau, 2019-2023 American Community Survey 5-Year Estimates

Foreign-born Population

Area	Any Foreign Country	Asia	Mexico	Europe	Caribbean	Central America[2]	South America	Africa	Canada
	Percent of Population Born in								
City	21.3	10.6	5.5	1.6	0.1	0.9	0.4	0.6	0.2
MSA[1]	18.9	9.4	4.2	2.8	0.1	0.7	0.4	0.5	0.3
U.S.	13.9	4.3	3.3	1.4	1.4	1.2	1.2	0.8	0.2

Note: (1) Figures cover the Sacramento-Roseville-Folsom, CA Metropolitan Statistical Area; (2) Excludes Mexico.
Source: U.S. Census Bureau, 2019-2023 American Community Survey 5-Year Estimates

Household Size

Area	One	Two	Three	Four	Five	Six	Seven or More	Average Household Size
	Persons in Household (%)							
City	31.7	29.8	14.4	12.4	6.6	2.6	2.5	2.58
MSA[1]	25.1	32.7	16.0	14.5	7.1	2.7	2.0	2.70
U.S.	28.5	33.8	15.4	12.7	5.9	2.3	1.4	2.54

Note: (1) Figures cover the Sacramento-Roseville-Folsom, CA Metropolitan Statistical Area
Source: U.S. Census Bureau, 2019-2023 American Community Survey 5-Year Estimates

Household Relationships

Area	House-holder	Opposite-sex Spouse	Same-sex Spouse	Opposite-sex Unmarried Partner	Same-sex Unmarried Partner	Child[2]	Grand-child	Other Relatives	Non-relatives
City	36.7	13.5	0.4	3.0	0.3	28.0	2.6	7.5	4.7
MSA[1]	36.2	17.1	0.3	2.4	0.2	29.4	2.2	6.0	4.2
U.S.	38.3	17.5	0.2	2.5	0.2	28.3	2.4	4.8	3.4

Note: Figures are percent of the total population; (1) Figures cover the Sacramento-Roseville-Folsom, CA Metropolitan Statistical Area; (2) Includes biological, adopted, and stepchildren of the householder
Source: U.S. Census Bureau, 2020 Census

Gender

Area	Males	Females	Males per 100 Females
City	260,163	264,639	98.3
MSA[1]	1,184,908	1,221,655	97.0
U.S.	164,545,087	167,842,453	98.0

Note: (1) Figures cover the Sacramento-Roseville-Folsom, CA Metropolitan Statistical Area
Source: U.S. Census Bureau, 2019-2023 American Community Survey 5-Year Estimates

Marital Status

Area	Never Married	Now Married[2]	Separated	Widowed	Divorced
City	41.5	40.8	2.3	4.7	10.7
MSA[1]	34.2	48.5	1.8	4.9	10.5
U.S.	34.1	47.9	1.7	5.6	10.7

Note: Figures are percentages and cover the population 15 years of age and older; (1) Figures cover the Sacramento-Roseville-Folsom, CA Metropolitan Statistical Area; (2) Excludes separated
Source: U.S. Census Bureau, 2019-2023 American Community Survey 5-Year Estimates

Religious Groups by Family

Area	Catholic	Baptist	Methodist	LDS[2]	Pentecostal	Lutheran	Islam	Adventist	Other
MSA[1]	17.1	1.9	1.1	3.1	2.2	0.6	1.9	1.9	8.2
U.S.	18.7	7.3	3.0	2.0	1.8	1.7	1.3	1.3	11.6

Note: Figures are the number of adherents as a percentage of the total population and cover the eight largest religious groups in the U.S; (1) Figures cover the Sacramento-Roseville-Folsom, CA Metropolitan Statistical Area; (2) Church of Jesus Christ of Latter-day Saints
Sources: 2020 U.S. Religion Census, Association of Statisticians of American Religious Bodies; The Association of Religion Data Archives (ARDA)

Religious Groups by Tradition

Area	Catholic	Evangelical Protestant	Mainline Protestant	Black Protestant	Islam	Judaism	Hinduism	Orthodox	Buddhism
MSA[1]	17.1	10.4	1.4	1.1	1.9	0.2	0.4	0.3	0.5
U.S.	18.7	16.5	5.2	2.3	1.3	0.6	0.4	0.4	0.3

Note: Figures are the number of adherents as a percentage of the total population; (1) Figures cover the Sacramento-Roseville-Folsom, CA Metropolitan Statistical Area
Sources: 2020 U.S. Religion Census, Association of Statisticians of American Religious Bodies; The Association of Religion Data Archives (ARDA)

ECONOMY

Real Gross Domestic Product (GDP)

Area	2017	2018	2019	2020	2021	2022	2023	Rank[3]
MSA[1]	131.2	136.9	141.9	138.9	147.4	150.4	153.8	31
U.S.[2]	17,619.1	18,160.7	18,642.5	18,238.9	19,387.6	19,896.6	20,436.3	–

Note: Figures are in billions of chained 2017 dollars; (1) Figures cover the Sacramento-Roseville-Folsom, CA Metropolitan Statistical Area; (2) Figures cover real GDP within metropolitan areas; (3) Rank is based on 2023 data and ranges from 1 to 384
Source: U.S. Bureau of Economic Analysis

Economic Growth

Area	2014	2015	2016	2017	2018	2019	2020	2021	2022	2023
MSA[1]	2.8	4.3	2.1	2.9	4.4	3.6	-2.1	6.1	2.1	2.2
U.S.[2]	2.6	3.2	2.0	2.7	3.1	2.7	-2.2	6.3	2.6	2.7

Note: Figures are real gross domestic product growth rates and represent percent change from preceding period; (1) Figures cover the Sacramento-Roseville-Folsom, CA Metropolitan Statistical Area; (2) Figures are the average growth rates within metropolitan areas
Source: U.S. Bureau of Economic Analysis

Metropolitan Area Exports

Area	2018	2019	2020	2021	2022	2023	Rank[2]
MSA[1]	6,222.8	5,449.2	4,980.9	5,682.3	5,716.7	7,586.6	50
U.S.	1,664,056.1	1,645,173.7	1,431,406.6	1,753,941.4	2,062,937.4	2,019,160.5	–

Note: Figures are in millions of dollars; (1) Figures cover the Sacramento-Roseville-Folsom, CA Metropolitan Statistical Area; (2) Rank is based on 2023 data and ranges from 1 to 386
Source: U.S. Department of Commerce, International Trade Administration, Office of Trade and Economic Analysis, Industry and Analysis, Exports by Metropolitan Area, data extracted April 2, 2025

Building Permits

Area	Single-Family			Multi-Family			Total		
	2023	2024	Pct. Chg.	2023	2024	Pct. Chg.	2023	2024	Pct. Chg.
City	653	708	8.4	1,864	1,335	-28.4	2,517	2,043	-18.8
MSA[1]	7,931	8,579	8.2	4,010	3,034	-24.3	11,941	11,613	-2.7
U.S.	920,000	981,900	6.7	591,100	496,100	-16.1	1,511,100	1,478,000	-2.2

Note: (1) Figures cover the Sacramento-Roseville-Folsom, CA Metropolitan Statistical Area; Figures represent new, privately-owned housing units authorized (unadjusted data)
Source: U.S. Census Bureau, Building Permits Survey (BPS), 2023, 2024

Bankruptcy Filings

Area	Business Filings			Nonbusiness Filings		
	2023	2024	% Chg.	2023	2024	% Chg.
Sacramento County	96	163	69.8	1,675	2,259	34.9
U.S.	18,926	23,107	22.1	434,064	494,201	13.9

Note: Business filings include Chapter 7, Chapter 9, Chapter 11, Chapter 12, Chapter 13, Chapter 15, and Section 304; Nonbusiness filings include Chapter 7, Chapter 11, and Chapter 13
Source: Administrative Office of the U.S. Courts, Business and Nonbusiness Bankruptcy, County Cases Commenced by Chapter of the Bankruptcy Code, During the 12-Month Period Ending December 31, 2023 and Business and Nonbusiness Bankruptcy, County Cases Commenced by Chapter of the Bankruptcy Code, During the 12-Month Period Ending December 31, 2024

Housing Vacancy Rates

Area	Gross Vacancy Rate[3] (%)			Year-Round Vacancy Rate[4] (%)			Rental Vacancy Rate[5] (%)			Homeowner Vacancy Rate[6] (%)		
	2022	2023	2024	2022	2023	2024	2022	2023	2024	2022	2023	2024
MSA[1]	6.3	6.4	8.0	6.1	6.2	7.6	2.3	4.2	3.9	0.6	0.6	0.9
U.S.[2]	9.1	9.0	9.1	7.5	7.5	7.6	5.7	6.5	6.8	0.8	0.8	1.0

Note: (1) Figures cover the Sacramento-Roseville-Folsom, CA Metropolitan Statistical Area; (2) Figures cover the 75 largest Metropolitan Statistical Areas; (3) The percentage of the total housing inventory that is vacant; (4) The percentage of the housing inventory (excluding seasonal units) that is year-round vacant; (5) The percentage of rental inventory that is vacant for rent; (6) The percentage of homeowner inventory that is vacant for sale
Source: U.S. Census Bureau, Housing Vacancies and Homeownership Annual Statistics: 2022, 2023, 2024

INCOME

Income

Area	Per Capita ($)	Median Household ($)	Average Household ($)
City	42,300	83,753	108,939
MSA[1]	45,964	93,986	123,767
U.S.	43,289	78,538	110,491

Note: (1) Figures cover the Sacramento-Roseville-Folsom, CA Metropolitan Statistical Area
Source: U.S. Census Bureau, 2019-2023 American Community Survey 5-Year Estimates

Household Income Distribution

Area	Percent of Households Earning							
	Under $15,000	$15,000 -$24,999	$25,000 -$34,999	$35,000 -$49,999	$50,000 -$74,999	$75,000 -$99,999	$100,000 -$149,999	$150,000 and up
City	9.1	6.1	5.2	9.5	15.1	13.6	18.7	22.7
MSA[1]	7.3	5.2	5.3	8.5	13.9	12.7	19.3	27.9
U.S.	8.5	6.6	6.8	10.4	15.7	12.7	17.4	21.9

Note: (1) Figures cover the Sacramento-Roseville-Folsom, CA Metropolitan Statistical Area
Source: U.S. Census Bureau, 2019-2023 American Community Survey 5-Year Estimates

Poverty Rate

Area	All Ages	Under 18 Years Old	18 to 64 Years Old	65 Years and Over
City	14.4	17.9	13.5	12.8
MSA[1]	11.6	13.6	11.4	9.3
U.S.	12.4	16.3	11.6	10.4

Note: Figures are percentage of people whose income during the past 12 months was below the poverty level;
(1) Figures cover the Sacramento-Roseville-Folsom, CA Metropolitan Statistical Area
Source: U.S. Census Bureau, 2019-2023 American Community Survey 5-Year Estimates

EMPLOYMENT

Labor Force and Employment

Area	Civilian Labor Force			Workers Employed		
	Dec. 2023	Dec. 2024	% Chg.	Dec. 2023	Dec. 2024	% Chg.
City	246,247	248,837	1.1	234,662	236,718	0.9
MSA[1]	1,144,784	1,156,797	1.0	1,094,502	1,103,633	0.8
U.S.	166,661,000	167,746,000	0.7	160,754,000	161,294,000	0.3

Note: Data is not seasonally adjusted and covers workers 16 years of age and older; (1) Figures cover the
Sacramento-Roseville-Folsom, CA Metropolitan Statistical Area
Source: Bureau of Labor Statistics, Local Area Unemployment Statistics

Unemployment Rate

Area	2024											
	Jan.	Feb.	Mar.	Apr.	May	Jun.	Jul.	Aug.	Sep.	Oct.	Nov.	Dec.
City	5.2	5.2	4.9	4.5	4.3	5.1	5.5	5.6	5.0	5.1	5.2	4.9
MSA[1]	4.9	4.9	4.7	4.2	4.0	4.8	5.1	5.2	4.6	4.7	4.8	4.6
U.S.	4.1	4.2	3.9	3.5	3.7	4.3	4.5	4.4	3.9	3.9	4.0	3.8

Note: Data is not seasonally adjusted and covers workers 16 years of age and older; (1) Figures cover the
Sacramento-Roseville-Folsom, CA Metropolitan Statistical Area
Source: Bureau of Labor Statistics, Local Area Unemployment Statistics

Average Wages

Occupation	$/Hr.	Occupation	$/Hr.
Accountants and Auditors	45.29	Maintenance and Repair Workers	27.33
Automotive Mechanics	31.97	Marketing Managers	84.16
Bookkeepers	28.08	Network and Computer Systems Admin.	52.73
Carpenters	37.87	Nurses, Licensed Practical	39.66
Cashiers	18.42	Nurses, Registered	78.37
Computer Programmers	56.85	Nursing Assistants	23.25
Computer Systems Analysts	57.48	Office Clerks, General	25.08
Computer User Support Specialists	47.62	Physical Therapists	60.12
Construction Laborers	31.16	Physicians	165.05
Cooks, Restaurant	20.88	Plumbers, Pipefitters and Steamfitters	35.78
Customer Service Representatives	24.98	Police and Sheriff's Patrol Officers	53.46
Dentists	89.82	Postal Service Mail Carriers	29.98
Electricians	39.30	Real Estate Sales Agents	35.09
Engineers, Electrical	65.09	Retail Salespersons	20.50
Fast Food and Counter Workers	19.02	Sales Representatives, Technical/Scientific	56.67
Financial Managers	82.16	Secretaries, Exc. Legal/Medical/Executive	26.05
First-Line Supervisors of Office Workers	37.86	Security Guards	21.11
General and Operations Managers	67.60	Surgeons	n/a
Hairdressers/Cosmetologists	20.39	Teacher Assistants, Exc. Postsecondary[1]	21.20
Home Health and Personal Care Aides	16.89	Teachers, Secondary School, Exc. Sp. Ed.[1]	45.34
Janitors and Cleaners	20.72	Telemarketers	19.22
Landscaping/Groundskeeping Workers	22.37	Truck Drivers, Heavy/Tractor-Trailer	29.27
Lawyers	97.12	Truck Drivers, Light/Delivery Services	24.31
Maids and Housekeeping Cleaners	21.69	Waiters and Waitresses	21.77

Note: Wage data covers the Sacramento-Roseville-Folsom, CA Metropolitan Statistical Area; (1) Hourly wages
were calculated from annual wage data based on a 40 hour work week
Source: Bureau of Labor Statistics, Metro Area Occupational Employment & Wage Estimates, May 2024

Employment by Industry

Sector	MSA[1]		U.S.
	Number of Employees	Percent of Total	Percent of Total
Construction	75,400	6.8	5.1
Financial Activities	46,800	4.2	5.8
Government	265,000	24.0	14.9
Information	9,400	0.9	1.9
Leisure and Hospitality	111,800	10.1	10.4
Manufacturing	40,000	3.6	8.0
Mining and Logging	400	<0.1	0.4
Other Services	38,600	3.5	3.7
Private Education and Health Services	206,000	18.7	16.9
Professional and Business Services	134,600	12.2	14.2
Retail Trade	101,500	9.2	10.0
Transportation, Warehousing, and Utilities	44,600	4.0	4.8
Wholesale Trade	28,600	2.6	3.9

Note: Figures are non-farm employment as of December 2024. Figures are not seasonally adjusted and include workers 16 years of age and older; (1) Figures cover the Sacramento-Roseville-Folsom, CA Metropolitan Statistical Area
Source: Bureau of Labor Statistics, Current Employment Statistics, Employment, Hours, and Earnings

Employment by Occupation

Occupation Classification	City (%)	MSA[1] (%)	U.S. (%)
Management, Business, Science, and Arts	43.0	43.8	42.0
Natural Resources, Construction, and Maintenance	7.4	7.5	8.6
Production, Transportation, and Material Moving	11.6	10.2	13.0
Sales and Office	20.8	20.7	19.9
Service	17.2	17.7	16.5

Note: Figures cover employed civilians 16 years of age and older; (1) Figures cover the Sacramento-Roseville-Folsom, CA Metropolitan Statistical Area
Source: U.S. Census Bureau, 2019-2023 American Community Survey 5-Year Estimates

Occupations with Greatest Projected Employment Growth: 2022 – 2032

Occupation[1]	2022 Employment	2032 Projected Employment	Numeric Employment Change	Percent Employment Change
Home Health and Personal Care Aides	796,900	1,060,200	263,300	33.0
Software Developers	313,700	388,000	74,300	23.7
Registered Nurses	333,700	376,900	43,200	12.9
Cooks, Restaurant	142,100	184,000	41,900	29.5
Laborers and Freight, Stock, and Material Movers, Hand	399,500	437,300	37,800	9.5
Janitors and Cleaners, Except Maids and Housekeeping Cleaners	262,900	300,200	37,300	14.2
Fast Food and Counter Workers	419,100	455,200	36,100	8.6
Stockers and Order Fillers	289,900	322,900	33,000	11.4
Medical Assistants	108,000	135,700	27,700	25.6
Landscaping and Groundskeeping Workers	135,200	162,100	26,900	19.9

Note: Projections cover California; (1) Sorted by numeric employment change
Source: www.projectionscentral.org, State Occupational Projections, 2022–2032 Long-Term Projections

Fastest-Growing Occupations: 2022 – 2032

Occupation[1]	2022 Employment	2032 Projected Employment	Numeric Employment Change	Percent Employment Change
Nurse Practitioners	21,500	34,100	12,600	58.6
Physical Therapist Assistants	7,900	11,200	3,300	41.8
Solar Photovoltaic Installers	7,900	11,200	3,300	41.8
Physician Assistants	13,000	18,200	5,200	40.0
Medical and Health Services Managers	58,300	81,400	23,100	39.6
Statisticians	2,800	3,900	1,100	39.3
Taxi Drivers	48,100	66,800	18,700	38.9
Occupational Therapy Assistants	2,700	3,600	900	33.3
Home Health and Personal Care Aides	796,900	1,060,200	263,300	33.0
Data Scientists	33,900	45,000	11,100	32.7

Note: Projections cover California; (1) Sorted by percent employment change and excludes occupations with numeric employment change less than 50
Source: www.projectionscentral.org, State Occupational Projections, 2022–2032 Long-Term Projections

CITY FINANCES

City Government Finances

Component	2022 ($000)	2022 ($ per capita)
Total Revenues	1,550,842	3,024
Total Expenditures	1,943,698	3,790
Debt Outstanding	1,990,208	3,881

Source: U.S. Census Bureau, State & Local Government Finances 2022

City Government Revenue by Source

Source	2022 ($000)	2022 ($ per capita)	2022 (%)
General Revenue			
From Federal Government	176,457	344	11.4
From State Government	95,417	186	6.2
From Local Governments	993	2	0.1
Taxes			
Property	212,015	413	13.7
Sales and Gross Receipts	340,560	664	22.0
Personal Income	0	0	0.0
Corporate Income	0	0	0.0
Motor Vehicle License	0	0	0.0
Other Taxes	89,551	175	5.8
Current Charges	390,681	762	25.2
Liquor Store	0	0	0.0
Utility	136,613	266	8.8

Source: U.S. Census Bureau, State & Local Government Finances 2022

City Government Expenditures by Function

Function	2022 ($000)	2022 ($ per capita)	2022 (%)
General Direct Expenditures			
Air Transportation	0	0	0.0
Corrections	0	0	0.0
Education	0	0	0.0
Employment Security Administration	0	0	0.0
Financial Administration	15,024	29	0.8
Fire Protection	171,673	334	8.8
General Public Buildings	432	< 1	< 0.1
Governmental Administration, Other	151,175	294	7.8
Health	39,017	76	2.0
Highways	87,302	170	4.5
Hospitals	0	0	0.0
Housing and Community Development	209,006	407	10.8
Interest on General Debt	51,386	100	2.6
Judicial and Legal	8,877	17	0.5
Libraries	26,073	50	1.3
Parking	19,409	37	1.0
Parks and Recreation	131,416	256	6.8
Police Protection	245,619	478	12.6
Public Welfare	5,635	11	0.3
Sewerage	74,513	145	3.8
Solid Waste Management	64,747	126	3.3
Veterans' Services	0	0	0.0
Liquor Store	0	0	0.0
Utility	90,827	177	4.7

Source: U.S. Census Bureau, State & Local Government Finances 2022

TAXES

State Corporate Income Tax Rates

State	Tax Rate (%)	Income Brackets ($)	Num. of Brackets	Financial Institution Tax Rate (%)[a]	Federal Income Tax Ded.
California	8.84 (b)	Flat rate	1	10.84 (b)	No

Note: Tax rates for tax year 2024; (a) Rates listed are the corporate income tax rate applied to financial institutions or excise taxes based on income. Some states have other taxes based upon the value of deposits or shares; (b) Minimum tax is $800 in California, $250 in District of Columbia, $50 in Arizona and North Dakota (banks), $400 ($100 banks) in Rhode Island, $200 per location in South Dakota (banks), $100 in Utah, in Vermont, simplified entity business tax for residents only at $250, otherwise minimum tax ($100 - $100,000) is based upon gross receipts.
Source: Federation of Tax Administrators, State Corporate Income Tax Rates, January 1, 2025

State Individual Income Tax Rates

State	Tax Rate (%)	Income Brackets ($)	Personal Exemptions ($) Single	Married	Depend.	Standard Ded. ($) Single	Married
California (a)	1.0 - 13.3 (g)	10,099 - 677,276 (b)	134	268	367 (c)	5,202	10,404 (a)

Note: Tax rates for tax year 2024; Local- and county-level taxes are not included; Federal income tax is not deductible on state income tax returns; (a) 16 states have statutory provision for automatically adjusting to the rate of inflation the dollar values of the income tax brackets, standard deductions, and/or personal exemptions. Oregon does not index the income brackets for $125,000 and over See: INFL and SPEC above; (b) For joint returns, taxes are twice the tax on half the couple's income. California brackets violate this formula at the two highest tax brackets in 2024; (c) The personal exemption takes the form of a tax credit instead of a deduction; (g) California imposes an additional 1% tax on taxable income over $1 million, making the maximum rate 13.3% over $1 million in 2023. Unreleased projections indicate 14.4% in 2024.
Source: Federation of Tax Administrators, State Individual Income Tax Rates, January 1, 2025

Various State Sales and Excise Tax Rates

State	State Sales Tax (%)	Gasoline[1] ($/gal.)	Cigarette[2] ($/pack)	Spirits[3] ($/gal.)	Wine[4] ($/gal.)	Beer[5] ($/gal.)	Recreational Marijuana (%)
California	7.25	0.70	2.87	3.30	0.20	0.20	(c)

Note: All tax rates as of January 1, 2025; (1) The American Petroleum Institute has developed a methodology for determining the average tax rate on a gallon of fuel. Rates may include any of the following: excise taxes, environmental fees, storage tank fees, other fees or taxes, general sales tax, and local taxes; (2) The federal excise tax of $1.0066 per pack and local taxes are not included; (3) Rates are those applicable to off-premise sales of 40% alcohol by volume (a.b.v.) distilled spirits in 750ml containers. Local excise taxes are excluded; (4) Rates are those applicable to off-premise sales of 11% a.b.v. non-carbonated wine in 750ml containers; (5) Rates are those applicable to off-premise sales of 4.7% a.b.v. beer in 12 ounce containers; (c) 15% excise tax (retail gross receipts)
Source: Tax Foundation, 2025 Facts & Figures: How Does Your State Compare?

State Tax Competitiveness Index

State	Overall Rank	Corporate Tax Rank	Individual Income Tax Rank	Sales Tax Rank	Property Tax Rank	Unemployment Insurance Tax Rank
California	48	41	49	46	23	25

Note: The Tax Foundation's State Tax Competitiveness Index enables policymakers, taxpayers, and business leaders to gauge how their states' tax systems compare. A rank of 1 is best, 50 is worst. Rankings do not average to the total. States without a tax rank equally as 1. DC's scores and rankings do not affect other states. The report shows tax systems as of July 1, 2024 (the beginning of Fiscal Year 2025).
Source: Tax Foundation, State Tax Competitiveness Index 2025

TRANSPORTATION

Means of Transportation to Work

Area	Car/Truck/Van Drove Alone	Car-pooled	Public Transportation Bus	Subway	Railroad	Bicycle	Walked	Other Means	Worked at Home
City	65.5	9.0	1.0	0.2	0.1	1.4	2.7	2.4	17.7
MSA[1]	67.7	8.6	0.8	0.1	0.1	1.1	1.8	1.9	17.9
U.S.	70.2	8.5	1.7	1.3	0.4	0.4	2.4	1.6	13.5

Note: Figures are percentages and cover workers 16 years of age and older; (1) Figures cover the Sacramento-Roseville-Folsom, CA Metropolitan Statistical Area
Source: U.S. Census Bureau, 2019-2023 American Community Survey 5-Year Estimates

Travel Time to Work

Area	Less Than 10 Minutes	10 to 19 Minutes	20 to 29 Minutes	30 to 44 Minutes	45 to 59 Minutes	60 to 89 Minutes	90 Minutes or More
City	8.9	32.2	25.8	21.3	5.1	3.5	3.2
MSA[1]	10.3	28.8	22.7	22.9	7.1	4.4	3.8
U.S.	12.6	28.6	21.2	20.8	8.1	6.0	2.8

Note: Note: Figures are percentages and include workers 16 years old and over; (1) Figures cover the Sacramento-Roseville-Folsom, CA Metropolitan Statistical Area
Source: U.S. Census Bureau, 2019-2023 American Community Survey 5-Year Estimates

Key Congestion Measures

Measure	2000	2010	2015	2020	2022
Annual Hours of Delay, Total (000)	37,073	59,264	68,922	47,492	73,841
Annual Hours of Delay, Per Auto Commuter	37	46	55	38	61
Annual Congestion Cost, Per Auto Commuter ($)	908	1,154	1,239	894	1,403

Note: Figures cover the Sacramento CA urban area
Source: Texas A&M Transportation Institute, 2023 Urban Mobility Report

Freeway Travel Time Index

Measure	1985	1990	1995	2000	2005	2010	2015	2020	2022
Urban Area Index[1]	1.10	1.14	1.17	1.20	1.23	1.24	1.27	1.11	1.25
Urban Area Rank[1,2]	27	26	29	29	28	24	20	20	19

Note: Freeway Travel Time Index—the ratio of travel time in the peak period to the travel time at free-flow conditions. For example, a value of 1.30 indicates a 20-minute free-flow trip takes 26 minutes in the peak (20 minutes x 1.30 = 26 minutes); (1) Covers the Sacramento CA urban area; (2) Rank is based on 101 larger urban areas (#1 = highest travel time index)
Source: Texas A&M Transportation Institute, 2023 Urban Mobility Report

Public Transportation

Agency Name / Mode of Transportation	Vehicles Operated in Maximum Service[1]	Annual Unlinked Passenger Trips[2] (in thous.)	Annual Passenger Miles[3] (in thous.)
Sacramento Regional Transit District (Sacramento RT)			
Bus (directly operated)	193	7,715.1	27,520.0
Demand Response (directly operated)	115	429.3	2,545.0
Demand Response - Transportation Network Company	23	64.3	584.0
Light Rail (directly operated)	43	6,140.9	35,062.1

Note: (1) Number of revenue vehicles operated by the given mode and type of service to meet the annual maximum service requirement. This is the revenue vehicle count during the peak season of the year; on the week and day that maximum service is provided. Vehicles operated in maximum service (VOMS) exclude atypical days and one-time special events; (2) Number of passengers who boarded public transportation vehicles. Passengers are counted each time they board a vehicle no matter how many vehicles they use to travel from their origin to their destination. (3) Sum of the distances ridden by all passengers during the entire fiscal year.
Source: Federal Transit Administration, National Transit Database, 2023

Air Transportation

Airport Name and Code / Type of Service	Passenger Airlines[1]	Passenger Enplanements	Freight Carriers[2]	Freight (lbs)
Sacramento International (SMF)				
Domestic service (U.S. carriers only)	19	6,469,089	11	98,207,616
International service (U.S. carriers only)	5	12,679	0	0

Note: (1) Includes all U.S.-based major, minor and commuter airlines that carried at least one passenger during the year; (2) Includes all U.S.-based airlines and freight carriers that transported at least one pound of freight during the year.
Source: Bureau of Transportation Statistics, The Intermodal Transportation Database, Air Carriers: T-100 Domestic Market (U.S. carriers only), 2024; Bureau of Transportation Statistics, The Intermodal Transportation Database, Air Carriers: T-100 International Market (U.S. carriers only), 2024

BUSINESSES

Major Business Headquarters

Company Name	Industry	Rankings	
		Fortune[1]	Forbes[2]
No companies listed	-	-	-

Note: (1) Companies that produce a 10-K are ranked 1 to 500 based on 2023 revenue; (2) All private companies with at least $2 billion in annual revenue through the end of their most current fiscal year are ranked 1 to 275; companies listed are headquartered in the city; dashes indicate no ranking
Source: Fortune, "Fortune 500," 2024; Forbes, "America's Largest Private Companies," 2024

Fastest-Growing Businesses

According to *Inc.*, Sacramento is home to two of America's 500 fastest-growing private companies: **Coral port** (#422); **Rhombus Systems** (#492). Criteria: must be an independent, privately-held, for-profit, U.S. corporation, proprietorship or partnership as of December 31, 2023; revenues must be at least $100,000 in 2020 and $2 million in 2023; must have four-year operating/sales history. *Inc., "America's 500 Fastest-Growing Private Companies," 2024*

Living Environment

COST OF LIVING

Cost of Living Index

Composite Index	Groceries	Housing	Utilities	Trans-portation	Health Care	Misc. Goods/Services
128.8	106.9	139.2	174.4	152.0	99.7	116.9

Note: The Cost of Living Index measures regional differences in the cost of consumer goods and services, excluding taxes and non-consumer expenditures, for professional and managerial households in the top income quintile. It is based on more than 50,000 prices covering almost 60 different items for which prices are collected three times a year by chambers of commerce, economic development organizations or university applied economic centers in each participating urban area. The numbers shown should be read as a percentage above or below the national average of 100. For example, a value of 115.4 in the groceries column indicates that grocery prices are 15.4% higher than the national average. Small differences in the index numbers should not be interpreted as significant; Figures cover the Sacramento CA urban area.
Source: The Council for Community and Economic Research, Cost of Living Index, 2024

Grocery Prices

Area[1]	T-Bone Steak ($/pound)	Frying Chicken ($/pound)	Whole Milk ($/half gal.)	Eggs ($/dozen)	Orange Juice ($/64 oz.)	Coffee ($/11.5 oz.)
City[2]	15.53	2.13	5.01	2.90	4.40	6.44
Avg.	15.42	1.55	4.69	3.25	4.41	5.46
Min.	14.50	1.16	4.43	2.75	4.00	4.85
Max.	17.56	2.89	5.49	4.78	5.54	7.89

*Note: (1) Values for the local area are compared with the average, minimum and maximum values for all 276 areas in the Cost of Living Index; (2) Figures cover the Sacramento CA urban area; **T-Bone Steak** (price per pound); **Frying Chicken** (price per pound, whole fryer); **Whole Milk** (half gallon carton); **Eggs** (price per dozen, Grade A, large); **Orange Juice** (64 oz. Tropicana or Florida Natural); **Coffee** (11.5 oz. can, vacuum-packed, Maxwell House, Hills Bros, or Folgers).*
Source: The Council for Community and Economic Research, Cost of Living Index, 2024

Housing and Utility Costs

Area[1]	New Home Price ($)	Apartment Rent ($/month)	All Electric ($/month)	Part Electric ($/month)	Other Energy ($/month)	Telephone ($/month)
City[2]	718,604	2,241	-	397.28	53.75	191.51
Avg.	515,975	1,550	210.99	123.07	82.07	194.99
Min.	265,375	692	104.33	53.68	36.26	179.42
Max.	2,775,821	5,719	529.02	397.28	361.63	223.33

*Note: (1) Values for the local area are compared with the average, minimum and maximum values for all 276 areas in the Cost of Living Index; (2) Figures cover the Sacramento CA urban area; **New Home Price** (2,400 sf living area, 8,000 sf lot, in urban area with full utilities); **Apartment Rent** (950 sf 2 bedroom/1.5 or 2 bath, unfurnished, excluding all utilities except water); **All Electric** (average monthly cost for an all-electric home); **Part Electric** (average monthly cost for a part-electric home); **Other Energy** (average monthly cost for natural gas, fuel oil, coal, wood, and any other forms of energy except electricity); **Telephone** (price includes the base monthly rate plus taxes and fees for three lines of mobile phone service).*
Source: The Council for Community and Economic Research, Cost of Living Index, 2024

Health Care, Transportation, and Other Costs

Area[1]	Doctor ($/visit)	Dentist ($/visit)	Optometrist ($/visit)	Gasoline ($/gallon)	Beauty Salon ($/visit)	Men's Shirt ($)
City[2]	151.58	121.82	173.55	5.28	71.49	36.48
Avg.	143.77	117.51	129.23	3.32	48.57	38.14
Min.	36.74	58.67	67.33	2.80	24.00	13.41
Max.	270.44	216.82	307.33	5.28	94.00	63.89

*Note: (1) Values for the local area are compared with the average, minimum and maximum values for all 276 areas in the Cost of Living Index; (2) Figures cover the Sacramento CA urban area; **Doctor** (general practitioners routine exam of an established patient); **Dentist** (adult teeth cleaning and periodic oral examination); **Optometrist** (full vision eye exam for established adult patient); **Gasoline** (one gallon regular unleaded, national brand, including all taxes, cash price at self-service pump if available); **Beauty Salon** (woman's shampoo, trim, and blow-dry); **Men's Shirt** (cotton/polyester dress shirt, pinpoint weave, long sleeves).*
Source: The Council for Community and Economic Research, Cost of Living Index, 2024

HOUSING

Homeownership Rate

Area	2017 (%)	2018 (%)	2019 (%)	2020 (%)	2021 (%)	2022 (%)	2023 (%)	2024 (%)
MSA[1]	60.1	64.1	61.6	63.4	63.2	63.5	64.4	63.0
U.S.	63.9	64.4	64.6	66.6	65.5	65.8	65.9	65.6

Note: (1) Figures cover the Sacramento-Roseville-Folsom, CA Metropolitan Statistical Area
Source: U.S. Census Bureau, Housing Vacancies and Homeownership Annual Statistics: 2017-2024

House Price Index (HPI)

Area	National Ranking[2]	Quarterly Change (%)	One-Year Change (%)	Five-Year Change (%)	Since 1991Q1 (%)
MSA[1]	198	0.32	3.19	42.05	255.25
U.S.[3]	–	1.43	4.51	57.13	327.82

Note: The HPI is a weighted repeat sales index. It measures average price changes in repeat sales or refinancings on the same properties. This information is obtained by reviewing repeat mortgage transactions on single-family properties whose mortgages have been purchased or securitized by Fannie Mae or Freddie Mac since January 1975; (1) Figures cover the Sacramento—Roseville—Arden-Arcade, CA Metropolitan Statistical Area; (2) Rankings are based on annual percentage change for all metro areas containing at least 15,000 transactions over the last 10 years and ranges from 1 to 241; (3) figures based on a weighted average of Census Division estimates using a seasonally adjusted, purchase-only index; all figures are for the period ending December 31, 2024
Source: Federal Housing Finance Agency, Change in FHFA Metropolitan Area House Price Indexes, All Transactions Index, 2024Q4

Home Value

Area	Under $100,000	$100,000 -$199,999	$200,000 -$299,999	$300,000 -$399,999	$400,000 -$499,999	$500,000 -$999,999	$1,000,000 or more	Median ($)
City	4.3	2.4	7.6	17.7	21.3	41.5	5.2	484,600
MSA[1]	4.1	2.1	5.1	12.0	18.3	49.6	8.8	559,000
U.S.	12.1	17.8	19.5	14.4	10.5	19.1	6.5	303,400

Note: Figures are percentages except for median and cover owner-occupied housing units; (1) Figures cover the Sacramento-Roseville-Folsom, CA Metropolitan Statistical Area
Source: U.S. Census Bureau, 2019-2023 American Community Survey 5-Year Estimates

Year Housing Structure Built

Area	2020 or Later	2010 -2019	2000 -2009	1990 -1999	1980 -1989	1970 -1979	1960 -1969	1950 -1959	1940 -1949	Before 1940	Median Year
City	0.9	6.3	15.0	7.8	15.2	13.3	11.3	11.9	7.2	11.0	1976
MSA[1]	1.2	6.8	17.1	14.0	16.3	17.3	10.4	9.3	3.3	4.2	1983
U.S.	1.2	8.9	13.6	12.8	13.0	14.4	10.0	9.7	4.5	11.9	1980

Note: Figures are percentages except for Median Year; Note: (1) Figures cover the Sacramento-Roseville-Folsom, CA Metropolitan Statistical Area
Source: U.S. Census Bureau, 2019-2023 American Community Survey 5-Year Estimates

Gross Monthly Rent

Area	Under $500	$500 -$999	$1,000 -$1,499	$1,500 -$1,999	$2,000 -$2,499	$2,500 -$2,999	$3,000 and up	Median ($)
City	4.4	10.1	23.1	31.7	19.4	7.9	3.3	1,694
MSA[1]	3.6	8.3	24.6	29.4	19.8	8.6	5.7	1,729
U.S.	6.5	22.3	29.5	20.2	10.8	4.8	5.9	1,348

Note: Figures are percentages except for median; Gross rent is the contract rent plus the estimated average monthly cost of utilities (electricity, gas, and water and sewer) and fuels (oil, coal, kerosene, wood, etc.) if these are paid by the renter (or paid for the renter by someone else); (1) Figures cover the Sacramento-Roseville-Folsom, CA Metropolitan Statistical Area
Source: U.S. Census Bureau, 2019-2023 American Community Survey 5-Year Estimates

HEALTH

Health Risk Factors

Category	MSA[1] (%)	U.S. (%)
Adults aged 18–64 who have any kind of health care coverage	94.3	90.8
Adults who reported being in good or better health	81.3	81.8
Adults who have been told they have high blood cholesterol	33.6	36.9
Adults who have been told they have high blood pressure	28.0	34.0
Adults who are current smokers	5.8	12.1
Adults who currently use e-cigarettes	4.9	7.7
Adults who currently use chewing tobacco, snuff, or snus	1.7	3.2
Adults who are heavy drinkers[2]	4.7	6.1
Adults who are binge drinkers[3]	14.0	15.2
Adults who are overweight (BMI 25.0 - 29.9)	36.0	34.4
Adults who are obese (BMI 30.0 - 99.8)	30.1	34.3
Adults who participated in any physical activities in the past month	78.7	75.8

Note: All figures are crude prevalence; (1) Figures cover the Sacramento—Roseville—Arden-Arcade, CA Metropolitan Statistical Area; (2) Heavy drinkers are classified as adult men having more than 14 drinks per week and adult women having more than 7 drinks per week; (3) Binge drinkers are classified as males having five or more drinks on one occasion or females having four or more drinks on one occasion
Source: Centers for Disease Control and Prevention, Behaviorial Risk Factor Surveillance System, SMART: Selected Metropolitan Area Risk Trends, 2023

Acute and Chronic Health Conditions

Category	MSA[1] (%)	U.S. (%)
Adults who have ever been told they had a heart attack	3.4	4.2
Adults who have ever been told they have angina or coronary heart disease	2.4	4.0
Adults who have ever been told they had a stroke	1.9	3.3
Adults who have ever been told they have asthma	20.3	15.7
Adults who have ever been told they have arthritis	26.7	26.3
Adults who have ever been told they have diabetes[2]	8.8	11.5
Adults who have ever been told they had skin cancer	4.4	5.6
Adults who have ever been told they had any other types of cancer	6.9	8.4
Adults who have ever been told they have COPD	n/a	6.4
Adults who have ever been told they have kidney disease	2.9	3.7
Adults who have ever been told they have a form of depression	18.5	22.0

Note: All figures are crude prevalence; (1) Figures cover the Sacramento—Roseville—Arden-Arcade, CA Metropolitan Statistical Area; (2) Figures do not include pregnancy-related, borderline, or pre-diabetes
Source: Centers for Disease Control and Prevention, Behaviorial Risk Factor Surveillance System, SMART: Selected Metropolitan Area Risk Trends, 2023

Health Screening and Vaccination Rates

Category	MSA[1] (%)	U.S. (%)
Adults who have ever been tested for HIV	39.5	37.5
Adults who have had their blood cholesterol checked within the last five years	87.8	87.0
Adults aged 65+ who have had flu shot within the past year	58.7	63.4
Adults aged 65+ who have ever had a pneumonia vaccination	78.2	71.9

Note: All figures are crude prevalence; (1) Figures cover the Sacramento—Roseville—Arden-Arcade, CA Metropolitan Statistical Area.
Source: Centers for Disease Control and Prevention, Behaviorial Risk Factor Surveillance System, SMART: Selected Metropolitan Area Risk Trends, 2023

Disability Status

Category	MSA[1] (%)	U.S. (%)
Adults who reported being deaf	6.7	7.4
Are you blind or have serious difficulty seeing, even when wearing glasses?	5.5	4.9
Do you have difficulty doing errands alone?	9.4	7.8
Do you have difficulty dressing or bathing?	4.6	3.6
Do you have serious difficulty concentrating/remembering/making decisions?	13.7	13.7
Do you have serious difficulty walking or climbing stairs?	13.7	13.2

Note: All figures are crude prevalence; (1) Figures cover the Sacramento—Roseville—Arden-Arcade, CA Metropolitan Statistical Area.
Source: Centers for Disease Control and Prevention, Behaviorial Risk Factor Surveillance System, SMART: Selected Metropolitan Area Risk Trends, 2023

Mortality Rates for the Top 10 Causes of Death in the U.S.

ICD-10[a] Sub-Chapter	ICD-10[a] Code	Crude Mortality Rate[2] per 100,000 population	
		County[3]	U.S.
Malignant neoplasms	C00-C97	166.2	182.7
Ischaemic heart diseases	I20-I25	86.6	109.6
Provisional assignment of new diseases of uncertain etiology[1]	U00-U49	47.2	65.3
Other forms of heart disease	I30-I51	47.8	65.1
Other degenerative diseases of the nervous system	G30-G31	56.1	52.4
Other external causes of accidental injury	W00-X59	49.0	52.3
Cerebrovascular diseases	I60-I69	59.0	49.1
Chronic lower respiratory diseases	J40-J47	31.7	43.5
Hypertensive diseases	I10-I15	40.6	38.9
Organic, including symptomatic, mental disorders	F01-F09	24.2	33.9

Note: (a) ICD-10 = International Classification of Diseases 10th Revision; (1) Includes COVID-19, adverse effects to COVID-19 vaccines, SARS, and vaping-related disorders; (2) Crude mortality rates are a three-year average covering 2021-2023; (3) Figures cover Sacramento County.
Source: Centers for Disease Control and Prevention, National Center for Health Statistics. National Vital Statistics System, Mortality 2018-2023 on CDC WONDER Online Database

Mortality Rates for Selected Causes of Death

Cause of Death	ICD-10[a] Code	Crude Mortality Rate[1] per 100,000 population	
		County[2]	U.S.
Accidental poisoning and exposure to noxious substances	X40-X49	34.6	30.5
Alzheimer disease	G30	47.5	35.4
Assault	X85-Y09	6.4	7.3
COVID-19	U07.1	47.2	65.3
Diabetes mellitus	E10-E14	30.4	30.0
Diseases of the liver	K70-K76	19.4	20.8
Human immunodeficiency virus (HIV) disease	B20-B24	1.3	1.5
Influenza and pneumonia	J09-J18	10.7	13.4
Intentional self-harm	X60-X84	12.4	14.7
Malnutrition	E40-E46	7.3	6.0
Obesity and other hyperalimentation	E65-E68	3.1	3.1
Renal failure	N17-N19	11.0	16.4
Transport accidents	V01-V99	15.6	14.4

Note: (a) ICD-10 = International Classification of Diseases 10th Revision; (1) Crude mortality rates are a three-year average covering 2021-2023; (2) Figures cover Sacramento County; Data are suppressed when the data meet the criteria for confidentiality constraints; Crude mortality rates are flagged as unreliable when the rate would be calculated with a numerator of 20 or less.
Source: Centers for Disease Control and Prevention, National Center for Health Statistics. National Vital Statistics System, Mortality 2018-2023 on CDC WONDER Online Database

Health Insurance Coverage

Area	With Health Insurance	With Private Health Insurance	With Public Health Insurance	Without Health Insurance	Population Under Age 19 Without Health Insurance
City	94.5	65.3	40.5	5.5	3.2
MSA[1]	95.3	70.1	38.7	4.7	2.7
U.S.	91.4	67.3	36.3	8.6	5.4

Note: Figures are percentages that cover the civilian noninstitutionalized population; (1) Figures cover the Sacramento-Roseville-Folsom, CA Metropolitan Statistical Area
Source: U.S. Census Bureau, 2019-2023 American Community Survey 5-Year Estimates

Number of Medical Professionals

Area	MDs[3]	DOs[3,4]	Dentists	Podiatrists	Chiropractors	Optometrists
County[1] (number)	5,460	322	1,336	72	348	307
County[1] (rate[2])	344.7	20.3	84.3	4.5	22.0	19.4
U.S. (rate[2])	302.5	29.2	74.6	6.4	29.5	18.0

Note: Data as of 2023 unless noted; (1) Data covers Sacramento County; (2) Number of medical professionals per 100,000 population; (3) Data as of 2022 and includes all active, non-federal physicians; (4) Doctor of Osteopathic Medicine
Source: U.S. Department of Health and Human Services, Health Resources and Services Administration, Bureau of Health Professions, Area Resource File (ARF) 2023-2024

Best Hospitals

According to *U.S. News,* the Sacramento-Roseville-Folsom, CA metro area is home to three of the best hospitals in the U.S.: **Sutter Medical Center-Sacramento** (1 adult specialty); **Sutter Roseville Medical Center** (1 adult specialty); **UC Davis Medical Center** (8 adult specialties and 5 pediatric specialties). The hospitals listed were nationally ranked in at least one of 15 adult or 11 pediatric specialties. The number of specialties shown cover the parent hospital. Only 160 U.S. hospitals performed well enough to be nationally ranked in one or more specialties. Twenty hospitals in the U.S. made the Honor Roll. The Best Hospitals Honor Roll takes both the national rankings and the procedure and condition ratings into account. Hospitals received points if they were nationally ranked in one of the 15 adult specialties—the higher they ranked, the more points they got—and how many ratings of "high performing" they earned in the 20 procedures and conditions. *U.S. News Online, "America's Best Hospitals 2024-25"*

According to *U.S. News,* the Sacramento-Roseville-Folsom, CA metro area is home to two of the best children's hospitals in the U.S.: **UC Davis Children's Hospital** (5 pediatric specialties); **UC Davis Children's Hospital/Shriners Children's Northern California** (5 pediatric specialties). The hospitals listed were highly ranked in at least one of 11 pediatric specialties. One hundred five children's hospitals in the U.S. were nationally ranked in at least one specialty. Hospitals received points for being ranked in a specialty, and the 10 hospitals with the most points across the 11 specialties make up the Honor Roll. *U.S. News Online, "America's Best Children's Hospitals 2024-25"*

EDUCATION

Public School District Statistics

District Name	Schls	Pupils	Pupil/ Teacher Ratio	Minority Pupils[1] (%)	Total Rev. per Pupil ($)	Total Exp. per Pupil ($)
California Innovative Career Acad. Dist.	1	3,180	31.0	46.1	21,964	14,340
Highlands Community Charter District	1	9,069	73.4	46.6	12,909	11,693
Natomas Unified	20	14,950	22.2	87.4	17,407	20,128
Sacramento City Unified	73	38,268	22.5	82.9	19,384	18,556

Note: Table includes school districts with 2,000 or more students; (1) Percentage of students that are not non-Hispanic white.
Source: U.S. Department of Education, National Center for Education Statistics, Common Core of Data, Local Education Agency (School District) Universe Survey: School Year 2023-2024; U.S. Department of Education, National Center for Education Statistics, Common Core of Data, School District Finance Survey (F-33): School Year 2021–22

Best High Schools

According to *U.S. News,* Sacramento is home to one of the top 500 high schools in the U.S.: **West Campus High School** (#142). Nearly 25,000 public, magnet and charter schools were ranked based on their performance on state assessments and how well they prepare students for college. *U.S. News & World Report, "Best High Schools 2024"*

Highest Level of Education

Area	Less than H.S.	H.S. Diploma	Some College, No Deg.	Associate Degree	Bachelor's Degree	Master's Degree	Prof. School Degree	Doctorate Degree
City	13.1	20.5	21.6	8.4	22.9	8.7	3.3	1.6
MSA[1]	9.9	20.6	23.3	9.9	23.0	8.7	3.0	1.6
U.S.	10.6	26.2	19.4	8.8	21.3	9.8	2.3	1.6

Note: Figures cover persons age 25 and over; (1) Figures cover the Sacramento-Roseville-Folsom, CA Metropolitan Statistical Area
Source: U.S. Census Bureau, 2019-2023 American Community Survey 5-Year Estimates

Educational Attainment by Race

Area	High School Graduate or Higher (%)					Bachelor's Degree or Higher (%)				
	Total	White	Black	Asian	Hisp.[2]	Total	White	Black	Asian	Hisp.[2]
City	86.9	93.0	91.4	82.5	76.4	36.4	45.2	24.4	38.9	23.7
MSA[1]	90.1	94.4	91.4	85.1	78.1	36.3	39.2	26.0	45.0	22.0
U.S.	89.4	92.9	88.1	88.0	72.5	35.0	37.7	24.7	57.0	19.9

Note: Figures shown cover persons 25 years old and over; (1) Figures cover the Sacramento-Roseville-Folsom, CA Metropolitan Statistical Area; (2) People of Hispanic origin can be of any race
Source: U.S. Census Bureau, 2019-2023 American Community Survey 5-Year Estimates

School Enrollment by Grade and Control

Area	Preschool (%)		Kindergarten (%)		Grades 1 - 4 (%)		Grades 5 - 8 (%)		Grades 9 - 12 (%)	
	Public	Private	Public	Private	Public	Private	Public	Private	Public	Private
City	56.9	43.1	92.4	7.6	91.3	8.7	92.3	7.7	89.5	10.5
MSA[1]	55.0	45.0	87.3	12.7	89.8	10.2	90.5	9.5	90.7	9.3
U.S.	58.7	41.3	85.2	14.8	87.2	12.8	87.9	12.1	89.0	11.0

Note: Figures shown cover persons 3 years old and over; (1) Figures cover the Sacramento-Roseville-Folsom, CA Metropolitan Statistical Area
Source: U.S. Census Bureau, 2019-2023 American Community Survey 5-Year Estimates

Higher Education

Four-Year Colleges			Two-Year Colleges			Medical Schools[1]	Law Schools[2]	Voc/ Tech[3]
Public	Private Non-profit	Private For-profit	Public	Private Non-profit	Private For-profit			
2	3	3	7	0	5	2	4	12

Note: Figures cover institutions located within the Sacramento-Roseville-Folsom, CA Metropolitan Statistical Area and include main campuses only; (1) includes schools accredited by the Liaison Committee on Medical Education and the American Osteopathic Association's Commission on Osteopathic College Accreditation; (2) includes ABA-accredited schools, schools with provisional ABA accreditation, and state accredited schools; (3) includes all schools with programs that are less than 2 years.
Source: National Center for Education Statistics, Integrated Postsecondary Education System (IPEDS), 2023-24; Wikipedia, List of Medical Schools in the United States, accessed May 2, 2025; Wikipedia, List of Law Schools in the United States, accessed May 2, 2025

According to *U.S. News & World Report,* the Sacramento-Roseville-Folsom, CA metro area is home to one of the top 200 national universities in the U.S.: **University of California, Davis** (#33 tie). The indicators used to capture academic quality fall into a number of categories: assessment by administrators at peer institutions; retention of students; faculty resources; student selectivity; financial resources; alumni giving; high school counselor ratings of colleges; and graduation rate. *U.S. News & World Report, "America's Best Colleges 2025"*

According to *U.S. News & World Report,* the Sacramento-Roseville-Folsom, CA metro area is home to one of the top 100 law schools in the U.S.: **University of California—Davis** (#50 tie). The rankings are based on a weighted average of 12 measures of quality: peer assessment score; assessment score by lawyers/judges; median LSAT scores; median undergrad GPA; acceptance rate; employment rates for graduates; placement success; bar passage rate; faculty resources; expenditures per student; student/faculty ratio; and library resources. *U.S. News & World Report, "America's Best Graduate Schools, Law, 2025"*

According to *U.S. News & World Report,* the Sacramento-Roseville-Folsom, CA metro area is home to one of the top medical schools for research in the U.S.: **University of California—Davis** (Tier 2). *U.S. News* placed medical and osteopathic schools into tiers based on their research productivity, faculty and admissions data. Each school's tier was derived from its overall score, calculated by summing the weighted normalized values generated across several factors of academic quality, outlined below. There are four tiers, with tier 1 medical schools as the highest-performing and tier 4 as the lowest-performing. Only tier 1 and 2 schools are shown. Because of the tier presentation, *U.S. News* calculated overall scores based on their percentile performance among all rated schools instead of dividing against the rescaled score of the No. 1-performing schools. Tier 1 included schools with overall scores of 85 to 99. The cutoffs for tiers 2 through 4 were schools scoring 50 to 84, 15 to 49 and 1 to 14, respectively. The rankings are based on a weighted average of the following measures of quality: total research activity; average research activity per faculty member; total NIH research grants at the medical school and its affiliated hospitals; average NIH research grants per faculty; median MCAT total score; median undergraduate GPA; acceptance rate; and faculty resources. *U.S. News & World Report, "America's Best Graduate Schools, Medical, 2025"*

According to *U.S. News & World Report,* the Sacramento-Roseville-Folsom, CA metro area is home to one of the top medical schools for primary care in the U.S.: **University of California—Davis** (Tier 1). *U.S. News* placed medical and osteopathic schools into tiers based on their research productivity, faculty and admissions data. Each school's tier was derived from its overall score, calculated by summing the weighted normalized values generated across several factors of academic quality, outlined below. There are four tiers, with tier 1 medical schools as the highest-performing and tier 4 as the lowest-performing. Only tier 1 and 2 schools are shown. Because of the tier presentation, *U.S. News* calculated overall scores based on their percentile performance among all rated schools instead of dividing against the rescaled score of the No. 1-performing schools. Tier 1 included schools with overall scores of 85 to 99. The cutoffs for tiers 2 through 4 were schools scoring 50 to 84, 15 to 49 and 1 to 14, respectively. The rankings are based on a weighted average of the following measures of quality: graduates practicing in primary care specialties; graduates entering primary care residencies; median MCAT total score; median undergraduate GPA; acceptance rate; and faculty resources. *U.S. News & World Report, "America's Best Graduate Schools, Medical, 2025"*

According to *U.S. News & World Report,* the Sacramento-Roseville-Folsom, CA metro area is home to one of the top 75 business schools in the U.S.: **University of California—Davis** (#65). The rankings are based on a weighted average of the following nine measures: quality assessment; peer assessment; recruiter assessment; placement success; mean starting salary and bonus; student selectivity; mean GMAT and GRE scores; mean undergraduate GPA; and acceptance rate. *U.S. News & World Report, "America's Best Graduate Schools, Business, 2025"*

EMPLOYERS

Major Employers

Company Name	Industry
Aerojet Rocketdyne	Aerospace industries, mfg
Agreeya Solutions	Information technology services
Ampac Fine Chemicals	Electronic equipment & supplies, mfg
Apple Distribution Center	Distribution centers, wholesale
California Department of Corrections	State government
California State University Sacramento	Higher education
Colliers International Ltd	Real estate
Disabled American Veterans	Veterans' & military organizations
Intel Corp	Semiconductors & related devices
Kaiser Permanente	Hospitals
LA Care Health Plan	Health plans
Mercy General Hospital	Hospitals
Mercy San Juan Medical Center	Hospitals
Sacramento Municipal Utility	Electric companies
State of California	Government
Summit Funding Inc	Real estate agents & managers
Sutter Medical Center	Hospitals
UC Davis Health	Healthcare
Villara	Building contractors
Water Resource Dept	Government offices, state

Note: Companies shown are located within the Sacramento-Roseville-Folsom, CA Metropolitan Statistical Area.
Source: Chambers of Commerce; State Departments of Labor; Wikipedia

PUBLIC SAFETY

Crime Rate

Area	Total Crime Rate	Violent Crime Rate				Property Crime Rate		
		Murder	Rape	Robbery	Aggrav. Assault	Burglary	Larceny -Theft	Motor Vehicle Theft
City	3,692.9	7.7	32.1	225.3	535.6	520.1	1,672.4	699.8
U.S.	2,290.9	5.7	38.0	66.5	264.1	250.7	1,347.2	318.7

Note: Figures are crimes per 100,000 population.
Source: FBI, Table 8, Offenses Known to Law Enforcement, by State by City, 2023

Hate Crimes

Area	Number of Quarters Reported	Number of Incidents per Bias Motivation					
		Race/Ethnicity/ Ancestry	Religion	Sexual Orientation	Disability	Gender	Gender Identity
City[1]	4	30	8	28	2	0	0
U.S.	4	5,900	2,699	2,077	187	92	492

Note: (1) Figures include at least one incident reported with more than one bias motivation.
Source: Federal Bureau of Investigation, Hate Crime Statistics 2023

Identity Theft Consumer Reports

Area	Reports	Reports per 100,000 Population	Rank[2]
MSA[1]	6,483	269	89
U.S.	1,135,291	339	-

Note: (1) Figures cover the Sacramento-Roseville-Folsom, CA Metropolitan Statistical Area; (2) Rank ranges from 1 to 401 where 1 indicates greatest number of identity theft reports per 100,000 population
Source: Federal Trade Commission, Consumer Sentinel Network Data Book 2024

Fraud and Other Consumer Reports

Area	Reports	Reports per 100,000 Population	Rank[2]
MSA[1]	33,026	1,372	80
U.S.	5,360,641	1,601	-

Note: (1) Figures cover the Sacramento-Roseville-Folsom, CA Metropolitan Statistical Area; (2) Rank ranges from 1 to 401 where 1 indicates greatest number of fraud and other consumer reports per 100,000 population
Source: Federal Trade Commission, Consumer Sentinel Network Data Book 2024

POLITICS

2024 Presidential Election Results

Area	Trump (Rep.)	Harris (Dem.)	Stein (Green)	Kennedy (Ind.)	Oliver (Lib.)	Other
Sacramento County	38.4	58.1	1.2	1.4	0.5	0.5
U.S.	49.7	48.2	0.6	0.5	0.4	0.6

Note: Results are percentages and may not add to 100% due to rounding
Source: Dave Leip's Atlas of U.S. Presidential Elections

SPORTS

Professional Sports Teams

Team Name	League	Year Established
Sacramento Kings	National Basketball Association (NBA)	1985
Sacramento Republic FC	Major League Soccer (MLS)	2012

Note: Includes teams located in the Sacramento-Roseville-Folsom, CA Metropolitan Statistical Area.
Source: Wikipedia, Major Professional Sports Teams of the United States and Canada, May 1, 2025

CLIMATE

Average and Extreme Temperatures

Temperature	Jan	Feb	Mar	Apr	May	Jun	Jul	Aug	Sep	Oct	Nov	Dec	Yr.
Extreme High (°F)	70	76	88	93	105	115	114	109	108	101	87	72	115
Average High (°F)	53	60	64	71	80	87	93	91	87	78	63	53	73
Average Temp. (°F)	45	51	54	59	65	72	76	75	72	64	53	46	61
Average Low (°F)	38	41	43	46	50	55	58	58	56	50	43	38	48
Extreme Low (°F)	20	23	26	32	34	41	48	48	43	35	26	18	18

Note: Figures cover the years 1947-1990
Source: National Climatic Data Center, International Station Meteorological Climate Summary, 9/96

Average Precipitation/Snowfall/Humidity

Precip./Humidity	Jan	Feb	Mar	Apr	May	Jun	Jul	Aug	Sep	Oct	Nov	Dec	Yr.
Avg. Precip. (in.)	3.6	2.8	2.4	1.3	0.4	0.1	Tr	0.1	0.3	1.0	2.4	2.8	17.3
Avg. Snowfall (in.)	Tr	Tr	Tr	Tr	0	0	0	0	0	0	0	Tr	Tr
Avg. Rel. Hum. 7am (%)	90	88	84	78	71	67	68	73	75	80	87	90	79
Avg. Rel. Hum. 4pm (%)	70	59	51	43	36	31	28	29	31	39	57	70	45

Note: Figures cover the years 1947-1990; Tr = Trace amounts (<0.05 in. of rain; <0.5 in. of snow)
Source: National Climatic Data Center, International Station Meteorological Climate Summary, 9/96

Weather Conditions

Temperature			Daytime Sky			Precipitation		
10°F & below	32°F & below	90°F & above	Clear	Partly cloudy	Cloudy	0.01 inch or more precip.	0.1 inch or more snow/ice	Thunder-storms
0	21	73	175	111	79	58	< 1	2

Note: Figures are average number of days per year and cover the years 1947-1990
Source: National Climatic Data Center, International Station Meteorological Climate Summary, 9/96

HAZARDOUS WASTE

Superfund Sites

The Sacramento-Roseville-Folsom, CA metro area is home to five sites on the EPA's Superfund National Priorities List (NPL) or Superfund Alternative Approach (SAA) list: **Aerojet General Corp.** (Final NPL); **Frontier Fertilizer** (Final NPL); **Mather Air Force Base (AC&W Disposal Site)** (Final NPL); **McClellan Air Force Base (Ground Water Contamination)** (Final NPL); **Sacramento Army Depot** (Final NPL). The Superfund alternative approach uses the same investigation and cleanup process and standards that are used for sites listed on the National Priorities List. The SAA is an alternative to listing a site on the NPL; it is not an alternative to Superfund or the Superfund process. There are a total of 1,445 Superfund sites with a status of proposed or final on both lists in the United States. *U.S. Environmental Protection Agency, National Priorities List, May 1, 2025; U.S. Environmental Protection Agency, Superfund Alternative Approach Sites, May 1, 2025*

AIR QUALITY

Air Quality Trends: Ozone

	1990	1995	2000	2005	2010	2015	2020	2021	2022	2023
MSA[1]	0.087	0.092	0.085	0.084	0.072	0.073	0.072	0.072	0.067	0.069
U.S.	0.087	0.089	0.081	0.080	0.072	0.068	0.066	0.067	0.067	0.070

Note: (1) Data covers the Sacramento-Roseville-Folsom, CA Metropolitan Statistical Area. The values shown are the composite ozone concentration averages among trend sites based on the highest fourth daily maximum 8-hour concentration in parts per million. These trends are based on sites having an adequate record of monitoring data during the trend period. Data from exceptional events are included.
Source: U.S. Environmental Protection Agency, Air Quality Monitoring Information, "Air Quality Trends by City, 1990-2023"

Air Quality Index

Area	Percent of Days when Air Quality was...[2]					AQI Statistics[2]	
	Good	Moderate	Unhealthy for Sensitive Groups	Unhealthy	Very Unhealthy	Maximum	Median
MSA[1]	35.3	60.8	3.8	0.0	0.0	143	58

Note: (1) Data covers the Sacramento-Roseville-Folsom, CA Metropolitan Statistical Area; (2) Based on 365 days with AQI data in 2023. Air Quality Index (AQI) is an index for reporting daily air quality. EPA calculates the AQI for five major air pollutants regulated by the Clean Air Act: ground-level ozone, particle pollution (aka particulate matter), carbon monoxide, sulfur dioxide, and nitrogen dioxide. The AQI runs from 0 to 500. The higher the AQI value, the greater the level of air pollution and the greater the health concern. There are six AQI categories: "Good" AQI is between 0 and 50. Air quality is considered satisfactory; "Moderate" AQI is between 51 and 100. Air quality is acceptable; "Unhealthy for Sensitive Groups" When AQI values are between 101 and 150, members of sensitive groups may experience health effects; "Unhealthy" When AQI values are between 151 and 200 everyone may begin to experience health effects; "Very Unhealthy" AQI values between 201 and 300 trigger a health alert; "Hazardous" AQI values over 300 trigger warnings of emergency conditions (not shown).
Source: U.S. Environmental Protection Agency, Air Quality Index Report, 2023

Air Quality Index Pollutants

Area	Percent of Days when AQI Pollutant was...[2]					
	Carbon Monoxide	Nitrogen Dioxide	Ozone	Sulfur Dioxide	Particulate Matter 2.5	Particulate Matter 10
MSA[1]	0.0	0.0	60.5	(3)	39.5	0.0

Note: (1) Data covers the Sacramento-Roseville-Folsom, CA Metropolitan Statistical Area; (2) Based on 365 days with AQI data in 2023. The Air Quality Index (AQI) is an index for reporting daily air quality. EPA calculates the AQI for five major air pollutants regulated by the Clean Air Act: ground-level ozone, particle pollution (also known as particulate matter), carbon monoxide, sulfur dioxide, and nitrogen dioxide. The AQI runs from 0 to 500. The higher the AQI value, the greater the level of air pollution and the greater the health concern; (3) Sulfur dioxide is no longer included in this table because SO_2 concentrations tend to be very localized and not necessarily representative of broad geographical areas like counties and CBSAs.
Source: U.S. Environmental Protection Agency, Air Quality Index Report, 2023

Maximum Air Pollutant Concentrations: Particulate Matter, Ozone, CO and Lead

	Particulate Matter 10 (ug/m^3)	Particulate Matter 2.5 Wtd AM (ug/m^3)	Particulate Matter 2.5 24-Hr (ug/m^3)	Ozone (ppm)	Carbon Monoxide (ppm)	Lead (ug/m^3)
MSA[1] Level	57	9.4	28	0.077	n/a	n/a
NAAQS[2]	150	15	35	0.075	9	0.15
Met NAAQS[2]	Yes	Yes	Yes	No	n/a	n/a

Note: (1) Data covers the Sacramento-Roseville-Folsom, CA Metropolitan Statistical Area; Data from exceptional events are included; (2) National Ambient Air Quality Standards; ppm = parts per million; ug/m^3 = micrograms per cubic meter; n/a not available.
Concentrations: Particulate Matter 10 (coarse particulate)—highest second maximum 24-hour concentration; Particulate Matter 2.5 Wtd AM (fine particulate)—highest weighted annual mean concentration; Particulate Matter 2.5 24-Hour (fine particulate)—highest 98th percentile 24-hour concentration; Ozone—highest fourth daily maximum 8-hour concentration; Carbon Monoxide—highest second maximum non-overlapping 8-hour concentration; Lead—maximum running 3-month average
Source: U.S. Environmental Protection Agency, Air Quality Monitoring Information, "Air Quality Statistics by City, 2023"

Maximum Air Pollutant Concentrations: Nitrogen Dioxide and Sulfur Dioxide

	Nitrogen Dioxide AM (ppb)	Nitrogen Dioxide 1-Hr (ppb)	Sulfur Dioxide AM (ppb)	Sulfur Dioxide 1-Hr (ppb)	Sulfur Dioxide 24-Hr (ppb)
MSA[1] Level	9	33	n/a	2	n/a
NAAQS[2]	53	100	30	75	140
Met NAAQS[2]	Yes	Yes	n/a	Yes	n/a

Note: (1) Data covers the Sacramento-Roseville-Folsom, CA Metropolitan Statistical Area; Data from exceptional events are included; (2) National Ambient Air Quality Standards; ppm = parts per million; ug/m^3 = micrograms per cubic meter; n/a not available.
Concentrations: Nitrogen Dioxide AM—highest arithmetic mean concentration; Nitrogen Dioxide 1-Hr—highest 98th percentile 1-hour daily maximum concentration; Sulfur Dioxide AM—highest annual mean concentration; Sulfur Dioxide 1-Hr—highest 99th percentile 1-hour daily maximum concentration; Sulfur Dioxide 24-Hr—highest second maximum 24-hour concentration
Source: U.S. Environmental Protection Agency, Air Quality Monitoring Information, "Air Quality Statistics by City, 2023"

Salem, Oregon

Background

Salem, the capital of Oregon, is in the center of the Willamette Valley, an hour west of the Cascade Mountains and an hour east of the Pacific Ocean. The first people to live in the region were the Kalapuya Native Americans, a semi-nomadic tribe who were master canoe-builders, travelling the intricate web of rivers and streams flowing through the Willamette countryside. In the early 19th century, sailors carried disease to the region and the native population declined rapidly.

The first non-native settlers to the area were Methodist ministers who established the Willamette Mission in 1834, ten miles north of Salem. The Methodist Mission became the Oregon Institute, the first white settlers school west of the Missouri River and, later, Willamette University.

By 1843, an influx of settlers arrived with the fervor of manifest destiny. They brought an agrarian lifestyle, planting wheat, raising sheep, and building lumber mills. By 1851, the steamboat "Hoosier" traveled the Willamette River south to Eugene, and north to Oregon City (near Portland), providing trade and transportation to the entire Willamette Valley. Oregon achieved statehood in 1859 with Salem as its capital and, although Oregon was a free state prohibiting slaves, it was illegal for black people to live there. Abraham Lincoln was a candidate for Oregon's first governor, but he turned down the job because his wife, Mary, had no interest in moving west.

The population tripled between 1900 and 1920. In 1903, Salem won the moniker "The Cherry City" in recognition of its past importance to the local cherry-growing industry. In 1920, the Oregon Pulp and Paper Company began operations, and Salem General Hospital opened its doors. By 1940, Salem's population topped 30,900.

After a disastrous flood in 1964, Salem reconstructed the downtown, and in 1970 Chemeketa Community College opened its doors. In the 1990s, Salem's economy transitioned from the lumber industry to high technology. Today, the city is home to Kettle Foods and Oregon Fruit Products, which have been canning fruits in Salem since 1935. Its top employers include the State of Oregon, Salem-Keizer School District, and Salem Health.

In 1962 Oscar Award-winner *One Flew Over the Cuckoo's Nest,*was filmed in the Oregon State Mental Hospital. Listed in the National Register of Historic Places, the hospital is now called the Oregon State Hospital Museum of Mental Health. In 2005, Oregonian writer Sarah Kershaw won a Pulitzer Prize for her series about the discovery of 5,000 copper urns in the hospital, containing the cremated remains of hospital patients.

In addition to the Oregon State Fair, Salem hosts numerous festivals and tours including the World Beat Festival at Riverfront Park, Salem Art Fair and Festival, Bite of Salem, and Salem Film Festival. The Capital Pride festival is hosted by Aundrea Smith, author of the 2019 *Your Local Queer*. Salem has been awarded Tree City USA status by the National Arbor Day Foundation for 30 consecutive years for its dedication to urban forestry, the first city in Oregon to receive the award.

Salem's downtown is home to the Willamette Heritage Center, the Hallie Ford Museum of Art, A.C. Gilbert's Discovery Village, and Prewitt-Allen Archaeological Museum. The city's park system is 2,338 acres with 30 miles of trails and 46 parks, the largest being Minto-Brown Island Park. The Peter Courtney pedestrian and bicycle bridge, completed in 2018, connects Minto-Brown with Riverfront Park, home to the Salem Carousel. Salem is also home to the smallest city park in the world, Waldo Park, which consists of a single Sequoia tree.

In 2023, Avelo Airlines began service from Salem-Willamette Valley Airport to Burbank CA and Las Vegas, NV. The city recently decided to shut down the airport's secondary runway, which is projected to be unusable by 2035.

Post secondary schools in Salem include Chemeketa Community College, Corban University, Tokyo International University of America, and Willamette University, the oldest university in the American west.

Salem has a Marine West Coast climate with some distinct characteristics of the Mediterranean climate. Rain is heaviest in late fall and throughout winter, but precipitation is spread from October until May, with a dry season from June through September. Light snowfall occurs in winter, but major snows are rare. Mostly cloudy skies, and low cloud ceilings are commonplace during the rainy season. Salem's mean annual temperature is 53.0 °F, annual precipitation is 39.64 inches, including an average 3.5 inches of snow.

Rankings

General Rankings

- In their annual survey, Livability.com looked at data for more than 2,000 mid-sized U.S. cities to assign a "Livability Score"for each. The top 100 scoring cities make up Livability's "Top 100 Best Places to Live in the U.S." in 2025. Salem was placed among the top 100 of the customizable list. Criteria: housing and economy; cost of living; environment; education; health care options; transportation; safety; and community amenities. *Livability.com, "Top 100 Best Places to Live in the U.S. in 2025" April 15, 2025*

Business/Finance Rankings

- The Salem metro area appeared on the Milken Institute "2025 Best Performing Cities" list. Rank: #68 out of 200 large metro areas (based on performance category). Criteria: job growth; wage growth; high-tech growth and impact; community resilience; housing affordability; household broadband access. *Milken Institute, "Best-Performing Cities 2025," January 14, 2025*

Education Rankings

- Personal finance website *WalletHub* analyzed the 150 largest U.S. metropolitan statistical areas to determine where the most educated Americans are putting their degrees to work. Criteria: education levels; percentage of workers with degrees; education quality and attainment gap; public school quality rankings; quality and enrollment of each metro area's universities. Salem was ranked #118 (#1 = most educated city). *WalletHub.com, "Most & Least Educated Cities in America, 2025" July 2, 2024*

Real Estate Rankings

- *WalletHub* compared the most populated U.S. cities to determine which had the best markets for real estate agents. Salem ranked #64 where demand was high and pay was the best. Criteria: sales per agent; annual median wage for real-estate agents; monthly average starting salary for real estate agents; real estate job density and competition; unemployment rate; home turnover rate; housing-market health index; and other relevant metrics. *WalletHub.com, "2021 Best Places to Be a Real Estate Agent," May 12, 2021*

- The Salem metro area was identified as one of the 20 worst housing markets in the U.S. in 2024. The area ranked #217 out of 226 markets. Criteria: year-over-year change of median sales price of existing single-family homes between the 4th quarter of 2023 and the 4th quarter of 2024. *National Association of Realtors®, Median Sales Price of Existing Single-Family Homes for Metropolitan Areas, 4th Quarter 2024*

- Salem was ranked #152 out of 176 metro areas in terms of cost of housing in 2024 by the National Association of Home Builders (#1 = most affordable). Criteria: the portion of an average family's income necessary to pay the mortgage on a median-priced home. *National Association of Home Builders®, NAHB-Wells Fargo Cost of Housing Index, 4th Quarter 2024*

Women/Minorities Rankings

- Personal finance website *WalletHub* compared more than 180 U.S. cities across two key dimensions, "Hispanic Business-Friendliness" and "Hispanic Purchasing Power," to arrive at the most favorable conditions for Hispanic entrepreneurs. Salem was ranked #128 out of 182. Criteria includes: share of Hispanic-Owned Businesses; average growth of Hispanic Business revenues; Small Business-Friendliness score; affordability; and number of Hispanics with at least a bachelor's degree. *WalletHub.com, "Best Cities for Hispanic Entrepreneurs," September 4, 2024*

Miscellaneous Rankings

- *WalletHub* compared 148 of the most populated U.S. cities to determine their operating efficiency. A "Quality of Services" score was constructed for each city and then measured against the total budget per capita to reveal which were managed the best. Salem ranked #41. Criteria: financial stability; economy; education; safety; health; infrastructure and pollution. *WalletHub.com, "2025's Best- & Worst-Run Cities in America," June 18, 2024*

Business Environment

DEMOGRAPHICS

Population Growth

Area	1990 Census	2000 Census	2010 Census	2020 Census	2023 Estimate[2]	Population Growth 1990-2023 (%)
City	112,046	136,924	154,637	175,535	176,666	57.7
MSA[1]	278,024	347,214	390,738	433,353	435,085	56.5
U.S.	248,709,873	281,421,906	308,745,538	331,449,281	332,387,540	33.6

Note: (1) Figures cover the Salem, OR Metropolitan Statistical Area; (2) 2019-2023 5-year ACS population estimate
Source: U.S. Census Bureau, 1990 Census, 2000 Census, 2010 Census, 2020 Census, 2019-2023 American Community Survey 5-Year Estimates

Race

Area	White Alone[2] (%)	Black Alone[2] (%)	Asian Alone[2] (%)	AIAN[3] Alone[2] (%)	NHOPI[4] Alone[2] (%)	Other Race Alone[2] (%)	Two or More Races (%)
City	69.8	1.6	3.5	1.2	1.6	8.2	14.1
MSA[1]	71.3	1.1	2.0	1.4	1.0	9.3	14.0
U.S.	63.4	12.4	5.8	0.9	0.2	6.6	10.7

Note: (1) Figures cover the Salem, OR Metropolitan Statistical Area; (2) Alone is defined as not being in combination with one or more other races; (3) American Indian and Alaska Native; (4) Native Hawaiian and Other Pacific Islander
Source: U.S. Census Bureau, 2019-2023 American Community Survey 5-Year Estimates

Hispanic or Latino Origin

Area	Total (%)	Mexican (%)	Puerto Rican (%)	Cuban (%)	Other (%)
City	23.4	20.0	0.4	0.1	2.9
MSA[1]	25.6	22.2	0.3	0.2	3.0
U.S.	19.0	11.3	1.8	0.7	5.2

Note: Persons of Hispanic or Latino origin can be of any race; (1) Figures cover the Salem, OR Metropolitan Statistical Area
Source: U.S. Census Bureau, 2019-2023 American Community Survey 5-Year Estimates

Age

Area	Percent of Population									Median Age
	Under Age 5	Age 5–19	Age 20–34	Age 35–44	Age 45–54	Age 55–64	Age 65–74	Age 75–84	Age 85+	
City	5.9	20.2	22.9	13.6	11.4	10.8	8.9	4.7	1.7	35.7
MSA[1]	5.9	20.5	20.5	13.0	11.6	11.6	10.1	4.9	1.9	37.3
U.S.	5.7	19.1	20.2	13.1	12.3	12.8	10.0	4.9	1.9	38.7

Note: (1) Figures cover the Salem, OR Metropolitan Statistical Area
Source: U.S. Census Bureau, 2019-2023 American Community Survey 5-Year Estimates

Disability by Age

Area	All Ages	Under 18 Years Old	18 to 64 Years Old	65 Years and Over
City	15.4	5.9	13.7	36.8
MSA[1]	15.8	5.8	13.8	36.9
U.S.	13.0	4.7	10.7	32.9

Note: Figures show percent of the civilian noninstitutionalized population that reported having a disability. Disability status is determined from six types of difficulty: vision, hearing, cognitive, ambulatory, self-care, and independent living. For children under 5 years old, hearing and vision difficulty are used to determine disability status. For children between the ages of 5 and 14, disability status is determined from hearing, vision, cognitive, ambulatory, and self-care difficulties. For people aged 15 years and older, they are considered to have a disability if they have difficulty with any one of the six difficulty types; Note: (1) Figures cover the Salem, OR Metropolitan Statistical Area
Source: U.S. Census Bureau, 2019-2023 American Community Survey 5-Year Estimates

Ancestry

Area	German	Irish	English	American	Italian	Polish	French[2]	European	Scottish
City	16.3	8.2	12.7	4.1	2.9	1.2	2.3	4.2	2.5
MSA[1]	16.6	8.4	12.1	3.9	2.6	1.4	2.3	3.6	2.6
U.S.	12.6	9.4	9.1	5.5	4.9	2.6	2.0	1.6	1.6

Note: Figures are the percentage of the total population reporting a particular ancestry. The nine most commonly reported ancestries in the U.S. are shown. Figures include multiple ancestries (e.g. if a person reported being Irish and Italian, they were included in both columns); (1) Figures cover the Salem, OR Metropolitan Statistical Area; (2) Excludes Basque
Source: U.S. Census Bureau, 2019-2023 American Community Survey 5-Year Estimates

Foreign-born Population

Area	Percent of Population Born in								
	Any Foreign Country	Asia	Mexico	Europe	Caribbean	Central America[2]	South America	Africa	Canada
City	12.2	2.5	6.2	1.0	0.0	0.8	0.2	0.4	0.2
MSA[1]	12.0	1.5	7.4	1.0	0.1	0.8	0.2	0.3	0.2
U.S.	13.9	4.3	3.3	1.4	1.4	1.2	1.2	0.8	0.2

Note: (1) Figures cover the Salem, OR Metropolitan Statistical Area; (2) Excludes Mexico.
Source: U.S. Census Bureau, 2019-2023 American Community Survey 5-Year Estimates

Household Size

Area	Persons in Household (%)							Average Household Size
	One	Two	Three	Four	Five	Six	Seven or More	
City	29.2	33.2	15.5	11.5	5.8	3.0	1.8	2.51
MSA[1]	25.5	33.8	15.8	12.5	6.7	3.3	2.3	2.67
U.S.	28.5	33.8	15.4	12.7	5.9	2.3	1.4	2.54

Note: (1) Figures cover the Salem, OR Metropolitan Statistical Area
Source: U.S. Census Bureau, 2019-2023 American Community Survey 5-Year Estimates

Household Relationships

Area	House-holder	Opposite-sex Spouse	Same-sex Spouse	Opposite-sex Unmarried Partner	Same-sex Unmarried Partner	Child[2]	Grand-child	Other Relatives	Non-relatives
City	36.6	16.0	0.2	3.1	0.2	28.1	1.9	4.6	4.2
MSA[1]	35.7	17.6	0.2	2.7	0.1	29.3	2.3	5.0	4.1
U.S.	38.3	17.5	0.2	2.5	0.2	28.3	2.4	4.8	3.4

Note: Figures are percent of the total population; (1) Figures cover the Salem, OR Metropolitan Statistical Area; (2) Includes biological, adopted, and stepchildren of the householder
Source: U.S. Census Bureau, 2020 Census

Gender

Area	Males	Females	Males per 100 Females
City	89,295	87,371	102.2
MSA[1]	217,233	217,852	99.7
U.S.	164,545,087	167,842,453	98.0

Note: (1) Figures cover the Salem, OR Metropolitan Statistical Area
Source: U.S. Census Bureau, 2019-2023 American Community Survey 5-Year Estimates

Marital Status

Area	Never Married	Now Married[2]	Separated	Widowed	Divorced
City	35.6	44.6	1.4	5.3	13.1
MSA[1]	32.4	48.5	1.6	5.4	12.1
U.S.	34.1	47.9	1.7	5.6	10.7

Note: Figures are percentages and cover the population 15 years of age and older; (1) Figures cover the Salem, OR Metropolitan Statistical Area; (2) Excludes separated
Source: U.S. Census Bureau, 2019-2023 American Community Survey 5-Year Estimates

Religious Groups by Family

Area	Catholic	Baptist	Methodist	LDS[2]	Pentecostal	Lutheran	Islam	Adventist	Other
MSA[1]	19.5	0.5	0.6	3.8	2.9	1.2	n/a	2.5	10.7
U.S.	18.7	7.3	3.0	2.0	1.8	1.7	1.3	1.3	11.6

Note: Figures are the number of adherents as a percentage of the total population and cover the eight largest religious groups in the U.S; (1) Figures cover the Salem, OR Metropolitan Statistical Area; (2) Church of Jesus Christ of Latter-day Saints
Sources: 2020 U.S. Religion Census, Association of Statisticians of American Religious Bodies; The Association of Religion Data Archives (ARDA)

Religious Groups by Tradition

Area	Catholic	Evangelical Protestant	Mainline Protestant	Black Protestant	Islam	Judaism	Hinduism	Orthodox	Buddhism
MSA[1]	19.5	14.4	2.0	0.2	n/a	0.1	<0.1	<0.1	<0.1
U.S.	18.7	16.5	5.2	2.3	1.3	0.6	0.4	0.4	0.3

Note: Figures are the number of adherents as a percentage of the total population; (1) Figures cover the Salem, OR Metropolitan Statistical Area
Sources: 2020 U.S. Religion Census, Association of Statisticians of American Religious Bodies; The Association of Religion Data Archives (ARDA)

ECONOMY

Real Gross Domestic Product (GDP)

Area	2017	2018	2019	2020	2021	2022	2023	Rank[3]
MSA[1]	17.1	18.0	18.6	18.6	19.8	20.1	20.6	147
U.S.[2]	17,619.1	18,160.7	18,642.5	18,238.9	19,387.6	19,896.6	20,436.3	–

Note: Figures are in billions of chained 2017 dollars; (1) Figures cover the Salem, OR Metropolitan Statistical Area; (2) Figures cover real GDP within metropolitan areas; (3) Rank is based on 2023 data and ranges from 1 to 384
Source: U.S. Bureau of Economic Analysis

Economic Growth

Area	2014	2015	2016	2017	2018	2019	2020	2021	2022	2023
MSA[1]	3.4	5.4	5.1	4.5	5.6	3.2	-0.3	6.4	1.7	2.6
U.S.[2]	2.6	3.2	2.0	2.7	3.1	2.7	-2.2	6.3	2.6	2.7

Note: Figures are real gross domestic product growth rates and represent percent change from preceding period; (1) Figures cover the Salem, OR Metropolitan Statistical Area; (2) Figures are the average growth rates within metropolitan areas
Source: U.S. Bureau of Economic Analysis

Metropolitan Area Exports

Area	2018	2019	2020	2021	2022	2023	Rank[2]
MSA[1]	410.2	405.7	350.5	372.0	422.3	404.8	244
U.S.	1,664,056.1	1,645,173.7	1,431,406.6	1,753,941.4	2,062,937.4	2,019,160.5	–

Note: Figures are in millions of dollars; (1) Figures cover the Salem, OR Metropolitan Statistical Area; (2) Rank is based on 2023 data and ranges from 1 to 386
Source: U.S. Department of Commerce, International Trade Administration, Office of Trade and Economic Analysis, Industry and Analysis, Exports by Metropolitan Area, data extracted April 2, 2025

Building Permits

Area	Single-Family			Multi-Family			Total		
	2023	2024	Pct. Chg.	2023	2024	Pct. Chg.	2023	2024	Pct. Chg.
City	360	392	8.9	326	513	57.4	686	905	31.9
MSA[1]	826	994	20.3	1,140	865	-24.1	1,966	1,859	-5.4
U.S.	920,000	981,900	6.7	591,100	496,100	-16.1	1,511,100	1,478,000	-2.2

Note: (1) Figures cover the Salem, OR Metropolitan Statistical Area; Figures represent new, privately-owned housing units authorized (unadjusted data)
Source: U.S. Census Bureau, Building Permits Survey (BPS), 2023, 2024

Bankruptcy Filings

Area	Business Filings			Nonbusiness Filings		
	2023	2024	% Chg.	2023	2024	% Chg.
Marion County	10	11	10.0	599	674	12.5
U.S.	18,926	23,107	22.1	434,064	494,201	13.9

Note: Business filings include Chapter 7, Chapter 9, Chapter 11, Chapter 12, Chapter 13, Chapter 15, and Section 304; Nonbusiness filings include Chapter 7, Chapter 11, and Chapter 13
Source: Administrative Office of the U.S. Courts, Business and Nonbusiness Bankruptcy, County Cases Commenced by Chapter of the Bankruptcy Code, During the 12-Month Period Ending December 31, 2023 and Business and Nonbusiness Bankruptcy, County Cases Commenced by Chapter of the Bankruptcy Code, During the 12-Month Period Ending December 31, 2024

Housing Vacancy Rates

Area	Gross Vacancy Rate[3] (%)			Year-Round Vacancy Rate[4] (%)			Rental Vacancy Rate[5] (%)			Homeowner Vacancy Rate[6] (%)		
	2022	2023	2024	2022	2023	2024	2022	2023	2024	2022	2023	2024
MSA[1]	n/a	n/a	n/a	n/a	n/a	n/a	n/a	n/a	n/a	n/a	n/a	n/a
U.S.[2]	9.1	9.0	9.1	7.5	7.5	7.6	5.7	6.5	6.8	0.8	0.8	1.0

Note: (1) Figures cover the Salem, OR Metropolitan Statistical Area; (2) Figures cover the 75 largest Metropolitan Statistical Areas; (3) The percentage of the total housing inventory that is vacant; (4) The percentage of the housing inventory (excluding seasonal units) that is year-round vacant; (5) The percentage of rental inventory that is vacant for rent; (6) The percentage of homeowner inventory that is vacant for sale; n/a not available
Source: U.S. Census Bureau, Housing Vacancies and Homeownership Annual Statistics: 2022, 2023, 2024

INCOME

Income

Area	Per Capita ($)	Median Household ($)	Average Household ($)
City	36,477	71,900	94,087
MSA[1]	36,260	76,010	97,771
U.S.	43,289	78,538	110,491

Note: (1) Figures cover the Salem, OR Metropolitan Statistical Area
Source: U.S. Census Bureau, 2019-2023 American Community Survey 5-Year Estimates

Household Income Distribution

Area	Percent of Households Earning							
	Under $15,000	$15,000 -$24,999	$25,000 -$34,999	$35,000 -$49,999	$50,000 -$74,999	$75,000 -$99,999	$100,000 -$149,999	$150,000 and up
City	9.0	6.5	7.5	11.2	17.5	12.6	19.0	16.5
MSA[1]	7.7	6.4	6.9	11.0	17.3	13.4	19.7	17.5
U.S.	8.5	6.6	6.8	10.4	15.7	12.7	17.4	21.9

Note: (1) Figures cover the Salem, OR Metropolitan Statistical Area
Source: U.S. Census Bureau, 2019-2023 American Community Survey 5-Year Estimates

Poverty Rate

Area	All Ages	Under 18 Years Old	18 to 64 Years Old	65 Years and Over
City	14.7	17.2	14.4	11.8
MSA[1]	12.9	16.0	12.5	10.2
U.S.	12.4	16.3	11.6	10.4

Note: Figures are percentage of people whose income during the past 12 months was below the poverty level;
(1) Figures cover the Salem, OR Metropolitan Statistical Area
Source: U.S. Census Bureau, 2019-2023 American Community Survey 5-Year Estimates

EMPLOYMENT

Labor Force and Employment

Area	Civilian Labor Force			Workers Employed		
	Dec. 2023	Dec. 2024	% Chg.	Dec. 2023	Dec. 2024	% Chg.
City	86,857	88,580	2.0	83,316	84,776	1.8
MSA[1]	215,316	219,611	2.0	206,688	210,311	1.8
U.S.	166,661,000	167,746,000	0.7	160,754,000	161,294,000	0.3

Note: Data is not seasonally adjusted and covers workers 16 years of age and older; (1) Figures cover the Salem, OR Metropolitan Statistical Area
Source: Bureau of Labor Statistics, Local Area Unemployment Statistics

Unemployment Rate

Area	2024											
	Jan.	Feb.	Mar.	Apr.	May	Jun.	Jul.	Aug.	Sep.	Oct.	Nov.	Dec.
City	4.7	4.6	4.5	3.8	3.7	4.2	4.6	4.5	4.0	4.0	4.1	4.3
MSA[1]	4.7	4.6	4.3	3.6	3.6	4.0	4.6	4.6	3.9	3.9	4.0	4.2
U.S.	4.1	4.2	3.9	3.5	3.7	4.3	4.5	4.4	3.9	3.9	4.0	3.8

Note: Data is not seasonally adjusted and covers workers 16 years of age and older; (1) Figures cover the Salem, OR Metropolitan Statistical Area
Source: Bureau of Labor Statistics, Local Area Unemployment Statistics

Average Wages

Occupation	$/Hr.	Occupation	$/Hr.
Accountants and Auditors	42.14	Maintenance and Repair Workers	25.44
Automotive Mechanics	27.01	Marketing Managers	64.66
Bookkeepers	26.35	Network and Computer Systems Admin.	52.82
Carpenters	27.76	Nurses, Licensed Practical	35.99
Cashiers	16.54	Nurses, Registered	58.70
Computer Programmers	52.83	Nursing Assistants	24.31
Computer Systems Analysts	53.95	Office Clerks, General	23.22
Computer User Support Specialists	31.51	Physical Therapists	46.55
Construction Laborers	25.90	Physicians	156.96
Cooks, Restaurant	18.91	Plumbers, Pipefitters and Steamfitters	38.33
Customer Service Representatives	22.72	Police and Sheriff's Patrol Officers	41.55
Dentists	104.28	Postal Service Mail Carriers	28.32
Electricians	40.07	Real Estate Sales Agents	31.93
Engineers, Electrical	55.99	Retail Salespersons	18.59
Fast Food and Counter Workers	16.51	Sales Representatives, Technical/Scientific	51.43
Financial Managers	80.64	Secretaries, Exc. Legal/Medical/Executive	25.45
First-Line Supervisors of Office Workers	34.43	Security Guards	21.67
General and Operations Managers	56.23	Surgeons	n/a
Hairdressers/Cosmetologists	22.06	Teacher Assistants, Exc. Postsecondary[1]	18.55
Home Health and Personal Care Aides	20.60	Teachers, Secondary School, Exc. Sp. Ed.[1]	36.88
Janitors and Cleaners	19.35	Telemarketers	n/a
Landscaping/Groundskeeping Workers	20.37	Truck Drivers, Heavy/Tractor-Trailer	29.67
Lawyers	76.23	Truck Drivers, Light/Delivery Services	22.75
Maids and Housekeeping Cleaners	19.11	Waiters and Waitresses	20.45

Note: Wage data covers the Salem, OR Metropolitan Statistical Area; (1) Hourly wages were calculated from annual wage data based on a 40 hour work week
Source: Bureau of Labor Statistics, Metro Area Occupational Employment & Wage Estimates, May 2024

Employment by Industry

Sector	MSA[1]		U.S.
	Number of Employees	Percent of Total	Percent of Total
Construction	13,300	7.1	5.1
Financial Activities	6,000	3.2	5.8
Government	46,200	24.5	14.9
Information	1,800	1.0	1.9
Leisure and Hospitality	16,000	8.5	10.4
Manufacturing	11,700	6.2	8.0
Mining and Logging	600	0.3	0.4
Other Services	5,700	3.0	3.7
Private Education and Health Services	37,500	19.9	16.9
Professional and Business Services	18,800	10.0	14.2
Retail Trade	19,100	10.1	10.0
Transportation, Warehousing, and Utilities	7,400	3.9	4.8
Wholesale Trade	4,200	2.2	3.9

Note: Figures are non-farm employment as of December 2024. Figures are not seasonally adjusted and include workers 16 years of age and older; (1) Figures cover the Salem, OR Metropolitan Statistical Area
Source: Bureau of Labor Statistics, Current Employment Statistics, Employment, Hours, and Earnings

Employment by Occupation

Occupation Classification	City (%)	MSA[1] (%)	U.S. (%)
Management, Business, Science, and Arts	39.4	35.7	42.0
Natural Resources, Construction, and Maintenance	9.2	11.8	8.6
Production, Transportation, and Material Moving	11.6	13.5	13.0
Sales and Office	20.8	20.0	19.9
Service	19.1	19.1	16.5

Note: Figures cover employed civilians 16 years of age and older; (1) Figures cover the Salem, OR Metropolitan Statistical Area
Source: U.S. Census Bureau, 2019-2023 American Community Survey 5-Year Estimates

Occupations with Greatest Projected Employment Growth: 2022 – 2032

Occupation[1]	2022 Employment	2032 Projected Employment	Numeric Employment Change	Percent Employment Change
Home Health and Personal Care Aides	36,900	46,170	9,270	25.1
Fast Food and Counter Workers	61,880	70,300	8,420	13.6
Software Developers	20,630	26,850	6,220	30.2
General and Operations Managers	44,700	50,550	5,850	13.1
Cooks, Restaurant	20,480	25,960	5,480	26.8
Stockers and Order Fillers	44,430	49,500	5,070	11.4
Registered Nurses	42,720	47,680	4,960	11.6
Laborers and Freight, Stock, and Material Movers, Hand	25,990	29,120	3,130	12.0
Personal Care and Service Workers, All Other	21,590	24,720	3,130	14.5
Construction Laborers	18,310	21,420	3,110	17.0

Note: Projections cover Oregon; (1) Sorted by numeric employment change
Source: www.projectionscentral.org, State Occupational Projections, 2022–2032 Long-Term Projections

Fastest-Growing Occupations: 2022 – 2032

Occupation[1]	2022 Employment	2032 Projected Employment	Numeric Employment Change	Percent Employment Change
Nurse Practitioners	2,240	3,420	1,180	52.7
Physical Therapist Assistants	840	1,160	320	38.1
Data Scientists	1,420	1,960	540	38.0
Curators	190	260	70	36.8
Information Security Analysts (SOC 2018)	1,390	1,900	510	36.7
Physician Assistants	1,420	1,930	510	35.9
Medical and Health Services Managers	5,080	6,880	1,800	35.4
Wind Turbine Service Technicians	290	390	100	34.5
Solar Photovoltaic Installers	350	470	120	34.3
Statisticians	570	760	190	33.3

Note: Projections cover Oregon; (1) Sorted by percent employment change and excludes occupations with numeric employment change less than 50
Source: www.projectionscentral.org, State Occupational Projections, 2022–2032 Long-Term Projections

CITY FINANCES

City Government Finances

Component	2022 ($000)	2022 ($ per capita)
Total Revenues	479,882	2,728
Total Expenditures	365,310	2,077
Debt Outstanding	241,407	1,372

Source: U.S. Census Bureau, State & Local Government Finances 2022

City Government Revenue by Source

Source	2022 ($000)	2022 ($ per capita)	2022 (%)
General Revenue			
From Federal Government	34,526	196	7.2
From State Government	87,400	497	18.2
From Local Governments	13,690	78	2.9
Taxes			
Property	111,829	636	23.3
Sales and Gross Receipts	26,267	149	5.5
Personal Income	0	0	0.0
Corporate Income	0	0	0.0
Motor Vehicle License	0	0	0.0
Other Taxes	22,515	128	4.7
Current Charges	89,705	510	18.7
Liquor Store	0	0	0.0
Utility	40,993	233	8.5

Source: U.S. Census Bureau, State & Local Government Finances 2022

City Government Expenditures by Function

Function	2022 ($000)	2022 ($ per capita)	2022 (%)
General Direct Expenditures			
Air Transportation	1,206	6	0.3
Corrections	0	0	0.0
Education	0	0	0.0
Employment Security Administration	0	0	0.0
Financial Administration	3,888	22	1.1
Fire Protection	40,527	230	11.1
General Public Buildings	7,070	40	1.9
Governmental Administration, Other	3,748	21	1.0
Health	1,893	10	0.5
Highways	15,647	89	4.3
Hospitals	0	0	0.0
Housing and Community Development	49,770	283	13.6
Interest on General Debt	6,924	39	1.9
Judicial and Legal	3,878	22	1.1
Libraries	5,164	29	1.4
Parking	1,240	7	0.3
Parks and Recreation	15,710	89	4.3
Police Protection	51,415	292	14.1
Public Welfare	0	0	0.0
Sewerage	66,933	380	18.3
Solid Waste Management	0	0	0.0
Veterans' Services	0	0	0.0
Liquor Store	0	0	0.0
Utility	46,138	262	12.6

Source: U.S. Census Bureau, State & Local Government Finances 2022

TAXES

State Corporate Income Tax Rates

State	Tax Rate (%)	Income Brackets ($)	Num. of Brackets	Financial Institution Tax Rate (%)[a]	Federal Income Tax Ded.
Oregon	6.6 - 7.6 (s)	1 million	2	6.6 - 7.6 (s)	No

Note: Tax rates for tax year 2024; (a) Rates listed are the corporate income tax rate applied to financial institutions or excise taxes based on income. Some states have other taxes based upon the value of deposits or shares; (s) Oregon's minimum tax for C corporations depends on the Oregon sales of the filing group. The minimum tax ranges from $150 for corporations with sales under $500,000, up to $100,000 for companies with sales of $100 million or above. Oregon also imposes Corporate Activity Tax [CAT] of $250 plus 0.57% of activity in excess of $1 million.
Source: Federation of Tax Administrators, State Corporate Income Tax Rates, January 1, 2025

State Individual Income Tax Rates

State	Tax Rate (%)	Income Brackets ($)	Personal Exemptions ($)			Standard Ded. ($)	
			Single	Married	Depend.	Single	Married
Oregon (a)	4.75 - 9.9	4,050 -125,000 (b)	236	472	236 (c)	2,745	5,495

Note: Tax rates for tax year 2024; Local- and county-level taxes are not included; The deduction for federal SALT deductions is limited to $5,000 for individuals and $10,000 for joint returns in Missouri and Montana, and to $7,800 for all filers in Oregon; (a) 16 states have statutory provision for automatically adjusting to the rate of inflation the dollar values of the income tax brackets, standard deductions, and/or personal exemptions. Oregon does not index the income brackets for $125,000 and over See: INFL and SPEC above; (b) For joint returns, taxes are twice the tax on half the couple's income. California brackets violate this formula at the two highest tax brackets in 2024; (c) The personal exemption takes the form of a tax credit instead of a deduction
Source: Federation of Tax Administrators, State Individual Income Tax Rates, January 1, 2025

Various State Sales and Excise Tax Rates

State	State Sales Tax (%)	Gasoline[1] ($/gal.)	Cigarette[2] ($/pack)	Spirits[3] ($/gal.)	Wine[4] ($/gal.)	Beer[5] ($/gal.)	Recreational Marijuana (%)
Oregon	None	0.40	3.33	22.86	0.67	0.08	(t)

Note: All tax rates as of January 1, 2025; (1) The American Petroleum Institute has developed a methodology for determining the average tax rate on a gallon of fuel. Rates may include any of the following: excise taxes, environmental fees, storage tank fees, other fees or taxes, general sales tax, and local taxes; (2) The federal excise tax of $1.0066 per pack and local taxes are not included; (3) Rates are those applicable to off-premise sales of 40% alcohol by volume (a.b.v.) distilled spirits in 750ml containers. Local excise taxes are excluded; (4) Rates are those applicable to off-premise sales of 11% a.b.v. non-carbonated wine in 750ml containers; (5) Rates are those applicable to off-premise sales of 4.7% a.b.v. beer in 12 ounce containers; (t) 17% excise tax (retail price)
Source: Tax Foundation, 2025 Facts & Figures: How Does Your State Compare?

State Tax Competitiveness Index

State	Overall Rank	Corporate Tax Rank	Individual Income Tax Rank	Sales Tax Rank	Property Tax Rank	Unemployment Insurance Tax Rank
Oregon	30	49	40	4	31	41

Note: The Tax Foundation's State Tax Competitiveness Index enables policymakers, taxpayers, and business leaders to gauge how their states' tax systems compare. A rank of 1 is best, 50 is worst. Rankings do not average to the total. States without a tax rank equally as 1. DC's scores and rankings do not affect other states. The report shows tax systems as of July 1, 2024 (the beginning of Fiscal Year 2025).
Source: Tax Foundation, State Tax Competitiveness Index 2025

TRANSPORTATION

Means of Transportation to Work

Area	Car/Truck/Van		Public Transportation			Bicycle	Walked	Other Means	Worked at Home
	Drove Alone	Car-pooled	Bus	Subway	Railroad				
City	68.4	10.4	1.8	0.0	0.0	1.1	3.0	1.4	14.0
MSA[1]	70.9	11.0	1.1	0.0	0.0	0.7	2.4	1.3	12.6
U.S.	70.2	8.5	1.7	1.3	0.4	0.4	2.4	1.6	13.5

Note: Figures are percentages and cover workers 16 years of age and older; (1) Figures cover the Salem, OR Metropolitan Statistical Area
Source: U.S. Census Bureau, 2019-2023 American Community Survey 5-Year Estimates

Travel Time to Work

Area	Less Than 10 Minutes	10 to 19 Minutes	20 to 29 Minutes	30 to 44 Minutes	45 to 59 Minutes	60 to 89 Minutes	90 Minutes or More
City	14.6	41.5	18.2	12.3	5.5	6.3	1.6
MSA[1]	15.0	32.4	19.8	17.1	7.4	6.5	1.8
U.S.	12.6	28.6	21.2	20.8	8.1	6.0	2.8

Note: Note: Figures are percentages and include workers 16 years old and over; (1) Figures cover the Salem, OR Metropolitan Statistical Area
Source: U.S. Census Bureau, 2019-2023 American Community Survey 5-Year Estimates

Key Congestion Measures

Measure	2000	2010	2015	2020	2022
Annual Hours of Delay, Total (000)	3,677	5,706	6,319	2,541	6,481
Annual Hours of Delay, Per Auto Commuter	31	37	39	15	40
Annual Congestion Cost, Per Auto Commuter ($)	646	802	817	338	886

Note: Figures cover the Salem OR urban area
Source: Texas A&M Transportation Institute, 2023 Urban Mobility Report

Freeway Travel Time Index

Measure	1985	1990	1995	2000	2005	2010	2015	2020	2022
Urban Area Index[1]	1.04	1.10	1.12	1.15	1.19	1.17	1.15	1.05	1.13
Urban Area Rank[1,2]	81	47	57	53	38	41	67	85	71

Note: Freeway Travel Time Index—the ratio of travel time in the peak period to the travel time at free-flow conditions. For example, a value of 1.30 indicates a 20-minute free-flow trip takes 26 minutes in the peak (20 minutes x 1.30 = 26 minutes); (1) Covers the Salem OR urban area; (2) Rank is based on 101 larger urban areas (#1 = highest travel time index)
Source: Texas A&M Transportation Institute, 2023 Urban Mobility Report

Public Transportation

Agency Name / Mode of Transportation	Vehicles Operated in Maximum Service[1]	Annual Unlinked Passenger Trips[2] (in thous.)	Annual Passenger Miles[3] (in thous.)
Salem Area Mass Transit District			
Bus (directly operated)	53	2,762.6	7,138.1
Bus (purchased transportation)	13	85.0	1,164.4
Demand Response (purchased transportation)	31	84.8	501.8
Vanpool (purchased transportation)	53	94.8	2,441.8

Note: (1) Number of revenue vehicles operated by the given mode and type of service to meet the annual maximum service requirement. This is the revenue vehicle count during the peak season of the year; on the week and day that maximum service is provided. Vehicles operated in maximum service (VOMS) exclude atypical days and one-time special events; (2) Number of passengers who boarded public transportation vehicles. Passengers are counted each time they board a vehicle no matter how many vehicles they use to travel from their origin to their destination. (3) Sum of the distances ridden by all passengers during the entire fiscal year.
Source: Federal Transit Administration, National Transit Database, 2023

Air Transportation

Airport Name and Code / Type of Service	Passenger Airlines[1]	Passenger Enplanements	Freight Carriers[2]	Freight (lbs)
Portland International Airport (60 miles) (PDX)				
Domestic service (U.S. carriers only)	24	8,223,580	15	223,047,020
International service (U.S. carriers only)	7	138,121	4	12,619,586

Note: (1) Includes all U.S.-based major, minor and commuter airlines that carried at least one passenger during the year; (2) Includes all U.S.-based airlines and freight carriers that transported at least one pound of freight during the year.
Source: Bureau of Transportation Statistics, The Intermodal Transportation Database, Air Carriers: T-100 Domestic Market (U.S. carriers only), 2024; Bureau of Transportation Statistics, The Intermodal Transportation Database, Air Carriers: T-100 International Market (U.S. carriers only), 2024

BUSINESSES

Major Business Headquarters

Company Name	Industry	Rankings	
		Fortune[1]	Forbes[2]
No companies listed	-	-	-

Note: (1) Companies that produce a 10-K are ranked 1 to 500 based on 2023 revenue; (2) All private companies with at least $2 billion in annual revenue through the end of their most current fiscal year are ranked 1 to 275; companies listed are headquartered in the city; dashes indicate no ranking
Source: Fortune, "Fortune 500," 2024; Forbes, "America's Largest Private Companies," 2024

Fastest-Growing Businesses

According to *Inc.*, Salem is home to one of America's 500 fastest-growing private companies: **DSP Connections** (#172). Criteria: must be an independent, privately-held, for-profit, U.S. corporation, proprietorship or partnership as of December 31, 2023; revenues must be at least $100,000 in 2020 and $2 million in 2023; must have four-year operating/sales history. *Inc., "America's 500 Fastest-Growing Private Companies," 2024*

Living Environment

COST OF LIVING

Cost of Living Index

Composite Index	Groceries	Housing	Utilities	Transportation	Health Care	Misc. Goods/ Services
n/a	n/a	n/a	n/a	n/a	n/a	n/a

Note: The Cost of Living Index measures regional differences in the cost of consumer goods and services, excluding taxes and non-consumer expenditures, for professional and managerial households in the top income quintile. It is based on more than 50,000 prices covering almost 60 different items for which prices are collected three times a year by chambers of commerce, economic development organizations or university applied economic centers in each participating urban area. The numbers shown should be read as a percentage above or below the national average of 100. For example, a value of 115.4 in the groceries column indicates that grocery prices are 15.4% higher than the national average. Small differences in the index numbers should not be interpreted as significant; n/a not available.
Source: The Council for Community and Economic Research, Cost of Living Index, 2024

Grocery Prices

Area[1]	T-Bone Steak ($/pound)	Frying Chicken ($/pound)	Whole Milk ($/half gal.)	Eggs ($/dozen)	Orange Juice ($/64 oz.)	Coffee ($/11.5 oz.)
City[2]	n/a	n/a	n/a	n/a	n/a	n/a
Avg.	15.42	1.55	4.69	3.25	4.41	5.46
Min.	14.50	1.16	4.43	2.75	4.00	4.85
Max.	17.56	2.89	5.49	4.78	5.54	7.89

*Note: (1) Values for the local area are compared with the average, minimum and maximum values for all 276 areas in the Cost of Living Index; (2) Figures cover the Salem OR urban area; n/a not available; **T-Bone Steak** (price per pound); **Frying Chicken** (price per pound, whole fryer); **Whole Milk** (half gallon carton); **Eggs** (price per dozen, Grade A, large); **Orange Juice** (64 oz. Tropicana or Florida Natural); **Coffee** (11.5 oz. can, vacuum-packed, Maxwell House, Hills Bros, or Folgers).*
Source: The Council for Community and Economic Research, Cost of Living Index, 2024

Housing and Utility Costs

Area[1]	New Home Price ($)	Apartment Rent ($/month)	All Electric ($/month)	Part Electric ($/month)	Other Energy ($/month)	Telephone ($/month)
City[2]	n/a	n/a	n/a	n/a	n/a	n/a
Avg.	515,975	1,550	210.99	123.07	82.07	194.99
Min.	265,375	692	104.33	53.68	36.26	179.42
Max.	2,775,821	5,719	529.02	397.28	361.63	223.33

*Note: (1) Values for the local area are compared with the average, minimum and maximum values for all 276 areas in the Cost of Living Index; (2) Figures cover the Salem OR urban area; n/a not available; **New Home Price** (2,400 sf living area, 8,000 sf lot, in urban area with full utilities); **Apartment Rent** (950 sf 2 bedroom/1.5 or 2 bath, unfurnished, excluding all utilities except water); **All Electric** (average monthly cost for an all-electric home); **Part Electric** (average monthly cost for a part-electric home); **Other Energy** (average monthly cost for natural gas, fuel oil, coal, wood, and any other forms of energy except electricity); **Telephone** (price includes the base monthly rate plus taxes and fees for three lines of mobile phone service).*
Source: The Council for Community and Economic Research, Cost of Living Index, 2024

Health Care, Transportation, and Other Costs

Area[1]	Doctor ($/visit)	Dentist ($/visit)	Optometrist ($/visit)	Gasoline ($/gallon)	Beauty Salon ($/visit)	Men's Shirt ($)
City[2]	n/a	n/a	n/a	n/a	n/a	n/a
Avg.	143.77	117.51	129.23	3.32	48.57	38.14
Min.	36.74	58.67	67.33	2.80	24.00	13.41
Max.	270.44	216.82	307.33	5.28	94.00	63.89

*Note: (1) Values for the local area are compared with the average, minimum and maximum values for all 276 areas in the Cost of Living Index; (2) Figures cover the Salem OR urban area; n/a not available; **Doctor** (general practitioners routine exam of an established patient); **Dentist** (adult teeth cleaning and periodic oral examination); **Optometrist** (full vision eye exam for established adult patient); **Gasoline** (one gallon regular unleaded, national brand, including all taxes, cash price at self-service pump if available); **Beauty Salon** (woman's shampoo, trim, and blow-dry); **Men's Shirt** (cotton/polyester dress shirt, pinpoint weave, long sleeves).*
Source: The Council for Community and Economic Research, Cost of Living Index, 2024

HOUSING

Homeownership Rate

Area	2017 (%)	2018 (%)	2019 (%)	2020 (%)	2021 (%)	2022 (%)	2023 (%)	2024 (%)
MSA[1]	n/a	n/a	n/a	n/a	n/a	n/a	n/a	n/a
U.S.	63.9	64.4	64.6	66.6	65.5	65.8	65.9	65.6

Note: (1) Figures cover the Salem, OR Metropolitan Statistical Area; n/a not available
Source: U.S. Census Bureau, Housing Vacancies and Homeownership Annual Statistics: 2017-2024

House Price Index (HPI)

Area	National Ranking[2]	Quarterly Change (%)	One-Year Change (%)	Five-Year Change (%)	Since 1991Q1 (%)
MSA[1]	209	0.85	2.90	48.54	494.72
U.S.[3]	–	1.43	4.51	57.13	327.82

Note: The HPI is a weighted repeat sales index. It measures average price changes in repeat sales or refinancings on the same properties. This information is obtained by reviewing repeat mortgage transactions on single-family properties whose mortgages have been purchased or securitized by Fannie Mae or Freddie Mac since January 1975; (1) Figures cover the Salem, OR Metropolitan Statistical Area; (2) Rankings are based on annual percentage change for all metro areas containing at least 15,000 transactions over the last 10 years and ranges from 1 to 241; (3) figures based on a weighted average of Census Division estimates using a seasonally adjusted, purchase-only index; all figures are for the period ending December 31, 2024
Source: Federal Housing Finance Agency, Change in FHFA Metropolitan Area House Price Indexes, All Transactions Index, 2024Q4

Home Value

Area	Under $100,000	$100,000 -$199,999	$200,000 -$299,999	$300,000 -$399,999	$400,000 -$499,999	$500,000 -$999,999	$1,000,000 or more	Median ($)
City	6.8	5.2	14.1	29.1	22.7	21.4	0.8	382,400
MSA[1]	7.5	5.1	14.2	25.9	20.5	24.2	2.7	389,800
U.S.	12.1	17.8	19.5	14.4	10.5	19.1	6.5	303,400

Note: Figures are percentages except for median and cover owner-occupied housing units; (1) Figures cover the Salem, OR Metropolitan Statistical Area
Source: U.S. Census Bureau, 2019-2023 American Community Survey 5-Year Estimates

Year Housing Structure Built

Area	2020 or Later	2010 -2019	2000 -2009	1990 -1999	1980 -1989	1970 -1979	1960 -1969	1950 -1959	1940 -1949	Before 1940	Median Year
City	1.8	9.1	13.5	15.9	9.5	18.5	9.3	9.3	4.5	8.6	1980
MSA[1]	1.6	8.1	14.1	16.7	9.7	21.1	9.8	7.1	3.9	7.9	1980
U.S.	1.2	8.9	13.6	12.8	13.0	14.4	10.0	9.7	4.5	11.9	1980

Note: Figures are percentages except for Median Year; Note: (1) Figures cover the Salem, OR Metropolitan Statistical Area
Source: U.S. Census Bureau, 2019-2023 American Community Survey 5-Year Estimates

Gross Monthly Rent

Area	Under $500	$500 -$999	$1,000 -$1,499	$1,500 -$1,999	$2,000 -$2,499	$2,500 -$2,999	$3,000 and up	Median ($)
City	5.6	16.1	43.1	24.0	8.2	1.8	1.2	1,323
MSA[1]	4.9	16.5	43.8	24.6	7.3	1.8	1.1	1,324
U.S.	6.5	22.3	29.5	20.2	10.8	4.8	5.9	1,348

Note: Figures are percentages except for median; Gross rent is the contract rent plus the estimated average monthly cost of utilities (electricity, gas, and water and sewer) and fuels (oil, coal, kerosene, wood, etc.) if these are paid by the renter (or paid for the renter by someone else); (1) Figures cover the Salem, OR Metropolitan Statistical Area
Source: U.S. Census Bureau, 2019-2023 American Community Survey 5-Year Estimates

HEALTH

Health Risk Factors

Category	MSA[1] (%)	U.S. (%)
Adults aged 18–64 who have any kind of health care coverage	87.5	90.8
Adults who reported being in good or better health	83.6	81.8
Adults who have been told they have high blood cholesterol	36.6	36.9
Adults who have been told they have high blood pressure	35.4	34.0
Adults who are current smokers	8.5	12.1
Adults who currently use e-cigarettes	7.8	7.7
Adults who currently use chewing tobacco, snuff, or snus	3.4	3.2
Adults who are heavy drinkers[2]	6.3	6.1
Adults who are binge drinkers[3]	13.7	15.2
Adults who are overweight (BMI 25.0 - 29.9)	31.2	34.4
Adults who are obese (BMI 30.0 - 99.8)	42.3	34.3
Adults who participated in any physical activities in the past month	82.6	75.8

Note: All figures are crude prevalence; (1) Figures cover the Salem, OR Metropolitan Statistical Area; (2) Heavy drinkers are classified as adult men having more than 14 drinks per week and adult women having more than 7 drinks per week; (3) Binge drinkers are classified as males having five or more drinks on one occasion or females having four or more drinks on one occasion
Source: Centers for Disease Control and Prevention, Behaviorial Risk Factor Surveillance System, SMART: Selected Metropolitan Area Risk Trends, 2023

Acute and Chronic Health Conditions

Category	MSA[1] (%)	U.S. (%)
Adults who have ever been told they had a heart attack	3.7	4.2
Adults who have ever been told they have angina or coronary heart disease	3.4	4.0
Adults who have ever been told they had a stroke	2.8	3.3
Adults who have ever been told they have asthma	17.5	15.7
Adults who have ever been told they have arthritis	28.4	26.3
Adults who have ever been told they have diabetes[2]	13.6	11.5
Adults who have ever been told they had skin cancer	7.5	5.6
Adults who have ever been told they had any other types of cancer	8.6	8.4
Adults who have ever been told they have COPD	7.7	6.4
Adults who have ever been told they have kidney disease	3.1	3.7
Adults who have ever been told they have a form of depression	27.9	22.0

Note: All figures are crude prevalence; (1) Figures cover the Salem, OR Metropolitan Statistical Area; (2) Figures do not include pregnancy-related, borderline, or pre-diabetes
Source: Centers for Disease Control and Prevention, Behaviorial Risk Factor Surveillance System, SMART: Selected Metropolitan Area Risk Trends, 2023

Health Screening and Vaccination Rates

Category	MSA[1] (%)	U.S. (%)
Adults who have ever been tested for HIV	35.2	37.5
Adults who have had their blood cholesterol checked within the last five years	83.3	87.0
Adults aged 65+ who have had flu shot within the past year	70.6	63.4
Adults aged 65+ who have ever had a pneumonia vaccination	69.2	71.9

Note: All figures are crude prevalence; (1) Figures cover the Salem, OR Metropolitan Statistical Area.
Source: Centers for Disease Control and Prevention, Behaviorial Risk Factor Surveillance System, SMART: Selected Metropolitan Area Risk Trends, 2023

Disability Status

Category	MSA[1] (%)	U.S. (%)
Adults who reported being deaf	7.3	7.4
Are you blind or have serious difficulty seeing, even when wearing glasses?	3.5	4.9
Do you have difficulty doing errands alone?	7.2	7.8
Do you have difficulty dressing or bathing?	3.3	3.6
Do you have serious difficulty concentrating/remembering/making decisions?	14.7	13.7
Do you have serious difficulty walking or climbing stairs?	12.9	13.2

Note: All figures are crude prevalence; (1) Figures cover the Salem, OR Metropolitan Statistical Area.
Source: Centers for Disease Control and Prevention, Behaviorial Risk Factor Surveillance System, SMART: Selected Metropolitan Area Risk Trends, 2023

Mortality Rates for the Top 10 Causes of Death in the U.S.

ICD-10[a] Sub-Chapter	ICD-10[a] Code	Crude Mortality Rate[2] per 100,000 population	
		County[3]	U.S.
Malignant neoplasms	C00-C97	182.5	182.7
Ischaemic heart diseases	I20-I25	77.1	109.6
Provisional assignment of new diseases of uncertain etiology[1]	U00-U49	49.7	65.3
Other forms of heart disease	I30-I51	66.1	65.1
Other degenerative diseases of the nervous system	G30-G31	47.6	52.4
Other external causes of accidental injury	W00-X59	61.2	52.3
Cerebrovascular diseases	I60-I69	55.3	49.1
Chronic lower respiratory diseases	J40-J47	44.8	43.5
Hypertensive diseases	I10-I15	34.1	38.9
Organic, including symptomatic, mental disorders	F01-F09	57.7	33.9

Note: (a) ICD-10 = International Classification of Diseases 10th Revision; (1) Includes COVID-19, adverse effects to COVID-19 vaccines, SARS, and vaping-related disorders; (2) Crude mortality rates are a three-year average covering 2021-2023; (3) Figures cover Marion County.
Source: Centers for Disease Control and Prevention, National Center for Health Statistics. National Vital Statistics System, Mortality 2018-2023 on CDC WONDER Online Database

Mortality Rates for Selected Causes of Death

Cause of Death	ICD-10[a] Code	Crude Mortality Rate[1] per 100,000 population	
		County[2]	U.S.
Accidental poisoning and exposure to noxious substances	X40-X49	29.1	30.5
Alzheimer disease	G30	32.2	35.4
Assault	X85-Y09	4.1	7.3
COVID-19	U07.1	49.7	65.3
Diabetes mellitus	E10-E14	36.4	30.0
Diseases of the liver	K70-K76	25.5	20.8
Human immunodeficiency virus (HIV) disease	B20-B24	Suppressed	1.5
Influenza and pneumonia	J09-J18	9.8	13.4
Intentional self-harm	X60-X84	16.0	14.7
Malnutrition	E40-E46	4.5	6.0
Obesity and other hyperalimentation	E65-E68	3.7	3.1
Renal failure	N17-N19	12.0	16.4
Transport accidents	V01-V99	17.7	14.4

Note: (a) ICD-10 = International Classification of Diseases 10th Revision; (1) Crude mortality rates are a three-year average covering 2021-2023; (2) Figures cover Marion County; Data are suppressed when the data meet the criteria for confidentiality constraints; Crude mortality rates are flagged as unreliable when the rate would be calculated with a numerator of 20 or less.
Source: Centers for Disease Control and Prevention, National Center for Health Statistics. National Vital Statistics System, Mortality 2018-2023 on CDC WONDER Online Database

Health Insurance Coverage

Area	With Health Insurance	With Private Health Insurance	With Public Health Insurance	Without Health Insurance	Population Under Age 19 Without Health Insurance
City	92.6	63.9	41.9	7.4	1.9
MSA[1]	92.0	63.0	42.6	8.0	3.3
U.S.	91.4	67.3	36.3	8.6	5.4

Note: Figures are percentages that cover the civilian noninstitutionalized population; (1) Figures cover the Salem, OR Metropolitan Statistical Area
Source: U.S. Census Bureau, 2019-2023 American Community Survey 5-Year Estimates

Number of Medical Professionals

Area	MDs[3]	DOs[3,4]	Dentists	Podiatrists	Chiropractors	Optometrists
County[1] (number)	624	65	306	23	123	58
County[1] (rate[2])	180.0	18.7	88.3	6.6	35.5	16.7
U.S. (rate[2])	302.5	29.2	74.6	6.4	29.5	18.0

Note: Data as of 2023 unless noted; (1) Data covers Marion County; (2) Number of medical professionals per 100,000 population; (3) Data as of 2022 and includes all active, non-federal physicians; (4) Doctor of Osteopathic Medicine
Source: U.S. Department of Health and Human Services, Health Resources and Services Administration, Bureau of Health Professions, Area Resource File (ARF) 2023-2024

EDUCATION

Public School District Statistics

District Name	Schls	Pupils	Pupil/ Teacher Ratio	Minority Pupils[1] (%)	Total Rev. per Pupil ($)	Total Exp. per Pupil ($)
Salem-Keizer SD 24J	65	38,818	19.2	60.9	18,076	22,282

Note: Table includes school districts with 2,000 or more students; (1) Percentage of students that are not non-Hispanic white.
Source: U.S. Department of Education, National Center for Education Statistics, Common Core of Data, Local Education Agency (School District) Universe Survey: School Year 2023-2024; U.S. Department of Education, National Center for Education Statistics, Common Core of Data, School District Finance Survey (F-33): School Year 2021–22

Highest Level of Education

Area	Less than H.S.	H.S. Diploma	Some College, No Deg.	Associate Degree	Bachelor's Degree	Master's Degree	Prof. School Degree	Doctorate Degree
City	11.3	22.4	25.4	9.3	19.3	8.6	2.1	1.5
MSA[1]	12.8	24.9	25.6	9.8	17.4	6.9	1.6	1.0
U.S.	10.6	26.2	19.4	8.8	21.3	9.8	2.3	1.6

Note: Figures cover persons age 25 and over; (1) Figures cover the Salem, OR Metropolitan Statistical Area
Source: U.S. Census Bureau, 2019-2023 American Community Survey 5-Year Estimates

Educational Attainment by Race

Area	High School Graduate or Higher (%)					Bachelor's Degree or Higher (%)				
	Total	White	Black	Asian	Hisp.[2]	Total	White	Black	Asian	Hisp.[2]
City	88.7	93.5	94.1	86.4	63.7	31.4	35.1	27.7	46.3	12.8
MSA[1]	87.2	92.5	91.1	85.4	62.2	26.9	30.0	28.2	43.5	11.0
U.S.	89.4	92.9	88.1	88.0	72.5	35.0	37.7	24.7	57.0	19.9

Note: Figures shown cover persons 25 years old and over; (1) Figures cover the Salem, OR Metropolitan Statistical Area; (2) People of Hispanic origin can be of any race
Source: U.S. Census Bureau, 2019-2023 American Community Survey 5-Year Estimates

School Enrollment by Grade and Control

Area	Preschool (%)		Kindergarten (%)		Grades 1 - 4 (%)		Grades 5 - 8 (%)		Grades 9 - 12 (%)	
	Public	Private	Public	Private	Public	Private	Public	Private	Public	Private
City	70.2	29.8	88.8	11.2	88.5	11.5	91.6	8.4	97.2	2.8
MSA[1]	59.8	40.2	86.8	13.2	86.0	14.0	90.3	9.7	92.4	7.6
U.S.	58.7	41.3	85.2	14.8	87.2	12.8	87.9	12.1	89.0	11.0

Note: Figures shown cover persons 3 years old and over; (1) Figures cover the Salem, OR Metropolitan Statistical Area
Source: U.S. Census Bureau, 2019-2023 American Community Survey 5-Year Estimates

Higher Education

Four-Year Colleges			Two-Year Colleges			Medical Schools[1]	Law Schools[2]	Voc/ Tech[3]
Public	Private Non-profit	Private For-profit	Public	Private Non-profit	Private For-profit			
2	3	0	0	0	3	0	1	1

Note: Figures cover institutions located within the Salem, OR Metropolitan Statistical Area and include main campuses only; (1) includes schools accredited by the Liaison Committee on Medical Education and the American Osteopathic Association's Commission on Osteopathic College Accreditation; (2) includes ABA-accredited schools, schools with provisional ABA accreditation, and state accredited schools; (3) includes all schools with programs that are less than 2 years.
Source: National Center for Education Statistics, Integrated Postsecondary Education System (IPEDS), 2023-24; Wikipedia, List of Medical Schools in the United States, accessed May 2, 2025; Wikipedia, List of Law Schools in the United States, accessed May 2, 2025

According to *U.S. News & World Report*, the Salem, OR metro area is home to one of the top 100 liberal arts colleges in the U.S.: **Willamette University** (#77 tie). The indicators used to capture academic quality fall into a number of categories: assessment by administrators at peer institutions; retention of students; faculty resources; student selectivity; financial resources; alumni giving; high school counselor ratings of colleges; and graduation rate. *U.S. News & World Report, "America's Best Colleges 2025"*

EMPLOYERS

Major Employers

Company Name	Industry
Chemeketa Community College	Colleges & universities
City of Salem	Municipal government
Kaiser Permanente	Integrated managed care consortium
Liberty Tax Service	Accounting, auditing, & bookkeeping
Marion County	County government
NORPAC Foods	Farm cooperative
Safeway	Grocery stores
Salem Health Laboratories	Laboratory services
Salem Hospital	Health care
Salem-Keizer School District	School districts
Spirit Mountain Casino	Casinos
State Accident Insurance Fund	Insurance
State of Oregon	State government
T-Mobile USA	Telecomunications

Note: Companies shown are located within the Salem, OR Metropolitan Statistical Area.
Source: Chambers of Commerce; State Departments of Labor; Wikipedia

PUBLIC SAFETY

Crime Rate

Area	Total Crime Rate	Violent Crime Rate				Property Crime Rate		
		Murder	Rape	Robbery	Aggrav. Assault	Burglary	Larceny -Theft	Motor Vehicle Theft
City	3,650.5	5.0	15.1	98.7	328.7	384.2	2,312.7	506.0
U.S.	2,290.9	5.7	38.0	66.5	264.1	250.7	1,347.2	318.7

Note: Figures are crimes per 100,000 population.
Source: FBI, Table 8, Offenses Known to Law Enforcement, by State by City, 2023

Hate Crimes

Area	Number of Quarters Reported	Number of Incidents per Bias Motivation					
		Race/Ethnicity/ Ancestry	Religion	Sexual Orientation	Disability	Gender	Gender Identity
City[1]	4	18	0	4	1	0	2
U.S.	4	5,900	2,699	2,077	187	92	492

Note: (1) Figures include at least one incident reported with more than one bias motivation.
Source: Federal Bureau of Investigation, Hate Crime Statistics 2023

Identity Theft Consumer Reports

Area	Reports	Reports per 100,000 Population	Rank[2]
MSA[1]	653	150	263
U.S.	1,135,291	339	-

Note: (1) Figures cover the Salem, OR Metropolitan Statistical Area; (2) Rank ranges from 1 to 401 where 1 indicates greatest number of identity theft reports per 100,000 population
Source: Federal Trade Commission, Consumer Sentinel Network Data Book 2024

Fraud and Other Consumer Reports

Area	Reports	Reports per 100,000 Population	Rank[2]
MSA[1]	3,979	915	256
U.S.	5,360,641	1,601	-

Note: (1) Figures cover the Salem, OR Metropolitan Statistical Area; (2) Rank ranges from 1 to 401 where 1 indicates greatest number of fraud and other consumer reports per 100,000 population
Source: Federal Trade Commission, Consumer Sentinel Network Data Book 2024

POLITICS

2024 Presidential Election Results

Area	Trump (Rep.)	Harris (Dem.)	Stein (Green)	Kennedy (Ind.)	Oliver (Lib.)	Other
Marion County	49.2	47.2	0.6	1.7	0.4	0.9
U.S.	49.7	48.2	0.6	0.5	0.4	0.6

Note: Results are percentages and may not add to 100% due to rounding
Source: Dave Leip's Atlas of U.S. Presidential Elections

SPORTS

Professional Sports Teams

Team Name	League	Year Established

No teams are located in the metro area
Source: Wikipedia, Major Professional Sports Teams of the United States and Canada, May 1, 2025

CLIMATE

Average and Extreme Temperatures

Temperature	Jan	Feb	Mar	Apr	May	Jun	Jul	Aug	Sep	Oct	Nov	Dec	Yr.
Extreme High (°F)	65	72	75	88	100	102	106	108	104	93	72	66	108
Average High (°F)	46	51	55	61	67	74	82	81	76	64	53	47	63
Average Temp. (°F)	39	43	46	50	55	61	66	67	62	53	45	41	52
Average Low (°F)	32	34	36	38	43	48	51	51	47	41	37	34	41
Extreme Low (°F)	-10	-4	12	23	25	32	37	36	26	23	9	-12	-12

Note: Figures cover the years 1948-1990
Source: National Climatic Data Center, International Station Meteorological Climate Summary, 9/96

Average Precipitation/Snowfall/Humidity

Precip./Humidity	Jan	Feb	Mar	Apr	May	Jun	Jul	Aug	Sep	Oct	Nov	Dec	Yr.
Avg. Precip. (in.)	6.5	4.9	4.3	2.4	2.0	1.4	0.5	0.7	1.5	3.3	6.1	6.8	40.2
Avg. Snowfall (in.)	3	1	1	Tr	Tr	0	0	0	0	Tr	Tr	2	7
Avg. Rel. Hum. 7am (%)	87	89	89	85	81	77	75	79	86	92	90	89	85
Avg. Rel. Hum. 4pm (%)	76	70	62	56	53	50	40	40	45	61	76	81	59

Note: Figures cover the years 1948-1990; Tr = Trace amounts (<0.05 in. of rain; <0.5 in. of snow)
Source: National Climatic Data Center, International Station Meteorological Climate Summary, 9/96

Weather Conditions

Temperature			Daytime Sky			Precipitation		
5°F & below	32°F & below	90°F & above	Clear	Partly cloudy	Cloudy	0.01 inch or more precip.	0.1 inch or more snow/ice	Thunder-storms
< 1	66	16	78	118	169	146	6	5

Note: Figures are average number of days per year and cover the years 1948-1990
Source: National Climatic Data Center, International Station Meteorological Climate Summary, 9/96

HAZARDOUS WASTE

Superfund Sites

The Salem, OR metro area has no sites on the EPA's Superfund Final National Priorities List (NPL) or Superfund Alternative Approach (SAA) list. The Superfund alternative approach uses the same investigation and cleanup process and standards that are used for sites listed on the National Priorities List. The SAA is an alternative to listing a site on the NPL; it is not an alternative to Superfund or the Superfund process. There are a total of 1,445 Superfund sites with a status of proposed or final on both lists in the United States. *U.S. Environmental Protection Agency, National Priorities List, May 1, 2025; U.S. Environmental Protection Agency, Superfund Alternative Approach Sites, May 1, 2025*

AIR QUALITY

Air Quality Trends: Ozone

	1990	1995	2000	2005	2010	2015	2020	2021	2022	2023
MSA[1]	n/a	n/a	n/a	n/a	n/a	n/a	n/a	n/a	n/a	n/a
U.S.	0.087	0.089	0.081	0.080	0.072	0.068	0.066	0.067	0.067	0.070

Note: (1) Data covers the Salem, OR Metropolitan Statistical Area; n/a not available. The values shown are the composite ozone concentration averages among trend sites based on the highest fourth daily maximum 8-hour concentration in parts per million. These trends are based on sites having an adequate record of monitoring data during the trend period. Data from exceptional events are included.
Source: U.S. Environmental Protection Agency, Air Quality Monitoring Information, "Air Quality Trends by City, 1990-2023"

Air Quality Index

Area	Percent of Days when Air Quality was...[2]					AQI Statistics[2]	
	Good	Moderate	Unhealthy for Sensitive Groups	Unhealthy	Very Unhealthy	Maximum	Median
MSA[1]	73.4	25.5	1.1	0.0	0.0	128	38

Note: (1) Data covers the Salem, OR Metropolitan Statistical Area; (2) Based on 365 days with AQI data in 2023. Air Quality Index (AQI) is an index for reporting daily air quality. EPA calculates the AQI for five major air pollutants regulated by the Clean Air Act: ground-level ozone, particle pollution (aka particulate matter), carbon monoxide, sulfur dioxide, and nitrogen dioxide. The AQI runs from 0 to 500. The higher the AQI value, the greater the level of air pollution and the greater the health concern. There are six AQI categories: "Good" AQI is between 0 and 50. Air quality is considered satisfactory; "Moderate" AQI is between 51 and 100. Air quality is acceptable; "Unhealthy for Sensitive Groups" When AQI values are between 101 and 150, members of sensitive groups may experience health effects; "Unhealthy" When AQI values are between 151 and 200 everyone may begin to experience health effects; "Very Unhealthy" AQI values between 201 and 300 trigger a health alert; "Hazardous" AQI values over 300 trigger warnings of emergency conditions (not shown).
Source: U.S. Environmental Protection Agency, Air Quality Index Report, 2023

Air Quality Index Pollutants

Area	Percent of Days when AQI Pollutant was...[2]					
	Carbon Monoxide	Nitrogen Dioxide	Ozone	Sulfur Dioxide	Particulate Matter 2.5	Particulate Matter 10
MSA[1]	0.0	0.0	35.6	(3)	64.4	0.0

Note: (1) Data covers the Salem, OR Metropolitan Statistical Area; (2) Based on 365 days with AQI data in 2023. The Air Quality Index (AQI) is an index for reporting daily air quality. EPA calculates the AQI for five major air pollutants regulated by the Clean Air Act: ground-level ozone, particle pollution (also known as particulate matter), carbon monoxide, sulfur dioxide, and nitrogen dioxide. The AQI runs from 0 to 500. The higher the AQI value, the greater the level of air pollution and the greater the health concern; (3) Sulfur dioxide is no longer included in this table because SO_2 concentrations tend to be very localized and not necessarily representative of broad geographical areas like counties and CBSAs.
Source: U.S. Environmental Protection Agency, Air Quality Index Report, 2023

Maximum Air Pollutant Concentrations: Particulate Matter, Ozone, CO and Lead

	Particulate Matter 10 (ug/m³)	Particulate Matter 2.5 Wtd AM (ug/m³)	Particulate Matter 2.5 24-Hr (ug/m³)	Ozone (ppm)	Carbon Monoxide (ppm)	Lead (ug/m³)
MSA[1] Level	n/a	n/a	n/a	0.064	n/a	n/a
NAAQS[2]	150	15	35	0.075	9	0.15
Met NAAQS[2]	n/a	n/a	n/a	Yes	n/a	n/a

Note: (1) Data covers the Salem, OR Metropolitan Statistical Area; Data from exceptional events are included; (2) National Ambient Air Quality Standards; ppm = parts per million; ug/m³ = micrograms per cubic meter; n/a not available.
Concentrations: Particulate Matter 10 (coarse particulate)—highest second maximum 24-hour concentration; Particulate Matter 2.5 Wtd AM (fine particulate)—highest weighted annual mean concentration; Particulate Matter 2.5 24-Hour (fine particulate)—highest 98th percentile 24-hour concentration; Ozone—highest fourth daily maximum 8-hour concentration; Carbon Monoxide—highest second maximum non-overlapping 8-hour concentration; Lead—maximum running 3-month average
Source: U.S. Environmental Protection Agency, Air Quality Monitoring Information, "Air Quality Statistics by City, 2023"

Maximum Air Pollutant Concentrations: Nitrogen Dioxide and Sulfur Dioxide

	Nitrogen Dioxide AM (ppb)	Nitrogen Dioxide 1-Hr (ppb)	Sulfur Dioxide AM (ppb)	Sulfur Dioxide 1-Hr (ppb)	Sulfur Dioxide 24-Hr (ppb)
MSA[1] Level	n/a	n/a	n/a	n/a	n/a
NAAQS[2]	53	100	30	75	140
Met NAAQS[2]	n/a	n/a	n/a	n/a	n/a

Note: (1) Data covers the Salem, OR Metropolitan Statistical Area; Data from exceptional events are included; (2) National Ambient Air Quality Standards; ppm = parts per million; ug/m³ = micrograms per cubic meter; n/a not available.

Concentrations: Nitrogen Dioxide AM—highest arithmetic mean concentration; Nitrogen Dioxide 1-Hr—highest 98th percentile 1-hour daily maximum concentration; Sulfur Dioxide AM—highest annual mean concentration; Sulfur Dioxide 1-Hr—highest 99th percentile 1-hour daily maximum concentration; Sulfur Dioxide 24-Hr—highest second maximum 24-hour concentration

Source: U.S. Environmental Protection Agency, Air Quality Monitoring Information, "Air Quality Statistics by City, 2023"

Salt Lake City, Utah

Background

Salt Lake City, Utah's largest city and state capital, is known for its Church of Jesus Christ of Latter-day Saints (Mormon) origins. The city was founded by Brigham Young on July 24, 1847, as a place of refuge from mainstream ostracism for the Mormon's polygamous lifestyle.

Brigham Young led his people to a place where they could exercise their form of worship in peace. The site that was to be called Salt Lake City was breathtaking, bordered on the east and southwest by the dramatic peaks of the Wasatch Range, and on the northwest by the Great Salt Lake.

The land was too dry and hard for traditional farming, but Mormon industry diverted the flow of mountain streams to irrigate the land, and the valley turned into a prosperous agricultural region. More than 10 years after its incorporation as a city, the U.S. government was still suspicious of its Mormon residents. Fort Douglas, founded in 1862 and manned by federal troops, kept an eye on the Mormons and their polygamous practices. In 1869, the completion of the Transcontinental Railroad brought mining, industry, and other non-Mormon interests to Salt Lake City. As for polygamy, the Mormon Church made it illegal in 1890.

While mining played a major role in the early development of Salt Lake City, major industry sectors today include construction, trade, transportation, communications, finance, insurance, and real estate. The University of Utah Research Park, also known at Bionic Valley, is on the campus of the University of Utah in city university and houses 48 companies, 18 university departments, and employs more than 14,000. Updates to Research Park are ongoing, including additional student housing, research innovation hub and additional locations for businesses.

Top employers in the city include O.C. Tanner, America First Credit Union, HealthEquity, and Fidelity Investments.

Major efforts to revitalize the downtown area have included the $1 billion, 20-acre City Creek Center with residences, offices, and a mall; Salt Lake City Redevelopment Agency renovated retail space that is part of the Utah Theater, a former 1918 vaudeville theater on Main Street; Utah Performing Arts Center cost $116 million and holds 2,500 patrons.

The Utah Pride Festival is held in June each year. Since 1983, it has grown dramatically to a three-day festival with attendance over 20,000 and is one of the largest festivals in the country comprising hundreds of vendors, food, musical performers, a 5k run, a dyke and trans march, as well as an interfaith service by the Utah Pride Interfaith Coalition.

Redevelopment at Salt Lake City International Airport is ongoing. Ten new gates are schedule to open at the end of 2025 and 11 more in 2026 to be followed by a dozen new restaurants and shops. The airport's Central Tunnel includes an art installation called The River Tunnel.

Salt Lake City was designated as a Silver-level Bicycle Friendly Community in 2010 by the League of American Bicyclists. Many streets in the city have bike lanes, and the city has published a bicycle map.

The NBA's Utah Jazz plays at the Delta Center. The city is also home to Real Salt Lake of Major League Soccer.

The nearby mountain ranges and the Great Salt Lake greatly influence climatic conditions. Temperatures are moderated by the lake in winter, and storm activity is enhanced by both the lake and the mountains. Salt Lake City has a semi-arid continental climate with four well-defined seasons. Summers are hot and dry, while winters are cold, but not severe due to the mountains to the north and east that barricade the cold air. Periods of heavy fog can develop in winter and persist for several days.

Rankings

Business/Finance Rankings

- According to *Business Insider*, the Salt Lake City metro area is a prime place to run a startup or move an existing business to. The area ranked #19. More than 300 metro areas were analyzed for factors that were of top concern to new business owners. Data was based on the 2019 U.S. Census Bureau American Community Survey, statistics from the CDC, and University of Chicago analysis. Criteria: business formations; percentage of vaccinated population; percentage of households with internet subscriptions; median household income; and share of work that can be done from home. *BusinessInsider.com, "The 20 Best Cities for Starting a Business in 2022 Include Denver, Raleigh, and Olympia," June 7, 2022*

- The Salt Lake City metro area appeared on the Milken Institute "2025 Best Performing Cities" list. Rank: #3 out of 200 large metro areas (based on performance category). Criteria: job growth; wage growth; high-tech growth and impact; community resilience; housing affordability; household broadband access. *Milken Institute, "Best-Performing Cities 2025," January 14, 2025*

Culture/Performing Arts Rankings

- Salt Lake City was selected as one of the 25 best cities for moviemakers in North America. Great film cities are places where filmmaking dreams can come true, that offer more creative space, lower costs, and great outdoor locations. NYC & LA were intentionally excluded. Criteria: film industry presence and culture; tax incentives; affordability; and proximity of festivals and schools. The city was ranked #22. *MovieMaker Magazine, "Best Places to Live and Work as a Moviemaker, 2025," January 29, 2025*

Education Rankings

- Personal finance website *WalletHub* analyzed the 150 largest U.S. metropolitan statistical areas to determine where the most educated Americans are putting their degrees to work. Criteria: education levels; percentage of workers with degrees; education quality and attainment gap; public school quality rankings; quality and enrollment of each metro area's universities. Salt Lake City was ranked #35 (#1 = most educated city). *WalletHub.com, "Most & Least Educated Cities in America, 2025" July 2, 2024*

Environmental Rankings

- Sperling's *BestPlaces* assessed the 50 largest metropolitan areas of the United States for the likelihood of dangerously extreme weather events or earthquakes. In general the Southeast and South-Central regions have the highest risk of weather extremes and earthquakes, while the Pacific Northwest enjoys the lowest risk. Of the least risky metropolitan areas, the Salt Lake City metro area was ranked #2. *Bestplaces.net, "Avoid Natural Disasters: BestPlaces Reveals The Top 10 Safest Places to Live," October 25, 2017*

- The U.S. Environmental Protection Agency (EPA) released its list of mid-size U.S. metropolitan areas with the most ENERGY STAR certified buildings in 2023. The Salt Lake City metro area was ranked #10 out of 10. *U.S. Environmental Protection Agency, "2024 Energy Star Top Cities," May 22, 2024*

- Salt Lake City was highlighted as one of the 25 most ozone-polluted metro areas in the U.S. during 2021 through 2023. The area ranked #9. *American Lung Association, "State of the Air 2025," April 23, 2025*

- Salt Lake City was highlighted as one of the 25 metro areas most polluted by short-term particle pollution (24-hour PM 2.5) in the U.S. during 2021 through 2023. The area ranked #25. *American Lung Association, "State of the Air 2025," April 23, 2025*

Health/Fitness Rankings

- Salt Lake City was identified as a "2025 Allergy Capital." The area ranked #99 out of the nation's 100 largest metropolitan areas. Three groups of factors were used to identify the most challenging cities for people with allergies: annual tree, grass, and weed pollen scores; over the counter allergy medicine use; number of board-certified allergy specialists. *Asthma and Allergy Foundation of America, "2025 Allergy Capitals: The Most Challenging Places to Live with Allergies," March 18, 2025*

- Salt Lake City was identified as a "2024 Asthma Capital." The area ranked #86 out of the nation's 100 largest metropolitan areas. Criteria: estimated asthma prevalence; asthma-related mortality; and ER visits due to asthma. Risk factors analyzed but not factored in the rankings: annual air quality including pollution and ozone levels; public smoking laws; indoor air quality; access to asthma specialists; rescue and controller medication use; uninsured rate; pollen allergy; poverty rate. *Asthma and Allergy Foundation of America, "Asthma Capitals 2024: The Most Challenging Places to Live With Asthma," September 10, 2024*

Pet Rankings

- Salt Lake City was selected by *Sniffspot.com* as one of the most dog-friendly cities in the U.S., ranking #22 out of 50. Criteria: dog parks; hiking; sniffspots; public parks; dog-friendly businesses; housing; dog waste cleanliness; leash laws; dog services; and overall cost. *Sniffspot.com, "The Top 50 Most Dog-Friendly Cities in the U.S.," September 30, 2024*

Real Estate Rankings

- *WalletHub* compared the most populated U.S. cities to determine which had the best markets for real estate agents. Salt Lake City ranked #4 where demand was high and pay was the best. Criteria: sales per agent; annual median wage for real-estate agents; monthly average starting salary for real estate agents; real estate job density and competition; unemployment rate; home turnover rate; housing-market health index; and other relevant metrics. *WalletHub.com, "2021 Best Places to Be a Real Estate Agent," May 12, 2021*

- The Salt Lake City metro area was identified as one of the 10 worst condo markets in the U.S. in 2024. The area ranked #58 out of 63 markets. Criteria: year-over-year change of median sales price of existing apartment condo-coop homes between the 4th quarter of 2023 and the 4th quarter of 2024. *National Association of Realtors®, Median Sales Price of Existing Apartment Condo-Coops Homes for Metropolitan Areas, 4th Quarter 2024*

- Salt Lake City was ranked #145 out of 176 metro areas in terms of cost of housing in 2024 by the National Association of Home Builders (#1 = most affordable). Criteria: the portion of an average family's income necessary to pay the mortgage on a median-priced home. *National Association of Home Builders®, NAHB-Wells Fargo Cost of Housing Index, 4th Quarter 2024*

Safety Rankings

- Statistics drawn from the FBI's Uniform Crime Report were used to rank the cities where violent crime rose the most year over year from 2019 to 2020. Only cities with 25,000 or more residents were included. *24/7 Wall St.* found that Salt Lake City placed #26 of those with a notable surge in incidents of violent crime. *247wallst.com, "American Cities Where Crime Is Soaring," March 4, 2022*

- Allstate ranked the 100 most populous cities in America in terms of driver safety. Salt Lake City ranked #34. Criteria based on anonymized driving behavior data from Allstate's mobile app powered by Arity: high speed driving (over 80 mph), phone handling, and hard braking. The report helps increase the importance of safety and awareness behind the wheel. *Allstate, "16th Allstate America's Best Drivers Report®" July 11, 2024*

- Salt Lake City was identified as one of the most dangerous cities in America by NeighborhoodScout. The city ranked #78 out of 100 (#1 = most dangerous). Criteria: number of violent crimes per 1,000 residents. The editors evaluated cities with 25,000 or more residents. *NeighborhoodScout.com, "2023 Top 100 Most Dangerous Cities in the U.S.," January 12, 2023*

Women/Minorities Rankings

- Personal finance website *WalletHub* compared more than 180 U.S. cities across two key dimensions, "Hispanic Business-Friendliness" and "Hispanic Purchasing Power," to arrive at the most favorable conditions for Hispanic entrepreneurs. Salt Lake City was ranked #72 out of 182. Criteria includes: share of Hispanic-Owned Businesses; average growth of Hispanic Business revenues; Small Business-Friendliness score; affordability; and number of Hispanics with at least a bachelor's degree. *WalletHub.com, "Best Cities for Hispanic Entrepreneurs," September 4, 2024*

Miscellaneous Rankings

- *MoveHub* ranked 446 hipster cities across 20 countries, using its new and improved alternative Hipster Index and Salt Lake City came out as #3 among the top 50. Criteria: population over 150,000; number of vintage boutiques; density of tattoo parlors; vegan places to eat; coffee shops; and density of vinyl record stores. *MoveHub.com, "The Hipster Index: Brighton Pips Portland to Global Top Spot," July 28, 2021*

- *WalletHub* compared 148 of the most populated U.S. cities to determine their operating efficiency. A "Quality of Services" score was constructed for each city and then measured against the total budget per capita to reveal which were managed the best. Salt Lake City ranked #130. Criteria: financial stability; economy; education; safety; health; infrastructure and pollution. *WalletHub.com, "2025's Best- & Worst-Run Cities in America," June 18, 2024*

Business Environment

DEMOGRAPHICS

Population Growth

Area	1990 Census	2000 Census	2010 Census	2020 Census	2023 Estimate[2]	Population Growth 1990-2023 (%)
City	159,796	181,743	186,440	199,723	203,888	27.6
MSA[1]	768,075	968,858	1,124,197	1,257,936	1,261,337	64.2
U.S.	248,709,873	281,421,906	308,745,538	331,449,281	332,387,540	33.6

Note: (1) Figures cover the Salt Lake City-Murray, UT Metropolitan Statistical Area; (2) 2019-2023 5-year ACS population estimate
Source: U.S. Census Bureau, 1990 Census, 2000 Census, 2010 Census, 2020 Census, 2019-2023 American Community Survey 5-Year Estimates

Race

Area	White Alone[2] (%)	Black Alone[2] (%)	Asian Alone[2] (%)	AIAN[3] Alone[2] (%)	NHOPI[4] Alone[2] (%)	Other Race Alone[2] (%)	Two or More Races (%)
City	70.5	2.7	5.4	1.2	1.4	9.2	9.6
MSA[1]	73.6	1.7	3.9	0.9	1.5	8.7	9.6
U.S.	63.4	12.4	5.8	0.9	0.2	6.6	10.7

Note: (1) Figures cover the Salt Lake City-Murray, UT Metropolitan Statistical Area; (2) Alone is defined as not being in combination with one or more other races; (3) American Indian and Alaska Native; (4) Native Hawaiian and Other Pacific Islander
Source: U.S. Census Bureau, 2019-2023 American Community Survey 5-Year Estimates

Hispanic or Latino Origin

Area	Total (%)	Mexican (%)	Puerto Rican (%)	Cuban (%)	Other (%)
City	20.8	15.2	0.5	0.3	4.8
MSA[1]	19.6	13.7	0.4	0.1	5.3
U.S.	19.0	11.3	1.8	0.7	5.2

Note: Persons of Hispanic or Latino origin can be of any race; (1) Figures cover the Salt Lake City-Murray, UT Metropolitan Statistical Area
Source: U.S. Census Bureau, 2019-2023 American Community Survey 5-Year Estimates

Age

Area	Percent of Population									Median Age
	Under Age 5	Age 5–19	Age 20–34	Age 35–44	Age 45–54	Age 55–64	Age 65–74	Age 75–84	Age 85+	
City	4.9	15.8	32.5	14.0	10.9	9.6	7.5	3.3	1.3	33.0
MSA[1]	6.6	22.3	23.3	14.9	11.7	9.9	7.2	3.1	1.2	33.7
U.S.	5.7	19.1	20.2	13.1	12.3	12.8	10.0	4.9	1.9	38.7

Note: (1) Figures cover the Salt Lake City-Murray, UT Metropolitan Statistical Area
Source: U.S. Census Bureau, 2019-2023 American Community Survey 5-Year Estimates

Disability by Age

Area	All Ages	Under 18 Years Old	18 to 64 Years Old	65 Years and Over
City	12.1	5.0	9.9	34.9
MSA[1]	10.2	4.4	9.1	29.8
U.S.	13.0	4.7	10.7	32.9

Note: Figures show percent of the civilian noninstitutionalized population that reported having a disability. Disability status is determined from six types of difficulty: vision, hearing, cognitive, ambulatory, self-care, and independent living. For children under 5 years old, hearing and vision difficulty are used to determine disability status. For children between the ages of 5 and 14, disability status is determined from hearing, vision, cognitive, ambulatory, and self-care difficulties. For people aged 15 years and older, they are considered to have a disability if they have difficulty with any one of the six difficulty types; Note: (1) Figures cover the Salt Lake City-Murray, UT Metropolitan Statistical Area
Source: U.S. Census Bureau, 2019-2023 American Community Survey 5-Year Estimates

Ancestry

Area	German	Irish	English	American	Italian	Polish	French[2]	European	Scottish
City	11.5	7.7	19.4	3.1	4.0	1.4	2.1	3.0	3.4
MSA[1]	9.9	6.1	23.6	3.8	3.0	0.9	1.7	3.3	3.6
U.S.	12.6	9.4	9.1	5.5	4.9	2.6	2.0	1.6	1.6

Note: Figures are the percentage of the total population reporting a particular ancestry. The nine most commonly reported ancestries in the U.S. are shown. Figures include multiple ancestries (e.g. if a person reported being Irish and Italian, they were included in both columns); (1) Figures cover the Salt Lake City-Murray, UT Metropolitan Statistical Area; (2) Excludes Basque
Source: U.S. Census Bureau, 2019-2023 American Community Survey 5-Year Estimates

Foreign-born Population

Area	Any Foreign Country	Asia	Mexico	Europe	Caribbean	Central America[2]	South America	Africa	Canada
					Percent of Population Born in				
City	15.4	4.2	5.1	1.8	0.2	0.7	1.4	1.0	0.3
MSA[1]	12.4	3.0	4.2	1.2	0.1	0.6	1.9	0.6	0.2
U.S.	13.9	4.3	3.3	1.4	1.4	1.2	1.2	0.8	0.2

Note: (1) Figures cover the Salt Lake City-Murray, UT Metropolitan Statistical Area; (2) Excludes Mexico.
Source: U.S. Census Bureau, 2019-2023 American Community Survey 5-Year Estimates

Household Size

Area	One	Two	Three	Four	Five	Six	Seven or More	Average Household Size
	Persons in Household (%)							
City	39.3	34.1	11.6	8.2	3.8	1.8	1.3	2.19
MSA[1]	24.0	31.1	15.7	13.9	7.9	4.4	3.0	2.83
U.S.	28.5	33.8	15.4	12.7	5.9	2.3	1.4	2.54

Note: (1) Figures cover the Salt Lake City-Murray, UT Metropolitan Statistical Area
Source: U.S. Census Bureau, 2019-2023 American Community Survey 5-Year Estimates

Household Relationships

Area	House-holder	Opposite-sex Spouse	Same-sex Spouse	Opposite-sex Unmarried Partner	Same-sex Unmarried Partner	Child[2]	Grand-child	Other Relatives	Non-relatives
City	42.3	13.9	0.5	3.4	0.4	22.1	1.7	4.2	7.6
MSA[1]	34.0	17.4	0.3	2.1	0.2	32.4	2.5	5.3	4.4
U.S.	38.3	17.5	0.2	2.5	0.2	28.3	2.4	4.8	3.4

Note: Figures are percent of the total population; (1) Figures cover the Salt Lake City-Murray, UT Metropolitan Statistical Area; (2) Includes biological, adopted, and stepchildren of the householder
Source: U.S. Census Bureau, 2020 Census

Gender

Area	Males	Females	Males per 100 Females
City	105,049	98,839	106.3
MSA[1]	637,671	623,666	102.2
U.S.	164,545,087	167,842,453	98.0

Note: (1) Figures cover the Salt Lake City-Murray, UT Metropolitan Statistical Area
Source: U.S. Census Bureau, 2019-2023 American Community Survey 5-Year Estimates

Marital Status

Area	Never Married	Now Married[2]	Separated	Widowed	Divorced
City	45.4	39.1	1.6	2.9	10.9
MSA[1]	33.6	51.2	1.5	3.6	10.2
U.S.	34.1	47.9	1.7	5.6	10.7

Note: Figures are percentages and cover the population 15 years of age and older; (1) Figures cover the Salt Lake City-Murray, UT Metropolitan Statistical Area; (2) Excludes separated
Source: U.S. Census Bureau, 2019-2023 American Community Survey 5-Year Estimates

Religious Groups by Family

Area	Catholic	Baptist	Methodist	LDS[2]	Pentecostal	Lutheran	Islam	Adventist	Other
MSA[1]	9.0	0.6	0.2	52.0	0.7	0.2	1.6	0.7	2.6
U.S.	18.7	7.3	3.0	2.0	1.8	1.7	1.3	1.3	11.6

Note: Figures are the number of adherents as a percentage of the total population and cover the eight largest religious groups in the U.S; (1) Figures cover the Salt Lake City-Murray, UT Metropolitan Statistical Area; (2) Church of Jesus Christ of Latter-day Saints
Sources: 2020 U.S. Religion Census, Association of Statisticians of American Religious Bodies; The Association of Religion Data Archives (ARDA)

Religious Groups by Tradition

Area	Catholic	Evangelical Protestant	Mainline Protestant	Black Protestant	Islam	Judaism	Hinduism	Orthodox	Buddhism
MSA[1]	9.0	2.4	0.7	0.1	1.6	0.1	0.3	0.4	0.3
U.S.	18.7	16.5	5.2	2.3	1.3	0.6	0.4	0.4	0.3

Note: Figures are the number of adherents as a percentage of the total population; (1) Figures cover the Salt Lake City-Murray, UT Metropolitan Statistical Area
Sources: 2020 U.S. Religion Census, Association of Statisticians of American Religious Bodies; The Association of Religion Data Archives (ARDA)

ECONOMY

Real Gross Domestic Product (GDP)

Area	2017	2018	2019	2020	2021	2022	2023	Rank[3]
MSA[1]	92.0	97.2	103.0	102.5	111.3	114.3	118.0	37
U.S.[2]	17,619.1	18,160.7	18,642.5	18,238.9	19,387.6	19,896.6	20,436.3	–

Note: Figures are in billions of chained 2017 dollars; (1) Figures cover the Salt Lake City-Murray, UT Metropolitan Statistical Area; (2) Figures cover real GDP within metropolitan areas; (3) Rank is based on 2023 data and ranges from 1 to 384
Source: U.S. Bureau of Economic Analysis

Economic Growth

Area	2014	2015	2016	2017	2018	2019	2020	2021	2022	2023
MSA[1]	3.2	3.4	4.7	5.2	5.7	6.0	-0.5	8.6	2.7	3.2
U.S.[2]	2.6	3.2	2.0	2.7	3.1	2.7	-2.2	6.3	2.6	2.7

Note: Figures are real gross domestic product growth rates and represent percent change from preceding period; (1) Figures cover the Salt Lake City-Murray, UT Metropolitan Statistical Area; (2) Figures are the average growth rates within metropolitan areas
Source: U.S. Bureau of Economic Analysis

Metropolitan Area Exports

Area	2018	2019	2020	2021	2022	2023	Rank[2]
MSA[1]	9,748.6	13,273.9	13,565.5	13,469.1	12,340.1	12,775.2	32
U.S.	1,664,056.1	1,645,173.7	1,431,406.6	1,753,941.4	2,062,937.4	2,019,160.5	–

Note: Figures are in millions of dollars; (1) Figures cover the Salt Lake City-Murray, UT Metropolitan Statistical Area; (2) Rank is based on 2023 data and ranges from 1 to 386
Source: U.S. Department of Commerce, International Trade Administration, Office of Trade and Economic Analysis, Industry and Analysis, Exports by Metropolitan Area, data extracted April 2, 2025

Building Permits

Area	Single-Family			Multi-Family			Total		
	2023	2024	Pct. Chg.	2023	2024	Pct. Chg.	2023	2024	Pct. Chg.
City	243	397	63.4	2,929	886	-69.8	3,172	1,283	-59.6
MSA[1]	3,163	3,525	11.4	6,072	1,922	-68.3	9,235	5,447	-41.0
U.S.	920,000	981,900	6.7	591,100	496,100	-16.1	1,511,100	1,478,000	-2.2

Note: (1) Figures cover the Salt Lake City-Murray, UT Metropolitan Statistical Area; Figures represent new, privately-owned housing units authorized (unadjusted data)
Source: U.S. Census Bureau, Building Permits Survey (BPS), 2023, 2024

Bankruptcy Filings

Area	Business Filings			Nonbusiness Filings		
	2023	2024	% Chg.	2023	2024	% Chg.
Salt Lake County	58	58	0.0	2,508	2,763	10.2
U.S.	18,926	23,107	22.1	434,064	494,201	13.9

Note: Business filings include Chapter 7, Chapter 9, Chapter 11, Chapter 12, Chapter 13, Chapter 15, and Section 304; Nonbusiness filings include Chapter 7, Chapter 11, and Chapter 13
Source: Administrative Office of the U.S. Courts, Business and Nonbusiness Bankruptcy, County Cases Commenced by Chapter of the Bankruptcy Code, During the 12-Month Period Ending December 31, 2023 and Business and Nonbusiness Bankruptcy, County Cases Commenced by Chapter of the Bankruptcy Code, During the 12-Month Period Ending December 31, 2024

Housing Vacancy Rates

Area	Gross Vacancy Rate[3] (%)			Year-Round Vacancy Rate[4] (%)			Rental Vacancy Rate[5] (%)			Homeowner Vacancy Rate[6] (%)		
	2022	2023	2024	2022	2023	2024	2022	2023	2024	2022	2023	2024
MSA[1]	5.1	6.1	10.1	4.5	5.0	5.8	4.6	6.2	6.1	0.6	0.6	0.7
U.S.[2]	9.1	9.0	9.1	7.5	7.5	7.6	5.7	6.5	6.8	0.8	0.8	1.0

Note: (1) Figures cover the Salt Lake City-Murray, UT Metropolitan Statistical Area; (2) Figures cover the 75 largest Metropolitan Statistical Areas; (3) The percentage of the total housing inventory that is vacant; (4) The percentage of the housing inventory (excluding seasonal units) that is year-round vacant; (5) The percentage of rental inventory that is vacant for rent; (6) The percentage of homeowner inventory that is vacant for sale
Source: U.S. Census Bureau, Housing Vacancies and Homeownership Annual Statistics: 2022, 2023, 2024

INCOME

Income

Area	Per Capita ($)	Median Household ($)	Average Household ($)
City	49,642	74,925	111,189
MSA[1]	43,026	95,045	121,478
U.S.	43,289	78,538	110,491

Note: (1) Figures cover the Salt Lake City-Murray, UT Metropolitan Statistical Area
Source: U.S. Census Bureau, 2019-2023 American Community Survey 5-Year Estimates

Household Income Distribution

Area	Percent of Households Earning							
	Under $15,000	$15,000 -$24,999	$25,000 -$34,999	$35,000 -$49,999	$50,000 -$74,999	$75,000 -$99,999	$100,000 -$149,999	$150,000 and up
City	9.0	6.7	6.5	11.1	16.8	13.5	15.9	20.5
MSA[1]	5.3	4.0	4.7	8.8	15.3	14.6	21.5	25.8
U.S.	8.5	6.6	6.8	10.4	15.7	12.7	17.4	21.9

Note: (1) Figures cover the Salt Lake City-Murray, UT Metropolitan Statistical Area
Source: U.S. Census Bureau, 2019-2023 American Community Survey 5-Year Estimates

Poverty Rate

Area	All Ages	Under 18 Years Old	18 to 64 Years Old	65 Years and Over
City	13.4	12.3	14.1	11.0
MSA[1]	8.1	8.8	8.0	7.5
U.S.	12.4	16.3	11.6	10.4

Note: Figures are percentage of people whose income during the past 12 months was below the poverty level;
(1) Figures cover the Salt Lake City-Murray, UT Metropolitan Statistical Area
Source: U.S. Census Bureau, 2019-2023 American Community Survey 5-Year Estimates

EMPLOYMENT

Labor Force and Employment

Area	Civilian Labor Force			Workers Employed		
	Dec. 2023	Dec. 2024	% Chg.	Dec. 2023	Dec. 2024	% Chg.
City	128,957	131,406	1.9	125,261	127,540	1.8
MSA[1]	738,638	754,401	2.1	719,094	732,202	1.8
U.S.	166,661,000	167,746,000	0.7	160,754,000	161,294,000	0.3

Note: Data is not seasonally adjusted and covers workers 16 years of age and older; (1) Figures cover the Salt Lake City-Murray, UT Metropolitan Statistical Area
Source: Bureau of Labor Statistics, Local Area Unemployment Statistics

Unemployment Rate

Area	2024											
	Jan.	Feb.	Mar.	Apr.	May	Jun.	Jul.	Aug.	Sep.	Oct.	Nov.	Dec.
City	3.0	3.4	3.2	3.0	3.0	3.3	3.5	3.5	3.0	3.1	3.1	2.9
MSA[1]	3.0	3.4	3.2	3.0	3.1	3.5	3.5	3.6	3.0	3.1	3.0	2.9
U.S.	4.1	4.2	3.9	3.5	3.7	4.3	4.5	4.4	3.9	3.9	4.0	3.8

Note: Data is not seasonally adjusted and covers workers 16 years of age and older; (1) Figures cover the Salt Lake City-Murray, UT Metropolitan Statistical Area
Source: Bureau of Labor Statistics, Local Area Unemployment Statistics

Average Wages

Occupation	$/Hr.	Occupation	$/Hr.
Accountants and Auditors	41.61	Maintenance and Repair Workers	25.87
Automotive Mechanics	25.97	Marketing Managers	72.64
Bookkeepers	24.91	Network and Computer Systems Admin.	49.94
Carpenters	27.86	Nurses, Licensed Practical	31.60
Cashiers	15.51	Nurses, Registered	44.02
Computer Programmers	46.78	Nursing Assistants	19.66
Computer Systems Analysts	45.51	Office Clerks, General	22.49
Computer User Support Specialists	32.60	Physical Therapists	47.44
Construction Laborers	23.53	Physicians	112.68
Cooks, Restaurant	18.51	Plumbers, Pipefitters and Steamfitters	32.12
Customer Service Representatives	21.44	Police and Sheriff's Patrol Officers	40.23
Dentists	80.35	Postal Service Mail Carriers	29.32
Electricians	31.02	Real Estate Sales Agents	31.26
Engineers, Electrical	55.43	Retail Salespersons	19.37
Fast Food and Counter Workers	13.99	Sales Representatives, Technical/Scientific	49.93
Financial Managers	78.19	Secretaries, Exc. Legal/Medical/Executive	22.46
First-Line Supervisors of Office Workers	35.75	Security Guards	21.09
General and Operations Managers	60.12	Surgeons	n/a
Hairdressers/Cosmetologists	21.89	Teacher Assistants, Exc. Postsecondary[1]	15.41
Home Health and Personal Care Aides	18.64	Teachers, Secondary School, Exc. Sp. Ed.[1]	35.90
Janitors and Cleaners	16.02	Telemarketers	17.54
Landscaping/Groundskeeping Workers	20.01	Truck Drivers, Heavy/Tractor-Trailer	29.38
Lawyers	76.47	Truck Drivers, Light/Delivery Services	23.05
Maids and Housekeeping Cleaners	17.31	Waiters and Waitresses	16.60

Note: Wage data covers the Salt Lake City-Murray, UT Metropolitan Statistical Area; (1) Hourly wages were calculated from annual wage data based on a 40 hour work week
Source: Bureau of Labor Statistics, Metro Area Occupational Employment & Wage Estimates, May 2024

Employment by Industry

Sector	MSA[1]		U.S.
	Number of Employees	Percent of Total	Percent of Total
Construction, Mining, and Logging	59,900	7.2	5.5
Financial Activities	64,700	7.7	5.8
Government	119,300	14.3	14.9
Information	23,100	2.8	1.9
Leisure and Hospitality	69,700	8.3	10.4
Manufacturing	64,000	7.7	8.0
Other Services	22,800	2.7	3.7
Private Education and Health Services	101,500	12.2	16.9
Professional and Business Services	142,900	17.1	14.2
Retail Trade	76,600	9.2	10.0
Transportation, Warehousing, and Utilities	50,000	6.0	4.8
Wholesale Trade	40,800	4.9	3.9

Note: Figures are non-farm employment as of December 2024. Figures are not seasonally adjusted and include workers 16 years of age and older; (1) Figures cover the Salt Lake City-Murray, UT Metropolitan Statistical Area
Source: Bureau of Labor Statistics, Current Employment Statistics, Employment, Hours, and Earnings

Employment by Occupation

Occupation Classification	City (%)	MSA[1] (%)	U.S. (%)
Management, Business, Science, and Arts	51.1	43.1	42.0
Natural Resources, Construction, and Maintenance	6.0	8.5	8.6
Production, Transportation, and Material Moving	10.7	13.1	13.0
Sales and Office	17.8	21.9	19.9
Service	14.5	13.3	16.5

Note: Figures cover employed civilians 16 years of age and older; (1) Figures cover the Salt Lake City-Murray, UT Metropolitan Statistical Area
Source: U.S. Census Bureau, 2019-2023 American Community Survey 5-Year Estimates

Occupations with Greatest Projected Employment Growth: 2022 – 2032

Occupation[1]	2022 Employment	2032 Projected Employment	Numeric Employment Change	Percent Employment Change
Fast Food and Counter Workers	50,740	67,110	16,370	32.3
General and Operations Managers	59,210	75,020	15,810	26.7
Software Developers	20,260	29,920	9,660	47.7
Construction Laborers	27,050	36,570	9,520	35.2
Cooks, Restaurant	12,890	20,160	7,270	56.4
Stockers and Order Fillers	27,150	33,880	6,730	24.8
Registered Nurses	25,300	31,710	6,410	25.3
Janitors and Cleaners, Except Maids and Housekeeping Cleaners	25,050	31,380	6,330	25.3
Landscaping and Groundskeeping Workers	14,560	19,690	5,130	35.2
Laborers and Freight, Stock, and Material Movers, Hand	25,010	29,990	4,980	19.9

Note: Projections cover Utah; (1) Sorted by numeric employment change
Source: www.projectionscentral.org, State Occupational Projections, 2022–2032 Long-Term Projections

Fastest-Growing Occupations: 2022 – 2032

Occupation[1]	2022 Employment	2032 Projected Employment	Numeric Employment Change	Percent Employment Change
Solar Photovoltaic Installers	390	660	270	69.2
Physical Therapist Assistants	650	1,090	440	67.7
Chiropractors	480	800	320	66.7
Occupational Therapy Assistants	300	500	200	66.7
Statisticians	470	760	290	61.7
Nurse Practitioners	3,680	5,900	2,220	60.3
Ophthalmic Medical Technicians	270	430	160	59.3
Data Scientists	3,100	4,900	1,800	58.1
Information Security Analysts (SOC 2018)	1,650	2,600	950	57.6
Orthotists and Prosthetists	660	1,040	380	57.6

Note: Projections cover Utah; (1) Sorted by percent employment change and excludes occupations with numeric employment change less than 50
Source: www.projectionscentral.org, State Occupational Projections, 2022–2032 Long-Term Projections

CITY FINANCES

City Government Finances

Component	2022 ($000)	2022 ($ per capita)
Total Revenues	1,203,262	5,896
Total Expenditures	1,365,276	6,690
Debt Outstanding	4,106,723	20,122

Source: U.S. Census Bureau, State & Local Government Finances 2022

City Government Revenue by Source

Source	2022 ($000)	2022 ($ per capita)	2022 (%)
General Revenue			
From Federal Government	142,930	700	11.9
From State Government	1,355	7	0.1
From Local Governments	11,998	59	1.0
Taxes			
Property	151,550	743	12.6
Sales and Gross Receipts	153,631	753	12.8
Personal Income	0	0	0.0
Corporate Income	0	0	0.0
Motor Vehicle License	0	0	0.0
Other Taxes	19,649	96	1.6
Current Charges	572,374	2,805	47.6
Liquor Store	0	0	0.0
Utility	71,660	351	6.0

Source: U.S. Census Bureau, State & Local Government Finances 2022

City Government Expenditures by Function

Function	2022 ($000)	2022 ($ per capita)	2022 (%)
General Direct Expenditures			
Air Transportation	535,551	2,624	39.2
Corrections	0	0	0.0
Education	435	2	0.0
Employment Security Administration	0	0	0.0
Financial Administration	10,983	53	0.8
Fire Protection	49,817	244	3.6
General Public Buildings	19,511	95	1.4
Governmental Administration, Other	31,692	155	2.3
Health	7,774	38	0.6
Highways	58,878	288	4.3
Hospitals	0	0	0.0
Housing and Community Development	18,928	92	1.4
Interest on General Debt	85,562	419	6.3
Judicial and Legal	13,004	63	1.0
Libraries	20,375	99	1.5
Parking	1,714	8	0.1
Parks and Recreation	34,720	170	2.5
Police Protection	83,256	407	6.1
Public Welfare	1,733	8	0.1
Sewerage	103,834	508	7.6
Solid Waste Management	13,376	65	1.0
Veterans' Services	0	0	0.0
Liquor Store	0	0	0.0
Utility	115,966	568	8.5

Source: U.S. Census Bureau, State & Local Government Finances 2022

TAXES

State Corporate Income Tax Rates

State	Tax Rate (%)	Income Brackets ($)	Num. of Brackets	Financial Institution Tax Rate (%)[a]	Federal Income Tax Ded.
Utah	4.65 (b)	Flat rate	–	4.65 (b)	No

Note: Tax rates for tax year 2024; (a) Rates listed are the corporate income tax rate applied to financial institutions or excise taxes based on income. Some states have other taxes based upon the value of deposits or shares; (b) Minimum tax is $800 in California, $250 in District of Columbia, $50 in Arizona and North Dakota (banks), $400 ($100 banks) in Rhode Island, $200 per location in South Dakota (banks), $100 in Utah, in Vermont, simplified entity business tax for residents only at $250, otherwise minimum tax ($100 - $100,000) is based upon gross receipts.
Source: Federation of Tax Administrators, State Corporate Income Tax Rates, January 1, 2025

State Individual Income Tax Rates

State	Tax Rate (%)	Income Brackets ($)	Personal Exemptions ($)			Standard Ded. ($)	
			Single	Married	Depend.	Single	Married
Utah	4.8	Flat rate	None	None	1,750	(w)	(w)

Note: Tax rates for tax year 2024; Local- and county-level taxes are not included; Federal income tax is not deductible on state income tax returns; (w) Utah provides a tax credit equal to 6% of the federal personal exemption amounts (and applicable standard deduction). The tax credit is reduced by $.013 for each dollar by which a claimant's state taxable income exceeds: $15,095 - S; $22,643 - HOH; $30,190 - MFJ in 2023.
Source: Federation of Tax Administrators, State Individual Income Tax Rates, January 1, 2025

Various State Sales and Excise Tax Rates

State	State Sales Tax (%)	Gasoline[1] ($/gal.)	Cigarette[2] ($/pack)	Spirits[3] ($/gal.)	Wine[4] ($/gal.)	Beer[5] ($/gal.)	Recreational Marijuana (%)
Utah	6.1	0.39	1.70	16.07	0.00	0.43	Not legal

Note: All tax rates as of January 1, 2025; (1) The American Petroleum Institute has developed a methodology for determining the average tax rate on a gallon of fuel. Rates may include any of the following: excise taxes, environmental fees, storage tank fees, other fees or taxes, general sales tax, and local taxes; (2) The federal excise tax of $1.0066 per pack and local taxes are not included; (3) Rates are those applicable to off-premise sales of 40% alcohol by volume (a.b.v.) distilled spirits in 750ml containers. Local excise taxes are excluded; (4) Rates are those applicable to off-premise sales of 11% a.b.v. non-carbonated wine in 750ml containers; (5) Rates are those applicable to off-premise sales of 4.7% a.b.v. beer in 12 ounce containers.
Source: Tax Foundation, 2025 Facts & Figures: How Does Your State Compare?

State Tax Competitiveness Index

State	Overall Rank	Corporate Tax Rank	Individual Income Tax Rank	Sales Tax Rank	Property Tax Rank	Unemployment Insurance Tax Rank
Utah	16	17	9	27	12	29

Note: The Tax Foundation's State Tax Competitiveness Index enables policymakers, taxpayers, and business leaders to gauge how their states' tax systems compare. A rank of 1 is best, 50 is worst. Rankings do not average to the total. States without a tax rank equally as 1. DC's scores and rankings do not affect other states. The report shows tax systems as of July 1, 2024 (the beginning of Fiscal Year 2025).
Source: Tax Foundation, State Tax Competitiveness Index 2025

TRANSPORTATION

Means of Transportation to Work

Area	Car/Truck/Van		Public Transportation			Bicycle	Walked	Other Means	Worked at Home
	Drove Alone	Car-pooled	Bus	Subway	Railroad				
City	60.2	8.1	3.1	0.3	0.3	1.6	4.8	2.9	18.5
MSA[1]	67.0	10.0	1.2	0.2	0.2	0.5	1.7	1.7	17.5
U.S.	70.2	8.5	1.7	1.3	0.4	0.4	2.4	1.6	13.5

Note: Figures are percentages and cover workers 16 years of age and older; (1) Figures cover the Salt Lake City-Murray, UT Metropolitan Statistical Area
Source: U.S. Census Bureau, 2019-2023 American Community Survey 5-Year Estimates

Travel Time to Work

Area	Less Than 10 Minutes	10 to 19 Minutes	20 to 29 Minutes	30 to 44 Minutes	45 to 59 Minutes	60 to 89 Minutes	90 Minutes or More
City	14.6	45.2	20.6	12.7	3.5	2.1	1.3
MSA[1]	11.1	33.7	26.6	19.0	5.5	2.9	1.3
U.S.	12.6	28.6	21.2	20.8	8.1	6.0	2.8

Note: Note: Figures are percentages and include workers 16 years old and over; (1) Figures cover the Salt Lake City-Murray, UT Metropolitan Statistical Area
Source: U.S. Census Bureau, 2019-2023 American Community Survey 5-Year Estimates

Key Congestion Measures

Measure	2000	2010	2015	2020	2022
Annual Hours of Delay, Total (000)	14,974	22,524	27,472	17,124	31,614
Annual Hours of Delay, Per Auto Commuter	28	36	43	26	52
Annual Congestion Cost, Per Auto Commuter ($)	697	834	939	608	1,169

Note: Figures cover the Salt Lake City-West Valley City UT urban area
Source: Texas A&M Transportation Institute, 2023 Urban Mobility Report

Freeway Travel Time Index

Measure	1985	1990	1995	2000	2005	2010	2015	2020	2022
Urban Area Index[1]	1.06	1.07	1.10	1.14	1.17	1.17	1.18	1.06	1.18
Urban Area Rank[1,2]	53	74	72	62	49	41	41	75	40

Note: Freeway Travel Time Index—the ratio of travel time in the peak period to the travel time at free-flow conditions. For example, a value of 1.30 indicates a 20-minute free-flow trip takes 26 minutes in the peak (20 minutes x 1.30 = 26 minutes); (1) Covers the Salt Lake City-West Valley City UT urban area; (2) Rank is based on 101 larger urban areas (#1 = highest travel time index)
Source: Texas A&M Transportation Institute, 2023 Urban Mobility Report

Public Transportation

Agency Name / Mode of Transportation	Vehicles Operated in Maximum Service[1]	Annual Unlinked Passenger Trips[2] (in thous.)	Annual Passenger Miles[3] (in thous.)
Utah Transit Authority (UTA)			
Bus (directly operated)	302	17,797.2	69,048.6
Bus (purchased transportation)	7	98.0	578.6
Commuter Bus (directly operated)	38	592.6	9,082.3
Commuter Rail (directly operated)	40	3,736.6	107,783.0
Demand Response (directly operated)	52	212.7	2,050.2
Demand Response (purchased transportation)	89	545.9	3,288.6
Light Rail (directly operated)	74	11,043.7	48,914.3
Vanpool (directly operated)	442	1,033.1	38,627.4

Note: (1) Number of revenue vehicles operated by the given mode and type of service to meet the annual maximum service requirement. This is the revenue vehicle count during the peak season of the year; on the week and day that maximum service is provided. Vehicles operated in maximum service (VOMS) exclude atypical days and one-time special events; (2) Number of passengers who boarded public transportation vehicles. Passengers are counted each time they board a vehicle no matter how many vehicles they use to travel from their origin to their destination. (3) Sum of the distances ridden by all passengers during the entire fiscal year.
Source: Federal Transit Administration, National Transit Database, 2023

Air Transportation

Airport Name and Code / Type of Service	Passenger Airlines[1]	Passenger Enplanements	Freight Carriers[2]	Freight (lbs)
Salt Lake City International (SLC)				
Domestic service (U.S. carriers only)	29	12,883,266	15	153,520,130
International service (U.S. carriers only)	6	572,505	1	3,194,061

Note: (1) Includes all U.S.-based major, minor and commuter airlines that carried at least one passenger during the year; (2) Includes all U.S.-based airlines and freight carriers that transported at least one pound of freight during the year.
Source: Bureau of Transportation Statistics, The Intermodal Transportation Database, Air Carriers: T-100 Domestic Market (U.S. carriers only), 2024; Bureau of Transportation Statistics, The Intermodal Transportation Database, Air Carriers: T-100 International Market (U.S. carriers only), 2024

BUSINESSES

Major Business Headquarters

Company Name	Industry	Rankings Fortune[1]	Rankings Forbes[2]
FJ Management	Convenience stores & gas stations	-	89

Note: (1) Companies that produce a 10-K are ranked 1 to 500 based on 2023 revenue; (2) All private companies with at least $2 billion in annual revenue through the end of their most current fiscal year are ranked 1 to 275; companies listed are headquartered in the city; dashes indicate no ranking
Source: Fortune, "Fortune 500," 2024; Forbes, "America's Largest Private Companies," 2024

Fastest-Growing Businesses

According to Deloitte, Salt Lake City is home to three of North America's 500 fastest-growing high-technology companies: **Recursion** (#116); **Filevine** (#389); **Brex** (#416). Companies are ranked by percentage growth in revenue over a four-year period. Criteria for inclusion: company must be headquartered within North America; must own proprietary intellectual property or technology that is sold to customers in products that contributes to a significant portion of the company's operating revenue; must have been in business for a minumum of four years with 2020 operating revenues of at least $50,000 USD/CD and 2023 operating revenues of at least $5 million USD/CD. *Deloitte, 2024 Technology Fast 500*™

Living Environment

COST OF LIVING

Cost of Living Index

Composite Index	Groceries	Housing	Utilities	Trans-portation	Health Care	Misc. Goods/ Services
109.0	98.1	128.7	95.4	111.4	88.5	103.0

Note: The Cost of Living Index measures regional differences in the cost of consumer goods and services, excluding taxes and non-consumer expenditures, for professional and managerial households in the top income quintile. It is based on more than 50,000 prices covering almost 60 different items for which prices are collected three times a year by chambers of commerce, economic development organizations or university applied economic centers in each participating urban area. The numbers shown should be read as a percentage above or below the national average of 100. For example, a value of 115.4 in the groceries column indicates that grocery prices are 15.4% higher than the national average. Small differences in the index numbers should not be interpreted as significant; Figures cover the Salt Lake City UT urban area.
Source: The Council for Community and Economic Research, Cost of Living Index, 2024

Grocery Prices

Area[1]	T-Bone Steak ($/pound)	Frying Chicken ($/pound)	Whole Milk ($/half gal.)	Eggs ($/dozen)	Orange Juice ($/64 oz.)	Coffee ($/11.5 oz.)
City[2]	15.51	1.53	4.62	3.03	4.19	6.11
Avg.	15.42	1.55	4.69	3.25	4.41	5.46
Min.	14.50	1.16	4.43	2.75	4.00	4.85
Max.	17.56	2.89	5.49	4.78	5.54	7.89

*Note: (1) Values for the local area are compared with the average, minimum and maximum values for all 276 areas in the Cost of Living Index; (2) Figures cover the Salt Lake City UT urban area; **T-Bone Steak** (price per pound); **Frying Chicken** (price per pound, whole fryer); **Whole Milk** (half gallon carton); **Eggs** (price per dozen, Grade A, large); **Orange Juice** (64 oz. Tropicana or Florida Natural); **Coffee** (11.5 oz. can, vacuum-packed, Maxwell House, Hills Bros, or Folgers).*
Source: The Council for Community and Economic Research, Cost of Living Index, 2024

Housing and Utility Costs

Area[1]	New Home Price ($)	Apartment Rent ($/month)	All Electric ($/month)	Part Electric ($/month)	Other Energy ($/month)	Telephone ($/month)
City[2]	717,422	1,758	-	96.56	93.13	196.83
Avg.	515,975	1,550	210.99	123.07	82.07	194.99
Min.	265,375	692	104.33	53.68	36.26	179.42
Max.	2,775,821	5,719	529.02	397.28	361.63	223.33

*Note: (1) Values for the local area are compared with the average, minimum and maximum values for all 276 areas in the Cost of Living Index; (2) Figures cover the Salt Lake City UT urban area; **New Home Price** (2,400 sf living area, 8,000 sf lot, in urban area with full utilities); **Apartment Rent** (950 sf 2 bedroom/1.5 or 2 bath, unfurnished, excluding all utilities except water); **All Electric** (average monthly cost for an all-electric home); **Part Electric** (average monthly cost for a part-electric home); **Other Energy** (average monthly cost for natural gas, fuel oil, coal, wood, and any other forms of energy except electricity); **Telephone** (price includes the base monthly rate plus taxes and fees for three lines of mobile phone service).*
Source: The Council for Community and Economic Research, Cost of Living Index, 2024

Health Care, Transportation, and Other Costs

Area[1]	Doctor ($/visit)	Dentist ($/visit)	Optometrist ($/visit)	Gasoline ($/gallon)	Beauty Salon ($/visit)	Men's Shirt ($)
City[2]	129.02	100.40	125.47	3.38	56.68	44.66
Avg.	143.77	117.51	129.23	3.32	48.57	38.14
Min.	36.74	58.67	67.33	2.80	24.00	13.41
Max.	270.44	216.82	307.33	5.28	94.00	63.89

*Note: (1) Values for the local area are compared with the average, minimum and maximum values for all 276 areas in the Cost of Living Index; (2) Figures cover the Salt Lake City UT urban area; **Doctor** (general practitioners routine exam of an established patient); **Dentist** (adult teeth cleaning and periodic oral examination); **Optometrist** (full vision eye exam for established adult patient); **Gasoline** (one gallon regular unleaded, national brand, including all taxes, cash price at self-service pump if available); **Beauty Salon** (woman's shampoo, trim, and blow-dry); **Men's Shirt** (cotton/polyester dress shirt, pinpoint weave, long sleeves).*
Source: The Council for Community and Economic Research, Cost of Living Index, 2024

HOUSING

Homeownership Rate

Area	2017 (%)	2018 (%)	2019 (%)	2020 (%)	2021 (%)	2022 (%)	2023 (%)	2024 (%)
MSA[1]	68.1	69.5	69.2	68.0	64.1	66.6	62.9	61.0
U.S.	63.9	64.4	64.6	66.6	65.5	65.8	65.9	65.6

Note: (1) Figures cover the Salt Lake City-Murray, UT Metropolitan Statistical Area
Source: U.S. Census Bureau, Housing Vacancies and Homeownership Annual Statistics: 2017-2024

House Price Index (HPI)

Area	National Ranking[2]	Quarterly Change (%)	One-Year Change (%)	Five-Year Change (%)	Since 1991Q1 (%)
MSA[1]	115	0.53	5.58	59.66	644.94
U.S.[3]	–	1.43	4.51	57.13	327.82

Note: The HPI is a weighted repeat sales index. It measures average price changes in repeat sales or refinancings on the same properties. This information is obtained by reviewing repeat mortgage transactions on single-family properties whose mortgages have been purchased or securitized by Fannie Mae or Freddie Mac since January 1975; (1) Figures cover the Salt Lake City, UT Metropolitan Statistical Area; (2) Rankings are based on annual percentage change for all metro areas containing at least 15,000 transactions over the last 10 years and ranges from 1 to 241; (3) figures based on a weighted average of Census Division estimates using a seasonally adjusted, purchase-only index; all figures are for the period ending December 31, 2024
Source: Federal Housing Finance Agency, Change in FHFA Metropolitan Area House Price Indexes, All Transactions Index, 2024Q4

Home Value

Area	Under $100,000	$100,000 -$199,999	$200,000 -$299,999	$300,000 -$399,999	$400,000 -$499,999	$500,000 -$999,999	$1,000,000 or more	Median ($)
City	4.1	3.4	11.3	15.5	16.4	37.9	11.4	495,700
MSA[1]	4.0	2.6	9.9	17.6	20.3	38.7	6.9	478,200
U.S.	12.1	17.8	19.5	14.4	10.5	19.1	6.5	303,400

Note: Figures are percentages except for median and cover owner-occupied housing units; (1) Figures cover the Salt Lake City-Murray, UT Metropolitan Statistical Area
Source: U.S. Census Bureau, 2019-2023 American Community Survey 5-Year Estimates

Year Housing Structure Built

Area	2020 or Later	2010 -2019	2000 -2009	1990 -1999	1980 -1989	1970 -1979	1960 -1969	1950 -1959	1940 -1949	Before 1940	Median Year
City	1.8	10.6	6.8	5.5	7.4	11.4	9.8	12.2	8.2	26.3	1963
MSA[1]	1.9	14.7	14.4	14.0	11.3	16.8	8.3	8.1	3.2	7.2	1986
U.S.	1.2	8.9	13.6	12.8	13.0	14.4	10.0	9.7	4.5	11.9	1980

Note: Figures are percentages except for Median Year; Note: (1) Figures cover the Salt Lake City-Murray, UT Metropolitan Statistical Area
Source: U.S. Census Bureau, 2019-2023 American Community Survey 5-Year Estimates

Gross Monthly Rent

Area	Under $500	$500 -$999	$1,000 -$1,499	$1,500 -$1,999	$2,000 -$2,499	$2,500 -$2,999	$3,000 and up	Median ($)
City	6.7	16.6	37.5	23.0	10.1	3.7	2.5	1,343
MSA[1]	3.9	11.4	35.8	29.9	13.2	3.6	2.2	1,486
U.S.	6.5	22.3	29.5	20.2	10.8	4.8	5.9	1,348

Note: Figures are percentages except for median; Gross rent is the contract rent plus the estimated average monthly cost of utilities (electricity, gas, and water and sewer) and fuels (oil, coal, kerosene, wood, etc.) if these are paid by the renter (or paid for the renter by someone else); (1) Figures cover the Salt Lake City-Murray, UT Metropolitan Statistical Area
Source: U.S. Census Bureau, 2019-2023 American Community Survey 5-Year Estimates

HEALTH

Health Risk Factors

Category	MSA[1] (%)	U.S. (%)
Adults aged 18–64 who have any kind of health care coverage	88.6	90.8
Adults who reported being in good or better health	85.1	81.8
Adults who have been told they have high blood cholesterol	31.2	36.9
Adults who have been told they have high blood pressure	26.1	34.0
Adults who are current smokers	6.6	12.1
Adults who currently use e-cigarettes	8.0	7.7
Adults who currently use chewing tobacco, snuff, or snus	1.8	3.2
Adults who are heavy drinkers[2]	5.4	6.1
Adults who are binge drinkers[3]	16.8	15.2
Adults who are overweight (BMI 25.0 - 29.9)	35.0	34.4
Adults who are obese (BMI 30.0 - 99.8)	29.1	34.3
Adults who participated in any physical activities in the past month	81.9	75.8

Note: All figures are crude prevalence; (1) Figures cover the Salt Lake City, UT Metropolitan Statistical Area; (2) Heavy drinkers are classified as adult men having more than 14 drinks per week and adult women having more than 7 drinks per week; (3) Binge drinkers are classified as males having five or more drinks on one occasion or females having four or more drinks on one occasion
Source: Centers for Disease Control and Prevention, Behaviorial Risk Factor Surveillance System, SMART: Selected Metropolitan Area Risk Trends, 2023

Acute and Chronic Health Conditions

Category	MSA[1] (%)	U.S. (%)
Adults who have ever been told they had a heart attack	2.8	4.2
Adults who have ever been told they have angina or coronary heart disease	2.2	4.0
Adults who have ever been told they had a stroke	2.0	3.3
Adults who have ever been told they have asthma	16.8	15.7
Adults who have ever been told they have arthritis	21.2	26.3
Adults who have ever been told they have diabetes[2]	7.6	11.5
Adults who have ever been told they had skin cancer	5.5	5.6
Adults who have ever been told they had any other types of cancer	7.8	8.4
Adults who have ever been told they have COPD	3.5	6.4
Adults who have ever been told they have kidney disease	2.7	3.7
Adults who have ever been told they have a form of depression	26.6	22.0

Note: All figures are crude prevalence; (1) Figures cover the Salt Lake City, UT Metropolitan Statistical Area;
(2) Figures do not include pregnancy-related, borderline, or pre-diabetes
Source: Centers for Disease Control and Prevention, Behaviorial Risk Factor Surveillance System, SMART:
Selected Metropolitan Area Risk Trends, 2023

Health Screening and Vaccination Rates

Category	MSA[1] (%)	U.S. (%)
Adults who have ever been tested for HIV	34.2	37.5
Adults who have had their blood cholesterol checked within the last five years	82.5	87.0
Adults aged 65+ who have had flu shot within the past year	63.7	63.4
Adults aged 65+ who have ever had a pneumonia vaccination	77.3	71.9

Note: All figures are crude prevalence; (1) Figures cover the Salt Lake City, UT Metropolitan Statistical Area.
Source: Centers for Disease Control and Prevention, Behaviorial Risk Factor Surveillance System, SMART:
Selected Metropolitan Area Risk Trends, 2023

Disability Status

Category	MSA[1] (%)	U.S. (%)
Adults who reported being deaf	6.0	7.4
Are you blind or have serious difficulty seeing, even when wearing glasses?	4.3	4.9
Do you have difficulty doing errands alone?	6.7	7.8
Do you have difficulty dressing or bathing?	2.1	3.6
Do you have serious difficulty concentrating/remembering/making decisions?	14.3	13.7
Do you have serious difficulty walking or climbing stairs?	10.6	13.2

Note: All figures are crude prevalence; (1) Figures cover the Salt Lake City, UT Metropolitan Statistical Area.
Source: Centers for Disease Control and Prevention, Behaviorial Risk Factor Surveillance System, SMART:
Selected Metropolitan Area Risk Trends, 2023

Mortality Rates for the Top 10 Causes of Death in the U.S.

ICD-10[a] Sub-Chapter	ICD-10[a] Code	Crude Mortality Rate[2] per 100,000 population	
		County[3]	U.S.
Malignant neoplasms	C00-C97	105.2	182.7
Ischaemic heart diseases	I20-I25	54.7	109.6
Provisional assignment of new diseases of uncertain etiology[1]	U00-U49	29.3	65.3
Other forms of heart disease	I30-I51	50.5	65.1
Other degenerative diseases of the nervous system	G30-G31	45.0	52.4
Other external causes of accidental injury	W00-X59	40.0	52.3
Cerebrovascular diseases	I60-I69	27.6	49.1
Chronic lower respiratory diseases	J40-J47	25.2	43.5
Hypertensive diseases	I10-I15	22.4	38.9
Organic, including symptomatic, mental disorders	F01-F09	24.0	33.9

Note: (a) ICD-10 = International Classification of Diseases 10th Revision; (1) Includes COVID-19, adverse
effects to COVID-19 vaccines, SARS, and vaping-related disorders; (2) Crude mortality rates are a three-year
average covering 2021-2023; (3) Figures cover Salt Lake County.
Source: Centers for Disease Control and Prevention, National Center for Health Statistics. National Vital
Statistics System, Mortality 2018-2023 on CDC WONDER Online Database

Mortality Rates for Selected Causes of Death

Cause of Death	ICD-10[a] Code	Crude Mortality Rate[1] per 100,000 population	
		County[2]	U.S.
Accidental poisoning and exposure to noxious substances	X40-X49	21.7	30.5
Alzheimer disease	G30	29.7	35.4
Assault	X85-Y09	3.6	7.3
COVID-19	U07.1	29.2	65.3
Diabetes mellitus	E10-E14	23.8	30.0
Diseases of the liver	K70-K76	14.7	20.8
Human immunodeficiency virus (HIV) disease	B20-B24	0.7	1.5
Influenza and pneumonia	J09-J18	5.6	13.4
Intentional self-harm	X60-X84	21.2	14.7
Malnutrition	E40-E46	13.9	6.0
Obesity and other hyperalimentation	E65-E68	3.7	3.1
Renal failure	N17-N19	9.6	16.4
Transport accidents	V01-V99	10.1	14.4

Note: (a) ICD-10 = International Classification of Diseases 10th Revision; (1) Crude mortality rates are a three-year average covering 2021-2023; (2) Figures cover Salt Lake County; Data are suppressed when the data meet the criteria for confidentiality constraints; Crude mortality rates are flagged as unreliable when the rate would be calculated with a numerator of 20 or less.
Source: Centers for Disease Control and Prevention, National Center for Health Statistics. National Vital Statistics System, Mortality 2018-2023 on CDC WONDER Online Database

Health Insurance Coverage

Area	With Health Insurance	With Private Health Insurance	With Public Health Insurance	Without Health Insurance	Population Under Age 19 Without Health Insurance
City	89.0	73.9	22.8	11.0	10.2
MSA[1]	90.6	77.4	20.8	9.4	7.7
U.S.	91.4	67.3	36.3	8.6	5.4

Note: Figures are percentages that cover the civilian noninstitutionalized population; (1) Figures cover the Salt Lake City-Murray, UT Metropolitan Statistical Area
Source: U.S. Census Bureau, 2019-2023 American Community Survey 5-Year Estimates

Number of Medical Professionals

Area	MDs[3]	DOs[3,4]	Dentists	Podiatrists	Chiropractors	Optometrists
County[1] (number)	5,013	277	986	78	352	179
County[1] (rate[2])	422.6	23.4	83.1	6.6	29.7	15.1
U.S. (rate[2])	302.5	29.2	74.6	6.4	29.5	18.0

Note: Data as of 2023 unless noted; (1) Data covers Salt Lake County; (2) Number of medical professionals per 100,000 population; (3) Data as of 2022 and includes all active, non-federal physicians; (4) Doctor of Osteopathic Medicine
Source: U.S. Department of Health and Human Services, Health Resources and Services Administration, Bureau of Health Professions, Area Resource File (ARF) 2023-2024

Best Hospitals

According to *U.S. News,* the Salt Lake City-Murray, UT metro area is home to two of the best hospitals in the U.S.: **Craig H. Neilsen Rehabilitation Hospital, University of Utah Health** (2 adult specialties); **John A. Moran Eye Center, University of Utah Health** (2 adult specialties). The hospitals listed were nationally ranked in at least one of 15 adult or 11 pediatric specialties. The number of specialties shown cover the parent hospital. Only 160 U.S. hospitals performed well enough to be nationally ranked in one or more specialties. Twenty hospitals in the U.S. made the Honor Roll. The Best Hospitals Honor Roll takes both the national rankings and the procedure and condition ratings into account. Hospitals received points if they were nationally ranked in one of the 15 adult specialties—the higher they ranked, the more points they got—and how many ratings of "high performing" they earned in the 20 procedures and conditions. *U.S. News Online, "America's Best Hospitals 2024-25"*

According to *U.S. News,* the Salt Lake City-Murray, UT metro area is home to two of the best children's hospitals in the U.S.: **Intermountain Primary Children's Hospital-Shriners Hospitals for Children-University of Utah** (11 pediatric specialties); **Intermountain Primary Children's Hospital-University of Utah** (11 pediatric specialties). The hospitals listed were highly ranked in at least one of 11 pediatric specialties. One hundred five children's hospitals in the U.S. were nationally ranked in at least one specialty. Hospitals received points for being ranked in a specialty, and the 10 hospitals with the most points across the 11 specialties make up the Honor Roll. *U.S. News Online, "America's Best Children's Hospitals 2024-25"*

EDUCATION

Public School District Statistics

District Name	Schls	Pupils	Pupil/ Teacher Ratio	Minority Pupils[1] (%)	Total Rev. per Pupil ($)	Total Exp. per Pupil ($)
Ascent Academies of Utah	5	2,750	17.6	41.4	11,084	11,030
Granite District	86	60,270	19.9	48.6	11,995	12,342
Salt Lake District	40	19,477	17.1	59.8	14,872	14,329

Note: Table includes school districts with 2,000 or more students; (1) Percentage of students that are not non-Hispanic white.
Source: U.S. Department of Education, National Center for Education Statistics, Common Core of Data, Local Education Agency (School District) Universe Survey: School Year 2023-2024; U.S. Department of Education, National Center for Education Statistics, Common Core of Data, School District Finance Survey (F-33): School Year 2021–22

Highest Level of Education

Area	Less than H.S.	H.S. Diploma	Some College, No Deg.	Associate Degree	Bachelor's Degree	Master's Degree	Prof. School Degree	Doctorate Degree
City	8.4	17.1	16.9	6.7	28.9	13.6	4.7	3.7
MSA[1]	8.2	22.7	22.1	9.2	24.1	9.7	2.3	1.7
U.S.	10.6	26.2	19.4	8.8	21.3	9.8	2.3	1.6

Note: Figures cover persons age 25 and over; (1) Figures cover the Salt Lake City-Murray, UT Metropolitan Statistical Area
Source: U.S. Census Bureau, 2019-2023 American Community Survey 5-Year Estimates

Educational Attainment by Race

Area	High School Graduate or Higher (%)					Bachelor's Degree or Higher (%)				
	Total	White	Black	Asian	Hisp.[2]	Total	White	Black	Asian	Hisp.[2]
City	91.6	95.7	86.1	85.3	72.5	50.9	56.2	30.7	62.6	24.5
MSA[1]	91.8	95.2	84.3	86.9	74.6	37.8	40.9	25.4	52.0	18.6
U.S.	89.4	92.9	88.1	88.0	72.5	35.0	37.7	24.7	57.0	19.9

Note: Figures shown cover persons 25 years old and over; (1) Figures cover the Salt Lake City-Murray, UT Metropolitan Statistical Area; (2) People of Hispanic origin can be of any race
Source: U.S. Census Bureau, 2019-2023 American Community Survey 5-Year Estimates

School Enrollment by Grade and Control

Area	Preschool (%)		Kindergarten (%)		Grades 1 - 4 (%)		Grades 5 - 8 (%)		Grades 9 - 12 (%)	
	Public	Private	Public	Private	Public	Private	Public	Private	Public	Private
City	52.1	47.9	81.8	18.2	85.6	14.4	90.6	9.4	93.7	6.3
MSA[1]	57.4	42.6	84.7	15.3	89.9	10.1	93.4	6.6	93.9	6.1
U.S.	58.7	41.3	85.2	14.8	87.2	12.8	87.9	12.1	89.0	11.0

Note: Figures shown cover persons 3 years old and over; (1) Figures cover the Salt Lake City-Murray, UT Metropolitan Statistical Area
Source: U.S. Census Bureau, 2019-2023 American Community Survey 5-Year Estimates

Higher Education

Four-Year Colleges			Two-Year Colleges			Medical Schools[1]	Law Schools[2]	Voc/ Tech[3]
Public	Private Non-profit	Private For-profit	Public	Private Non-profit	Private For-profit			
1	4	5	1	0	2	1	1	13

Note: Figures cover institutions located within the Salt Lake City-Murray, UT Metropolitan Statistical Area and include main campuses only; (1) includes schools accredited by the Liaison Committee on Medical Education and the American Osteopathic Association's Commission on Osteopathic College Accreditation; (2) includes ABA-accredited schools, schools with provisional ABA accreditation, and state accredited schools; (3) includes all schools with programs that are less than 2 years.
Source: National Center for Education Statistics, Integrated Postsecondary Education System (IPEDS), 2023-24; Wikipedia, List of Medical Schools in the United States, accessed May 2, 2025; Wikipedia, List of Law Schools in the United States, accessed May 2, 2025

According to *U.S. News & World Report,* the Salt Lake City-Murray, UT metro area is home to one of the top 200 national universities in the U.S.: **University of Utah** (#136 tie). The indicators used to capture academic quality fall into a number of categories: assessment by administrators at peer institutions; retention of students; faculty resources; student selectivity; financial resources; alumni giving; high school counselor ratings of colleges; and graduation rate. *U.S. News & World Report, "America's Best Colleges 2025"*

According to *U.S. News & World Report,* the Salt Lake City-Murray, UT metro area is home to one of the top 100 law schools in the U.S.: **University of Utah (Quinney)** (#31 tie). The rankings are based on a weighted average of 12 measures of quality: peer assessment score; assessment score by lawyers/judges; median LSAT scores; median undergrad GPA; acceptance rate; employment rates for graduates; placement success; bar passage rate; faculty resources; expenditures per student; student/faculty ratio; and library resources. *U.S. News & World Report, "America's Best Graduate Schools, Law, 2025"*

According to *U.S. News & World Report,* the Salt Lake City-Murray, UT metro area is home to one of the top medical schools for research in the U.S.: **University of Utah** (Tier 2). *U.S. News* placed medical and osteopathic schools into tiers based on their research productivity, faculty and admissions data. Each school's tier was derived from its overall score, calculated by summing the weighted normalized values generated across several factors of academic quality, outlined below. There are four tiers, with tier 1 medical schools as the highest-performing and tier 4 as the lowest-performing. Only tier 1 and 2 schools are shown. Because of the tier presentation, *U.S. News* calculated overall scores based on their percentile performance among all rated schools instead of dividing against the rescaled score of the No. 1-performing schools. Tier 1 included schools with overall scores of 85 to 99. The cutoffs for tiers 2 through 4 were schools scoring 50 to 84, 15 to 49 and 1 to 14, respectively. The rankings are based on a weighted average of the following measures of quality: total research activity; average research activity per faculty member; total NIH research grants at the medical school and its affiliated hospitals; average NIH research grants per faculty; median MCAT total score; median undergraduate GPA; acceptance rate; and faculty resources. *U.S. News & World Report, "America's Best Graduate Schools, Medical, 2025"*

According to *U.S. News & World Report,* the Salt Lake City-Murray, UT metro area is home to one of the top medical schools for primary care in the U.S.: **University of Utah** (Tier 2). *U.S. News* placed medical and osteopathic schools into tiers based on their research productivity, faculty and admissions data. Each school's tier was derived from its overall score, calculated by summing the weighted normalized values generated across several factors of academic quality, outlined below. There are four tiers, with tier 1 medical schools as the highest-performing and tier 4 as the lowest-performing. Only tier 1 and 2 schools are shown. Because of the tier presentation, *U.S. News* calculated overall scores based on their percentile performance among all rated schools instead of dividing against the rescaled score of the No. 1-performing schools. Tier 1 included schools with overall scores of 85 to 99. The cutoffs for tiers 2 through 4 were schools scoring 50 to 84, 15 to 49 and 1 to 14, respectively. The rankings are based on a weighted average of the following measures of quality: graduates practicing in primary care specialties; graduates entering primary care residencies; median MCAT total score; median undergraduate GPA; acceptance rate; and faculty resources. *U.S. News & World Report, "America's Best Graduate Schools, Medical, 2025"*

According to *U.S. News & World Report,* the Salt Lake City-Murray, UT metro area is home to one of the top 75 business schools in the U.S.: **University of Utah (Eccles)** (#40 tie). The rankings are based on a weighted average of the following nine measures: quality assessment; peer assessment; recruiter assessment; placement success; mean starting salary and bonus; student selectivity; mean GMAT and GRE scores; mean undergraduate GPA; and acceptance rate. *U.S. News & World Report, "America's Best Graduate Schools, Business, 2025"*

EMPLOYERS

Major Employers

Company Name	Industry
ACS Commercial Solutions	Data entry service
Alsco	Laundry & garment services
Boart Longyear Company	Test boring for nonmetallic minerals
Church of Jesus Christ of LDS	Mormon church
Comenity Capital Bank	State commercial banks
County of Salt Lake	County government
EnergySolutions	Nonresidential construction
Executive Office of the State of Utah	Executive offices
Granite School District Aid Association	Public elementary & secondary schools
Huntsman Corporation	Plastics materials & resins
Huntsman Holdings	Polystyrene resins
Intermountain Health Care	General medical & surgical hospitals
Jordan School District	Public elementary & secondary schools
Longyear Holdings	Test boring for nonmetallic minerals
Sinclair Oil Corporation	Petroleum refining
Smith's Food & Drug Centers	Grocery stores
Sportsman's Warehouse Holdings	Hunting equipment
State of Utah	State government
The University of Utah	Colleges & universities
TPUSA	Telemarketing services

Note: Companies shown are located within the Salt Lake City-Murray, UT Metropolitan Statistical Area.
Source: Chambers of Commerce; State Departments of Labor; Wikipedia

Best Companies to Work For

TP, headquartered in Salt Lake City, is among "The 100 Best Companies to Work For." To pick the best companies, *Fortune* partnered with the Great Place to Work Institute. Using their proprietary Trust Index™ survey, the core of what creates great a workplace is measured—key behaviors that drive trust in management, connection with colleagues, and loyalty to the company. To be eligible for the *Fortune* 100 Best Companies to Work For list, employers must have 1,000 or more employees in the U.S. and cannot be a government agency. *Fortune, "The 100 Best Companies to Work For," 2025*

Waystar, headquartered in Salt Lake City, is among "Best Workplaces in Health Care." To determine the Best Workplaces in Health Care list, Great Place To Work analyzed the survey responses of over 185,000 employees from Great Place To Work-Certified companies in the health care industry. Survey data analysis and company-provided datapoints are then factored into a combined score to compare and rank the companies that create the most consistently positive experience for all employees in this industry. *Fortune, "Best Workplaces in Health Care," 2024*

PUBLIC SAFETY

Crime Rate

Area	Total Crime Rate	Violent Crime Rate				Property Crime Rate		
		Murder	Rape	Robbery	Aggrav. Assault	Burglary	Larceny -Theft	Motor Vehicle Theft
City	6,514.5	7.7	159.7	175.6	524.9	555.4	4,504.8	586.4
U.S.	2,290.9	5.7	38.0	66.5	264.1	250.7	1,347.2	318.7

Note: Figures are crimes per 100,000 population.
Source: FBI, Table 8, Offenses Known to Law Enforcement, by State by City, 2023

Hate Crimes

Area	Number of Quarters Reported	Number of Incidents per Bias Motivation					
		Race/Ethnicity/ Ancestry	Religion	Sexual Orientation	Disability	Gender	Gender Identity
City	4	2	2	13	0	0	1
U.S.	4	5,900	2,699	2,077	187	92	492

Source: Federal Bureau of Investigation, Hate Crime Statistics 2023

Identity Theft Consumer Reports

Area	Reports	Reports per 100,000 Population	Rank[2]
MSA[1]	2,212	175	214
U.S.	1,135,291	339	-

Note: (1) Figures cover the Salt Lake City-Murray, UT Metropolitan Statistical Area; (2) Rank ranges from 1 to 401 where 1 indicates greatest number of identity theft reports per 100,000 population
Source: Federal Trade Commission, Consumer Sentinel Network Data Book 2024

Fraud and Other Consumer Reports

Area	Reports	Reports per 100,000 Population	Rank[2]
MSA[1]	13,144	1,042	187
U.S.	5,360,641	1,601	-

Note: (1) Figures cover the Salt Lake City-Murray, UT Metropolitan Statistical Area; (2) Rank ranges from 1 to 401 where 1 indicates greatest number of fraud and other consumer reports per 100,000 population
Source: Federal Trade Commission, Consumer Sentinel Network Data Book 2024

POLITICS

2024 Presidential Election Results

Area	Trump (Rep.)	Harris (Dem.)	Stein (Green)	Kennedy (Ind.)	Oliver (Lib.)	Other
Salt Lake County	42.9	52.9	0.7	0.0	1.0	2.5
U.S.	49.7	48.2	0.6	0.5	0.4	0.6

Note: Results are percentages and may not add to 100% due to rounding
Source: Dave Leip's Atlas of U.S. Presidential Elections

SPORTS

Professional Sports Teams

Team Name	League	Year Established
Real Salt Lake	Major League Soccer (MLS)	2005
Utah Hockey Club	National Hockey League (NHL)	2024
Utah Jazz	National Basketball Association (NBA)	1979

Note: Includes teams located in the Salt Lake City-Murray, UT Metropolitan Statistical Area.
Source: Wikipedia, Major Professional Sports Teams of the United States and Canada, May 1, 2025

CLIMATE

Average and Extreme Temperatures

Temperature	Jan	Feb	Mar	Apr	May	Jun	Jul	Aug	Sep	Oct	Nov	Dec	Yr.
Extreme High (°F)	62	69	78	85	93	104	107	104	100	89	75	67	107
Average High (°F)	37	43	52	62	72	83	93	90	80	66	50	38	64
Average Temp. (°F)	28	34	41	50	59	69	78	76	65	53	40	30	52
Average Low (°F)	19	24	31	38	46	54	62	61	51	40	30	22	40
Extreme Low (°F)	-22	-14	2	15	25	35	40	37	27	16	-14	-15	-22

Note: Figures cover the years 1948-1990
Source: National Climatic Data Center, International Station Meteorological Climate Summary, 9/96

Average Precipitation/Snowfall/Humidity

Precip./Humidity	Jan	Feb	Mar	Apr	May	Jun	Jul	Aug	Sep	Oct	Nov	Dec	Yr.
Avg. Precip. (in.)	1.3	1.2	1.8	2.0	1.7	0.9	0.8	0.9	1.1	1.3	1.3	1.4	15.6
Avg. Snowfall (in.)	13	10	11	6	1	Tr	0	0	Tr	2	6	13	63
Avg. Rel. Hum. 5am (%)	79	77	71	67	66	60	53	54	60	68	75	79	67
Avg. Rel. Hum. 5pm (%)	69	59	47	38	33	26	22	23	28	40	59	71	43

Note: Figures cover the years 1948-1990; Tr = Trace amounts (<0.05 in. of rain; <0.5 in. of snow)
Source: National Climatic Data Center, International Station Meteorological Climate Summary, 9/96

Weather Conditions

Temperature			Daytime Sky			Precipitation		
5°F & below	32°F & below	90°F & above	Clear	Partly cloudy	Cloudy	0.01 inch or more precip.	0.1 inch or more snow/ice	Thunder-storms
7	128	56	94	152	119	92	38	38

Note: Figures are average number of days per year and cover the years 1948-1990
Source: National Climatic Data Center, International Station Meteorological Climate Summary, 9/96

HAZARDOUS WASTE

Superfund Sites

The Salt Lake City-Murray, UT metro area is home to 10 sites on the EPA's Superfund National Priorities List (NPL) or Superfund Alternative Approach (SAA) list: **700 South 1600 East Pce Plume** (Final NPL); **Jacobs Smelter** (Final NPL); **Kennecott (North Zone)** (Proposed NPL); **Kennecott (south Zone)** (Removed from NPL and SAA); **Murray Smelter** (Proposed NPL); **Portland Cement (Kiln Dust 2 & 3)** (Final NPL); **Tooele Army Depot (North Area)** (Final NPL); **US Magnesium** (Final NPL); **Utah Power & Light/american Barrel Co.** (Final NPL); **Wasatch Chemical Co. (Lot 6)** (Final NPL). The Superfund alternative approach uses the same investigation and cleanup process and standards that are used for sites listed on the National Priorities List. The SAA is an alternative to listing a site on the NPL; it is not an alternative to Superfund or the Superfund process. There are a total of 1,445 Superfund sites with a status of proposed or final on both lists in the United States. *U.S. Environmental Protection Agency, National Priorities List, May 1, 2025; U.S. Environmental Protection Agency, Superfund Alternative Approach Sites, May 1, 2025*

AIR QUALITY

Air Quality Trends: Ozone

	1990	1995	2000	2005	2010	2015	2020	2021	2022	2023
MSA[1]	n/a	n/a	n/a	n/a	n/a	n/a	n/a	n/a	n/a	n/a
U.S.	0.087	0.089	0.081	0.080	0.072	0.068	0.066	0.067	0.067	0.070

Note: (1) Data covers the Salt Lake City-Murray, UT Metropolitan Statistical Area; n/a not available. The values shown are the composite ozone concentration averages among trend sites based on the highest fourth daily maximum 8-hour concentration in parts per million. These trends are based on sites having an adequate record of monitoring data during the trend period. Data from exceptional events are included.
Source: U.S. Environmental Protection Agency, Air Quality Monitoring Information, "Air Quality Trends by City, 1990-2023"

Air Quality Index

Area	Percent of Days when Air Quality was...[2]					AQI Statistics[2]	
	Good	Moderate	Unhealthy for Sensitive Groups	Unhealthy	Very Unhealthy	Maximum	Median
MSA[1]	40.5	55.1	4.1	0.3	0.0	154	54

Note: (1) Data covers the Salt Lake City-Murray, UT Metropolitan Statistical Area; (2) Based on 365 days with AQI data in 2023. Air Quality Index (AQI) is an index for reporting daily air quality. EPA calculates the AQI for five major air pollutants regulated by the Clean Air Act: ground-level ozone, particle pollution (aka particulate matter), carbon monoxide, sulfur dioxide, and nitrogen dioxide. The AQI runs from 0 to 500. The higher the AQI value, the greater the level of air pollution and the greater the health concern. There are six AQI categories: "Good" AQI is between 0 and 50. Air quality is considered satisfactory; "Moderate" AQI is between 51 and 100. Air quality is acceptable; "Unhealthy for Sensitive Groups" When AQI values are between 101 and 150, members of sensitive groups may experience health effects; "Unhealthy" When AQI values are between 151 and 200 everyone may begin to experience health effects; "Very Unhealthy" AQI values between 201 and 300 trigger a health alert; "Hazardous" AQI values over 300 trigger warnings of emergency conditions (not shown).
Source: U.S. Environmental Protection Agency, Air Quality Index Report, 2023

Air Quality Index Pollutants

Area	Percent of Days when AQI Pollutant was...[2]					
	Carbon Monoxide	Nitrogen Dioxide	Ozone	Sulfur Dioxide	Particulate Matter 2.5	Particulate Matter 10
MSA[1]	0.0	5.5	60.0	(3)	32.3	2.2

Note: (1) Data covers the Salt Lake City-Murray, UT Metropolitan Statistical Area; (2) Based on 365 days with AQI data in 2023. The Air Quality Index (AQI) is an index for reporting daily air quality. EPA calculates the AQI for five major air pollutants regulated by the Clean Air Act: ground-level ozone, particle pollution (also known as particulate matter), carbon monoxide, sulfur dioxide, and nitrogen dioxide. The AQI runs from 0 to 500. The higher the AQI value, the greater the level of air pollution and the greater the health concern; (3) Sulfur dioxide is no longer included in this table because SO_2 concentrations tend to be very localized and not necessarily representative of broad geographical areas like counties and CBSAs.
Source: U.S. Environmental Protection Agency, Air Quality Index Report, 2023

Maximum Air Pollutant Concentrations: Particulate Matter, Ozone, CO and Lead

	Particulate Matter 10 (ug/m^3)	Particulate Matter 2.5 Wtd AM (ug/m^3)	Particulate Matter 2.5 24-Hr (ug/m^3)	Ozone (ppm)	Carbon Monoxide (ppm)	Lead (ug/m^3)
MSA[1] Level	79	8.6	31	0.076	1	n/a
NAAQS[2]	150	15	35	0.075	9	0.15
Met NAAQS[2]	Yes	Yes	Yes	No	Yes	n/a

Note: (1) Data covers the Salt Lake City-Murray, UT Metropolitan Statistical Area; Data from exceptional events are included; (2) National Ambient Air Quality Standards; ppm = parts per million; ug/m^3 = micrograms per cubic meter; n/a not available.
Concentrations: Particulate Matter 10 (coarse particulate)—highest second maximum 24-hour concentration; Particulate Matter 2.5 Wtd AM (fine particulate)—highest weighted annual mean concentration; Particulate Matter 2.5 24-Hour (fine particulate)—highest 98th percentile 24-hour concentration; Ozone—highest fourth daily maximum 8-hour concentration; Carbon Monoxide—highest second maximum non-overlapping 8-hour concentration; Lead—maximum running 3-month average
Source: U.S. Environmental Protection Agency, Air Quality Monitoring Information, "Air Quality Statistics by City, 2023"

Maximum Air Pollutant Concentrations: Nitrogen Dioxide and Sulfur Dioxide

	Nitrogen Dioxide AM (ppb)	Nitrogen Dioxide 1-Hr (ppb)	Sulfur Dioxide AM (ppb)	Sulfur Dioxide 1-Hr (ppb)	Sulfur Dioxide 24-Hr (ppb)
MSA[1] Level	16	57	n/a	5	n/a
NAAQS[2]	53	100	30	75	140
Met NAAQS[2]	Yes	Yes	n/a	Yes	n/a

Note: (1) Data covers the Salt Lake City-Murray, UT Metropolitan Statistical Area; Data from exceptional events are included; (2) National Ambient Air Quality Standards; ppm = parts per million; ug/m^3 = micrograms per cubic meter; n/a not available.
Concentrations: Nitrogen Dioxide AM—highest arithmetic mean concentration; Nitrogen Dioxide 1-Hr—highest 98th percentile 1-hour daily maximum concentration; Sulfur Dioxide AM—highest annual mean concentration; Sulfur Dioxide 1-Hr—highest 99th percentile 1-hour daily maximum concentration; Sulfur Dioxide 24-Hr—highest second maximum 24-hour concentration
Source: U.S. Environmental Protection Agency, Air Quality Monitoring Information, "Air Quality Statistics by City, 2023"

San Diego, California

Background

San Diego, 100 miles south of Los Angeles near the Mexican border, is characterized by sunny days, an excellent harbor, residents influenced by its Spanish heritage, and recreational activities based on ideal weather conditions.

San Diego was first claimed in 1542 for Spain by Juan Rodriguez Cabrillo, a Portuguese navigator in the service of the Spanish crown. The site remained uneventful until 1769, when Spanish colonizer, Gaspar de Portola, established the first European settlement in California. Accompanying de Portola was a Franciscan monk named Junipero Serra, who established the Mission Basilica San Diego de Alcala, the first of a chain of missions along the California coast.

After San Diego fell under the U.S. flag during the Mexican War of 1846, the city existed in relative isolation, deferring status and importance to its sister cities in the north, Los Angeles and San Francisco. Even when San Francisco businessman Alonzo Horton bought 1,000 acres of land near the harbor to establish a downtown there, San Diego remained secondary to both these cities, and saw a decrease in population from 40,000 in 1880 to 17,000 at the turn of the century.

World War II repopulated the city, when the Navy moved one of its bases from Pearl Harbor to San Diego. The naval base brought personnel and several related industries, such as nuclear and oceanographic research, and aviation development. In celebration of this past, the famed *Midway*, a 1,000-foot World War II aircraft carrier, has undergone a $6.5 million reconstruction and has been moved to Navy Pier, where it opened in 2004 as a floating museum.

Today, San Diego is the second most populous city in California, with plenty of outdoor activities, jobs, educational institutions, theaters, and museums. Its redevelopment agency has transformed what was largely an abandoned downtown into a glittering showcase of waterfront skyscrapers, live-work loft developments, five-star hotels, cafes, restaurants, and shops. The once-industrial East Village adjacent to PETCO ballpark is now the new frontier in San Diego's downtown urban renewal.

The western part of the U.S. has become the center for hot growth industries, specifically from Seattle to the Silicon Valley, and from San Diego to Denver. Telecommunications, biomedical products, software, and financial services are all prominent in these regions, with San Diego leading the country in biotechnology companies.

Expansion of the city's trolley service was completed in 2021 and that same year renovations to San Diego International Airport began; a new parking plaza opened in early 2025 and new access roads are under construction to be followed by a new terminal with 30 new gates by 2030. Plans for "Midway Rising," an ambitious over hall of San Diego's Sports Arena are in the works.

San Diego is a LGBTQ-friendly city, with the seventh-highest percentage of gay residents in the U.S. Additionally, San Diego State University (SDSU), one of the city's prominent universities, has been named one of the top LGBTQ-friendly campuses in the nation.

The city's Windansea Beach, known for its reef break and iconic palm frond shack, attracts some of the best surfers in the world. Windansea was the inspiration for the popular "Beach Party" movies in the 1960s. Today, the Windansea Surf Club continues to compete in surf contests and combines community involvement with its competitive heritage. Windansea's surf shack, originally built in 1946, has been rebuilt by surfers numerous times after storms destroyed it. Designated a Historical Landmark in 1998, it remains a symbol of San Diego's surfing heritage and Hawaiian roots.

San Diego summers are cool, and winters are warm in comparison with other locations along the same general latitude, due to the Pacific Ocean. A marked feature of the climate is the wide variation in temperature. In nearby valleys, daytime temperatures are much warmer in summer and noticeably cooler on winter nights than in the city proper. As is usual on the Pacific Coast, nighttime and early morning cloudiness is the norm. Considerable fog occurs along the coast, especially during the winter months.

Rankings

General Rankings

- To help military veterans find the best places in which to settle down, *WalletHub* compared the 100 largest U.S. cities across 19 key indicators of livability, affordability and veteran-friendliness. They range from the share of military skill-related jobs to veteran income growth to the availability of VA health facilities. San Diego ranked #17. *Wallethub.com, "Best & Worst Places for Veterans to Live (2025)," November 7, 2024*

- For its 37th annual "Readers' Choice Awards" survey, *Condé Nast Traveler* ranked its readers' favorite cities in the U.S. Whether it be a longed-for visit or the next big new thing, these are the places travelers loved best. The list was broken into large cities and cities under 250,000. San Diego ranked #2 in the big city category. *Condé Nast Traveler, Readers' Choice Awards 2024, "Best Big Cities in the U.S." October 1, 2024*

Business/Finance Rankings

- Payscale.com ranked the 32 largest metro areas in terms of wage growth. The San Diego metro area ranked #24. Criteria: quarterly changes in private industry employee and education professional wage growth from the previous year. *PayScale, "Wage Trends by Metro Area-4th Quarter," February 4, 2025*

- For its annual survey of the "Most Expensive U.S. Cities to Live In," Kiplinger applied Cost of Living Index statistics developed by the Council for Community and Economic Research to U.S. Census Bureau population and median household income data for 265 urban areas. San Diego ranked #10 among the most expensive in the country. *Kiplinger.com, "The 10 Most Expensive Cities to Live in the U.S.," February 3, 2025*

- The San Diego metro area appeared on the Milken Institute "2025 Best Performing Cities" list. Rank: #71 out of 200 large metro areas (based on performance category). Criteria: job growth; wage growth; high-tech growth and impact; community resilience; housing affordability; household broadband access. *Milken Institute, "Best-Performing Cities 2025," January 14, 2025*

Children/Family Rankings

- San Diego was selected as one of the best cities for newlyweds by *Rent.com*. The city ranked #9 of 15. Criteria: cost of living; availability of affordable rental inventory; annual household income; entertainment, culture and restaurant options; percentage of married couples; concentration of millennials; and safety. *Rent.com, "The 15 Best Cities for Newlyweds," September 2, 2021*

Dating/Romance Rankings

- *Apartment List* conducted its Annual Renter Satisfaction Survey and asked renters "how satisfied are you with opportunities for dating in your current city." The cities were ranked from highest to lowest based on their satisfaction scores. San Diego ranked #4 out of 10 cities. *Apartment List, "Best Cities for Dating 2022 with Local Dating Insights from Bumble," February 7, 2022*

Education Rankings

- Personal finance website *WalletHub* analyzed the 150 largest U.S. metropolitan statistical areas to determine where the most educated Americans are putting their degrees to work. Criteria: education levels; percentage of workers with degrees; education quality and attainment gap; public school quality rankings; quality and enrollment of each metro area's universities. San Diego was ranked #23 (#1 = most educated city). *WalletHub.com, "Most & Least Educated Cities in America, 2025" July 2, 2024*

Environmental Rankings

- The U.S. Environmental Protection Agency (EPA) released its list of U.S. metropolitan areas with the most ENERGY STAR certified buildings in 2023. The San Diego metro area was ranked #13 out of 25. *U.S. Environmental Protection Agency, "2024 Energy Star Top Cities," May 22, 2024*

- The U.S. Conference of Mayors and Walmart Stores sponsor the Mayors' Climate Protection Awards Program which recognize mayors for outstanding and innovative practices that address the climate crisis: increase energy efficiency in their cities, reduce carbon emissions and expand renewable energy. San Diego received an Honorable Mention in the large city category. *U.S. Conference of Mayors, "2024 Mayors' Climate Protection Awards," June 20, 2024*

- San Diego was highlighted as one of the 25 most ozone-polluted metro areas in the U.S. during 2021 through 2023. The area ranked #8. *American Lung Association, "State of the Air 2025," April 23, 2025*

Food/Drink Rankings

- WalletHub compared the 100 largest U.S. cities across 17 key indicators of vegan- and vegetarian-friendliness. San Diego was ranked #4. Cities were selected based on metrics such as the cost of groceries for vegetarians, the share of restaurants serving meatless options and the number of salad shops per capita. *WalletHub.com, "Best Cities for Vegans & Vegetarians (2025)," September 24, 2024*

Health/Fitness Rankings

- For each of the 100 largest cities in the United States, the American Fitness Index®, compiled in partnership between the American College of Sports Medicine and the Elevance Health Foundation, evaluated community infrastructure and more than 30 health behaviors including preventive health, levels of chronic disease conditions, food insecurity, pedestrian safety, air quality, and community/environment resources that support physical activity. San Diego ranked #11 for "community fitness." *americanfitnessindex.org, "2024 ACSM American Fitness Index Summary Report," July 23, 2024*

- San Diego was identified as a "2025 Allergy Capital." The area ranked #97 out of the nation's 100 largest metropolitan areas. Three groups of factors were used to identify the most challenging cities for people with allergies: annual tree, grass, and weed pollen scores; over the counter allergy medicine use; number of board-certified allergy specialists. *Asthma and Allergy Foundation of America, "2025 Allergy Capitals: The Most Challenging Places to Live with Allergies," March 18, 2025*

- San Diego was identified as a "2024 Asthma Capital." The area ranked #50 out of the nation's 100 largest metropolitan areas. Criteria: estimated asthma prevalence; asthma-related mortality; and ER visits due to asthma. Risk factors analyzed but not factored in the rankings: annual air quality including pollution and ozone levels; public smoking laws; indoor air quality; access to asthma specialists; rescue and controller medication use; uninsured rate; pollen allergy; poverty rate. *Asthma and Allergy Foundation of America, "Asthma Capitals 2024: The Most Challenging Places to Live With Asthma," September 10, 2024*

Pet Rankings

- San Diego was selected by *Sniffspot.com* as one of the most dog-friendly cities in the U.S., ranking #7 out of 50. Criteria: dog parks; hiking; sniffspots; public parks; dog-friendly businesses; housing; dog waste cleanliness; leash laws; dog services; and overall cost. *Sniffspot.com, "The Top 50 Most Dog-Friendly Cities in the U.S.," September 30, 2024*

Real Estate Rankings

- *WalletHub* compared the most populated U.S. cities to determine which had the best markets for real estate agents. San Diego ranked #17 where demand was high and pay was the best. Criteria: sales per agent; annual median wage for real-estate agents; monthly average starting salary for real estate agents; real estate job density and competition; unemployment rate; home turnover rate; housing-market health index; and other relevant metrics. *WalletHub.com, "2021 Best Places to Be a Real Estate Agent," May 12, 2021*

- The San Diego metro area was identified as one of the 10 worst condo markets in the U.S. in 2024. The area ranked #63 out of 63 markets. Criteria: year-over-year change of median sales price of existing apartment condo-coop homes between the 4th quarter of 2023 and the 4th quarter of 2024. *National Association of Realtors®, Median Sales Price of Existing Apartment Condo-Coops Homes for Metropolitan Areas, 4th Quarter 2024*

- The San Diego metro area was identified as one of the 20 least affordable housing markets in the U.S. in 2024. The area ranked #222 out of 226 markets. Criteria: qualification for a mortgage loan with a 10 percent down payment on a typical home. *National Association of Realtors®, Qualifying Income Based on Sales Price of Existing Single-Family Homes for Metropolitan Areas, February 6, 2025*

- San Diego was ranked #173 out of 176 metro areas in terms of cost of housing in 2024 by the National Association of Home Builders (#1 = most affordable). Criteria: the portion of an average family's income necessary to pay the mortgage on a median-priced home. *National Association of Home Builders®, NAHB-Wells Fargo Cost of Housing Index, 4th Quarter 2024*

Safety Rankings

- Allstate ranked the 100 most populous cities in America in terms of driver safety. San Diego ranked #70. Criteria based on anonymized driving behavior data from Allstate's mobile app powered by Arity: high speed driving (over 80 mph), phone handling, and hard braking. The report helps increase the importance of safety and awareness behind the wheel. *Allstate, "16th Allstate America's Best Drivers Report®" July 11, 2024*

Women/Minorities Rankings

- *Travel + Leisure* listed the best cities in and around the U.S. for a memorable and fun girls' trip, even on a budget. Whether it is for a special occasion, to make new memories or just to get away, San Diego is sure to have something for all the ladies in your tribe. *Travel + Leisure, "25 Affordable Girls Weekend Getaways That Won't Break the Bank," January 30, 2025*

- San Diego was listed as one of the most LGBTQ-friendly cities in America by *The Advocate*, as compiled by the real estate data site *Clever*. The city ranked #7 out of 15. Criteria, among many: Pride events; gay bars; LGBTQ-affirming healthcare options; state and local laws; number of PFLAG chapters; LGBTQ+ population. *The Advocate, "These Are the 15 Most LGBTQ-Friendly Cities in the U.S." November 1, 2023*

- Personal finance website *WalletHub* compared more than 180 U.S. cities across two key dimensions, "Hispanic Business-Friendliness" and "Hispanic Purchasing Power," to arrive at the most favorable conditions for Hispanic entrepreneurs. San Diego was ranked #126 out of 182. Criteria includes: share of Hispanic-Owned Businesses; average growth of Hispanic Business revenues; Small Business-Friendliness score; affordability; and number of Hispanics with at least a bachelor's degree. *WalletHub.com, "Best Cities for Hispanic Entrepreneurs," September 4, 2024*

Miscellaneous Rankings

- San Diego was selected as a 2024 Digital Cities Survey winner. The city ranked #1 in the large city (500,000 or more population) category. The survey examined and assessed how city governments are utilizing new technology and modernized applications to provide residents an array of contactless services and conveniences. Survey questions focused on ten initiatives: cybersecurity; citizen experience; disaster recovery; business intelligence; IT personnel retention; data governance; business automation; AI/machine learning; application modernization; and IT collaboration. *Center for Digital Government, "2024 Digital Cities Survey," November 5, 2024*

- In its roundup of St. Patrick's Day parades, *Gayot* listed the best festivals and parades of all things Irish. The festivities in San Diego as among the best in North America. *Gayot.com, "Best St. Patrick's Day Parades," March 2025*

- The financial planning site *SmartAsset* has compiled its annual study on the best places for Halloween in the U.S. for 2022. 146 cities were compared to determine that San Diego ranked #16 out of 35 for still being able to enjoy the festivities despite COVID-19. Metrics included: safety, family-friendliness, percentage of children in the population, concentration of candy and costume shops, weather and COVID infection rates. *SmartAsset.com, "2022 Edition-Best Places to Celebrate Halloween," October 19, 2022*

- *WalletHub* compared 148 of the most populated U.S. cities to determine their operating efficiency. A "Quality of Services" score was constructed for each city and then measured against the total budget per capita to reveal which were managed the best. San Diego ranked #79. Criteria: financial stability; economy; education; safety; health; infrastructure and pollution. *WalletHub.com, "2025's Best- & Worst-Run Cities in America," June 18, 2024*

Business Environment

DEMOGRAPHICS

Population Growth

Area	1990 Census	2000 Census	2010 Census	2020 Census	2023 Estimate[2]	Population Growth 1990-2023 (%)
City	1,111,048	1,223,400	1,307,402	1,386,932	1,385,061	24.7
MSA[1]	2,498,016	2,813,833	3,095,313	3,298,634	3,282,782	31.4
U.S.	248,709,873	281,421,906	308,745,538	331,449,281	332,387,540	33.6

Note: (1) Figures cover the San Diego-Chula Vista-Carlsbad, CA Metropolitan Statistical Area; (2) 2019-2023 5-year ACS population estimate
Source: U.S. Census Bureau, 1990 Census, 2000 Census, 2010 Census, 2020 Census, 2019-2023 American Community Survey 5-Year Estimates

Race

Area	White Alone[2] (%)	Black Alone[2] (%)	Asian Alone[2] (%)	AIAN[3] Alone[2] (%)	NHOPI[4] Alone[2] (%)	Other Race Alone[2] (%)	Two or More Races (%)
City	50.4	5.7	17.6	0.7	0.5	9.5	15.6
MSA[1]	53.0	4.7	12.2	0.9	0.4	10.6	18.1
U.S.	63.4	12.4	5.8	0.9	0.2	6.6	10.7

Note: (1) Figures cover the San Diego-Chula Vista-Carlsbad, CA Metropolitan Statistical Area; (2) Alone is defined as not being in combination with one or more other races; (3) American Indian and Alaska Native; (4) Native Hawaiian and Other Pacific Islander
Source: U.S. Census Bureau, 2019-2023 American Community Survey 5-Year Estimates

Hispanic or Latino Origin

Area	Total (%)	Mexican (%)	Puerto Rican (%)	Cuban (%)	Other (%)
City	29.6	24.9	0.8	0.3	3.6
MSA[1]	34.3	29.6	0.8	0.2	3.6
U.S.	19.0	11.3	1.8	0.7	5.2

Note: Persons of Hispanic or Latino origin can be of any race; (1) Figures cover the San Diego-Chula Vista-Carlsbad, CA Metropolitan Statistical Area
Source: U.S. Census Bureau, 2019-2023 American Community Survey 5-Year Estimates

Age

Area	Percent of Population									Median Age
	Under Age 5	Age 5–19	Age 20–34	Age 35–44	Age 45–54	Age 55–64	Age 65–74	Age 75–84	Age 85+	
City	5.3	16.6	26.4	14.7	12.0	10.9	8.2	4.3	1.7	36.0
MSA[1]	5.7	18.2	23.0	14.1	12.1	11.8	8.9	4.4	1.8	37.1
U.S.	5.7	19.1	20.2	13.1	12.3	12.8	10.0	4.9	1.9	38.7

Note: (1) Figures cover the San Diego-Chula Vista-Carlsbad, CA Metropolitan Statistical Area
Source: U.S. Census Bureau, 2019-2023 American Community Survey 5-Year Estimates

Disability by Age

Area	All Ages	Under 18 Years Old	18 to 64 Years Old	65 Years and Over
City	10.0	3.4	7.3	31.2
MSA[1]	10.7	3.6	8.2	31.3
U.S.	13.0	4.7	10.7	32.9

Note: Figures show percent of the civilian noninstitutionalized population that reported having a disability. Disability status is determined from six types of difficulty: vision, hearing, cognitive, ambulatory, self-care, and independent living. For children under 5 years old, hearing and vision difficulty are used to determine disability status. For children between the ages of 5 and 14, disability status is determined from hearing, vision, cognitive, ambulatory, and self-care difficulties. For people aged 15 years and older, they are considered to have a disability if they have difficulty with any one of the six difficulty types; Note: (1) Figures cover the San Diego-Chula Vista-Carlsbad, CA Metropolitan Statistical Area
Source: U.S. Census Bureau, 2019-2023 American Community Survey 5-Year Estimates

Ancestry

Area	German	Irish	English	American	Italian	Polish	French[2]	European	Scottish
City	8.7	7.3	7.0	2.3	4.2	1.8	1.7	1.7	1.3
MSA[1]	9.0	7.5	7.6	2.6	4.1	1.6	1.8	1.9	1.5
U.S.	12.6	9.4	9.1	5.5	4.9	2.6	2.0	1.6	1.6

Note: Figures are the percentage of the total population reporting a particular ancestry. The nine most commonly reported ancestries in the U.S. are shown. Figures include multiple ancestries (e.g. if a person reported being Irish and Italian, they were included in both columns); (1) Figures cover the San Diego-Chula Vista-Carlsbad, CA Metropolitan Statistical Area; (2) Excludes Basque
Source: U.S. Census Bureau, 2019-2023 American Community Survey 5-Year Estimates

Foreign-born Population

| Area | Any Foreign Country | Percent of Population Born in | | | | | | | |
		Asia	Mexico	Europe	Caribbean	Central America[2]	South America	Africa	Canada
City	24.8	11.8	7.5	2.3	0.2	0.5	0.9	1.0	0.4
MSA[1]	22.5	8.9	9.1	1.9	0.2	0.6	0.7	0.6	0.4
U.S.	13.9	4.3	3.3	1.4	1.4	1.2	1.2	0.8	0.2

Note: (1) Figures cover the San Diego-Chula Vista-Carlsbad, CA Metropolitan Statistical Area; (2) Excludes Mexico.
Source: U.S. Census Bureau, 2019-2023 American Community Survey 5-Year Estimates

Household Size

| Area | Persons in Household (%) | | | | | | | Average Household Size |
	One	Two	Three	Four	Five	Six	Seven or More	
City	28.8	34.2	15.5	12.8	5.4	2.0	1.4	2.55
MSA[1]	24.5	33.0	16.7	14.6	6.7	2.6	1.8	2.74
U.S.	28.5	33.8	15.4	12.7	5.9	2.3	1.4	2.54

Note: (1) Figures cover the San Diego-Chula Vista-Carlsbad, CA Metropolitan Statistical Area
Source: U.S. Census Bureau, 2019-2023 American Community Survey 5-Year Estimates

Household Relationships

Area	House-holder	Opposite-sex Spouse	Same-sex Spouse	Opposite-sex Unmarried Partner	Same-sex Unmarried Partner	Child[2]	Grand-child	Other Relatives	Non-relatives
City	37.2	15.7	0.4	2.6	0.3	25.0	2.0	6.2	6.1
MSA[1]	35.1	16.9	0.3	2.3	0.2	27.8	2.3	6.6	5.1
U.S.	38.3	17.5	0.2	2.5	0.2	28.3	2.4	4.8	3.4

Note: Figures are percent of the total population; (1) Figures cover the San Diego-Chula Vista-Carlsbad, CA Metropolitan Statistical Area; (2) Includes biological, adopted, and stepchildren of the householder
Source: U.S. Census Bureau, 2020 Census

Gender

Area	Males	Females	Males per 100 Females
City	703,091	681,970	103.1
MSA[1]	1,660,156	1,622,626	102.3
U.S.	164,545,087	167,842,453	98.0

Note: (1) Figures cover the San Diego-Chula Vista-Carlsbad, CA Metropolitan Statistical Area
Source: U.S. Census Bureau, 2019-2023 American Community Survey 5-Year Estimates

Marital Status

Area	Never Married	Now Married[2]	Separated	Widowed	Divorced
City	40.5	44.7	1.6	3.9	9.2
MSA[1]	36.3	48.1	1.6	4.4	9.6
U.S.	34.1	47.9	1.7	5.6	10.7

Note: Figures are percentages and cover the population 15 years of age and older; (1) Figures cover the San Diego-Chula Vista-Carlsbad, CA Metropolitan Statistical Area; (2) Excludes separated
Source: U.S. Census Bureau, 2019-2023 American Community Survey 5-Year Estimates

Religious Groups by Family

Area	Catholic	Baptist	Methodist	LDS[2]	Pentecostal	Lutheran	Islam	Adventist	Other
MSA[1]	22.9	1.5	0.6	2.1	1.0	0.6	1.5	1.9	9.4
U.S.	18.7	7.3	3.0	2.0	1.8	1.7	1.3	1.3	11.6

Note: Figures are the number of adherents as a percentage of the total population and cover the eight largest religious groups in the U.S; (1) Figures cover the San Diego-Chula Vista-Carlsbad, CA Metropolitan Statistical Area; (2) Church of Jesus Christ of Latter-day Saints
Sources: 2020 U.S. Religion Census, Association of Statisticians of American Religious Bodies; The Association of Religion Data Archives (ARDA)

Religious Groups by Tradition

Area	Catholic	Evangelical Protestant	Mainline Protestant	Black Protestant	Islam	Judaism	Hinduism	Orthodox	Buddhism
MSA[1]	22.9	9.5	1.5	0.6	1.5	0.4	0.3	0.4	0.7
U.S.	18.7	16.5	5.2	2.3	1.3	0.6	0.4	0.4	0.3

Note: Figures are the number of adherents as a percentage of the total population; (1) Figures cover the San Diego-Chula Vista-Carlsbad, CA Metropolitan Statistical Area
Sources: 2020 U.S. Religion Census, Association of Statisticians of American Religious Bodies; The Association of Religion Data Archives (ARDA)

ECONOMY

Real Gross Domestic Product (GDP)

Area	2017	2018	2019	2020	2021	2022	2023	Rank[3]
MSA[1]	224.8	230.5	236.6	233.3	250.4	258.0	261.7	17
U.S.[2]	17,619.1	18,160.7	18,642.5	18,238.9	19,387.6	19,896.6	20,436.3	–

Note: Figures are in billions of chained 2017 dollars; (1) Figures cover the San Diego-Chula Vista-Carlsbad, CA Metropolitan Statistical Area; (2) Figures cover real GDP within metropolitan areas; (3) Rank is based on 2023 data and ranges from 1 to 384
Source: U.S. Bureau of Economic Analysis

Economic Growth

Area	2014	2015	2016	2017	2018	2019	2020	2021	2022	2023
MSA[1]	3.1	3.3	1.3	3.7	2.6	2.7	-1.4	7.3	3.1	1.4
U.S.[2]	2.6	3.2	2.0	2.7	3.1	2.7	-2.2	6.3	2.6	2.7

Note: Figures are real gross domestic product growth rates and represent percent change from preceding period; (1) Figures cover the San Diego-Chula Vista-Carlsbad, CA Metropolitan Statistical Area; (2) Figures are the average growth rates within metropolitan areas
Source: U.S. Bureau of Economic Analysis

Metropolitan Area Exports

Area	2018	2019	2020	2021	2022	2023	Rank[2]
MSA[1]	20,156.8	19,774.1	18,999.7	23,687.8	24,657.9	22,975.3	22
U.S.	1,664,056.1	1,645,173.7	1,431,406.6	1,753,941.4	2,062,937.4	2,019,160.5	–

Note: Figures are in millions of dollars; (1) Figures cover the San Diego-Chula Vista-Carlsbad, CA Metropolitan Statistical Area; (2) Rank is based on 2023 data and ranges from 1 to 386
Source: U.S. Department of Commerce, International Trade Administration, Office of Trade and Economic Analysis, Industry and Analysis, Exports by Metropolitan Area, data extracted April 2, 2025

Building Permits

Area	Single-Family			Multi-Family			Total		
	2023	2024	Pct. Chg.	2023	2024	Pct. Chg.	2023	2024	Pct. Chg.
City	516	775	50.2	5,249	5,840	11.3	5,765	6,615	14.7
MSA[1]	3,049	3,377	10.8	8,420	8,195	-2.7	11,469	11,572	0.9
U.S.	920,000	981,900	6.7	591,100	496,100	-16.1	1,511,100	1,478,000	-2.2

Note: (1) Figures cover the San Diego-Chula Vista-Carlsbad, CA Metropolitan Statistical Area; Figures represent new, privately-owned housing units authorized (unadjusted data)
Source: U.S. Census Bureau, Building Permits Survey (BPS), 2023, 2024

Bankruptcy Filings

Area	Business Filings			Nonbusiness Filings		
	2023	2024	% Chg.	2023	2024	% Chg.
San Diego County	214	267	24.8	3,866	4,558	17.9
U.S.	18,926	23,107	22.1	434,064	494,201	13.9

Note: Business filings include Chapter 7, Chapter 9, Chapter 11, Chapter 12, Chapter 13, Chapter 15, and Section 304; Nonbusiness filings include Chapter 7, Chapter 11, and Chapter 13
Source: Administrative Office of the U.S. Courts, Business and Nonbusiness Bankruptcy, County Cases Commenced by Chapter of the Bankruptcy Code, During the 12-Month Period Ending December 31, 2023 and Business and Nonbusiness Bankruptcy, County Cases Commenced by Chapter of the Bankruptcy Code, During the 12-Month Period Ending December 31, 2024

Housing Vacancy Rates

Area	Gross Vacancy Rate[3] (%)			Year-Round Vacancy Rate[4] (%)			Rental Vacancy Rate[5] (%)			Homeowner Vacancy Rate[6] (%)		
	2022	2023	2024	2022	2023	2024	2022	2023	2024	2022	2023	2024
MSA[1]	6.9	6.8	6.4	6.6	6.2	6.0	3.6	4.1	5.2	0.6	0.2	0.5
U.S.[2]	9.1	9.0	9.1	7.5	7.5	7.6	5.7	6.5	6.8	0.8	0.8	1.0

Note: (1) Figures cover the San Diego-Chula Vista-Carlsbad, CA Metropolitan Statistical Area; (2) Figures cover the 75 largest Metropolitan Statistical Areas; (3) The percentage of the total housing inventory that is vacant; (4) The percentage of the housing inventory (excluding seasonal units) that is year-round vacant; (5) The percentage of rental inventory that is vacant for rent; (6) The percentage of homeowner inventory that is vacant for sale
Source: U.S. Census Bureau, Housing Vacancies and Homeownership Annual Statistics: 2022, 2023, 2024

INCOME

Income

Area	Per Capita ($)	Median Household ($)	Average Household ($)
City	54,678	104,321	139,707
MSA[1]	49,891	102,285	136,236
U.S.	43,289	78,538	110,491

Note: (1) Figures cover the San Diego-Chula Vista-Carlsbad, CA Metropolitan Statistical Area
Source: U.S. Census Bureau, 2019-2023 American Community Survey 5-Year Estimates

Household Income Distribution

Area	Percent of Households Earning							
	Under $15,000	$15,000 -$24,999	$25,000 -$34,999	$35,000 -$49,999	$50,000 -$74,999	$75,000 -$99,999	$100,000 -$149,999	$150,000 and up
City	6.7	4.4	4.8	7.3	12.5	12.4	19.4	32.5
MSA[1]	6.3	4.7	5.0	7.8	13.1	12.1	19.1	31.9
U.S.	8.5	6.6	6.8	10.4	15.7	12.7	17.4	21.9

Note: (1) Figures cover the San Diego-Chula Vista-Carlsbad, CA Metropolitan Statistical Area
Source: U.S. Census Bureau, 2019-2023 American Community Survey 5-Year Estimates

Poverty Rate

Area	All Ages	Under 18 Years Old	18 to 64 Years Old	65 Years and Over
City	11.1	12.3	11.0	10.2
MSA[1]	10.4	12.0	10.0	9.4
U.S.	12.4	16.3	11.6	10.4

Note: Figures are percentage of people whose income during the past 12 months was below the poverty level;
(1) Figures cover the San Diego-Chula Vista-Carlsbad, CA Metropolitan Statistical Area
Source: U.S. Census Bureau, 2019-2023 American Community Survey 5-Year Estimates

EMPLOYMENT

Labor Force and Employment

Area	Civilian Labor Force			Workers Employed		
	Dec. 2023	Dec. 2024	% Chg.	Dec. 2023	Dec. 2024	% Chg.
City	730,171	734,863	0.6	701,246	703,991	0.4
MSA[1]	1,608,713	1,619,332	0.7	1,543,490	1,549,532	0.4
U.S.	166,661,000	167,746,000	0.7	160,754,000	161,294,000	0.3

Note: Data is not seasonally adjusted and covers workers 16 years of age and older; (1) Figures cover the San Diego-Chula Vista-Carlsbad, CA Metropolitan Statistical Area
Source: Bureau of Labor Statistics, Local Area Unemployment Statistics

Unemployment Rate

Area	2024											
	Jan.	Feb.	Mar.	Apr.	May	Jun.	Jul.	Aug.	Sep.	Oct.	Nov.	Dec.
City	4.4	4.4	4.2	3.8	3.7	4.4	4.8	4.9	4.3	4.4	4.5	4.2
MSA[1]	4.5	4.5	4.2	3.9	3.7	4.6	4.9	5.0	4.5	4.6	4.6	4.3
U.S.	4.1	4.2	3.9	3.5	3.7	4.3	4.5	4.4	3.9	3.9	4.0	3.8

Note: Data is not seasonally adjusted and covers workers 16 years of age and older; (1) Figures cover the San Diego-Chula Vista-Carlsbad, CA Metropolitan Statistical Area
Source: Bureau of Labor Statistics, Local Area Unemployment Statistics

Average Wages

Occupation	$/Hr.	Occupation	$/Hr.
Accountants and Auditors	50.36	Maintenance and Repair Workers	27.48
Automotive Mechanics	29.84	Marketing Managers	93.41
Bookkeepers	28.01	Network and Computer Systems Admin.	50.55
Carpenters	36.37	Nurses, Licensed Practical	37.47
Cashiers	18.50	Nurses, Registered	67.00
Computer Programmers	60.74	Nursing Assistants	23.07
Computer Systems Analysts	57.81	Office Clerks, General	23.88
Computer User Support Specialists	35.01	Physical Therapists	52.74
Construction Laborers	30.44	Physicians	133.58
Cooks, Restaurant	21.15	Plumbers, Pipefitters and Steamfitters	36.03
Customer Service Representatives	24.53	Police and Sheriff's Patrol Officers	53.06
Dentists	87.88	Postal Service Mail Carriers	28.81
Electricians	39.61	Real Estate Sales Agents	33.54
Engineers, Electrical	65.99	Retail Salespersons	20.16
Fast Food and Counter Workers	18.39	Sales Representatives, Technical/Scientific	56.30
Financial Managers	92.64	Secretaries, Exc. Legal/Medical/Executive	26.29
First-Line Supervisors of Office Workers	36.65	Security Guards	21.29
General and Operations Managers	n/a	Surgeons	215.16
Hairdressers/Cosmetologists	22.37	Teacher Assistants, Exc. Postsecondary[1]	20.95
Home Health and Personal Care Aides	17.55	Teachers, Secondary School, Exc. Sp. Ed.[1]	54.30
Janitors and Cleaners	19.51	Telemarketers	19.47
Landscaping/Groundskeeping Workers	21.52	Truck Drivers, Heavy/Tractor-Trailer	28.38
Lawyers	93.11	Truck Drivers, Light/Delivery Services	23.68
Maids and Housekeeping Cleaners	20.83	Waiters and Waitresses	22.56

Note: Wage data covers the San Diego-Chula Vista-Carlsbad, CA Metropolitan Statistical Area; (1) Hourly wages were calculated from annual wage data based on a 40 hour work week
Source: Bureau of Labor Statistics, Metro Area Occupational Employment & Wage Estimates, May 2024

Employment by Industry

Sector	MSA[1]		U.S.
	Number of Employees	Percent of Total	Percent of Total
Construction	90,600	5.7	5.1
Financial Activities	71,800	4.5	5.8
Government	262,800	16.6	14.9
Information	20,800	1.3	1.9
Leisure and Hospitality	203,400	12.9	10.4
Manufacturing	111,200	7.0	8.0
Mining and Logging	300	<0.1	0.4
Other Services	57,000	3.6	3.7
Private Education and Health Services	261,800	16.6	16.9
Professional and Business Services	267,700	17.0	14.2
Retail Trade	143,100	9.1	10.0
Transportation, Warehousing, and Utilities	45,400	2.9	4.8
Wholesale Trade	42,700	2.7	3.9

Note: Figures are non-farm employment as of December 2024. Figures are not seasonally adjusted and include workers 16 years of age and older; (1) Figures cover the San Diego-Chula Vista-Carlsbad, CA Metropolitan Statistical Area
Source: Bureau of Labor Statistics, Current Employment Statistics, Employment, Hours, and Earnings

Employment by Occupation

Occupation Classification	City (%)	MSA[1] (%)	U.S. (%)
Management, Business, Science, and Arts	53.0	46.9	42.0
Natural Resources, Construction, and Maintenance	5.0	7.1	8.6
Production, Transportation, and Material Moving	8.3	9.6	13.0
Sales and Office	17.2	19.0	19.9
Service	16.5	17.4	16.5

Note: Figures cover employed civilians 16 years of age and older; (1) Figures cover the San Diego-Chula Vista-Carlsbad, CA Metropolitan Statistical Area
Source: U.S. Census Bureau, 2019-2023 American Community Survey 5-Year Estimates

Occupations with Greatest Projected Employment Growth: 2022 – 2032

Occupation[1]	2022 Employment	2032 Projected Employment	Numeric Employment Change	Percent Employment Change
Home Health and Personal Care Aides	796,900	1,060,200	263,300	33.0
Software Developers	313,700	388,000	74,300	23.7
Registered Nurses	333,700	376,900	43,200	12.9
Cooks, Restaurant	142,100	184,000	41,900	29.5
Laborers and Freight, Stock, and Material Movers, Hand	399,500	437,300	37,800	9.5
Janitors and Cleaners, Except Maids and Housekeeping Cleaners	262,900	300,200	37,300	14.2
Fast Food and Counter Workers	419,100	455,200	36,100	8.6
Stockers and Order Fillers	289,900	322,900	33,000	11.4
Medical Assistants	108,000	135,700	27,700	25.6
Landscaping and Groundskeeping Workers	135,200	162,100	26,900	19.9

Note: Projections cover California; (1) Sorted by numeric employment change
Source: www.projectionscentral.org, State Occupational Projections, 2022–2032 Long-Term Projections

Fastest-Growing Occupations: 2022 – 2032

Occupation[1]	2022 Employment	2032 Projected Employment	Numeric Employment Change	Percent Employment Change
Nurse Practitioners	21,500	34,100	12,600	58.6
Physical Therapist Assistants	7,900	11,200	3,300	41.8
Solar Photovoltaic Installers	7,900	11,200	3,300	41.8
Physician Assistants	13,000	18,200	5,200	40.0
Medical and Health Services Managers	58,300	81,400	23,100	39.6
Statisticians	2,800	3,900	1,100	39.3
Taxi Drivers	48,100	66,800	18,700	38.9
Occupational Therapy Assistants	2,700	3,600	900	33.3
Home Health and Personal Care Aides	796,900	1,060,200	263,300	33.0
Data Scientists	33,900	45,000	11,100	32.7

Note: Projections cover California; (1) Sorted by percent employment change and excludes occupations with numeric employment change less than 50
Source: www.projectionscentral.org, State Occupational Projections, 2022–2032 Long-Term Projections

CITY FINANCES

City Government Finances

Component	2022 ($000)	2022 ($ per capita)
Total Revenues	5,230,498	3,677
Total Expenditures	4,750,085	3,339
Debt Outstanding	5,585,303	3,927

Source: U.S. Census Bureau, State & Local Government Finances 2022

City Government Revenue by Source

Source	2022 ($000)	2022 ($ per capita)	2022 (%)
General Revenue			
From Federal Government	868,487	611	16.6
From State Government	82,200	58	1.6
From Local Governments	35,424	25	0.7
Taxes			
Property	679,409	478	13.0
Sales and Gross Receipts	870,838	612	16.6
Personal Income	0	0	0.0
Corporate Income	0	0	0.0
Motor Vehicle License	0	0	0.0
Other Taxes	71,379	50	1.4
Current Charges	1,655,646	1,164	31.7
Liquor Store	0	0	0.0
Utility	584,850	411	11.2

Source: U.S. Census Bureau, State & Local Government Finances 2022

City Government Expenditures by Function

Function	2022 ($000)	2022 ($ per capita)	2022 (%)
General Direct Expenditures			
Air Transportation	5,554	3	0.1
Corrections	0	0	0.0
Education	0	0	0.0
Employment Security Administration	0	0	0.0
Financial Administration	64,629	45	1.4
Fire Protection	240,115	168	5.1
General Public Buildings	104,573	73	2.2
Governmental Administration, Other	400,152	281	8.4
Health	5,719	4	0.1
Highways	306,459	215	6.5
Hospitals	0	0	0.0
Housing and Community Development	773,194	543	16.3
Interest on General Debt	142,417	100	3.0
Judicial and Legal	69,701	49	1.5
Libraries	49,608	34	1.0
Parking	0	0	0.0
Parks and Recreation	361,636	254	7.6
Police Protection	456,050	320	9.6
Public Welfare	0	0	0.0
Sewerage	323,643	227	6.8
Solid Waste Management	107,432	75	2.3
Veterans' Services	0	0	0.0
Liquor Store	0	0	0.0
Utility	646,349	454	13.6

Source: U.S. Census Bureau, State & Local Government Finances 2022

TAXES

State Corporate Income Tax Rates

State	Tax Rate (%)	Income Brackets ($)	Num. of Brackets	Financial Institution Tax Rate (%)[a]	Federal Income Tax Ded.
California	8.84 (b)	Flat rate	1	10.84 (b)	No

Note: Tax rates for tax year 2024; (a) Rates listed are the corporate income tax rate applied to financial institutions or excise taxes based on income. Some states have other taxes based upon the value of deposits or shares; (b) Minimum tax is $800 in California, $250 in District of Columbia, $50 in Arizona and North Dakota (banks), $400 ($100 banks) in Rhode Island, $200 per location in South Dakota (banks), $100 in Utah, in Vermont, simplified entity business tax for residents only at $250, otherwise minimum tax ($100 - $100,000) is based upon gross receipts.
Source: Federation of Tax Administrators, State Corporate Income Tax Rates, January 1, 2025

State Individual Income Tax Rates

State	Tax Rate (%)	Income Brackets ($)	Personal Exemptions ($)			Standard Ded. ($)	
			Single	Married	Depend.	Single	Married
California (a)	1.0 - 13.3 (g)	10,099 - 677,276 (b)	134	268	367 (c)	5,202	10,404 (a)

Note: Tax rates for tax year 2024; Local- and county-level taxes are not included; Federal income tax is not deductible on state income tax returns; (a) 16 states have statutory provision for automatically adjusting to the rate of inflation the dollar values of the income tax brackets, standard deductions, and/or personal exemptions. Oregon does not index the income brackets for $125,000 and over See: INFL and SPEC above; (b) For joint returns, taxes are twice the tax on half the couple's income. California brackets violate this formula at the two highest tax brackets in 2024; (c) The personal exemption takes the form of a tax credit instead of a deduction; (g) California imposes an additional 1% tax on taxable income over $1 million, making the maximum rate 13.3% over $1 million in 2023. Unreleased projections indicate 14.4% in 2024.
Source: Federation of Tax Administrators, State Individual Income Tax Rates, January 1, 2025

Various State Sales and Excise Tax Rates

State	State Sales Tax (%)	Gasoline[1] ($/gal.)	Cigarette[2] ($/pack)	Spirits[3] ($/gal.)	Wine[4] ($/gal.)	Beer[5] ($/gal.)	Recreational Marijuana (%)
California	7.25	0.70	2.87	3.30	0.20	0.20	(c)

Note: All tax rates as of January 1, 2025; (1) The American Petroleum Institute has developed a methodology for determining the average tax rate on a gallon of fuel. Rates may include any of the following: excise taxes, environmental fees, storage tank fees, other fees or taxes, general sales tax, and local taxes; (2) The federal excise tax of $1.0066 per pack and local taxes are not included; (3) Rates are those applicable to off-premise sales of 40% alcohol by volume (a.b.v.) distilled spirits in 750ml containers. Local excise taxes are excluded; (4) Rates are those applicable to off-premise sales of 11% a.b.v. non-carbonated wine in 750ml containers; (5) Rates are those applicable to off-premise sales of 4.7% a.b.v. beer in 12 ounce containers; (c) 15% excise tax (retail gross receipts)
Source: Tax Foundation, 2025 Facts & Figures: How Does Your State Compare?

State Tax Competitiveness Index

State	Overall Rank	Corporate Tax Rank	Individual Income Tax Rank	Sales Tax Rank	Property Tax Rank	Unemployment Insurance Tax Rank
California	48	41	49	46	23	25

Note: The Tax Foundation's State Tax Competitiveness Index enables policymakers, taxpayers, and business leaders to gauge how their states' tax systems compare. A rank of 1 is best, 50 is worst. Rankings do not average to the total. States without a tax rank equally as 1. DC's scores and rankings do not affect other states. The report shows tax systems as of July 1, 2024 (the beginning of Fiscal Year 2025).
Source: Tax Foundation, State Tax Competitiveness Index 2025

TRANSPORTATION

Means of Transportation to Work

Area	Car/Truck/Van		Public Transportation			Bicycle	Walked	Other Means	Worked at Home
	Drove Alone	Car-pooled	Bus	Subway	Railroad				
City	64.2	7.8	2.3	0.1	0.1	0.7	3.4	2.2	19.2
MSA[1]	67.6	8.2	1.6	0.1	0.1	0.5	3.1	2.0	16.9
U.S.	70.2	8.5	1.7	1.3	0.4	0.4	2.4	1.6	13.5

Note: Figures are percentages and cover workers 16 years of age and older; (1) Figures cover the San Diego-Chula Vista-Carlsbad, CA Metropolitan Statistical Area
Source: U.S. Census Bureau, 2019-2023 American Community Survey 5-Year Estimates

Travel Time to Work

Area	Less Than 10 Minutes	10 to 19 Minutes	20 to 29 Minutes	30 to 44 Minutes	45 to 59 Minutes	60 to 89 Minutes	90 Minutes or More
City	8.2	33.2	27.9	20.4	5.4	3.3	1.7
MSA[1]	8.5	29.3	25.1	23.4	7.1	4.5	2.1
U.S.	12.6	28.6	21.2	20.8	8.1	6.0	2.8

Note: Note: Figures are percentages and include workers 16 years old and over; (1) Figures cover the San Diego-Chula Vista-Carlsbad, CA Metropolitan Statistical Area
Source: U.S. Census Bureau, 2019-2023 American Community Survey 5-Year Estimates

Key Congestion Measures

Measure	2000	2010	2015	2020	2022
Annual Hours of Delay, Total (000)	85,177	115,240	138,187	55,433	142,070
Annual Hours of Delay, Per Auto Commuter	41	54	63	24	66
Annual Congestion Cost, Per Auto Commuter ($)	1,480	1,594	1,763	743	1,927

Note: Figures cover the San Diego CA urban area
Source: Texas A&M Transportation Institute, 2023 Urban Mobility Report

Freeway Travel Time Index

Measure	1985	1990	1995	2000	2005	2010	2015	2020	2022
Urban Area Index[1]	1.10	1.14	1.16	1.22	1.27	1.30	1.34	1.10	1.29
Urban Area Rank[1,2]	27	26	32	24	18	12	9	29	13

Note: Freeway Travel Time Index—the ratio of travel time in the peak period to the travel time at free-flow conditions. For example, a value of 1.30 indicates a 20-minute free-flow trip takes 26 minutes in the peak (20 minutes x 1.30 = 26 minutes); (1) Covers the San Diego CA urban area; (2) Rank is based on 101 larger urban areas (#1 = highest travel time index)
Source: Texas A&M Transportation Institute, 2023 Urban Mobility Report

Public Transportation

Agency Name / Mode of Transportation	Vehicles Operated in Maximum Service[1]	Annual Unlinked Passenger Trips[2] (in thous.)	Annual Passenger Miles[3] (in thous.)
San Diego Metropolitan Transit System (MTS)			
Bus (directly operated)	194	16,519.0	72,309.5
Bus (purchased transportation)	272	15,593.2	59,612.7
Commuter Bus (purchased transportation)	9	102.1	2,554.0
Demand Response (purchased transportation)	59	178.8	2,271.4
Demand Response - Taxi	126	70.8	863.1
Light Rail (directly operated)	114	36,047.4	248,512.1
North San Diego County Transit District (NCTD)			
Bus (purchased transportation)	135	4,541.5	28,489.6
Commuter Rail (directly operated)	30	813.2	22,553.7
Demand Response (purchased transportation)	16	93.1	1,546.9
Hybrid Rail (directly operated)	8	1,684.6	13,034.6
San Diego Association of Governments (SANDAG)			
Vanpool (purchased transportation)	413	1,048.6	52,485.4

Note: (1) Number of revenue vehicles operated by the given mode and type of service to meet the annual maximum service requirement. This is the revenue vehicle count during the peak season of the year; on the week and day that maximum service is provided. Vehicles operated in maximum service (VOMS) exclude atypical days and one-time special events; (2) Number of passengers who boarded public transportation vehicles. Passengers are counted each time they board a vehicle no matter how many vehicles they use to travel from their origin to their destination. (3) Sum of the distances ridden by all passengers during the entire fiscal year.
Source: Federal Transit Administration, National Transit Database, 2023

Air Transportation

Airport Name and Code / Type of Service	Passenger Airlines[1]	Passenger Enplanements	Freight Carriers[2]	Freight (lbs)
San Diego International-Lindbergh Field (SAN)				
Domestic service (U.S. carriers only)	27	12,277,942	12	99,729,718
International service (U.S. carriers only)	8	90,003	3	5,898,616

Note: (1) Includes all U.S.-based major, minor and commuter airlines that carried at least one passenger during the year; (2) Includes all U.S.-based airlines and freight carriers that transported at least one pound of freight during the year.
Source: Bureau of Transportation Statistics, The Intermodal Transportation Database, Air Carriers: T-100 Domestic Market (U.S. carriers only), 2024; Bureau of Transportation Statistics, The Intermodal Transportation Database, Air Carriers: T-100 International Market (U.S. carriers only), 2024

BUSINESSES

Major Business Headquarters

Company Name	Industry	Rankings Fortune[1]	Rankings Forbes[2]
LPL Financial Holdings	Securities	392	-
Qualcomm	Semiconductors and other electronic components	117	-
Sempra	Utilities: gas and electric	246	-

Note: (1) Companies that produce a 10-K are ranked 1 to 500 based on 2023 revenue; (2) All private companies with at least $2 billion in annual revenue through the end of their most current fiscal year are ranked 1 to 275; companies listed are headquartered in the city; dashes indicate no ranking
Source: Fortune, "Fortune 500," 2024; Forbes, "America's Largest Private Companies," 2024

Fastest-Growing Businesses

According to *Inc.*, San Diego is home to six of America's 500 fastest-growing private companies: **CourtAvenue** (#58); **REA.co** (#277); **Valoroo** (#290); **Virtual Latinos** (#311); **Crown Point Systems** (#336); **Cymbiotika** (#347). Criteria: must be an independent, privately-held, for-profit, U.S. corporation, proprietorship or partnership as of December 31, 2023; revenues must be at least $100,000 in 2020 and $2 million in 2023; must have four-year operating/sales history. *Inc., "America's 500 Fastest-Growing Private Companies," 2024*

According to Deloitte, San Diego is home to eight of North America's 500 fastest-growing high-technology companies: **Arcturus Therapeutics** (#87); **Mosaic.tech** (#97); **ClickUp** (#99); **Workiz** (#193); **Cloudbeds** (#248); **Gyre Therapeutics** (#261); **SOCi** (#345); **Verse.ai** (#491). Companies are ranked by percentage growth in revenue over a four-year period. Criteria for inclusion: company must be headquartered within North America; must own proprietary intellectual property or technology that is sold to customers in products that contributes to a significant portion of the company's operating revenue; must have been in business for a minumum of four years with 2020 operating revenues of at least $50,000 USD/CD and 2023 operating revenues of at least $5 million USD/CD.
Deloitte, 2024 Technology Fast 500[TM]

Living Environment

COST OF LIVING

Cost of Living Index

Composite Index	Groceries	Housing	Utilities	Trans-portation	Health Care	Misc. Goods/ Services
145.3	111.1	212.1	139.4	140.9	102.2	113.9

Note: The Cost of Living Index measures regional differences in the cost of consumer goods and services, excluding taxes and non-consumer expenditures, for professional and managerial households in the top income quintile. It is based on more than 50,000 prices covering almost 60 different items for which prices are collected three times a year by chambers of commerce, economic development organizations or university applied economic centers in each participating urban area. The numbers shown should be read as a percentage above or below the national average of 100. For example, a value of 115.4 in the groceries column indicates that grocery prices are 15.4% higher than the national average. Small differences in the index numbers should not be interpreted as significant; Figures cover the San Diego CA urban area.
Source: The Council for Community and Economic Research, Cost of Living Index, 2024

Grocery Prices

Area[1]	T-Bone Steak ($/pound)	Frying Chicken ($/pound)	Whole Milk ($/half gal.)	Eggs ($/dozen)	Orange Juice ($/64 oz.)	Coffee ($/11.5 oz.)
City[2]	15.56	2.40	5.07	3.17	4.63	6.78
Avg.	15.42	1.55	4.69	3.25	4.41	5.46
Min.	14.50	1.16	4.43	2.75	4.00	4.85
Max.	17.56	2.89	5.49	4.78	5.54	7.89

*Note: (1) Values for the local area are compared with the average, minimum and maximum values for all 276 areas in the Cost of Living Index; (2) Figures cover the San Diego CA urban area; **T-Bone Steak** (price per pound); **Frying Chicken** (price per pound, whole fryer); **Whole Milk** (half gallon carton); **Eggs** (price per dozen, Grade A, large); **Orange Juice** (64 oz. Tropicana or Florida Natural); **Coffee** (11.5 oz. can, vacuum-packed, Maxwell House, Hills Bros, or Folgers).*
Source: The Council for Community and Economic Research, Cost of Living Index, 2024

Housing and Utility Costs

Area[1]	New Home Price ($)	Apartment Rent ($/month)	All Electric ($/month)	Part Electric ($/month)	Other Energy ($/month)	Telephone ($/month)
City[2]	1,113,702	3,153	-	255.41	87.52	181.36
Avg.	515,975	1,550	210.99	123.07	82.07	194.99
Min.	265,375	692	104.33	53.68	36.26	179.42
Max.	2,775,821	5,719	529.02	397.28	361.63	223.33

*Note: (1) Values for the local area are compared with the average, minimum and maximum values for all 276 areas in the Cost of Living Index; (2) Figures cover the San Diego CA urban area; **New Home Price** (2,400 sf living area, 8,000 sf lot, in urban area with full utilities); **Apartment Rent** (950 sf 2 bedroom/1.5 or 2 bath, unfurnished, excluding all utilities except water); **All Electric** (average monthly cost for an all-electric home); **Part Electric** (average monthly cost for a part-electric home); **Other Energy** (average monthly cost for natural gas, fuel oil, coal, wood, and any other forms of energy except electricity); **Telephone** (price includes the base monthly rate plus taxes and fees for three lines of mobile phone service).*
Source: The Council for Community and Economic Research, Cost of Living Index, 2024

Health Care, Transportation, and Other Costs

Area[1]	Doctor ($/visit)	Dentist ($/visit)	Optometrist ($/visit)	Gasoline ($/gallon)	Beauty Salon ($/visit)	Men's Shirt ($)
City[2]	139.44	126.00	143.70	4.93	67.95	39.49
Avg.	143.77	117.51	129.23	3.32	48.57	38.14
Min.	36.74	58.67	67.33	2.80	24.00	13.41
Max.	270.44	216.82	307.33	5.28	94.00	63.89

*Note: (1) Values for the local area are compared with the average, minimum and maximum values for all 276 areas in the Cost of Living Index; (2) Figures cover the San Diego CA urban area; **Doctor** (general practitioners routine exam of an established patient); **Dentist** (adult teeth cleaning and periodic oral examination); **Optometrist** (full vision eye exam for established adult patient); **Gasoline** (one gallon regular unleaded, national brand, including all taxes, cash price at self-service pump if available); **Beauty Salon** (woman's shampoo, trim, and blow-dry); **Men's Shirt** (cotton/polyester dress shirt, pinpoint weave, long sleeves).*
Source: The Council for Community and Economic Research, Cost of Living Index, 2024

HOUSING

Homeownership Rate

Area	2017 (%)	2018 (%)	2019 (%)	2020 (%)	2021 (%)	2022 (%)	2023 (%)	2024 (%)
MSA[1]	56.0	56.1	56.7	57.8	52.6	51.6	54.5	51.4
U.S.	63.9	64.4	64.6	66.6	65.5	65.8	65.9	65.6

Note: (1) Figures cover the San Diego-Chula Vista-Carlsbad, CA Metropolitan Statistical Area
Source: U.S. Census Bureau, Housing Vacancies and Homeownership Annual Statistics: 2017-2024

House Price Index (HPI)

Area	National Ranking[2]	Quarterly Change (%)	One-Year Change (%)	Five-Year Change (%)	Since 1991Q1 (%)
MSA[1]	102	1.05	5.91	61.16	410.00
U.S.[3]	–	1.43	4.51	57.13	327.82

Note: The HPI is a weighted repeat sales index. It measures average price changes in repeat sales or refinancings on the same properties. This information is obtained by reviewing repeat mortgage transactions on single-family properties whose mortgages have been purchased or securitized by Fannie Mae or Freddie Mac since January 1975; (1) Figures cover the San Diego-Carlsbad, CA Metropolitan Statistical Area; (2) Rankings are based on annual percentage change for all metro areas containing at least 15,000 transactions over the last 10 years and ranges from 1 to 241; (3) figures based on a weighted average of Census Division estimates using a seasonally adjusted, purchase-only index; all figures are for the period ending December 31, 2024
Source: Federal Housing Finance Agency, Change in FHFA Metropolitan Area House Price Indexes, All Transactions Index, 2024Q4

Home Value

Area	Under $100,000	$100,000 -$199,999	$200,000 -$299,999	$300,000 -$399,999	$400,000 -$499,999	$500,000 -$999,999	$1,000,000 or more	Median ($)
City	2.6	1.2	1.5	3.4	7.1	48.7	35.6	848,500
MSA[1]	3.7	1.9	2.1	3.4	6.8	52.6	29.5	791,600
U.S.	12.1	17.8	19.5	14.4	10.5	19.1	6.5	303,400

Note: Figures are percentages except for median and cover owner-occupied housing units; (1) Figures cover the San Diego-Chula Vista-Carlsbad, CA Metropolitan Statistical Area
Source: U.S. Census Bureau, 2019-2023 American Community Survey 5-Year Estimates

Year Housing Structure Built

Area	2020 or Later	2010 -2019	2000 -2009	1990 -1999	1980 -1989	1970 -1979	1960 -1969	1950 -1959	1940 -1949	Before 1940	Median Year
City	0.8	7.1	10.2	10.6	17.7	20.2	12.2	11.0	3.7	6.6	1978
MSA[1]	0.8	6.5	12.0	11.5	18.6	21.7	11.6	10.1	3.1	4.1	1980
U.S.	1.2	8.9	13.6	12.8	13.0	14.4	10.0	9.7	4.5	11.9	1980

Note: Figures are percentages except for Median Year; Note: (1) Figures cover the San Diego-Chula Vista-Carlsbad, CA Metropolitan Statistical Area
Source: U.S. Census Bureau, 2019-2023 American Community Survey 5-Year Estimates

Gross Monthly Rent

Area	Under $500	$500 -$999	$1,000 -$1,499	$1,500 -$1,999	$2,000 -$2,499	$2,500 -$2,999	$3,000 and up	Median ($)
City	2.3	3.9	11.3	22.8	21.9	16.0	21.8	2,223
MSA[1]	2.2	4.0	12.0	24.8	22.5	14.8	19.6	2,154
U.S.	6.5	22.3	29.5	20.2	10.8	4.8	5.9	1,348

Note: Figures are percentages except for median; Gross rent is the contract rent plus the estimated average monthly cost of utilities (electricity, gas, and water and sewer) and fuels (oil, coal, kerosene, wood, etc.) if these are paid by the renter (or paid for the renter by someone else); (1) Figures cover the San Diego-Chula Vista-Carlsbad, CA Metropolitan Statistical Area
Source: U.S. Census Bureau, 2019-2023 American Community Survey 5-Year Estimates

HEALTH

Health Risk Factors

Category	MSA[1] (%)	U.S. (%)
Adults aged 18–64 who have any kind of health care coverage	n/a	90.8
Adults who reported being in good or better health	n/a	81.8
Adults who have been told they have high blood cholesterol	n/a	36.9
Adults who have been told they have high blood pressure	n/a	34.0
Adults who are current smokers	n/a	12.1
Adults who currently use e-cigarettes	n/a	7.7
Adults who currently use chewing tobacco, snuff, or snus	n/a	3.2
Adults who are heavy drinkers[2]	n/a	6.1
Adults who are binge drinkers[3]	n/a	15.2
Adults who are overweight (BMI 25.0 - 29.9)	n/a	34.4
Adults who are obese (BMI 30.0 - 99.8)	n/a	34.3
Adults who participated in any physical activities in the past month	n/a	75.8

Note: All figures are crude prevalence; (1) Figures for the San Diego-Chula Vista-Carlsbad, CA Metropolitan Statistical Area were not available.
(2) Heavy drinkers are classified as adult men having more than 14 drinks per week and adult women having more than 7 drinks per week; (3) Binge drinkers are classified as males having five or more drinks on one occasion or females having four or more drinks on one occasion
Source: Centers for Disease Control and Prevention, Behaviorial Risk Factor Surveillance System, SMART: Selected Metropolitan Area Risk Trends, 2023

Acute and Chronic Health Conditions

Category	MSA[1] (%)	U.S. (%)
Adults who have ever been told they had a heart attack	n/a	4.2
Adults who have ever been told they have angina or coronary heart disease	n/a	4.0
Adults who have ever been told they had a stroke	n/a	3.3
Adults who have ever been told they have asthma	n/a	15.7
Adults who have ever been told they have arthritis	n/a	26.3
Adults who have ever been told they have diabetes[2]	n/a	11.5
Adults who have ever been told they had skin cancer	n/a	5.6
Adults who have ever been told they had any other types of cancer	n/a	8.4
Adults who have ever been told they have COPD	n/a	6.4
Adults who have ever been told they have kidney disease	n/a	3.7
Adults who have ever been told they have a form of depression	n/a	22.0

Note: All figures are crude prevalence; (1) Figures for the San Diego-Chula Vista-Carlsbad, CA Metropolitan Statistical Area were not available.
(2) Figures do not include pregnancy-related, borderline, or pre-diabetes
Source: Centers for Disease Control and Prevention, Behaviorial Risk Factor Surveillance System, SMART: Selected Metropolitan Area Risk Trends, 2023

Health Screening and Vaccination Rates

Category	MSA[1] (%)	U.S. (%)
Adults who have ever been tested for HIV	n/a	37.5
Adults who have had their blood cholesterol checked within the last five years	n/a	87.0
Adults aged 65+ who have had flu shot within the past year	n/a	63.4
Adults aged 65+ who have ever had a pneumonia vaccination	n/a	71.9

Note: All figures are crude prevalence; (1) Figures for the San Diego-Chula Vista-Carlsbad, CA Metropolitan Statistical Area were not available.
Source: Centers for Disease Control and Prevention, Behaviorial Risk Factor Surveillance System, SMART: Selected Metropolitan Area Risk Trends, 2023

Disability Status

Category	MSA[1] (%)	U.S. (%)
Adults who reported being deaf	n/a	7.4
Are you blind or have serious difficulty seeing, even when wearing glasses?	n/a	4.9
Do you have difficulty doing errands alone?	n/a	7.8
Do you have difficulty dressing or bathing?	n/a	3.6
Do you have serious difficulty concentrating/remembering/making decisions?	n/a	13.7
Do you have serious difficulty walking or climbing stairs?	n/a	13.2

Note: All figures are crude prevalence; (1) Figures for the San Diego-Chula Vista-Carlsbad, CA Metropolitan Statistical Area were not available.
Source: Centers for Disease Control and Prevention, Behaviorial Risk Factor Surveillance System, SMART: Selected Metropolitan Area Risk Trends, 2023

Mortality Rates for the Top 10 Causes of Death in the U.S.

ICD-10[a] Sub-Chapter	ICD-10[a] Code	Crude Mortality Rate[2] per 100,000 population	
		County[3]	U.S.
Malignant neoplasms	C00-C97	156.7	182.7
Ischaemic heart diseases	I20-I25	76.2	109.6
Provisional assignment of new diseases of uncertain etiology[1]	U00-U49	46.7	65.3
Other forms of heart disease	I30-I51	52.6	65.1
Other degenerative diseases of the nervous system	G30-G31	65.2	52.4
Other external causes of accidental injury	W00-X59	44.5	52.3
Cerebrovascular diseases	I60-I69	49.4	49.1
Chronic lower respiratory diseases	J40-J47	27.8	43.5
Hypertensive diseases	I10-I15	33.8	38.9
Organic, including symptomatic, mental disorders	F01-F09	18.5	33.9

Note: (a) ICD-10 = International Classification of Diseases 10th Revision; (1) Includes COVID-19, adverse effects to COVID-19 vaccines, SARS, and vaping-related disorders; (2) Crude mortality rates are a three-year average covering 2021-2023; (3) Figures cover San Diego County.
Source: Centers for Disease Control and Prevention, National Center for Health Statistics. National Vital Statistics System, Mortality 2018-2023 on CDC WONDER Online Database

Mortality Rates for Selected Causes of Death

Cause of Death	ICD-10[a] Code	Crude Mortality Rate[1] per 100,000 population	
		County[2]	U.S.
Accidental poisoning and exposure to noxious substances	X40-X49	29.1	30.5
Alzheimer disease	G30	39.7	35.4
Assault	X85-Y09	3.1	7.3
COVID-19	U07.1	46.7	65.3
Diabetes mellitus	E10-E14	27.7	30.0
Diseases of the liver	K70-K76	16.6	20.8
Human immunodeficiency virus (HIV) disease	B20-B24	1.2	1.5
Influenza and pneumonia	J09-J18	6.3	13.4
Intentional self-harm	X60-X84	11.1	14.7
Malnutrition	E40-E46	4.0	6.0
Obesity and other hyperalimentation	E65-E68	2.2	3.1
Renal failure	N17-N19	2.8	16.4
Transport accidents	V01-V99	10.1	14.4

Note: (a) ICD-10 = International Classification of Diseases 10th Revision; (1) Crude mortality rates are a three-year average covering 2021-2023; (2) Figures cover San Diego County; Data are suppressed when the data meet the criteria for confidentiality constraints; Crude mortality rates are flagged as unreliable when the rate would be calculated with a numerator of 20 or less.
Source: Centers for Disease Control and Prevention, National Center for Health Statistics. National Vital Statistics System, Mortality 2018-2023 on CDC WONDER Online Database

Health Insurance Coverage

Area	With Health Insurance	With Private Health Insurance	With Public Health Insurance	Without Health Insurance	Population Under Age 19 Without Health Insurance
City	93.7	71.9	31.7	6.3	3.6
MSA[1]	93.2	69.6	34.3	6.8	3.8
U.S.	91.4	67.3	36.3	8.6	5.4

Note: Figures are percentages that cover the civilian noninstitutionalized population; (1) Figures cover the San Diego-Chula Vista-Carlsbad, CA Metropolitan Statistical Area
Source: U.S. Census Bureau, 2019-2023 American Community Survey 5-Year Estimates

Number of Medical Professionals

Area	MDs[3]	DOs[3,4]	Dentists	Podiatrists	Chiropractors	Optometrists
County[1] (number)	11,932	727	3,296	165	1,191	692
County[1] (rate[2])	364.2	22.2	100.8	5.0	36.4	21.2
U.S. (rate[2])	302.5	29.2	74.6	6.4	29.5	18.0

Note: Data as of 2023 unless noted; (1) Data covers San Diego County; (2) Number of medical professionals per 100,000 population; (3) Data as of 2022 and includes all active, non-federal physicians; (4) Doctor of Osteopathic Medicine
Source: U.S. Department of Health and Human Services, Health Resources and Services Administration, Bureau of Health Professions, Area Resource File (ARF) 2023-2024

Best Hospitals

According to U.S. News, the San Diego-Chula Vista-Carlsbad, CA metro area is home to six of the best hospitals in the U.S.: **Scripps La Jolla Hospitals** (6 adult specialties); **Sharp Memorial Hospital** (1 adult specialty); **UC San Diego Health-Cardiovascular Institute** (11 adult specialties); **UC San Diego Health-La Jolla, Hillcrest, and East Campus Medical Centers** (Honor Roll/11 adult specialties); **UC San Diego Health-Moores Cancer Center** (11 adult specialties); **UC San Diego Health-Shiley Eye Institute** (11 adult specialties). The hospitals listed were nationally ranked in at least one of 15 adult or 11 pediatric specialties. The number of specialties shown cover the parent hospital. Only 160 U.S. hospitals performed well enough to be nationally ranked in one or more specialties. Twenty hospitals in the U.S. made the Honor Roll. The Best Hospitals Honor Roll takes both the national rankings and the procedure and condition ratings into account. Hospitals received points if they were nationally ranked in one of the 15 adult specialties—the higher they ranked, the more points they got—and how many ratings of "high performing" they earned in the 20 procedures and conditions. U.S. News Online, "America's Best Hospitals 2024-25"

According to U.S. News, the San Diego-Chula Vista-Carlsbad, CA metro area is home to one of the best children's hospitals in the U.S.: **Rady Children's Hospital** (Honor Roll/11 pediatric specialties). The hospital listed was highly ranked in at least one of 11 pediatric specialties. One hundred five children's hospitals in the U.S. were nationally ranked in at least one specialty. Hospitals received points for being ranked in a specialty, and the 10 hospitals with the most points across the 11 specialties make up the Honor Roll. U.S. News Online, "America's Best Children's Hospitals 2024-25"

EDUCATION

Public School District Statistics

District Name	Schls	Pupils	Pupil/ Teacher Ratio	Minority Pupils[1] (%)	Total Rev. per Pupil ($)	Total Exp. per Pupil ($)
Del Mar Union Elementary	9	3,662	20.0	59.0	21,312	34,103
Poway Unified	39	34,935	23.3	62.1	17,020	15,877
San Diego Unified	175	95,492	22.3	75.8	26,705	26,901

Note: Table includes school districts with 2,000 or more students; (1) Percentage of students that are not non-Hispanic white.
Source: U.S. Department of Education, National Center for Education Statistics, Common Core of Data, Local Education Agency (School District) Universe Survey: School Year 2023-2024; U.S. Department of Education, National Center for Education Statistics, Common Core of Data, School District Finance Survey (F-33): School Year 2021–22

Best High Schools

According to *U.S. News,* San Diego is home to five of the top 500 high schools in the U.S.: **Canyon Crest Academy** (#140); **Preuss School UCSD** (#231); **Del Norte High School** (#329); **Westview High School** (#401); **Mt. Everest Academy** (#489). Nearly 25,000 public, magnet and charter schools were ranked based on their performance on state assessments and how well they prepare students for college. *U.S. News & World Report, "Best High Schools 2024"*

Highest Level of Education

Area	Less than H.S.	H.S. Diploma	Some College, No Deg.	Associate Degree	Bachelor's Degree	Master's Degree	Prof. School Degree	Doctorate Degree
City	9.8	15.0	17.8	7.5	28.8	13.6	3.6	3.8
MSA[1]	11.0	17.9	20.6	8.3	25.6	11.0	2.9	2.6
U.S.	10.6	26.2	19.4	8.8	21.3	9.8	2.3	1.6

Note: Figures cover persons age 25 and over; (1) Figures cover the San Diego-Chula Vista-Carlsbad, CA Metropolitan Statistical Area
Source: U.S. Census Bureau, 2019-2023 American Community Survey 5-Year Estimates

Educational Attainment by Race

Area	High School Graduate or Higher (%)					Bachelor's Degree or Higher (%)				
	Total	White	Black	Asian	Hisp.[2]	Total	White	Black	Asian	Hisp.[2]
City	90.2	95.2	90.0	90.2	76.2	49.9	57.6	31.3	57.3	25.4
MSA[1]	89.0	93.8	91.0	91.1	75.0	42.1	48.0	29.6	55.2	21.5
U.S.	89.4	92.9	88.1	88.0	72.5	35.0	37.7	24.7	57.0	19.9

Note: Figures shown cover persons 25 years old and over; (1) Figures cover the San Diego-Chula Vista-Carlsbad, CA Metropolitan Statistical Area; (2) People of Hispanic origin can be of any race
Source: U.S. Census Bureau, 2019-2023 American Community Survey 5-Year Estimates

School Enrollment by Grade and Control

Area	Preschool (%)		Kindergarten (%)		Grades 1 - 4 (%)		Grades 5 - 8 (%)		Grades 9 - 12 (%)	
	Public	Private	Public	Private	Public	Private	Public	Private	Public	Private
City	47.0	53.0	84.6	15.4	88.6	11.4	91.3	8.7	90.8	9.2
MSA[1]	50.7	49.3	86.1	13.9	89.3	10.7	90.8	9.2	91.9	8.1
U.S.	58.7	41.3	85.2	14.8	87.2	12.8	87.9	12.1	89.0	11.0

Note: Figures shown cover persons 3 years old and over; (1) Figures cover the San Diego-Chula Vista-Carlsbad, CA Metropolitan Statistical Area
Source: U.S. Census Bureau, 2019-2023 American Community Survey 5-Year Estimates

Higher Education

Four-Year Colleges			Two-Year Colleges			Medical Schools[1]	Law Schools[2]	Voc/ Tech[3]
Public	Private Non-profit	Private For-profit	Public	Private Non-profit	Private For-profit			
5	15	12	6	1	7	1	4	17

Note: Figures cover institutions located within the San Diego-Chula Vista-Carlsbad, CA Metropolitan Statistical Area and include main campuses only; (1) includes schools accredited by the Liaison Committee on Medical Education and the American Osteopathic Association's Commission on Osteopathic College Accreditation; (2) includes ABA-accredited schools, schools with provisional ABA accreditation, and state accredited schools; (3) includes all schools with programs that are less than 2 years.
Source: National Center for Education Statistics, Integrated Postsecondary Education System (IPEDS), 2023-24; Wikipedia, List of Medical Schools in the United States, accessed May 2, 2025; Wikipedia, List of Law Schools in the United States, accessed May 2, 2025

According to *U.S. News & World Report,* the San Diego-Chula Vista-Carlsbad, CA metro area is home to three of the top 200 national universities in the U.S.: **University of California, San Diego** (#29); **San Diego State University** (#109 tie); **University of San Diego** (#109 tie). The indicators used to capture academic quality fall into a number of categories: assessment by administrators at peer institutions; retention of students; faculty resources; student selectivity; financial resources;

alumni giving; high school counselor ratings of colleges; and graduation rate. *U.S. News & World Report*, "America's Best Colleges 2025"

According to *U.S. News & World Report*, the San Diego-Chula Vista-Carlsbad, CA metro area is home to one of the top 100 law schools in the U.S.: **University of San Diego** (#57 tie). The rankings are based on a weighted average of 12 measures of quality: peer assessment score; assessment score by lawyers/judges; median LSAT scores; median undergrad GPA; acceptance rate; employment rates for graduates; placement success; bar passage rate; faculty resources; expenditures per student; student/faculty ratio; and library resources. *U.S. News & World Report*, "America's Best Graduate Schools, Law, 2025"

According to *U.S. News & World Report*, the San Diego-Chula Vista-Carlsbad, CA metro area is home to one of the top medical schools for research in the U.S.: **University of California—San Diego** (Tier 1). *U.S. News* placed medical and osteopathic schools into tiers based on their research productivity, faculty and admissions data. Each school's tier was derived from its overall score, calculated by summing the weighted normalized values generated across several factors of academic quality, outlined below. There are four tiers, with tier 1 medical schools as the highest-performing and tier 4 as the lowest-performing. Only tier 1 and 2 schools are shown. Because of the tier presentation, *U.S. News* calculated overall scores based on their percentile performance among all rated schools instead of dividing against the rescaled score of the No. 1-performing schools. Tier 1 included schools with overall scores of 85 to 99. The cutoffs for tiers 2 through 4 were schools scoring 50 to 84, 15 to 49 and 1 to 14, respectively. The rankings are based on a weighted average of the following measures of quality: total research activity; average research activity per faculty member; total NIH research grants at the medical school and its affiliated hospitals; average NIH research grants per faculty; median MCAT total score; median undergraduate GPA; acceptance rate; and faculty resources. *U.S. News & World Report*, "America's Best Graduate Schools, Medical, 2025"

According to *U.S. News & World Report*, the San Diego-Chula Vista-Carlsbad, CA metro area is home to one of the top medical schools for primary care in the U.S.: **University of California—San Diego** (Tier 2). *U.S. News* placed medical and osteopathic schools into tiers based on their research productivity, faculty and admissions data. Each school's tier was derived from its overall score, calculated by summing the weighted normalized values generated across several factors of academic quality, outlined below. There are four tiers, with tier 1 medical schools as the highest-performing and tier 4 as the lowest-performing. Only tier 1 and 2 schools are shown. Because of the tier presentation, *U.S. News* calculated overall scores based on their percentile performance among all rated schools instead of dividing against the rescaled score of the No. 1-performing schools. Tier 1 included schools with overall scores of 85 to 99. The cutoffs for tiers 2 through 4 were schools scoring 50 to 84, 15 to 49 and 1 to 14, respectively. The rankings are based on a weighted average of the following measures of quality: graduates practicing in primary care specialties; graduates entering primary care residencies; median MCAT total score; median undergraduate GPA; acceptance rate; and faculty resources. *U.S. News & World Report*, "America's Best Graduate Schools, Medical, 2025"

According to *U.S. News & World Report*, the San Diego-Chula Vista-Carlsbad, CA metro area is home to one of the top 75 business schools in the U.S.: **University of California—San Diego (Rady)** (#68 tie). The rankings are based on a weighted average of the following nine measures: quality assessment; peer assessment; recruiter assessment; placement success; mean starting salary and bonus; student selectivity; mean GMAT and GRE scores; mean undergraduate GPA; and acceptance rate. *U.S. News & World Report*, "America's Best Graduate Schools, Business, 2025"

EMPLOYERS

Major Employers

Company Name	Industry
Barona Resort and Casino	Resort hotels
Collins Aerospace	Aircraft components, mfg
Kaiser Permanente Vandever Medical Ctr	Hospitals
San Diego Community College	Education
San Diego County Sheriff	Law enforcement
Scripps Mercy Hospital San Diego	Hospitals
Scripps Research Institute	Education
Seaworld San Diego	Recreation, animal life
Sharp Grossmont Hospital	Hospitals
Sharp Grossmonth Rehab Ctr	Healthcare
Sharp Mary Birch Hospital	Hospitals
Sharp Memorial Hospital	Hospitals
Sony Electronics Inc	Electronics
University of California	Higher education
VA San Diego Healthcare System	Healthcare

Note: Companies shown are located within the San Diego-Chula Vista-Carlsbad, CA Metropolitan Statistical Area.
Source: Chambers of Commerce; State Departments of Labor; Wikipedia

Best Companies to Work For

Scripps Health, headquartered in San Diego, is among "The 100 Best Companies to Work For." To pick the best companies, *Fortune* partnered with the Great Place to Work Institute. Using their proprietary Trust Index™ survey, the core of what creates great a workplace is measured—key behaviors that drive trust in management, connection with colleagues, and loyalty to the company. To be eligible for the *Fortune* 100 Best Companies to Work For list, employers must have 1,000 or more employees in the U.S. and cannot be a government agency. *Fortune, "The 100 Best Companies to Work For," 2025*

Seismic; WestPac Wealth Partners, headquartered in San Diego, are among "Fortune's Best Workplaces for Parents." To pick the best companies, *Fortune* partnered with the Great Place to Work Institute. To be considered for the list, companies must be Great Place To Work-Certified and have at least 50 responses from parents in the US. The survey enables employees to share confidential quantitative and qualitative feedback about their organization's culture by responding to 60 statements on a 5-point scale and answering two open-ended questions. Collectively, these statements describe a great employee experience, defined by high levels of trust, respect, credibility, fairness, pride, and camaraderie. In addition, companies provide organizational data like size, location, industry, demographics, roles, and levels; and provide information about parental leave, adoption, flexible schedule, childcare and dependent health care benefits. *Fortune, "Best Workplaces for Parents," 2024*

Aya Healthcare; WestPac Wealth Partners, headquartered in San Diego, are among "Fortune's Best Workplaces for Women." To pick the best companies, *Fortune* partnered with the Great Place to Work Institute. To be considered for the list, companies must be Great Place To Work-Certified. Companies must also employ at least 50 women, at least 20% of their non-executive managers must be female, and at least one executive must be female. To determine the Best Workplaces for Women, Great Place To Work measured the differences in women's survey responses to those of their peers and assesses the impact of demographics and roles on the quality and consistency of women's experiences. Great Place To Work also analyzed the gender balance of each workplace, how it compared to each company's industry, and patterns in representation as women rise from front-line positions to the board of directors. *Fortune, "Best Workplaces for Women," 2024*

Aya Healthcare; Scripps Health, headquartered in San Diego, are among "Best Workplaces in Health Care." To determine the Best Workplaces in Health Care list, Great Place To Work analyzed the survey responses of over 185,000 employees from Great Place To Work-Certified companies in the health care industry. Survey data analysis and company-provided datapoints are then factored into a combined score to compare and rank the companies that create the most consistently positive experience for all employees in this industry. *Fortune, "Best Workplaces in Health Care," 2024*

Qualcomm; San Diego Gas & Electric and Southern California Gas Company, headquartered in San Diego, are among the "Best Places to Work in IT." To qualify, companies had to have a minimum of 100 total employees and five IT employees. The best places to work were selected based on DEI (diversity, equity, and inclusion) practices; IT turnover, promotions, and growth; IT retention and engagement programs; remote/hybrid working; benefits and perks (such as elder care and child care, flextime, and reimbursement for college tuition); and training and career development opportunities. *Computerworld, "Best Places to Work in IT," 2025*

PUBLIC SAFETY

Crime Rate

Area	Total Crime Rate	Violent Crime Rate				Property Crime Rate		
		Murder	Rape	Robbery	Aggrav. Assault	Burglary	Larceny -Theft	Motor Vehicle Theft
City	2,229.6	2.9	21.5	87.4	306.1	201.5	1,118.7	491.6
U.S.	2,290.9	5.7	38.0	66.5	264.1	250.7	1,347.2	318.7

Note: Figures are crimes per 100,000 population.
Source: FBI, Table 8, Offenses Known to Law Enforcement, by State by City, 2023

Hate Crimes

Area	Number of Quarters Reported	Number of Incidents per Bias Motivation					
		Race/Ethnicity/ Ancestry	Religion	Sexual Orientation	Disability	Gender	Gender Identity
City[1]	4	23	18	18	0	0	4
U.S.	4	5,900	2,699	2,077	187	92	492

Note: (1) Figures include at least one incident reported with more than one bias motivation.
Source: Federal Bureau of Investigation, Hate Crime Statistics 2023

Identity Theft Consumer Reports

Area	Reports	Reports per 100,000 Population	Rank[2]
MSA[1]	10,260	313	60
U.S.	1,135,291	339	-

Note: (1) Figures cover the San Diego-Chula Vista-Carlsbad, CA Metropolitan Statistical Area; (2) Rank ranges from 1 to 401 where 1 indicates greatest number of identity theft reports per 100,000 population
Source: Federal Trade Commission, Consumer Sentinel Network Data Book 2024

Fraud and Other Consumer Reports

Area	Reports	Reports per 100,000 Population	Rank[2]
MSA[1]	43,651	1,330	89
U.S.	5,360,641	1,601	-

Note: (1) Figures cover the San Diego-Chula Vista-Carlsbad, CA Metropolitan Statistical Area; (2) Rank ranges from 1 to 401 where 1 indicates greatest number of fraud and other consumer reports per 100,000 population
Source: Federal Trade Commission, Consumer Sentinel Network Data Book 2024

POLITICS

2024 Presidential Election Results

Area	Trump (Rep.)	Harris (Dem.)	Stein (Green)	Kennedy (Ind.)	Oliver (Lib.)	Other
San Diego County	40.1	56.9	1.0	1.1	0.5	0.4
U.S.	49.7	48.2	0.6	0.5	0.4	0.6

Note: Results are percentages and may not add to 100% due to rounding
Source: Dave Leip's Atlas of U.S. Presidential Elections

SPORTS

Professional Sports Teams

Team Name	League	Year Established
San Diego FC	Major League Soccer (MLS)	2023
San Diego Padres	Major League Baseball (MLB)	1969

Note: Includes teams located in the San Diego-Chula Vista-Carlsbad, CA Metropolitan Statistical Area.
Source: Wikipedia, Major Professional Sports Teams of the United States and Canada, May 1, 2025

CLIMATE

Average and Extreme Temperatures

Temperature	Jan	Feb	Mar	Apr	May	Jun	Jul	Aug	Sep	Oct	Nov	Dec	Yr.
Extreme High (°F)	88	88	93	98	96	101	95	98	111	107	97	88	111
Average High (°F)	65	66	66	68	69	72	76	77	77	74	71	66	71
Average Temp. (°F)	57	58	59	62	64	67	71	72	71	67	62	58	64
Average Low (°F)	48	50	52	55	58	61	65	66	65	60	53	49	57
Extreme Low (°F)	29	36	39	44	48	51	55	58	51	43	38	34	29

Note: Figures cover the years 1948-1990
Source: National Climatic Data Center, International Station Meteorological Climate Summary, 9/96

Average Precipitation/Snowfall/Humidity

Precip./Humidity	Jan	Feb	Mar	Apr	May	Jun	Jul	Aug	Sep	Oct	Nov	Dec	Yr.
Avg. Precip. (in.)	1.9	1.4	1.7	0.8	0.2	0.1	Tr	0.1	0.2	0.4	1.2	1.4	9.5
Avg. Snowfall (in.)	Tr	0	0	0	0	0	0	0	0	0	0	Tr	Tr
Avg. Rel. Hum. 7am (%)	70	72	73	72	73	77	79	79	78	74	69	68	74
Avg. Rel. Hum. 4pm (%)	57	58	59	59	63	66	65	66	65	63	60	58	62

Note: Figures cover the years 1948-1990; Tr = Trace amounts (<0.05 in. of rain; <0.5 in. of snow)
Source: National Climatic Data Center, International Station Meteorological Climate Summary, 9/96

Weather Conditions

Temperature			Daytime Sky			Precipitation		
10°F & below	32°F & below	90°F & above	Clear	Partly cloudy	Cloudy	0.01 inch or more precip.	0.1 inch or more snow/ice	Thunder-storms
0	< 1	4	115	126	124	40	0	5

Note: Figures are average number of days per year and cover the years 1948-1990
Source: National Climatic Data Center, International Station Meteorological Climate Summary, 9/96

HAZARDOUS WASTE

Superfund Sites

The San Diego-Chula Vista-Carlsbad, CA metro area is home to one site on the EPA's Superfund National Priorities List (NPL) or Superfund Alternative Approach (SAA) list: **Camp Pendleton Marine Corps Base** (Final NPL). The Superfund alternative approach uses the same investigation and cleanup process and standards that are used for sites listed on the National Priorities List. The SAA is an alternative to listing a site on the NPL; it is not an alternative to Superfund or the Superfund process. There are a total of 1,445 Superfund sites with a status of proposed or final on both lists in the United States. *U.S. Environmental Protection Agency, National Priorities List, May 1, 2025; U.S. Environmental Protection Agency, Superfund Alternative Approach Sites, May 1, 2025*

AIR QUALITY

Air Quality Trends: Ozone

	1990	1995	2000	2005	2010	2015	2020	2021	2022	2023
MSA[1]	0.110	0.085	0.079	0.074	0.073	0.068	0.078	0.068	0.067	0.072
U.S.	0.087	0.089	0.081	0.080	0.072	0.068	0.066	0.067	0.067	0.070

Note: (1) Data covers the San Diego-Chula Vista-Carlsbad, CA Metropolitan Statistical Area. The values shown are the composite ozone concentration averages among trend sites based on the highest fourth daily maximum 8-hour concentration in parts per million. These trends are based on sites having an adequate record of monitoring data during the trend period. Data from exceptional events are included.
Source: U.S. Environmental Protection Agency, Air Quality Monitoring Information, "Air Quality Trends by City, 1990-2023"

Air Quality Index

Area	\multicolumn{5}{c}{Percent of Days when Air Quality was...[2]}					\multicolumn{2}{c}{AQI Statistics[2]}	
	Good	Moderate	Unhealthy for Sensitive Groups	Unhealthy	Very Unhealthy	Maximum	Median
MSA[1]	16.7	71.2	12.1	0.0	0.0	150	67

Note: (1) Data covers the San Diego-Chula Vista-Carlsbad, CA Metropolitan Statistical Area; (2) Based on 365 days with AQI data in 2023. Air Quality Index (AQI) is an index for reporting daily air quality. EPA calculates the AQI for five major air pollutants regulated by the Clean Air Act: ground-level ozone, particle pollution (aka particulate matter), carbon monoxide, sulfur dioxide, and nitrogen dioxide. The AQI runs from 0 to 500. The higher the AQI value, the greater the level of air pollution and the greater the health concern. There are six AQI categories: "Good" AQI is between 0 and 50. Air quality is considered satisfactory; "Moderate" AQI is between 51 and 100. Air quality is acceptable; "Unhealthy for Sensitive Groups" When AQI values are between 101 and 150, members of sensitive groups may experience health effects; "Unhealthy" When AQI values are between 151 and 200 everyone may begin to experience health effects; "Very Unhealthy" AQI values between 201 and 300 trigger a health alert; "Hazardous" AQI values over 300 trigger warnings of emergency conditions (not shown).
Source: U.S. Environmental Protection Agency, Air Quality Index Report, 2023

Air Quality Index Pollutants

Area	\multicolumn{6}{c}{Percent of Days when AQI Pollutant was...[2]}					
	Carbon Monoxide	Nitrogen Dioxide	Ozone	Sulfur Dioxide	Particulate Matter 2.5	Particulate Matter 10
MSA[1]	0.0	0.3	50.7	(3)	41.4	7.7

Note: (1) Data covers the San Diego-Chula Vista-Carlsbad, CA Metropolitan Statistical Area; (2) Based on 365 days with AQI data in 2023. The Air Quality Index (AQI) is an index for reporting daily air quality. EPA calculates the AQI for five major air pollutants regulated by the Clean Air Act: ground-level ozone, particle pollution (also known as particulate matter), carbon monoxide, sulfur dioxide, and nitrogen dioxide. The AQI runs from 0 to 500. The higher the AQI value, the greater the level of air pollution and the greater the health concern; (3) Sulfur dioxide is no longer included in this table because SO_2 concentrations tend to be very localized and not necessarily representative of broad geographical areas like counties and CBSAs.
Source: U.S. Environmental Protection Agency, Air Quality Index Report, 2023

Maximum Air Pollutant Concentrations: Particulate Matter, Ozone, CO and Lead

	Particulate Matter 10 (ug/m^3)	Particulate Matter 2.5 Wtd AM (ug/m^3)	Particulate Matter 2.5 24-Hr (ug/m^3)	Ozone (ppm)	Carbon Monoxide (ppm)	Lead (ug/m^3)
MSA[1] Level	142	12.5	24	0.08	1	0.02
NAAQS[2]	150	15	35	0.075	9	0.15
Met NAAQS[2]	Yes	Yes	Yes	No	Yes	Yes

Note: (1) Data covers the San Diego-Chula Vista-Carlsbad, CA Metropolitan Statistical Area; Data from exceptional events are included; (2) National Ambient Air Quality Standards; ppm = parts per million; ug/m^3 = micrograms per cubic meter; n/a not available.
Concentrations: Particulate Matter 10 (coarse particulate)—highest second maximum 24-hour concentration; Particulate Matter 2.5 Wtd AM (fine particulate)—highest weighted annual mean concentration; Particulate Matter 2.5 24-Hour (fine particulate)—highest 98th percentile 24-hour concentration; Ozone—highest fourth daily maximum 8-hour concentration; Carbon Monoxide—highest second maximum non-overlapping 8-hour concentration; Lead—maximum running 3-month average
Source: U.S. Environmental Protection Agency, Air Quality Monitoring Information, "Air Quality Statistics by City, 2023"

Maximum Air Pollutant Concentrations: Nitrogen Dioxide and Sulfur Dioxide

	Nitrogen Dioxide AM (ppb)	Nitrogen Dioxide 1-Hr (ppb)	Sulfur Dioxide AM (ppb)	Sulfur Dioxide 1-Hr (ppb)	Sulfur Dioxide 24-Hr (ppb)
MSA[1] Level	14	49	n/a	n/a	n/a
NAAQS[2]	53	100	30	75	140
Met NAAQS[2]	Yes	Yes	n/a	n/a	n/a

Note: (1) Data covers the San Diego-Chula Vista-Carlsbad, CA Metropolitan Statistical Area; Data from exceptional events are included; (2) National Ambient Air Quality Standards; ppm = parts per million; ug/m³ = micrograms per cubic meter; n/a not available.
Concentrations: Nitrogen Dioxide AM—highest arithmetic mean concentration; Nitrogen Dioxide 1-Hr—highest 98th percentile 1-hour daily maximum concentration; Sulfur Dioxide AM—highest annual mean concentration; Sulfur Dioxide 1-Hr—highest 99th percentile 1-hour daily maximum concentration; Sulfur Dioxide 24-Hr—highest second maximum 24-hour concentration
Source: U.S. Environmental Protection Agency, Air Quality Monitoring Information, "Air Quality Statistics by City, 2023"

San Francisco, California

Background

San Francisco, in northern California sits between the Pacific Ocean and the San Francisco Bay, boasts a mild climate, one of the best landlocked harbors in the world, and a strong sense of civic pride shaped by its unique history.

The hilly peninsula known today as San Francisco and its bay was largely ignored by explorers during the sixteenth and seventeenth centuries. Until the 1760s, Europeans had not seen the "Golden Gate" or the narrow strip of water leading into what was to become one of the greatest harbors in the world. San Francisco remained a quiet and pastoral settlement until the discovery of gold in the Sierra Nevada foothills in 1848, which changed San Francisco forever. Every hopeful adventurer from around the world docked in San Francisco, aspiring to make his fortune, creating a rowdy, frontier, gold-prospecting town, with plenty of gambling houses and saloons.

When the supply of gold dwindled around 1855, many gold miners went back to their native countries. Those that stayed continued to live in the ethnic neighborhoods they had created—neighborhoods that still exist today, such as Chinatown, the Italian District, and Japan Center.

The present-day charm of San Francisco lies in its cosmopolitan, yet cohesive, flavor. The city has long embraced a significant gay community. It's home to the first lesbian-rights organization in the United States, Daughters of Bilitis; the first openly gay person to run for public office in the United States, Jose Sarria; the first openly gay man to be elected to public office in California, Harvey Milk; the first openly lesbian judge appointed in the U.S., Mary C. Morgan; and the first transgender police commissioner, Theresa Sparks.

The San Francisco Bay Area is part of the Silicon Valley—the region in Northern California that serves as a global center for high technology and innovation. As such, it is one of the major economic regions of the United States, with one of the highest percentages of college-educated adults and per-capita income in the nation. The Bay Area is home to 44 Fortune 500 companies, and major employers include Salesforce, Google, Apple, UCSF Health and Sutter Health. Twenty percent of California's environmental companies live in San Francisco, which has the largest concentration of biotech companies in the state. A former warehouse district in San Francisco has become the center for hundreds of multimedia and technology companies. Silicon Valley accounts for about one-third of the nation's high-technology exports

Oracle Park is home of the San Francisco Giants major league baseball team, winners of the World Series in 2010, 2012, and 2014. The Golden State Warriors won the 2022 NBA championship. The city offers excellent convention facilities with its Moscone Center, which comprises 770,000 square feet of exhibit space. The center was named for Mayor George Moscone, who championed controversial causes and who was murdered in office in 1978, along with gay activist Harvey Milk. The film, *The Times of Harvey Milk* won the 2008 Academy Award for best picture.

The Fine Arts Museums of San Francisco include the de Young, the city's oldest museum, and the Legion of Honor, home to Rodin's *Thinker*. In 2005, the de Young reopened in a new space in Golden Gate Park, replacing a structure damaged by the 1989 earthquake.

Also damaged in that quake was the main facility of the California Academy of Sciences, which oversees the Steinhart Aquarium, the Morrison Planetarium, and the Natural History Museum and which also reopened in Golden Gate Park in 2008. Architect Renzo Piano designed the building to be seismically safe, green, and sustainable, which allows outside views from nearly anywhere inside.

The early 2020s featured an exodus of tech companies from downtown San Francisco in the wake of the COVID-19 pandemic and the city struggles with homelessness.

San Francisco has a warm-summer Mediterranean climate, characteristic of California's coast, with moist winters and dry summers. San Francisco's weather is strongly influenced by the cool currents of the Pacific Ocean on the west side of the city, and the water of San Francisco Bay to the north and east. This moderates temperature swings and produces a remarkably mild year-round climate with little seasonal temperature variation. San Francisco has the cool daily temperatures for June, July, and August and foggy conditions are caused by rising hot air in California's interior valleys.

Rankings

General Rankings

- To help military veterans find the best places in which to settle down, *WalletHub* compared the 100 largest U.S. cities across 19 key indicators of livability, affordability and veteran-friendliness. They range from the share of military skill-related jobs to veteran income growth to the availability of VA health facilities. San Francisco ranked #42. *Wallethub.com, "Best & Worst Places for Veterans to Live (2025)," November 7, 2024*

- *US News & World Report* conducted a survey of more than 3,500 people and analyzed the 150 largest metropolitan areas to determine what matters most when selecting the next place to live. San Francisco ranked #22 out of the top 25 as having the best combination of desirable factors. Criteria: cost of living; quality of life and education; climate; job market; desirability; and other factors. *realestate.usnews.com, "Best Places to Live in the U.S. in 2024-2025," May 21, 2024*

- *Insider* listed 23 places in the U.S. that travel industry trends reveal would be popular destinations in 2023. This year the list trends towards cultural and historical happenings, sports events, wellness experiences and invigorating outdoor escapes. According to the website insider.com San Francisco is a place to visit in 2023. *Insider, "23 of the Best Places You Should Travel to in the U.S. in 2023," December 17, 2022*

- The human resources consulting firm Mercer ranked 241 major cities worldwide in terms of overall quality of life. San Francisco ranked #36. Criteria: political and personal safety, social, and economic factors; medical and health considerations; schools and education; public services and transportation; recreation; connectivity; housing and infrastructure; and climate. *Mercer, "Mercer 2024 Quality of Living Survey," December 2024*

- For its 37th annual "Readers' Choice Awards" survey, *Condé Nast Traveler* ranked its readers' favorite cities in the U.S. Whether it be a longed-for visit or the next big new thing, these are the places travelers loved best. The list was broken into large cities and cities under 250,000. San Francisco ranked #6 in the big city category. *Condé Nast Traveler, Readers' Choice Awards 2024, "Best Big Cities in the U.S." October 1, 2024*

Business/Finance Rankings

- According to *Business Insider*, the San Francisco metro area is a prime place to run a startup or move an existing business to. The area ranked #2. More than 300 metro areas were analyzed for factors that were of top concern to new business owners. Data was based on the 2019 U.S. Census Bureau American Community Survey, statistics from the CDC, and University of Chicago analysis. Criteria: business formations; percentage of vaccinated population; percentage of households with internet subscriptions; median household income; and share of work that can be done from home. *BusinessInsider.com, "The 20 Best Cities for Starting a Business in 2022 Include Denver, Raleigh, and Olympia," June 7, 2022*

- WalletHub's latest report ranked 182 cities by the average credit score of its residents. San Francisco was ranked #4 among the ten cities with the highest average credit score, based on WalletHub's 2024 fourth quarter data. *WalletHub.com, "2025's Cities With the Highest & Lowest Credit Scores," March 6, 2025*

- Payscale.com ranked the 32 largest metro areas in terms of wage growth. The San Francisco metro area ranked #28. Criteria: quarterly changes in private industry employee and education professional wage growth from the previous year. *PayScale, "Wage Trends by Metro Area-4th Quarter," February 4, 2025*

- For its annual survey of the "Most Expensive U.S. Cities to Live In," Kiplinger applied Cost of Living Index statistics developed by the Council for Community and Economic Research to U.S. Census Bureau population and median household income data for 265 urban areas. San Francisco ranked #4 among the most expensive in the country. *Kiplinger.com, "The 10 Most Expensive Cities to Live in the U.S.," February 3, 2025*

- The San Francisco metro area appeared on the Milken Institute "2025 Best Performing Cities" list. Rank: #126 out of 200 large metro areas (based on performance category). Criteria: job growth; wage growth; high-tech growth and impact; community resilience; housing affordability; household broadband access. *Milken Institute, "Best-Performing Cities 2025," January 14, 2025*

- Mercer Human Resources Consulting ranked 226 cities worldwide in terms of cost-of-living. San Francisco ranked #13 (the lower the ranking, the higher the cost-of-living). The survey measured the comparative cost of over 200 items (such as housing, food, clothing, domestic supplies, transportation, and recreation/entertainment) in each location. *Mercer, "2024 Cost of Living City Ranking," June 17, 2024*

Education Rankings

- Personal finance website *WalletHub* analyzed the 150 largest U.S. metropolitan statistical areas to determine where the most educated Americans are putting their degrees to work. Criteria: education levels; percentage of workers with degrees; education quality and attainment gap; public school quality rankings; quality and enrollment of each metro area's universities. San Francisco was ranked #6 (#1 = most educated city). *WalletHub.com, "Most & Least Educated Cities in America, 2025" July 2, 2024*

Environmental Rankings

- Sperling's *BestPlaces* assessed the 50 largest metropolitan areas of the United States for the likelihood of dangerously extreme weather events or earthquakes. In general the Southeast and South-Central regions have the highest risk of weather extremes and earthquakes, while the Pacific Northwest enjoys the lowest risk. Of the least risky metropolitan areas, the San Francisco metro area was ranked #4. *Bestplaces.net, "Avoid Natural Disasters: BestPlaces Reveals The Top 10 Safest Places to Live," October 25, 2017*

- The U.S. Environmental Protection Agency (EPA) released its list of U.S. metropolitan areas with the most ENERGY STAR certified buildings in 2023. The San Francisco metro area was ranked #5 out of 25. *U.S. Environmental Protection Agency, "2024 Energy Star Top Cities," May 22, 2024*

Food/Drink Rankings

- WalletHub compared the 100 largest U.S. cities across 17 key indicators of vegan- and vegetarian-friendliness. San Francisco was ranked #7. Cities were selected based on metrics such as the cost of groceries for vegetarians, the share of restaurants serving meatless options and the number of salad shops per capita. *WalletHub.com, "Best Cities for Vegans & Vegetarians (2025)," September 24, 2024*

Health/Fitness Rankings

- For each of the 100 largest cities in the United States, the American Fitness Index®, compiled in partnership between the American College of Sports Medicine and the Elevance Health Foundation, evaluated community infrastructure and more than 30 health behaviors including preventive health, levels of chronic disease conditions, food insecurity, pedestrian safety, air quality, and community/environment resources that support physical activity. San Francisco ranked #4 for "community fitness." *americanfitnessindex.org, "2024 ACSM American Fitness Index Summary Report," July 23, 2024*

- San Francisco was identified as one of the 10 most walkable cities in the U.S. by Walk Score. The city ranked #2. Walk Score measures walkability by analyzing hundreds of walking routes to nearby amenities, and also measures pedestrian friendliness by analyzing population density and road metrics such as block length and intersection density. *WalkScore.com, April 13, 2021*

- The San Francisco metro area was identified as one of the worst cities for bed bugs in America by pest control company Orkin. The area ranked #41 out of 50 based on the number of bed bug treatments Orkin performed from December 2022 to November 2023. *Orkin, "Chicago Joins Paris In Global Bed Bug Spotlight Ranking As The Worst City On Orkin's U.S. Bed Bug Cities List," January 22, 2024*

- San Francisco was identified as a "2025 Allergy Capital." The area ranked #53 out of the nation's 100 largest metropolitan areas. Three groups of factors were used to identify the most challenging cities for people with allergies: annual tree, grass, and weed pollen scores; over the counter allergy medicine use; number of board-certified allergy specialists. *Asthma and Allergy Foundation of America, "2025 Allergy Capitals: The Most Challenging Places to Live with Allergies," March 18, 2025*

- San Francisco was identified as a "2024 Asthma Capital." The area ranked #64 out of the nation's 100 largest metropolitan areas. Criteria: estimated asthma prevalence; asthma-related mortality; and ER visits due to asthma. Risk factors analyzed but not factored in the rankings: annual air quality including pollution and ozone levels; public smoking laws; indoor air quality; access to asthma specialists; rescue and controller medication use; uninsured rate; pollen allergy; poverty rate. *Asthma and Allergy Foundation of America, "Asthma Capitals 2024: The Most Challenging Places to Live With Asthma," September 10, 2024*

- The Sharecare Community Well-Being Index evaluates 10 individual and social health factors in order to measure what matters to Americans in the communities in which they live. The San Francisco metro area ranked #1 in the top 10 across all 10 domains. Criteria: access to healthcare, food, and community resources; housing and transportation; economic security; feeling of purpose; and physical, financial, social, and community well-being. *Sharecare.com, "Community Well-Being Index: 2020 Metro Area & County Rankings Report," August 30, 2021*

Pet Rankings

- San Francisco was selected by *Sniffspot.com* as one of the most dog-friendly cities in the U.S., ranking #46 out of 50. Criteria: dog parks; hiking; sniffspots; public parks; dog-friendly businesses; housing; dog waste cleanliness; leash laws; dog services; and overall cost. *Sniffspot.com, "The Top 50 Most Dog-Friendly Cities in the U.S.," September 30, 2024*

Real Estate Rankings

- *WalletHub* compared the most populated U.S. cities to determine which had the best markets for real estate agents. San Francisco ranked #24 where demand was high and pay was the best. Criteria: sales per agent; annual median wage for real-estate agents; monthly average starting salary for real estate agents; real estate job density and competition; unemployment rate; home turnover rate; housing-market health index; and other relevant metrics. *WalletHub.com, "2021 Best Places to Be a Real Estate Agent," May 12, 2021*

- The San Francisco metro area was identified as one of the 10 worst condo markets in the U.S. in 2024. The area ranked #62 out of 63 markets. Criteria: year-over-year change of median sales price of existing apartment condo-coop homes between the 4th quarter of 2023 and the 4th quarter of 2024. *National Association of Realtors®, Median Sales Price of Existing Apartment Condo-Coops Homes for Metropolitan Areas, 4th Quarter 2024*

- The San Francisco metro area was identified as one of the 20 least affordable housing markets in the U.S. in 2024. The area ranked #224 out of 226 markets. Criteria: qualification for a mortgage loan with a 10 percent down payment on a typical home. *National Association of Realtors®, Qualifying Income Based on Sales Price of Existing Single-Family Homes for Metropolitan Areas, February 6, 2025*

- San Francisco was ranked #173 out of 176 metro areas in terms of cost of housing in 2024 by the National Association of Home Builders (#1 = most affordable). Criteria: the portion of an average family's income necessary to pay the mortgage on a median-priced home. *National Association of Home Builders®, NAHB-Wells Fargo Cost of Housing Index, 4th Quarter 2024*

Safety Rankings

- Allstate ranked the 100 most populous cities in America in terms of driver safety. San Francisco ranked #29. Criteria based on anonymized driving behavior data from Allstate's mobile app powered by Arity: high speed driving (over 80 mph), phone handling, and hard braking. The report helps increase the importance of safety and awareness behind the wheel. *Allstate, "16th Allstate America's Best Drivers Report®" July 11, 2024*

- The National Insurance Crime Bureau ranked the largest metro areas in the U.S. in terms of per capita rates of vehicle theft. The San Francisco metro area ranked #2 out of the top 10 (#1 = highest rate). Criteria: number of vehicle theft offenses per 100,000 inhabitants in 2023. *National Insurance Crime Bureau, "Vehicle Thefts Surge Nationwide in 2023," April 9, 2024*

Transportation Rankings

- San Francisco was identified as one of the most congested metro areas in the U.S. The area ranked #2 out of 10. Criteria: yearly delay per auto commuter in hours. *Texas A&M Transportation Institute, "2023 Urban Mobility Report," June 2024*

Women/Minorities Rankings

- San Francisco was listed as one of the most LGBTQ-friendly cities in America by *The Advocate*, as compiled by the real estate data site *Clever*. The city ranked #1 out of 15. Criteria, among many: Pride events; gay bars; LGBTQ-affirming healthcare options; state and local laws; number of PFLAG chapters; LGBTQ+ population. *The Advocate, "These Are the 15 Most LGBTQ-Friendly Cities in the U.S." November 1, 2023*

- Personal finance website *WalletHub* compared more than 180 U.S. cities across two key dimensions, "Hispanic Business-Friendliness" and "Hispanic Purchasing Power," to arrive at the most favorable conditions for Hispanic entrepreneurs. San Francisco was ranked #149 out of 182. Criteria includes: share of Hispanic-Owned Businesses; average growth of Hispanic Business revenues; Small Business-Friendliness score; affordability; and number of Hispanics with at least a bachelor's degree. *WalletHub.com, "Best Cities for Hispanic Entrepreneurs," September 4, 2024*

Miscellaneous Rankings

- *MoveHub* ranked 446 hipster cities across 20 countries, using its new and improved alternative Hipster Index and San Francisco came out as #15 among the top 50. Criteria: population over 150,000; number of vintage boutiques; density of tattoo parlors; vegan places to eat; coffee shops; and density of vinyl record stores. *MoveHub.com, "The Hipster Index: Brighton Pips Portland to Global Top Spot," July 28, 2021*

- In its roundup of St. Patrick's Day parades, *Gayot* listed the best festivals and parades of all things Irish. The festivities in San Francisco as among the best in North America. *Gayot.com, "Best St. Patrick's Day Parades," March 2025*

- *WalletHub* compared 148 of the most populated U.S. cities to determine their operating efficiency. A "Quality of Services" score was constructed for each city and then measured against the total budget per capita to reveal which were managed the best. San Francisco ranked #148. Criteria: financial stability; economy; education; safety; health; infrastructure and pollution. *WalletHub.com, "2025's Best- & Worst-Run Cities in America," June 18, 2024*

Business Environment

DEMOGRAPHICS

Population Growth

Area	1990 Census	2000 Census	2010 Census	2020 Census	2023 Estimate[2]	Population Growth 1990-2023 (%)
City	723,959	776,733	805,235	873,965	836,321	15.5
MSA[1]	3,686,592	4,123,740	4,335,391	4,749,008	4,653,593	26.2
U.S.	248,709,873	281,421,906	308,745,538	331,449,281	332,387,540	33.6

Note: (1) Figures cover the San Francisco-Oakland-Fremont, CA Metropolitan Statistical Area; (2) 2019-2023 5-year ACS population estimate
Source: U.S. Census Bureau, 1990 Census, 2000 Census, 2010 Census, 2020 Census, 2019-2023 American Community Survey 5-Year Estimates

Race

Area	White Alone[2] (%)	Black Alone[2] (%)	Asian Alone[2] (%)	AIAN[3] Alone[2] (%)	NHOPI[4] Alone[2] (%)	Other Race Alone[2] (%)	Two or More Races (%)
City	40.5	5.1	35.0	0.7	0.4	7.7	10.7
MSA[1]	39.9	7.0	27.6	0.9	0.6	11.8	12.2
U.S.	63.4	12.4	5.8	0.9	0.2	6.6	10.7

Note: (1) Figures cover the San Francisco-Oakland-Fremont, CA Metropolitan Statistical Area; (2) Alone is defined as not being in combination with one or more other races; (3) American Indian and Alaska Native; (4) Native Hawaiian and Other Pacific Islander
Source: U.S. Census Bureau, 2019-2023 American Community Survey 5-Year Estimates

Hispanic or Latino Origin

Area	Total (%)	Mexican (%)	Puerto Rican (%)	Cuban (%)	Other (%)
City	15.9	7.8	0.7	0.2	7.2
MSA[1]	23.0	14.5	0.7	0.2	7.6
U.S.	19.0	11.3	1.8	0.7	5.2

Note: Persons of Hispanic or Latino origin can be of any race; (1) Figures cover the San Francisco-Oakland-Fremont, CA Metropolitan Statistical Area
Source: U.S. Census Bureau, 2019-2023 American Community Survey 5-Year Estimates

Age

Area	Percent of Population									Median Age
	Under Age 5	Age 5–19	Age 20–34	Age 35–44	Age 45–54	Age 55–64	Age 65–74	Age 75–84	Age 85+	
City	4.2	11.0	26.1	16.3	13.2	12.0	9.8	4.8	2.6	39.7
MSA[1]	5.1	16.5	20.6	15.0	13.5	12.7	9.6	4.8	2.1	40.0
U.S.	5.7	19.1	20.2	13.1	12.3	12.8	10.0	4.9	1.9	38.7

Note: (1) Figures cover the San Francisco-Oakland-Fremont, CA Metropolitan Statistical Area
Source: U.S. Census Bureau, 2019-2023 American Community Survey 5-Year Estimates

Disability by Age

Area	All Ages	Under 18 Years Old	18 to 64 Years Old	65 Years and Over
City	11.2	2.7	7.3	34.1
MSA[1]	10.3	3.2	7.3	30.4
U.S.	13.0	4.7	10.7	32.9

Note: Figures show percent of the civilian noninstitutionalized population that reported having a disability. Disability status is determined from six types of difficulty: vision, hearing, cognitive, ambulatory, self-care, and independent living. For children under 5 years old, hearing and vision difficulty are used to determine disability status. For children between the ages of 5 and 14, disability status is determined from hearing, vision, cognitive, ambulatory, and self-care difficulties. For people aged 15 years and older, they are considered to have a disability if they have difficulty with any one of the six difficulty types; Note: (1) Figures cover the San Francisco-Oakland-Fremont, CA Metropolitan Statistical Area
Source: U.S. Census Bureau, 2019-2023 American Community Survey 5-Year Estimates

Ancestry

Area	German	Irish	English	American	Italian	Polish	French[2]	European	Scottish
City	7.1	7.5	6.0	2.1	4.5	1.8	2.2	2.1	1.3
MSA[1]	7.1	6.8	6.6	2.2	4.2	1.4	1.7	2.0	1.3
U.S.	12.6	9.4	9.1	5.5	4.9	2.6	2.0	1.6	1.6

Note: Figures are the percentage of the total population reporting a particular ancestry. The nine most commonly reported ancestries in the U.S. are shown. Figures include multiple ancestries (e.g. if a person reported being Irish and Italian, they were included in both columns); (1) Figures cover the San Francisco-Oakland-Fremont, CA Metropolitan Statistical Area; (2) Excludes Basque
Source: U.S. Census Bureau, 2019-2023 American Community Survey 5-Year Estimates

Foreign-born Population

Area	Any Foreign Country	Asia	Mexico	Europe	Caribbean	Central America[2]	South America	Africa	Canada
					Percent of Population Born in				
City	34.2	21.9	2.4	4.4	0.1	2.4	1.3	0.6	0.7
MSA[1]	31.6	18.0	4.9	2.8	0.2	2.7	1.2	0.9	0.5
U.S.	13.9	4.3	3.3	1.4	1.4	1.2	1.2	0.8	0.2

Note: (1) Figures cover the San Francisco-Oakland-Fremont, CA Metropolitan Statistical Area; (2) Excludes Mexico.
Source: U.S. Census Bureau, 2019-2023 American Community Survey 5-Year Estimates

Household Size

Area	Persons in Household (%)							Average Household Size
	One	Two	Three	Four	Five	Six	Seven or More	
City	38.0	32.3	13.4	9.9	3.5	1.6	1.2	2.24
MSA[1]	27.2	31.8	16.7	14.5	5.9	2.3	1.6	2.63
U.S.	28.5	33.8	15.4	12.7	5.9	2.3	1.4	2.54

Note: (1) Figures cover the San Francisco-Oakland-Fremont, CA Metropolitan Statistical Area
Source: U.S. Census Bureau, 2019-2023 American Community Survey 5-Year Estimates

Household Relationships

Area	House-holder	Opposite-sex Spouse	Same-sex Spouse	Opposite-sex Unmarried Partner	Same-sex Unmarried Partner	Child[2]	Grand-child	Other Relatives	Non-relatives
City	42.6	13.6	0.8	3.3	0.6	17.6	1.3	6.8	10.3
MSA[1]	36.7	17.0	0.4	2.3	0.3	26.3	1.8	6.9	5.9
U.S.	38.3	17.5	0.2	2.5	0.2	28.3	2.4	4.8	3.4

Note: Figures are percent of the total population; (1) Figures cover the San Francisco-Oakland-Fremont, CA Metropolitan Statistical Area; (2) Includes biological, adopted, and stepchildren of the householder
Source: U.S. Census Bureau, 2020 Census

Gender

Area	Males	Females	Males per 100 Females
City	429,837	406,484	105.7
MSA[1]	2,318,841	2,334,752	99.3
U.S.	164,545,087	167,842,453	98.0

Note: (1) Figures cover the San Francisco-Oakland-Fremont, CA Metropolitan Statistical Area
Source: U.S. Census Bureau, 2019-2023 American Community Survey 5-Year Estimates

Marital Status

Area	Never Married	Now Married[2]	Separated	Widowed	Divorced
City	45.6	40.7	1.4	4.5	7.8
MSA[1]	36.8	48.8	1.4	4.6	8.4
U.S.	34.1	47.9	1.7	5.6	10.7

Note: Figures are percentages and cover the population 15 years of age and older; (1) Figures cover the San Francisco-Oakland-Fremont, CA Metropolitan Statistical Area; (2) Excludes separated
Source: U.S. Census Bureau, 2019-2023 American Community Survey 5-Year Estimates

Religious Groups by Family

Area	Catholic	Baptist	Methodist	LDS[2]	Pentecostal	Lutheran	Islam	Adventist	Other
MSA[1]	21.5	2.2	0.9	1.5	1.4	0.4	2.0	1.0	7.7
U.S.	18.7	7.3	3.0	2.0	1.8	1.7	1.3	1.3	11.6

Note: Figures are the number of adherents as a percentage of the total population and cover the eight largest religious groups in the U.S; (1) Figures cover the San Francisco-Oakland-Fremont, CA Metropolitan Statistical Area; (2) Church of Jesus Christ of Latter-day Saints
Sources: 2020 U.S. Religion Census, Association of Statisticians of American Religious Bodies; The Association of Religion Data Archives (ARDA)

Religious Groups by Tradition

Area	Catholic	Evangelical Protestant	Mainline Protestant	Black Protestant	Islam	Judaism	Hinduism	Orthodox	Buddhism
MSA[1]	21.5	5.2	2.2	1.8	2.0	0.7	1.1	0.7	1.1
U.S.	18.7	16.5	5.2	2.3	1.3	0.6	0.4	0.4	0.3

Note: Figures are the number of adherents as a percentage of the total population; (1) Figures cover the San Francisco-Oakland-Fremont, CA Metropolitan Statistical Area
Sources: 2020 U.S. Religion Census, Association of Statisticians of American Religious Bodies; The Association of Religion Data Archives (ARDA)

ECONOMY

Real Gross Domestic Product (GDP)

Area	2017	2018	2019	2020	2021	2022	2023	Rank[3]
MSA[1]	526.6	560.6	594.3	596.5	662.4	659.3	681.9	4
U.S.[2]	17,619.1	18,160.7	18,642.5	18,238.9	19,387.6	19,896.6	20,436.3	–

Note: Figures are in billions of chained 2017 dollars; (1) Figures cover the San Francisco-Oakland-Fremont, CA Metropolitan Statistical Area; (2) Figures cover real GDP within metropolitan areas; (3) Rank is based on 2023 data and ranges from 1 to 384
Source: U.S. Bureau of Economic Analysis

Economic Growth

Area	2014	2015	2016	2017	2018	2019	2020	2021	2022	2023
MSA[1]	6.1	6.0	5.7	9.3	6.5	6.0	0.4	11.0	-0.5	3.4
U.S.[2]	2.6	3.2	2.0	2.7	3.1	2.7	-2.2	6.3	2.6	2.7

Note: Figures are real gross domestic product growth rates and represent percent change from preceding period; (1) Figures cover the San Francisco-Oakland-Fremont, CA Metropolitan Statistical Area; (2) Figures are the average growth rates within metropolitan areas
Source: U.S. Bureau of Economic Analysis

Metropolitan Area Exports

Area	2018	2019	2020	2021	2022	2023	Rank[2]
MSA[1]	27,417.0	28,003.8	23,864.5	29,972.0	30,649.0	24,253.0	19
U.S.	1,664,056.1	1,645,173.7	1,431,406.6	1,753,941.4	2,062,937.4	2,019,160.5	–

Note: Figures are in millions of dollars; (1) Figures cover the San Francisco-Oakland-Fremont, CA Metropolitan Statistical Area; (2) Rank is based on 2023 data and ranges from 1 to 386
Source: U.S. Department of Commerce, International Trade Administration, Office of Trade and Economic Analysis, Industry and Analysis, Exports by Metropolitan Area, data extracted April 2, 2025

Building Permits

Area	Single-Family			Multi-Family			Total		
	2023	2024	Pct. Chg.	2023	2024	Pct. Chg.	2023	2024	Pct. Chg.
City	29	27	-6.9	1,107	743	-32.9	1,136	770	-32.2
MSA[1]	3,015	2,776	-7.9	4,515	3,138	-30.5	7,530	5,914	-21.5
U.S.	920,000	981,900	6.7	591,100	496,100	-16.1	1,511,100	1,478,000	-2.2

Note: (1) Figures cover the San Francisco-Oakland-Fremont, CA Metropolitan Statistical Area; Figures represent new, privately-owned housing units authorized (unadjusted data)
Source: U.S. Census Bureau, Building Permits Survey (BPS), 2023, 2024

Bankruptcy Filings

Area	Business Filings			Nonbusiness Filings		
	2023	2024	% Chg.	2023	2024	% Chg.
San Francisco County	68	140	105.9	348	417	19.8
U.S.	18,926	23,107	22.1	434,064	494,201	13.9

Note: Business filings include Chapter 7, Chapter 9, Chapter 11, Chapter 12, Chapter 13, Chapter 15, and Section 304; Nonbusiness filings include Chapter 7, Chapter 11, and Chapter 13
Source: Administrative Office of the U.S. Courts, Business and Nonbusiness Bankruptcy, County Cases Commenced by Chapter of the Bankruptcy Code, During the 12-Month Period Ending December 31, 2023 and Business and Nonbusiness Bankruptcy, County Cases Commenced by Chapter of the Bankruptcy Code, During the 12-Month Period Ending December 31, 2024

Housing Vacancy Rates

Area	Gross Vacancy Rate[3] (%)			Year-Round Vacancy Rate[4] (%)			Rental Vacancy Rate[5] (%)			Homeowner Vacancy Rate[6] (%)		
	2022	2023	2024	2022	2023	2024	2022	2023	2024	2022	2023	2024
MSA[1]	7.9	8.1	8.3	7.7	8.0	8.1	5.4	6.6	6.3	1.3	0.5	0.7
U.S.[2]	9.1	9.0	9.1	7.5	7.5	7.6	5.7	6.5	6.8	0.8	0.8	1.0

Note: (1) Figures cover the San Francisco-Oakland-Fremont, CA Metropolitan Statistical Area; (2) Figures cover the 75 largest Metropolitan Statistical Areas; (3) The percentage of the total housing inventory that is vacant; (4) The percentage of the housing inventory (excluding seasonal units) that is year-round vacant; (5) The percentage of rental inventory that is vacant for rent; (6) The percentage of homeowner inventory that is vacant for sale
Source: U.S. Census Bureau, Housing Vacancies and Homeownership Annual Statistics: 2022, 2023, 2024

INCOME

Income

Area	Per Capita ($)	Median Household ($)	Average Household ($)
City	90,285	141,446	204,625
MSA[1]	72,306	133,780	190,258
U.S.	43,289	78,538	110,491

Note: (1) Figures cover the San Francisco-Oakland-Fremont, CA Metropolitan Statistical Area
Source: U.S. Census Bureau, 2019-2023 American Community Survey 5-Year Estimates

Household Income Distribution

Area	Percent of Households Earning							
	Under $15,000	$15,000 -$24,999	$25,000 -$34,999	$35,000 -$49,999	$50,000 -$74,999	$75,000 -$99,999	$100,000 -$149,999	$150,000 and up
City	8.5	4.8	3.9	5.2	8.1	8.4	13.4	47.7
MSA[1]	6.3	3.8	3.8	5.9	9.6	9.3	15.9	45.4
U.S.	8.5	6.6	6.8	10.4	15.7	12.7	17.4	21.9

Note: (1) Figures cover the San Francisco-Oakland-Fremont, CA Metropolitan Statistical Area
Source: U.S. Census Bureau, 2019-2023 American Community Survey 5-Year Estimates

Poverty Rate

Area	All Ages	Under 18 Years Old	18 to 64 Years Old	65 Years and Over
City	10.6	8.2	9.6	16.4
MSA[1]	8.7	8.8	8.2	10.4
U.S.	12.4	16.3	11.6	10.4

Note: Figures are percentage of people whose income during the past 12 months was below the poverty level;
(1) Figures cover the San Francisco-Oakland-Fremont, CA Metropolitan Statistical Area
Source: U.S. Census Bureau, 2019-2023 American Community Survey 5-Year Estimates

EMPLOYMENT

Labor Force and Employment

Area	Civilian Labor Force			Workers Employed		
	Dec. 2023	Dec. 2024	% Chg.	Dec. 2023	Dec. 2024	% Chg.
City	564,822	561,032	-0.7	545,573	541,446	-0.8
MD[1]	1,011,370	1,004,815	-0.6	978,032	970,469	-0.8
U.S.	166,661,000	167,746,000	0.7	160,754,000	161,294,000	0.3

Note: Data is not seasonally adjusted and covers workers 16 years of age and older; (1) Figures cover the San Francisco-San Mateo-Redwood City, CA Metropolitan Division
Source: Bureau of Labor Statistics, Local Area Unemployment Statistics

Unemployment Rate

Area	2024											
	Jan.	Feb.	Mar.	Apr.	May	Jun.	Jul.	Aug.	Sep.	Oct.	Nov.	Dec.
City	3.8	3.6	3.5	3.3	3.1	3.7	4.0	4.1	3.6	3.7	3.7	3.5
MD[1]	3.7	3.6	3.4	3.2	3.1	3.6	3.9	4.0	3.5	3.6	3.7	3.4
U.S.	4.1	4.2	3.9	3.5	3.7	4.3	4.5	4.4	3.9	3.9	4.0	3.8

Note: Data is not seasonally adjusted and covers workers 16 years of age and older; (1) Figures cover the San Francisco-San Mateo-Redwood City, CA Metropolitan Division
Source: Bureau of Labor Statistics, Local Area Unemployment Statistics

Average Wages

Occupation	$/Hr.	Occupation	$/Hr.
Accountants and Auditors	57.63	Maintenance and Repair Workers	33.69
Automotive Mechanics	35.20	Marketing Managers	109.71
Bookkeepers	32.85	Network and Computer Systems Admin.	64.21
Carpenters	41.44	Nurses, Licensed Practical	43.56
Cashiers	20.07	Nurses, Registered	85.79
Computer Programmers	62.74	Nursing Assistants	27.59
Computer Systems Analysts	71.92	Office Clerks, General	27.96
Computer User Support Specialists	43.40	Physical Therapists	65.53
Construction Laborers	36.32	Physicians	127.97
Cooks, Restaurant	22.87	Plumbers, Pipefitters and Steamfitters	41.48
Customer Service Representatives	29.30	Police and Sheriff's Patrol Officers	61.75
Dentists	109.18	Postal Service Mail Carriers	29.93
Electricians	50.12	Real Estate Sales Agents	39.65
Engineers, Electrical	77.50	Retail Salespersons	22.87
Fast Food and Counter Workers	20.67	Sales Representatives, Technical/Scientific	70.21
Financial Managers	117.20	Secretaries, Exc. Legal/Medical/Executive	31.24
First-Line Supervisors of Office Workers	43.48	Security Guards	24.81
General and Operations Managers	85.95	Surgeons	n/a
Hairdressers/Cosmetologists	23.49	Teacher Assistants, Exc. Postsecondary[1]	24.02
Home Health and Personal Care Aides	18.28	Teachers, Secondary School, Exc. Sp. Ed.[1]	55.15
Janitors and Cleaners	23.06	Telemarketers	23.72
Landscaping/Groundskeeping Workers	25.75	Truck Drivers, Heavy/Tractor-Trailer	32.89
Lawyers	132.29	Truck Drivers, Light/Delivery Services	27.39
Maids and Housekeeping Cleaners	25.07	Waiters and Waitresses	22.18

Note: Wage data covers the San Francisco-Oakland-Fremont, CA Metropolitan Statistical Area; (1) Hourly wages were calculated from annual wage data based on a 40 hour work week
Source: Bureau of Labor Statistics, Metro Area Occupational Employment & Wage Estimates, May 2024

Employment by Industry

Sector	MD[1]		U.S.
	Number of Employees	Percent of Total	Percent of Total
Construction	38,700	3.3	5.1
Financial Activities	78,000	6.7	5.8
Government	142,900	12.4	14.9
Information	111,800	9.7	1.9
Leisure and Hospitality	122,900	10.6	10.4
Manufacturing	29,600	2.6	8.0
Mining and Logging	100	<0.1	0.4
Other Services	38,600	3.3	3.7
Private Education and Health Services	165,600	14.3	16.9
Professional and Business Services	290,600	25.1	14.2
Retail Trade	63,800	5.5	10.0
Transportation, Warehousing, and Utilities	50,300	4.4	4.8
Wholesale Trade	23,300	2.0	3.9

Note: Figures are non-farm employment as of December 2024. Figures are not seasonally adjusted and include workers 16 years of age and older; (1) Figures cover the San Francisco-San Mateo-Redwood City, CA Metropolitan Division
Source: Bureau of Labor Statistics, Current Employment Statistics, Employment, Hours, and Earnings

Employment by Occupation

Occupation Classification	City (%)	MSA[1] (%)	U.S. (%)
Management, Business, Science, and Arts	63.4	55.0	42.0
Natural Resources, Construction, and Maintenance	2.9	5.6	8.6
Production, Transportation, and Material Moving	5.4	8.0	13.0
Sales and Office	15.3	17.0	19.9
Service	13.0	14.5	16.5

Note: Figures cover employed civilians 16 years of age and older; (1) Figures cover the San Francisco-Oakland-Fremont, CA Metropolitan Statistical Area
Source: U.S. Census Bureau, 2019-2023 American Community Survey 5-Year Estimates

Occupations with Greatest Projected Employment Growth: 2022 – 2032

Occupation[1]	2022 Employment	2032 Projected Employment	Numeric Employment Change	Percent Employment Change
Home Health and Personal Care Aides	796,900	1,060,200	263,300	33.0
Software Developers	313,700	388,000	74,300	23.7
Registered Nurses	333,700	376,900	43,200	12.9
Cooks, Restaurant	142,100	184,000	41,900	29.5
Laborers and Freight, Stock, and Material Movers, Hand	399,500	437,300	37,800	9.5
Janitors and Cleaners, Except Maids and Housekeeping Cleaners	262,900	300,200	37,300	14.2
Fast Food and Counter Workers	419,100	455,200	36,100	8.6
Stockers and Order Fillers	289,900	322,900	33,000	11.4
Medical Assistants	108,000	135,700	27,700	25.6
Landscaping and Groundskeeping Workers	135,200	162,100	26,900	19.9

Note: Projections cover California; (1) Sorted by numeric employment change
Source: www.projectionscentral.org, State Occupational Projections, 2022–2032 Long-Term Projections

Fastest-Growing Occupations: 2022 – 2032

Occupation[1]	2022 Employment	2032 Projected Employment	Numeric Employment Change	Percent Employment Change
Nurse Practitioners	21,500	34,100	12,600	58.6
Physical Therapist Assistants	7,900	11,200	3,300	41.8
Solar Photovoltaic Installers	7,900	11,200	3,300	41.8
Physician Assistants	13,000	18,200	5,200	40.0
Medical and Health Services Managers	58,300	81,400	23,100	39.6
Statisticians	2,800	3,900	1,100	39.3
Taxi Drivers	48,100	66,800	18,700	38.9
Occupational Therapy Assistants	2,700	3,600	900	33.3
Home Health and Personal Care Aides	796,900	1,060,200	263,300	33.0
Data Scientists	33,900	45,000	11,100	32.7

Note: Projections cover California; (1) Sorted by percent employment change and excludes occupations with numeric employment change less than 50
Source: www.projectionscentral.org, State Occupational Projections, 2022–2032 Long-Term Projections

CITY FINANCES

City Government Finances

Component	2022 ($000)	2022 ($ per capita)
Total Revenues	15,989,397	18,451
Total Expenditures	15,794,091	18,225
Debt Outstanding	23,054,687	26,603

Source: U.S. Census Bureau, State & Local Government Finances 2022

City Government Revenue by Source

Source	2022 ($000)	2022 ($ per capita)	2022 (%)
General Revenue			
From Federal Government	1,659,948	1,915	10.4
From State Government	2,003,924	2,312	12.5
From Local Governments	836,285	965	5.2
Taxes			
Property	2,972,973	3,431	18.6
Sales and Gross Receipts	860,676	993	5.4
Personal Income	0	0	0.0
Corporate Income	0	0	0.0
Motor Vehicle License	4,652	5	0.0
Other Taxes	2,081,444	2,402	13.0
Current Charges	4,032,007	4,653	25.2
Liquor Store	0	0	0.0
Utility	1,039,778	1,200	6.5

Source: U.S. Census Bureau, State & Local Government Finances 2022

City Government Expenditures by Function

Function	2022 ($000)	2022 ($ per capita)	2022 (%)
General Direct Expenditures			
Air Transportation	737,630	851	4.7
Corrections	274,196	316	1.7
Education	0	0	0.0
Employment Security Administration	0	0	0.0
Financial Administration	164,684	190	1.0
Fire Protection	425,040	490	2.7
General Public Buildings	2,373	2	0.0
Governmental Administration, Other	518,394	598	3.3
Health	2,749,283	3,172	17.4
Highways	276,247	318	1.7
Hospitals	1,139,667	1,315	7.2
Housing and Community Development	515,557	594	3.3
Interest on General Debt	505,143	582	3.2
Judicial and Legal	163,007	188	1.0
Libraries	139,008	160	0.9
Parking	165,512	191	1.0
Parks and Recreation	331,951	383	2.1
Police Protection	659,302	760	4.2
Public Welfare	1,532,018	1,767	9.7
Sewerage	166,221	191	1.1
Solid Waste Management	0	0	0.0
Veterans' Services	0	0	0.0
Liquor Store	0	0	0.0
Utility	2,433,881	2,808	15.4

Source: U.S. Census Bureau, State & Local Government Finances 2022

TAXES

State Corporate Income Tax Rates

State	Tax Rate (%)	Income Brackets ($)	Num. of Brackets	Financial Institution Tax Rate (%)[a]	Federal Income Tax Ded.
California	8.84 (b)	Flat rate	1	10.84 (b)	No

Note: Tax rates for tax year 2024; (a) Rates listed are the corporate income tax rate applied to financial institutions or excise taxes based on income. Some states have other taxes based upon the value of deposits or shares; (b) Minimum tax is $800 in California, $250 in District of Columbia, $50 in Arizona and North Dakota (banks), $400 ($100 banks) in Rhode Island, $200 per location in South Dakota (banks), $100 in Utah, in Vermont, simplified entity business tax for residents only at $250, otherwise minimum tax ($100 - $100,000) is based upon gross receipts.
Source: Federation of Tax Administrators, State Corporate Income Tax Rates, January 1, 2025

State Individual Income Tax Rates

State	Tax Rate (%)	Income Brackets ($)	Personal Exemptions ($) Single	Married	Depend.	Standard Ded. ($) Single	Married
California (a)	1.0 - 13.3 (g)	10,099 - 677,276 (b)	134	268	367 (c)	5,202	10,404 (a)

Note: Tax rates for tax year 2024; Local- and county-level taxes are not included; Federal income tax is not deductible on state income tax returns; (a) 16 states have statutory provision for automatically adjusting to the rate of inflation the dollar values of the income tax brackets, standard deductions, and/or personal exemptions. Oregon does not index the income brackets for $125,000 and over See: INFL and SPEC above; (b) For joint returns, taxes are twice the tax on half the couple's income. California brackets violate this formula at the two highest tax brackets in 2024; (c) The personal exemption takes the form of a tax credit instead of a deduction; (g) California imposes an additional 1% tax on taxable income over $1 million, making the maximum rate 13.3% over $1 million in 2023. Unreleased projections indicate 14.4% in 2024.
Source: Federation of Tax Administrators, State Individual Income Tax Rates, January 1, 2025

Various State Sales and Excise Tax Rates

State	State Sales Tax (%)	Gasoline[1] ($/gal.)	Cigarette[2] ($/pack)	Spirits[3] ($/gal.)	Wine[4] ($/gal.)	Beer[5] ($/gal.)	Recreational Marijuana (%)
California	7.25	0.70	2.87	3.30	0.20	0.20	(c)

Note: All tax rates as of January 1, 2025; (1) The American Petroleum Institute has developed a methodology for determining the average tax rate on a gallon of fuel. Rates may include any of the following: excise taxes, environmental fees, storage tank fees, other fees or taxes, general sales tax, and local taxes; (2) The federal excise tax of $1.0066 per pack and local taxes are not included; (3) Rates are those applicable to off-premise sales of 40% alcohol by volume (a.b.v.) distilled spirits in 750ml containers. Local excise taxes are excluded; (4) Rates are those applicable to off-premise sales of 11% a.b.v. non-carbonated wine in 750ml containers; (5) Rates are those applicable to off-premise sales of 4.7% a.b.v. beer in 12 ounce containers; (c) 15% excise tax (retail gross receipts)
Source: Tax Foundation, 2025 Facts & Figures: How Does Your State Compare?

State Tax Competitiveness Index

State	Overall Rank	Corporate Tax Rank	Individual Income Tax Rank	Sales Tax Rank	Property Tax Rank	Unemployment Insurance Tax Rank
California	48	41	49	46	23	25

Note: The Tax Foundation's State Tax Competitiveness Index enables policymakers, taxpayers, and business leaders to gauge how their states' tax systems compare. A rank of 1 is best, 50 is worst. Rankings do not average to the total. States without a tax rank equally as 1. DC's scores and rankings do not affect other states. The report shows tax systems as of July 1, 2024 (the beginning of Fiscal Year 2025).
Source: Tax Foundation, State Tax Competitiveness Index 2025

TRANSPORTATION

Means of Transportation to Work

Area	Car/Truck/Van Drove Alone	Car-pooled	Public Transportation Bus	Subway	Railroad	Bicycle	Walked	Other Means	Worked at Home
City	28.6	6.0	14.1	4.8	1.1	3.3	10.0	4.5	27.5
MSA[1]	50.9	8.2	4.7	3.9	1.1	1.5	3.9	2.6	23.2
U.S.	70.2	8.5	1.7	1.3	0.4	0.4	2.4	1.6	13.5

Note: Figures are percentages and cover workers 16 years of age and older; (1) Figures cover the San Francisco-Oakland-Fremont, CA Metropolitan Statistical Area
Source: U.S. Census Bureau, 2019-2023 American Community Survey 5-Year Estimates

Travel Time to Work

Area	Less Than 10 Minutes	10 to 19 Minutes	20 to 29 Minutes	30 to 44 Minutes	45 to 59 Minutes	60 to 89 Minutes	90 Minutes or More
City	5.3	21.2	22.1	28.8	10.6	8.9	3.1
MSA[1]	7.5	24.2	18.7	23.7	11.0	10.8	4.1
U.S.	12.6	28.6	21.2	20.8	8.1	6.0	2.8

Note: Note: Figures are percentages and include workers 16 years old and over; (1) Figures cover the San Francisco-Oakland-Fremont, CA Metropolitan Statistical Area
Source: U.S. Census Bureau, 2019-2023 American Community Survey 5-Year Estimates

Key Congestion Measures

Measure	2000	2010	2015	2020	2022
Annual Hours of Delay, Total (000)	182,881	208,286	245,689	112,507	248,889
Annual Hours of Delay, Per Auto Commuter	79	90	101	46	109
Annual Congestion Cost, Per Auto Commuter ($)	3,033	2,746	2,991	1,455	3,148

Note: Figures cover the San Francisco-Oakland CA urban area
Source: Texas A&M Transportation Institute, 2023 Urban Mobility Report

Freeway Travel Time Index

Measure	1985	1990	1995	2000	2005	2010	2015	2020	2022
Urban Area Index[1]	1.30	1.32	1.36	1.38	1.40	1.41	1.49	1.16	1.48
Urban Area Rank[1,2]	2	2	2	2	2	2	1	2	2

Note: Freeway Travel Time Index—the ratio of travel time in the peak period to the travel time at free-flow conditions. For example, a value of 1.30 indicates a 20-minute free-flow trip takes 26 minutes in the peak (20 minutes x 1.30 = 26 minutes); (1) Covers the San Francisco-Oakland CA urban area; (2) Rank is based on 101 larger urban areas (#1 = highest travel time index)
Source: Texas A&M Transportation Institute, 2023 Urban Mobility Report

Public Transportation

Agency Name / Mode of Transportation	Vehicles Operated in Maximum Service[1]	Annual Unlinked Passenger Trips[2] (in thous.)	Annual Passenger Miles[3] (in thous.)
San Francisco Municipal Railway (MUNI)			
Bus (directly operated)	354	71,851.9	144,667.6
Cable Car (directly operated)	26	2,926.5	3,879.7
Demand Response (purchased transportation)	111	237.4	1,376.4
Light Rail (directly operated)	115	23,281.3	56,446.7
Streetcar Rail (directly operated)	12	3,136.1	4,445.9
Trolleybus (directly operated)	156	37,694.5	55,160.1
San Francisco Bay Area Rapid Transit District (BART)			
Heavy Rail (directly operated)	566	49,043.3	670,728.3
Hybrid Rail (directly operated)	14	1,263.7	9,189.8
Monorail and Automated Guideway (purchased transportation)	2	457.4	1,397.2

Note: (1) Number of revenue vehicles operated by the given mode and type of service to meet the annual maximum service requirement. This is the revenue vehicle count during the peak season of the year; on the week and day that maximum service is provided. Vehicles operated in maximum service (VOMS) exclude atypical days and one-time special events; (2) Number of passengers who boarded public transportation vehicles. Passengers are counted each time they board a vehicle no matter how many vehicles they use to travel from their origin to their destination. (3) Sum of the distances ridden by all passengers during the entire fiscal year.
Source: Federal Transit Administration, National Transit Database, 2023

Air Transportation

Airport Name and Code / Type of Service	Passenger Airlines[1]	Passenger Enplanements	Freight Carriers[2]	Freight (lbs)
San Francisco International (SFO)				
Domestic service (U.S. carriers only)	19	17,631,272	15	217,963,509
International service (U.S. carriers only)	6	3,090,264	5	88,989,548

Note: (1) Includes all U.S.-based major, minor and commuter airlines that carried at least one passenger during the year; (2) Includes all U.S.-based airlines and freight carriers that transported at least one pound of freight during the year.
Source: Bureau of Transportation Statistics, The Intermodal Transportation Database, Air Carriers: T-100 Domestic Market (U.S. carriers only), 2024; Bureau of Transportation Statistics, The Intermodal Transportation Database, Air Carriers: T-100 International Market (U.S. carriers only), 2024

BUSINESSES

Major Business Headquarters

Company Name	Industry	Rankings Fortune[1]	Rankings Forbes[2]
Airbnb	Internet services and retailing	396	-
DoorDash	Internet services and retailing	443	-
Gap	Specialty retailers: apparel	278	-
Prologis	Real estate	463	-
Salesforce	Computer software	123	-
Stripe	Business services & supplies	-	183
Swinerton	Construction	-	157
Uber Technologies	Internet services and retailing	113	-
Visa	Financial data services	135	-
Wells Fargo	Commercial banks	34	-
Wilbur-Ellis	Chemicals	-	184
Williams-Sonoma	Specialty retailers: other	474	-
X (formerly Twitter)	IT software & services	-	185

Note: (1) Companies that produce a 10-K are ranked 1 to 500 based on 2023 revenue; (2) All private companies with at least $2 billion in annual revenue through the end of their most current fiscal year are ranked 1 to 275; companies listed are headquartered in the city; dashes indicate no ranking
Source: Fortune, "Fortune 500," 2024; Forbes, "America's Largest Private Companies," 2024

Fastest-Growing Businesses

According to *Inc.*, San Francisco is home to 16 of America's 500 fastest-growing private companies: **Bounce** (#8); **Amara** (#44); **Empower Finance** (#65); **SparkPlug Applications** (#137); **Lively** (#148); **Invisible Technologies** (#152); **At-Bay** (#198); **Arine** (#236); **Aura Bora** (#257); **UserGems** (#319); **InnoActive Group** (#350); **Suite Experience Group** (#374); **Raydiant** (#385); **WorkWhile** (#412); **Enable** (#454); **Embarc Advisors** (#477). Criteria: must be an independent, privately-held, for-profit, U.S. corporation, proprietorship or partnership as of December 31, 2023; revenues must be at least $100,000 in 2020 and $2 million in 2023; must have four-year operating/sales history. *Inc., "America's 500 Fastest-Growing Private Companies," 2024*

According to *Initiative for a Competitive Inner City (ICIC)*, San Francisco is home to one of America's 100 fastest-growing "inner city" companies: **Reva Murphy Associates** (#65). To be eligible for the IC100, companies have to be independently operated, privately held, for-profit businesses with revenues of at least $50,000 in 2019 and $500,000 in 2023, and headquartered in an under-resourced community. Recognizing that concentrated poverty exists within metropolitan areas outside of big cities (and that poverty overall is suburbanizing), ICIC defines under-resourced communities as large low-income, high-poverty areas located in the urban and suburban parts of all but the smallest metropolitan areas. Companies were ranked overall by revenue growth over the five-year period between 2019 and 2023. *Initiative for a Competitive Inner City (ICIC), "Inner City 100 Companies," 2024*

According to Deloitte, San Francisco is home to 40 of North America's 500 fastest-growing high-technology companies: **Deel** (#5); **Wisetack** (#15); **Rad AI** (#19); **Cribl** (#27); **TRM Labs** (#39); **MaintainX** (#48); **Miro** (#53); **Invisible** (#61); **At-Bay** (#68); **Retool** (#100); **Laurel** (#122); **Apollo.io** (#125); **Apollo GraphQL** (#148); **Canary Technologies** (#163); **Vontive** (#178); **Lattice** (#184); **Nova Credit** (#199); **Aurora Solar** (#233); **Censia Talent Intelligence** (#240); **6sense** (#246); **Samsara** (#257); **Gitlab** (#272); **Upgrade** (#280); **Sense** (#334); **Ouster** (#341); **Nurix Therapeutics** (#350); **Yodeck** (#354); **Pipefy** (#358); **Discord** (#362); **Nabis** (#376); **Innovaccer** (#381); **Asana** (#384); **Tesorio** (#391); **People.ai** (#398); **Super.com** (#410); **Armis** (#438); **Karbon** (#442); **Okta** (#477); **Eventbrite** (#486); **Cloudflare** (#499). Companies are ranked by percentage growth in revenue over a four-year period. Criteria for inclusion: company must be headquartered within North America; must own proprietary intellectual property or technology that is sold to customers in products that contributes to a significant portion of the company's operating revenue; must have been in business for a minumum of four years with 2020 operating revenues of at least $50,000 USD/CD and 2023 operating revenues of at least $5 million USD/CD. *Deloitte, 2024 Technology Fast 500*[TM]

Living Environment

COST OF LIVING

Cost of Living Index

Composite Index	Groceries	Housing	Utilities	Trans-portation	Health Care	Misc. Goods/ Services
166.8	123.6	263.3	160.1	143.6	127.6	119.3

Note: The Cost of Living Index measures regional differences in the cost of consumer goods and services, excluding taxes and non-consumer expenditures, for professional and managerial households in the top income quintile. It is based on more than 50,000 prices covering almost 60 different items for which prices are collected three times a year by chambers of commerce, economic development organizations or university applied economic centers in each participating urban area. The numbers shown should be read as a percentage above or below the national average of 100. For example, a value of 115.4 in the groceries column indicates that grocery prices are 15.4% higher than the national average. Small differences in the index numbers should not be interpreted as significant; Figures cover the San Francisco CA urban area.
Source: The Council for Community and Economic Research, Cost of Living Index, 2024

Grocery Prices

Area[1]	T-Bone Steak ($/pound)	Frying Chicken ($/pound)	Whole Milk ($/half gal.)	Eggs ($/dozen)	Orange Juice ($/64 oz.)	Coffee ($/11.5 oz.)
City[2]	15.55	2.66	5.03	3.35	4.86	7.53
Avg.	15.42	1.55	4.69	3.25	4.41	5.46
Min.	14.50	1.16	4.43	2.75	4.00	4.85
Max.	17.56	2.89	5.49	4.78	5.54	7.89

*Note: (1) Values for the local area are compared with the average, minimum and maximum values for all 276 areas in the Cost of Living Index; (2) Figures cover the San Francisco CA urban area; **T-Bone Steak** (price per pound); **Frying Chicken** (price per pound, whole fryer); **Whole Milk** (half gallon carton); **Eggs** (price per dozen, Grade A, large); **Orange Juice** (64 oz. Tropicana or Florida Natural); **Coffee** (11.5 oz. can, vacuum-packed, Maxwell House, Hills Bros, or Folgers).*
Source: The Council for Community and Economic Research, Cost of Living Index, 2024

Housing and Utility Costs

Area[1]	New Home Price ($)	Apartment Rent ($/month)	All Electric ($/month)	Part Electric ($/month)	Other Energy ($/month)	Telephone ($/month)
City[2]	1,383,739	3,749	-	264.12	131.73	205.06
Avg.	515,975	1,550	210.99	123.07	82.07	194.99
Min.	265,375	692	104.33	53.68	36.26	179.42
Max.	2,775,821	5,719	529.02	397.28	361.63	223.33

*Note: (1) Values for the local area are compared with the average, minimum and maximum values for all 276 areas in the Cost of Living Index; (2) Figures cover the San Francisco CA urban area; **New Home Price** (2,400 sf living area, 8,000 sf lot, in urban area with full utilities); **Apartment Rent** (950 sf 2 bedroom/1.5 or 2 bath, unfurnished, excluding all utilities except water); **All Electric** (average monthly cost for an all-electric home); **Part Electric** (average monthly cost for a part-electric home); **Other Energy** (average monthly cost for natural gas, fuel oil, coal, wood, and any other forms of energy except electricity); **Telephone** (price includes the base monthly rate plus taxes and fees for three lines of mobile phone service).*
Source: The Council for Community and Economic Research, Cost of Living Index, 2024

Health Care, Transportation, and Other Costs

Area[1]	Doctor ($/visit)	Dentist ($/visit)	Optometrist ($/visit)	Gasoline ($/gallon)	Beauty Salon ($/visit)	Men's Shirt ($)
City[2]	183.65	160.37	168.34	5.07	86.22	48.81
Avg.	143.77	117.51	129.23	3.32	48.57	38.14
Min.	36.74	58.67	67.33	2.80	24.00	13.41
Max.	270.44	216.82	307.33	5.28	94.00	63.89

*Note: (1) Values for the local area are compared with the average, minimum and maximum values for all 276 areas in the Cost of Living Index; (2) Figures cover the San Francisco CA urban area; **Doctor** (general practitioners routine exam of an established patient); **Dentist** (adult teeth cleaning and periodic oral examination); **Optometrist** (full vision eye exam for established adult patient); **Gasoline** (one gallon regular unleaded, national brand, including all taxes, cash price at self-service pump if available); **Beauty Salon** (woman's shampoo, trim, and blow-dry); **Men's Shirt** (cotton/polyester dress shirt, pinpoint weave, long sleeves).*
Source: The Council for Community and Economic Research, Cost of Living Index, 2024

HOUSING

Homeownership Rate

Area	2017 (%)	2018 (%)	2019 (%)	2020 (%)	2021 (%)	2022 (%)	2023 (%)	2024 (%)
MSA[1]	55.7	55.6	52.8	53.0	54.7	56.4	55.0	56.4
U.S.	63.9	64.4	64.6	66.6	65.5	65.8	65.9	65.6

Note: (1) Figures cover the San Francisco-Oakland-Fremont, CA Metropolitan Statistical Area
Source: U.S. Census Bureau, Housing Vacancies and Homeownership Annual Statistics: 2017-2024

House Price Index (HPI)

Area	National Ranking[2]	Quarterly Change (%)	One-Year Change (%)	Five-Year Change (%)	Since 1991Q1 (%)
MD[1]	191	0.32	3.50	15.70	376.10
U.S.[3]	–	1.43	4.51	57.13	327.82

Note: The HPI is a weighted repeat sales index. It measures average price changes in repeat sales or refinancings on the same properties. This information is obtained by reviewing repeat mortgage transactions on single-family properties whose mortgages have been purchased or securitized by Fannie Mae or Freddie Mac since January 1975; (1) Figures cover the San Francisco-Redwood City-South San Francisco, CA Metropolitan Division; (2) Rankings are based on annual percentage change for all metro areas containing at least 15,000 transactions over the last 10 years and ranges from 1 to 241; (3) figures based on a weighted average of Census Division estimates using a seasonally adjusted, purchase-only index; all figures are for the period ending December 31, 2024
Source: Federal Housing Finance Agency, Change in FHFA Metropolitan Area House Price Indexes, All Transactions Index, 2024Q4

Home Value

Area	Under $100,000	$100,000 -$199,999	$200,000 -$299,999	$300,000 -$399,999	$400,000 -$499,999	$500,000 -$999,999	$1,000,000 or more	Median ($)
City	1.5	1.2	0.7	1.3	1.6	16.0	77.8	1,380,500
MSA[1]	2.1	1.4	1.3	1.7	3.4	31.8	58.4	1,113,800
U.S.	12.1	17.8	19.5	14.4	10.5	19.1	6.5	303,400

Note: Figures are percentages except for median and cover owner-occupied housing units; (1) Figures cover the San Francisco-Oakland-Fremont, CA Metropolitan Statistical Area
Source: U.S. Census Bureau, 2019-2023 American Community Survey 5-Year Estimates

Year Housing Structure Built

Area	2020 or Later	2010 -2019	2000 -2009	1990 -1999	1980 -1989	1970 -1979	1960 -1969	1950 -1959	1940 -1949	Before 1940	Median Year
City	0.7	6.4	6.5	4.0	5.3	7.1	8.1	7.9	8.7	45.4	1945
MSA[1]	0.7	5.6	7.7	7.8	10.6	14.2	12.8	13.4	7.7	19.5	1967
U.S.	1.2	8.9	13.6	12.8	13.0	14.4	10.0	9.7	4.5	11.9	1980

Note: Figures are percentages except for Median Year; Note: (1) Figures cover the San Francisco-Oakland-Fremont, CA Metropolitan Statistical Area
Source: U.S. Census Bureau, 2019-2023 American Community Survey 5-Year Estimates

Gross Monthly Rent

Area	Under $500	$500 -$999	$1,000 -$1,499	$1,500 -$1,999	$2,000 -$2,499	$2,500 -$2,999	$3,000 and up	Median ($)
City	7.8	8.1	11.1	11.9	13.2	10.9	36.9	2,419
MSA[1]	5.1	5.6	9.5	14.1	18.4	15.0	32.3	2,426
U.S.	6.5	22.3	29.5	20.2	10.8	4.8	5.9	1,348

Note: Figures are percentages except for median; Gross rent is the contract rent plus the estimated average monthly cost of utilities (electricity, gas, and water and sewer) and fuels (oil, coal, kerosene, wood, etc.) if these are paid by the renter (or paid for the renter by someone else); (1) Figures cover the San Francisco-Oakland-Fremont, CA Metropolitan Statistical Area
Source: U.S. Census Bureau, 2019-2023 American Community Survey 5-Year Estimates

HEALTH

Health Risk Factors

Category	MSA[1] (%)	U.S. (%)
Adults aged 18–64 who have any kind of health care coverage	n/a	90.8
Adults who reported being in good or better health	n/a	81.8
Adults who have been told they have high blood cholesterol	n/a	36.9
Adults who have been told they have high blood pressure	n/a	34.0
Adults who are current smokers	n/a	12.1
Adults who currently use e-cigarettes	n/a	7.7
Adults who currently use chewing tobacco, snuff, or snus	n/a	3.2
Adults who are heavy drinkers[2]	n/a	6.1
Adults who are binge drinkers[3]	n/a	15.2
Adults who are overweight (BMI 25.0 - 29.9)	n/a	34.4
Adults who are obese (BMI 30.0 - 99.8)	n/a	34.3
Adults who participated in any physical activities in the past month	n/a	75.8

Note: All figures are crude prevalence; (1) Figures for the San Francisco-Oakland-Fremont, CA Metropolitan Statistical Area were not available.
(2) Heavy drinkers are classified as adult men having more than 14 drinks per week and adult women having more than 7 drinks per week; (3) Binge drinkers are classified as males having five or more drinks on one occasion or females having four or more drinks on one occasion
Source: Centers for Disease Control and Prevention, Behaviorial Risk Factor Surveillance System, SMART: Selected Metropolitan Area Risk Trends, 2023

Acute and Chronic Health Conditions

Category	MSA[1] (%)	U.S. (%)
Adults who have ever been told they had a heart attack	n/a	4.2
Adults who have ever been told they have angina or coronary heart disease	n/a	4.0
Adults who have ever been told they had a stroke	n/a	3.3
Adults who have ever been told they have asthma	n/a	15.7
Adults who have ever been told they have arthritis	n/a	26.3
Adults who have ever been told they have diabetes[2]	n/a	11.5
Adults who have ever been told they had skin cancer	n/a	5.6
Adults who have ever been told they had any other types of cancer	n/a	8.4
Adults who have ever been told they have COPD	n/a	6.4
Adults who have ever been told they have kidney disease	n/a	3.7
Adults who have ever been told they have a form of depression	n/a	22.0

Note: All figures are crude prevalence; (1) Figures for the San Francisco-Oakland-Fremont, CA Metropolitan Statistical Area were not available.
(2) Figures do not include pregnancy-related, borderline, or pre-diabetes
Source: Centers for Disease Control and Prevention, Behaviorial Risk Factor Surveillance System, SMART: Selected Metropolitan Area Risk Trends, 2023

Health Screening and Vaccination Rates

Category	MSA[1] (%)	U.S. (%)
Adults who have ever been tested for HIV	n/a	37.5
Adults who have had their blood cholesterol checked within the last five years	n/a	87.0
Adults aged 65+ who have had flu shot within the past year	n/a	63.4
Adults aged 65+ who have ever had a pneumonia vaccination	n/a	71.9

Note: All figures are crude prevalence; (1) Figures for the San Francisco-Oakland-Fremont, CA Metropolitan Statistical Area were not available.
Source: Centers for Disease Control and Prevention, Behaviorial Risk Factor Surveillance System, SMART: Selected Metropolitan Area Risk Trends, 2023

Disability Status

Category	MSA[1] (%)	U.S. (%)
Adults who reported being deaf	n/a	7.4
Are you blind or have serious difficulty seeing, even when wearing glasses?	n/a	4.9
Do you have difficulty doing errands alone?	n/a	7.8
Do you have difficulty dressing or bathing?	n/a	3.6
Do you have serious difficulty concentrating/remembering/making decisions?	n/a	13.7
Do you have serious difficulty walking or climbing stairs?	n/a	13.2

Note: All figures are crude prevalence; (1) Figures for the San Francisco-Oakland-Fremont, CA Metropolitan Statistical Area were not available.
Source: Centers for Disease Control and Prevention, Behaviorial Risk Factor Surveillance System, SMART: Selected Metropolitan Area Risk Trends, 2023

Mortality Rates for the Top 10 Causes of Death in the U.S.

ICD-10[a] Sub-Chapter	ICD-10[a] Code	Crude Mortality Rate[2] per 100,000 population	
		County[3]	U.S.
Malignant neoplasms	C00-C97	156.4	182.7
Ischaemic heart diseases	I20-I25	107.3	109.6
Provisional assignment of new diseases of uncertain etiology[1]	U00-U49	28.8	65.3
Other forms of heart disease	I30-I51	46.4	65.1
Other degenerative diseases of the nervous system	G30-G31	41.9	52.4
Other external causes of accidental injury	W00-X59	82.2	52.3
Cerebrovascular diseases	I60-I69	53.4	49.1
Chronic lower respiratory diseases	J40-J47	21.0	43.5
Hypertensive diseases	I10-I15	33.5	38.9
Organic, including symptomatic, mental disorders	F01-F09	21.2	33.9

Note: (a) ICD-10 = International Classification of Diseases 10th Revision; (1) Includes COVID-19, adverse effects to COVID-19 vaccines, SARS, and vaping-related disorders; (2) Crude mortality rates are a three-year average covering 2021-2023; (3) Figures cover San Francisco County.
Source: Centers for Disease Control and Prevention, National Center for Health Statistics. National Vital Statistics System, Mortality 2018-2023 on CDC WONDER Online Database

Mortality Rates for Selected Causes of Death

Cause of Death	ICD-10[a] Code	Crude Mortality Rate[1] per 100,000 population	
		County[2]	U.S.
Accidental poisoning and exposure to noxious substances	X40-X49	66.4	30.5
Alzheimer disease	G30	33.1	35.4
Assault	X85-Y09	5.3	7.3
COVID-19	U07.1	28.8	65.3
Diabetes mellitus	E10-E14	24.9	30.0
Diseases of the liver	K70-K76	12.5	20.8
Human immunodeficiency virus (HIV) disease	B20-B24	4.2	1.5
Influenza and pneumonia	J09-J18	8.8	13.4
Intentional self-harm	X60-X84	9.8	14.7
Malnutrition	E40-E46	3.4	6.0
Obesity and other hyperalimentation	E65-E68	1.2	3.1
Renal failure	N17-N19	11.5	16.4
Transport accidents	V01-V99	6.5	14.4

Note: (a) ICD-10 = International Classification of Diseases 10th Revision; (1) Crude mortality rates are a three-year average covering 2021-2023; (2) Figures cover San Francisco County; Data are suppressed when the data meet the criteria for confidentiality constraints; Crude mortality rates are flagged as unreliable when the rate would be calculated with a numerator of 20 or less.
Source: Centers for Disease Control and Prevention, National Center for Health Statistics. National Vital Statistics System, Mortality 2018-2023 on CDC WONDER Online Database

Health Insurance Coverage

Area	With Health Insurance	With Private Health Insurance	With Public Health Insurance	Without Health Insurance	Population Under Age 19 Without Health Insurance
City	96.5	75.8	30.7	3.5	2.0
MSA[1]	95.9	75.5	31.5	4.1	2.4
U.S.	91.4	67.3	36.3	8.6	5.4

Note: Figures are percentages that cover the civilian noninstitutionalized population; (1) Figures cover the San Francisco-Oakland-Fremont, CA Metropolitan Statistical Area
Source: U.S. Census Bureau, 2019-2023 American Community Survey 5-Year Estimates

Number of Medical Professionals

Area	MDs[3]	DOs[3,4]	Dentists	Podiatrists	Chiropractors	Optometrists
County[1] (number)	7,619	135	1,423	92	356	280
County[1] (rate[2])	942.4	16.7	175.9	11.4	44.0	34.6
U.S. (rate[2])	302.5	29.2	74.6	6.4	29.5	18.0

Note: Data as of 2023 unless noted; (1) Data covers San Francisco County; (2) Number of medical professionals per 100,000 population; (3) Data as of 2022 and includes all active, non-federal physicians; (4) Doctor of Osteopathic Medicine
Source: U.S. Department of Health and Human Services, Health Resources and Services Administration, Bureau of Health Professions, Area Resource File (ARF) 2023-2024

Best Hospitals

According to *U.S. News,* the San Francisco-Oakland-Fremont, CA metro area is home to three of the best hospitals in the U.S.: **California Pacific Medical Center-Van Ness Campus** (1 adult specialty); **John Muir Health-Walnut Creek Medical Center** (1 adult specialty); **UCSF Health-UCSF Medical Center** (Honor Roll/13 adult specialties and 11 pediatric specialties). The hospitals listed were nationally ranked in at least one of 15 adult or 11 pediatric specialties. The number of specialties shown cover the parent hospital. Only 160 U.S. hospitals performed well enough to be nationally ranked in one or more specialties. Twenty hospitals in the U.S. made the Honor Roll. The Best Hospitals Honor Roll takes both the national rankings and the procedure and condition ratings into account. Hospitals received points if they were nationally ranked in one of the 15 adult specialties—the higher they ranked, the more points they got—and how many ratings of "high performing" they earned in the 20 procedures and conditions. *U.S. News Online, "America's Best Hospitals 2024-25"*

According to *U.S. News,* the San Francisco-Oakland-Fremont, CA metro area is home to one of the best children's hospitals in the U.S.: **UCSF Benioff Children's Hospitals, San Francisco and Oakland** (11 pediatric specialties). The hospital listed was highly ranked in at least one of 11 pediatric specialties. One hundred five children's hospitals in the U.S. were nationally ranked in at least one specialty. Hospitals received points for being ranked in a specialty, and the 10 hospitals with the most points across the 11 specialties make up the Honor Roll. *U.S. News Online, "America's Best Children's Hospitals 2024-25"*

EDUCATION

Public School District Statistics

District Name	Schls	Pupils	Pupil/ Teacher Ratio	Minority Pupils[1] (%)	Total Rev. per Pupil ($)	Total Exp. per Pupil ($)
Five Keys Independence HSD	1	3,172	34.3	92.6	16,261	14,421
San Francisco Unified	113	48,736	20.6	86.5	31,147	27,074

Note: Table includes school districts with 2,000 or more students; (1) Percentage of students that are not non-Hispanic white.
Source: U.S. Department of Education, National Center for Education Statistics, Common Core of Data, Local Education Agency (School District) Universe Survey: School Year 2023-2024; U.S. Department of Education, National Center for Education Statistics, Common Core of Data, School District Finance Survey (F-33): School Year 2021–22

Best High Schools

According to *U.S. News,* San Francisco is home to two of the top 500 high schools in the U.S.: **Lowell High School** (#74); **Ruth Asawa San Francisco School of the Arts** (#448). Nearly 25,000 public, magnet and charter schools were ranked based on their performance on state assessments and how well they prepare students for college. *U.S. News & World Report, "Best High Schools 2024"*

Highest Level of Education

Area	Less than H.S.	H.S. Diploma	Some College, No Deg.	Associate Degree	Bachelor's Degree	Master's Degree	Prof. School Degree	Doctorate Degree
City	11.2	11.3	12.0	5.3	35.1	16.7	4.9	3.4
MSA[1]	10.5	15.0	15.5	6.6	30.0	15.1	3.9	3.4
U.S.	10.6	26.2	19.4	8.8	21.3	9.8	2.3	1.6

Note: Figures cover persons age 25 and over; (1) Figures cover the San Francisco-Oakland-Fremont, CA Metropolitan Statistical Area
Source: U.S. Census Bureau, 2019-2023 American Community Survey 5-Year Estimates

Educational Attainment by Race

Area	High School Graduate or Higher (%)					Bachelor's Degree or Higher (%)				
	Total	White	Black	Asian	Hisp.[2]	Total	White	Black	Asian	Hisp.[2]
City	88.8	97.5	88.8	80.8	80.1	60.1	76.3	30.9	51.0	40.1
MSA[1]	89.5	96.2	91.4	88.4	73.3	52.4	61.6	32.3	59.9	25.1
U.S.	89.4	92.9	88.1	88.0	72.5	35.0	37.7	24.7	57.0	19.9

Note: Figures shown cover persons 25 years old and over; (1) Figures cover the San Francisco-Oakland-Fremont, CA Metropolitan Statistical Area; (2) People of Hispanic origin can be of any race
Source: U.S. Census Bureau, 2019-2023 American Community Survey 5-Year Estimates

School Enrollment by Grade and Control

Area	Preschool (%)		Kindergarten (%)		Grades 1 - 4 (%)		Grades 5 - 8 (%)		Grades 9 - 12 (%)	
	Public	Private	Public	Private	Public	Private	Public	Private	Public	Private
City	25.0	75.0	67.5	32.5	69.1	30.9	68.5	31.5	72.8	27.2
MSA[1]	38.9	61.1	81.4	18.6	84.7	15.3	83.8	16.2	85.8	14.2
U.S.	58.7	41.3	85.2	14.8	87.2	12.8	87.9	12.1	89.0	11.0

Note: Figures shown cover persons 3 years old and over; (1) Figures cover the San Francisco-Oakland-Fremont, CA Metropolitan Statistical Area
Source: U.S. Census Bureau, 2019-2023 American Community Survey 5-Year Estimates

Higher Education

Four-Year Colleges			Two-Year Colleges			Medical Schools[1]	Law Schools[2]	Voc/ Tech[3]
Public	Private Non-profit	Private For-profit	Public	Private Non-profit	Private For-profit			
6	29	2	14	0	6	1	7	14

Note: Figures cover institutions located within the San Francisco-Oakland-Fremont, CA Metropolitan Statistical Area and include main campuses only; (1) includes schools accredited by the Liaison Committee on Medical Education and the American Osteopathic Association's Commission on Osteopathic College Accreditation; (2) includes ABA-accredited schools, schools with provisional ABA accreditation, and state accredited schools; (3) includes all schools with programs that are less than 2 years.
Source: National Center for Education Statistics, Integrated Postsecondary Education System (IPEDS), 2023-24; Wikipedia, List of Medical Schools in the United States, accessed May 2, 2025; Wikipedia, List of Law Schools in the United States, accessed May 2, 2025

According to *U.S. News & World Report,* the San Francisco-Oakland-Fremont, CA metro area is home to two of the top 200 national universities in the U.S.: **University of California, Berkeley** (#17); **University of San Francisco** (#109 tie). The indicators used to capture academic quality fall into a number of categories: assessment by administrators at peer institutions; retention of students; faculty resources; student selectivity; financial resources; alumni giving; high school counselor ratings of colleges; and graduation rate. *U.S. News & World Report, "America's Best Colleges 2025"*

According to *U.S. News & World Report,* the San Francisco-Oakland-Fremont, CA metro area is home to two of the top 100 law schools in the U.S.: **University of California, Berkeley 1** (#13); **University of California—San Francisco 1** (#88 tie). The rankings are based on a weighted average of 12 measures of quality: peer assessment score; assessment score by lawyers/judges; median LSAT scores; median undergrad GPA; acceptance rate; employment rates for graduates; placement success; bar passage rate; faculty resources; expenditures per student; student/faculty ratio; and library resources. *U.S. News & World Report, "America's Best Graduate Schools, Law, 2025"*

According to *U.S. News & World Report,* the San Francisco-Oakland-Fremont, CA metro area is home to one of the top medical schools for research in the U.S.: **University of California—San Francisco** (Tier 1). *U.S. News* placed medical and osteopathic schools into tiers based on their research productivity, faculty and admissions data. Each school's tier was derived from its overall score, calculated by summing the weighted normalized values generated across several factors of academic quality, outlined below. There are four tiers, with tier 1 medical schools as the highest-performing and tier 4 as the lowest-performing. Only tier 1 and 2 schools are shown. Because of the tier presentation, *U.S. News* calculated overall scores based on their percentile performance among all rated schools instead of dividing against the rescaled score of the No. 1-performing schools. Tier 1 included schools with overall scores of 85 to 99. The cutoffs for tiers 2 through 4 were schools scoring 50 to 84, 15 to 49 and 1 to 14, respectively. The rankings are based on a weighted average of the following measures of quality: total research activity; average research activity per faculty member; total NIH research grants at the medical school and its affiliated hospitals; average NIH research grants per faculty; median MCAT total score; median undergraduate GPA; acceptance rate; and faculty resources. *U.S. News & World Report, "America's Best Graduate Schools, Medical, 2025"*

According to *U.S. News & World Report,* the San Francisco-Oakland-Fremont, CA metro area is home to one of the top medical schools for primary care in the U.S.: **University of California—San Francisco** (Tier 1). *U.S. News* placed medical and osteopathic schools into tiers based on their research productivity, faculty and admissions data. Each school's tier was derived from its overall score, calculated by summing the weighted normalized values generated across several factors of academic quality, outlined below. There are four tiers, with tier 1 medical schools as the highest-performing and tier 4 as the lowest-performing. Only tier 1 and 2 schools are shown. Because of the tier presentation, *U.S. News* calculated overall scores based on their percentile performance among all rated schools instead of dividing against the rescaled score of the No. 1-performing schools. Tier 1 included schools with overall scores of 85 to 99. The cutoffs for tiers 2 through 4 were schools scoring 50 to 84, 15 to 49 and 1 to 14, respectively. The rankings are based on a weighted average of the following measures of quality: graduates practicing in primary care specialties; graduates entering primary care residencies; median MCAT total score; median undergraduate GPA; acceptance rate; and faculty resources. *U.S. News & World Report, "America's Best Graduate Schools, Medical, 2025"*

According to *U.S. News & World Report,* the San Francisco-Oakland-Fremont, CA metro area is home to one of the top 75 business schools in the U.S.: **University of California, Berkeley (Haas)** (#11 tie). The rankings are based on a weighted average of the following nine measures: quality assessment; peer assessment; recruiter assessment; placement success; mean starting salary and bonus; student selectivity; mean GMAT and GRE scores; mean undergraduate GPA; and acceptance rate. *U.S. News & World Report, "America's Best Graduate Schools, Business, 2025"*

EMPLOYERS

Major Employers

Company Name	Industry
California Pacific Medical Center	General medical & surgical hospitals
City & County of San Francisco	Public welfare administration: nonoperating, govt.
Github	Software/application developers
Kaiser Permanente Medical Center	Healthcare
Laguna Honda Hosp & Rehab Ctr	Healthcare
Levi Strauss & Co	Clothing, retail
Oracle America	Minicomputers
Oracle Park	Stadiums, arenas & athletic fields
Oracle Systems Corporation	Prepackaged software
Pacific Gas and Electric Company	Electric & other services combined
Salesforce Inc.	Software
San Francisco Municipal Transportation Sys	Transportation
San Francisco Unified School District	Education
St. Francis Memorial Hospital	Healthcare
UCSF Health	Healthcare
United Airlines	Aerospace
University of California, Berkeley	University
Veterans Health Administration	Administration of veterans' affairs
Wells Fargo	National commercial banks
Williams-Sonoma	Home goods, retail

Note: Companies shown are located within the San Francisco-Oakland-Fremont, CA Metropolitan Statistical Area.
Source: Chambers of Commerce; State Departments of Labor; Wikipedia

Best Companies to Work For

Atlassian; Salesforce; Visa, headquartered in San Francisco, are among "The 100 Best Companies to Work For." To pick the best companies, *Fortune* partnered with the Great Place to Work Institute. Using their proprietary Trust Index™ survey, the core of what creates great a workplace is measured—key behaviors that drive trust in management, connection with colleagues, and loyalty to the company. To be eligible for the *Fortune* 100 Best Companies to Work For list, employers must have 1,000 or more employees in the U.S. and cannot be a government agency. *Fortune, "The 100 Best Companies to Work For," 2025*

Demandbase; Mercury; NerdWallet; PagerDuty; Ripple Labs; Samsara; Visa, headquartered in San Francisco, are among "Fortune's Best Workplaces for Parents." To pick the best companies, *Fortune* partnered with the Great Place to Work Institute. To be considered for the list, companies must be Great Place To Work-Certified and have at least 50 responses from parents in the US. The survey enables employees to share confidential quantitative and qualitative feedback about their organization's culture by responding to 60 statements on a 5-point scale and answering two open-ended questions. Collectively, these statements describe a great employee experience, defined by high levels of trust, respect, credibility, fairness, pride, and camaraderie. In addition, companies provide organizational data like size, location, industry, demographics, roles, and levels; and provide information about parental leave, adoption, flexible schedule, childcare and dependent health care benefits. *Fortune, "Best Workplaces for Parents," 2024*

Mercury; PagerDuty, headquartered in San Francisco, are among "Fortune's Best Workplaces for Women." To pick the best companies, *Fortune* partnered with the Great Place to Work Institute. To be considered for the list, companies must be Great Place To Work-Certified. Companies must also employ at least 50 women, at least 20% of their non-executive managers must be female, and at least one executive must be female. To determine the Best Workplaces for Women, Great Place To Work measured the differences in women's survey responses to those of their peers and assesses the impact of demographics and roles on the quality and consistency of women's experiences. Great Place To Work also analyzed the gender balance of each workplace, how it compared to each company's industry, and patterns in representation as women rise from front-line positions to the board of directors. *Fortune, "Best Workplaces for Women," 2024*

Homeward; Omada Health; Two Chairs, headquartered in San Francisco, are among "Best Workplaces in Health Care." To determine the Best Workplaces in Health Care list, Great Place To Work analyzed the survey responses of over 185,000 employees from Great Place To Work-Certified companies in the health care industry. Survey data analysis and company-provided datapoints are then factored into a combined score to compare and rank the companies that create the most consistently positive experience for all employees in this industry. *Fortune, "Best Workplaces in Health Care," 2024*

Divvy Homes; Opendoor Technologies; Pacaso, headquartered in San Francisco, are among "Best Workplaces in Real Estate." To determine the Best Workplaces in Real Estate list, Great Place To Work analyzed the survey responses of over 29,000 employees from Great Place To Work-Certified companies in the real estate industry. Survey data analysis and company-provided datapoints are then factored into a combined score to compare and rank the companies that create the most consistently positive experience for all employees in this industry. *Fortune, "Best Workplaces in Real Estate," 2024*

PUBLIC SAFETY

Crime Rate

Area	Total Crime Rate	Violent Crime Rate				Property Crime Rate		
		Murder	Rape	Robbery	Aggrav. Assault	Burglary	Larceny -Theft	Motor Vehicle Theft
City	6,422.7	6.6	37.3	349.7	316.5	720.8	4,135.3	856.4
U.S.	2,290.9	5.7	38.0	66.5	264.1	250.7	1,347.2	318.7

Note: Figures are crimes per 100,000 population.
Source: FBI, Table 8, Offenses Known to Law Enforcement, by State by City, 2023

Hate Crimes

Area	Number of Quarters Reported	Number of Incidents per Bias Motivation					
		Race/Ethnicity/ Ancestry	Religion	Sexual Orientation	Disability	Gender	Gender Identity
City[1]	4	23	25	8	0	0	6
U.S.	4	5,900	2,699	2,077	187	92	492

Note: (1) Figures include at least one incident reported with more than one bias motivation.
Source: Federal Bureau of Investigation, Hate Crime Statistics 2023

Identity Theft Consumer Reports

Area	Reports	Reports per 100,000 Population	Rank[2]
MSA[1]	11,641	250	100
U.S.	1,135,291	339	-

Note: (1) Figures cover the San Francisco-Oakland-Fremont, CA Metropolitan Statistical Area; (2) Rank ranges from 1 to 401 where 1 indicates greatest number of identity theft reports per 100,000 population
Source: Federal Trade Commission, Consumer Sentinel Network Data Book 2024

Fraud and Other Consumer Reports

Area	Reports	Reports per 100,000 Population	Rank[2]
MSA[1]	60,059	1,291	99
U.S.	5,360,641	1,601	-

Note: (1) Figures cover the San Francisco-Oakland-Fremont, CA Metropolitan Statistical Area; (2) Rank ranges from 1 to 401 where 1 indicates greatest number of fraud and other consumer reports per 100,000 population
Source: Federal Trade Commission, Consumer Sentinel Network Data Book 2024

POLITICS

2024 Presidential Election Results

Area	Trump (Rep.)	Harris (Dem.)	Stein (Green)	Kennedy (Ind.)	Oliver (Lib.)	Other
San Francisco County	15.5	80.3	1.7	1.1	0.5	0.9
U.S.	49.7	48.2	0.6	0.5	0.4	0.6

Note: Results are percentages and may not add to 100% due to rounding
Source: Dave Leip's Atlas of U.S. Presidential Elections

SPORTS

Professional Sports Teams

Team Name	League	Year Established
Golden State Warriors	National Basketball Association (NBA)	1962
Oakland Athletics	Major League Baseball (MLB)	1968
San Francisco 49ers	National Football League (NFL)	1946
San Francisco Giants	Major League Baseball (MLB)	1958

Note: Includes teams located in the San Francisco-Oakland-Fremont, CA Metropolitan Statistical Area.
Source: Wikipedia, Major Professional Sports Teams of the United States and Canada, May 1, 2025

CLIMATE

Average and Extreme Temperatures

Temperature	Jan	Feb	Mar	Apr	May	Jun	Jul	Aug	Sep	Oct	Nov	Dec	Yr.
Extreme High (°F)	72	77	85	92	97	106	105	98	103	99	85	75	106
Average High (°F)	56	59	61	64	66	70	71	72	73	70	63	56	65
Average Temp. (°F)	49	52	53	56	58	61	63	63	64	61	55	50	57
Average Low (°F)	42	44	45	47	49	52	53	54	54	51	47	42	49
Extreme Low (°F)	26	30	31	36	39	43	44	45	41	37	31	24	24

Note: Figures cover the years 1948-1990
Source: National Climatic Data Center, International Station Meteorological Climate Summary, 9/96

Average Precipitation/Snowfall/Humidity

Precip./Humidity	Jan	Feb	Mar	Apr	May	Jun	Jul	Aug	Sep	Oct	Nov	Dec	Yr.
Avg. Precip. (in.)	4.3	3.1	2.9	1.4	0.3	0.1	Tr	Tr	0.2	1.0	2.5	3.4	19.3
Avg. Snowfall (in.)	Tr	Tr	Tr	0	0	0	0	0	0	0	0	Tr	Tr
Avg. Rel. Hum. 7am (%)	86	85	82	79	78	77	81	83	83	83	85	86	82
Avg. Rel. Hum. 4pm (%)	67	65	63	61	61	60	60	62	60	60	64	68	63

Note: Figures cover the years 1948-1990; Tr = Trace amounts (<0.05 in. of rain; <0.5 in. of snow)
Source: National Climatic Data Center, International Station Meteorological Climate Summary, 9/96

Weather Conditions

Temperature			Daytime Sky			Precipitation		
10°F & below	32°F & below	90°F & above	Clear	Partly cloudy	Cloudy	0.01 inch or more precip.	0.1 inch or more snow/ice	Thunder-storms
0	6	4	136	130	99	63	< 1	5

Note: Figures are average number of days per year and cover the years 1948-1990
Source: National Climatic Data Center, International Station Meteorological Climate Summary, 9/96

HAZARDOUS WASTE   ### Superfund Sites

The San Francisco-San Mateo-Redwood City, CA metro division is home to one site on the EPA's Superfund National Priorities List (NPL) or Superfund Alternative Approach (SAA) list: **Treasure**

Island Naval Station-Hunters Point Annex (Final NPL). The Superfund alternative approach uses the same investigation and cleanup process and standards that are used for sites listed on the National Priorities List. The SAA is an alternative to listing a site on the NPL; it is not an alternative to Superfund or the Superfund process. There are a total of 1,445 Superfund sites with a status of proposed or final on both lists in the United States. *U.S. Environmental Protection Agency, National Priorities List, May 1, 2025; U.S. Environmental Protection Agency, Superfund Alternative Approach Sites, May 1, 2025*

AIR QUALITY

Air Quality Trends: Ozone

	1990	1995	2000	2005	2010	2015	2020	2021	2022	2023
MSA[1]	0.062	0.077	0.060	0.060	0.063	0.064	0.062	0.064	0.057	0.053
U.S.	0.087	0.089	0.081	0.080	0.072	0.068	0.066	0.067	0.067	0.070

Note: (1) Data covers the San Francisco-Oakland-Fremont, CA Metropolitan Statistical Area. The values shown are the composite ozone concentration averages among trend sites based on the highest fourth daily maximum 8-hour concentration in parts per million. These trends are based on sites having an adequate record of monitoring data during the trend period. Data from exceptional events are included.
Source: U.S. Environmental Protection Agency, Air Quality Monitoring Information, "Air Quality Trends by City, 1990-2023"

Air Quality Index

Area	Percent of Days when Air Quality was...[2]					AQI Statistics[2]	
	Good	Moderate	Unhealthy for Sensitive Groups	Unhealthy	Very Unhealthy	Maximum	Median
MSA[1]	34.0	62.5	3.6	0.0	0.0	130	54

Note: (1) Data covers the San Francisco-Oakland-Fremont, CA Metropolitan Statistical Area; (2) Based on 365 days with AQI data in 2023. Air Quality Index (AQI) is an index for reporting daily air quality. EPA calculates the AQI for five major air pollutants regulated by the Clean Air Act: ground-level ozone, particle pollution (aka particulate matter), carbon monoxide, sulfur dioxide, and nitrogen dioxide. The AQI runs from 0 to 500. The higher the AQI value, the greater the level of air pollution and the greater the health concern. There are six AQI categories: "Good" AQI is between 0 and 50. Air quality is considered satisfactory; "Moderate" AQI is between 51 and 100. Air quality is acceptable; "Unhealthy for Sensitive Groups" When AQI values are between 101 and 150, members of sensitive groups may experience health effects; "Unhealthy" When AQI values are between 151 and 200 everyone may begin to experience health effects; "Very Unhealthy" AQI values between 201 and 300 trigger a health alert; "Hazardous" AQI values over 300 trigger warnings of emergency conditions (not shown).
Source: U.S. Environmental Protection Agency, Air Quality Index Report, 2023

Air Quality Index Pollutants

Area	Percent of Days when AQI Pollutant was...[2]					
	Carbon Monoxide	Nitrogen Dioxide	Ozone	Sulfur Dioxide	Particulate Matter 2.5	Particulate Matter 10
MSA[1]	0.3	4.4	17.8	(3)	77.5	0.0

Note: (1) Data covers the San Francisco-Oakland-Fremont, CA Metropolitan Statistical Area; (2) Based on 365 days with AQI data in 2023. The Air Quality Index (AQI) is an index for reporting daily air quality. EPA calculates the AQI for five major air pollutants regulated by the Clean Air Act: ground-level ozone, particle pollution (also known as particulate matter), carbon monoxide, sulfur dioxide, and nitrogen dioxide. The AQI runs from 0 to 500. The higher the AQI value, the greater the level of air pollution and the greater the health concern; (3) Sulfur dioxide is no longer included in this table because SO_2 concentrations tend to be very localized and not necessarily representative of broad geographical areas like counties and CBSAs.
Source: U.S. Environmental Protection Agency, Air Quality Index Report, 2023

Maximum Air Pollutant Concentrations: Particulate Matter, Ozone, CO and Lead

	Particulate Matter 10 (ug/m³)	Particulate Matter 2.5 Wtd AM (ug/m³)	Particulate Matter 2.5 24-Hr (ug/m³)	Ozone (ppm)	Carbon Monoxide (ppm)	Lead (ug/m³)
MSA[1] Level	48	9.9	23	0.069	4	n/a
NAAQS[2]	150	15	35	0.075	9	0.15
Met NAAQS[2]	Yes	Yes	Yes	Yes	Yes	n/a

Note: (1) Data covers the San Francisco-Oakland-Fremont, CA Metropolitan Statistical Area; Data from exceptional events are included; (2) National Ambient Air Quality Standards; ppm = parts per million; ug/m³ = micrograms per cubic meter; n/a not available.
Concentrations: Particulate Matter 10 (coarse particulate)—highest second maximum 24-hour concentration; Particulate Matter 2.5 Wtd AM (fine particulate)—highest weighted annual mean concentration; Particulate Matter 2.5 24-Hour (fine particulate)—highest 98th percentile 24-hour concentration; Ozone—highest fourth daily maximum 8-hour concentration; Carbon Monoxide—highest second maximum non-overlapping 8-hour concentration; Lead—maximum running 3-month average
Source: U.S. Environmental Protection Agency, Air Quality Monitoring Information, "Air Quality Statistics by City, 2023"

Maximum Air Pollutant Concentrations: Nitrogen Dioxide and Sulfur Dioxide

	Nitrogen Dioxide AM (ppb)	Nitrogen Dioxide 1-Hr (ppb)	Sulfur Dioxide AM (ppb)	Sulfur Dioxide 1-Hr (ppb)	Sulfur Dioxide 24-Hr (ppb)
MSA[1] Level	11	102	n/a	18	n/a
NAAQS[2]	53	100	30	75	140
Met NAAQS[2]	Yes	No	n/a	Yes	n/a

Note: (1) Data covers the San Francisco-Oakland-Fremont, CA Metropolitan Statistical Area; Data from exceptional events are included; (2) National Ambient Air Quality Standards; ppm = parts per million; ug/m³ = micrograms per cubic meter; n/a not available.

Concentrations: Nitrogen Dioxide AM—highest arithmetic mean concentration; Nitrogen Dioxide 1-Hr—highest 98th percentile 1-hour daily maximum concentration; Sulfur Dioxide AM—highest annual mean concentration; Sulfur Dioxide 1-Hr—highest 99th percentile 1-hour daily maximum concentration; Sulfur Dioxide 24-Hr—highest second maximum 24-hour concentration

Source: U.S. Environmental Protection Agency, Air Quality Monitoring Information, "Air Quality Statistics by City, 2023"

San Jose, California

Background

Like many cities in the valleys of northern California, San Jose is an abundant cornucopia of wine grapes and produce. It is part of the high-tech Silicon Valley, situated only seven miles from the southernmost tip of San Francisco Bay, flanked by the Santa Cruz Mountains to the west, and the Mount Hamilton arm of the Diablo Range to the east. The Coyote and Guadalupe rivers gently cut through this landscape, carrying water only in the spring.

The oldest civic settlement in California, San Jose was founded on November 29, 1777 by Spanish colonizers to be a produce and cattle supplier to the nearby communities and presidios of San Francisco and Monterey, a role that it still enjoys today. After U.S. troops wrested the territory of California from Mexican rule, San Jose became its state capital, also serving as a supply base to gold prospectors.

Today, San Jose retains much of its history, still a major shipping and processing center for agricultural produce, and producing some of the best table wines in the country. A replica of the Mission of Santa Clara stands on the grounds of the University of Santa Clara—a reminder of its Spanish heritage.

Due to annexation of surrounding communities after World War II, the population of San Jose increased more than tenfold, attracting residents with industries that included NASA research, electronic components, and motors production. San Jose rapidly became a family-oriented community of housing developments and shopping malls.

During the 1990s, San Jose was home to more than half of Silicon Valley's leading semiconductor, networking, and telecommunications companies, earning the nickname "Capital of Silicon Valley." At the turn of the 21st century, San Jose suffered from a downturn in electronics and computer industries, but the city has since rebounded, and today is home to 6,600 technology companies including Adobe, Cisco, Brocade, Netflix, eBay, PayPal and Tivo. The region has been cited as the happiest place to work in the United States, noting that technology jobs typically offer a high salary and opportunity for growth, and that tech companies usually provide a fun and innovative work environment.

The HP Pavilion, home of the San Jose Sharks hockey team, is one of the most active venues for non-sporting events in the world. The city is partnering in 2025 with the San Jose Earthquakes soccer team to sponsor Saturday Night Lights, a program designed to offer middle and high schools students more opportunities to play sports.

Public art is an evolving attraction in the city, one of the first to adopt a public art ordinance at 2 percent of capital improvement building project budgets. This commitment has affected the visual landscape of the city with a considerable number of public art projects throughout the downtown area, and a growing collection in civic locations in neighborhoods including libraries, parks, and fire stations. Of note, San Jose's Mineta Airport has incorporated a program of Art & Technology that includes a series of platforms for projection-based, digital and data-driven artwork throughout the airport, designed to be changed over time in keeping up with technological advances.

San Jose, like most of the Bay Area, has a Mediterranean climate with warm to hot, dry summers and cool, wet winters. San Jose has an average of 298 days of sunshine and an annual mean temperature of about 61 degrees F. It lies inland, surrounded on three sides by mountains, and does not front the Pacific Ocean like San Francisco. As a result, the city is somewhat more sheltered from rain, barely avoiding a cold semi-arid climate. Like most of the Bay Area, San Jose is made up of dozens of microclimates. Because of a more prominent rain shadow from the Santa Cruz Mountains, downtown San Jose experiences the lightest rainfall in the city, while South San Jose, only 10 miles distant, experiences more rainfall, and somewhat more extreme temperatures.

Rankings

General Rankings

- To help military veterans find the best places in which to settle down, *WalletHub* compared the 100 largest U.S. cities across 19 key indicators of livability, affordability and veteran-friendliness. They range from the share of military skill-related jobs to veteran income growth to the availability of VA health facilities. San Jose ranked #40. *Wallethub.com, "Best & Worst Places for Veterans to Live (2025)," November 7, 2024*

Business/Finance Rankings

- According to *Business Insider*, the San Jose metro area is a prime place to run a startup or move an existing business to. The area ranked #1. More than 300 metro areas were analyzed for factors that were of top concern to new business owners. Data was based on the 2019 U.S. Census Bureau American Community Survey, statistics from the CDC, and University of Chicago analysis. Criteria: business formations; percentage of vaccinated population; percentage of households with internet subscriptions; median household income; and share of work that can be done from home. *BusinessInsider.com, "The 20 Best Cities for Starting a Business in 2022 Include Denver, Raleigh, and Olympia," June 7, 2022*

- Payscale.com ranked the 32 largest metro areas in terms of wage growth. The San Jose metro area ranked #24. Criteria: quarterly changes in private industry employee and education professional wage growth from the previous year. *PayScale, "Wage Trends by Metro Area-4th Quarter," February 4, 2025*

- For its annual survey of the "Most Expensive U.S. Cities to Live In," Kiplinger applied Cost of Living Index statistics developed by the Council for Community and Economic Research to U.S. Census Bureau population and median household income data for 265 urban areas. San Jose ranked #3 among the most expensive in the country. *Kiplinger.com, "The 10 Most Expensive Cities to Live in the U.S.," February 3, 2025*

- The San Jose metro area appeared on the Milken Institute "2025 Best Performing Cities" list. Rank: #108 out of 200 large metro areas (based on performance category). Criteria: job growth; wage growth; high-tech growth and impact; community resilience; housing affordability; household broadband access. *Milken Institute, "Best-Performing Cities 2025," January 14, 2025*

Education Rankings

- Personal finance website *WalletHub* analyzed the 150 largest U.S. metropolitan statistical areas to determine where the most educated Americans are putting their degrees to work. Criteria: education levels; percentage of workers with degrees; education quality and attainment gap; public school quality rankings; quality and enrollment of each metro area's universities. San Jose was ranked #2 (#1 = most educated city). *WalletHub.com, "Most & Least Educated Cities in America, 2025" July 2, 2024*

Environmental Rankings

- Sperling's *BestPlaces* assessed the 50 largest metropolitan areas of the United States for the likelihood of dangerously extreme weather events or earthquakes. In general the Southeast and South-Central regions have the highest risk of weather extremes and earthquakes, while the Pacific Northwest enjoys the lowest risk. Of the least risky metropolitan areas, the San Jose metro area was ranked #6. *Bestplaces.net, "Avoid Natural Disasters: BestPlaces Reveals The Top 10 Safest Places to Live," October 25, 2017*

- The U.S. Environmental Protection Agency (EPA) released its list of U.S. metropolitan areas with the most ENERGY STAR certified buildings in 2023. The San Jose metro area was ranked #18 out of 25. *U.S. Environmental Protection Agency, "2024 Energy Star Top Cities," May 22, 2024*

- San Jose was highlighted as one of the 25 most ozone-polluted metro areas in the U.S. during 2021 through 2023. The area ranked #14. *American Lung Association, "State of the Air 2025," April 23, 2025*

- San Jose was highlighted as one of the 25 metro areas most polluted by year-round particle pollution (Annual PM 2.5) in the U.S. during 2021 through 2023. The area ranked #6. *American Lung Association, "State of the Air 2025," April 23, 2025*

- San Jose was highlighted as one of the 25 metro areas most polluted by short-term particle pollution (24-hour PM 2.5) in the U.S. during 2021 through 2023. The area ranked #11. *American Lung Association, "State of the Air 2025," April 23, 2025*

Health/Fitness Rankings

- For each of the 100 largest cities in the United States, the American Fitness Index®, compiled in partnership between the American College of Sports Medicine and the Elevance Health Foundation, evaluated community infrastructure and more than 30 health behaviors including preventive health, levels of chronic disease conditions, food insecurity, pedestrian safety, air quality, and community/environment resources that support physical activity. San Jose ranked #21 for "community fitness." *americanfitnessindex.org, "2024 ACSM American Fitness Index Summary Report," July 23, 2024*

- San Jose was identified as a "2025 Allergy Capital." The area ranked #41 out of the nation's 100 largest metropolitan areas. Three groups of factors were used to identify the most challenging cities for people with allergies: annual tree, grass, and weed pollen scores; over the counter allergy medicine use; number of board-certified allergy specialists. *Asthma and Allergy Foundation of America, "2025 Allergy Capitals: The Most Challenging Places to Live with Allergies," March 18, 2025*

- San Jose was identified as a "2024 Asthma Capital." The area ranked #77 out of the nation's 100 largest metropolitan areas. Criteria: estimated asthma prevalence; asthma-related mortality; and ER visits due to asthma. Risk factors analyzed but not factored in the rankings: annual air quality including pollution and ozone levels; public smoking laws; indoor air quality; access to asthma specialists; rescue and controller medication use; uninsured rate; pollen allergy; poverty rate. *Asthma and Allergy Foundation of America, "Asthma Capitals 2024: The Most Challenging Places to Live With Asthma," September 10, 2024*

- The Sharecare Community Well-Being Index evaluates 10 individual and social health factors in order to measure what matters to Americans in the communities in which they live. The San Jose metro area ranked #2 in the top 10 across all 10 domains. Criteria: access to healthcare, food, and community resources; housing and transportation; economic security; feeling of purpose; and physical, financial, social, and community well-being. *Sharecare.com, "Community Well-Being Index: 2020 Metro Area & County Rankings Report," August 30, 2021*

Real Estate Rankings

- *WalletHub* compared the most populated U.S. cities to determine which had the best markets for real estate agents. San Jose ranked #10 where demand was high and pay was the best. Criteria: sales per agent; annual median wage for real-estate agents; monthly average starting salary for real estate agents; real estate job density and competition; unemployment rate; home turnover rate; housing-market health index; and other relevant metrics. *WalletHub.com, "2021 Best Places to Be a Real Estate Agent," May 12, 2021*

- The San Jose metro area was identified as one of the 20 least affordable housing markets in the U.S. in 2024. The area ranked #226 out of 226 markets. Criteria: qualification for a mortgage loan with a 10 percent down payment on a typical home. *National Association of Realtors®, Qualifying Income Based on Sales Price of Existing Single-Family Homes for Metropolitan Areas, February 6, 2025*

- San Jose was ranked #176 out of 176 metro areas in terms of cost of housing in 2024 by the National Association of Home Builders (#1 = most affordable). Criteria: the portion of an average family's income necessary to pay the mortgage on a median-priced home. *National Association of Home Builders®, NAHB-Wells Fargo Cost of Housing Index, 4th Quarter 2024*

Safety Rankings

- Allstate ranked the 100 most populous cities in America in terms of driver safety. San Jose ranked #51. Criteria based on anonymized driving behavior data from Allstate's mobile app powered by Arity: high speed driving (over 80 mph), phone handling, and hard braking. The report helps increase the importance of safety and awareness behind the wheel. *Allstate, "16th Allstate America's Best Drivers Report®" July 11, 2024*

Transportation Rankings

- San Jose was identified as one of the most congested metro areas in the U.S. The area ranked #8 out of 10. Criteria: yearly delay per auto commuter in hours. *Texas A&M Transportation Institute, "2023 Urban Mobility Report," June 2024*

Women/Minorities Rankings

- San Jose was listed as one of the most LGBTQ-friendly cities in America by *The Advocate*, as compiled by the real estate data site *Clever*. The city ranked #11 out of 15. Criteria, among many: Pride events; gay bars; LGBTQ-affirming healthcare options; state and local laws; number of PFLAG chapters; LGBTQ+ population. *The Advocate, "These Are the 15 Most LGBTQ-Friendly Cities in the U.S." November 1, 2023*

- Personal finance website *WalletHub* compared more than 180 U.S. cities across two key dimensions, "Hispanic Business-Friendliness" and "Hispanic Purchasing Power," to arrive at the most favorable conditions for Hispanic entrepreneurs. San Jose was ranked #142 out of 182. Criteria includes: share of Hispanic-Owned Businesses; average growth of Hispanic Business revenues; Small Business-Friendliness score; affordability; and number of Hispanics with at least a bachelor's degree. *WalletHub.com, "Best Cities for Hispanic Entrepreneurs," September 4, 2024*

Miscellaneous Rankings

- San Jose was selected as a 2024 Digital Cities Survey winner. The city ranked #2 in the large city (500,000 or more population) category. The survey examined and assessed how city governments are utilizing new technology and modernized applications to provide residents an array of contactless services and conveniences. Survey questions focused on ten initiatives: cybersecurity; citizen experience; disaster recovery; business intelligence; IT personnel retention; data governance; business automation; AI/machine learning; application modernization; and IT collaboration. *Center for Digital Government, "2024 Digital Cities Survey," November 5, 2024*

- *WalletHub* compared 148 of the most populated U.S. cities to determine their operating efficiency. A "Quality of Services" score was constructed for each city and then measured against the total budget per capita to reveal which were managed the best. San Jose ranked #111. Criteria: financial stability; economy; education; safety; health; infrastructure and pollution. *WalletHub.com, "2025's Best- & Worst-Run Cities in America," June 18, 2024*

Business Environment

DEMOGRAPHICS

Population Growth

Area	1990 Census	2000 Census	2010 Census	2020 Census	2023 Estimate[2]	Population Growth 1990-2023 (%)
City	784,324	894,943	945,942	1,013,240	990,054	26.2
MSA[1]	1,534,280	1,735,819	1,836,911	2,000,468	1,969,353	28.4
U.S.	248,709,873	281,421,906	308,745,538	331,449,281	332,387,540	33.6

Note: (1) Figures cover the San Jose-Sunnyvale-Santa Clara, CA Metropolitan Statistical Area; (2) 2019-2023 5-year ACS population estimate
Source: U.S. Census Bureau, 1990 Census, 2000 Census, 2010 Census, 2020 Census, 2019-2023 American Community Survey 5-Year Estimates

Race

Area	White Alone[2] (%)	Black Alone[2] (%)	Asian Alone[2] (%)	AIAN[3] Alone[2] (%)	NHOPI[4] Alone[2] (%)	Other Race Alone[2] (%)	Two or More Races (%)
City	29.0	2.9	38.6	1.0	0.5	13.6	14.4
MSA[1]	33.6	2.3	38.3	0.8	0.4	10.7	13.9
U.S.	63.4	12.4	5.8	0.9	0.2	6.6	10.7

Note: (1) Figures cover the San Jose-Sunnyvale-Santa Clara, CA Metropolitan Statistical Area; (2) Alone is defined as not being in combination with one or more other races; (3) American Indian and Alaska Native; (4) Native Hawaiian and Other Pacific Islander
Source: U.S. Census Bureau, 2019-2023 American Community Survey 5-Year Estimates

Hispanic or Latino Origin

Area	Total (%)	Mexican (%)	Puerto Rican (%)	Cuban (%)	Other (%)
City	31.0	25.4	0.5	0.2	4.9
MSA[1]	26.3	21.2	0.4	0.2	4.5
U.S.	19.0	11.3	1.8	0.7	5.2

Note: Persons of Hispanic or Latino origin can be of any race; (1) Figures cover the San Jose-Sunnyvale-Santa Clara, CA Metropolitan Statistical Area
Source: U.S. Census Bureau, 2019-2023 American Community Survey 5-Year Estimates

Age

Area	Percent of Population									Median Age
	Under Age 5	Age 5–19	Age 20–34	Age 35–44	Age 45–54	Age 55–64	Age 65–74	Age 75–84	Age 85+	
City	5.2	18.3	21.9	14.6	13.8	12.1	8.2	4.1	1.8	38.1
MSA[1]	5.4	18.3	22.1	14.4	13.4	12.1	8.1	4.3	2.0	37.8
U.S.	5.7	19.1	20.2	13.1	12.3	12.8	10.0	4.9	1.9	38.7

Note: (1) Figures cover the San Jose-Sunnyvale-Santa Clara, CA Metropolitan Statistical Area
Source: U.S. Census Bureau, 2019-2023 American Community Survey 5-Year Estimates

Disability by Age

Area	All Ages	Under 18 Years Old	18 to 64 Years Old	65 Years and Over
City	9.6	3.6	6.3	34.3
MSA[1]	8.8	3.1	5.7	31.3
U.S.	13.0	4.7	10.7	32.9

Note: Figures show percent of the civilian noninstitutionalized population that reported having a disability. Disability status is determined from six types of difficulty: vision, hearing, cognitive, ambulatory, self-care, and independent living. For children under 5 years old, hearing and vision difficulty are used to determine disability status. For children between the ages of 5 and 14, disability status is determined from hearing, vision, cognitive, ambulatory, and self-care difficulties. For people aged 15 years and older, they are considered to have a disability if they have difficulty with any one of the six difficulty types; Note: (1) Figures cover the San Jose-Sunnyvale-Santa Clara, CA Metropolitan Statistical Area
Source: U.S. Census Bureau, 2019-2023 American Community Survey 5-Year Estimates

Ancestry

Area	German	Irish	English	American	Italian	Polish	French[2]	European	Scottish
City	4.4	4.0	4.0	1.5	3.2	0.8	1.0	1.2	0.7
MSA[1]	5.6	4.6	4.9	1.8	3.5	1.0	1.2	1.6	0.9
U.S.	12.6	9.4	9.1	5.5	4.9	2.6	2.0	1.6	1.6

Note: Figures are the percentage of the total population reporting a particular ancestry. The nine most commonly reported ancestries in the U.S. are shown. Figures include multiple ancestries (e.g. if a person reported being Irish and Italian, they were included in both columns); (1) Figures cover the San Jose-Sunnyvale-Santa Clara, CA Metropolitan Statistical Area; (2) Excludes Basque
Source: U.S. Census Bureau, 2019-2023 American Community Survey 5-Year Estimates

Foreign-born Population

Area	Percent of Population Born in								
	Any Foreign Country	Asia	Mexico	Europe	Caribbean	Central America[2]	South America	Africa	Canada
City	41.6	27.3	8.4	2.2	0.1	1.3	1.0	0.7	0.3
MSA[1]	40.3	27.1	6.5	3.0	0.1	1.0	1.1	0.7	0.5
U.S.	13.9	4.3	3.3	1.4	1.4	1.2	1.2	0.8	0.2

Note: (1) Figures cover the San Jose-Sunnyvale-Santa Clara, CA Metropolitan Statistical Area; (2) Excludes Mexico.
Source: U.S. Census Bureau, 2019-2023 American Community Survey 5-Year Estimates

Household Size

Area	Persons in Household (%)							Average Household Size
	One	Two	Three	Four	Five	Six	Seven or More	
City	20.7	29.4	18.8	17.6	7.6	3.0	2.9	2.98
MSA[1]	21.4	31.1	18.8	17.2	6.9	2.6	2.1	2.86
U.S.	28.5	33.8	15.4	12.7	5.9	2.3	1.4	2.54

Note: (1) Figures cover the San Jose-Sunnyvale-Santa Clara, CA Metropolitan Statistical Area
Source: U.S. Census Bureau, 2019-2023 American Community Survey 5-Year Estimates

Household Relationships

Area	House-holder	Opposite-sex Spouse	Same-sex Spouse	Opposite-sex Unmarried Partner	Same-sex Unmarried Partner	Child[2]	Grand-child	Other Relatives	Non-relatives
City	32.4	17.1	0.2	1.9	0.1	28.6	2.3	9.8	6.1
MSA[1]	33.8	18.4	0.2	1.8	0.1	28.3	1.9	7.9	5.6
U.S.	38.3	17.5	0.2	2.5	0.2	28.3	2.4	4.8	3.4

Note: Figures are percent of the total population; (1) Figures cover the San Jose-Sunnyvale-Santa Clara, CA Metropolitan Statistical Area; (2) Includes biological, adopted, and stepchildren of the householder
Source: U.S. Census Bureau, 2020 Census

Gender

Area	Males	Females	Males per 100 Females
City	504,179	485,875	103.8
MSA[1]	1,003,282	966,071	103.9
U.S.	164,545,087	167,842,453	98.0

Note: (1) Figures cover the San Jose-Sunnyvale-Santa Clara, CA Metropolitan Statistical Area
Source: U.S. Census Bureau, 2019-2023 American Community Survey 5-Year Estimates

Marital Status

Area	Never Married	Now Married[2]	Separated	Widowed	Divorced
City	37.2	49.3	1.6	4.4	7.5
MSA[1]	35.5	51.7	1.4	4.2	7.1
U.S.	34.1	47.9	1.7	5.6	10.7

Note: Figures are percentages and cover the population 15 years of age and older; (1) Figures cover the San Jose-Sunnyvale-Santa Clara, CA Metropolitan Statistical Area; (2) Excludes separated
Source: U.S. Census Bureau, 2019-2023 American Community Survey 5-Year Estimates

Religious Groups by Family

Area	Catholic	Baptist	Methodist	LDS[2]	Pentecostal	Lutheran	Islam	Adventist	Other
MSA[1]	27.2	1.2	0.6	1.4	0.9	0.4	2.0	1.3	11.4
U.S.	18.7	7.3	3.0	2.0	1.8	1.7	1.3	1.3	11.6

Note: Figures are the number of adherents as a percentage of the total population and cover the eight largest religious groups in the U.S; (1) Figures cover the San Jose-Sunnyvale-Santa Clara, CA Metropolitan Statistical Area; (2) Church of Jesus Christ of Latter-day Saints
Sources: 2020 U.S. Religion Census, Association of Statisticians of American Religious Bodies; The Association of Religion Data Archives (ARDA)

Religious Groups by Tradition

Area	Catholic	Evangelical Protestant	Mainline Protestant	Black Protestant	Islam	Judaism	Hinduism	Orthodox	Buddhism
MSA[1]	27.2	8.4	1.4	0.3	2.0	0.6	2.4	0.6	1.2
U.S.	18.7	16.5	5.2	2.3	1.3	0.6	0.4	0.4	0.3

Note: Figures are the number of adherents as a percentage of the total population; (1) Figures cover the San Jose-Sunnyvale-Santa Clara, CA Metropolitan Statistical Area
Sources: 2020 U.S. Religion Census, Association of Statisticians of American Religious Bodies; The Association of Religion Data Archives (ARDA)

ECONOMY

Real Gross Domestic Product (GDP)

Area	2017	2018	2019	2020	2021	2022	2023	Rank[3]
MSA[1]	282.7	304.6	319.4	339.4	381.6	379.7	392.5	13
U.S.[2]	17,619.1	18,160.7	18,642.5	18,238.9	19,387.6	19,896.6	20,436.3	–

Note: Figures are in billions of chained 2017 dollars; (1) Figures cover the San Jose-Sunnyvale-Santa Clara, CA Metropolitan Statistical Area; (2) Figures cover real GDP within metropolitan areas; (3) Rank is based on 2023 data and ranges from 1 to 384
Source: U.S. Bureau of Economic Analysis

Economic Growth

Area	2014	2015	2016	2017	2018	2019	2020	2021	2022	2023
MSA[1]	7.2	8.9	6.1	4.9	7.8	4.8	6.3	12.4	-0.5	3.4
U.S.[2]	2.6	3.2	2.0	2.7	3.1	2.7	-2.2	6.3	2.6	2.7

Note: Figures are real gross domestic product growth rates and represent percent change from preceding period; (1) Figures cover the San Jose-Sunnyvale-Santa Clara, CA Metropolitan Statistical Area; (2) Figures are the average growth rates within metropolitan areas
Source: U.S. Bureau of Economic Analysis

Metropolitan Area Exports

Area	2018	2019	2020	2021	2022	2023	Rank[2]
MSA[1]	22,224.2	20,909.4	19,534.5	22,293.6	24,342.2	22,985.4	21
U.S.	1,664,056.1	1,645,173.7	1,431,406.6	1,753,941.4	2,062,937.4	2,019,160.5	–

Note: Figures are in millions of dollars; (1) Figures cover the San Jose-Sunnyvale-Santa Clara, CA Metropolitan Statistical Area; (2) Rank is based on 2023 data and ranges from 1 to 386
Source: U.S. Department of Commerce, International Trade Administration, Office of Trade and Economic Analysis, Industry and Analysis, Exports by Metropolitan Area, data extracted April 2, 2025

Building Permits

Area	Single-Family			Multi-Family			Total		
	2023	2024	Pct. Chg.	2023	2024	Pct. Chg.	2023	2024	Pct. Chg.
City	581	642	10.5	2,069	1,356	-34.5	2,650	1,998	-24.6
MSA[1]	2,037	2,207	8.3	4,190	1,908	-54.5	6,227	4,115	-33.9
U.S.	920,000	981,900	6.7	591,100	496,100	-16.1	1,511,100	1,478,000	-2.2

Note: (1) Figures cover the San Jose-Sunnyvale-Santa Clara, CA Metropolitan Statistical Area; Figures represent new, privately-owned housing units authorized (unadjusted data)
Source: U.S. Census Bureau, Building Permits Survey (BPS), 2023, 2024

Bankruptcy Filings

Area	Business Filings			Nonbusiness Filings		
	2023	2024	% Chg.	2023	2024	% Chg.
Santa Clara County	86	105	22.1	782	1,008	28.9
U.S.	18,926	23,107	22.1	434,064	494,201	13.9

Note: Business filings include Chapter 7, Chapter 9, Chapter 11, Chapter 12, Chapter 13, Chapter 15, and Section 304; Nonbusiness filings include Chapter 7, Chapter 11, and Chapter 13
Source: Administrative Office of the U.S. Courts, Business and Nonbusiness Bankruptcy, County Cases Commenced by Chapter of the Bankruptcy Code, During the 12-Month Period Ending December 31, 2023 and Business and Nonbusiness Bankruptcy, County Cases Commenced by Chapter of the Bankruptcy Code, During the 12-Month Period Ending December 31, 2024

Housing Vacancy Rates

Area	Gross Vacancy Rate[3] (%)			Year-Round Vacancy Rate[4] (%)			Rental Vacancy Rate[5] (%)			Homeowner Vacancy Rate[6] (%)		
	2022	2023	2024	2022	2023	2024	2022	2023	2024	2022	2023	2024
MSA[1]	5.8	4.5	4.7	5.8	4.5	4.7	4.7	3.3	3.3	0.4	0.3	1.0
U.S.[2]	9.1	9.0	9.1	7.5	7.5	7.6	5.7	6.5	6.8	0.8	0.8	1.0

Note: (1) Figures cover the San Jose-Sunnyvale-Santa Clara, CA Metropolitan Statistical Area; (2) Figures cover the 75 largest Metropolitan Statistical Areas; (3) The percentage of the total housing inventory that is vacant; (4) The percentage of the housing inventory (excluding seasonal units) that is year-round vacant; (5) The percentage of rental inventory that is vacant for rent; (6) The percentage of homeowner inventory that is vacant for sale
Source: U.S. Census Bureau, Housing Vacancies and Homeownership Annual Statistics: 2022, 2023, 2024

INCOME

Income

Area	Per Capita ($)	Median Household ($)	Average Household ($)
City	63,253	141,565	187,711
MSA[1]	75,895	157,444	217,226
U.S.	43,289	78,538	110,491

Note: (1) Figures cover the San Jose-Sunnyvale-Santa Clara, CA Metropolitan Statistical Area
Source: U.S. Census Bureau, 2019-2023 American Community Survey 5-Year Estimates

Household Income Distribution

Area	Percent of Households Earning							
	Under $15,000	$15,000 -$24,999	$25,000 -$34,999	$35,000 -$49,999	$50,000 -$74,999	$75,000 -$99,999	$100,000 -$149,999	$150,000 and up
City	4.9	3.6	3.5	5.5	9.2	9.3	16.6	47.3
MSA[1]	4.6	3.0	3.1	4.8	8.4	8.5	15.5	52.0
U.S.	8.5	6.6	6.8	10.4	15.7	12.7	17.4	21.9

Note: (1) Figures cover the San Jose-Sunnyvale-Santa Clara, CA Metropolitan Statistical Area
Source: U.S. Census Bureau, 2019-2023 American Community Survey 5-Year Estimates

Poverty Rate

Area	All Ages	Under 18 Years Old	18 to 64 Years Old	65 Years and Over
City	7.8	7.6	7.4	10.5
MSA[1]	6.9	6.6	6.5	9.0
U.S.	12.4	16.3	11.6	10.4

Note: Figures are percentage of people whose income during the past 12 months was below the poverty level;
(1) Figures cover the San Jose-Sunnyvale-Santa Clara, CA Metropolitan Statistical Area
Source: U.S. Census Bureau, 2019-2023 American Community Survey 5-Year Estimates

EMPLOYMENT

Labor Force and Employment

Area	Civilian Labor Force			Workers Employed		
	Dec. 2023	Dec. 2024	% Chg.	Dec. 2023	Dec. 2024	% Chg.
City	550,266	551,509	0.2	528,718	529,659	0.2
MSA[1]	1,075,900	1,078,520	0.2	1,034,963	1,036,708	0.2
U.S.	166,661,000	167,746,000	0.7	160,754,000	161,294,000	0.3

Note: Data is not seasonally adjusted and covers workers 16 years of age and older; (1) Figures cover the San Jose-Sunnyvale-Santa Clara, CA Metropolitan Statistical Area
Source: Bureau of Labor Statistics, Local Area Unemployment Statistics

Unemployment Rate

Area	2024											
	Jan.	Feb.	Mar.	Apr.	May	Jun.	Jul.	Aug.	Sep.	Oct.	Nov.	Dec.
City	4.3	4.2	4.1	3.8	3.6	4.4	4.7	4.7	4.2	4.3	4.3	4.0
MSA[1]	4.2	4.2	4.0	3.7	3.6	4.2	4.5	4.5	4.1	4.1	4.1	3.9
U.S.	4.1	4.2	3.9	3.5	3.7	4.3	4.5	4.4	3.9	3.9	4.0	3.8

Note: Data is not seasonally adjusted and covers workers 16 years of age and older; (1) Figures cover the San Jose-Sunnyvale-Santa Clara, CA Metropolitan Statistical Area
Source: Bureau of Labor Statistics, Local Area Unemployment Statistics

Average Wages

Occupation	$/Hr.	Occupation	$/Hr.
Accountants and Auditors	61.89	Maintenance and Repair Workers	33.50
Automotive Mechanics	39.24	Marketing Managers	137.00
Bookkeepers	32.88	Network and Computer Systems Admin.	63.55
Carpenters	41.63	Nurses, Licensed Practical	44.06
Cashiers	20.75	Nurses, Registered	91.29
Computer Programmers	76.50	Nursing Assistants	27.97
Computer Systems Analysts	77.64	Office Clerks, General	28.51
Computer User Support Specialists	43.29	Physical Therapists	68.75
Construction Laborers	35.06	Physicians	89.33
Cooks, Restaurant	24.13	Plumbers, Pipefitters and Steamfitters	49.42
Customer Service Representatives	30.67	Police and Sheriff's Patrol Officers	69.86
Dentists	90.06	Postal Service Mail Carriers	29.61
Electricians	49.71	Real Estate Sales Agents	49.32
Engineers, Electrical	90.89	Retail Salespersons	23.09
Fast Food and Counter Workers	20.83	Sales Representatives, Technical/Scientific	78.15
Financial Managers	142.60	Secretaries, Exc. Legal/Medical/Executive	31.07
First-Line Supervisors of Office Workers	46.77	Security Guards	24.80
General and Operations Managers	94.44	Surgeons	n/a
Hairdressers/Cosmetologists	21.94	Teacher Assistants, Exc. Postsecondary[1]	24.13
Home Health and Personal Care Aides	18.62	Teachers, Secondary School, Exc. Sp. Ed.[1]	52.38
Janitors and Cleaners	21.80	Telemarketers	23.11
Landscaping/Groundskeeping Workers	25.28	Truck Drivers, Heavy/Tractor-Trailer	33.44
Lawyers	151.17	Truck Drivers, Light/Delivery Services	26.28
Maids and Housekeeping Cleaners	27.28	Waiters and Waitresses	24.41

Note: Wage data covers the San Jose-Sunnyvale-Santa Clara, CA Metropolitan Statistical Area; (1) Hourly wages were calculated from annual wage data based on a 40 hour work week
Source: Bureau of Labor Statistics, Metro Area Occupational Employment & Wage Estimates, May 2024

Employment by Industry

Sector	MSA[1]		U.S.
	Number of Employees	Percent of Total	Percent of Total
Construction	52,700	4.5	5.1
Financial Activities	36,400	3.1	5.8
Government	102,400	8.8	14.9
Information	94,100	8.1	1.9
Leisure and Hospitality	104,100	9.0	10.4
Manufacturing	123,700	10.6	8.0
Mining and Logging	200	<0.1	0.4
Other Services	27,500	2.4	3.7
Private Education and Health Services	213,600	18.4	16.9
Professional and Business Services	285,900	24.6	14.2
Retail Trade	75,300	6.5	10.0
Transportation, Warehousing, and Utilities	17,100	1.5	4.8
Wholesale Trade	28,900	2.5	3.9

Note: Figures are non-farm employment as of December 2024. Figures are not seasonally adjusted and include workers 16 years of age and older; (1) Figures cover the San Jose-Sunnyvale-Santa Clara, CA Metropolitan Statistical Area
Source: Bureau of Labor Statistics, Current Employment Statistics, Employment, Hours, and Earnings

Employment by Occupation

Occupation Classification	City (%)	MSA[1] (%)	U.S. (%)
Management, Business, Science, and Arts	50.8	57.8	42.0
Natural Resources, Construction, and Maintenance	6.8	5.8	8.6
Production, Transportation, and Material Moving	9.3	7.8	13.0
Sales and Office	16.6	14.9	19.9
Service	16.6	13.6	16.5

Note: Figures cover employed civilians 16 years of age and older; (1) Figures cover the San Jose-Sunnyvale-Santa Clara, CA Metropolitan Statistical Area
Source: U.S. Census Bureau, 2019-2023 American Community Survey 5-Year Estimates

Occupations with Greatest Projected Employment Growth: 2022 – 2032

Occupation[1]	2022 Employment	2032 Projected Employment	Numeric Employment Change	Percent Employment Change
Home Health and Personal Care Aides	796,900	1,060,200	263,300	33.0
Software Developers	313,700	388,000	74,300	23.7
Registered Nurses	333,700	376,900	43,200	12.9
Cooks, Restaurant	142,100	184,000	41,900	29.5
Laborers and Freight, Stock, and Material Movers, Hand	399,500	437,300	37,800	9.5
Janitors and Cleaners, Except Maids and Housekeeping Cleaners	262,900	300,200	37,300	14.2
Fast Food and Counter Workers	419,100	455,200	36,100	8.6
Stockers and Order Fillers	289,900	322,900	33,000	11.4
Medical Assistants	108,000	135,700	27,700	25.6
Landscaping and Groundskeeping Workers	135,200	162,100	26,900	19.9

Note: Projections cover California; (1) Sorted by numeric employment change
Source: www.projectionscentral.org, State Occupational Projections, 2022–2032 Long-Term Projections

Fastest-Growing Occupations: 2022 – 2032

Occupation[1]	2022 Employment	2032 Projected Employment	Numeric Employment Change	Percent Employment Change
Nurse Practitioners	21,500	34,100	12,600	58.6
Physical Therapist Assistants	7,900	11,200	3,300	41.8
Solar Photovoltaic Installers	7,900	11,200	3,300	41.8
Physician Assistants	13,000	18,200	5,200	40.0
Medical and Health Services Managers	58,300	81,400	23,100	39.6
Statisticians	2,800	3,900	1,100	39.3
Taxi Drivers	48,100	66,800	18,700	38.9
Occupational Therapy Assistants	2,700	3,600	900	33.3
Home Health and Personal Care Aides	796,900	1,060,200	263,300	33.0
Data Scientists	33,900	45,000	11,100	32.7

Note: Projections cover California; (1) Sorted by percent employment change and excludes occupations with numeric employment change less than 50
Source: www.projectionscentral.org, State Occupational Projections, 2022–2032 Long-Term Projections

CITY FINANCES

City Government Finances

Component	2022 ($000)	2022 ($ per capita)
Total Revenues	3,329,079	3,284
Total Expenditures	2,395,921	2,364
Debt Outstanding	3,813,607	3,762

Source: U.S. Census Bureau, State & Local Government Finances 2022

City Government Revenue by Source

Source	2022 ($000)	2022 ($ per capita)	2022 (%)
General Revenue			
From Federal Government	242,017	239	7.3
From State Government	83,579	82	2.5
From Local Governments	54,210	53	1.6
Taxes			
Property	653,455	645	19.6
Sales and Gross Receipts	469,411	463	14.1
Personal Income	0	0	0.0
Corporate Income	0	0	0.0
Motor Vehicle License	0	0	0.0
Other Taxes	451,727	446	13.6
Current Charges	838,155	827	25.2
Liquor Store	0	0	0.0
Utility	406,449	401	12.2

Source: U.S. Census Bureau, State & Local Government Finances 2022

City Government Expenditures by Function

Function	2022 ($000)	2022 ($ per capita)	2022 (%)
General Direct Expenditures			
Air Transportation	109,077	107	4.6
Corrections	0	0	0.0
Education	0	0	0.0
Employment Security Administration	0	0	0.0
Financial Administration	0	0	0.0
Fire Protection	181,883	179	7.6
General Public Buildings	0	0	0.0
Governmental Administration, Other	226,095	223	9.4
Health	200	< 1	< 0.1
Highways	210,833	208	8.8
Hospitals	0	0	0.0
Housing and Community Development	182,172	179	7.6
Interest on General Debt	86,991	85	3.6
Judicial and Legal	0	0	0.0
Libraries	41,549	41	1.7
Parking	11,131	11	0.5
Parks and Recreation	194,559	191	8.1
Police Protection	376,857	371	15.7
Public Welfare	0	0	0.0
Sewerage	152,461	150	6.4
Solid Waste Management	172,495	170	7.2
Veterans' Services	0	0	0.0
Liquor Store	0	0	0.0
Utility	376,104	371	15.7

Source: U.S. Census Bureau, State & Local Government Finances 2022

TAXES

State Corporate Income Tax Rates

State	Tax Rate (%)	Income Brackets ($)	Num. of Brackets	Financial Institution Tax Rate (%)[a]	Federal Income Tax Ded.
California	8.84 (b)	Flat rate	1	10.84 (b)	No

Note: Tax rates for tax year 2024; (a) Rates listed are the corporate income tax rate applied to financial institutions or excise taxes based on income. Some states have other taxes based upon the value of deposits or shares; (b) Minimum tax is $800 in California, $250 in District of Columbia, $50 in Arizona and North Dakota (banks), $400 ($100 banks) in Rhode Island, $200 per location in South Dakota (banks), $100 in Utah, in Vermont, simplified entity business tax for residents only at $250, otherwise minimum tax ($100 - $100,000) is based upon gross receipts.
Source: Federation of Tax Administrators, State Corporate Income Tax Rates, January 1, 2025

State Individual Income Tax Rates

State	Tax Rate (%)	Income Brackets ($)	Personal Exemptions ($)			Standard Ded. ($)	
			Single	Married	Depend.	Single	Married
California (a)	1.0 - 13.3 (g)	10,099 - 677,276 (b)	134	268	367 (c)	5,202	10,404 (a)

Note: Tax rates for tax year 2024; Local- and county-level taxes are not included; Federal income tax is not deductible on state income tax returns; (a) 16 states have statutory provision for automatically adjusting to the rate of inflation the dollar values of the income tax brackets, standard deductions, and/or personal exemptions. Oregon does not index the income brackets for $125,000 and over See: INFL and SPEC above; (b) For joint returns, taxes are twice the tax on half the couple's income. California brackets violate this formula at the two highest tax brackets in 2024; (c) The personal exemption takes the form of a tax credit instead of a deduction; (g) California imposes an additional 1% tax on taxable income over $1 million, making the maximum rate 13.3% over $1 million in 2023. Unreleased projections indicate 14.4% in 2024.
Source: Federation of Tax Administrators, State Individual Income Tax Rates, January 1, 2025

Various State Sales and Excise Tax Rates

State	State Sales Tax (%)	Gasoline[1] ($/gal.)	Cigarette[2] ($/pack)	Spirits[3] ($/gal.)	Wine[4] ($/gal.)	Beer[5] ($/gal.)	Recreational Marijuana (%)
California	7.25	0.70	2.87	3.30	0.20	0.20	(c)

Note: All tax rates as of January 1, 2025; (1) The American Petroleum Institute has developed a methodology for determining the average tax rate on a gallon of fuel. Rates may include any of the following: excise taxes, environmental fees, storage tank fees, other fees or taxes, general sales tax, and local taxes; (2) The federal excise tax of $1.0066 per pack and local taxes are not included; (3) Rates are those applicable to off-premise sales of 40% alcohol by volume (a.b.v.) distilled spirits in 750ml containers. Local excise taxes are excluded; (4) Rates are those applicable to off-premise sales of 11% a.b.v. non-carbonated wine in 750ml containers; (5) Rates are those applicable to off-premise sales of 4.7% a.b.v. beer in 12 ounce containers; (c) 15% excise tax (retail gross receipts)
Source: Tax Foundation, 2025 Facts & Figures: How Does Your State Compare?

State Tax Competitiveness Index

State	Overall Rank	Corporate Tax Rank	Individual Income Tax Rank	Sales Tax Rank	Property Tax Rank	Unemployment Insurance Tax Rank
California	48	41	49	46	23	25

Note: The Tax Foundation's State Tax Competitiveness Index enables policymakers, taxpayers, and business leaders to gauge how their states' tax systems compare. A rank of 1 is best, 50 is worst. Rankings do not average to the total. States without a tax rank equally as 1. DC's scores and rankings do not affect other states. The report shows tax systems as of July 1, 2024 (the beginning of Fiscal Year 2025).
Source: Tax Foundation, State Tax Competitiveness Index 2025

TRANSPORTATION

Means of Transportation to Work

Area	Car/Truck/Van		Public Transportation			Bicycle	Walked	Other Means	Worked at Home
	Drove Alone	Car-pooled	Bus	Subway	Railroad				
City	64.6	10.5	1.6	0.2	0.5	0.5	1.8	1.7	18.5
MSA[1]	62.1	9.0	1.5	0.2	0.6	1.3	2.0	1.7	21.5
U.S.	70.2	8.5	1.7	1.3	0.4	0.4	2.4	1.6	13.5

Note: Figures are percentages and cover workers 16 years of age and older; (1) Figures cover the San Jose-Sunnyvale-Santa Clara, CA Metropolitan Statistical Area
Source: U.S. Census Bureau, 2019-2023 American Community Survey 5-Year Estimates

Travel Time to Work

Area	Less Than 10 Minutes	10 to 19 Minutes	20 to 29 Minutes	30 to 44 Minutes	45 to 59 Minutes	60 to 89 Minutes	90 Minutes or More
City	5.9	26.5	25.5	25.0	8.6	5.7	2.7
MSA[1]	7.5	28.4	24.3	23.1	8.2	5.8	2.7
U.S.	12.6	28.6	21.2	20.8	8.1	6.0	2.8

Note: Note: Figures are percentages and include workers 16 years old and over; (1) Figures cover the San Jose-Sunnyvale-Santa Clara, CA Metropolitan Statistical Area
Source: U.S. Census Bureau, 2019-2023 American Community Survey 5-Year Estimates

Key Congestion Measures

Measure	2000	2010	2015	2020	2022
Annual Hours of Delay, Total (000)	59,026	87,229	114,375	46,377	100,700
Annual Hours of Delay, Per Auto Commuter	49	63	78	31	77
Annual Congestion Cost, Per Auto Commuter ($)	1,282	1,506	1,822	796	1,790

Note: Figures cover the San Jose CA urban area
Source: Texas A&M Transportation Institute, 2023 Urban Mobility Report

Freeway Travel Time Index

Measure	1985	1990	1995	2000	2005	2010	2015	2020	2022
Urban Area Index[1]	1.15	1.21	1.23	1.28	1.32	1.34	1.43	1.12	1.35
Urban Area Rank[1,2]	15	7	8	9	8	6	3	10	5

Note: Freeway Travel Time Index—the ratio of travel time in the peak period to the travel time at free-flow conditions. For example, a value of 1.30 indicates a 20-minute free-flow trip takes 26 minutes in the peak (20 minutes x 1.30 = 26 minutes); (1) Covers the San Jose CA urban area; (2) Rank is based on 101 larger urban areas (#1 = highest travel time index)
Source: Texas A&M Transportation Institute, 2023 Urban Mobility Report

Public Transportation

Agency Name / Mode of Transportation	Vehicles Operated in Maximum Service[1]	Annual Unlinked Passenger Trips[2] (in thous.)	Annual Passenger Miles[3] (in thous.)
Santa Clara Valley Transportation Authority (VTA)			
Bus (directly operated)	330	19,267.0	91,725.9
Bus (purchased transportation)	12	114.7	466.4
Demand Response (purchased transportation)	116	324.4	3,438.2
Light Rail (directly operated)	54	4,147.8	22,191.6

Note: (1) Number of revenue vehicles operated by the given mode and type of service to meet the annual maximum service requirement. This is the revenue vehicle count during the peak season of the year; on the week and day that maximum service is provided. Vehicles operated in maximum service (VOMS) exclude atypical days and one-time special events; (2) Number of passengers who boarded public transportation vehicles. Passengers are counted each time they board a vehicle no matter how many vehicles they use to travel from their origin to their destination. (3) Sum of the distances ridden by all passengers during the entire fiscal year.
Source: Federal Transit Administration, National Transit Database, 2023

Air Transportation

Airport Name and Code / Type of Service	Passenger Airlines[1]	Passenger Enplanements	Freight Carriers[2]	Freight (lbs)
San Jose International (SJC)				
Domestic service (U.S. carriers only)	27	5,502,643	12	34,212,742
International service (U.S. carriers only)	8	99,732	1	43,457

Note: (1) Includes all U.S.-based major, minor and commuter airlines that carried at least one passenger during the year; (2) Includes all U.S.-based airlines and freight carriers that transported at least one pound of freight during the year.
Source: Bureau of Transportation Statistics, The Intermodal Transportation Database, Air Carriers: T-100 Domestic Market (U.S. carriers only), 2024; Bureau of Transportation Statistics, The Intermodal Transportation Database, Air Carriers: T-100 International Market (U.S. carriers only), 2024

BUSINESSES

Major Business Headquarters

Company Name	Industry	Rankings Fortune[1]	Rankings Forbes[2]
Adobe	Computer software	210	-
Cisco Systems	Network and other communications equipment	74	-
Ebay	Internet services and retailing	390	-
PayPal Holdings	Financial data services	145	-
Sanmina	Semiconductors and other electronic components	433	-
Super Micro Computer	Computers, office equipment	498	-
Western Digital	Computers, office equipment	334	-

Note: (1) Companies that produce a 10-K are ranked 1 to 500 based on 2023 revenue; (2) All private companies with at least $2 billion in annual revenue through the end of their most current fiscal year are ranked 1 to 275; companies listed are headquartered in the city; dashes indicate no ranking
Source: Fortune, "Fortune 500," 2024; Forbes, "America's Largest Private Companies," 2024

Fastest-Growing Businesses

According to *Inc.*, San Jose is home to one of America's 500 fastest-growing private companies: **Element5** (#177). Criteria: must be an independent, privately-held, for-profit, U.S. corporation, proprietorship or partnership as of December 31, 2023; revenues must be at least $100,000 in 2020 and $2 million in 2023; must have four-year operating/sales history. *Inc., "America's 500 Fastest-Growing Private Companies," 2024*

According to Deloitte, San Jose is home to five of North America's 500 fastest-growing high-technology companies: **Alkira** (#25); **Zoom Video Communications** (#192); **BILL** (#205); **Whatfix** (#369); **Zscaler** (#397). Companies are ranked by percentage growth in revenue over a four-year period. Criteria for inclusion: company must be headquartered within North America; must own proprietary intellectual property or technology that is sold to customers in products that contributes to a significant portion of the company's operating revenue; must have been in business for a minumum of four years with 2020 operating revenues of at least $50,000 USD/CD and 2023 operating revenues of at least $5 million USD/CD. *Deloitte, 2024 Technology Fast 500*[TM]

Living Environment

COST OF LIVING

Cost of Living Index

Composite Index	Groceries	Housing	Utilities	Trans-portation	Health Care	Misc. Goods/Services
180.6	115.0	321.1	158.6	140.7	120.1	117.9

Note: The Cost of Living Index measures regional differences in the cost of consumer goods and services, excluding taxes and non-consumer expenditures, for professional and managerial households in the top income quintile. It is based on more than 50,000 prices covering almost 60 different items for which prices are collected three times a year by chambers of commerce, economic development organizations or university applied economic centers in each participating urban area. The numbers shown should be read as a percentage above or below the national average of 100. For example, a value of 115.4 in the groceries column indicates that grocery prices are 15.4% higher than the national average. Small differences in the index numbers should not be interpreted as significant; Figures cover the San Jose CA urban area.
Source: The Council for Community and Economic Research, Cost of Living Index, 2024

Grocery Prices

Area[1]	T-Bone Steak ($/pound)	Frying Chicken ($/pound)	Whole Milk ($/half gal.)	Eggs ($/dozen)	Orange Juice ($/64 oz.)	Coffee ($/11.5 oz.)
City[2]	15.54	2.57	5.09	3.10	4.64	6.92
Avg.	15.42	1.55	4.69	3.25	4.41	5.46
Min.	14.50	1.16	4.43	2.75	4.00	4.85
Max.	17.56	2.89	5.49	4.78	5.54	7.89

*Note: (1) Values for the local area are compared with the average, minimum and maximum values for all 276 areas in the Cost of Living Index; (2) Figures cover the San Jose CA urban area; **T-Bone Steak** (price per pound); **Frying Chicken** (price per pound, whole fryer); **Whole Milk** (half gallon carton); **Eggs** (price per dozen, Grade A, large); **Orange Juice** (64 oz. Tropicana or Florida Natural); **Coffee** (11.5 oz. can, vacuum-packed, Maxwell House, Hills Bros, or Folgers).*
Source: The Council for Community and Economic Research, Cost of Living Index, 2024

Housing and Utility Costs

Area[1]	New Home Price ($)	Apartment Rent ($/month)	All Electric ($/month)	Part Electric ($/month)	Other Energy ($/month)	Telephone ($/month)
City[2]	1,860,932	3,311	-	267.58	131.25	192.30
Avg.	515,975	1,550	210.99	123.07	82.07	194.99
Min.	265,375	692	104.33	53.68	36.26	179.42
Max.	2,775,821	5,719	529.02	397.28	361.63	223.33

*Note: (1) Values for the local area are compared with the average, minimum and maximum values for all 276 areas in the Cost of Living Index; (2) Figures cover the San Jose CA urban area; **New Home Price** (2,400 sf living area, 8,000 sf lot, in urban area with full utilities); **Apartment Rent** (950 sf 2 bedroom/1.5 or 2 bath, unfurnished, excluding all utilities except water); **All Electric** (average monthly cost for an all-electric home); **Part Electric** (average monthly cost for a part-electric home); **Other Energy** (average monthly cost for natural gas, fuel oil, coal, wood, and any other forms of energy except electricity); **Telephone** (price includes the base monthly rate plus taxes and fees for three lines of mobile phone service).*
Source: The Council for Community and Economic Research, Cost of Living Index, 2024

Health Care, Transportation, and Other Costs

Area[1]	Doctor ($/visit)	Dentist ($/visit)	Optometrist ($/visit)	Gasoline ($/gallon)	Beauty Salon ($/visit)	Men's Shirt ($)
City[2]	212.00	131.83	166.92	5.00	65.28	32.93
Avg.	143.77	117.51	129.23	3.32	48.57	38.14
Min.	36.74	58.67	67.33	2.80	24.00	13.41
Max.	270.44	216.82	307.33	5.28	94.00	63.89

*Note: (1) Values for the local area are compared with the average, minimum and maximum values for all 276 areas in the Cost of Living Index; (2) Figures cover the San Jose CA urban area; **Doctor** (general practitioners routine exam of an established patient); **Dentist** (adult teeth cleaning and periodic oral examination); **Optometrist** (full vision eye exam for established adult patient); **Gasoline** (one gallon regular unleaded, national brand, including all taxes, cash price at self-service pump if available); **Beauty Salon** (woman's shampoo, trim, and blow-dry); **Men's Shirt** (cotton/polyester dress shirt, pinpoint weave, long sleeves).*
Source: The Council for Community and Economic Research, Cost of Living Index, 2024

HOUSING

Homeownership Rate

Area	2017 (%)	2018 (%)	2019 (%)	2020 (%)	2021 (%)	2022 (%)	2023 (%)	2024 (%)
MSA[1]	50.4	50.4	52.4	52.6	48.4	53.1	53.5	52.3
U.S.	63.9	64.4	64.6	66.6	65.5	65.8	65.9	65.6

Note: (1) Figures cover the San Jose-Sunnyvale-Santa Clara, CA Metropolitan Statistical Area
Source: U.S. Census Bureau, Housing Vacancies and Homeownership Annual Statistics: 2017-2024

House Price Index (HPI)

Area	National Ranking[2]	Quarterly Change (%)	One-Year Change (%)	Five-Year Change (%)	Since 1991Q1 (%)
MSA[1]	221	-0.52	2.35	36.42	433.00
U.S.[3]	–	1.43	4.51	57.13	327.82

Note: The HPI is a weighted repeat sales index. It measures average price changes in repeat sales or refinancings on the same properties. This information is obtained by reviewing repeat mortgage transactions on single-family properties whose mortgages have been purchased or securitized by Fannie Mae or Freddie Mac since January 1975; (1) Figures cover the San Jose-Sunnyvale-Santa Clara, CA Metropolitan Statistical Area; (2) Rankings are based on annual percentage change for all metro areas containing at least 15,000 transactions over the last 10 years and ranges from 1 to 241; (3) figures based on a weighted average of Census Division estimates using a seasonally adjusted, purchase-only index; all figures are for the period ending December 31, 2024
Source: Federal Housing Finance Agency, Change in FHFA Metropolitan Area House Price Indexes, All Transactions Index, 2024Q4

Home Value

Area	Under $100,000	$100,000 -$199,999	$200,000 -$299,999	$300,000 -$399,999	$400,000 -$499,999	$500,000 -$999,999	$1,000,000 or more	Median ($)
City	2.2	2.2	2.3	1.5	1.3	22.4	68.0	1,187,800
MSA[1]	2.1	1.7	1.8	1.3	1.2	19.3	72.6	1,342,700
U.S.	12.1	17.8	19.5	14.4	10.5	19.1	6.5	303,400

Note: Figures are percentages except for median and cover owner-occupied housing units; (1) Figures cover the San Jose-Sunnyvale-Santa Clara, CA Metropolitan Statistical Area
Source: U.S. Census Bureau, 2019-2023 American Community Survey 5-Year Estimates

Year Housing Structure Built

Area	2020 or Later	2010 -2019	2000 -2009	1990 -1999	1980 -1989	1970 -1979	1960 -1969	1950 -1959	1940 -1949	Before 1940	Median Year
City	0.6	7.3	9.6	9.6	12.1	23.6	18.5	10.9	2.7	5.2	1975
MSA[1]	0.9	8.8	9.2	9.6	11.7	20.4	17.4	13.7	3.4	4.8	1975
U.S.	1.2	8.9	13.6	12.8	13.0	14.4	10.0	9.7	4.5	11.9	1980

Note: Figures are percentages except for Median Year; Note: (1) Figures cover the San Jose-Sunnyvale-Santa Clara, CA Metropolitan Statistical Area
Source: U.S. Census Bureau, 2019-2023 American Community Survey 5-Year Estimates

Gross Monthly Rent

Area	Under $500	$500 -$999	$1,000 -$1,499	$1,500 -$1,999	$2,000 -$2,499	$2,500 -$2,999	$3,000 and up	Median ($)
City	3.7	4.7	6.6	12.7	18.3	17.6	36.5	2,617
MSA[1]	2.7	3.7	5.4	10.8	16.8	17.6	42.7	2,794
U.S.	6.5	22.3	29.5	20.2	10.8	4.8	5.9	1,348

Note: Figures are percentages except for median; Gross rent is the contract rent plus the estimated average monthly cost of utilities (electricity, gas, and water and sewer) and fuels (oil, coal, kerosene, wood, etc.) if these are paid by the renter (or paid for the renter by someone else); (1) Figures cover the San Jose-Sunnyvale-Santa Clara, CA Metropolitan Statistical Area
Source: U.S. Census Bureau, 2019-2023 American Community Survey 5-Year Estimates

HEALTH

Health Risk Factors

Category	MSA[1] (%)	U.S. (%)
Adults aged 18–64 who have any kind of health care coverage	93.6	90.8
Adults who reported being in good or better health	84.5	81.8
Adults who have been told they have high blood cholesterol	36.0	36.9
Adults who have been told they have high blood pressure	28.7	34.0
Adults who are current smokers	7.7	12.1
Adults who currently use e-cigarettes	5.7	7.7
Adults who currently use chewing tobacco, snuff, or snus	0.9	3.2
Adults who are heavy drinkers[2]	n/a	6.1
Adults who are binge drinkers[3]	11.5	15.2
Adults who are overweight (BMI 25.0 - 29.9)	31.2	34.4
Adults who are obese (BMI 30.0 - 99.8)	24.6	34.3
Adults who participated in any physical activities in the past month	80.4	75.8

Note: All figures are crude prevalence; (1) Figures cover the San Jose-Sunnyvale-Santa Clara, CA Metropolitan Statistical Area; (2) Heavy drinkers are classified as adult men having more than 14 drinks per week and adult women having more than 7 drinks per week; (3) Binge drinkers are classified as males having five or more drinks on one occasion or females having four or more drinks on one occasion
Source: Centers for Disease Control and Prevention, Behaviorial Risk Factor Surveillance System, SMART: Selected Metropolitan Area Risk Trends, 2023

Acute and Chronic Health Conditions

Category	MSA[1] (%)	U.S. (%)
Adults who have ever been told they had a heart attack	1.5	4.2
Adults who have ever been told they have angina or coronary heart disease	n/a	4.0
Adults who have ever been told they had a stroke	n/a	3.3
Adults who have ever been told they have asthma	14.6	15.7
Adults who have ever been told they have arthritis	17.3	26.3
Adults who have ever been told they have diabetes[2]	10.4	11.5
Adults who have ever been told they had skin cancer	4.3	5.6
Adults who have ever been told they had any other types of cancer	5.0	8.4
Adults who have ever been told they have COPD	n/a	6.4
Adults who have ever been told they have kidney disease	n/a	3.7
Adults who have ever been told they have a form of depression	16.0	22.0

Note: All figures are crude prevalence; (1) Figures cover the San Jose-Sunnyvale-Santa Clara, CA Metropolitan Statistical Area; (2) Figures do not include pregnancy-related, borderline, or pre-diabetes
Source: Centers for Disease Control and Prevention, Behaviorial Risk Factor Surveillance System, SMART: Selected Metropolitan Area Risk Trends, 2023

Health Screening and Vaccination Rates

Category	MSA[1] (%)	U.S. (%)
Adults who have ever been tested for HIV	34.5	37.5
Adults who have had their blood cholesterol checked within the last five years	87.8	87.0
Adults aged 65+ who have had flu shot within the past year	69.2	63.4
Adults aged 65+ who have ever had a pneumonia vaccination	79.7	71.9

Note: All figures are crude prevalence; (1) Figures cover the San Jose-Sunnyvale-Santa Clara, CA Metropolitan Statistical Area.
Source: Centers for Disease Control and Prevention, Behaviorial Risk Factor Surveillance System, SMART: Selected Metropolitan Area Risk Trends, 2023

Disability Status

Category	MSA[1] (%)	U.S. (%)
Adults who reported being deaf	5.6	7.4
Are you blind or have serious difficulty seeing, even when wearing glasses?	2.8	4.9
Do you have difficulty doing errands alone?	3.8	7.8
Do you have difficulty dressing or bathing?	1.9	3.6
Do you have serious difficulty concentrating/remembering/making decisions?	9.6	13.7
Do you have serious difficulty walking or climbing stairs?	8.4	13.2

Note: All figures are crude prevalence; (1) Figures cover the San Jose-Sunnyvale-Santa Clara, CA Metropolitan Statistical Area.
Source: Centers for Disease Control and Prevention, Behaviorial Risk Factor Surveillance System, SMART: Selected Metropolitan Area Risk Trends, 2023

Mortality Rates for the Top 10 Causes of Death in the U.S.

ICD-10[a] Sub-Chapter	ICD-10[a] Code	Crude Mortality Rate[2] per 100,000 population	
		County[3]	U.S.
Malignant neoplasms	C00-C97	125.8	182.7
Ischaemic heart diseases	I20-I25	59.5	109.6
Provisional assignment of new diseases of uncertain etiology[1]	U00-U49	35.5	65.3
Other forms of heart disease	I30-I51	24.7	65.1
Other degenerative diseases of the nervous system	G30-G31	61.3	52.4
Other external causes of accidental injury	W00-X59	30.5	52.3
Cerebrovascular diseases	I60-I69	38.6	49.1
Chronic lower respiratory diseases	J40-J47	16.2	43.5
Hypertensive diseases	I10-I15	47.6	38.9
Organic, including symptomatic, mental disorders	F01-F09	3.5	33.9

Note: (a) ICD-10 = International Classification of Diseases 10th Revision; (1) Includes COVID-19, adverse effects to COVID-19 vaccines, SARS, and vaping-related disorders; (2) Crude mortality rates are a three-year average covering 2021-2023; (3) Figures cover Santa Clara County.
Source: Centers for Disease Control and Prevention, National Center for Health Statistics. National Vital Statistics System, Mortality 2018-2023 on CDC WONDER Online Database

Mortality Rates for Selected Causes of Death

Cause of Death	ICD-10[a] Code	Crude Mortality Rate[1] per 100,000 population	
		County[2]	U.S.
Accidental poisoning and exposure to noxious substances	X40-X49	17.1	30.5
Alzheimer disease	G30	30.2	35.4
Assault	X85-Y09	2.4	7.3
COVID-19	U07.1	35.5	65.3
Diabetes mellitus	E10-E14	23.2	30.0
Diseases of the liver	K70-K76	11.4	20.8
Human immunodeficiency virus (HIV) disease	B20-B24	0.5	1.5
Influenza and pneumonia	J09-J18	6.0	13.4
Intentional self-harm	X60-X84	8.4	14.7
Malnutrition	E40-E46	1.3	6.0
Obesity and other hyperalimentation	E65-E68	1.4	3.1
Renal failure	N17-N19	6.4	16.4
Transport accidents	V01-V99	8.4	14.4

Note: (a) ICD-10 = International Classification of Diseases 10th Revision; (1) Crude mortality rates are a three-year average covering 2021-2023; (2) Figures cover Santa Clara County; Data are suppressed when the data meet the criteria for confidentiality constraints; Crude mortality rates are flagged as unreliable when the rate would be calculated with a numerator of 20 or less.
Source: Centers for Disease Control and Prevention, National Center for Health Statistics. National Vital Statistics System, Mortality 2018-2023 on CDC WONDER Online Database

Health Insurance Coverage

Area	With Health Insurance	With Private Health Insurance	With Public Health Insurance	Without Health Insurance	Population Under Age 19 Without Health Insurance
City	95.1	72.5	30.6	4.9	1.8
MSA[1]	95.9	77.1	27.4	4.1	1.8
U.S.	91.4	67.3	36.3	8.6	5.4

Note: Figures are percentages that cover the civilian noninstitutionalized population; (1) Figures cover the San Jose-Sunnyvale-Santa Clara, CA Metropolitan Statistical Area
Source: U.S. Census Bureau, 2019-2023 American Community Survey 5-Year Estimates

Number of Medical Professionals

Area	MDs[3]	DOs[3,4]	Dentists	Podiatrists	Chiropractors	Optometrists
County[1] (number)	9,051	272	2,430	139	882	577
County[1] (rate[2])	483.8	14.5	129.4	7.4	47.0	30.7
U.S. (rate[2])	302.5	29.2	74.6	6.4	29.5	18.0

Note: Data as of 2023 unless noted; (1) Data covers Santa Clara County; (2) Number of medical professionals per 100,000 population; (3) Data as of 2022 and includes all active, non-federal physicians; (4) Doctor of Osteopathic Medicine
Source: U.S. Department of Health and Human Services, Health Resources and Services Administration, Bureau of Health Professions, Area Resource File (ARF) 2023-2024

Best Hospitals

According to *U.S. News,* the San Jose-Sunnyvale-Santa Clara, CA metro area is home to three of the best hospitals in the U.S.: **Byers Eye Institute, Stanford Health Care** (11 adult specialties); **Santa Clara Valley Medical Center** (1 adult specialty); **Stanford Health Care-Stanford Hospital** (Honor Roll/11 adult specialties). The hospitals listed were nationally ranked in at least one of 15 adult or 11 pediatric specialties. The number of specialties shown cover the parent hospital. Only 160 U.S. hospitals performed well enough to be nationally ranked in one or more specialties. Twenty hospitals in the U.S. made the Honor Roll. The Best Hospitals Honor Roll takes both the national rankings and the procedure and condition ratings into account. Hospitals received points if they were nationally ranked in one of the 15 adult specialties—the higher they ranked, the more points they got—and how many ratings of "high performing" they earned in the 20 procedures and conditions. *U.S. News Online, "America's Best Hospitals 2024-25"*

According to *U.S. News,* the San Jose-Sunnyvale-Santa Clara, CA metro area is home to one of the best children's hospitals in the U.S.: **Lucile Packard Children's Hospital Stanford** (11 pediatric specialties). The hospital listed was highly ranked in at least one of 11 pediatric specialties. One hundred five children's hospitals in the U.S. were nationally ranked in at least one specialty. Hospitals received points for being ranked in a specialty, and the 10 hospitals with the most points across the 11 specialties make up the Honor Roll. *U.S. News Online, "America's Best Children's Hospitals 2024-25"*

EDUCATION

Public School District Statistics

District Name	Schls	Pupils	Pupil/ Teacher Ratio	Minority Pupils[1] (%)	Total Rev. per Pupil ($)	Total Exp. per Pupil ($)
Alum Rock Union Elementary	22	7,367	19.6	98.5	22,377	19,026
Berryessa Union Elementary	14	6,026	23.8	95.6	16,379	18,676
Cambrian	6	3,014	22.6	69.3	18,503	17,376
Campbell Union High	6	8,613	21.8	70.8	24,422	26,391
East Side Union High	16	20,471	21.5	95.3	21,623	21,090
Evergreen Elementary	16	8,779	23.3	96.0	16,469	16,624
Franklin-Mckinley Elementary	16	5,766	19.7	98.2	23,199	21,746
Moreland	7	3,863	20.3	81.3	21,070	19,773
Oak Grove Elementary	18	8,714	24.1	87.2	19,182	16,643
San Jose Unified	41	25,059	21.1	79.0	20,728	17,538
Union Elementary	8	5,371	23.7	67.9	17,236	16,544

Note: Table includes school districts with 2,000 or more students; (1) Percentage of students that are not non-Hispanic white.
Source: U.S. Department of Education, National Center for Education Statistics, Common Core of Data, Local Education Agency (School District) Universe Survey: School Year 2023-2024; U.S. Department of Education, National Center for Education Statistics, Common Core of Data, School District Finance Survey (F-33): School Year 2021–22

Best High Schools

According to *U.S. News,* San Jose is home to six of the top 500 high schools in the U.S.: **Lynbrook High School** (#82); **University Preparatory Academy Charter** (#247); **Evergreen Valley High School** (#369); **Leland High School** (#375); **Kipp Navigate College Prep** (#415); **KIPP San Jose Collegiate** (#477). Nearly 25,000 public, magnet and charter schools were ranked based on their performance on state assessments and how well they prepare students for college. *U.S. News & World Report, "Best High Schools 2024"*

Highest Level of Education

Area	Less than H.S.	H.S. Diploma	Some College, No Deg.	Associate Degree	Bachelor's Degree	Master's Degree	Prof. School Degree	Doctorate Degree
City	14.5	16.4	15.5	7.1	26.2	15.1	2.1	3.1
MSA[1]	10.9	13.9	13.9	6.5	27.8	19.3	2.9	4.8
U.S.	10.6	26.2	19.4	8.8	21.3	9.8	2.3	1.6

Note: Figures cover persons age 25 and over; (1) Figures cover the San Jose-Sunnyvale-Santa Clara, CA Metropolitan Statistical Area
Source: U.S. Census Bureau, 2019-2023 American Community Survey 5-Year Estimates

Educational Attainment by Race

Area	High School Graduate or Higher (%)					Bachelor's Degree or Higher (%)				
	Total	White	Black	Asian	Hisp.[2]	Total	White	Black	Asian	Hisp.[2]
City	85.5	93.1	90.1	88.3	69.6	46.5	51.5	37.5	59.7	17.5
MSA[1]	89.1	94.7	92.0	91.9	72.1	54.8	57.5	42.1	69.5	20.2
U.S.	89.4	92.9	88.1	88.0	72.5	35.0	37.7	24.7	57.0	19.9

Note: Figures shown cover persons 25 years old and over; (1) Figures cover the San Jose-Sunnyvale-Santa Clara, CA Metropolitan Statistical Area; (2) People of Hispanic origin can be of any race
Source: U.S. Census Bureau, 2019-2023 American Community Survey 5-Year Estimates

School Enrollment by Grade and Control

Area	Preschool (%)		Kindergarten (%)		Grades 1 - 4 (%)		Grades 5 - 8 (%)		Grades 9 - 12 (%)	
	Public	Private	Public	Private	Public	Private	Public	Private	Public	Private
City	43.5	56.5	83.1	16.9	86.1	13.9	87.4	12.6	87.1	12.9
MSA[1]	36.2	63.8	80.1	19.9	84.7	15.3	85.9	14.1	86.5	13.5
U.S.	58.7	41.3	85.2	14.8	87.2	12.8	87.9	12.1	89.0	11.0

Note: Figures shown cover persons 3 years old and over; (1) Figures cover the San Jose-Sunnyvale-Santa Clara, CA Metropolitan Statistical Area
Source: U.S. Census Bureau, 2019-2023 American Community Survey 5-Year Estimates

Higher Education

Four-Year Colleges			Two-Year Colleges			Medical Schools[1]	Law Schools[2]	Voc/ Tech[3]
Public	Private Non-profit	Private For-profit	Public	Private Non-profit	Private For-profit			
2	5	0	6	2	0	1	3	3

Note: Figures cover institutions located within the San Jose-Sunnyvale-Santa Clara, CA Metropolitan Statistical Area and include main campuses only; (1) includes schools accredited by the Liaison Committee on Medical Education and the American Osteopathic Association's Commission on Osteopathic College Accreditation; (2) includes ABA-accredited schools, schools with provisional ABA accreditation, and state accredited schools; (3) includes all schools with programs that are less than 2 years.
Source: National Center for Education Statistics, Integrated Postsecondary Education System (IPEDS), 2023-24; Wikipedia, List of Medical Schools in the United States, accessed May 2, 2025; Wikipedia, List of Law Schools in the United States, accessed May 2, 2025

According to *U.S. News & World Report,* the San Jose-Sunnyvale-Santa Clara, CA metro area is home to two of the top 200 national universities in the U.S.: **Stanford University** (#4); **Santa Clara University** (#63 tie). The indicators used to capture academic quality fall into a number of categories: assessment by administrators at peer institutions; retention of students; faculty resources; student selectivity; financial resources; alumni giving; high school counselor ratings of colleges; and graduation rate. *U.S. News & World Report, "America's Best Colleges 2025"*

According to *U.S. News & World Report,* the San Jose-Sunnyvale-Santa Clara, CA metro area is home to one of the top 100 law schools in the U.S.: **Stanford University** 1 (#1 tie). The rankings are based on a weighted average of 12 measures of quality: peer assessment score; assessment score by lawyers/judges; median LSAT scores; median undergrad GPA; acceptance rate; employment rates for graduates; placement success; bar passage rate; faculty resources; expenditures per student; student/faculty ratio; and library resources. *U.S. News & World Report, "America's Best Graduate Schools, Law, 2025"*

According to *U.S. News & World Report,* the San Jose-Sunnyvale-Santa Clara, CA metro area is home to one of the top 75 business schools in the U.S.: **Stanford University** (#2 tie). The rankings are based on a weighted average of the following nine measures: quality assessment; peer assessment; recruiter assessment; placement success; mean starting salary and bonus; student selectivity; mean GMAT and GRE scores; mean undergraduate GPA; and acceptance rate. *U.S. News & World Report, "America's Best Graduate Schools, Business, 2025"*

EMPLOYERS

Major Employers

Company Name	Industry
Adobe Systems Inc	Publishers-computer software, mfg
Advanced Micro Devices Inc	Semiconductor devices, mfg
Apple Inc	Computers-electronic-manufacturers
Applied Materials	Semiconductor manufacturing equip, mfg
California's Great America	Amusement & theme parks
Christopher Ranch	Garlic manufacturers
Cisco Systems Inc	Computer peripherals
Ebay	E-commerce
Flextronics	Solar energy equipment-manufacturers
General Motors Advanced Tech	Automobile manufacturing
Google	Information & technology
Hewlett-Packard Co.	Computers-electronic-manufacturers
Intel Corporation	Semiconductor devices, mfg
Kaiser Permanente Medical Center	General medical & surgical hospitals
Lockheed Martin Space Systems	Satellite equipment & systems, mfg
Microsoft	Computer software-manufacturers
NASA	Government offices, federal
Net App Inc	Computer storage devices
PayPal	Software and tech services
Western Digital	Computer storage

Note: Companies shown are located within the San Jose-Sunnyvale-Santa Clara, CA Metropolitan Statistical Area.
Source: Chambers of Commerce; State Departments of Labor; Wikipedia

Best Companies to Work For

Adobe; Cadence; Cisco, headquartered in San Jose, are among "The 100 Best Companies to Work For." To pick the best companies, *Fortune* partnered with the Great Place to Work Institute. Using their proprietary Trust Index™ survey, the core of what creates great a workplace is measured—key behaviors that drive trust in management, connection with colleagues, and loyalty to the company. To be eligible for the *Fortune* 100 Best Companies to Work For list, employers must have 1,000 or more employees in the U.S. and cannot be a government agency. *Fortune, "The 100 Best Companies to Work For," 2025*

Adobe; Calix; Cisco, headquartered in San Jose, are among "Fortune's Best Workplaces for Parents." To pick the best companies, *Fortune* partnered with the Great Place to Work Institute. To be considered for the list, companies must be Great Place To Work-Certified and have at least 50 responses from parents in the US. The survey enables employees to share confidential quantitative and qualitative feedback about their organization's culture by responding to 60 statements on a 5-point scale and answering two open-ended questions. Collectively, these statements describe a great employee experience, defined by high levels of trust, respect, credibility, fairness, pride, and camaraderie. In addition, companies provide organizational data like size, location, industry, demographics, roles, and levels; and provide information about parental leave, adoption, flexible schedule, childcare and dependent health care benefits. *Fortune, "Best Workplaces for Parents," 2024*

Cisco, headquartered in San Jose, is among "Fortune's Best Workplaces for Women." To pick the best companies, *Fortune* partnered with the Great Place to Work Institute. To be considered for the list, companies must be Great Place To Work-Certified. Companies must also employ at least 50 women, at least 20% of their non-executive managers must be female, and at least one executive must be female. To determine the Best Workplaces for Women, Great Place To Work measured the differences in women's survey responses to those of their peers and assesses the impact of demographics and roles on the quality and consistency of women's experiences. Great Place To Work also analyzed the gender balance of each workplace, how it compared to each company's industry, and patterns in representation as women rise from front-line positions to the board of directors. *Fortune, "Best Workplaces for Women," 2024*

PUBLIC SAFETY

Crime Rate

Area	Total Crime Rate	Violent Crime Rate				Property Crime Rate		
		Murder	Rape	Robbery	Aggrav. Assault	Burglary	Larceny -Theft	Motor Vehicle Theft
City	3,178.2	3.7	93.4	132.1	298.2	405.9	1,568.7	676.1
U.S.	2,362.5	6.5	42.1	67.1	273.0	272.7	1,416.6	284.5

Note: Figures are crimes per 100,000 population and cover 2022. Data for 2023 was not available.
Source: FBI, Table 8, Offenses Known to Law Enforcement, by State by City, 2022

Hate Crimes

Area	Number of Quarters Reported	Number of Incidents per Bias Motivation					
		Race/Ethnicity/ Ancestry	Religion	Sexual Orientation	Disability	Gender	Gender Identity
City[1]	4	38	6	20	2	1	1
U.S.	4	5,900	2,699	2,077	187	92	492

Note: (1) Figures include at least one incident reported with more than one bias motivation.
Source: Federal Bureau of Investigation, Hate Crime Statistics 2023

Identity Theft Consumer Reports

Area	Reports	Reports per 100,000 Population	Rank[2]
MSA[1]	4,515	229	119
U.S.	1,135,291	339	-

Note: (1) Figures cover the San Jose-Sunnyvale-Santa Clara, CA Metropolitan Statistical Area; (2) Rank ranges from 1 to 401 where 1 indicates greatest number of identity theft reports per 100,000 population
Source: Federal Trade Commission, Consumer Sentinel Network Data Book 2024

Fraud and Other Consumer Reports

Area	Reports	Reports per 100,000 Population	Rank[2]
MSA[1]	22,452	1,140	148
U.S.	5,360,641	1,601	-

Note: (1) Figures cover the San Jose-Sunnyvale-Santa Clara, CA Metropolitan Statistical Area; (2) Rank ranges from 1 to 401 where 1 indicates greatest number of fraud and other consumer reports per 100,000 population
Source: Federal Trade Commission, Consumer Sentinel Network Data Book 2024

POLITICS

2024 Presidential Election Results

Area	Trump (Rep.)	Harris (Dem.)	Stein (Green)	Kennedy (Ind.)	Oliver (Lib.)	Other
Santa Clara County	28.1	68.0	1.6	1.2	0.5	0.5
U.S.	49.7	48.2	0.6	0.5	0.4	0.6

Note: Results are percentages and may not add to 100% due to rounding
Source: Dave Leip's Atlas of U.S. Presidential Elections

SPORTS

Professional Sports Teams

Team Name	League	Year Established
San Jose Earthquakes	Major League Soccer (MLS)	1996
San Jose Sharks	National Hockey League (NHL)	1991

Note: Includes teams located in the San Jose-Sunnyvale-Santa Clara, CA Metropolitan Statistical Area.
Source: Wikipedia, Major Professional Sports Teams of the United States and Canada, May 1, 2025

CLIMATE

Average and Extreme Temperatures

Temperature	Jan	Feb	Mar	Apr	May	Jun	Jul	Aug	Sep	Oct	Nov	Dec	Yr.
Extreme High (°F)	76	82	83	95	103	104	105	101	105	100	87	76	105
Average High (°F)	57	61	63	67	70	74	75	75	76	72	65	58	68
Average Temp. (°F)	50	53	55	58	61	65	66	67	66	63	56	50	59
Average Low (°F)	42	45	46	48	51	55	57	58	57	53	47	42	50
Extreme Low (°F)	21	26	30	32	38	43	45	47	41	33	29	23	21

Note: Figures cover the years 1945-1993
Source: National Climatic Data Center, International Station Meteorological Climate Summary, 9/96

Average Precipitation/Snowfall/Humidity

Precip./Humidity	Jan	Feb	Mar	Apr	May	Jun	Jul	Aug	Sep	Oct	Nov	Dec	Yr.
Avg. Precip. (in.)	2.7	2.3	2.2	0.9	0.3	0.1	Tr	Tr	0.2	0.7	1.7	2.3	13.5
Avg. Snowfall (in.)	Tr	Tr	Tr	0	0	0	0	0	0	0	0	Tr	Tr
Avg. Rel. Hum. 7am (%)	82	82	80	76	74	73	77	79	79	79	81	82	79
Avg. Rel. Hum. 4pm (%)	62	59	56	52	53	54	58	58	55	54	59	63	57

Note: Figures cover the years 1945-1993; Tr = Trace amounts (<0.05 in. of rain; <0.5 in. of snow)
Source: National Climatic Data Center, International Station Meteorological Climate Summary, 9/96

Weather Conditions

Temperature			Daytime Sky			Precipitation		
10°F & below	32°F & below	90°F & above	Clear	Partly cloudy	Cloudy	0.01 inch or more precip.	0.1 inch or more snow/ice	Thunder-storms
0	5	5	106	180	79	57	< 1	6

Note: Figures are average number of days per year and cover the years 1945-1993
Source: National Climatic Data Center, International Station Meteorological Climate Summary, 9/96

HAZARDOUS WASTE

Superfund Sites

The San Jose-Sunnyvale-Santa Clara, CA metro area is home to 22 sites on the EPA's Superfund National Priorities List (NPL) or Superfund Alternative Approach (SAA) list: **Advanced Micro Devices, Inc.** (Final NPL); **Advanced Micro Devices, Inc. (Building 915)** (Final NPL); **Applied Materials** (Final NPL); **CTS Printex, Inc.** (Final NPL); **Fairchild Semiconductor Corp. (Mountain View Plant)** (Final NPL); **Fairchild Semiconductor Corp. (South San Jose Plant)** (Final NPL); **Hewlett-Packard (620-640 Page Mill Road)** (Final NPL); **Intel Corp. (Mountain View Plant)** (Final NPL); **Intel Magnetics** (Final NPL); **Intersil Inc./Siemens Components** (Final NPL); **Lorentz Barrel & Drum Co.** (Final NPL); **Moffett Field Naval Air Station** (Final NPL); **Monolithic Memories** (Final NPL); **National Semiconductor Corp.** (Final NPL); **New Idria Mercury Mine** (Final NPL); **Raytheon Corp.** (Final NPL); **South Bay Asbestos Area** (Final NPL); **Spectra-physics, Inc.** (Final NPL); **Synertek, Inc. (Building 1)** (Final NPL); **Teledyne Semiconductor** (Final NPL); **Trw Microwave, Inc (Building 825)** (Final NPL); **Westinghouse Electric Corp. (Sunnyvale Plant)** (Final NPL). The Superfund alternative approach uses the same investigation and cleanup process and standards that are used for sites listed on the National Priorities List. The SAA is an alternative to listing a site on the NPL; it is not an alternative to Superfund or the Superfund process. There are a total of 1,445 Superfund sites with a status of proposed or final on both lists in the United States. *U.S. Environmental Protection Agency, National Priorities List, May 1, 2025; U.S. Environmental Protection Agency, Superfund Alternative Approach Sites, May 1, 2025*

AIR QUALITY

Air Quality Trends: Ozone

	1990	1995	2000	2005	2010	2015	2020	2021	2022	2023
MSA[1]	0.078	0.084	0.065	0.063	0.072	0.067	0.066	0.067	0.062	0.057
U.S.	0.087	0.089	0.081	0.080	0.072	0.068	0.066	0.067	0.067	0.070

Note: (1) Data covers the San Jose-Sunnyvale-Santa Clara, CA Metropolitan Statistical Area. The values shown are the composite ozone concentration averages among trend sites based on the highest fourth daily maximum 8-hour concentration in parts per million. These trends are based on sites having an adequate record of monitoring data during the trend period. Data from exceptional events are included.
Source: U.S. Environmental Protection Agency, Air Quality Monitoring Information, "Air Quality Trends by City, 1990-2023"

Air Quality Index

Area	Percent of Days when Air Quality was...[2]					AQI Statistics[2]	
	Good	Moderate	Unhealthy for Sensitive Groups	Unhealthy	Very Unhealthy	Maximum	Median
MSA[1]	61.6	37.3	1.1	0.0	0.0	134	45

Note: (1) Data covers the San Jose-Sunnyvale-Santa Clara, CA Metropolitan Statistical Area; (2) Based on 365 days with AQI data in 2023. Air Quality Index (AQI) is an index for reporting daily air quality. EPA calculates the AQI for five major air pollutants regulated by the Clean Air Act: ground-level ozone, particle pollution (aka particulate matter), carbon monoxide, sulfur dioxide, and nitrogen dioxide. The AQI runs from 0 to 500. The higher the AQI value, the greater the level of air pollution and the greater the health concern. There are six AQI categories: "Good" AQI is between 0 and 50. Air quality is considered satisfactory; "Moderate" AQI is between 51 and 100. Air quality is acceptable; "Unhealthy for Sensitive Groups" When AQI values are between 101 and 150, members of sensitive groups may experience health effects; "Unhealthy" When AQI values are between 151 and 200 everyone may begin to experience health effects; "Very Unhealthy" AQI values between 201 and 300 trigger a health alert; "Hazardous" AQI values over 300 trigger warnings of emergency conditions (not shown).
Source: U.S. Environmental Protection Agency, Air Quality Index Report, 2023

Air Quality Index Pollutants

Area	Percent of Days when AQI Pollutant was...[2]					
	Carbon Monoxide	Nitrogen Dioxide	Ozone	Sulfur Dioxide	Particulate Matter 2.5	Particulate Matter 10
MSA[1]	0.0	0.0	57.5	(3)	41.9	0.5

Note: (1) Data covers the San Jose-Sunnyvale-Santa Clara, CA Metropolitan Statistical Area; (2) Based on 365 days with AQI data in 2023. The Air Quality Index (AQI) is an index for reporting daily air quality. EPA calculates the AQI for five major air pollutants regulated by the Clean Air Act: ground-level ozone, particle pollution (also known as particulate matter), carbon monoxide, sulfur dioxide, and nitrogen dioxide. The AQI runs from 0 to 500. The higher the AQI value, the greater the level of air pollution and the greater the health concern; (3) Sulfur dioxide is no longer included in this table because SO_2 concentrations tend to be very localized and not necessarily representative of broad geographical areas like counties and CBSAs.
Source: U.S. Environmental Protection Agency, Air Quality Index Report, 2023

Maximum Air Pollutant Concentrations: Particulate Matter, Ozone, CO and Lead

	Particulate Matter 10 (ug/m³)	Particulate Matter 2.5 Wtd AM (ug/m³)	Particulate Matter 2.5 24-Hr (ug/m³)	Ozone (ppm)	Carbon Monoxide (ppm)	Lead (ug/m³)
MSA[1] Level	59	8.2	25	0.067	1	0.02
NAAQS[2]	150	15	35	0.075	9	0.15
Met NAAQS[2]	Yes	Yes	Yes	Yes	Yes	Yes

Note: (1) Data covers the San Jose-Sunnyvale-Santa Clara, CA Metropolitan Statistical Area; Data from exceptional events are included; (2) National Ambient Air Quality Standards; ppm = parts per million; ug/m³ = micrograms per cubic meter; n/a not available.
Concentrations: Particulate Matter 10 (coarse particulate)—highest second maximum 24-hour concentration; Particulate Matter 2.5 Wtd AM (fine particulate)—highest weighted annual mean concentration; Particulate Matter 2.5 24-Hour (fine particulate)—highest 98th percentile 24-hour concentration; Ozone—highest fourth daily maximum 8-hour concentration; Carbon Monoxide—highest second maximum non-overlapping 8-hour concentration; Lead—maximum running 3-month average
Source: U.S. Environmental Protection Agency, Air Quality Monitoring Information, "Air Quality Statistics by City, 2023"

Maximum Air Pollutant Concentrations: Nitrogen Dioxide and Sulfur Dioxide

	Nitrogen Dioxide AM (ppb)	Nitrogen Dioxide 1-Hr (ppb)	Sulfur Dioxide AM (ppb)	Sulfur Dioxide 1-Hr (ppb)	Sulfur Dioxide 24-Hr (ppb)
MSA[1] Level	13	44	n/a	2	n/a
NAAQS[2]	53	100	30	75	140
Met NAAQS[2]	Yes	Yes	n/a	Yes	n/a

Note: (1) Data covers the San Jose-Sunnyvale-Santa Clara, CA Metropolitan Statistical Area; Data from exceptional events are included; (2) National Ambient Air Quality Standards; ppm = parts per million; ug/m³ = micrograms per cubic meter; n/a not available.
Concentrations: Nitrogen Dioxide AM—highest arithmetic mean concentration; Nitrogen Dioxide 1-Hr—highest 98th percentile 1-hour daily maximum concentration; Sulfur Dioxide AM—highest annual mean concentration; Sulfur Dioxide 1-Hr—highest 99th percentile 1-hour daily maximum concentration; Sulfur Dioxide 24-Hr—highest second maximum 24-hour concentration
Source: U.S. Environmental Protection Agency, Air Quality Monitoring Information, "Air Quality Statistics by City, 2023"

Santa Rosa, California

Background

Santa Rosa is located 55 miles north of San Francisco in the county seat of Sonoma County and home to one-third of the county's residents. The city is part of both the San Francisco Bay Area and the California wine country. The popularity of the vineyards, especially among tourists, has helped the city evolve from a small farming town during the California gold rush to a thriving, modern city known for its climate, location, and natural beauty.

During the early days of European exploration, the area that is now Santa Rosa was a homestead for wealthy and prominent families, both under Mexican and Spanish rule. In 1852, the Mexican American War ended, and the territory of California became part of the United States. Around this time, the California Gold Rush brought large numbers of new settlers to the area. As the gold rush waned, explorers found they could make more money farming than they could digging for gold. The community began to grow, and Santa Rosa was officially incorporated 1868. That same year, the first railroad line reached the city, a main reason for its population to increase tenfold in just seven years.

During the twentieth century, population began to level off, and Santa Rosa settled into a medium-sized city that affords residents the benefits of a larger urban center. At the end of the twentieth century, population began increasing rapidly. To plan for future growth, the city launched the *Santa Rosa 2030 Vision* and in 2017 annexed the community of Roseland in its quest for more land.

The city has two Sonoma-Marin Area Rail transit (SMART) stations—one downtown and the other in North Santa Rosa—enhancing pedestrian-friendly neighborhoods.

Downtown Santa Rosa includes the central Old Courthouse Square and historic Railroad Square area of shopping, restaurants, nightclubs, and theaters. The city's health major employers include Keysight Technologies, Kaiser Permanente, Santa Rosa Community Junior College, Santa Rose Schools, and Sutter Health.

The city's natural beauty and highly regarded vineyards make Santa Rosa a popular destination for tourists and wine enthusiasts. In addition to wine production, major attractions in Santa Rosa include the Luther Burbank Home and Gardens, Redwood Empire Ice Arena, Sonoma County Museum, and 6th Street Playhouse. The city is also home to the Charles M. Schulz Museum and Research Center, which celebrates the life and work of the Peanuts comic strip and its creator, who lived in Santa Rosa for over 30 years. In 2000, the city renamed its airport "Charles M. Schulz Sonoma County Airport," which is served by Alaska Airlines, with destinations that include San Diego, Los Angeles, Portland, and Seattle.

Institutions of higher learning in the city include the University of San Francisco Santa Rosa, Empire College, and Santa Rosa Junior College.

Santa Rosa has a warm-summer climate with cool, wet winters and warm, dry summers. In the summer, fog and low overcast often move in from the Pacific Ocean during the evenings and mornings. They usually clear up to very warm, sunny weather by late morning, occasionally lingering all day. In October 2017, five percent of the city's homes were destroyed and 19 people died in the Tubbs Fire, a major section of one of the most destructive firestorms in California history. Average annual rainfall is about 32 inches. Measurable snowfall is extremely rare in the lowlands, with light snowfall sometimes falling in the nearby mountains.

Rankings

Business/Finance Rankings

- According to *Business Insider*, the Santa Rosa metro area is a prime place to run a startup or move an existing business to. The area ranked #8. More than 300 metro areas were analyzed for factors that were of top concern to new business owners. Data was based on the 2019 U.S. Census Bureau American Community Survey, statistics from the CDC, and University of Chicago analysis. Criteria: business formations; percentage of vaccinated population; percentage of households with internet subscriptions; median household income; and share of work that can be done from home. *BusinessInsider.com, "The 20 Best Cities for Starting a Business in 2022 Include Denver, Raleigh, and Olympia," June 7, 2022*

- The Santa Rosa metro area appeared on the Milken Institute "2025 Best Performing Cities" list. Rank: #132 out of 200 large metro areas (based on performance category). Criteria: job growth; wage growth; high-tech growth and impact; community resilience; housing affordability; household broadband access. *Milken Institute, "Best-Performing Cities 2025," January 14, 2025*

Education Rankings

- Personal finance website *WalletHub* analyzed the 150 largest U.S. metropolitan statistical areas to determine where the most educated Americans are putting their degrees to work. Criteria: education levels; percentage of workers with degrees; education quality and attainment gap; public school quality rankings; quality and enrollment of each metro area's universities. Santa Rosa was ranked #52 (#1 = most educated city). *WalletHub.com, "Most & Least Educated Cities in America, 2025" July 2, 2024*

Environmental Rankings

- Santa Rosa was highlighted as one of the cleanest metro areas for ozone air pollution in the U.S. during 2021 through 2023. The list represents cities with no monitored ozone air pollution in unhealthful ranges. *American Lung Association, "State of the Air 2025," April 23, 2025*

- Santa Rosa was highlighted as one of the top 25 cleanest metro areas for year-round particle pollution (Annual PM 2.5) in the U.S. during 2021 through 2023. The area ranked #19. *American Lung Association, "State of the Air 2025," April 23, 2025*

Pet Rankings

- Santa Rosa was selected by *Sniffspot.com* as one of the most dog-friendly cities in the U.S., ranking #29 out of 50. Criteria: dog parks; hiking; sniffspots; public parks; dog-friendly businesses; housing; dog waste cleanliness; leash laws; dog services; and overall cost. *Sniffspot.com, "The Top 50 Most Dog-Friendly Cities in the U.S.," September 30, 2024*

Real Estate Rankings

- *WalletHub* compared the most populated U.S. cities to determine which had the best markets for real estate agents. Santa Rosa ranked #43 where demand was high and pay was the best. Criteria: sales per agent; annual median wage for real-estate agents; monthly average starting salary for real estate agents; real estate job density and competition; unemployment rate; home turnover rate; housing-market health index; and other relevant metrics. *WalletHub.com, "2021 Best Places to Be a Real Estate Agent," May 12, 2021*

Women/Minorities Rankings

- Personal finance website *WalletHub* compared more than 180 U.S. cities across two key dimensions, "Hispanic Business-Friendliness" and "Hispanic Purchasing Power," to arrive at the most favorable conditions for Hispanic entrepreneurs. Santa Rosa was ranked #75 out of 182. Criteria includes: share of Hispanic-Owned Businesses; average growth of Hispanic Business revenues; Small Business-Friendliness score; affordability; and number of Hispanics with at least a bachelor's degree. *WalletHub.com, "Best Cities for Hispanic Entrepreneurs," September 4, 2024*

Business Environment

DEMOGRAPHICS

Population Growth

Area	1990 Census	2000 Census	2010 Census	2020 Census	2023 Estimate[2]	Population Growth 1990-2023 (%)
City	123,297	147,595	167,815	178,127	177,216	43.7
MSA[1]	388,222	458,614	483,878	488,863	485,642	25.1
U.S.	248,709,873	281,421,906	308,745,538	331,449,281	332,387,540	33.6

Note: (1) Figures cover the Santa Rosa-Petaluma, CA Metropolitan Statistical Area; (2) 2019-2023 5-year ACS population estimate
Source: U.S. Census Bureau, 1990 Census, 2000 Census, 2010 Census, 2020 Census, 2019-2023 American Community Survey 5-Year Estimates

Race

Area	White Alone[2] (%)	Black Alone[2] (%)	Asian Alone[2] (%)	AIAN[3] Alone[2] (%)	NHOPI[4] Alone[2] (%)	Other Race Alone[2] (%)	Two or More Races (%)
City	56.2	1.9	6.5	1.4	0.6	20.0	13.4
MSA[1]	64.5	1.6	4.4	1.3	0.4	14.1	13.7
U.S.	63.4	12.4	5.8	0.9	0.2	6.6	10.7

Note: (1) Figures cover the Santa Rosa-Petaluma, CA Metropolitan Statistical Area; (2) Alone is defined as not being in combination with one or more other races; (3) American Indian and Alaska Native; (4) Native Hawaiian and Other Pacific Islander
Source: U.S. Census Bureau, 2019-2023 American Community Survey 5-Year Estimates

Hispanic or Latino Origin

Area	Total (%)	Mexican (%)	Puerto Rican (%)	Cuban (%)	Other (%)
City	35.8	30.3	0.5	0.1	4.9
MSA[1]	29.4	23.7	0.4	0.2	5.1
U.S.	19.0	11.3	1.8	0.7	5.2

Note: Persons of Hispanic or Latino origin can be of any race; (1) Figures cover the Santa Rosa-Petaluma, CA Metropolitan Statistical Area
Source: U.S. Census Bureau, 2019-2023 American Community Survey 5-Year Estimates

Age

Area	Under Age 5	Age 5–19	Age 20–34	Age 35–44	Age 45–54	Age 55–64	Age 65–74	Age 75–84	Age 85+	Median Age
City	4.9	17.9	19.3	14.1	12.9	12.1	11.2	5.1	2.4	40.5
MSA[1]	4.7	17.1	17.8	13.2	12.4	14.0	12.8	5.8	2.4	42.7
U.S.	5.7	19.1	20.2	13.1	12.3	12.8	10.0	4.9	1.9	38.7

Note: (1) Figures cover the Santa Rosa-Petaluma, CA Metropolitan Statistical Area
Source: U.S. Census Bureau, 2019-2023 American Community Survey 5-Year Estimates

Disability by Age

Area	All Ages	Under 18 Years Old	18 to 64 Years Old	65 Years and Over
City	12.7	4.3	10.3	30.0
MSA[1]	12.1	4.0	9.1	28.2
U.S.	13.0	4.7	10.7	32.9

Note: Figures show percent of the civilian noninstitutionalized population that reported having a disability. Disability status is determined from six types of difficulty: vision, hearing, cognitive, ambulatory, self-care, and independent living. For children under 5 years old, hearing and vision difficulty are used to determine disability status. For children between the ages of 5 and 14, disability status is determined from hearing, vision, cognitive, ambulatory, and self-care difficulties. For people aged 15 years and older, they are considered to have a disability if they have difficulty with any one of the six difficulty types; Note: (1) Figures cover the Santa Rosa-Petaluma, CA Metropolitan Statistical Area
Source: U.S. Census Bureau, 2019-2023 American Community Survey 5-Year Estimates

Ancestry

Area	German	Irish	English	American	Italian	Polish	French[2]	European	Scottish
City	11.1	10.1	10.4	2.2	6.3	1.6	2.4	2.4	1.9
MSA[1]	12.4	12.2	11.8	2.4	7.9	1.8	2.9	3.7	2.5
U.S.	12.6	9.4	9.1	5.5	4.9	2.6	2.0	1.6	1.6

Note: Figures are the percentage of the total population reporting a particular ancestry. The nine most commonly reported ancestries in the U.S. are shown. Figures include multiple ancestries (e.g. if a person reported being Irish and Italian, they were included in both columns); (1) Figures cover the Santa Rosa-Petaluma, CA Metropolitan Statistical Area; (2) Excludes Basque
Source: U.S. Census Bureau, 2019-2023 American Community Survey 5-Year Estimates

Foreign-born Population

Area	Any Foreign Country	Percent of Population Born in							
		Asia	Mexico	Europe	Caribbean	Central America[2]	South America	Africa	Canada
City	20.8	4.7	11.5	1.5	0.1	1.4	0.3	0.6	0.3
MSA[1]	16.6	3.1	9.1	1.8	0.1	1.0	0.5	0.4	0.4
U.S.	13.9	4.3	3.3	1.4	1.4	1.2	1.2	0.8	0.2

Note: (1) Figures cover the Santa Rosa-Petaluma, CA Metropolitan Statistical Area; (2) Excludes Mexico.
Source: U.S. Census Bureau, 2019-2023 American Community Survey 5-Year Estimates

Household Size

Area	Persons in Household (%)							Average Household Size
	One	Two	Three	Four	Five	Six	Seven or More	
City	28.0	33.1	16.1	13.7	5.7	2.2	1.2	2.54
MSA[1]	27.5	35.1	15.1	13.5	5.5	2.0	1.2	2.50
U.S.	28.5	33.8	15.4	12.7	5.9	2.3	1.4	2.54

Note: (1) Figures cover the Santa Rosa-Petaluma, CA Metropolitan Statistical Area
Source: U.S. Census Bureau, 2019-2023 American Community Survey 5-Year Estimates

Household Relationships

Area	House-holder	Opposite-sex Spouse	Same-sex Spouse	Opposite-sex Unmarried Partner	Same-sex Unmarried Partner	Child[2]	Grand-child	Other Relatives	Non-relatives
City	37.6	16.2	0.4	3.0	0.2	27.3	1.8	6.2	5.5
MSA[1]	38.4	17.6	0.4	2.9	0.2	26.1	1.9	5.2	5.5
U.S.	38.3	17.5	0.2	2.5	0.2	28.3	2.4	4.8	3.4

Note: Figures are percent of the total population; (1) Figures cover the Santa Rosa-Petaluma, CA Metropolitan Statistical Area; (2) Includes biological, adopted, and stepchildren of the householder
Source: U.S. Census Bureau, 2020 Census

Gender

Area	Males	Females	Males per 100 Females
City	86,188	91,028	94.7
MSA[1]	238,817	246,825	96.8
U.S.	164,545,087	167,842,453	98.0

Note: (1) Figures cover the Santa Rosa-Petaluma, CA Metropolitan Statistical Area
Source: U.S. Census Bureau, 2019-2023 American Community Survey 5-Year Estimates

Marital Status

Area	Never Married	Now Married[2]	Separated	Widowed	Divorced
City	34.6	45.9	2.0	5.6	12.0
MSA[1]	32.7	48.5	1.4	5.2	12.2
U.S.	34.1	47.9	1.7	5.6	10.7

Note: Figures are percentages and cover the population 15 years of age and older; (1) Figures cover the Santa Rosa-Petaluma, CA Metropolitan Statistical Area; (2) Excludes separated
Source: U.S. Census Bureau, 2019-2023 American Community Survey 5-Year Estimates

Religious Groups by Family

Area	Catholic	Baptist	Methodist	LDS[2]	Pentecostal	Lutheran	Islam	Adventist	Other
MSA[1]	23.5	1.1	0.5	1.4	0.5	0.5	0.2	1.8	6.9
U.S.	18.7	7.3	3.0	2.0	1.8	1.7	1.3	1.3	11.6

Note: Figures are the number of adherents as a percentage of the total population and cover the eight largest religious groups in the U.S; (1) Figures cover the Santa Rosa-Petaluma, CA Metropolitan Statistical Area; (2) Church of Jesus Christ of Latter-day Saints
Sources: 2020 U.S. Religion Census, Association of Statisticians of American Religious Bodies; The Association of Religion Data Archives (ARDA)

Religious Groups by Tradition

Area	Catholic	Evangelical Protestant	Mainline Protestant	Black Protestant	Islam	Judaism	Hinduism	Orthodox	Buddhism
MSA[1]	23.5	5.3	1.5	<0.1	0.2	0.4	0.3	0.4	1.7
U.S.	18.7	16.5	5.2	2.3	1.3	0.6	0.4	0.4	0.3

Note: Figures are the number of adherents as a percentage of the total population; (1) Figures cover the Santa Rosa-Petaluma, CA Metropolitan Statistical Area
Sources: 2020 U.S. Religion Census, Association of Statisticians of American Religious Bodies; The Association of Religion Data Archives (ARDA)

ECONOMY

Real Gross Domestic Product (GDP)

Area	2017	2018	2019	2020	2021	2022	2023	Rank[3]
MSA[1]	28.9	30.2	30.5	29.6	31.7	31.0	31.0	106
U.S.[2]	17,619.1	18,160.7	18,642.5	18,238.9	19,387.6	19,896.6	20,436.3	–

Note: Figures are in billions of chained 2017 dollars; (1) Figures cover the Santa Rosa-Petaluma, CA Metropolitan Statistical Area; (2) Figures cover real GDP within metropolitan areas; (3) Rank is based on 2023 data and ranges from 1 to 384
Source: U.S. Bureau of Economic Analysis

Economic Growth

Area	2014	2015	2016	2017	2018	2019	2020	2021	2022	2023
MSA[1]	4.1	4.8	2.5	1.6	4.7	0.9	-3.0	7.0	-2.2	0.2
U.S.[2]	2.6	3.2	2.0	2.7	3.1	2.7	-2.2	6.3	2.6	2.7

Note: Figures are real gross domestic product growth rates and represent percent change from preceding period; (1) Figures cover the Santa Rosa-Petaluma, CA Metropolitan Statistical Area; (2) Figures are the average growth rates within metropolitan areas
Source: U.S. Bureau of Economic Analysis

Metropolitan Area Exports

Area	2018	2019	2020	2021	2022	2023	Rank[2]
MSA[1]	1,231.7	1,234.5	1,131.4	1,301.8	1,297.3	1,121.8	161
U.S.	1,664,056.1	1,645,173.7	1,431,406.6	1,753,941.4	2,062,937.4	2,019,160.5	–

Note: Figures are in millions of dollars; (1) Figures cover the Santa Rosa-Petaluma, CA Metropolitan Statistical Area; (2) Rank is based on 2023 data and ranges from 1 to 386
Source: U.S. Department of Commerce, International Trade Administration, Office of Trade and Economic Analysis, Industry and Analysis, Exports by Metropolitan Area, data extracted April 2, 2025

Building Permits

Area	Single-Family			Multi-Family			Total		
	2023	2024	Pct. Chg.	2023	2024	Pct. Chg.	2023	2024	Pct. Chg.
City	441	292	-33.8	905	0	-100.0	1,346	292	-78.3
MSA[1]	1,020	832	-18.4	1,333	180	-86.5	2,353	1,012	-57.0
U.S.	920,000	981,900	6.7	591,100	496,100	-16.1	1,511,100	1,478,000	-2.2

Note: (1) Figures cover the Santa Rosa-Petaluma, CA Metropolitan Statistical Area; Figures represent new, privately-owned housing units authorized (unadjusted data)
Source: U.S. Census Bureau, Building Permits Survey (BPS), 2023, 2024

Bankruptcy Filings

Area	Business Filings			Nonbusiness Filings		
	2023	2024	% Chg.	2023	2024	% Chg.
Sonoma County	17	56	229.4	338	378	11.8
U.S.	18,926	23,107	22.1	434,064	494,201	13.9

Note: Business filings include Chapter 7, Chapter 9, Chapter 11, Chapter 12, Chapter 13, Chapter 15, and Section 304; Nonbusiness filings include Chapter 7, Chapter 11, and Chapter 13
Source: Administrative Office of the U.S. Courts, Business and Nonbusiness Bankruptcy, County Cases Commenced by Chapter of the Bankruptcy Code, During the 12-Month Period Ending December 31, 2023 and Business and Nonbusiness Bankruptcy, County Cases Commenced by Chapter of the Bankruptcy Code, During the 12-Month Period Ending December 31, 2024

Housing Vacancy Rates

Area	Gross Vacancy Rate[3] (%)			Year-Round Vacancy Rate[4] (%)			Rental Vacancy Rate[5] (%)			Homeowner Vacancy Rate[6] (%)		
	2022	2023	2024	2022	2023	2024	2022	2023	2024	2022	2023	2024
MSA[1]	n/a	n/a	n/a	n/a	n/a	n/a	n/a	n/a	n/a	n/a	n/a	n/a
U.S.[2]	9.1	9.0	9.1	7.5	7.5	7.6	5.7	6.5	6.8	0.8	0.8	1.0

Note: (1) Figures cover the Santa Rosa-Petaluma, CA Metropolitan Statistical Area; (2) Figures cover the 75 largest Metropolitan Statistical Areas; (3) The percentage of the total housing inventory that is vacant; (4) The percentage of the housing inventory (excluding seasonal units) that is year-round vacant; (5) The percentage of rental inventory that is vacant for rent; (6) The percentage of homeowner inventory that is vacant for sale; n/a not available
Source: U.S. Census Bureau, Housing Vacancies and Homeownership Annual Statistics: 2022, 2023, 2024

INCOME

Income

Area	Per Capita ($)	Median Household ($)	Average Household ($)
City	50,520	97,410	129,680
MSA[1]	54,941	102,840	138,572
U.S.	43,289	78,538	110,491

Note: (1) Figures cover the Santa Rosa-Petaluma, CA Metropolitan Statistical Area
Source: U.S. Census Bureau, 2019-2023 American Community Survey 5-Year Estimates

Household Income Distribution

Area	Percent of Households Earning							
	Under $15,000	$15,000 -$24,999	$25,000 -$34,999	$35,000 -$49,999	$50,000 -$74,999	$75,000 -$99,999	$100,000 -$149,999	$150,000 and up
City	6.3	4.1	4.4	7.7	15.6	13.4	19.5	29.1
MSA[1]	5.9	4.1	4.7	7.8	13.4	12.7	19.3	32.2
U.S.	8.5	6.6	6.8	10.4	15.7	12.7	17.4	21.9

Note: (1) Figures cover the Santa Rosa-Petaluma, CA Metropolitan Statistical Area
Source: U.S. Census Bureau, 2019-2023 American Community Survey 5-Year Estimates

Poverty Rate

Area	All Ages	Under 18 Years Old	18 to 64 Years Old	65 Years and Over
City	9.5	10.8	9.1	9.5
MSA[1]	8.6	9.3	8.4	8.4
U.S.	12.4	16.3	11.6	10.4

Note: Figures are percentage of people whose income during the past 12 months was below the poverty level;
(1) Figures cover the Santa Rosa-Petaluma, CA Metropolitan Statistical Area
Source: U.S. Census Bureau, 2019-2023 American Community Survey 5-Year Estimates

EMPLOYMENT

Labor Force and Employment

Area	Civilian Labor Force			Workers Employed		
	Dec. 2023	Dec. 2024	% Chg.	Dec. 2023	Dec. 2024	% Chg.
City	87,410	88,152	0.8	84,056	84,516	0.5
MSA[1]	249,694	251,825	0.9	240,531	241,848	0.5
U.S.	166,661,000	167,746,000	0.7	160,754,000	161,294,000	0.3

Note: Data is not seasonally adjusted and covers workers 16 years of age and older; (1) Figures cover the Santa Rosa-Petaluma, CA Metropolitan Statistical Area
Source: Bureau of Labor Statistics, Local Area Unemployment Statistics

Unemployment Rate

Area	2024											
	Jan.	Feb.	Mar.	Apr.	May	Jun.	Jul.	Aug.	Sep.	Oct.	Nov.	Dec.
City	4.5	4.3	4.2	3.8	3.6	4.3	4.7	4.7	4.1	4.3	4.4	4.1
MSA[1]	4.3	4.2	4.0	3.6	3.4	4.1	4.4	4.5	3.9	4.1	4.2	4.0
U.S.	4.1	4.2	3.9	3.5	3.7	4.3	4.5	4.4	3.9	3.9	4.0	3.8

Note: Data is not seasonally adjusted and covers workers 16 years of age and older; (1) Figures cover the Santa Rosa-Petaluma, CA Metropolitan Statistical Area
Source: Bureau of Labor Statistics, Local Area Unemployment Statistics

Average Wages

Occupation	$/Hr.	Occupation	$/Hr.
Accountants and Auditors	47.74	Maintenance and Repair Workers	28.52
Automotive Mechanics	31.99	Marketing Managers	80.50
Bookkeepers	29.51	Network and Computer Systems Admin.	50.04
Carpenters	40.36	Nurses, Licensed Practical	41.93
Cashiers	19.48	Nurses, Registered	82.45
Computer Programmers	48.16	Nursing Assistants	23.29
Computer Systems Analysts	55.29	Office Clerks, General	26.18
Computer User Support Specialists	37.08	Physical Therapists	62.99
Construction Laborers	32.20	Physicians	96.04
Cooks, Restaurant	21.98	Plumbers, Pipefitters and Steamfitters	38.02
Customer Service Representatives	25.04	Police and Sheriff's Patrol Officers	53.85
Dentists	82.86	Postal Service Mail Carriers	28.63
Electricians	42.00	Real Estate Sales Agents	39.71
Engineers, Electrical	63.20	Retail Salespersons	21.77
Fast Food and Counter Workers	19.46	Sales Representatives, Technical/Scientific	56.13
Financial Managers	82.80	Secretaries, Exc. Legal/Medical/Executive	27.28
First-Line Supervisors of Office Workers	36.40	Security Guards	22.66
General and Operations Managers	66.12	Surgeons	n/a
Hairdressers/Cosmetologists	22.13	Teacher Assistants, Exc. Postsecondary[1]	22.92
Home Health and Personal Care Aides	18.18	Teachers, Secondary School, Exc. Sp. Ed.[1]	47.05
Janitors and Cleaners	21.32	Telemarketers	n/a
Landscaping/Groundskeeping Workers	23.68	Truck Drivers, Heavy/Tractor-Trailer	29.46
Lawyers	124.30	Truck Drivers, Light/Delivery Services	25.70
Maids and Housekeeping Cleaners	22.21	Waiters and Waitresses	21.12

Note: Wage data covers the Santa Rosa-Petaluma, CA Metropolitan Statistical Area; (1) Hourly wages were calculated from annual wage data based on a 40 hour work week
Source: Bureau of Labor Statistics, Metro Area Occupational Employment & Wage Estimates, May 2024

Employment by Industry

Sector	MSA[1]		U.S.
	Number of Employees	Percent of Total	Percent of Total
Construction	16,200	7.9	5.1
Financial Activities	6,800	3.3	5.8
Government	28,500	13.9	14.9
Information	2,600	1.3	1.9
Leisure and Hospitality	25,400	12.4	10.4
Manufacturing	21,600	10.5	8.0
Mining and Logging	200	0.1	0.4
Other Services	7,800	3.8	3.7
Private Education and Health Services	38,300	18.6	16.9
Professional and Business Services	23,700	11.5	14.2
Retail Trade	23,100	11.2	10.0
Transportation, Warehousing, and Utilities	4,800	2.3	4.8
Wholesale Trade	6,500	3.2	3.9

Note: Figures are non-farm employment as of December 2024. Figures are not seasonally adjusted and include workers 16 years of age and older; (1) Figures cover the Santa Rosa-Petaluma, CA Metropolitan Statistical Area
Source: Bureau of Labor Statistics, Current Employment Statistics, Employment, Hours, and Earnings

Employment by Occupation

Occupation Classification	City (%)	MSA[1] (%)	U.S. (%)
Management, Business, Science, and Arts	39.9	41.9	42.0
Natural Resources, Construction, and Maintenance	10.6	10.1	8.6
Production, Transportation, and Material Moving	10.7	9.5	13.0
Sales and Office	19.2	19.7	19.9
Service	19.6	18.8	16.5

Note: Figures cover employed civilians 16 years of age and older; (1) Figures cover the Santa Rosa-Petaluma, CA Metropolitan Statistical Area
Source: U.S. Census Bureau, 2019-2023 American Community Survey 5-Year Estimates

Occupations with Greatest Projected Employment Growth: 2022 – 2032

Occupation[1]	2022 Employment	2032 Projected Employment	Numeric Employment Change	Percent Employment Change
Home Health and Personal Care Aides	796,900	1,060,200	263,300	33.0
Software Developers	313,700	388,000	74,300	23.7
Registered Nurses	333,700	376,900	43,200	12.9
Cooks, Restaurant	142,100	184,000	41,900	29.5
Laborers and Freight, Stock, and Material Movers, Hand	399,500	437,300	37,800	9.5
Janitors and Cleaners, Except Maids and Housekeeping Cleaners	262,900	300,200	37,300	14.2
Fast Food and Counter Workers	419,100	455,200	36,100	8.6
Stockers and Order Fillers	289,900	322,900	33,000	11.4
Medical Assistants	108,000	135,700	27,700	25.6
Landscaping and Groundskeeping Workers	135,200	162,100	26,900	19.9

Note: Projections cover California; (1) Sorted by numeric employment change
Source: www.projectionscentral.org, State Occupational Projections, 2022–2032 Long-Term Projections

Fastest-Growing Occupations: 2022 – 2032

Occupation[1]	2022 Employment	2032 Projected Employment	Numeric Employment Change	Percent Employment Change
Nurse Practitioners	21,500	34,100	12,600	58.6
Physical Therapist Assistants	7,900	11,200	3,300	41.8
Solar Photovoltaic Installers	7,900	11,200	3,300	41.8
Physician Assistants	13,000	18,200	5,200	40.0
Medical and Health Services Managers	58,300	81,400	23,100	39.6
Statisticians	2,800	3,900	1,100	39.3
Taxi Drivers	48,100	66,800	18,700	38.9
Occupational Therapy Assistants	2,700	3,600	900	33.3
Home Health and Personal Care Aides	796,900	1,060,200	263,300	33.0
Data Scientists	33,900	45,000	11,100	32.7

Note: Projections cover California; (1) Sorted by percent employment change and excludes occupations with numeric employment change less than 50
Source: www.projectionscentral.org, State Occupational Projections, 2022–2032 Long-Term Projections

CITY FINANCES

City Government Finances

Component	2022 ($000)	2022 ($ per capita)
Total Revenues	431,743	2,473
Total Expenditures	370,916	2,124
Debt Outstanding	318,668	1,825

Source: U.S. Census Bureau, State & Local Government Finances 2022

City Government Revenue by Source

Source	2022 ($000)	2022 ($ per capita)	2022 (%)
General Revenue			
From Federal Government	20,393	117	4.7
From State Government	42,394	243	9.8
From Local Governments	5,598	32	1.3
Taxes			
Property	49,892	286	11.6
Sales and Gross Receipts	115,132	659	26.7
Personal Income	0	0	0.0
Corporate Income	0	0	0.0
Motor Vehicle License	0	0	0.0
Other Taxes	15,733	90	3.6
Current Charges	117,554	673	27.2
Liquor Store	0	0	0.0
Utility	47,641	273	11.0

Source: U.S. Census Bureau, State & Local Government Finances 2022

City Government Expenditures by Function

Function	2022 ($000)	2022 ($ per capita)	2022 (%)
General Direct Expenditures			
Air Transportation	0	0	0.0
Corrections	0	0	0.0
Education	0	0	0.0
Employment Security Administration	0	0	0.0
Financial Administration	0	0	0.0
Fire Protection	50,895	291	13.7
General Public Buildings	0	0	0.0
Governmental Administration, Other	38,181	218	10.3
Health	3,047	17	0.8
Highways	15,413	88	4.2
Hospitals	0	0	0.0
Housing and Community Development	32,389	185	8.7
Interest on General Debt	9,143	52	2.5
Judicial and Legal	0	0	0.0
Libraries	0	0	0.0
Parking	4,984	28	1.3
Parks and Recreation	18,671	106	5.0
Police Protection	72,343	414	19.5
Public Welfare	0	0	0.0
Sewerage	47,973	274	12.9
Solid Waste Management	0	0	0.0
Veterans' Services	0	0	0.0
Liquor Store	0	0	0.0
Utility	59,536	341	16.1

Source: U.S. Census Bureau, State & Local Government Finances 2022

TAXES

State Corporate Income Tax Rates

State	Tax Rate (%)	Income Brackets ($)	Num. of Brackets	Financial Institution Tax Rate (%)[a]	Federal Income Tax Ded.
California	8.84 (b)	Flat rate	1	10.84 (b)	No

Note: Tax rates for tax year 2024; (a) Rates listed are the corporate income tax rate applied to financial institutions or excise taxes based on income. Some states have other taxes based upon the value of deposits or shares; (b) Minimum tax is $800 in California, $250 in District of Columbia, $50 in Arizona and North Dakota (banks), $400 ($100 banks) in Rhode Island, $200 per location in South Dakota (banks), $100 in Utah, in Vermont, simplified entity business tax for residents only at $250, otherwise minimum tax ($100 - $100,000) is based upon gross receipts.
Source: Federation of Tax Administrators, State Corporate Income Tax Rates, January 1, 2025

State Individual Income Tax Rates

State	Tax Rate (%)	Income Brackets ($)	Personal Exemptions ($)			Standard Ded. ($)	
			Single	Married	Depend.	Single	Married
California (a)	1.0 - 13.3 (g)	10,099 - 677,276 (b)	134	268	367 (c)	5,202	10,404 (a)

Note: Tax rates for tax year 2024; Local- and county-level taxes are not included; Federal income tax is not deductible on state income tax returns; (a) 16 states have statutory provision for automatically adjusting to the rate of inflation the dollar values of the income tax brackets, standard deductions, and/or personal exemptions. Oregon does not index the income brackets for $125,000 and over See: INFL and SPEC above; (b) For joint returns, taxes are twice the tax on half the couple's income. California brackets violate this formula at the two highest tax brackets in 2024; (c) The personal exemption takes the form of a tax credit instead of a deduction; (g) California imposes an additional 1% tax on taxable income over $1 million, making the maximum rate 13.3% over $1 million in 2023. Unreleased projections indicate 14.4% in 2024.
Source: Federation of Tax Administrators, State Individual Income Tax Rates, January 1, 2025

Various State Sales and Excise Tax Rates

State	State Sales Tax (%)	Gasoline[1] ($/gal.)	Cigarette[2] ($/pack)	Spirits[3] ($/gal.)	Wine[4] ($/gal.)	Beer[5] ($/gal.)	Recreational Marijuana (%)
California	7.25	0.70	2.87	3.30	0.20	0.20	(c)

Note: All tax rates as of January 1, 2025; (1) The American Petroleum Institute has developed a methodology for determining the average tax rate on a gallon of fuel. Rates may include any of the following: excise taxes, environmental fees, storage tank fees, other fees or taxes, general sales tax, and local taxes; (2) The federal excise tax of $1.0066 per pack and local taxes are not included; (3) Rates are those applicable to off-premise sales of 40% alcohol by volume (a.b.v.) distilled spirits in 750ml containers. Local excise taxes are excluded; (4) Rates are those applicable to off-premise sales of 11% a.b.v. non-carbonated wine in 750ml containers; (5) Rates are those applicable to off-premise sales of 4.7% a.b.v. beer in 12 ounce containers; (c) 15% excise tax (retail gross receipts)
Source: Tax Foundation, 2025 Facts & Figures: How Does Your State Compare?

State Tax Competitiveness Index

State	Overall Rank	Corporate Tax Rank	Individual Income Tax Rank	Sales Tax Rank	Property Tax Rank	Unemployment Insurance Tax Rank
California	48	41	49	46	23	25

Note: The Tax Foundation's State Tax Competitiveness Index enables policymakers, taxpayers, and business leaders to gauge how their states' tax systems compare. A rank of 1 is best, 50 is worst. Rankings do not average to the total. States without a tax rank equally as 1. DC's scores and rankings do not affect other states. The report shows tax systems as of July 1, 2024 (the beginning of Fiscal Year 2025).
Source: Tax Foundation, State Tax Competitiveness Index 2025

TRANSPORTATION

Means of Transportation to Work

Area	Car/Truck/Van		Public Transportation			Bicycle	Walked	Other Means	Worked at Home
	Drove Alone	Car-pooled	Bus	Subway	Railroad				
City	73.1	11.1	0.9	0.0	0.2	0.6	2.3	1.3	10.5
MSA[1]	71.0	9.2	0.7	0.1	0.2	0.7	2.4	1.4	14.4
U.S.	70.2	8.5	1.7	1.3	0.4	0.4	2.4	1.6	13.5

Note: Figures are percentages and cover workers 16 years of age and older; (1) Figures cover the Santa Rosa-Petaluma, CA Metropolitan Statistical Area
Source: U.S. Census Bureau, 2019-2023 American Community Survey 5-Year Estimates

Travel Time to Work

Area	Less Than 10 Minutes	10 to 19 Minutes	20 to 29 Minutes	30 to 44 Minutes	45 to 59 Minutes	60 to 89 Minutes	90 Minutes or More
City	13.1	42.1	19.4	14.4	4.5	3.6	2.9
MSA[1]	14.0	34.1	19.3	17.3	6.3	5.6	3.4
U.S.	12.6	28.6	21.2	20.8	8.1	6.0	2.8

Note: Note: Figures are percentages and include workers 16 years old and over; (1) Figures cover the Santa Rosa-Petaluma, CA Metropolitan Statistical Area
Source: U.S. Census Bureau, 2019-2023 American Community Survey 5-Year Estimates

Key Congestion Measures

Measure	2000	2010	2015	2020	2022
Annual Hours of Delay, Total (000)	n/a	n/a	18,462	7,830	14,041
Annual Hours of Delay, Per Auto Commuter	n/a	n/a	53	22	41
Annual Congestion Cost, Per Auto Commuter ($)	n/a	n/a	1,230	572	968

Note: n/a not available
Source: Texas A&M Transportation Institute, 2023 Urban Mobility Report

Freeway Travel Time Index

Measure	1985	1990	1995	2000	2005	2010	2015	2020	2022
Urban Area Index[1]	n/a	n/a	n/a	n/a	n/a	n/a	1.22	1.11	1.19
Urban Area Rank[1,2]	n/a	n/a	n/a	n/a	n/a	n/a	n/a	n/a	n/a

Note: Freeway Travel Time Index—the ratio of travel time in the peak period to the travel time at free-flow conditions. For example, a value of 1.30 indicates a 20-minute free-flow trip takes 26 minutes in the peak (20 minutes x 1.30 = 26 minutes); (1) Covers the Santa Rosa CA urban area; (2) Rank is based on 101 larger urban areas (#1 = highest travel time index); n/a not available
Source: Texas A&M Transportation Institute, 2023 Urban Mobility Report

Public Transportation

Agency Name / Mode of Transportation	Vehicles Operated in Maximum Service[1]	Annual Unlinked Passenger Trips[2] (in thous.)	Annual Passenger Miles[3] (in thous.)
City of Santa Rosa (Santa Rosa CityBus)			
Bus (directly operated)	18	1,289.0	3,006.0
Bus (purchased transportation)	1	4.8	17.1
Demand Response (purchased transportation)	10	26.0	133.3
Sonoma County Transit			
Bus (purchased transportation)	30	613.0	6,644.6
Demand Response (purchased transportation)	17	36.8	479.5

Note: (1) Number of revenue vehicles operated by the given mode and type of service to meet the annual maximum service requirement. This is the revenue vehicle count during the peak season of the year; on the week and day that maximum service is provided. Vehicles operated in maximum service (VOMS) exclude atypical days and one-time special events; (2) Number of passengers who boarded public transportation vehicles. Passengers are counted each time they board a vehicle no matter how many vehicles they use to travel from their origin to their destination. (3) Sum of the distances ridden by all passengers during the entire fiscal year.
Source: Federal Transit Administration, National Transit Database, 2023

Air Transportation

Airport Name and Code / Type of Service	Passenger Airlines[1]	Passenger Enplanements	Freight Carriers[2]	Freight (lbs)
San Francisco International (SFO)				
Domestic service (U.S. carriers only)	19	17,631,272	15	217,963,509
International service (U.S. carriers only)	6	3,090,264	5	88,989,548

Note: (1) Includes all U.S.-based major, minor and commuter airlines that carried at least one passenger during the year; (2) Includes all U.S.-based airlines and freight carriers that transported at least one pound of freight during the year.
Source: Bureau of Transportation Statistics, The Intermodal Transportation Database, Air Carriers: T-100 Domestic Market (U.S. carriers only), 2024; Bureau of Transportation Statistics, The Intermodal Transportation Database, Air Carriers: T-100 International Market (U.S. carriers only), 2024

BUSINESSES

Major Business Headquarters

Company Name	Industry	Rankings	
		Fortune[1]	Forbes[2]
No companies listed	-	-	-

Note: (1) Companies that produce a 10-K are ranked 1 to 500 based on 2023 revenue; (2) All private companies with at least $2 billion in annual revenue through the end of their most current fiscal year are ranked 1 to 275; companies listed are headquartered in the city; dashes indicate no ranking
Source: Fortune, "Fortune 500," 2024; Forbes, "America's Largest Private Companies," 2024

Living Environment

COST OF LIVING

Cost of Living Index

Composite Index	Groceries	Housing	Utilities	Trans- portation	Health Care	Misc. Goods/ Services
n/a	n/a	n/a	n/a	n/a	n/a	n/a

Note: The Cost of Living Index measures regional differences in the cost of consumer goods and services, excluding taxes and non-consumer expenditures, for professional and managerial households in the top income quintile. It is based on more than 50,000 prices covering almost 60 different items for which prices are collected three times a year by chambers of commerce, economic development organizations or university applied economic centers in each participating urban area. The numbers shown should be read as a percentage above or below the national average of 100. For example, a value of 115.4 in the groceries column indicates that grocery prices are 15.4% higher than the national average. Small differences in the index numbers should not be interpreted as significant; n/a not available.
Source: The Council for Community and Economic Research, Cost of Living Index, 2024

Grocery Prices

Area[1]	T-Bone Steak ($/pound)	Frying Chicken ($/pound)	Whole Milk ($/half gal.)	Eggs ($/dozen)	Orange Juice ($/64 oz.)	Coffee ($/11.5 oz.)
City[2]	n/a	n/a	n/a	n/a	n/a	n/a
Avg.	15.42	1.55	4.69	3.25	4.41	5.46
Min.	14.50	1.16	4.43	2.75	4.00	4.85
Max.	17.56	2.89	5.49	4.78	5.54	7.89

Note: (1) Values for the local area are compared with the average, minimum and maximum values for all 276 areas in the Cost of Living Index; (2) Figures cover the Santa Rosa CA urban area; n/a not available; **T-Bone Steak** (price per pound); **Frying Chicken** (price per pound, whole fryer); **Whole Milk** (half gallon carton); **Eggs** (price per dozen, Grade A, large); **Orange Juice** (64 oz. Tropicana or Florida Natural); **Coffee** (11.5 oz. can, vacuum-packed, Maxwell House, Hills Bros, or Folgers).
Source: The Council for Community and Economic Research, Cost of Living Index, 2024

Housing and Utility Costs

Area[1]	New Home Price ($)	Apartment Rent ($/month)	All Electric ($/month)	Part Electric ($/month)	Other Energy ($/month)	Telephone ($/month)
City[2]	n/a	n/a	n/a	n/a	n/a	n/a
Avg.	515,975	1,550	210.99	123.07	82.07	194.99
Min.	265,375	692	104.33	53.68	36.26	179.42
Max.	2,775,821	5,719	529.02	397.28	361.63	223.33

Note: (1) Values for the local area are compared with the average, minimum and maximum values for all 276 areas in the Cost of Living Index; (2) Figures cover the Santa Rosa CA urban area; n/a not available; **New Home Price** (2,400 sf living area, 8,000 sf lot, in urban area with full utilities); **Apartment Rent** (950 sf 2 bedroom/1.5 or 2 bath, unfurnished, excluding all utilities except water); **All Electric** (average monthly cost for an all-electric home); **Part Electric** (average monthly cost for a part-electric home); **Other Energy** (average monthly cost for natural gas, fuel oil, coal, wood, and any other forms of energy except electricity); **Telephone** (price includes the base monthly rate plus taxes and fees for three lines of mobile phone service).
Source: The Council for Community and Economic Research, Cost of Living Index, 2024

Health Care, Transportation, and Other Costs

Area[1]	Doctor ($/visit)	Dentist ($/visit)	Optometrist ($/visit)	Gasoline ($/gallon)	Beauty Salon ($/visit)	Men's Shirt ($)
City[2]	n/a	n/a	n/a	n/a	n/a	n/a
Avg.	143.77	117.51	129.23	3.32	48.57	38.14
Min.	36.74	58.67	67.33	2.80	24.00	13.41
Max.	270.44	216.82	307.33	5.28	94.00	63.89

Note: (1) Values for the local area are compared with the average, minimum and maximum values for all 276 areas in the Cost of Living Index; (2) Figures cover the Santa Rosa CA urban area; n/a not available; **Doctor** (general practitioners routine exam of an established patient); **Dentist** (adult teeth cleaning and periodic oral examination); **Optometrist** (full vision eye exam for established adult patient); **Gasoline** (one gallon regular unleaded, national brand, including all taxes, cash price at self-service pump if available); **Beauty Salon** (woman's shampoo, trim, and blow-dry); **Men's Shirt** (cotton/polyester dress shirt, pinpoint weave, long sleeves).
Source: The Council for Community and Economic Research, Cost of Living Index, 2024

HOUSING

Homeownership Rate

Area	2017 (%)	2018 (%)	2019 (%)	2020 (%)	2021 (%)	2022 (%)	2023 (%)	2024 (%)
MSA[1]	n/a	n/a	n/a	n/a	n/a	n/a	n/a	n/a
U.S.	63.9	64.4	64.6	66.6	65.5	65.8	65.9	65.6

Note: (1) Figures cover the Santa Rosa-Petaluma, CA Metropolitan Statistical Area; n/a not available
Source: U.S. Census Bureau, Housing Vacancies and Homeownership Annual Statistics: 2017-2024

House Price Index (HPI)

Area	National Ranking[2]	Quarterly Change (%)	One-Year Change (%)	Five-Year Change (%)	Since 1991Q1 (%)
MSA[1]	192	-0.37	3.47	28.24	304.85
U.S.[3]	–	1.43	4.51	57.13	327.82

Note: The HPI is a weighted repeat sales index. It measures average price changes in repeat sales or refinancings on the same properties. This information is obtained by reviewing repeat mortgage transactions on single-family properties whose mortgages have been purchased or securitized by Fannie Mae or Freddie Mac since January 1975; (1) Figures cover the Santa Rosa, CA Metropolitan Statistical Area; (2) Rankings are based on annual percentage change for all metro areas containing at least 15,000 transactions over the last 10 years and ranges from 1 to 241; (3) figures based on a weighted average of Census Division estimates using a seasonally adjusted, purchase-only index; all figures are for the period ending December 31, 2024
Source: Federal Housing Finance Agency, Change in FHFA Metropolitan Area House Price Indexes, All Transactions Index, 2024Q4

Home Value

Area	Under $100,000	$100,000 -$199,999	$200,000 -$299,999	$300,000 -$399,999	$400,000 -$499,999	$500,000 -$999,999	$1,000,000 or more	Median ($)
City	3.7	2.8	2.7	3.8	7.2	65.4	14.3	685,000
MSA[1]	3.3	3.1	2.4	2.7	5.4	57.0	26.2	779,000
U.S.	12.1	17.8	19.5	14.4	10.5	19.1	6.5	303,400

Note: Figures are percentages except for median and cover owner-occupied housing units; (1) Figures cover the Santa Rosa-Petaluma, CA Metropolitan Statistical Area
Source: U.S. Census Bureau, 2019-2023 American Community Survey 5-Year Estimates

Year Housing Structure Built

Area	2020 or Later	2010 -2019	2000 -2009	1990 -1999	1980 -1989	1970 -1979	1960 -1969	1950 -1959	1940 -1949	Before 1940	Median Year
City	1.0	6.2	12.3	12.5	17.9	20.9	11.9	8.1	4.4	4.9	1980
MSA[1]	1.0	5.3	10.1	13.2	18.0	19.8	11.8	8.5	4.2	8.0	1979
U.S.	1.2	8.9	13.6	12.8	13.0	14.4	10.0	9.7	4.5	11.9	1980

Note: Figures are percentages except for Median Year; Note: (1) Figures cover the Santa Rosa-Petaluma, CA Metropolitan Statistical Area
Source: U.S. Census Bureau, 2019-2023 American Community Survey 5-Year Estimates

Gross Monthly Rent

Area	Under $500	$500 -$999	$1,000 -$1,499	$1,500 -$1,999	$2,000 -$2,499	$2,500 -$2,999	$3,000 and up	Median ($)
City	4.1	5.1	12.9	24.0	23.2	15.4	15.3	2,084
MSA[1]	4.1	6.8	13.4	21.5	22.3	14.4	17.4	2,093
U.S.	6.5	22.3	29.5	20.2	10.8	4.8	5.9	1,348

Note: Figures are percentages except for median; Gross rent is the contract rent plus the estimated average monthly cost of utilities (electricity, gas, and water and sewer) and fuels (oil, coal, kerosene, wood, etc.) if these are paid by the renter (or paid for the renter by someone else); (1) Figures cover the Santa Rosa-Petaluma, CA Metropolitan Statistical Area
Source: U.S. Census Bureau, 2019-2023 American Community Survey 5-Year Estimates

HEALTH

Health Risk Factors

Category	MSA[1] (%)	U.S. (%)
Adults aged 18–64 who have any kind of health care coverage	n/a	90.8
Adults who reported being in good or better health	n/a	81.8
Adults who have been told they have high blood cholesterol	n/a	36.9
Adults who have been told they have high blood pressure	n/a	34.0
Adults who are current smokers	n/a	12.1
Adults who currently use e-cigarettes	n/a	7.7
Adults who currently use chewing tobacco, snuff, or snus	n/a	3.2
Adults who are heavy drinkers[2]	n/a	6.1
Adults who are binge drinkers[3]	n/a	15.2
Adults who are overweight (BMI 25.0 - 29.9)	n/a	34.4
Adults who are obese (BMI 30.0 - 99.8)	n/a	34.3
Adults who participated in any physical activities in the past month	n/a	75.8

Note: All figures are crude prevalence; (1) Figures for the Santa Rosa-Petaluma, CA Metropolitan Statistical Area were not available.
(2) Heavy drinkers are classified as adult men having more than 14 drinks per week and adult women having more than 7 drinks per week; (3) Binge drinkers are classified as males having five or more drinks on one occasion or females having four or more drinks on one occasion
Source: Centers for Disease Control and Prevention, Behaviorial Risk Factor Surveillance System, SMART: Selected Metropolitan Area Risk Trends, 2023

Acute and Chronic Health Conditions

Category	MSA[1] (%)	U.S. (%)
Adults who have ever been told they had a heart attack	n/a	4.2
Adults who have ever been told they have angina or coronary heart disease	n/a	4.0
Adults who have ever been told they had a stroke	n/a	3.3
Adults who have ever been told they have asthma	n/a	15.7
Adults who have ever been told they have arthritis	n/a	26.3
Adults who have ever been told they have diabetes[2]	n/a	11.5
Adults who have ever been told they had skin cancer	n/a	5.6
Adults who have ever been told they had any other types of cancer	n/a	8.4
Adults who have ever been told they have COPD	n/a	6.4
Adults who have ever been told they have kidney disease	n/a	3.7
Adults who have ever been told they have a form of depression	n/a	22.0

Note: All figures are crude prevalence; (1) Figures for the Santa Rosa-Petaluma, CA Metropolitan Statistical Area were not available.
(2) Figures do not include pregnancy-related, borderline, or pre-diabetes
Source: Centers for Disease Control and Prevention, Behaviorial Risk Factor Surveillance System, SMART: Selected Metropolitan Area Risk Trends, 2023

Health Screening and Vaccination Rates

Category	MSA[1] (%)	U.S. (%)
Adults who have ever been tested for HIV	n/a	37.5
Adults who have had their blood cholesterol checked within the last five years	n/a	87.0
Adults aged 65+ who have had flu shot within the past year	n/a	63.4
Adults aged 65+ who have ever had a pneumonia vaccination	n/a	71.9

Note: All figures are crude prevalence; (1) Figures for the Santa Rosa-Petaluma, CA Metropolitan Statistical Area were not available.
Source: Centers for Disease Control and Prevention, Behaviorial Risk Factor Surveillance System, SMART: Selected Metropolitan Area Risk Trends, 2023

Disability Status

Category	MSA[1] (%)	U.S. (%)
Adults who reported being deaf	n/a	7.4
Are you blind or have serious difficulty seeing, even when wearing glasses?	n/a	4.9
Do you have difficulty doing errands alone?	n/a	7.8
Do you have difficulty dressing or bathing?	n/a	3.6
Do you have serious difficulty concentrating/remembering/making decisions?	n/a	13.7
Do you have serious difficulty walking or climbing stairs?	n/a	13.2

Note: All figures are crude prevalence; (1) Figures for the Santa Rosa-Petaluma, CA Metropolitan Statistical Area were not available.
Source: Centers for Disease Control and Prevention, Behaviorial Risk Factor Surveillance System, SMART: Selected Metropolitan Area Risk Trends, 2023

Mortality Rates for the Top 10 Causes of Death in the U.S.

ICD-10[a] Sub-Chapter	ICD-10[a] Code	Crude Mortality Rate[2] per 100,000 population	
		County[3]	U.S.
Malignant neoplasms	C00-C97	213.7	182.7
Ischaemic heart diseases	I20-I25	94.4	109.6
Provisional assignment of new diseases of uncertain etiology[1]	U00-U49	30.3	65.3
Other forms of heart disease	I30-I51	59.9	65.1
Other degenerative diseases of the nervous system	G30-G31	52.3	52.4
Other external causes of accidental injury	W00-X59	39.3	52.3
Cerebrovascular diseases	I60-I69	57.6	49.1
Chronic lower respiratory diseases	J40-J47	39.4	43.5
Hypertensive diseases	I10-I15	37.1	38.9
Organic, including symptomatic, mental disorders	F01-F09	45.0	33.9

Note: (a) ICD-10 = International Classification of Diseases 10th Revision; (1) Includes COVID-19, adverse effects to COVID-19 vaccines, SARS, and vaping-related disorders; (2) Crude mortality rates are a three-year average covering 2021-2023; (3) Figures cover Sonoma County.
Source: Centers for Disease Control and Prevention, National Center for Health Statistics. National Vital Statistics System, Mortality 2018-2023 on CDC WONDER Online Database

Mortality Rates for Selected Causes of Death

Cause of Death	ICD-10[a] Code	Crude Mortality Rate[1] per 100,000 population	
		County[2]	U.S.
Accidental poisoning and exposure to noxious substances	X40-X49	27.6	30.5
Alzheimer disease	G30	40.7	35.4
Assault	X85-Y09	3.0	7.3
COVID-19	U07.1	30.3	65.3
Diabetes mellitus	E10-E14	23.9	30.0
Diseases of the liver	K70-K76	22.3	20.8
Human immunodeficiency virus (HIV) disease	B20-B24	Unreliable	1.5
Influenza and pneumonia	J09-J18	9.6	13.4
Intentional self-harm	X60-X84	15.6	14.7
Malnutrition	E40-E46	14.5	6.0
Obesity and other hyperalimentation	E65-E68	2.8	3.1
Renal failure	N17-N19	6.5	16.4
Transport accidents	V01-V99	10.2	14.4

Note: (a) ICD-10 = International Classification of Diseases 10th Revision; (1) Crude mortality rates are a three-year average covering 2021-2023; (2) Figures cover Sonoma County; Data are suppressed when the data meet the criteria for confidentiality constraints; Crude mortality rates are flagged as unreliable when the rate would be calculated with a numerator of 20 or less.
Source: Centers for Disease Control and Prevention, National Center for Health Statistics. National Vital Statistics System, Mortality 2018-2023 on CDC WONDER Online Database

Health Insurance Coverage

Area	With Health Insurance	With Private Health Insurance	With Public Health Insurance	Without Health Insurance	Population Under Age 19 Without Health Insurance
City	93.6	67.8	39.1	6.4	3.9
MSA[1]	94.6	71.3	38.3	5.4	3.2
U.S.	91.4	67.3	36.3	8.6	5.4

Note: Figures are percentages that cover the civilian noninstitutionalized population; (1) Figures cover the Santa Rosa-Petaluma, CA Metropolitan Statistical Area
Source: U.S. Census Bureau, 2019-2023 American Community Survey 5-Year Estimates

Number of Medical Professionals

Area	MDs[3]	DOs[3,4]	Dentists	Podiatrists	Chiropractors	Optometrists
County[1] (number)	1,395	103	480	33	216	91
County[1] (rate[2])	289.0	21.3	99.6	6.8	44.8	18.9
U.S. (rate[2])	302.5	29.2	74.6	6.4	29.5	18.0

Note: Data as of 2023 unless noted; (1) Data covers Sonoma County; (2) Number of medical professionals per 100,000 population; (3) Data as of 2022 and includes all active, non-federal physicians; (4) Doctor of Osteopathic Medicine
Source: U.S. Department of Health and Human Services, Health Resources and Services Administration, Bureau of Health Professions, Area Resource File (ARF) 2023-2024

EDUCATION

Public School District Statistics

District Name	Schls	Pupils	Pupil/ Teacher Ratio	Minority Pupils[1] (%)	Total Rev. per Pupil ($)	Total Exp. per Pupil ($)
Rincon Valley Union Elementary	9	3,112	20.3	53.6	18,671	18,022
Santa Rosa Elementary	13	4,741	19.4	76.7	n/a	n/a
Santa Rosa High	12	9,941	19.8	70.7	n/a	n/a

Note: Table includes school districts with 2,000 or more students; (1) Percentage of students that are not non-Hispanic white.
Source: U.S. Department of Education, National Center for Education Statistics, Common Core of Data, Local Education Agency (School District) Universe Survey: School Year 2023-2024; U.S. Department of Education, National Center for Education Statistics, Common Core of Data, School District Finance Survey (F-33): School Year 2021–22

Highest Level of Education

Area	Less than H.S.	H.S. Diploma	Some College, No Deg.	Associate Degree	Bachelor's Degree	Master's Degree	Prof. School Degree	Doctorate Degree
City	14.5	19.2	21.9	9.7	21.3	9.0	3.2	1.2
MSA[1]	11.1	18.6	23.0	9.4	23.5	9.4	3.4	1.5
U.S.	10.6	26.2	19.4	8.8	21.3	9.8	2.3	1.6

Note: Figures cover persons age 25 and over; (1) Figures cover the Santa Rosa-Petaluma, CA Metropolitan Statistical Area
Source: U.S. Census Bureau, 2019-2023 American Community Survey 5-Year Estimates

Educational Attainment by Race

Area	High School Graduate or Higher (%)					Bachelor's Degree or Higher (%)				
	Total	White	Black	Asian	Hisp.[2]	Total	White	Black	Asian	Hisp.[2]
City	85.5	94.7	85.7	83.6	63.0	34.8	42.5	21.8	45.8	14.6
MSA[1]	88.9	95.8	88.8	86.2	66.2	37.8	44.2	29.4	46.1	16.0
U.S.	89.4	92.9	88.1	88.0	72.5	35.0	37.7	24.7	57.0	19.9

Note: Figures shown cover persons 25 years old and over; (1) Figures cover the Santa Rosa-Petaluma, CA Metropolitan Statistical Area; (2) People of Hispanic origin can be of any race
Source: U.S. Census Bureau, 2019-2023 American Community Survey 5-Year Estimates

School Enrollment by Grade and Control

Area	Preschool (%)		Kindergarten (%)		Grades 1 - 4 (%)		Grades 5 - 8 (%)		Grades 9 - 12 (%)	
	Public	Private	Public	Private	Public	Private	Public	Private	Public	Private
City	55.2	44.8	90.3	9.7	92.4	7.6	88.6	11.4	92.8	7.2
MSA[1]	53.1	46.9	91.2	8.8	92.9	7.1	89.9	10.1	91.1	8.9
U.S.	58.7	41.3	85.2	14.8	87.2	12.8	87.9	12.1	89.0	11.0

Note: Figures shown cover persons 3 years old and over; (1) Figures cover the Santa Rosa-Petaluma, CA Metropolitan Statistical Area
Source: U.S. Census Bureau, 2019-2023 American Community Survey 5-Year Estimates

Higher Education

Four-Year Colleges			Two-Year Colleges			Medical Schools[1]	Law Schools[2]	Voc/ Tech[3]
Public	Private Non-profit	Private For-profit	Public	Private Non-profit	Private For-profit			
1	1	2	1	0	0	0	1	1

Note: Figures cover institutions located within the Santa Rosa-Petaluma, CA Metropolitan Statistical Area and include main campuses only; (1) includes schools accredited by the Liaison Committee on Medical Education and the American Osteopathic Association's Commission on Osteopathic College Accreditation; (2) includes ABA-accredited schools, schools with provisional ABA accreditation, and state accredited schools; (3) includes all schools with programs that are less than 2 years.
Source: National Center for Education Statistics, Integrated Postsecondary Education System (IPEDS), 2023-24; Wikipedia, List of Medical Schools in the United States, accessed May 2, 2025; Wikipedia, List of Law Schools in the United States, accessed May 2, 2025

EMPLOYERS

Major Employers

Company Name	Industry
Amy's Kitchen	Food manufacturing
City of Santa Rosa	Government
County of Sonoma	Government
Kaiser Permanente Medical Center	Healthcare
Keysight Technologies	Electronics
Medtronic CardioVascular	Medical devices
Santa Rosa City Schools	Education
Santa Rosa Junior College	Education
St. Joseph Health System	Healthcare
Sutter Regional Hospital	Healthcare

Note: Companies shown are located within the Santa Rosa-Petaluma, CA Metropolitan Statistical Area.
Source: Chambers of Commerce; State Departments of Labor; Wikipedia

PUBLIC SAFETY

Crime Rate

Area	Total Crime Rate	Violent Crime Rate				Property Crime Rate		
		Murder	Rape	Robbery	Aggrav. Assault	Burglary	Larceny -Theft	Motor Vehicle Theft
City	1,799.8	5.7	65.0	63.9	196.2	257.8	1,004.2	206.9
U.S.	2,290.9	5.7	38.0	66.5	264.1	250.7	1,347.2	318.7

Note: Figures are crimes per 100,000 population.
Source: FBI, Table 8, Offenses Known to Law Enforcement, by State by City, 2023

Hate Crimes

Area	Number of Quarters Reported	Number of Incidents per Bias Motivation					
		Race/Ethnicity/ Ancestry	Religion	Sexual Orientation	Disability	Gender	Gender Identity
City[1]	4	4	3	1	0	0	0
U.S.	4	5,900	2,699	2,077	187	92	492

Note: (1) Figures include at least one incident reported with more than one bias motivation.
Source: Federal Bureau of Investigation, Hate Crime Statistics 2023

Identity Theft Consumer Reports

Area	Reports	Reports per 100,000 Population	Rank[2]
MSA[1]	681	140	298
U.S.	1,135,291	339	-

Note: (1) Figures cover the Santa Rosa-Petaluma, CA Metropolitan Statistical Area; (2) Rank ranges from 1 to 401 where 1 indicates greatest number of identity theft reports per 100,000 population
Source: Federal Trade Commission, Consumer Sentinel Network Data Book 2024

Fraud and Other Consumer Reports

Area	Reports	Reports per 100,000 Population	Rank[2]
MSA[1]	4,928	1,015	195
U.S.	5,360,641	1,601	-

Note: (1) Figures cover the Santa Rosa-Petaluma, CA Metropolitan Statistical Area; (2) Rank ranges from 1 to 401 where 1 indicates greatest number of fraud and other consumer reports per 100,000 population
Source: Federal Trade Commission, Consumer Sentinel Network Data Book 2024

POLITICS

2024 Presidential Election Results

Area	Trump (Rep.)	Harris (Dem.)	Stein (Green)	Kennedy (Ind.)	Oliver (Lib.)	Other
Sonoma County	25.2	71.4	0.9	1.5	0.4	0.4
U.S.	49.7	48.2	0.6	0.5	0.4	0.6

Note: Results are percentages and may not add to 100% due to rounding
Source: Dave Leip's Atlas of U.S. Presidential Elections

SPORTS

Professional Sports Teams

Team Name	League	Year Established

No teams are located in the metro area
Source: Wikipedia, Major Professional Sports Teams of the United States and Canada, May 1, 2025

CLIMATE

Average and Extreme Temperatures

Temperature	Jan	Feb	Mar	Apr	May	Jun	Jul	Aug	Sep	Oct	Nov	Dec	Yr.
Extreme High (°F)	69	72	83	89	99	102	103	105	109	94	85	73	109
Average High (°F)	56	61	65	69	74	79	81	84	84	75	65	58	71
Average Temp. (°F)	46	50	51	55	60	63	65	66	65	60	52	47	57
Average Low (°F)	35	38	36	41	45	47	49	47	46	44	39	35	42
Extreme Low (°F)	24	26	25	29	32	36	41	40	36	32	28	23	23

Note: Figures cover the years 1948-1990
Source: National Climatic Data Center, International Station Meteorological Climate Summary, 9/96

Average Precipitation/Snowfall/Humidity

Precip./Humidity	Jan	Feb	Mar	Apr	May	Jun	Jul	Aug	Sep	Oct	Nov	Dec	Yr.
Avg. Precip. (in.)	5.6	6.2	4.5	0.7	0.9	0.1	0.0	0.0	0.0	2.3	4.7	4.0	29.0
Avg. Snowfall (in.)	n/a	n/a	n/a	0	0	0	0	0	0	0	n/a	n/a	n/a
Avg. Rel. Hum. (%)	85	74	70	69	68	63	71	68	66	74	81	82	73

Note: Figures cover the years 1948-1990
Source: National Climatic Data Center, International Station Meteorological Climate Summary, 9/96

Weather Conditions

Temperature			Daytime Sky			Precipitation		
0°F & below	32°F & below	90°F & above	Clear	Partly cloudy	Cloudy	0.01 inch or more precip.	0.1 inch or more snow/ice	Thunder-storms
0	43	30	n/a	n/a	n/a	n/a	n/a	2

Note: Figures are average number of days per year and cover the years 1948-1990
Source: National Climatic Data Center, International Station Meteorological Climate Summary, 9/96

HAZARDOUS WASTE

Superfund Sites

The Santa Rosa-Petaluma, CA metro area has no sites on the EPA's Superfund Final National Priorities List (NPL) or Superfund Alternative Approach (SAA) list. The Superfund alternative approach uses the same investigation and cleanup process and standards that are used for sites listed on the National Priorities List. The SAA is an alternative to listing a site on the NPL; it is not an alternative to Superfund or the Superfund process. There are a total of 1,445 Superfund sites with a status of proposed or final on both lists in the United States. *U.S. Environmental Protection Agency, National Pri-*

orities List, May 1, 2025; U.S. Environmental Protection Agency, Superfund Alternative Approach Sites, May 1, 2025

AIR QUALITY

Air Quality Trends: Ozone

	1990	1995	2000	2005	2010	2015	2020	2021	2022	2023
MSA[1]	n/a	n/a	n/a	n/a	n/a	n/a	n/a	n/a	n/a	n/a
U.S.	0.087	0.089	0.081	0.080	0.072	0.068	0.066	0.067	0.067	0.070

Note: (1) Data covers the Santa Rosa-Petaluma, CA Metropolitan Statistical Area; n/a not available. The values shown are the composite ozone concentration averages among trend sites based on the highest fourth daily maximum 8-hour concentration in parts per million. These trends are based on sites having an adequate record of monitoring data during the trend period. Data from exceptional events are included.
Source: U.S. Environmental Protection Agency, Air Quality Monitoring Information, "Air Quality Trends by City, 1990-2023"

Air Quality Index

Area	Percent of Days when Air Quality was...[2]					AQI Statistics[2]	
	Good	Moderate	Unhealthy for Sensitive Groups	Unhealthy	Very Unhealthy	Maximum	Median
MSA[1]	88.5	11.0	0.5	0.0	0.0	117	33

Note: (1) Data covers the Santa Rosa-Petaluma, CA Metropolitan Statistical Area; (2) Based on 365 days with AQI data in 2023. Air Quality Index (AQI) is an index for reporting daily air quality. EPA calculates the AQI for five major air pollutants regulated by the Clean Air Act: ground-level ozone, particle pollution (aka particulate matter), carbon monoxide, sulfur dioxide, and nitrogen dioxide. The AQI runs from 0 to 500. The higher the AQI value, the greater the level of air pollution and the greater the health concern. There are six AQI categories: "Good" AQI is between 0 and 50. Air quality is considered satisfactory; "Moderate" AQI is between 51 and 100. Air quality is acceptable; "Unhealthy for Sensitive Groups" When AQI values are between 101 and 150, members of sensitive groups may experience health effects; "Unhealthy" When AQI values are between 151 and 200 everyone may begin to experience health effects; "Very Unhealthy" AQI values between 201 and 300 trigger a health alert; "Hazardous" AQI values over 300 trigger warnings of emergency conditions (not shown).
Source: U.S. Environmental Protection Agency, Air Quality Index Report, 2023

Air Quality Index Pollutants

Area	Percent of Days when AQI Pollutant was...[2]					
	Carbon Monoxide	Nitrogen Dioxide	Ozone	Sulfur Dioxide	Particulate Matter 2.5	Particulate Matter 10
MSA[1]	0.3	0.0	64.9	(3)	34.5	0.3

Note: (1) Data covers the Santa Rosa-Petaluma, CA Metropolitan Statistical Area; (2) Based on 365 days with AQI data in 2023. The Air Quality Index (AQI) is an index for reporting daily air quality. EPA calculates the AQI for five major air pollutants regulated by the Clean Air Act: ground-level ozone, particle pollution (also known as particulate matter), carbon monoxide, sulfur dioxide, and nitrogen dioxide. The AQI runs from 0 to 500. The higher the AQI value, the greater the level of air pollution and the greater the health concern; (3) Sulfur dioxide is no longer included in this table because SO_2 concentrations tend to be very localized and not necessarily representative of broad geographical areas like counties and CBSAs.
Source: U.S. Environmental Protection Agency, Air Quality Index Report, 2023

Maximum Air Pollutant Concentrations: Particulate Matter, Ozone, CO and Lead

	Particulate Matter 10 (ug/m^3)	Particulate Matter 2.5 Wtd AM (ug/m^3)	Particulate Matter 2.5 24-Hr (ug/m^3)	Ozone (ppm)	Carbon Monoxide (ppm)	Lead (ug/m^3)
MSA[1] Level	48	5	17	0.046	1	n/a
NAAQS[2]	150	15	35	0.075	9	0.15
Met NAAQS[2]	Yes	Yes	Yes	Yes	Yes	n/a

Note: (1) Data covers the Santa Rosa-Petaluma, CA Metropolitan Statistical Area; Data from exceptional events are included; (2) National Ambient Air Quality Standards; ppm = parts per million; ug/m^3 = micrograms per cubic meter; n/a not available.
Concentrations: Particulate Matter 10 (coarse particulate)—highest second maximum 24-hour concentration; Particulate Matter 2.5 Wtd AM (fine particulate)—highest weighted annual mean concentration; Particulate Matter 2.5 24-Hour (fine particulate)—highest 98th percentile 24-hour concentration; Ozone—highest fourth daily maximum 8-hour concentration; Carbon Monoxide—highest second maximum non-overlapping 8-hour concentration; Lead—maximum running 3-month average
Source: U.S. Environmental Protection Agency, Air Quality Monitoring Information, "Air Quality Statistics by City, 2023"

Maximum Air Pollutant Concentrations: Nitrogen Dioxide and Sulfur Dioxide

	Nitrogen Dioxide AM (ppb)	Nitrogen Dioxide 1-Hr (ppb)	Sulfur Dioxide AM (ppb)	Sulfur Dioxide 1-Hr (ppb)	Sulfur Dioxide 24-Hr (ppb)
MSA[1] Level	3	25	n/a	n/a	n/a
NAAQS[2]	53	100	30	75	140
Met NAAQS[2]	Yes	Yes	n/a	n/a	n/a

Note: (1) Data covers the Santa Rosa-Petaluma, CA Metropolitan Statistical Area; Data from exceptional events are included; (2) National Ambient Air Quality Standards; ppm = parts per million; ug/m³ = micrograms per cubic meter; n/a not available.

Concentrations: Nitrogen Dioxide AM—highest arithmetic mean concentration; Nitrogen Dioxide 1-Hr—highest 98th percentile 1-hour daily maximum concentration; Sulfur Dioxide AM—highest annual mean concentration; Sulfur Dioxide 1-Hr—highest 99th percentile 1-hour daily maximum concentration; Sulfur Dioxide 24-Hr—highest second maximum 24-hour concentration

Source: U.S. Environmental Protection Agency, Air Quality Monitoring Information, "Air Quality Statistics by City, 2023"

Seattle, Washington

Background

Once named New York, the virgin hinterlands and wide curving arch of Elliot Bay was renamed Seattle in 1853, for the Native American Indian Chief Seattle, two years after its first five families from Illinois had settled into the narrow strip of land between Puget Sound and Lake Washington.

The lush, green forests of the "Emerald City," created by frequent rain and its many natural waterways, gave birth to Seattle's first major industry—lumber, which also bred a society of bearded, rabble-rousing bachelors. To alleviate that problem, Asa Mercer, president of the Territorial University, which later became the University of Washington, trekked back east, and recruited marriageable women, aka "Mercer girls."

Today, the city does not rely on lumber as its major industry, but boasts commercial aircraft production and missile research, importing and exporting, and technology. As the closest U.S. mainland port to Asia, Seattle has become a key trade center for goods such as cars, forest products, electronic equipment, bananas, and petroleum products. The Seattle area continues to move toward becoming the next Silicon Valley. It is predominantly a software town dominated by Microsoft, located in nearby Redmond. The city is home to ten Fortune 500 companies including Amazon, Costco, Microsoft, Paccar, Starbucks, and Nordstrom.

The Seattle Seaport Terminal Project, comprised of small-and-large-scale projects designed to improve the port's facilities for businesses, passengers, residents, and tourists, included a major renovation of Terminal 5, construction of a Cruise Ship Terminal improvement, and port facilities improvements. Seattle is the fourth largest container port in North America.

Seattle has undergone a cultural and commercial reemergence of its downtown. Tourists and locals are drawn by luxury hotels, restaurants, a multi-screen movie theater, and other entertainment-oriented businesses, including the first in a nationwide chain of Game Works, computerized playgrounds for adults. Center City Seattle continues to see renovation and development projects, as city planners deal with more people living, working, and visiting in the city. Popular attractions in Center City are Chihuly Garden and Glass, showing the work of artist Dale Chihuly, and the Space Needle, built for the 1962 World's Fair and offering visitors Seattle's only 360 degree indoor and outdoor panoramic views of downtown and surrounding natural beauty from 605 feet up.

The arts are a vital part of Seattle life. The world-famous Seattle Opera, founded in 1963, performs at Marion Oliver McCaw Hall. The Seattle Philharmonic Orchestra celebrates its 81st anniversary in 2025; its annual Bushnell Concerto Competition features promising new area musicians. The city's jazz scene developed the early careers of Ray Charles and Quincy Jones, and is the birthplace of rocker Jimi Hendrix, the bands Nirvana, Pearl Jam, Soundgarden, and Foo Fighters, and the alternative rock movement grunge.

Seattle has four major professional sports teams: the National Football League's (NFL) Seattle Seahawks, Major League Baseball's (MLB) Seattle Mariners, the National Hockey League's (NHL) Seattle Kraken, and Major League Soccer's (MLS) Seattle Sounders FC. Other professional sports teams include the Women's National Basketball Association's (WNBA) Seattle Storm, the National Women's Soccer League's (NWSL) Seattle Reign FC, and Major League Rugby's (MLR) Seattle Seawolves.

Seattle is classified as having both a warm-summer climate, and an oceanic climate. It has cool, wet winters and mild, relatively dry summers, characteristics of both. Temperature extremes are moderated by the adjacent Puget Sound, greater Pacific Ocean, and Lake Washington. Thus extreme heat waves are rare in the Seattle area, as are very cold temperatures. It is the cloudiest region of the United States, due in part to frequent storms and lows moving in from the adjacent Pacific Ocean. It has many more "rain days" than other major American cities, with at least 0.01 inches (0.25 mm) of precipitation falling on 150 days. However, because it often has merely a light drizzle falling from the sky for many days, Seattle actually receives significantly less rainfall (or other precipitation) overall than many other U.S. cities. The city is cloudy 201 days out of the year and partly cloudy 93 days.

Rankings

General Rankings

- To help military veterans find the best places in which to settle down, *WalletHub* compared the 100 largest U.S. cities across 19 key indicators of livability, affordability and veteran-friendliness. They range from the share of military skill-related jobs to veteran income growth to the availability of VA health facilities. Seattle ranked #76. *Wallethub.com, "Best & Worst Places for Veterans to Live (2025)," November 7, 2024*

- The human resources consulting firm Mercer ranked 241 major cities worldwide in terms of overall quality of life. Seattle ranked #52. Criteria: political and personal safety, social, and economic factors; medical and health considerations; schools and education; public services and transportation; recreation; connectivity; housing and infrastructure; and climate. *Mercer, "Mercer 2024 Quality of Living Survey," December 2024*

- Seattle was selected as an "All-America City" by the National Civic League. The All-America City Award recognizes civic excellence and in 2024 honored 10 communities that best exemplify the spirit of citizen engagement and cross-sector collaborative problem solving to address pressing and complex issues and create stronger community connections. This year's theme was: "Strengthening Democracy Through Local Action and Innovation." *National Civic League, "2024 All-America City Awards," June 7-9, 2024*

Business/Finance Rankings

- According to *Business Insider*, the Seattle metro area is a prime place to run a startup or move an existing business to. The area ranked #5. More than 300 metro areas were analyzed for factors that were of top concern to new business owners. Data was based on the 2019 U.S. Census Bureau American Community Survey, statistics from the CDC, and University of Chicago analysis. Criteria: business formations; percentage of vaccinated population; percentage of households with internet subscriptions; median household income; and share of work that can be done from home. *BusinessInsider.com, "The 20 Best Cities for Starting a Business in 2022 Include Denver, Raleigh, and Olympia," June 7, 2022*

- WalletHub's latest report ranked 182 cities by the average credit score of its residents. Seattle was ranked #6 among the ten cities with the highest average credit score, based on WalletHub's 2024 fourth quarter data. *WalletHub.com, "2025's Cities With the Highest & Lowest Credit Scores," March 6, 2025*

- Payscale.com ranked the 32 largest metro areas in terms of wage growth. The Seattle metro area ranked #11. Criteria: quarterly changes in private industry employee and education professional wage growth from the previous year. *PayScale, "Wage Trends by Metro Area-4th Quarter," February 4, 2025*

- The Seattle metro area appeared on the Milken Institute "2025 Best Performing Cities" list. Rank: #25 out of 200 large metro areas (based on performance category). Criteria: job growth; wage growth; high-tech growth and impact; community resilience; housing affordability; household broadband access. *Milken Institute, "Best-Performing Cities 2025," January 14, 2025*

- Mercer Human Resources Consulting ranked 226 cities worldwide in terms of cost-of-living. Seattle ranked #28 (the lower the ranking, the higher the cost-of-living). The survey measured the comparative cost of over 200 items (such as housing, food, clothing, domestic supplies, transportation, and recreation/entertainment) in each location. *Mercer, "2024 Cost of Living City Ranking," June 17, 2024*

Education Rankings

- Personal finance website *WalletHub* analyzed the 150 largest U.S. metropolitan statistical areas to determine where the most educated Americans are putting their degrees to work. Criteria: education levels; percentage of workers with degrees; education quality and attainment gap; public school quality rankings; quality and enrollment of each metro area's universities. Seattle was ranked #10 (#1 = most educated city). *WalletHub.com, "Most & Least Educated Cities in America, 2025" July 2, 2024*

Environmental Rankings

- Sperling's *BestPlaces* assessed the 50 largest metropolitan areas of the United States for the likelihood of dangerously extreme weather events or earthquakes. In general the Southeast and South-Central regions have the highest risk of weather extremes and earthquakes, while the Pacific Northwest enjoys the lowest risk. Of the least risky metropolitan areas, the Seattle metro area was ranked #5. *Bestplaces.net, "Avoid Natural Disasters: BestPlaces Reveals The Top 10 Safest Places to Live," October 25, 2017*

- The U.S. Environmental Protection Agency (EPA) released its list of U.S. metropolitan areas with the most ENERGY STAR certified buildings in 2023. The Seattle metro area was ranked #14 out of 25. *U.S. Environmental Protection Agency, "2024 Energy Star Top Cities," May 22, 2024*

- Seattle was highlighted as one of the 25 metro areas most polluted by short-term particle pollution (24-hour PM 2.5) in the U.S. during 2021 through 2023. The area ranked #9. *American Lung Association, "State of the Air 2025," April 23, 2025*

Food/Drink Rankings

- WalletHub compared the 100 largest U.S. cities across 17 key indicators of vegan- and vegetarian-friendliness. Seattle was ranked #5. Cities were selected based on metrics such as the cost of groceries for vegetarians, the share of restaurants serving meatless options and the number of salad shops per capita. *WalletHub.com, "Best Cities for Vegans & Vegetarians (2025)," September 24, 2024*

Health/Fitness Rankings

- For each of the 100 largest cities in the United States, the American Fitness Index®, compiled in partnership between the American College of Sports Medicine and the Elevance Health Foundation, evaluated community infrastructure and more than 30 health behaviors including preventive health, levels of chronic disease conditions, food insecurity, pedestrian safety, air quality, and community/environment resources that support physical activity. Seattle ranked #3 for "community fitness." *americanfitnessindex.org, "2024 ACSM American Fitness Index Summary Report," July 23, 2024*

- Seattle was identified as one of the 10 most walkable cities in the U.S. by Walk Score. The city ranked #8. Walk Score measures walkability by analyzing hundreds of walking routes to nearby amenities, and also measures pedestrian friendliness by analyzing population density and road metrics such as block length and intersection density. *WalkScore.com, April 13, 2021*

- The Seattle metro area was identified as one of the worst cities for bed bugs in America by pest control company Orkin. The area ranked #44 out of 50 based on the number of bed bug treatments Orkin performed from December 2022 to November 2023. *Orkin, "Chicago Joins Paris In Global Bed Bug Spotlight Ranking As The Worst City On Orkin's U.S. Bed Bug Cities List," January 22, 2024*

- Seattle was identified as a "2025 Allergy Capital." The area ranked #68 out of the nation's 100 largest metropolitan areas. Three groups of factors were used to identify the most challenging cities for people with allergies: annual tree, grass, and weed pollen scores; over the counter allergy medicine use; number of board-certified allergy specialists. *Asthma and Allergy Foundation of America, "2025 Allergy Capitals: The Most Challenging Places to Live with Allergies," March 18, 2025*

- Seattle was identified as a "2024 Asthma Capital." The area ranked #59 out of the nation's 100 largest metropolitan areas. Criteria: estimated asthma prevalence; asthma-related mortality; and ER visits due to asthma. Risk factors analyzed but not factored in the rankings: annual air quality including pollution and ozone levels; public smoking laws; indoor air quality; access to asthma specialists; rescue and controller medication use; uninsured rate; pollen allergy; poverty rate. *Asthma and Allergy Foundation of America, "Asthma Capitals 2024: The Most Challenging Places to Live With Asthma," September 10, 2024*

- The Sharecare Community Well-Being Index evaluates 10 individual and social health factors in order to measure what matters to Americans in the communities in which they live. The Seattle metro area ranked #9 in the top 10 across all 10 domains. Criteria: access to healthcare, food, and community resources; housing and transportation; economic security; feeling of purpose; and physical, financial, social, and community well-being. *Sharecare.com, "Community Well-Being Index: 2020 Metro Area & County Rankings Report," August 30, 2021*

Pet Rankings

- Seattle was selected by *Sniffspot.com* as one of the most dog-friendly cities in the U.S., ranking #16 out of 50. Criteria: dog parks; hiking; sniffspots; public parks; dog-friendly businesses; housing; dog waste cleanliness; leash laws; dog services; and overall cost. *Sniffspot.com, "The Top 50 Most Dog-Friendly Cities in the U.S.," September 30, 2024*

Real Estate Rankings

- *WalletHub* compared the most populated U.S. cities to determine which had the best markets for real estate agents. Seattle ranked #1 where demand was high and pay was the best. Criteria: sales per agent; annual median wage for real-estate agents; monthly average starting salary for real estate agents; real estate job density and competition; unemployment rate; home turnover rate; housing-market health index; and other relevant metrics. *WalletHub.com, "2021 Best Places to Be a Real Estate Agent," May 12, 2021*

- The Seattle metro area was identified as one of the 20 least affordable housing markets in the U.S. in 2024. The area ranked #216 out of 226 markets. Criteria: qualification for a mortgage loan with a 10 percent down payment on a typical home. *National Association of Realtors®, Qualifying Income Based on Sales Price of Existing Single-Family Homes for Metropolitan Areas, February 6, 2025*

- Seattle was ranked #165 out of 176 metro areas in terms of cost of housing in 2024 by the National Association of Home Builders (#1 = most affordable). Criteria: the portion of an average family's income necessary to pay the mortgage on a median-priced home. *National Association of Home Builders®, NAHB-Wells Fargo Cost of Housing Index, 4th Quarter 2024*

Safety Rankings

- Allstate ranked the 100 most populous cities in America in terms of driver safety. Seattle ranked #3. Criteria based on anonymized driving behavior data from Allstate's mobile app powered by Arity: high speed driving (over 80 mph), phone handling, and hard braking. The report helps increase the importance of safety and awareness behind the wheel. *Allstate, "16th Allstate America's Best Drivers Report®" July 11, 2024*

- The National Insurance Crime Bureau ranked the largest metro areas in the U.S. in terms of per capita rates of vehicle theft. The Seattle metro area ranked #7 out of the top 10 (#1 = highest rate). Criteria: number of vehicle theft offenses per 100,000 inhabitants in 2023. *National Insurance Crime Bureau, "Vehicle Thefts Surge Nationwide in 2023," April 9, 2024*

Transportation Rankings

- Seattle was identified as one of the most congested metro areas in the U.S. The area ranked #5 out of 10. Criteria: yearly delay per auto commuter in hours. *Texas A&M Transportation Institute, "2023 Urban Mobility Report," June 2024*

- According to the INRIX "2024 Global Traffic Scorecard," Seattle was identified as one of the most congested metro areas in the U.S. The area ranked #10 out of 10 in the country and among the top 25 most congested in the world. Criteria: average annual time spent in traffic and average cost of congestion per motorist. *Inrix.com, "Employees & Consumers Returned to Downtowns, Traffic Delays & Costs Grew," January 6, 2025*

Women/Minorities Rankings

- Personal finance website *WalletHub* compared more than 180 U.S. cities across two key dimensions, "Hispanic Business-Friendliness" and "Hispanic Purchasing Power," to arrive at the most favorable conditions for Hispanic entrepreneurs. Seattle was ranked #121 out of 182. Criteria includes: share of Hispanic-Owned Businesses; average growth of Hispanic Business revenues; Small Business-Friendliness score; affordability; and number of Hispanics with at least a bachelor's degree. *WalletHub.com, "Best Cities for Hispanic Entrepreneurs," September 4, 2024*

Miscellaneous Rankings

- *MoveHub* ranked 446 hipster cities across 20 countries, using its new and improved alternative Hipster Index and Seattle came out as #4 among the top 50. Criteria: population over 150,000; number of vintage boutiques; density of tattoo parlors; vegan places to eat; coffee shops; and density of vinyl record stores. *MoveHub.com, "The Hipster Index: Brighton Pips Portland to Global Top Spot," July 28, 2021*

- Seattle was selected as a 2024 Digital Cities Survey winner. The city ranked #3 in the large city (500,000 or more population) category. The survey examined and assessed how city governments are utilizing new technology and modernized applications to provide residents an array of contactless services and conveniences. Survey questions focused on ten initiatives: cybersecurity; citizen experience; disaster recovery; business intelligence; IT personnel retention; data governance; business automation; AI/machine learning; application modernization; and IT collaboration. *Center for Digital Government, "2024 Digital Cities Survey," November 5, 2024*

- *WalletHub* compared 148 of the most populated U.S. cities to determine their operating efficiency. A "Quality of Services" score was constructed for each city and then measured against the total budget per capita to reveal which were managed the best. Seattle ranked #123. Criteria: financial stability; economy; education; safety; health; infrastructure and pollution. *WalletHub.com, "2025's Best- & Worst-Run Cities in America," June 18, 2024*

Business Environment

DEMOGRAPHICS

Population Growth

Area	1990 Census	2000 Census	2010 Census	2020 Census	2023 Estimate[2]	Population Growth 1990-2023 (%)
City	516,262	563,374	608,660	737,015	741,440	43.6
MSA[1]	2,559,164	3,043,878	3,439,809	4,018,762	4,021,467	57.1
U.S.	248,709,873	281,421,906	308,745,538	331,449,281	332,387,540	33.6

Note: (1) Figures cover the Seattle-Tacoma-Bellevue, WA Metropolitan Statistical Area; (2) 2019-2023 5-year ACS population estimate
Source: U.S. Census Bureau, 1990 Census, 2000 Census, 2010 Census, 2020 Census, 2019-2023 American Community Survey 5-Year Estimates

Race

Area	White Alone[2] (%)	Black Alone[2] (%)	Asian Alone[2] (%)	AIAN[3] Alone[2] (%)	NHOPI[4] Alone[2] (%)	Other Race Alone[2] (%)	Two or More Races (%)
City	61.8	6.6	17.2	0.6	0.3	3.0	10.5
MSA[1]	60.9	6.1	15.4	0.8	0.9	4.6	11.4
U.S.	63.4	12.4	5.8	0.9	0.2	6.6	10.7

Note: (1) Figures cover the Seattle-Tacoma-Bellevue, WA Metropolitan Statistical Area; (2) Alone is defined as not being in combination with one or more other races; (3) American Indian and Alaska Native; (4) Native Hawaiian and Other Pacific Islander
Source: U.S. Census Bureau, 2019-2023 American Community Survey 5-Year Estimates

Hispanic or Latino Origin

Area	Total (%)	Mexican (%)	Puerto Rican (%)	Cuban (%)	Other (%)
City	8.2	4.8	0.4	0.2	2.8
MSA[1]	11.4	7.7	0.6	0.2	2.9
U.S.	19.0	11.3	1.8	0.7	5.2

Note: Persons of Hispanic or Latino origin can be of any race; (1) Figures cover the Seattle-Tacoma-Bellevue, WA Metropolitan Statistical Area
Source: U.S. Census Bureau, 2019-2023 American Community Survey 5-Year Estimates

Age

Area	Percent of Population									Median Age
	Under Age 5	Age 5–19	Age 20–34	Age 35–44	Age 45–54	Age 55–64	Age 65–74	Age 75–84	Age 85+	
City	4.2	12.2	32.7	16.3	12.2	9.7	7.7	3.4	1.6	35.5
MSA[1]	5.7	17.5	22.8	15.4	12.7	11.9	8.6	3.8	1.6	37.4
U.S.	5.7	19.1	20.2	13.1	12.3	12.8	10.0	4.9	1.9	38.7

Note: (1) Figures cover the Seattle-Tacoma-Bellevue, WA Metropolitan Statistical Area
Source: U.S. Census Bureau, 2019-2023 American Community Survey 5-Year Estimates

Disability by Age

Area	All Ages	Under 18 Years Old	18 to 64 Years Old	65 Years and Over
City	10.0	2.8	8.0	30.3
MSA[1]	11.4	4.2	9.2	32.6
U.S.	13.0	4.7	10.7	32.9

Note: Figures show percent of the civilian noninstitutionalized population that reported having a disability. Disability status is determined from six types of difficulty: vision, hearing, cognitive, ambulatory, self-care, and independent living. For children under 5 years old, hearing and vision difficulty are used to determine disability status. For children between the ages of 5 and 14, disability status is determined from hearing, vision, cognitive, ambulatory, and self-care difficulties. For people aged 15 years and older, they are considered to have a disability if they have difficulty with any one of the six difficulty types; Note: (1) Figures cover the Seattle-Tacoma-Bellevue, WA Metropolitan Statistical Area
Source: U.S. Census Bureau, 2019-2023 American Community Survey 5-Year Estimates

Ancestry

Area	German	Irish	English	American	Italian	Polish	French[2]	European	Scottish
City	14.0	10.8	12.2	2.4	4.7	2.6	2.8	3.9	2.7
MSA[1]	13.2	9.0	10.9	2.9	3.4	1.7	2.4	3.2	2.3
U.S.	12.6	9.4	9.1	5.5	4.9	2.6	2.0	1.6	1.6

Note: Figures are the percentage of the total population reporting a particular ancestry. The nine most commonly reported ancestries in the U.S. are shown. Figures include multiple ancestries (e.g. if a person reported being Irish and Italian, they were included in both columns); (1) Figures cover the Seattle-Tacoma-Bellevue, WA Metropolitan Statistical Area; (2) Excludes Basque
Source: U.S. Census Bureau, 2019-2023 American Community Survey 5-Year Estimates

Foreign-born Population

Area	Any Foreign Country	Asia	Mexico	Europe	Caribbean	Central America[2]	South America	Africa	Canada
	Percent of Population Born in								
City	19.9	11.4	1.4	2.5	0.2	0.4	0.7	2.1	1.1
MSA[1]	20.4	11.0	2.4	2.8	0.2	0.6	0.7	1.7	0.7
U.S.	13.9	4.3	3.3	1.4	1.4	1.2	1.2	0.8	0.2

Note: (1) Figures cover the Seattle-Tacoma-Bellevue, WA Metropolitan Statistical Area; (2) Excludes Mexico.
Source: U.S. Census Bureau, 2019-2023 American Community Survey 5-Year Estimates

Household Size

Area	One	Two	Three	Four	Five	Six	Seven or More	Average Household Size
	Persons in Household (%)							
City	41.3	35.4	11.2	8.5	2.5	0.7	0.5	2.03
MSA[1]	28.0	34.0	15.8	13.6	5.4	1.9	1.3	2.49
U.S.	28.5	33.8	15.4	12.7	5.9	2.3	1.4	2.54

Note: (1) Figures cover the Seattle-Tacoma-Bellevue, WA Metropolitan Statistical Area
Source: U.S. Census Bureau, 2019-2023 American Community Survey 5-Year Estimates

Household Relationships

Area	House-holder	Opposite-sex Spouse	Same-sex Spouse	Opposite-sex Unmarried Partner	Same-sex Unmarried Partner	Child[2]	Grand-child	Other Relatives	Non-relatives
City	46.9	15.2	0.8	4.3	0.6	17.5	0.7	2.8	7.3
MSA[1]	38.9	18.3	0.3	2.9	0.2	26.7	1.5	4.6	4.7
U.S.	38.3	17.5	0.2	2.5	0.2	28.3	2.4	4.8	3.4

Note: Figures are percent of the total population; (1) Figures cover the Seattle-Tacoma-Bellevue, WA Metropolitan Statistical Area; (2) Includes biological, adopted, and stepchildren of the householder
Source: U.S. Census Bureau, 2020 Census

Gender

Area	Males	Females	Males per 100 Females
City	378,278	363,162	104.2
MSA[1]	2,031,168	1,990,299	102.1
U.S.	164,545,087	167,842,453	98.0

Note: (1) Figures cover the Seattle-Tacoma-Bellevue, WA Metropolitan Statistical Area
Source: U.S. Census Bureau, 2019-2023 American Community Survey 5-Year Estimates

Marital Status

Area	Never Married	Now Married[2]	Separated	Widowed	Divorced
City	46.1	40.3	1.1	3.0	9.5
MSA[1]	33.8	50.4	1.3	4.0	10.5
U.S.	34.1	47.9	1.7	5.6	10.7

Note: Figures are percentages and cover the population 15 years of age and older; (1) Figures cover the Seattle-Tacoma-Bellevue, WA Metropolitan Statistical Area; (2) Excludes separated
Source: U.S. Census Bureau, 2019-2023 American Community Survey 5-Year Estimates

Religious Groups by Family

Area	Catholic	Baptist	Methodist	LDS[2]	Pentecostal	Lutheran	Islam	Adventist	Other
MSA[1]	11.0	1.0	0.7	2.6	2.8	1.2	0.6	1.4	19.8
U.S.	18.7	7.3	3.0	2.0	1.8	1.7	1.3	1.3	11.6

Note: Figures are the number of adherents as a percentage of the total population and cover the eight largest religious groups in the U.S; (1) Figures cover the Seattle-Tacoma-Bellevue, WA Metropolitan Statistical Area; (2) Church of Jesus Christ of Latter-day Saints
Sources: 2020 U.S. Religion Census, Association of Statisticians of American Religious Bodies; The Association of Religion Data Archives (ARDA)

Religious Groups by Tradition

Area	Catholic	Evangelical Protestant	Mainline Protestant	Black Protestant	Islam	Judaism	Hinduism	Orthodox	Buddhism
MSA[1]	11.0	19.5	2.7	0.6	0.6	0.4	0.4	0.6	1.6
U.S.	18.7	16.5	5.2	2.3	1.3	0.6	0.4	0.4	0.3

Note: Figures are the number of adherents as a percentage of the total population; (1) Figures cover the Seattle-Tacoma-Bellevue, WA Metropolitan Statistical Area
Sources: 2020 U.S. Religion Census, Association of Statisticians of American Religious Bodies; The Association of Religion Data Archives (ARDA)

ECONOMY

Real Gross Domestic Product (GDP)

Area	2017	2018	2019	2020	2021	2022	2023	Rank[3]
MSA[1]	368.2	395.7	417.4	418.4	449.5	459.5	487.8	9
U.S.[2]	17,619.1	18,160.7	18,642.5	18,238.9	19,387.6	19,896.6	20,436.3	–

Note: Figures are in billions of chained 2017 dollars; (1) Figures cover the Seattle-Tacoma-Bellevue, WA Metropolitan Statistical Area; (2) Figures cover real GDP within metropolitan areas; (3) Rank is based on 2023 data and ranges from 1 to 384
Source: U.S. Bureau of Economic Analysis

Economic Growth

Area	2014	2015	2016	2017	2018	2019	2020	2021	2022	2023
MSA[1]	4.9	4.6	4.1	8.2	7.5	5.5	0.2	7.4	2.2	6.2
U.S.[2]	2.6	3.2	2.0	2.7	3.1	2.7	-2.2	6.3	2.6	2.7

Note: Figures are real gross domestic product growth rates and represent percent change from preceding period; (1) Figures cover the Seattle-Tacoma-Bellevue, WA Metropolitan Statistical Area; (2) Figures are the average growth rates within metropolitan areas
Source: U.S. Bureau of Economic Analysis

Metropolitan Area Exports

Area	2018	2019	2020	2021	2022	2023	Rank[2]
MSA[1]	59,742.9	41,249.0	23,851.0	28,866.7	34,159.9	36,267.3	10
U.S.	1,664,056.1	1,645,173.7	1,431,406.6	1,753,941.4	2,062,937.4	2,019,160.5	–

Note: Figures are in millions of dollars; (1) Figures cover the Seattle-Tacoma-Bellevue, WA Metropolitan Statistical Area; (2) Rank is based on 2023 data and ranges from 1 to 386
Source: U.S. Department of Commerce, International Trade Administration, Office of Trade and Economic Analysis, Industry and Analysis, Exports by Metropolitan Area, data extracted April 2, 2025

Building Permits

Area	Single-Family			Multi-Family			Total		
	2023	2024	Pct. Chg.	2023	2024	Pct. Chg.	2023	2024	Pct. Chg.
City	473	405	-14.4	4,826	5,490	13.8	5,299	5,895	11.2
MSA[1]	6,296	6,489	3.1	10,927	11,431	4.6	17,223	17,920	4.0
U.S.	920,000	981,900	6.7	591,100	496,100	-16.1	1,511,100	1,478,000	-2.2

Note: (1) Figures cover the Seattle-Tacoma-Bellevue, WA Metropolitan Statistical Area; Figures represent new, privately-owned housing units authorized (unadjusted data)
Source: U.S. Census Bureau, Building Permits Survey (BPS), 2023, 2024

Bankruptcy Filings

Area	Business Filings			Nonbusiness Filings		
	2023	2024	% Chg.	2023	2024	% Chg.
King County	92	113	22.8	1,134	1,459	28.7
U.S.	18,926	23,107	22.1	434,064	494,201	13.9

Note: Business filings include Chapter 7, Chapter 9, Chapter 11, Chapter 12, Chapter 13, Chapter 15, and Section 304; Nonbusiness filings include Chapter 7, Chapter 11, and Chapter 13
Source: Administrative Office of the U.S. Courts, Business and Nonbusiness Bankruptcy, County Cases Commenced by Chapter of the Bankruptcy Code, During the 12-Month Period Ending December 31, 2023 and Business and Nonbusiness Bankruptcy, County Cases Commenced by Chapter of the Bankruptcy Code, During the 12-Month Period Ending December 31, 2024

Housing Vacancy Rates

Area	Gross Vacancy Rate[3] (%)			Year-Round Vacancy Rate[4] (%)			Rental Vacancy Rate[5] (%)			Homeowner Vacancy Rate[6] (%)		
	2022	2023	2024	2022	2023	2024	2022	2023	2024	2022	2023	2024
MSA[1]	5.7	5.1	6.2	5.2	4.7	5.9	4.9	4.0	6.5	0.7	0.6	1.1
U.S.[2]	9.1	9.0	9.1	7.5	7.5	7.6	5.7	6.5	6.8	0.8	0.8	1.0

Note: (1) Figures cover the Seattle-Tacoma-Bellevue, WA Metropolitan Statistical Area; (2) Figures cover the 75 largest Metropolitan Statistical Areas; (3) The percentage of the total housing inventory that is vacant; (4) The percentage of the housing inventory (excluding seasonal units) that is year-round vacant; (5) The percentage of rental inventory that is vacant for rent; (6) The percentage of homeowner inventory that is vacant for sale
Source: U.S. Census Bureau, Housing Vacancies and Homeownership Annual Statistics: 2022, 2023, 2024

INCOME

Income

Area	Per Capita ($)	Median Household ($)	Average Household ($)
City	82,508	121,984	170,038
MSA[1]	61,286	112,594	152,753
U.S.	43,289	78,538	110,491

Note: (1) Figures cover the Seattle-Tacoma-Bellevue, WA Metropolitan Statistical Area
Source: U.S. Census Bureau, 2019-2023 American Community Survey 5-Year Estimates

Household Income Distribution

Area	Percent of Households Earning							
	Under $15,000	$15,000 -$24,999	$25,000 -$34,999	$35,000 -$49,999	$50,000 -$74,999	$75,000 -$99,999	$100,000 -$149,999	$150,000 and up
City	7.3	3.9	4.0	6.5	11.4	9.5	16.3	41.1
MSA[1]	5.6	3.8	4.2	7.0	12.6	11.5	19.2	36.1
U.S.	8.5	6.6	6.8	10.4	15.7	12.7	17.4	21.9

Note: (1) Figures cover the Seattle-Tacoma-Bellevue, WA Metropolitan Statistical Area
Source: U.S. Census Bureau, 2019-2023 American Community Survey 5-Year Estimates

Poverty Rate

Area	All Ages	Under 18 Years Old	18 to 64 Years Old	65 Years and Over
City	9.9	8.6	9.7	12.3
MSA[1]	8.4	9.5	7.9	8.8
U.S.	12.4	16.3	11.6	10.4

Note: Figures are percentage of people whose income during the past 12 months was below the poverty level;
(1) Figures cover the Seattle-Tacoma-Bellevue, WA Metropolitan Statistical Area
Source: U.S. Census Bureau, 2019-2023 American Community Survey 5-Year Estimates

EMPLOYMENT

Labor Force and Employment

Area	Civilian Labor Force			Workers Employed		
	Dec. 2023	Dec. 2024	% Chg.	Dec. 2023	Dec. 2024	% Chg.
City	511,941	526,448	2.8	495,245	511,570	3.3
MD[1]	1,366,721	1,405,582	2.8	1,318,947	1,362,424	3.3
U.S.	166,661,000	167,746,000	0.7	160,754,000	161,294,000	0.3

Note: Data is not seasonally adjusted and covers workers 16 years of age and older; (1) Figures cover the Seattle-Bellevue-Kent, WA Metropolitan Division
Source: Bureau of Labor Statistics, Local Area Unemployment Statistics

Unemployment Rate

Area	2024											
	Jan.	Feb.	Mar.	Apr.	May	Jun.	Jul.	Aug.	Sep.	Oct.	Nov.	Dec.
City	4.0	3.6	3.5	3.5	3.7	4.5	4.2	4.1	3.9	3.7	3.4	2.8
MD[1]	4.2	3.8	3.7	3.7	3.8	4.7	4.4	4.2	4.1	4.0	3.7	3.1
U.S.	4.1	4.2	3.9	3.5	3.7	4.3	4.5	4.4	3.9	3.9	4.0	3.8

Note: Data is not seasonally adjusted and covers workers 16 years of age and older; (1) Figures cover the Seattle-Bellevue-Kent, WA Metropolitan Division
Source: Bureau of Labor Statistics, Local Area Unemployment Statistics

Average Wages

Occupation	$/Hr.	Occupation	$/Hr.
Accountants and Auditors	51.01	Maintenance and Repair Workers	30.02
Automotive Mechanics	30.63	Marketing Managers	94.44
Bookkeepers	28.45	Network and Computer Systems Admin.	55.61
Carpenters	39.76	Nurses, Licensed Practical	39.88
Cashiers	20.63	Nurses, Registered	57.82
Computer Programmers	80.47	Nursing Assistants	25.24
Computer Systems Analysts	66.53	Office Clerks, General	26.95
Computer User Support Specialists	37.28	Physical Therapists	50.63
Construction Laborers	31.08	Physicians	142.83
Cooks, Restaurant	22.67	Plumbers, Pipefitters and Steamfitters	45.49
Customer Service Representatives	27.52	Police and Sheriff's Patrol Officers	53.76
Dentists	97.55	Postal Service Mail Carriers	29.52
Electricians	48.19	Real Estate Sales Agents	40.04
Engineers, Electrical	67.55	Retail Salespersons	21.76
Fast Food and Counter Workers	19.74	Sales Representatives, Technical/Scientific	71.82
Financial Managers	96.69	Secretaries, Exc. Legal/Medical/Executive	28.37
First-Line Supervisors of Office Workers	42.38	Security Guards	25.48
General and Operations Managers	82.62	Surgeons	164.19
Hairdressers/Cosmetologists	33.56	Teacher Assistants, Exc. Postsecondary[1]	24.88
Home Health and Personal Care Aides	23.17	Teachers, Secondary School, Exc. Sp. Ed.[1]	47.37
Janitors and Cleaners	22.62	Telemarketers	21.66
Landscaping/Groundskeeping Workers	24.35	Truck Drivers, Heavy/Tractor-Trailer	33.99
Lawyers	88.39	Truck Drivers, Light/Delivery Services	26.42
Maids and Housekeeping Cleaners	20.95	Waiters and Waitresses	27.97

Note: Wage data covers the Seattle-Tacoma-Bellevue, WA Metropolitan Statistical Area; (1) Hourly wages were calculated from annual wage data based on a 40 hour work week
Source: Bureau of Labor Statistics, Metro Area Occupational Employment & Wage Estimates, May 2024

Employment by Industry

Sector	MD[1]		U.S.
	Number of Employees	Percent of Total	Percent of Total
Construction	71,700	4.8	5.1
Financial Activities	74,600	4.9	5.8
Government	192,500	12.8	14.9
Information	131,200	8.7	1.9
Leisure and Hospitality	139,900	9.3	10.4
Manufacturing	93,100	6.2	8.0
Mining and Logging	400	<0.1	0.4
Other Services	48,100	3.2	3.7
Private Education and Health Services	206,000	13.7	16.9
Professional and Business Services	315,100	20.9	14.2
Retail Trade	108,700	7.2	10.0
Transportation, Warehousing, and Utilities	68,100	4.5	4.8
Wholesale Trade	59,700	4.0	3.9

Note: Figures are non-farm employment as of December 2024. Figures are not seasonally adjusted and include workers 16 years of age and older; (1) Figures cover the Seattle-Bellevue-Kent, WA Metropolitan Division
Source: Bureau of Labor Statistics, Current Employment Statistics, Employment, Hours, and Earnings

Employment by Occupation

Occupation Classification	City (%)	MSA[1] (%)	U.S. (%)
Management, Business, Science, and Arts	66.2	51.0	42.0
Natural Resources, Construction, and Maintenance	2.8	7.2	8.6
Production, Transportation, and Material Moving	5.4	10.3	13.0
Sales and Office	14.0	17.3	19.9
Service	11.6	14.2	16.5

Note: Figures cover employed civilians 16 years of age and older; (1) Figures cover the Seattle-Tacoma-Bellevue, WA Metropolitan Statistical Area
Source: U.S. Census Bureau, 2019-2023 American Community Survey 5-Year Estimates

Occupations with Greatest Projected Employment Growth: 2022 – 2032

Occupation[1]	2022 Employment	2032 Projected Employment	Numeric Employment Change	Percent Employment Change
Software Developers and Software Quality Assurance Analysts and Testers	103,910	134,850	30,940	29.8
Fast Food and Counter Workers	107,310	126,380	19,070	17.8
Business Operations Specialists, All Other	57,360	68,560	11,200	19.5
Management Analysts	34,490	45,290	10,800	31.3
Construction Laborers	53,710	64,190	10,480	19.5
Retail Salespersons	109,670	118,630	8,960	8.2
Office Clerks, General	76,900	85,300	8,400	10.9
Registered Nurses	61,030	69,180	8,150	13.4
General and Operations Managers	50,860	58,430	7,570	14.9
Janitors and Cleaners, Except Maids and Housekeeping Cleaners	49,840	57,160	7,320	14.7

Note: Projections cover Washington; (1) Sorted by numeric employment change
Source: www.projectionscentral.org, State Occupational Projections, 2022–2032 Long-Term Projections

Fastest-Growing Occupations: 2022 – 2032

Occupation[1]	2022 Employment	2032 Projected Employment	Numeric Employment Change	Percent Employment Change
Museum Technicians and Conservators	230	340	110	47.8
Nuclear Technicians	130	190	60	46.2
Nurse Practitioners	4,150	6,020	1,870	45.1
Data Scientists and Mathematical Science Occupations, All Other	2,490	3,570	1,080	43.4
Solar Photovoltaic Installers	280	400	120	42.9
Transportation Attendants, Except Flight Attendants	700	970	270	38.6
Wind Turbine Service Technicians	260	360	100	38.5
Massage Therapists	8,630	11,840	3,210	37.2
Multimedia Artists and Animators	3,040	4,130	1,090	35.9
Information Security Analysts (SOC 2018)	4,310	5,840	1,530	35.5

Note: Projections cover Washington; (1) Sorted by percent employment change and excludes occupations with numeric employment change less than 50
Source: www.projectionscentral.org, State Occupational Projections, 2022–2032 Long-Term Projections

CITY FINANCES

City Government Finances

Component	2022 ($000)	2022 ($ per capita)
Total Revenues	5,244,066	6,813
Total Expenditures	4,361,603	5,667
Debt Outstanding	5,513,696	7,163

Source: U.S. Census Bureau, State & Local Government Finances 2022

City Government Revenue by Source

Source	2022 ($000)	2022 ($ per capita)	2022 (%)
General Revenue			
From Federal Government	235,578	306	4.5
From State Government	203,976	265	3.9
From Local Governments	14,029	18	0.3
Taxes			
Property	761,662	990	14.5
Sales and Gross Receipts	782,643	1,017	14.9
Personal Income	0	0	0.0
Corporate Income	0	0	0.0
Motor Vehicle License	53,260	69	1.0
Other Taxes	531,421	690	10.1
Current Charges	1,061,875	1,380	20.2
Liquor Store	0	0	0.0
Utility	1,393,399	1,810	26.6

Source: U.S. Census Bureau, State & Local Government Finances 2022

City Government Expenditures by Function

Function	2022 ($000)	2022 ($ per capita)	2022 (%)
General Direct Expenditures			
Air Transportation	0	0	0.0
Corrections	0	0	0.0
Education	105,967	137	2.4
Employment Security Administration	0	0	0.0
Financial Administration	13,120	17	0.3
Fire Protection	240,572	312	5.5
General Public Buildings	0	0	0.0
Governmental Administration, Other	93,096	120	2.1
Health	17,559	22	0.4
Highways	435,839	566	10.0
Hospitals	0	0	0.0
Housing and Community Development	95,296	123	2.2
Interest on General Debt	87,574	113	2.0
Judicial and Legal	58,074	75	1.3
Libraries	80,948	105	1.9
Parking	8,659	11	0.2
Parks and Recreation	311,506	404	7.1
Police Protection	264,217	343	6.1
Public Welfare	169,152	219	3.9
Sewerage	256,412	333	5.9
Solid Waste Management	155,665	202	3.6
Veterans' Services	0	0	0.0
Liquor Store	0	0	0.0
Utility	1,382,708	1,796	31.7

Source: U.S. Census Bureau, State & Local Government Finances 2022

TAXES

State Corporate Income Tax Rates

State	Tax Rate (%)	Income Brackets ($)	Num. of Brackets	Financial Institution Tax Rate (%)[a]	Federal Income Tax Ded.
Washington	None	–	–	–	–

Note: Tax rates for tax year 2024; (a) Rates listed are the corporate income tax rate applied to financial institutions or excise taxes based on income. Some states have other taxes based upon the value of deposits or shares.
Source: Federation of Tax Administrators, State Corporate Income Tax Rates, January 1, 2025

State Individual Income Tax Rates

State	Tax Rate (%)	Income Brackets ($)	Personal Exemptions ($)			Standard Ded. ($)	
			Single	Married	Depend.	Single	Married
Washington			– No state income tax –				

Note: Tax rates for tax year 2024; Local- and county-level taxes are not included
Source: Federation of Tax Administrators, State Individual Income Tax Rates, January 1, 2025

Various State Sales and Excise Tax Rates

State	State Sales Tax (%)	Gasoline[1] ($/gal.)	Cigarette[2] ($/pack)	Spirits[3] ($/gal.)	Wine[4] ($/gal.)	Beer[5] ($/gal.)	Recreational Marijuana (%)
Washington	6.5	0.53	3.03	36.98	0.87	0.26	(x)

Note: All tax rates as of January 1, 2025; (1) The American Petroleum Institute has developed a methodology for determining the average tax rate on a gallon of fuel. Rates may include any of the following: excise taxes, environmental fees, storage tank fees, other fees or taxes, general sales tax, and local taxes; (2) The federal excise tax of $1.0066 per pack and local taxes are not included; (3) Rates are those applicable to off-premise sales of 40% alcohol by volume (a.b.v.) distilled spirits in 750ml containers. Local excise taxes are excluded; (4) Rates are those applicable to off-premise sales of 11% a.b.v. non-carbonated wine in 750ml containers; (5) Rates are those applicable to off-premise sales of 4.7% a.b.v. beer in 12 ounce containers; (x) 37% excise tax (retail price)
Source: Tax Foundation, 2025 Facts & Figures: How Does Your State Compare?

State Tax Competitiveness Index

State	Overall Rank	Corporate Tax Rank	Individual Income Tax Rank	Sales Tax Rank	Property Tax Rank	Unemployment Insurance Tax Rank
Washington	45	47	15	50	25	44

Note: The Tax Foundation's State Tax Competitiveness Index enables policymakers, taxpayers, and business leaders to gauge how their states' tax systems compare. A rank of 1 is best, 50 is worst. Rankings do not average to the total. States without a tax rank equally as 1. DC's scores and rankings do not affect other states. The report shows tax systems as of July 1, 2024 (the beginning of Fiscal Year 2025).
Source: Tax Foundation, State Tax Competitiveness Index 2025

TRANSPORTATION

Means of Transportation to Work

Area	Car/Truck/Van		Public Transportation			Bicycle	Walked	Other Means	Worked at Home
	Drove Alone	Car-pooled	Bus	Subway	Railroad				
City	37.6	5.1	11.2	0.5	0.0	2.5	8.3	3.5	31.3
MSA[1]	59.1	8.2	4.7	0.1	0.3	0.8	3.3	1.8	21.6
U.S.	70.2	8.5	1.7	1.3	0.4	0.4	2.4	1.6	13.5

Note: Figures are percentages and cover workers 16 years of age and older; (1) Figures cover the Seattle-Tacoma-Bellevue, WA Metropolitan Statistical Area
Source: U.S. Census Bureau, 2019-2023 American Community Survey 5-Year Estimates

Travel Time to Work

Area	Less Than 10 Minutes	10 to 19 Minutes	20 to 29 Minutes	30 to 44 Minutes	45 to 59 Minutes	60 to 89 Minutes	90 Minutes or More
City	8.0	26.0	24.5	26.4	9.2	4.4	1.4
MSA[1]	8.7	23.7	21.6	24.7	10.5	7.8	3.0
U.S.	12.6	28.6	21.2	20.8	8.1	6.0	2.8

Note: Note: Figures are percentages and include workers 16 years old and over; (1) Figures cover the Seattle-Tacoma-Bellevue, WA Metropolitan Statistical Area
Source: U.S. Census Bureau, 2019-2023 American Community Survey 5-Year Estimates

Key Congestion Measures

Measure	2000	2010	2015	2020	2022
Annual Hours of Delay, Total (000)	92,925	137,010	162,517	69,016	168,916
Annual Hours of Delay, Per Auto Commuter	55	64	74	31	82
Annual Congestion Cost, Per Auto Commuter ($)	1,376	1,612	1,766	766	1,874

Note: Figures cover the Seattle WA urban area
Source: Texas A&M Transportation Institute, 2023 Urban Mobility Report

Freeway Travel Time Index

Measure	1985	1990	1995	2000	2005	2010	2015	2020	2022
Urban Area Index[1]	1.22	1.26	1.29	1.33	1.37	1.36	1.37	1.11	1.32
Urban Area Rank[1,2]	4	3	3	3	3	4	5	20	8

Note: Freeway Travel Time Index—the ratio of travel time in the peak period to the travel time at free-flow conditions. For example, a value of 1.30 indicates a 20-minute free-flow trip takes 26 minutes in the peak (20 minutes x 1.30 = 26 minutes); (1) Covers the Seattle WA urban area; (2) Rank is based on 101 larger urban areas (#1 = highest travel time index)
Source: Texas A&M Transportation Institute, 2023 Urban Mobility Report

Public Transportation

Agency Name / Mode of Transportation	Vehicles Operated in Maximum Service[1]	Annual Unlinked Passenger Trips[2] (in thous.)	Annual Passenger Miles[3] (in thous.)
King County Department of Transportation (KC Metro)			
Bus (directly operated)	715	63,485.2	244,710.1
Bus (purchased transportation)	58	623.9	2,376.4
Demand Response (purchased transportation)	317	888.7	6,470.6
Demand Response - Taxi	81	121.5	1,509.5
Ferryboat (directly operated)	2	399.7	1,479.7
Streetcar Rail (directly operated)	10	1,411.8	1,556.4
Trolleybus (directly operated)	110	10,851.6	20,078.7
Vanpool (directly operated)	977	1,104.5	23,349.0
Central Puget Sound Regional Transit Authority (Sound Transit)			
Commuter Bus (directly operated)	143	6,918.1	94,155.8
Commuter Bus (purchased transportation)	32	1,650.0	22,716.8
Commuter Rail (purchased transportation)	57	1,755.8	43,432.0
Light Rail (directly operated)	84	26,867.8	185,378.0
Streetcar Rail (directly operated)	3	380.0	623.4
Washington State Ferries			
Ferryboat (directly operated)	15	18,241.1	131,769.1
City of Seattle (Seattle Center Monorail)			
Monorail and Automated Guideway (purchased transportation)	8	2,135.0	1,921.5

Note: (1) Number of revenue vehicles operated by the given mode and type of service to meet the annual maximum service requirement. This is the revenue vehicle count during the peak season of the year; on the week and day that maximum service is provided. Vehicles operated in maximum service (VOMS) exclude atypical days and one-time special events; (2) Number of passengers who boarded public transportation vehicles. Passengers are counted each time they board a vehicle no matter how many vehicles they use to travel from their origin to their destination. (3) Sum of the distances ridden by all passengers during the entire fiscal year.
Source: Federal Transit Administration, National Transit Database, 2023

Air Transportation

Airport Name and Code / Type of Service	Passenger Airlines[1]	Passenger Enplanements	Freight Carriers[2]	Freight (lbs)
Seattle-Tacoma International (SEA)				
Domestic service (U.S. carriers only)	16	22,279,609	19	339,775,806
International service (U.S. carriers only)	8	1,351,572	6	8,749,804

Note: (1) Includes all U.S.-based major, minor and commuter airlines that carried at least one passenger during the year; (2) Includes all U.S.-based airlines and freight carriers that transported at least one pound of freight during the year.
Source: Bureau of Transportation Statistics, The Intermodal Transportation Database, Air Carriers: T-100 Domestic Market (U.S. carriers only), 2024; Bureau of Transportation Statistics, The Intermodal Transportation Database, Air Carriers: T-100 International Market (U.S. carriers only), 2024

BUSINESSES

Major Business Headquarters

Company Name	Industry	Rankings	
		Fortune[1]	Forbes[2]
Alaska Air Group	Airlines	385	-
Amazon	Internet services and retailing	2	-
Coupang	Internet services and retailing	168	-
Expedia Group	Internet services and retailing	315	-
Expeditors International of Washington	Transportation and logistics	420	-
Nordstrom	General merchandisers	286	-
Saltchuk	Transportation	-	142
Starbucks	Food services	116	-
Trident Seafoods	Food, drink & tobacco	-	235
Weyerhaeuser	Forest and paper products	476	-

Note: (1) Companies that produce a 10-K are ranked 1 to 500 based on 2023 revenue; (2) All private companies with at least $2 billion in annual revenue through the end of their most current fiscal year are ranked 1 to 275; companies listed are headquartered in the city; dashes indicate no ranking
Source: Fortune, "Fortune 500," 2024; Forbes, "America's Largest Private Companies," 2024

Fastest-Growing Businesses

According to *Inc.*, Seattle is home to four of America's 500 fastest-growing private companies: **Vouched** (#141); **Deako** (#182); **ThirstySprout** (#247); **Gamesight** (#392). Criteria: must be an independent, privately-held, for-profit, U.S. corporation, proprietorship or partnership as of December 31, 2023; revenues must be at least $100,000 in 2020 and $2 million in 2023; must have four-year operating/sales history. *Inc., "America's 500 Fastest-Growing Private Companies," 2024*

According to Deloitte, Seattle is home to 11 of North America's 500 fastest-growing high-technology companies: **Vouched** (#55); **Pulumi Corporation** (#96); **Gamesight** (#106); **Curi Bio** (#123); **FlavorCloud** (#166); **Porch Group** (#239); **Flexe** (#370); **Amperity** (#373); **Remitly** (#407); **Omnidian** (#436); **Highspot** (#444). Companies are ranked by percentage growth in revenue over a four-year period. Criteria for inclusion: company must be headquartered within North America; must own proprietary intellectual property or technology that is sold to customers in products that contributes to a significant portion of the company's operating revenue; must have been in business for a minumum of four years with 2020 operating revenues of at least $50,000 USD/CD and 2023 operating revenues of at least $5 million USD/CD. *Deloitte, 2024 Technology Fast 500*[TM]

Living Environment

COST OF LIVING

Cost of Living Index

Composite Index	Groceries	Housing	Utilities	Trans-portation	Health Care	Misc. Goods/ Services
145.1	110.3	212.2	101.4	128.4	128.5	122.4

Note: The Cost of Living Index measures regional differences in the cost of consumer goods and services, excluding taxes and non-consumer expenditures, for professional and managerial households in the top income quintile. It is based on more than 50,000 prices covering almost 60 different items for which prices are collected three times a year by chambers of commerce, economic development organizations or university applied economic centers in each participating urban area. The numbers shown should be read as a percentage above or below the national average of 100. For example, a value of 115.4 in the groceries column indicates that grocery prices are 15.4% higher than the national average. Small differences in the index numbers should not be interpreted as significant; Figures cover the Seattle WA urban area.
Source: The Council for Community and Economic Research, Cost of Living Index, 2024

Grocery Prices

Area[1]	T-Bone Steak ($/pound)	Frying Chicken ($/pound)	Whole Milk ($/half gal.)	Eggs ($/dozen)	Orange Juice ($/64 oz.)	Coffee ($/11.5 oz.)
City[2]	15.51	1.98	4.94	3.87	4.58	7.06
Avg.	15.42	1.55	4.69	3.25	4.41	5.46
Min.	14.50	1.16	4.43	2.75	4.00	4.85
Max.	17.56	2.89	5.49	4.78	5.54	7.89

*Note: (1) Values for the local area are compared with the average, minimum and maximum values for all 276 areas in the Cost of Living Index; (2) Figures cover the Seattle WA urban area; **T-Bone Steak** (price per pound); **Frying Chicken** (price per pound, whole fryer); **Whole Milk** (half gallon carton); **Eggs** (price per dozen, Grade A, large); **Orange Juice** (64 oz. Tropicana or Florida Natural); **Coffee** (11.5 oz. can, vacuum-packed, Maxwell House, Hills Bros, or Folgers).*
Source: The Council for Community and Economic Research, Cost of Living Index, 2024

Housing and Utility Costs

Area[1]	New Home Price ($)	Apartment Rent ($/month)	All Electric ($/month)	Part Electric ($/month)	Other Energy ($/month)	Telephone ($/month)
City[2]	1,093,157	3,259	204.50	-	-	204.74
Avg.	515,975	1,550	210.99	123.07	82.07	194.99
Min.	265,375	692	104.33	53.68	36.26	179.42
Max.	2,775,821	5,719	529.02	397.28	361.63	223.33

*Note: (1) Values for the local area are compared with the average, minimum and maximum values for all 276 areas in the Cost of Living Index; (2) Figures cover the Seattle WA urban area; **New Home Price** (2,400 sf living area, 8,000 sf lot, in urban area with full utilities); **Apartment Rent** (950 sf 2 bedroom/1.5 or 2 bath, unfurnished, excluding all utilities except water); **All Electric** (average monthly cost for an all-electric home); **Part Electric** (average monthly cost for a part-electric home); **Other Energy** (average monthly cost for natural gas, fuel oil, coal, wood, and any other forms of energy except electricity); **Telephone** (price includes the base monthly rate plus taxes and fees for three lines of mobile phone service).*
Source: The Council for Community and Economic Research, Cost of Living Index, 2024

Health Care, Transportation, and Other Costs

Area[1]	Doctor ($/visit)	Dentist ($/visit)	Optometrist ($/visit)	Gasoline ($/gallon)	Beauty Salon ($/visit)	Men's Shirt ($)
City[2]	208.77	157.05	179.39	4.49	85.33	49.17
Avg.	143.77	117.51	129.23	3.32	48.57	38.14
Min.	36.74	58.67	67.33	2.80	24.00	13.41
Max.	270.44	216.82	307.33	5.28	94.00	63.89

*Note: (1) Values for the local area are compared with the average, minimum and maximum values for all 276 areas in the Cost of Living Index; (2) Figures cover the Seattle WA urban area; **Doctor** (general practitioners routine exam of an established patient); **Dentist** (adult teeth cleaning and periodic oral examination); **Optometrist** (full vision eye exam for established adult patient); **Gasoline** (one gallon regular unleaded, national brand, including all taxes, cash price at self-service pump if available); **Beauty Salon** (woman's shampoo, trim, and blow-dry); **Men's Shirt** (cotton/polyester dress shirt, pinpoint weave, long sleeves).*
Source: The Council for Community and Economic Research, Cost of Living Index, 2024

HOUSING

Homeownership Rate

Area	2017 (%)	2018 (%)	2019 (%)	2020 (%)	2021 (%)	2022 (%)	2023 (%)	2024 (%)
MSA[1]	59.5	62.5	61.5	59.4	58.0	62.7	62.7	61.1
U.S.	63.9	64.4	64.6	66.6	65.5	65.8	65.9	65.6

Note: (1) Figures cover the Seattle-Tacoma-Bellevue, WA Metropolitan Statistical Area
Source: U.S. Census Bureau, Housing Vacancies and Homeownership Annual Statistics: 2017-2024

House Price Index (HPI)

Area	National Ranking[2]	Quarterly Change (%)	One-Year Change (%)	Five-Year Change (%)	Since 1991Q1 (%)
MD[1]	91	-0.16	6.14	47.96	484.10
U.S.[3]	–	1.43	4.51	57.13	327.82

Note: The HPI is a weighted repeat sales index. It measures average price changes in repeat sales or refinancings on the same properties. This information is obtained by reviewing repeat mortgage transactions on single-family properties whose mortgages have been purchased or securitized by Fannie Mae or Freddie Mac since January 1975; (1) Figures cover the Seattle-Bellevue-Everett, WA Metropolitan Division; (2) Rankings are based on annual percentage change for all metro areas containing at least 15,000 transactions over the last 10 years and ranges from 1 to 241; (3) figures based on a weighted average of Census Division estimates using a seasonally adjusted, purchase-only index; all figures are for the period ending December 31, 2024
Source: Federal Housing Finance Agency, Change in FHFA Metropolitan Area House Price Indexes, All Transactions Index, 2024Q4

Home Value

Area	Under $100,000	$100,000 -$199,999	$200,000 -$299,999	$300,000 -$399,999	$400,000 -$499,999	$500,000 -$999,999	$1,000,000 or more	Median ($)
City	1.1	0.6	1.2	3.6	5.2	47.4	40.8	912,100
MSA[1]	3.2	1.7	3.9	8.3	12.9	46.7	23.2	673,500
U.S.	12.1	17.8	19.5	14.4	10.5	19.1	6.5	303,400

Note: Figures are percentages except for median and cover owner-occupied housing units; (1) Figures cover the Seattle-Tacoma-Bellevue, WA Metropolitan Statistical Area
Source: U.S. Census Bureau, 2019-2023 American Community Survey 5-Year Estimates

Year Housing Structure Built

Area	2020 or Later	2010 -2019	2000 -2009	1990 -1999	1980 -1989	1970 -1979	1960 -1969	1950 -1959	1940 -1949	Before 1940	Median Year
City	1.2	17.6	12.0	7.4	7.5	7.2	7.7	8.4	7.4	23.4	1974
MSA[1]	1.3	12.4	14.7	14.0	13.7	12.9	10.5	6.8	3.9	9.7	1985
U.S.	1.2	8.9	13.6	12.8	13.0	14.4	10.0	9.7	4.5	11.9	1980

Note: Figures are percentages except for Median Year; Note: (1) Figures cover the Seattle-Tacoma-Bellevue, WA Metropolitan Statistical Area
Source: U.S. Census Bureau, 2019-2023 American Community Survey 5-Year Estimates

Gross Monthly Rent

Area	Under $500	$500 -$999	$1,000 -$1,499	$1,500 -$1,999	$2,000 -$2,499	$2,500 -$2,999	$3,000 and up	Median ($)
City	5.0	4.2	15.6	25.4	21.5	13.0	15.5	1,998
MSA[1]	4.0	4.8	16.7	28.3	22.6	11.5	12.2	1,932
U.S.	6.5	22.3	29.5	20.2	10.8	4.8	5.9	1,348

Note: Figures are percentages except for median; Gross rent is the contract rent plus the estimated average monthly cost of utilities (electricity, gas, and water and sewer) and fuels (oil, coal, kerosene, wood, etc.) if these are paid by the renter (or paid for the renter by someone else); (1) Figures cover the Seattle-Tacoma-Bellevue, WA Metropolitan Statistical Area
Source: U.S. Census Bureau, 2019-2023 American Community Survey 5-Year Estimates

HEALTH

Health Risk Factors

Category	MD[1] (%)	U.S. (%)
Adults aged 18–64 who have any kind of health care coverage	92.2	90.8
Adults who reported being in good or better health	87.2	81.8
Adults who have been told they have high blood cholesterol	35.6	36.9
Adults who have been told they have high blood pressure	27.7	34.0
Adults who are current smokers	6.6	12.1
Adults who currently use e-cigarettes	5.6	7.7
Adults who currently use chewing tobacco, snuff, or snus	1.7	3.2
Adults who are heavy drinkers[2]	6.5	6.1
Adults who are binge drinkers[3]	15.7	15.2
Adults who are overweight (BMI 25.0 - 29.9)	36.1	34.4
Adults who are obese (BMI 30.0 - 99.8)	24.9	34.3
Adults who participated in any physical activities in the past month	85.3	75.8

Note: All figures are crude prevalence; (1) Figures cover the Seattle-Bellevue-Everett, WA Metropolitan Division; (2) Heavy drinkers are classified as adult men having more than 14 drinks per week and adult women having more than 7 drinks per week; (3) Binge drinkers are classified as males having five or more drinks on one occasion or females having four or more drinks on one occasion
Source: Centers for Disease Control and Prevention, Behaviorial Risk Factor Surveillance System, SMART: Selected Metropolitan Area Risk Trends, 2023

Acute and Chronic Health Conditions

Category	MD[1] (%)	U.S. (%)
Adults who have ever been told they had a heart attack	2.7	4.2
Adults who have ever been told they have angina or coronary heart disease	2.6	4.0
Adults who have ever been told they had a stroke	1.9	3.3
Adults who have ever been told they have asthma	15.6	15.7
Adults who have ever been told they have arthritis	20.5	26.3
Adults who have ever been told they have diabetes[2]	7.6	11.5
Adults who have ever been told they had skin cancer	4.7	5.6
Adults who have ever been told they had any other types of cancer	7.1	8.4
Adults who have ever been told they have COPD	3.2	6.4
Adults who have ever been told they have kidney disease	3.1	3.7
Adults who have ever been told they have a form of depression	22.3	22.0

Note: All figures are crude prevalence; (1) Figures cover the Seattle-Bellevue-Everett, WA Metropolitan Division; (2) Figures do not include pregnancy-related, borderline, or pre-diabetes
Source: Centers for Disease Control and Prevention, Behaviorial Risk Factor Surveillance System, SMART: Selected Metropolitan Area Risk Trends, 2023

Health Screening and Vaccination Rates

Category	MD[1] (%)	U.S. (%)
Adults who have ever been tested for HIV	41.7	37.5
Adults who have had their blood cholesterol checked within the last five years	87.3	87.0
Adults aged 65+ who have had flu shot within the past year	74.0	63.4
Adults aged 65+ who have ever had a pneumonia vaccination	78.1	71.9

Note: All figures are crude prevalence; (1) Figures cover the Seattle-Bellevue-Everett, WA Metropolitan Division.
Source: Centers for Disease Control and Prevention, Behaviorial Risk Factor Surveillance System, SMART: Selected Metropolitan Area Risk Trends, 2023

Disability Status

Category	MD[1] (%)	U.S. (%)
Adults who reported being deaf	4.8	7.4
Are you blind or have serious difficulty seeing, even when wearing glasses?	2.9	4.9
Do you have difficulty doing errands alone?	5.0	7.8
Do you have difficulty dressing or bathing?	2.0	3.6
Do you have serious difficulty concentrating/remembering/making decisions?	11.3	13.7
Do you have serious difficulty walking or climbing stairs?	7.7	13.2

Note: All figures are crude prevalence; (1) Figures cover the Seattle-Bellevue-Everett, WA Metropolitan Division.
Source: Centers for Disease Control and Prevention, Behaviorial Risk Factor Surveillance System, SMART: Selected Metropolitan Area Risk Trends, 2023

Mortality Rates for the Top 10 Causes of Death in the U.S.

ICD-10[a] Sub-Chapter	ICD-10[a] Code	Crude Mortality Rate[2] per 100,000 population	
		County[3]	U.S.
Malignant neoplasms	C00-C97	134.4	182.7
Ischaemic heart diseases	I20-I25	72.8	109.6
Provisional assignment of new diseases of uncertain etiology[1]	U00-U49	21.7	65.3
Other forms of heart disease	I30-I51	30.0	65.1
Other degenerative diseases of the nervous system	G30-G31	57.2	52.4
Other external causes of accidental injury	W00-X59	57.3	52.3
Cerebrovascular diseases	I60-I69	30.6	49.1
Chronic lower respiratory diseases	J40-J47	19.0	43.5
Hypertensive diseases	I10-I15	28.3	38.9
Organic, including symptomatic, mental disorders	F01-F09	20.0	33.9

Note: (a) ICD-10 = International Classification of Diseases 10th Revision; (1) Includes COVID-19, adverse effects to COVID-19 vaccines, SARS, and vaping-related disorders; (2) Crude mortality rates are a three-year average covering 2021-2023; (3) Figures cover King County.
Source: Centers for Disease Control and Prevention, National Center for Health Statistics. National Vital Statistics System, Mortality 2018-2023 on CDC WONDER Online Database

Mortality Rates for Selected Causes of Death

Cause of Death	ICD-10[a] Code	Crude Mortality Rate[1] per 100,000 population	
		County[2]	U.S.
Accidental poisoning and exposure to noxious substances	X40-X49	40.1	30.5
Alzheimer disease	G30	40.0	35.4
Assault	X85-Y09	5.3	7.3
COVID-19	U07.1	21.7	65.3
Diabetes mellitus	E10-E14	20.5	30.0
Diseases of the liver	K70-K76	15.5	20.8
Human immunodeficiency virus (HIV) disease	B20-B24	1.0	1.5
Influenza and pneumonia	J09-J18	6.5	13.4
Intentional self-harm	X60-X84	13.3	14.7
Malnutrition	E40-E46	4.0	6.0
Obesity and other hyperalimentation	E65-E68	2.1	3.1
Renal failure	N17-N19	4.6	16.4
Transport accidents	V01-V99	8.3	14.4

Note: (a) ICD-10 = International Classification of Diseases 10th Revision; (1) Crude mortality rates are a three-year average covering 2021-2023; (2) Figures cover King County; Data are suppressed when the data meet the criteria for confidentiality constraints; Crude mortality rates are flagged as unreliable when the rate would be calculated with a numerator of 20 or less.
Source: Centers for Disease Control and Prevention, National Center for Health Statistics. National Vital Statistics System, Mortality 2018-2023 on CDC WONDER Online Database

Health Insurance Coverage

Area	With Health Insurance	With Private Health Insurance	With Public Health Insurance	Without Health Insurance	Population Under Age 19 Without Health Insurance
City	95.6	80.5	23.5	4.4	1.8
MSA[1]	94.4	75.5	29.6	5.6	2.7
U.S.	91.4	67.3	36.3	8.6	5.4

Note: Figures are percentages that cover the civilian noninstitutionalized population; (1) Figures cover the Seattle-Tacoma-Bellevue, WA Metropolitan Statistical Area
Source: U.S. Census Bureau, 2019-2023 American Community Survey 5-Year Estimates

Number of Medical Professionals

Area	MDs[3]	DOs[3,4]	Dentists	Podiatrists	Chiropractors	Optometrists
County[1] (number)	11,823	430	2,688	145	1,100	552
County[1] (rate[2])	521.6	19.0	118.3	6.4	48.4	24.3
U.S. (rate[2])	302.5	29.2	74.6	6.4	29.5	18.0

Note: Data as of 2023 unless noted; (1) Data covers King County; (2) Number of medical professionals per 100,000 population; (3) Data as of 2022 and includes all active, non-federal physicians; (4) Doctor of Osteopathic Medicine
Source: U.S. Department of Health and Human Services, Health Resources and Services Administration, Bureau of Health Professions, Area Resource File (ARF) 2023-2024

Best Hospitals

According to *U.S. News,* the Seattle-Tacoma-Bellevue, WA metro area is home to two of the best hospitals in the U.S.: **Fred Hutchinson Cancer Center/University of Washington Medical Center** (1 adult specialty); **UW Medicine-University of Washington Medical Center** (2 adult specialties). The hospitals listed were nationally ranked in at least one of 15 adult or 11 pediatric specialties. The number of specialties shown cover the parent hospital. Only 160 U.S. hospitals performed well enough to be nationally ranked in one or more specialties. Twenty hospitals in the U.S. made the Honor Roll. The Best Hospitals Honor Roll takes both the national rankings and the procedure and condition ratings into account. Hospitals received points if they were nationally ranked in one of the 15 adult specialties—the higher they ranked, the more points they got—and how many ratings of "high performing" they earned in the 20 procedures and conditions. *U.S. News Online, "America's Best Hospitals 2024-25"*

According to *U.S. News,* the Seattle-Tacoma-Bellevue, WA metro area is home to one of the best children's hospitals in the U.S.: **Seattle Children's Hospital** (Honor Roll/11 pediatric specialties). The hospital listed was highly ranked in at least one of 11 pediatric specialties. One hundred five children's hospitals in the U.S. were nationally ranked in at least one specialty. Hospitals received points for being ranked in a specialty, and the 10 hospitals with the most points across the 11 specialties make up the Honor Roll. *U.S. News Online, "America's Best Children's Hospitals 2024-25"*

EDUCATION

Public School District Statistics

District Name	Schls	Pupils	Pupil/ Teacher Ratio	Minority Pupils[1] (%)	Total Rev. per Pupil ($)	Total Exp. per Pupil ($)
Seattle Public Schools	109	50,770	16.5	55.6	26,438	25,927

Note: Table includes school districts with 2,000 or more students; (1) Percentage of students that are not non-Hispanic white.
Source: U.S. Department of Education, National Center for Education Statistics, Common Core of Data, Local Education Agency (School District) Universe Survey: School Year 2023-2024; U.S. Department of Education, National Center for Education Statistics, Common Core of Data, School District Finance Survey (F-33): School Year 2021–22

Highest Level of Education

Area	Less than H.S.	H.S. Diploma	Some College, No Deg.	Associate Degree	Bachelor's Degree	Master's Degree	Prof. School Degree	Doctorate Degree
City	4.3	9.5	12.9	5.8	37.6	20.5	5.3	4.2
MSA[1]	6.7	18.8	19.2	9.1	27.8	13.5	2.8	2.2
U.S.	10.6	26.2	19.4	8.8	21.3	9.8	2.3	1.6

Note: Figures cover persons age 25 and over; (1) Figures cover the Seattle-Tacoma-Bellevue, WA Metropolitan Statistical Area
Source: U.S. Census Bureau, 2019-2023 American Community Survey 5-Year Estimates

Educational Attainment by Race

Area	High School Graduate or Higher (%)					Bachelor's Degree or Higher (%)				
	Total	White	Black	Asian	Hisp.[2]	Total	White	Black	Asian	Hisp.[2]
City	95.7	98.4	89.9	91.2	87.8	67.5	72.6	33.8	69.8	49.3
MSA[1]	93.3	96.0	90.4	91.0	77.4	46.3	47.0	28.6	61.7	27.5
U.S.	89.4	92.9	88.1	88.0	72.5	35.0	37.7	24.7	57.0	19.9

Note: Figures shown cover persons 25 years old and over; (1) Figures cover the Seattle-Tacoma-Bellevue, WA Metropolitan Statistical Area; (2) People of Hispanic origin can be of any race
Source: U.S. Census Bureau, 2019-2023 American Community Survey 5-Year Estimates

School Enrollment by Grade and Control

Area	Preschool (%)		Kindergarten (%)		Grades 1 - 4 (%)		Grades 5 - 8 (%)		Grades 9 - 12 (%)	
	Public	Private	Public	Private	Public	Private	Public	Private	Public	Private
City	35.0	65.0	76.0	24.0	77.9	22.1	74.8	25.2	78.3	21.7
MSA[1]	40.8	59.2	79.5	20.5	85.6	14.4	86.7	13.3	90.0	10.0
U.S.	58.7	41.3	85.2	14.8	87.2	12.8	87.9	12.1	89.0	11.0

Note: Figures shown cover persons 3 years old and over; (1) Figures cover the Seattle-Tacoma-Bellevue, WA Metropolitan Statistical Area
Source: U.S. Census Bureau, 2019-2023 American Community Survey 5-Year Estimates

Higher Education

Four-Year Colleges			Two-Year Colleges			Medical Schools[1]	Law Schools[2]	Voc/ Tech[3]
Public	Private Non-profit	Private For-profit	Public	Private Non-profit	Private For-profit			
17	13	3	2	1	3	1	2	7

Note: Figures cover institutions located within the Seattle-Tacoma-Bellevue, WA Metropolitan Statistical Area and include main campuses only; (1) includes schools accredited by the Liaison Committee on Medical Education and the American Osteopathic Association's Commission on Osteopathic College Accreditation; (2) includes ABA-accredited schools, schools with provisional ABA accreditation, and state accredited schools; (3) includes all schools with programs that are less than 2 years.
Source: National Center for Education Statistics, Integrated Postsecondary Education System (IPEDS), 2023-24; Wikipedia, List of Medical Schools in the United States, accessed May 2, 2025; Wikipedia, List of Law Schools in the United States, accessed May 2, 2025

According to *U.S. News & World Report,* the Seattle-Tacoma-Bellevue, WA metro area is home to two of the top 200 national universities in the U.S.: **University of Washington** (#46 tie); **Seattle University** (#152 tie). The indicators used to capture academic quality fall into a number of categories: assessment by administrators at peer institutions; retention of students; faculty resources; student selectivity; financial resources; alumni giving; high school counselor ratings of colleges; and graduation rate. *U.S. News & World Report, "America's Best Colleges 2025"*

According to *U.S. News & World Report,* the Seattle-Tacoma-Bellevue, WA metro area is home to one of the top 100 liberal arts colleges in the U.S.: **University of Puget Sound** (#95 tie). The indicators used to capture academic quality fall into a number of categories: assessment by administrators at peer institutions; retention of students; faculty resources; student selectivity; financial resources; alumni giving; high school counselor ratings of colleges; and graduation rate. *U.S. News & World Report, "America's Best Colleges 2025"*

According to *U.S. News & World Report,* the Seattle-Tacoma-Bellevue, WA metro area is home to one of the top 100 law schools in the U.S.: **University of Washington 1** (#50 tie). The rankings are based on a weighted average of 12 measures of quality: peer assessment score; assessment score by lawyers/judges; median LSAT scores; median undergrad GPA; acceptance rate; employment rates for graduates; placement success; bar passage rate; faculty resources; expenditures per student; student/faculty ratio; and library resources. *U.S. News & World Report, "America's Best Graduate Schools, Law, 2025"*

According to *U.S. News & World Report,* the Seattle-Tacoma-Bellevue, WA metro area is home to one of the top 75 business schools in the U.S.: **University of Washington (Foster)** (#22 tie). The rankings are based on a weighted average of the following nine measures: quality assessment; peer assessment; recruiter assessment; placement success; mean starting salary and bonus; student selectivity; mean GMAT and GRE scores; mean undergraduate GPA; and acceptance rate. *U.S. News & World Report, "America's Best Graduate Schools, Business, 2025"*

EMPLOYERS

Major Employers

Company Name	Industry
Amazon.com	Online retail
City of Seattle	Municipal government
Costco Wholesale Corporation	Miscellaneous general merchandise stores
County of Snohomish	County government
Evergreen Healthcare	General medical & surgical hospitals
Harborview Medical Center	General medical & surgical hospitals
King County Public Hospital Dist No. 2	Hospital & health services consultant
Microsoft	Prepackaged software
Providence Health & Services	General medical & surgical hospitals
R U Corporation	American restaurant
SNC-Lavalin Constructors	Heavy construction
Starbucks	Coffee/food services
T-Mobile USA	Radio, telephone communication
The Boeing Company	Airplanes, fixed or rotary wing
Tulalip Resort Casino	Casino hotels
United States Department of the Army	Medical centers
University of Washington	Colleges & universities
Virginia Mason Medical Center	General medical & surgical hospitals
Virginia Mason Seattle Main Clinic	Clinic, operated by physicians
Washington Dept of Social & Health Svcs	General medical & surgical hospitals

Note: Companies shown are located within the Seattle-Tacoma-Bellevue, WA Metropolitan Statistical Area.
Source: Chambers of Commerce; State Departments of Labor; Wikipedia

Best Companies to Work For

Perkins Coie; Zillow Group, headquartered in Seattle, are among "The 100 Best Companies to Work For." To pick the best companies, *Fortune* partnered with the Great Place to Work Institute. Using their proprietary Trust Index™ survey, the core of what creates great a workplace is measured—key behaviors that drive trust in management, connection with colleagues, and loyalty to the company. To be eligible for the *Fortune* 100 Best Companies to Work For list, employers must have 1,000 or more employees in the U.S. and cannot be a government agency. *Fortune, "The 100 Best Companies to Work For," 2025*

Zillow Group, headquartered in Seattle, is among "Fortune's Best Workplaces for Parents." To pick the best companies, *Fortune* partnered with the Great Place to Work Institute. To be considered for the list, companies must be Great Place To Work-Certified and have at least 50 responses from parents in the US. The survey enables employees to share confidential quantitative and qualitative feedback about their organization's culture by responding to 60 statements on a 5-point scale and answering two open-ended questions. Collectively, these statements describe a great employee experience, defined by high levels of trust, respect, credibility, fairness, pride, and camaraderie. In addition, companies provide organizational data like size, location, industry, demographics, roles, and levels; and provide information about parental leave, adoption, flexible schedule, childcare and dependent health care benefits. *Fortune, "Best Workplaces for Parents," 2024*

Zillow Group, headquartered in Seattle, is among "Fortune's Best Workplaces for Women." To pick the best companies, *Fortune* partnered with the Great Place to Work Institute. To be considered for the list, companies must be Great Place To Work-Certified. Companies must also employ at least 50 women, at least 20% of their non-executive managers must be female, and at least one executive must be female. To determine the Best Workplaces for Women, Great Place To Work measured the differences in women's survey responses to those of their peers and assesses the impact of demographics and roles on the quality and consistency of women's experiences. Great Place To Work also analyzed the gender balance of each workplace, how it compared to each company's industry, and patterns in representation as women rise from front-line positions to the board of directors. *Fortune, "Best Workplaces for Women," 2024*

SkinSpirit, headquartered in Seattle, is among "Best Workplaces in Health Care." To determine the Best Workplaces in Health Care list, Great Place To Work analyzed the survey responses of over 185,000 employees from Great Place To Work-Certified companies in the health care industry. Survey data analysis and company-provided datapoints are then factored into a combined score to compare and rank the companies that create the most consistently positive experience for all employees in this industry. *Fortune, "Best Workplaces in Health Care," 2024*

Avenue5 Residential; Horizon Realty Advisors; Zillow Group, headquartered in Seattle, are among "Best Workplaces in Real Estate." To determine the Best Workplaces in Real Estate list, Great Place To Work analyzed the survey responses of over 29,000 employees from Great Place To Work-Certified companies in the real estate industry. Survey data analysis and company-provided datapoints are then factored into a combined score to compare and rank the companies that create the most consistently positive experience for all employees in this industry. *Fortune, "Best Workplaces in Real Estate," 2024*

Avanade, headquartered in Seattle, is among the "Best Places to Work in IT." To qualify, companies had to have a minimum of 100 total employees and five IT employees. The best places to work were selected based on DEI (diversity, equity, and inclusion) practices; IT turnover, promotions, and growth; IT retention and engagement programs; remote/hybrid working; benefits and perks (such as elder care and child care, flextime, and reimbursement for college tuition); and training and career development opportunities. *Computerworld, "Best Places to Work in IT," 2025*

PUBLIC SAFETY

Crime Rate

Area	Total Crime Rate	Violent Crime Rate				Property Crime Rate		
		Murder	Rape	Robbery	Aggrav. Assault	Burglary	Larceny -Theft	Motor Vehicle Theft
City	5,789.3	9.0	36.2	221.7	510.2	1,126.3	2,662.2	1,223.7
U.S.	2,290.9	5.7	38.0	66.5	264.1	250.7	1,347.2	318.7

Note: Figures are crimes per 100,000 population.
Source: FBI, Table 8, Offenses Known to Law Enforcement, by State by City, 2023

Hate Crimes

Area	Number of Quarters Reported	Number of Incidents per Bias Motivation					
		Race/Ethnicity/ Ancestry	Religion	Sexual Orientation	Disability	Gender	Gender Identity
City[1]	4	66	20	34	0	10	5
U.S.	4	5,900	2,699	2,077	187	92	492

Note: (1) Figures include at least one incident reported with more than one bias motivation.
Source: Federal Bureau of Investigation, Hate Crime Statistics 2023

Identity Theft Consumer Reports

Area	Reports	Reports per 100,000 Population	Rank[2]
MSA[1]	7,838	195	166
U.S.	1,135,291	339	-

Note: (1) Figures cover the Seattle-Tacoma-Bellevue, WA Metropolitan Statistical Area; (2) Rank ranges from 1 to 401 where 1 indicates greatest number of identity theft reports per 100,000 population
Source: Federal Trade Commission, Consumer Sentinel Network Data Book 2024

Fraud and Other Consumer Reports

Area	Reports	Reports per 100,000 Population	Rank[2]
MSA[1]	50,609	1,258	110
U.S.	5,360,641	1,601	-

Note: (1) Figures cover the Seattle-Tacoma-Bellevue, WA Metropolitan Statistical Area; (2) Rank ranges from 1 to 401 where 1 indicates greatest number of fraud and other consumer reports per 100,000 population
Source: Federal Trade Commission, Consumer Sentinel Network Data Book 2024

POLITICS

2024 Presidential Election Results

Area	Trump (Rep.)	Harris (Dem.)	Stein (Green)	Kennedy (Ind.)	Oliver (Lib.)	Other
King County	22.3	73.6	1.2	1.0	0.4	1.4
U.S.	49.7	48.2	0.6	0.5	0.4	0.6

Note: Results are percentages and may not add to 100% due to rounding
Source: Dave Leip's Atlas of U.S. Presidential Elections

SPORTS

Professional Sports Teams

Team Name	League	Year Established
Seattle Kraken	National Hockey League (NHL)	2021
Seattle Mariners	Major League Baseball (MLB)	1977
Seattle Seahawks	National Football League (NFL)	1976
Seattle Sounders FC	Major League Soccer (MLS)	2009

Note: Includes teams located in the Seattle-Tacoma-Bellevue, WA Metropolitan Statistical Area.
Source: Wikipedia, Major Professional Sports Teams of the United States and Canada, May 1, 2025

CLIMATE

Average and Extreme Temperatures

Temperature	Jan	Feb	Mar	Apr	May	Jun	Jul	Aug	Sep	Oct	Nov	Dec	Yr.
Extreme High (°F)	64	70	75	85	93	96	98	99	98	89	74	63	99
Average High (°F)	44	48	52	57	64	69	75	74	69	59	50	45	59
Average Temp. (°F)	39	43	45	49	55	61	65	65	60	52	45	41	52
Average Low (°F)	34	36	38	41	46	51	54	55	51	45	39	36	44
Extreme Low (°F)	0	1	11	29	28	38	43	44	35	28	6	6	0

Note: Figures cover the years 1948-1990
Source: National Climatic Data Center, International Station Meteorological Climate Summary, 9/96

Average Precipitation/Snowfall/Humidity

Precip./Humidity	Jan	Feb	Mar	Apr	May	Jun	Jul	Aug	Sep	Oct	Nov	Dec	Yr.
Avg. Precip. (in.)	5.7	4.2	3.7	2.4	1.7	1.4	0.8	1.1	1.9	3.5	5.9	5.9	38.4
Avg. Snowfall (in.)	5	2	1	Tr	Tr	0	0	0	0	Tr	1	3	13
Avg. Rel. Hum. 7am (%)	83	83	84	83	80	79	79	84	87	88	85	85	83
Avg. Rel. Hum. 4pm (%)	76	69	63	57	54	54	49	51	57	68	76	79	63

Note: Figures cover the years 1948-1990; Tr = Trace amounts (<0.05 in. of rain; <0.5 in. of snow)
Source: National Climatic Data Center, International Station Meteorological Climate Summary, 9/96

Weather Conditions

Temperature			Daytime Sky			Precipitation		
5°F & below	32°F & below	90°F & above	Clear	Partly cloudy	Cloudy	0.01 inch or more precip.	0.1 inch or more snow/ice	Thunder-storms
< 1	38	3	57	120	188	157	8	8

Note: Figures are average number of days per year and cover the years 1948-1990
Source: National Climatic Data Center, International Station Meteorological Climate Summary, 9/96

HAZARDOUS WASTE

Superfund Sites

The Seattle-Bellevue-Kent, WA metro division is home to 10 sites on the EPA's Superfund National Priorities List (NPL) or Superfund Alternative Approach (SAA) list: **Harbor Island (Lead)** (Final NPL); **Lockheed West Seattle** (Final NPL); **Lower Duwamish Waterway** (Final NPL); **Midway Landfill** (Final NPL); **Pacific Car & Foundry Co.** (Final NPL); **Pacific Sound Resources** (Final NPL); **Queen City Farms** (Final NPL); **Quendall Terminals** (Final NPL); **Seattle Municipal Landfill (Kent Highlands)** (Final NPL); **Western Processing Co., Inc.** (Final NPL). The Superfund alternative approach uses the same investigation and cleanup process and standards that are used for sites listed on the National Priorities List. The SAA is an alternative to listing a site on the NPL; it is not an alternative to Superfund or the Superfund process. There are a total of 1,445 Superfund sites with a status of proposed or final on both lists in the United States. *U.S. Environmental Protection Agency, National Priorities List, May 1, 2025; U.S. Environmental Protection Agency, Superfund Alternative Approach Sites, May 1, 2025*

AIR QUALITY

Air Quality Trends: Ozone

	1990	1995	2000	2005	2010	2015	2020	2021	2022	2023
MSA[1]	0.082	0.062	0.056	0.053	0.053	0.059	0.056	0.061	0.065	0.056
U.S.	0.087	0.089	0.081	0.080	0.072	0.068	0.066	0.067	0.067	0.070

Note: (1) Data covers the Seattle-Tacoma-Bellevue, WA Metropolitan Statistical Area. The values shown are the composite ozone concentration averages among trend sites based on the highest fourth daily maximum 8-hour concentration in parts per million. These trends are based on sites having an adequate record of monitoring data during the trend period. Data from exceptional events are included.
Source: U.S. Environmental Protection Agency, Air Quality Monitoring Information, "Air Quality Trends by City, 1990-2023"

Air Quality Index

Area	Percent of Days when Air Quality was...[2]					AQI Statistics[2]	
	Good	Moderate	Unhealthy for Sensitive Groups	Unhealthy	Very Unhealthy	Maximum	Median
MSA[1]	51.0	47.1	1.1	0.8	0.0	195	50

Note: (1) Data covers the Seattle-Tacoma-Bellevue, WA Metropolitan Statistical Area; (2) Based on 365 days with AQI data in 2023. Air Quality Index (AQI) is an index for reporting daily air quality. EPA calculates the AQI for five major air pollutants regulated by the Clean Air Act: ground-level ozone, particle pollution (aka particulate matter), carbon monoxide, sulfur dioxide, and nitrogen dioxide. The AQI runs from 0 to 500. The higher the AQI value, the greater the level of air pollution and the greater the health concern. There are six AQI categories: "Good" AQI is between 0 and 50. Air quality is considered satisfactory; "Moderate" AQI is between 51 and 100. Air quality is acceptable; "Unhealthy for Sensitive Groups" When AQI values are between 101 and 150, members of sensitive groups may experience health effects; "Unhealthy" When AQI values are between 151 and 200 everyone may begin to experience health effects; "Very Unhealthy" AQI values between 201 and 300 trigger a health alert; "Hazardous" AQI values over 300 trigger warnings of emergency conditions (not shown).
Source: U.S. Environmental Protection Agency, Air Quality Index Report, 2023

Air Quality Index Pollutants

Area	Percent of Days when AQI Pollutant was...[2]					
	Carbon Monoxide	Nitrogen Dioxide	Ozone	Sulfur Dioxide	Particulate Matter 2.5	Particulate Matter 10
MSA[1]	0.0	0.8	32.9	(3)	66.3	0.0

Note: (1) Data covers the Seattle-Tacoma-Bellevue, WA Metropolitan Statistical Area; (2) Based on 365 days with AQI data in 2023. The Air Quality Index (AQI) is an index for reporting daily air quality. EPA calculates the AQI for five major air pollutants regulated by the Clean Air Act: ground-level ozone, particle pollution (also known as particulate matter), carbon monoxide, sulfur dioxide, and nitrogen dioxide. The AQI runs from 0 to 500. The higher the AQI value, the greater the level of air pollution and the greater the health concern; (3) Sulfur dioxide is no longer included in this table because SO_2 concentrations tend to be very localized and not necessarily representative of broad geographical areas like counties and CBSAs.
Source: U.S. Environmental Protection Agency, Air Quality Index Report, 2023

Maximum Air Pollutant Concentrations: Particulate Matter, Ozone, CO and Lead

	Particulate Matter 10 (ug/m³)	Particulate Matter 2.5 Wtd AM (ug/m³)	Particulate Matter 2.5 24-Hr (ug/m³)	Ozone (ppm)	Carbon Monoxide (ppm)	Lead (ug/m³)
MSA[1] Level	17	8.5	29	0.068	1	n/a
NAAQS[2]	150	15	35	0.075	9	0.15
Met NAAQS[2]	Yes	Yes	Yes	Yes	Yes	n/a

Note: (1) Data covers the Seattle-Tacoma-Bellevue, WA Metropolitan Statistical Area; Data from exceptional events are included; (2) National Ambient Air Quality Standards; ppm = parts per million; ug/m³ = micrograms per cubic meter; n/a not available.
Concentrations: Particulate Matter 10 (coarse particulate)—highest second maximum 24-hour concentration; Particulate Matter 2.5 Wtd AM (fine particulate)—highest weighted annual mean concentration; Particulate Matter 2.5 24-Hour (fine particulate)—highest 98th percentile 24-hour concentration; Ozone—highest fourth daily maximum 8-hour concentration; Carbon Monoxide—highest second maximum non-overlapping 8-hour concentration; Lead—maximum running 3-month average
Source: U.S. Environmental Protection Agency, Air Quality Monitoring Information, "Air Quality Statistics by City, 2023"

Maximum Air Pollutant Concentrations: Nitrogen Dioxide and Sulfur Dioxide

	Nitrogen Dioxide AM (ppb)	Nitrogen Dioxide 1-Hr (ppb)	Sulfur Dioxide AM (ppb)	Sulfur Dioxide 1-Hr (ppb)	Sulfur Dioxide 24-Hr (ppb)
MSA[1] Level	15	50	n/a	3	n/a
NAAQS[2]	53	100	30	75	140
Met NAAQS[2]	Yes	Yes	n/a	Yes	n/a

Note: (1) Data covers the Seattle-Tacoma-Bellevue, WA Metropolitan Statistical Area; Data from exceptional events are included; (2) National Ambient Air Quality Standards; ppm = parts per million; ug/m³ = micrograms per cubic meter; n/a not available.
Concentrations: Nitrogen Dioxide AM—highest arithmetic mean concentration; Nitrogen Dioxide 1-Hr—highest 98th percentile 1-hour daily maximum concentration; Sulfur Dioxide AM—highest annual mean concentration; Sulfur Dioxide 1-Hr—highest 99th percentile 1-hour daily maximum concentration; Sulfur Dioxide 24-Hr—highest second maximum 24-hour concentration
Source: U.S. Environmental Protection Agency, Air Quality Monitoring Information, "Air Quality Statistics by City, 2023"

Tucson, Arizona

Background

Tucson lies in a high desert valley that was once the floor of an ancient inland sea. Its name derives from the Native American term for the ancient settlement, Stukshon, which in Spanish is Tuquison. It is believed that the Spanish Jesuit Eusebio Francesco Kino, who established the San Xavier Mission, was the first European to visit the area in 1700. Spanish prospectors who came after Father Kino were driven out by Native Americans trying to protect their territory.

Tucson came under Mexican jurisdiction in 1821, when Mexico was no longer ruled by Spain. In 1853 Mexico sold the area to the U.S. and soon after overland stage service from San Antonio was instituted. The Civil War interrupted travel along this route to California. After the war, Tucson continued as a supply and distribution point, first for the army and then for miners. From 1867 to 1877, it was the capital of the territory.

Tucson grew slowly until World War II when it became more industrialized. Today, the city is both an industrial center and a health resort. Aircraft and missile manufacturing, optics, electronics research, tourism, and education are chief industries. Top employers in the city are the U.S. Air Force, the University of Arizona, and Raytheon Company.

Recreation in Tucson revolves around its breathtaking natural beauty. Attractions include the Arizona-Sonoran Desert Museum—21 acres of wild desert inhabited by over 300 animal species and 1,200 types of plants—and Kitt Peak National Observatory atop a 6,882-foot mountain, where visitors can peek through its many optical and radio telescopes and enjoy exhibits and tours. Saguaro National Park is a 91,000-acre park featuring one of the world's largest saguaro, or tall cactus. Mount Lemmon, over 9,000 feet high, offers hiking, camping, picnicking, and skiing. Biosphere 2, the world's largest controlled environment dedicated to understanding the impact of climate change is in nearby Oracle. This 3.14-acre laboratory is home to world-class research and education programs under the stewardship of the University of Arizona and a popular tourist attraction.

In an attempt to combat the water scarcity in the city due to climate change, the city provides financial incentives for residents to harvest their rainwater. Tucson's water supply, like many Western cities, is drawn from surface water that is pumped more than 300 miles from the Colorado River, and groundwater. The pump expends a significant amount of energy and the Colorado River is diminishing as a result of climate change and overuse. Since 2012, Tucson has been rebating residents up to $2,000 for the purchase of water harvesting systems. The system harvests rainwater from building surfaces, and storm runoff from streets and earth to be used for irrigation, landscaping and other uses. The city is working to become carbon-neutral by 2030.

Arizona State Museum features extensive basketry and fiber arts exhibits, celebrating the country's Southwest ancient fiber-weaving traditions. The unparalleled collections of basketry and pottery have been named National Treasures by the National Endowment for the Humanities. Other notable museums include the University of Arizona Museum of Art, Arizona-Sonora Desert Museum, and Pima Air & Space Museum. The city is home to numerous annual events, including the Tucson Gem & Mineral Show, the Tucson Festival of Books, the Tucson Folk Festival, and the All-Souls Procession Weekend.

The college scene in Tucson includes the University of Arizona, one of the top research universities in the U.S., with 45,000 national and international students, and Pima Community College, serving students on five campuses in the city. Tucson's sports focuses on the University of Arizona, with competitive men's basketball women's softball teams. A 2018 addition to the city was the Indoor Football League expansion team, the Tucson Sugar Skulls, playing in the renovated Tucson Arena.

Nightlife in Tucson abounds with music of all kinds—blues, jazz, country, folk, Latino, and reggae. The diverse restaurant scene, including Japanese, Southwestern, and Italian, is world-renowned.

Tucson has a desert climate, with two major seasons, a hot summer and mild winter. Tucson averages 10.6 inches of precipitation per year, concentrated during the Pacific storms of winter and the North American Monsoon of summer. Fall and spring tend to be sunny and dry. Despite being at a more southerly latitude than Phoenix, Tucson is slightly cooler and wetter due to a variety of factors, including elevation and orographic lift in surrounding mountains, though Tucson does occasionally see warmer daytime temperatures in the winter.

Rankings

General Rankings

- To help military veterans find the best places in which to settle down, *WalletHub* compared the 100 largest U.S. cities across 19 key indicators of livability, affordability and veteran-friendliness. They range from the share of military skill-related jobs to veteran income growth to the availability of VA health facilities. Tucson ranked #62. *Wallethub.com, "Best & Worst Places for Veterans to Live (2025)," November 7, 2024*

Business/Finance Rankings

- The Tucson metro area appeared on the Milken Institute "2025 Best Performing Cities" list. Rank: #110 out of 200 large metro areas (based on performance category). Criteria: job growth; wage growth; high-tech growth and impact; community resilience; housing affordability; household broadband access. *Milken Institute, "Best-Performing Cities 2025," January 14, 2025*

Education Rankings

- Personal finance website *WalletHub* analyzed the 150 largest U.S. metropolitan statistical areas to determine where the most educated Americans are putting their degrees to work. Criteria: education levels; percentage of workers with degrees; education quality and attainment gap; public school quality rankings; quality and enrollment of each metro area's universities. Tucson was ranked #46 (#1 = most educated city). *WalletHub.com, "Most & Least Educated Cities in America, 2025" July 2, 2024*

Health/Fitness Rankings

- For each of the 100 largest cities in the United States, the American Fitness Index®, compiled in partnership between the American College of Sports Medicine and the Elevance Health Foundation, evaluated community infrastructure and more than 30 health behaviors including preventive health, levels of chronic disease conditions, food insecurity, pedestrian safety, air quality, and community/environment resources that support physical activity. Tucson ranked #56 for "community fitness." *americanfitnessindex.org, "2024 ACSM American Fitness Index Summary Report," July 23, 2024*

- Tucson was identified as a "2025 Allergy Capital." The area ranked #59 out of the nation's 100 largest metropolitan areas. Three groups of factors were used to identify the most challenging cities for people with allergies: annual tree, grass, and weed pollen scores; over the counter allergy medicine use; number of board-certified allergy specialists. *Asthma and Allergy Foundation of America, "2025 Allergy Capitals: The Most Challenging Places to Live with Allergies," March 18, 2025*

- Tucson was identified as a "2024 Asthma Capital." The area ranked #27 out of the nation's 100 largest metropolitan areas. Criteria: estimated asthma prevalence; asthma-related mortality; and ER visits due to asthma. Risk factors analyzed but not factored in the rankings: annual air quality including pollution and ozone levels; public smoking laws; indoor air quality; access to asthma specialists; rescue and controller medication use; uninsured rate; pollen allergy; poverty rate. *Asthma and Allergy Foundation of America, "Asthma Capitals 2024: The Most Challenging Places to Live With Asthma," September 10, 2024*

Real Estate Rankings

- *WalletHub* compared the most populated U.S. cities to determine which had the best markets for real estate agents. Tucson ranked #67 where demand was high and pay was the best. Criteria: sales per agent; annual median wage for real-estate agents; monthly average starting salary for real estate agents; real estate job density and competition; unemployment rate; home turnover rate; housing-market health index; and other relevant metrics. *WalletHub.com, "2021 Best Places to Be a Real Estate Agent," May 12, 2021*

- Tucson was ranked #125 out of 176 metro areas in terms of cost of housing in 2024 by the National Association of Home Builders (#1 = most affordable). Criteria: the portion of an average family's income necessary to pay the mortgage on a median-priced home. *National Association of Home Builders®, NAHB-Wells Fargo Cost of Housing Index, 4th Quarter 2024*

Safety Rankings

- Allstate ranked the 100 most populous cities in America in terms of driver safety. Tucson ranked #91. Criteria based on anonymized driving behavior data from Allstate's mobile app powered by Arity: high speed driving (over 80 mph), phone handling, and hard braking. The report helps increase the importance of safety and awareness behind the wheel. *Allstate, "16th Allstate America's Best Drivers Report®" July 11, 2024*

Seniors/Retirement Rankings

- Tucson made the 2024 *Forbes* list of "25 Best Places to Retire." Criteria, focused on overall affordability as well as quality of life indicators, include: housing/living costs compared to the national average and taxes; air quality; crime rates; median home prices; risk associated with climate-change/natural hazards; availability of medical care; bikeability; walkability; healthy living. *Forbes.com, "The Best Places to Retire in 2024: Las Cruces and Other Unexpected Hot Spots," May 10, 2024*

Women/Minorities Rankings

- Personal finance website *WalletHub* compared more than 180 U.S. cities across two key dimensions, "Hispanic Business-Friendliness" and "Hispanic Purchasing Power," to arrive at the most favorable conditions for Hispanic entrepreneurs. Tucson was ranked #103 out of 182. Criteria includes: share of Hispanic-Owned Businesses; average growth of Hispanic Business revenues; Small Business-Friendliness score; affordability; and number of Hispanics with at least a bachelor's degree. *WalletHub.com, "Best Cities for Hispanic Entrepreneurs," September 4, 2024*

Miscellaneous Rankings

- *WalletHub* compared 148 of the most populated U.S. cities to determine their operating efficiency. A "Quality of Services" score was constructed for each city and then measured against the total budget per capita to reveal which were managed the best. Tucson ranked #31. Criteria: financial stability; economy; education; safety; health; infrastructure and pollution. *WalletHub.com, "2025's Best- & Worst-Run Cities in America," June 18, 2024*

Business Environment

DEMOGRAPHICS

Population Growth

Area	1990 Census	2000 Census	2010 Census	2020 Census	2023 Estimate[2]	Population Growth 1990-2023 (%)
City	417,942	486,699	520,116	542,629	543,348	30.0
MSA[1]	666,880	843,746	980,263	1,043,433	1,049,947	57.4
U.S.	248,709,873	281,421,906	308,745,538	331,449,281	332,387,540	33.6

Note: (1) Figures cover the Tucson, AZ Metropolitan Statistical Area; (2) 2019-2023 5-year ACS population estimate
Source: U.S. Census Bureau, 1990 Census, 2000 Census, 2010 Census, 2020 Census, 2019-2023 American Community Survey 5-Year Estimates

Race

Area	White Alone[2] (%)	Black Alone[2] (%)	Asian Alone[2] (%)	AIAN[3] Alone[2] (%)	NHOPI[4] Alone[2] (%)	Other Race Alone[2] (%)	Two or More Races (%)
City	58.2	5.0	3.1	2.7	0.2	11.6	19.1
MSA[1]	63.2	3.6	3.0	3.1	0.2	9.9	17.0
U.S.	63.4	12.4	5.8	0.9	0.2	6.6	10.7

Note: (1) Figures cover the Tucson, AZ Metropolitan Statistical Area; (2) Alone is defined as not being in combination with one or more other races; (3) American Indian and Alaska Native; (4) Native Hawaiian and Other Pacific Islander
Source: U.S. Census Bureau, 2019-2023 American Community Survey 5-Year Estimates

Hispanic or Latino Origin

Area	Total (%)	Mexican (%)	Puerto Rican (%)	Cuban (%)	Other (%)
City	42.7	38.1	0.8	0.3	3.5
MSA[1]	36.1	32.1	0.9	0.2	3.0
U.S.	19.0	11.3	1.8	0.7	5.2

Note: Persons of Hispanic or Latino origin can be of any race; (1) Figures cover the Tucson, AZ Metropolitan Statistical Area
Source: U.S. Census Bureau, 2019-2023 American Community Survey 5-Year Estimates

Age

Area	Under Age 5	Age 5–19	Age 20–34	Age 35–44	Age 45–54	Age 55–64	Age 65–74	Age 75–84	Age 85+	Median Age
City	5.3	18.5	26.7	12.2	10.4	11.0	9.0	4.8	2.0	34.6
MSA[1]	5.0	18.0	21.4	11.6	10.8	12.2	12.0	6.8	2.4	39.7
U.S.	5.7	19.1	20.2	13.1	12.3	12.8	10.0	4.9	1.9	38.7

Note: (1) Figures cover the Tucson, AZ Metropolitan Statistical Area
Source: U.S. Census Bureau, 2019-2023 American Community Survey 5-Year Estimates

Disability by Age

Area	All Ages	Under 18 Years Old	18 to 64 Years Old	65 Years and Over
City	15.5	6.1	13.2	36.8
MSA[1]	15.1	5.6	12.2	32.3
U.S.	13.0	4.7	10.7	32.9

Note: Figures show percent of the civilian noninstitutionalized population that reported having a disability. Disability status is determined from six types of difficulty: vision, hearing, cognitive, ambulatory, self-care, and independent living. For children under 5 years old, hearing and vision difficulty are used to determine disability status. For children between the ages of 5 and 14, disability status is determined from hearing, vision, cognitive, ambulatory, and self-care difficulties. For people aged 15 years and older, they are considered to have a disability if they have difficulty with any one of the six difficulty types; Note: (1) Figures cover the Tucson, AZ Metropolitan Statistical Area
Source: U.S. Census Bureau, 2019-2023 American Community Survey 5-Year Estimates

Ancestry

Area	German	Irish	English	American	Italian	Polish	French[2]	European	Scottish
City	11.5	8.4	8.0	2.9	3.7	1.9	1.8	1.5	1.7
MSA[1]	13.2	9.0	10.1	3.5	4.1	2.2	2.1	1.7	2.0
U.S.	12.6	9.4	9.1	5.5	4.9	2.6	2.0	1.6	1.6

Note: Figures are the percentage of the total population reporting a particular ancestry. The nine most commonly reported ancestries in the U.S. are shown. Figures include multiple ancestries (e.g. if a person reported being Irish and Italian, they were included in both columns); (1) Figures cover the Tucson, AZ Metropolitan Statistical Area; (2) Excludes Basque
Source: U.S. Census Bureau, 2019-2023 American Community Survey 5-Year Estimates

Foreign-born Population

Area	Any Foreign Country	Asia	Mexico	Europe	Caribbean	Central America[2]	South America	Africa	Canada
City	13.7	2.4	8.3	1.0	0.1	0.4	0.3	0.8	0.2
MSA[1]	11.9	2.3	6.6	1.3	0.2	0.3	0.3	0.6	0.3
U.S.	13.9	4.3	3.3	1.4	1.4	1.2	1.2	0.8	0.2

Note: (1) Figures cover the Tucson, AZ Metropolitan Statistical Area; (2) Excludes Mexico.
Source: U.S. Census Bureau, 2019-2023 American Community Survey 5-Year Estimates

Household Size

Area	Persons in Household (%)							Average Household Size
	One	Two	Three	Four	Five	Six	Seven or More	
City	36.3	31.0	13.7	10.7	5.2	2.0	1.1	2.30
MSA[1]	31.8	35.4	13.2	11.1	5.1	2.3	1.2	2.37
U.S.	28.5	33.8	15.4	12.7	5.9	2.3	1.4	2.54

Note: (1) Figures cover the Tucson, AZ Metropolitan Statistical Area
Source: U.S. Census Bureau, 2019-2023 American Community Survey 5-Year Estimates

Household Relationships

Area	House-holder	Opposite-sex Spouse	Same-sex Spouse	Opposite-sex Unmarried Partner	Same-sex Unmarried Partner	Child[2]	Grand-child	Other Relatives	Non-relatives
City	41.1	13.3	0.3	3.3	0.3	25.4	2.8	4.8	4.5
MSA[1]	40.9	17.2	0.3	2.9	0.2	25.5	2.6	4.4	3.4
U.S.	38.3	17.5	0.2	2.5	0.2	28.3	2.4	4.8	3.4

Note: Figures are percent of the total population; (1) Figures cover the Tucson, AZ Metropolitan Statistical Area; (2) Includes biological, adopted, and stepchildren of the householder
Source: U.S. Census Bureau, 2020 Census

Gender

Area	Males	Females	Males per 100 Females
City	270,198	273,150	98.9
MSA[1]	518,998	530,949	97.7
U.S.	164,545,087	167,842,453	98.0

Note: (1) Figures cover the Tucson, AZ Metropolitan Statistical Area
Source: U.S. Census Bureau, 2019-2023 American Community Survey 5-Year Estimates

Marital Status

Area	Never Married	Now Married[2]	Separated	Widowed	Divorced
City	42.9	36.0	1.8	5.2	14.1
MSA[1]	35.1	44.8	1.5	5.8	12.9
U.S.	34.1	47.9	1.7	5.6	10.7

Note: Figures are percentages and cover the population 15 years of age and older; (1) Figures cover the Tucson, AZ Metropolitan Statistical Area; (2) Excludes separated
Source: U.S. Census Bureau, 2019-2023 American Community Survey 5-Year Estimates

Religious Groups by Family

Area	Catholic	Baptist	Methodist	LDS[2]	Pentecostal	Lutheran	Islam	Adventist	Other
MSA[1]	18.9	1.9	0.6	2.8	1.3	1.1	1.0	1.4	9.7
U.S.	18.7	7.3	3.0	2.0	1.8	1.7	1.3	1.3	11.6

Note: Figures are the number of adherents as a percentage of the total population and cover the eight largest religious groups in the U.S; (1) Figures cover the Tucson, AZ Metropolitan Statistical Area; (2) Church of Jesus Christ of Latter-day Saints
Sources: 2020 U.S. Religion Census, Association of Statisticians of American Religious Bodies; The Association of Religion Data Archives (ARDA)

Religious Groups by Tradition

Area	Catholic	Evangelical Protestant	Mainline Protestant	Black Protestant	Islam	Judaism	Hinduism	Orthodox	Buddhism
MSA[1]	18.9	10.4	2.4	0.6	1.0	0.4	0.4	0.2	0.3
U.S.	18.7	16.5	5.2	2.3	1.3	0.6	0.4	0.4	0.3

Note: Figures are the number of adherents as a percentage of the total population; (1) Figures cover the Tucson, AZ Metropolitan Statistical Area
Sources: 2020 U.S. Religion Census, Association of Statisticians of American Religious Bodies; The Association of Religion Data Archives (ARDA)

ECONOMY

Real Gross Domestic Product (GDP)

Area	2017	2018	2019	2020	2021	2022	2023	Rank[3]
MSA[1]	42.3	43.9	45.4	45.3	47.9	48.6	50.8	68
U.S.[2]	17,619.1	18,160.7	18,642.5	18,238.9	19,387.6	19,896.6	20,436.3	–

Note: Figures are in billions of chained 2017 dollars; (1) Figures cover the Tucson, AZ Metropolitan Statistical Area; (2) Figures cover real GDP within metropolitan areas; (3) Rank is based on 2023 data and ranges from 1 to 384
Source: U.S. Bureau of Economic Analysis

Economic Growth

Area	2014	2015	2016	2017	2018	2019	2020	2021	2022	2023
MSA[1]	0.2	-0.5	3.4	3.5	3.7	3.5	-0.3	5.7	1.4	4.6
U.S.[2]	2.6	3.2	2.0	2.7	3.1	2.7	-2.2	6.3	2.6	2.7

Note: Figures are real gross domestic product growth rates and represent percent change from preceding period; (1) Figures cover the Tucson, AZ Metropolitan Statistical Area; (2) Figures are the average growth rates within metropolitan areas
Source: U.S. Bureau of Economic Analysis

Metropolitan Area Exports

Area	2018	2019	2020	2021	2022	2023	Rank[2]
MSA[1]	2,824.8	2,943.7	2,640.7	2,846.1	3,779.4	4,503.0	68
U.S.	1,664,056.1	1,645,173.7	1,431,406.6	1,753,941.4	2,062,937.4	2,019,160.5	–

Note: Figures are in millions of dollars; (1) Figures cover the Tucson, AZ Metropolitan Statistical Area; (2) Rank is based on 2023 data and ranges from 1 to 386
Source: U.S. Department of Commerce, International Trade Administration, Office of Trade and Economic Analysis, Industry and Analysis, Exports by Metropolitan Area, data extracted April 2, 2025

Building Permits

Area	Single-Family			Multi-Family			Total		
	2023	2024	Pct. Chg.	2023	2024	Pct. Chg.	2023	2024	Pct. Chg.
City	839	923	10.0	829	582	-29.8	1,668	1,505	-9.8
MSA[1]	3,688	4,150	12.5	1,567	1,100	-29.8	5,255	5,250	-0.1
U.S.	920,000	981,900	6.7	591,100	496,100	-16.1	1,511,100	1,478,000	-2.2

Note: (1) Figures cover the Tucson, AZ Metropolitan Statistical Area; Figures represent new, privately-owned housing units authorized (unadjusted data)
Source: U.S. Census Bureau, Building Permits Survey (BPS), 2023, 2024

Bankruptcy Filings

Area	Business Filings			Nonbusiness Filings		
	2023	2024	% Chg.	2023	2024	% Chg.
Pima County	28	27	-3.6	1,402	1,638	16.8
U.S.	18,926	23,107	22.1	434,064	494,201	13.9

Note: Business filings include Chapter 7, Chapter 9, Chapter 11, Chapter 12, Chapter 13, Chapter 15, and Section 304; Nonbusiness filings include Chapter 7, Chapter 11, and Chapter 13
Source: Administrative Office of the U.S. Courts, Business and Nonbusiness Bankruptcy, County Cases Commenced by Chapter of the Bankruptcy Code, During the 12-Month Period Ending December 31, 2023 and Business and Nonbusiness Bankruptcy, County Cases Commenced by Chapter of the Bankruptcy Code, During the 12-Month Period Ending December 31, 2024

Housing Vacancy Rates

Area	Gross Vacancy Rate[3] (%)			Year-Round Vacancy Rate[4] (%)			Rental Vacancy Rate[5] (%)			Homeowner Vacancy Rate[6] (%)		
	2022	2023	2024	2022	2023	2024	2022	2023	2024	2022	2023	2024
MSA[1]	13.5	14.2	10.1	10.3	11.2	8.7	8.0	10.2	9.3	1.4	1.3	1.1
U.S.[2]	9.1	9.0	9.1	7.5	7.5	7.6	5.7	6.5	6.8	0.8	0.8	1.0

Note: (1) Figures cover the Tucson, AZ Metropolitan Statistical Area; (2) Figures cover the 75 largest Metropolitan Statistical Areas; (3) The percentage of the total housing inventory that is vacant; (4) The percentage of the housing inventory (excluding seasonal units) that is year-round vacant; (5) The percentage of rental inventory that is vacant for rent; (6) The percentage of homeowner inventory that is vacant for sale
Source: U.S. Census Bureau, Housing Vacancies and Homeownership Annual Statistics: 2022, 2023, 2024

INCOME

Income

Area	Per Capita ($)	Median Household ($)	Average Household ($)
City	31,152	54,546	73,528
MSA[1]	38,564	67,929	92,561
U.S.	43,289	78,538	110,491

Note: (1) Figures cover the Tucson, AZ Metropolitan Statistical Area
Source: U.S. Census Bureau, 2019-2023 American Community Survey 5-Year Estimates

Household Income Distribution

Area	Percent of Households Earning							
	Under $15,000	$15,000 -$24,999	$25,000 -$34,999	$35,000 -$49,999	$50,000 -$74,999	$75,000 -$99,999	$100,000 -$149,999	$150,000 and up
City	12.0	9.6	10.2	14.6	17.5	12.7	14.1	9.5
MSA[1]	9.3	7.6	8.5	12.3	16.7	12.8	16.7	16.0
U.S.	8.5	6.6	6.8	10.4	15.7	12.7	17.4	21.9

Note: (1) Figures cover the Tucson, AZ Metropolitan Statistical Area
Source: U.S. Census Bureau, 2019-2023 American Community Survey 5-Year Estimates

Poverty Rate

Area	All Ages	Under 18 Years Old	18 to 64 Years Old	65 Years and Over
City	18.8	24.3	18.7	12.5
MSA[1]	14.4	18.7	14.9	8.9
U.S.	12.4	16.3	11.6	10.4

Note: Figures are percentage of people whose income during the past 12 months was below the poverty level;
(1) Figures cover the Tucson, AZ Metropolitan Statistical Area
Source: U.S. Census Bureau, 2019-2023 American Community Survey 5-Year Estimates

EMPLOYMENT

Labor Force and Employment

Area	Civilian Labor Force			Workers Employed		
	Dec. 2023	Dec. 2024	% Chg.	Dec. 2023	Dec. 2024	% Chg.
City	263,211	266,440	1.2	254,477	256,864	0.9
MSA[1]	493,139	499,226	1.2	477,781	482,263	0.9
U.S.	166,661,000	167,746,000	0.7	160,754,000	161,294,000	0.3

Note: Data is not seasonally adjusted and covers workers 16 years of age and older; (1) Figures cover the
Tucson, AZ Metropolitan Statistical Area
Source: Bureau of Labor Statistics, Local Area Unemployment Statistics

Unemployment Rate

Area	2024											
	Jan.	Feb.	Mar.	Apr.	May	Jun.	Jul.	Aug.	Sep.	Oct.	Nov.	Dec.
City	3.5	3.4	3.1	2.9	3.4	4.2	4.4	4.3	3.9	3.8	3.9	3.6
MSA[1]	3.3	3.3	3.0	2.8	3.3	4.0	4.3	4.0	3.7	3.7	3.6	3.4
U.S.	4.1	4.2	3.9	3.5	3.7	4.3	4.5	4.4	3.9	3.9	4.0	3.8

Note: Data is not seasonally adjusted and covers workers 16 years of age and older; (1) Figures cover the
Tucson, AZ Metropolitan Statistical Area
Source: Bureau of Labor Statistics, Local Area Unemployment Statistics

Average Wages

Occupation	$/Hr.	Occupation	$/Hr.
Accountants and Auditors	39.27	Maintenance and Repair Workers	22.70
Automotive Mechanics	26.22	Marketing Managers	65.42
Bookkeepers	24.08	Network and Computer Systems Admin.	44.42
Carpenters	25.46	Nurses, Licensed Practical	34.81
Cashiers	15.74	Nurses, Registered	44.18
Computer Programmers	46.55	Nursing Assistants	20.24
Computer Systems Analysts	51.81	Office Clerks, General	22.28
Computer User Support Specialists	28.35	Physical Therapists	47.48
Construction Laborers	21.11	Physicians	134.43
Cooks, Restaurant	17.71	Plumbers, Pipefitters and Steamfitters	27.72
Customer Service Representatives	19.74	Police and Sheriff's Patrol Officers	37.95
Dentists	92.54	Postal Service Mail Carriers	29.27
Electricians	28.60	Real Estate Sales Agents	30.47
Engineers, Electrical	62.08	Retail Salespersons	18.32
Fast Food and Counter Workers	15.89	Sales Representatives, Technical/Scientific	47.81
Financial Managers	66.97	Secretaries, Exc. Legal/Medical/Executive	21.86
First-Line Supervisors of Office Workers	29.60	Security Guards	18.88
General and Operations Managers	57.34	Surgeons	n/a
Hairdressers/Cosmetologists	19.10	Teacher Assistants, Exc. Postsecondary[1]	16.88
Home Health and Personal Care Aides	16.54	Teachers, Secondary School, Exc. Sp. Ed.[1]	25.54
Janitors and Cleaners	17.29	Telemarketers	n/a
Landscaping/Groundskeeping Workers	18.04	Truck Drivers, Heavy/Tractor-Trailer	25.42
Lawyers	67.35	Truck Drivers, Light/Delivery Services	23.43
Maids and Housekeeping Cleaners	16.29	Waiters and Waitresses	20.95

Note: Wage data covers the Tucson, AZ Metropolitan Statistical Area; (1) Hourly wages were calculated from
annual wage data based on a 40 hour work week
Source: Bureau of Labor Statistics, Metro Area Occupational Employment & Wage Estimates, May 2024

Employment by Industry

Sector	MSA[1]		U.S.
	Number of Employees	Percent of Total	Percent of Total
Construction	20,400	5.0	5.1
Financial Activities	17,400	4.3	5.8
Government	80,700	19.9	14.9
Information	5,100	1.3	1.9
Leisure and Hospitality	45,400	11.2	10.4
Manufacturing	28,400	7.0	8.0
Mining and Logging	2,600	0.6	0.4
Other Services	14,900	3.7	3.7
Private Education and Health Services	72,400	17.9	16.9
Professional and Business Services	44,900	11.1	14.2
Retail Trade	44,000	10.9	10.0
Transportation, Warehousing, and Utilities	20,600	5.1	4.8
Wholesale Trade	8,100	2.0	3.9

Note: Figures are non-farm employment as of December 2024. Figures are not seasonally adjusted and include workers 16 years of age and older; (1) Figures cover the Tucson, AZ Metropolitan Statistical Area
Source: Bureau of Labor Statistics, Current Employment Statistics, Employment, Hours, and Earnings

Employment by Occupation

Occupation Classification	City (%)	MSA[1] (%)	U.S. (%)
Management, Business, Science, and Arts	37.3	41.6	42.0
Natural Resources, Construction, and Maintenance	8.5	8.4	8.6
Production, Transportation, and Material Moving	10.1	9.2	13.0
Sales and Office	22.4	21.5	19.9
Service	21.7	19.3	16.5

Note: Figures cover employed civilians 16 years of age and older; (1) Figures cover the Tucson, AZ Metropolitan Statistical Area
Source: U.S. Census Bureau, 2019-2023 American Community Survey 5-Year Estimates

Occupations with Greatest Projected Employment Growth: 2022 – 2032

Occupation[1]	2022 Employment	2032 Projected Employment	Numeric Employment Change	Percent Employment Change
Home Health and Personal Care Aides	68,550	96,120	27,570	40.2
Laborers and Freight, Stock, and Material Movers, Hand	72,140	89,140	17,000	23.6
General and Operations Managers	96,240	111,360	15,120	15.7
Software Developers	39,420	53,530	14,110	35.8
Stockers and Order Fillers	60,920	74,660	13,740	22.6
Registered Nurses	59,110	72,050	12,940	21.9
Fast Food and Counter Workers	85,580	98,010	12,430	14.5
Retail Salespersons	85,240	96,850	11,610	13.6
Heavy and Tractor-Trailer Truck Drivers	43,020	53,850	10,830	25.2
Cooks, Restaurant	28,890	38,830	9,940	34.4

Note: Projections cover Arizona; (1) Sorted by numeric employment change
Source: www.projectionscentral.org, State Occupational Projections, 2022–2032 Long-Term Projections

Fastest-Growing Occupations: 2022 – 2032

Occupation[1]	2022 Employment	2032 Projected Employment	Numeric Employment Change	Percent Employment Change
Nurse Practitioners	6,540	11,200	4,660	71.3
Physician Assistants	3,440	5,180	1,740	50.6
Medical and Health Services Managers	9,580	14,390	4,810	50.2
Data Scientists	2,960	4,380	1,420	48.0
Physical Therapist Assistants	1,480	2,180	700	47.3
Occupational Therapy Assistants	1,140	1,670	530	46.5
Statisticians	1,010	1,460	450	44.6
Solar Photovoltaic Installers	750	1,070	320	42.7
Home Health and Personal Care Aides	68,550	96,120	27,570	40.2
Information Security Analysts (SOC 2018)	3,660	5,110	1,450	39.6

Note: Projections cover Arizona; (1) Sorted by percent employment change and excludes occupations with numeric employment change less than 50
Source: www.projectionscentral.org, State Occupational Projections, 2022–2032 Long-Term Projections

CITY FINANCES

City Government Finances

Component	2022 ($000)	2022 ($ per capita)
Total Revenues	1,378,028	2,540
Total Expenditures	974,474	1,796
Debt Outstanding	903,012	1,664

Source: U.S. Census Bureau, State & Local Government Finances 2022

City Government Revenue by Source

Source	2022 ($000)	2022 ($ per capita)	2022 (%)
General Revenue			
From Federal Government	113,792	210	8.3
From State Government	242,953	448	17.6
From Local Governments	0	0	0.0
Taxes			
Property	71,092	131	5.2
Sales and Gross Receipts	350,054	645	25.4
Personal Income	0	0	0.0
Corporate Income	0	0	0.0
Motor Vehicle License	0	0	0.0
Other Taxes	32,397	60	2.4
Current Charges	163,208	301	11.8
Liquor Store	0	0	0.0
Utility	260,644	480	18.9

Source: U.S. Census Bureau, State & Local Government Finances 2022

City Government Expenditures by Function

Function	2022 ($000)	2022 ($ per capita)	2022 (%)
General Direct Expenditures			
Air Transportation	51,737	95	5.3
Corrections	0	0	0.0
Education	0	0	0.0
Employment Security Administration	0	0	0.0
Financial Administration	22,000	40	2.3
Fire Protection	118,304	218	12.1
General Public Buildings	0	0	0.0
Governmental Administration, Other	22,376	41	2.3
Health	0	0	0.0
Highways	49,076	90	5.0
Hospitals	0	0	0.0
Housing and Community Development	45,813	84	4.7
Interest on General Debt	9,638	17	1.0
Judicial and Legal	30,191	55	3.1
Libraries	0	0	0.0
Parking	4,543	8	0.5
Parks and Recreation	14,283	26	1.5
Police Protection	283,044	521	29.0
Public Welfare	0	0	0.0
Sewerage	0	0	0.0
Solid Waste Management	44,486	82	4.6
Veterans' Services	0	0	0.0
Liquor Store	0	0	0.0
Utility	257,404	474	26.4

Source: U.S. Census Bureau, State & Local Government Finances 2022

TAXES

State Corporate Income Tax Rates

State	Tax Rate (%)	Income Brackets ($)	Num. of Brackets	Financial Institution Tax Rate (%)[a]	Federal Income Tax Ded.
Arizona	4.9 (b)	Flat rate	1	4.9 (b)	No

Note: Tax rates for tax year 2024; (a) Rates listed are the corporate income tax rate applied to financial institutions or excise taxes based on income. Some states have other taxes based upon the value of deposits or shares; (b) Minimum tax is $800 in California, $250 in District of Columbia, $50 in Arizona and North Dakota (banks), $400 ($100 banks) in Rhode Island, $200 per location in South Dakota (banks), $100 in Utah, in Vermont, simplified entity business tax for residents only at $250, otherwise minimum tax ($100 - $100,000) is based upon gross receipts.
Source: Federation of Tax Administrators, State Corporate Income Tax Rates, January 1, 2025

State Individual Income Tax Rates

State	Tax Rate (%)	Income Brackets ($)	Personal Exemptions ($)			Standard Ded. ($)	
			Single	Married	Depend.	Single	Married
Arizona	2.5	Flat rate	–	–	100 (c)	14,600	29,200

Note: Tax rates for tax year 2024; Local- and county-level taxes are not included; Federal income tax is not deductible on state income tax returns; (c) The personal exemption takes the form of a tax credit instead of a deduction
Source: Federation of Tax Administrators, State Individual Income Tax Rates, January 1, 2025

Various State Sales and Excise Tax Rates

State	State Sales Tax (%)	Gasoline[1] ($/gal.)	Cigarette[2] ($/pack)	Spirits[3] ($/gal.)	Wine[4] ($/gal.)	Beer[5] ($/gal.)	Recreational Marijuana (%)
Arizona	5.6	0.19	2.00	3.00	0.84	0.16	(b)

Note: All tax rates as of January 1, 2025; (1) The American Petroleum Institute has developed a methodology for determining the average tax rate on a gallon of fuel. Rates may include any of the following: excise taxes, environmental fees, storage tank fees, other fees or taxes, general sales tax, and local taxes; (2) The federal excise tax of $1.0066 per pack and local taxes are not included; (3) Rates are those applicable to off-premise sales of 40% alcohol by volume (a.b.v.) distilled spirits in 750ml containers. Local excise taxes are excluded; (4) Rates are those applicable to off-premise sales of 11% a.b.v. non-carbonated wine in 750ml containers; (5) Rates are those applicable to off-premise sales of 4.7% a.b.v. beer in 12 ounce containers; (b) 16% excise tax (retail price)
Source: Tax Foundation, 2025 Facts & Figures: How Does Your State Compare?

State Tax Competitiveness Index

State	Overall Rank	Corporate Tax Rank	Individual Income Tax Rank	Sales Tax Rank	Property Tax Rank	Unemployment Insurance Tax Rank
Arizona	15	13	8	45	13	2

Note: The Tax Foundation's State Tax Competitiveness Index enables policymakers, taxpayers, and business leaders to gauge how their states' tax systems compare. A rank of 1 is best, 50 is worst. Rankings do not average to the total. States without a tax rank equally as 1. DC's scores and rankings do not affect other states. The report shows tax systems as of July 1, 2024 (the beginning of Fiscal Year 2025).
Source: Tax Foundation, State Tax Competitiveness Index 2025

TRANSPORTATION

Means of Transportation to Work

Area	Car/Truck/Van		Public Transportation			Bicycle	Walked	Other Means	Worked at Home
	Drove Alone	Car-pooled	Bus	Subway	Railroad				
City	69.5	9.9	2.3	0.0	0.0	1.6	2.7	1.6	12.4
MSA[1]	70.7	9.6	1.5	0.0	0.0	1.0	1.9	1.5	13.8
U.S.	70.2	8.5	1.7	1.3	0.4	0.4	2.4	1.6	13.5

Note: Figures are percentages and cover workers 16 years of age and older; (1) Figures cover the Tucson, AZ Metropolitan Statistical Area
Source: U.S. Census Bureau, 2019-2023 American Community Survey 5-Year Estimates

Travel Time to Work

Area	Less Than 10 Minutes	10 to 19 Minutes	20 to 29 Minutes	30 to 44 Minutes	45 to 59 Minutes	60 to 89 Minutes	90 Minutes or More
City	12.3	34.4	25.8	19.3	4.6	2.1	1.4
MSA[1]	11.0	29.4	25.2	23.2	6.8	2.6	1.7
U.S.	12.6	28.6	21.2	20.8	8.1	6.0	2.8

Note: Note: Figures are percentages and include workers 16 years old and over; (1) Figures cover the Tucson, AZ Metropolitan Statistical Area
Source: U.S. Census Bureau, 2019-2023 American Community Survey 5-Year Estimates

Key Congestion Measures

Measure	2000	2010	2015	2020	2022
Annual Hours of Delay, Total (000)	18,225	27,738	30,850	13,189	23,388
Annual Hours of Delay, Per Auto Commuter	40	43	49	21	39
Annual Congestion Cost, Per Auto Commuter ($)	752	912	935	426	741

Note: Figures cover the Tucson AZ urban area
Source: Texas A&M Transportation Institute, 2023 Urban Mobility Report

Freeway Travel Time Index

Measure	1985	1990	1995	2000	2005	2010	2015	2020	2022
Urban Area Index[1]	1.10	1.14	1.16	1.20	1.21	1.20	1.21	1.07	1.14
Urban Area Rank[1,2]	27	26	32	29	35	36	36	57	64

Note: Freeway Travel Time Index—the ratio of travel time in the peak period to the travel time at free-flow conditions. For example, a value of 1.30 indicates a 20-minute free-flow trip takes 26 minutes in the peak (20 minutes x 1.30 = 26 minutes); (1) Covers the Tucson AZ urban area; (2) Rank is based on 101 larger urban areas (#1 = highest travel time index)
Source: Texas A&M Transportation Institute, 2023 Urban Mobility Report

Public Transportation

Agency Name / Mode of Transportation	Vehicles Operated in Maximum Service[1]	Annual Unlinked Passenger Trips[2] (in thous.)	Annual Passenger Miles[3] (in thous.)
City of Tucson (COT)			
Bus (purchased transportation)	155	14,615.3	52,311.0
Demand Response (purchased transportation)	106	476.8	4,290.8
Streetcar Rail (purchased transportation)	6	1,667.2	1,384.5

Note: (1) Number of revenue vehicles operated by the given mode and type of service to meet the annual maximum service requirement. This is the revenue vehicle count during the peak season of the year; on the week and day that maximum service is provided. Vehicles operated in maximum service (VOMS) exclude atypical days and one-time special events; (2) Number of passengers who boarded public transportation vehicles. Passengers are counted each time they board a vehicle no matter how many vehicles they use to travel from their origin to their destination. (3) Sum of the distances ridden by all passengers during the entire fiscal year.
Source: Federal Transit Administration, National Transit Database, 2023

Air Transportation

Airport Name and Code / Type of Service	Passenger Airlines[1]	Passenger Enplanements	Freight Carriers[2]	Freight (lbs)
Tucson International (TUS)				
Domestic service (U.S. carriers only)	25	1,956,368	12	25,336,015
International service (U.S. carriers only)	4	3,202	1	11,090

Note: (1) Includes all U.S.-based major, minor and commuter airlines that carried at least one passenger during the year; (2) Includes all U.S.-based airlines and freight carriers that transported at least one pound of freight during the year.
Source: Bureau of Transportation Statistics, The Intermodal Transportation Database, Air Carriers: T-100 Domestic Market (U.S. carriers only), 2024; Bureau of Transportation Statistics, The Intermodal Transportation Database, Air Carriers: T-100 International Market (U.S. carriers only), 2024

BUSINESSES

Major Business Headquarters

Company Name	Industry	Rankings	
		Fortune[1]	Forbes[2]
No companies listed	-	-	-

Note: (1) Companies that produce a 10-K are ranked 1 to 500 based on 2023 revenue; (2) All private companies with at least $2 billion in annual revenue through the end of their most current fiscal year are ranked 1 to 275; companies listed are headquartered in the city; dashes indicate no ranking
Source: Fortune, "Fortune 500," 2024; Forbes, "America's Largest Private Companies," 2024

Living Environment

COST OF LIVING

Cost of Living Index

Composite Index	Groceries	Housing	Utilities	Trans-portation	Health Care	Misc. Goods/ Services
n/a	n/a	n/a	n/a	n/a	n/a	n/a

Note: The Cost of Living Index measures regional differences in the cost of consumer goods and services, excluding taxes and non-consumer expenditures, for professional and managerial households in the top income quintile. It is based on more than 50,000 prices covering almost 60 different items for which prices are collected three times a year by chambers of commerce, economic development organizations or university applied economic centers in each participating urban area. The numbers shown should be read as a percentage above or below the national average of 100. For example, a value of 115.4 in the groceries column indicates that grocery prices are 15.4% higher than the national average. Small differences in the index numbers should not be interpreted as significant; n/a not available.
Source: The Council for Community and Economic Research, Cost of Living Index, 2024

Grocery Prices

Area[1]	T-Bone Steak ($/pound)	Frying Chicken ($/pound)	Whole Milk ($/half gal.)	Eggs ($/dozen)	Orange Juice ($/64 oz.)	Coffee ($/11.5 oz.)
City[2]	n/a	n/a	n/a	n/a	n/a	n/a
Avg.	15.42	1.55	4.69	3.25	4.41	5.46
Min.	14.50	1.16	4.43	2.75	4.00	4.85
Max.	17.56	2.89	5.49	4.78	5.54	7.89

Note: (1) Values for the local area are compared with the average, minimum and maximum values for all 276 areas in the Cost of Living Index; (2) Figures cover the Tucson AZ urban area; n/a not available; T-Bone Steak (price per pound); Frying Chicken (price per pound, whole fryer); Whole Milk (half gallon carton); Eggs (price per dozen, Grade A, large); Orange Juice (64 oz. Tropicana or Florida Natural); Coffee (11.5 oz. can, vacuum-packed, Maxwell House, Hills Bros, or Folgers).
Source: The Council for Community and Economic Research, Cost of Living Index, 2024

Housing and Utility Costs

Area[1]	New Home Price ($)	Apartment Rent ($/month)	All Electric ($/month)	Part Electric ($/month)	Other Energy ($/month)	Telephone ($/month)
City[2]	n/a	n/a	n/a	n/a	n/a	n/a
Avg.	515,975	1,550	210.99	123.07	82.07	194.99
Min.	265,375	692	104.33	53.68	36.26	179.42
Max.	2,775,821	5,719	529.02	397.28	361.63	223.33

Note: (1) Values for the local area are compared with the average, minimum and maximum values for all 276 areas in the Cost of Living Index; (2) Figures cover the Tucson AZ urban area; n/a not available; New Home Price (2,400 sf living area, 8,000 sf lot, in urban area with full utilities); Apartment Rent (950 sf 2 bedroom/1.5 or 2 bath, unfurnished, excluding all utilities except water); All Electric (average monthly cost for an all-electric home); Part Electric (average monthly cost for a part-electric home); Other Energy (average monthly cost for natural gas, fuel oil, coal, wood, and any other forms of energy except electricity); Telephone (price includes the base monthly rate plus taxes and fees for three lines of mobile phone service).
Source: The Council for Community and Economic Research, Cost of Living Index, 2024

Health Care, Transportation, and Other Costs

Area[1]	Doctor ($/visit)	Dentist ($/visit)	Optometrist ($/visit)	Gasoline ($/gallon)	Beauty Salon ($/visit)	Men's Shirt ($)
City[2]	n/a	n/a	n/a	n/a	n/a	n/a
Avg.	143.77	117.51	129.23	3.32	48.57	38.14
Min.	36.74	58.67	67.33	2.80	24.00	13.41
Max.	270.44	216.82	307.33	5.28	94.00	63.89

Note: (1) Values for the local area are compared with the average, minimum and maximum values for all 276 areas in the Cost of Living Index; (2) Figures cover the Tucson AZ urban area; n/a not available; Doctor (general practitioners routine exam of an established patient); Dentist (adult teeth cleaning and periodic oral examination); Optometrist (full vision eye exam for established adult patient); Gasoline (one gallon regular unleaded, national brand, including all taxes, cash price at self-service pump if available); Beauty Salon (woman's shampoo, trim, and blow-dry); Men's Shirt (cotton/polyester dress shirt, pinpoint weave, long sleeves).
Source: The Council for Community and Economic Research, Cost of Living Index, 2024

HOUSING

Homeownership Rate

Area	2017 (%)	2018 (%)	2019 (%)	2020 (%)	2021 (%)	2022 (%)	2023 (%)	2024 (%)
MSA[1]	60.1	63.8	60.1	67.1	63.5	71.6	73.3	66.4
U.S.	63.9	64.4	64.6	66.6	65.5	65.8	65.9	65.6

Note: (1) Figures cover the Tucson, AZ Metropolitan Statistical Area
Source: U.S. Census Bureau, Housing Vacancies and Homeownership Annual Statistics: 2017-2024

House Price Index (HPI)

Area	National Ranking[2]	Quarterly Change (%)	One-Year Change (%)	Five-Year Change (%)	Since 1991Q1 (%)
MSA[1]	223	-1.32	2.30	65.72	364.15
U.S.[3]	–	1.43	4.51	57.13	327.82

Note: The HPI is a weighted repeat sales index. It measures average price changes in repeat sales or refinancings on the same properties. This information is obtained by reviewing repeat mortgage transactions on single-family properties whose mortgages have been purchased or securitized by Fannie Mae or Freddie Mac since January 1975; (1) Figures cover the Tucson, AZ Metropolitan Statistical Area; (2) Rankings are based on annual percentage change for all metro areas containing at least 15,000 transactions over the last 10 years and ranges from 1 to 241; (3) figures based on a weighted average of Census Division estimates using a seasonally adjusted, purchase-only index; all figures are for the period ending December 31, 2024
Source: Federal Housing Finance Agency, Change in FHFA Metropolitan Area House Price Indexes, All Transactions Index, 2024Q4

Home Value

Area	Under $100,000	$100,000 -$199,999	$200,000 -$299,999	$300,000 -$399,999	$400,000 -$499,999	$500,000 -$999,999	$1,000,000 or more	Median ($)
City	12.9	21.2	34.4	17.5	7.6	5.4	1.1	242,200
MSA[1]	11.2	15.2	26.9	19.0	11.6	13.4	2.6	286,900
U.S.	12.1	17.8	19.5	14.4	10.5	19.1	6.5	303,400

Note: Figures are percentages except for median and cover owner-occupied housing units; (1) Figures cover the Tucson, AZ Metropolitan Statistical Area
Source: U.S. Census Bureau, 2019-2023 American Community Survey 5-Year Estimates

Year Housing Structure Built

Area	2020 or Later	2010 -2019	2000 -2009	1990 -1999	1980 -1989	1970 -1979	1960 -1969	1950 -1959	1940 -1949	Before 1940	Median Year
City	0.7	4.6	13.0	12.7	16.5	20.2	11.0	13.4	4.8	3.2	1979
MSA[1]	1.2	7.5	18.2	16.5	17.1	18.6	8.3	7.9	2.8	1.9	1986
U.S.	1.2	8.9	13.6	12.8	13.0	14.4	10.0	9.7	4.5	11.9	1980

Note: Figures are percentages except for Median Year; Note: (1) Figures cover the Tucson, AZ Metropolitan Statistical Area
Source: U.S. Census Bureau, 2019-2023 American Community Survey 5-Year Estimates

Gross Monthly Rent

Area	Under $500	$500 -$999	$1,000 -$1,499	$1,500 -$1,999	$2,000 -$2,499	$2,500 -$2,999	$3,000 and up	Median ($)
City	4.5	38.5	36.3	15.0	3.5	0.8	1.3	1,079
MSA[1]	4.3	32.8	35.8	18.7	4.9	1.4	2.1	1,154
U.S.	6.5	22.3	29.5	20.2	10.8	4.8	5.9	1,348

Note: Figures are percentages except for median; Gross rent is the contract rent plus the estimated average monthly cost of utilities (electricity, gas, and water and sewer) and fuels (oil, coal, kerosene, wood, etc.) if these are paid by the renter (or paid for the renter by someone else); (1) Figures cover the Tucson, AZ Metropolitan Statistical Area
Source: U.S. Census Bureau, 2019-2023 American Community Survey 5-Year Estimates

HEALTH

Health Risk Factors

Category	MSA[1] (%)	U.S. (%)
Adults aged 18–64 who have any kind of health care coverage	n/a	90.8
Adults who reported being in good or better health	n/a	81.8
Adults who have been told they have high blood cholesterol	n/a	36.9
Adults who have been told they have high blood pressure	n/a	34.0
Adults who are current smokers	n/a	12.1
Adults who currently use e-cigarettes	n/a	7.7
Adults who currently use chewing tobacco, snuff, or snus	n/a	3.2
Adults who are heavy drinkers[2]	n/a	6.1
Adults who are binge drinkers[3]	n/a	15.2
Adults who are overweight (BMI 25.0 - 29.9)	n/a	34.4
Adults who are obese (BMI 30.0 - 99.8)	n/a	34.3
Adults who participated in any physical activities in the past month	n/a	75.8

Note: All figures are crude prevalence; (1) Figures for the Tucson, AZ Metropolitan Statistical Area were not available.
(2) Heavy drinkers are classified as adult men having more than 14 drinks per week and adult women having more than 7 drinks per week; (3) Binge drinkers are classified as males having five or more drinks on one occasion or females having four or more drinks on one occasion
Source: Centers for Disease Control and Prevention, Behaviorial Risk Factor Surveillance System, SMART: Selected Metropolitan Area Risk Trends, 2023

Acute and Chronic Health Conditions

Category	MSA[1] (%)	U.S. (%)
Adults who have ever been told they had a heart attack	n/a	4.2
Adults who have ever been told they have angina or coronary heart disease	n/a	4.0
Adults who have ever been told they had a stroke	n/a	3.3
Adults who have ever been told they have asthma	n/a	15.7
Adults who have ever been told they have arthritis	n/a	26.3
Adults who have ever been told they have diabetes[2]	n/a	11.5
Adults who have ever been told they had skin cancer	n/a	5.6
Adults who have ever been told they had any other types of cancer	n/a	8.4
Adults who have ever been told they have COPD	n/a	6.4
Adults who have ever been told they have kidney disease	n/a	3.7
Adults who have ever been told they have a form of depression	n/a	22.0

Note: All figures are crude prevalence; (1) Figures for the Tucson, AZ Metropolitan Statistical Area were not available.
(2) Figures do not include pregnancy-related, borderline, or pre-diabetes
Source: Centers for Disease Control and Prevention, Behavioral Risk Factor Surveillance System, SMART: Selected Metropolitan Area Risk Trends, 2023

Health Screening and Vaccination Rates

Category	MSA[1] (%)	U.S. (%)
Adults who have ever been tested for HIV	n/a	37.5
Adults who have had their blood cholesterol checked within the last five years	n/a	87.0
Adults aged 65+ who have had flu shot within the past year	n/a	63.4
Adults aged 65+ who have ever had a pneumonia vaccination	n/a	71.9

Note: All figures are crude prevalence; (1) Figures for the Tucson, AZ Metropolitan Statistical Area were not available.
Source: Centers for Disease Control and Prevention, Behavioral Risk Factor Surveillance System, SMART: Selected Metropolitan Area Risk Trends, 2023

Disability Status

Category	MSA[1] (%)	U.S. (%)
Adults who reported being deaf	n/a	7.4
Are you blind or have serious difficulty seeing, even when wearing glasses?	n/a	4.9
Do you have difficulty doing errands alone?	n/a	7.8
Do you have difficulty dressing or bathing?	n/a	3.6
Do you have serious difficulty concentrating/remembering/making decisions?	n/a	13.7
Do you have serious difficulty walking or climbing stairs?	n/a	13.2

Note: All figures are crude prevalence; (1) Figures for the Tucson, AZ Metropolitan Statistical Area were not available.
Source: Centers for Disease Control and Prevention, Behavioral Risk Factor Surveillance System, SMART: Selected Metropolitan Area Risk Trends, 2023

Mortality Rates for the Top 10 Causes of Death in the U.S.

ICD-10[a] Sub-Chapter	ICD-10[a] Code	Crude Mortality Rate[2] per 100,000 population	
		County[3]	U.S.
Malignant neoplasms	C00-C97	196.9	182.7
Ischaemic heart diseases	I20-I25	110.5	109.6
Provisional assignment of new diseases of uncertain etiology[1]	U00-U49	79.7	65.3
Other forms of heart disease	I30-I51	58.7	65.1
Other degenerative diseases of the nervous system	G30-G31	88.9	52.4
Other external causes of accidental injury	W00-X59	70.3	52.3
Cerebrovascular diseases	I60-I69	55.1	49.1
Chronic lower respiratory diseases	J40-J47	50.6	43.5
Hypertensive diseases	I10-I15	48.9	38.9
Organic, including symptomatic, mental disorders	F01-F09	18.5	33.9

Note: (a) ICD-10 = International Classification of Diseases 10th Revision; (1) Includes COVID-19, adverse effects to COVID-19 vaccines, SARS, and vaping-related disorders; (2) Crude mortality rates are a three-year average covering 2021-2023; (3) Figures cover Pima County.
Source: Centers for Disease Control and Prevention, National Center for Health Statistics. National Vital Statistics System, Mortality 2018-2023 on CDC WONDER Online Database

Mortality Rates for Selected Causes of Death

Cause of Death	ICD-10[a] Code	Crude Mortality Rate[1] per 100,000 population	
		County[2]	U.S.
Accidental poisoning and exposure to noxious substances	X40-X49	42.2	30.5
Alzheimer disease	G30	39.1	35.4
Assault	X85-Y09	8.4	7.3
COVID-19	U07.1	79.7	65.3
Diabetes mellitus	E10-E14	35.9	30.0
Diseases of the liver	K70-K76	28.7	20.8
Human immunodeficiency virus (HIV) disease	B20-B24	1.4	1.5
Influenza and pneumonia	J09-J18	14.5	13.4
Intentional self-harm	X60-X84	21.4	14.7
Malnutrition	E40-E46	11.7	6.0
Obesity and other hyperalimentation	E65-E68	3.8	3.1
Renal failure	N17-N19	15.4	16.4
Transport accidents	V01-V99	18.7	14.4

Note: (a) ICD-10 = International Classification of Diseases 10th Revision; (1) Crude mortality rates are a three-year average covering 2021-2023; (2) Figures cover Pima County; Data are suppressed when the data meet the criteria for confidentiality constraints; Crude mortality rates are flagged as unreliable when the rate would be calculated with a numerator of 20 or less.
Source: Centers for Disease Control and Prevention, National Center for Health Statistics. National Vital Statistics System, Mortality 2018-2023 on CDC WONDER Online Database

Health Insurance Coverage

Area	With Health Insurance	With Private Health Insurance	With Public Health Insurance	Without Health Insurance	Population Under Age 19 Without Health Insurance
City	89.0	57.0	42.7	11.0	7.4
MSA[1]	91.1	62.8	42.8	8.9	7.0
U.S.	91.4	67.3	36.3	8.6	5.4

Note: Figures are percentages that cover the civilian noninstitutionalized population; (1) Figures cover the Tucson, AZ Metropolitan Statistical Area
Source: U.S. Census Bureau, 2019-2023 American Community Survey 5-Year Estimates

Number of Medical Professionals

Area	MDs[3]	DOs[3,4]	Dentists	Podiatrists	Chiropractors	Optometrists
County[1] (number)	4,102	376	721	60	206	187
County[1] (rate[2])	387.9	35.6	67.8	5.6	19.4	17.6
U.S. (rate[2])	302.5	29.2	74.6	6.4	29.5	18.0

Note: Data as of 2023 unless noted; (1) Data covers Pima County; (2) Number of medical professionals per 100,000 population; (3) Data as of 2022 and includes all active, non-federal physicians; (4) Doctor of Osteopathic Medicine
Source: U.S. Department of Health and Human Services, Health Resources and Services Administration, Bureau of Health Professions, Area Resource File (ARF) 2023-2024

EDUCATION

Public School District Statistics

District Name	Schls	Pupils	Pupil/ Teacher Ratio	Minority Pupils[1] (%)	Total Rev. per Pupil ($)	Total Exp. per Pupil ($)
Academy of Math and Science South	6	6,151	n/a	92.9	12,510	10,426
Amphitheater Unified District	23	11,835	15.2	56.7	13,276	11,759
Arizona Community Development Corp.	3	2,031	n/a	79.9	12,454	10,136
Catalina Foothills Unified District	8	5,164	17.2	45.3	11,939	11,052
Flowing Wells Unified District	11	5,287	17.3	77.6	11,953	11,350
Leman Academy of Excellence	7	4,775	n/a	53.2	10,375	8,230
Sunnyside Unified District	22	14,144	19.5	96.7	12,022	11,046
Tanque Verde Unified District	4	2,211	16.4	28.4	24,202	18,731
Tucson Unified District	102	40,929	14.4	82.0	13,810	13,118

Note: Table includes school districts with 2,000 or more students; (1) Percentage of students that are not non-Hispanic white.
Source: U.S. Department of Education, National Center for Education Statistics, Common Core of Data, Local Education Agency (School District) Universe Survey: School Year 2023-2024; U.S. Department of Education, National Center for Education Statistics, Common Core of Data, School District Finance Survey (F-33): School Year 2021–22

Best High Schools

According to *U.S. News,* Tucson is home to two of the top 500 high schools in the U.S.: **BASIS Tucson North** (#33); **University High School (Tucson)** (#81). Nearly 25,000 public, magnet and charter schools were ranked based on their performance on state assessments and how well they prepare students for college. *U.S. News & World Report, "Best High Schools 2024"*

Highest Level of Education

Area	Less than H.S.	H.S. Diploma	Some College, No Deg.	Associate Degree	Bachelor's Degree	Master's Degree	Prof. School Degree	Doctorate Degree
City	12.7	23.0	25.2	9.0	17.7	9.0	1.6	1.9
MSA[1]	10.1	21.2	23.9	9.0	20.4	10.7	2.4	2.4
U.S.	10.6	26.2	19.4	8.8	21.3	9.8	2.3	1.6

Note: Figures cover persons age 25 and over; (1) Figures cover the Tucson, AZ Metropolitan Statistical Area
Source: U.S. Census Bureau, 2019-2023 American Community Survey 5-Year Estimates

Educational Attainment by Race

Area	High School Graduate or Higher (%)					Bachelor's Degree or Higher (%)				
	Total	White	Black	Asian	Hisp.[2]	Total	White	Black	Asian	Hisp.[2]
City	87.3	91.8	87.3	88.4	76.7	30.2	35.6	17.5	51.9	17.3
MSA[1]	89.9	93.9	89.2	89.8	78.6	35.9	41.0	25.7	56.3	19.7
U.S.	89.4	92.9	88.1	88.0	72.5	35.0	37.7	24.7	57.0	19.9

Note: Figures shown cover persons 25 years old and over; (1) Figures cover the Tucson, AZ Metropolitan Statistical Area; (2) People of Hispanic origin can be of any race
Source: U.S. Census Bureau, 2019-2023 American Community Survey 5-Year Estimates

School Enrollment by Grade and Control

Area	Preschool (%)		Kindergarten (%)		Grades 1 - 4 (%)		Grades 5 - 8 (%)		Grades 9 - 12 (%)	
	Public	Private	Public	Private	Public	Private	Public	Private	Public	Private
City	71.7	28.3	90.3	9.7	88.2	11.8	88.1	11.9	91.9	8.1
MSA[1]	71.3	28.7	88.0	12.0	87.2	12.8	87.8	12.2	89.8	10.2
U.S.	58.7	41.3	85.2	14.8	87.2	12.8	87.9	12.1	89.0	11.0

Note: Figures shown cover persons 3 years old and over; (1) Figures cover the Tucson, AZ Metropolitan Statistical Area
Source: U.S. Census Bureau, 2019-2023 American Community Survey 5-Year Estimates

Higher Education

Four-Year Colleges			Two-Year Colleges			Medical Schools[1]	Law Schools[2]	Voc/ Tech[3]
Public	Private Non-profit	Private For-profit	Public	Private Non-profit	Private For-profit			
1	0	3	2	0	2	1	1	7

Note: Figures cover institutions located within the Tucson, AZ Metropolitan Statistical Area and include main campuses only; (1) includes schools accredited by the Liaison Committee on Medical Education and the American Osteopathic Association's Commission on Osteopathic College Accreditation; (2) includes ABA-accredited schools, schools with provisional ABA accreditation, and state accredited schools; (3) includes all schools with programs that are less than 2 years.
Source: National Center for Education Statistics, Integrated Postsecondary Education System (IPEDS), 2023-24; Wikipedia, List of Medical Schools in the United States, accessed May 2, 2025; Wikipedia, List of Law Schools in the United States, accessed May 2, 2025

According to *U.S. News & World Report,* the Tucson, AZ metro area is home to one of the top 200 national universities in the U.S.: **University of Arizona** (#109 tie). The indicators used to capture academic quality fall into a number of categories: assessment by administrators at peer institutions; retention of students; faculty resources; student selectivity; financial resources; alumni giving; high school counselor ratings of colleges; and graduation rate. *U.S. News & World Report, "America's Best Colleges 2025"*

According to *U.S. News & World Report,* the Tucson, AZ metro area is home to one of the top 100 law schools in the U.S.: **University of Arizona (Rogers)** (#59 tie). The rankings are based on a weighted average of 12 measures of quality: peer assessment score; assessment score by lawyers/judges; median LSAT scores; median undergrad GPA; acceptance rate; employment rates for graduates; placement success; bar passage rate; faculty resources; expenditures per student; student/faculty ratio; and library resources. *U.S. News & World Report, "America's Best Graduate Schools, Law, 2025"*

According to *U.S. News & World Report,* the Tucson, AZ metro area is home to one of the top medical schools for research in the U.S.: **University of Arizona—Tucson** (Tier 2). *U.S. News* placed medical and osteopathic schools into tiers based on their research productivity, faculty and admissions data. Each school's tier was derived from its overall score, calculated by summing the weighted normalized values generated across several factors of academic quality, outlined below. There are four tiers, with tier 1 medical schools as the highest-performing and tier 4 as the lowest-performing. Only tier 1 and 2 schools are shown. Because of the tier presentation, *U.S. News* calculated overall scores based on their percentile performance among all rated schools instead of dividing against the rescaled score of the No. 1-performing schools. Tier 1 included schools with overall scores of 85 to 99. The cutoffs for tiers 2 through 4 were schools scoring 50 to 84, 15 to 49 and 1 to 14, respectively. The rankings are based on a weighted average of the following measures of quality: total research activity; average research activity per faculty member; total NIH research grants at the medical school and its affiliated hospitals; average NIH research grants per faculty; median MCAT total score; median undergraduate GPA; acceptance rate; and faculty resources. *U.S. News & World Report, "America's Best Graduate Schools, Medical, 2025"*

According to *U.S. News & World Report,* the Tucson, AZ metro area is home to one of the top medical schools for primary care in the U.S.: **University of Arizona—Tucson** (Tier 1). *U.S. News* placed medical and osteopathic schools into tiers based on their research productivity, faculty and admissions data. Each school's tier was derived from its overall score, calculated by summing the weighted normalized values generated across several factors of academic quality, outlined below. There are four tiers, with tier 1 medical schools as the highest-performing and tier 4 as the lowest-performing. Only tier 1 and 2 schools are shown. Because of the tier presentation, *U.S. News* calculated overall scores based on their percentile performance among all rated schools instead of dividing against the rescaled score of the No. 1-performing schools. Tier 1 included schools with overall scores of 85 to 99. The cutoffs for tiers 2 through 4 were schools scoring 50 to 84, 15 to 49 and 1 to 14, respectively. The rankings are based on a weighted average of the following measures of quality: graduates practicing in primary care specialties; graduates entering primary care residencies; median MCAT total score; median undergraduate GPA; acceptance rate; and faculty resources. *U.S. News & World Report, "America's Best Graduate Schools, Medical, 2025"*

According to *U.S. News & World Report,* the Tucson, AZ metro area is home to one of the top 75 business schools in the U.S.: **University of Arizona (Eller)** (#66 tie). The rankings are based on a weighted average of the following nine measures: quality assessment; peer assessment; recruiter assessment; placement success; mean starting salary and bonus; student selectivity; mean GMAT and GRE scores; mean undergraduate GPA; and acceptance rate. *U.S. News & World Report, "America's Best Graduate Schools, Business, 2025"*

EMPLOYERS

Major Employers

Company Name	Industry
Banner University Medical Center Tucson	General medical & surgical hospitals
City of Tuscon	Local government
Davis-Monthan Air Force Base	U.S. military
Freeport-McMoran Copper & Gold	Mining
Fry's Food Stores of Arizona Inc.	Grocery
Pima Community College	Education
Pima County	County government
Raytheon Missile Systems	Missile systems
State of Arizona	State government
TMC HealthCare	Healthcare
Tohono O'odham Nation	Reservation
Tucson Unified School District	School districts
U.S. Customs and Border Protection	Federal government
University of Arizona	Public research university
Wal-Mart Stores	Retail stores

Note: Companies shown are located within the Tucson, AZ Metropolitan Statistical Area.
Source: Chambers of Commerce; State Departments of Labor; Wikipedia

PUBLIC SAFETY

Crime Rate

Area	Total Crime Rate	Violent Crime Rate				Property Crime Rate		
		Murder	Rape	Robbery	Aggrav. Assault	Burglary	Larceny -Theft	Motor Vehicle Theft
City	n/a	n/a	n/a	n/a	n/a	n/a	n/a	n/a
U.S.	2,290.9	5.7	38.0	66.5	264.1	250.7	1,347.2	318.7

Note: Figures are crimes per 100,000 population; n/a not available.
Source: FBI, Table 8, Offenses Known to Law Enforcement, by State by City, 2023

Hate Crimes

Area	Number of Quarters Reported	Number of Incidents per Bias Motivation					
		Race/Ethnicity/ Ancestry	Religion	Sexual Orientation	Disability	Gender	Gender Identity
City	n/a	n/a	n/a	n/a	n/a	n/a	n/a
U.S.	4	5,900	2,699	2,077	187	92	492

Note: n/a not available.
Source: Federal Bureau of Investigation, Hate Crime Statistics 2023

Identity Theft Consumer Reports

Area	Reports	Reports per 100,000 Population	Rank[2]
MSA[1]	2,146	204	152
U.S.	1,135,291	339	-

Note: (1) Figures cover the Tucson, AZ Metropolitan Statistical Area; (2) Rank ranges from 1 to 401 where 1 indicates greatest number of identity theft reports per 100,000 population
Source: Federal Trade Commission, Consumer Sentinel Network Data Book 2024

Fraud and Other Consumer Reports

Area	Reports	Reports per 100,000 Population	Rank[2]
MSA[1]	14,321	1,364	82
U.S.	5,360,641	1,601	-

Note: (1) Figures cover the Tucson, AZ Metropolitan Statistical Area; (2) Rank ranges from 1 to 401 where 1 indicates greatest number of fraud and other consumer reports per 100,000 population
Source: Federal Trade Commission, Consumer Sentinel Network Data Book 2024

POLITICS

2024 Presidential Election Results

Area	Trump (Rep.)	Harris (Dem.)	Stein (Green)	Kennedy (Ind.)	Oliver (Lib.)	Other
Pima County	41.7	56.8	0.6	0.0	0.6	0.4
U.S.	49.7	48.2	0.6	0.5	0.4	0.6

Note: Results are percentages and may not add to 100% due to rounding
Source: Dave Leip's Atlas of U.S. Presidential Elections

SPORTS

Professional Sports Teams

Team Name	League	Year Established
No teams are located in the metro area		

Source: Wikipedia, Major Professional Sports Teams of the United States and Canada, May 1, 2025

CLIMATE

Average and Extreme Temperatures

Temperature	Jan	Feb	Mar	Apr	May	Jun	Jul	Aug	Sep	Oct	Nov	Dec	Yr.
Extreme High (°F)	87	92	99	104	107	117	114	108	107	101	90	84	117
Average High (°F)	64	68	73	81	89	99	99	96	94	84	73	65	82
Average Temp. (°F)	51	54	59	66	74	84	86	84	81	71	59	52	69
Average Low (°F)	38	40	44	51	58	68	74	72	67	57	45	39	55
Extreme Low (°F)	16	20	20	33	38	47	62	61	44	26	24	16	16

Note: Figures cover the years 1946-1990
Source: National Climatic Data Center, International Station Meteorological Climate Summary, 9/96

Average Precipitation/Snowfall/Humidity

Precip./Humidity	Jan	Feb	Mar	Apr	May	Jun	Jul	Aug	Sep	Oct	Nov	Dec	Yr.
Avg. Precip. (in.)	0.9	0.7	0.7	0.3	0.1	0.2	2.5	2.2	1.4	0.9	0.6	0.9	11.6
Avg. Snowfall (in.)	Tr	Tr	Tr	Tr	0	0	0	0	0	0	Tr	Tr	2
Avg. Rel. Hum. 5am (%)	62	58	52	41	34	32	58	65	55	52	54	61	52
Avg. Rel. Hum. 5pm (%)	31	26	22	16	13	13	29	32	26	24	27	33	24

Note: Figures cover the years 1946-1990; Tr = Trace amounts (<0.05 in. of rain; <0.5 in. of snow)
Source: National Climatic Data Center, International Station Meteorological Climate Summary, 9/96

Weather Conditions

Temperature			Daytime Sky			Precipitation		
10°F & below	32°F & below	90°F & above	Clear	Partly cloudy	Cloudy	0.01 inch or more precip.	0.1 inch or more snow/ice	Thunder-storms
0	18	140	177	119	69	54	2	42

Note: Figures are average number of days per year and cover the years 1946-1990
Source: National Climatic Data Center, International Station Meteorological Climate Summary, 9/96

HAZARDOUS WASTE

Superfund Sites

The Tucson, AZ metro area is home to one site on the EPA's Superfund National Priorities List (NPL) or Superfund Alternative Approach (SAA) list: **Tucson International Airport Area** (Final NPL). The Superfund alternative approach uses the same investigation and cleanup process and standards that are used for sites listed on the National Priorities List. The SAA is an alternative to listing a site on the NPL; it is not an alternative to Superfund or the Superfund process. There are a total of 1,445 Superfund sites with a status of proposed or final on both lists in the United States. *U.S. Envi-*

ronmental Protection Agency, National Priorities List, May 1, 2025; U.S. Environmental Protection Agency, Superfund Alternative Approach Sites, May 1, 2025

AIR QUALITY

Air Quality Trends: Ozone

	1990	1995	2000	2005	2010	2015	2020	2021	2022	2023
MSA[1]	0.073	0.078	0.074	0.075	0.068	0.065	0.070	0.068	0.069	0.069
U.S.	0.087	0.089	0.081	0.080	0.072	0.068	0.066	0.067	0.067	0.070

Note: (1) Data covers the Tucson, AZ Metropolitan Statistical Area. The values shown are the composite ozone concentration averages among trend sites based on the highest fourth daily maximum 8-hour concentration in parts per million. These trends are based on sites having an adequate record of monitoring data during the trend period. Data from exceptional events are included.
Source: U.S. Environmental Protection Agency, Air Quality Monitoring Information, "Air Quality Trends by City, 1990-2023"

Air Quality Index

Area	Percent of Days when Air Quality was...[2]					AQI Statistics[2]	
	Good	Moderate	Unhealthy for Sensitive Groups	Unhealthy	Very Unhealthy	Maximum	Median
MSA[1]	33.7	64.4	1.9	0.0	0.0	147	54

Note: (1) Data covers the Tucson, AZ Metropolitan Statistical Area; (2) Based on 365 days with AQI data in 2023. Air Quality Index (AQI) is an index for reporting daily air quality. EPA calculates the AQI for five major air pollutants regulated by the Clean Air Act: ground-level ozone, particle pollution (aka particulate matter), carbon monoxide, sulfur dioxide, and nitrogen dioxide. The AQI runs from 0 to 500. The higher the AQI value, the greater the level of air pollution and the greater the health concern. There are six AQI categories: "Good" AQI is between 0 and 50. Air quality is considered satisfactory; "Moderate" AQI is between 51 and 100. Air quality is acceptable; "Unhealthy for Sensitive Groups" When AQI values are between 101 and 150, members of sensitive groups may experience health effects; "Unhealthy" When AQI values are between 151 and 200 everyone may begin to experience health effects; "Very Unhealthy" AQI values between 201 and 300 trigger a health alert; "Hazardous" AQI values over 300 trigger warnings of emergency conditions (not shown).
Source: U.S. Environmental Protection Agency, Air Quality Index Report, 2023

Air Quality Index Pollutants

Area	Percent of Days when AQI Pollutant was...[2]					
	Carbon Monoxide	Nitrogen Dioxide	Ozone	Sulfur Dioxide	Particulate Matter 2.5	Particulate Matter 10
MSA[1]	0.0	0.0	49.0	(3)	33.7	17.3

Note: (1) Data covers the Tucson, AZ Metropolitan Statistical Area; (2) Based on 365 days with AQI data in 2023. The Air Quality Index (AQI) is an index for reporting daily air quality. EPA calculates the AQI for five major air pollutants regulated by the Clean Air Act: ground-level ozone, particle pollution (also known as particulate matter), carbon monoxide, sulfur dioxide, and nitrogen dioxide. The AQI runs from 0 to 500. The higher the AQI value, the greater the level of air pollution and the greater the health concern; (3) Sulfur dioxide is no longer included in this table because SO_2 concentrations tend to be very localized and not necessarily representative of broad geographical areas like counties and CBSAs.
Source: U.S. Environmental Protection Agency, Air Quality Index Report, 2023

Maximum Air Pollutant Concentrations: Particulate Matter, Ozone, CO and Lead

	Particulate Matter 10 (ug/m^3)	Particulate Matter 2.5 Wtd AM (ug/m^3)	Particulate Matter 2.5 24-Hr (ug/m^3)	Ozone (ppm)	Carbon Monoxide (ppm)	Lead (ug/m^3)
MSA[1] Level	201	7.8	16	0.07	1	n/a
NAAQS[2]	150	15	35	0.075	9	0.15
Met NAAQS[2]	No	Yes	Yes	Yes	Yes	n/a

Note: (1) Data covers the Tucson, AZ Metropolitan Statistical Area; Data from exceptional events are included; (2) National Ambient Air Quality Standards; ppm = parts per million; ug/m^3 = micrograms per cubic meter; n/a not available.
Concentrations: Particulate Matter 10 (coarse particulate)—highest second maximum 24-hour concentration; Particulate Matter 2.5 Wtd AM (fine particulate)—highest weighted annual mean concentration; Particulate Matter 2.5 24-Hour (fine particulate)—highest 98th percentile 24-hour concentration; Ozone—highest fourth daily maximum 8-hour concentration; Carbon Monoxide—highest second maximum non-overlapping 8-hour concentration; Lead—maximum running 3-month average
Source: U.S. Environmental Protection Agency, Air Quality Monitoring Information, "Air Quality Statistics by City, 2023"

Maximum Air Pollutant Concentrations: Nitrogen Dioxide and Sulfur Dioxide

	Nitrogen Dioxide AM (ppb)	Nitrogen Dioxide 1-Hr (ppb)	Sulfur Dioxide AM (ppb)	Sulfur Dioxide 1-Hr (ppb)	Sulfur Dioxide 24-Hr (ppb)
MSA[1] Level	13	39	n/a	1	n/a
NAAQS[2]	53	100	30	75	140
Met NAAQS[2]	Yes	Yes	n/a	Yes	n/a

Note: (1) Data covers the Tucson, AZ Metropolitan Statistical Area; Data from exceptional events are included; (2) National Ambient Air Quality Standards; ppm = parts per million; ug/m³ = micrograms per cubic meter; n/a not available.
Concentrations: Nitrogen Dioxide AM—highest arithmetic mean concentration; Nitrogen Dioxide 1-Hr—highest 98th percentile 1-hour daily maximum concentration; Sulfur Dioxide AM—highest annual mean concentration; Sulfur Dioxide 1-Hr—highest 99th percentile 1-hour daily maximum concentration; Sulfur Dioxide 24-Hr—highest second maximum 24-hour concentration
Source: U.S. Environmental Protection Agency, Air Quality Monitoring Information, "Air Quality Statistics by City, 2023"

Appendixes

Appendix A: Comparative Statistics

Table of Contents

Population Growth: City

City	1990 Census	2000 Census	2010 Census	2020 Census	Current Estimate[1]	Population Growth 1990-2023 (%)
Albuquerque, NM	388,375	448,607	545,852	564,559	562,488	44.8
Anchorage, AK	226,338	260,283	291,826	291,247	289,069	27.7
Ann Arbor, MI	111,018	114,024	113,934	123,851	121,179	9.2
Athens, GA	86,561	100,266	115,452	127,315	126,987	46.7
Atlanta, GA	394,092	416,474	420,003	498,715	499,287	26.7
Austin, TX	499,053	656,562	790,390	961,855	967,862	93.9
Baltimore, MD	736,014	651,154	620,961	585,708	577,193	-21.6
Billings, MT	81,812	89,847	104,170	117,116	118,321	44.6
Boise City, ID	144,317	185,787	205,671	235,684	235,701	63.3
Boston, MA	574,283	589,141	617,594	675,647	663,972	15.6
Boulder, CO	87,737	94,673	97,385	108,250	106,274	21.1
Cape Coral, FL	75,507	102,286	154,305	194,016	206,387	173.3
Cedar Rapids, IA	110,829	120,758	126,326	137,710	136,859	23.5
Charleston, SC	96,102	96,650	120,083	150,227	152,014	58.2
Charlotte, NC	428,283	540,828	731,424	874,579	886,283	106.9
Chicago, IL	2,783,726	2,896,016	2,695,598	2,746,388	2,707,648	-2.7
Cincinnati, OH	363,974	331,285	296,943	309,317	309,595	-14.9
Clarksville, TN	78,569	103,455	132,929	166,722	171,897	118.8
Cleveland, OH	505,333	478,403	396,815	372,624	367,523	-27.3
College Station, TX	53,318	67,890	93,857	120,511	122,280	129.3
Colorado Springs, CO	283,798	360,890	416,427	478,961	483,099	70.2
Columbia, MO	71,069	84,531	108,500	126,254	127,200	79.0
Columbia, SC	115,475	116,278	129,272	136,632	138,019	19.5
Columbus, OH	648,656	711,470	787,033	905,748	906,480	39.7
Dallas, TX	1,006,971	1,188,580	1,197,816	1,304,379	1,299,553	29.1
Davenport, IA	95,705	98,359	99,685	101,724	101,083	5.6
Denver, CO	467,153	554,636	600,158	715,522	713,734	52.8
Des Moines, IA	193,569	198,682	203,433	214,133	212,464	9.8
Detroit, MI	1,027,974	951,270	713,777	639,111	636,644	-38.1
Durham, NC	151,737	187,035	228,330	283,506	288,465	90.1
El Paso, TX	515,541	563,662	649,121	678,815	678,147	31.5
Eugene, OR	118,073	137,893	156,185	176,654	177,520	50.3
Fargo, ND	74,372	90,599	105,549	125,990	129,064	73.5
Fort Collins, CO	89,555	118,652	143,986	169,810	169,705	89.5
Fort Wayne, IN	205,671	205,727	253,691	263,886	266,235	29.4
Fort Worth, TX	448,311	534,694	741,206	918,915	941,311	110.0
Gainesville, FL	90,519	95,447	124,354	141,085	143,611	58.7
Green Bay, WI	96,466	102,313	104,057	107,395	106,585	10.5
Greensboro, NC	193,389	223,891	269,666	299,035	298,564	54.4
Honolulu, HI	376,465	371,657	337,256	350,964	346,323	-8.0
Houston, TX	1,697,610	1,953,631	2,099,451	2,304,580	2,300,419	35.5
Huntsville, AL	161,842	158,216	180,105	215,006	218,814	35.2
Indianapolis, IN	730,993	781,870	820,445	887,642	882,043	20.7
Jacksonville, FL	635,221	735,617	821,784	949,611	961,739	51.4
Kansas City, MO	434,967	441,545	459,787	508,090	508,233	16.8
Lafayette, LA	104,735	110,257	120,623	121,374	121,537	16.0
Las Vegas, NV	261,374	478,434	583,756	641,903	650,873	149.0
Lexington, KY	225,366	260,512	295,803	322,570	321,122	42.5
Lincoln, NE	193,629	225,581	258,379	291,082	291,932	50.8
Little Rock, AR	177,519	183,133	193,524	202,591	202,739	14.2
Los Angeles, CA	3,487,671	3,694,820	3,792,621	3,898,747	3,857,897	10.6
Louisville, KY	269,160	256,231	597,337	386,884	627,210	133.0
Madison, WI	193,451	208,054	233,209	269,840	275,568	42.4
Manchester, NH	99,567	107,006	109,565	115,644	115,415	15.9
McAllen, TX	86,145	106,414	129,877	142,210	143,789	66.9

Table continued on following page.

City	1990 Census	2000 Census	2010 Census	2020 Census	Current Estimate[1]	Population Growth 1990-2023 (%)
Memphis, TN	660,536	650,100	646,889	633,104	629,063	-4.8
Miami, FL	358,843	362,470	399,457	442,241	446,663	24.5
Midland, TX	89,358	94,996	111,147	132,524	133,998	50.0
Milwaukee, WI	628,095	596,974	594,833	577,222	569,756	-9.3
Minneapolis, MN	368,383	382,618	382,578	429,954	426,845	15.9
Nashville, TN	488,364	545,524	601,222	689,447	684,298	40.1
New Orleans, LA	496,938	484,674	343,829	383,997	376,035	-24.3
New York, NY	7,322,552	8,008,278	8,175,133	8,804,190	8,516,202	16.3
Oklahoma City, OK	445,065	506,132	579,999	681,054	688,693	54.7
Omaha, NE	371,972	390,007	408,958	486,051	488,197	31.2
Orlando, FL	161,172	185,951	238,300	307,573	311,732	93.4
Philadelphia, PA	1,585,577	1,517,550	1,526,006	1,603,797	1,582,432	-0.2
Phoenix, AZ	989,873	1,321,045	1,445,632	1,608,139	1,624,832	64.1
Pittsburgh, PA	369,785	334,563	305,704	302,971	303,620	-17.9
Portland, OR	485,833	529,121	583,776	652,503	642,715	32.3
Providence, RI	160,734	173,618	178,042	190,934	190,214	18.3
Provo, UT	87,148	105,166	112,488	115,162	114,303	31.2
Raleigh, NC	226,841	276,093	403,892	467,665	470,763	107.5
Reno, NV	139,950	180,480	225,221	264,165	268,959	92.2
Richmond, VA	202,783	197,790	204,214	226,610	227,595	12.2
Rochester, MN	74,151	85,806	106,769	121,395	121,638	64.0
Sacramento, CA	368,923	407,018	466,488	524,943	524,802	42.3
Saint Louis, MO	396,685	348,189	319,294	301,578	293,109	-26.1
Saint Paul, MN	272,235	287,151	285,068	311,527	307,762	13.1
Salem, OR	112,046	136,924	154,637	175,535	176,666	57.7
Salt Lake City, UT	159,796	181,743	186,440	199,723	203,888	27.6
San Antonio, TX	997,258	1,144,646	1,327,407	1,434,625	1,458,954	46.3
San Diego, CA	1,111,048	1,223,400	1,307,402	1,386,932	1,385,061	24.7
San Francisco, CA	723,959	776,733	805,235	873,965	836,321	15.5
San Jose, CA	784,324	894,943	945,942	1,013,240	990,054	26.2
Santa Rosa, CA	123,297	147,595	167,815	178,127	177,216	43.7
Savannah, GA	138,038	131,510	136,286	147,780	147,546	6.9
Seattle, WA	516,262	563,374	608,660	737,015	741,440	43.6
Sioux Falls, SD	102,262	123,975	153,888	192,517	197,642	93.3
Tampa, FL	279,960	303,447	335,709	384,959	393,389	40.5
Tucson, AZ	417,942	486,699	520,116	542,629	543,348	30.0
Tulsa, OK	367,241	393,049	391,906	413,066	412,322	12.3
Virginia Beach, VA	393,069	425,257	437,994	459,470	457,066	16.3
Washington, DC	606,900	572,059	601,723	689,545	672,079	10.7
Wichita, KS	313,693	344,284	382,368	397,532	396,488	26.4
Wilmington, NC	64,609	75,838	106,476	115,451	118,578	83.5
Winston-Salem, NC	168,139	185,776	229,617	249,545	250,887	49.2
U.S.	248,709,873	281,421,906	308,745,538	331,449,281	332,387,540	33.6

Note: (1) 2019-2023 5-year estimated population
Source: U.S. Census Bureau: 1990 Census, Census 2000, Census 2010, Census 2020, 2019-2023 American Community Survey 5-Year Estimates

Population Growth: Metro Area

Metro Area	1990 Census	2000 Census	2010 Census	2020 Census	Current Estimate[1]	Population Growth 1990-2023 (%)
Albuquerque, NM	599,416	729,649	887,077	916,528	918,567	53.2
Anchorage, AK	266,021	319,605	380,821	398,328	399,746	50.3
Ann Arbor, MI	282,937	322,895	344,791	372,258	368,394	30.2
Athens, GA	136,025	166,079	192,541	215,415	218,190	60.4
Atlanta, GA	3,069,411	4,247,981	5,268,860	6,089,815	6,176,937	101.2
Austin, TX	846,217	1,249,763	1,716,289	2,283,371	2,357,497	178.6
Baltimore, MD	2,382,172	2,552,994	2,710,489	2,844,510	2,839,409	19.2
Billings, MT	121,499	138,904	158,050	184,167	187,269	54.1
Boise City, ID	319,596	464,840	616,561	764,718	790,640	147.4
Boston, MA	4,133,895	4,391,344	4,552,402	4,941,632	4,917,661	19.0
Boulder, CO	208,898	269,758	294,567	330,758	328,317	57.2
Cape Coral, FL	335,113	440,888	618,754	760,822	792,692	136.5
Cedar Rapids, IA	210,640	237,230	257,940	276,520	275,960	31.0
Charleston, SC	506,875	549,033	664,607	799,636	817,756	61.3
Charlotte, NC	1,024,331	1,330,448	1,758,038	2,660,329	2,712,818	164.8
Chicago, IL	8,182,076	9,098,316	9,461,105	9,618,502	9,359,555	14.4
Cincinnati, OH	1,844,917	2,009,632	2,130,151	2,256,884	2,255,257	22.2
Clarksville, TN	189,277	232,000	273,949	320,535	328,626	73.6
Cleveland, OH	2,102,219	2,148,143	2,077,240	2,088,251	2,171,978	3.3
College Station, TX	150,998	184,885	228,660	268,248	273,280	81.0
Colorado Springs, CO	409,482	537,484	645,613	755,105	760,782	85.8
Columbia, MO	122,010	145,666	172,786	210,864	212,850	74.5
Columbia, SC	548,325	647,158	767,598	829,470	839,868	53.2
Columbus, OH	1,405,176	1,612,694	1,836,536	2,138,926	2,151,847	53.1
Dallas, TX	3,989,294	5,161,544	6,371,773	7,637,387	7,807,555	95.7
Davenport, IA	368,151	376,019	379,690	384,324	381,864	3.7
Denver, CO	1,666,935	2,179,296	2,543,482	2,963,821	2,977,085	78.6
Des Moines, IA	416,346	481,394	569,633	709,466	720,331	73.0
Detroit, MI	4,248,699	4,452,557	4,296,250	4,392,041	4,367,620	2.8
Durham, NC	344,646	426,493	504,357	649,903	594,291	72.4
El Paso, TX	591,610	679,622	800,647	868,859	869,606	47.0
Eugene, OR	282,912	322,959	351,715	382,971	382,628	35.2
Fargo, ND	153,296	174,367	208,777	249,843	254,914	66.3
Fort Collins, CO	186,136	251,494	299,630	359,066	363,561	95.3
Fort Wayne, IN	354,435	390,156	416,257	419,601	451,440	27.4
Fort Worth, TX	3,989,294	5,161,544	6,371,773	7,637,387	7,807,555	95.7
Gainesville, FL	191,263	232,392	264,275	339,247	344,521	80.1
Green Bay, WI	243,698	282,599	306,241	328,268	329,375	35.2
Greensboro, NC	540,257	643,430	723,801	776,566	779,894	44.4
Honolulu, HI	836,231	876,156	953,207	1,016,508	1,003,666	20.0
Houston, TX	3,767,335	4,715,407	5,946,800	7,122,240	7,274,714	93.1
Huntsville, AL	293,047	342,376	417,593	491,723	504,712	72.2
Indianapolis, IN	1,294,217	1,525,104	1,756,241	2,111,040	2,106,327	62.7
Jacksonville, FL	925,213	1,122,750	1,345,596	1,605,848	1,645,707	77.9
Kansas City, MO	1,636,528	1,836,038	2,035,334	2,192,035	2,202,006	34.6
Lafayette, LA	208,740	239,086	273,738	478,384	410,883	96.8
Las Vegas, NV	741,459	1,375,765	1,951,269	2,265,461	2,293,764	209.4
Lexington, KY	348,428	408,326	472,099	516,811	517,378	48.5
Lincoln, NE	229,091	266,787	302,157	340,217	341,309	49.0
Little Rock, AR	535,034	610,518	699,757	748,031	753,605	40.9
Los Angeles, CA	11,273,720	12,365,627	12,828,837	13,200,998	13,012,469	15.4
Louisville, KY	1,055,973	1,161,975	1,283,566	1,285,439	1,361,847	29.0
Madison, WI	432,323	501,774	568,593	680,796	683,967	58.2
Manchester, NH	336,073	380,841	400,721	422,937	424,732	26.4
McAllen, TX	383,545	569,463	774,769	870,781	880,921	129.7

Table continued on following page.

Metro Area	1990 Census	2000 Census	2010 Census	2020 Census	Current Estimate[1]	Population Growth 1990-2023 (%)
Memphis, TN	1,067,263	1,205,204	1,316,100	1,337,779	1,341,606	25.7
Miami, FL	4,056,100	5,007,564	5,564,635	6,138,333	6,138,876	51.3
Midland, TX	106,611	116,009	136,872	175,220	176,726	65.8
Milwaukee, WI	1,432,149	1,500,741	1,555,908	1,574,731	1,566,361	9.4
Minneapolis, MN	2,538,834	2,968,806	3,279,833	3,690,261	3,693,351	45.5
Nashville, TN	1,048,218	1,311,789	1,589,934	1,989,519	2,043,713	95.0
New Orleans, LA	1,264,391	1,316,510	1,167,764	1,271,845	988,763	-21.8
New York, NY	16,845,992	18,323,002	18,897,109	20,140,470	19,756,722	17.3
Oklahoma City, OK	971,042	1,095,421	1,252,987	1,425,695	1,445,122	48.8
Omaha, NE	685,797	767,041	865,350	967,604	972,840	41.9
Orlando, FL	1,224,852	1,644,561	2,134,411	2,673,376	2,721,022	122.2
Philadelphia, PA	5,435,470	5,687,147	5,965,343	6,245,051	6,241,882	14.8
Phoenix, AZ	2,238,480	3,251,876	4,192,887	4,845,832	4,941,206	120.7
Pittsburgh, PA	2,468,289	2,431,087	2,356,285	2,370,930	2,443,921	-1.0
Portland, OR	1,523,741	1,927,881	2,226,009	2,512,859	2,510,529	64.8
Providence, RI	1,509,789	1,582,997	1,600,852	1,676,579	1,673,807	10.9
Provo, UT	269,407	376,774	526,810	671,185	695,895	158.3
Raleigh, NC	541,081	797,071	1,130,490	1,413,982	1,449,594	167.9
Reno, NV	257,193	342,885	425,417	490,596	556,539	116.4
Richmond, VA	949,244	1,096,957	1,258,251	1,314,434	1,327,321	39.8
Rochester, MN	141,945	163,618	186,011	226,329	227,252	60.1
Sacramento, CA	1,481,126	1,796,857	2,149,127	2,397,382	2,406,563	62.5
Saint Louis, MO	2,580,897	2,698,687	2,812,896	2,820,253	2,809,414	8.9
Saint Paul, MN	2,538,834	2,968,806	3,279,833	3,690,261	3,693,351	45.5
Salem, OR	278,024	347,214	390,738	433,353	435,085	56.5
Salt Lake City, UT	768,075	968,858	1,124,197	1,257,936	1,261,337	64.2
San Antonio, TX	1,407,745	1,711,703	2,142,508	2,558,143	2,612,802	85.6
San Diego, CA	2,498,016	2,813,833	3,095,313	3,298,634	3,282,782	31.4
San Francisco, CA	3,686,592	4,123,740	4,335,391	4,749,008	4,653,593	26.2
San Jose, CA	1,534,280	1,735,819	1,836,911	2,000,468	1,969,353	28.4
Santa Rosa, CA	388,222	458,614	483,878	488,863	485,642	25.1
Savannah, GA	258,060	293,000	347,611	404,798	412,089	59.7
Seattle, WA	2,559,164	3,043,878	3,439,809	4,018,762	4,021,467	57.1
Sioux Falls, SD	153,500	187,093	228,261	276,730	293,107	90.9
Tampa, FL	2,067,959	2,395,997	2,783,243	3,175,275	3,240,469	56.7
Tucson, AZ	666,880	843,746	980,263	1,043,433	1,049,947	57.4
Tulsa, OK	761,019	859,532	937,478	1,015,331	1,026,209	34.8
Virginia Beach, VA	1,449,389	1,576,370	1,671,683	1,799,674	1,782,590	23.0
Washington, DC	4,122,914	4,796,183	5,582,170	6,385,162	6,263,796	51.9
Wichita, KS	511,111	571,166	623,061	647,610	648,935	27.0
Wilmington, NC	200,124	274,532	362,315	285,905	440,578	120.2
Winston-Salem, NC	361,091	421,961	477,717	675,966	683,637	89.3
U.S.	248,709,873	281,421,906	308,745,538	331,449,281	332,387,540	33.6

Note: (1) 2019-2023 5-year estimated population; Figures cover the Metropolitan Statistical Area (MSA)
Source: U.S. Census Bureau: 1990 Census, Census 2000, Census 2010, Census 2020, 2019-2023 American Community Survey 5-Year Estimates

Male/Female Ratio: City

City	Males	Females	Males per 100 Females
Albuquerque, NM	275,413	287,075	95.9
Anchorage, AK	147,620	141,449	104.4
Ann Arbor, MI	60,397	60,782	99.4
Athens, GA	60,237	66,750	90.2
Atlanta, GA	242,994	256,293	94.8
Austin, TX	495,563	472,299	104.9
Baltimore, MD	268,932	308,261	87.2
Billings, MT	58,615	59,706	98.2
Boise City, ID	118,294	117,407	100.8
Boston, MA	319,182	344,790	92.6
Boulder, CO	55,022	51,252	107.4
Cape Coral, FL	103,313	103,074	100.2
Cedar Rapids, IA	67,551	69,308	97.5
Charleston, SC	72,280	79,734	90.7
Charlotte, NC	427,869	458,414	93.3
Chicago, IL	1,314,256	1,393,392	94.3
Cincinnati, OH	148,944	160,651	92.7
Clarksville, TN	86,129	85,768	100.4
Cleveland, OH	177,863	189,660	93.8
College Station, TX	62,870	59,410	105.8
Colorado Springs, CO	241,781	241,318	100.2
Columbia, MO	61,139	66,061	92.5
Columbia, SC	68,245	69,774	97.8
Columbus, OH	445,564	460,916	96.7
Dallas, TX	647,372	652,181	99.3
Davenport, IA	50,102	50,981	98.3
Denver, CO	359,969	353,765	101.8
Des Moines, IA	105,131	107,333	97.9
Detroit, MI	302,503	334,141	90.5
Durham, NC	136,368	152,097	89.7
El Paso, TX	333,802	344,345	96.9
Eugene, OR	87,095	90,425	96.3
Fargo, ND	65,129	63,935	101.9
Fort Collins, CO	84,686	85,019	99.6
Fort Wayne, IN	129,959	136,276	95.4
Fort Worth, TX	461,317	479,994	96.1
Gainesville, FL	68,593	75,018	91.4
Green Bay, WI	52,829	53,756	98.3
Greensboro, NC	138,079	160,485	86.0
Honolulu, HI	173,028	173,295	99.8
Houston, TX	1,138,504	1,161,915	98.0
Huntsville, AL	107,036	111,778	95.8
Indianapolis, IN	428,660	453,383	94.5
Jacksonville, FL	466,421	495,318	94.2
Kansas City, MO	245,780	262,453	93.6
Lafayette, LA	58,993	62,544	94.3
Las Vegas, NV	325,629	325,244	100.1
Lexington, KY	158,152	162,970	97.0
Lincoln, NE	146,855	145,077	101.2
Little Rock, AR	95,597	107,142	89.2
Los Angeles, CA	1,921,735	1,936,162	99.3
Louisville, KY	305,342	321,868	94.9
Madison, WI	137,655	137,913	99.8
Manchester, NH	57,084	58,331	97.9
McAllen, TX	71,212	72,577	98.1

Table continued on following page.

City	Males	Females	Males per 100 Females
Memphis, TN	298,855	330,208	90.5
Miami, FL	226,349	220,314	102.7
Midland, TX	68,527	65,471	104.7
Milwaukee, WI	275,637	294,119	93.7
Minneapolis, MN	218,753	208,092	105.1
Nashville, TN	331,646	352,652	94.0
New Orleans, LA	177,299	198,736	89.2
New York, NY	4,088,026	4,428,176	92.3
Oklahoma City, OK	340,327	348,366	97.7
Omaha, NE	242,508	245,689	98.7
Orlando, FL	153,714	158,018	97.3
Philadelphia, PA	749,410	833,022	90.0
Phoenix, AZ	815,308	809,524	100.7
Pittsburgh, PA	149,240	154,380	96.7
Portland, OR	319,454	323,261	98.8
Providence, RI	93,138	97,076	95.9
Provo, UT	56,107	58,196	96.4
Raleigh, NC	228,452	242,311	94.3
Reno, NV	136,341	132,618	102.8
Richmond, VA	108,090	119,505	90.4
Rochester, MN	59,099	62,539	94.5
Sacramento, CA	260,163	264,639	98.3
Saint Louis, MO	142,190	150,919	94.2
Saint Paul, MN	151,659	156,103	97.2
Salem, OR	89,295	87,371	102.2
Salt Lake City, UT	105,049	98,839	106.3
San Antonio, TX	722,875	736,079	98.2
San Diego, CA	703,091	681,970	103.1
San Francisco, CA	429,837	406,484	105.7
San Jose, CA	504,179	485,875	103.8
Santa Rosa, CA	86,188	91,028	94.7
Savannah, GA	69,345	78,201	88.7
Seattle, WA	378,278	363,162	104.2
Sioux Falls, SD	99,791	97,851	102.0
Tampa, FL	197,565	195,824	100.9
Tucson, AZ	270,198	273,150	98.9
Tulsa, OK	201,524	210,798	95.6
Virginia Beach, VA	224,463	232,603	96.5
Washington, DC	320,001	352,078	90.9
Wichita, KS	197,295	199,193	99.0
Wilmington, NC	55,595	62,983	88.3
Winston-Salem, NC	116,981	133,906	87.4
U.S.	164,545,087	167,842,453	98.0

Source: U.S. Census Bureau, 2019-2023 American Community Survey 5-Year Estimates

Male/Female Ratio: Metro Area

Metro Area	Males	Females	Males per 100 Females
Albuquerque, NM	452,929	465,638	97.3
Anchorage, AK	205,511	194,235	105.8
Ann Arbor, MI	183,761	184,633	99.5
Athens, GA	105,119	113,071	93.0
Atlanta, GA	2,998,312	3,178,625	94.3
Austin, TX	1,190,277	1,167,220	102.0
Baltimore, MD	1,371,348	1,468,061	93.4
Billings, MT	92,957	94,312	98.6
Boise City, ID	397,370	393,270	101.0
Boston, MA	2,405,154	2,512,507	95.7
Boulder, CO	165,677	162,640	101.9
Cape Coral, FL	389,853	402,839	96.8
Cedar Rapids, IA	137,287	138,673	99.0
Charleston, SC	400,382	417,374	95.9
Charlotte, NC	1,323,612	1,389,206	95.3
Chicago, IL	4,607,366	4,752,189	97.0
Cincinnati, OH	1,113,237	1,142,020	97.5
Clarksville, TN	165,784	162,842	101.8
Cleveland, OH	1,057,990	1,113,988	95.0
College Station, TX	137,218	136,062	100.8
Colorado Springs, CO	386,799	373,983	103.4
Columbia, MO	103,590	109,260	94.8
Columbia, SC	407,291	432,577	94.2
Columbus, OH	1,066,090	1,085,757	98.2
Dallas, TX	3,864,152	3,943,403	98.0
Davenport, IA	189,025	192,839	98.0
Denver, CO	1,499,649	1,477,436	101.5
Des Moines, IA	359,219	361,112	99.5
Detroit, MI	2,140,962	2,226,658	96.2
Durham, NC	285,396	308,895	92.4
El Paso, TX	432,470	437,136	98.9
Eugene, OR	189,067	193,561	97.7
Fargo, ND	128,561	126,353	101.7
Fort Collins, CO	181,725	181,836	99.9
Fort Wayne, IN	222,504	228,936	97.2
Fort Worth, TX	3,864,152	3,943,403	98.0
Gainesville, FL	166,988	177,533	94.1
Green Bay, WI	165,274	164,101	100.7
Greensboro, NC	374,844	405,050	92.5
Honolulu, HI	507,355	496,311	102.2
Houston, TX	3,616,570	3,658,144	98.9
Huntsville, AL	249,354	255,358	97.6
Indianapolis, IN	1,034,791	1,071,536	96.6
Jacksonville, FL	804,019	841,688	95.5
Kansas City, MO	1,087,932	1,114,074	97.7
Lafayette, LA	200,575	210,308	95.4
Las Vegas, NV	1,148,112	1,145,652	100.2
Lexington, KY	254,019	263,359	96.5
Lincoln, NE	172,052	169,257	101.7
Little Rock, AR	365,071	388,534	94.0
Los Angeles, CA	6,447,486	6,564,983	98.2
Louisville, KY	669,908	691,939	96.8
Madison, WI	343,409	340,558	100.8
Manchester, NH	212,913	211,819	100.5
McAllen, TX	434,784	446,137	97.5

Table continued on following page.

Metro Area	Males	Females	Males per 100 Females
Memphis, TN	642,599	699,007	91.9
Miami, FL	3,005,200	3,133,676	95.9
Midland, TX	90,328	86,398	104.5
Milwaukee, WI	768,160	798,201	96.2
Minneapolis, MN	1,842,197	1,851,154	99.5
Nashville, TN	1,004,473	1,039,240	96.7
New Orleans, LA	476,985	511,778	93.2
New York, NY	9,622,708	10,134,014	95.0
Oklahoma City, OK	714,932	730,190	97.9
Omaha, NE	485,489	487,351	99.6
Orlando, FL	1,336,264	1,384,758	96.5
Philadelphia, PA	3,031,854	3,210,028	94.4
Phoenix, AZ	2,466,995	2,474,211	99.7
Pittsburgh, PA	1,200,522	1,243,399	96.6
Portland, OR	1,251,055	1,259,474	99.3
Providence, RI	819,607	854,200	96.0
Provo, UT	353,303	342,592	103.1
Raleigh, NC	711,279	738,315	96.3
Reno, NV	283,387	273,152	103.7
Richmond, VA	645,193	682,128	94.6
Rochester, MN	112,416	114,836	97.9
Sacramento, CA	1,184,908	1,221,655	97.0
Saint Louis, MO	1,370,976	1,438,438	95.3
Saint Paul, MN	1,842,197	1,851,154	99.5
Salem, OR	217,233	217,852	99.7
Salt Lake City, UT	637,671	623,666	102.2
San Antonio, TX	1,298,427	1,314,375	98.8
San Diego, CA	1,660,156	1,622,626	102.3
San Francisco, CA	2,318,841	2,334,752	99.3
San Jose, CA	1,003,282	966,071	103.9
Santa Rosa, CA	238,817	246,825	96.8
Savannah, GA	200,060	212,029	94.4
Seattle, WA	2,031,168	1,990,299	102.1
Sioux Falls, SD	148,246	144,861	102.3
Tampa, FL	1,583,138	1,657,331	95.5
Tucson, AZ	518,998	530,949	97.7
Tulsa, OK	506,779	519,430	97.6
Virginia Beach, VA	875,910	906,680	96.6
Washington, DC	3,081,518	3,182,278	96.8
Wichita, KS	323,191	325,744	99.2
Wilmington, NC	212,689	227,889	93.3
Winston-Salem, NC	330,177	353,460	93.4
U.S.	164,545,087	167,842,453	98.0

Note: Figures cover the Metropolitan Statistical Area (MSA)
Source: U.S. Census Bureau, 2019-2023 American Community Survey 5-Year Estimates

Race: City

City	White Alone[1] (%)	Black Alone[1] (%)	Asian Alone[1] (%)	AIAN[2] Alone[1] (%)	NHOPI[3] Alone[1] (%)	Other Race Alone[1] (%)	Two or More Races (%)
Albuquerque, NM	55.3	3.3	3.3	5.0	0.1	11.1	21.9
Anchorage, AK	58.3	5.3	9.8	7.3	3.1	3.1	13.1
Ann Arbor, MI	68.8	7.2	15.2	0.3	0.0	1.2	7.3
Athens, GA	57.6	26.2	4.3	0.4	0.0	3.4	8.1
Atlanta, GA	39.9	46.9	5.0	0.3	0.1	2.1	5.8
Austin, TX	59.9	7.5	8.6	0.7	0.1	7.7	15.5
Baltimore, MD	27.4	60.0	2.5	0.4	0.0	4.4	5.2
Billings, MT	86.3	1.0	0.9	4.4	0.1	1.4	6.1
Boise City, ID	83.6	1.4	3.3	0.7	0.3	3.0	7.6
Boston, MA	47.8	21.5	10.0	0.3	0.1	7.1	13.2
Boulder, CO	81.8	1.1	5.8	0.3	0.1	1.8	9.2
Cape Coral, FL	72.9	4.5	1.5	0.1	0.0	4.1	16.9
Cedar Rapids, IA	79.7	8.5	2.6	0.2	0.0	1.4	7.6
Charleston, SC	72.9	17.4	2.2	0.6	0.2	1.9	5.0
Charlotte, NC	41.5	34.1	6.4	0.4	0.0	8.8	8.9
Chicago, IL	39.0	28.4	7.1	0.9	0.1	12.4	12.0
Cincinnati, OH	49.4	38.7	2.8	0.1	0.0	2.0	7.0
Clarksville, TN	59.4	23.0	2.5	0.4	0.3	2.8	11.7
Cleveland, OH	36.7	46.8	2.3	0.4	0.0	4.6	9.2
College Station, TX	67.0	8.8	9.6	0.3	0.1	3.3	10.9
Colorado Springs, CO	72.3	5.8	3.0	1.0	0.2	4.9	12.8
Columbia, MO	74.3	12.1	6.1	0.1	0.1	1.2	6.1
Columbia, SC	49.9	39.5	2.7	0.2	0.2	1.7	5.9
Columbus, OH	53.3	29.0	5.8	0.3	0.0	3.4	8.2
Dallas, TX	41.9	23.7	3.7	0.8	0.1	12.5	17.3
Davenport, IA	75.9	11.2	2.0	0.3	0.1	2.1	8.5
Denver, CO	62.9	8.8	3.6	0.9	0.1	8.2	15.5
Des Moines, IA	66.9	12.0	6.2	0.5	0.0	5.2	9.1
Detroit, MI	11.7	76.8	1.6	0.4	0.0	4.6	4.8
Durham, NC	43.9	34.4	5.6	0.5	0.1	6.8	8.6
El Paso, TX	39.3	3.6	1.5	0.9	0.2	16.0	38.6
Eugene, OR	78.9	1.8	3.9	0.8	0.4	3.8	10.5
Fargo, ND	80.8	8.3	3.9	1.0	0.0	1.1	5.0
Fort Collins, CO	81.7	1.4	3.3	0.8	0.1	2.2	10.5
Fort Wayne, IN	66.4	14.6	5.8	0.4	0.0	4.3	8.4
Fort Worth, TX	47.7	19.5	5.2	0.6	0.1	10.4	16.4
Gainesville, FL	59.2	21.6	6.2	0.2	0.1	3.0	9.7
Green Bay, WI	69.9	3.8	4.1	3.3	0.0	7.1	11.8
Greensboro, NC	40.4	42.2	5.0	0.5	0.0	4.5	7.5
Honolulu, HI	17.0	1.8	52.9	0.2	8.5	1.2	18.4
Houston, TX	35.5	22.9	6.9	0.9	0.1	14.6	19.2
Huntsville, AL	58.4	29.7	2.0	0.6	0.1	2.9	6.2
Indianapolis, IN	53.6	28.1	4.1	0.5	0.0	5.7	8.0
Jacksonville, FL	51.2	30.1	4.9	0.2	0.1	3.9	9.6
Kansas City, MO	57.8	25.8	2.7	0.4	0.3	4.5	8.6
Lafayette, LA	59.1	28.6	2.1	0.1	0.1	1.2	8.8
Las Vegas, NV	49.2	11.9	6.9	1.1	0.8	13.9	16.2
Lexington, KY	69.9	14.4	4.2	0.2	0.0	3.5	7.8
Lincoln, NE	80.9	4.2	4.5	0.7	0.1	2.3	7.4
Little Rock, AR	46.3	39.4	3.0	0.3	0.1	4.2	6.6
Los Angeles, CA	37.3	8.5	12.0	1.2	0.1	25.1	15.7
Louisville, KY	63.1	23.7	2.6	0.1	0.0	2.1	8.4
Madison, WI	73.0	7.1	8.0	0.4	0.0	2.1	9.4
Manchester, NH	76.7	5.3	4.6	0.2	0.0	3.2	10.0

Table continued on following page.

City	White Alone[1] (%)	Black Alone[1] (%)	Asian Alone[1] (%)	AIAN[2] Alone[1] (%)	NHOPI[3] Alone[1] (%)	Other Race Alone[1] (%)	Two or More Races (%)
McAllen, TX	43.1	0.9	2.9	0.6	0.0	17.5	35.1
Memphis, TN	25.0	62.9	1.7	0.5	0.1	5.1	4.6
Miami, FL	34.2	13.7	1.6	0.4	0.0	7.5	42.6
Midland, TX	58.8	8.6	2.1	0.7	0.0	12.0	17.9
Milwaukee, WI	36.5	38.6	4.8	0.7	0.0	6.9	12.4
Minneapolis, MN	61.6	18.3	5.2	1.1	0.1	4.9	8.9
Nashville, TN	56.5	25.5	3.5	0.3	0.1	4.9	9.2
New Orleans, LA	31.6	55.2	2.8	0.3	0.0	2.8	7.3
New York, NY	35.9	22.7	14.6	0.7	0.1	15.5	10.5
Oklahoma City, OK	58.4	13.4	4.5	3.4	0.1	5.8	14.4
Omaha, NE	68.8	11.8	4.0	0.8	0.0	5.0	9.7
Orlando, FL	43.2	22.9	4.4	0.1	0.1	8.4	21.0
Philadelphia, PA	36.1	39.9	7.8	0.4	0.1	8.4	7.3
Phoenix, AZ	53.7	7.8	3.9	2.3	0.2	11.4	20.8
Pittsburgh, PA	63.7	22.5	5.8	0.2	0.0	1.6	6.2
Portland, OR	70.1	5.8	8.1	0.8	0.5	3.3	11.3
Providence, RI	40.7	13.3	5.9	1.0	0.1	20.4	18.7
Provo, UT	78.6	1.1	2.2	1.0	1.4	5.4	10.2
Raleigh, NC	53.8	27.5	4.7	0.4	0.0	5.5	8.0
Reno, NV	63.5	3.2	7.0	1.0	0.7	11.1	13.5
Richmond, VA	43.2	42.0	2.1	0.2	0.0	5.3	7.1
Rochester, MN	74.3	9.4	8.0	0.2	0.1	2.1	5.9
Sacramento, CA	36.8	12.4	19.7	1.0	1.7	13.4	15.0
Saint Louis, MO	45.7	43.1	3.4	0.2	0.0	1.6	5.9
Saint Paul, MN	53.2	16.2	17.9	0.7	0.0	3.5	8.4
Salem, OR	69.8	1.6	3.5	1.2	1.6	8.2	14.1
Salt Lake City, UT	70.5	2.7	5.4	1.2	1.4	9.2	9.6
San Antonio, TX	48.3	6.9	3.1	1.1	0.1	10.9	29.6
San Diego, CA	50.4	5.7	17.6	0.7	0.5	9.5	15.6
San Francisco, CA	40.5	5.1	35.0	0.7	0.4	7.7	10.7
San Jose, CA	29.0	2.9	38.6	1.0	0.5	13.6	14.4
Santa Rosa, CA	56.2	1.9	6.5	1.4	0.6	20.0	13.4
Savannah, GA	37.2	52.2	2.9	0.2	0.2	2.0	5.4
Seattle, WA	61.8	6.6	17.2	0.6	0.3	3.0	10.5
Sioux Falls, SD	79.9	7.0	2.3	1.9	0.0	2.0	7.0
Tampa, FL	51.8	21.3	4.8	0.3	0.1	4.8	17.0
Tucson, AZ	58.2	5.0	3.1	2.7	0.2	11.6	19.1
Tulsa, OK	57.0	14.2	3.5	4.3	0.2	5.9	14.9
Virginia Beach, VA	61.6	18.9	7.3	0.2	0.2	2.4	9.4
Washington, DC	39.1	43.3	4.1	0.3	0.1	4.8	8.4
Wichita, KS	66.6	9.7	4.9	0.9	0.0	5.5	12.4
Wilmington, NC	72.9	14.9	1.3	0.3	0.0	4.8	5.9
Winston-Salem, NC	48.7	32.4	2.3	0.5	0.0	7.3	8.8
U.S.	63.4	12.4	5.8	0.9	0.2	6.6	10.7

Note: (1) Alone is defined as not being in combination with one or more other races; (2) American Indian and Alaska Native; (3) Native Hawaiian and Other Pacific Islander
Source: U.S. Census Bureau, 2019-2023 American Community Survey 5-Year Estimates

Race: Metro Area

Metro Area	White Alone[1] (%)	Black Alone[1] (%)	Asian Alone[1] (%)	AIAN[2] Alone[1] (%)	NHOPI[3] Alone[1] (%)	Other Race Alone[1] (%)	Two or More Races (%)
Albuquerque, NM	55.2	2.7	2.5	6.2	0.1	10.9	22.3
Anchorage, AK	63.8	4.2	7.6	6.9	2.4	2.7	12.5
Ann Arbor, MI	69.9	11.6	8.9	0.3	0.0	1.6	7.7
Athens, GA	67.1	18.6	3.7	0.4	0.2	3.0	7.1
Atlanta, GA	46.3	34.0	6.4	0.4	0.1	4.9	7.9
Austin, TX	61.4	7.2	6.9	0.7	0.1	7.3	16.5
Baltimore, MD	54.8	29.0	5.8	0.3	0.0	3.6	6.4
Billings, MT	87.5	0.8	0.8	3.6	0.0	1.6	5.7
Boise City, ID	81.5	1.0	1.9	0.8	0.2	5.6	9.0
Boston, MA	69.2	7.5	8.5	0.2	0.0	5.5	9.1
Boulder, CO	80.7	0.8	4.7	0.3	0.1	2.9	10.6
Cape Coral, FL	70.5	8.0	1.7	0.6	0.0	4.3	15.0
Cedar Rapids, IA	86.2	5.0	2.0	0.3	0.0	1.1	5.5
Charleston, SC	64.6	23.9	2.0	0.4	0.2	3.3	5.7
Charlotte, NC	60.2	22.2	4.2	0.4	0.0	5.5	7.5
Chicago, IL	55.7	16.2	7.1	0.6	0.0	9.5	10.8
Cincinnati, OH	78.0	11.9	2.9	0.1	0.1	1.7	5.5
Clarksville, TN	67.3	18.5	2.1	0.3	0.3	2.2	9.5
Cleveland, OH	70.5	18.6	2.3	0.2	0.0	1.9	6.4
College Station, TX	66.6	11.4	5.1	0.6	0.1	4.4	11.8
Colorado Springs, CO	73.1	5.8	2.8	0.9	0.3	4.3	12.8
Columbia, MO	79.2	9.0	4.1	0.2	0.1	1.3	6.1
Columbia, SC	55.4	33.3	2.3	0.2	0.1	2.7	5.9
Columbus, OH	70.3	15.8	4.8	0.2	0.0	2.2	6.7
Dallas, TX	52.7	16.2	7.8	0.6	0.1	8.0	14.5
Davenport, IA	79.4	7.7	2.4	0.2	0.1	2.8	7.5
Denver, CO	69.1	5.6	4.3	0.9	0.2	6.4	13.6
Des Moines, IA	81.5	5.7	4.2	0.3	0.0	2.5	5.8
Detroit, MI	65.6	21.5	4.8	0.2	0.0	1.9	5.9
Durham, NC	56.6	24.0	5.1	0.5	0.0	5.9	7.8
El Paso, TX	39.2	3.3	1.3	0.9	0.2	16.3	38.9
Eugene, OR	82.0	1.2	2.6	1.0	0.2	3.6	9.5
Fargo, ND	84.2	6.1	2.7	0.9	0.1	0.9	5.1
Fort Collins, CO	84.1	1.0	2.1	0.6	0.1	2.6	9.5
Fort Wayne, IN	75.6	9.5	4.3	0.3	0.0	3.2	7.1
Fort Worth, TX	52.7	16.2	7.8	0.6	0.1	8.0	14.5
Gainesville, FL	66.6	17.1	4.9	0.2	0.0	2.5	8.7
Green Bay, WI	82.9	2.2	2.7	1.7	0.0	3.3	7.1
Greensboro, NC	57.7	26.9	3.8	0.4	0.0	4.3	6.9
Honolulu, HI	18.8	2.4	42.6	0.2	9.9	1.6	24.4
Houston, TX	45.3	17.3	8.2	0.7	0.1	10.7	17.8
Huntsville, AL	66.6	21.8	2.4	0.7	0.1	2.2	6.2
Indianapolis, IN	70.8	15.1	3.8	0.3	0.0	3.4	6.5
Jacksonville, FL	62.8	20.7	4.0	0.2	0.1	3.2	9.0
Kansas City, MO	73.0	11.9	2.9	0.4	0.2	3.7	7.8
Lafayette, LA	68.0	22.7	1.5	0.2	0.1	1.1	6.4
Las Vegas, NV	47.1	12.1	10.5	1.1	0.8	12.9	15.5
Lexington, KY	76.6	10.6	2.9	0.2	0.0	2.9	6.7
Lincoln, NE	83.0	3.6	3.9	0.7	0.1	2.0	6.8
Little Rock, AR	65.9	23.5	1.6	0.3	0.0	2.8	5.8
Los Angeles, CA	38.1	6.3	16.7	1.1	0.2	21.2	16.2
Louisville, KY	75.2	14.2	2.1	0.1	0.0	1.6	6.7
Madison, WI	81.4	4.5	5.0	0.3	0.1	1.7	7.1
Manchester, NH	83.3	2.6	4.2	0.1	0.0	2.1	7.7

Table continued on following page.

Metro Area	White Alone[1] (%)	Black Alone[1] (%)	Asian Alone[1] (%)	AIAN[2] Alone[1] (%)	NHOPI[3] Alone[1] (%)	Other Race Alone[1] (%)	Two or More Races (%)
McAllen, TX	39.5	0.7	1.0	0.4	0.0	10.8	47.6
Memphis, TN	42.5	46.8	2.2	0.3	0.1	3.4	4.7
Miami, FL	43.7	20.3	2.6	0.2	0.0	6.6	26.6
Midland, TX	60.4	7.1	2.1	0.6	0.0	12.8	17.1
Milwaukee, WI	67.4	16.1	4.0	0.4	0.0	3.8	8.3
Minneapolis, MN	73.8	8.9	6.9	0.5	0.0	3.0	6.8
Nashville, TN	71.6	14.3	2.9	0.2	0.1	3.4	7.6
New Orleans, LA	45.0	38.5	3.2	0.6	0.0	4.4	8.4
New York, NY	48.4	16.3	11.8	0.5	0.0	12.3	10.6
Oklahoma City, OK	66.5	9.8	3.3	3.6	0.1	3.9	12.8
Omaha, NE	77.1	7.4	3.2	0.6	0.1	3.7	7.9
Orlando, FL	52.5	16.0	4.5	0.3	0.1	9.5	17.2
Philadelphia, PA	61.4	20.2	6.3	0.2	0.0	4.9	6.9
Phoenix, AZ	63.2	5.7	4.1	2.2	0.2	8.4	16.1
Pittsburgh, PA	84.1	7.9	2.5	0.1	0.0	0.8	4.6
Portland, OR	73.0	3.0	7.0	0.8	0.5	4.5	11.2
Providence, RI	74.5	5.3	3.1	0.4	0.1	6.6	10.0
Provo, UT	83.9	0.7	1.4	0.6	0.8	4.0	8.6
Raleigh, NC	60.7	19.1	6.6	0.4	0.0	5.4	7.8
Reno, NV	66.9	2.3	5.1	1.4	0.6	10.0	13.7
Richmond, VA	56.8	28.5	4.1	0.3	0.1	4.0	6.2
Rochester, MN	83.0	5.4	4.7	0.2	0.1	1.7	4.9
Sacramento, CA	54.8	6.9	14.8	0.8	0.8	8.7	13.2
Saint Louis, MO	72.1	17.5	2.8	0.1	0.0	1.3	6.1
Saint Paul, MN	73.8	8.9	6.9	0.5	0.0	3.0	6.8
Salem, OR	71.3	1.1	2.0	1.4	1.0	9.3	14.0
Salt Lake City, UT	73.6	1.7	3.9	0.9	1.5	8.7	9.6
San Antonio, TX	53.5	7.0	2.8	0.9	0.1	9.5	26.2
San Diego, CA	53.0	4.7	12.2	0.9	0.4	10.6	18.1
San Francisco, CA	39.9	7.0	27.6	0.9	0.6	11.8	12.2
San Jose, CA	33.6	2.3	38.3	0.8	0.4	10.7	13.9
Santa Rosa, CA	64.5	1.6	4.4	1.3	0.4	14.1	13.7
Savannah, GA	55.2	32.4	2.5	0.2	0.1	3.1	6.5
Seattle, WA	60.9	6.1	15.4	0.8	0.9	4.6	11.4
Sioux Falls, SD	84.2	5.1	1.6	1.5	0.0	1.6	6.0
Tampa, FL	66.0	11.8	3.8	0.3	0.1	4.8	13.2
Tucson, AZ	63.2	3.6	3.0	3.1	0.2	9.9	17.0
Tulsa, OK	65.3	7.6	2.8	7.2	0.1	3.5	13.4
Virginia Beach, VA	55.0	29.7	4.1	0.3	0.1	2.4	8.4
Washington, DC	45.5	24.9	10.7	0.5	0.0	8.3	10.1
Wichita, KS	74.4	6.7	3.7	0.8	0.1	4.3	10.1
Wilmington, NC	78.8	10.4	1.0	0.3	0.0	3.5	5.9
Winston-Salem, NC	68.8	17.4	1.8	0.3	0.0	4.4	7.3
U.S.	63.4	12.4	5.8	0.9	0.2	6.6	10.7

Note: Figures cover the Metropolitan Statistical Area (MSA); (1) Alone is defined as not being in combination with one or more other races; (2) American Indian and Alaska Native; (3) Native Hawaiian & Other Pacific Islander
Source: U.S. Census Bureau, 2019-2023 American Community Survey 5-Year Estimates

Hispanic Origin: City

City	Hispanic or Latino (%)	Mexican (%)	Puerto Rican (%)	Cuban (%)	Other Hispanic or Latino (%)
Albuquerque, NM	47.9	28.9	0.7	0.5	17.9
Anchorage, AK	9.3	4.2	1.4	0.5	3.1
Ann Arbor, MI	5.4	2.3	0.7	0.2	2.3
Athens, GA	11.5	6.1	0.4	0.7	4.2
Atlanta, GA	6.3	2.0	0.9	0.3	3.0
Austin, TX	32.2	23.7	1.0	0.9	6.7
Baltimore, MD	7.9	1.6	1.0	0.4	4.8
Billings, MT	7.2	5.0	0.3	0.2	1.8
Boise City, ID	9.5	7.0	0.4	0.1	2.1
Boston, MA	18.9	1.2	4.4	0.4	13.0
Boulder, CO	11.2	6.6	0.3	0.5	3.8
Cape Coral, FL	25.0	1.9	4.9	10.7	7.5
Cedar Rapids, IA	5.1	3.5	0.4	0.1	1.2
Charleston, SC	5.9	2.6	0.7	0.2	2.4
Charlotte, NC	17.0	6.0	1.2	0.5	9.3
Chicago, IL	29.6	21.6	3.5	0.4	4.2
Cincinnati, OH	5.4	1.6	0.9	0.2	2.6
Clarksville, TN	12.5	6.0	3.0	0.3	3.2
Cleveland, OH	12.8	1.7	8.8	0.2	2.2
College Station, TX	18.4	12.9	0.7	0.5	4.3
Colorado Springs, CO	18.7	12.0	1.2	0.2	5.3
Columbia, MO	4.3	2.5	0.2	0.2	1.3
Columbia, SC	5.7	2.0	1.3	0.2	2.2
Columbus, OH	7.9	3.7	1.1	0.1	3.0
Dallas, TX	41.9	33.6	0.6	0.4	7.4
Davenport, IA	9.1	8.0	0.4	0.1	0.6
Denver, CO	27.9	20.9	0.7	0.3	6.1
Des Moines, IA	16.0	11.4	0.6	0.3	3.8
Detroit, MI	8.0	5.5	0.9	0.2	1.3
Durham, NC	14.7	6.6	0.9	0.5	6.7
El Paso, TX	81.3	76.1	1.1	0.2	3.9
Eugene, OR	11.4	8.0	0.4	0.2	2.8
Fargo, ND	3.7	2.2	0.6	0.0	0.8
Fort Collins, CO	12.3	8.2	0.7	0.2	3.3
Fort Wayne, IN	10.5	7.7	0.7	0.1	2.2
Fort Worth, TX	34.6	28.7	1.3	0.4	4.2
Gainesville, FL	13.4	1.3	2.9	2.9	6.3
Green Bay, WI	18.1	13.8	2.3	0.1	1.9
Greensboro, NC	10.5	4.5	1.7	0.2	4.1
Honolulu, HI	6.6	2.3	1.8	0.1	2.4
Houston, TX	44.1	28.5	0.8	0.8	14.0
Huntsville, AL	8.1	4.3	1.0	0.2	2.5
Indianapolis, IN	13.3	8.7	0.8	0.3	3.5
Jacksonville, FL	12.0	2.0	3.9	1.8	4.3
Kansas City, MO	12.3	8.3	0.6	0.4	3.0
Lafayette, LA	7.6	1.9	0.4	0.5	4.8
Las Vegas, NV	34.1	24.7	1.2	1.6	6.6
Lexington, KY	9.2	5.9	0.7	0.3	2.4
Lincoln, NE	8.8	5.7	0.4	0.2	2.5
Little Rock, AR	10.4	6.8	0.2	0.1	3.3
Los Angeles, CA	47.2	30.0	0.5	0.4	16.3
Louisville, KY	8.6	2.9	0.4	3.4	1.9
Madison, WI	9.3	5.7	0.7	0.2	2.8
Manchester, NH	13.4	1.5	4.4	0.1	7.4
McAllen, TX	86.5	81.1	0.5	0.1	4.8

Table continued on following page.

City	Hispanic or Latino (%)	Mexican (%)	Puerto Rican (%)	Cuban (%)	Other Hispanic or Latino (%)
Memphis, TN	10.2	5.7	0.3	0.2	3.9
Miami, FL	71.2	2.2	3.3	31.0	34.8
Midland, TX	44.3	38.1	0.6	1.3	4.3
Milwaukee, WI	20.7	13.7	4.9	0.1	1.9
Minneapolis, MN	10.5	5.9	0.4	0.2	4.0
Nashville, TN	13.8	6.8	0.7	0.6	5.7
New Orleans, LA	7.9	1.5	0.4	0.8	5.3
New York, NY	28.4	3.9	7.1	0.5	17.0
Oklahoma City, OK	21.7	17.3	0.5	0.1	3.8
Omaha, NE	15.6	11.4	0.5	0.2	3.5
Orlando, FL	35.6	2.0	15.2	2.6	15.8
Philadelphia, PA	15.2	1.4	8.4	0.2	5.2
Phoenix, AZ	41.8	36.7	0.7	0.4	4.0
Pittsburgh, PA	4.2	1.4	0.8	0.1	2.0
Portland, OR	11.3	7.6	0.5	0.4	2.8
Providence, RI	44.3	1.6	6.8	0.3	35.6
Provo, UT	18.9	11.4	0.7	0.2	6.6
Raleigh, NC	12.7	5.0	1.4	0.4	5.9
Reno, NV	24.6	17.9	0.7	0.3	5.7
Richmond, VA	10.3	2.1	1.1	0.3	6.8
Rochester, MN	6.2	3.9	0.4	0.1	1.8
Sacramento, CA	29.5	24.1	0.9	0.1	4.4
Saint Louis, MO	5.1	3.1	0.3	0.3	1.4
Saint Paul, MN	9.1	5.9	0.4	0.2	2.7
Salem, OR	23.4	20.0	0.4	0.1	2.9
Salt Lake City, UT	20.8	15.2	0.5	0.3	4.8
San Antonio, TX	64.4	54.1	1.4	0.4	8.6
San Diego, CA	29.6	24.9	0.8	0.3	3.6
San Francisco, CA	15.9	7.8	0.7	0.2	7.2
San Jose, CA	31.0	25.4	0.5	0.2	4.9
Santa Rosa, CA	35.8	30.3	0.5	0.1	4.9
Savannah, GA	7.1	2.2	2.0	0.5	2.4
Seattle, WA	8.2	4.8	0.4	0.2	2.8
Sioux Falls, SD	6.4	2.7	0.3	0.1	3.3
Tampa, FL	26.2	3.2	6.1	7.8	9.1
Tucson, AZ	42.7	38.1	0.8	0.3	3.5
Tulsa, OK	19.2	14.5	0.7	0.1	4.0
Virginia Beach, VA	8.9	2.8	2.5	0.3	3.3
Washington, DC	11.6	2.1	0.8	0.4	8.2
Wichita, KS	18.4	15.1	0.8	0.1	2.5
Wilmington, NC	8.9	3.6	1.4	0.4	3.5
Winston-Salem, NC	17.9	10.1	1.7	0.3	5.8
U.S.	19.0	11.3	1.8	0.7	5.2

Note: Persons of Hispanic or Latino origin can be of any race
Source: U.S. Census Bureau, 2019-2023 American Community Survey 5-Year Estimates

Hispanic Origin: Metro Area

Metro Area	Hispanic or Latino (%)	Mexican (%)	Puerto Rican (%)	Cuban (%)	Other Hispanic or Latino (%)
Albuquerque, NM	48.3	28.5	0.7	0.4	18.6
Anchorage, AK	8.2	3.8	1.2	0.4	2.8
Ann Arbor, MI	5.6	2.8	0.6	0.2	2.1
Athens, GA	9.3	5.1	0.4	0.5	3.3
Atlanta, GA	12.1	5.7	1.2	0.4	4.7
Austin, TX	32.0	24.8	1.0	0.6	5.6
Baltimore, MD	7.8	1.6	1.2	0.3	4.7
Billings, MT	6.1	4.4	0.2	0.1	1.3
Boise City, ID	14.7	11.8	0.4	0.1	2.4
Boston, MA	12.0	0.8	2.7	0.3	8.3
Boulder, CO	14.6	9.8	0.5	0.3	3.9
Cape Coral, FL	23.6	4.7	4.5	6.7	7.8
Cedar Rapids, IA	3.7	2.6	0.2	0.0	0.8
Charleston, SC	7.5	3.5	1.1	0.3	2.7
Charlotte, NC	12.0	4.9	1.1	0.4	5.6
Chicago, IL	23.8	18.3	2.3	0.3	2.9
Cincinnati, OH	4.3	1.8	0.5	0.2	1.9
Clarksville, TN	9.7	5.0	2.3	0.2	2.2
Cleveland, OH	6.5	1.5	3.6	0.1	1.3
College Station, TX	26.4	21.9	0.5	0.5	3.6
Colorado Springs, CO	18.0	10.8	1.5	0.3	5.3
Columbia, MO	4.1	2.7	0.2	0.1	1.0
Columbia, SC	6.8	3.2	1.1	0.3	2.3
Columbus, OH	5.3	2.5	0.8	0.1	2.0
Dallas, TX	29.4	23.1	0.9	0.4	5.1
Davenport, IA	9.5	8.3	0.4	0.1	0.8
Denver, CO	23.6	17.5	0.7	0.2	5.3
Des Moines, IA	8.4	5.7	0.4	0.1	2.2
Detroit, MI	5.1	3.4	0.6	0.1	1.0
Durham, NC	13.2	6.3	0.8	0.4	5.8
El Paso, TX	82.6	77.5	1.0	0.2	4.0
Eugene, OR	10.2	7.3	0.4	0.2	2.3
Fargo, ND	3.8	2.5	0.4	0.0	0.8
Fort Collins, CO	12.7	9.0	0.5	0.2	3.0
Fort Wayne, IN	8.0	5.7	0.6	0.1	1.7
Fort Worth, TX	29.4	23.1	0.9	0.4	5.1
Gainesville, FL	11.6	1.8	2.8	2.1	4.9
Green Bay, WI	8.7	6.2	1.0	0.1	1.3
Greensboro, NC	10.2	5.9	1.2	0.2	2.8
Honolulu, HI	9.3	3.1	3.1	0.2	3.0
Houston, TX	37.8	26.1	0.8	0.8	10.1
Huntsville, AL	6.7	3.6	0.9	0.2	1.9
Indianapolis, IN	8.6	5.4	0.6	0.2	2.4
Jacksonville, FL	10.6	1.8	3.3	1.5	4.0
Kansas City, MO	10.6	7.5	0.5	0.3	2.3
Lafayette, LA	5.3	1.9	0.2	0.2	3.0
Las Vegas, NV	31.4	22.7	1.1	1.5	6.1
Lexington, KY	7.8	4.9	0.5	0.3	2.0
Lincoln, NE	8.0	5.2	0.4	0.2	2.2
Little Rock, AR	7.1	4.6	0.3	0.1	2.1
Los Angeles, CA	44.8	33.8	0.5	0.4	10.2
Louisville, KY	6.5	2.7	0.5	1.8	1.5
Madison, WI	6.9	4.2	0.6	0.1	1.9
Manchester, NH	8.3	1.2	2.6	0.2	4.2
McAllen, TX	91.9	87.6	0.3	0.1	3.9

Table continued on following page.

Metro Area	Hispanic or Latino (%)	Mexican (%)	Puerto Rican (%)	Cuban (%)	Other Hispanic or Latino (%)
Memphis, TN	7.2	4.2	0.3	0.2	2.5
Miami, FL	46.0	2.5	3.7	18.4	21.5
Midland, TX	44.8	39.3	0.6	1.2	3.8
Milwaukee, WI	11.8	7.7	2.6	0.1	1.4
Minneapolis, MN	6.7	4.1	0.3	0.1	2.1
Nashville, TN	9.7	5.1	0.7	0.4	3.5
New Orleans, LA	12.6	2.0	0.7	0.9	9.1
New York, NY	25.4	3.0	5.6	0.8	16.0
Oklahoma City, OK	15.3	11.9	0.5	0.1	2.8
Omaha, NE	11.9	8.7	0.4	0.2	2.6
Orlando, FL	32.5	2.7	14.3	2.6	12.9
Philadelphia, PA	10.4	2.0	4.6	0.3	3.6
Phoenix, AZ	30.8	26.2	0.7	0.3	3.6
Pittsburgh, PA	2.3	0.8	0.5	0.1	0.9
Portland, OR	13.5	10.2	0.4	0.2	2.6
Providence, RI	14.6	1.0	4.3	0.2	9.1
Provo, UT	13.7	8.1	0.4	0.1	5.1
Raleigh, NC	12.1	6.0	1.4	0.4	4.4
Reno, NV	24.7	18.9	0.6	0.3	5.0
Richmond, VA	8.1	1.9	1.2	0.3	4.7
Rochester, MN	5.1	3.2	0.3	0.1	1.5
Sacramento, CA	22.6	17.9	0.7	0.2	3.8
Saint Louis, MO	3.8	2.3	0.3	0.1	1.1
Saint Paul, MN	6.7	4.1	0.3	0.1	2.1
Salem, OR	25.6	22.2	0.3	0.2	3.0
Salt Lake City, UT	19.6	13.7	0.4	0.1	5.3
San Antonio, TX	54.5	45.5	1.5	0.3	7.2
San Diego, CA	34.3	29.6	0.8	0.2	3.6
San Francisco, CA	23.0	14.5	0.7	0.2	7.6
San Jose, CA	26.3	21.2	0.4	0.2	4.5
Santa Rosa, CA	29.4	23.7	0.4	0.2	5.1
Savannah, GA	7.7	2.9	1.9	0.5	2.4
Seattle, WA	11.4	7.7	0.6	0.2	2.9
Sioux Falls, SD	5.3	2.4	0.2	0.1	2.6
Tampa, FL	21.1	3.7	6.0	4.5	6.9
Tucson, AZ	36.1	32.1	0.9	0.2	3.0
Tulsa, OK	12.0	8.9	0.5	0.1	2.5
Virginia Beach, VA	7.8	2.6	2.2	0.3	2.8
Washington, DC	17.6	2.5	1.2	0.3	13.6
Wichita, KS	14.5	11.8	0.6	0.1	2.0
Wilmington, NC	7.1	3.4	0.9	0.3	2.5
Winston-Salem, NC	11.8	7.0	1.1	0.3	3.4
U.S.	19.0	11.3	1.8	0.7	5.2

Note: Persons of Hispanic or Latino origin can be of any race; Figures cover the Metropolitan Statistical Area (MSA)
Source: U.S. Census Bureau, 2019-2023 American Community Survey 5-Year Estimates

Household Size: City

City	Persons in Household (%)							Average Household Size
	One	Two	Three	Four	Five	Six	Seven or More	
Albuquerque, NM	37.3	32.4	13.7	9.8	4.6	1.4	0.8	2.29
Anchorage, AK	28.5	33.7	14.8	13.5	5.4	2.3	1.8	2.61
Ann Arbor, MI	34.0	35.9	14.5	9.9	3.2	1.8	0.7	2.19
Athens, GA	33.6	35.1	15.3	10.6	4.0	0.9	0.6	2.18
Atlanta, GA	47.0	32.0	10.6	6.5	2.3	1.0	0.6	2.01
Austin, TX	36.9	34.0	13.4	10.0	3.4	1.5	0.7	2.14
Baltimore, MD	43.4	29.6	13.4	7.7	3.7	1.3	1.0	2.22
Billings, MT	34.0	35.0	13.2	10.8	4.7	1.2	1.1	2.29
Boise City, ID	30.1	37.7	15.0	10.9	4.2	1.5	0.7	2.30
Boston, MA	36.9	33.2	14.6	8.9	4.0	1.5	0.9	2.22
Boulder, CO	34.9	36.6	13.9	10.9	2.5	0.6	0.7	2.16
Cape Coral, FL	24.2	44.1	13.7	10.3	5.5	1.3	0.8	2.59
Cedar Rapids, IA	34.4	35.4	13.5	9.4	5.0	1.1	1.3	2.27
Charleston, SC	34.5	40.1	12.4	8.7	3.2	0.8	0.3	2.20
Charlotte, NC	35.1	31.7	14.8	11.2	4.7	1.5	1.0	2.42
Chicago, IL	39.2	29.4	13.1	9.9	4.8	2.1	1.5	2.32
Cincinnati, OH	44.9	30.5	10.7	8.5	3.0	1.4	1.0	2.07
Clarksville, TN	25.7	33.0	18.0	13.6	5.5	2.5	1.6	2.59
Cleveland, OH	46.4	28.4	11.9	7.4	3.4	1.7	0.9	2.11
College Station, TX	31.1	32.3	15.1	15.1	3.5	2.4	0.6	2.42
Colorado Springs, CO	28.2	36.1	15.4	11.8	5.3	2.2	1.0	2.39
Columbia, MO	34.5	33.8	13.4	12.2	4.6	1.0	0.5	2.29
Columbia, SC	39.3	33.0	14.2	8.3	3.7	1.2	0.3	2.16
Columbus, OH	36.5	32.2	13.4	9.7	4.9	2.0	1.3	2.29
Dallas, TX	37.1	29.7	12.7	10.1	6.1	2.6	1.6	2.43
Davenport, IA	34.9	35.3	13.1	9.5	5.1	1.4	0.7	2.25
Denver, CO	40.0	33.5	11.4	9.0	3.7	1.5	1.0	2.12
Des Moines, IA	37.1	30.7	13.2	10.3	4.8	2.1	1.8	2.30
Detroit, MI	42.5	25.3	13.8	8.9	4.8	2.7	1.9	2.47
Durham, NC	36.1	34.1	13.9	9.9	4.0	1.4	0.6	2.25
El Paso, TX	25.8	28.2	18.0	15.5	8.0	2.8	1.7	2.77
Eugene, OR	34.3	35.7	13.6	10.6	4.0	1.2	0.5	2.23
Fargo, ND	41.1	33.0	11.6	9.3	3.4	1.1	0.5	2.10
Fort Collins, CO	26.6	37.8	17.6	12.5	4.1	1.0	0.4	2.27
Fort Wayne, IN	33.5	33.1	13.3	10.7	5.4	2.5	1.4	2.39
Fort Worth, TX	27.7	29.8	15.6	14.1	7.6	3.1	2.0	2.76
Gainesville, FL	39.2	33.2	14.6	8.8	3.1	0.5	0.6	2.17
Green Bay, WI	35.7	32.4	12.0	11.7	4.8	2.0	1.3	2.35
Greensboro, NC	36.4	30.7	15.3	9.8	4.8	1.5	1.5	2.33
Honolulu, HI	35.0	31.1	14.6	9.7	4.5	2.1	3.0	2.47
Houston, TX	34.1	29.2	15.6	11.6	5.7	2.3	1.5	2.47
Huntsville, AL	36.9	35.6	13.6	8.6	3.8	1.2	0.4	2.21
Indianapolis, IN	36.6	31.9	13.1	9.8	5.4	1.9	1.3	2.41
Jacksonville, FL	32.2	33.3	16.2	10.6	5.0	1.8	0.9	2.44
Kansas City, MO	37.7	31.3	12.3	10.8	4.7	2.1	1.0	2.28
Lafayette, LA	33.8	36.5	13.4	9.1	5.0	1.4	0.9	2.25
Las Vegas, NV	30.3	31.2	15.8	11.9	6.3	2.7	1.9	2.63
Lexington, KY	34.8	33.4	14.3	10.8	4.0	1.7	0.9	2.24
Lincoln, NE	32.7	34.1	13.7	11.0	4.9	2.5	1.0	2.31
Little Rock, AR	39.4	31.1	13.5	9.1	4.3	1.4	1.1	2.28
Los Angeles, CA	31.5	28.9	15.5	12.5	6.4	2.6	2.5	2.64
Louisville, KY	34.5	32.8	15.3	10.3	4.6	1.7	0.9	2.34
Madison, WI	39.0	35.2	12.0	9.1	3.3	0.8	0.7	2.09
Manchester, NH	34.5	34.2	14.7	10.7	3.7	1.7	0.5	2.27

Table continued on following page.

City	Persons in Household (%)							Average Household Size
	One	Two	Three	Four	Five	Six	Seven or More	
McAllen, TX	21.4	28.2	18.3	16.3	10.9	2.4	2.5	2.96
Memphis, TN	38.9	29.6	14.5	9.4	4.3	1.8	1.5	2.42
Miami, FL	36.5	32.1	15.8	9.5	3.8	1.1	1.2	2.30
Midland, TX	29.9	27.2	15.3	16.3	7.6	2.6	1.1	2.51
Milwaukee, WI	38.7	29.0	13.7	9.4	5.6	2.1	1.6	2.40
Minneapolis, MN	42.0	30.8	11.5	9.2	3.5	1.5	1.4	2.16
Nashville, TN	36.9	33.0	13.6	9.2	4.6	1.5	1.2	2.19
New Orleans, LA	44.7	29.3	13.2	8.0	3.3	1.0	0.5	2.34
New York, NY	33.4	28.8	16.1	11.7	5.6	2.5	1.9	2.51
Oklahoma City, OK	31.6	31.7	15.5	11.5	6.3	2.3	1.1	2.46
Omaha, NE	34.5	31.5	13.1	10.7	6.0	2.5	1.7	2.39
Orlando, FL	32.4	33.5	15.9	11.2	4.5	1.4	1.1	2.44
Philadelphia, PA	37.6	29.9	14.9	9.6	4.8	1.7	1.4	2.29
Phoenix, AZ	28.3	30.6	15.2	12.8	7.3	3.3	2.5	2.66
Pittsburgh, PA	43.9	33.0	11.6	7.1	2.9	0.8	0.7	2.03
Portland, OR	36.4	34.8	13.8	9.9	3.2	1.1	0.7	2.18
Providence, RI	33.8	28.4	15.4	11.7	7.0	2.3	1.4	2.48
Provo, UT	14.0	36.9	17.7	14.4	7.6	6.5	3.0	2.98
Raleigh, NC	35.3	33.7	13.8	11.4	4.2	1.1	0.5	2.30
Reno, NV	31.9	34.1	14.9	12.1	4.5	1.3	1.2	2.35
Richmond, VA	42.9	32.7	12.2	7.7	2.6	1.2	0.6	2.13
Rochester, MN	31.6	34.6	13.4	12.5	5.0	1.8	1.1	2.35
Sacramento, CA	31.7	29.8	14.4	12.4	6.6	2.6	2.5	2.58
Saint Louis, MO	47.9	30.1	10.3	6.9	3.0	1.0	0.8	1.96
Saint Paul, MN	37.1	29.8	12.5	9.6	5.1	2.9	3.1	2.42
Salem, OR	29.2	33.2	15.5	11.5	5.8	3.0	1.8	2.51
Salt Lake City, UT	39.3	34.1	11.6	8.2	3.8	1.8	1.3	2.19
San Antonio, TX	31.3	29.4	15.5	12.5	6.7	2.8	1.8	2.62
San Diego, CA	28.8	34.2	15.5	12.8	5.4	2.0	1.4	2.55
San Francisco, CA	38.0	32.3	13.4	9.9	3.5	1.6	1.2	2.24
San Jose, CA	20.7	29.4	18.8	17.6	7.6	3.0	2.9	2.98
Santa Rosa, CA	28.0	33.1	16.1	13.7	5.7	2.2	1.2	2.54
Savannah, GA	35.4	34.5	14.8	9.4	3.7	1.1	1.1	2.35
Seattle, WA	41.3	35.4	11.2	8.5	2.5	0.7	0.5	2.03
Sioux Falls, SD	33.9	33.0	12.9	10.3	6.9	1.8	1.2	2.32
Tampa, FL	35.7	32.1	15.4	10.9	4.1	1.4	0.5	2.35
Tucson, AZ	36.3	31.0	13.7	10.7	5.2	2.0	1.1	2.30
Tulsa, OK	35.9	31.9	13.4	10.3	4.9	2.4	1.3	2.36
Virginia Beach, VA	26.1	35.6	17.3	12.7	5.9	1.7	0.8	2.50
Washington, DC	46.7	30.2	11.1	7.4	2.8	1.2	0.7	1.99
Wichita, KS	33.2	32.6	13.2	10.8	5.7	2.7	1.7	2.47
Wilmington, NC	38.5	38.5	12.3	6.8	2.8	0.8	0.3	2.06
Winston-Salem, NC	35.2	32.7	14.2	9.8	4.8	2.3	1.0	2.40
U.S.	28.5	33.8	15.4	12.7	5.9	2.3	1.4	2.54

U.S. Census Bureau, 2019-2023 American Community Survey 5-Year Estimates

Household Size: Metro Area

Metro Area	Persons in Household (%)							Average Household Size
	One	Two	Three	Four	Five	Six	Seven or More	
Albuquerque, NM	33.0	33.6	14.6	10.8	5.0	1.9	1.2	2.44
Anchorage, AK	27.2	33.9	14.5	13.6	6.1	2.7	2.1	2.64
Ann Arbor, MI	30.6	36.1	14.9	11.5	4.2	1.9	0.9	2.34
Athens, GA	28.1	35.1	16.5	12.8	5.1	1.7	0.7	2.43
Atlanta, GA	27.1	32.0	17.0	13.7	6.2	2.4	1.5	2.67
Austin, TX	28.7	33.8	15.6	13.2	5.3	2.3	1.1	2.44
Baltimore, MD	30.0	32.8	15.7	13.0	5.3	2.1	1.2	2.51
Billings, MT	31.0	36.9	13.2	11.3	4.8	1.5	1.3	2.36
Boise City, ID	23.2	36.6	15.4	13.4	6.5	3.3	1.7	2.62
Boston, MA	28.0	33.2	16.7	14.0	5.5	1.7	0.9	2.47
Boulder, CO	29.8	37.0	14.5	12.6	4.2	1.3	0.6	2.33
Cape Coral, FL	28.3	44.7	11.6	8.8	4.4	1.5	0.7	2.44
Cedar Rapids, IA	29.8	37.2	13.8	11.3	5.4	1.4	1.1	2.38
Charleston, SC	29.3	36.3	15.3	11.8	5.0	1.6	0.7	2.45
Charlotte, NC	28.0	34.2	15.9	13.2	5.6	1.9	1.1	2.55
Chicago, IL	29.9	31.0	15.4	13.5	6.4	2.3	1.5	2.55
Cincinnati, OH	29.7	34.2	14.5	12.8	5.6	2.1	1.2	2.46
Clarksville, TN	26.0	33.6	17.5	12.8	5.8	2.4	1.9	2.63
Cleveland, OH	35.3	33.7	13.6	10.5	4.4	1.6	0.9	2.29
College Station, TX	30.3	32.8	14.7	13.5	5.3	2.3	1.1	2.48
Colorado Springs, CO	24.8	36.1	16.2	13.0	6.1	2.4	1.4	2.51
Columbia, MO	31.1	36.1	13.7	12.2	5.0	1.2	0.8	2.37
Columbia, SC	30.6	34.0	15.5	11.9	5.2	1.9	0.9	2.42
Columbus, OH	29.4	33.6	15.1	12.7	5.8	2.2	1.2	2.46
Dallas, TX	25.9	30.9	16.4	14.7	7.5	2.9	1.7	2.73
Davenport, IA	31.5	35.8	13.6	11.3	5.3	1.8	0.8	2.32
Denver, CO	29.2	34.9	14.8	12.7	5.0	2.2	1.2	2.45
Des Moines, IA	29.6	33.9	14.0	12.8	6.4	2.1	1.1	2.44
Detroit, MI	31.9	32.8	15.0	11.9	5.3	1.9	1.2	2.46
Durham, NC	31.7	35.8	14.8	10.9	4.6	1.5	0.6	2.33
El Paso, TX	23.9	27.3	18.2	16.3	9.0	3.5	1.8	2.88
Eugene, OR	29.5	38.4	14.1	10.8	4.8	1.5	0.9	2.34
Fargo, ND	35.2	33.4	13.1	11.0	5.0	1.5	0.8	2.28
Fort Collins, CO	25.5	39.2	16.4	12.1	4.5	1.4	0.9	2.33
Fort Wayne, IN	29.7	34.7	13.4	11.7	6.1	2.7	1.6	2.48
Fort Worth, TX	25.9	30.9	16.4	14.7	7.5	2.9	1.7	2.73
Gainesville, FL	32.9	35.5	15.3	10.3	3.9	1.2	0.9	2.36
Green Bay, WI	29.3	37.6	13.1	12.1	5.2	1.8	0.8	2.38
Greensboro, NC	31.0	33.8	15.5	11.4	5.2	2.0	1.1	2.42
Honolulu, HI	24.9	30.8	16.7	13.1	6.8	3.5	4.1	2.88
Houston, TX	24.8	29.9	17.2	15.3	8.0	3.0	1.8	2.76
Huntsville, AL	29.4	36.4	15.1	12.1	4.8	1.5	0.6	2.42
Indianapolis, IN	29.6	33.8	14.7	12.7	6.1	1.9	1.1	2.50
Jacksonville, FL	27.8	35.6	16.4	11.8	5.5	1.9	1.0	2.51
Kansas City, MO	29.8	34.3	14.1	12.6	5.8	2.3	1.2	2.46
Lafayette, LA	29.1	33.5	16.1	12.4	5.4	2.1	1.2	2.49
Las Vegas, NV	28.0	32.7	15.8	12.3	6.8	2.8	1.8	2.68
Lexington, KY	31.6	34.5	15.2	11.6	4.3	1.9	0.9	2.35
Lincoln, NE	30.8	35.3	13.6	11.4	5.2	2.5	1.1	2.35
Little Rock, AR	31.7	34.1	15.2	11.0	5.3	1.7	1.0	2.41
Los Angeles, CA	25.1	29.0	17.0	15.1	7.7	3.2	2.8	2.86
Louisville, KY	30.6	34.4	15.5	11.8	5.1	1.8	0.9	2.43
Madison, WI	32.9	36.5	13.2	11.1	4.3	1.4	0.7	2.25
Manchester, NH	27.2	35.8	16.5	13.1	4.9	1.7	0.8	2.48

Table continued on following page.

Metro Area	Persons in Household (%)							Average Household Size
	One	Two	Three	Four	Five	Six	Seven or More	
McAllen, TX	18.5	25.1	16.9	17.1	12.2	5.6	4.5	3.30
Memphis, TN	31.2	31.7	16.4	11.7	5.5	2.0	1.5	2.55
Miami, FL	27.9	32.2	17.3	13.3	6.0	2.1	1.3	2.62
Midland, TX	28.9	27.1	15.8	16.0	8.2	2.7	1.4	2.53
Milwaukee, WI	33.0	34.4	13.7	11.3	5.1	1.7	0.9	2.37
Minneapolis, MN	28.9	34.2	14.3	13.3	5.8	2.1	1.4	2.49
Nashville, TN	28.0	34.5	16.1	12.7	5.7	1.9	1.1	2.49
New Orleans, LA	36.4	30.5	15.4	10.8	4.4	1.6	0.9	2.44
New York, NY	28.6	29.6	16.8	14.1	6.3	2.6	1.9	2.63
Oklahoma City, OK	29.0	33.1	15.7	12.4	6.3	2.3	1.2	2.51
Omaha, NE	29.6	33.1	14.3	12.3	6.6	2.5	1.5	2.49
Orlando, FL	24.5	34.1	17.0	14.3	6.5	2.2	1.3	2.71
Philadelphia, PA	29.7	32.3	16.0	13.2	5.7	1.9	1.1	2.49
Phoenix, AZ	26.0	34.8	14.8	12.6	6.7	3.0	2.1	2.62
Pittsburgh, PA	34.1	35.8	13.7	10.6	4.1	1.2	0.6	2.25
Portland, OR	27.6	35.7	15.6	12.8	5.2	1.9	1.2	2.47
Providence, RI	29.5	33.7	16.3	12.9	5.1	1.6	0.9	2.41
Provo, UT	12.3	29.0	16.2	16.6	12.5	8.1	5.3	3.40
Raleigh, NC	25.9	34.7	16.1	14.5	6.0	1.9	0.9	2.57
Reno, NV	27.5	35.2	15.5	12.9	5.6	2.1	1.3	2.49
Richmond, VA	29.5	34.7	15.8	12.2	5.1	1.8	1.0	2.47
Rochester, MN	27.9	36.9	13.2	13.3	5.9	1.8	1.1	2.42
Sacramento, CA	25.1	32.7	16.0	14.5	7.1	2.7	2.0	2.70
Saint Louis, MO	31.3	34.4	14.6	11.9	5.2	1.6	0.9	2.38
Saint Paul, MN	28.9	34.2	14.3	13.3	5.8	2.1	1.4	2.49
Salem, OR	25.5	33.8	15.8	12.5	6.7	3.3	2.3	2.67
Salt Lake City, UT	24.0	31.1	15.7	13.9	7.9	4.4	3.0	2.83
San Antonio, TX	26.8	31.1	16.3	13.8	7.3	2.8	1.9	2.71
San Diego, CA	24.5	33.0	16.7	14.6	6.7	2.6	1.8	2.74
San Francisco, CA	27.2	31.8	16.7	14.5	5.9	2.3	1.6	2.63
San Jose, CA	21.4	31.1	18.8	17.2	6.9	2.6	2.1	2.86
Santa Rosa, CA	27.5	35.1	15.1	13.5	5.5	2.0	1.2	2.50
Savannah, GA	28.1	36.4	15.7	12.1	5.2	1.5	1.1	2.52
Seattle, WA	28.0	34.0	15.8	13.6	5.4	1.9	1.3	2.49
Sioux Falls, SD	30.0	34.4	13.6	11.4	7.3	2.1	1.2	2.41
Tampa, FL	30.8	36.3	15.0	10.9	4.6	1.6	0.8	2.44
Tucson, AZ	31.8	35.4	13.2	11.1	5.1	2.3	1.2	2.37
Tulsa, OK	29.2	33.6	15.2	12.3	5.9	2.5	1.4	2.53
Virginia Beach, VA	28.6	34.6	16.5	12.2	5.5	1.9	0.9	2.46
Washington, DC	28.6	30.4	15.9	14.3	6.5	2.6	1.7	2.62
Wichita, KS	30.1	33.6	14.0	11.7	6.2	2.8	1.7	2.52
Wilmington, NC	29.9	42.0	14.0	8.9	3.6	1.2	0.4	2.26
Winston-Salem, NC	30.3	35.6	15.4	11.1	4.7	2.0	0.9	2.43
U.S.	28.5	33.8	15.4	12.7	5.9	2.3	1.4	2.54

Note: Figures cover the Metropolitan Statistical Area (MSA)
Source: U.S. Census Bureau, 2019-2023 American Community Survey 5-Year Estimates

Household Relationships: City

City	House-holder	Opposite-sex Spouse	Same-sex Spouse	Opposite-sex Unmarried Partner	Same-sex Unmarried Partner	Child[1]	Grand-child	Other Relatives	Non-relatives
Albuquerque, NM	42.1	15.1	0.3	3.4	0.3	27.0	2.5	4.6	3.2
Anchorage, AK	37.5	17.0	0.2	3.0	0.2	28.3	1.9	4.6	4.2
Ann Arbor, MI	40.3	13.3	0.3	2.4	0.2	17.1	0.5	1.6	11.5
Athens, GA	40.1	11.6	0.2	2.7	0.2	20.8	2.0	3.7	10.7
Atlanta, GA	45.7	10.4	0.5	3.1	0.6	20.7	2.1	3.9	5.9
Austin, TX	42.7	14.5	0.4	3.6	0.4	23.2	1.5	4.1	6.4
Baltimore, MD	42.9	9.6	0.3	3.3	0.3	24.9	3.7	5.8	6.1
Billings, MT	42.2	17.7	0.2	3.1	0.1	26.0	1.7	2.5	3.5
Boise City, ID	41.4	17.8	0.2	3.2	0.2	24.7	1.3	2.9	5.4
Boston, MA	41.4	10.4	0.5	3.1	0.4	20.6	1.7	5.3	9.7
Boulder, CO	40.2	13.0	0.3	3.1	0.2	16.4	0.3	1.6	12.3
Cape Coral, FL	39.5	21.2	0.3	3.2	0.1	25.5	2.1	4.8	2.8
Cedar Rapids, IA	42.2	16.7	0.2	3.5	0.2	26.8	1.3	2.9	3.4
Charleston, SC	45.0	17.0	0.3	3.1	0.2	21.8	1.4	2.7	5.3
Charlotte, NC	40.6	15.2	0.2	2.8	0.2	28.0	2.1	4.9	4.2
Chicago, IL	41.6	12.2	0.3	3.0	0.3	26.6	3.0	6.4	4.8
Cincinnati, OH	45.1	10.2	0.3	3.4	0.3	24.6	2.2	3.4	5.3
Clarksville, TN	36.6	16.9	0.2	2.5	0.1	31.2	2.4	3.9	3.5
Cleveland, OH	45.0	8.5	0.2	3.5	0.3	27.0	3.3	5.0	3.8
College Station, TX	35.2	11.2	0.2	1.8	0.1	19.7	0.7	2.7	13.7
Colorado Springs, CO	39.7	18.3	0.3	2.6	0.2	27.5	1.9	3.6	4.3
Columbia, MO	40.5	14.1	0.2	2.8	0.2	22.4	1.0	2.5	7.8
Columbia, SC	39.2	10.5	0.2	2.1	0.2	19.5	1.6	2.8	5.8
Columbus, OH	42.2	12.9	0.3	3.6	0.3	26.2	2.1	4.4	5.2
Dallas, TX	40.1	13.4	0.4	2.6	0.3	28.6	3.2	6.2	4.0
Davenport, IA	41.9	15.9	0.2	3.7	0.2	27.0	2.0	3.0	3.2
Denver, CO	44.4	14.0	0.5	4.1	0.4	22.3	1.9	4.4	5.9
Des Moines, IA	41.1	14.2	0.3	3.5	0.2	27.9	2.0	4.4	3.9
Detroit, MI	39.8	7.3	0.1	2.9	0.2	32.0	4.8	7.3	3.9
Durham, NC	42.0	14.8	0.4	2.9	0.3	24.6	1.8	4.4	4.6
El Paso, TX	35.9	15.8	0.2	1.8	0.1	32.7	3.9	6.4	2.0
Eugene, OR	41.6	14.7	0.3	3.8	0.3	20.7	1.1	2.7	8.3
Fargo, ND	44.5	15.5	0.1	3.6	0.2	23.5	0.7	2.5	5.0
Fort Collins, CO	39.9	16.0	0.2	3.3	0.2	22.1	0.9	2.4	9.0
Fort Wayne, IN	40.7	15.6	0.2	3.1	0.2	29.7	2.0	3.4	3.0
Fort Worth, TX	35.2	15.8	0.2	2.1	0.1	33.0	3.1	5.6	3.0
Gainesville, FL	41.0	9.4	0.3	3.0	0.3	17.0	1.5	3.4	12.5
Green Bay, WI	40.7	15.2	0.2	4.0	0.2	28.6	1.6	3.4	3.0
Greensboro, NC	40.9	13.6	0.2	2.6	0.2	26.4	2.0	4.1	3.6
Honolulu, HI	39.1	15.0	0.3	2.4	0.2	22.2	3.1	9.1	5.6
Houston, TX	38.9	14.0	0.3	2.4	0.2	29.5	2.9	6.5	3.6
Huntsville, AL	42.8	16.5	0.2	2.2	0.2	25.1	2.1	3.5	3.1
Indianapolis, IN	40.7	14.0	0.3	3.4	0.3	28.6	2.5	4.5	3.9
Jacksonville, FL	39.9	15.6	0.2	2.8	0.2	27.7	2.8	4.9	3.6
Kansas City, MO	42.6	14.5	0.3	3.3	0.3	27.2	2.3	4.0	3.8
Lafayette, LA	43.0	15.3	0.2	2.8	0.2	27.0	2.3	3.5	3.8
Las Vegas, NV	37.5	15.2	0.3	2.9	0.2	29.3	2.7	6.7	4.3
Lexington, KY	41.7	16.0	0.3	2.9	0.3	25.3	1.6	3.4	4.4
Lincoln, NE	40.1	16.9	0.2	2.8	0.1	26.6	1.1	2.7	4.6
Little Rock, AR	43.5	14.5	0.3	2.4	0.3	27.1	2.3	3.9	3.1
Los Angeles, CA	36.2	13.1	0.3	2.8	0.3	26.5	2.8	9.0	6.3
Louisville, KY	40.0	18.0	0.2	2.9	0.2	28.8	2.6	4.2	2.7
Madison, WI	44.8	14.5	0.4	3.8	0.3	19.7	0.7	2.4	8.2
Manchester, NH	42.5	14.9	0.3	4.3	0.2	24.3	1.6	4.3	4.7
McAllen, TX	34.3	16.0	0.1	1.7	0.1	34.6	3.5	6.8	2.0

Table continued on following page.

City	House-holder	Opposite-sex Spouse	Same-sex Spouse	Opposite-sex Unmarried Partner	Same-sex Unmarried Partner	Child[1]	Grand-child	Other Relatives	Non-relatives
Memphis, TN	40.4	10.9	0.2	2.7	0.2	29.7	4.3	6.1	3.7
Miami, FL	42.4	12.6	0.5	3.3	0.3	22.5	2.4	8.7	5.8
Midland, TX	36.4	18.5	0.1	2.1	0.1	31.9	3.0	4.2	2.5
Milwaukee, WI	40.8	10.2	0.2	3.6	0.2	30.2	2.7	4.9	4.4
Minneapolis, MN	43.7	12.0	0.6	3.9	0.5	22.1	1.1	3.5	8.0
Nashville, TN	42.1	14.3	0.3	3.0	0.3	24.0	1.9	4.7	5.7
New Orleans, LA	43.0	11.0	0.3	3.1	0.4	26.1	3.2	4.6	4.3
New York, NY	38.3	12.7	0.3	2.2	0.2	27.6	2.5	8.3	5.3
Oklahoma City, OK	39.4	16.6	0.2	2.6	0.2	29.4	2.3	4.3	3.1
Omaha, NE	39.8	16.0	0.2	2.8	0.2	29.6	1.8	3.7	3.6
Orlando, FL	41.7	13.7	0.5	3.5	0.4	26.1	2.0	5.9	5.0
Philadelphia, PA	41.0	10.9	0.3	3.1	0.3	26.8	3.6	5.9	5.2
Phoenix, AZ	36.3	14.4	0.3	3.1	0.3	30.2	2.9	6.6	4.2
Pittsburgh, PA	46.1	11.5	0.3	3.6	0.4	19.3	1.7	3.1	6.7
Portland, OR	43.2	14.9	0.7	4.4	0.6	21.2	1.1	3.7	7.2
Providence, RI	36.5	10.5	0.3	2.9	0.3	27.3	1.9	5.7	6.1
Provo, UT	29.6	15.9	0.1	0.6	0.0	25.7	1.6	4.0	12.7
Raleigh, NC	41.8	15.1	0.2	2.9	0.2	25.5	1.4	3.9	5.0
Reno, NV	41.1	15.2	0.3	3.8	0.2	24.8	1.7	4.7	5.7
Richmond, VA	45.2	10.4	0.4	4.0	0.4	20.8	2.1	4.3	7.4
Rochester, MN	41.1	18.5	0.2	2.8	0.1	27.8	0.9	2.8	3.3
Sacramento, CA	36.7	13.5	0.4	3.0	0.3	28.0	2.6	7.5	4.7
Saint Louis, MO	48.0	10.3	0.4	3.7	0.4	22.5	2.6	4.0	4.3
Saint Paul, MN	38.7	12.7	0.4	3.3	0.3	28.8	1.7	5.6	4.8
Salem, OR	36.6	16.0	0.2	3.1	0.2	28.1	1.9	4.6	4.2
Salt Lake City, UT	42.3	13.9	0.5	3.4	0.4	22.1	1.7	4.2	7.6
San Antonio, TX	37.5	14.7	0.3	2.7	0.2	30.3	3.8	5.5	3.2
San Diego, CA	37.2	15.7	0.4	2.6	0.3	25.0	2.0	6.2	6.1
San Francisco, CA	42.6	13.6	0.8	3.3	0.6	17.6	1.3	6.8	10.3
San Jose, CA	32.4	17.1	0.2	1.9	0.1	28.6	2.3	9.8	6.1
Santa Rosa, CA	37.6	16.2	0.4	3.0	0.2	27.3	1.8	6.2	5.5
Savannah, GA	39.9	11.2	0.3	2.7	0.3	24.9	3.2	4.4	5.0
Seattle, WA	46.9	15.2	0.8	4.3	0.6	17.5	0.7	2.8	7.3
Sioux Falls, SD	40.7	18.0	0.1	3.2	0.1	28.4	1.1	2.7	3.1
Tampa, FL	40.9	13.8	0.3	3.2	0.3	25.8	2.3	4.9	4.5
Tucson, AZ	41.1	13.3	0.3	3.3	0.3	25.4	2.8	4.8	4.5
Tulsa, OK	41.6	14.8	0.2	2.9	0.2	27.8	2.3	4.3	3.4
Virginia Beach, VA	38.8	18.6	0.2	2.4	0.1	28.7	2.2	4.0	3.5
Washington, DC	45.3	10.3	0.6	3.1	0.5	20.4	2.4	4.2	7.1
Wichita, KS	40.0	16.4	0.2	2.7	0.2	29.1	2.2	3.7	3.1
Wilmington, NC	45.7	14.9	0.3	3.4	0.3	21.2	1.5	3.0	5.9
Winston-Salem, NC	40.9	14.6	0.2	2.5	0.2	28.1	2.4	4.3	2.7
U.S.	38.3	17.5	0.2	2.5	0.2	28.3	2.4	4.8	3.4

Note: Figures are percent of the total population; (1) Includes biological, adopted, and stepchildren of the householder
Source: U.S. Census Bureau, 2020 Census

Household Relationships: Metro Area

Metro Area	House-holder	Opposite-sex Spouse	Same-sex Spouse	Opposite-sex Unmarried Partner	Same-sex Unmarried Partner	Child[1]	Grand-child	Other Relatives	Non-relatives
Albuquerque, NM	40.1	16.3	0.3	3.1	0.3	27.7	3.1	4.6	2.9
Anchorage, AK	37.1	17.6	0.2	2.9	0.1	29.1	1.9	4.2	4.0
Ann Arbor, MI	39.7	17.0	0.3	2.4	0.2	24.3	1.3	2.5	5.8
Athens, GA	38.6	15.6	0.2	2.3	0.2	25.1	2.3	3.7	7.3
Atlanta, GA	37.1	16.7	0.2	2.1	0.2	30.4	2.7	5.7	3.5
Austin, TX	38.6	17.3	0.3	2.7	0.3	27.8	1.9	4.4	4.6
Baltimore, MD	38.7	16.8	0.2	2.4	0.2	28.7	2.5	4.8	3.5
Billings, MT	41.3	19.5	0.1	2.8	0.1	26.5	1.8	2.5	3.1
Boise City, ID	36.6	19.5	0.2	2.5	0.1	29.7	1.9	3.5	3.8
Boston, MA	38.7	17.4	0.3	2.5	0.2	27.1	1.6	4.5	4.4
Boulder, CO	40.1	18.0	0.3	2.8	0.2	23.8	1.0	2.6	6.8
Cape Coral, FL	41.8	20.9	0.3	3.0	0.2	22.4	1.8	4.4	3.3
Cedar Rapids, IA	40.9	19.3	0.1	3.0	0.1	27.9	1.2	2.3	2.5
Charleston, SC	39.9	18.1	0.2	2.4	0.1	27.3	2.6	3.8	3.5
Charlotte, NC	38.9	18.3	0.2	2.4	0.2	29.2	2.4	4.2	2.8
Chicago, IL	38.2	17.1	0.2	2.3	0.1	30.3	2.4	5.1	2.8
Cincinnati, OH	39.5	18.1	0.2	2.7	0.1	28.9	2.3	3.2	2.9
Clarksville, TN	36.7	18.2	0.2	2.2	0.1	30.5	2.5	3.6	3.0
Cleveland, OH	42.5	17.1	0.1	2.7	0.1	27.7	2.1	3.3	2.3
College Station, TX	36.9	14.6	0.1	2.0	0.1	24.7	1.9	3.5	8.3
Colorado Springs, CO	37.5	19.3	0.2	2.2	0.1	28.5	2.0	3.6	3.8
Columbia, MO	39.8	16.5	0.2	2.8	0.2	24.9	1.4	2.5	5.7
Columbia, SC	39.9	17.0	0.2	2.1	0.2	27.5	2.7	3.8	3.0
Columbus, OH	39.4	17.4	0.2	2.9	0.2	28.5	2.0	3.5	3.3
Dallas, TX	36.2	17.6	0.2	2.0	0.2	31.7	2.7	5.5	2.9
Davenport, IA	41.4	18.8	0.2	2.9	0.1	27.9	1.8	2.5	2.2
Denver, CO	39.4	17.9	0.3	2.9	0.2	27.4	1.9	4.4	4.3
Des Moines, IA	39.6	19.2	0.2	2.7	0.1	29.6	1.3	2.8	2.6
Detroit, MI	40.1	17.2	0.1	2.5	0.1	30.1	2.3	4.2	2.4
Durham, NC	40.3	17.2	0.3	2.5	0.2	25.1	1.9	3.8	3.9
El Paso, TX	34.2	15.8	0.2	1.7	0.1	33.5	4.2	6.5	1.8
Eugene, OR	40.9	17.0	0.3	3.7	0.2	22.7	1.8	3.5	6.6
Fargo, ND	41.5	17.7	0.1	3.2	0.1	27.0	0.7	2.2	3.9
Fort Collins, CO	40.2	19.4	0.2	2.8	0.2	24.0	1.2	2.7	6.0
Fort Wayne, IN	39.5	18.0	0.2	2.7	0.1	30.5	1.9	2.9	2.5
Fort Worth, TX	36.2	17.6	0.2	2.0	0.2	31.7	2.7	5.5	2.9
Gainesville, FL	40.4	14.9	0.2	2.8	0.2	22.9	2.2	3.9	6.9
Green Bay, WI	40.5	19.8	0.1	3.3	0.1	28.1	1.2	2.2	2.2
Greensboro, NC	40.2	17.1	0.2	2.4	0.2	27.4	2.3	3.9	2.6
Honolulu, HI	33.1	16.3	0.2	1.9	0.1	26.2	4.5	9.2	4.9
Houston, TX	35.2	17.1	0.2	2.0	0.1	32.7	2.8	6.1	2.6
Huntsville, AL	40.1	19.3	0.1	1.9	0.1	27.8	2.3	3.4	2.3
Indianapolis, IN	39.2	17.9	0.2	2.8	0.2	29.6	2.1	3.5	2.8
Jacksonville, FL	39.1	17.9	0.2	2.6	0.2	28.0	2.6	4.3	3.2
Kansas City, MO	39.6	18.4	0.2	2.6	0.2	29.4	2.0	3.3	2.7
Lafayette, LA	39.5	17.1	0.2	2.7	0.2	30.4	2.9	3.5	2.5
Las Vegas, NV	37.3	15.5	0.3	3.0	0.2	28.7	2.6	7.0	4.4
Lexington, KY	40.5	17.4	0.2	2.8	0.2	26.5	2.0	3.4	3.7
Lincoln, NE	39.5	17.9	0.2	2.6	0.1	27.2	1.1	2.6	4.1
Little Rock, AR	40.8	17.7	0.2	2.3	0.2	27.9	2.6	3.6	2.7
Los Angeles, CA	34.0	15.2	0.2	2.3	0.2	29.0	3.0	9.1	5.1
Louisville, KY	40.5	17.7	0.2	2.8	0.2	27.6	2.5	3.6	2.9
Madison, WI	42.2	18.6	0.3	3.3	0.2	25.0	0.8	2.1	4.5
Manchester, NH	39.7	19.2	0.3	3.2	0.1	27.2	1.6	3.5	3.2
McAllen, TX	29.7	15.0	0.1	1.6	0.1	38.3	5.2	7.5	1.6

Table continued on following page.

Metro Area	House-holder	Opposite-sex Spouse	Same-sex Spouse	Opposite-sex Unmarried Partner	Same-sex Unmarried Partner	Child[1]	Grand-child	Other Relatives	Non-relatives
Memphis, TN	38.6	15.1	0.1	2.2	0.1	30.4	3.9	5.2	2.7
Miami, FL	38.0	16.0	0.3	2.6	0.2	27.6	2.5	7.8	3.7
Midland, TX	35.8	18.6	0.1	2.0	0.1	32.3	3.2	4.4	2.6
Milwaukee, WI	41.3	17.5	0.2	2.9	0.2	28.7	1.6	3.1	2.7
Minneapolis, MN	38.9	18.7	0.2	2.8	0.2	29.4	1.2	3.3	3.3
Nashville, TN	38.8	18.2	0.2	2.4	0.2	28.1	2.2	4.1	3.8
New Orleans, LA	40.3	15.3	0.2	2.7	0.2	28.8	3.1	4.6	2.9
New York, NY	36.8	15.8	0.2	2.0	0.2	29.7	2.1	7.1	4.1
Oklahoma City, OK	38.8	17.7	0.2	2.4	0.2	29.0	2.3	3.8	3.1
Omaha, NE	38.8	18.4	0.2	2.6	0.1	30.6	1.6	3.1	2.8
Orlando, FL	37.0	17.0	0.3	2.7	0.2	28.4	2.4	6.0	4.2
Philadelphia, PA	38.7	16.9	0.2	2.5	0.2	29.2	2.5	4.4	3.0
Phoenix, AZ	36.9	17.2	0.2	2.8	0.2	29.0	2.5	5.4	3.7
Pittsburgh, PA	43.2	19.0	0.2	2.8	0.2	25.6	1.6	2.6	2.4
Portland, OR	39.0	18.1	0.4	3.2	0.3	26.7	1.6	4.2	4.9
Providence, RI	40.0	16.9	0.2	3.0	0.2	27.2	1.9	4.1	3.0
Provo, UT	28.0	18.8	0.1	0.7	0.0	39.0	2.1	4.0	4.8
Raleigh, NC	38.4	19.2	0.2	2.2	0.2	30.0	1.5	3.7	3.0
Reno, NV	39.5	17.2	0.2	3.4	0.2	26.1	2.1	5.0	4.9
Richmond, VA	39.5	17.3	0.2	2.5	0.2	27.7	2.4	4.0	3.3
Rochester, MN	40.1	20.5	0.1	2.7	0.1	28.9	1.0	2.2	2.5
Sacramento, CA	36.2	17.1	0.3	2.4	0.2	29.4	2.2	6.0	4.2
Saint Louis, MO	40.8	18.2	0.2	2.6	0.2	28.5	2.2	3.0	2.4
Saint Paul, MN	38.9	18.7	0.2	2.8	0.2	29.4	1.2	3.3	3.3
Salem, OR	35.7	17.6	0.2	2.7	0.1	29.3	2.3	5.0	4.1
Salt Lake City, UT	34.0	17.4	0.3	2.1	0.2	32.4	2.5	5.3	4.4
San Antonio, TX	36.2	16.9	0.2	2.3	0.2	31.0	3.5	5.1	2.8
San Diego, CA	35.1	16.9	0.3	2.3	0.2	27.8	2.3	6.6	5.1
San Francisco, CA	36.7	17.0	0.4	2.3	0.3	26.3	1.8	6.9	5.9
San Jose, CA	33.8	18.4	0.2	1.8	0.1	28.3	1.9	7.9	5.6
Santa Rosa, CA	38.4	17.6	0.4	2.9	0.2	26.1	1.9	5.2	5.5
Savannah, GA	38.7	16.6	0.2	2.4	0.2	28.0	2.8	4.1	3.4
Seattle, WA	38.9	18.3	0.3	2.9	0.2	26.7	1.5	4.6	4.7
Sioux Falls, SD	39.5	19.4	0.1	2.9	0.1	29.8	1.1	2.3	2.6
Tampa, FL	41.2	17.6	0.3	3.1	0.2	25.5	2.2	4.6	3.4
Tucson, AZ	40.9	17.2	0.3	2.9	0.2	25.5	2.6	4.4	3.4
Tulsa, OK	39.1	18.2	0.2	2.4	0.1	29.0	2.6	3.9	2.7
Virginia Beach, VA	39.0	17.4	0.2	2.3	0.1	27.7	2.5	4.0	3.3
Washington, DC	37.0	17.3	0.3	2.0	0.2	29.3	2.0	5.9	4.4
Wichita, KS	39.0	18.2	0.1	2.4	0.1	29.8	2.1	3.2	2.6
Wilmington, NC	42.3	18.7	0.2	2.9	0.2	24.4	1.9	3.1	3.9
Winston-Salem, NC	40.9	18.6	0.2	2.3	0.1	27.5	2.4	3.7	2.2
U.S.	38.3	17.5	0.2	2.5	0.2	28.3	2.4	4.8	3.4

Note: Figures are percent of the total population; Figures cover the Metropolitan Statistical Area (MSA); (1) Includes biological, adopted, and stepchildren of the householder
Source: U.S. Census Bureau, 2020 Census

Age: City

City	Percent of Population									Median Age
	Under Age 5	Age 5–19	Age 20–34	Age 35–44	Age 45–54	Age 55–64	Age 65–74	Age 75–84	Age 85+	
Albuquerque, NM	5.1	18.0	21.5	13.9	11.7	12.5	10.4	4.7	2.1	38.7
Anchorage, AK	6.5	19.6	24.0	14.2	11.6	11.6	8.2	3.4	0.9	34.9
Ann Arbor, MI	3.8	18.7	38.6	10.1	8.2	7.9	7.3	4.0	1.4	27.7
Athens, GA	4.8	19.9	33.9	11.5	9.1	8.9	7.4	3.5	1.1	29.2
Atlanta, GA	5.1	15.7	31.0	14.7	11.4	9.8	7.5	3.5	1.3	34.0
Austin, TX	5.4	15.7	29.9	17.3	12.0	9.6	6.4	2.6	1.1	34.5
Baltimore, MD	6.1	17.5	24.5	13.7	10.7	12.5	9.3	4.0	1.6	36.1
Billings, MT	5.9	18.9	21.1	14.0	10.2	11.6	10.3	5.4	2.6	38.1
Boise City, ID	4.4	17.8	23.2	14.2	12.6	12.5	9.2	4.6	1.6	38.2
Boston, MA	4.6	15.3	33.4	13.3	10.2	10.5	7.6	3.4	1.7	33.2
Boulder, CO	2.0	20.2	36.8	10.3	10.0	8.4	7.4	3.2	1.8	28.8
Cape Coral, FL	4.5	14.5	15.7	10.8	13.4	15.9	14.6	7.9	2.5	48.7
Cedar Rapids, IA	5.7	18.7	22.7	13.5	11.4	11.8	9.3	4.7	2.3	36.9
Charleston, SC	5.1	15.6	27.7	14.1	10.2	11.3	9.5	4.5	2.1	36.1
Charlotte, NC	6.5	19.1	25.5	14.8	12.8	10.7	6.7	2.8	1.2	34.4
Chicago, IL	5.6	16.6	26.7	14.6	11.8	11.2	8.1	3.9	1.7	35.7
Cincinnati, OH	6.3	18.7	28.1	12.5	10.0	11.1	8.2	3.4	1.7	33.0
Clarksville, TN	8.5	21.0	29.2	14.0	9.6	9.0	5.8	2.3	0.7	30.4
Cleveland, OH	5.6	18.2	24.4	12.2	11.2	13.4	9.3	4.1	1.6	36.3
College Station, TX	4.8	25.3	40.0	10.3	6.8	6.2	4.2	1.9	0.6	22.9
Colorado Springs, CO	5.9	18.5	24.7	13.7	11.2	11.2	8.7	4.3	1.7	35.6
Columbia, MO	5.4	20.7	32.4	12.5	8.9	8.8	6.4	3.3	1.6	29.2
Columbia, SC	5.4	21.9	32.9	10.9	9.5	8.4	6.8	3.2	1.0	28.7
Columbus, OH	6.7	18.6	28.6	13.8	10.9	10.5	6.9	2.9	1.2	33.0
Dallas, TX	7.0	19.5	26.0	13.8	11.6	10.7	7.0	3.1	1.3	33.4
Davenport, IA	6.1	17.9	22.1	13.4	11.1	12.9	9.8	4.6	2.2	37.8
Denver, CO	5.5	14.8	29.4	16.9	11.7	9.5	7.6	3.3	1.4	35.2
Des Moines, IA	6.8	19.2	24.7	13.0	11.8	11.9	7.7	3.3	1.5	34.6
Detroit, MI	6.8	20.8	22.2	11.8	11.8	11.8	9.0	4.1	1.7	35.1
Durham, NC	6.1	17.6	26.8	14.3	11.5	10.7	8.1	3.5	1.4	34.8
El Paso, TX	6.5	21.6	23.2	12.5	11.5	10.8	8.1	4.1	1.8	34.1
Eugene, OR	3.9	17.1	28.5	12.4	10.4	10.1	10.4	5.2	2.1	35.4
Fargo, ND	6.0	18.4	30.1	12.8	9.0	10.1	7.9	3.9	1.8	32.2
Fort Collins, CO	3.9	18.9	33.6	12.6	9.4	9.4	7.3	3.3	1.6	30.6
Fort Wayne, IN	7.0	20.0	22.9	12.5	11.4	11.3	8.8	4.1	2.0	35.0
Fort Worth, TX	7.3	22.1	23.3	14.4	12.0	10.3	6.5	2.9	1.0	33.4
Gainesville, FL	3.7	19.7	40.6	9.6	7.3	7.3	6.7	3.3	1.7	26.5
Green Bay, WI	6.5	20.5	21.8	13.5	11.6	12.2	8.3	3.7	1.7	35.7
Greensboro, NC	5.7	21.4	24.2	12.4	11.6	10.8	8.2	3.9	1.9	34.1
Honolulu, HI	4.5	13.9	20.6	13.8	12.8	12.7	11.5	6.5	3.6	42.9
Houston, TX	6.7	19.4	25.1	14.5	11.7	10.6	7.3	3.4	1.3	34.3
Huntsville, AL	5.6	17.5	24.7	12.3	10.9	12.5	9.2	5.2	2.1	36.4
Indianapolis, IN	7.0	20.5	23.8	13.2	11.2	11.4	8.1	3.3	1.5	34.1
Jacksonville, FL	6.5	18.7	22.6	13.4	11.8	12.5	9.0	4.1	1.6	36.4
Kansas City, MO	6.2	18.7	24.1	13.7	11.4	11.8	8.8	3.6	1.7	35.7
Lafayette, LA	6.1	18.0	22.9	12.8	10.2	12.9	10.9	4.5	1.8	37.1
Las Vegas, NV	5.8	19.1	20.4	13.7	13.0	12.4	9.3	4.8	1.5	38.5
Lexington, KY	5.7	18.8	25.1	13.1	11.6	11.2	8.8	4.2	1.4	35.2
Lincoln, NE	5.9	20.0	26.1	12.8	10.4	10.4	8.8	4.0	1.7	33.4
Little Rock, AR	6.7	19.9	21.8	13.4	12.1	11.0	9.2	4.0	2.0	36.4
Los Angeles, CA	5.2	16.8	24.8	14.8	13.0	11.6	8.1	3.8	1.9	36.9
Louisville, KY	6.2	18.8	21.1	13.1	12.1	12.8	9.9	4.5	1.6	37.7
Madison, WI	4.8	16.9	33.7	12.8	9.6	9.5	7.7	3.6	1.4	31.8
Manchester, NH	4.9	15.1	25.7	13.8	11.6	13.7	8.7	4.6	2.0	37.9

Table continued on following page.

City	Percent of Population									Median Age
	Under Age 5	Age 5–19	Age 20–34	Age 35–44	Age 45–54	Age 55–64	Age 65–74	Age 75–84	Age 85+	
McAllen, TX	7.0	23.3	21.2	13.3	12.4	9.4	8.1	3.8	1.5	34.0
Memphis, TN	7.2	20.2	23.7	12.1	11.1	11.6	8.9	3.9	1.3	34.3
Miami, FL	5.3	12.8	23.8	15.4	13.5	12.8	8.5	5.2	2.6	39.7
Midland, TX	8.8	22.6	24.9	14.7	9.6	8.9	6.0	2.9	1.6	31.6
Milwaukee, WI	6.9	22.2	25.1	13.0	10.6	10.4	7.4	3.0	1.4	32.2
Minneapolis, MN	5.7	17.1	30.9	14.9	10.7	9.9	7.0	2.7	1.1	33.0
Nashville, TN	6.6	16.9	27.6	14.5	11.2	10.8	7.9	3.4	1.2	34.4
New Orleans, LA	5.5	16.9	22.0	14.9	11.5	12.7	10.4	4.3	1.7	38.4
New York, NY	5.9	16.7	22.9	13.9	12.4	12.2	9.2	4.8	2.0	38.0
Oklahoma City, OK	6.8	20.5	22.6	14.2	11.4	11.1	8.3	3.8	1.2	35.0
Omaha, NE	6.8	20.5	22.4	13.6	11.2	11.4	8.7	3.9	1.5	35.3
Orlando, FL	6.2	16.8	26.7	16.5	12.4	10.2	6.6	3.2	1.3	35.1
Philadelphia, PA	6.1	18.4	25.5	13.4	10.9	11.6	8.6	4.1	1.6	35.1
Phoenix, AZ	6.1	20.7	23.4	14.1	12.5	11.2	7.4	3.2	1.2	34.8
Pittsburgh, PA	4.4	16.1	32.1	12.5	9.0	10.8	9.0	4.0	2.0	33.5
Portland, OR	4.3	14.5	24.5	18.0	13.8	10.7	8.8	3.9	1.5	38.6
Providence, RI	5.4	20.3	28.3	12.6	11.9	10.0	6.8	3.3	1.5	32.9
Provo, UT	5.8	20.1	48.3	8.2	5.7	5.3	3.7	1.9	0.9	23.7
Raleigh, NC	5.7	17.8	27.0	14.4	13.0	10.4	7.1	3.3	1.3	34.7
Reno, NV	5.3	17.2	23.9	13.8	11.0	12.3	10.1	4.6	1.6	37.3
Richmond, VA	5.9	15.4	29.6	13.5	10.1	11.9	8.7	3.5	1.4	34.5
Rochester, MN	6.8	18.9	22.4	14.1	10.3	11.5	8.8	4.9	2.3	36.4
Sacramento, CA	5.9	18.4	24.4	14.7	11.6	11.0	8.5	3.8	1.7	35.7
Saint Louis, MO	5.8	15.0	26.2	14.2	11.1	12.6	9.6	3.7	1.6	36.6
Saint Paul, MN	6.3	20.3	25.8	13.9	10.7	10.7	7.9	3.0	1.3	33.5
Salem, OR	5.9	20.2	22.9	13.6	11.4	10.8	8.9	4.7	1.7	35.7
Salt Lake City, UT	4.9	15.8	32.5	14.0	10.9	9.6	7.5	3.3	1.3	33.0
San Antonio, TX	6.3	20.5	23.7	13.8	11.8	10.7	7.9	3.7	1.6	34.6
San Diego, CA	5.3	16.6	26.4	14.7	12.0	10.9	8.2	4.3	1.7	36.0
San Francisco, CA	4.2	11.0	26.1	16.3	13.2	12.0	9.8	4.8	2.6	39.7
San Jose, CA	5.2	18.3	21.9	14.6	13.8	12.1	8.2	4.1	1.8	38.1
Santa Rosa, CA	4.9	17.9	19.3	14.1	12.9	12.1	11.2	5.1	2.4	40.5
Savannah, GA	6.1	18.1	28.1	11.9	10.3	11.4	8.1	4.5	1.4	33.7
Seattle, WA	4.2	12.2	32.7	16.3	12.2	9.7	7.7	3.4	1.6	35.5
Sioux Falls, SD	7.0	20.0	22.8	14.4	10.8	11.4	8.8	3.4	1.4	35.1
Tampa, FL	5.8	18.5	24.6	14.2	12.5	11.2	7.8	4.1	1.3	35.6
Tucson, AZ	5.3	18.5	26.7	12.2	10.4	11.0	9.0	4.8	2.0	34.6
Tulsa, OK	6.7	20.3	22.3	13.2	11.2	11.3	9.1	4.2	1.7	35.5
Virginia Beach, VA	6.0	18.3	22.1	14.1	11.7	12.6	9.2	4.5	1.6	37.4
Washington, DC	6.1	15.2	29.0	16.4	10.7	9.8	7.4	3.8	1.5	34.9
Wichita, KS	6.3	20.7	22.0	12.9	11.0	11.7	9.4	4.1	1.9	35.7
Wilmington, NC	4.3	17.0	25.9	11.7	10.8	12.6	10.2	5.3	2.3	37.5
Winston-Salem, NC	5.9	21.7	21.6	12.1	11.9	12.0	8.5	4.3	1.9	35.6
U.S.	5.7	19.1	20.2	13.1	12.3	12.8	10.0	4.9	1.9	38.7

Source: U.S. Census Bureau, 2019-2023 American Community Survey 5-Year Estimates

Age: Metro Area

Metro Area	Percent of Population									Median Age
	Under Age 5	Age 5–19	Age 20–34	Age 35–44	Age 45–54	Age 55–64	Age 65–74	Age 75–84	Age 85+	
Albuquerque, NM	5.0	18.5	20.0	13.4	11.8	12.9	11.1	5.1	2.0	39.6
Anchorage, AK	6.5	20.2	22.8	14.2	11.7	11.9	8.5	3.3	0.9	35.4
Ann Arbor, MI	4.6	19.1	26.4	11.9	11.3	11.3	9.2	4.5	1.5	34.8
Athens, GA	5.0	20.7	26.4	12.2	11.0	10.6	8.8	4.1	1.3	33.2
Atlanta, GA	5.9	20.6	20.5	13.9	13.7	12.2	8.2	3.7	1.2	37.0
Austin, TX	5.8	19.0	23.8	16.3	13.0	10.5	7.5	3.1	1.1	35.9
Baltimore, MD	5.8	18.8	19.8	13.5	12.3	13.4	9.7	4.7	1.9	38.9
Billings, MT	5.5	19.3	18.9	13.2	11.4	12.9	11.3	5.2	2.2	39.7
Boise City, ID	5.7	20.8	19.9	13.9	12.2	11.8	9.6	4.6	1.4	37.4
Boston, MA	5.1	17.2	21.6	13.2	12.6	13.5	9.8	4.7	2.1	39.3
Boulder, CO	4.0	19.1	23.8	12.6	12.6	12.2	9.8	4.2	1.8	37.5
Cape Coral, FL	4.5	14.9	15.7	10.6	11.3	14.2	15.4	10.2	3.3	49.3
Cedar Rapids, IA	5.8	19.3	19.1	13.2	12.1	13.1	10.1	5.1	2.2	39.3
Charleston, SC	5.9	18.2	21.0	14.1	12.0	12.6	10.0	4.5	1.6	38.1
Charlotte, NC	5.9	19.9	20.1	13.9	13.7	12.2	8.7	4.1	1.4	37.9
Chicago, IL	5.6	19.2	20.4	13.6	12.8	12.7	9.3	4.4	1.8	38.4
Cincinnati, OH	6.0	20.0	19.7	12.8	12.1	13.1	9.9	4.5	1.8	38.2
Clarksville, TN	8.1	21.2	25.9	13.1	10.3	10.0	7.1	3.3	1.1	31.9
Cleveland, OH	5.3	17.9	18.9	12.1	12.2	14.2	11.5	5.6	2.4	41.6
College Station, TX	5.6	22.3	30.9	11.6	9.2	9.0	6.9	3.0	1.4	28.4
Colorado Springs, CO	6.1	19.7	23.6	13.5	11.3	11.7	8.7	3.9	1.4	35.4
Columbia, MO	5.5	20.2	26.9	12.3	10.3	10.9	8.5	3.9	1.5	33.1
Columbia, SC	5.6	20.1	21.2	12.8	12.1	12.5	9.8	4.5	1.5	37.5
Columbus, OH	6.3	19.8	21.6	14.0	12.4	11.9	8.7	3.9	1.5	36.6
Dallas, TX	6.4	21.6	21.3	14.4	13.0	11.4	7.4	3.3	1.1	35.5
Davenport, IA	5.7	19.6	17.9	12.9	11.8	13.2	11.1	5.6	2.3	40.2
Denver, CO	5.5	18.2	22.7	15.4	12.8	11.6	8.6	3.8	1.4	37.2
Des Moines, IA	6.5	20.7	20.4	14.4	12.1	11.7	8.6	4.0	1.7	36.7
Detroit, MI	5.6	18.4	19.6	12.2	12.9	14.0	10.5	4.8	2.0	40.2
Durham, NC	5.3	18.5	22.6	13.0	12.2	12.1	10.0	4.7	1.7	37.6
El Paso, TX	6.8	22.6	23.1	12.8	11.4	10.4	7.6	3.7	1.6	33.3
Eugene, OR	4.4	16.8	22.2	12.5	11.2	12.5	12.5	5.8	2.2	40.2
Fargo, ND	6.5	20.6	26.1	13.8	10.0	9.9	7.7	3.6	1.7	33.0
Fort Collins, CO	4.5	18.2	24.9	12.9	11.0	11.7	10.5	4.5	1.8	36.6
Fort Wayne, IN	6.7	21.0	20.2	12.6	11.7	12.1	9.5	4.3	1.9	36.8
Fort Worth, TX	6.4	21.6	21.3	14.4	13.0	11.4	7.4	3.3	1.1	35.5
Gainesville, FL	4.9	18.6	27.4	11.4	10.1	11.2	9.9	4.7	2.0	34.3
Green Bay, WI	5.7	19.6	18.8	12.9	12.1	13.9	10.4	4.8	1.7	39.2
Greensboro, NC	5.6	20.1	19.7	12.0	12.9	13.0	9.9	4.8	1.9	38.9
Honolulu, HI	5.8	17.0	21.0	13.3	11.8	12.0	10.3	5.8	3.0	39.4
Houston, TX	6.7	22.0	20.8	14.5	12.8	11.1	7.7	3.3	1.1	35.3
Huntsville, AL	5.6	18.9	20.4	13.1	12.5	14.0	9.2	4.7	1.5	38.8
Indianapolis, IN	6.3	20.6	20.5	13.7	12.4	12.2	8.8	3.9	1.6	36.7
Jacksonville, FL	5.8	18.7	19.8	13.3	12.4	13.2	10.2	4.8	1.7	39.1
Kansas City, MO	6.1	20.1	19.9	13.7	12.2	12.6	9.4	4.4	1.8	37.8
Lafayette, LA	6.6	20.1	20.1	13.6	11.7	12.8	9.5	4.2	1.4	37.2
Las Vegas, NV	5.8	19.0	20.5	14.1	13.0	12.1	9.5	4.7	1.3	38.3
Lexington, KY	5.8	19.3	22.7	12.9	12.1	11.9	9.2	4.4	1.5	36.6
Lincoln, NE	5.9	20.6	24.1	12.8	10.7	10.9	9.3	4.0	1.7	34.4
Little Rock, AR	6.1	19.8	20.8	13.3	11.9	12.2	9.7	4.6	1.7	37.4
Los Angeles, CA	5.3	18.2	21.9	13.8	13.3	12.6	8.7	4.3	2.0	38.2
Louisville, KY	5.9	18.8	19.6	13.1	12.6	13.4	10.3	4.7	1.7	39.3
Madison, WI	5.2	18.3	23.8	13.6	11.6	12.0	9.6	4.2	1.7	36.9
Manchester, NH	5.1	17.1	20.1	12.9	13.2	15.0	10.1	4.8	1.8	41.0

Table continued on following page.

Metro Area	Percent of Population									Median Age
	Under Age 5	Age 5–19	Age 20–34	Age 35–44	Age 45–54	Age 55–64	Age 65–74	Age 75–84	Age 85+	
McAllen, TX	8.0	26.8	21.3	12.3	11.4	8.6	6.5	3.8	1.2	30.3
Memphis, TN	6.5	20.8	20.4	12.9	12.2	12.4	9.3	4.1	1.4	36.7
Miami, FL	5.4	16.9	18.5	13.2	13.6	13.4	10.2	6.1	2.7	41.9
Midland, TX	8.3	23.1	22.7	15.3	10.2	9.9	6.5	2.7	1.4	32.7
Milwaukee, WI	5.9	19.3	19.8	13.1	11.9	13.2	10.0	4.5	2.1	38.5
Minneapolis, MN	6.1	19.7	20.0	14.1	12.2	12.8	9.1	4.2	1.7	37.8
Nashville, TN	6.1	19.3	21.9	14.2	12.6	12.1	8.6	4.0	1.2	36.8
New Orleans, LA	5.9	18.1	20.2	13.9	11.8	13.3	10.5	4.5	1.9	38.9
New York, NY	5.8	17.9	20.4	13.3	12.9	13.2	9.6	4.9	2.1	39.4
Oklahoma City, OK	6.3	21.0	21.7	13.7	11.4	11.5	8.9	4.2	1.4	35.8
Omaha, NE	6.6	21.3	20.0	13.9	11.7	12.0	8.9	4.0	1.6	36.5
Orlando, FL	5.5	18.5	21.4	14.2	12.9	12.0	9.1	4.7	1.8	38.3
Philadelphia, PA	5.5	18.6	20.2	13.1	12.3	13.4	10.0	4.8	2.0	39.1
Phoenix, AZ	5.7	19.6	20.9	13.3	12.3	11.8	9.5	5.2	1.8	37.7
Pittsburgh, PA	4.9	16.6	18.7	12.4	12.0	14.5	12.4	5.9	2.8	42.8
Portland, OR	5.1	17.7	20.9	15.2	13.2	12.0	9.8	4.4	1.7	39.1
Providence, RI	5.0	17.6	20.1	12.6	12.6	14.2	10.6	5.2	2.2	40.6
Provo, UT	8.7	27.7	27.3	12.5	9.2	6.7	4.8	2.3	0.8	25.6
Raleigh, NC	5.9	20.4	20.2	14.8	14.1	11.9	8.0	3.6	1.3	37.5
Reno, NV	5.4	17.8	20.9	13.0	11.8	13.1	11.3	5.1	1.6	39.4
Richmond, VA	5.7	18.4	20.5	13.5	12.4	13.1	10.0	4.6	1.7	38.7
Rochester, MN	6.2	20.1	18.7	13.6	11.1	12.9	9.8	5.2	2.3	38.8
Sacramento, CA	5.6	19.3	20.3	13.8	12.2	12.3	9.7	4.6	2.0	38.3
Saint Louis, MO	5.6	18.8	19.2	13.2	12.0	13.8	10.5	4.9	2.0	39.8
Saint Paul, MN	6.1	19.7	20.0	14.1	12.2	12.8	9.1	4.2	1.7	37.8
Salem, OR	5.9	20.5	20.5	13.0	11.6	11.6	10.1	4.9	1.9	37.3
Salt Lake City, UT	6.6	22.3	23.3	14.9	11.7	9.9	7.2	3.1	1.2	33.7
San Antonio, TX	6.3	21.1	21.5	14.1	12.2	11.2	8.3	3.8	1.5	35.7
San Diego, CA	5.7	18.2	23.0	14.1	12.1	11.8	8.9	4.4	1.8	37.1
San Francisco, CA	5.1	16.5	20.6	15.0	13.5	12.7	9.6	4.8	2.1	40.0
San Jose, CA	5.4	18.3	22.1	14.4	13.4	12.1	8.1	4.3	2.0	37.8
Santa Rosa, CA	4.7	17.1	17.8	13.2	12.4	14.0	12.8	5.8	2.4	42.7
Savannah, GA	6.1	19.5	22.0	13.8	11.7	11.8	9.2	4.4	1.5	36.7
Seattle, WA	5.7	17.5	22.8	15.4	12.7	11.9	8.6	3.8	1.6	37.4
Sioux Falls, SD	6.9	21.1	20.4	14.3	11.2	11.8	9.1	3.7	1.5	36.1
Tampa, FL	5.0	16.7	18.7	12.9	12.8	13.7	11.4	6.4	2.4	42.2
Tucson, AZ	5.0	18.0	21.4	11.6	10.8	12.2	12.0	6.8	2.4	39.7
Tulsa, OK	6.3	20.7	19.9	13.1	11.9	12.2	9.6	4.7	1.7	37.3
Virginia Beach, VA	6.0	18.8	22.1	13.3	11.3	12.8	9.4	4.6	1.6	37.2
Washington, DC	6.1	19.2	20.3	14.8	13.4	12.3	8.3	4.0	1.5	37.9
Wichita, KS	6.3	21.5	20.2	12.8	11.2	12.3	9.6	4.3	2.0	36.6
Wilmington, NC	4.5	15.5	18.1	11.8	11.8	14.9	14.8	6.6	2.0	45.1
Winston-Salem, NC	5.5	19.2	18.7	11.8	13.0	13.8	10.7	5.4	2.0	40.6
U.S.	5.7	19.1	20.2	13.1	12.3	12.8	10.0	4.9	1.9	38.7

Note: Figures cover the Metropolitan Statistical Area (MSA)
Source: U.S. Census Bureau, 2019-2023 American Community Survey 5-Year Estimates

Ancestry: City

City	German	Irish	English	American	Italian	Polish	French[1]	European	Scottish
Albuquerque, NM	9.8	7.9	9.1	3.1	3.4	1.4	1.8	1.6	1.5
Anchorage, AK	13.5	9.0	9.9	3.6	3.1	1.9	1.9	2.1	1.8
Ann Arbor, MI	16.5	10.7	9.7	2.1	4.5	6.2	2.2	2.7	2.3
Athens, GA	9.0	8.9	12.2	3.9	3.1	1.8	1.6	2.7	2.7
Atlanta, GA	7.1	6.4	9.3	3.8	2.9	1.4	1.7	1.7	1.4
Austin, TX	11.5	8.7	10.2	2.8	3.2	1.9	2.4	2.4	2.2
Baltimore, MD	5.8	5.7	3.7	2.7	2.9	2.0	0.9	0.7	0.7
Billings, MT	27.7	13.2	13.3	3.7	3.1	1.7	2.6	2.0	2.8
Boise City, ID	18.2	11.5	17.8	3.9	4.2	1.7	2.4	3.7	3.1
Boston, MA	4.8	13.2	5.4	2.2	7.3	2.2	1.7	1.1	1.1
Boulder, CO	16.0	11.3	11.4	2.6	5.2	3.4	2.4	4.2	3.2
Cape Coral, FL	13.4	11.5	8.5	10.4	9.2	3.3	2.2	1.5	1.3
Cedar Rapids, IA	26.8	13.3	10.4	3.3	1.7	1.4	1.8	1.5	1.6
Charleston, SC	11.7	11.0	13.6	13.0	4.8	2.4	2.8	1.9	2.4
Charlotte, NC	7.4	6.7	7.7	4.7	3.5	1.5	1.2	1.1	1.6
Chicago, IL	7.4	7.2	3.2	2.0	3.8	5.0	0.9	0.9	0.7
Cincinnati, OH	17.5	9.8	6.9	3.0	3.7	1.4	1.2	1.2	1.0
Clarksville, TN	12.5	8.8	8.3	6.0	3.6	1.0	1.6	3.7	1.5
Cleveland, OH	9.4	8.4	3.5	2.5	4.4	3.7	0.8	0.5	0.7
College Station, TX	14.8	8.0	9.8	3.2	3.3	2.3	1.9	1.8	1.6
Colorado Springs, CO	17.8	11.4	12.8	4.2	4.7	2.6	2.4	2.9	2.6
Columbia, MO	24.0	12.1	13.5	5.1	3.4	1.6	1.9	2.2	2.3
Columbia, SC	9.0	7.2	8.8	5.3	3.0	1.1	1.7	1.9	2.0
Columbus, OH	14.9	10.0	8.0	3.4	4.6	2.1	1.3	1.5	1.6
Dallas, TX	5.4	4.4	6.0	3.8	1.7	0.8	1.2	1.2	1.1
Davenport, IA	28.1	14.7	8.7	3.0	2.6	1.9	1.3	1.1	1.8
Denver, CO	14.0	10.9	10.4	3.0	5.5	2.8	2.1	2.5	2.0
Des Moines, IA	19.1	12.4	9.2	3.1	3.5	1.0	1.4	1.5	1.3
Detroit, MI	1.8	1.6	1.1	4.4	0.8	1.1	0.5	0.2	0.3
Durham, NC	8.2	6.7	10.0	3.8	3.4	1.8	1.5	1.7	1.8
El Paso, TX	3.8	2.4	2.2	2.2	1.3	0.5	0.6	0.5	0.4
Eugene, OR	18.4	12.9	14.5	3.1	5.2	1.9	3.1	3.8	3.9
Fargo, ND	32.9	8.1	5.2	2.9	1.3	2.2	3.4	0.8	1.4
Fort Collins, CO	23.1	12.3	14.9	3.2	5.6	3.4	3.1	3.6	3.5
Fort Wayne, IN	22.5	9.0	9.2	5.0	2.1	1.9	2.4	2.3	1.9
Fort Worth, TX	7.1	6.0	7.4	3.7	1.8	0.8	1.3	1.4	1.5
Gainesville, FL	10.6	8.9	10.5	3.4	5.1	2.5	1.6	1.3	2.6
Green Bay, WI	26.6	8.2	4.6	3.6	2.0	7.2	3.0	1.6	1.0
Greensboro, NC	6.5	5.3	9.4	4.5	2.4	0.8	1.2	1.6	1.7
Honolulu, HI	4.5	3.4	3.6	1.4	1.3	0.9	1.0	0.5	0.7
Houston, TX	5.0	3.6	5.0	3.1	1.6	0.9	1.4	1.0	0.9
Huntsville, AL	9.2	8.5	13.0	10.2	2.4	1.3	1.8	2.2	2.1
Indianapolis, IN	12.8	7.9	8.0	4.5	2.0	1.4	1.4	1.4	1.5
Jacksonville, FL	7.8	7.7	7.6	6.3	3.6	1.4	1.4	2.2	1.6
Kansas City, MO	15.2	10.0	9.5	4.1	3.7	1.6	1.5	2.3	1.4
Lafayette, LA	9.2	5.6	6.7	5.2	3.8	0.5	16.7	0.7	1.1
Las Vegas, NV	8.0	7.2	7.2	2.9	4.9	1.8	1.5	1.6	1.3
Lexington, KY	12.7	10.8	13.8	7.7	2.7	1.4	1.6	2.4	2.4
Lincoln, NE	30.2	11.0	9.3	3.4	1.9	2.2	1.7	1.8	1.4
Little Rock, AR	7.5	6.5	10.4	4.6	1.2	0.7	1.3	1.7	1.7
Los Angeles, CA	3.9	3.7	3.5	3.8	2.7	1.3	1.1	1.3	0.7
Louisville, KY	14.8	11.3	10.8	5.8	2.5	1.1	1.5	1.6	1.6
Madison, WI	28.4	12.2	9.2	1.9	4.0	5.5	2.0	2.0	1.9
Manchester, NH	6.5	18.5	10.0	3.0	8.7	3.6	10.5	0.8	2.3
McAllen, TX	2.6	1.6	1.9	3.1	0.9	0.4	1.0	0.3	0.2
Memphis, TN	3.3	3.6	4.9	3.3	1.5	0.5	0.7	1.6	0.9

Table continued on following page.

City	German	Irish	English	American	Italian	Polish	French[1]	European	Scottish
Miami, FL	1.9	1.3	1.3	2.6	3.0	0.7	0.9	0.6	0.2
Midland, TX	6.6	6.1	7.8	4.6	0.9	0.4	1.3	1.1	1.5
Milwaukee, WI	15.1	5.4	2.2	1.4	2.4	5.5	1.2	1.0	0.5
Minneapolis, MN	21.0	10.7	7.4	1.7	2.6	3.9	2.7	2.0	1.4
Nashville, TN	8.7	7.9	10.2	5.9	2.7	1.4	1.5	1.7	1.9
New Orleans, LA	6.4	6.0	5.3	2.3	4.0	0.9	5.4	1.2	1.1
New York, NY	2.9	4.4	2.1	3.7	5.8	2.1	0.8	0.9	0.5
Oklahoma City, OK	10.1	7.8	9.5	5.3	1.5	0.7	1.2	1.9	1.7
Omaha, NE	24.8	12.8	8.4	2.7	3.7	3.3	1.9	1.6	1.8
Orlando, FL	6.4	5.4	5.9	6.1	4.5	1.6	1.5	0.8	0.9
Philadelphia, PA	7.0	9.6	3.2	2.2	6.7	3.0	0.7	0.7	0.7
Phoenix, AZ	9.6	7.4	6.8	2.7	3.9	1.8	1.4	1.5	1.3
Pittsburgh, PA	17.1	13.2	6.1	2.7	11.4	6.6	1.2	1.2	1.4
Portland, OR	15.2	11.6	12.9	4.3	4.5	2.4	2.6	4.4	3.1
Providence, RI	3.3	8.1	4.4	2.4	6.9	1.7	2.7	0.7	0.9
Provo, UT	10.4	4.9	28.2	2.2	2.2	0.7	1.3	4.0	3.6
Raleigh, NC	9.2	8.5	11.8	5.7	3.8	1.9	1.7	1.6	2.2
Reno, NV	12.3	11.0	11.1	4.4	5.9	1.6	2.2	2.6	2.0
Richmond, VA	8.2	7.9	9.9	3.9	3.8	1.4	1.5	1.3	1.8
Rochester, MN	28.8	9.8	7.1	2.6	1.8	2.6	1.8	1.6	1.4
Sacramento, CA	6.5	5.8	6.0	2.3	3.4	1.0	1.4	1.4	1.0
Saint Louis, MO	15.9	9.7	6.4	6.3	4.0	1.7	2.5	1.2	1.3
Saint Paul, MN	19.5	9.9	5.6	1.9	2.5	2.6	2.6	1.5	1.2
Salem, OR	16.3	8.2	12.7	4.1	2.9	1.2	2.3	4.2	2.5
Salt Lake City, UT	11.5	7.7	19.4	3.1	4.0	1.4	2.1	3.0	3.4
San Antonio, TX	7.2	4.6	4.7	3.4	2.0	0.9	1.2	0.8	0.9
San Diego, CA	8.7	7.3	7.0	2.3	4.2	1.8	1.7	1.7	1.3
San Francisco, CA	7.1	7.5	6.0	2.1	4.5	1.8	2.2	2.1	1.3
San Jose, CA	4.4	4.0	4.0	1.5	3.2	0.8	1.0	1.2	0.7
Santa Rosa, CA	11.1	10.1	10.4	2.2	6.3	1.6	2.4	2.4	1.9
Savannah, GA	6.6	7.3	6.3	3.8	3.2	1.1	1.3	0.8	1.4
Seattle, WA	14.0	10.8	12.2	2.4	4.7	2.6	2.8	3.9	2.7
Sioux Falls, SD	31.7	10.1	7.4	4.3	1.5	1.4	1.6	1.3	0.8
Tampa, FL	8.8	7.6	7.6	6.2	6.2	2.0	1.6	1.1	1.4
Tucson, AZ	11.5	8.4	8.0	2.9	3.7	1.9	1.8	1.5	1.7
Tulsa, OK	10.4	8.5	10.6	6.0	2.0	0.9	1.6	1.6	2.1
Virginia Beach, VA	11.2	10.5	11.3	7.5	5.5	2.3	1.9	1.6	2.2
Washington, DC	7.7	7.8	6.8	2.8	4.5	2.2	1.7	1.7	1.4
Wichita, KS	19.2	9.8	10.4	4.8	1.7	0.9	1.8	1.6	1.6
Wilmington, NC	10.8	10.8	13.8	4.7	5.6	2.2	2.1	2.3	2.7
Winston-Salem, NC	7.9	6.3	9.5	5.3	2.5	0.8	1.0	1.7	1.9
U.S.	12.6	9.4	9.1	5.5	4.9	2.6	2.0	1.6	1.6

Note: Figures are the percentage of the total population reporting a particular ancestry. The nine most commonly reported ancestries in the U.S. are shown. Figures include multiple ancestries (e.g. if a person reported being Irish and Italian, they were included in both columns); (1) Excludes Basque
Source: U.S. Census Bureau, 2019-2023 American Community Survey 5-Year Estimates

Ancestry: Metro Area

Metro Area	German	Irish	English	American	Italian	Polish	French[1]	European	Scottish
Albuquerque, NM	9.7	7.6	8.9	3.7	3.3	1.4	1.8	1.6	1.7
Anchorage, AK	14.5	9.7	10.1	4.2	2.9	1.9	1.9	2.1	1.9
Ann Arbor, MI	17.8	10.2	11.1	5.1	4.5	6.2	2.5	2.3	2.8
Athens, GA	8.8	10.4	13.5	6.1	2.8	1.4	1.5	2.4	2.5
Atlanta, GA	6.3	6.3	9.1	6.8	2.5	1.2	1.2	1.5	1.6
Austin, TX	12.4	8.3	10.4	3.6	2.9	1.7	2.3	2.4	2.2
Baltimore, MD	13.7	10.9	8.6	4.4	5.5	3.6	1.3	1.4	1.4
Billings, MT	29.0	13.1	12.6	4.2	3.2	1.5	2.6	2.1	2.6
Boise City, ID	17.0	10.2	18.2	4.8	3.5	1.4	2.4	3.1	3.1
Boston, MA	5.7	19.8	10.0	3.2	12.0	3.0	3.9	1.3	2.0
Boulder, CO	18.0	12.1	14.5	3.0	5.1	3.0	2.8	3.2	2.9
Cape Coral, FL	13.1	10.6	9.0	10.2	7.9	3.1	2.0	1.4	1.6
Cedar Rapids, IA	31.4	14.1	10.6	4.0	1.6	1.2	1.8	1.7	1.8
Charleston, SC	10.5	9.6	12.6	8.7	4.1	1.8	2.1	1.8	2.2
Charlotte, NC	10.2	8.4	10.3	8.3	3.9	1.7	1.4	1.5	2.0
Chicago, IL	12.9	10.2	4.8	2.5	6.1	8.0	1.2	1.2	0.9
Cincinnati, OH	25.7	12.9	11.4	5.6	3.9	1.6	1.6	1.6	1.8
Clarksville, TN	11.5	8.6	9.9	7.4	2.8	1.0	1.5	3.5	1.7
Cleveland, OH	18.5	13.3	8.6	4.1	9.1	6.9	1.4	1.1	1.5
College Station, TX	13.5	7.5	9.3	3.8	2.6	2.0	2.1	1.5	1.6
Colorado Springs, CO	17.6	11.0	12.3	4.5	4.5	2.4	2.3	3.0	2.7
Columbia, MO	24.4	11.8	13.9	6.4	2.8	1.4	1.9	2.2	2.1
Columbia, SC	9.5	7.3	9.5	6.5	2.5	1.3	1.5	1.6	1.9
Columbus, OH	20.0	12.4	11.1	5.3	5.1	2.2	1.6	1.8	2.1
Dallas, TX	8.1	6.4	8.7	5.3	2.2	1.0	1.4	1.4	1.5
Davenport, IA	25.2	13.0	9.4	3.8	2.5	1.9	1.5	1.5	1.5
Denver, CO	16.9	11.0	11.7	3.3	5.2	2.5	2.2	2.6	2.2
Des Moines, IA	25.8	13.5	11.3	3.8	3.1	1.2	1.6	2.3	1.7
Detroit, MI	14.3	9.1	7.9	4.0	5.8	8.9	2.8	1.5	2.0
Durham, NC	9.3	8.2	12.5	5.0	3.7	1.9	1.7	1.9	2.3
El Paso, TX	3.5	2.2	2.0	2.3	1.2	0.4	0.5	0.5	0.3
Eugene, OR	18.3	13.1	14.6	3.9	4.4	1.6	3.3	3.4	3.3
Fargo, ND	33.8	7.6	5.1	2.5	1.4	2.2	3.2	0.9	1.3
Fort Collins, CO	24.4	12.6	16.0	4.2	5.1	2.9	3.2	3.5	3.5
Fort Wayne, IN	26.1	9.0	9.8	5.8	2.2	2.0	2.8	2.6	1.8
Fort Worth, TX	8.1	6.4	8.7	5.3	2.2	1.0	1.4	1.4	1.5
Gainesville, FL	11.6	10.3	12.1	4.6	4.5	2.1	2.0	1.7	2.9
Green Bay, WI	33.7	9.3	4.9	4.0	2.2	9.4	3.5	1.6	0.7
Greensboro, NC	8.4	6.9	11.0	7.4	2.4	1.0	1.3	1.8	2.1
Honolulu, HI	5.2	4.0	4.1	1.3	1.8	0.8	1.0	0.6	0.7
Houston, TX	7.1	5.0	6.6	3.6	2.0	1.1	1.8	1.2	1.1
Huntsville, AL	9.4	9.3	13.8	11.4	2.3	1.2	1.5	2.2	2.1
Indianapolis, IN	16.6	9.4	10.9	7.3	2.5	1.7	1.5	1.7	1.8
Jacksonville, FL	9.6	9.6	10.2	7.5	4.5	1.8	1.8	2.1	2.0
Kansas City, MO	19.5	11.8	12.5	4.6	3.0	1.5	1.9	3.4	1.8
Lafayette, LA	7.1	4.5	5.3	6.2	3.0	0.6	17.1	0.7	0.7
Las Vegas, NV	7.9	6.8	7.0	2.9	4.7	1.7	1.4	1.3	1.2
Lexington, KY	12.3	11.3	14.6	10.4	2.5	1.3	1.5	2.3	2.3
Lincoln, NE	32.0	10.9	9.3	3.6	1.8	2.1	1.6	1.7	1.3
Little Rock, AR	8.5	8.4	11.7	6.6	1.4	0.8	1.4	1.6	1.8
Los Angeles, CA	5.1	4.3	4.5	3.5	2.8	1.1	1.1	1.2	0.8
Louisville, KY	16.6	12.4	12.6	7.6	2.6	1.1	1.7	1.7	1.9
Madison, WI	34.3	12.8	9.8	2.6	3.5	5.0	2.3	1.9	1.7
Manchester, NH	8.0	20.6	14.5	3.4	9.9	3.8	10.8	1.3	3.0
McAllen, TX	1.7	1.0	1.1	2.1	0.4	0.2	0.4	0.2	0.2
Memphis, TN	5.1	5.9	7.7	6.6	2.0	0.7	1.0	1.6	1.2

Table continued on following page.

Metro Area	German	Irish	English	American	Italian	Polish	French[1]	European	Scottish
Miami, FL	4.2	4.1	3.1	5.6	4.9	1.8	1.1	0.9	0.6
Midland, TX	7.0	5.8	7.6	5.2	0.9	0.3	1.3	1.0	1.4
Milwaukee, WI	31.6	9.3	5.0	2.4	4.3	9.8	2.1	1.4	0.9
Minneapolis, MN	27.4	10.7	6.9	3.1	2.5	4.0	2.9	2.0	1.2
Nashville, TN	9.6	8.9	12.9	10.5	2.6	1.2	1.6	2.3	2.2
New Orleans, LA	8.2	6.6	5.2	3.8	6.7	0.6	9.1	0.9	0.8
New York, NY	5.7	8.6	3.0	3.9	11.0	3.4	0.8	0.9	0.6
Oklahoma City, OK	11.8	9.0	11.2	6.2	1.7	0.8	1.5	2.0	1.9
Omaha, NE	27.8	12.9	9.7	3.5	3.7	3.5	1.8	1.7	1.6
Orlando, FL	8.2	7.2	7.1	9.1	5.0	1.7	1.6	1.1	1.2
Philadelphia, PA	13.7	16.9	7.8	3.2	12.2	4.6	1.2	1.0	1.2
Phoenix, AZ	12.6	8.7	9.5	4.2	4.5	2.2	1.8	1.8	1.6
Pittsburgh, PA	24.5	16.9	9.2	3.3	15.1	7.8	1.4	1.1	1.8
Portland, OR	16.0	10.5	12.8	4.4	3.5	1.7	2.4	3.8	2.8
Providence, RI	4.5	16.5	10.8	3.4	12.8	3.2	7.9	0.7	1.5
Provo, UT	10.0	4.9	32.1	4.1	2.1	0.5	1.4	4.8	4.1
Raleigh, NC	9.7	8.8	12.8	6.8	4.6	2.0	1.8	2.0	2.3
Reno, NV	12.7	10.9	11.6	4.0	6.0	1.6	2.3	3.5	2.0
Richmond, VA	9.1	8.2	12.7	6.6	3.7	1.5	1.4	1.7	1.8
Rochester, MN	32.8	10.3	7.3	3.6	1.5	2.5	1.7	1.8	1.3
Sacramento, CA	10.1	8.0	9.4	2.6	4.5	1.2	1.8	2.4	1.7
Saint Louis, MO	25.5	12.6	9.6	5.5	4.5	2.3	2.8	1.6	1.5
Saint Paul, MN	27.4	10.7	6.9	3.1	2.5	4.0	2.9	2.0	1.2
Salem, OR	16.6	8.4	12.1	3.9	2.6	1.4	2.3	3.6	2.6
Salt Lake City, UT	9.9	6.1	23.6	3.8	3.0	0.9	1.7	3.3	3.6
San Antonio, TX	10.0	5.8	6.6	3.8	2.2	1.4	1.5	1.1	1.3
San Diego, CA	9.0	7.5	7.6	2.6	4.1	1.6	1.8	1.9	1.5
San Francisco, CA	7.1	6.8	6.6	2.2	4.2	1.4	1.7	2.0	1.3
San Jose, CA	5.6	4.6	4.9	1.8	3.5	1.0	1.2	1.6	0.9
Santa Rosa, CA	12.4	12.2	11.8	2.4	7.9	1.8	2.9	3.7	2.5
Savannah, GA	9.4	9.4	10.2	6.8	3.7	1.2	1.5	1.2	1.8
Seattle, WA	13.2	9.0	10.9	2.9	3.4	1.7	2.4	3.2	2.3
Sioux Falls, SD	33.6	9.6	6.6	5.0	1.4	1.3	1.5	1.3	0.8
Tampa, FL	11.3	9.8	9.2	8.6	7.2	2.8	2.1	1.3	1.6
Tucson, AZ	13.2	9.0	10.1	3.5	4.1	2.2	2.1	1.7	2.0
Tulsa, OK	12.4	10.2	11.7	5.6	1.9	0.9	1.7	1.7	2.1
Virginia Beach, VA	9.4	8.6	10.8	8.0	4.1	1.7	1.7	1.6	1.8
Washington, DC	8.8	8.1	8.0	3.7	4.1	2.1	1.4	1.8	1.5
Wichita, KS	21.4	9.8	11.1	5.5	1.8	0.9	1.8	1.9	1.8
Wilmington, NC	12.2	12.4	14.8	5.9	5.9	2.4	2.1	1.8	2.8
Winston-Salem, NC	10.9	8.3	13.1	7.8	2.6	1.0	1.1	1.7	2.1
U.S.	12.6	9.4	9.1	5.5	4.9	2.6	2.0	1.6	1.6

Note: Figures are the percentage of the total population reporting a particular ancestry. The nine most commonly reported ancestries in the U.S. are shown. Figures include multiple ancestries (e.g. if a person reported being Irish and Italian, they were included in both columns); Figures cover the Metropolitan Statistical Area (MSA); (1) Excludes Basque
Source: U.S. Census Bureau, 2019-2023 American Community Survey 5-Year Estimates

Foreign-born Population: City

City	Any Foreign Country	Percent of Population Born in							
		Asia	Mexico	Europe	Caribbean	Central America[1]	South America	Africa	Canada
Albuquerque, NM	10.4	2.7	5.0	1.0	0.4	0.2	0.5	0.4	0.1
Anchorage, AK	10.9	6.0	0.6	1.2	0.5	0.2	0.6	0.5	0.4
Ann Arbor, MI	18.7	11.8	0.5	2.9	0.1	0.3	0.6	1.6	0.7
Athens, GA	9.8	3.2	2.3	0.9	0.4	1.3	0.8	0.7	0.2
Atlanta, GA	8.6	3.1	0.7	1.3	0.9	0.3	0.9	1.1	0.3
Austin, TX	18.1	6.2	5.2	1.6	0.8	2.0	0.9	1.0	0.3
Baltimore, MD	8.8	2.1	0.4	0.9	1.3	1.6	0.6	1.7	0.1
Billings, MT	2.0	0.7	0.2	0.6	0.0	0.0	0.1	0.0	0.3
Boise City, ID	7.2	3.0	1.3	1.3	0.1	0.1	0.3	0.6	0.5
Boston, MA	27.5	7.8	0.4	3.0	8.1	2.3	2.3	3.0	0.4
Boulder, CO	10.2	4.2	1.0	3.0	0.2	0.4	0.6	0.3	0.6
Cape Coral, FL	17.9	1.3	0.4	2.2	9.2	1.2	2.8	0.1	0.7
Cedar Rapids, IA	7.1	2.6	0.7	0.5	0.1	0.3	0.2	2.5	0.1
Charleston, SC	5.4	1.6	0.6	1.2	0.3	0.3	0.8	0.3	0.2
Charlotte, NC	18.1	4.9	2.7	1.5	1.2	3.8	1.7	2.1	0.2
Chicago, IL	20.7	5.2	8.2	3.3	0.4	0.9	1.4	1.1	0.2
Cincinnati, OH	7.1	2.1	0.3	0.7	0.2	1.0	0.3	2.2	0.1
Clarksville, TN	6.8	1.9	1.2	1.0	0.6	0.6	0.6	0.6	0.2
Cleveland, OH	6.1	2.3	0.4	1.1	0.5	0.5	0.3	0.9	0.1
College Station, TX	12.3	7.1	1.5	0.9	0.1	1.0	1.0	0.5	0.1
Colorado Springs, CO	7.4	2.0	1.7	1.5	0.2	0.6	0.4	0.5	0.3
Columbia, MO	8.1	4.9	0.6	0.4	0.3	0.2	0.5	1.1	0.0
Columbia, SC	5.1	2.0	0.2	0.7	0.8	0.3	0.5	0.4	0.1
Columbus, OH	14.4	4.7	1.3	0.8	0.7	0.9	0.7	5.1	0.1
Dallas, TX	23.4	2.9	12.8	0.8	0.4	3.3	1.0	2.0	0.1
Davenport, IA	4.6	1.5	1.5	0.5	0.0	0.1	0.0	0.6	0.2
Denver, CO	13.8	2.7	5.8	1.5	0.3	0.5	1.2	1.5	0.3
Des Moines, IA	14.0	4.4	3.6	0.8	0.2	1.6	0.1	3.2	0.1
Detroit, MI	6.0	2.4	1.7	0.2	0.3	0.5	0.1	0.5	0.2
Durham, NC	15.3	4.1	2.8	1.4	0.8	3.4	0.8	1.7	0.3
El Paso, TX	22.3	1.0	19.5	0.6	0.2	0.3	0.2	0.3	0.1
Eugene, OR	6.8	2.7	1.5	1.2	0.1	0.4	0.2	0.4	0.3
Fargo, ND	9.7	3.2	0.1	0.6	0.1	0.0	0.1	4.9	0.4
Fort Collins, CO	6.6	2.5	1.2	1.3	0.1	0.3	0.6	0.3	0.2
Fort Wayne, IN	9.0	4.4	2.1	0.5	0.2	1.0	0.2	0.5	0.2
Fort Worth, TX	17.0	4.1	8.9	0.5	0.3	0.8	0.6	1.6	0.1
Gainesville, FL	12.1	4.6	0.2	1.7	1.7	0.4	2.3	0.8	0.4
Green Bay, WI	8.8	2.1	4.5	0.4	0.2	0.5	0.3	0.6	0.2
Greensboro, NC	12.7	4.0	1.9	1.0	0.6	0.9	0.8	3.4	0.2
Honolulu, HI	27.8	22.9	0.2	1.0	0.1	0.1	0.3	0.2	0.2
Houston, TX	28.8	5.7	9.9	1.2	1.0	6.8	1.9	2.0	0.2
Huntsville, AL	6.6	1.7	1.6	0.8	0.7	0.5	0.3	0.5	0.2
Indianapolis, IN	11.6	3.1	3.2	0.5	0.7	1.3	0.6	2.2	0.1
Jacksonville, FL	12.2	4.1	0.5	1.7	2.5	0.8	1.7	0.8	0.1
Kansas City, MO	8.5	2.2	2.2	0.6	0.5	0.9	0.4	1.5	0.1
Lafayette, LA	6.6	2.1	0.5	0.4	0.2	1.8	0.8	0.4	0.1
Las Vegas, NV	20.9	5.3	8.5	1.6	1.3	2.2	1.0	0.4	0.4
Lexington, KY	11.0	3.8	2.3	1.0	0.4	0.8	0.5	2.0	0.2
Lincoln, NE	9.2	4.9	1.3	0.9	0.4	0.6	0.3	0.8	0.1
Little Rock, AR	7.9	2.7	2.1	0.6	0.1	1.6	0.3	0.4	0.1
Los Angeles, CA	35.8	11.2	11.2	2.4	0.3	8.3	1.2	0.7	0.4
Louisville, KY	9.8	2.5	1.0	0.8	2.8	0.6	0.4	1.6	0.1
Madison, WI	11.6	5.5	1.9	1.4	0.2	0.2	1.1	1.0	0.2
Manchester, NH	14.7	3.8	0.4	2.2	2.0	2.1	1.0	2.1	1.0

Table continued on following page.

City	Percent of Population Born in								
	Any Foreign Country	Asia	Mexico	Europe	Caribbean	Central America[1]	South America	Africa	Canada
McAllen, TX	25.7	2.2	22.0	0.2	0.3	0.5	0.4	0.1	0.0
Memphis, TN	7.4	1.3	2.3	0.3	0.3	1.9	0.5	0.7	0.1
Miami, FL	57.7	1.5	1.2	2.2	28.5	11.8	11.9	0.4	0.2
Midland, TX	13.7	2.0	7.1	0.4	1.0	0.5	1.1	1.0	0.6
Milwaukee, WI	10.8	2.8	5.1	0.6	0.3	0.4	0.3	1.0	0.1
Minneapolis, MN	14.1	3.2	1.8	1.0	0.2	0.3	1.5	5.7	0.3
Nashville, TN	15.1	3.6	3.1	0.8	0.6	3.1	0.6	2.9	0.3
New Orleans, LA	6.6	2.0	0.4	0.6	0.6	1.9	0.5	0.3	0.2
New York, NY	36.5	11.0	1.8	5.1	9.7	1.4	5.1	1.9	0.3
Oklahoma City, OK	12.0	3.1	5.4	0.5	0.2	1.3	0.5	0.7	0.2
Omaha, NE	11.0	3.3	3.4	0.6	0.2	1.5	0.3	1.5	0.2
Orlando, FL	24.1	3.0	0.8	1.8	6.5	1.2	10.1	0.5	0.2
Philadelphia, PA	14.6	5.6	0.5	2.2	2.8	0.7	1.0	1.7	0.1
Phoenix, AZ	19.0	3.1	11.3	1.3	0.4	0.9	0.4	1.1	0.3
Pittsburgh, PA	9.3	4.5	0.3	1.8	0.4	0.2	0.6	1.0	0.3
Portland, OR	12.4	5.5	2.0	2.3	0.2	0.4	0.3	0.8	0.5
Providence, RI	32.8	3.9	0.5	2.2	15.3	5.9	1.2	3.4	0.3
Provo, UT	12.2	1.6	3.8	0.7	0.4	1.0	3.3	0.5	0.4
Raleigh, NC	13.6	3.8	2.4	1.3	1.1	1.4	1.1	2.2	0.2
Reno, NV	16.1	5.4	5.3	1.4	0.3	2.2	0.4	0.5	0.3
Richmond, VA	8.6	1.5	0.9	0.8	0.7	3.5	0.4	0.6	0.1
Rochester, MN	14.1	5.9	1.0	1.2	0.1	0.3	0.4	4.9	0.2
Sacramento, CA	21.3	10.6	5.5	1.6	0.1	0.9	0.4	0.6	0.2
Saint Louis, MO	6.6	2.7	0.8	1.0	0.3	0.3	0.3	0.9	0.1
Saint Paul, MN	18.7	9.3	1.8	0.7	0.2	0.9	0.4	4.9	0.3
Salem, OR	12.2	2.5	6.2	1.0	0.0	0.8	0.2	0.4	0.2
Salt Lake City, UT	15.4	4.2	5.1	1.8	0.2	0.7	1.4	1.0	0.3
San Antonio, TX	14.3	2.6	8.8	0.6	0.3	1.0	0.6	0.4	0.1
San Diego, CA	24.8	11.8	7.5	2.3	0.2	0.5	0.9	1.0	0.4
San Francisco, CA	34.2	21.9	2.4	4.4	0.1	2.4	1.3	0.6	0.7
San Jose, CA	41.6	27.3	8.4	2.2	0.1	1.3	1.0	0.7	0.3
Santa Rosa, CA	20.8	4.7	11.5	1.5	0.1	1.4	0.3	0.6	0.3
Savannah, GA	6.7	2.6	0.8	0.8	0.9	0.7	0.5	0.4	0.2
Seattle, WA	19.9	11.4	1.4	2.5	0.2	0.4	0.7	2.1	1.1
Sioux Falls, SD	9.0	2.0	0.6	1.1	0.1	1.7	0.2	3.2	0.1
Tampa, FL	19.0	4.0	1.1	1.8	7.4	1.3	2.4	0.6	0.3
Tucson, AZ	13.7	2.4	8.3	1.0	0.1	0.4	0.3	0.8	0.2
Tulsa, OK	12.0	2.6	5.5	0.7	0.3	1.3	0.7	0.6	0.1
Virginia Beach, VA	9.1	5.0	0.3	1.4	0.5	0.4	0.8	0.5	0.2
Washington, DC	13.3	2.8	0.6	2.3	1.2	2.2	1.7	2.2	0.3
Wichita, KS	10.0	3.5	4.4	0.5	0.1	0.5	0.4	0.6	0.1
Wilmington, NC	5.7	1.2	1.5	1.0	0.2	0.8	0.7	0.2	0.1
Winston-Salem, NC	10.7	2.0	4.1	0.6	0.6	1.7	1.0	0.6	0.1
U.S.	13.9	4.3	3.3	1.4	1.4	1.2	1.2	0.8	0.2

Note: (1) Excludes Mexico
Source: U.S. Census Bureau, 2019-2023 American Community Survey 5-Year Estimates

Foreign-born Population: Metro Area

Metro Area	Any Foreign Country	Percent of Population Born in							
		Asia	Mexico	Europe	Caribbean	Central America[1]	South America	Africa	Canada
Albuquerque, NM	9.2	2.0	4.9	0.8	0.3	0.2	0.4	0.4	0.1
Anchorage, AK	8.7	4.6	0.5	1.2	0.4	0.2	0.5	0.4	0.3
Ann Arbor, MI	12.8	7.3	0.7	2.2	0.1	0.5	0.4	0.9	0.5
Athens, GA	8.0	2.7	1.7	0.7	0.2	1.1	0.5	0.7	0.2
Atlanta, GA	14.8	4.8	2.3	1.1	1.7	1.4	1.4	1.8	0.2
Austin, TX	15.5	5.1	5.1	1.3	0.5	1.4	0.8	0.8	0.3
Baltimore, MD	11.2	4.4	0.4	1.2	0.8	1.5	0.7	2.1	0.1
Billings, MT	1.8	0.5	0.2	0.5	0.0	0.0	0.1	0.1	0.2
Boise City, ID	6.6	1.5	2.6	1.1	0.0	0.3	0.3	0.3	0.3
Boston, MA	19.7	6.4	0.2	3.1	3.5	1.7	2.5	1.8	0.4
Boulder, CO	10.0	3.4	2.0	2.5	0.1	0.4	0.7	0.3	0.5
Cape Coral, FL	17.9	1.4	1.7	1.9	7.0	2.4	2.2	0.2	1.0
Cedar Rapids, IA	4.5	1.8	0.5	0.4	0.1	0.2	0.1	1.3	0.1
Charleston, SC	6.3	1.5	1.1	1.1	0.4	0.7	1.0	0.3	0.2
Charlotte, NC	11.4	3.2	2.0	1.2	0.7	1.8	1.2	1.0	0.2
Chicago, IL	18.3	5.4	6.5	3.7	0.3	0.6	0.8	0.7	0.2
Cincinnati, OH	5.7	2.3	0.5	0.7	0.2	0.6	0.2	0.9	0.2
Clarksville, TN	5.4	1.6	0.9	0.8	0.4	0.4	0.4	0.6	0.2
Cleveland, OH	5.8	2.2	0.3	2.0	0.2	0.2	0.3	0.5	0.2
College Station, TX	11.7	3.8	4.9	0.7	0.2	0.9	0.7	0.4	0.1
Colorado Springs, CO	6.7	1.8	1.5	1.4	0.3	0.5	0.4	0.4	0.3
Columbia, MO	5.8	3.4	0.6	0.4	0.2	0.1	0.3	0.7	0.0
Columbia, SC	5.6	1.8	1.0	0.7	0.5	0.7	0.5	0.3	0.1
Columbus, OH	9.5	3.8	0.8	0.7	0.4	0.5	0.4	2.7	0.1
Dallas, TX	19.0	6.0	7.4	0.8	0.3	1.7	0.8	1.7	0.2
Davenport, IA	5.4	1.8	1.7	0.4	0.1	0.1	0.1	1.1	0.1
Denver, CO	12.1	3.1	4.5	1.4	0.2	0.5	0.8	1.2	0.3
Des Moines, IA	8.6	3.1	1.6	1.0	0.1	0.8	0.3	1.6	0.1
Detroit, MI	10.3	6.0	0.8	1.9	0.2	0.2	0.2	0.4	0.5
Durham, NC	13.2	3.7	2.7	1.6	0.5	2.4	0.8	1.1	0.2
El Paso, TX	23.1	0.9	20.6	0.5	0.2	0.4	0.2	0.3	0.1
Eugene, OR	5.4	1.7	1.6	0.8	0.1	0.2	0.1	0.3	0.4
Fargo, ND	6.9	2.4	0.2	0.5	0.1	0.0	0.1	3.2	0.3
Fort Collins, CO	5.4	1.6	1.4	1.1	0.1	0.3	0.4	0.2	0.2
Fort Wayne, IN	6.9	3.3	1.4	0.5	0.1	0.7	0.2	0.4	0.2
Fort Worth, TX	19.0	6.0	7.4	0.8	0.3	1.7	0.8	1.7	0.2
Gainesville, FL	10.2	3.7	0.5	1.5	1.3	0.6	1.7	0.5	0.4
Green Bay, WI	4.8	1.5	1.9	0.5	0.1	0.3	0.2	0.2	0.1
Greensboro, NC	9.5	2.9	2.3	0.7	0.4	0.7	0.5	1.7	0.1
Honolulu, HI	19.6	15.7	0.2	0.7	0.1	0.1	0.2	0.1	0.3
Houston, TX	23.8	6.2	8.0	1.0	1.0	3.9	1.8	1.6	0.3
Huntsville, AL	5.4	1.8	1.1	0.8	0.4	0.4	0.3	0.3	0.2
Indianapolis, IN	8.4	2.8	1.8	0.6	0.4	0.7	0.5	1.5	0.1
Jacksonville, FL	10.0	3.2	0.5	1.7	1.8	0.6	1.4	0.5	0.2
Kansas City, MO	7.2	2.2	2.0	0.6	0.3	0.8	0.3	0.8	0.1
Lafayette, LA	3.8	1.2	0.5	0.2	0.2	1.0	0.4	0.1	0.0
Las Vegas, NV	21.7	7.4	7.3	1.6	1.3	1.8	0.9	0.9	0.4
Lexington, KY	8.2	2.6	1.8	0.9	0.3	0.7	0.4	1.3	0.2
Lincoln, NE	8.1	4.3	1.1	0.8	0.3	0.5	0.3	0.7	0.1
Little Rock, AR	4.6	1.3	1.4	0.4	0.1	0.9	0.2	0.2	0.1
Los Angeles, CA	32.5	13.0	11.1	1.7	0.3	4.3	1.0	0.6	0.3
Louisville, KY	6.7	1.9	0.9	0.6	1.5	0.4	0.3	1.0	0.1
Madison, WI	7.6	3.3	1.3	1.0	0.1	0.2	0.8	0.6	0.2
Manchester, NH	10.4	3.4	0.4	1.7	1.4	0.8	0.9	0.9	0.8

Table continued on following page.

Metro Area	Percent of Population Born in								
	Any Foreign Country	Asia	Mexico	Europe	Caribbean	Central America[1]	South America	Africa	Canada
McAllen, TX	26.0	0.8	24.1	0.1	0.1	0.5	0.2	0.1	0.1
Memphis, TN	6.1	1.7	1.6	0.4	0.2	1.0	0.4	0.6	0.1
Miami, FL	41.9	2.2	1.1	2.4	20.6	4.3	10.2	0.4	0.5
Midland, TX	13.0	1.9	7.2	0.3	0.9	0.4	0.9	0.8	0.5
Milwaukee, WI	7.6	2.7	2.4	1.1	0.2	0.2	0.3	0.6	0.1
Minneapolis, MN	10.7	4.0	1.2	1.0	0.2	0.4	0.6	3.1	0.2
Nashville, TN	9.4	2.4	2.1	0.7	0.4	1.6	0.5	1.4	0.3
New Orleans, LA	9.5	2.4	0.6	0.5	1.1	3.9	0.5	0.4	0.1
New York, NY	29.8	8.9	1.4	4.2	6.8	2.0	4.7	1.5	0.3
Oklahoma City, OK	8.2	2.3	3.4	0.5	0.1	0.8	0.4	0.5	0.2
Omaha, NE	7.9	2.6	2.4	0.6	0.2	0.9	0.3	1.0	0.1
Orlando, FL	20.3	3.1	0.9	1.6	5.9	1.2	6.8	0.6	0.3
Philadelphia, PA	11.5	4.7	0.8	1.8	1.5	0.5	0.8	1.2	0.2
Phoenix, AZ	13.9	3.3	6.6	1.3	0.3	0.6	0.4	0.7	0.6
Pittsburgh, PA	4.1	2.0	0.2	0.9	0.2	0.1	0.2	0.4	0.1
Portland, OR	12.5	5.0	3.0	2.3	0.2	0.5	0.4	0.6	0.4
Providence, RI	14.4	2.3	0.3	3.8	2.9	1.7	1.3	1.7	0.2
Provo, UT	7.7	1.0	2.5	0.5	0.2	0.6	2.0	0.3	0.3
Raleigh, NC	13.1	5.0	2.5	1.3	0.8	1.0	0.8	1.3	0.3
Reno, NV	13.4	3.6	5.5	1.1	0.2	1.6	0.4	0.3	0.3
Richmond, VA	8.7	3.2	0.7	1.0	0.5	1.8	0.7	0.8	0.1
Rochester, MN	8.8	3.5	0.8	0.9	0.1	0.2	0.4	2.7	0.2
Sacramento, CA	18.9	9.4	4.2	2.8	0.1	0.7	0.4	0.5	0.3
Saint Louis, MO	5.0	2.3	0.5	1.0	0.1	0.3	0.2	0.5	0.1
Saint Paul, MN	10.7	4.0	1.2	1.0	0.2	0.4	0.6	3.1	0.2
Salem, OR	12.0	1.5	7.4	1.0	0.1	0.8	0.2	0.3	0.2
Salt Lake City, UT	12.4	3.0	4.2	1.2	0.1	0.6	1.9	0.6	0.2
San Antonio, TX	11.8	2.2	6.8	0.6	0.3	0.8	0.5	0.4	0.1
San Diego, CA	22.5	8.9	9.1	1.9	0.2	0.6	0.7	0.6	0.4
San Francisco, CA	31.6	18.0	4.9	2.8	0.2	2.7	1.2	0.9	0.5
San Jose, CA	40.3	27.1	6.5	3.0	0.1	1.0	1.1	0.7	0.5
Santa Rosa, CA	16.6	3.1	9.1	1.8	0.1	1.0	0.5	0.4	0.4
Savannah, GA	6.9	2.1	1.1	0.9	0.8	0.6	0.7	0.5	0.2
Seattle, WA	20.4	11.0	2.4	2.8	0.2	0.6	0.7	1.7	0.7
Sioux Falls, SD	6.7	1.5	0.5	0.9	0.1	1.2	0.1	2.2	0.1
Tampa, FL	15.0	2.9	1.2	2.2	4.3	0.8	2.4	0.5	0.6
Tucson, AZ	11.9	2.3	6.6	1.3	0.2	0.3	0.3	0.6	0.3
Tulsa, OK	7.2	2.0	2.9	0.6	0.2	0.7	0.4	0.4	0.1
Virginia Beach, VA	6.8	2.9	0.4	1.1	0.6	0.6	0.4	0.5	0.2
Washington, DC	24.0	8.4	0.9	1.8	1.1	5.2	2.5	3.8	0.2
Wichita, KS	7.4	2.6	3.1	0.5	0.1	0.4	0.3	0.4	0.1
Wilmington, NC	4.9	0.9	1.2	1.0	0.1	0.7	0.7	0.2	0.2
Winston-Salem, NC	7.3	1.4	2.8	0.7	0.3	1.0	0.7	0.3	0.1
U.S.	13.9	4.3	3.3	1.4	1.4	1.2	1.2	0.8	0.2

Note: Figures cover the Metropolitan Statistical Area (MSA); (1) Excludes Mexico
Source: U.S. Census Bureau, 2019-2023 American Community Survey 5-Year Estimates

Marital Status: City

City	Never Married	Now Married[1]	Separated	Widowed	Divorced
Albuquerque, NM	38.6	39.4	1.5	5.5	15.1
Anchorage, AK	34.6	47.7	1.9	3.5	12.2
Ann Arbor, MI	55.4	35.4	0.6	2.3	6.3
Athens, GA	53.9	31.2	1.3	4.3	9.3
Atlanta, GA	55.0	28.9	1.5	4.1	10.5
Austin, TX	44.0	41.7	1.3	3.0	9.9
Baltimore, MD	52.7	27.1	2.9	5.9	11.4
Billings, MT	31.9	47.2	1.0	5.6	14.3
Boise City, ID	35.2	46.8	1.0	4.3	12.7
Boston, MA	55.7	31.0	2.2	3.8	7.4
Boulder, CO	57.8	30.4	0.5	2.2	9.0
Cape Coral, FL	24.7	52.6	1.5	7.8	13.4
Cedar Rapids, IA	36.8	44.3	1.5	5.0	12.3
Charleston, SC	39.4	44.3	1.6	4.8	10.0
Charlotte, NC	42.9	41.1	2.1	3.8	10.1
Chicago, IL	49.1	35.6	2.2	5.0	8.1
Cincinnati, OH	53.4	29.8	1.8	4.5	10.6
Clarksville, TN	30.0	50.9	2.2	4.2	12.7
Cleveland, OH	53.7	23.7	2.8	6.1	13.7
College Station, TX	60.3	31.2	1.2	2.4	5.0
Colorado Springs, CO	30.7	50.8	1.5	4.5	12.5
Columbia, MO	49.8	37.9	1.0	3.4	8.0
Columbia, SC	55.8	29.7	2.0	3.9	8.6
Columbus, OH	45.8	36.3	2.0	4.2	11.7
Dallas, TX	43.0	40.2	2.5	4.0	10.2
Davenport, IA	37.3	44.0	1.0	5.6	12.0
Denver, CO	44.4	39.3	1.3	3.4	11.5
Des Moines, IA	40.8	38.8	2.3	5.7	12.5
Detroit, MI	57.0	22.0	2.9	6.3	11.9
Durham, NC	44.1	40.5	1.8	3.7	9.8
El Paso, TX	35.5	44.8	3.3	5.6	10.9
Eugene, OR	44.6	37.5	1.3	4.2	12.4
Fargo, ND	44.3	41.2	1.0	3.8	9.6
Fort Collins, CO	46.5	41.1	0.7	3.0	8.8
Fort Wayne, IN	37.2	42.9	1.5	5.9	12.5
Fort Worth, TX	35.8	46.5	2.2	4.6	10.7
Gainesville, FL	62.8	24.3	1.3	2.9	8.8
Green Bay, WI	39.4	41.0	1.1	4.9	13.5
Greensboro, NC	45.1	36.4	2.4	5.8	10.3
Honolulu, HI	38.0	44.0	1.2	6.6	10.1
Houston, TX	42.2	40.5	2.8	4.4	10.0
Huntsville, AL	37.9	42.7	1.9	6.0	11.6
Indianapolis, IN	41.1	40.4	1.7	4.8	12.0
Jacksonville, FL	36.2	42.5	2.1	5.5	13.6
Kansas City, MO	39.5	40.6	1.9	4.8	13.2
Lafayette, LA	40.0	42.8	2.2	5.1	9.9
Las Vegas, NV	36.4	42.8	1.8	5.3	13.5
Lexington, KY	38.8	43.1	1.4	4.6	12.0
Lincoln, NE	39.6	45.4	0.8	4.2	10.0
Little Rock, AR	38.6	41.0	1.5	5.5	13.4
Los Angeles, CA	46.5	38.6	2.3	4.5	8.0
Louisville, KY	37.2	41.9	2.0	6.1	12.8
Madison, WI	50.7	37.5	0.8	3.0	8.0
Manchester, NH	39.0	39.6	1.6	5.5	14.3
McAllen, TX	35.1	48.8	2.1	5.6	8.4
Memphis, TN	48.1	30.9	3.3	5.9	11.7

Table continued on following page.

City	Never Married	Now Married[1]	Separated	Widowed	Divorced
Miami, FL	40.4	37.0	3.3	5.7	13.5
Midland, TX	29.3	54.5	1.9	4.8	9.6
Milwaukee, WI	54.7	29.2	1.9	4.3	9.9
Minneapolis, MN	52.0	33.9	1.2	2.9	9.9
Nashville, TN	41.6	41.4	1.7	4.3	11.0
New Orleans, LA	49.2	30.8	2.3	5.2	12.5
New York, NY	44.0	39.8	2.8	5.2	8.2
Oklahoma City, OK	34.2	46.4	2.1	5.2	12.2
Omaha, NE	37.9	45.3	1.2	4.7	11.0
Orlando, FL	42.9	38.6	2.4	3.7	12.5
Philadelphia, PA	50.7	31.9	2.8	5.5	9.1
Phoenix, AZ	40.2	42.0	1.9	4.0	11.9
Pittsburgh, PA	54.4	30.6	1.7	5.0	8.3
Portland, OR	42.9	39.8	1.3	3.5	12.6
Providence, RI	53.4	32.1	2.0	4.1	8.5
Provo, UT	49.3	43.5	0.7	2.2	4.3
Raleigh, NC	43.1	40.5	1.9	3.9	10.6
Reno, NV	37.7	41.7	1.5	4.9	14.2
Richmond, VA	51.4	30.0	2.7	4.6	11.2
Rochester, MN	34.2	51.3	0.9	4.8	8.8
Sacramento, CA	41.5	40.8	2.3	4.7	10.7
Saint Louis, MO	49.7	30.2	2.7	5.3	12.2
Saint Paul, MN	46.4	37.8	1.5	3.6	10.6
Salem, OR	35.6	44.6	1.4	5.3	13.1
Salt Lake City, UT	45.4	39.1	1.6	2.9	10.9
San Antonio, TX	39.1	40.8	2.9	5.3	12.0
San Diego, CA	40.5	44.7	1.6	3.9	9.2
San Francisco, CA	45.6	40.7	1.4	4.5	7.8
San Jose, CA	37.2	49.3	1.6	4.4	7.5
Santa Rosa, CA	34.6	45.9	2.0	5.6	12.0
Savannah, GA	48.6	31.4	2.6	5.4	12.0
Seattle, WA	46.1	40.3	1.1	3.0	9.5
Sioux Falls, SD	34.5	48.4	1.4	4.3	11.4
Tampa, FL	43.1	38.1	2.2	4.7	11.8
Tucson, AZ	42.9	36.0	1.8	5.2	14.1
Tulsa, OK	36.5	41.7	2.4	5.5	14.0
Virginia Beach, VA	31.2	50.6	2.0	5.0	11.2
Washington, DC	55.2	31.5	1.4	3.4	8.5
Wichita, KS	35.0	45.2	1.8	5.2	12.8
Wilmington, NC	42.2	38.8	2.3	5.3	11.4
Winston-Salem, NC	42.5	39.6	2.4	5.2	10.3
U.S.	34.1	47.9	1.7	5.6	10.7

Note: Figures are percentages and cover the population 15 years of age and older; (1) Excludes separated
Source: U.S. Census Bureau, 2019-2023 American Community Survey 5-Year Estimates

Marital Status: Metro Area

Metro Area	Never Married	Now Married[1]	Separated	Widowed	Divorced
Albuquerque, NM	36.1	43.1	1.4	5.4	13.9
Anchorage, AK	33.3	49.3	1.8	3.7	11.9
Ann Arbor, MI	42.3	44.6	0.9	3.8	8.4
Athens, GA	43.0	41.4	1.3	4.7	9.5
Atlanta, GA	36.2	47.1	1.7	4.4	10.6
Austin, TX	35.9	49.4	1.3	3.5	9.8
Baltimore, MD	36.4	46.2	1.8	5.7	9.9
Billings, MT	28.7	51.5	1.0	5.5	13.3
Boise City, ID	28.9	54.0	1.0	4.4	11.8
Boston, MA	37.5	47.6	1.5	4.9	8.6
Boulder, CO	39.2	45.4	0.7	3.7	11.1
Cape Coral, FL	26.5	51.8	1.5	7.8	12.3
Cedar Rapids, IA	30.9	51.1	1.3	5.2	11.5
Charleston, SC	33.2	48.9	2.0	5.4	10.5
Charlotte, NC	33.6	49.4	2.0	4.9	10.0
Chicago, IL	37.6	46.7	1.6	5.3	8.8
Cincinnati, OH	33.2	49.0	1.3	5.5	11.0
Clarksville, TN	29.2	51.6	1.9	5.2	12.0
Cleveland, OH	35.7	44.2	1.5	6.4	12.1
College Station, TX	46.7	39.5	1.6	4.3	7.9
Colorado Springs, CO	29.4	53.8	1.3	4.1	11.5
Columbia, MO	41.1	44.4	1.1	4.3	9.2
Columbia, SC	36.0	45.7	2.3	5.7	10.2
Columbus, OH	35.0	47.4	1.6	4.8	11.2
Dallas, TX	33.4	50.6	1.7	4.2	10.0
Davenport, IA	31.1	50.1	1.2	6.2	11.5
Denver, CO	34.5	49.4	1.3	3.7	11.0
Des Moines, IA	31.7	51.3	1.3	5.0	10.7
Detroit, MI	35.9	45.7	1.2	6.0	11.2
Durham, NC	38.3	46.2	1.7	4.5	9.3
El Paso, TX	35.5	45.7	3.2	5.4	10.2
Eugene, OR	35.8	44.3	1.3	5.4	13.2
Fargo, ND	38.8	47.3	0.9	3.9	9.1
Fort Collins, CO	35.3	50.3	0.8	3.9	9.7
Fort Wayne, IN	31.8	49.9	1.3	5.5	11.5
Fort Worth, TX	33.4	50.6	1.7	4.2	10.0
Gainesville, FL	43.5	39.6	1.3	5.1	10.4
Green Bay, WI	31.8	51.2	0.6	5.2	11.1
Greensboro, NC	35.2	45.3	2.3	6.2	11.0
Honolulu, HI	34.6	49.5	1.1	6.0	8.7
Houston, TX	34.3	50.1	2.1	4.3	9.2
Huntsville, AL	30.6	51.3	1.4	5.5	11.2
Indianapolis, IN	32.7	49.7	1.2	4.9	11.5
Jacksonville, FL	31.4	48.4	1.8	5.6	12.7
Kansas City, MO	31.3	50.3	1.5	5.1	11.8
Lafayette, LA	33.9	47.8	2.0	5.4	10.9
Las Vegas, NV	35.6	44.3	2.0	5.1	13.1
Lexington, KY	34.4	46.7	1.5	5.1	12.3
Lincoln, NE	37.2	48.2	0.8	4.2	9.6
Little Rock, AR	31.5	48.0	1.7	5.9	12.9
Los Angeles, CA	40.7	44.3	2.0	4.7	8.3
Louisville, KY	31.8	47.6	1.7	6.0	12.9
Madison, WI	37.6	48.1	0.7	4.1	9.5
Manchester, NH	32.0	49.8	1.1	5.2	11.8
McAllen, TX	36.7	47.8	3.0	4.9	7.6
Memphis, TN	38.5	42.0	2.5	5.9	11.1

Table continued on following page.

Metro Area	Never Married	Now Married[1]	Separated	Widowed	Divorced
Miami, FL	34.0	44.7	2.4	6.1	12.8
Midland, TX	28.6	55.2	1.6	4.9	9.8
Milwaukee, WI	37.7	45.9	1.2	5.1	10.1
Minneapolis, MN	34.1	50.7	0.9	4.3	10.0
Nashville, TN	32.8	50.3	1.4	4.9	10.6
New Orleans, LA	40.3	38.9	2.3	6.0	12.4
New York, NY	38.3	46.0	2.1	5.4	8.1
Oklahoma City, OK	32.3	48.6	1.8	5.5	11.9
Omaha, NE	32.4	51.2	1.1	4.6	10.8
Orlando, FL	35.1	47.0	1.8	4.9	11.2
Philadelphia, PA	37.7	45.7	1.8	5.6	9.1
Phoenix, AZ	34.3	47.9	1.4	4.9	11.5
Pittsburgh, PA	33.1	48.4	1.5	7.0	10.0
Portland, OR	33.7	48.9	1.3	4.3	11.8
Providence, RI	36.7	45.0	1.5	5.8	11.0
Provo, UT	33.4	57.7	0.8	2.6	5.5
Raleigh, NC	32.4	52.4	1.8	4.2	9.3
Reno, NV	32.6	47.1	1.4	5.1	13.8
Richmond, VA	35.0	47.0	2.0	5.5	10.4
Rochester, MN	29.3	55.9	0.7	4.9	9.1
Sacramento, CA	34.2	48.5	1.8	4.9	10.5
Saint Louis, MO	32.9	48.4	1.6	5.8	11.2
Saint Paul, MN	34.1	50.7	0.9	4.3	10.0
Salem, OR	32.4	48.5	1.6	5.4	12.1
Salt Lake City, UT	33.6	51.2	1.5	3.6	10.2
San Antonio, TX	34.3	47.2	2.3	5.1	11.1
San Diego, CA	36.3	48.1	1.6	4.4	9.6
San Francisco, CA	36.8	48.8	1.4	4.6	8.4
San Jose, CA	35.5	51.7	1.4	4.2	7.1
Santa Rosa, CA	32.7	48.5	1.4	5.2	12.2
Savannah, GA	35.8	45.9	2.1	5.1	11.2
Seattle, WA	33.8	50.4	1.3	4.0	10.5
Sioux Falls, SD	30.7	53.1	1.1	4.3	10.8
Tampa, FL	32.1	46.3	1.8	6.8	13.1
Tucson, AZ	35.1	44.8	1.5	5.8	12.9
Tulsa, OK	29.9	49.5	1.8	6.1	12.7
Virginia Beach, VA	33.7	47.7	2.2	5.5	10.8
Washington, DC	36.7	48.8	1.6	4.2	8.7
Wichita, KS	31.2	50.0	1.4	5.4	12.0
Wilmington, NC	28.5	52.5	1.9	6.2	10.9
Winston-Salem, NC	31.7	48.8	2.2	6.3	11.1
U.S.	34.1	47.9	1.7	5.6	10.7

Note: Figures are percentages and cover the population 15 years of age and older; Figures cover the Metropolitan Statistical Area (MSA); (1) Excludes separated
Source: U.S. Census Bureau, 2019-2023 American Community Survey 5-Year Estimates

Disability by Age: City

City	All Ages	Under 18 Years Old	18 to 64 Years Old	65 Years and Over
Albuquerque, NM	15.2	4.8	13.2	35.2
Anchorage, AK	12.2	4.9	10.7	33.7
Ann Arbor, MI	8.1	4.7	6.1	23.8
Athens, GA	12.2	5.9	10.1	34.0
Atlanta, GA	11.6	5.4	9.6	32.3
Austin, TX	9.5	3.8	8.4	28.3
Baltimore, MD	16.5	5.7	14.6	40.0
Billings, MT	14.5	4.4	11.8	36.3
Boise City, ID	12.1	5.3	10.2	29.4
Boston, MA	12.1	5.8	9.1	37.2
Boulder, CO	7.5	2.9	6.1	20.9
Cape Coral, FL	14.0	3.8	10.0	30.5
Cedar Rapids, IA	11.6	4.9	10.0	27.3
Charleston, SC	9.7	3.2	6.7	29.6
Charlotte, NC	8.3	2.8	7.0	28.3
Chicago, IL	11.9	3.8	9.6	35.4
Cincinnati, OH	13.6	6.0	12.6	31.7
Clarksville, TN	14.8	5.7	15.1	41.8
Cleveland, OH	19.9	9.8	18.5	40.7
College Station, TX	8.2	6.2	6.8	29.3
Colorado Springs, CO	13.2	5.7	11.9	30.1
Columbia, MO	11.9	5.4	10.5	32.2
Columbia, SC	12.7	3.9	10.7	38.0
Columbus, OH	12.2	5.3	10.9	34.7
Dallas, TX	11.4	4.7	9.8	34.9
Davenport, IA	13.9	5.5	11.8	33.3
Denver, CO	10.1	3.3	8.3	30.7
Des Moines, IA	14.3	5.8	13.4	35.2
Detroit, MI	19.6	6.0	19.7	42.6
Durham, NC	9.9	3.6	8.0	29.6
El Paso, TX	14.3	5.5	12.0	40.2
Eugene, OR	15.1	4.8	13.2	31.7
Fargo, ND	11.4	5.4	9.0	32.6
Fort Collins, CO	8.9	3.0	7.7	24.0
Fort Wayne, IN	13.6	5.3	12.5	32.5
Fort Worth, TX	10.2	3.7	9.0	34.4
Gainesville, FL	10.5	3.9	8.3	33.6
Green Bay, WI	15.0	7.1	13.9	34.3
Greensboro, NC	11.8	5.4	9.9	31.4
Honolulu, HI	12.5	3.9	7.9	32.1
Houston, TX	11.0	4.7	8.9	35.1
Huntsville, AL	14.3	5.4	11.8	34.8
Indianapolis, IN	13.5	5.1	12.6	34.6
Jacksonville, FL	13.5	5.0	11.8	34.1
Kansas City, MO	12.8	3.7	11.6	33.3
Lafayette, LA	12.9	3.5	10.3	33.9
Las Vegas, NV	13.3	4.5	11.3	34.2
Lexington, KY	12.8	4.9	11.0	32.4
Lincoln, NE	12.0	4.8	10.6	29.5
Little Rock, AR	13.9	6.8	12.0	33.8
Los Angeles, CA	11.1	3.5	8.3	36.3
Louisville, KY	14.7	5.3	13.3	34.1
Madison, WI	9.1	4.1	7.5	24.6
Manchester, NH	13.6	7.4	11.5	31.1
McAllen, TX	13.0	6.1	9.4	43.8

Table continued on following page.

City	All Ages	Under 18 Years Old	18 to 64 Years Old	65 Years and Over
Memphis, TN	13.6	4.6	12.5	34.6
Miami, FL	11.5	3.7	7.0	38.2
Midland, TX	10.4	3.4	8.7	40.3
Milwaukee, WI	13.2	4.8	12.5	35.3
Minneapolis, MN	11.6	4.8	10.7	30.5
Nashville, TN	11.0	4.5	8.8	33.8
New Orleans, LA	14.1	5.7	11.6	34.2
New York, NY	11.7	3.9	8.5	34.6
Oklahoma City, OK	13.9	5.6	12.5	36.6
Omaha, NE	11.1	3.8	9.8	30.2
Orlando, FL	10.3	5.2	8.3	33.4
Philadelphia, PA	17.4	7.7	15.6	40.8
Phoenix, AZ	11.5	4.6	10.2	32.5
Pittsburgh, PA	14.2	7.4	11.5	34.3
Portland, OR	13.2	4.9	10.9	34.3
Providence, RI	13.7	6.0	12.4	37.3
Provo, UT	10.2	4.2	8.9	42.2
Raleigh, NC	9.6	4.4	7.9	29.1
Reno, NV	12.1	4.0	9.8	31.2
Richmond, VA	14.0	7.0	12.0	33.1
Rochester, MN	10.1	3.8	7.8	28.9
Sacramento, CA	12.4	4.0	10.1	35.8
Saint Louis, MO	16.6	6.5	14.4	39.0
Saint Paul, MN	12.5	4.7	11.9	31.3
Salem, OR	15.4	5.9	13.7	36.8
Salt Lake City, UT	12.1	5.0	9.9	34.9
San Antonio, TX	15.5	6.7	13.5	41.8
San Diego, CA	10.0	3.4	7.3	31.2
San Francisco, CA	11.2	2.7	7.3	34.1
San Jose, CA	9.6	3.6	6.3	34.3
Santa Rosa, CA	12.7	4.3	10.3	30.0
Savannah, GA	15.9	7.0	13.5	40.7
Seattle, WA	10.0	2.8	8.0	30.3
Sioux Falls, SD	10.0	3.4	8.7	28.4
Tampa, FL	11.9	4.1	9.3	38.0
Tucson, AZ	15.5	6.1	13.2	36.8
Tulsa, OK	14.4	5.3	13.3	34.2
Virginia Beach, VA	11.7	4.4	10.1	28.7
Washington, DC	11.0	4.5	8.8	32.3
Wichita, KS	14.9	5.9	13.6	34.7
Wilmington, NC	12.9	3.7	10.4	31.1
Winston-Salem, NC	12.6	4.7	10.9	32.8
U.S.	13.0	4.7	10.7	32.9

Note: Figures show percent of the civilian noninstitutionalized population that reported having a disability. Disability status is determined from from six types of difficulty: vision, hearing, cognitive, ambulatory, self-care, and independent living. For children under 5 years old, hearing and vision difficulty are used to determine disability status. For children between the ages of 5 and 14, disability status is determined from hearing, vision, cognitive, ambulatory, and self-care difficulties. For people aged 15 years and older, they are considered to have a disability if they have difficulty with any one of the six difficulty types.
Source: U.S. Census Bureau, 2019-2023 American Community Survey 5-Year Estimates

Disability by Age: Metro Area

Metro Area	All Ages	Under 18 Years Old	18 to 64 Years Old	65 Years and Over
Albuquerque, NM	16.1	4.7	14.1	36.3
Anchorage, AK	12.6	4.8	11.3	34.0
Ann Arbor, MI	10.3	4.1	8.3	26.9
Athens, GA	12.8	4.9	11.0	32.7
Atlanta, GA	10.8	4.5	9.0	31.3
Austin, TX	10.0	4.3	8.5	29.1
Baltimore, MD	12.0	4.5	9.8	30.7
Billings, MT	14.3	4.4	11.6	35.1
Boise City, ID	12.7	4.9	11.0	31.0
Boston, MA	10.9	4.5	8.2	29.6
Boulder, CO	8.8	2.9	6.9	23.8
Cape Coral, FL	13.7	4.0	9.6	27.1
Cedar Rapids, IA	11.5	5.0	9.5	27.3
Charleston, SC	12.1	4.5	9.8	31.5
Charlotte, NC	10.6	3.4	8.7	31.0
Chicago, IL	10.7	3.6	8.4	30.2
Cincinnati, OH	12.7	5.1	10.8	31.5
Clarksville, TN	16.4	6.5	16.1	41.9
Cleveland, OH	14.6	5.6	12.2	32.1
College Station, TX	10.9	5.5	8.8	33.8
Colorado Springs, CO	12.5	5.4	11.3	29.7
Columbia, MO	13.0	5.3	11.5	31.9
Columbia, SC	14.3	5.1	12.3	35.3
Columbus, OH	12.1	5.0	10.4	32.3
Dallas, TX	10.1	4.0	8.5	32.0
Davenport, IA	13.5	5.7	10.9	30.9
Denver, CO	10.2	3.7	8.4	29.1
Des Moines, IA	10.8	3.8	9.3	29.8
Detroit, MI	14.0	4.6	11.9	33.5
Durham, NC	10.4	3.7	8.1	28.1
El Paso, TX	13.9	5.5	11.7	41.5
Eugene, OR	17.1	6.2	15.0	33.4
Fargo, ND	11.0	4.1	9.3	32.1
Fort Collins, CO	10.3	3.3	8.2	26.6
Fort Wayne, IN	12.4	4.7	11.1	30.4
Fort Worth, TX	10.1	4.0	8.5	32.0
Gainesville, FL	13.3	5.4	10.2	34.6
Green Bay, WI	12.0	4.4	10.6	27.3
Greensboro, NC	13.4	4.9	11.2	32.9
Honolulu, HI	12.2	3.6	8.5	32.8
Houston, TX	10.4	4.3	8.6	32.8
Huntsville, AL	13.5	4.5	11.5	34.9
Indianapolis, IN	12.4	5.0	10.9	32.1
Jacksonville, FL	13.1	4.8	11.1	31.8
Kansas City, MO	12.0	4.4	10.3	31.1
Lafayette, LA	14.5	4.7	12.9	37.2
Las Vegas, NV	13.0	4.4	10.7	34.3
Lexington, KY	13.9	5.4	12.2	33.8
Lincoln, NE	11.8	4.5	10.2	29.6
Little Rock, AR	15.5	5.7	13.6	37.4
Los Angeles, CA	10.5	3.5	7.7	32.8
Louisville, KY	14.4	5.0	12.5	34.4
Madison, WI	9.4	3.8	7.6	24.3
Manchester, NH	11.7	4.7	9.6	28.3
McAllen, TX	12.5	5.5	9.7	45.5

Table continued on following page.

Metro Area	All Ages	Under 18 Years Old	18 to 64 Years Old	65 Years and Over
Memphis, TN	13.5	5.0	12.1	34.6
Miami, FL	11.0	4.0	7.2	30.9
Midland, TX	10.9	3.5	9.3	40.7
Milwaukee, WI	11.3	4.0	9.4	28.9
Minneapolis, MN	10.4	4.0	8.6	27.9
Nashville, TN	11.4	4.2	9.4	32.9
New Orleans, LA	15.3	6.1	12.9	36.3
New York, NY	10.6	3.5	7.7	30.9
Oklahoma City, OK	14.7	5.2	13.0	38.3
Omaha, NE	11.2	3.8	9.7	31.0
Orlando, FL	12.3	5.6	9.5	33.1
Philadelphia, PA	13.2	5.5	11.0	31.5
Phoenix, AZ	12.3	4.9	10.1	31.1
Pittsburgh, PA	14.7	5.7	11.7	31.9
Portland, OR	12.9	4.5	10.8	32.6
Providence, RI	13.9	5.6	11.7	31.4
Provo, UT	8.7	3.9	8.3	31.3
Raleigh, NC	10.0	3.9	8.3	30.1
Reno, NV	13.0	4.7	10.4	31.7
Richmond, VA	12.8	5.3	10.7	30.4
Rochester, MN	10.1	3.6	7.8	27.2
Sacramento, CA	12.3	4.0	9.6	33.8
Saint Louis, MO	13.3	4.7	11.2	32.1
Saint Paul, MN	10.4	4.0	8.6	27.9
Salem, OR	15.8	5.8	13.8	36.9
Salt Lake City, UT	10.2	4.4	9.1	29.8
San Antonio, TX	14.6	6.3	12.6	39.1
San Diego, CA	10.7	3.6	8.2	31.3
San Francisco, CA	10.3	3.2	7.3	30.4
San Jose, CA	8.8	3.1	5.7	31.3
Santa Rosa, CA	12.1	4.0	9.1	28.2
Savannah, GA	14.5	5.3	12.8	35.7
Seattle, WA	11.4	4.2	9.2	32.6
Sioux Falls, SD	9.9	3.3	8.5	28.5
Tampa, FL	14.4	5.3	11.1	33.5
Tucson, AZ	15.1	5.6	12.2	32.3
Tulsa, OK	15.0	5.2	13.4	37.0
Virginia Beach, VA	13.6	5.4	11.6	32.5
Washington, DC	9.1	3.5	7.0	27.9
Wichita, KS	14.6	5.6	13.0	35.1
Wilmington, NC	13.5	5.5	10.7	26.6
Winston-Salem, NC	14.2	4.9	12.0	33.1
U.S.	13.0	4.7	10.7	32.9

Note: Figures show percent of the civilian noninstitutionalized population that reported having a disability. Disability status is determined from from six types of difficulty: vision, hearing, cognitive, ambulatory, self-care, and independent living. For children under 5 years old, hearing and vision difficulty are used to determine disability status. For children between the ages of 5 and 14, disability status is determined from hearing, vision, cognitive, ambulatory, and self-care difficulties. For people aged 15 years and older, they are considered to have a disability if they have difficulty with any one of the six difficulty types; Figures cover the Metropolitan Statistical Area (MSA)
Source: U.S. Census Bureau, 2019-2023 American Community Survey 5-Year Estimates

Religious Groups by Family

Metro Area	Catholic	Baptist	Methodist	LDS[1]	Pentecostal	Lutheran	Islam	Adventist	Other
Albuquerque, NM	32.6	3.2	0.9	2.7	1.7	0.4	0.7	1.5	10.8
Anchorage, AK	4.9	3.4	1.0	5.1	1.7	1.5	0.1	1.7	16.3
Ann Arbor, MI	9.7	2.0	2.4	0.8	1.5	2.3	2.2	0.9	10.0
Athens, GA	6.4	12.8	5.7	1.0	2.4	0.3	0.2	1.3	7.9
Atlanta, GA	10.7	14.7	6.7	0.8	2.0	0.4	1.9	1.9	12.4
Austin, TX	18.8	6.5	2.2	1.3	0.7	1.1	1.0	1.0	9.9
Baltimore, MD	12.4	3.2	4.4	0.6	1.2	1.4	3.3	1.2	11.7
Billings, MT	7.4	1.9	1.1	5.2	3.6	4.9	n/a	1.2	7.8
Boise City, ID	13.0	0.8	2.5	15.0	1.6	0.8	0.3	1.7	10.0
Boston, MA	37.0	1.0	0.7	0.5	0.7	0.2	2.2	0.9	7.1
Boulder, CO	16.0	0.3	0.7	0.7	0.5	1.7	0.4	0.9	15.2
Cape Coral, FL	18.8	2.5	1.7	0.6	3.0	0.7	0.2	2.0	12.2
Cedar Rapids, IA	16.8	1.0	5.3	1.0	1.3	8.1	1.3	0.6	9.6
Charleston, SC	11.5	7.7	8.0	0.8	1.9	0.7	0.2	1.0	12.8
Charlotte, NC	12.1	13.9	7.0	0.7	2.2	1.1	1.7	1.4	15.9
Chicago, IL	28.6	3.4	1.4	0.3	1.5	2.1	4.7	1.1	9.2
Cincinnati, OH	17.0	5.7	2.3	0.6	1.5	0.8	1.1	0.7	21.8
Clarksville, TN	4.6	23.2	4.4	1.4	3.2	0.5	0.1	0.8	12.4
Cleveland, OH	26.1	4.3	2.3	0.4	1.5	1.8	1.1	1.3	16.8
College Station, TX	17.2	10.6	4.3	1.7	0.5	1.1	0.6	0.5	6.8
Colorado Springs, CO	16.4	2.6	1.3	3.0	1.0	1.2	0.1	1.0	16.2
Columbia, MO	7.1	9.0	3.5	1.7	1.1	1.6	1.4	1.2	12.4
Columbia, SC	6.6	15.1	8.5	1.2	3.8	2.3	0.3	1.3	15.4
Columbus, OH	11.7	3.4	3.0	0.8	1.9	1.7	2.1	0.9	17.5
Dallas, TX	14.2	14.3	4.7	1.4	2.2	0.5	1.8	1.3	13.8
Davenport, IA	13.2	3.2	3.6	0.8	1.5	6.6	0.7	0.8	6.7
Denver, CO	16.1	1.5	1.0	2.1	0.6	1.4	0.3	1.1	10.4
Des Moines, IA	12.1	1.8	4.0	0.9	2.5	6.6	1.6	0.8	8.7
Detroit, MI	18.6	4.8	1.7	0.3	2.1	2.2	4.5	1.0	8.5
Durham, NC	8.5	12.3	6.5	0.9	1.3	0.3	1.5	1.1	13.7
El Paso, TX	47.9	2.5	0.4	1.2	1.1	0.2	0.1	2.1	6.9
Eugene, OR	5.6	0.7	0.5	2.8	2.5	0.8	<0.1	2.0	9.0
Fargo, ND	14.2	0.2	1.0	0.6	1.3	24.0	<0.1	0.6	8.1
Fort Collins, CO	9.9	1.2	1.3	4.0	2.7	2.5	<0.1	1.2	12.1
Fort Wayne, IN	13.1	8.1	3.9	0.4	1.1	7.1	1.0	0.9	17.6
Fort Worth, TX	14.2	14.3	4.7	1.4	2.2	0.5	1.8	1.3	13.8
Gainesville, FL	8.5	10.6	4.8	1.4	3.2	0.3	0.4	1.3	14.5
Green Bay, WI	31.8	0.3	1.4	0.5	1.1	10.8	0.4	0.9	7.0
Greensboro, NC	7.9	10.0	8.0	0.7	2.8	0.4	1.5	1.4	17.8
Honolulu, HI	18.0	1.4	0.5	4.1	2.6	0.2	<0.1	1.9	9.8
Houston, TX	18.3	13.1	3.7	1.2	1.6	0.7	1.7	1.5	13.1
Huntsville, AL	7.5	23.6	6.6	1.4	1.2	0.4	0.8	2.7	17.5
Indianapolis, IN	11.5	6.2	3.3	0.7	1.3	1.1	1.1	1.0	17.4
Jacksonville, FL	13.0	14.5	3.0	1.0	1.4	0.4	0.6	1.3	20.5
Kansas City, MO	11.3	9.1	5.0	1.6	2.7	1.7	1.0	1.0	12.1
Lafayette, LA	44.3	9.3	2.0	0.4	1.8	0.1	0.1	0.8	7.0
Las Vegas, NV	26.2	1.9	0.3	5.8	1.5	0.6	0.3	1.3	5.5
Lexington, KY	5.8	14.9	5.5	1.2	1.6	0.3	0.5	1.2	16.6
Lincoln, NE	13.2	1.0	5.7	1.2	3.1	9.1	0.1	1.8	10.0
Little Rock, AR	4.9	23.5	6.2	0.8	3.7	0.4	0.4	1.0	13.6
Los Angeles, CA	31.1	2.6	0.8	1.5	2.4	0.4	1.4	1.5	9.1
Louisville, KY	11.9	14.5	3.2	0.8	0.9	0.5	1.0	1.0	12.4
Madison, WI	14.4	0.5	2.0	0.7	0.2	9.2	1.2	0.7	8.4
Manchester, NH	16.3	0.6	0.6	0.6	0.3	0.3	0.1	0.8	8.1
McAllen, TX	46.6	2.2	0.8	1.2	1.0	0.3	0.2	3.2	6.0
Memphis, TN	4.8	26.6	6.0	0.7	5.1	0.3	1.3	1.3	18.4

Table continued on following page.

Metro Area	Catholic	Baptist	Methodist	LDS[1]	Pentecostal	Lutheran	Islam	Adventist	Other
Miami, FL	23.8	5.1	0.9	0.5	1.3	0.3	0.8	2.4	11.1
Midland, TX	15.4	25.5	2.5	2.0	1.2	0.3	0.4	1.3	16.5
Milwaukee, WI	24.5	3.0	1.0	0.4	2.8	9.1	2.8	0.9	10.7
Minneapolis, MN	19.8	0.8	1.4	0.5	2.5	10.7	2.9	0.7	7.4
Nashville, TN	6.2	16.4	4.8	0.9	1.6	0.4	0.8	1.3	19.4
New Orleans, LA	42.1	9.3	2.5	0.5	2.1	0.5	1.4	1.0	8.0
New York, NY	32.5	1.7	1.2	0.3	0.9	0.5	4.5	1.4	10.6
Oklahoma City, OK	10.0	16.6	6.2	1.3	3.9	0.6	0.6	0.9	21.4
Omaha, NE	19.9	2.8	2.8	1.6	1.0	6.1	0.2	1.0	9.0
Orlando, FL	17.6	5.7	2.1	0.9	2.7	0.6	1.3	2.8	14.6
Philadelphia, PA	26.8	3.3	2.4	0.3	1.0	1.2	2.6	1.0	10.5
Phoenix, AZ	22.9	1.7	0.6	6.2	1.5	1.0	1.9	1.5	9.3
Pittsburgh, PA	30.6	1.9	4.3	0.4	1.3	2.5	0.6	0.6	12.5
Portland, OR	11.8	0.8	0.6	3.3	1.4	1.1	0.2	2.0	14.4
Providence, RI	37.9	0.9	0.6	0.3	0.6	0.3	0.5	0.9	6.1
Provo, UT	4.9	0.1	<0.1	82.6	0.1	<0.1	0.3	0.3	0.4
Raleigh, NC	12.4	9.8	5.4	1.2	1.9	0.7	3.2	1.5	12.8
Reno, NV	24.4	1.4	0.5	4.0	0.9	0.5	0.3	1.4	5.3
Richmond, VA	12.3	14.2	4.8	0.9	3.2	0.5	2.1	1.2	14.8
Rochester, MN	15.6	0.4	2.8	1.5	1.9	19.3	1.0	0.7	10.1
Sacramento, CA	17.1	1.9	1.1	3.1	2.2	0.6	1.9	1.9	8.2
Saint Louis, MO	21.2	8.6	2.9	0.7	1.4	3.2	1.3	0.8	11.1
Saint Paul, MN	19.8	0.8	1.4	0.5	2.5	10.7	2.9	0.7	7.4
Salem, OR	19.5	0.5	0.6	3.8	2.9	1.2	n/a	2.5	10.7
Salt Lake City, UT	9.0	0.6	0.2	52.0	0.7	0.2	1.6	0.7	2.6
San Antonio, TX	27.3	6.4	2.1	1.4	1.6	1.1	0.5	1.5	11.0
San Diego, CA	22.9	1.5	0.6	2.1	1.0	0.6	1.5	1.9	9.4
San Francisco, CA	21.5	2.2	0.9	1.5	1.4	0.4	2.0	1.0	7.7
San Jose, CA	27.2	1.2	0.6	1.4	0.9	0.4	2.0	1.3	11.4
Santa Rosa, CA	23.5	1.1	0.5	1.4	0.5	0.5	0.2	1.8	6.9
Savannah, GA	5.5	11.9	4.8	0.8	1.5	1.1	0.2	1.4	12.3
Seattle, WA	11.0	1.0	0.7	2.6	2.8	1.2	0.6	1.4	19.8
Sioux Falls, SD	13.1	0.7	2.9	0.7	1.7	16.4	0.1	0.6	20.3
Tampa, FL	23.1	6.3	2.9	0.5	1.9	0.6	0.7	1.8	12.1
Tucson, AZ	18.9	1.9	0.6	2.8	1.3	1.1	1.0	1.4	9.7
Tulsa, OK	5.6	15.5	7.7	1.2	2.5	0.5	0.5	1.2	22.2
Virginia Beach, VA	8.3	9.5	4.8	0.7	2.0	0.5	1.0	0.9	16.1
Washington, DC	16.1	6.0	4.1	1.1	1.3	0.8	3.3	1.5	12.6
Wichita, KS	12.7	23.5	4.5	1.5	1.4	1.3	0.1	1.1	15.0
Wilmington, NC	13.2	9.9	8.1	1.0	1.0	0.7	0.7	1.4	12.6
Winston-Salem, NC	9.3	12.8	11.4	0.5	1.0	0.6	0.8	1.4	22.5
U.S.	18.7	7.3	3.0	2.0	1.8	1.7	1.3	1.3	11.6

Note: Figures are the number of adherents as a percentage of the total population; Figures cover the Metropolitan Statistical Area (MSA);
(1) Church of Jesus Christ of Latter-day Saints
Source: 2020 U.S. Religion Census, Association of Statisticians of American Religious Bodies; The Association of Religion Data Archives

Religious Groups by Tradition

Metro Area	Catholic	Evangelical Protestant	Mainline Protestant	Black Protestant	Islam	Judaism	Hinduism	Orthodox	Buddhism
Albuquerque, NM	32.6	13.4	2.2	0.5	0.7	0.2	0.2	0.1	0.6
Anchorage, AK	4.9	19.2	2.4	0.9	0.1	0.1	0.1	0.5	1.3
Ann Arbor, MI	9.7	8.1	5.6	2.5	2.2	0.8	0.5	0.4	0.3
Athens, GA	6.4	19.1	7.2	2.6	0.2	0.2	0.2	0.1	<0.1
Atlanta, GA	10.7	22.3	7.4	5.3	1.9	0.5	0.7	0.3	0.2
Austin, TX	18.8	13.5	4.0	1.7	1.0	0.2	0.6	0.2	0.3
Baltimore, MD	12.4	10.6	5.9	3.3	3.3	1.7	0.1	0.5	0.1
Billings, MT	7.4	13.9	5.2	0.1	n/a	n/a	n/a	0.1	n/a
Boise City, ID	13.0	11.9	3.9	<0.1	0.3	0.1	0.2	0.1	0.1
Boston, MA	37.0	3.4	3.2	0.3	2.2	1.1	0.3	0.9	0.4
Boulder, CO	16.0	12.7	3.4	n/a	0.4	0.7	0.5	0.2	1.0
Cape Coral, FL	18.8	16.4	3.0	0.6	0.2	0.2	0.2	0.1	0.1
Cedar Rapids, IA	16.8	11.9	12.2	0.4	1.3	0.1	0.7	0.1	<0.1
Charleston, SC	11.5	17.1	6.8	6.6	0.2	0.4	<0.1	0.2	n/a
Charlotte, NC	12.1	26.4	9.5	3.4	1.7	0.2	0.2	0.4	0.1
Chicago, IL	28.6	8.2	3.7	3.6	4.7	0.7	0.4	0.7	0.4
Cincinnati, OH	17.0	24.9	4.1	2.0	1.1	0.4	0.3	0.3	0.1
Clarksville, TN	4.6	35.7	4.8	3.4	0.1	n/a	n/a	0.1	n/a
Cleveland, OH	26.1	15.1	5.6	3.5	1.1	1.3	0.3	0.8	0.2
College Station, TX	17.2	16.1	5.3	1.8	0.6	n/a	0.1	0.1	n/a
Colorado Springs, CO	16.4	18.3	2.9	0.9	0.1	<0.1	<0.1	0.1	0.3
Columbia, MO	7.1	19.4	6.3	1.9	1.4	0.2	0.1	0.1	<0.1
Columbia, SC	6.6	27.9	10.7	5.6	0.3	0.2	0.4	0.1	0.3
Columbus, OH	11.7	18.1	6.8	1.5	2.1	0.4	0.4	0.5	0.2
Dallas, TX	14.2	25.4	5.9	3.3	1.8	0.3	0.5	0.3	0.2
Davenport, IA	13.2	8.5	10.6	1.9	0.7	0.1	0.2	0.1	n/a
Denver, CO	16.1	9.6	2.8	0.6	0.3	0.4	0.5	0.4	0.5
Des Moines, IA	12.1	10.3	12.2	1.0	1.6	<0.1	0.2	0.1	0.1
Detroit, MI	18.6	9.1	3.3	5.1	4.5	0.8	0.3	0.8	0.2
Durham, NC	8.5	20.0	8.8	4.3	1.5	0.5	0.1	0.3	0.1
El Paso, TX	47.9	9.9	0.6	0.4	0.1	0.2	<0.1	<0.1	0.2
Eugene, OR	5.6	10.3	2.3	0.1	<0.1	0.4	0.3	0.1	0.5
Fargo, ND	14.2	11.1	23.4	n/a	<0.1	<0.1	n/a	0.1	n/a
Fort Collins, CO	9.9	15.6	3.3	0.4	<0.1	n/a	0.1	0.1	0.1
Fort Wayne, IN	13.1	24.7	6.1	6.5	1.0	0.1	0.1	0.2	0.4
Fort Worth, TX	14.2	25.4	5.9	3.3	1.8	0.3	0.5	0.3	0.2
Gainesville, FL	8.5	25.3	5.4	2.0	0.4	0.3	0.3	<0.1	0.3
Green Bay, WI	31.8	14.6	6.2	<0.1	0.4	n/a	n/a	<0.1	<0.1
Greensboro, NC	7.9	24.9	10.1	3.5	1.5	0.3	0.3	0.1	0.1
Honolulu, HI	18.0	8.1	2.3	0.2	<0.1	0.1	0.2	<0.1	4.0
Houston, TX	18.3	23.8	4.7	2.3	1.7	0.3	0.7	0.3	0.3
Huntsville, AL	7.5	34.8	8.2	7.2	0.8	0.1	0.9	0.1	0.1
Indianapolis, IN	11.5	16.8	7.6	4.2	1.1	0.4	0.2	0.3	0.1
Jacksonville, FL	13.0	29.8	3.5	5.6	0.6	0.3	0.3	0.3	0.2
Kansas City, MO	11.3	19.1	7.1	3.6	1.0	0.3	0.4	0.1	0.2
Lafayette, LA	44.3	12.6	2.4	5.0	0.1	n/a	<0.1	<0.1	0.1
Las Vegas, NV	26.2	6.6	1.0	0.5	0.3	0.3	0.2	0.6	0.7
Lexington, KY	5.8	26.9	8.1	3.5	0.5	0.3	0.1	0.2	<0.1
Lincoln, NE	13.2	16.6	12.9	0.3	0.1	0.1	0.1	0.1	0.1
Little Rock, AR	4.9	32.1	6.6	8.5	0.4	0.1	<0.1	0.1	0.1
Los Angeles, CA	31.1	9.3	1.5	1.7	1.4	0.8	0.4	0.9	0.9
Louisville, KY	11.9	21.1	5.0	4.6	1.0	0.2	0.4	0.2	0.2
Madison, WI	14.4	8.0	10.6	0.2	1.2	0.4	0.1	0.1	0.9
Manchester, NH	16.3	5.8	2.7	n/a	0.1	0.3	<0.1	0.9	n/a
McAllen, TX	46.6	10.0	1.1	0.1	0.2	<0.1	<0.1	<0.1	n/a

Table continued on following page.

Metro Area	Catholic	Evangelical Protestant	Mainline Protestant	Black Protestant	Islam	Judaism	Hinduism	Orthodox	Buddhism
Memphis, TN	4.8	32.4	5.8	17.2	1.3	0.6	0.4	0.1	0.1
Miami, FL	23.8	13.7	1.6	2.2	0.8	1.2	0.3	0.2	0.3
Midland, TX	15.4	35.5	3.0	7.6	0.4	n/a	0.2	n/a	n/a
Milwaukee, WI	24.5	16.3	5.4	3.3	2.8	0.4	0.4	0.5	0.4
Minneapolis, MN	19.8	10.6	10.3	0.5	2.9	0.6	0.2	0.3	0.3
Nashville, TN	6.2	30.1	6.0	5.2	0.8	0.2	0.4	1.1	0.2
New Orleans, LA	42.1	13.5	3.0	4.9	1.4	0.4	0.3	0.1	0.3
New York, NY	32.5	4.4	3.0	1.5	4.5	4.4	1.0	0.8	0.3
Oklahoma City, OK	10.0	38.7	7.1	2.2	0.6	0.1	0.4	0.1	0.4
Omaha, NE	19.9	10.8	7.9	1.5	0.2	0.3	1.0	0.2	0.2
Orlando, FL	17.6	20.6	2.5	2.7	1.3	0.2	0.5	0.3	0.3
Philadelphia, PA	26.8	7.3	6.6	2.2	2.6	1.1	0.6	0.4	0.4
Phoenix, AZ	22.9	11.0	1.6	0.3	1.9	0.3	0.5	0.4	0.2
Pittsburgh, PA	30.6	8.8	10.1	1.3	0.6	0.6	1.2	0.6	0.1
Portland, OR	11.8	14.6	2.3	0.4	0.2	0.3	0.7	0.3	0.4
Providence, RI	37.9	4.0	3.2	0.1	0.5	0.6	0.1	0.5	0.2
Provo, UT	4.9	0.4	<0.1	n/a	0.3	n/a	0.1	n/a	n/a
Raleigh, NC	12.4	19.3	7.4	2.8	3.2	0.2	0.4	0.3	0.4
Reno, NV	24.4	6.8	1.3	0.2	0.3	0.1	0.1	0.1	0.2
Richmond, VA	12.3	23.1	9.3	3.1	2.1	0.3	1.3	0.4	0.2
Rochester, MN	15.6	15.0	19.1	n/a	1.0	0.1	0.1	0.2	0.2
Sacramento, CA	17.1	10.4	1.4	1.1	1.9	0.2	0.4	0.3	0.5
Saint Louis, MO	21.2	16.1	5.7	3.9	1.3	0.6	0.2	0.2	0.3
Saint Paul, MN	19.8	10.6	10.3	0.5	2.9	0.6	0.2	0.3	0.3
Salem, OR	19.5	14.4	2.0	0.2	n/a	0.1	<0.1	<0.1	<0.1
Salt Lake City, UT	9.0	2.4	0.7	0.1	1.6	0.1	0.3	0.4	0.3
San Antonio, TX	27.3	17.7	3.1	0.8	0.5	0.2	0.1	0.1	0.3
San Diego, CA	22.9	9.5	1.5	0.6	1.5	0.4	0.3	0.4	0.7
San Francisco, CA	21.5	5.2	2.2	1.8	2.0	0.7	1.1	0.7	1.1
San Jose, CA	27.2	8.4	1.4	0.3	2.0	0.6	2.4	0.6	1.2
Santa Rosa, CA	23.5	5.3	1.5	<0.1	0.2	0.4	0.3	0.4	1.7
Savannah, GA	5.5	19.0	5.7	5.9	0.2	0.7	0.5	0.1	n/a
Seattle, WA	11.0	19.5	2.7	0.6	0.6	0.4	0.4	0.6	1.6
Sioux Falls, SD	13.1	21.0	20.2	0.1	0.1	n/a	n/a	0.8	<0.1
Tampa, FL	23.1	16.9	3.8	1.7	0.7	0.4	0.3	0.8	0.4
Tucson, AZ	18.9	10.4	2.4	0.6	1.0	0.4	0.4	0.2	0.3
Tulsa, OK	5.6	37.8	8.6	1.7	0.5	0.2	0.1	0.1	<0.1
Virginia Beach, VA	8.3	21.3	6.9	3.7	1.0	0.3	0.2	0.3	0.3
Washington, DC	16.1	12.3	6.5	3.3	3.3	1.0	0.9	0.9	0.5
Wichita, KS	12.7	19.4	23.2	2.6	0.1	<0.1	0.1	0.2	0.5
Wilmington, NC	13.2	17.9	9.3	4.6	0.7	0.3	0.1	0.3	n/a
Winston-Salem, NC	9.3	31.4	13.6	3.4	0.8	n/a	<0.1	0.3	0.1
U.S.	18.7	16.5	5.2	2.3	1.3	0.6	0.4	0.4	0.3

Note: Figures are the number of adherents as a percentage of the total population; Figures cover the Metropolitan Statistical Area (MSA)
Source: 2020 U.S. Religion Census, Association of Statisticians of American Religious Bodies; The Association of Religion Data Archives

Real Gross Domestic Product (GDP)

Metro Area	2017	2018	2019	2020	2021	2022	2023	Rank[1]
Albuquerque, NM	41.9	42.7	43.9	43.3	45.7	47.4	48.6	70
Anchorage, AK	25.8	26.0	26.0	25.3	25.9	26.3	27.3	116
Ann Arbor, MI	24.0	24.6	25.6	25.0	26.3	27.0	27.8	114
Athens, GA	10.0	10.3	10.3	9.8	10.4	10.8	11.0	211
Atlanta, GA	398.2	413.0	429.7	416.6	444.7	462.0	471.7	10
Austin, TX	141.1	149.3	159.1	163.6	181.1	198.5	207.5	20
Baltimore, MD	198.3	200.4	201.6	194.8	204.8	210.2	213.5	19
Billings, MT	10.2	10.3	10.0	9.8	10.5	10.5	10.9	215
Boise City, ID	32.3	34.8	36.4	37.0	40.4	43.4	44.6	76
Boston, MA	433.8	451.3	467.4	463.3	495.9	507.8	515.4	8
Boulder, CO	26.3	27.2	29.7	29.1	31.3	31.9	32.9	100
Cape Coral, FL	31.3	32.6	33.3	33.2	36.0	38.8	40.4	84
Cedar Rapids, IA	18.3	18.7	18.3	18.0	19.2	19.0	18.8	155
Charleston, SC	41.7	43.4	45.5	44.2	46.6	49.6	52.1	65
Charlotte, NC	168.1	171.6	177.5	179.1	190.5	197.3	206.5	21
Chicago, IL	674.6	691.2	697.5	659.6	698.0	715.6	725.7	3
Cincinnati, OH	145.2	145.3	152.3	149.5	155.9	157.4	160.1	29
Clarksville, TN	12.3	12.4	12.7	12.9	13.6	13.9	14.2	189
Cleveland, OH	128.6	130.6	134.0	129.2	136.3	139.1	139.9	36
College Station, TX	12.5	13.0	13.6	13.5	14.2	14.7	15.8	171
Colorado Springs, CO	35.1	36.2	37.7	38.8	41.1	41.8	43.6	79
Columbia, MO	10.0	10.0	10.4	10.1	10.6	10.7	11.0	213
Columbia, SC	41.0	41.7	42.7	42.2	44.6	45.5	47.0	73
Columbus, OH	129.9	131.5	135.7	134.2	143.6	145.5	148.0	34
Dallas, TX	483.7	506.2	526.2	520.2	562.1	594.5	613.4	5
Davenport, IA	21.6	21.4	21.6	21.0	21.6	22.0	22.4	136
Denver, CO	202.2	211.2	222.5	222.8	239.1	250.3	259.0	18
Des Moines, IA	51.8	51.9	54.2	55.6	60.7	59.8	60.4	57
Detroit, MI	256.2	261.5	262.7	249.7	263.7	271.7	276.5	16
Durham, NC	46.4	48.7	50.1	51.5	55.1	57.0	59.0	58
El Paso, TX	30.4	31.4	33.1	32.9	35.3	35.9	38.1	87
Eugene, OR	15.9	16.3	16.4	16.3	17.4	17.7	18.1	157
Fargo, ND	15.0	15.1	15.4	14.9	15.7	15.8	16.3	167
Fort Collins, CO	18.6	19.5	20.3	20.2	21.3	21.7	22.0	139
Fort Wayne, IN	22.4	23.3	23.5	21.8	23.4	24.3	24.7	120
Fort Worth, TX	483.7	506.2	526.2	520.2	562.1	594.5	613.4	5
Gainesville, FL	14.5	15.0	15.4	15.4	16.4	17.0	17.7	159
Green Bay, WI	20.0	20.6	20.7	20.1	20.5	20.8	21.1	144
Greensboro, NC	41.2	41.4	41.0	39.5	41.1	42.2	42.5	80
Honolulu, HI	65.8	66.0	65.6	60.1	62.8	64.5	66.0	55
Houston, TX	470.7	491.2	486.9	478.0	501.2	522.6	550.8	7
Huntsville, AL	27.5	28.6	30.2	30.7	32.6	34.1	36.1	92
Indianapolis, IN	135.9	140.7	143.8	142.8	152.5	158.8	161.8	28
Jacksonville, FL	80.3	83.0	86.5	87.7	94.4	100.4	104.7	40
Kansas City, MO	133.8	136.4	139.5	136.8	141.7	148.9	152.8	32
Lafayette, LA	21.1	22.0	21.8	20.8	21.8	21.8	22.6	132
Las Vegas, NV	116.3	122.7	128.2	117.3	130.1	138.5	142.8	35
Lexington, KY	28.7	29.5	30.0	28.7	29.6	30.6	31.4	105
Lincoln, NE	19.6	19.9	20.3	20.2	21.1	22.1	22.8	130
Little Rock, AR	36.5	37.1	37.4	37.7	39.4	39.9	41.3	82
Los Angeles, CA	965.3	991.3	1,026.5	982.0	1,041.7	1,065.3	1,075.1	2
Louisville, KY	70.8	71.6	74.3	72.8	76.4	77.9	79.2	49
Madison, WI	47.4	49.3	50.6	49.4	52.3	53.4	55.1	59
Manchester, NH	26.0	26.5	27.2	27.0	29.5	30.0	30.5	108
McAllen, TX	20.7	21.2	22.0	21.5	22.7	23.1	24.0	124
Memphis, TN	75.3	76.0	76.6	75.7	79.9	79.7	81.2	47

Table continued on following page.

Metro Area	2017	2018	2019	2020	2021	2022	2023	Rank[1]
Miami, FL	347.0	359.9	367.6	353.8	391.4	415.2	431.9	12
Midland, TX	21.9	27.6	33.1	31.1	31.7	31.0	44.2	78
Milwaukee, WI	99.3	100.8	102.3	98.2	102.4	105.2	106.6	39
Minneapolis, MN	257.8	265.7	270.1	260.6	275.7	281.3	286.7	15
Nashville, TN	130.5	134.6	139.3	138.4	154.0	163.2	168.2	27
New Orleans, LA	78.2	78.1	79.8	73.4	76.8	75.7	79.6	48
New York, NY	1,714.1	1,766.3	1,801.1	1,744.7	1,834.5	1,875.1	1,905.2	1
Oklahoma City, OK	74.4	77.0	78.4	76.1	76.7	76.3	81.6	46
Omaha, NE	64.3	65.7	66.4	65.2	68.9	73.7	75.3	50
Orlando, FL	136.2	141.2	146.8	140.3	156.9	167.8	175.3	26
Philadelphia, PA	425.4	432.3	437.0	420.4	438.8	450.2	459.5	11
Phoenix, AZ	246.1	257.4	269.4	274.6	299.1	313.6	322.8	14
Pittsburgh, PA	150.7	154.3	155.9	147.7	153.2	155.0	159.6	30
Portland, OR	155.8	162.7	166.7	164.9	174.8	178.8	182.0	25
Providence, RI	84.6	84.7	86.8	84.2	88.5	89.3	90.4	45
Provo, UT	25.5	27.6	30.1	31.5	34.1	35.8	37.4	90
Raleigh, NC	84.9	89.5	92.3	92.4	101.0	105.8	110.6	38
Reno, NV	29.4	28.8	29.9	30.1	33.2	33.6	34.1	96
Richmond, VA	84.5	86.5	88.6	87.2	91.8	93.9	94.8	44
Rochester, MN	13.1	13.6	13.8	13.6	14.1	14.4	14.9	182
Sacramento, CA	131.2	136.9	141.9	138.9	147.4	150.4	153.8	31
Saint Louis, MO	164.4	166.6	169.5	165.7	175.8	180.2	184.8	24
Saint Paul, MN	257.8	265.7	270.1	260.6	275.7	281.3	286.7	15
Salem, OR	17.1	18.0	18.6	18.6	19.8	20.1	20.6	147
Salt Lake City, UT	92.0	97.2	103.0	102.5	111.3	114.3	118.0	37
San Antonio, TX	118.9	124.5	129.0	127.4	134.2	143.7	150.3	33
San Diego, CA	224.8	230.5	236.6	233.3	250.4	258.0	261.7	17
San Francisco, CA	526.6	560.6	594.3	596.5	662.4	659.3	681.9	4
San Jose, CA	282.7	304.6	319.4	339.4	381.6	379.7	392.5	13
Santa Rosa, CA	28.9	30.2	30.5	29.6	31.7	31.0	31.0	106
Savannah, GA	21.2	21.5	22.3	22.2	23.9	24.5	25.7	118
Seattle, WA	368.2	395.7	417.4	418.4	449.5	459.5	487.8	9
Sioux Falls, SD	22.2	21.9	22.8	22.0	23.2	22.8	23.2	128
Tampa, FL	152.7	158.0	163.9	165.5	180.0	190.7	198.9	23
Tucson, AZ	42.3	43.9	45.4	45.3	47.9	48.6	50.8	68
Tulsa, OK	51.6	53.1	52.0	49.2	51.1	51.6	53.9	61
Virginia Beach, VA	94.9	93.9	94.9	94.3	99.0	100.9	104.0	41
Washington, DC	528.9	542.4	551.9	543.4	571.1	584.2	600.2	6
Wichita, KS	35.9	35.8	35.8	34.7	35.7	36.7	37.7	89
Wilmington, NC	14.1	14.5	15.1	15.1	16.5	17.1	17.7	160
Winston-Salem, NC	34.9	34.2	34.7	32.6	34.8	35.7	36.1	91
U.S.[2]	17,619.1	18,160.7	18,642.5	18,238.9	19,387.6	19,896.6	20,436.3	–

Note: Figures are in billions of chained 2017 dollars; Figures cover the Metropolitan Statistical Area (MSA); (1) Rank is based on 2023 data and ranges from 1 to 384; (2) Figures cover real GDP within metropolitan areas
Source: U.S. Bureau of Economic Analysis

Economic Growth

Metro Area	2014	2015	2016	2017	2018	2019	2020	2021	2022	2023
Albuquerque, NM	2.0	1.2	1.7	0.4	1.9	2.9	-1.3	5.4	3.9	2.4
Anchorage, AK	0.3	4.3	1.2	-1.5	0.7	-0.3	-2.6	2.6	1.4	3.7
Ann Arbor, MI	1.7	3.7	2.2	3.3	2.5	4.0	-2.5	5.2	2.6	2.9
Athens, GA	2.4	4.3	2.2	5.7	3.5	-0.7	-4.3	5.7	4.5	1.5
Atlanta, GA	4.6	5.3	5.3	4.8	3.7	4.0	-3.0	6.7	3.9	2.1
Austin, TX	5.7	7.7	4.2	4.5	5.8	6.5	2.8	10.7	9.6	4.5
Baltimore, MD	1.6	2.0	3.4	2.1	1.0	0.6	-3.4	5.1	2.6	1.6
Billings, MT	5.4	4.6	-5.8	7.2	0.6	-2.4	-2.3	7.3	0.1	3.5
Boise City, ID	4.5	1.6	4.2	5.5	7.8	4.7	1.6	9.1	7.5	2.9
Boston, MA	2.1	4.0	1.7	2.3	4.0	3.6	-0.9	7.0	2.4	1.5
Boulder, CO	3.3	3.9	3.5	4.9	3.7	9.0	-1.9	7.5	1.9	3.4
Cape Coral, FL	5.0	6.1	7.5	0.6	4.1	2.4	-0.5	8.5	7.8	4.2
Cedar Rapids, IA	4.4	4.0	3.1	0.1	1.8	-1.9	-1.8	6.7	-1.0	-0.9
Charleston, SC	2.8	4.7	5.6	2.0	4.0	4.8	-2.7	5.4	6.4	5.2
Charlotte, NC	3.3	4.2	3.0	3.7	2.1	3.4	0.9	6.4	3.6	4.7
Chicago, IL	2.3	2.4	0.8	1.4	2.5	0.9	-5.4	5.8	2.5	1.4
Cincinnati, OH	3.6	2.9	3.7	3.1	0.0	4.8	-1.8	4.3	1.0	1.7
Clarksville, TN	-1.2	0.5	-1.0	0.0	1.1	2.0	1.4	5.9	2.1	1.9
Cleveland, OH	2.3	0.8	0.1	2.4	1.6	2.6	-3.6	5.5	2.1	0.6
College Station, TX	6.3	6.2	-0.3	1.7	4.3	4.5	-0.2	4.6	4.0	7.4
Colorado Springs, CO	0.9	1.1	2.0	4.2	3.3	4.2	2.9	5.8	1.7	4.4
Columbia, MO	0.4	2.1	0.4	2.4	0.6	4.0	-2.9	5.1	0.5	2.8
Columbia, SC	3.6	2.9	2.9	0.3	1.6	2.4	-1.0	5.6	2.0	3.4
Columbus, OH	3.6	2.1	2.1	4.4	1.2	3.2	-1.1	7.0	1.3	1.8
Dallas, TX	3.8	4.8	2.3	3.6	4.6	3.9	-1.1	8.1	5.8	3.2
Davenport, IA	0.4	-1.4	-0.7	1.0	-0.7	0.8	-2.4	2.8	1.6	2.1
Denver, CO	4.5	5.3	2.2	3.8	4.4	5.3	0.1	7.3	4.7	3.5
Des Moines, IA	12.6	8.5	3.8	-1.3	0.2	4.3	2.6	9.3	-1.5	1.0
Detroit, MI	1.4	1.7	1.9	0.9	2.1	0.4	-4.9	5.6	3.0	1.8
Durham, NC	-1.9	-1.7	-0.7	-0.5	4.9	2.8	2.8	7.0	3.4	3.5
El Paso, TX	-1.5	1.5	0.9	2.1	3.1	5.4	-0.5	7.2	1.9	6.1
Eugene, OR	1.5	5.0	3.0	3.8	2.7	0.4	-0.7	7.0	1.9	2.3
Fargo, ND	7.0	3.5	-0.3	3.3	0.7	2.5	-3.4	5.3	0.4	3.6
Fort Collins, CO	5.3	4.6	4.0	7.7	4.8	4.4	-0.9	5.8	1.9	1.3
Fort Wayne, IN	7.7	4.3	3.2	3.8	3.8	0.7	-7.1	7.2	4.2	1.4
Fort Worth, TX	3.8	4.8	2.3	3.6	4.6	3.9	-1.1	8.1	5.8	3.2
Gainesville, FL	3.2	1.9	2.1	3.8	3.3	2.9	0.1	6.5	3.4	4.5
Green Bay, WI	6.3	2.8	1.0	-0.2	3.2	0.4	-2.8	1.9	1.4	1.3
Greensboro, NC	-0.4	2.5	-1.1	0.5	0.5	-1.1	-3.6	4.0	2.8	0.5
Honolulu, HI	0.9	2.7	1.9	2.1	0.4	-0.6	-8.5	4.5	2.6	2.4
Houston, TX	1.7	5.5	-2.1	0.7	4.4	-0.9	-1.8	4.8	4.3	5.4
Huntsville, AL	0.3	1.8	3.1	3.8	3.9	5.7	1.6	6.0	4.6	6.0
Indianapolis, IN	2.1	-2.5	2.4	2.4	3.6	2.2	-0.7	6.8	4.1	1.9
Jacksonville, FL	2.4	4.2	3.8	4.5	3.3	4.3	1.3	7.7	6.3	4.3
Kansas City, MO	2.7	3.8	0.5	3.3	2.0	2.3	-1.9	3.6	5.0	2.7
Lafayette, LA	1.4	-7.6	-9.3	0.0	4.4	-1.0	-4.5	4.6	0.1	3.8
Las Vegas, NV	1.5	4.4	3.2	3.6	5.5	4.5	-8.5	10.9	6.4	3.2
Lexington, KY	2.6	3.9	2.2	1.2	2.8	1.9	-4.5	3.1	3.6	2.7
Lincoln, NE	4.9	3.5	1.7	5.3	2.0	1.9	-0.7	4.5	4.6	3.3
Little Rock, AR	1.1	1.4	1.1	-0.8	1.5	0.8	0.8	4.6	1.1	3.5
Los Angeles, CA	2.7	4.3	1.8	3.7	2.7	3.6	-4.3	6.1	2.3	0.9
Louisville, KY	1.3	2.6	1.9	1.7	1.2	3.8	-2.0	4.9	2.0	1.6
Madison, WI	5.0	3.7	3.3	1.5	3.9	2.7	-2.4	5.9	2.2	3.2
Manchester, NH	2.2	3.4	1.6	0.4	1.9	3.0	-0.9	9.3	1.7	1.6
McAllen, TX	1.7	1.1	-0.4	0.5	2.2	3.8	-2.1	5.4	1.9	3.8
Memphis, TN	-0.2	2.0	1.3	1.8	0.8	0.9	-1.2	5.5	-0.2	1.9

Table continued on following page.

Metro Area	2014	2015	2016	2017	2018	2019	2020	2021	2022	2023
Miami, FL	3.4	4.4	3.1	4.5	3.7	2.1	-3.7	10.6	6.1	4.0
Midland, TX	9.0	9.5	-1.7	14.0	25.9	20.3	-6.1	1.8	-2.3	42.9
Milwaukee, WI	0.6	1.2	0.5	1.5	1.6	1.5	-4.0	4.3	2.7	1.4
Minneapolis, MN	3.8	2.2	1.6	1.9	3.1	1.6	-3.5	5.8	2.0	2.0
Nashville, TN	4.6	6.7	3.7	4.6	3.1	3.6	-0.7	11.3	6.0	3.1
New Orleans, LA	1.2	0.3	0.8	5.8	-0.1	2.1	-8.0	4.6	-1.3	5.0
New York, NY	1.9	2.2	1.7	2.0	3.0	2.0	-3.1	5.1	2.2	1.6
Oklahoma City, OK	6.4	4.2	0.3	3.1	3.5	1.7	-2.8	0.7	-0.5	6.9
Omaha, NE	6.2	3.3	0.5	4.6	2.1	1.1	-1.8	5.6	7.0	2.2
Orlando, FL	3.8	5.5	3.8	5.5	3.7	4.0	-4.4	11.9	6.9	4.5
Philadelphia, PA	2.5	1.7	1.4	-0.3	1.6	1.1	-3.8	4.4	2.6	2.1
Phoenix, AZ	1.6	3.1	3.6	4.6	4.6	4.7	1.9	8.9	4.8	2.9
Pittsburgh, PA	1.8	3.1	0.2	4.4	2.4	1.0	-5.3	3.7	1.2	2.9
Portland, OR	3.4	5.7	4.7	5.7	4.4	2.5	-1.1	6.0	2.3	1.8
Providence, RI	1.6	2.5	0.2	0.5	0.1	2.4	-3.0	5.1	0.9	1.2
Provo, UT	4.7	8.2	7.0	6.8	8.3	9.1	4.6	8.3	4.9	4.4
Raleigh, NC	6.1	7.4	6.5	4.6	5.4	3.1	0.2	9.3	4.7	4.6
Reno, NV	0.4	7.7	4.1	7.1	-2.0	3.9	0.8	10.2	1.4	1.4
Richmond, VA	1.2	3.9	1.5	1.8	2.4	2.4	-1.6	5.3	2.3	1.0
Rochester, MN	1.6	2.9	1.4	3.6	3.5	2.0	-1.6	3.9	2.0	3.2
Sacramento, CA	2.8	4.3	2.1	2.9	4.4	3.6	-2.1	6.1	2.1	2.2
Saint Louis, MO	1.4	0.8	0.1	-0.4	1.3	1.7	-2.2	6.1	2.5	2.5
Saint Paul, MN	3.8	2.2	1.6	1.9	3.1	1.6	-3.5	5.8	2.0	2.0
Salem, OR	3.4	5.4	5.1	4.5	5.6	3.2	-0.3	6.4	1.7	2.6
Salt Lake City, UT	3.2	3.4	4.7	5.2	5.7	6.0	-0.5	8.6	2.7	3.2
San Antonio, TX	5.3	5.7	0.9	0.3	4.7	3.6	-1.3	5.4	7.1	4.6
San Diego, CA	3.1	3.3	1.3	3.7	2.6	2.7	-1.4	7.3	3.1	1.4
San Francisco, CA	6.1	6.0	5.7	9.3	6.5	6.0	0.4	11.0	-0.5	3.4
San Jose, CA	7.2	8.9	6.1	4.9	7.8	4.8	6.3	12.4	-0.5	3.4
Santa Rosa, CA	4.1	4.8	2.5	1.6	4.7	0.9	-3.0	7.0	-2.2	0.2
Savannah, GA	4.3	3.0	3.9	2.5	1.4	4.0	-0.5	7.7	2.6	4.9
Seattle, WA	4.9	4.6	4.1	8.2	7.5	5.5	0.2	7.4	2.2	6.2
Sioux Falls, SD	5.5	1.3	1.4	1.5	-1.2	4.3	-3.5	5.4	-2.0	2.0
Tampa, FL	2.0	4.2	3.3	2.1	3.5	3.7	1.0	8.8	5.9	4.3
Tucson, AZ	0.2	-0.5	3.4	3.5	3.7	3.5	-0.3	5.7	1.4	4.6
Tulsa, OK	5.4	1.7	-5.9	3.5	2.9	-2.1	-5.4	3.9	1.0	4.4
Virginia Beach, VA	-1.0	1.7	1.1	0.7	-1.2	1.2	-0.7	5.0	1.9	3.2
Washington, DC	1.2	2.1	2.5	2.4	2.5	1.8	-1.6	5.1	2.3	2.7
Wichita, KS	6.2	5.6	8.2	0.4	-0.1	-0.2	-2.9	2.8	2.9	2.8
Wilmington, NC	4.1	1.5	5.1	0.6	3.0	4.2	0.1	9.2	3.6	3.5
Winston-Salem, NC	2.6	1.0	1.4	2.6	-2.1	1.4	-6.0	6.9	2.5	1.3
U.S.[1]	2.6	3.2	2.0	2.7	3.1	2.7	-2.2	6.3	2.6	2.7

Note: Figures are real gross domestic product growth rates and represent percent change from preceding period; Figures cover the Metropolitan Statistical Area (MSA); (1) Figures are the average growth rates within metropolitan areas
Source: U.S. Bureau of Economic Analysis

Metropolitan Area Exports

Metro Area	2018	2019	2020	2021	2022	2023	Rank[1]
Albuquerque, NM	771.5	1,629.7	1,265.3	2,215.0	939.7	789.4	195
Anchorage, AK	1,510.8	1,348.0	990.9	n/a	n/a	n/a	n/a
Ann Arbor, MI	1,538.7	1,432.7	1,183.1	1,230.7	1,334.2	1,196.2	156
Athens, GA	378.1	442.1	338.7	448.1	489.9	533.9	217
Atlanta, GA	24,091.6	25,800.8	25,791.0	28,116.4	30,833.1	32,336.4	13
Austin, TX	12,929.9	12,509.0	13,041.5	15,621.9	17,290.7	17,251.5	27
Baltimore, MD	6,039.2	7,081.8	6,084.6	8,200.6	7,820.0	10,196.2	43
Billings, MT	114.3	141.9	116.0	173.8	156.0	119.2	349
Boise City, ID	2,771.7	2,062.8	1,632.9	1,937.1	2,156.7	1,922.6	121
Boston, MA	24,450.1	23,505.8	23,233.8	32,084.2	33,101.8	34,519.4	12
Boulder, CO	1,044.1	1,014.9	1,110.4	1,078.0	1,201.9	1,213.1	153
Cape Coral, FL	668.0	694.9	654.8	797.5	886.9	935.4	177
Cedar Rapids, IA	1,025.0	1,028.4	832.0	980.0	1,018.7	1,175.4	159
Charleston, SC	10,943.2	16,337.9	6,110.5	3,381.6	4,256.0	9,497.6	44
Charlotte, NC	14,083.2	13,892.4	8,225.6	10,554.3	12,223.1	11,470.3	34
Chicago, IL	47,287.8	42,438.8	41,279.4	54,498.1	63,374.6	56,656.6	5
Cincinnati, OH	27,396.3	28,778.3	21,002.2	23,198.7	29,285.0	31,216.2	14
Clarksville, TN	435.5	341.8	246.8	288.7	376.7	445.6	236
Cleveland, OH	9,382.9	8,829.9	7,415.8	8,560.4	9,561.2	10,206.2	42
College Station, TX	153.0	160.5	114.9	110.3	136.2	180.0	323
Colorado Springs, CO	850.6	864.2	979.2	866.9	1,209.5	1,425.7	137
Columbia, MO	238.6	291.4	256.2	335.4	368.7	474.1	230
Columbia, SC	2,083.8	2,184.6	2,058.8	2,100.2	2,351.3	2,160.3	112
Columbus, OH	7,529.5	7,296.6	6,304.8	6,557.9	7,597.3	8,418.9	47
Dallas, TX	36,260.9	39,474.0	35,642.0	43,189.0	50,632.9	51,863.7	6
Davenport, IA	6,761.9	6,066.3	5,097.5	6,341.0	8,173.6	6,050.0	57
Denver, CO	4,544.3	4,555.6	4,604.4	4,670.8	5,761.7	5,724.2	59
Des Moines, IA	1,293.7	1,437.8	1,414.0	1,706.6	1,706.8	2,175.7	110
Detroit, MI	44,131.4	41,070.4	30,715.1	35,433.2	40,395.3	45,591.4	7
Durham, NC	3,945.8	4,452.9	3,359.3	3,326.4	4,071.8	4,898.7	65
El Paso, TX	30,052.0	32,749.6	27,154.4	32,397.9	36,488.3	35,223.0	11
Eugene, OR	400.1	360.0	340.6	426.7	434.9	415.2	241
Fargo, ND	553.5	515.0	438.3	539.4	518.7	880.1	185
Fort Collins, CO	1,021.8	1,060.0	1,092.5	1,132.5	1,178.8	1,180.5	157
Fort Wayne, IN	1,593.3	1,438.5	1,144.6	1,592.7	1,787.5	2,032.1	115
Fort Worth, TX	36,260.9	39,474.0	35,642.0	43,189.0	50,632.9	51,863.7	6
Gainesville, FL	370.2	297.2	260.9	320.7	307.2	306.6	274
Green Bay, WI	1,044.3	928.2	736.4	765.6	855.1	835.1	190
Greensboro, NC	3,053.5	2,561.8	2,007.3	2,356.2	2,375.6	2,239.4	108
Honolulu, HI	438.9	308.6	169.0	164.3	258.8	450.6	234
Houston, TX	120,714.3	129,656.0	104,538.2	140,750.4	191,846.9	175,470.1	1
Huntsville, AL	1,608.7	1,534.2	1,263.0	1,579.5	1,558.7	1,762.1	125
Indianapolis, IN	11,069.9	11,148.7	11,100.4	12,740.4	14,671.5	23,080.6	20
Jacksonville, FL	2,406.7	2,975.5	2,473.3	2,683.7	3,007.8	2,730.8	92
Kansas City, MO	7,316.9	7,652.6	7,862.7	9,177.6	9,623.5	10,627.2	40
Lafayette, LA	1,001.7	1,086.2	946.2	895.7	911.8	836.2	189
Las Vegas, NV	2,240.6	2,430.8	1,705.9	1,866.2	2,116.3	2,762.3	91
Lexington, KY	2,148.0	2,093.8	1,586.3	1,880.0	2,677.2	3,343.3	81
Lincoln, NE	885.6	807.0	726.3	872.6	1,161.3	1,082.2	165
Little Rock, AR	1,607.4	1,642.5	n/a	1,370.6	1,373.7	1,464.0	134
Los Angeles, CA	64,814.6	61,041.1	50,185.4	58,588.4	60,979.7	59,561.6	4
Louisville, KY	8,987.0	9,105.5	8,360.3	10,262.8	10,618.7	11,072.0	37
Madison, WI	2,460.2	2,337.6	2,450.5	2,756.3	2,893.8	2,822.9	90
Manchester, NH	1,651.4	1,587.1	1,704.9	2,077.6	2,349.8	2,416.7	101
McAllen, TX	6,627.9	5,234.1	4,087.6	5,164.6	5,677.1	7,072.4	51
Memphis, TN	12,695.4	13,751.7	13,350.3	16,761.5	17,835.3	17,853.5	25

Table continued on following page.

Metro Area	2018	2019	2020	2021	2022	2023	Rank[1]
Miami, FL	35,650.2	35,498.9	29,112.1	36,011.3	41,517.8	44,256.4	8
Midland, TX	63.6	63.7	57.7	49.9	76.2	72.4	365
Milwaukee, WI	7,337.6	6,896.3	6,624.0	7,282.8	8,742.5	9,352.5	45
Minneapolis, MN	20,016.2	18,633.0	17,109.5	21,098.8	21,964.3	22,209.4	23
Nashville, TN	8,723.7	7,940.7	6,569.9	8,256.1	9,347.5	10,385.4	41
New Orleans, LA	36,570.4	34,109.6	31,088.4	35,773.5	52,912.9	38,978.6	9
New York, NY	97,692.4	87,365.7	75,745.4	103,930.9	120,643.7	106,209.0	2
Oklahoma City, OK	1,489.4	1,434.5	1,326.6	1,773.2	2,019.1	2,277.7	107
Omaha, NE	4,371.6	3,725.7	3,852.5	4,595.1	4,585.5	3,411.0	80
Orlando, FL	3,131.7	3,363.9	2,849.8	3,313.6	4,096.9	4,443.5	71
Philadelphia, PA	23,663.2	24,721.3	23,022.1	28,724.4	29,352.1	28,760.2	16
Phoenix, AZ	13,614.9	15,136.6	11,073.9	14,165.1	16,658.8	17,553.6	26
Pittsburgh, PA	9,824.2	9,672.9	7,545.1	9,469.6	11,188.3	11,538.4	33
Portland, OR	21,442.9	23,761.9	27,824.7	33,787.5	34,368.0	26,973.2	18
Providence, RI	6,236.6	7,424.8	6,685.2	6,708.2	7,179.7	6,517.8	53
Provo, UT	1,788.1	1,783.7	1,888.5	2,053.8	1,318.4	1,416.7	140
Raleigh, NC	3,193.2	3,546.8	3,372.0	3,962.7	4,714.1	5,965.8	58
Reno, NV	2,631.7	2,598.3	4,553.3	4,503.0	3,864.0	3,434.1	78
Richmond, VA	3,535.0	3,203.2	2,719.1	3,010.7	3,283.5	2,579.8	95
Rochester, MN	537.6	390.1	194.0	224.9	215.9	258.7	293
Sacramento, CA	6,222.8	5,449.2	4,980.9	5,682.3	5,716.7	7,586.6	50
Saint Louis, MO	10,866.8	10,711.1	9,089.4	10,486.1	14,215.6	13,817.0	30
Saint Paul, MN	20,016.2	18,633.0	17,109.5	21,098.8	21,964.3	22,209.4	23
Salem, OR	410.2	405.7	350.5	372.0	422.3	404.8	244
Salt Lake City, UT	9,748.6	13,273.9	13,565.5	13,469.1	12,340.1	12,775.2	32
San Antonio, TX	11,678.1	11,668.0	10,987.9	13,086.4	13,173.6	12,821.8	31
San Diego, CA	20,156.8	19,774.1	18,999.7	23,687.8	24,657.9	22,975.3	22
San Francisco, CA	27,417.0	28,003.8	23,864.5	29,972.0	30,649.0	24,253.0	19
San Jose, CA	22,224.2	20,909.4	19,534.5	22,293.6	24,342.2	22,985.4	21
Santa Rosa, CA	1,231.7	1,234.5	1,131.4	1,301.8	1,297.3	1,121.8	161
Savannah, GA	5,407.8	4,925.5	4,557.0	5,520.5	6,171.2	6,206.1	56
Seattle, WA	59,742.9	41,249.0	23,851.0	28,866.7	34,159.9	36,267.3	10
Sioux Falls, SD	400.0	431.5	524.9	547.3	371.3	510.9	224
Tampa, FL	4,966.7	6,219.7	5,082.2	5,754.7	9,588.2	7,923.6	49
Tucson, AZ	2,824.8	2,943.7	2,640.7	2,846.1	3,779.4	4,503.0	68
Tulsa, OK	3,351.7	3,399.2	2,567.8	3,064.8	3,379.2	3,234.5	84
Virginia Beach, VA	3,950.6	3,642.4	4,284.3	4,566.3	5,750.1	6,338.3	54
Washington, DC	13,602.7	14,563.8	13,537.3	12,210.8	14,001.9	14,758.9	29
Wichita, KS	3,817.0	3,494.7	2,882.1	3,615.3	4,550.4	4,475.1	69
Wilmington, NC	634.4	526.4	553.6	497.8	593.6	671.5	206
Winston-Salem, NC	1,107.5	1,209.1	913.1	918.2	1,012.1	1,071.1	166
U.S.	1,664,056.1	1,645,173.7	1,431,406.6	1,753,941.4	2,062,937.4	2,019,160.5	—

Note: Figures are in millions of dollars; Figures cover the Metropolitan Statistical Area (MSA); (1) Rank is based on 2023 data and ranges from 1 to 386
Source: U.S. Department of Commerce, International Trade Administration, Office of Trade and Economic Analysis, Industry and Analysis, Exports by Metropolitan Area, data extracted April 2, 2025

Building Permits: City

City	Single-Family			Multi-Family			Total		
	2023	2024	Pct. Chg.	2023	2024	Pct. Chg.	2023	2024	Pct. Chg.
Albuquerque, NM	587	525	-10.6	512	574	12.1	1,099	1,099	0.0
Anchorage, AK	271	161	-40.6	28	180	542.9	299	341	14.0
Ann Arbor, MI	161	28	-82.6	61	266	336.1	222	294	32.4
Athens, GA	168	212	26.2	238	960	303.4	406	1,172	188.7
Atlanta, GA	1,139	791	-30.6	6,482	7,318	12.9	7,621	8,109	6.4
Austin, TX	1,799	1,946	8.2	11,885	7,498	-36.9	13,684	9,444	-31.0
Baltimore, MD	92	165	79.3	1,751	1,108	-36.7	1,843	1,273	-30.9
Billings, MT	259	327	26.3	0	328	—	259	655	152.9
Boise City, ID	447	468	4.7	1,450	273	-81.2	1,897	741	-60.9
Boston, MA	108	72	-33.3	1,943	1,717	-11.6	2,051	1,789	-12.8
Boulder, CO	30	35	16.7	225	371	64.9	255	406	59.2
Cape Coral, FL	2,023	2,671	32.0	1,972	726	-63.2	3,995	3,397	-15.0
Cedar Rapids, IA	145	143	-1.4	229	465	103.1	374	608	62.6
Charleston, SC	891	878	-1.5	363	266	-26.7	1,254	1,144	-8.8
Charlotte, NC	n/a	n/a	n/a	n/a	n/a	n/a	n/a	n/a	n/a
Chicago, IL	290	325	12.1	3,326	4,046	21.6	3,616	4,371	20.9
Cincinnati, OH	117	110	-6.0	514	114	-77.8	631	224	-64.5
Clarksville, TN	805	1,366	69.7	1,455	703	-51.7	2,260	2,069	-8.5
Cleveland, OH	161	234	45.3	644	662	2.8	805	896	11.3
College Station, TX	448	650	45.1	293	462	57.7	741	1,112	50.1
Colorado Springs, CO	n/a	n/a	n/a	n/a	n/a	n/a	n/a	n/a	n/a
Columbia, MO	314	461	46.8	56	549	880.4	370	1,010	173.0
Columbia, SC	883	833	-5.7	718	1,315	83.1	1,601	2,148	34.2
Columbus, OH	943	828	-12.2	4,340	5,256	21.1	5,283	6,084	15.2
Dallas, TX	1,995	1,957	-1.9	4,429	4,081	-7.9	6,424	6,038	-6.0
Davenport, IA	94	149	58.5	121	162	33.9	215	311	44.7
Denver, CO	1,174	872	-25.7	4,551	3,122	-31.4	5,725	3,994	-30.2
Des Moines, IA	248	218	-12.1	321	400	24.6	569	618	8.6
Detroit, MI	397	483	21.7	828	1,436	73.4	1,225	1,919	56.7
Durham, NC	1,687	1,822	8.0	2,678	971	-63.7	4,365	2,793	-36.0
El Paso, TX	1,572	1,644	4.6	280	243	-13.2	1,852	1,887	1.9
Eugene, OR	171	309	80.7	422	693	64.2	593	1,002	69.0
Fargo, ND	292	241	-17.5	980	410	-58.2	1,272	651	-48.8
Fort Collins, CO	372	371	-0.3	631	314	-50.2	1,003	685	-31.7
Fort Wayne, IN	n/a	n/a	n/a	n/a	n/a	n/a	n/a	n/a	n/a
Fort Worth, TX	6,631	6,257	-5.6	3,429	6,891	101.0	10,060	13,148	30.7
Gainesville, FL	236	296	25.4	544	922	69.5	780	1,218	56.2
Green Bay, WI	37	42	13.5	0	434	—	37	476	1,186.5
Greensboro, NC	704	618	-12.2	1,063	1,336	25.7	1,767	1,954	10.6
Honolulu, HI	n/a	n/a	n/a	n/a	n/a	n/a	n/a	n/a	n/a
Houston, TX	6,609	6,808	3.0	9,821	5,090	-48.2	16,430	11,898	-27.6
Huntsville, AL	1,403	1,245	-11.3	1,197	240	-79.9	2,600	1,485	-42.9
Indianapolis, IN	896	1,170	30.6	1,517	653	-57.0	2,413	1,823	-24.5
Jacksonville, FL	4,223	5,037	19.3	5,485	1,361	-75.2	9,708	6,398	-34.1
Kansas City, MO	776	429	-44.7	458	2,449	434.7	1,234	2,878	133.2
Lafayette, LA	n/a	n/a	n/a	n/a	n/a	n/a	n/a	n/a	n/a
Las Vegas, NV	2,590	2,655	2.5	1,026	935	-8.9	3,616	3,590	-0.7
Lexington, KY	624	492	-21.2	774	544	-29.7	1,398	1,036	-25.9
Lincoln, NE	699	937	34.0	1,282	793	-38.1	1,981	1,730	-12.7
Little Rock, AR	703	468	-33.4	230	18	-92.2	933	486	-47.9
Los Angeles, CA	2,918	3,041	4.2	10,236	7,447	-27.2	13,154	10,488	-20.3
Louisville, KY	1,014	1,168	15.2	2,686	1,690	-37.1	3,700	2,858	-22.8
Madison, WI	332	250	-24.7	2,288	2,562	12.0	2,620	2,812	7.3
Manchester, NH	99	26	-73.7	280	167	-40.4	379	193	-49.1

Table continued on following page.

City	Single-Family			Multi-Family			Total		
	2023	2024	Pct. Chg.	2023	2024	Pct. Chg.	2023	2024	Pct. Chg.
McAllen, TX	428	669	56.3	753	1,053	39.8	1,181	1,722	45.8
Memphis, TN	n/a	n/a	n/a	n/a	n/a	n/a	n/a	n/a	n/a
Miami, FL	113	145	28.3	5,307	5,878	10.8	5,420	6,023	11.1
Midland, TX	805	1,504	86.8	0	0	0.0	805	1,504	86.8
Milwaukee, WI	61	72	18.0	36	164	355.6	97	236	143.3
Minneapolis, MN	70	65	-7.1	1,458	387	-73.5	1,528	452	-70.4
Nashville, TN	3,106	2,662	-14.3	8,052	4,137	-48.6	11,158	6,799	-39.1
New Orleans, LA	249	202	-18.9	818	508	-37.9	1,067	710	-33.5
New York, NY	232	197	-15.1	31,733	27,044	-14.8	31,965	27,241	-14.8
Oklahoma City, OK	3,339	3,460	3.6	805	938	16.5	4,144	4,398	6.1
Omaha, NE	1,294	1,692	30.8	1,756	2,668	51.9	3,050	4,360	43.0
Orlando, FL	887	914	3.0	1,514	1,056	-30.3	2,401	1,970	-18.0
Philadelphia, PA	405	539	33.1	3,458	2,423	-29.9	3,863	2,962	-23.3
Phoenix, AZ	4,200	4,062	-3.3	10,268	4,935	-51.9	14,468	8,997	-37.8
Pittsburgh, PA	229	229	0.0	2,283	1,435	-37.1	2,512	1,664	-33.8
Portland, OR	877	815	-7.1	2,212	885	-60.0	3,089	1,700	-45.0
Providence, RI	0	31	–	5	238	4,660.0	5	269	5,280.0
Provo, UT	147	133	-9.5	80	153	91.3	227	286	26.0
Raleigh, NC	1,762	1,653	-6.2	4,626	3,391	-26.7	6,388	5,044	-21.0
Reno, NV	1,059	1,087	2.6	2,176	1,636	-24.8	3,235	2,723	-15.8
Richmond, VA	387	380	-1.8	1,896	2,160	13.9	2,283	2,540	11.3
Rochester, MN	241	193	-19.9	551	925	67.9	792	1,118	41.2
Sacramento, CA	653	708	8.4	1,864	1,335	-28.4	2,517	2,043	-18.8
Saint Louis, MO	51	56	9.8	227	238	4.8	278	294	5.8
Saint Paul, MN	48	75	56.3	1,156	329	-71.5	1,204	404	-66.4
Salem, OR	360	392	8.9	326	513	57.4	686	905	31.9
Salt Lake City, UT	243	397	63.4	2,929	886	-69.8	3,172	1,283	-59.6
San Antonio, TX	4,299	5,000	16.3	4,860	1,258	-74.1	9,159	6,258	-31.7
San Diego, CA	516	775	50.2	5,249	5,840	11.3	5,765	6,615	14.7
San Francisco, CA	29	27	-6.9	1,107	743	-32.9	1,136	770	-32.2
San Jose, CA	581	642	10.5	2,069	1,356	-34.5	2,650	1,998	-24.6
Santa Rosa, CA	441	292	-33.8	905	0	-100.0	1,346	292	-78.3
Savannah, GA	589	565	-4.1	12	14	16.7	601	579	-3.7
Seattle, WA	473	405	-14.4	4,826	5,490	13.8	5,299	5,895	11.2
Sioux Falls, SD	750	880	17.3	1,986	1,239	-37.6	2,736	2,119	-22.6
Tampa, FL	738	912	23.6	2,415	1,634	-32.3	3,153	2,546	-19.3
Tucson, AZ	839	923	10.0	829	582	-29.8	1,668	1,505	-9.8
Tulsa, OK	524	424	-19.1	352	299	-15.1	876	723	-17.5
Virginia Beach, VA	201	319	58.7	341	347	1.8	542	666	22.9
Washington, DC	166	146	-12.0	2,854	1,591	-44.3	3,020	1,737	-42.5
Wichita, KS	605	558	-7.8	1,173	742	-36.7	1,778	1,300	-26.9
Wilmington, NC	n/a	n/a	n/a	n/a	n/a	n/a	n/a	n/a	n/a
Winston-Salem, NC	860	1,168	35.8	1,281	966	-24.6	2,141	2,134	-0.3
U.S.	920,000	981,900	6.7	591,100	496,100	-16.1	1,511,100	1,478,000	-2.2

Note: Figures represent new, privately-owned housing units authorized (unadjusted data)
Source: U.S. Census Bureau, Building Permits Survey (BPS), 2023, 2024

Building Permits: Metro Area

Metro Area	Single-Family			Multi-Family			Total		
	2023	2024	Pct. Chg.	2023	2024	Pct. Chg.	2023	2024	Pct. Chg.
Albuquerque, NM	2,057	2,064	0.3	777	812	4.5	2,834	2,876	1.5
Anchorage, AK	338	198	-41.4	119	228	91.6	457	426	-6.8
Ann Arbor, MI	485	557	14.8	1,112	636	-42.8	1,597	1,193	-25.3
Athens, GA	776	863	11.2	250	972	288.8	1,026	1,835	78.8
Atlanta, GA	24,022	25,773	7.3	14,617	14,914	2.0	38,639	40,687	5.3
Austin, TX	16,532	16,435	-0.6	22,241	15,859	-28.7	38,773	32,294	-16.7
Baltimore, MD	3,798	3,849	1.3	3,741	2,435	-34.9	7,539	6,284	-16.6
Billings, MT	343	896	161.2	6	629	10,383.3	349	1,525	337.0
Boise City, ID	6,508	8,252	26.8	3,383	811	-76.0	9,891	9,063	-8.4
Boston, MA	3,396	3,734	10.0	7,426	7,501	1.0	10,822	11,235	3.8
Boulder, CO	791	441	-44.2	851	1,239	45.6	1,642	1,680	2.3
Cape Coral, FL	8,654	10,554	22.0	4,902	4,857	-0.9	13,556	15,411	13.7
Cedar Rapids, IA	467	494	5.8	301	593	97.0	768	1,087	41.5
Charleston, SC	6,184	6,817	10.2	2,389	1,697	-29.0	8,573	8,514	-0.7
Charlotte, NC	19,146	18,954	-1.0	10,273	6,981	-32.0	29,419	25,935	-11.8
Chicago, IL	8,452	9,509	12.5	6,576	8,555	30.1	15,028	18,064	20.2
Cincinnati, OH	3,714	4,025	8.4	2,527	3,064	21.3	6,241	7,089	13.6
Clarksville, TN	1,385	1,975	42.6	1,554	823	-47.0	2,939	2,798	-4.8
Cleveland, OH	2,500	2,980	19.2	991	1,309	32.1	3,491	4,289	22.9
College Station, TX	1,155	1,482	28.3	307	839	173.3	1,462	2,321	58.8
Colorado Springs, CO	2,670	2,878	7.8	2,607	1,116	-57.2	5,277	3,994	-24.3
Columbia, MO	609	763	25.3	72	568	688.9	681	1,331	95.4
Columbia, SC	4,634	4,469	-3.6	831	1,423	71.2	5,465	5,892	7.8
Columbus, OH	5,364	6,094	13.6	6,076	7,868	29.5	11,440	13,962	22.0
Dallas, TX	44,366	46,440	4.7	23,663	25,348	7.1	68,029	71,788	5.5
Davenport, IA	366	401	9.6	248	564	127.4	614	965	57.2
Denver, CO	9,012	9,012	0.0	11,638	6,558	-43.7	20,650	15,570	-24.6
Des Moines, IA	3,689	3,717	0.8	1,311	1,347	2.7	5,000	5,064	1.3
Detroit, MI	4,541	4,878	7.4	2,193	2,826	28.9	6,734	7,704	14.4
Durham, NC	3,127	2,815	-10.0	4,083	1,043	-74.5	7,210	3,858	-46.5
El Paso, TX	1,967	2,077	5.6	280	243	-13.2	2,247	2,320	3.2
Eugene, OR	732	799	9.2	507	1,015	100.2	1,239	1,814	46.4
Fargo, ND	885	832	-6.0	1,204	660	-45.2	2,089	1,492	-28.6
Fort Collins, CO	1,289	1,370	6.3	1,397	416	-70.2	2,686	1,786	-33.5
Fort Wayne, IN	1,680	1,409	-16.1	756	625	-17.3	2,436	2,034	-16.5
Fort Worth, TX	44,366	46,440	4.7	23,663	25,348	7.1	68,029	71,788	5.5
Gainesville, FL	1,247	1,115	-10.6	698	928	33.0	1,945	2,043	5.0
Green Bay, WI	578	717	24.0	415	1,108	167.0	993	1,825	83.8
Greensboro, NC	2,368	2,337	-1.3	1,139	2,639	131.7	3,507	4,976	41.9
Honolulu, HI	657	706	7.5	1,194	932	-21.9	1,851	1,638	-11.5
Houston, TX	50,444	52,703	4.5	18,311	13,044	-28.8	68,755	65,747	-4.4
Huntsville, AL	3,908	3,972	1.6	2,032	1,234	-39.3	5,940	5,206	-12.4
Indianapolis, IN	7,252	9,168	26.4	5,302	2,620	-50.6	12,554	11,788	-6.1
Jacksonville, FL	12,479	12,936	3.7	7,847	2,066	-73.7	20,326	15,002	-26.2
Kansas City, MO	4,299	4,875	13.4	3,215	4,273	32.9	7,514	9,148	21.7
Lafayette, LA	2,008	2,001	-0.3	378	18	-95.2	2,386	2,019	-15.4
Las Vegas, NV	10,087	12,277	21.7	2,986	2,477	-17.0	13,073	14,754	12.9
Lexington, KY	1,319	1,392	5.5	1,123	809	-28.0	2,442	2,201	-9.9
Lincoln, NE	849	1,077	26.9	1,288	959	-25.5	2,137	2,036	-4.7
Little Rock, AR	1,932	2,055	6.4	732	551	-24.7	2,664	2,606	-2.2
Los Angeles, CA	12,035	11,777	-2.1	18,732	15,004	-19.9	30,767	26,781	-13.0
Louisville, KY	2,914	3,690	26.6	3,817	2,106	-44.8	6,731	5,796	-13.9
Madison, WI	1,534	1,679	9.5	3,827	4,159	8.7	5,361	5,838	8.9
Manchester, NH	532	427	-19.7	850	445	-47.6	1,382	872	-36.9

Table continued on following page.

Metro Area	Single-Family			Multi-Family			Total		
	2023	2024	Pct. Chg.	2023	2024	Pct. Chg.	2023	2024	Pct. Chg.
McAllen, TX	4,143	4,336	4.7	2,756	2,956	7.3	6,899	7,292	5.7
Memphis, TN	3,062	2,773	-9.4	996	1,467	47.3	4,058	4,240	4.5
Miami, FL	5,512	5,825	5.7	15,808	10,527	-33.4	21,320	16,352	-23.3
Midland, TX	810	1,505	85.8	8	4	-50.0	818	1,509	84.5
Milwaukee, WI	1,408	1,712	21.6	1,436	2,346	63.4	2,844	4,058	42.7
Minneapolis, MN	8,245	9,300	12.8	10,388	4,722	-54.5	18,633	14,022	-24.7
Nashville, TN	13,842	14,465	4.5	9,716	5,573	-42.6	23,558	20,038	-14.9
New Orleans, LA	1,865	1,007	-46.0	1,207	604	-50.0	3,072	1,611	-47.6
New York, NY	11,734	12,530	6.8	51,296	45,399	-11.5	63,030	57,929	-8.1
Oklahoma City, OK	5,573	6,014	7.9	1,163	1,693	45.6	6,736	7,707	14.4
Omaha, NE	2,763	3,505	26.9	1,956	3,692	88.8	4,719	7,197	52.5
Orlando, FL	17,049	15,364	-9.9	8,366	8,771	4.8	25,415	24,135	-5.0
Philadelphia, PA	6,255	8,324	33.1	5,764	5,890	2.2	12,019	14,214	18.3
Phoenix, AZ	24,708	30,277	22.5	20,908	15,607	-25.4	45,616	45,884	0.6
Pittsburgh, PA	3,332	3,530	5.9	2,962	1,882	-36.5	6,294	5,412	-14.0
Portland, OR	6,326	6,345	0.3	5,056	3,108	-38.5	11,382	9,453	-16.9
Providence, RI	1,255	1,339	6.7	675	1,281	89.8	1,930	2,620	35.8
Provo, UT	4,663	5,246	12.5	1,518	1,182	-22.1	6,181	6,428	4.0
Raleigh, NC	12,147	13,343	9.8	8,472	5,636	-33.5	20,619	18,979	-8.0
Reno, NV	1,992	2,474	24.2	2,279	1,917	-15.9	4,271	4,391	2.8
Richmond, VA	4,590	5,023	9.4	5,383	3,619	-32.8	9,973	8,642	-13.3
Rochester, MN	604	491	-18.7	570	993	74.2	1,174	1,484	26.4
Sacramento, CA	7,931	8,579	8.2	4,010	3,034	-24.3	11,941	11,613	-2.7
Saint Louis, MO	4,599	4,653	1.2	2,508	2,364	-5.7	7,107	7,017	-1.3
Saint Paul, MN	8,245	9,300	12.8	10,388	4,722	-54.5	18,633	14,022	-24.7
Salem, OR	826	994	20.3	1,140	865	-24.1	1,966	1,859	-5.4
Salt Lake City, UT	3,163	3,525	11.4	6,072	1,922	-68.3	9,235	5,447	-41.0
San Antonio, TX	8,718	10,999	26.2	7,767	3,858	-50.3	16,485	14,857	-9.9
San Diego, CA	3,049	3,377	10.8	8,420	8,195	-2.7	11,469	11,572	0.9
San Francisco, CA	3,015	2,776	-7.9	4,515	3,138	-30.5	7,530	5,914	-21.5
San Jose, CA	2,037	2,207	8.3	4,190	1,908	-54.5	6,227	4,115	-33.9
Santa Rosa, CA	1,020	832	-18.4	1,333	180	-86.5	2,353	1,012	-57.0
Savannah, GA	2,620	2,936	12.1	768	1,101	43.4	3,388	4,037	19.2
Seattle, WA	6,296	6,489	3.1	10,927	11,431	4.6	17,223	17,920	4.0
Sioux Falls, SD	1,155	1,270	10.0	2,284	1,532	-32.9	3,439	2,802	-18.5
Tampa, FL	14,852	13,205	-11.1	10,534	7,745	-26.5	25,386	20,950	-17.5
Tucson, AZ	3,688	4,150	12.5	1,567	1,100	-29.8	5,255	5,250	-0.1
Tulsa, OK	3,393	3,602	6.2	1,616	709	-56.1	5,009	4,311	-13.9
Virginia Beach, VA	3,393	3,544	4.5	2,721	862	-68.3	6,114	4,406	-27.9
Washington, DC	10,936	11,743	7.4	12,557	9,744	-22.4	23,493	21,487	-8.5
Wichita, KS	1,470	1,479	0.6	2,063	1,560	-24.4	3,533	3,039	-14.0
Wilmington, NC	2,228	7,263	226.0	1,737	2,355	35.6	3,965	9,618	142.6
Winston-Salem, NC	3,567	4,010	12.4	1,507	1,446	-4.0	5,074	5,456	7.5
U.S.	920,000	981,900	6.7	591,100	496,100	-16.1	1,511,100	1,478,000	-2.2

Note: Figures cover the Metropolitan Statistical Area (MSA); Figures represent new, privately-owned housing units authorized (unadjusted data)
Source: U.S. Census Bureau, Building Permits Survey (BPS), 2023, 2024

Housing Vacancy Rates

Metro Area	Gross Vacancy Rate[1] (%)			Year-Round Vacancy Rate[2] (%)			Rental Vacancy Rate[3] (%)			Homeowner Vacancy Rate[4] (%)		
	2022	2023	2024	2022	2023	2024	2022	2023	2024	2022	2023	2024
Albuquerque, NM	5.3	5.6	6.4	5.1	5.4	6.1	5.5	6.1	6.7	1.0	0.7	1.6
Anchorage, AK	n/a	n/a	n/a	n/a	n/a	n/a	n/a	n/a	n/a	n/a	n/a	n/a
Ann Arbor, MI	n/a	n/a	n/a	n/a	n/a	n/a	n/a	n/a	n/a	n/a	n/a	n/a
Athens, GA	n/a	n/a	n/a	n/a	n/a	n/a	n/a	n/a	n/a	n/a	n/a	n/a
Atlanta, GA	5.9	6.6	6.8	5.7	6.4	6.6	6.7	8.7	9.3	0.8	1.2	0.9
Austin, TX	5.5	8.5	8.6	4.9	8.2	8.3	5.6	9.0	8.2	0.6	1.3	1.7
Baltimore, MD	5.9	6.6	7.0	5.7	6.5	6.5	5.3	9.4	6.1	0.5	0.6	0.9
Billings, MT	n/a	n/a	n/a	n/a	n/a	n/a	n/a	n/a	n/a	n/a	n/a	n/a
Boise City, ID	n/a	n/a	n/a	n/a	n/a	n/a	n/a	n/a	n/a	n/a	n/a	n/a
Boston, MA	6.2	6.1	5.7	5.4	5.3	4.8	2.5	2.5	3.0	0.7	0.6	0.6
Boulder, CO	n/a	n/a	n/a	n/a	n/a	n/a	n/a	n/a	n/a	n/a	n/a	n/a
Cape Coral, FL	38.2	38.7	34.1	16.9	16.1	14.7	11.6	15.3	10.1	3.9	2.3	3.0
Cedar Rapids, IA	n/a	n/a	n/a	n/a	n/a	n/a	n/a	n/a	n/a	n/a	n/a	n/a
Charleston, SC	10.6	12.6	11.9	7.5	10.2	9.8	8.8	12.0	12.8	0.4	0.5	0.9
Charlotte, NC	7.4	7.6	8.1	7.0	7.4	7.7	5.9	6.6	6.7	0.7	0.4	0.9
Chicago, IL	7.3	6.0	5.8	7.1	5.8	5.6	6.1	5.6	5.1	1.1	0.5	0.6
Cincinnati, OH	6.8	5.4	5.8	6.3	5.2	5.5	6.3	7.2	6.1	0.3	0.2	0.8
Clarksville, TN	n/a	n/a	n/a	n/a	n/a	n/a	n/a	n/a	n/a	n/a	n/a	n/a
Cleveland, OH	7.0	7.6	7.5	6.8	7.2	7.4	3.2	4.7	5.8	1.0	0.5	0.4
College Station, TX	n/a	n/a	n/a	n/a	n/a	n/a	n/a	n/a	n/a	n/a	n/a	n/a
Colorado Springs, CO	n/a	n/a	n/a	n/a	n/a	n/a	n/a	n/a	n/a	n/a	n/a	n/a
Columbia, MO	n/a	n/a	n/a	n/a	n/a	n/a	n/a	n/a	n/a	n/a	n/a	n/a
Columbia, SC	12.0	12.7	8.8	12.0	12.6	8.8	6.1	8.5	6.8	0.6	1.0	0.5
Columbus, OH	5.6	6.6	7.4	5.4	6.5	7.3	3.8	5.8	7.3	0.8	0.8	0.3
Dallas, TX	6.6	7.6	7.9	6.3	7.2	7.6	6.8	8.4	8.9	0.7	0.8	1.3
Davenport, IA	n/a	n/a	n/a	n/a	n/a	n/a	n/a	n/a	n/a	n/a	n/a	n/a
Denver, CO	5.8	6.0	4.9	5.2	5.5	4.4	5.1	5.3	4.7	0.3	0.7	0.7
Des Moines, IA	n/a	n/a	n/a	n/a	n/a	n/a	n/a	n/a	n/a	n/a	n/a	n/a
Detroit, MI	7.1	9.0	9.4	6.6	8.7	9.3	4.5	9.3	8.7	0.9	1.0	1.1
Durham, NC	n/a	n/a	n/a	n/a	n/a	n/a	n/a	n/a	n/a	n/a	n/a	n/a
El Paso, TX	n/a	n/a	n/a	n/a	n/a	n/a	n/a	n/a	n/a	n/a	n/a	n/a
Eugene, OR	n/a	n/a	n/a	n/a	n/a	n/a	n/a	n/a	n/a	n/a	n/a	n/a
Fargo, ND	n/a	n/a	n/a	n/a	n/a	n/a	n/a	n/a	n/a	n/a	n/a	n/a
Fort Collins, CO	n/a	n/a	n/a	n/a	n/a	n/a	n/a	n/a	n/a	n/a	n/a	n/a
Fort Wayne, IN	n/a	n/a	n/a	n/a	n/a	n/a	n/a	n/a	n/a	n/a	n/a	n/a
Fort Worth, TX	6.6	7.6	7.9	6.3	7.2	7.6	6.8	8.4	8.9	0.7	0.8	1.3
Gainesville, FL	n/a	n/a	n/a	n/a	n/a	n/a	n/a	n/a	n/a	n/a	n/a	n/a
Green Bay, WI	n/a	n/a	n/a	n/a	n/a	n/a	n/a	n/a	n/a	n/a	n/a	n/a
Greensboro, NC	8.7	6.1	7.8	8.7	5.7	6.0	10.2	5.7	5.5	0.7	0.1	0.5
Honolulu, HI	10.6	11.5	11.9	10.0	10.7	11.1	5.7	6.8	6.2	0.6	0.5	0.9
Houston, TX	6.9	7.9	7.8	6.3	7.3	7.2	8.9	10.9	9.8	0.6	1.4	1.2
Huntsville, AL	n/a	n/a	n/a	n/a	n/a	n/a	n/a	n/a	n/a	n/a	n/a	n/a
Indianapolis, IN	7.7	6.2	6.7	7.2	5.6	5.8	11.0	8.8	9.2	1.0	0.8	0.8
Jacksonville, FL	8.9	8.6	9.2	7.7	7.8	8.5	6.2	9.4	8.8	1.7	0.7	1.0
Kansas City, MO	7.1	7.0	6.9	7.1	6.6	6.3	7.8	7.6	8.9	0.6	1.2	0.9
Lafayette, LA	n/a	n/a	n/a	n/a	n/a	n/a	n/a	n/a	n/a	n/a	n/a	n/a
Las Vegas, NV	9.2	9.6	9.7	8.3	8.8	9.3	5.7	7.2	8.3	0.9	1.1	1.1
Lexington, KY	n/a	n/a	n/a	n/a	n/a	n/a	n/a	n/a	n/a	n/a	n/a	n/a
Lincoln, NE	n/a	n/a	n/a	n/a	n/a	n/a	n/a	n/a	n/a	n/a	n/a	n/a
Little Rock, AR	9.4	10.1	10.7	9.2	9.8	9.9	11.4	10.8	11.7	0.7	0.9	0.6
Los Angeles, CA	5.9	5.8	6.2	5.5	5.7	6.1	4.1	4.0	4.8	0.5	0.6	0.7
Louisville, KY	5.7	6.3	6.7	5.7	6.2	6.5	5.3	3.6	7.1	0.5	0.4	1.2
Madison, WI	n/a	n/a	n/a	n/a	n/a	n/a	n/a	n/a	n/a	n/a	n/a	n/a
Manchester, NH	n/a	n/a	n/a	n/a	n/a	n/a	n/a	n/a	n/a	n/a	n/a	n/a

Table continued on following page.

Metro Area	Gross Vacancy Rate[1] (%)			Year-Round Vacancy Rate[2] (%)			Rental Vacancy Rate[3] (%)			Homeowner Vacancy Rate[4] (%)		
	2022	2023	2024	2022	2023	2024	2022	2023	2024	2022	2023	2024
McAllen, TX	n/a	n/a	n/a	n/a	n/a	n/a	n/a	n/a	n/a	n/a	n/a	n/a
Memphis, TN	6.2	7.0	7.4	6.1	6.9	7.2	6.4	11.4	12.0	0.4	0.4	0.9
Miami, FL	12.6	14.7	14.8	7.5	8.9	9.3	6.3	8.4	9.5	1.1	0.9	1.4
Midland, TX	n/a	n/a	n/a	n/a	n/a	n/a	n/a	n/a	n/a	n/a	n/a	n/a
Milwaukee, WI	5.2	6.7	5.6	5.1	6.6	5.1	5.9	4.1	4.8	0.1	0.8	0.4
Minneapolis, MN	4.8	5.5	4.9	4.5	5.3	4.6	6.7	8.1	5.2	0.8	0.5	0.4
Nashville, TN	7.6	7.5	7.0	7.1	7.0	6.4	6.4	9.3	8.6	0.9	0.9	1.5
New Orleans, LA	13.4	10.9	11.9	11.5	9.8	10.8	6.6	9.2	9.1	1.6	1.6	1.4
New York, NY	8.2	7.8	8.3	7.0	6.7	7.4	3.5	3.9	4.7	1.0	0.9	1.0
Oklahoma City, OK	8.6	7.8	7.0	8.5	7.6	6.7	10.6	10.6	9.0	0.9	1.6	1.2
Omaha, NE	5.4	5.4	5.1	5.0	5.1	5.1	4.2	4.3	5.3	0.8	0.9	0.3
Orlando, FL	9.6	9.5	9.8	7.4	7.6	8.4	6.5	7.0	9.4	1.4	1.1	1.5
Philadelphia, PA	5.5	5.3	5.3	5.4	5.2	5.2	4.2	5.2	6.3	1.0	0.9	0.5
Phoenix, AZ	10.9	11.0	12.6	6.7	7.2	7.9	6.4	8.0	7.9	0.9	0.7	1.0
Pittsburgh, PA	11.5	10.0	10.5	11.0	9.2	9.7	8.3	6.3	8.9	0.7	0.9	0.8
Portland, OR	5.4	5.4	5.7	5.1	5.1	5.5	4.0	6.8	5.7	1.2	0.8	1.0
Providence, RI	9.5	9.4	8.5	7.6	7.6	6.8	4.5	3.7	3.2	0.4	0.3	0.4
Provo, UT	n/a	n/a	n/a	n/a	n/a	n/a	n/a	n/a	n/a	n/a	n/a	n/a
Raleigh, NC	7.4	6.7	6.3	7.3	6.6	6.2	7.1	8.8	8.8	0.5	0.5	0.7
Reno, NV	n/a	n/a	n/a	n/a	n/a	n/a	n/a	n/a	n/a	n/a	n/a	n/a
Richmond, VA	6.1	5.9	7.7	6.1	5.9	7.7	3.0	5.2	7.9	0.7	0.2	0.7
Rochester, MN	n/a	n/a	n/a	n/a	n/a	n/a	n/a	n/a	n/a	n/a	n/a	n/a
Sacramento, CA	6.3	6.4	8.0	6.1	6.2	7.6	2.3	4.2	3.9	0.6	0.6	0.9
Saint Louis, MO	7.2	7.4	7.7	7.1	7.3	7.6	6.8	7.8	7.9	1.4	0.6	0.9
Saint Paul, MN	4.8	5.5	4.9	4.5	5.3	4.6	6.7	8.1	5.2	0.8	0.5	0.4
Salem, OR	n/a	n/a	n/a	n/a	n/a	n/a	n/a	n/a	n/a	n/a	n/a	n/a
Salt Lake City, UT	5.1	6.1	10.1	4.5	5.0	5.8	4.6	6.2	6.1	0.6	0.6	0.7
San Antonio, TX	7.5	7.4	9.9	7.1	6.9	7.9	8.1	8.8	10.0	0.9	1.3	1.9
San Diego, CA	6.9	6.8	6.4	6.6	6.2	6.0	3.6	4.1	5.2	0.6	0.2	0.5
San Francisco, CA	7.9	8.1	8.3	7.7	8.0	8.1	5.4	6.6	6.3	1.3	0.5	0.7
San Jose, CA	5.8	4.5	4.7	5.8	4.5	4.7	4.7	3.3	3.3	0.4	0.3	1.0
Santa Rosa, CA	n/a	n/a	n/a	n/a	n/a	n/a	n/a	n/a	n/a	n/a	n/a	n/a
Savannah, GA	n/a	n/a	n/a	n/a	n/a	n/a	n/a	n/a	n/a	n/a	n/a	n/a
Seattle, WA	5.7	5.1	6.2	5.2	4.7	5.9	4.9	4.0	6.5	0.7	0.6	1.1
Sioux Falls, SD	n/a	n/a	n/a	n/a	n/a	n/a	n/a	n/a	n/a	n/a	n/a	n/a
Tampa, FL	13.3	13.3	14.2	9.9	9.1	10.9	8.1	8.5	8.7	1.2	1.0	2.0
Tucson, AZ	13.5	14.2	10.1	10.3	11.2	8.7	8.0	10.2	9.3	1.4	1.3	1.1
Tulsa, OK	8.9	8.3	7.5	8.5	7.9	6.8	5.6	6.7	7.2	0.7	0.8	0.7
Virginia Beach, VA	8.1	5.9	9.2	7.3	5.4	8.5	6.3	5.1	9.1	1.0	0.5	1.4
Washington, DC	5.2	5.1	5.5	5.0	5.0	5.4	5.3	5.5	4.7	0.6	0.3	0.4
Wichita, KS	n/a	n/a	n/a	n/a	n/a	n/a	n/a	n/a	n/a	n/a	n/a	n/a
Wilmington, NC	n/a	n/a	n/a	n/a	n/a	n/a	n/a	n/a	n/a	n/a	n/a	n/a
Winston-Salem, NC	n/a	n/a	n/a	n/a	n/a	n/a	n/a	n/a	n/a	n/a	n/a	n/a
U.S.[5]	9.1	9.0	9.1	7.5	7.5	7.6	5.7	6.5	6.8	0.8	0.8	1.0

Note: Figures cover the Metropolitan Statistical Area (MSA); (1) The percentage of the total housing inventory that is vacant; (2) The percentage of the housing inventory (excluding seasonal units) that is year-round vacant; (3) The percentage of rental inventory that is vacant for rent; (4) The percentage of homeowner inventory that is vacant for sale; (5) Figures cover the 75 largest Metropolitan Statistical Areas; n/a not available
Source: U.S. Census Bureau, Housing Vacancies and Homeownership Annual Statistics: 2022, 2023, 2024

Bankruptcy Filings

City	Area Covered	Business Filings			Nonbusiness Filings		
		2023	2024	% Chg.	2023	2024	% Chg.
Albuquerque, NM	Bernalillo County	24	33	37.5	373	454	21.7
Anchorage, AK	Anchorage Borough	9	7	-22.2	113	90	-20.4
Ann Arbor, MI	Washtenaw County	7	8	14.3	396	404	2.0
Athens, GA	Clarke County	2	5	150.0	176	189	7.4
Atlanta, GA	Fulton County	318	251	-21.1	2,723	2,846	4.5
Austin, TX	Travis County	133	121	-9.0	408	619	51.7
Baltimore, MD	Baltimore City	35	43	22.9	1,502	1,656	10.3
Billings, MT	Yellowstone County	5	9	80.0	111	153	37.8
Boise City, ID	Ada County	18	26	44.4	350	466	33.1
Boston, MA	Suffolk County	53	63	18.9	233	316	35.6
Boulder, CO	Boulder County	25	35	40.0	228	247	8.3
Cape Coral, FL	Lee County	97	64	-34.0	860	1,216	41.4
Cedar Rapids, IA	Linn County	9	7	-22.2	224	278	24.1
Charleston, SC	Charleston County	7	13	85.7	195	215	10.3
Charlotte, NC	Mecklenburg County	69	60	-13.0	577	689	19.4
Chicago, IL	Cook County	361	479	32.7	12,419	13,840	11.4
Cincinnati, OH	Hamilton County	32	42	31.3	1,286	1,619	25.9
Clarksville, TN	Montgomery County	4	11	175.0	475	513	8.0
Cleveland, OH	Cuyahoga County	37	60	62.2	3,437	4,054	18.0
College Station, TX	Brazos County	5	7	40.0	65	80	23.1
Colorado Springs, CO	El Paso County	23	50	117.4	784	973	24.1
Columbia, MO	Boone County	3	5	66.7	191	201	5.2
Columbia, SC	Richland County	7	10	42.9	453	584	28.9
Columbus, OH	Franklin County	43	81	88.4	2,330	2,671	14.6
Dallas, TX	Dallas County	296	496	67.6	2,363	3,025	28.0
Davenport, IA	Scott County	9	4	-55.6	157	158	0.6
Denver, CO	Denver County	61	79	29.5	669	854	27.7
Des Moines, IA	Polk County	15	13	-13.3	566	594	4.9
Detroit, MI	Wayne County	43	58	34.9	6,087	6,501	6.8
Durham, NC	Durham County	14	42	200.0	162	195	20.4
El Paso, TX	El Paso County	65	72	10.8	1,351	1,512	11.9
Eugene, OR	Lane County	12	18	50.0	535	707	32.1
Fargo, ND	Cass County	5	14	180.0	129	132	2.3
Fort Collins, CO	Larimer County	21	28	33.3	347	417	20.2
Fort Wayne, IN	Allen County	17	17	0.0	924	959	3.8
Fort Worth, TX	Tarrant County	200	198	-1.0	2,934	3,513	19.7
Gainesville, FL	Alachua County	11	30	172.7	153	177	15.7
Green Bay, WI	Brown County	5	10	100.0	320	408	27.5
Greensboro, NC	Guilford County	11	16	45.5	375	473	26.1
Honolulu, HI	Honolulu County	36	38	5.6	757	840	11.0
Houston, TX	Harris County	356	426	19.7	3,285	3,853	17.3
Huntsville, AL	Madison County	20	35	75.0	902	946	4.9
Indianapolis, IN	Marion County	45	43	-4.4	2,601	3,166	21.7
Jacksonville, FL	Duval County	73	83	13.7	1,514	1,784	17.8
Kansas City, MO	Jackson County	22	27	22.7	1,186	1,166	-1.7
Lafayette, LA	Lafayette Parish	19	44	131.6	335	410	22.4
Las Vegas, NV	Clark County	194	178	-8.2	5,622	6,690	19.0
Lexington, KY	Fayette County	13	14	7.7	468	540	15.4
Lincoln, NE	Lancaster County	11	15	36.4	367	405	10.4
Little Rock, AR	Pulaski County	17	29	70.6	1,436	1,390	-3.2
Los Angeles, CA	Los Angeles County	815	977	19.9	10,059	12,169	21.0
Louisville, KY	Jefferson County	28	35	25.0	2,280	2,258	-1.0
Madison, WI	Dane County	25	21	-16.0	437	494	13.0
Manchester, NH	Hillsborough County	8	21	162.5	235	298	26.8
McAllen, TX	Hidalgo County	13	11	-15.4	263	274	4.2

Table continued on following page.

City	Area Covered	Business Filings			Nonbusiness Filings		
		2023	2024	% Chg.	2023	2024	% Chg.
Memphis, TN	Shelby County	48	45	-6.3	5,959	6,030	1.2
Miami, FL	Miami-Dade County	242	413	70.7	5,320	6,779	27.4
Midland, TX	Midland County	14	17	21.4	66	93	40.9
Milwaukee, WI	Milwaukee County	24	40	66.7	2,881	3,306	14.8
Minneapolis, MN	Hennepin County	64	77	20.3	1,473	1,952	32.5
Nashville, TN	Davidson County	303	123	-59.4	1,109	1,195	7.8
New Orleans, LA	Orleans Parish	28	35	25.0	388	446	14.9
New York, NY	Bronx County	25	44	76.0	1,071	1,319	23.2
New York, NY	Kings County	394	457	16.0	1,781	2,036	14.3
New York, NY	New York County	750	361	-51.9	684	793	15.9
New York, NY	Queens County	215	209	-2.8	1,921	2,120	10.4
New York, NY	Richmond County	23	29	26.1	490	494	0.8
Oklahoma City, OK	Oklahoma County	46	54	17.4	1,374	1,526	11.1
Omaha, NE	Douglas County	21	26	23.8	687	802	16.7
Orlando, FL	Orange County	152	231	52.0	1,832	2,279	24.4
Philadelphia, PA	Philadelphia County	227	131	-42.3	940	1,094	16.4
Phoenix, AZ	Maricopa County	252	355	40.9	6,085	7,026	15.5
Pittsburgh, PA	Allegheny County	59	111	88.1	1,217	1,424	17.0
Portland, OR	Multnomah County	35	61	74.3	938	1,078	14.9
Providence, RI	Providence County	13	22	69.2	520	581	11.7
Provo, UT	Utah County	33	36	9.1	925	1,070	15.7
Raleigh, NC	Wake County	51	76	49.0	653	830	27.1
Reno, NV	Washoe County	35	59	68.6	610	860	41.0
Richmond, VA	Richmond city	2	14	600.0	620	678	9.4
Rochester, MN	Olmsted County	8	6	-25.0	137	161	17.5
Sacramento, CA	Sacramento County	96	163	69.8	1,675	2,259	34.9
Saint Louis, MO	Saint Louis City	12	23	91.7	1,497	1,311	-12.4
Saint Paul, MN	Ramsey County	20	19	-5.0	694	840	21.0
Salem, OR	Marion County	10	11	10.0	599	674	12.5
Salt Lake City, UT	Salt Lake County	58	58	0.0	2,508	2,763	10.2
San Antonio, TX	Bexar County	126	169	34.1	1,270	1,813	42.8
San Diego, CA	San Diego County	214	267	24.8	3,866	4,558	17.9
San Francisco, CA	San Francisco County	68	140	105.9	348	417	19.8
San Jose, CA	Santa Clara County	86	105	22.1	782	1,008	28.9
Santa Rosa, CA	Sonoma County	17	56	229.4	338	378	11.8
Savannah, GA	Chatham County	8	3	-62.5	732	695	-5.1
Seattle, WA	King County	92	113	22.8	1,134	1,459	28.7
Sioux Falls, SD	Minnehaha County	10	8	-20.0	220	220	0.0
Tampa, FL	Hillsborough County	121	158	30.6	1,822	2,440	33.9
Tucson, AZ	Pima County	28	27	-3.6	1,402	1,638	16.8
Tulsa, OK	Tulsa County	46	44	-4.3	867	1,065	22.8
Virginia Beach, VA	Virginia Beach City	10	20	100.0	822	966	17.5
Washington, DC	District of Columbia	78	81	3.8	293	347	18.4
Wichita, KS	Sedgwick County	24	27	12.5	757	777	2.6
Wilmington, NC	New Hanover County	29	19	-34.5	145	183	26.2
Winston-Salem, NC	Forsyth County	7	18	157.1	263	330	25.5
U.S.	U.S.	18,926	23,107	22.1	434,064	494,201	13.9

Note: Business filings include Chapter 7, Chapter 9, Chapter 11, Chapter 12, Chapter 13, Chapter 15, and Section 304; Nonbusiness filings include Chapter 7, Chapter 11, and Chapter 13
Source: Administrative Office of the U.S. Courts, Business and Nonbusiness Bankruptcy, County Cases Commenced by Chapter of the Bankruptcy Code, During the 12-Month Period Ending December 31, 2023 and Business and Nonbusiness Bankruptcy, County Cases Commenced by Chapter of the Bankruptcy Code, During the 12-Month Period Ending December 31, 2024

Income: City

City	Per Capita ($)	Median Household ($)	Average Household ($)
Albuquerque, NM	39,117	65,604	88,262
Anchorage, AK	49,338	98,152	127,598
Ann Arbor, MI	54,604	81,089	121,561
Athens, GA	31,836	51,655	76,375
Atlanta, GA	64,063	81,938	135,218
Austin, TX	59,427	91,461	130,163
Baltimore, MD	39,195	59,623	87,339
Billings, MT	42,639	71,855	98,655
Boise City, ID	48,274	81,308	112,482
Boston, MA	60,001	94,755	140,807
Boulder, CO	59,450	85,364	140,662
Cape Coral, FL	39,603	76,062	97,070
Cedar Rapids, IA	39,824	67,859	91,040
Charleston, SC	58,583	90,038	129,666
Charlotte, NC	49,991	78,438	119,473
Chicago, IL	48,148	75,134	112,443
Cincinnati, OH	38,878	51,707	83,146
Clarksville, TN	31,266	66,786	79,769
Cleveland, OH	27,078	39,187	56,900
College Station, TX	32,123	51,776	84,849
Colorado Springs, CO	44,893	83,198	108,459
Columbia, MO	37,359	64,488	91,425
Columbia, SC	38,087	55,653	90,935
Columbus, OH	37,189	65,327	85,919
Dallas, TX	44,138	67,760	106,979
Davenport, IA	36,583	64,497	83,699
Denver, CO	61,202	91,681	131,349
Des Moines, IA	36,459	63,966	83,728
Detroit, MI	24,029	39,575	56,528
Durham, NC	47,246	79,234	108,538
El Paso, TX	28,942	58,734	78,842
Eugene, OR	41,035	63,836	94,063
Fargo, ND	42,212	66,029	91,129
Fort Collins, CO	46,341	83,598	110,629
Fort Wayne, IN	32,884	60,293	78,764
Fort Worth, TX	37,157	76,602	101,838
Gainesville, FL	30,282	45,611	71,640
Green Bay, WI	34,514	62,546	81,363
Greensboro, NC	35,858	58,884	85,861
Honolulu, HI	48,465	85,428	120,718
Houston, TX	41,142	62,894	101,848
Huntsville, AL	44,733	70,778	101,671
Indianapolis, IN	36,194	62,995	86,913
Jacksonville, FL	37,269	66,981	90,429
Kansas City, MO	40,112	67,449	91,703
Lafayette, LA	39,861	61,454	91,871
Las Vegas, NV	38,421	70,723	98,664
Lexington, KY	42,272	67,631	98,429
Lincoln, NE	39,187	69,991	94,181
Little Rock, AR	43,242	60,583	98,728
Los Angeles, CA	46,270	80,366	122,610
Louisville, KY	38,890	64,731	91,264
Madison, WI	48,557	76,983	104,969
Manchester, NH	44,220	77,415	100,102
McAllen, TX	29,406	60,165	86,175
Memphis, TN	32,314	51,211	77,102

Table continued on following page.

City	Per Capita ($)	Median Household ($)	Average Household ($)
Miami, FL	42,528	59,390	97,643
Midland, TX	49,327	91,169	126,317
Milwaukee, WI	29,679	51,888	70,559
Minneapolis, MN	50,605	80,269	112,607
Nashville, TN	46,820	75,197	106,483
New Orleans, LA	39,698	55,339	89,943
New York, NY	50,776	79,713	127,894
Oklahoma City, OK	37,109	66,702	91,131
Omaha, NE	42,515	72,708	103,010
Orlando, FL	41,985	69,268	100,135
Philadelphia, PA	37,669	60,698	88,307
Phoenix, AZ	40,309	77,041	106,845
Pittsburgh, PA	43,590	64,137	93,301
Portland, OR	55,312	88,792	122,267
Providence, RI	36,694	66,772	95,112
Provo, UT	26,755	62,800	86,072
Raleigh, NC	49,948	82,424	116,724
Reno, NV	45,180	78,448	107,386
Richmond, VA	44,249	62,671	94,647
Rochester, MN	49,727	87,767	119,510
Sacramento, CA	42,300	83,753	108,939
Saint Louis, MO	38,947	55,279	78,097
Saint Paul, MN	41,594	73,055	102,197
Salem, OR	36,477	71,900	94,087
Salt Lake City, UT	49,642	74,925	111,189
San Antonio, TX	32,983	62,917	85,107
San Diego, CA	54,678	104,321	139,707
San Francisco, CA	90,285	141,446	204,625
San Jose, CA	63,253	141,565	187,711
Santa Rosa, CA	50,520	97,410	129,680
Savannah, GA	32,004	56,782	77,786
Seattle, WA	82,508	121,984	170,038
Sioux Falls, SD	43,231	74,714	102,058
Tampa, FL	49,513	71,302	117,408
Tucson, AZ	31,152	54,546	73,528
Tulsa, OK	37,533	58,407	88,998
Virginia Beach, VA	47,372	90,685	118,081
Washington, DC	75,253	106,287	157,604
Wichita, KS	35,958	63,072	87,820
Wilmington, NC	46,062	63,900	98,401
Winston-Salem, NC	35,074	57,673	85,278
U.S.	43,289	78,538	110,491

Source: U.S. Census Bureau, 2019-2023 American Community Survey 5-Year Estimates

Income: Metro Area

Metro Area	Per Capita ($)	Median Household ($)	Average Household ($)
Albuquerque, NM	38,300	67,995	91,376
Anchorage, AK	47,015	95,918	123,232
Ann Arbor, MI	51,746	87,156	122,847
Athens, GA	36,105	62,897	91,841
Atlanta, GA	44,798	86,338	118,625
Austin, TX	53,550	97,638	132,189
Baltimore, MD	51,146	97,300	128,719
Billings, MT	43,176	74,599	102,275
Boise City, ID	41,793	82,694	110,044
Boston, MA	61,389	112,484	155,005
Boulder, CO	60,272	102,772	144,869
Cape Coral, FL	43,365	73,099	102,290
Cedar Rapids, IA	41,820	77,084	100,451
Charleston, SC	46,863	82,272	114,464
Charlotte, NC	44,995	80,201	113,387
Chicago, IL	48,107	88,850	122,980
Cincinnati, OH	43,371	79,490	107,457
Clarksville, TN	31,813	66,210	82,303
Cleveland, OH	41,791	68,507	96,273
College Station, TX	34,136	59,691	88,300
Colorado Springs, CO	44,315	87,180	112,662
Columbia, MO	37,799	69,463	93,435
Columbia, SC	37,159	66,146	90,520
Columbus, OH	43,665	79,847	108,257
Dallas, TX	44,447	87,155	120,397
Davenport, IA	39,357	71,925	93,006
Denver, CO	55,529	102,339	135,703
Des Moines, IA	44,796	84,209	109,864
Detroit, MI	42,145	75,123	102,705
Durham, NC	48,827	81,017	116,697
El Paso, TX	27,509	58,800	77,734
Eugene, OR	38,563	69,311	91,348
Fargo, ND	43,099	75,523	100,645
Fort Collins, CO	49,323	91,364	118,812
Fort Wayne, IN	36,444	69,378	90,705
Fort Worth, TX	44,447	87,155	120,397
Gainesville, FL	36,810	58,946	89,302
Green Bay, WI	40,606	77,459	98,052
Greensboro, NC	35,569	63,083	87,043
Honolulu, HI	46,361	104,264	133,753
Houston, TX	41,559	80,458	115,043
Huntsville, AL	45,250	83,529	110,607
Indianapolis, IN	42,522	77,065	106,219
Jacksonville, FL	41,987	77,013	104,828
Kansas City, MO	44,205	81,927	108,186
Lafayette, LA	34,845	60,910	86,057
Las Vegas, NV	38,654	73,845	101,010
Lexington, KY	41,230	70,717	99,405
Lincoln, NE	40,527	73,095	99,081
Little Rock, AR	37,678	65,309	90,691
Los Angeles, CA	46,385	93,525	132,022
Louisville, KY	40,019	71,737	97,103
Madison, WI	49,799	86,827	113,809
Manchester, NH	52,243	100,436	128,567
McAllen, TX	22,005	52,281	71,722
Memphis, TN	36,519	64,743	92,389

Table continued on following page.

Metro Area	Per Capita ($)	Median Household ($)	Average Household ($)
Miami, FL	42,369	73,481	109,356
Midland, TX	48,843	93,442	126,152
Milwaukee, WI	44,476	76,404	104,403
Minneapolis, MN	51,500	98,180	128,647
Nashville, TN	45,266	82,499	113,441
New Orleans, LA	37,547	62,271	90,627
New York, NY	54,510	97,334	144,032
Oklahoma City, OK	38,240	70,499	95,891
Omaha, NE	44,338	83,023	111,142
Orlando, FL	38,776	75,611	103,312
Philadelphia, PA	49,178	89,273	123,454
Phoenix, AZ	43,395	84,703	113,623
Pittsburgh, PA	44,726	73,942	101,289
Portland, OR	50,158	94,573	124,372
Providence, RI	45,170	85,646	111,377
Provo, UT	35,045	96,745	121,112
Raleigh, NC	49,462	96,066	126,566
Reno, NV	45,849	84,684	114,037
Richmond, VA	46,237	84,405	114,424
Rochester, MN	48,977	89,675	120,598
Sacramento, CA	45,964	93,986	123,767
Saint Louis, MO	44,689	78,225	107,013
Saint Paul, MN	51,500	98,180	128,647
Salem, OR	36,260	76,010	97,771
Salt Lake City, UT	43,026	95,045	121,478
San Antonio, TX	37,425	74,297	100,400
San Diego, CA	49,891	102,285	136,236
San Francisco, CA	72,306	133,780	190,258
San Jose, CA	75,895	157,444	217,226
Santa Rosa, CA	54,941	102,840	138,572
Savannah, GA	39,158	74,632	99,643
Seattle, WA	61,286	112,594	152,753
Sioux Falls, SD	43,434	81,418	106,253
Tampa, FL	42,023	71,254	100,901
Tucson, AZ	38,564	67,929	92,561
Tulsa, OK	37,865	67,823	94,114
Virginia Beach, VA	42,791	80,533	105,690
Washington, DC	62,026	123,896	162,905
Wichita, KS	36,529	68,930	91,559
Wilmington, NC	44,459	73,687	100,847
Winston-Salem, NC	35,829	64,282	87,020
U.S.	43,289	78,538	110,491

Note: Figures cover the Metropolitan Statistical Area (MSA)
Source: U.S. Census Bureau, 2019-2023 American Community Survey 5-Year Estimates

Household Income Distribution: City

City	Percent of Households Earning							
	Under $15,000	$15,000 -$24,999	$25,000 -$34,999	$35,000 -$49,999	$50,000 -$74,999	$75,000 -$99,999	$100,000 -$149,999	$150,000 and up
Albuquerque, NM	10.9	8.5	7.9	11.5	17.5	12.6	16.0	15.2
Anchorage, AK	5.2	4.6	4.4	8.3	14.6	13.7	19.5	29.7
Ann Arbor, MI	12.8	5.7	5.8	8.8	14.4	10.6	15.2	26.8
Athens, GA	15.5	10.4	10.3	12.4	16.1	10.9	12.9	11.6
Atlanta, GA	13.2	6.7	6.1	8.2	12.8	11.5	15.0	26.5
Austin, TX	7.8	4.6	4.9	9.3	15.1	12.4	17.2	28.7
Baltimore, MD	15.7	8.4	7.4	11.4	16.6	11.3	13.5	15.7
Billings, MT	7.2	7.0	7.4	12.6	18.1	13.0	17.9	16.9
Boise City, ID	5.7	6.0	6.3	11.2	16.6	15.1	17.4	21.6
Boston, MA	12.9	6.5	5.1	7.1	10.6	9.9	15.5	32.5
Boulder, CO	12.4	6.7	7.3	7.7	11.5	9.5	14.0	30.9
Cape Coral, FL	6.2	5.0	7.7	10.6	19.9	15.6	19.3	15.7
Cedar Rapids, IA	7.3	6.6	8.9	14.1	18.3	14.2	16.0	14.8
Charleston, SC	7.7	6.1	4.3	9.6	14.7	12.7	18.6	26.4
Charlotte, NC	7.0	5.6	6.2	11.6	17.6	12.7	16.9	22.5
Chicago, IL	12.1	7.2	6.9	9.8	14.0	11.7	16.0	22.4
Cincinnati, OH	16.9	10.2	8.7	12.9	15.0	10.3	11.8	14.2
Clarksville, TN	7.7	5.7	7.7	13.4	21.0	16.7	17.8	10.0
Cleveland, OH	22.1	12.6	10.7	14.2	16.0	9.2	8.9	6.4
College Station, TX	18.3	8.3	9.5	12.9	12.2	11.0	12.2	15.6
Colorado Springs, CO	6.2	5.3	5.8	10.4	17.7	13.6	19.8	21.3
Columbia, MO	12.4	8.3	8.5	10.8	17.1	11.8	14.3	17.0
Columbia, SC	16.5	8.6	8.2	11.7	16.7	10.7	11.7	15.8
Columbus, OH	10.0	7.1	7.4	13.3	18.5	13.5	16.6	13.5
Dallas, TX	10.2	6.8	7.7	12.3	17.9	12.5	13.7	18.8
Davenport, IA	10.8	7.0	8.8	11.5	19.0	13.5	17.4	12.0
Denver, CO	7.8	5.2	5.1	8.6	14.4	12.6	17.9	28.4
Des Moines, IA	8.8	7.7	7.2	14.3	19.3	15.4	15.2	12.1
Detroit, MI	22.8	12.2	10.2	15.2	15.1	9.5	9.2	5.8
Durham, NC	7.7	5.8	6.4	10.6	16.9	12.9	17.9	21.7
El Paso, TX	12.9	9.1	8.9	12.8	18.2	12.6	14.2	11.5
Eugene, OR	11.3	7.8	7.6	13.2	15.5	12.5	15.8	16.3
Fargo, ND	8.5	7.3	9.2	12.9	18.1	13.8	15.2	15.0
Fort Collins, CO	9.5	5.7	5.5	10.0	14.9	12.5	18.4	23.5
Fort Wayne, IN	9.3	7.9	9.6	14.5	19.5	14.1	15.2	9.9
Fort Worth, TX	7.4	5.9	6.9	11.1	17.3	13.7	18.1	19.4
Gainesville, FL	18.0	10.4	11.2	14.8	14.8	10.2	10.4	10.2
Green Bay, WI	9.5	8.6	7.4	13.6	19.7	14.6	16.2	10.4
Greensboro, NC	11.7	8.0	9.0	13.8	17.8	12.2	15.0	12.6
Honolulu, HI	8.8	5.7	5.1	9.4	15.2	12.7	17.4	25.7
Houston, TX	10.9	8.2	8.5	12.6	17.4	11.6	13.1	17.7
Huntsville, AL	9.2	8.0	8.7	11.3	15.0	12.6	15.6	19.6
Indianapolis, IN	10.7	7.5	8.2	13.5	18.7	12.5	15.0	13.8
Jacksonville, FL	10.0	7.3	7.5	12.7	17.9	13.3	16.9	14.5
Kansas City, MO	10.3	7.2	7.5	12.5	17.2	12.6	16.9	15.7
Lafayette, LA	13.8	8.8	8.0	11.5	14.6	12.8	14.9	15.6
Las Vegas, NV	10.0	6.7	7.5	11.4	17.3	12.9	16.8	17.4
Lexington, KY	9.8	7.2	8.6	11.9	16.8	11.9	15.7	18.1
Lincoln, NE	8.1	6.4	8.2	12.5	18.3	14.0	17.1	15.6
Little Rock, AR	10.7	8.2	9.9	13.9	15.6	11.3	13.1	17.2
Los Angeles, CA	10.8	6.7	6.5	9.4	14.0	11.5	16.0	25.1
Louisville, KY	10.6	7.6	8.2	12.7	17.2	12.8	15.9	15.0
Madison, WI	9.4	6.2	7.2	10.3	15.5	12.8	17.6	20.9
Manchester, NH	6.0	6.9	5.7	11.7	18.0	14.3	19.3	18.1

Table continued on following page.

City	Percent of Households Earning							
	Under $15,000	$15,000 -$24,999	$25,000 -$34,999	$35,000 -$49,999	$50,000 -$74,999	$75,000 -$99,999	$100,000 -$149,999	$150,000 and up
McAllen, TX	11.9	10.2	9.3	11.4	16.1	11.7	15.7	13.7
Memphis, TN	14.7	9.9	10.1	14.4	17.9	10.9	11.6	10.5
Miami, FL	14.4	9.3	8.1	11.9	15.7	10.2	13.1	17.4
Midland, TX	9.1	4.8	5.8	9.2	14.3	10.1	18.0	28.6
Milwaukee, WI	14.5	9.7	10.4	13.8	18.0	12.0	12.7	8.9
Minneapolis, MN	9.5	6.6	6.2	9.7	15.2	12.3	17.3	23.1
Nashville, TN	8.5	5.6	6.6	11.8	17.4	13.6	17.2	19.3
New Orleans, LA	18.7	9.7	7.7	10.8	14.8	9.6	12.8	15.8
New York, NY	12.3	7.0	6.3	8.9	13.3	10.8	15.3	26.1
Oklahoma City, OK	10.0	7.0	7.9	12.4	18.1	13.3	15.9	15.4
Omaha, NE	8.8	6.5	7.2	11.4	17.6	13.1	17.1	18.2
Orlando, FL	9.5	7.0	8.7	11.7	17.1	12.5	16.3	17.2
Philadelphia, PA	15.1	8.7	8.2	11.0	15.8	11.8	14.0	15.3
Phoenix, AZ	7.7	5.6	6.7	11.5	17.3	13.7	17.4	20.1
Pittsburgh, PA	14.2	8.1	7.4	11.0	16.6	11.4	14.6	16.8
Portland, OR	8.8	5.3	5.6	9.2	14.2	11.9	17.6	27.3
Providence, RI	13.7	8.4	6.6	10.7	16.0	11.7	15.8	17.1
Provo, UT	9.4	8.2	9.2	13.5	17.7	13.6	14.5	13.8
Raleigh, NC	7.0	5.6	6.0	11.2	15.9	13.0	17.2	24.1
Reno, NV	7.9	6.4	6.9	10.2	16.6	13.2	18.7	19.9
Richmond, VA	13.0	8.4	7.7	12.7	16.6	12.0	12.4	17.1
Rochester, MN	5.2	5.8	5.7	9.1	16.3	13.5	19.9	24.5
Sacramento, CA	9.1	6.1	5.2	9.5	15.1	13.6	18.7	22.7
Saint Louis, MO	15.5	8.8	9.1	12.5	17.5	11.3	13.1	12.4
Saint Paul, MN	9.0	6.6	6.9	10.4	18.4	13.2	16.1	19.4
Salem, OR	9.0	6.5	7.5	11.2	17.5	12.6	19.0	16.5
Salt Lake City, UT	9.0	6.7	6.5	11.1	16.8	13.5	15.9	20.5
San Antonio, TX	10.3	7.9	9.2	12.4	18.6	13.4	15.0	13.4
San Diego, CA	6.7	4.4	4.8	7.3	12.5	12.4	19.4	32.5
San Francisco, CA	8.5	4.8	3.9	5.2	8.1	8.4	13.4	47.7
San Jose, CA	4.9	3.6	3.5	5.5	9.2	9.3	16.6	47.3
Santa Rosa, CA	6.3	4.1	4.4	7.7	15.6	13.4	19.5	29.1
Savannah, GA	13.4	8.3	9.8	13.0	18.8	11.7	13.9	11.2
Seattle, WA	7.3	3.9	4.0	6.5	11.4	9.5	16.3	41.1
Sioux Falls, SD	6.0	5.5	7.5	12.3	18.8	14.3	18.6	16.9
Tampa, FL	11.1	7.2	7.2	11.2	15.6	11.2	14.4	22.1
Tucson, AZ	12.0	9.6	10.2	14.6	17.5	12.7	14.1	9.5
Tulsa, OK	11.9	7.6	10.1	13.5	17.8	11.5	13.4	14.2
Virginia Beach, VA	5.7	3.9	5.1	8.5	18.1	13.7	20.8	24.2
Washington, DC	10.5	4.6	3.8	6.8	11.4	10.4	15.7	36.9
Wichita, KS	9.5	7.6	9.6	13.0	18.1	13.3	15.6	13.3
Wilmington, NC	11.3	6.8	8.3	13.0	17.6	11.9	14.2	16.8
Winston-Salem, NC	11.3	8.9	10.0	13.2	17.2	12.5	13.8	13.0
U.S.	8.5	6.6	6.8	10.4	15.7	12.7	17.4	21.9

Source: U.S. Census Bureau, 2019-2023 American Community Survey 5-Year Estimates

Household Income Distribution: Metro Area

Metro Area	Percent of Households Earning							
	Under $15,000	$15,000 -$24,999	$25,000 -$34,999	$35,000 -$49,999	$50,000 -$74,999	$75,000 -$99,999	$100,000 -$149,999	$150,000 and up
Albuquerque, NM	10.3	7.9	7.6	11.2	17.5	12.8	16.6	16.0
Anchorage, AK	5.4	4.9	4.7	8.5	14.6	13.8	19.8	28.2
Ann Arbor, MI	8.8	5.3	5.8	9.3	14.9	11.8	17.5	26.6
Athens, GA	12.6	8.5	9.0	11.3	15.5	12.1	14.8	16.2
Atlanta, GA	6.9	5.4	6.0	9.8	15.4	13.4	18.3	24.8
Austin, TX	6.3	4.1	4.8	8.6	14.8	12.4	19.2	29.9
Baltimore, MD	7.6	4.9	5.0	8.3	13.3	12.0	18.8	30.1
Billings, MT	6.6	6.8	7.6	11.5	17.6	13.4	18.1	18.2
Boise City, ID	5.3	5.3	5.6	10.5	18.4	15.3	19.7	19.8
Boston, MA	7.2	4.9	4.5	6.7	11.2	10.5	17.7	37.2
Boulder, CO	7.5	5.3	5.2	7.4	12.4	11.1	17.3	33.9
Cape Coral, FL	7.9	6.2	7.5	11.7	18.0	14.2	17.3	17.2
Cedar Rapids, IA	6.1	6.2	7.2	12.0	17.3	14.5	18.2	18.5
Charleston, SC	7.2	6.1	6.1	10.0	16.8	13.0	19.2	21.6
Charlotte, NC	6.8	6.1	6.5	10.9	16.7	13.0	17.7	22.2
Chicago, IL	8.1	5.6	5.9	9.0	14.2	12.5	18.4	26.4
Cincinnati, OH	8.4	6.5	6.7	10.4	15.5	13.0	18.7	20.9
Clarksville, TN	9.1	6.6	8.1	12.3	20.0	15.2	17.1	11.5
Cleveland, OH	10.1	7.6	7.8	11.6	16.9	12.5	16.0	17.3
College Station, TX	14.7	7.7	8.7	12.5	14.6	12.2	14.2	15.4
Colorado Springs, CO	5.7	4.8	5.6	9.8	16.9	13.7	20.3	23.3
Columbia, MO	10.3	7.4	7.6	11.1	17.3	13.3	16.6	16.2
Columbia, SC	10.1	7.3	8.1	12.5	17.5	13.0	15.8	15.7
Columbus, OH	7.6	5.8	6.4	11.0	16.6	12.9	18.2	21.5
Dallas, TX	6.3	4.9	5.8	10.0	16.1	13.1	18.5	25.2
Davenport, IA	9.0	6.9	7.5	11.5	17.0	13.6	18.6	16.0
Denver, CO	5.7	4.1	4.5	7.9	14.0	12.8	19.7	31.4
Des Moines, IA	5.6	5.4	6.1	11.0	16.5	14.0	19.1	22.4
Detroit, MI	9.3	6.7	7.0	11.1	15.7	12.8	17.0	20.2
Durham, NC	7.8	6.2	6.4	10.3	16.0	12.0	17.3	23.9
El Paso, TX	12.8	8.9	8.9	12.8	18.6	12.6	14.4	11.1
Eugene, OR	10.0	7.3	7.5	12.5	16.2	14.2	17.8	14.6
Fargo, ND	7.8	6.5	7.5	11.4	16.5	13.8	18.0	18.5
Fort Collins, CO	7.2	5.1	5.3	8.9	14.9	13.5	19.9	25.2
Fort Wayne, IN	7.2	6.9	7.9	12.8	18.9	15.0	17.0	14.1
Fort Worth, TX	6.3	4.9	5.8	10.0	16.1	13.1	18.5	25.2
Gainesville, FL	13.2	8.5	9.1	12.6	16.2	11.1	14.0	15.2
Green Bay, WI	6.7	5.6	7.0	11.1	17.9	14.8	20.8	16.1
Greensboro, NC	10.1	8.0	8.3	13.7	17.6	12.6	16.3	13.5
Honolulu, HI	6.3	4.2	4.2	7.9	12.9	12.6	20.4	31.6
Houston, TX	7.7	6.2	6.7	10.5	15.9	12.5	16.9	23.6
Huntsville, AL	7.3	6.6	6.8	10.1	15.1	12.5	18.2	23.4
Indianapolis, IN	7.7	6.0	6.6	11.2	17.3	13.2	17.5	20.5
Jacksonville, FL	8.0	6.1	6.7	11.1	16.9	13.3	18.3	19.7
Kansas City, MO	6.9	5.7	6.4	10.4	16.6	13.3	19.1	21.3
Lafayette, LA	13.1	9.6	8.3	12.0	14.7	12.2	15.8	14.3
Las Vegas, NV	8.6	6.4	7.2	11.3	17.2	13.6	17.4	18.2
Lexington, KY	9.1	6.8	8.1	11.7	17.0	12.5	17.0	17.6
Lincoln, NE	7.4	6.1	7.7	12.0	17.9	13.8	18.0	17.1
Little Rock, AR	9.9	7.9	8.8	12.9	17.0	12.7	16.1	14.8
Los Angeles, CA	8.3	5.4	5.6	8.5	13.4	11.7	17.9	29.3
Louisville, KY	8.5	6.8	7.4	12.0	17.2	13.5	17.6	17.0
Madison, WI	6.5	5.2	6.1	9.4	16.1	13.5	19.4	23.8
Manchester, NH	4.5	4.5	4.6	8.8	14.6	12.8	19.9	30.3

Table continued on following page.

Metro Area	Percent of Households Earning							
	Under $15,000	$15,000 -$24,999	$25,000 -$34,999	$35,000 -$49,999	$50,000 -$74,999	$75,000 -$99,999	$100,000 -$149,999	$150,000 and up
McAllen, TX	14.0	11.7	10.0	12.6	16.7	11.7	13.8	9.5
Memphis, TN	10.9	8.0	8.2	12.2	16.7	12.1	16.0	15.9
Miami, FL	9.3	7.1	7.4	10.9	16.1	12.6	16.3	20.1
Midland, TX	8.0	4.3	5.9	9.4	13.7	11.6	18.6	28.4
Milwaukee, WI	8.5	6.5	7.4	10.4	16.3	13.1	17.8	20.0
Minneapolis, MN	5.5	4.5	4.9	8.5	14.5	13.0	20.3	28.9
Nashville, TN	6.6	5.5	5.8	10.7	16.8	13.9	19.0	21.7
New Orleans, LA	13.6	8.8	8.5	11.2	15.6	11.7	14.6	15.9
New York, NY	9.0	5.6	5.4	7.9	12.4	10.7	16.7	32.4
Oklahoma City, OK	8.9	6.7	7.8	11.9	17.6	13.5	17.0	16.6
Omaha, NE	6.9	5.6	6.3	10.1	16.6	13.2	19.6	21.7
Orlando, FL	7.3	6.3	7.3	11.1	17.7	13.5	18.0	18.9
Philadelphia, PA	8.4	5.8	6.0	8.9	14.0	11.9	17.9	27.1
Phoenix, AZ	6.6	5.0	5.9	10.1	16.6	13.9	19.3	22.5
Pittsburgh, PA	8.8	7.3	7.3	10.9	16.2	12.9	17.2	19.3
Portland, OR	6.4	4.7	5.1	8.8	14.6	13.1	19.7	27.6
Providence, RI	8.7	6.7	6.0	9.1	14.0	12.6	19.0	23.8
Provo, UT	4.4	4.1	4.6	8.5	15.1	15.0	22.7	25.6
Raleigh, NC	5.6	4.9	5.4	9.0	14.6	12.1	19.5	28.8
Reno, NV	6.9	5.4	6.0	9.9	16.4	13.4	20.5	21.6
Richmond, VA	7.2	5.6	5.9	10.0	16.3	12.7	18.9	23.4
Rochester, MN	5.2	5.4	5.6	9.0	16.3	13.4	20.4	24.7
Sacramento, CA	7.3	5.2	5.3	8.5	13.9	12.7	19.3	27.9
Saint Louis, MO	7.6	6.2	6.8	11.1	16.4	13.1	18.1	20.7
Saint Paul, MN	5.5	4.5	4.9	8.5	14.5	13.0	20.3	28.9
Salem, OR	7.7	6.4	6.9	11.0	17.3	13.4	19.7	17.5
Salt Lake City, UT	5.3	4.0	4.7	8.8	15.3	14.6	21.5	25.8
San Antonio, TX	8.2	6.5	7.5	10.9	17.2	13.3	17.4	18.9
San Diego, CA	6.3	4.7	5.0	7.8	13.1	12.1	19.1	31.9
San Francisco, CA	6.3	3.8	3.8	5.9	9.6	9.3	15.9	45.4
San Jose, CA	4.6	3.0	3.1	4.8	8.4	8.5	15.5	52.0
Santa Rosa, CA	5.9	4.1	4.7	7.8	13.4	12.7	19.3	32.2
Savannah, GA	8.5	6.0	7.5	11.0	17.3	13.8	18.5	17.4
Seattle, WA	5.6	3.8	4.2	7.0	12.6	11.5	19.2	36.1
Sioux Falls, SD	5.4	5.2	6.6	11.6	17.7	14.7	20.0	18.9
Tampa, FL	8.6	6.9	7.6	11.6	17.6	12.8	16.6	18.3
Tucson, AZ	9.3	7.6	8.5	12.3	16.7	12.8	16.7	16.0
Tulsa, OK	8.9	7.1	8.4	12.3	17.8	12.9	16.9	15.8
Virginia Beach, VA	7.5	5.5	6.6	10.0	17.3	13.3	19.2	20.7
Washington, DC	5.4	3.2	3.5	5.9	11.0	11.0	18.9	41.0
Wichita, KS	8.3	6.6	8.7	12.2	18.3	13.9	17.0	14.8
Wilmington, NC	8.2	6.4	6.8	11.5	18.0	13.4	17.6	18.0
Winston-Salem, NC	9.2	8.1	9.0	12.8	18.0	13.7	15.4	13.9
U.S.	8.5	6.6	6.8	10.4	15.7	12.7	17.4	21.9

Note: Figures cover the Metropolitan Statistical Area (MSA)
Source: U.S. Census Bureau, 2019-2023 American Community Survey 5-Year Estimates

Poverty Rate: City

City	All Ages	Under 18 Years Old	18 to 64 Years Old	65 Years and Over
Albuquerque, NM	16.0	20.8	15.3	12.6
Anchorage, AK	9.3	11.3	8.8	7.8
Ann Arbor, MI	23.0	13.5	27.9	6.0
Athens, GA	26.3	24.3	29.5	11.7
Atlanta, GA	17.9	25.9	15.6	18.7
Austin, TX	12.3	15.7	11.6	10.9
Baltimore, MD	20.1	26.4	17.8	20.9
Billings, MT	10.6	13.0	10.2	8.9
Boise City, ID	10.6	12.7	10.8	7.3
Boston, MA	16.9	21.8	15.0	21.0
Boulder, CO	21.8	9.7	26.8	6.2
Cape Coral, FL	9.8	13.1	9.1	9.2
Cedar Rapids, IA	11.8	14.3	11.9	7.8
Charleston, SC	12.0	15.4	12.2	7.3
Charlotte, NC	11.7	16.9	10.1	10.4
Chicago, IL	16.8	24.0	14.6	17.1
Cincinnati, OH	24.5	34.2	22.8	17.1
Clarksville, TN	12.8	16.8	11.8	7.7
Cleveland, OH	30.8	45.3	27.4	24.5
College Station, TX	28.6	14.8	34.5	5.8
Colorado Springs, CO	9.3	10.8	9.2	7.7
Columbia, MO	20.0	13.4	23.5	10.7
Columbia, SC	23.3	29.4	22.6	17.2
Columbus, OH	17.8	25.9	16.1	12.1
Dallas, TX	17.2	25.7	14.3	15.0
Davenport, IA	15.6	20.7	15.0	11.3
Denver, CO	11.2	14.9	10.2	11.5
Des Moines, IA	14.9	22.1	13.1	10.8
Detroit, MI	31.5	44.2	28.8	20.9
Durham, NC	12.2	16.9	11.5	8.2
El Paso, TX	18.4	24.8	15.4	20.0
Eugene, OR	18.2	15.1	21.4	9.4
Fargo, ND	12.8	14.6	13.7	6.0
Fort Collins, CO	16.0	9.2	19.1	8.0
Fort Wayne, IN	15.6	22.5	14.3	9.1
Fort Worth, TX	12.9	18.0	11.1	10.2
Gainesville, FL	28.0	18.0	32.8	11.4
Green Bay, WI	16.5	23.4	15.0	11.0
Greensboro, NC	18.4	26.0	16.5	14.2
Honolulu, HI	11.9	15.0	11.1	11.7
Houston, TX	19.7	29.9	16.6	16.0
Huntsville, AL	13.8	19.5	13.3	8.9
Indianapolis, IN	15.7	21.2	14.3	11.5
Jacksonville, FL	15.0	20.9	13.1	14.2
Kansas City, MO	14.6	20.5	12.9	12.4
Lafayette, LA	19.1	28.3	17.1	14.8
Las Vegas, NV	14.2	18.8	13.2	11.7
Lexington, KY	15.7	19.3	16.3	7.7
Lincoln, NE	12.6	13.0	13.6	8.0
Little Rock, AR	16.4	25.1	15.1	7.8
Los Angeles, CA	16.5	22.1	14.8	16.9
Louisville, KY	16.1	23.2	14.9	10.8
Madison, WI	16.2	13.1	18.7	7.0
Manchester, NH	10.7	17.2	9.3	9.5
McAllen, TX	20.2	27.2	17.6	17.0

Table continued on following page.

City	All Ages	Under 18 Years Old	18 to 64 Years Old	65 Years and Over
Memphis, TN	22.5	34.7	18.9	16.4
Miami, FL	19.2	23.4	15.3	31.4
Midland, TX	11.7	14.0	10.6	11.5
Milwaukee, WI	23.3	32.5	20.7	16.7
Minneapolis, MN	16.4	19.8	15.7	14.2
Nashville, TN	14.1	21.2	12.5	11.2
New Orleans, LA	22.6	32.2	20.1	20.7
New York, NY	17.4	23.2	15.1	18.9
Oklahoma City, OK	15.2	20.6	14.2	9.4
Omaha, NE	12.8	15.9	12.3	9.3
Orlando, FL	15.5	23.0	12.9	16.8
Philadelphia, PA	22.0	30.1	19.5	21.1
Phoenix, AZ	14.3	20.3	12.5	11.7
Pittsburgh, PA	19.5	29.5	18.4	14.1
Portland, OR	12.8	14.5	12.5	11.8
Providence, RI	20.1	26.0	18.2	19.9
Provo, UT	22.3	12.8	26.3	9.4
Raleigh, NC	11.4	14.6	10.9	9.1
Reno, NV	12.5	13.9	12.2	11.8
Richmond, VA	18.8	28.3	17.2	14.6
Rochester, MN	9.1	9.0	9.4	7.6
Sacramento, CA	14.4	17.9	13.5	12.8
Saint Louis, MO	19.8	26.9	18.2	17.8
Saint Paul, MN	15.7	22.9	13.8	11.7
Salem, OR	14.7	17.2	14.4	11.8
Salt Lake City, UT	13.4	12.3	14.1	11.0
San Antonio, TX	17.1	24.8	14.8	14.2
San Diego, CA	11.1	12.3	11.0	10.2
San Francisco, CA	10.6	8.2	9.6	16.4
San Jose, CA	7.8	7.6	7.4	10.5
Santa Rosa, CA	9.5	10.8	9.1	9.5
Savannah, GA	19.5	28.9	17.6	14.0
Seattle, WA	9.9	8.6	9.7	12.3
Sioux Falls, SD	9.6	12.3	9.1	7.1
Tampa, FL	15.9	20.3	13.5	21.2
Tucson, AZ	18.8	24.3	18.7	12.5
Tulsa, OK	18.6	27.0	17.3	10.4
Virginia Beach, VA	8.4	11.2	8.0	5.9
Washington, DC	14.5	20.4	12.9	14.6
Wichita, KS	15.9	21.6	15.0	10.3
Wilmington, NC	16.3	18.1	17.3	11.0
Winston-Salem, NC	17.9	27.1	16.0	10.7
U.S.	12.4	16.3	11.6	10.4

Note: Figures are percentage of people whose income during the past 12 months was below the poverty level
Source: U.S. Census Bureau, 2019-2023 American Community Survey 5-Year Estimates

Poverty Rate: Metro Area

Metro Area	All Ages	Under 18 Years Old	18 to 64 Years Old	65 Years and Over
Albuquerque, NM	15.1	19.6	14.5	12.0
Anchorage, AK	9.6	11.6	9.1	7.9
Ann Arbor, MI	13.8	12.5	16.2	5.9
Athens, GA	19.7	19.0	22.1	10.1
Atlanta, GA	11.0	15.0	9.7	9.3
Austin, TX	9.9	11.5	9.6	8.7
Baltimore, MD	9.9	12.0	9.0	10.2
Billings, MT	10.0	12.0	9.9	8.2
Boise City, ID	9.1	10.7	8.9	7.7
Boston, MA	8.9	9.7	8.3	10.3
Boulder, CO	11.4	7.5	13.7	7.1
Cape Coral, FL	11.7	17.1	11.2	9.5
Cedar Rapids, IA	9.7	11.5	9.7	7.5
Charleston, SC	11.2	15.6	10.3	9.0
Charlotte, NC	10.5	14.2	9.4	9.3
Chicago, IL	11.1	14.8	10.0	10.2
Cincinnati, OH	11.6	14.7	11.1	9.2
Clarksville, TN	13.2	16.4	12.3	10.5
Cleveland, OH	13.6	19.3	12.6	10.6
College Station, TX	22.6	19.9	26.0	8.5
Colorado Springs, CO	8.5	10.2	8.2	6.9
Columbia, MO	16.5	14.6	18.8	9.0
Columbia, SC	14.7	19.8	13.9	10.6
Columbus, OH	12.2	16.5	11.4	8.7
Dallas, TX	10.5	14.5	9.2	9.3
Davenport, IA	12.4	16.9	12.0	8.3
Denver, CO	8.2	10.3	7.6	7.6
Des Moines, IA	8.9	11.0	8.5	7.1
Detroit, MI	13.2	19.1	12.0	10.2
Durham, NC	12.3	16.2	12.2	7.9
El Paso, TX	18.9	25.1	15.8	20.6
Eugene, OR	15.3	14.3	17.4	9.7
Fargo, ND	11.4	11.8	12.2	6.7
Fort Collins, CO	11.1	8.5	12.9	7.1
Fort Wayne, IN	11.8	16.1	11.1	7.3
Fort Worth, TX	10.5	14.5	9.2	9.3
Gainesville, FL	18.9	16.3	21.8	10.7
Green Bay, WI	9.5	11.6	9.3	7.5
Greensboro, NC	15.3	21.4	14.1	11.6
Honolulu, HI	9.1	11.4	8.5	8.7
Houston, TX	13.6	19.1	11.7	11.3
Huntsville, AL	10.4	13.1	9.8	9.1
Indianapolis, IN	10.5	13.6	9.8	8.3
Jacksonville, FL	12.1	16.9	10.9	10.2
Kansas City, MO	10.0	13.2	9.2	8.5
Lafayette, LA	18.5	25.0	16.8	14.8
Las Vegas, NV	13.2	18.1	12.1	10.6
Lexington, KY	14.0	17.4	14.1	8.6
Lincoln, NE	11.4	11.3	12.5	7.6
Little Rock, AR	14.2	19.7	13.5	8.7
Los Angeles, CA	12.6	16.0	11.4	13.1
Louisville, KY	12.3	17.0	11.4	9.2
Madison, WI	10.0	8.5	11.4	6.1
Manchester, NH	6.5	8.1	6.0	6.7
McAllen, TX	27.2	37.1	22.6	22.9

Table continued on following page.

Metro Area	All Ages	Under 18 Years Old	18 to 64 Years Old	65 Years and Over
Memphis, TN	16.3	24.2	14.0	12.2
Miami, FL	13.1	16.9	11.0	15.9
Midland, TX	10.6	12.7	9.3	11.6
Milwaukee, WI	12.4	17.0	11.2	10.3
Minneapolis, MN	8.2	9.6	7.7	7.7
Nashville, TN	10.4	13.6	9.5	8.9
New Orleans, LA	18.3	25.6	16.5	14.9
New York, NY	12.4	16.4	10.9	13.0
Oklahoma City, OK	13.9	18.3	13.3	8.8
Omaha, NE	9.5	11.2	9.1	8.1
Orlando, FL	11.8	15.0	11.0	10.5
Philadelphia, PA	11.7	15.7	10.6	10.3
Phoenix, AZ	11.2	15.1	10.3	9.2
Pittsburgh, PA	10.9	14.4	10.5	8.9
Portland, OR	9.5	10.5	9.4	9.0
Providence, RI	11.2	14.2	10.3	10.6
Provo, UT	8.7	7.2	10.0	5.5
Raleigh, NC	8.6	10.3	8.0	7.9
Reno, NV	10.7	12.1	10.3	10.3
Richmond, VA	10.0	13.4	9.3	8.0
Rochester, MN	7.8	8.3	7.8	7.1
Sacramento, CA	11.6	13.6	11.4	9.3
Saint Louis, MO	10.3	13.3	9.7	8.7
Saint Paul, MN	8.2	9.6	7.7	7.7
Salem, OR	12.9	16.0	12.5	10.2
Salt Lake City, UT	8.1	8.8	8.0	7.5
San Antonio, TX	13.4	18.5	11.9	11.4
San Diego, CA	10.4	12.0	10.0	9.4
San Francisco, CA	8.7	8.8	8.2	10.4
San Jose, CA	6.9	6.6	6.5	9.0
Santa Rosa, CA	8.6	9.3	8.4	8.4
Savannah, GA	12.4	16.6	11.4	9.9
Seattle, WA	8.4	9.5	7.9	8.8
Sioux Falls, SD	8.1	9.7	7.7	6.8
Tampa, FL	12.2	15.5	11.3	11.9
Tucson, AZ	14.4	18.7	14.9	8.9
Tulsa, OK	13.7	18.9	12.9	8.9
Virginia Beach, VA	10.9	15.4	9.9	8.4
Washington, DC	7.9	9.8	7.2	7.6
Wichita, KS	13.1	17.4	12.4	8.8
Wilmington, NC	11.1	13.9	11.9	7.0
Winston-Salem, NC	13.9	21.2	12.5	9.7
U.S.	12.4	16.3	11.6	10.4

Note: Figures are percentage of people whose income during the past 12 months was below the poverty level; Figures cover the Metropolitan Statistical Area (MSA)
Source: U.S. Census Bureau, 2019-2023 American Community Survey 5-Year Estimates

Employment by Industry

Metro Area	(A)	(B)	(C)	(D)	(E)	(F)	(G)	(H)	(I)	(J)	(K)	(L)	(M)	(N)
Albuquerque, NM	6.6	n/a	4.6	19.8	1.3	10.4	4.0	n/a	3.1	17.3	16.0	10.3	3.9	2.7
Anchorage, AK	7.3	6.2	4.0	19.3	1.7	10.9	1.3	1.1	3.7	19.1	11.0	10.9	8.0	2.8
Ann Arbor, MI	2.2	n/a	2.9	37.3	2.5	7.1	5.1	n/a	2.8	15.0	12.4	7.3	2.2	3.1
Athens, GA	3.9	n/a	3.3	28.7	0.7	11.4	6.7	n/a	3.6	16.0	8.8	11.1	1.8	4.0
Atlanta, GA[1]	4.2	4.1	7.0	11.9	3.8	9.7	5.3	0.1	3.6	14.6	18.3	9.4	7.1	5.1
Austin, TX	6.5	n/a	6.5	15.3	3.6	10.7	5.3	n/a	3.9	12.0	20.5	9.0	2.7	4.1
Baltimore, MD	5.4	n/a	5.3	16.6	1.1	8.4	3.9	n/a	3.7	20.0	17.5	9.0	5.3	3.7
Billings, MT	8.0	n/a	5.4	11.1	0.9	14.6	4.3	n/a	4.2	18.0	9.8	12.6	5.0	6.0
Boise City, ID	9.1	n/a	5.8	13.3	1.1	10.0	7.6	n/a	3.5	15.4	14.6	10.0	4.6	4.7
Boston, MA[1]	4.1	n/a	9.6	12.2	2.6	10.5	2.8	n/a	3.6	24.6	16.3	7.8	3.4	2.5
Boulder, CO	2.7	n/a	3.3	19.7	4.0	9.6	10.0	n/a	4.3	13.2	20.1	8.2	1.1	3.7
Cape Coral, FL	13.6	n/a	4.9	15.3	1.1	13.0	2.6	n/a	4.0	11.5	14.2	14.3	2.5	3.0
Cedar Rapids, IA	6.3	n/a	6.6	11.9	2.0	8.4	14.2	n/a	3.6	16.3	11.1	10.4	5.1	4.1
Charleston, SC	5.7	n/a	5.1	16.7	1.8	12.4	8.1	n/a	3.9	11.9	15.8	10.9	4.7	3.0
Charlotte, NC	5.9	n/a	8.8	12.9	1.9	10.9	7.7	n/a	4.0	11.1	16.2	10.0	6.1	4.7
Chicago, IL[1]	3.4	3.4	7.2	11.2	1.8	9.8	7.3	<0.1	4.1	17.0	18.0	8.7	6.5	4.9
Cincinnati, OH	4.6	n/a	6.8	11.6	1.1	10.6	10.4	n/a	3.6	15.9	15.3	9.0	5.8	5.3
Clarksville, TN	4.5	n/a	3.8	20.6	1.3	12.1	12.9	n/a	3.3	13.1	8.4	13.2	4.5	2.3
Cleveland, OH	3.7	n/a	6.5	12.5	1.3	9.5	11.6	n/a	3.5	19.7	13.9	9.1	3.8	4.9
College Station, TX	5.3	n/a	3.3	35.1	1.1	14.4	4.2	n/a	2.8	10.9	9.8	9.1	1.9	2.2
Colorado Springs, CO	5.4	n/a	5.8	17.9	1.5	12.4	3.6	n/a	7.0	14.6	16.0	10.2	3.8	2.0
Columbia, MO	3.6	3.5	7.6	31.5	1.1	10.6	4.7	0.1	2.8	13.9	9.1	10.1	2.6	2.5
Columbia, SC	4.3	n/a	8.3	19.4	1.1	9.4	7.4	n/a	4.2	13.9	13.6	10.5	4.2	3.7
Columbus, OH	4.5	n/a	6.9	16.6	1.5	9.1	6.5	n/a	3.8	15.5	16.3	9.2	6.7	3.6
Dallas, TX[1]	5.4	n/a	10.0	11.3	2.5	9.4	6.6	n/a	3.1	11.5	20.2	9.0	5.4	5.6
Davenport, IA	5.7	n/a	4.1	14.4	0.8	9.7	12.8	n/a	3.7	15.0	11.3	11.7	4.2	6.5
Denver, CO	6.9	n/a	7.1	13.7	3.0	10.4	4.0	n/a	4.2	12.9	19.4	8.5	5.3	4.7
Des Moines, IA	5.9	n/a	13.6	12.8	1.5	8.8	5.4	n/a	3.3	15.2	13.4	10.6	4.8	4.8
Detroit, MI[1]	4.0	n/a	6.2	9.6	1.4	9.1	12.1	n/a	3.8	16.2	18.4	9.9	5.2	4.1
Durham, NC	3.1	n/a	4.8	19.3	1.6	7.8	7.9	n/a	3.7	21.8	17.8	6.9	2.4	2.8
El Paso, TX	4.5	n/a	4.1	20.8	1.8	11.6	4.8	n/a	2.8	15.5	12.6	11.4	6.0	4.0
Eugene, OR	5.0	4.4	5.2	19.8	1.2	10.1	8.5	0.6	3.1	18.6	10.9	11.7	2.3	3.5
Fargo, ND	6.0	n/a	7.1	14.0	1.5	9.6	8.0	n/a	3.3	19.6	9.5	10.3	5.2	5.9
Fort Collins, CO	6.0	n/a	3.8	26.3	1.3	12.1	8.0	n/a	3.6	11.3	11.6	10.5	2.5	3.2
Fort Wayne, IN	5.5	n/a	5.1	9.6	0.8	8.8	15.8	n/a	5.6	19.2	9.6	10.4	5.0	4.6
Fort Worth, TX[1]	7.1	n/a	6.4	11.7	1.0	11.1	8.9	n/a	3.5	12.9	12.8	10.9	8.7	5.0
Gainesville, FL	4.3	n/a	4.0	28.7	1.2	10.5	3.1	n/a	3.0	19.7	10.7	10.0	2.8	2.1
Green Bay, WI	4.8	n/a	4.7	11.8	0.9	9.8	18.1	n/a	4.4	15.8	10.5	9.5	4.8	4.9
Greensboro, NC	5.3	n/a	4.3	12.6	1.0	9.9	12.8	n/a	3.7	14.9	12.6	11.3	5.7	5.8
Honolulu, HI	6.0	n/a	4.5	21.0	1.5	15.8	2.1	n/a	4.4	14.9	12.1	9.3	5.5	2.9
Houston, TX	9.0	6.7	5.2	13.4	0.9	10.4	6.9	2.3	3.9	13.3	16.4	9.6	5.8	5.2
Huntsville, AL	4.0	n/a	3.1	20.8	1.0	8.4	12.4	n/a	3.3	9.0	23.6	9.9	2.2	2.5
Indianapolis, IN	5.5	5.5	6.3	12.6	1.0	9.1	8.1	0.1	4.1	15.8	15.7	8.8	8.3	4.7
Jacksonville, FL	6.6	6.6	9.0	10.1	1.8	11.3	4.5	<0.1	3.6	16.3	14.9	11.0	7.3	3.7
Kansas City, MO	5.3	5.2	6.9	13.4	1.5	9.6	7.9	0.1	3.7	15.3	16.0	9.9	6.0	4.6
Lafayette, LA	9.6	5.5	4.7	12.6	0.8	11.1	7.7	4.1	3.6	18.3	11.3	12.6	3.3	4.4
Las Vegas, NV	6.8	6.8	5.3	10.7	1.3	25.8	2.6	<0.1	3.0	11.4	14.3	9.8	6.7	2.3
Lexington, KY	4.9	n/a	4.0	19.6	1.0	10.7	10.5	n/a	4.8	13.2	13.5	9.6	4.2	3.9
Lincoln, NE	5.4	n/a	5.4	21.8	2.0	9.7	7.4	n/a	4.3	17.0	10.3	9.3	5.3	2.2
Little Rock, AR	5.4	n/a	7.1	17.8	1.3	8.5	5.4	n/a	4.8	16.9	12.4	10.0	6.0	4.6
Los Angeles, CA[1]	3.2	3.2	4.5	12.9	4.1	11.6	6.5	<0.1	3.4	21.4	14.4	8.9	4.9	4.2
Louisville, KY	5.1	n/a	6.4	10.6	1.1	9.6	11.8	n/a	3.8	15.4	12.2	9.5	9.8	4.7
Madison, WI	4.6	n/a	5.5	22.4	5.0	8.4	8.7	n/a	5.0	13.1	12.2	9.1	2.5	3.6
Manchester, NH	4.3	n/a	5.6	10.8	2.4	9.0	12.0	n/a	3.8	20.1	14.1	12.5	2.4	3.1
McAllen, TX	3.0	n/a	3.3	20.3	1.0	9.8	2.3	n/a	2.2	30.1	8.9	12.7	3.3	3.1
Memphis, TN	3.8	n/a	4.5	13.2	0.8	9.3	6.1	n/a	4.2	15.2	13.5	9.4	14.1	5.8

Table continued on following page.

Metro Area	(A)	(B)	(C)	(D)	(E)	(F)	(G)	(H)	(I)	(J)	(K)	(L)	(M)	(N)
Miami, FL[1]	4.5	4.5	7.1	10.6	1.7	11.4	3.5	<0.1	3.7	16.6	15.7	11.2	7.8	6.2
Midland, TX	33.1	n/a	5.0	8.7	0.8	9.2	3.7	n/a	3.4	7.7	9.5	7.9	5.2	5.8
Milwaukee, WI	4.3	4.2	5.5	9.6	1.3	9.2	12.8	0.1	5.1	20.8	14.0	9.0	4.0	4.5
Minneapolis, MN	4.3	n/a	7.2	13.2	1.4	8.9	10.0	n/a	3.9	19.0	14.4	9.2	4.4	4.2
Nashville, TN	5.5	n/a	6.8	11.2	2.7	11.2	7.4	n/a	4.2	15.1	16.1	9.2	6.4	4.2
New Orleans, LA	6.0	5.6	5.0	11.6	1.4	14.5	5.5	0.4	4.3	20.3	12.9	9.3	5.6	3.6
New York, NY[1]	3.3	n/a	9.8	12.5	4.0	9.0	2.1	n/a	3.8	25.2	16.1	7.3	3.7	3.3
Oklahoma City, OK	6.5	5.0	5.2	19.0	0.9	11.4	4.9	1.4	4.3	16.7	12.7	10.2	4.7	3.5
Omaha, NE	6.2	n/a	7.7	13.5	1.7	10.7	6.9	n/a	3.5	17.6	13.6	10.2	5.2	3.2
Orlando, FL	6.3	6.3	6.1	8.9	1.8	19.2	3.5	<0.1	3.7	12.9	19.1	10.5	4.5	3.5
Philadelphia, PA[1]	2.4	n/a	6.1	13.0	1.8	9.3	3.1	n/a	4.2	32.9	14.4	6.7	3.9	2.2
Phoenix, AZ	7.3	7.2	8.5	10.5	1.6	10.7	6.0	0.1	3.2	16.9	15.6	10.3	5.3	4.1
Pittsburgh, PA	5.3	4.7	6.5	9.9	1.7	9.8	7.1	0.7	4.1	22.2	15.4	10.0	4.5	3.5
Portland, OR	6.4	6.3	5.8	12.9	2.1	9.4	9.6	0.1	3.5	16.6	15.5	9.3	4.3	4.6
Providence, RI	4.5	4.5	5.5	13.3	1.0	10.7	8.5	<0.1	4.2	21.6	12.1	11.0	3.6	3.8
Provo, UT	9.5	n/a	4.0	11.9	3.9	9.1	7.8	n/a	2.3	22.1	14.4	10.8	2.0	2.2
Raleigh, NC	7.0	n/a	5.5	14.4	3.3	10.5	4.5	n/a	4.4	13.8	19.4	10.1	3.5	3.8
Reno, NV	8.8	8.5	4.2	12.8	1.4	14.2	10.6	0.3	2.7	11.6	12.1	9.4	8.8	3.5
Richmond, VA	5.9	n/a	7.9	15.7	0.9	9.3	4.4	n/a	4.6	15.3	17.0	9.2	6.0	3.8
Rochester, MN	4.1	n/a	2.2	10.5	0.8	8.2	6.9	n/a	3.0	45.2	5.3	9.6	2.1	2.1
Sacramento, CA	6.9	6.8	4.2	24.0	0.9	10.1	3.6	<0.1	3.5	18.7	12.2	9.2	4.0	2.6
Saint Louis, MO	5.4	n/a	6.7	11.2	2.0	9.7	8.2	n/a	3.6	19.5	14.9	9.6	4.8	4.6
Saint Paul, MN	4.3	n/a	7.2	13.2	1.4	8.9	10.0	n/a	3.9	19.0	14.4	9.2	4.4	4.2
Salem, OR	7.4	7.1	3.2	24.5	1.0	8.5	6.2	0.3	3.0	19.9	10.0	10.1	3.9	2.2
Salt Lake City, UT	7.2	n/a	7.7	14.3	2.8	8.3	7.7	n/a	2.7	12.2	17.1	9.2	6.0	4.9
San Antonio, TX	6.3	5.7	8.5	16.1	1.6	12.2	5.2	0.6	3.5	15.2	13.3	10.7	4.0	3.2
San Diego, CA	5.8	5.7	4.5	16.6	1.3	12.9	7.0	<0.1	3.6	16.6	17.0	9.1	2.9	2.7
San Francisco, CA[1]	3.4	3.3	6.7	12.4	9.7	10.6	2.6	<0.1	3.3	14.3	25.1	5.5	4.4	2.0
San Jose, CA	4.6	4.5	3.1	8.8	8.1	9.0	10.6	<0.1	2.4	18.4	24.6	6.5	1.5	2.5
Santa Rosa, CA	8.0	7.9	3.3	13.9	1.3	12.4	10.5	0.1	3.8	18.6	11.5	11.2	2.3	3.2
Savannah, GA	4.8	n/a	3.7	12.3	0.7	13.1	11.0	n/a	4.1	14.2	11.2	11.5	9.8	3.7
Seattle, WA[1]	4.8	4.8	4.9	12.8	8.7	9.3	6.2	<0.1	3.2	13.7	20.9	7.2	4.5	4.0
Sioux Falls, SD	6.8	n/a	8.2	9.5	1.5	9.1	8.7	n/a	3.7	21.6	9.7	11.4	4.6	5.2
Tampa, FL[1]	n/a	6.6	10.2	10.4	1.8	10.3	3.7	n/a	3.3	16.0	18.1	10.9	4.3	4.3
Tucson, AZ	5.7	5.0	4.3	19.9	1.3	11.2	7.0	0.6	3.7	17.9	11.1	10.9	5.1	2.0
Tulsa, OK	6.4	5.7	5.1	13.2	1.0	9.9	11.1	0.7	4.5	17.0	13.2	10.3	4.6	3.7
Virginia Beach, VA	5.0	n/a	4.9	20.1	1.0	11.1	7.0	n/a	4.3	15.4	14.8	10.0	3.9	2.4
Washington, DC[1]	4.2	n/a	3.3	30.2	1.8	9.9	0.8	n/a	6.7	14.8	19.4	5.6	1.9	1.4
Wichita, KS	5.5	n/a	4.1	14.0	1.1	10.2	16.7	n/a	4.0	15.9	10.8	10.1	4.4	3.2
Wilmington, NC	7.3	n/a	4.9	12.9	1.6	15.5	4.5	n/a	4.6	16.9	12.2	13.3	3.6	2.8
Winston-Salem, NC	4.7	n/a	4.5	12.3	0.7	10.7	11.7	n/a	3.9	21.5	11.9	11.4	3.6	3.2
U.S.	5.5	5.1	5.8	14.9	1.9	10.4	8.0	0.4	3.7	16.9	14.2	10.0	4.8	3.9

Note: All figures are percentages covering non-farm employment as of December 2024 and are not seasonally adjusted; Figures cover the Metropolitan Statistical Area (MSA) except where noted; (1) Metropolitan Division; (A) Construction, Mining, and Logging (some areas report Construction separate from Mining and Logging); (B) Construction; (C) Financial Activities; (D) Government; (E) Information; (F) Leisure and Hospitality; (G) Manufacturing; (H) Mining and Logging; (I) Other Services; (J) Private Education and Health Services; (K) Professional and Business Services; (L) Retail Trade; (M) Transportation and Utilities; (N) Wholesale Trade; n/a not available
Source: Bureau of Labor Statistics, Current Employment Statistics, Employment, Hours, and Earnings, December 2024

Labor Force, Employment and Job Growth: City

City	Civilian Labor Force			Workers Employed		
	Dec. 2023	Dec. 2024	% Chg.	Dec. 2023	Dec. 2024	% Chg.
Albuquerque, NM	295,286	297,348	0.7	286,112	286,738	0.2
Anchorage, AK	153,020	155,068	1.3	147,538	149,604	1.4
Ann Arbor, MI	66,518	68,304	2.6	64,986	66,059	1.6
Athens, GA	61,309	61,837	0.8	59,338	59,852	0.8
Atlanta, GA	278,364	279,245	0.3	268,161	267,879	-0.1
Austin, TX	692,732	711,010	2.6	671,863	690,459	2.7
Baltimore, MD	276,136	279,771	1.3	267,011	268,805	0.6
Billings, MT	59,483	58,785	-1.1	57,662	57,121	-0.9
Boise City, ID	146,113	151,831	3.9	142,029	147,110	3.5
Boston, MA	403,771	411,958	2.0	390,365	395,765	1.3
Boulder, CO	68,299	68,728	0.6	66,297	66,171	-0.1
Cape Coral, FL	100,486	101,752	1.2	97,397	98,477	1.1
Cedar Rapids, IA	70,086	70,636	0.7	67,783	68,276	0.7
Charleston, SC	81,443	83,687	2.7	79,209	80,914	2.1
Charlotte, NC	531,420	537,158	1.0	513,465	519,577	1.1
Chicago, IL	1,391,216	1,432,019	2.9	1,330,946	1,363,159	2.4
Cincinnati, OH	150,446	153,060	1.7	145,104	146,196	0.7
Clarksville, TN	65,211	66,900	2.5	62,910	64,067	1.8
Cleveland, OH	154,882	158,055	2.0	148,680	151,454	1.8
College Station, TX	70,826	73,610	3.9	68,915	71,605	3.9
Colorado Springs, CO	254,636	258,951	1.6	245,377	247,188	0.7
Columbia, MO	69,206	70,699	2.1	67,566	68,998	2.1
Columbia, SC	59,838	60,914	1.8	57,599	58,055	0.7
Columbus, OH	490,638	493,589	0.6	474,627	473,223	-0.3
Dallas, TX	753,950	773,828	2.6	727,021	746,370	2.6
Davenport, IA	49,490	49,873	0.7	47,766	47,656	-0.2
Denver, CO	439,297	444,521	1.1	421,359	422,120	0.1
Des Moines, IA	113,506	113,721	0.1	109,944	109,495	-0.4
Detroit, MI	252,407	254,935	1.0	235,064	230,371	-2.0
Durham, NC	161,695	163,549	1.1	156,943	158,778	1.1
El Paso, TX	321,869	330,289	2.6	309,686	317,905	2.6
Eugene, OR	86,438	87,547	1.2	82,952	83,877	1.1
Fargo, ND	75,385	76,672	1.7	73,971	74,762	1.0
Fort Collins, CO	104,877	106,076	1.1	101,643	102,156	0.5
Fort Wayne, IN	130,643	133,106	1.8	126,751	127,554	0.6
Fort Worth, TX	492,810	506,338	2.7	474,900	487,778	2.7
Gainesville, FL	71,265	72,407	1.6	68,797	69,722	1.3
Green Bay, WI	53,842	54,171	0.6	52,558	52,661	0.2
Greensboro, NC	145,300	143,645	-1.1	139,667	137,971	-1.2
Honolulu, HI	458,516	467,102	1.8	447,781	454,669	1.5
Houston, TX	1,221,575	1,251,524	2.4	1,168,408	1,201,001	2.7
Huntsville, AL	110,121	113,202	2.8	107,585	109,886	2.1
Indianapolis, IN	468,727	483,276	3.1	453,754	464,036	2.2
Jacksonville, FL	491,737	495,209	0.7	476,373	479,227	0.6
Kansas City, MO	261,274	264,629	1.2	252,452	255,316	1.1
Lafayette, LA	59,760	59,993	0.3	57,644	57,720	0.1
Las Vegas, NV	330,736	337,672	2.1	312,658	317,296	1.4
Lexington, KY	178,351	182,353	2.2	172,195	175,041	1.6
Lincoln, NE	164,857	168,647	2.3	161,204	164,571	2.0
Little Rock, AR	100,778	102,786	1.9	97,463	99,326	1.9
Los Angeles, CA	2,074,549	2,094,633	0.9	1,964,638	1,972,226	0.3
Louisville, KY	394,849	401,525	1.6	379,511	382,789	0.8
Madison, WI	167,700	168,775	0.6	164,752	165,214	0.2
Manchester, NH	64,039	66,140	3.2	62,588	64,103	2.4
McAllen, TX	72,499	74,052	2.1	69,572	71,063	2.1

Table continued on following page.

City	Civilian Labor Force			Workers Employed		
	Dec. 2023	Dec. 2024	% Chg.	Dec. 2023	Dec. 2024	% Chg.
Memphis, TN	283,933	286,196	0.8	271,779	271,426	-0.1
Miami, FL	247,114	249,197	0.8	242,276	243,343	0.4
Midland, TX	93,937	96,111	2.3	91,915	93,872	2.1
Milwaukee, WI	273,443	274,723	0.4	264,071	263,797	-0.1
Minneapolis, MN	244,672	245,657	0.4	238,965	239,886	0.3
Nashville, TN	421,198	426,189	1.1	411,304	413,569	0.5
New Orleans, LA	173,294	173,800	0.2	165,506	165,809	0.1
New York, NY	4,197,201	4,289,830	2.2	4,004,371	4,065,287	1.5
Oklahoma City, OK	352,331	357,109	1.3	341,478	346,634	1.5
Omaha, NE	251,851	256,156	1.7	245,154	248,481	1.3
Orlando, FL	181,418	181,948	0.2	176,377	176,719	0.1
Philadelphia, PA	750,976	745,485	-0.7	719,837	713,546	-0.8
Phoenix, AZ	913,817	927,572	1.5	887,451	898,365	1.2
Pittsburgh, PA	152,654	151,757	-0.5	148,435	147,774	-0.4
Portland, OR	386,871	388,825	0.5	372,067	372,849	0.2
Providence, RI	90,820	92,307	1.6	86,757	87,271	0.5
Provo, UT	73,763	74,411	0.8	72,156	72,484	0.4
Raleigh, NC	276,576	277,882	0.4	267,801	269,378	0.5
Reno, NV	144,664	147,939	2.2	138,887	141,134	1.6
Richmond, VA	123,724	126,447	2.2	120,027	122,541	2.0
Rochester, MN	68,874	73,886	7.2	67,640	72,557	7.2
Sacramento, CA	246,247	248,837	1.0	234,662	236,718	0.8
Saint Louis, MO	150,472	152,715	1.4	144,679	146,505	1.2
Saint Paul, MN	156,382	157,144	0.4	152,569	153,219	0.4
Salem, OR	86,857	88,580	1.9	83,316	84,776	1.7
Salt Lake City, UT	128,957	131,406	1.9	125,261	127,540	1.8
San Antonio, TX	780,314	813,666	4.2	753,069	786,995	4.5
San Diego, CA	730,171	734,863	0.6	701,246	703,991	0.3
San Francisco, CA	564,822	561,032	-0.6	545,573	541,446	-0.7
San Jose, CA	550,266	551,509	0.2	528,718	529,659	0.1
Santa Rosa, CA	87,410	88,152	0.8	84,056	84,516	0.5
Savannah, GA	69,925	69,887	0.0	67,803	67,610	-0.2
Seattle, WA	511,941	526,448	2.8	495,245	511,570	3.3
Sioux Falls, SD	113,602	115,243	1.4	111,615	112,947	1.1
Tampa, FL	222,684	223,321	0.2	215,665	215,892	0.1
Tucson, AZ	263,211	266,440	1.2	254,477	256,864	0.9
Tulsa, OK	206,897	209,496	1.2	199,811	203,133	1.6
Virginia Beach, VA	237,550	239,534	0.8	231,972	233,678	0.7
Washington, DC	411,135	417,094	1.4	391,912	396,492	1.1
Wichita, KS	194,170	197,795	1.8	188,497	190,038	0.8
Wilmington, NC	69,827	69,943	0.1	67,604	67,846	0.3
Winston-Salem, NC	118,508	118,217	-0.2	114,267	114,055	-0.1
U.S.	166,661,000	167,746,000	0.7	160,754,000	161,294,000	0.3

Note: Data is not seasonally adjusted and covers workers 16 years of age and older
Source: Bureau of Labor Statistics, Local Area Unemployment Statistics

Labor Force, Employment and Job Growth: Metro Area

Metro Area	Civilian Labor Force			Workers Employed		
	Dec. 2023	Dec. 2024	% Chg.	Dec. 2023	Dec. 2024	% Chg.
Albuquerque, NM	459,168	462,519	0.7	444,472	445,570	0.2
Anchorage, AK	203,512	206,186	1.3	195,498	198,110	1.3
Ann Arbor, MI	201,644	207,512	2.9	195,986	199,223	1.6
Athens, GA	103,836	104,775	0.9	100,776	101,698	0.9
Atlanta, GA[1]	2,520,105	2,525,607	0.2	2,441,223	2,439,016	0.0
Austin, TX	1,480,563	1,521,172	2.7	1,434,717	1,474,387	2.7
Baltimore, MD	1,496,175	1,509,109	0.8	1,460,563	1,468,370	0.5
Billings, MT	99,307	98,165	-1.1	96,370	95,349	-1.0
Boise City, ID	432,273	448,781	3.8	418,731	433,330	3.4
Boston, MA[1]	1,158,650	1,182,153	2.0	1,119,472	1,135,105	1.4
Boulder, CO	204,348	205,677	0.6	197,756	197,382	-0.1
Cape Coral, FL	376,769	381,593	1.2	365,271	369,323	1.1
Cedar Rapids, IA	141,248	142,473	0.8	136,873	137,885	0.7
Charleston, SC	433,190	445,523	2.8	421,406	430,483	2.1
Charlotte, NC	1,472,294	1,492,625	1.3	1,424,686	1,443,425	1.3
Chicago, IL[1]	3,780,647	3,890,015	2.8	3,630,697	3,719,159	2.4
Cincinnati, OH	1,154,630	1,170,746	1.4	1,116,229	1,123,236	0.6
Clarksville, TN	126,537	129,924	2.6	121,844	124,244	1.9
Cleveland, OH	1,067,052	1,088,179	1.9	1,033,451	1,051,761	1.7
College Station, TX	154,708	160,796	3.9	150,546	156,418	3.9
Colorado Springs, CO	380,947	387,217	1.6	366,679	369,336	0.7
Columbia, MO	113,118	115,648	2.2	110,484	112,817	2.1
Columbia, SC	419,770	426,736	1.6	406,945	410,354	0.8
Columbus, OH	1,134,646	1,141,335	0.5	1,099,340	1,096,249	-0.2
Dallas, TX[1]	3,019,102	3,099,037	2.6	2,914,521	2,992,023	2.6
Davenport, IA	184,725	184,714	0.0	177,254	176,542	-0.4
Denver, CO	1,731,722	1,751,255	1.1	1,667,215	1,670,077	0.1
Des Moines, IA	394,185	394,876	0.1	384,347	382,847	-0.3
Detroit, MI[1]	816,930	814,679	-0.2	784,713	769,048	-2.0
Durham, NC	323,131	326,577	1.0	313,852	317,268	1.0
El Paso, TX	388,422	398,643	2.6	372,959	382,859	2.6
Eugene, OR	184,890	187,239	1.2	177,117	179,091	1.1
Fargo, ND	149,293	152,175	1.9	146,516	148,732	1.5
Fort Collins, CO	216,529	219,305	1.2	209,634	210,691	0.5
Fort Wayne, IN	220,472	224,223	1.7	214,223	215,591	0.6
Fort Worth, TX[1]	1,397,596	1,435,889	2.7	1,349,809	1,386,446	2.7
Gainesville, FL	168,667	171,235	1.5	163,355	165,582	1.3
Green Bay, WI	174,722	175,808	0.6	170,734	171,226	0.2
Greensboro, NC	366,503	362,230	-1.1	353,122	348,882	-1.2
Honolulu, HI	458,516	467,102	1.8	447,781	454,669	1.5
Houston, TX	3,704,314	3,811,882	2.9	3,557,779	3,657,192	2.7
Huntsville, AL	257,532	264,722	2.7	252,062	257,486	2.1
Indianapolis, IN	1,114,296	1,147,341	2.9	1,082,623	1,106,085	2.1
Jacksonville, FL	845,904	852,367	0.7	820,842	825,781	0.6
Kansas City, MO	1,160,004	1,182,211	1.9	1,127,092	1,144,249	1.5
Lafayette, LA	185,004	185,747	0.4	178,352	178,532	0.1
Las Vegas, NV	1,199,294	1,224,775	2.1	1,135,389	1,152,230	1.4
Lexington, KY	278,181	284,384	2.2	268,513	272,804	1.6
Lincoln, NE	191,591	195,942	2.2	187,422	191,304	2.0
Little Rock, AR	371,026	378,813	2.1	359,838	366,941	1.9
Los Angeles, CA[1]	5,037,643	5,091,130	1.0	4,782,176	4,800,645	0.3
Louisville, KY	691,184	703,358	1.7	666,258	672,517	0.9
Madison, WI	410,987	413,894	0.7	403,502	404,881	0.3
Manchester, NH	238,986	245,151	2.5	233,791	237,759	1.7
McAllen, TX	385,693	394,540	2.2	362,243	370,007	2.1

Table continued on following page.

Metro Area	Civilian Labor Force			Workers Employed		
	Dec. 2023	Dec. 2024	% Chg.	Dec. 2023	Dec. 2024	% Chg.
Memphis, TN	620,716	627,549	1.1	598,585	600,246	0.2
Miami, FL[1]	1,433,283	1,445,779	0.8	1,404,765	1,410,954	0.4
Midland, TX	116,721	119,415	2.3	114,162	116,595	2.1
Milwaukee, WI	822,104	825,110	0.3	800,656	800,116	0.0
Minneapolis, MN	2,005,284	2,015,070	0.4	1,956,084	1,964,999	0.4
Nashville, TN	1,150,386	1,163,681	1.1	1,123,659	1,129,538	0.5
New Orleans, LA	461,088	463,007	0.4	442,552	443,450	0.2
New York, NY[1]	6,077,969	6,169,474	1.5	5,813,964	5,874,694	1.0
Oklahoma City, OK	752,168	762,662	1.4	729,908	740,966	1.5
Omaha, NE	505,378	514,350	1.7	492,693	499,953	1.4
Orlando, FL	1,476,354	1,481,986	0.3	1,432,973	1,435,926	0.2
Philadelphia, PA[1]	1,055,097	1,047,116	-0.7	1,014,794	1,006,018	-0.8
Phoenix, AZ	2,660,126	2,699,326	1.4	2,583,768	2,614,930	1.2
Pittsburgh, PA	1,218,768	1,213,214	-0.4	1,179,001	1,172,526	-0.5
Portland, OR	1,358,801	1,358,994	0.0	1,305,393	1,301,850	-0.2
Providence, RI	887,464	901,729	1.6	854,672	862,458	0.9
Provo, UT	363,569	366,874	0.9	354,453	356,068	0.4
Raleigh, NC	799,354	803,302	0.4	775,484	780,100	0.6
Reno, NV	291,520	298,309	2.3	279,599	284,384	1.7
Richmond, VA	703,806	718,292	2.0	685,441	699,371	2.0
Rochester, MN	128,702	138,168	7.3	126,091	135,339	7.3
Sacramento, CA	1,144,784	1,156,797	1.0	1,094,502	1,103,633	0.8
Saint Louis, MO	1,476,468	1,495,860	1.3	1,428,392	1,447,762	1.3
Saint Paul, MN	2,005,284	2,015,070	0.4	1,956,084	1,964,999	0.4
Salem, OR	215,316	219,611	1.9	206,688	210,311	1.7
Salt Lake City, UT	738,638	754,401	2.1	719,094	732,202	1.8
San Antonio, TX	1,308,187	1,349,973	3.1	1,265,057	1,304,101	3.0
San Diego, CA	1,608,713	1,619,332	0.6	1,543,490	1,549,532	0.3
San Francisco, CA[1]	1,011,370	1,004,815	-0.6	978,032	970,469	-0.7
San Jose, CA	1,075,900	1,078,520	0.2	1,034,963	1,036,708	0.1
Santa Rosa, CA	249,694	251,825	0.8	240,531	241,848	0.5
Savannah, GA	202,550	202,333	-0.1	197,273	196,748	-0.2
Seattle, WA[1]	1,366,721	1,405,582	2.8	1,318,947	1,362,424	3.3
Sioux Falls, SD	171,226	173,604	1.3	168,466	170,431	1.1
Tampa, FL[1]	1,167,354	1,171,736	0.3	1,130,613	1,132,522	0.1
Tucson, AZ	493,139	499,226	1.2	477,781	482,263	0.9
Tulsa, OK	510,676	517,614	1.3	494,038	502,372	1.6
Virginia Beach, VA	883,468	890,934	0.8	860,628	866,842	0.7
Washington, DC[1]	1,000,003	1,013,650	1.3	966,020	974,957	0.9
Wichita, KS	320,952	326,697	1.7	311,687	314,280	0.8
Wilmington, NC	222,997	222,642	-0.1	215,630	215,604	0.0
Winston-Salem, NC	329,205	328,631	-0.1	318,577	317,977	-0.1
U.S.	166,661,000	167,746,000	0.7	160,754,000	161,294,000	0.3

Note: Data is not seasonally adjusted and covers workers 16 years of age and older; Figures cover the Metropolitan Statistical Area (MSA) except where noted; (1) Metropolitan Division
Source: Bureau of Labor Statistics, Local Area Unemployment Statistics

Unemployment Rate: City

City	2024											
	Jan.	Feb.	Mar.	Apr.	May	Jun.	Jul.	Aug.	Sep.	Oct.	Nov.	Dec.
Albuquerque, NM	3.5	3.4	3.1	3.1	3.5	4.4	4.9	4.3	3.8	3.9	3.9	3.6
Anchorage, AK	4.0	4.2	3.8	3.7	3.6	4.2	3.8	3.5	3.5	3.6	3.8	3.5
Ann Arbor, MI	2.5	2.7	2.8	2.6	3.2	3.8	4.2	3.7	3.2	3.1	3.2	3.3
Athens, GA	3.7	3.5	3.6	2.8	3.7	4.6	4.5	4.5	3.8	4.0	3.3	3.2
Atlanta, GA	3.9	3.9	3.8	3.6	4.0	4.5	4.5	4.6	4.1	4.2	4.2	4.1
Austin, TX	3.3	3.5	3.2	2.9	3.1	3.5	3.5	3.5	3.3	3.2	3.2	2.9
Baltimore, MD	4.2	4.2	4.0	3.6	3.8	4.5	4.8	4.8	4.0	4.3	4.2	3.9
Billings, MT	3.5	3.3	3.0	2.6	2.6	3.2	3.1	3.0	2.5	2.5	2.6	2.8
Boise City, ID	3.3	3.4	3.3	2.9	3.0	3.3	3.5	3.3	3.1	3.1	3.3	3.1
Boston, MA	3.7	3.7	3.5	3.2	3.8	4.3	4.6	4.4	3.8	3.9	3.9	3.9
Boulder, CO	3.3	3.5	3.4	3.2	4.0	4.5	4.5	4.5	4.1	4.1	4.4	3.7
Cape Coral, FL	3.4	3.2	3.2	3.0	3.2	3.8	3.9	3.9	3.6	3.5	3.6	3.2
Cedar Rapids, IA	3.9	4.3	3.2	2.7	3.6	4.5	4.2	4.0	3.3	3.5	3.6	3.3
Charleston, SC	3.0	3.3	3.0	2.7	3.2	3.9	4.0	4.1	3.5	3.7	3.6	3.3
Charlotte, NC	3.8	3.9	3.6	3.2	3.4	3.8	4.1	3.9	3.2	3.3	3.5	3.3
Chicago, IL	5.0	5.5	5.1	5.1	5.6	6.9	6.7	6.4	5.8	5.8	5.4	4.8
Cincinnati, OH	4.3	4.4	4.3	4.1	4.5	5.2	5.3	5.0	4.6	4.3	4.6	4.5
Clarksville, TN	4.0	3.7	3.8	3.3	3.5	4.6	4.6	4.4	4.2	4.2	4.3	4.2
Cleveland, OH	5.0	5.8	5.2	4.7	5.0	5.5	5.5	4.7	4.1	3.8	4.0	4.2
College Station, TX	3.4	3.6	3.0	2.5	3.0	3.7	3.8	3.7	3.3	3.2	3.1	2.7
Colorado Springs, CO	4.1	4.2	3.8	3.7	3.9	4.4	4.7	4.6	4.3	4.4	4.7	4.5
Columbia, MO	3.1	2.9	3.2	2.7	3.3	3.6	3.8	3.4	2.4	2.7	2.8	2.4
Columbia, SC	4.1	4.4	4.1	3.8	5.0	5.8	6.1	5.8	4.9	5.7	5.3	4.7
Columbus, OH	4.0	4.0	4.0	3.8	4.0	4.5	4.5	4.3	4.2	3.9	4.2	4.1
Dallas, TX	4.0	4.1	3.9	3.5	3.7	4.3	4.3	4.3	4.0	4.0	4.0	3.5
Davenport, IA	4.2	3.6	3.5	3.0	3.8	4.5	4.8	4.9	5.1	4.9	4.9	4.4
Denver, CO	4.5	4.5	4.0	4.1	4.1	4.5	4.9	4.9	4.6	4.8	5.0	5.0
Des Moines, IA	4.3	3.8	3.5	2.6	3.1	3.6	4.1	4.4	3.5	3.7	3.9	3.7
Detroit, MI	8.3	8.3	8.1	7.4	8.6	10.0	12.7	9.7	9.6	10.8	10.6	9.6
Durham, NC	3.3	3.3	3.2	2.8	3.1	3.4	3.6	3.5	2.9	2.9	3.1	2.9
El Paso, TX	4.3	4.5	4.1	3.7	3.9	4.5	4.5	4.5	4.2	4.2	4.2	3.7
Eugene, OR	4.6	4.5	4.2	3.6	3.6	4.1	4.5	4.4	4.0	3.9	3.8	4.2
Fargo, ND	2.5	2.6	2.7	2.3	2.0	2.5	2.2	2.3	1.9	1.9	2.2	2.5
Fort Collins, CO	3.5	3.6	3.3	3.1	3.5	3.9	4.1	4.1	3.8	3.7	4.1	3.7
Fort Wayne, IN	3.9	4.3	4.1	3.4	3.9	4.4	6.0	4.4	4.0	4.1	4.4	4.2
Fort Worth, TX	4.1	4.3	4.1	3.6	3.9	4.6	4.6	4.4	4.1	4.1	4.1	3.7
Gainesville, FL	3.8	3.6	4.0	3.4	3.8	4.6	4.4	4.6	3.9	4.2	4.4	3.7
Green Bay, WI	2.7	3.2	3.3	2.8	2.8	3.3	3.1	2.8	2.5	2.5	2.6	2.8
Greensboro, NC	4.4	4.4	4.3	3.7	4.0	4.8	5.2	4.9	4.0	3.9	4.2	4.0
Honolulu, HI	2.5	2.5	2.4	2.4	2.3	3.2	3.0	3.1	3.1	2.9	3.0	2.7
Houston, TX	4.4	4.4	4.2	3.8	4.0	4.7	5.1	4.9	4.5	4.4	4.5	4.0
Huntsville, AL	2.8	2.8	2.6	2.1	2.1	2.9	3.1	3.1	2.7	2.8	2.9	2.9
Indianapolis, IN	3.9	4.3	4.2	3.6	4.0	4.4	4.7	4.5	4.1	4.0	4.2	4.0
Jacksonville, FL	3.5	3.4	3.3	3.1	3.3	3.9	4.1	4.0	3.6	3.6	3.5	3.2
Kansas City, MO	3.9	4.1	4.1	3.5	4.0	4.1	4.6	4.2	3.3	3.6	3.6	3.5
Lafayette, LA	4.0	3.9	3.8	3.4	3.6	4.5	4.4	4.4	4.3	4.3	4.1	3.8
Las Vegas, NV	5.7	5.8	5.7	5.5	5.6	6.2	6.5	6.3	5.9	6.0	6.1	6.0
Lexington, KY	3.9	4.3	4.2	3.5	3.9	4.5	4.7	4.4	4.1	4.0	4.1	4.0
Lincoln, NE	2.5	2.7	2.5	2.2	2.5	3.0	2.7	2.8	2.4	2.6	2.6	2.4
Little Rock, AR	3.8	3.8	3.6	3.3	3.4	3.8	4.0	3.6	3.3	3.3	3.4	3.4
Los Angeles, CA	5.8	5.5	5.4	5.1	5.5	6.2	6.8	6.8	6.1	6.1	6.1	5.8
Louisville, KY	4.5	4.9	4.7	4.2	4.3	4.9	5.9	4.9	4.6	4.7	4.7	4.7
Madison, WI	1.9	2.2	2.4	2.2	2.3	2.8	2.6	2.3	2.2	2.1	2.1	2.1
Manchester, NH	2.8	3.1	2.9	2.5	2.4	2.7	3.0	2.9	2.5	2.6	3.2	3.1
McAllen, TX	4.5	4.6	4.3	4.0	4.2	4.9	4.9	4.8	4.3	4.2	4.3	4.0

Table continued on following page.

City	2024											
	Jan.	Feb.	Mar.	Apr.	May	Jun.	Jul.	Aug.	Sep.	Oct.	Nov.	Dec.
Memphis, TN	4.9	4.5	4.7	4.2	4.4	5.8	6.2	5.8	5.3	5.4	5.3	5.2
Miami, FL	1.8	2.0	2.2	2.2	2.2	2.4	2.8	2.8	2.4	2.4	2.3	2.3
Midland, TX	2.6	2.8	2.4	2.2	2.4	2.8	2.8	2.9	2.6	2.7	2.7	2.3
Milwaukee, WI	3.9	4.5	4.6	4.2	4.0	4.9	4.9	4.8	3.8	3.9	4.1	4.0
Minneapolis, MN	2.8	3.0	2.8	2.6	2.5	3.3	3.4	3.4	2.9	2.7	2.5	2.3
Nashville, TN	2.6	2.5	2.6	2.4	2.5	3.1	3.2	3.1	2.9	3.0	3.1	3.0
New Orleans, LA	5.3	4.8	4.7	4.3	4.4	5.7	5.8	5.5	5.2	5.3	4.9	4.6
New York, NY	4.8	5.1	4.8	4.6	4.9	5.4	6.1	6.1	5.3	5.5	5.5	5.2
Oklahoma City, OK	3.4	3.4	3.1	2.7	3.2	3.4	3.4	3.3	3.1	3.1	3.1	2.9
Omaha, NE	3.2	3.5	3.2	3.1	3.1	3.5	3.6	3.3	3.0	3.2	3.0	3.0
Orlando, FL	3.0	2.8	2.7	2.7	2.9	3.3	3.5	3.5	3.2	3.1	3.1	2.9
Philadelphia, PA	4.7	4.9	4.4	4.0	4.4	4.9	5.5	5.7	4.4	4.6	4.5	4.3
Phoenix, AZ	3.0	3.0	2.7	2.5	2.9	3.5	3.8	3.7	3.4	3.4	3.4	3.1
Pittsburgh, PA	3.2	3.2	3.1	2.5	3.0	3.5	3.7	4.0	2.8	3.0	2.9	2.6
Portland, OR	4.5	4.4	4.3	3.6	3.6	4.0	4.4	4.3	3.9	3.9	4.0	4.1
Providence, RI	5.7	6.4	5.6	4.7	5.4	5.4	6.3	6.7	5.2	5.3	5.8	5.5
Provo, UT	2.6	2.6	2.4	2.4	3.2	3.8	3.2	3.4	2.9	2.6	2.8	2.6
Raleigh, NC	3.5	3.6	3.5	3.0	3.2	3.6	3.8	3.6	3.0	3.0	3.3	3.1
Reno, NV	4.5	4.6	4.6	4.4	4.6	4.9	5.1	4.9	4.4	4.6	4.5	4.6
Richmond, VA	3.4	3.4	3.4	3.0	3.4	3.6	3.8	3.9	3.5	3.4	3.4	3.1
Rochester, MN	2.2	2.5	2.1	2.0	1.9	2.6	2.6	2.5	2.0	1.9	1.9	1.8
Sacramento, CA	5.2	5.2	4.9	4.5	4.3	5.1	5.5	5.6	5.0	5.1	5.2	4.9
Saint Louis, MO	4.4	4.8	4.6	3.9	4.3	4.6	4.9	4.8	3.8	4.0	4.0	4.1
Saint Paul, MN	3.0	3.3	3.1	2.8	2.7	3.6	3.7	3.7	3.1	2.8	2.6	2.5
Salem, OR	4.7	4.6	4.5	3.8	3.7	4.2	4.6	4.5	4.0	4.0	4.1	4.3
Salt Lake City, UT	3.0	3.4	3.2	3.0	3.0	3.3	3.5	3.5	3.0	3.1	3.1	2.9
San Antonio, TX	3.9	4.1	3.6	3.4	3.4	4.5	4.3	4.2	3.8	3.8	4.0	3.3
San Diego, CA	4.4	4.4	4.2	3.8	3.7	4.4	4.8	4.9	4.3	4.4	4.5	4.2
San Francisco, CA	3.8	3.6	3.5	3.3	3.1	3.7	4.0	4.1	3.6	3.7	3.7	3.5
San Jose, CA	4.3	4.2	4.1	3.8	3.6	4.4	4.7	4.7	4.2	4.3	4.3	4.0
Santa Rosa, CA	4.5	4.3	4.2	3.8	3.6	4.3	4.7	4.7	4.1	4.3	4.4	4.1
Savannah, GA	3.5	3.5	3.5	3.0	3.6	4.1	4.0	4.2	3.5	3.6	3.4	3.3
Seattle, WA	4.0	3.6	3.5	3.5	3.7	4.5	4.2	4.1	3.9	3.7	3.4	2.8
Sioux Falls, SD	1.9	2.2	1.7	1.7	1.6	1.8	1.6	1.8	1.4	1.6	1.6	2.0
Tampa, FL	3.5	3.3	3.4	3.1	3.3	3.8	3.9	4.0	3.6	3.7	3.8	3.3
Tucson, AZ	3.5	3.4	3.1	2.9	3.4	4.2	4.4	4.3	3.9	3.8	3.9	3.6
Tulsa, OK	4.0	4.0	3.3	3.0	3.5	3.7	3.7	3.6	3.2	3.3	3.3	3.0
Virginia Beach, VA	2.6	2.7	2.5	2.3	2.7	2.9	3.0	3.1	2.8	2.7	2.8	2.4
Washington, DC	5.1	5.3	5.0	4.5	5.0	5.7	6.0	6.0	5.2	5.2	5.0	4.9
Wichita, KS	3.7	4.1	3.9	3.5	3.9	4.4	5.1	4.7	3.9	4.4	4.5	3.9
Wilmington, NC	3.6	3.5	3.3	2.8	3.1	3.5	3.7	3.5	2.9	2.9	3.2	3.0
Winston-Salem, NC	4.0	4.0	4.0	3.4	3.8	4.3	4.6	4.4	3.5	3.6	3.8	3.5
U.S.	4.1	4.2	3.9	3.5	3.7	4.3	4.5	4.4	3.9	3.9	4.0	3.8

Note: Data is not seasonally adjusted and covers workers 16 years of age and older; All figures are percentages
Source: Bureau of Labor Statistics, Local Area Unemployment Statistics

Unemployment Rate: Metro Area

Metro Area	2024											
	Jan.	Feb.	Mar.	Apr.	May	Jun.	Jul.	Aug.	Sep.	Oct.	Nov.	Dec.
Albuquerque, NM	3.6	3.5	3.2	3.3	3.6	4.6	5.1	4.4	3.9	4.0	4.1	3.7
Anchorage, AK	4.4	4.6	4.2	4.0	3.9	4.5	4.1	3.7	3.7	3.9	4.2	3.9
Ann Arbor, MI	3.1	3.3	3.4	3.2	3.9	4.6	5.1	4.5	3.9	3.8	3.8	4.0
Athens, GA	3.4	3.2	3.3	2.6	3.4	4.1	4.0	4.1	3.4	3.6	3.1	2.9
Atlanta, GA[1]	3.4	3.4	3.4	3.1	3.5	4.0	3.9	4.0	3.5	3.6	3.6	3.4
Austin, TX	3.5	3.6	3.4	3.0	3.2	3.7	3.7	3.7	3.5	3.4	3.4	3.1
Baltimore, MD	3.0	3.1	2.9	2.5	2.7	3.4	3.5	3.5	2.9	3.1	3.0	2.7
Billings, MT	3.3	3.3	2.9	2.6	2.5	3.1	3.0	2.9	2.4	2.3	2.4	2.9
Boise City, ID	3.8	3.9	3.7	3.2	3.3	3.6	3.8	3.7	3.3	3.4	3.6	3.4
Boston, MA[1]	3.9	4.0	3.7	3.2	3.8	4.2	4.5	4.3	3.7	3.9	3.9	4.0
Boulder, CO	3.6	3.7	3.4	3.3	3.7	4.2	4.4	4.3	4.0	4.1	4.3	4.0
Cape Coral, FL	3.4	3.3	3.2	3.0	3.2	3.7	4.0	3.9	3.7	3.6	3.6	3.2
Cedar Rapids, IA	3.9	4.0	3.2	2.5	3.2	3.8	3.8	3.7	3.0	3.3	3.4	3.2
Charleston, SC	3.1	3.4	3.1	2.7	3.3	4.0	4.2	4.3	3.6	3.8	3.6	3.4
Charlotte, NC	3.6	3.8	3.5	3.1	3.4	3.8	4.0	3.9	3.3	3.4	3.5	3.3
Chicago, IL[1]	4.7	5.2	4.8	4.6	5.1	6.2	6.0	5.7	5.1	5.1	4.8	4.4
Cincinnati, OH	4.1	4.2	4.2	3.8	4.0	4.6	4.6	4.3	4.1	3.9	4.1	4.1
Clarksville, TN	4.2	4.1	4.1	3.6	3.8	4.8	4.9	4.6	4.4	4.4	4.5	4.4
Cleveland, OH	4.0	4.7	4.2	3.6	3.9	4.4	4.4	3.7	3.3	3.0	3.2	3.3
College Station, TX	3.3	3.4	3.0	2.6	3.0	3.6	3.7	3.6	3.2	3.1	3.1	2.7
Colorado Springs, CO	4.2	4.3	3.9	3.8	4.0	4.5	4.8	4.8	4.4	4.5	4.8	4.6
Columbia, MO	3.2	3.0	3.2	2.7	3.2	3.5	3.7	3.3	2.4	2.7	2.7	2.4
Columbia, SC	3.5	3.7	3.5	3.1	3.8	4.5	4.7	4.8	4.1	4.3	4.1	3.8
Columbus, OH	3.9	3.9	3.9	3.6	3.8	4.3	4.3	4.1	4.0	3.7	4.0	4.0
Dallas, TX[1]	3.9	4.0	3.8	3.4	3.6	4.2	4.2	4.2	3.9	3.8	3.8	3.5
Davenport, IA	5.2	4.8	4.5	4.0	4.2	4.7	4.8	4.9	5.2	5.0	4.8	4.4
Denver, CO	4.1	4.2	3.8	3.8	3.9	4.4	4.6	4.7	4.3	4.5	4.7	4.6
Des Moines, IA	3.3	2.9	2.7	2.1	2.6	3.1	3.5	3.6	3.0	3.1	3.2	3.0
Detroit, MI[1]	4.8	4.8	4.7	4.3	5.0	5.8	7.5	5.6	5.6	6.3	6.2	5.6
Durham, NC	3.2	3.2	3.2	2.8	3.0	3.4	3.6	3.4	2.8	2.9	3.1	2.9
El Paso, TX	4.5	4.7	4.3	3.9	4.1	4.8	4.8	4.7	4.4	4.4	4.4	4.0
Eugene, OR	4.9	4.7	4.4	3.8	3.8	4.2	4.7	4.6	4.1	4.1	4.1	4.4
Fargo, ND	2.5	2.7	2.7	2.2	2.0	2.6	2.3	2.3	1.8	1.8	2.0	2.3
Fort Collins, CO	3.6	3.8	3.4	3.3	3.5	3.9	4.1	4.2	3.8	3.9	4.2	3.9
Fort Wayne, IN	3.8	4.1	3.9	3.2	3.7	4.2	5.8	4.1	3.7	3.8	4.1	3.8
Fort Worth, TX[1]	3.9	4.1	3.8	3.4	3.6	4.2	4.3	4.2	3.9	3.9	3.9	3.4
Gainesville, FL	3.5	3.3	3.5	3.1	3.4	4.0	4.0	4.0	3.5	3.7	3.8	3.3
Green Bay, WI	2.6	3.1	3.1	2.6	2.6	3.0	2.9	2.6	2.3	2.3	2.4	2.6
Greensboro, NC	4.2	4.2	4.0	3.5	3.9	4.5	4.8	4.5	3.7	3.7	4.0	3.7
Honolulu, HI	2.5	2.5	2.4	2.4	2.3	3.2	3.0	3.1	3.1	2.9	3.0	2.7
Houston, TX	4.4	4.5	4.1	3.8	4.0	4.7	5.0	4.8	4.5	4.4	4.4	4.1
Huntsville, AL	2.6	2.7	2.4	2.0	2.0	2.7	2.9	3.0	2.6	2.7	2.8	2.7
Indianapolis, IN	3.6	3.9	3.9	3.2	3.6	4.0	4.3	4.0	3.6	3.6	3.9	3.6
Jacksonville, FL	3.3	3.2	3.2	2.9	3.1	3.7	3.9	3.8	3.4	3.4	3.5	3.1
Kansas City, MO	3.5	3.8	3.8	3.2	3.6	3.8	4.2	3.9	3.2	3.5	3.3	3.2
Lafayette, LA	4.1	4.0	3.8	3.4	3.6	4.5	4.4	4.4	4.3	4.3	4.2	3.9
Las Vegas, NV	5.6	5.6	5.5	5.4	5.5	6.1	6.4	6.2	5.8	5.9	6.0	5.9
Lexington, KY	4.0	4.4	4.2	3.5	3.9	4.6	4.7	4.5	4.1	4.1	4.2	4.1
Lincoln, NE	2.4	2.6	2.4	2.2	2.5	3.0	2.6	2.7	2.4	2.6	2.5	2.4
Little Rock, AR	3.5	3.5	3.2	2.9	3.1	3.5	3.7	3.3	3.0	2.9	3.0	3.1
Los Angeles, CA[1]	5.6	5.3	5.3	5.0	5.4	6.1	6.7	6.7	6.0	6.0	6.0	5.7
Louisville, KY	4.3	4.7	4.4	3.9	4.1	4.7	5.6	4.6	4.3	4.4	4.5	4.4
Madison, WI	2.1	2.5	2.5	2.2	2.3	2.7	2.6	2.3	2.1	2.1	2.2	2.2
Manchester, NH	2.7	3.0	2.9	2.4	2.3	2.6	3.0	2.9	2.5	2.6	3.1	3.0
McAllen, TX	6.5	6.0	5.8	5.4	5.7	6.9	6.9	6.5	5.9	5.4	6.0	6.2

Table continued on following page.

Metro Area	2024											
	Jan.	Feb.	Mar.	Apr.	May	Jun.	Jul.	Aug.	Sep.	Oct.	Nov.	Dec.
Memphis, TN	4.0	3.7	3.8	3.4	3.7	4.9	5.0	4.8	4.4	4.5	4.5	4.4
Miami, FL[1]	1.9	2.0	2.3	2.3	2.3	2.6	2.8	2.9	2.4	2.4	2.4	2.4
Midland, TX	2.6	2.8	2.5	2.2	2.5	2.8	2.9	2.9	2.7	2.7	2.7	2.4
Milwaukee, WI	3.0	3.5	3.6	3.2	3.1	3.8	3.7	3.4	2.9	2.9	3.1	3.0
Minneapolis, MN	3.1	3.3	3.1	2.7	2.6	3.5	3.4	3.4	2.7	2.4	2.4	2.5
Nashville, TN	2.6	2.5	2.5	2.3	2.4	3.1	3.2	3.1	2.9	3.0	3.0	2.9
New Orleans, LA	4.6	4.3	4.2	3.8	3.9	5.0	5.0	4.9	4.7	4.7	4.5	4.2
New York, NY[1]	4.6	4.9	4.6	4.3	4.6	5.1	5.7	5.6	4.8	5.0	5.0	4.8
Oklahoma City, OK	3.3	3.4	3.0	2.6	3.0	3.3	3.3	3.2	3.0	3.0	3.0	2.8
Omaha, NE	3.1	3.2	2.9	2.7	2.9	3.3	3.4	3.1	2.8	3.0	2.9	2.8
Orlando, FL	3.2	3.1	3.1	2.9	3.1	3.6	3.8	3.8	3.4	3.4	3.5	3.1
Philadelphia, PA[1]	4.3	4.6	4.1	3.7	4.1	4.5	5.1	5.3	4.1	4.2	4.2	3.9
Phoenix, AZ	3.0	3.0	2.7	2.6	3.0	3.5	3.8	3.6	3.4	3.4	3.3	3.1
Pittsburgh, PA	3.9	4.1	3.6	3.1	3.3	3.9	4.2	4.4	3.1	3.4	3.3	3.4
Portland, OR	4.4	4.5	4.2	3.6	3.7	3.9	4.4	4.3	3.9	3.9	4.0	4.2
Providence, RI	4.8	5.2	4.5	3.8	4.1	4.3	4.9	5.0	4.0	4.2	4.4	4.4
Provo, UT	3.0	3.2	3.0	2.9	3.2	3.7	3.6	3.7	3.1	3.0	3.1	2.9
Raleigh, NC	3.3	3.4	3.2	2.9	3.1	3.4	3.6	3.5	2.9	2.9	3.1	2.9
Reno, NV	4.7	4.8	4.7	4.5	4.6	5.0	5.1	4.9	4.5	4.6	4.6	4.7
Richmond, VA	3.0	3.0	2.9	2.6	2.9	3.2	3.3	3.4	3.0	2.9	3.0	2.6
Rochester, MN	2.8	3.0	2.6	2.2	2.2	2.8	2.7	2.6	2.0	1.8	1.9	2.0
Sacramento, CA	4.9	4.9	4.7	4.2	4.0	4.8	5.1	5.2	4.6	4.7	4.8	4.6
Saint Louis, MO	3.9	4.1	3.9	3.4	3.7	4.0	4.2	3.9	3.2	3.3	3.3	3.2
Saint Paul, MN	3.1	3.3	3.1	2.7	2.6	3.5	3.4	3.4	2.7	2.4	2.4	2.5
Salem, OR	4.7	4.6	4.3	3.6	3.6	4.0	4.6	4.4	3.9	3.9	4.0	4.2
Salt Lake City, UT	3.0	3.4	3.2	3.0	3.1	3.5	3.5	3.6	3.0	3.1	3.0	2.9
San Antonio, TX	3.8	4.0	3.6	3.3	3.5	4.1	4.2	4.1	3.8	3.8	3.8	3.4
San Diego, CA	4.5	4.5	4.2	3.9	3.7	4.6	4.9	5.0	4.5	4.6	4.6	4.3
San Francisco, CA[1]	3.7	3.6	3.4	3.2	3.1	3.6	3.9	4.0	3.5	3.6	3.7	3.4
San Jose, CA	4.2	4.2	4.0	3.7	3.6	4.2	4.5	4.5	4.1	4.1	4.1	3.9
Santa Rosa, CA	4.3	4.2	4.0	3.6	3.4	4.1	4.4	4.5	3.9	4.1	4.2	4.0
Savannah, GA	2.9	3.0	3.0	2.5	3.1	3.5	3.4	3.7	2.9	3.0	2.9	2.8
Seattle, WA[1]	4.2	3.8	3.7	3.7	3.8	4.7	4.4	4.2	4.1	4.0	3.7	3.1
Sioux Falls, SD	1.8	2.1	1.6	1.6	1.6	1.8	1.5	1.8	1.3	1.5	1.5	1.8
Tampa, FL[1]	3.5	3.4	3.3	3.1	3.3	3.8	4.0	4.0	3.7	3.7	3.8	3.3
Tucson, AZ	3.3	3.3	3.0	2.8	3.3	4.0	4.3	4.0	3.7	3.7	3.6	3.4
Tulsa, OK	3.8	3.8	3.2	2.8	3.3	3.6	3.5	3.4	3.1	3.2	3.2	2.9
Virginia Beach, VA	3.0	3.0	2.9	2.6	3.0	3.2	3.4	3.4	3.1	3.0	3.1	2.7
Washington, DC[1]	3.9	4.1	3.9	3.4	3.7	4.4	4.6	4.7	4.0	4.1	4.1	3.8
Wichita, KS	3.6	3.8	3.7	3.4	3.7	4.2	5.0	4.6	3.8	4.2	4.3	3.8
Wilmington, NC	3.8	3.8	3.4	3.0	3.3	3.6	3.7	3.7	3.1	3.2	3.4	3.2
Winston-Salem, NC	3.6	3.7	3.6	3.1	3.4	3.9	4.1	4.0	3.3	3.3	3.6	3.2
U.S.	4.1	4.2	3.9	3.5	3.7	4.3	4.5	4.4	3.9	3.9	4.0	3.8

Note: Data is not seasonally adjusted and covers workers 16 years of age and older; All figures are percentages; (1) Figures cover the Metropolitan Statistical Area (MSA) except where noted; (1) Metropolitan Division
Source: Bureau of Labor Statistics, Local Area Unemployment Statistics

Average Hourly Wages: Occupations A – C

Metro Area	Accountants/ Auditors	Automotive Mechanics	Book-keepers	Carpenters	Cashiers	Computer Program-mers	Computer Systems Analysts
Albuquerque, NM	40.90	25.69	23.51	26.42	14.93	43.80	46.83
Anchorage, AK	42.24	31.29	26.96	36.09	17.64	44.68	45.88
Ann Arbor, MI	41.19	27.70	24.68	30.96	15.32	39.67	53.91
Athens, GA	39.24	25.81	21.79	22.39	12.95	36.03	36.11
Atlanta, GA	46.20	28.17	24.88	24.84	13.99	49.60	53.95
Austin, TX	44.19	27.17	26.04	24.84	15.10	45.82	53.57
Baltimore, MD	44.96	27.65	26.87	28.13	16.18	52.85	56.04
Billings, MT	39.29	28.20	22.49	27.02	14.91	48.63	46.01
Boise City, ID	35.88	24.94	23.92	24.55	15.24	43.27	44.48
Boston, MA	49.79	29.49	28.51	38.40	17.37	57.83	60.98
Boulder, CO[2]	46.39	28.81	26.63	29.94	17.71	71.62	67.66
Cape Coral, FL	39.76	25.28	24.21	23.36	14.53	43.02	46.99
Cedar Rapids, IA	39.80	26.02	24.03	27.03	14.47	39.50	44.19
Charleston, SC	44.26	24.26	23.80	25.54	13.77	53.17	52.43
Charlotte, NC	47.13	27.27	24.68	25.51	14.02	44.72	57.50
Chicago, IL	44.28	28.71	25.75	38.11	16.33	46.08	48.09
Cincinnati, OH	41.81	24.64	24.76	27.72	14.23	56.17	52.48
Clarksville, TN	35.41	23.62	22.04	24.61	13.04	n/a	39.08
Cleveland, OH	41.49	26.14	24.08	29.35	14.16	44.94	47.53
College Station, TX	36.32	24.82	21.78	22.38	13.30	39.46	42.81
Colorado Springs, CO[2]	41.44	26.83	23.32	26.46	16.36	53.50	54.60
Columbia, MO	35.97	23.99	23.55	26.93	14.42	n/a	44.38
Columbia, SC	34.91	23.93	22.33	24.28	12.66	54.49	41.80
Columbus, OH	44.22	27.22	24.48	29.44	14.46	48.11	49.66
Dallas, TX	45.03	27.86	25.94	24.01	14.32	47.68	57.86
Davenport, IA	39.77	25.81	23.07	28.79	14.78	38.43	42.15
Denver, CO[2]	46.80	28.10	26.85	27.44	17.46	54.01	56.16
Des Moines, IA	40.26	26.59	24.64	28.46	14.74	45.02	47.37
Detroit, MI	43.77	27.01	25.39	31.70	14.88	39.07	50.95
Durham, NC	46.33	26.94	26.20	24.03	14.15	51.55	54.64
El Paso, TX	35.86	22.04	20.35	20.00	12.41	34.05	44.84
Eugene, OR	40.17	26.31	23.97	29.35	16.41	44.82	51.80
Fargo, ND	36.22	26.79	24.09	29.49	15.21	43.27	50.62
Fort Collins, CO[2]	43.11	27.93	24.64	26.93	16.61	54.48	53.23
Fort Wayne, IN	38.36	24.39	22.76	27.40	13.68	39.45	44.73
Fort Worth, TX	45.03	27.86	25.94	24.01	14.32	47.68	57.86
Gainesville, FL	38.54	24.87	23.70	23.37	14.25	44.12	41.84
Green Bay, WI	40.76	27.11	23.58	30.80	14.24	45.19	48.58
Greensboro, NC	41.27	25.40	22.80	21.70	13.29	43.91	50.14
Honolulu, HI	36.77	27.01	23.29	42.67	17.05	50.07	44.25
Houston, TX	45.33	27.12	24.69	24.93	14.10	n/a	56.46
Huntsville, AL	41.06	25.69	22.10	23.65	13.43	52.24	59.51
Indianapolis, IN	41.42	25.35	23.97	30.07	13.91	47.00	50.67
Jacksonville, FL	41.72	25.10	23.66	24.55	14.62	50.71	50.41
Kansas City, MO	41.41	26.51	24.38	31.38	15.02	46.73	48.94
Lafayette, LA	35.63	23.75	20.97	22.46	11.84	40.56	49.57
Las Vegas, NV	39.57	25.88	24.90	32.87	14.94	44.52	47.58
Lexington, KY	36.98	22.15	23.60	25.79	13.44	52.20	41.98
Lincoln, NE	34.67	25.66	22.74	25.07	14.50	43.25	40.47
Little Rock, AR	36.16	23.85	22.54	23.06	13.71	45.30	29.95
Los Angeles, CA	48.45	30.20	28.58	36.97	18.47	50.36	59.72
Louisville, KY	39.40	23.99	24.07	26.54	14.14	52.89	45.74
Madison, WI	41.87	28.99	25.40	32.44	15.63	42.40	46.04
Manchester, NH	42.84	28.99	25.41	28.98	14.89	41.19	52.98
McAllen, TX	33.75	22.30	19.81	18.97	12.40	38.07	37.09

Table continued on following page.

Metro Area	Accountants/ Auditors	Automotive Mechanics	Book- keepers	Carpenters	Cashiers	Computer Program- mers	Computer Systems Analysts
Memphis, TN	39.28	25.26	23.48	25.20	13.30	43.86	48.38
Miami, FL	43.02	26.45	24.75	24.57	14.99	57.85	54.87
Midland, TX	47.51	26.20	25.44	24.81	14.69	42.10	57.62
Milwaukee, WI	43.31	28.74	24.38	32.43	14.53	43.19	50.52
Minneapolis, MN	45.40	29.52	26.89	35.62	16.35	50.83	53.62
Nashville, TN	41.77	26.05	24.43	25.67	14.57	n/a	42.96
New Orleans, LA	40.08	24.79	22.70	25.98	13.04	39.98	48.21
New York, NY	58.64	29.75	29.11	37.32	17.91	58.71	61.28
Oklahoma City, OK	41.96	23.62	22.88	25.29	13.24	57.04	47.08
Omaha, NE	37.98	26.58	24.02	26.11	14.93	46.38	46.14
Orlando, FL	42.38	25.24	23.73	24.25	15.21	46.42	49.67
Philadelphia, PA	46.34	27.57	26.12	32.62	15.31	46.77	51.52
Phoenix, AZ	42.29	28.52	25.59	28.74	16.53	40.51	51.41
Pittsburgh, PA	39.21	24.59	23.05	31.17	14.11	42.07	47.00
Portland, OR	44.95	29.63	26.60	35.28	17.91	57.44	60.32
Providence, RI	46.37	26.05	26.20	32.98	16.12	49.33	57.45
Provo, UT	38.12	23.63	23.58	25.60	15.11	43.63	48.54
Raleigh, NC	44.26	26.71	24.19	23.43	13.98	41.74	52.76
Reno, NV	41.47	27.04	25.86	32.80	15.27	49.79	47.77
Richmond, VA	42.37	27.70	24.33	24.90	15.01	46.29	51.27
Rochester, MN	46.22	27.15	27.32	32.24	15.88	n/a	n/a
Sacramento, CA	45.29	31.97	28.08	37.87	18.42	56.85	57.48
Saint Louis, MO	40.41	25.56	25.12	33.56	15.63	48.91	46.89
Saint Paul, MN	45.40	29.52	26.89	35.62	16.35	50.83	53.62
Salem, OR	42.14	27.01	26.35	27.76	16.54	52.83	53.95
Salt Lake City, UT	41.61	25.97	24.91	27.86	15.51	46.78	45.51
San Antonio, TX	41.41	25.74	23.19	23.06	14.39	62.03	51.53
San Diego, CA	50.36	29.84	28.01	36.37	18.50	60.74	57.81
San Francisco, CA	57.63	35.20	32.85	41.44	20.07	62.74	71.92
San Jose, CA	61.89	39.24	32.88	41.63	20.75	76.50	77.64
Santa Rosa, CA	47.74	31.99	29.51	40.36	19.48	48.16	55.29
Savannah, GA	40.41	27.16	23.06	24.58	13.64	46.30	52.25
Seattle, WA	51.01	30.63	28.45	39.76	20.63	80.47	66.53
Sioux Falls, SD	40.80	28.20	21.98	23.96	14.91	n/a	48.25
Tampa, FL	42.37	25.41	25.17	24.57	14.51	46.54	53.50
Tucson, AZ	39.27	26.22	24.08	25.46	15.74	46.55	51.81
Tulsa, OK	40.70	24.36	23.49	24.64	13.45	47.67	55.21
Virginia Beach, VA	41.24	26.43	23.13	24.88	14.28	50.07	50.99
Washington, DC	52.24	31.94	28.25	30.71	17.17	54.17	62.36
Wichita, KS	37.74	24.13	21.79	25.64	13.10	50.82	48.92
Wilmington, NC	37.67	23.96	22.76	24.06	13.23	37.74	46.73
Winston-Salem, NC	40.27	25.20	22.66	23.60	13.15	44.83	50.74

Notes: Figures cover the Metropolitan Statistical Area (MSA); (1) Data is from 2023 due to data quality issues in the state of Colorado and its substate areas in 2024; n/a not available
Source: Bureau of Labor Statistics, Metro Area Occupational Employment and Wage Estimates, May 2024

Average Hourly Wages: Occupations C – E

Metro Area	Comp. User Support Specialists	Construction Laborers	Cooks, Restaurant	Customer Service Reps.	Dentists	Electricians	Engineers, Electrical
Albuquerque, NM	24.18	20.58	16.62	20.23	92.52	28.48	71.65
Anchorage, AK	30.11	30.31	19.67	22.30	96.63	38.60	57.20
Ann Arbor, MI	27.63	24.45	18.17	20.90	n/a	37.90	52.52
Athens, GA	24.25	19.20	15.36	17.62	86.37	28.38	52.45
Atlanta, GA	31.11	20.30	16.66	21.35	102.19	30.62	56.08
Austin, TX	29.47	20.17	17.40	20.72	105.18	28.24	67.90
Baltimore, MD	33.50	22.42	18.38	21.60	108.70	33.58	59.60
Billings, MT	26.60	24.46	18.09	21.17	118.06	34.75	51.14
Boise City, ID	26.79	22.50	16.50	21.14	85.60	29.13	65.01
Boston, MA	37.62	33.95	21.98	25.48	n/a	40.10	64.82
Boulder, CO[1]	36.17	22.30	20.42	22.82	85.12	31.85	63.49
Cape Coral, FL	28.07	21.08	17.88	19.48	132.27	25.82	49.73
Cedar Rapids, IA	28.20	23.76	16.74	21.95	76.51	26.89	53.76
Charleston, SC	28.38	21.91	17.47	20.80	78.30	28.18	56.11
Charlotte, NC	30.08	21.52	17.64	21.55	106.87	27.55	58.48
Chicago, IL	30.31	34.99	18.66	23.30	89.54	44.39	57.06
Cincinnati, OH	28.23	26.28	15.92	21.20	103.59	30.46	51.81
Clarksville, TN	25.48	20.62	15.08	18.84	87.66	28.77	45.74
Cleveland, OH	28.26	27.82	17.24	22.13	81.41	32.62	49.77
College Station, TX	24.10	17.72	14.89	17.74	103.68	25.02	50.62
Colorado Springs, CO[1]	30.73	21.28	19.05	20.87	88.76	28.83	56.23
Columbia, MO	27.69	28.79	16.00	20.94	105.42	30.08	n/a
Columbia, SC	27.54	21.14	16.57	19.31	120.35	29.62	51.67
Columbus, OH	30.19	27.99	16.81	22.27	78.07	31.75	49.68
Dallas, TX	29.72	19.90	17.09	21.47	96.90	28.56	56.38
Davenport, IA	27.46	27.61	16.58	20.62	95.43	34.34	54.36
Denver, CO[1]	36.27	22.62	20.14	22.82	64.29	30.65	55.39
Des Moines, IA	29.14	24.89	17.75	24.02	93.83	32.28	69.53
Detroit, MI	29.25	26.26	18.06	22.70	93.92	36.41	53.76
Durham, NC	32.70	22.51	17.45	22.07	96.79	29.52	58.62
El Paso, TX	22.07	17.25	14.12	17.31	101.96	23.92	44.54
Eugene, OR	30.29	24.26	18.28	21.66	107.76	40.45	54.89
Fargo, ND	30.52	25.14	17.42	21.49	100.00	33.30	50.36
Fort Collins, CO[1]	32.68	21.53	18.75	20.21	100.41	29.77	55.88
Fort Wayne, IN	26.58	23.81	15.90	21.57	98.97	31.08	49.63
Fort Worth, TX	29.72	19.90	17.09	21.47	96.90	28.56	56.38
Gainesville, FL	25.88	19.68	16.92	19.63	98.53	25.55	51.00
Green Bay, WI	28.66	26.49	17.71	22.50	81.11	33.62	47.47
Greensboro, NC	26.94	20.44	16.19	20.71	85.23	26.42	53.13
Honolulu, HI	28.29	33.27	21.30	21.38	65.12	42.47	50.66
Houston, TX	29.02	20.13	15.99	20.40	115.55	28.39	57.48
Huntsville, AL	25.12	18.37	16.05	19.29	n/a	27.47	63.59
Indianapolis, IN	29.12	25.60	16.96	22.07	89.99	32.56	53.74
Jacksonville, FL	28.60	20.35	16.89	20.86	86.80	27.03	52.71
Kansas City, MO	28.37	26.74	18.07	21.64	89.46	35.72	51.97
Lafayette, LA	30.51	20.27	13.44	18.01	82.38	26.35	47.69
Las Vegas, NV	27.07	24.69	19.59	19.65	69.07	34.73	51.25
Lexington, KY	27.96	21.98	15.85	20.23	86.12	27.82	50.32
Lincoln, NE	28.07	21.86	17.81	19.65	85.28	29.82	47.88
Little Rock, AR	26.42	18.42	15.24	19.85	92.76	24.62	51.32
Los Angeles, CA	35.73	31.23	21.28	25.04	83.74	39.39	65.77
Louisville, KY	27.34	23.10	16.46	20.93	90.25	30.65	47.48
Madison, WI	29.81	27.12	18.70	23.53	98.38	36.51	51.89
Manchester, NH	34.06	22.66	18.60	23.92	77.22	30.59	70.89
McAllen, TX	21.73	15.75	13.57	17.73	106.72	21.99	46.39

Table continued on following page.

Metro Area	Comp. User Support Specialists	Construction Laborers	Cooks, Restaurant	Customer Service Reps.	Dentists	Electricians	Engineers, Electrical
Memphis, TN	28.25	22.21	16.20	21.10	91.70	27.81	53.37
Miami, FL	32.66	21.69	17.30	20.41	89.88	27.58	53.23
Midland, TX	27.70	20.63	16.62	20.78	n/a	28.92	61.86
Milwaukee, WI	30.47	28.30	18.61	23.48	97.31	35.83	50.13
Minneapolis, MN	33.76	30.67	20.11	24.54	108.57	41.70	54.81
Nashville, TN	29.95	22.45	18.35	21.72	97.05	29.83	55.61
New Orleans, LA	28.92	21.90	15.42	19.43	97.54	29.41	56.07
New York, NY	35.37	34.43	20.82	25.80	89.32	41.08	60.31
Oklahoma City, OK	26.99	20.63	17.14	20.02	112.93	30.47	53.72
Omaha, NE	29.50	23.84	18.03	21.38	103.65	31.36	48.89
Orlando, FL	28.57	21.13	18.25	19.99	85.11	26.17	56.13
Philadelphia, PA	31.66	28.19	17.84	23.03	87.74	38.14	61.83
Phoenix, AZ	32.43	23.17	19.56	22.50	98.52	29.58	59.00
Pittsburgh, PA	29.05	25.52	15.76	21.46	78.26	34.21	53.62
Portland, OR	31.89	27.95	20.13	23.78	94.71	46.08	57.53
Providence, RI	30.62	30.51	19.97	22.77	n/a	34.24	54.44
Provo, UT	28.65	22.38	17.58	19.85	66.32	29.16	60.54
Raleigh, NC	29.83	22.02	17.14	21.36	104.78	26.83	65.68
Reno, NV	28.19	27.64	18.27	20.68	74.31	32.97	57.15
Richmond, VA	29.64	19.84	17.56	20.92	103.90	29.24	56.26
Rochester, MN	33.24	28.42	18.68	23.08	122.85	39.75	50.77
Sacramento, CA	47.62	31.16	20.88	24.98	89.82	39.30	65.09
Saint Louis, MO	29.80	31.00	18.07	22.36	n/a	36.65	56.55
Saint Paul, MN	33.76	30.67	20.11	24.54	108.57	41.70	54.81
Salem, OR	31.51	25.90	18.91	22.72	104.28	40.07	55.99
Salt Lake City, UT	32.60	23.53	18.51	21.44	80.35	31.02	55.43
San Antonio, TX	27.32	19.44	15.83	20.34	78.33	26.69	55.23
San Diego, CA	35.01	30.44	21.15	24.53	87.88	39.61	65.99
San Francisco, CA	43.40	36.32	22.87	29.30	109.18	50.12	77.50
San Jose, CA	43.29	35.06	24.13	30.67	90.06	49.71	90.89
Santa Rosa, CA	37.08	32.20	21.98	25.04	82.86	42.00	63.20
Savannah, GA	31.48	19.01	16.30	18.64	98.92	28.43	57.20
Seattle, WA	37.28	31.08	22.67	27.52	97.55	48.19	67.55
Sioux Falls, SD	23.81	20.75	17.44	21.01	89.53	28.14	48.75
Tampa, FL	29.29	21.37	17.47	20.59	112.24	26.80	55.02
Tucson, AZ	28.35	21.11	17.71	19.74	92.54	28.60	62.08
Tulsa, OK	27.43	21.54	16.20	19.80	97.17	30.23	53.92
Virginia Beach, VA	29.01	19.76	17.15	19.47	87.77	29.26	53.55
Washington, DC	38.26	23.15	20.33	23.55	109.72	37.78	67.24
Wichita, KS	24.62	20.29	15.63	19.26	82.76	31.51	46.39
Wilmington, NC	28.36	21.81	16.50	19.57	104.98	26.12	54.21
Winston-Salem, NC	27.29	21.31	15.89	19.29	77.83	26.05	42.46

Notes: Figures cover the Metropolitan Statistical Area (MSA); (1) Data is from 2023 due to data quality issues in the state of Colorado and its substate areas in 2024; n/a not available
Source: Bureau of Labor Statistics, Metro Area Occupational Employment and Wage Estimates, May 2024

Average Hourly Wages: Occupations F – J

Metro Area	Fast Food and Counter Workers	Financial Managers	First-Line Supervisors/ of Office Workers	General and Operations Managers	Hair-dressers/ Cosme-tologists	Home Health and Personal Care Aides	Janitors/ Cleaners
Albuquerque, NM	14.78	67.06	31.40	59.24	18.37	14.44	16.27
Anchorage, AK	16.07	66.10	34.12	67.82	n/a	18.20	19.57
Ann Arbor, MI	15.01	78.28	33.10	66.91	21.16	17.05	18.60
Athens, GA	12.25	70.43	29.73	48.33	20.63	13.58	14.96
Atlanta, GA	13.55	92.61	34.57	65.51	22.26	14.69	16.89
Austin, TX	14.09	89.92	36.88	68.18	20.93	13.82	16.90
Baltimore, MD	15.89	80.29	35.89	61.48	20.61	18.43	18.03
Billings, MT	14.42	73.01	31.75	52.57	21.23	16.16	18.70
Boise City, ID	13.54	68.45	30.86	47.05	15.23	16.17	16.90
Boston, MA	17.43	100.73	38.59	78.73	24.97	19.58	21.75
Boulder, CO[1]	17.78	93.87	36.12	81.98	25.46	19.56	19.68
Cape Coral, FL	14.23	82.00	32.80	57.19	17.77	16.30	16.54
Cedar Rapids, IA	13.79	67.28	31.58	49.70	22.37	17.35	17.85
Charleston, SC	13.83	72.75	33.77	59.32	18.76	15.46	15.59
Charlotte, NC	14.27	91.39	33.22	66.57	20.12	15.34	16.27
Chicago, IL	16.05	88.31	35.22	68.58	20.23	17.79	19.25
Cincinnati, OH	14.06	77.39	32.81	58.30	20.06	15.99	17.45
Clarksville, TN	12.79	65.73	29.27	48.25	16.23	15.17	15.39
Cleveland, OH	14.06	76.95	33.00	57.91	17.62	15.55	17.41
College Station, TX	12.43	70.24	29.93	51.36	16.38	12.18	15.33
Colorado Springs, CO[1]	15.91	84.63	32.60	70.11	22.98	17.68	17.57
Columbia, MO	14.25	67.68	31.10	46.12	20.40	17.18	16.98
Columbia, SC	12.71	64.62	33.15	54.00	16.41	14.20	15.80
Columbus, OH	14.24	75.71	33.43	60.59	18.45	15.89	17.74
Dallas, TX	13.48	83.96	36.12	67.98	17.46	13.45	16.43
Davenport, IA	14.11	69.21	30.67	52.32	21.43	16.37	17.91
Denver, CO[1]	16.95	93.78	36.61	79.34	23.38	18.27	18.56
Des Moines, IA	14.21	77.18	33.94	54.24	22.00	17.30	17.35
Detroit, MI	14.34	77.60	33.92	65.30	21.26	15.95	17.41
Durham, NC	14.66	87.22	34.76	68.52	24.56	15.58	17.12
El Paso, TX	11.61	67.83	27.70	46.07	15.79	11.14	13.49
Eugene, OR	16.00	72.01	33.88	52.88	21.53	19.39	18.09
Fargo, ND	14.66	75.72	33.25	56.75	20.05	18.76	18.02
Fort Collins, CO[1]	16.21	90.82	32.90	67.45	28.72	18.19	18.27
Fort Wayne, IN	13.24	65.40	33.46	64.53	16.40	15.55	16.97
Fort Worth, TX	13.48	83.96	36.12	67.98	17.46	13.45	16.43
Gainesville, FL	14.25	67.20	30.71	55.75	15.92	15.70	16.07
Green Bay, WI	13.45	72.06	32.86	64.79	18.07	15.70	16.94
Greensboro, NC	13.39	82.48	31.23	58.89	18.93	14.32	15.59
Honolulu, HI	16.01	67.37	32.34	60.89	24.25	17.39	18.20
Houston, TX	12.78	88.07	35.05	66.82	19.05	12.11	15.20
Huntsville, AL	13.10	78.84	31.88	74.54	15.09	13.34	15.09
Indianapolis, IN	14.01	75.66	36.11	72.23	17.77	15.78	16.98
Jacksonville, FL	13.94	80.15	33.12	59.57	17.54	15.94	16.39
Kansas City, MO	14.34	76.99	34.02	53.13	20.28	15.65	17.70
Lafayette, LA	12.06	57.76	27.80	57.89	12.82	10.36	13.40
Las Vegas, NV	14.78	68.81	30.93	60.08	16.64	14.71	18.25
Lexington, KY	13.35	70.52	31.52	48.11	21.66	16.98	16.37
Lincoln, NE	14.42	68.94	30.73	50.12	17.48	16.47	16.83
Little Rock, AR	13.24	60.66	28.31	42.89	14.46	13.31	15.15
Los Angeles, CA	18.75	96.29	37.23	81.25	27.74	17.43	19.78
Louisville, KY	13.57	71.03	33.66	51.34	24.77	17.39	16.81
Madison, WI	14.40	77.53	36.80	69.40	17.58	17.03	18.27
Manchester, NH	14.45	76.66	37.63	74.48	18.36	18.05	18.24

Table continued on following page.

Metro Area	Fast Food and Counter Workers	Financial Managers	First-Line Supervisors/ of Office Workers	General and Operations Managers	Hair-dressers/ Cosme-tologists	Home Health and Personal Care Aides	Janitors/ Cleaners
McAllen, TX	11.81	63.80	28.02	44.25	14.51	11.34	14.44
Memphis, TN	13.12	76.07	34.04	61.94	17.10	15.01	15.76
Miami, FL	14.62	85.42	34.06	64.93	18.78	16.09	15.94
Midland, TX	13.82	87.54	36.53	69.94	n/a	12.83	16.27
Milwaukee, WI	13.86	78.61	35.29	68.07	19.57	15.84	17.69
Minneapolis, MN	16.17	85.12	37.88	59.75	22.01	17.88	19.66
Nashville, TN	14.12	79.15	35.70	66.64	20.68	16.69	17.04
New Orleans, LA	13.66	67.51	30.04	62.93	14.33	11.68	14.73
New York, NY	17.50	119.16	39.92	89.97	24.83	19.02	21.61
Oklahoma City, OK	12.18	71.53	32.48	52.56	18.80	13.47	15.40
Omaha, NE	14.83	75.03	31.66	51.15	21.52	17.13	17.41
Orlando, FL	14.19	78.11	32.58	58.33	17.70	16.03	16.19
Philadelphia, PA	15.05	85.35	35.52	66.76	19.65	15.40	18.54
Phoenix, AZ	16.50	75.51	33.09	59.06	19.33	17.28	18.02
Pittsburgh, PA	13.48	73.83	32.42	57.41	17.44	14.92	17.29
Portland, OR	17.61	86.12	36.29	70.26	25.82	21.37	20.22
Providence, RI	15.96	82.12	36.46	63.72	19.74	19.36	19.58
Provo, UT	13.85	75.16	33.39	54.43	18.78	17.59	15.34
Raleigh, NC	14.64	85.21	31.78	66.79	22.26	15.48	16.07
Reno, NV	15.29	67.77	32.24	59.24	23.92	16.38	17.04
Richmond, VA	14.48	88.63	33.36	63.23	25.31	14.98	16.42
Rochester, MN	15.53	77.53	34.14	50.21	22.80	17.71	20.40
Sacramento, CA	19.02	82.16	37.86	67.60	20.39	16.89	20.72
Saint Louis, MO	15.19	76.57	34.31	53.75	20.57	15.72	17.54
Saint Paul, MN	16.17	85.12	37.88	59.75	22.01	17.88	19.66
Salem, OR	16.51	80.64	34.43	56.23	22.06	20.60	19.35
Salt Lake City, UT	13.99	78.19	35.75	60.12	21.89	18.64	16.02
San Antonio, TX	13.32	77.30	32.68	57.15	16.98	12.52	15.75
San Diego, CA	18.39	92.64	36.65	n/a	22.37	17.55	19.51
San Francisco, CA	20.67	117.20	43.48	85.95	23.49	18.28	23.06
San Jose, CA	20.83	142.60	46.77	94.44	21.94	18.62	21.80
Santa Rosa, CA	19.46	82.80	36.40	66.12	22.13	18.18	21.32
Savannah, GA	13.18	76.60	32.20	55.21	19.33	14.47	15.78
Seattle, WA	19.74	96.69	42.38	82.62	33.56	23.17	22.62
Sioux Falls, SD	15.01	86.95	31.03	76.69	23.12	18.16	16.68
Tampa, FL	14.40	81.07	32.48	65.80	18.35	16.19	16.47
Tucson, AZ	15.89	66.97	29.60	57.34	19.10	16.54	17.29
Tulsa, OK	12.63	71.47	31.71	53.60	17.42	13.24	15.65
Virginia Beach, VA	14.30	78.26	32.80	57.87	23.44	14.33	16.05
Washington, DC	16.65	93.22	38.57	77.26	25.20	18.26	18.52
Wichita, KS	12.56	75.40	30.36	48.65	17.46	14.72	15.77
Wilmington, NC	13.68	73.03	29.78	55.43	19.37	14.82	16.04
Winston-Salem, NC	13.91	77.03	30.59	59.42	18.68	14.44	15.37

Notes: Figures cover the Metropolitan Statistical Area (MSA); (1) Data is from 2023 due to data quality issues in the state of Colorado and its substate areas in 2024; n/a not available
Source: Bureau of Labor Statistics, Metro Area Occupational Employment and Wage Estimates, May 2024

Average Hourly Wages: Occupations L – N

Metro Area	Landscapers	Lawyers	Maids/ House- keepers	Main- tenance/ Repairers	Marketing Managers	Network Admin.	Nurses, Licensed Practical
Albuquerque, NM	18.15	67.75	15.65	23.82	62.50	44.51	26.25
Anchorage, AK	21.86	65.58	18.49	27.18	60.07	45.18	37.16
Ann Arbor, MI	19.91	80.54	17.03	24.12	70.18	46.70	33.06
Athens, GA	17.53	49.61	13.10	20.51	72.47	40.57	27.62
Atlanta, GA	18.84	98.50	15.44	25.02	82.69	48.68	29.80
Austin, TX	18.93	83.20	15.47	24.12	79.43	50.49	30.98
Baltimore, MD	19.36	76.50	16.48	25.58	76.43	60.34	34.04
Billings, MT	19.81	52.20	17.08	22.86	66.97	39.58	26.99
Boise City, ID	20.23	67.91	16.90	24.14	62.17	49.66	30.70
Boston, MA	24.09	109.06	21.01	28.49	98.23	53.85	37.85
Boulder, CO[1]	23.16	120.91	18.76	28.09	89.78	53.52	32.93
Cape Coral, FL	17.78	72.21	16.09	23.30	65.95	46.21	29.34
Cedar Rapids, IA	18.72	61.80	15.71	26.12	66.98	41.23	29.02
Charleston, SC	18.21	62.85	15.15	23.84	66.50	46.44	29.19
Charlotte, NC	18.72	89.69	16.06	25.50	77.80	48.36	30.80
Chicago, IL	21.26	89.56	19.33	27.90	78.03	49.76	34.69
Cincinnati, OH	18.59	69.29	15.43	26.32	72.86	48.96	29.78
Clarksville, TN	17.20	67.51	13.62	22.72	56.80	57.61	26.97
Cleveland, OH	18.91	71.42	15.21	25.41	67.80	46.55	30.00
College Station, TX	16.48	67.99	13.30	20.21	61.86	38.10	26.76
Colorado Springs, CO[1]	20.66	69.39	16.92	23.63	81.56	49.17	30.52
Columbia, MO	17.79	71.41	15.77	22.42	59.28	43.70	28.34
Columbia, SC	17.37	65.86	13.97	23.42	63.36	43.01	28.97
Columbus, OH	19.22	72.24	15.53	25.88	70.72	48.31	30.09
Dallas, TX	18.42	85.71	15.45	24.02	74.76	50.61	30.36
Davenport, IA	18.79	67.21	15.51	25.55	69.88	40.45	28.99
Denver, CO[1]	21.35	95.55	18.17	26.82	89.00	51.25	31.94
Des Moines, IA	19.53	64.42	15.83	25.62	70.53	44.92	30.46
Detroit, MI	19.93	69.97	16.33	24.30	72.83	48.72	32.31
Durham, NC	19.05	73.55	17.00	25.50	82.71	53.21	30.26
El Paso, TX	15.24	61.03	12.61	19.68	55.59	39.84	27.06
Eugene, OR	19.74	68.79	17.08	24.77	64.41	45.54	35.15
Fargo, ND	20.93	60.13	16.65	25.20	66.41	40.53	28.38
Fort Collins, CO[1]	20.58	104.22	17.22	24.61	88.03	47.68	30.10
Fort Wayne, IN	17.85	65.81	14.93	25.25	n/a	39.62	29.69
Fort Worth, TX	18.42	85.71	15.45	24.02	74.76	50.61	30.36
Gainesville, FL	17.73	53.79	15.37	23.13	64.71	41.00	27.62
Green Bay, WI	19.50	69.46	16.12	25.64	75.74	41.79	28.26
Greensboro, NC	17.87	68.03	14.93	23.70	80.15	41.61	30.11
Honolulu, HI	20.46	58.87	25.07	27.07	63.78	48.37	32.75
Houston, TX	17.42	78.80	14.99	23.29	75.23	48.11	30.16
Huntsville, AL	17.69	69.83	13.23	22.69	67.44	48.12	25.96
Indianapolis, IN	18.81	82.32	15.57	25.58	64.61	43.51	30.93
Jacksonville, FL	17.93	62.65	15.49	23.93	69.06	44.92	28.41
Kansas City, MO	20.15	84.26	16.32	25.52	69.71	44.91	30.67
Lafayette, LA	15.75	66.98	12.04	19.43	52.19	45.64	24.52
Las Vegas, NV	19.84	n/a	20.07	26.40	59.85	49.09	34.18
Lexington, KY	18.10	57.22	14.59	22.68	59.96	41.66	28.18
Lincoln, NE	18.75	54.48	15.57	24.63	54.33	42.93	28.51
Little Rock, AR	16.67	65.50	13.80	22.43	55.96	40.49	26.10
Los Angeles, CA	21.42	130.10	21.39	27.74	87.09	53.71	37.14
Louisville, KY	18.54	58.69	15.46	25.41	68.75	43.31	29.46
Madison, WI	21.04	69.54	16.72	26.12	67.95	41.94	30.71
Manchester, NH	21.01	90.60	16.93	26.41	79.04	50.29	34.71
McAllen, TX	14.92	57.98	12.70	17.79	54.38	37.41	24.78

Table continued on following page.

Metro Area	Landscapers	Lawyers	Maids/House-keepers	Main-tenance/Repairers	Marketing Managers	Network Admin.	Nurses, Licensed Practical
Memphis, TN	18.30	71.60	15.17	23.77	70.27	43.88	25.70
Miami, FL	18.25	78.54	16.01	23.66	69.64	47.57	30.32
Midland, TX	18.44	95.87	14.15	23.89	73.71	47.24	30.11
Milwaukee, WI	19.82	86.63	17.09	26.01	71.02	46.35	30.73
Minneapolis, MN	22.32	79.57	19.15	28.72	85.36	48.14	30.75
Nashville, TN	19.47	80.00	15.97	24.27	70.23	54.49	28.30
New Orleans, LA	16.51	66.68	14.95	22.29	60.16	47.36	28.31
New York, NY	21.91	103.90	24.09	28.95	96.08	57.33	34.69
Oklahoma City, OK	17.06	59.75	13.86	21.81	69.08	41.11	26.98
Omaha, NE	20.04	68.96	16.54	25.08	63.75	45.55	29.24
Orlando, FL	17.82	68.56	16.98	23.02	75.25	45.79	28.81
Philadelphia, PA	19.86	82.76	16.94	26.00	81.62	49.02	32.87
Phoenix, AZ	19.42	81.05	17.66	25.41	74.34	46.72	35.33
Pittsburgh, PA	18.69	72.59	15.75	24.30	63.96	44.03	28.96
Portland, OR	21.90	76.99	19.20	28.31	81.04	50.92	38.94
Providence, RI	21.36	73.53	17.71	25.96	82.62	50.61	35.27
Provo, UT	20.19	70.82	16.07	24.23	70.63	46.73	28.85
Raleigh, NC	19.00	71.98	15.98	24.47	81.03	50.43	30.60
Reno, NV	21.79	96.52	18.19	25.86	73.52	48.59	35.06
Richmond, VA	18.50	80.01	15.53	25.46	84.07	49.36	30.78
Rochester, MN	21.83	65.23	18.18	26.25	80.62	52.13	29.80
Sacramento, CA	22.37	97.12	21.69	27.33	84.16	52.73	39.66
Saint Louis, MO	19.80	73.53	16.55	26.56	66.03	43.67	30.72
Saint Paul, MN	22.32	79.57	19.15	28.72	85.36	48.14	30.75
Salem, OR	20.37	76.23	19.11	25.44	64.66	52.82	35.99
Salt Lake City, UT	20.01	76.47	17.31	25.87	72.64	49.94	31.60
San Antonio, TX	17.39	73.65	14.28	22.06	67.10	43.87	29.23
San Diego, CA	21.52	93.11	20.83	27.48	93.41	50.55	37.47
San Francisco, CA	25.75	132.29	25.07	33.69	109.71	64.21	43.56
San Jose, CA	25.28	151.17	27.28	33.50	137.00	63.55	44.06
Santa Rosa, CA	23.68	124.30	22.21	28.52	80.50	50.04	41.93
Savannah, GA	17.56	67.70	13.59	23.15	75.38	45.56	27.56
Seattle, WA	24.35	88.39	20.95	30.02	94.44	55.61	39.88
Sioux Falls, SD	17.48	64.81	15.77	23.21	78.00	37.26	24.52
Tampa, FL	17.89	67.66	16.79	22.66	73.93	48.19	29.09
Tucson, AZ	18.04	67.35	16.29	22.70	65.42	44.42	34.81
Tulsa, OK	17.01	57.59	13.86	22.39	70.25	51.21	27.71
Virginia Beach, VA	17.88	71.39	15.26	24.23	77.38	47.60	29.68
Washington, DC	20.84	105.48	18.53	27.76	91.27	60.06	34.17
Wichita, KS	18.31	60.10	14.70	22.57	67.18	39.93	27.76
Wilmington, NC	17.61	60.44	14.71	22.36	72.18	42.11	29.97
Winston-Salem, NC	17.78	83.92	15.70	24.06	74.45	43.84	28.98

Notes: Figures cover the Metropolitan Statistical Area (MSA); (1) Data is from 2023 due to data quality issues in the state of Colorado and its substate areas in 2024; n/a not available
Source: Bureau of Labor Statistics, Metro Area Occupational Employment and Wage Estimates, May 2024

Average Hourly Wages: Occupations N – P

Metro Area	Nurses, Registered	Nursing Assistants	Office Clerks	Physical Therapists	Physicians	Plumbers	Police Officers
Albuquerque, NM	45.99	18.59	18.52	48.32	146.53	30.61	33.46
Anchorage, AK	54.49	22.44	25.42	54.28	n/a	40.27	52.82
Ann Arbor, MI	46.65	19.82	21.46	47.54	117.60	35.47	37.47
Athens, GA	40.42	17.28	20.80	45.86	148.79	26.20	28.56
Atlanta, GA	46.46	18.72	20.88	50.04	128.59	29.64	30.37
Austin, TX	44.74	18.68	21.24	50.22	140.23	30.87	40.67
Baltimore, MD	46.70	20.15	22.45	50.65	111.79	32.84	38.57
Billings, MT	43.06	20.43	21.25	46.45	n/a	37.35	35.12
Boise City, ID	44.68	18.92	21.13	46.02	150.09	28.71	36.96
Boston, MA	55.63	22.73	25.39	49.54	104.76	42.81	39.16
Boulder, CO[1]	47.77	22.19	27.23	47.73	157.65	33.25	43.85
Cape Coral, FL	41.84	18.75	22.60	46.75	178.53	25.11	36.26
Cedar Rapids, IA	37.78	19.56	21.03	42.76	148.31	33.30	35.70
Charleston, SC	42.57	18.63	20.56	47.07	142.06	26.91	30.52
Charlotte, NC	42.86	19.15	20.94	48.26	150.06	27.07	32.47
Chicago, IL	45.47	21.85	23.22	52.46	109.22	44.43	47.28
Cincinnati, OH	41.93	19.66	21.56	48.99	137.38	32.13	38.17
Clarksville, TN	37.88	17.59	18.67	45.46	154.95	31.80	26.37
Cleveland, OH	43.24	19.22	22.21	48.56	117.07	33.28	37.16
College Station, TX	40.15	16.34	n/a	49.86	118.72	26.89	36.08
Colorado Springs, CO[1]	41.57	20.55	25.08	47.11	145.41	29.44	40.85
Columbia, MO	39.72	18.73	20.78	43.86	149.57	30.64	28.96
Columbia, SC	40.80	17.13	19.07	45.02	172.10	25.12	32.54
Columbus, OH	42.87	19.72	22.35	47.24	129.01	32.38	42.38
Dallas, TX	46.50	18.80	21.12	52.68	105.52	30.24	41.90
Davenport, IA	36.47	18.90	20.19	45.91	133.88	34.59	34.22
Denver, CO[1]	44.80	21.50	27.01	47.63	148.66	32.33	44.76
Des Moines, IA	38.30	20.34	21.64	46.36	117.95	32.51	39.83
Detroit, MI	44.56	19.58	22.38	47.96	79.84	36.88	36.19
Durham, NC	n/a	19.70	21.79	44.30	69.93	28.13	30.46
El Paso, TX	42.08	16.41	16.95	46.74	120.70	25.72	36.19
Eugene, OR	54.25	23.01	22.54	47.48	165.85	40.25	42.81
Fargo, ND	39.76	19.70	24.78	43.52	165.27	31.67	36.83
Fort Collins, CO[1]	43.16	20.38	25.12	44.64	119.01	30.07	44.59
Fort Wayne, IN	39.85	18.10	21.10	46.11	144.14	35.26	36.57
Fort Worth, TX	46.50	18.80	21.12	52.68	105.52	30.24	41.90
Gainesville, FL	42.66	18.80	21.26	46.21	130.80	24.73	29.02
Green Bay, WI	41.77	19.98	21.47	47.00	196.56	39.90	39.06
Greensboro, NC	41.93	18.27	19.68	44.25	144.60	25.64	30.89
Honolulu, HI	60.17	21.81	21.33	48.19	152.85	40.69	45.53
Houston, TX	46.51	18.77	19.64	53.94	123.51	29.30	35.97
Huntsville, AL	35.22	16.31	16.03	47.20	140.44	26.63	30.79
Indianapolis, IN	42.93	18.85	22.26	47.40	154.93	33.46	38.34
Jacksonville, FL	41.31	18.27	21.57	46.05	130.38	26.34	33.29
Kansas City, MO	41.12	20.02	22.34	46.79	76.04	36.37	33.12
Lafayette, LA	38.87	14.75	15.09	45.77	127.73	26.64	26.21
Las Vegas, NV	49.23	21.32	21.50	55.52	108.49	31.52	41.22
Lexington, KY	40.98	19.39	19.89	44.65	134.53	31.89	32.13
Lincoln, NE	39.04	19.33	18.58	44.86	136.23	30.39	40.64
Little Rock, AR	39.00	16.82	19.51	45.58	113.68	25.08	28.58
Los Angeles, CA	66.35	23.03	23.99	56.57	82.19	37.49	52.17
Louisville, KY	42.06	19.38	18.96	44.32	137.23	33.07	31.32
Madison, WI	46.09	21.62	21.81	47.86	156.17	42.99	38.38
Manchester, NH	44.26	22.36	24.15	44.89	148.76	31.71	36.87
McAllen, TX	36.77	15.66	16.04	50.03	144.98	22.61	29.67

Table continued on following page.

Metro Area	Nurses, Registered	Nursing Assistants	Office Clerks	Physical Therapists	Physicians	Plumbers	Police Officers
Memphis, TN	40.79	17.76	19.17	48.19	143.52	28.45	32.26
Miami, FL	44.26	19.01	22.54	42.79	117.21	27.27	50.84
Midland, TX	42.82	18.39	23.20	54.19	n/a	27.83	40.49
Milwaukee, WI	43.77	21.00	21.09	48.16	115.37	41.81	41.03
Minneapolis, MN	49.42	22.60	24.20	47.65	159.99	42.95	42.99
Nashville, TN	42.71	19.32	20.60	47.86	134.22	29.46	30.96
New Orleans, LA	43.12	16.45	16.23	51.00	147.27	29.90	27.76
New York, NY	55.60	23.60	24.07	52.54	125.08	43.78	44.53
Oklahoma City, OK	41.29	17.28	19.03	48.05	113.07	27.59	35.39
Omaha, NE	40.84	20.08	19.65	45.26	132.45	34.64	39.22
Orlando, FL	41.57	17.96	21.36	47.77	152.34	26.02	32.01
Philadelphia, PA	46.88	20.72	22.87	50.29	103.98	38.73	41.45
Phoenix, AZ	46.26	21.03	24.26	50.72	101.37	33.45	42.24
Pittsburgh, PA	41.36	19.62	21.43	45.46	106.62	34.88	39.89
Portland, OR	59.41	24.32	24.99	51.26	145.16	46.10	45.23
Providence, RI	47.85	20.93	23.21	47.81	115.77	36.48	37.31
Provo, UT	40.74	18.10	20.61	47.91	138.71	27.75	34.98
Raleigh, NC	43.18	18.76	20.44	45.60	140.88	27.06	31.94
Reno, NV	49.60	21.66	22.82	51.17	119.36	34.61	40.69
Richmond, VA	43.52	19.49	22.18	49.10	124.83	28.27	33.25
Rochester, MN	50.31	21.62	23.84	46.20	142.26	41.69	38.02
Sacramento, CA	78.37	23.25	25.08	60.12	165.05	35.78	53.46
Saint Louis, MO	40.74	19.04	21.94	46.78	n/a	37.26	34.71
Saint Paul, MN	49.42	22.60	24.20	47.65	159.99	42.95	42.99
Salem, OR	58.70	24.31	23.22	46.55	156.96	38.33	41.55
Salt Lake City, UT	44.02	19.66	22.49	47.44	112.68	32.12	40.23
San Antonio, TX	42.93	17.50	19.72	48.60	148.25	28.13	33.62
San Diego, CA	67.00	23.07	23.88	52.74	133.58	36.03	53.06
San Francisco, CA	85.79	27.59	27.96	65.53	127.97	41.48	61.75
San Jose, CA	91.29	27.97	28.51	68.75	89.33	49.42	69.86
Santa Rosa, CA	82.45	23.29	26.18	62.99	96.04	38.02	53.85
Savannah, GA	41.90	17.49	19.60	47.93	140.56	29.86	30.08
Seattle, WA	57.82	25.24	26.95	50.63	142.83	45.49	53.76
Sioux Falls, SD	34.16	18.18	18.51	42.66	n/a	27.31	37.35
Tampa, FL	43.40	18.54	21.94	47.43	143.21	26.24	37.66
Tucson, AZ	44.18	20.24	22.28	47.48	134.43	27.72	37.95
Tulsa, OK	43.20	17.41	19.08	46.55	83.29	28.27	31.70
Virginia Beach, VA	42.13	18.43	21.17	48.12	125.27	27.83	32.02
Washington, DC	49.29	20.85	26.37	53.25	100.51	34.13	41.76
Wichita, KS	36.06	17.82	16.54	46.81	100.27	29.54	28.31
Wilmington, NC	39.17	18.20	18.96	41.99	129.60	25.08	26.40
Winston-Salem, NC	42.11	18.13	19.25	47.50	n/a	25.08	27.78

Notes: Figures cover the Metropolitan Statistical Area (MSA); (1) Data is from 2023 due to data quality issues in the state of Colorado and its substate areas in 2024; n/a not available
Source: Bureau of Labor Statistics, Metro Area Occupational Employment and Wage Estimates, May 2024

Average Hourly Wages: Occupations P – S

Metro Area	Postal Mail Carriers	R.E. Sales Agents	Retail Sales-persons	Sales Reps., Technical/ Scientific	Secretaries, Exc. Leg./ Med./Exec.	Security Guards	Surgeons
Albuquerque, NM	28.74	40.95	16.73	41.73	21.86	21.72	219.96
Anchorage, AK	27.61	43.45	19.57	40.10	21.78	26.71	n/a
Ann Arbor, MI	28.15	31.11	18.46	105.25	24.23	21.89	n/a
Athens, GA	28.08	27.38	14.88	n/a	17.77	21.83	n/a
Atlanta, GA	28.20	34.66	16.55	55.13	20.91	19.64	216.10
Austin, TX	29.21	41.46	17.04	45.57	22.22	19.26	n/a
Baltimore, MD	28.82	27.82	17.59	44.15	23.24	20.69	171.05
Billings, MT	28.52	37.77	17.80	49.31	21.21	19.51	n/a
Boise City, ID	28.72	n/a	18.06	59.59	20.77	20.32	n/a
Boston, MA	29.71	46.11	19.71	54.45	27.63	22.25	161.25
Boulder, CO[1]	29.62	37.36	20.20	68.73	23.54	25.69	n/a
Cape Coral, FL	29.05	37.59	16.92	57.39	20.71	17.45	n/a
Cedar Rapids, IA	28.91	21.00	16.36	49.65	21.59	19.04	n/a
Charleston, SC	29.37	n/a	16.45	50.27	21.83	18.35	n/a
Charlotte, NC	29.03	30.17	16.65	63.70	20.49	19.12	248.26
Chicago, IL	29.11	29.28	18.67	58.57	25.84	21.16	161.04
Cincinnati, OH	29.19	24.40	17.19	57.27	23.98	19.14	n/a
Clarksville, TN	27.83	25.11	16.33	34.76	19.85	19.00	n/a
Cleveland, OH	28.67	23.45	17.25	47.42	22.52	19.46	n/a
College Station, TX	27.95	29.01	15.01	41.37	19.66	16.89	n/a
Colorado Springs, CO[1]	27.18	33.25	18.80	53.78	21.04	19.20	n/a
Columbia, MO	28.47	24.50	16.22	46.86	20.78	18.70	n/a
Columbia, SC	27.58	25.47	15.69	55.80	20.60	16.75	n/a
Columbus, OH	29.11	25.57	17.40	54.37	23.47	19.81	n/a
Dallas, TX	29.14	35.39	16.85	49.39	22.33	19.16	172.43
Davenport, IA	28.67	31.72	16.82	46.92	21.95	19.78	n/a
Denver, CO[1]	29.38	n/a	20.04	57.52	23.31	22.24	n/a
Des Moines, IA	30.06	20.22	17.08	60.11	22.86	19.84	207.59
Detroit, MI	28.48	32.41	19.31	68.16	23.38	19.17	n/a
Durham, NC	29.34	28.62	16.63	57.68	23.09	21.40	n/a
El Paso, TX	28.75	31.06	14.45	41.79	18.76	14.38	n/a
Eugene, OR	27.06	26.12	18.58	52.14	23.51	19.91	186.25
Fargo, ND	30.03	34.07	18.57	54.80	21.50	20.01	n/a
Fort Collins, CO[1]	28.36	32.17	18.87	52.65	21.68	19.32	n/a
Fort Wayne, IN	28.41	37.39	16.08	52.60	20.58	20.23	n/a
Fort Worth, TX	29.14	35.39	16.85	49.39	22.33	19.16	172.43
Gainesville, FL	28.67	29.50	16.05	48.82	21.09	17.73	n/a
Green Bay, WI	29.14	28.56	17.47	31.64	22.49	20.67	n/a
Greensboro, NC	29.19	31.36	15.70	47.29	21.42	17.81	n/a
Honolulu, HI	27.98	33.03	19.06	58.17	25.07	20.40	n/a
Houston, TX	28.58	36.58	16.26	50.66	22.14	18.23	n/a
Huntsville, AL	27.93	22.98	16.48	52.53	21.47	19.04	n/a
Indianapolis, IN	29.29	36.12	16.89	55.71	21.53	21.17	222.23
Jacksonville, FL	29.28	35.39	16.85	47.51	21.36	17.65	n/a
Kansas City, MO	29.08	40.62	17.76	57.49	21.49	22.78	n/a
Lafayette, LA	28.33	20.17	14.62	53.76	19.61	15.29	n/a
Las Vegas, NV	28.67	32.12	17.32	51.43	22.21	19.00	n/a
Lexington, KY	28.80	31.80	16.41	45.46	21.53	17.37	n/a
Lincoln, NE	30.57	27.17	16.38	40.00	22.03	20.05	n/a
Little Rock, AR	29.24	n/a	15.97	38.95	19.79	18.85	n/a
Los Angeles, CA	29.11	36.15	20.52	56.19	26.51	21.76	181.61
Louisville, KY	28.87	25.01	16.47	51.44	22.05	18.78	n/a
Madison, WI	29.38	32.13	17.90	43.29	24.50	21.74	n/a
Manchester, NH	29.69	25.56	18.32	57.21	22.59	22.02	n/a
McAllen, TX	30.28	28.28	14.03	39.87	18.47	13.98	n/a

Table continued on following page.

Metro Area	Postal Mail Carriers	R.E. Sales Agents	Retail Sales-persons	Sales Reps., Technical/ Scientific	Secretaries, Exc. Leg./ Med./Exec.	Security Guards	Surgeons
Memphis, TN	28.14	27.09	16.86	48.33	21.52	18.00	n/a
Miami, FL	28.58	35.78	17.72	72.39	22.74	19.47	n/a
Midland, TX	27.68	57.72	17.23	n/a	22.14	23.02	n/a
Milwaukee, WI	28.92	36.71	17.62	43.52	23.21	21.24	n/a
Minneapolis, MN	29.62	34.01	18.56	50.40	25.28	24.99	180.26
Nashville, TN	29.67	24.17	17.69	49.18	22.79	20.23	n/a
New Orleans, LA	28.47	24.83	15.83	70.24	20.08	17.58	n/a
New York, NY	28.97	50.92	21.03	71.17	25.44	21.96	153.50
Oklahoma City, OK	28.83	n/a	16.29	44.00	19.75	20.95	n/a
Omaha, NE	29.45	23.46	16.96	41.73	22.46	21.05	165.50
Orlando, FL	28.68	33.44	16.93	50.60	21.59	18.05	n/a
Philadelphia, PA	28.61	31.43	17.58	57.13	23.47	20.88	n/a
Phoenix, AZ	29.45	33.31	18.61	47.67	23.90	20.06	201.58
Pittsburgh, PA	28.52	31.38	16.07	51.43	20.70	18.83	n/a
Portland, OR	28.58	33.65	20.03	60.80	26.92	23.38	n/a
Providence, RI	29.03	31.86	18.21	51.21	24.94	19.43	n/a
Provo, UT	29.07	24.11	17.69	38.31	20.88	20.05	n/a
Raleigh, NC	29.38	33.92	16.98	55.52	22.71	20.01	n/a
Reno, NV	28.83	27.04	18.04	54.60	23.35	20.48	n/a
Richmond, VA	29.19	34.95	17.09	54.94	22.38	21.69	n/a
Rochester, MN	30.26	32.82	18.61	63.87	25.11	23.45	n/a
Sacramento, CA	29.98	35.09	20.50	56.67	26.05	21.11	n/a
Saint Louis, MO	28.63	22.92	17.47	49.86	21.95	21.78	n/a
Saint Paul, MN	29.62	34.01	18.56	50.40	25.28	24.99	180.26
Salem, OR	28.32	31.93	18.59	51.43	25.45	21.67	n/a
Salt Lake City, UT	29.32	31.26	19.37	49.93	22.46	21.09	n/a
San Antonio, TX	28.61	27.84	16.14	48.30	21.21	17.26	n/a
San Diego, CA	28.81	33.54	20.16	56.30	26.29	21.29	215.16
San Francisco, CA	29.93	39.65	22.87	70.21	31.24	24.81	n/a
San Jose, CA	29.61	49.32	23.09	78.15	31.07	24.80	n/a
Santa Rosa, CA	28.63	39.71	21.77	56.13	27.28	22.66	n/a
Savannah, GA	28.40	31.87	15.49	43.92	19.62	17.54	n/a
Seattle, WA	29.52	40.04	21.76	71.82	28.37	25.48	164.19
Sioux Falls, SD	29.60	44.83	20.29	72.14	19.77	19.11	n/a
Tampa, FL	28.84	34.03	16.81	55.31	22.08	18.32	210.11
Tucson, AZ	29.27	30.47	18.32	47.81	21.86	18.88	n/a
Tulsa, OK	29.17	29.25	16.41	43.73	19.75	19.04	n/a
Virginia Beach, VA	28.31	31.93	16.44	52.97	21.87	20.46	n/a
Washington, DC	29.66	34.90	18.96	54.33	26.32	26.46	178.95
Wichita, KS	28.32	n/a	16.72	58.23	19.03	18.73	n/a
Wilmington, NC	29.33	24.73	16.08	51.06	21.11	21.00	n/a
Winston-Salem, NC	28.87	23.59	15.88	51.83	21.50	20.24	n/a

Notes: Figures cover the Metropolitan Statistical Area (MSA); (1) Data is from 2023 due to data quality issues in the state of Colorado and its substate areas in 2024; n/a not available
Source: Bureau of Labor Statistics, Metro Area Occupational Employment and Wage Estimates, May 2024

Average Hourly Wages: Occupations T – W

Metro Area	Teacher Assistants[2]	Teachers, Secondary School[2]	Telemarketers	Truck Drivers, Heavy	Truck Drivers, Light	Waiters/ Waitresses
Albuquerque, NM	15.58	32.70	33.59	25.68	20.59	18.83
Anchorage, AK	16.43	39.21	n/a	31.27	29.20	20.08
Ann Arbor, MI	16.34	35.96	n/a	28.12	23.79	20.05
Athens, GA	12.66	31.86	n/a	26.99	22.11	12.40
Atlanta, GA	14.65	35.49	16.14	28.06	23.97	13.74
Austin, TX	15.99	29.94	16.65	28.00	23.95	17.05
Baltimore, MD	18.88	36.16	16.80	28.16	23.74	19.68
Billings, MT	15.66	31.64	n/a	29.65	24.41	14.05
Boise City, ID	15.78	32.07	18.37	27.48	27.08	16.87
Boston, MA	20.03	42.74	18.61	29.10	25.46	22.07
Boulder, CO[1]	19.34	37.59	n/a	28.09	24.74	22.52
Cape Coral, FL	17.30	27.48	17.59	24.75	21.61	18.95
Cedar Rapids, IA	14.24	28.68	15.78	29.58	24.80	14.45
Charleston, SC	13.41	31.47	n/a	27.48	22.40	12.20
Charlotte, NC	14.49	27.70	19.21	27.14	21.73	16.65
Chicago, IL	18.41	42.55	17.05	31.25	25.40	16.76
Cincinnati, OH	17.09	33.20	16.50	30.56	24.16	18.39
Clarksville, TN	15.35	26.88	n/a	26.20	18.98	13.57
Cleveland, OH	17.13	37.67	15.51	28.14	21.75	18.81
College Station, TX	14.65	28.00	n/a	24.31	25.81	15.16
Colorado Springs, CO[1]	16.56	28.08	25.27	26.24	21.53	21.16
Columbia, MO	15.25	26.79	n/a	26.84	22.33	15.03
Columbia, SC	14.58	28.10	13.70	26.77	22.11	11.85
Columbus, OH	16.73	38.26	15.60	30.84	23.64	19.12
Dallas, TX	14.37	31.75	17.73	28.88	23.68	15.52
Davenport, IA	15.98	32.25	15.38	26.97	22.49	14.76
Denver, CO[1]	18.20	34.07	24.12	29.22	24.04	18.83
Des Moines, IA	15.17	29.25	15.86	29.34	22.55	15.00
Detroit, MI	15.96	34.65	16.11	27.01	21.91	19.88
Durham, NC	14.99	27.78	17.39	26.62	21.88	16.09
El Paso, TX	13.36	29.30	n/a	25.51	19.26	13.84
Eugene, OR	18.52	38.08	n/a	28.02	23.03	18.82
Fargo, ND	18.13	29.54	n/a	27.21	24.35	16.96
Fort Collins, CO[1]	17.53	31.75	n/a	26.38	22.67	21.70
Fort Wayne, IN	15.68	30.99	n/a	28.99	21.73	14.84
Fort Worth, TX	14.37	31.75	17.73	28.88	23.68	15.52
Gainesville, FL	15.81	33.04	n/a	24.90	21.27	18.15
Green Bay, WI	17.43	29.58	n/a	27.16	22.51	14.93
Greensboro, NC	13.56	25.65	16.15	26.84	21.55	15.80
Honolulu, HI	17.06	30.19	n/a	27.42	23.32	25.96
Houston, TX	14.01	31.15	18.64	27.49	23.30	15.23
Huntsville, AL	11.76	30.28	n/a	27.09	22.62	12.42
Indianapolis, IN	16.14	32.97	18.55	30.71	24.66	15.51
Jacksonville, FL	16.11	33.35	17.68	27.47	22.53	18.38
Kansas City, MO	15.24	29.47	18.48	28.62	23.71	17.04
Lafayette, LA	12.65	24.74	n/a	26.47	19.63	11.17
Las Vegas, NV	15.55	31.27	16.68	28.15	22.31	15.55
Lexington, KY	17.74	30.50	n/a	29.78	22.45	14.52
Lincoln, NE	13.52	29.94	14.12	38.54	22.72	19.50
Little Rock, AR	15.65	27.84	n/a	28.31	21.58	14.13
Los Angeles, CA	21.70	49.74	19.37	28.59	24.21	20.65
Louisville, KY	16.51	31.82	n/a	30.63	24.78	14.86
Madison, WI	18.13	30.40	17.61	27.62	23.52	17.52
Manchester, NH	18.04	34.04	15.89	27.49	22.94	21.07
McAllen, TX	13.28	30.53	n/a	24.00	19.17	13.40

Table continued on following page.

Metro Area	Teacher Assistants[2]	Teachers, Secondary School[2]	Telemarketers	Truck Drivers, Heavy	Truck Drivers, Light	Waiters/ Waitresses
Memphis, TN	14.32	28.90	13.76	29.58	29.29	13.80
Miami, FL	15.86	28.86	18.31	26.65	23.18	18.71
Midland, TX	15.30	31.99	n/a	28.32	23.98	15.93
Milwaukee, WI	17.98	34.09	17.30	28.14	22.92	16.18
Minneapolis, MN	20.05	35.70	22.16	31.39	25.01	13.95
Nashville, TN	14.83	29.56	15.16	28.95	23.69	15.99
New Orleans, LA	14.58	28.89	n/a	25.97	22.33	12.40
New York, NY	19.26	48.38	19.76	33.26	25.01	25.65
Oklahoma City, OK	14.11	27.06	16.04	27.43	20.70	14.43
Omaha, NE	14.60	29.23	14.96	27.64	23.61	19.47
Orlando, FL	15.02	27.08	17.71	26.28	22.34	18.62
Philadelphia, PA	16.42	37.57	18.66	29.70	23.32	19.57
Phoenix, AZ	17.41	33.10	25.15	27.04	25.25	23.73
Pittsburgh, PA	15.48	37.69	18.78	27.85	20.24	16.99
Portland, OR	19.63	42.02	19.64	31.98	24.55	22.74
Providence, RI	17.96	39.10	18.03	28.07	23.04	20.77
Provo, UT	15.72	32.55	19.36	27.39	21.30	16.73
Raleigh, NC	15.69	26.95	n/a	26.45	20.95	16.07
Reno, NV	17.00	36.97	16.27	31.35	24.02	13.93
Richmond, VA	16.87	30.92	n/a	29.88	21.77	19.74
Rochester, MN	18.97	34.45	n/a	30.88	23.86	12.89
Sacramento, CA	21.20	45.34	19.22	29.27	24.31	21.77
Saint Louis, MO	16.42	31.39	15.91	27.24	23.38	15.95
Saint Paul, MN	20.05	35.70	22.16	31.39	25.01	13.95
Salem, OR	18.55	36.88	n/a	29.67	22.75	20.45
Salt Lake City, UT	15.41	35.90	17.54	29.38	23.05	16.60
San Antonio, TX	12.78	29.49	16.58	25.47	21.43	15.16
San Diego, CA	20.95	54.30	19.47	28.38	23.68	22.56
San Francisco, CA	24.02	55.15	23.72	32.89	27.39	22.18
San Jose, CA	24.13	52.38	23.11	33.44	26.28	24.41
Santa Rosa, CA	22.92	47.05	n/a	29.46	25.70	21.12
Savannah, GA	13.88	32.08	13.85	27.26	24.37	13.65
Seattle, WA	24.88	47.37	21.66	33.99	26.42	27.97
Sioux Falls, SD	13.44	24.78	n/a	28.36	21.88	15.30
Tampa, FL	14.20	30.50	17.64	25.87	21.83	19.64
Tucson, AZ	16.88	25.54	n/a	25.42	23.43	20.95
Tulsa, OK	13.50	28.84	16.76	27.89	20.63	14.21
Virginia Beach, VA	18.39	34.95	20.17	24.69	20.85	19.88
Washington, DC	20.42	38.87	19.03	29.14	24.85	22.84
Wichita, KS	14.38	28.72	n/a	26.88	19.57	17.67
Wilmington, NC	14.70	25.61	16.58	24.77	19.92	14.23
Winston-Salem, NC	13.12	26.41	n/a	25.99	20.43	14.25

Notes: Figures cover the Metropolitan Statistical Area (MSA); (1) Data is from 2023 due to data quality issues in the state of Colorado and its substate areas in 2024; (2) Hourly wages were calculated from annual wage data based on a 40 hour work week; n/a not available
Source: Bureau of Labor Statistics, Metro Area Occupational Employment and Wage Estimates, May 2024

Means of Transportation to Work: City

City	Car/Truck/Van		Public Transportation			Bicycle	Walked	Other Means	Worked at Home
	Drove Alone	Car-pooled	Bus	Subway	Railroad				
Albuquerque, NM	73.2	8.8	1.2	0.0	0.1	0.9	1.9	1.2	12.8
Anchorage, AK	71.0	12.4	1.3	0.0	0.0	0.6	2.6	2.5	9.6
Ann Arbor, MI	45.6	5.0	7.3	0.1	0.0	2.4	13.1	0.5	26.2
Athens, GA	72.0	7.8	2.1	0.0	0.0	0.9	4.5	0.8	11.9
Atlanta, GA	55.2	4.6	3.6	2.5	0.1	0.7	4.2	2.4	26.6
Austin, TX	58.8	6.9	1.9	0.0	0.0	0.8	2.4	1.6	27.5
Baltimore, MD	56.8	6.9	9.3	1.0	0.8	0.6	5.6	3.1	15.9
Billings, MT	78.5	9.1	1.0	0.0	0.0	0.7	2.0	1.0	7.6
Boise City, ID	68.6	7.6	0.5	0.0	0.0	2.3	3.4	1.6	15.8
Boston, MA	34.1	5.4	8.6	13.6	1.2	2.1	13.8	2.4	18.8
Boulder, CO	41.9	3.6	5.8	0.0	0.0	7.6	8.6	0.9	31.6
Cape Coral, FL	76.0	8.1	0.2	0.0	0.0	0.1	1.0	1.4	13.1
Cedar Rapids, IA	77.0	6.5	0.6	0.0	0.0	0.3	2.2	0.8	12.6
Charleston, SC	68.1	6.5	0.9	0.0	0.0	1.5	4.1	1.2	17.6
Charlotte, NC	61.0	8.1	1.4	0.1	0.0	0.2	1.7	2.0	25.5
Chicago, IL	46.0	7.4	9.5	8.5	1.2	1.4	5.7	2.1	18.3
Cincinnati, OH	66.2	7.5	5.7	0.0	0.0	0.3	5.3	1.8	13.2
Clarksville, TN	81.0	8.7	0.5	0.0	0.0	0.0	1.2	1.5	7.1
Cleveland, OH	65.4	10.0	6.3	0.4	0.0	0.5	5.3	1.9	10.1
College Station, TX	70.8	8.0	2.3	0.0	0.0	1.9	3.9	1.1	12.1
Colorado Springs, CO	71.1	9.0	0.4	0.0	0.0	0.5	1.8	1.1	16.1
Columbia, MO	74.1	7.6	1.1	0.0	0.0	1.0	5.6	0.9	9.6
Columbia, SC	62.9	6.9	1.4	0.0	0.0	0.3	16.4	2.2	9.8
Columbus, OH	70.1	7.5	2.1	0.0	0.0	0.4	2.6	1.2	16.1
Dallas, TX	68.5	11.4	1.7	0.2	0.1	0.2	2.2	1.7	14.0
Davenport, IA	78.8	7.3	0.8	0.0	0.1	0.2	2.7	1.1	8.9
Denver, CO	57.7	6.5	2.8	0.3	0.1	1.6	3.9	2.7	24.4
Des Moines, IA	72.3	11.2	1.1	0.0	0.0	0.4	2.2	1.3	11.4
Detroit, MI	66.3	11.0	5.9	0.0	0.0	0.5	3.1	3.1	10.1
Durham, NC	65.2	8.0	2.2	0.0	0.0	0.5	2.3	1.4	20.6
El Paso, TX	76.5	11.1	1.0	0.0	0.0	0.1	1.1	2.3	7.8
Eugene, OR	63.0	7.9	2.6	0.0	0.0	4.7	5.3	1.1	15.3
Fargo, ND	78.7	6.6	0.7	0.0	0.1	0.3	3.5	2.0	8.1
Fort Collins, CO	63.3	5.6	1.4	0.0	0.0	4.2	4.2	1.0	20.2
Fort Wayne, IN	78.1	9.9	1.1	0.0	0.0	0.3	1.5	0.8	8.2
Fort Worth, TX	72.9	10.9	0.4	0.0	0.1	0.2	1.2	1.5	12.9
Gainesville, FL	62.9	9.0	4.9	0.0	0.0	3.5	5.0	2.3	12.4
Green Bay, WI	75.9	10.7	1.0	0.0	0.0	0.4	2.3	1.1	8.5
Greensboro, NC	73.7	8.2	2.4	0.0	0.0	0.2	2.3	1.4	11.8
Honolulu, HI	55.7	14.2	7.9	0.0	0.0	1.8	7.7	3.7	8.9
Houston, TX	69.7	10.1	2.9	0.1	0.0	0.4	1.9	3.1	11.7
Huntsville, AL	77.5	6.8	0.3	0.0	0.0	0.0	1.3	1.0	13.1
Indianapolis, IN	73.7	9.6	1.4	0.0	0.0	0.4	1.8	0.9	12.3
Jacksonville, FL	72.8	9.0	1.2	0.0	0.0	0.4	1.2	2.0	13.5
Kansas City, MO	72.7	7.4	1.9	0.0	0.0	0.2	1.5	1.5	14.8
Lafayette, LA	80.4	5.6	0.6	0.0	0.0	0.5	2.2	1.2	9.5
Las Vegas, NV	72.6	10.0	2.4	0.0	0.0	0.3	1.3	2.9	10.5
Lexington, KY	74.8	8.4	1.3	0.0	0.0	0.5	3.0	1.0	10.9
Lincoln, NE	75.7	8.6	0.9	0.0	0.0	0.9	3.2	0.8	10.0
Little Rock, AR	76.5	8.9	1.0	0.0	0.0	0.2	1.8	0.9	10.8
Los Angeles, CA	61.4	8.8	5.7	0.6	0.1	0.7	3.1	2.3	17.3
Louisville, KY	73.5	8.7	2.2	0.0	0.0	0.3	2.0	1.7	11.6
Madison, WI	57.6	5.9	5.6	0.0	0.1	3.1	8.2	1.3	18.2
Manchester, NH	74.2	9.1	0.4	0.1	0.0	0.3	2.4	1.5	12.1

Table continued on following page.

City	Car/Truck/Van		Public Transportation			Bicycle	Walked	Other Means	Worked at Home
	Drove Alone	Car-pooled	Bus	Subway	Railroad				
McAllen, TX	72.2	10.4	0.4	0.0	0.0	0.3	0.9	4.3	11.5
Memphis, TN	77.8	10.0	0.8	0.0	0.0	0.2	1.7	1.5	8.0
Miami, FL	61.7	7.9	5.4	1.1	0.1	0.8	5.4	3.5	14.2
Midland, TX	79.9	12.2	0.4	0.0	0.0	0.2	0.7	1.0	5.6
Milwaukee, WI	67.8	10.0	5.3	0.0	0.0	0.5	4.0	1.2	11.2
Minneapolis, MN	53.4	5.9	6.3	0.2	0.0	2.3	6.0	2.5	23.3
Nashville, TN	68.1	8.3	1.6	0.0	0.0	0.3	1.9	1.5	18.3
New Orleans, LA	63.2	8.7	3.8	0.1	0.0	1.9	5.6	3.0	13.7
New York, NY	21.9	4.3	9.8	34.4	1.0	1.5	9.4	2.7	15.0
Oklahoma City, OK	77.0	9.6	0.4	0.0	0.0	0.2	1.4	1.6	9.8
Omaha, NE	73.3	8.7	1.1	0.0	0.0	0.2	1.8	1.3	13.6
Orlando, FL	69.5	8.9	1.8	0.0	0.0	0.5	1.6	2.5	15.1
Philadelphia, PA	46.7	7.6	10.9	4.7	1.6	1.9	7.5	2.8	16.4
Phoenix, AZ	66.1	10.9	1.8	0.0	0.0	0.4	1.6	2.2	16.9
Pittsburgh, PA	48.2	6.2	11.6	0.3	0.0	1.1	9.8	2.3	20.4
Portland, OR	50.5	7.0	5.4	0.2	0.1	3.7	4.8	3.0	25.3
Providence, RI	62.6	9.8	3.1	0.0	1.1	0.8	7.3	2.6	12.7
Provo, UT	57.4	10.4	4.3	0.1	0.9	1.4	10.3	1.1	14.2
Raleigh, NC	65.1	6.6	1.3	0.0	0.0	0.4	1.6	1.6	23.4
Reno, NV	67.6	12.6	2.4	0.0	0.0	0.6	3.2	2.8	10.8
Richmond, VA	64.9	7.8	3.6	0.0	0.0	1.1	4.2	1.5	16.9
Rochester, MN	65.5	11.1	4.1	0.0	0.0	0.8	4.3	1.3	12.9
Sacramento, CA	65.5	9.0	1.0	0.2	0.1	1.4	2.7	2.4	17.7
Saint Louis, MO	66.6	6.7	4.4	0.4	0.1	0.9	4.0	1.9	15.0
Saint Paul, MN	59.3	10.0	5.0	0.1	0.0	0.8	3.7	2.7	18.3
Salem, OR	68.4	10.4	1.8	0.0	0.0	1.1	3.0	1.4	14.0
Salt Lake City, UT	60.2	8.1	3.1	0.3	0.3	1.6	4.8	2.9	18.5
San Antonio, TX	70.5	12.1	2.1	0.0	0.0	0.2	1.7	1.6	11.8
San Diego, CA	64.2	7.8	2.3	0.1	0.1	0.7	3.4	2.2	19.2
San Francisco, CA	28.6	6.0	14.1	4.8	1.1	3.3	10.0	4.5	27.5
San Jose, CA	64.6	10.5	1.6	0.2	0.5	0.5	1.8	1.7	18.5
Santa Rosa, CA	73.1	11.1	0.9	0.0	0.2	0.6	2.3	1.3	10.5
Savannah, GA	70.4	10.3	2.5	0.1	0.0	1.5	3.8	1.4	10.1
Seattle, WA	37.6	5.1	11.2	0.5	0.0	2.5	8.3	3.5	31.3
Sioux Falls, SD	79.4	7.7	0.7	0.0	0.0	0.2	1.9	0.9	9.4
Tampa, FL	66.1	8.2	1.3	0.0	0.0	0.8	2.3	2.1	19.3
Tucson, AZ	69.5	9.9	2.3	0.0	0.0	1.6	2.7	1.6	12.4
Tulsa, OK	75.4	10.2	0.5	0.0	0.0	0.3	1.7	1.8	10.1
Virginia Beach, VA	75.3	7.5	0.8	0.0	0.0	0.4	1.8	1.6	12.7
Washington, DC	28.2	4.3	8.1	13.8	0.3	3.3	10.0	2.7	29.4
Wichita, KS	80.0	9.6	0.6	0.0	0.0	0.4	0.9	1.5	6.9
Wilmington, NC	70.9	7.0	0.4	0.0	0.0	0.8	2.2	1.0	17.7
Winston-Salem, NC	73.2	9.5	1.1	0.0	0.0	0.3	2.0	1.6	12.3
U.S.	70.2	8.5	1.7	1.3	0.4	0.4	2.4	1.6	13.5

Note: Figures are percentages and cover workers 16 years of age and older
Source: U.S. Census Bureau, 2019-2023 American Community Survey 5-Year Estimates

Means of Transportation to Work: Metro Area

Metro Area	Car/Truck/Van		Public Transportation			Bicycle	Walked	Other Means	Worked at Home
	Drove Alone	Car-pooled	Bus	Subway	Railroad				
Albuquerque, NM	73.5	9.1	0.8	0.0	0.1	0.6	1.6	1.3	12.9
Anchorage, AK	71.3	11.7	1.1	0.0	0.0	0.5	2.4	3.1	9.8
Ann Arbor, MI	61.9	6.3	3.7	0.0	0.0	1.0	5.8	0.8	20.3
Athens, GA	74.7	7.3	1.3	0.0	0.0	0.6	3.3	0.9	12.1
Atlanta, GA	68.0	8.7	1.2	0.5	0.1	0.1	1.2	1.8	18.5
Austin, TX	63.4	7.7	1.0	0.0	0.0	0.4	1.8	1.4	24.2
Baltimore, MD	69.2	6.9	2.7	0.5	0.5	0.2	2.2	1.6	16.1
Billings, MT	76.5	10.5	1.0	0.0	0.0	0.5	2.3	1.0	8.2
Boise City, ID	71.7	8.3	0.3	0.0	0.0	1.1	2.2	1.4	15.1
Boston, MA	58.6	6.3	2.6	4.6	1.4	1.0	4.7	2.0	18.7
Boulder, CO	55.6	5.7	3.1	0.0	0.0	3.0	3.8	0.9	27.9
Cape Coral, FL	72.7	9.4	0.4	0.0	0.0	0.6	1.1	1.8	13.8
Cedar Rapids, IA	76.8	6.5	0.5	0.0	0.0	0.2	1.9	0.8	13.3
Charleston, SC	75.3	7.8	0.6	0.0	0.0	0.5	1.7	1.2	12.9
Charlotte, NC	69.3	8.1	0.7	0.1	0.0	0.1	1.2	1.5	19.0
Chicago, IL	63.6	7.8	3.3	2.9	2.0	0.6	2.8	1.6	15.6
Cincinnati, OH	75.0	7.7	1.3	0.0	0.0	0.2	1.8	1.1	12.9
Clarksville, TN	79.6	9.5	0.4	0.0	0.0	0.2	2.4	1.5	6.5
Cleveland, OH	74.3	7.4	1.9	0.1	0.0	0.2	2.1	1.3	12.6
College Station, TX	75.1	9.5	1.3	0.0	0.0	1.0	2.1	1.3	9.7
Colorado Springs, CO	70.5	9.0	0.3	0.0	0.0	0.4	3.3	1.1	15.4
Columbia, MO	76.0	8.8	0.7	0.0	0.0	0.7	3.8	1.0	8.9
Columbia, SC	76.2	8.1	0.5	0.0	0.0	0.1	3.5	1.7	9.9
Columbus, OH	72.2	6.8	1.1	0.0	0.0	0.2	1.9	1.1	16.6
Dallas, TX	71.2	9.4	0.5	0.1	0.1	0.1	1.2	1.5	15.9
Davenport, IA	80.1	7.2	0.8	0.0	0.0	0.1	2.4	0.9	8.4
Denver, CO	65.0	7.3	1.6	0.1	0.1	0.7	2.0	2.0	21.2
Des Moines, IA	74.3	7.9	0.4	0.0	0.0	0.2	1.6	1.2	14.3
Detroit, MI	74.8	7.6	1.0	0.0	0.0	0.2	1.3	1.2	13.8
Durham, NC	65.1	7.4	2.2	0.0	0.0	0.7	2.5	1.5	20.6
El Paso, TX	76.3	11.4	0.9	0.0	0.0	0.1	1.5	2.0	7.8
Eugene, OR	67.4	8.9	1.9	0.0	0.0	2.8	4.1	1.1	13.9
Fargo, ND	78.5	6.8	0.7	0.0	0.0	0.3	2.8	1.6	9.3
Fort Collins, CO	68.4	5.6	0.9	0.0	0.0	2.4	2.8	1.1	18.9
Fort Wayne, IN	79.9	9.1	0.7	0.0	0.0	0.3	1.2	0.7	8.1
Fort Worth, TX	71.2	9.4	0.5	0.1	0.1	0.1	1.2	1.5	15.9
Gainesville, FL	71.5	8.8	2.4	0.0	0.0	1.6	2.9	1.5	11.2
Green Bay, WI	78.7	7.8	0.4	0.0	0.0	0.2	1.7	0.9	10.4
Greensboro, NC	76.6	8.9	1.0	0.0	0.0	0.1	1.6	1.6	10.3
Honolulu, HI	64.0	13.7	5.2	0.0	0.0	1.0	5.0	2.6	8.4
Houston, TX	73.5	9.7	1.4	0.0	0.0	0.2	1.2	2.0	11.9
Huntsville, AL	78.3	6.8	0.2	0.0	0.0	0.0	0.8	1.1	12.7
Indianapolis, IN	74.5	8.4	0.6	0.0	0.0	0.3	1.3	0.9	14.0
Jacksonville, FL	72.1	8.2	0.7	0.0	0.0	0.4	1.1	1.8	15.6
Kansas City, MO	75.0	6.9	0.6	0.0	0.0	0.1	1.1	1.1	15.2
Lafayette, LA	82.4	6.3	0.3	0.0	0.0	0.3	1.8	1.3	7.7
Las Vegas, NV	72.6	10.3	2.3	0.0	0.0	0.2	1.2	2.6	10.7
Lexington, KY	76.1	8.6	0.9	0.0	0.0	0.4	2.5	0.8	10.7
Lincoln, NE	76.3	8.5	0.8	0.0	0.0	0.8	3.0	0.7	9.9
Little Rock, AR	79.2	8.8	0.5	0.0	0.0	0.1	1.2	1.0	9.1
Los Angeles, CA	67.1	9.2	2.9	0.3	0.1	0.6	2.3	1.9	15.5
Louisville, KY	76.0	8.4	1.1	0.0	0.0	0.2	1.5	1.2	11.6
Madison, WI	67.3	5.9	2.6	0.0	0.0	1.6	4.8	1.1	16.7
Manchester, NH	72.9	7.4	0.4	0.1	0.1	0.2	1.7	1.1	16.1

Table continued on following page.

Metro Area	Car/Truck/Van		Public Transportation			Bicycle	Walked	Other Means	Worked at Home
	Drove Alone	Car-pooled	Bus	Subway	Railroad				
McAllen, TX	75.8	10.3	0.2	0.0	0.0	0.1	1.2	3.7	8.6
Memphis, TN	79.5	9.2	0.4	0.0	0.0	0.1	1.0	1.1	8.6
Miami, FL	71.3	9.2	2.0	0.2	0.1	0.4	1.6	2.3	12.9
Midland, TX	79.8	12.0	0.3	0.0	0.0	0.2	1.1	1.3	5.2
Milwaukee, WI	73.8	7.1	2.1	0.0	0.0	0.3	2.2	0.9	13.5
Minneapolis, MN	67.7	7.1	2.2	0.0	0.0	0.5	2.0	1.4	19.0
Nashville, TN	72.4	8.2	0.7	0.0	0.0	0.1	1.1	1.2	16.3
New Orleans, LA	73.0	9.7	1.8	0.0	0.0	0.9	3.1	1.9	9.6
New York, NY	45.5	6.1	6.4	15.6	2.6	0.8	5.4	2.7	14.9
Oklahoma City, OK	78.1	9.0	0.3	0.0	0.0	0.2	1.6	1.3	9.5
Omaha, NE	75.8	7.8	0.6	0.0	0.0	0.1	1.5	1.1	13.0
Orlando, FL	70.8	9.2	1.0	0.0	0.1	0.3	1.2	1.8	15.6
Philadelphia, PA	64.4	7.0	3.4	1.5	1.3	0.6	3.2	1.7	16.8
Phoenix, AZ	66.9	9.7	1.0	0.0	0.0	0.5	1.4	2.0	18.5
Pittsburgh, PA	69.9	6.9	3.2	0.2	0.0	0.2	2.9	1.4	15.4
Portland, OR	62.7	7.7	2.6	0.2	0.1	1.4	3.1	2.0	20.4
Providence, RI	74.9	8.1	1.1	0.1	0.7	0.3	2.6	1.5	10.9
Provo, UT	66.7	10.1	1.2	0.0	0.6	0.5	2.9	1.0	17.1
Raleigh, NC	67.0	6.5	0.5	0.0	0.0	0.2	1.1	1.3	23.4
Reno, NV	70.2	12.5	1.8	0.0	0.0	0.4	2.2	2.1	10.8
Richmond, VA	71.6	7.3	1.0	0.0	0.1	0.3	1.7	1.2	16.7
Rochester, MN	69.6	9.9	2.4	0.0	0.0	0.6	3.5	1.1	12.8
Sacramento, CA	67.7	8.6	0.8	0.1	0.1	1.1	1.8	1.9	17.9
Saint Louis, MO	75.6	6.6	1.1	0.1	0.0	0.2	1.5	1.1	13.8
Saint Paul, MN	67.7	7.1	2.2	0.0	0.0	0.5	2.0	1.4	19.0
Salem, OR	70.9	11.0	1.1	0.0	0.0	0.7	2.4	1.3	12.6
Salt Lake City, UT	67.0	10.0	1.2	0.2	0.2	0.5	1.7	1.7	17.5
San Antonio, TX	71.5	10.9	1.3	0.0	0.0	0.2	1.5	1.5	13.0
San Diego, CA	67.6	8.2	1.6	0.1	0.1	0.5	3.1	2.0	16.9
San Francisco, CA	50.9	8.2	4.7	3.9	1.1	1.5	3.9	2.6	23.2
San Jose, CA	62.1	9.0	1.5	0.2	0.6	1.3	2.0	1.7	21.5
Santa Rosa, CA	71.0	9.2	0.7	0.1	0.2	0.7	2.4	1.4	14.4
Savannah, GA	76.6	9.4	1.0	0.0	0.0	0.7	1.7	1.5	9.0
Seattle, WA	59.1	8.2	4.7	0.1	0.3	0.8	3.3	1.8	21.6
Sioux Falls, SD	79.3	7.2	0.5	0.0	0.0	0.1	2.0	0.8	10.1
Tampa, FL	69.7	8.1	0.8	0.0	0.0	0.5	1.2	1.8	17.8
Tucson, AZ	70.7	9.6	1.5	0.0	0.0	1.0	1.9	1.5	13.8
Tulsa, OK	78.2	9.0	0.3	0.0	0.0	0.2	1.2	1.2	9.8
Virginia Beach, VA	75.8	8.2	1.0	0.0	0.0	0.3	2.4	1.6	10.7
Washington, DC	56.4	8.0	2.9	4.4	0.4	0.7	2.7	1.9	22.6
Wichita, KS	80.6	8.6	0.4	0.0	0.0	0.3	1.4	1.3	7.3
Wilmington, NC	73.9	7.8	0.2	0.0	0.0	0.3	1.2	1.1	15.5
Winston-Salem, NC	77.9	8.7	0.5	0.0	0.0	0.1	1.2	1.1	10.6
U.S.	70.2	8.5	1.7	1.3	0.4	0.4	2.4	1.6	13.5

Note: Figures are percentages and cover workers 16 years of age and older; Figures cover the Metropolitan Statistical Area (MSA)
Source: U.S. Census Bureau, 2019-2023 American Community Survey 5-Year Estimates

Travel Time to Work: City

City	Less Than 10 Minutes	10 to 19 Minutes	20 to 29 Minutes	30 to 44 Minutes	45 to 59 Minutes	60 to 89 Minutes	90 Minutes or More
Albuquerque, NM	11.7	36.0	27.6	17.3	3.0	2.5	1.9
Anchorage, AK	15.6	44.8	23.3	11.1	2.3	1.4	1.5
Ann Arbor, MI	12.9	45.8	18.9	13.6	5.8	2.3	0.7
Athens, GA	17.2	45.0	17.6	10.5	3.8	3.6	2.3
Atlanta, GA	7.8	29.8	25.5	22.5	6.3	5.1	3.0
Austin, TX	9.6	33.4	24.5	21.5	6.1	3.5	1.4
Baltimore, MD	7.2	24.8	24.3	24.3	8.5	6.9	4.0
Billings, MT	19.3	51.9	18.3	6.8	1.2	1.2	1.2
Boise City, ID	14.3	44.2	25.5	11.5	1.7	1.6	1.2
Boston, MA	6.9	21.3	20.7	28.8	11.4	8.6	2.3
Boulder, CO	20.2	44.2	16.9	9.4	5.0	2.9	1.3
Cape Coral, FL	7.8	24.9	22.7	24.9	10.5	6.5	2.7
Cedar Rapids, IA	19.8	47.9	17.9	8.7	1.8	2.5	1.4
Charleston, SC	11.8	32.8	24.8	19.0	7.2	2.5	1.8
Charlotte, NC	9.1	29.7	27.1	23.2	6.1	3.0	1.9
Chicago, IL	5.2	17.2	19.2	29.8	14.6	10.9	3.0
Cincinnati, OH	11.2	34.5	26.3	19.1	3.8	2.8	2.2
Clarksville, TN	10.5	32.6	25.9	13.1	7.3	8.3	2.3
Cleveland, OH	10.5	35.0	27.3	19.4	3.3	2.6	1.9
College Station, TX	17.5	54.7	15.3	7.9	1.4	1.8	1.5
Colorado Springs, CO	11.6	35.7	27.6	16.9	3.0	3.0	2.1
Columbia, MO	19.5	54.4	14.3	7.2	2.1	1.2	1.3
Columbia, SC	27.7	37.4	19.1	10.0	2.7	1.2	1.8
Columbus, OH	10.3	35.1	31.0	17.2	3.1	2.1	1.3
Dallas, TX	8.8	28.5	23.6	24.7	7.4	5.6	1.5
Davenport, IA	15.3	45.9	24.3	8.4	2.9	2.0	1.1
Denver, CO	8.6	28.3	25.3	25.9	6.5	3.9	1.5
Des Moines, IA	14.1	43.0	25.7	11.9	2.0	1.9	1.5
Detroit, MI	8.1	30.2	27.0	22.3	6.0	4.0	2.3
Durham, NC	10.2	37.8	25.1	17.8	4.8	2.6	1.6
El Paso, TX	9.3	33.5	28.5	20.1	4.3	2.4	1.9
Eugene, OR	16.3	50.9	19.5	7.2	2.2	2.1	1.9
Fargo, ND	20.1	56.1	15.1	4.6	1.5	1.7	0.9
Fort Collins, CO	15.6	45.7	19.3	10.1	4.6	3.3	1.4
Fort Wayne, IN	13.1	38.1	27.8	13.7	2.9	2.2	2.2
Fort Worth, TX	7.4	29.2	23.5	23.5	8.9	5.7	1.8
Gainesville, FL	16.1	43.8	23.4	11.6	2.6	1.6	0.9
Green Bay, WI	18.1	47.5	18.0	9.1	3.9	1.9	1.5
Greensboro, NC	13.4	40.9	22.3	14.6	3.5	3.0	2.4
Honolulu, HI	9.0	39.2	22.3	20.5	4.5	3.4	1.2
Houston, TX	7.5	25.3	23.6	27.7	8.6	5.5	1.8
Huntsville, AL	13.9	39.8	27.2	14.9	2.2	1.2	0.7
Indianapolis, IN	9.8	29.6	28.6	23.1	4.5	2.5	2.0
Jacksonville, FL	8.7	29.0	28.0	24.9	5.6	2.5	1.3
Kansas City, MO	11.7	35.0	28.3	18.3	3.5	1.8	1.4
Lafayette, LA	16.4	44.8	19.9	11.5	2.3	3.6	1.6
Las Vegas, NV	7.3	24.0	30.9	27.3	6.0	2.6	1.9
Lexington, KY	13.0	40.1	26.4	13.7	2.7	2.3	1.9
Lincoln, NE	16.8	46.0	22.5	8.9	2.9	2.1	1.0
Little Rock, AR	15.3	46.6	22.6	10.7	2.2	1.7	0.9
Los Angeles, CA	6.3	22.2	19.9	28.5	10.4	9.4	3.3
Louisville, KY	10.1	31.8	31.9	19.1	3.6	2.0	1.4
Madison, WI	14.4	40.3	25.5	14.3	3.2	1.7	0.6
Manchester, NH	12.9	35.1	23.0	16.0	6.2	5.1	1.9
McAllen, TX	14.6	39.5	23.9	15.2	2.9	2.1	1.7

Table continued on following page.

City	Less Than 10 Minutes	10 to 19 Minutes	20 to 29 Minutes	30 to 44 Minutes	45 to 59 Minutes	60 to 89 Minutes	90 Minutes or More
Memphis, TN	11.2	31.8	33.7	18.2	2.7	1.5	1.0
Miami, FL	6.4	24.1	25.7	27.6	8.7	6.0	1.5
Midland, TX	16.2	45.2	18.6	11.9	4.0	2.3	1.9
Milwaukee, WI	10.6	36.2	26.5	18.9	3.4	2.9	1.6
Minneapolis, MN	8.3	36.1	28.8	19.2	4.2	2.4	1.0
Nashville, TN	9.2	28.7	26.8	23.2	7.0	3.8	1.3
New Orleans, LA	11.9	35.1	24.3	18.7	5.2	3.1	1.7
New York, NY	4.4	12.7	14.0	27.0	16.1	18.7	7.1
Oklahoma City, OK	10.4	35.0	28.8	19.2	3.6	1.5	1.6
Omaha, NE	14.6	41.3	26.4	12.4	2.3	1.8	1.2
Orlando, FL	7.5	26.1	27.4	26.5	6.4	3.9	2.2
Philadelphia, PA	6.7	19.7	20.8	28.1	12.0	9.2	3.5
Phoenix, AZ	9.0	26.7	26.8	24.6	7.1	4.2	1.6
Pittsburgh, PA	10.3	34.0	26.0	20.5	4.6	3.2	1.5
Portland, OR	9.3	29.9	27.1	22.5	6.1	3.7	1.5
Providence, RI	11.0	36.1	20.6	16.8	6.7	6.1	2.7
Provo, UT	20.5	44.9	16.6	10.2	4.4	2.3	1.1
Raleigh, NC	10.3	33.4	26.8	19.9	5.4	2.5	1.7
Reno, NV	15.1	39.7	23.5	13.2	4.9	2.4	1.2
Richmond, VA	11.4	37.4	27.0	16.8	2.9	2.8	1.7
Rochester, MN	18.3	54.5	14.7	6.1	2.8	2.7	0.9
Sacramento, CA	8.9	32.2	25.8	21.3	5.1	3.5	3.2
Saint Louis, MO	9.9	36.2	27.2	19.5	3.2	2.5	1.6
Saint Paul, MN	10.5	35.0	27.6	19.0	4.4	2.1	1.4
Salem, OR	14.6	41.5	18.2	12.3	5.5	6.3	1.6
Salt Lake City, UT	14.6	45.2	20.6	12.7	3.5	2.1	1.3
San Antonio, TX	9.5	30.7	26.1	22.2	5.9	3.7	1.8
San Diego, CA	8.2	33.2	27.9	20.4	5.4	3.3	1.7
San Francisco, CA	5.3	21.2	22.1	28.8	10.6	8.9	3.1
San Jose, CA	5.9	26.5	25.5	25.0	8.6	5.7	2.7
Santa Rosa, CA	13.1	42.1	19.4	14.4	4.5	3.6	2.9
Savannah, GA	14.0	40.1	23.5	14.7	4.4	2.3	1.0
Seattle, WA	8.0	26.0	24.5	26.4	9.2	4.4	1.4
Sioux Falls, SD	15.9	52.2	22.0	6.2	1.5	1.0	1.2
Tampa, FL	10.8	31.4	22.8	22.5	6.5	4.2	1.8
Tucson, AZ	12.3	34.4	25.8	19.3	4.6	2.1	1.4
Tulsa, OK	14.0	46.0	25.7	9.8	1.8	1.4	1.3
Virginia Beach, VA	10.2	31.3	27.8	21.8	5.4	2.1	1.4
Washington, DC	5.2	19.2	22.5	33.1	11.8	6.3	1.9
Wichita, KS	14.0	46.0	25.9	9.5	1.8	1.4	1.4
Wilmington, NC	16.7	46.7	20.7	10.2	2.9	1.2	1.6
Winston-Salem, NC	14.4	39.6	23.0	14.0	4.1	2.9	2.0
U.S.	12.6	28.6	21.2	20.8	8.1	6.0	2.8

Note: Figures are percentages and include workers 16 years old and over
Source: U.S. Census Bureau, 2019-2023 American Community Survey 5-Year Estimates

Travel Time to Work: Metro Area

Metro Area	Less Than 10 Minutes	10 to 19 Minutes	20 to 29 Minutes	30 to 44 Minutes	45 to 59 Minutes	60 to 89 Minutes	90 Minutes or More
Albuquerque, NM	11.5	31.1	25.0	20.6	5.8	3.8	2.3
Anchorage, AK	14.7	40.5	21.8	11.4	5.1	4.0	2.6
Ann Arbor, MI	11.2	33.3	25.2	18.5	7.2	3.5	1.2
Athens, GA	13.4	38.2	22.3	13.7	5.2	4.1	3.0
Atlanta, GA	7.3	22.7	20.1	25.5	12.0	9.0	3.3
Austin, TX	9.5	27.1	21.8	24.0	9.7	6.0	1.9
Baltimore, MD	8.2	24.1	21.7	24.6	10.7	7.5	3.1
Billings, MT	18.7	42.7	20.8	11.0	2.7	2.1	2.0
Boise City, ID	13.4	31.8	25.2	19.9	5.8	2.3	1.5
Boston, MA	9.4	22.9	19.3	24.4	11.2	9.6	3.1
Boulder, CO	15.0	34.3	20.7	17.0	6.9	4.4	1.6
Cape Coral, FL	8.8	24.5	22.6	25.2	10.2	6.3	2.4
Cedar Rapids, IA	19.1	39.1	20.6	13.0	4.3	2.6	1.3
Charleston, SC	9.1	26.3	23.3	24.0	9.9	5.4	2.1
Charlotte, NC	9.8	27.9	22.9	23.4	9.2	4.9	2.0
Chicago, IL	8.9	22.3	19.5	25.3	11.9	9.3	2.9
Cincinnati, OH	10.7	28.7	25.2	23.3	6.9	3.4	1.7
Clarksville, TN	14.1	30.9	22.8	15.1	7.2	6.9	3.0
Cleveland, OH	12.0	28.7	25.7	22.7	6.4	2.8	1.7
College Station, TX	16.2	48.4	17.1	11.0	3.2	2.3	1.9
Colorado Springs, CO	12.1	32.3	26.6	19.0	4.3	3.5	2.2
Columbia, MO	17.1	44.0	20.2	11.8	3.4	1.7	1.8
Columbia, SC	12.7	28.9	23.6	22.0	7.3	3.2	2.3
Columbus, OH	11.7	29.8	27.5	20.7	5.8	3.1	1.5
Dallas, TX	8.8	25.5	21.7	25.3	10.2	6.5	2.0
Davenport, IA	18.0	35.9	26.0	12.4	3.7	2.6	1.4
Denver, CO	8.8	25.1	23.7	26.4	9.0	5.1	1.9
Des Moines, IA	15.2	35.6	26.7	15.6	3.8	1.7	1.3
Detroit, MI	10.0	27.0	23.7	24.2	8.5	4.8	1.7
Durham, NC	10.6	32.7	25.3	20.0	6.2	3.8	1.5
El Paso, TX	9.7	32.0	27.4	21.6	4.9	2.4	2.0
Eugene, OR	16.0	43.1	21.9	11.6	3.0	2.6	1.8
Fargo, ND	17.7	51.4	18.0	7.1	2.4	1.9	1.5
Fort Collins, CO	13.9	36.1	21.5	15.8	6.0	4.6	2.1
Fort Wayne, IN	13.8	34.9	28.2	15.9	3.4	1.9	2.0
Fort Worth, TX	8.8	25.5	21.7	25.3	10.2	6.5	2.0
Gainesville, FL	12.2	32.8	25.2	19.2	5.7	3.2	1.7
Green Bay, WI	16.8	39.6	22.4	13.1	4.3	2.1	1.7
Greensboro, NC	13.3	34.4	23.7	18.1	5.0	3.2	2.2
Honolulu, HI	9.9	27.1	20.0	25.2	9.1	6.5	2.1
Houston, TX	7.7	22.9	20.7	26.9	11.5	7.9	2.5
Huntsville, AL	10.8	30.8	28.1	22.2	4.9	1.9	1.2
Indianapolis, IN	11.3	27.6	24.2	24.6	7.2	3.3	1.9
Jacksonville, FL	9.2	26.2	24.8	26.0	8.2	3.9	1.7
Kansas City, MO	12.4	30.9	26.3	20.9	5.7	2.4	1.4
Lafayette, LA	13.7	32.9	21.8	19.4	5.2	3.8	3.2
Las Vegas, NV	7.9	27.2	29.2	25.9	5.3	2.6	2.0
Lexington, KY	14.4	35.7	24.4	16.8	4.4	2.5	1.8
Lincoln, NE	17.0	42.8	23.2	10.6	3.2	2.3	1.0
Little Rock, AR	13.2	32.4	22.2	21.1	6.6	3.1	1.5
Los Angeles, CA	7.3	25.0	20.8	25.4	9.7	8.5	3.3
Louisville, KY	10.6	29.6	28.4	20.9	6.1	2.9	1.5
Madison, WI	15.8	32.4	25.5	17.6	5.0	2.5	1.1
Manchester, NH	11.5	29.3	21.6	19.8	8.2	6.9	2.8
McAllen, TX	15.4	33.5	24.2	18.6	3.8	2.4	2.2

Table continued on following page.

Metro Area	Less Than 10 Minutes	10 to 19 Minutes	20 to 29 Minutes	30 to 44 Minutes	45 to 59 Minutes	60 to 89 Minutes	90 Minutes or More
Memphis, TN	11.0	26.8	27.9	23.6	6.6	2.6	1.4
Miami, FL	6.8	23.2	23.1	27.1	9.9	7.2	2.6
Midland, TX	15.7	40.3	20.4	14.4	4.2	2.3	2.7
Milwaukee, WI	12.3	32.4	26.0	20.7	4.7	2.5	1.4
Minneapolis, MN	11.1	29.6	25.3	22.3	6.9	3.5	1.4
Nashville, TN	9.6	26.0	21.1	24.2	10.7	6.6	1.8
New Orleans, LA	11.4	31.5	22.9	21.7	6.6	3.9	2.0
New York, NY	7.3	19.0	16.6	23.9	12.6	14.2	6.4
Oklahoma City, OK	12.2	31.4	25.4	21.2	5.6	2.6	1.7
Omaha, NE	14.0	36.2	27.4	15.9	3.5	1.8	1.2
Orlando, FL	7.1	23.4	22.2	27.8	10.6	6.3	2.5
Philadelphia, PA	10.0	24.4	20.8	24.1	10.6	7.3	2.8
Phoenix, AZ	10.2	26.0	24.3	23.7	8.7	5.3	1.8
Pittsburgh, PA	12.3	27.5	21.7	22.5	8.7	5.3	2.0
Portland, OR	11.5	29.0	23.7	21.7	7.7	4.5	1.8
Providence, RI	11.7	30.0	21.3	20.3	7.9	6.1	2.9
Provo, UT	17.2	34.7	19.9	17.0	6.2	3.7	1.3
Raleigh, NC	9.0	26.8	23.5	24.3	9.6	5.0	1.8
Reno, NV	12.8	34.1	24.2	17.6	6.0	3.6	1.6
Richmond, VA	9.7	28.3	26.8	23.2	6.5	3.2	2.2
Rochester, MN	18.1	41.6	18.7	12.5	4.6	2.9	1.6
Sacramento, CA	10.3	28.8	22.7	22.9	7.1	4.4	3.8
Saint Louis, MO	11.3	28.2	24.6	23.4	7.3	3.5	1.6
Saint Paul, MN	11.1	29.6	25.3	22.3	6.9	3.5	1.4
Salem, OR	15.0	32.4	19.8	17.1	7.4	6.5	1.8
Salt Lake City, UT	11.1	33.7	26.6	19.0	5.5	2.9	1.3
San Antonio, TX	9.5	27.1	24.0	23.8	8.3	5.1	2.3
San Diego, CA	8.5	29.3	25.1	23.4	7.1	4.5	2.1
San Francisco, CA	7.5	24.2	18.7	23.7	11.0	10.8	4.1
San Jose, CA	7.5	28.4	24.3	23.1	8.2	5.8	2.7
Santa Rosa, CA	14.0	34.1	19.3	17.3	6.3	5.6	3.4
Savannah, GA	10.5	29.3	23.7	22.8	8.5	3.7	1.5
Seattle, WA	8.7	23.7	21.6	24.7	10.5	7.8	3.0
Sioux Falls, SD	17.3	43.1	23.9	10.5	2.5	1.3	1.3
Tampa, FL	9.6	26.6	20.9	23.8	10.2	6.5	2.5
Tucson, AZ	11.0	29.4	25.2	23.2	6.8	2.6	1.7
Tulsa, OK	13.4	34.0	26.6	17.7	4.7	2.2	1.5
Virginia Beach, VA	10.5	31.2	24.1	21.7	6.9	3.9	1.8
Washington, DC	6.5	20.1	19.2	26.3	13.2	11.0	3.6
Wichita, KS	15.7	38.0	25.6	14.9	2.8	1.6	1.4
Wilmington, NC	12.4	35.0	23.4	18.2	5.8	3.0	2.3
Winston-Salem, NC	12.5	32.1	24.5	19.3	5.8	3.5	2.2
U.S.	12.6	28.6	21.2	20.8	8.1	6.0	2.8

Note: Figures are percentages and include workers 16 years old and over; Figures cover the Metropolitan Statistical Area (MSA)
Source: U.S. Census Bureau, 2019-2023 American Community Survey 5-Year Estimates

2024 Presidential Election Results

City	Area Covered	Trump (Rep.)	Harris (Dem.)	Stein (Green)	Kennedy (Ind.)	Oliver (Lib.)	Other
Albuquerque, NM	Bernalillo County	38.2	59.2	0.7	1.0	0.5	0.5
Anchorage, AK	State of Alaska	54.5	41.4	0.7	1.7	0.9	0.8
Ann Arbor, MI	Washtenaw County	26.5	70.7	1.3	0.4	0.4	0.7
Athens, GA	Clarke County	30.2	68.3	0.5	0.0	0.6	0.4
Atlanta, GA	Fulton County	26.8	71.3	0.6	0.0	0.5	0.8
Austin, TX	Travis County	29.2	68.3	1.0	0.0	0.8	0.6
Baltimore, MD	Baltimore City	12.1	84.6	1.4	0.8	0.4	0.7
Billings, MT	Yellowstone County	62.0	34.9	0.4	1.9	0.8	0.0
Boise City, ID	Ada County	53.8	43.4	0.4	1.3	0.6	0.5
Boston, MA	Suffolk County	22.2	74.3	1.1	0.0	0.4	2.0
Boulder, CO	Boulder County	20.8	76.5	0.8	0.9	0.6	0.4
Cape Coral, FL	Lee County	63.6	35.3	0.2	0.0	0.2	0.6
Cedar Rapids, IA	Linn County	44.1	54.0	0.0	0.8	0.5	0.6
Charleston, SC	Charleston County	46.3	51.9	0.5	0.0	0.8	0.6
Charlotte, NC	Mecklenburg County	32.5	65.2	0.7	0.0	0.5	1.1
Chicago, IL	Cook County	28.1	69.6	0.9	1.2	0.1	0.2
Cincinnati, OH	Hamilton County	41.7	56.5	0.4	0.0	0.6	0.8
Clarksville, TN	Montgomery County	58.3	39.9	0.3	0.8	0.0	0.7
Cleveland, OH	Cuyahoga County	33.6	64.7	0.5	0.0	0.4	0.8
College Station, TX	Brazos County	61.6	36.8	0.6	0.0	0.9	0.1
Colorado Springs, CO	El Paso County	53.5	43.7	0.5	1.1	0.8	0.4
Columbia, MO	Boone County	43.9	53.6	0.9	0.0	1.1	0.4
Columbia, SC	Richland County	31.8	66.4	0.4	0.0	0.5	0.9
Columbus, OH	Franklin County	34.9	63.0	0.6	0.0	0.6	0.9
Dallas, TX	Dallas County	37.8	59.9	1.1	0.0	0.7	0.5
Davenport, IA	Scott County	51.0	47.1	0.0	0.8	0.5	0.6
Denver, CO	Denver County	20.6	76.6	0.9	0.8	0.6	0.5
Des Moines, IA	Polk County	43.7	54.5	0.0	0.6	0.5	0.7
Detroit, MI	Wayne County	33.6	62.5	2.4	0.4	0.3	0.8
Durham, NC	Durham County	18.2	79.8	0.7	0.0	0.4	0.8
El Paso, TX	El Paso County	41.7	56.8	0.6	0.0	0.6	0.3
Eugene, OR	Lane County	36.6	59.5	0.9	1.5	0.4	1.1
Fargo, ND	Cass County	52.7	44.4	0.0	0.0	1.8	1.1
Fort Collins, CO	Larimer County	39.7	57.3	0.5	1.2	0.8	0.5
Fort Wayne, IN	Allen County	55.2	42.7	0.0	0.9	0.8	0.4
Fort Worth, TX	Tarrant County	51.8	46.7	0.7	0.0	0.7	0.1
Gainesville, FL	Alachua County	38.6	59.4	0.6	0.0	0.5	0.9
Green Bay, WI	Brown County	53.0	45.5	0.2	0.5	0.3	0.5
Greensboro, NC	Guilford County	38.3	60.0	0.5	0.0	0.4	0.8
Honolulu, HI	Honolulu County	38.3	59.9	0.7	0.0	0.5	0.5
Houston, TX	Harris County	46.4	51.9	1.0	0.0	0.6	0.1
Huntsville, AL	Madison County	53.4	44.4	0.3	0.8	0.5	0.6
Indianapolis, IN	Marion County	35.1	62.6	0.0	0.9	0.8	0.7
Jacksonville, FL	Duval County	49.9	48.5	0.5	0.0	0.4	0.7
Kansas City, MO	Jackson County	39.3	58.5	0.8	0.0	0.8	0.6
Lafayette, LA	Lafayette Parish	64.8	33.5	0.4	0.4	0.4	0.5
Las Vegas, NV	Clark County	47.8	50.4	0.0	0.0	0.4	1.4
Lexington, KY	Fayette County	39.8	57.9	0.7	0.9	0.5	0.2
Lincoln, NE	Lancaster County	46.8	51.0	0.4	0.0	0.8	1.1
Little Rock, AR	Pulaski County	37.7	59.8	0.6	1.1	0.5	0.3
Los Angeles, CA	Los Angeles County	31.9	64.8	1.1	1.2	0.3	0.6
Louisville, KY	Jefferson County	40.6	57.1	0.6	0.7	0.3	0.6
Madison, WI	Dane County	23.4	74.9	0.5	0.4	0.3	0.6
Manchester, NH	Hillsborough County	47.8	50.7	0.5	0.0	0.5	0.5
McAllen, TX	Hidalgo County	51.0	48.1	0.5	0.0	0.4	0.0

Table continued on following page.

City	Area Covered	Trump (Rep.)	Harris (Dem.)	Stein (Green)	Kennedy (Ind.)	Oliver (Lib.)	Other
Memphis, TN	Shelby County	36.2	61.5	0.6	0.8	0.0	1.0
Miami, FL	Miami-Dade County	55.2	43.8	0.3	0.0	0.2	0.5
Midland, TX	Midland County	79.6	19.2	0.2	0.0	0.6	0.3
Milwaukee, WI	Milwaukee County	29.7	68.2	0.7	0.4	0.2	0.7
Minneapolis, MN	Hennepin County	27.4	69.8	0.8	0.6	0.5	1.0
Nashville, TN	Davidson County	35.0	62.2	0.6	0.9	0.0	1.2
New Orleans, LA	Orleans Parish	15.2	82.2	0.9	0.3	0.5	1.0
New York, NY	New York City	30.0	68.1	0.9	0.0	0.0	1.0
New York, NY	Bronx County	27.0	71.9	0.6	0.0	0.0	0.5
New York, NY	Kings County	27.4	70.4	1.1	0.0	0.0	1.1
New York, NY	New York County	17.2	80.8	0.7	0.0	0.0	1.3
New York, NY	Queens County	37.0	61.1	1.2	0.0	0.0	0.7
New York, NY	Richmond County	63.9	34.6	0.9	0.0	0.0	0.6
Oklahoma City, OK	Oklahoma County	49.7	48.0	0.0	1.1	0.8	0.4
Omaha, NE	Douglas County	43.9	54.1	0.4	0.0	0.6	1.0
Orlando, FL	Orange County	42.4	55.9	0.7	0.0	0.3	0.7
Philadelphia, PA	Philadelphia County	19.9	78.6	0.9	0.0	0.3	0.3
Phoenix, AZ	Maricopa County	51.0	47.5	0.6	0.0	0.5	0.4
Pittsburgh, PA	Allegheny County	39.2	59.4	0.5	0.0	0.5	0.5
Portland, OR	Multnomah County	17.1	78.7	1.5	1.0	0.3	1.4
Providence, RI	Providence County	41.7	55.7	0.6	0.9	0.3	0.8
Provo, UT	Utah County	66.7	27.8	0.5	0.0	1.4	3.6
Raleigh, NC	Wake County	36.2	61.7	0.8	0.0	0.5	0.8
Reno, NV	Washoe County	48.3	49.3	0.0	0.0	0.5	1.8
Richmond, VA	Richmond City	64.7	34.5	0.2	0.0	0.2	0.3
Rochester, MN	Olmsted County	43.4	54.0	0.6	0.8	0.5	0.7
Sacramento, CA	Sacramento County	38.4	58.1	1.2	1.4	0.5	0.5
Saint Louis, MO	St. Louis City	16.5	80.7	1.2	0.0	0.7	0.8
Saint Paul, MN	Ramsey County	27.1	70.2	0.8	0.5	0.5	0.9
Salem, OR	Marion County	49.2	47.2	0.6	1.7	0.4	0.9
Salt Lake City, UT	Salt Lake County	42.9	52.9	0.7	0.0	1.0	2.5
San Antonio, TX	Bexar County	44.4	54.1	0.6	0.0	0.6	0.4
San Diego, CA	San Diego County	40.1	56.9	1.0	1.1	0.5	0.4
San Francisco, CA	San Francisco County	15.5	80.3	1.7	1.1	0.5	0.9
San Jose, CA	Santa Clara County	28.1	68.0	1.6	1.2	0.5	0.5
Santa Rosa, CA	Sonoma County	25.2	71.4	0.9	1.5	0.4	0.4
Savannah, GA	Chatham County	40.4	58.3	0.3	0.0	0.4	0.7
Seattle, WA	King County	22.3	73.6	1.2	1.0	0.4	1.4
Sioux Falls, SD	Minnehaha County	55.2	42.5	0.0	1.6	0.7	0.0
Tampa, FL	Hillsborough County	50.7	47.6	0.6	0.0	0.4	0.7
Tucson, AZ	Pima County	41.7	56.8	0.6	0.0	0.6	0.4
Tulsa, OK	Tulsa County	56.5	41.3	0.0	1.1	0.7	0.4
Virginia Beach, VA	Virginia Beach City	47.8	50.4	0.4	0.0	0.5	0.9
Washington, DC	District of Columbia	6.5	90.3	0.0	0.9	0.0	2.4
Wichita, KS	Sedgwick County	55.7	42.0	0.1	1.1	0.6	0.5
Wilmington, NC	New Hanover County	49.0	49.6	0.4	0.0	0.4	0.6
Winston-Salem, NC	Forsyth County	42.6	55.8	0.4	0.0	0.4	0.8
U.S.	U.S.	49.7	48.2	0.6	0.5	0.4	0.6

Note: Results are percentages and may not add to 100% due to rounding
Source: Dave Leip's Atlas of U.S. Presidential Elections

House Price Index (HPI)

Metro Area	National Ranking[2]	Quarterly Change (%)	One-Year Change (%)	Five-Year Change (%)	Since 1991Q1 (%)
Albuquerque, NM	152	0.28	4.68	60.38	291.99
Anchorage, AK	120	-2.19	5.44	38.20	272.70
Ann Arbor, MI	111	0.79	5.63	45.12	265.98
Athens, GA	145	0.95	4.82	77.54	363.29
Atlanta, GA	169	-0.09	4.19	66.19	310.49
Austin, TX	237	-1.06	-0.80	47.35	579.98
Baltimore, MD	113	0.13	5.59	41.90	246.61
Billings, MT	211	-0.95	2.58	54.45	434.47
Boise City, ID	156	0.77	4.58	63.16	546.52
Boston, MA[1]	123	0.36	5.29	50.28	365.78
Boulder, CO	218	0.54	2.49	40.60	618.40
Cape Coral, FL	240	-0.39	-2.44	67.84	353.01
Cedar Rapids, IA	204	-0.20	3.04	39.04	206.71
Charleston, SC	84	2.18	6.43	77.86	536.36
Charlotte, NC	175	0.39	4.07	71.74	349.74
Chicago, IL[1]	70	0.05	6.77	43.67	208.59
Cincinnati, OH	93	0.82	6.08	61.42	247.18
Clarksville, TN	(a)	n/a	3.55	67.67	n/a
Cleveland, OH	71	0.34	6.77	57.08	194.72
College Station, TX	(a)	n/a	1.96	50.70	n/a
Colorado Springs, CO	196	-0.38	3.24	49.58	453.42
Columbia, MO	24	0.09	8.46	58.84	279.40
Columbia, SC	61	0.87	6.97	64.02	248.40
Columbus, OH	63	1.20	6.96	61.81	293.84
Dallas, TX[1]	181	0.68	3.91	56.27	350.14
Davenport, IA	143	-0.86	4.87	39.11	236.99
Denver, CO	193	0.30	3.30	43.23	580.34
Des Moines, IA	174	-0.70	4.10	43.67	253.81
Detroit, MI[1]	40	0.25	7.71	52.17	227.11
Durham, NC	150	0.26	4.76	67.43	344.03
El Paso, TX	67	1.00	6.86	63.01	237.09
Eugene, OR	220	-1.37	2.45	48.27	459.38
Fargo, ND	214	-1.86	2.52	33.66	292.25
Fort Collins, CO	215	-0.72	2.52	44.72	544.83
Fort Wayne, IN	32	1.26	7.98	72.59	239.64
Fort Worth, TX[1]	194	0.54	3.30	53.69	324.24
Gainesville, FL	(a)	n/a	5.55	65.26	n/a
Green Bay, WI	103	-1.16	5.89	63.68	299.15
Greensboro, NC	65	0.24	6.92	68.92	226.57
Honolulu, HI	183	-0.33	3.85	35.89	242.48
Houston, TX	195	0.35	3.29	44.19	326.50
Huntsville, AL	76	-1.12	6.65	66.60	239.11
Indianapolis, IN	136	1.08	4.99	59.79	247.41
Jacksonville, FL	168	-0.18	4.19	65.48	401.54
Kansas City, MO	149	-0.76	4.78	56.68	300.63
Lafayette, LA	132	3.26	5.15	25.86	238.79
Las Vegas, NV	44	1.27	7.43	58.90	295.91
Lexington, KY	147	-0.02	4.79	58.94	282.27
Lincoln, NE	60	0.91	6.97	52.28	300.89
Little Rock, AR	197	-1.14	3.23	47.11	222.55
Los Angeles, CA[1]	114	0.65	5.59	48.41	341.40
Louisville, KY	81	0.59	6.45	50.59	291.73
Madison, WI	118	0.61	5.50	54.87	369.35
Manchester, NH	25	-0.15	8.25	67.31	310.83
McAllen, TX	(a)	n/a	8.58	59.26	n/a

Table continued on following page.

Metro Area	National Ranking[2]	Quarterly Change (%)	One-Year Change (%)	Five-Year Change (%)	Since 1991Q1 (%)
Memphis, TN	206	-0.64	2.99	49.80	207.31
Miami, FL[1]	19	2.12	8.69	89.36	668.91
Midland, TX	(a)	n/a	1.09	21.00	n/a
Milwaukee, WI	49	0.11	7.27	55.07	296.31
Minneapolis, MN	153	0.20	4.68	37.75	302.55
Nashville, TN	164	-0.12	4.28	65.94	467.10
New Orleans, LA	233	0.13	0.85	25.47	285.27
New York, NY[1]	34	0.62	7.86	43.82	309.75
Oklahoma City, OK	129	-0.57	5.22	50.62	294.07
Omaha, NE	154	0.12	4.63	51.76	295.39
Orlando, FL	56	2.87	7.06	70.73	377.10
Philadelphia, PA[1]	110	0.84	5.64	41.74	286.32
Phoenix, AZ	200	0.13	3.14	69.09	488.41
Pittsburgh, PA	104	0.17	5.87	45.46	262.85
Portland, OR	182	0.32	3.88	37.41	518.30
Providence, RI	41	0.25	7.70	64.34	289.70
Provo, UT	139	-1.41	4.94	59.50	545.94
Raleigh, NC	185	0.14	3.78	65.05	335.12
Reno, NV	121	0.31	5.40	49.95	361.77
Richmond, VA	98	0.07	5.98	59.60	306.38
Rochester, MN	160	-1.25	4.39	42.16	268.82
Sacramento, CA	198	0.32	3.19	42.05	255.25
Saint Louis, MO	92	1.02	6.12	48.75	237.26
Saint Paul, MN	153	0.20	4.68	37.75	302.55
Salem, OR	209	0.85	2.90	48.54	494.72
Salt Lake City, UT	115	0.53	5.58	59.66	644.94
San Antonio, TX	228	4.07	1.99	49.58	357.13
San Diego, CA	102	1.05	5.91	61.16	410.00
San Francisco, CA[1]	191	0.32	3.50	15.70	376.10
San Jose, CA	221	-0.52	2.35	36.42	433.00
Santa Rosa, CA	192	-0.37	3.47	28.24	304.85
Savannah, GA	225	-1.45	2.18	77.13	438.29
Seattle, WA[1]	91	-0.16	6.14	47.96	484.10
Sioux Falls, SD	224	0.06	2.21	52.27	347.79
Tampa, FL	229	-0.90	1.88	77.61	480.18
Tucson, AZ	223	-1.32	2.30	65.72	364.15
Tulsa, OK	116	1.84	5.52	56.84	272.73
Virginia Beach, VA	64	1.54	6.94	53.57	289.47
Washington, DC[1]	106	-0.50	5.79	38.73	288.38
Wichita, KS	170	-0.42	4.15	57.02	241.93
Wilmington, NC	137	0.32	4.98	74.07	421.24
Winston-Salem, NC	33	1.41	7.91	70.24	245.21
U.S.[3]	–	1.43	4.51	57.13	327.82

Note: The HPI is a weighted repeat sales index. It measures average price changes in repeat sales or refinancings on the same properties. This information is obtained by reviewing repeat mortgage transactions on single-family properties whose mortgages have been purchased or securitized by Fannie Mae or Freddie Mac since January 1975; all figures are for the period ended December 31, 2024; Figures cover the Metropolitan Statistical Area (MSA) unless noted otherwise; (1) Metropolitan Division; (2) Rankings are based on annual percentage change, for all MSAs containing at least 15,000 transactions over the last 10 years and ranges from 1 to 241; (3) Figures based on a weighted division average; (a) Not ranked because of increased index variability due to smaller sample size; n/a not available
Source: Federal Housing Finance Agency, Change in FHFA Metropolitan Area House Price Indexes, All Transactions Index, 2024Q4

Home Value: City

City	Under $100,000	$100,000 -$199,999	$200,000 -$299,999	$300,000 -$399,999	$400,000 -$499,999	$500,000 -$999,999	$1,000,000 or more	Median ($)
Albuquerque, NM	6.9	18.8	34.6	19.9	10.2	8.7	0.9	266,700
Anchorage, AK	5.3	7.4	17.7	25.8	19.8	21.8	2.2	375,900
Ann Arbor, MI	1.8	5.6	14.3	20.1	23.3	29.4	5.4	435,100
Athens, GA	8.3	18.2	31.4	20.3	9.1	11.0	1.8	271,800
Atlanta, GA	4.8	10.7	17.8	14.5	11.2	27.8	13.3	420,600
Austin, TX	2.9	2.8	11.0	14.7	17.1	39.2	12.2	512,700
Baltimore, MD	15.5	28.6	26.5	13.5	6.5	7.8	1.5	219,300
Billings, MT	6.6	10.2	30.1	25.7	15.5	10.6	1.3	311,800
Boise City, ID	4.2	3.9	12.0	18.2	21.0	33.8	6.9	456,000
Boston, MA	3.4	0.7	3.2	5.8	9.4	53.3	24.2	710,400
Boulder, CO	4.3	2.6	2.6	3.9	4.0	33.9	48.6	982,600
Cape Coral, FL	3.1	8.9	28.1	25.5	15.2	16.3	3.0	339,200
Cedar Rapids, IA	12.5	47.4	24.5	8.5	3.9	2.7	0.5	177,100
Charleston, SC	2.0	3.6	12.8	18.9	18.2	31.3	13.1	469,100
Charlotte, NC	4.4	13.0	22.8	19.2	12.6	20.8	7.2	351,500
Chicago, IL	6.6	16.0	24.7	17.7	11.1	18.1	5.8	315,200
Cincinnati, OH	14.9	31.5	20.8	12.4	7.1	10.7	2.6	215,300
Clarksville, TN	7.4	25.5	40.9	15.0	6.3	4.1	0.7	236,100
Cleveland, OH	53.4	31.8	8.1	3.0	1.6	1.7	0.5	94,100
College Station, TX	2.4	7.5	32.9	27.0	15.6	12.5	2.1	326,500
Colorado Springs, CO	4.1	3.5	14.0	23.8	22.3	29.5	2.8	420,700
Columbia, MO	6.6	23.2	30.2	18.4	10.8	10.1	0.8	268,300
Columbia, SC	12.4	26.0	23.5	11.7	8.3	14.7	3.5	243,500
Columbus, OH	11.3	27.4	31.0	18.0	6.6	4.9	0.8	234,500
Dallas, TX	9.9	20.3	20.7	12.2	8.8	19.9	8.2	295,300
Davenport, IA	18.4	45.7	19.6	9.4	3.8	2.8	0.3	162,900
Denver, CO	2.3	2.1	6.6	11.4	17.3	44.6	15.7	586,700
Des Moines, IA	13.7	44.2	27.4	8.7	2.6	2.7	0.7	183,700
Detroit, MI	63.8	21.8	7.7	3.4	1.3	1.6	0.4	76,800
Durham, NC	3.1	10.7	22.2	25.3	16.4	20.2	2.1	355,300
El Paso, TX	14.2	47.6	24.4	7.7	2.7	2.8	0.7	171,700
Eugene, OR	6.5	3.0	11.6	20.1	24.6	31.0	3.0	435,400
Fargo, ND	6.0	16.7	36.1	22.1	9.0	8.7	1.4	269,800
Fort Collins, CO	3.7	1.7	4.2	9.6	22.7	52.5	5.6	548,400
Fort Wayne, IN	19.8	42.0	25.3	7.7	2.8	2.0	0.3	169,700
Fort Worth, TX	8.5	18.0	31.0	21.0	10.5	8.9	2.0	277,300
Gainesville, FL	7.9	27.4	35.1	16.9	5.7	6.3	0.7	235,000
Green Bay, WI	8.5	46.2	29.0	8.4	4.0	3.6	0.3	191,500
Greensboro, NC	10.1	33.8	25.7	14.3	6.6	8.2	1.4	221,300
Honolulu, HI	2.1	1.6	3.1	8.6	10.6	35.0	39.0	834,100
Houston, TX	11.1	24.9	22.9	12.3	8.6	14.1	6.1	253,400
Huntsville, AL	11.8	23.6	22.4	17.3	9.3	12.8	2.7	263,100
Indianapolis, IN	14.2	33.3	28.5	11.6	5.2	6.1	1.1	207,000
Jacksonville, FL	11.0	20.4	27.6	19.5	10.1	9.1	2.2	266,100
Kansas City, MO	16.8	25.8	25.2	14.7	8.5	7.8	1.2	227,000
Lafayette, LA	11.2	23.8	28.6	14.9	9.3	10.0	2.2	251,300
Las Vegas, NV	3.9	4.5	17.2	25.6	19.7	24.9	4.2	395,300
Lexington, KY	5.4	22.4	29.2	18.8	10.0	11.8	2.4	272,100
Lincoln, NE	5.9	26.1	34.7	18.1	7.5	6.6	1.1	248,200
Little Rock, AR	15.5	28.7	22.6	12.2	8.1	10.2	2.6	221,200
Los Angeles, CA	2.5	1.2	1.2	2.5	5.7	47.7	39.2	879,500
Louisville, KY	11.8	32.0	25.5	13.2	7.6	8.4	1.5	221,500
Madison, WI	2.9	9.1	25.1	27.7	16.5	17.0	1.8	346,900
Manchester, NH	3.9	10.2	24.0	32.7	19.8	8.6	0.7	336,300
McAllen, TX	20.0	40.0	22.5	10.6	3.3	3.0	0.8	173,800

Table continued on following page.

City	Under $100,000	$100,000 -$199,999	$200,000 -$299,999	$300,000 -$399,999	$400,000 -$499,999	$500,000 -$999,999	$1,000,000 or more	Median ($)
Memphis, TN	31.7	28.3	18.4	8.8	4.5	6.3	1.9	157,100
Miami, FL	2.9	5.9	12.9	14.6	18.1	31.4	14.1	475,200
Midland, TX	7.8	12.9	29.7	24.9	10.4	11.8	2.5	298,600
Milwaukee, WI	19.7	43.3	25.1	5.9	2.6	2.6	0.8	172,000
Minneapolis, MN	2.9	10.4	25.0	25.6	14.0	18.1	4.0	345,600
Nashville, TN	3.4	6.6	21.4	22.5	16.9	22.1	7.1	383,100
New Orleans, LA	6.4	21.2	23.1	13.8	9.7	19.4	6.4	296,400
New York, NY	4.7	2.9	4.7	5.6	7.1	44.9	30.1	751,700
Oklahoma City, OK	14.8	30.5	27.8	13.1	5.7	6.6	1.6	215,100
Omaha, NE	9.8	29.2	31.6	14.2	7.4	6.7	1.2	230,100
Orlando, FL	3.5	15.0	19.9	19.6	14.5	22.0	5.4	359,000
Philadelphia, PA	14.0	26.4	26.8	14.6	6.6	9.5	2.0	232,400
Phoenix, AZ	5.7	6.6	20.5	21.1	16.0	24.9	5.2	381,900
Pittsburgh, PA	22.7	29.2	19.5	10.3	5.6	10.3	2.2	193,200
Portland, OR	2.5	1.5	4.8	11.9	21.2	50.0	8.1	557,600
Providence, RI	4.1	9.3	30.8	25.2	11.6	14.5	4.4	322,800
Provo, UT	5.1	1.8	10.4	24.4	22.4	31.3	4.6	437,100
Raleigh, NC	3.1	7.7	22.7	21.2	15.2	24.4	5.7	377,800
Reno, NV	6.1	3.0	6.9	14.9	19.3	42.7	7.1	498,600
Richmond, VA	4.9	17.9	22.4	17.1	13.0	19.0	5.7	328,100
Rochester, MN	4.4	16.0	33.6	19.2	12.2	13.4	1.1	287,500
Sacramento, CA	4.3	2.4	7.6	17.7	21.3	41.5	5.2	484,600
Saint Louis, MO	22.9	31.6	22.8	11.1	5.1	5.2	1.2	185,100
Saint Paul, MN	3.5	15.9	37.6	19.5	9.9	11.4	2.0	280,300
Salem, OR	6.8	5.2	14.1	29.1	22.7	21.4	0.8	382,400
Salt Lake City, UT	4.1	3.4	11.3	15.5	16.4	37.9	11.4	495,700
San Antonio, TX	13.7	29.8	29.2	14.1	6.3	5.9	1.0	219,700
San Diego, CA	2.6	1.2	1.5	3.4	7.1	48.7	35.6	848,500
San Francisco, CA	1.5	1.2	0.7	1.3	1.6	16.0	77.8	1,380,500
San Jose, CA	2.2	2.2	2.3	1.5	1.3	22.4	68.0	1,187,800
Santa Rosa, CA	3.7	2.8	2.7	3.8	7.2	65.4	14.3	685,000
Savannah, GA	12.1	29.9	27.2	12.5	6.6	9.4	2.4	225,200
Seattle, WA	1.1	0.6	1.2	3.6	5.2	47.4	40.8	912,100
Sioux Falls, SD	7.9	18.0	32.8	18.7	10.0	10.5	2.2	271,400
Tampa, FL	4.8	12.4	20.8	16.0	12.1	24.0	10.0	375,300
Tucson, AZ	12.9	21.2	34.4	17.5	7.6	5.4	1.1	242,200
Tulsa, OK	20.0	33.1	20.0	10.7	5.6	8.3	2.3	189,600
Virginia Beach, VA	3.1	7.5	23.9	23.4	16.1	21.5	4.5	366,300
Washington, DC	1.4	1.8	4.6	9.1	11.2	41.8	30.1	724,600
Wichita, KS	21.6	34.9	24.3	9.6	4.5	4.2	0.9	179,500
Wilmington, NC	3.3	13.2	23.0	21.1	14.2	19.1	6.2	350,300
Winston-Salem, NC	12.9	34.6	25.9	12.1	4.6	8.3	1.7	208,200
U.S.	12.1	17.8	19.5	14.4	10.5	19.1	6.5	303,400

Note: Figures are percentages except for median and cover owner-occupied housing units.
Source: U.S. Census Bureau, 2019-2023 American Community Survey 5-Year Estimates

Home Value: Metro Area

Metro Area	Under $100,000	$100,000 -$199,999	$200,000 -$299,999	$300,000 -$399,999	$400,000 -$499,999	$500,000 -$999,999	$1,000,000 or more	Median ($)
Albuquerque, NM	9.6	19.3	31.5	17.9	9.9	10.1	1.6	263,500
Anchorage, AK	5.4	8.2	21.3	25.5	18.1	19.7	1.8	358,900
Ann Arbor, MI	7.1	11.0	21.8	19.2	16.2	21.4	3.4	353,000
Athens, GA	10.5	18.0	26.3	18.0	10.1	14.3	2.8	280,900
Atlanta, GA	5.5	13.6	23.9	19.8	13.6	19.9	3.6	335,100
Austin, TX	5.1	5.2	15.7	18.2	16.6	30.5	8.6	434,800
Baltimore, MD	5.5	10.2	19.7	19.9	15.1	25.5	4.1	373,300
Billings, MT	8.9	10.1	25.9	22.6	14.8	15.5	2.2	322,700
Boise City, ID	5.0	4.9	13.8	19.8	19.1	31.9	5.6	434,400
Boston, MA	2.6	1.9	5.8	10.4	15.0	48.7	15.6	610,900
Boulder, CO	3.9	1.2	2.5	6.2	10.6	49.6	25.9	713,900
Cape Coral, FL	8.7	12.9	23.1	19.9	12.6	17.6	5.1	326,300
Cedar Rapids, IA	11.7	37.7	25.8	12.6	6.1	5.0	1.0	202,100
Charleston, SC	8.4	11.0	22.2	18.2	12.1	19.8	8.1	345,400
Charlotte, NC	8.7	15.9	21.8	18.3	12.5	18.3	4.4	319,400
Chicago, IL	6.2	16.9	26.5	19.9	12.0	15.0	3.5	301,900
Cincinnati, OH	10.2	28.0	26.6	15.7	8.7	9.3	1.5	240,200
Clarksville, TN	13.8	25.6	31.2	14.6	7.2	6.3	1.2	229,400
Cleveland, OH	16.6	33.1	23.9	12.6	6.4	6.4	1.0	201,000
College Station, TX	15.0	18.5	26.1	17.3	9.5	11.2	2.3	261,900
Colorado Springs, CO	4.0	3.9	13.2	22.2	21.5	31.2	4.1	431,600
Columbia, MO	11.1	26.8	26.5	15.4	9.6	9.0	1.6	242,500
Columbia, SC	15.7	30.4	25.4	12.9	6.5	7.4	1.7	213,400
Columbus, OH	9.2	20.9	26.3	18.4	10.8	12.8	1.6	274,300
Dallas, TX	6.8	13.3	23.8	20.1	13.1	18.8	4.1	330,300
Davenport, IA	20.4	38.7	21.3	9.7	5.0	4.2	0.7	170,000
Denver, CO	3.2	1.7	5.1	11.3	18.6	49.8	10.3	570,300
Des Moines, IA	8.7	25.7	28.2	18.3	9.0	9.0	1.1	252,400
Detroit, MI	16.3	23.8	24.2	15.1	9.2	9.8	1.5	237,100
Durham, NC	6.8	12.7	19.0	19.3	14.3	23.7	4.1	359,400
El Paso, TX	17.9	45.6	23.7	7.1	2.7	2.4	0.6	167,000
Eugene, OR	7.7	4.1	16.6	22.5	19.7	25.8	3.5	395,800
Fargo, ND	6.0	16.9	33.8	21.7	10.4	9.8	1.5	276,600
Fort Collins, CO	4.8	1.6	4.6	11.8	22.6	47.6	6.9	532,200
Fort Wayne, IN	16.3	35.8	25.6	11.4	5.1	5.0	0.7	194,000
Fort Worth, TX	6.8	13.3	23.8	20.1	13.1	18.8	4.1	330,300
Gainesville, FL	13.9	23.8	25.3	16.2	9.0	10.1	1.6	245,800
Green Bay, WI	7.8	29.2	31.1	15.7	8.0	7.3	0.9	238,700
Greensboro, NC	15.0	33.0	23.9	13.1	6.3	7.9	1.0	207,600
Honolulu, HI	2.2	1.5	2.2	5.1	7.6	43.9	37.6	873,000
Houston, TX	9.2	18.8	28.6	17.5	10.0	12.4	3.6	275,200
Huntsville, AL	10.6	22.2	26.0	17.6	10.3	11.7	1.6	265,000
Indianapolis, IN	10.9	25.6	27.2	15.9	8.9	9.9	1.7	244,000
Jacksonville, FL	8.7	15.7	24.0	19.1	12.4	16.2	4.0	308,900
Kansas City, MO	10.8	22.1	25.5	17.5	10.4	11.8	1.8	265,400
Lafayette, LA	22.9	24.9	27.1	12.6	6.3	5.2	1.0	206,900
Las Vegas, NV	4.7	4.8	15.2	25.2	21.6	24.5	4.1	400,800
Lexington, KY	6.9	24.4	28.6	17.8	9.1	10.7	2.5	258,900
Lincoln, NE	5.8	24.3	32.7	18.0	8.9	8.9	1.3	257,500
Little Rock, AR	17.5	32.8	24.9	11.9	5.4	6.1	1.5	199,300
Los Angeles, CA	3.2	1.7	1.8	3.2	6.3	50.5	33.3	825,300
Louisville, KY	10.5	28.4	27.1	15.9	8.1	8.6	1.3	236,400
Madison, WI	3.7	11.6	24.1	23.9	16.0	18.4	2.3	344,600
Manchester, NH	3.8	6.2	18.2	25.4	21.4	23.3	1.5	385,500
McAllen, TX	39.7	34.5	16.0	5.7	2.2	1.6	0.4	124,000

Table continued on following page.

Metro Area	Under $100,000	$100,000 -$199,999	$200,000 -$299,999	$300,000 -$399,999	$400,000 -$499,999	$500,000 -$999,999	$1,000,000 or more	Median ($)
Memphis, TN	18.7	24.3	22.8	15.3	8.1	9.3	1.6	228,100
Miami, FL	6.3	9.6	15.7	17.5	16.5	26.1	8.3	405,600
Midland, TX	12.7	13.2	26.8	21.6	10.8	12.6	2.4	290,300
Milwaukee, WI	7.4	19.6	27.2	19.0	11.7	13.0	2.1	283,800
Minneapolis, MN	4.0	7.4	24.9	25.1	16.1	19.6	2.9	354,400
Nashville, TN	4.8	8.7	20.9	20.4	15.0	23.6	6.7	376,800
New Orleans, LA	8.9	25.9	28.3	15.3	7.8	10.8	3.0	248,000
New York, NY	3.6	3.3	7.3	11.1	14.3	44.4	16.0	587,400
Oklahoma City, OK	14.4	31.1	26.8	12.7	6.2	7.1	1.7	214,700
Omaha, NE	8.7	25.0	29.9	16.9	9.6	8.7	1.3	248,100
Orlando, FL	7.9	10.2	22.8	23.6	15.2	17.1	3.2	338,500
Philadelphia, PA	7.1	14.6	23.2	19.2	13.4	19.5	3.0	326,700
Phoenix, AZ	6.7	5.9	16.8	20.3	17.5	26.9	5.9	401,400
Pittsburgh, PA	19.2	29.5	23.7	12.0	6.6	7.6	1.3	204,500
Portland, OR	3.9	2.2	5.4	12.8	22.0	46.6	7.0	526,500
Providence, RI	3.3	4.7	20.9	24.5	18.9	24.2	3.4	385,900
Provo, UT	3.5	1.6	7.4	18.5	22.0	41.2	6.0	487,200
Raleigh, NC	5.3	9.2	19.3	20.0	16.2	26.2	3.9	381,000
Reno, NV	5.5	4.0	9.4	17.0	18.9	36.5	8.6	474,000
Richmond, VA	4.9	12.5	26.9	22.4	13.5	17.3	2.6	325,800
Rochester, MN	6.7	18.1	29.5	17.4	11.9	14.4	2.0	284,600
Sacramento, CA	4.1	2.1	5.1	12.0	18.3	49.6	8.8	559,000
Saint Louis, MO	14.9	26.3	25.0	14.9	8.2	8.9	1.8	232,100
Saint Paul, MN	4.0	7.4	24.9	25.1	16.1	19.6	2.9	354,400
Salem, OR	7.5	5.1	14.2	25.9	20.5	24.2	2.7	389,800
Salt Lake City, UT	4.0	2.6	9.9	17.6	20.3	38.7	6.9	478,200
San Antonio, TX	11.7	21.6	27.6	16.5	9.1	11.3	2.2	258,700
San Diego, CA	3.7	1.9	2.1	3.4	6.8	52.6	29.5	791,600
San Francisco, CA	2.1	1.4	1.3	1.7	3.4	31.8	58.4	1,113,800
San Jose, CA	2.1	1.7	1.8	1.3	1.2	19.3	72.6	1,342,700
Santa Rosa, CA	3.3	3.1	2.4	2.7	5.4	57.0	26.2	779,000
Savannah, GA	9.6	21.3	26.2	16.7	9.8	13.3	3.2	271,100
Seattle, WA	3.2	1.7	3.9	8.3	12.9	46.7	23.2	673,500
Sioux Falls, SD	8.4	18.3	30.7	18.5	10.4	11.8	1.9	274,800
Tampa, FL	11.5	14.4	22.9	19.3	12.1	16.0	3.8	306,100
Tucson, AZ	11.2	15.2	26.9	19.0	11.6	13.4	2.6	286,900
Tulsa, OK	17.5	31.2	25.4	12.1	5.9	6.5	1.4	204,400
Virginia Beach, VA	5.2	13.4	27.6	21.5	14.3	15.6	2.5	318,000
Washington, DC	2.5	2.4	8.4	14.5	16.2	42.5	13.4	553,000
Wichita, KS	20.1	33.8	25.4	10.2	4.8	4.9	0.8	188,200
Wilmington, NC	7.5	14.3	22.8	19.4	13.3	19.0	3.8	328,000
Winston-Salem, NC	14.0	32.0	26.0	13.0	6.5	7.3	1.2	213,300
U.S.	12.1	17.8	19.5	14.4	10.5	19.1	6.5	303,400

Note: Figures are percentages except for median and cover owner-occupied housing units; Figures cover the Metropolitan Statistical Area (MSA)
Source: U.S. Census Bureau, 2019-2023 American Community Survey 5-Year Estimates

Homeownership Rate

Metro Area	2017	2018	2019	2020	2021	2022	2023	2024
Albuquerque, NM	67.0	67.9	70.0	69.5	66.5	67.3	69.1	71.8
Anchorage, AK	n/a	n/a	n/a	n/a	n/a	n/a	n/a	n/a
Ann Arbor, MI	n/a	n/a	n/a	n/a	n/a	n/a	n/a	n/a
Athens, GA	n/a	n/a	n/a	n/a	n/a	n/a	n/a	n/a
Atlanta, GA	62.4	64.0	64.2	66.4	64.2	64.4	67.5	67.5
Austin, TX	55.6	56.1	59.0	65.4	62.2	62.4	60.3	56.2
Baltimore, MD	67.5	63.5	66.5	70.7	67.5	70.4	72.9	70.0
Billings, MT	n/a	n/a	n/a	n/a	n/a	n/a	n/a	n/a
Boise City, ID	n/a	n/a	n/a	n/a	n/a	n/a	n/a	n/a
Boston, MA	58.8	61.0	60.9	61.2	60.7	59.4	59.9	60.7
Boulder, CO	n/a	n/a	n/a	n/a	n/a	n/a	n/a	n/a
Cape Coral, FL	65.5	75.1	72.0	77.4	76.1	70.8	78.5	77.1
Cedar Rapids, IA	n/a	n/a	n/a	n/a	n/a	n/a	n/a	n/a
Charleston, SC	67.7	68.8	70.7	75.5	73.2	71.9	69.6	68.1
Charlotte, NC	64.6	67.9	72.3	73.3	70.0	68.7	64.8	62.7
Chicago, IL	64.1	64.6	63.4	66.0	67.5	66.8	67.3	68.0
Cincinnati, OH	65.7	67.3	67.4	71.1	72.1	67.1	69.6	72.3
Clarksville, TN	n/a	n/a	n/a	n/a	n/a	n/a	n/a	n/a
Cleveland, OH	66.6	66.7	64.4	66.3	64.7	63.0	63.1	65.6
College Station, TX	n/a	n/a	n/a	n/a	n/a	n/a	n/a	n/a
Colorado Springs, CO	n/a	n/a	n/a	n/a	n/a	n/a	n/a	n/a
Columbia, MO	n/a	n/a	n/a	n/a	n/a	n/a	n/a	n/a
Columbia, SC	70.7	69.3	65.9	69.7	69.4	70.9	69.2	73.4
Columbus, OH	57.9	64.8	65.7	65.6	64.6	61.5	58.6	61.5
Dallas, TX	61.8	62.0	60.6	64.7	61.8	60.4	61.7	61.1
Davenport, IA	n/a	n/a	n/a	n/a	n/a	n/a	n/a	n/a
Denver, CO	59.3	60.1	63.5	62.9	62.8	64.6	65.9	61.6
Des Moines, IA	n/a	n/a	n/a	n/a	n/a	n/a	n/a	n/a
Detroit, MI	70.2	70.9	70.2	71.8	71.6	71.9	73.5	72.0
Durham, NC	n/a	n/a	n/a	n/a	n/a	n/a	n/a	n/a
El Paso, TX	n/a	n/a	n/a	n/a	n/a	n/a	n/a	n/a
Eugene, OR	n/a	n/a	n/a	n/a	n/a	n/a	n/a	n/a
Fargo, ND	n/a	n/a	n/a	n/a	n/a	n/a	n/a	n/a
Fort Collins, CO	n/a	n/a	n/a	n/a	n/a	n/a	n/a	n/a
Fort Wayne, IN	n/a	n/a	n/a	n/a	n/a	n/a	n/a	n/a
Fort Worth, TX	61.8	62.0	60.6	64.7	61.8	60.4	61.7	61.1
Gainesville, FL	n/a	n/a	n/a	n/a	n/a	n/a	n/a	n/a
Green Bay, WI	n/a	n/a	n/a	n/a	n/a	n/a	n/a	n/a
Greensboro, NC	61.9	63.2	61.7	65.8	61.9	70.0	69.4	67.0
Honolulu, HI	53.8	57.7	59.0	56.9	55.9	57.7	60.4	58.5
Houston, TX	58.9	60.1	61.3	65.3	64.1	63.7	61.8	61.6
Huntsville, AL	n/a	n/a	n/a	n/a	n/a	n/a	n/a	n/a
Indianapolis, IN	63.9	64.3	66.2	70.0	70.1	68.8	70.2	69.6
Jacksonville, FL	65.2	61.4	63.1	64.8	68.1	70.6	72.9	67.0
Kansas City, MO	62.4	64.3	65.0	66.7	63.8	63.8	64.1	65.3
Lafayette, LA	n/a	n/a	h/a	n/a	n/a	n/a	n/a	n/a
Las Vegas, NV	54.4	58.1	56.0	57.3	57.7	58.7	58.9	58.5
Lexington, KY	n/a	n/a	n/a	n/a	n/a	n/a	n/a	n/a
Lincoln, NE	n/a	n/a	n/a	n/a	n/a	n/a	n/a	n/a
Little Rock, AR	61.0	62.2	65.0	67.7	64.6	64.4	62.6	61.7
Los Angeles, CA	49.1	49.5	48.2	48.5	47.9	48.3	48.0	48.3
Louisville, KY	71.7	67.9	64.9	69.3	71.4	71.7	68.3	67.0
Madison, WI	n/a	n/a	n/a	n/a	n/a	n/a	n/a	n/a
Manchester, NH	n/a	n/a	n/a	n/a	n/a	n/a	n/a	n/a
McAllen, TX	n/a	n/a	n/a	n/a	n/a	n/a	n/a	n/a
Memphis, TN	62.4	63.5	63.7	62.5	60.7	59.7	63.2	60.1

Table continued on following page.

Metro Area	2017	2018	2019	2020	2021	2022	2023	2024
Miami, FL	57.9	59.9	60.4	60.6	59.4	58.3	58.6	60.8
Midland, TX	n/a	n/a	n/a	n/a	n/a	n/a	n/a	n/a
Milwaukee, WI	63.9	62.3	56.9	58.5	56.8	57.3	60.0	62.7
Minneapolis, MN	70.1	67.8	70.2	73.0	75.0	73.0	72.0	67.8
Nashville, TN	69.4	68.3	69.8	69.8	65.7	70.4	70.7	71.6
New Orleans, LA	61.7	62.6	61.1	66.3	66.2	66.3	63.2	63.2
New York, NY	49.9	49.7	50.4	50.9	50.7	50.5	50.2	49.4
Oklahoma City, OK	64.7	64.6	64.3	68.3	61.9	64.8	68.1	65.0
Omaha, NE	65.5	67.8	66.9	68.6	68.6	67.9	67.0	67.4
Orlando, FL	59.5	58.5	56.1	64.2	63.0	62.1	61.9	62.6
Philadelphia, PA	65.6	67.4	67.4	69.2	69.8	68.2	67.4	69.6
Phoenix, AZ	64.0	65.3	65.9	67.9	65.2	68.0	69.7	69.4
Pittsburgh, PA	72.7	71.7	71.5	69.8	69.1	72.7	72.4	71.7
Portland, OR	61.1	59.2	60.0	62.5	64.1	65.2	65.6	61.1
Providence, RI	58.6	61.3	63.5	64.8	64.1	66.3	65.4	63.2
Provo, UT	n/a	n/a	n/a	n/a	n/a	n/a	n/a	n/a
Raleigh, NC	68.2	64.9	63.0	68.2	62.7	65.1	68.8	65.0
Reno, NV	n/a	n/a	n/a	n/a	n/a	n/a	n/a	n/a
Richmond, VA	63.1	62.9	66.4	66.5	64.9	66.3	64.9	65.4
Rochester, MN	n/a	n/a	n/a	n/a	n/a	n/a	n/a	n/a
Sacramento, CA	60.1	64.1	61.6	63.4	63.2	63.5	64.4	63.0
Saint Louis, MO	65.6	65.8	68.1	71.1	73.8	69.9	69.4	68.2
Saint Paul, MN	70.1	67.8	70.2	73.0	75.0	73.0	72.0	67.8
Salem, OR	n/a	n/a	n/a	n/a	n/a	n/a	n/a	n/a
Salt Lake City, UT	68.1	69.5	69.2	68.0	64.1	66.6	62.9	61.0
San Antonio, TX	62.5	64.4	62.6	64.2	62.7	62.9	66.9	63.3
San Diego, CA	56.0	56.1	56.7	57.8	52.6	51.6	54.5	51.4
San Francisco, CA	55.7	55.6	52.8	53.0	54.7	56.4	55.0	56.4
San Jose, CA	50.4	50.4	52.4	52.6	48.4	53.1	53.5	52.3
Santa Rosa, CA	n/a	n/a	n/a	n/a	n/a	n/a	n/a	n/a
Savannah, GA	n/a	n/a	n/a	n/a	n/a	n/a	n/a	n/a
Seattle, WA	59.5	62.5	61.5	59.4	58.0	62.7	62.7	61.1
Sioux Falls, SD	n/a	n/a	n/a	n/a	n/a	n/a	n/a	n/a
Tampa, FL	60.4	64.9	68.0	72.2	68.3	68.4	66.9	68.9
Tucson, AZ	60.1	63.8	60.1	67.1	63.5	71.6	73.3	66.4
Tulsa, OK	66.8	68.3	70.5	70.1	63.8	63.7	62.8	65.3
Virginia Beach, VA	65.3	62.8	63.0	65.8	64.4	61.4	67.8	69.8
Washington, DC	63.3	62.9	64.7	67.9	65.8	66.2	65.1	64.0
Wichita, KS	n/a	n/a	n/a	n/a	n/a	n/a	n/a	n/a
Wilmington, NC	n/a	n/a	n/a	n/a	n/a	n/a	n/a	n/a
Winston-Salem, NC	n/a	n/a	n/a	n/a	n/a	n/a	n/a	n/a
U.S.	63.9	64.4	64.6	66.6	65.5	65.8	65.9	65.6

Note: Figures are percentages and cover the Metropolitan Statistical Area (MSA); n/a not available
Source: U.S. Census Bureau, Housing Vacancies and Homeownership Annual Statistics: 2017-2024

Year Housing Structure Built: City

City	2020 or Later	2010 -2019	2000 -2009	1990 -1999	1980 -1989	1970 -1979	1960 -1969	1950 -1959	1940 -1949	Before 1940	Median Year
Albuquerque, NM	0.7	6.9	16.2	14.2	14.1	19.2	9.5	12.3	3.9	3.0	1982
Anchorage, AK	0.2	6.6	12.1	11.6	24.8	27.5	9.7	5.8	0.9	0.8	1982
Ann Arbor, MI	1.3	6.5	6.8	11.2	9.9	16.0	17.9	10.6	4.8	15.2	1971
Athens, GA	1.6	8.9	19.0	16.3	14.5	14.3	12.0	5.8	2.7	4.9	1987
Atlanta, GA	2.3	15.8	21.0	8.9	7.8	7.8	10.2	8.8	5.3	12.1	1987
Austin, TX	2.5	20.7	17.2	13.0	17.3	13.7	7.2	4.1	2.0	2.3	1993
Baltimore, MD	0.3	4.3	4.1	4.1	4.6	5.8	8.6	15.3	11.6	41.1	1948
Billings, MT	2.3	12.7	10.6	11.9	11.3	16.3	9.0	13.1	5.5	7.4	1979
Boise City, ID	1.3	10.8	11.4	19.6	14.4	17.8	7.8	7.2	3.7	6.3	1985
Boston, MA	0.9	9.2	6.5	4.3	5.6	7.6	7.2	7.1	4.9	46.8	1947
Boulder, CO	0.5	8.5	8.8	12.4	15.5	19.8	16.2	9.0	1.5	7.7	1978
Cape Coral, FL	2.0	11.6	34.3	15.2	21.1	10.3	4.5	0.8	0.3	0.0	1999
Cedar Rapids, IA	0.8	9.6	11.3	10.9	7.5	14.7	13.9	12.4	4.3	14.7	1973
Charleston, SC	2.6	22.7	19.1	10.1	10.5	7.5	8.2	5.6	3.0	10.8	1994
Charlotte, NC	1.8	16.9	20.9	17.3	13.9	10.2	8.2	5.8	2.4	2.6	1994
Chicago, IL	0.4	5.1	8.2	4.9	5.0	7.9	9.7	11.6	8.2	39.1	1952
Cincinnati, OH	0.5	4.4	4.1	4.0	6.3	9.3	12.0	10.9	8.3	40.3	1951
Clarksville, TN	3.3	18.0	21.2	18.8	12.9	11.3	6.2	4.2	2.3	1.7	1996
Cleveland, OH	0.6	3.8	3.8	2.9	3.0	5.6	7.8	12.1	10.8	49.6	1940
College Station, TX	2.4	23.2	20.3	16.5	18.5	12.2	3.9	1.7	0.5	0.7	1998
Colorado Springs, CO	1.9	11.6	14.9	14.2	17.5	16.8	9.3	7.0	1.7	5.3	1986
Columbia, MO	0.8	17.5	20.3	17.0	12.3	9.9	10.3	4.5	2.4	5.0	1993
Columbia, SC	1.0	12.9	14.8	9.8	9.6	9.6	10.1	13.3	8.9	10.1	1978
Columbus, OH	1.0	9.6	11.8	13.7	13.3	14.4	10.7	9.6	4.0	12.0	1980
Dallas, TX	1.0	12.0	11.0	10.0	16.3	15.0	12.0	12.7	4.6	5.2	1980
Davenport, IA	0.6	4.8	9.1	8.4	6.9	15.3	12.8	11.8	6.0	24.2	1966
Denver, CO	2.3	15.5	10.9	6.6	7.4	12.0	9.9	13.0	5.2	17.2	1974
Des Moines, IA	0.6	6.9	7.3	6.8	6.4	12.8	9.5	14.6	7.3	27.8	1960
Detroit, MI	0.1	1.5	2.7	2.3	3.2	4.9	7.8	21.8	20.4	35.2	1947
Durham, NC	2.6	21.5	17.1	14.2	14.0	9.6	7.1	5.3	3.4	5.2	1994
El Paso, TX	0.9	14.1	13.5	11.7	14.9	15.9	10.2	10.9	3.2	4.7	1983
Eugene, OR	0.7	10.2	13.3	15.0	9.2	19.9	11.7	8.5	5.5	6.0	1979
Fargo, ND	1.3	20.3	14.9	14.5	11.5	13.7	5.8	7.7	2.5	7.9	1991
Fort Collins, CO	1.5	15.0	18.9	19.0	14.5	15.7	6.5	3.0	1.3	4.5	1992
Fort Wayne, IN	0.5	3.4	7.4	12.9	11.3	16.9	15.5	12.0	5.7	14.4	1971
Fort Worth, TX	2.4	17.7	20.8	11.1	13.2	8.7	6.9	9.3	4.5	5.6	1992
Gainesville, FL	1.3	6.5	14.0	14.2	19.5	20.2	11.8	7.0	2.7	2.9	1983
Green Bay, WI	0.4	3.2	7.3	9.8	12.5	17.9	12.6	16.1	5.9	14.4	1971
Greensboro, NC	0.8	9.8	14.7	14.5	15.6	13.9	11.0	10.1	3.8	5.7	1983
Honolulu, HI	0.5	7.5	6.7	7.8	10.5	25.9	19.6	11.6	5.1	4.8	1973
Houston, TX	1.4	14.0	13.0	9.3	14.1	19.0	12.1	9.4	3.7	4.1	1981
Huntsville, AL	2.3	15.6	12.4	10.8	14.8	11.9	20.1	7.8	1.8	2.6	1984
Indianapolis, IN	0.6	6.5	9.9	12.0	11.2	12.1	13.4	12.1	6.0	16.1	1972
Jacksonville, FL	2.4	10.6	17.4	13.1	15.9	11.9	9.3	10.3	4.1	5.0	1986
Kansas City, MO	1.0	8.2	10.1	8.5	8.6	11.4	12.0	13.2	5.5	21.6	1968
Lafayette, LA	0.8	12.4	11.5	9.3	18.6	21.5	12.8	8.7	2.7	1.6	1981
Las Vegas, NV	1.4	8.8	21.4	29.3	16.3	10.2	7.0	4.1	1.0	0.5	1994
Lexington, KY	1.1	10.0	14.5	15.6	13.0	14.5	13.4	8.5	2.7	6.7	1983
Lincoln, NE	1.0	11.9	14.2	13.6	10.1	14.5	8.7	10.3	3.2	12.4	1981
Little Rock, AR	0.4	9.7	11.7	11.8	13.1	17.9	14.7	8.5	4.9	7.2	1978
Los Angeles, CA	0.8	6.1	5.6	5.7	10.8	13.4	13.2	16.2	9.1	19.2	1964
Louisville, KY	0.8	7.7	11.8	10.4	6.9	13.0	12.7	14.2	6.6	15.9	1970
Madison, WI	0.9	11.8	14.3	11.8	9.5	12.8	11.9	9.2	4.3	13.4	1979
Manchester, NH	0.5	3.5	6.5	7.7	15.5	11.5	8.1	10.7	6.6	29.4	1964
McAllen, TX	1.2	13.0	24.8	16.8	18.5	15.3	5.0	2.3	1.2	1.9	1993

Table continued on following page.

City	2020 or Later	2010 -2019	2000 -2009	1990 -1999	1980 -1989	1970 -1979	1960 -1969	1950 -1959	1940 -1949	Before 1940	Median Year
Memphis, TN	0.5	3.6	6.5	9.7	12.4	17.3	14.6	20.0	7.7	7.7	1970
Miami, FL	1.8	15.4	17.0	6.0	7.4	11.9	10.0	13.5	9.1	7.9	1978
Midland, TX	2.2	21.9	10.1	9.7	17.3	10.9	7.7	16.6	2.5	1.1	1986
Milwaukee, WI	0.3	3.5	3.7	3.5	3.8	9.2	11.6	18.8	10.9	34.7	1952
Minneapolis, MN	1.0	8.8	6.2	4.2	6.8	8.2	6.8	8.2	6.2	43.6	1950
Nashville, TN	3.2	15.4	13.9	11.0	14.2	12.8	10.9	9.0	3.4	6.2	1985
New Orleans, LA	0.4	5.7	7.6	3.0	7.8	13.9	10.2	12.0	7.1	32.1	1959
New York, NY	0.4	5.5	5.5	3.7	5.0	7.0	12.2	12.8	9.4	38.4	1952
Oklahoma City, OK	1.6	13.7	13.3	9.3	13.4	15.6	11.3	9.2	5.0	7.4	1981
Omaha, NE	0.4	6.4	8.7	11.9	10.8	15.1	13.9	10.5	4.2	18.1	1972
Orlando, FL	1.3	16.1	21.0	13.1	15.1	12.7	7.2	8.4	2.6	2.6	1991
Philadelphia, PA	0.6	4.8	3.2	2.7	4.5	7.8	10.9	15.0	10.7	39.9	1949
Phoenix, AZ	1.1	8.6	16.4	14.3	17.3	18.9	9.5	9.6	2.4	1.9	1984
Pittsburgh, PA	0.5	4.8	3.7	3.4	4.2	6.5	7.9	13.0	7.6	48.4	1942
Portland, OR	0.9	11.0	10.1	7.3	6.4	10.5	8.4	11.0	7.2	27.1	1966
Providence, RI	0.4	2.2	4.9	4.5	5.6	7.8	5.4	7.5	6.3	55.6	1938
Provo, UT	1.1	7.6	11.6	18.7	14.7	17.7	9.7	7.3	5.0	6.6	1982
Raleigh, NC	1.6	17.5	23.5	17.1	16.0	9.6	6.8	3.7	1.3	2.9	1996
Reno, NV	3.0	11.6	19.1	15.0	13.3	17.7	8.5	5.7	3.1	2.9	1989
Richmond, VA	1.1	8.6	5.9	5.7	7.3	8.7	11.1	14.1	9.0	28.6	1959
Rochester, MN	1.2	12.9	18.5	14.1	11.1	12.4	9.9	9.0	3.7	7.2	1987
Sacramento, CA	0.9	6.3	15.0	7.8	15.2	13.3	11.3	11.9	7.2	11.0	1976
Saint Louis, MO	0.2	3.2	4.0	3.0	3.7	4.3	6.1	9.7	7.6	58.3	1938
Saint Paul, MN	0.7	4.5	5.1	3.5	7.3	9.8	9.4	11.7	6.7	41.2	1952
Salem, OR	1.8	9.1	13.5	15.9	9.5	18.5	9.3	9.3	4.5	8.6	1980
Salt Lake City, UT	1.8	10.6	6.8	5.5	7.4	11.4	9.8	12.2	8.2	26.3	1963
San Antonio, TX	1.6	11.9	15.2	11.3	16.2	13.8	10.1	9.5	5.2	5.2	1984
San Diego, CA	0.8	7.1	10.2	10.6	17.7	20.2	12.2	11.0	3.7	6.6	1978
San Francisco, CA	0.7	6.4	6.5	4.0	5.3	7.1	8.1	7.9	8.7	45.4	1945
San Jose, CA	0.6	7.3	9.6	9.6	12.1	23.6	18.5	10.9	2.7	5.2	1975
Santa Rosa, CA	1.0	6.2	12.3	12.5	17.9	20.9	11.9	8.1	4.4	4.9	1980
Savannah, GA	1.3	11.9	9.0	6.3	11.5	11.7	10.7	13.9	6.9	16.7	1971
Seattle, WA	1.2	17.6	12.0	7.4	7.5	7.2	7.7	8.4	7.4	23.4	1974
Sioux Falls, SD	2.0	19.1	18.4	13.3	10.6	10.4	6.5	8.0	3.0	8.6	1992
Tampa, FL	1.8	13.8	16.5	10.7	11.7	10.3	9.1	12.9	4.9	8.3	1984
Tucson, AZ	0.7	4.6	13.0	12.7	16.5	20.2	11.0	13.4	4.8	3.2	1979
Tulsa, OK	0.4	6.0	6.5	8.2	13.8	20.0	14.5	15.5	6.2	8.9	1972
Virginia Beach, VA	0.4	8.2	10.9	13.1	27.2	19.7	12.3	5.7	1.3	1.1	1984
Washington, DC	1.7	12.5	7.7	3.0	4.7	6.7	9.9	11.6	10.3	31.7	1957
Wichita, KS	0.7	6.9	10.1	11.2	12.8	13.3	9.1	18.0	7.7	10.3	1974
Wilmington, NC	2.3	13.1	14.9	16.2	15.2	11.1	6.2	6.3	5.7	9.1	1988
Winston-Salem, NC	1.1	8.6	13.2	12.5	15.0	14.4	11.0	12.2	4.1	7.7	1980
U.S.	1.2	8.9	13.6	12.8	13.0	14.4	10.0	9.7	4.5	11.9	1980

Note: Figures are percentages except for median year
Source: U.S. Census Bureau, 2019-2023 American Community Survey 5-Year Estimates

Year Housing Structure Built: Metro Area

Metro Area	2020 or Later	2010 -2019	2000 -2009	1990 -1999	1980 -1989	1970 -1979	1960 -1969	1950 -1959	1940 -1949	Before 1940	Median Year
Albuquerque, NM	0.9	7.5	17.4	16.2	15.7	17.7	8.6	9.5	3.3	3.2	1985
Anchorage, AK	0.5	9.5	16.8	12.5	23.9	22.9	7.8	4.6	0.8	0.7	1986
Ann Arbor, MI	1.2	6.4	13.0	16.0	10.5	15.4	12.3	9.1	4.3	11.8	1978
Athens, GA	1.8	10.2	19.4	18.1	15.0	14.1	9.5	4.6	2.2	5.1	1990
Atlanta, GA	1.7	11.8	23.5	19.3	16.7	11.5	6.8	4.2	1.7	2.8	1993
Austin, TX	4.0	25.5	21.4	14.6	14.3	9.7	4.5	2.8	1.3	2.0	2000
Baltimore, MD	0.6	7.2	9.6	13.0	13.4	12.8	10.3	12.4	6.0	14.6	1975
Billings, MT	2.1	12.3	12.8	12.9	11.6	16.7	7.7	10.1	4.8	9.1	1981
Boise City, ID	3.5	17.3	22.2	17.7	8.9	13.4	4.7	4.2	2.8	5.2	1996
Boston, MA	0.8	7.1	7.5	7.1	10.5	10.6	9.8	10.4	4.8	31.5	1963
Boulder, CO	1.5	11.2	12.5	18.7	14.7	19.1	9.9	5.0	1.4	6.2	1986
Cape Coral, FL	1.9	11.4	29.2	16.2	20.5	12.9	5.0	1.8	0.4	0.6	1995
Cedar Rapids, IA	0.9	10.2	13.2	12.8	7.4	13.6	11.6	10.2	3.6	16.6	1976
Charleston, SC	2.9	19.5	20.3	14.1	14.6	11.3	7.2	4.5	2.2	3.4	1995
Charlotte, NC	2.2	16.8	21.6	17.2	12.3	10.0	7.2	5.8	2.9	4.1	1994
Chicago, IL	0.5	4.6	11.5	10.7	9.2	13.9	11.6	12.4	5.5	20.1	1970
Cincinnati, OH	0.9	6.6	12.1	13.5	10.7	13.4	10.4	11.3	4.7	16.5	1975
Clarksville, TN	2.6	16.3	19.0	18.9	12.1	12.6	7.3	5.5	2.6	3.0	1994
Cleveland, OH	0.5	4.0	7.0	8.8	7.1	12.5	13.3	17.0	7.3	22.6	1962
College Station, TX	2.6	20.0	19.0	15.1	17.1	12.3	5.7	3.9	2.1	2.2	1994
Colorado Springs, CO	1.9	12.9	17.5	15.2	16.4	15.8	8.0	5.9	1.4	4.9	1988
Columbia, MO	1.0	14.0	17.9	16.8	13.2	13.1	9.7	4.6	2.4	7.3	1990
Columbia, SC	1.6	13.8	18.3	16.7	13.5	14.1	8.8	6.7	2.8	3.7	1990
Columbus, OH	1.4	9.5	14.1	14.9	11.5	13.7	10.1	9.2	3.5	12.1	1981
Dallas, TX	2.6	16.9	18.6	14.3	16.5	12.2	7.6	6.6	2.2	2.5	1992
Davenport, IA	0.6	5.3	8.4	7.9	7.0	16.0	13.7	12.1	6.9	22.1	1966
Denver, CO	1.9	13.0	15.6	13.8	13.5	16.4	8.7	8.4	2.4	6.3	1986
Des Moines, IA	2.2	15.6	15.3	12.1	7.8	12.5	7.5	8.3	3.5	15.3	1984
Detroit, MI	0.5	4.0	8.7	11.1	9.0	14.5	12.4	18.3	8.8	12.8	1968
Durham, NC	2.3	17.4	17.1	16.3	14.5	11.4	7.5	5.9	2.9	4.7	1992
El Paso, TX	1.4	16.4	15.2	12.8	14.7	14.6	8.7	9.3	2.8	4.1	1987
Eugene, OR	0.8	7.5	12.2	14.5	9.1	21.0	13.2	8.5	6.7	6.4	1977
Fargo, ND	1.9	19.2	17.1	13.2	9.8	14.3	6.5	7.4	2.2	8.2	1991
Fort Collins, CO	2.2	16.8	18.4	17.5	12.3	16.7	5.8	3.2	1.8	5.3	1993
Fort Wayne, IN	1.0	7.6	11.5	13.5	10.2	14.7	12.3	9.9	4.7	14.5	1976
Fort Worth, TX	2.6	16.9	18.6	14.3	16.5	12.2	7.6	6.6	2.2	2.5	1992
Gainesville, FL	1.8	9.8	17.7	17.7	18.9	16.6	8.4	4.7	1.9	2.5	1988
Green Bay, WI	1.0	8.5	13.4	15.1	11.6	15.5	9.9	9.3	4.0	11.7	1980
Greensboro, NC	0.9	9.0	15.8	16.5	14.4	14.3	10.1	8.9	4.1	6.0	1985
Honolulu, HI	0.6	7.7	9.6	11.4	12.8	23.9	17.3	10.0	3.8	3.0	1977
Houston, TX	2.3	18.1	19.6	12.8	14.7	15.1	7.6	5.4	2.1	2.3	1992
Huntsville, AL	2.9	16.7	18.5	15.2	14.9	9.8	12.7	5.5	1.4	2.3	1992
Indianapolis, IN	1.4	10.4	14.9	15.5	9.9	11.7	10.3	9.4	4.3	12.2	1982
Jacksonville, FL	3.2	13.5	20.2	14.3	16.1	11.4	7.3	7.2	2.9	3.8	1991
Kansas City, MO	1.2	8.8	13.5	13.3	12.0	14.1	11.2	10.6	4.0	11.4	1979
Lafayette, LA	1.4	15.7	15.9	12.0	15.0	15.9	9.4	8.3	3.2	3.4	1987
Las Vegas, NV	1.9	12.3	28.8	25.5	13.7	10.1	4.7	2.0	0.6	0.4	1997
Lexington, KY	1.2	10.3	15.9	16.7	13.1	14.2	10.8	7.5	2.8	7.5	1985
Lincoln, NE	1.1	11.9	14.3	13.5	9.6	14.7	8.9	9.5	3.2	13.1	1981
Little Rock, AR	1.3	13.5	17.7	15.3	13.9	15.3	9.9	6.3	3.2	3.7	1988
Los Angeles, CA	0.6	5.3	6.3	7.4	12.6	15.9	15.0	17.6	7.8	11.5	1969
Louisville, KY	1.1	8.4	13.5	13.4	9.3	14.8	11.1	11.7	5.1	11.6	1977
Madison, WI	1.2	11.5	15.9	14.2	10.4	13.6	9.2	7.5	3.3	13.1	1983
Manchester, NH	0.5	5.4	9.6	10.5	20.2	15.3	9.2	7.3	3.6	18.6	1977
McAllen, TX	1.6	18.0	27.8	19.0	15.8	9.7	3.9	2.1	1.1	1.1	1999

Table continued on following page.

Metro Area	2020 or Later	2010 -2019	2000 -2009	1990 -1999	1980 -1989	1970 -1979	1960 -1969	1950 -1959	1940 -1949	Before 1940	Median Year
Memphis, TN	0.9	7.4	15.0	16.1	13.3	15.3	10.5	11.7	4.8	4.9	1982
Miami, FL	1.0	7.4	12.8	13.8	19.0	20.4	11.5	9.6	2.6	2.0	1982
Midland, TX	2.4	24.0	11.8	9.7	17.4	10.3	6.8	13.7	2.4	1.3	1989
Milwaukee, WI	0.7	5.5	8.2	10.4	7.6	13.1	11.6	15.3	7.0	20.7	1966
Minneapolis, MN	1.3	8.6	13.3	13.4	13.8	13.9	9.3	9.1	3.6	13.6	1980
Nashville, TN	3.1	17.7	18.1	15.3	13.0	11.9	8.2	6.0	2.5	4.3	1993
New Orleans, LA	0.4	5.1	9.9	6.8	13.1	19.6	13.9	10.8	5.1	15.2	1973
New York, NY	0.5	5.3	6.6	5.9	7.8	9.6	13.3	15.3	8.3	27.3	1959
Oklahoma City, OK	1.7	13.5	14.4	10.3	13.8	16.5	11.2	8.6	4.3	5.6	1983
Omaha, NE	1.3	10.7	14.3	11.8	9.6	13.9	11.2	8.2	3.4	15.6	1978
Orlando, FL	2.1	15.3	21.5	17.9	18.5	11.6	5.5	4.9	1.1	1.5	1994
Philadelphia, PA	0.7	5.3	7.9	8.9	9.9	12.2	11.7	14.9	7.0	21.5	1966
Phoenix, AZ	1.9	12.2	23.7	17.9	16.2	14.9	6.3	4.8	1.1	0.9	1993
Pittsburgh, PA	0.6	4.6	6.4	7.3	7.7	11.8	11.3	16.3	8.2	25.8	1960
Portland, OR	1.4	11.1	14.0	16.3	10.9	16.0	8.0	6.7	4.2	11.3	1983
Providence, RI	0.4	3.6	6.3	7.6	11.6	11.9	10.3	11.6	5.9	30.8	1962
Provo, UT	3.7	22.3	22.9	16.1	8.5	11.7	4.3	4.2	2.6	3.9	1999
Raleigh, NC	2.9	20.7	23.7	19.4	13.7	8.2	4.8	3.0	1.2	2.5	1999
Reno, NV	2.3	10.8	21.1	16.9	14.2	17.6	7.9	4.6	2.3	2.3	1991
Richmond, VA	1.3	10.3	14.2	14.3	15.3	13.7	9.3	8.5	4.2	8.8	1984
Rochester, MN	1.2	10.4	18.3	13.5	10.5	13.0	8.9	7.5	3.4	13.3	1984
Sacramento, CA	1.2	6.8	17.1	14.0	16.3	17.3	10.4	9.3	3.3	4.2	1983
Saint Louis, MO	0.8	6.3	11.4	11.6	11.1	12.8	12.2	12.3	5.4	16.1	1973
Saint Paul, MN	1.3	8.6	13.3	13.4	13.8	13.9	9.3	9.1	3.6	13.6	1980
Salem, OR	1.6	8.1	14.1	16.7	9.7	21.1	9.8	7.1	3.9	7.9	1980
Salt Lake City, UT	1.9	14.7	14.4	14.0	11.3	16.8	8.3	8.1	3.2	7.2	1986
San Antonio, TX	3.0	18.3	18.5	12.4	13.9	11.8	7.6	6.7	3.7	4.0	1992
San Diego, CA	0.8	6.5	12.0	11.5	18.6	21.7	11.6	10.1	3.1	4.1	1980
San Francisco, CA	0.7	5.6	7.7	7.8	10.6	14.2	12.8	13.4	7.7	19.5	1967
San Jose, CA	0.9	8.8	9.2	9.6	11.7	20.4	17.4	13.7	3.4	4.8	1975
Santa Rosa, CA	1.0	5.3	10.1	13.2	18.0	19.8	11.8	8.5	4.2	8.0	1979
Savannah, GA	2.2	15.8	19.4	13.1	12.7	11.0	6.7	7.5	3.8	7.7	1990
Seattle, WA	1.3	12.4	14.7	14.0	13.7	12.9	10.5	6.8	3.9	9.7	1985
Sioux Falls, SD	1.9	17.3	17.9	13.6	9.2	11.2	6.3	7.4	3.1	12.2	1990
Tampa, FL	1.6	10.2	15.4	13.0	19.8	18.9	8.7	7.9	1.9	2.5	1985
Tucson, AZ	1.2	7.5	18.2	16.5	17.1	18.6	8.3	7.9	2.8	1.9	1986
Tulsa, OK	1.2	11.0	13.9	11.1	13.9	18.2	10.3	9.8	4.1	6.7	1981
Virginia Beach, VA	1.0	9.6	12.6	14.0	18.1	14.3	11.5	9.1	4.2	5.6	1983
Washington, DC	1.2	10.7	14.1	12.9	15.2	13.0	11.5	8.7	4.7	8.1	1983
Wichita, KS	0.9	7.8	12.0	12.8	12.5	13.0	8.1	15.9	6.1	10.7	1977
Wilmington, NC	2.7	17.1	23.5	18.8	14.4	9.9	4.4	3.2	2.4	3.6	1996
Winston-Salem, NC	1.0	8.7	15.6	15.9	14.5	15.5	10.1	9.0	3.7	6.1	1984
U.S.	1.2	8.9	13.6	12.8	13.0	14.4	10.0	9.7	4.5	11.9	1980

Note: Figures are percentages except for median year; Figures cover the Metropolitan Statistical Area (MSA)
Source: U.S. Census Bureau, 2019-2023 American Community Survey 5-Year Estimates

Gross Monthly Rent: City

City	Under $500	$500 -$999	$1,000 -$1,499	$1,500 -$1,999	$2,000 -$2,499	$2,500 -$2,999	$3,000 and up	Median ($)
Albuquerque, NM	5.3	37.7	35.1	16.1	3.9	0.8	1.1	1,085
Anchorage, AK	3.5	14.0	35.7	25.6	12.6	5.5	3.0	1,453
Ann Arbor, MI	3.0	11.6	32.6	26.6	14.6	4.9	6.7	1,552
Athens, GA	3.8	33.4	37.8	17.1	5.0	1.5	1.3	1,162
Atlanta, GA	9.7	10.8	22.9	28.6	16.1	6.4	5.6	1,617
Austin, TX	2.5	4.7	32.4	33.5	15.4	6.4	5.0	1,655
Baltimore, MD	13.0	15.9	35.9	21.5	8.9	2.8	2.0	1,290
Billings, MT	7.9	34.2	37.7	14.4	3.3	0.7	1.7	1,097
Boise City, ID	4.1	15.0	41.7	26.5	9.3	1.9	1.6	1,359
Boston, MA	12.2	9.1	9.8	15.4	18.7	13.2	21.6	2,093
Boulder, CO	2.9	4.3	17.5	29.8	18.2	10.7	16.5	1,924
Cape Coral, FL	0.8	4.6	24.6	39.7	20.2	6.3	3.7	1,751
Cedar Rapids, IA	7.5	49.3	31.3	8.7	0.9	0.3	2.0	925
Charleston, SC	4.4	7.5	29.8	31.4	16.4	4.4	6.1	1,632
Charlotte, NC	2.7	10.1	36.9	33.9	10.9	3.2	2.3	1,504
Chicago, IL	7.2	17.6	32.2	20.1	11.6	5.4	5.9	1,380
Cincinnati, OH	11.8	43.6	26.9	11.1	3.9	1.5	1.3	953
Clarksville, TN	2.4	26.4	43.4	20.7	6.1	0.8	0.3	1,215
Cleveland, OH	17.2	43.0	26.0	9.4	2.6	0.9	0.8	894
College Station, TX	2.3	31.8	36.6	18.4	6.6	3.1	1.1	1,168
Colorado Springs, CO	2.7	10.7	32.8	30.0	15.9	4.3	3.6	1,562
Columbia, MO	4.0	39.3	38.9	9.8	5.8	1.4	0.8	1,067
Columbia, SC	8.4	26.7	42.3	16.5	5.4	0.5	0.2	1,158
Columbus, OH	4.5	22.1	46.5	19.4	5.3	1.2	0.9	1,224
Dallas, TX	3.1	12.2	42.5	25.9	9.5	3.4	3.4	1,403
Davenport, IA	7.1	52.5	29.5	6.8	1.6	0.1	2.4	930
Denver, CO	5.7	6.3	22.4	28.8	19.9	9.0	7.9	1,770
Des Moines, IA	5.4	39.0	40.2	12.9	2.0	0.2	0.3	1,054
Detroit, MI	11.7	35.1	39.5	10.0	2.5	0.8	0.4	1,034
Durham, NC	4.9	15.5	37.1	29.7	8.9	2.1	1.8	1,412
El Paso, TX	8.8	37.4	37.3	12.4	3.1	0.6	0.5	1,041
Eugene, OR	4.5	22.0	34.3	25.4	8.7	2.5	2.6	1,347
Fargo, ND	4.3	56.5	27.7	8.1	1.6	0.7	1.1	916
Fort Collins, CO	2.5	10.8	26.1	33.0	19.7	6.0	1.9	1,661
Fort Wayne, IN	6.7	48.7	37.3	5.3	1.4	0.4	0.3	959
Fort Worth, TX	2.6	13.5	40.6	25.3	12.3	3.4	2.2	1,412
Gainesville, FL	3.6	27.6	37.8	20.0	7.3	2.2	1.6	1,214
Green Bay, WI	6.7	55.0	31.7	5.1	0.7	0.1	0.6	904
Greensboro, NC	4.8	31.8	45.3	12.5	3.2	0.8	1.5	1,114
Honolulu, HI	5.7	7.6	21.8	26.2	16.6	7.5	14.5	1,783
Houston, TX	2.7	21.1	39.5	23.4	8.1	2.6	2.7	1,313
Huntsville, AL	4.8	38.7	37.7	14.0	2.9	0.5	1.3	1,078
Indianapolis, IN	4.8	32.8	43.9	13.7	3.2	1.0	0.6	1,112
Jacksonville, FL	4.9	16.1	38.9	26.9	9.7	2.3	1.2	1,375
Kansas City, MO	6.7	25.9	41.6	18.6	4.6	1.5	1.2	1,186
Lafayette, LA	6.5	37.0	39.7	13.7	2.6	0.2	0.4	1,065
Las Vegas, NV	3.1	14.4	35.9	29.4	11.7	3.5	1.9	1,456
Lexington, KY	4.4	36.0	40.3	13.9	3.8	1.2	0.5	1,101
Lincoln, NE	4.7	41.3	37.3	12.0	3.0	0.5	1.4	1,045
Little Rock, AR	5.2	38.1	39.8	12.0	2.8	0.8	1.2	1,067
Los Angeles, CA	4.6	7.2	20.1	23.9	18.3	10.6	15.3	1,879
Louisville, KY	9.7	34.0	39.6	12.5	2.8	0.7	0.7	1,069
Madison, WI	3.6	15.5	41.6	26.0	8.2	2.4	2.7	1,364
Manchester, NH	5.5	12.8	34.2	31.7	12.5	1.9	1.3	1,465
McAllen, TX	8.3	40.3	37.2	11.2	2.0	0.9	0.0	1,017

Table continued on following page.

City	Under $500	$500 -$999	$1,000 -$1,499	$1,500 -$1,999	$2,000 -$2,499	$2,500 -$2,999	$3,000 and up	Median ($)
Memphis, TN	4.9	32.5	43.3	15.2	2.8	0.7	0.6	1,123
Miami, FL	8.4	9.2	25.4	22.3	16.1	8.1	10.5	1,657
Midland, TX	3.2	15.5	38.6	24.4	11.7	4.2	2.3	1,407
Milwaukee, WI	7.0	39.6	38.2	10.7	2.4	1.0	1.1	1,033
Minneapolis, MN	8.7	16.4	35.0	22.5	10.8	3.3	3.3	1,329
Nashville, TN	6.2	10.7	34.1	28.4	12.8	4.5	3.3	1,486
New Orleans, LA	10.0	21.7	38.2	19.5	6.2	2.7	1.7	1,211
New York, NY	8.3	10.0	19.2	22.4	16.2	8.5	15.4	1,779
Oklahoma City, OK	5.3	36.3	40.4	13.3	2.8	1.1	0.7	1,083
Omaha, NE	4.4	29.7	43.5	16.1	4.3	0.8	1.3	1,150
Orlando, FL	3.1	6.0	30.0	36.5	17.1	4.7	2.6	1,650
Philadelphia, PA	8.5	18.1	35.8	22.6	8.7	3.1	3.2	1,323
Phoenix, AZ	3.5	13.5	36.2	29.1	12.0	3.7	2.0	1,458
Pittsburgh, PA	10.6	21.9	35.1	18.4	8.3	3.3	2.4	1,221
Portland, OR	4.6	9.6	30.1	29.6	15.0	6.3	4.8	1,596
Providence, RI	16.9	11.3	33.2	22.3	10.5	3.4	2.4	1,333
Provo, UT	5.6	28.6	40.3	16.6	6.4	1.9	0.5	1,152
Raleigh, NC	2.5	9.3	41.1	33.8	8.8	2.7	1.8	1,468
Reno, NV	4.9	15.0	33.3	26.7	13.4	4.0	2.7	1,453
Richmond, VA	9.4	14.9	41.0	24.1	7.9	1.9	0.8	1,314
Rochester, MN	6.3	23.1	32.8	23.3	8.8	1.7	4.0	1,316
Sacramento, CA	4.4	10.1	23.1	31.7	19.4	7.9	3.3	1,694
Saint Louis, MO	9.1	43.5	33.0	9.9	3.0	0.9	0.7	978
Saint Paul, MN	9.5	16.7	41.4	20.1	9.0	1.6	1.7	1,248
Salem, OR	5.6	16.1	43.1	24.0	8.2	1.8	1.2	1,323
Salt Lake City, UT	6.7	16.6	37.5	23.0	10.1	3.7	2.5	1,343
San Antonio, TX	4.8	21.4	43.5	21.8	5.7	1.6	1.2	1,258
San Diego, CA	2.3	3.9	11.3	22.8	21.9	16.0	21.8	2,223
San Francisco, CA	7.8	8.1	11.1	11.9	13.2	10.9	36.9	2,419
San Jose, CA	3.7	4.7	6.6	12.7	18.3	17.6	36.5	2,617
Santa Rosa, CA	4.1	5.1	12.9	24.0	23.2	15.4	15.3	2,084
Savannah, GA	6.6	17.0	41.8	23.1	7.7	1.9	2.0	1,302
Seattle, WA	5.0	4.2	15.6	25.4	21.5	13.0	15.5	1,998
Sioux Falls, SD	4.5	46.5	36.9	8.1	2.4	0.3	1.2	993
Tampa, FL	6.5	11.9	27.9	27.1	14.9	6.8	4.9	1,567
Tucson, AZ	4.5	38.5	36.3	15.0	3.5	0.8	1.3	1,079
Tulsa, OK	7.3	42.9	36.4	9.1	2.1	1.0	1.2	998
Virginia Beach, VA	1.9	5.3	31.3	38.7	14.9	3.9	4.0	1,649
Washington, DC	7.4	7.8	17.8	21.2	16.8	11.4	17.6	1,900
Wichita, KS	4.8	50.2	34.2	7.8	2.1	0.3	0.7	960
Wilmington, NC	6.3	17.3	40.7	25.1	7.1	1.9	1.5	1,311
Winston-Salem, NC	6.7	40.1	36.5	11.4	3.5	0.8	1.0	1,033
U.S.	6.5	22.3	29.5	20.2	10.8	4.8	5.9	1,348

Note: Figures are percentages except for Median; Gross rent is the contract rent plus the estimated average monthly cost of utilities (electricity, gas, and water and sewer) and fuels (oil, coal, kerosene, wood, etc.) if these are paid by the renter (or paid for the renter by someone else).
Source: U.S. Census Bureau, 2019-2023 American Community Survey 5-Year Estimates

Gross Monthly Rent: Metro Area

Metro Area	Under $500	$500 -$999	$1,000 -$1,499	$1,500 -$1,999	$2,000 -$2,499	$2,500 -2,999	$3,000 and up	Median ($)
Albuquerque, NM	5.5	36.2	35.3	16.7	4.3	0.9	1.1	1,102
Anchorage, AK	3.9	15.2	36.0	25.1	12.2	4.8	2.7	1,422
Ann Arbor, MI	4.3	14.9	39.0	23.1	10.3	3.5	4.7	1,400
Athens, GA	4.0	34.6	36.7	16.4	4.9	2.0	1.4	1,144
Atlanta, GA	3.5	10.4	31.9	33.0	14.4	4.1	2.7	1,563
Austin, TX	2.2	6.5	32.0	32.0	16.4	6.3	4.6	1,646
Baltimore, MD	6.9	10.5	29.1	28.1	15.8	5.6	3.9	1,562
Billings, MT	8.5	35.8	36.1	14.7	2.8	0.7	1.4	1,072
Boise City, ID	4.7	16.9	37.0	26.4	10.2	2.7	2.2	1,383
Boston, MA	9.4	8.3	13.6	21.1	19.8	12.2	15.5	1,940
Boulder, CO	3.0	4.7	17.7	31.3	20.8	10.0	12.5	1,893
Cape Coral, FL	2.9	8.6	31.7	34.5	14.0	4.2	4.1	1,597
Cedar Rapids, IA	7.8	50.9	29.5	8.0	1.3	0.3	2.2	899
Charleston, SC	3.1	11.1	36.7	27.9	13.4	4.0	3.8	1,488
Charlotte, NC	3.8	18.7	36.7	27.1	9.1	2.5	2.0	1,377
Chicago, IL	5.8	16.7	35.4	21.8	11.0	4.6	4.6	1,378
Cincinnati, OH	8.2	37.8	34.1	12.7	4.4	1.5	1.4	1,047
Clarksville, TN	4.4	33.0	39.4	17.7	4.4	0.6	0.5	1,141
Cleveland, OH	9.8	40.6	34.0	10.8	2.6	0.9	1.3	996
College Station, TX	4.0	32.0	38.0	16.6	5.7	2.2	1.4	1,146
Colorado Springs, CO	2.7	10.6	30.1	29.6	18.6	5.0	3.4	1,611
Columbia, MO	4.7	41.2	38.4	9.2	4.6	1.1	0.8	1,041
Columbia, SC	5.2	31.0	41.5	15.6	5.0	0.9	0.9	1,145
Columbus, OH	5.1	24.3	43.9	18.5	5.5	1.4	1.2	1,208
Dallas, TX	2.1	9.7	37.7	28.7	13.8	4.7	3.3	1,509
Davenport, IA	11.1	50.2	27.2	7.3	1.5	0.8	1.9	899
Denver, CO	3.6	5.3	21.2	32.6	21.1	9.5	6.7	1,805
Des Moines, IA	4.6	33.5	42.0	15.1	3.4	0.5	0.9	1,113
Detroit, MI	7.5	26.8	41.4	16.4	4.7	1.3	1.8	1,162
Durham, NC	5.0	18.6	36.6	26.5	8.7	2.4	2.3	1,374
El Paso, TX	8.7	37.2	37.0	13.0	3.1	0.5	0.4	1,045
Eugene, OR	5.4	23.6	36.5	23.0	7.6	1.9	1.9	1,287
Fargo, ND	4.7	52.7	29.3	9.2	2.5	0.8	0.9	940
Fort Collins, CO	2.6	10.0	25.7	33.1	18.9	6.6	3.1	1,677
Fort Wayne, IN	6.6	48.2	36.5	6.1	1.7	0.5	0.4	963
Fort Worth, TX	2.1	9.7	37.7	28.7	13.8	4.7	3.3	1,509
Gainesville, FL	3.9	27.5	36.4	20.0	7.2	2.6	2.3	1,219
Green Bay, WI	4.8	50.7	35.3	6.6	1.4	0.4	0.8	959
Greensboro, NC	7.6	37.7	39.7	10.5	2.6	0.7	1.2	1,045
Honolulu, HI	4.7	6.3	16.7	20.6	15.8	11.3	24.6	2,054
Houston, TX	2.6	17.5	39.1	24.9	10.1	3.2	2.6	1,378
Huntsville, AL	4.8	37.6	36.8	14.6	4.3	0.6	1.2	1,091
Indianapolis, IN	4.8	30.7	41.9	15.6	4.7	1.4	0.9	1,142
Jacksonville, FL	4.3	15.8	36.2	27.0	11.0	2.9	2.7	1,416
Kansas City, MO	5.4	25.3	41.7	18.9	5.6	1.4	1.6	1,201
Lafayette, LA	11.3	44.1	33.2	9.1	1.7	0.3	0.2	954
Las Vegas, NV	1.8	12.2	34.8	31.6	13.6	3.7	2.2	1,518
Lexington, KY	5.5	38.0	38.7	13.0	3.1	1.1	0.5	1,070
Lincoln, NE	4.8	41.4	37.2	11.8	2.9	0.5	1.4	1,043
Little Rock, AR	6.2	43.2	37.0	10.4	1.7	0.6	0.9	1,007
Los Angeles, CA	3.5	5.8	16.8	24.5	21.1	12.0	16.3	1,987
Louisville, KY	9.1	34.6	40.1	12.2	2.6	0.7	0.8	1,064
Madison, WI	3.9	19.6	41.6	23.8	6.9	1.9	2.2	1,300
Manchester, NH	5.5	11.2	31.2	31.7	14.5	3.8	2.0	1,532
McAllen, TX	11.1	48.5	30.9	7.4	1.4	0.5	0.2	925

Table continued on following page.

Metro Area	Under $500	$500 -$999	$1,000 -$1,499	$1,500 -$1,999	$2,000 -$2,499	$2,500 -2,999	$3,000 and up	Median ($)
Memphis, TN	4.9	30.4	42.2	16.0	4.3	1.2	1.0	1,153
Miami, FL	3.9	6.5	23.2	30.3	19.3	8.6	8.2	1,770
Midland, TX	3.7	17.8	38.4	23.7	10.7	3.8	2.0	1,377
Milwaukee, WI	6.0	33.5	39.6	14.3	3.8	1.5	1.3	1,105
Minneapolis, MN	6.6	14.0	36.6	25.6	10.8	3.3	3.2	1,396
Nashville, TN	5.4	15.0	34.3	27.1	11.6	3.7	2.8	1,434
New Orleans, LA	7.3	24.9	41.7	18.2	5.0	1.7	1.1	1,182
New York, NY	7.3	9.0	20.0	24.4	16.9	8.6	13.8	1,780
Oklahoma City, OK	5.3	36.8	39.1	13.4	3.1	1.1	1.1	1,081
Omaha, NE	5.0	29.1	42.6	16.6	4.3	0.9	1.5	1,152
Orlando, FL	2.1	8.2	28.7	34.6	18.0	5.3	3.0	1,659
Philadelphia, PA	6.4	14.6	35.3	25.2	11.2	3.7	3.7	1,413
Phoenix, AZ	2.7	10.8	31.5	30.9	15.3	5.2	3.5	1,581
Pittsburgh, PA	11.8	37.3	32.0	11.5	4.4	1.5	1.6	1,011
Portland, OR	3.4	7.7	28.4	33.9	16.2	6.3	4.1	1,654
Providence, RI	12.9	18.9	35.1	20.9	7.8	2.5	1.9	1,236
Provo, UT	3.1	16.5	34.5	27.9	12.6	3.7	1.8	1,434
Raleigh, NC	3.4	13.4	36.5	31.2	10.0	3.4	2.1	1,459
Reno, NV	4.2	14.7	31.6	27.3	14.8	4.0	3.4	1,491
Richmond, VA	5.5	14.0	39.6	27.9	9.1	1.8	2.0	1,388
Rochester, MN	7.9	29.2	31.6	19.9	7.1	1.3	3.0	1,195
Sacramento, CA	3.6	8.3	24.6	29.4	19.8	8.6	5.7	1,729
Saint Louis, MO	6.4	36.8	37.9	12.7	3.4	1.2	1.8	1,073
Saint Paul, MN	6.6	14.0	36.6	25.6	10.8	3.3	3.2	1,396
Salem, OR	4.9	16.5	43.8	24.6	7.3	1.8	1.1	1,324
Salt Lake City, UT	3.9	11.4	35.8	29.9	13.2	3.6	2.2	1,486
San Antonio, TX	4.4	19.8	41.8	22.8	7.7	2.0	1.4	1,299
San Diego, CA	2.2	4.0	12.0	24.8	22.5	14.8	19.6	2,154
San Francisco, CA	5.1	5.6	9.5	14.1	18.4	15.0	32.3	2,426
San Jose, CA	2.7	3.7	5.4	10.8	16.8	17.8	42.7	2,794
Santa Rosa, CA	4.1	6.8	13.4	21.5	22.3	14.4	17.4	2,093
Savannah, GA	4.2	17.2	38.3	28.2	8.4	1.9	1.8	1,370
Seattle, WA	4.0	4.8	16.7	28.3	22.6	11.5	12.2	1,932
Sioux Falls, SD	5.6	46.3	36.0	8.1	2.6	0.3	1.1	987
Tampa, FL	3.2	13.0	34.1	27.7	13.7	4.8	3.5	1,497
Tucson, AZ	4.3	32.8	35.8	18.7	4.9	1.4	2.1	1,154
Tulsa, OK	7.1	39.7	37.8	10.4	2.9	1.0	1.1	1,034
Virginia Beach, VA	5.0	13.8	37.7	28.0	10.3	2.6	2.7	1,416
Washington, DC	3.7	4.7	14.3	28.7	23.5	12.3	12.9	1,975
Wichita, KS	5.7	48.1	34.1	8.5	2.5	0.5	0.6	969
Wilmington, NC	5.1	19.5	40.4	23.1	7.7	2.0	2.3	1,313
Winston-Salem, NC	7.6	45.5	32.7	10.3	2.5	0.7	0.6	973
U.S.	6.5	22.3	29.5	20.2	10.8	4.8	5.9	1,348

Note: Figures are percentages except for Median; Gross rent is the contract rent plus the estimated average monthly cost of utilities (electricity, gas, and water and sewer) and fuels (oil, coal, kerosene, wood, etc.) if these are paid by the renter (or paid for the renter by someone else); Figures cover the Metropolitan Statistical Area (MSA)
Source: U.S. Census Bureau, 2019-2023 American Community Survey 5-Year Estimates

Highest Level of Education: City

City	Less than H.S.	H.S. Diploma	Some College, No Deg.	Associate Degree	Bachelors Degree	Masters Degree	Profess. School Degree	Doctorate Degree
Albuquerque, NM	9.1	21.6	21.2	9.5	20.9	12.0	2.8	2.9
Anchorage, AK	6.0	24.5	23.2	8.6	23.4	9.9	2.7	1.7
Ann Arbor, MI	2.4	7.0	8.9	4.0	30.5	26.4	8.7	12.1
Athens, GA	10.1	17.7	16.5	7.0	24.3	15.3	2.9	6.2
Atlanta, GA	7.0	16.0	13.6	5.0	32.8	16.8	5.7	3.0
Austin, TX	8.4	13.2	14.8	5.4	36.2	15.9	3.6	2.5
Baltimore, MD	12.8	27.9	18.4	5.5	18.1	11.7	3.1	2.5
Billings, MT	4.5	27.6	22.5	8.3	25.0	7.7	2.6	1.7
Boise City, ID	5.2	19.3	21.5	7.3	29.2	12.0	3.1	2.2
Boston, MA	11.1	18.3	11.6	4.9	28.5	16.4	5.2	3.9
Boulder, CO	3.1	6.4	10.2	3.5	36.9	25.7	5.1	9.1
Cape Coral, FL	6.8	35.3	22.6	9.5	16.7	6.0	1.7	1.3
Cedar Rapids, IA	5.9	25.9	22.4	12.9	22.2	7.8	2.1	0.8
Charleston, SC	4.1	15.4	16.0	6.8	35.5	13.8	5.2	3.2
Charlotte, NC	10.4	16.6	17.5	8.0	30.4	12.8	2.9	1.3
Chicago, IL	13.2	21.3	16.4	5.8	24.9	12.8	3.6	2.0
Cincinnati, OH	10.3	24.1	17.0	7.3	23.2	11.7	3.8	2.5
Clarksville, TN	5.8	27.4	24.2	12.0	18.9	9.4	1.2	1.1
Cleveland, OH	16.5	33.5	21.6	7.1	12.5	5.8	2.2	0.9
College Station, TX	5.4	14.4	16.9	6.2	29.5	16.1	2.0	9.5
Colorado Springs, CO	5.4	19.2	23.0	10.6	25.2	12.8	2.1	1.9
Columbia, MO	4.7	16.9	15.7	6.2	30.1	15.7	4.8	5.9
Columbia, SC	9.1	19.2	18.2	7.4	25.2	12.7	5.0	3.1
Columbus, OH	10.2	25.2	19.2	7.2	24.1	10.2	2.1	1.8
Dallas, TX	19.2	21.5	16.7	5.1	22.9	9.7	3.4	1.4
Davenport, IA	7.4	28.8	22.1	11.7	18.9	8.2	1.8	1.1
Denver, CO	8.6	14.8	15.7	5.3	33.8	15.0	4.7	2.2
Des Moines, IA	12.7	29.1	20.0	9.1	19.9	6.3	1.8	0.9
Detroit, MI	16.6	33.2	25.4	7.2	10.5	5.4	1.0	0.7
Durham, NC	8.6	15.4	13.7	6.6	28.8	16.9	4.5	5.5
El Paso, TX	18.1	24.4	21.3	8.8	18.3	6.7	1.4	1.0
Eugene, OR	5.2	17.4	24.3	8.8	23.7	13.5	3.6	3.5
Fargo, ND	4.7	18.7	20.7	12.7	29.0	9.9	2.0	2.3
Fort Collins, CO	2.4	13.5	16.1	8.2	34.3	18.9	2.8	3.9
Fort Wayne, IN	11.1	28.7	21.8	9.9	19.4	7.2	1.1	0.9
Fort Worth, TX	15.7	24.7	20.5	7.4	20.6	8.4	1.6	1.1
Gainesville, FL	5.7	17.7	14.9	10.0	25.7	15.1	4.2	6.8
Green Bay, WI	11.0	31.4	20.4	11.7	18.4	5.3	1.2	0.7
Greensboro, NC	9.9	21.5	20.1	8.7	24.2	11.3	2.3	2.1
Honolulu, HI	9.1	22.8	17.2	10.1	25.2	9.9	3.4	2.2
Houston, TX	19.7	21.5	16.6	6.2	21.3	9.6	3.2	1.9
Huntsville, AL	8.4	17.3	20.8	7.3	26.7	14.8	2.3	2.3
Indianapolis, IN	12.5	26.8	18.9	7.7	21.7	8.8	2.3	1.4
Jacksonville, FL	9.2	28.2	20.7	10.0	21.6	7.4	1.7	1.1
Kansas City, MO	8.2	25.0	21.6	7.4	23.8	10.1	2.7	1.2
Lafayette, LA	9.1	25.3	18.9	6.0	27.1	7.7	4.0	1.9
Las Vegas, NV	14.2	26.7	23.7	8.1	17.3	6.9	2.1	1.0
Lexington, KY	7.6	19.0	18.5	7.6	26.5	12.9	4.3	3.6
Lincoln, NE	7.0	20.4	20.3	11.4	26.4	9.8	2.3	2.5
Little Rock, AR	7.7	21.2	20.7	6.5	25.0	11.7	4.7	2.6
Los Angeles, CA	20.7	18.5	16.6	6.3	24.5	8.7	3.1	1.6
Louisville, KY	9.5	27.7	21.0	8.4	19.9	9.6	2.4	1.5
Madison, WI	4.3	14.6	14.4	7.5	33.5	16.0	3.7	6.0
Manchester, NH	11.3	29.1	18.1	8.0	22.5	8.8	1.3	0.9
McAllen, TX	20.1	20.7	20.6	6.5	20.3	7.6	2.9	1.2

Table continued on following page.

City	Less than H.S.	H.S. Diploma	Some College, No Deg.	Associate Degree	Bachelors Degree	Masters Degree	Profess. School Degree	Doctorate Degree
Memphis, TN	12.6	30.6	22.5	6.1	16.9	7.9	2.0	1.4
Miami, FL	20.0	25.2	11.6	7.5	21.5	8.8	4.1	1.3
Midland, TX	13.5	22.5	22.4	8.0	23.9	7.4	1.4	1.0
Milwaukee, WI	14.5	30.8	20.9	7.3	17.2	7.0	1.4	1.0
Minneapolis, MN	8.9	13.8	15.7	7.2	32.7	14.8	4.1	2.9
Nashville, TN	9.8	20.2	17.0	6.0	29.1	11.7	3.4	2.7
New Orleans, LA	10.9	21.3	20.7	5.2	22.5	12.0	4.8	2.6
New York, NY	16.3	23.0	13.2	6.5	23.6	12.4	3.3	1.7
Oklahoma City, OK	12.2	24.5	21.3	8.0	21.5	8.5	2.6	1.3
Omaha, NE	9.5	21.3	21.3	7.7	25.6	9.7	3.2	1.8
Orlando, FL	8.1	23.1	15.7	10.9	26.1	11.2	3.2	1.8
Philadelphia, PA	12.6	29.8	16.4	6.5	19.4	10.2	3.0	2.1
Phoenix, AZ	15.6	23.1	21.1	7.9	19.9	8.9	2.3	1.3
Pittsburgh, PA	5.7	23.7	14.7	8.0	24.6	14.1	4.5	4.6
Portland, OR	6.7	14.7	18.5	6.7	32.1	14.2	4.5	2.7
Providence, RI	18.1	27.5	14.8	4.9	18.3	9.7	3.5	3.3
Provo, UT	7.5	14.4	24.4	8.7	31.1	9.5	1.7	2.6
Raleigh, NC	7.5	15.9	16.2	7.4	32.5	14.3	3.5	2.6
Reno, NV	10.7	22.8	22.6	8.3	21.4	9.4	2.8	2.2
Richmond, VA	10.7	21.2	18.8	5.3	26.0	12.3	3.5	2.2
Rochester, MN	5.5	18.9	14.9	10.6	27.7	13.2	5.2	3.9
Sacramento, CA	13.1	20.5	21.6	8.4	22.9	8.7	3.3	1.6
Saint Louis, MO	9.5	24.5	19.7	6.1	22.0	12.1	3.4	2.7
Saint Paul, MN	11.1	20.8	16.9	7.7	25.2	12.3	3.3	2.8
Salem, OR	11.3	22.4	25.4	9.3	19.3	8.6	2.1	1.5
Salt Lake City, UT	8.4	17.1	16.9	6.7	28.9	13.6	4.7	3.7
San Antonio, TX	15.7	25.6	21.8	8.2	17.7	7.7	2.1	1.3
San Diego, CA	9.8	15.0	17.8	7.5	28.8	13.6	3.6	3.8
San Francisco, CA	11.2	11.3	12.0	5.3	35.1	16.7	4.9	3.4
San Jose, CA	14.5	16.4	15.5	7.1	26.2	15.1	2.1	3.1
Santa Rosa, CA	14.5	19.2	21.9	9.7	21.3	9.0	3.2	1.2
Savannah, GA	10.1	27.0	23.7	7.2	20.6	8.1	2.0	1.3
Seattle, WA	4.3	9.5	12.9	5.8	37.6	20.5	5.3	4.2
Sioux Falls, SD	6.9	24.3	20.1	11.2	25.4	8.2	2.5	1.3
Tampa, FL	10.2	22.5	14.7	8.0	26.3	11.7	4.4	2.2
Tucson, AZ	12.7	23.0	25.2	9.0	17.7	9.0	1.6	1.9
Tulsa, OK	12.4	25.0	21.2	8.2	20.8	8.0	3.0	1.5
Virginia Beach, VA	5.3	21.3	22.4	10.5	25.0	11.4	2.3	1.8
Washington, DC	7.2	14.5	11.8	2.9	26.1	22.7	10.3	4.6
Wichita, KS	12.0	26.0	23.0	8.1	19.7	8.5	1.6	1.1
Wilmington, NC	6.5	18.0	18.9	10.8	29.2	11.1	3.3	2.3
Winston-Salem, NC	11.6	23.7	19.5	7.9	21.6	10.2	2.8	2.6
U.S.	10.6	26.2	19.4	8.8	21.3	9.8	2.3	1.6

Note: Figures cover persons age 25 and over
Source: U.S. Census Bureau, 2019-2023 American Community Survey 5-Year Estimates

Highest Level of Education: Metro Area

Metro Area	Less than H.S.	H.S. Diploma	Some College, No Deg.	Associate Degree	Bachelors Degree	Masters Degree	Profess. School Degree	Doctorate Degree
Albuquerque, NM	9.7	23.6	22.0	9.7	19.2	11.0	2.4	2.5
Anchorage, AK	5.9	27.1	23.6	9.4	21.3	9.0	2.3	1.4
Ann Arbor, MI	4.2	14.2	16.8	6.7	27.1	19.4	5.1	6.5
Athens, GA	10.2	21.4	17.5	7.5	21.9	13.4	3.3	4.9
Atlanta, GA	9.2	23.0	18.4	7.9	25.4	11.7	2.6	1.8
Austin, TX	8.4	17.1	18.0	6.6	31.6	13.6	2.7	2.1
Baltimore, MD	7.9	23.6	18.2	7.0	23.4	14.4	3.1	2.5
Billings, MT	4.8	30.1	22.7	9.0	22.8	7.0	2.2	1.5
Boise City, ID	7.5	23.3	24.0	8.6	24.3	8.8	2.1	1.4
Boston, MA	7.7	20.8	13.3	7.0	27.5	16.4	3.6	3.7
Boulder, CO	4.5	11.0	14.5	6.1	34.5	20.0	3.8	5.6
Cape Coral, FL	9.6	30.0	19.8	9.8	18.8	8.2	2.3	1.4
Cedar Rapids, IA	4.8	27.8	20.7	13.9	22.2	8.0	1.7	0.9
Charleston, SC	8.1	22.9	19.8	9.3	24.9	10.7	2.8	1.6
Charlotte, NC	9.6	22.6	19.4	9.5	25.4	10.4	2.1	1.1
Chicago, IL	10.3	23.2	18.4	7.3	24.4	12.1	2.8	1.6
Cincinnati, OH	7.7	28.8	18.0	8.6	22.7	10.4	2.2	1.6
Clarksville, TN	7.7	29.5	23.6	11.2	17.4	8.2	1.3	1.1
Cleveland, OH	8.3	29.0	20.4	8.8	20.0	9.6	2.5	1.4
College Station, TX	11.7	23.8	18.7	6.8	22.2	10.2	1.7	5.0
Colorado Springs, CO	4.9	19.7	23.4	11.0	24.9	12.6	1.8	1.7
Columbia, MO	6.0	22.6	16.6	7.3	26.7	13.0	3.5	4.2
Columbia, SC	8.9	25.3	21.2	9.6	20.8	10.2	2.2	1.8
Columbus, OH	7.9	26.7	18.4	7.5	24.4	10.8	2.5	1.7
Dallas, TX	12.7	21.7	19.7	7.4	24.5	10.7	2.0	1.3
Davenport, IA	7.6	29.3	22.7	11.1	18.6	8.2	1.5	1.1
Denver, CO	7.7	18.4	18.2	7.3	30.3	13.3	2.9	1.9
Des Moines, IA	6.5	25.0	19.0	10.4	26.4	9.0	2.1	1.5
Detroit, MI	8.8	26.0	22.0	9.2	20.4	10.3	2.2	1.1
Durham, NC	8.9	17.0	14.3	7.5	26.3	15.5	4.8	5.6
El Paso, TX	19.4	24.9	21.1	9.2	17.1	6.1	1.2	0.9
Eugene, OR	6.9	22.8	27.0	9.9	19.7	9.4	2.3	2.1
Fargo, ND	4.4	19.1	20.8	13.5	28.4	9.7	1.9	2.3
Fort Collins, CO	3.4	16.8	19.3	8.8	31.0	14.9	2.7	3.1
Fort Wayne, IN	9.3	29.7	20.7	10.6	20.0	7.3	1.5	0.9
Fort Worth, TX	12.7	21.7	19.7	7.4	24.5	10.7	2.0	1.3
Gainesville, FL	7.3	24.2	16.4	11.1	20.3	11.8	4.0	4.8
Green Bay, WI	6.7	31.3	19.1	13.0	21.0	6.8	1.3	0.8
Greensboro, NC	11.7	26.5	20.8	9.6	20.0	8.5	1.5	1.4
Honolulu, HI	7.1	25.2	19.0	11.0	23.7	9.4	2.8	1.8
Houston, TX	14.9	22.7	19.5	7.5	22.1	9.3	2.3	1.7
Huntsville, AL	8.5	20.7	20.4	8.0	25.3	13.5	1.7	1.9
Indianapolis, IN	8.9	26.7	18.4	8.1	24.1	9.9	2.4	1.5
Jacksonville, FL	7.9	26.4	20.5	10.0	23.0	8.9	2.0	1.3
Kansas City, MO	6.9	24.9	21.1	7.9	24.4	11.0	2.5	1.3
Lafayette, LA	13.0	34.8	17.9	7.3	19.0	5.3	1.8	0.9
Las Vegas, NV	13.2	27.6	23.4	8.5	18.0	6.6	1.7	1.0
Lexington, KY	8.1	23.5	19.2	8.1	23.4	11.4	3.5	2.8
Lincoln, NE	6.4	20.9	20.1	11.9	26.2	9.8	2.1	2.4
Little Rock, AR	7.9	29.1	21.7	8.4	20.3	8.8	2.4	1.4
Los Angeles, CA	17.8	19.5	18.1	7.1	23.9	9.2	2.8	1.6
Louisville, KY	8.7	29.4	20.8	8.9	19.5	9.2	2.2	1.3
Madison, WI	4.1	20.2	16.6	9.7	29.9	12.7	2.9	3.8
Manchester, NH	7.0	25.6	17.2	9.6	25.4	12.1	1.6	1.5
McAllen, TX	30.7	25.2	18.3	5.6	13.9	4.8	1.0	0.6

Table continued on following page.

Metro Area	Less than H.S.	H.S. Diploma	Some College, No Deg.	Associate Degree	Bachelors Degree	Masters Degree	Profess. School Degree	Doctorate Degree
Memphis, TN	10.5	29.1	22.1	7.6	18.5	8.9	2.0	1.4
Miami, FL	13.1	25.7	16.0	9.5	21.8	9.0	3.4	1.4
Midland, TX	13.8	24.0	23.3	8.2	20.9	7.4	1.4	0.8
Milwaukee, WI	7.3	25.6	19.3	9.0	25.2	9.8	2.2	1.5
Minneapolis, MN	5.8	20.2	18.7	10.5	29.1	11.3	2.7	1.9
Nashville, TN	8.5	25.7	18.7	7.3	25.6	10.0	2.4	1.9
New Orleans, LA	12.5	26.2	21.5	6.7	19.6	8.7	3.1	1.6
New York, NY	12.4	23.2	14.0	6.8	24.9	13.3	3.5	1.8
Oklahoma City, OK	10.1	26.2	22.3	8.0	21.3	8.4	2.2	1.5
Omaha, NE	7.3	22.5	21.7	9.4	24.9	10.2	2.5	1.5
Orlando, FL	9.3	25.1	18.5	11.2	23.2	9.2	2.1	1.3
Philadelphia, PA	7.9	27.0	16.1	7.5	24.1	12.2	3.0	2.2
Phoenix, AZ	10.5	22.7	23.0	9.2	21.6	9.4	2.1	1.4
Pittsburgh, PA	5.1	31.4	15.5	10.6	22.6	10.6	2.3	1.9
Portland, OR	7.2	19.8	22.1	8.8	26.0	11.1	2.8	2.1
Providence, RI	11.6	27.8	17.2	8.4	21.3	9.9	2.1	1.7
Provo, UT	4.7	17.1	24.8	10.1	30.1	9.9	1.7	1.6
Raleigh, NC	7.1	17.3	16.6	8.8	30.8	14.4	2.6	2.4
Reno, NV	11.4	24.4	24.0	8.8	19.2	8.4	2.2	1.6
Richmond, VA	8.1	24.4	19.5	7.8	24.4	11.7	2.5	1.7
Rochester, MN	5.2	23.0	17.1	12.5	24.7	10.8	4.1	2.7
Sacramento, CA	9.9	20.6	23.3	9.9	23.0	8.7	3.0	1.6
Saint Louis, MO	6.7	25.5	21.0	9.3	22.3	11.2	2.3	1.7
Saint Paul, MN	5.8	20.2	18.7	10.5	29.1	11.3	2.7	1.9
Salem, OR	12.8	24.9	25.6	9.8	17.4	6.9	1.6	1.0
Salt Lake City, UT	8.2	22.7	22.1	9.2	24.1	9.7	2.3	1.7
San Antonio, TX	12.7	25.0	21.8	8.6	20.0	8.7	1.9	1.3
San Diego, CA	11.0	17.9	20.6	8.3	25.6	11.0	2.9	2.6
San Francisco, CA	10.5	15.0	15.5	6.6	30.0	15.1	3.9	3.4
San Jose, CA	10.9	13.9	13.9	6.5	27.8	19.3	2.9	4.8
Santa Rosa, CA	11.1	18.6	23.0	9.4	23.5	9.4	3.4	1.5
Savannah, GA	8.7	25.9	22.4	8.0	21.6	9.6	2.3	1.5
Seattle, WA	6.7	18.8	19.2	9.1	27.8	13.5	2.8	2.2
Sioux Falls, SD	6.3	25.7	19.7	12.6	24.8	7.7	2.0	1.2
Tampa, FL	9.1	27.4	19.4	10.0	21.5	8.9	2.2	1.3
Tucson, AZ	10.1	21.2	23.9	9.0	20.4	10.7	2.4	2.4
Tulsa, OK	9.9	28.6	22.4	9.4	19.7	7.0	1.9	1.1
Virginia Beach, VA	7.2	25.1	22.8	9.8	21.2	10.4	1.9	1.6
Washington, DC	8.5	17.3	14.6	5.8	27.0	18.7	4.7	3.4
Wichita, KS	9.7	26.4	23.4	9.0	20.2	8.8	1.5	1.0
Wilmington, NC	6.9	22.3	20.8	11.4	24.9	9.7	2.5	1.4
Winston-Salem, NC	10.8	28.4	21.4	9.8	18.9	7.3	1.9	1.5
U.S.	10.6	26.2	19.4	8.8	21.3	9.8	2.3	1.6

Note: Figures cover persons age 25 and over; Figures cover the Metropolitan Statistical Area (MSA)
Source: U.S. Census Bureau, 2019-2023 American Community Survey 5-Year Estimates

School Enrollment by Grade and Control: City

City	Preschool (%)		Kindergarten (%)		Grades 1 - 4 (%)		Grades 5 - 8 (%)		Grades 9 - 12 (%)	
	Public	Private	Public	Private	Public	Private	Public	Private	Public	Private
Albuquerque, NM	51.7	48.3	85.1	14.9	87.2	12.8	89.7	10.3	91.4	8.6
Anchorage, AK	53.5	46.5	89.2	10.8	84.1	15.9	87.8	12.2	91.8	8.2
Ann Arbor, MI	44.3	55.7	86.7	13.3	89.6	10.4	87.0	13.0	91.2	8.8
Athens, GA	65.1	34.9	95.8	4.2	88.4	11.6	86.4	13.6	89.2	10.8
Atlanta, GA	44.5	55.5	67.2	32.8	82.9	17.1	77.0	23.0	78.1	21.9
Austin, TX	51.1	48.9	85.1	14.9	87.7	12.3	86.7	13.3	90.3	9.7
Baltimore, MD	65.6	34.4	85.0	15.0	83.9	16.1	85.1	14.9	85.3	14.7
Billings, MT	39.2	60.8	80.1	19.9	84.7	15.3	84.3	15.7	86.1	13.9
Boise City, ID	34.8	65.2	80.0	20.0	85.7	14.3	89.3	10.7	86.4	13.6
Boston, MA	46.4	53.6	83.7	16.3	86.5	13.5	85.2	14.8	85.4	14.6
Boulder, CO	43.0	57.0	93.0	7.0	86.9	13.1	92.7	7.3	90.7	9.3
Cape Coral, FL	65.1	34.9	94.7	5.3	84.1	15.9	91.1	8.9	88.5	11.5
Cedar Rapids, IA	73.1	26.9	85.9	14.1	88.2	11.8	87.2	12.8	86.4	13.6
Charleston, SC	55.1	44.9	79.8	20.2	86.0	14.0	85.5	14.5	80.9	19.1
Charlotte, NC	50.8	49.2	86.8	13.2	88.6	11.4	87.4	12.6	88.8	11.2
Chicago, IL	56.4	43.6	81.6	18.4	82.8	17.2	83.6	16.4	85.2	14.8
Cincinnati, OH	60.9	39.1	77.2	22.8	78.5	21.5	78.9	21.1	81.8	18.2
Clarksville, TN	65.2	34.8	88.2	11.8	93.2	6.8	91.6	8.4	88.3	11.7
Cleveland, OH	68.9	31.1	68.7	31.3	78.2	21.8	77.9	22.1	77.6	22.4
College Station, TX	57.7	42.3	82.6	17.4	90.0	10.0	87.4	12.6	86.2	13.8
Colorado Springs, CO	64.6	35.4	88.0	12.0	87.3	12.7	88.4	11.6	90.7	9.3
Columbia, MO	49.7	50.3	85.6	14.4	87.0	13.0	89.5	10.5	91.0	9.0
Columbia, SC	33.0	67.0	81.8	18.2	76.7	23.3	85.6	14.4	84.0	16.0
Columbus, OH	64.5	35.5	79.2	20.8	84.3	15.7	85.7	14.3	87.2	12.8
Dallas, TX	69.0	31.0	88.5	11.5	89.5	10.5	91.1	8.9	89.8	10.2
Davenport, IA	52.6	47.4	86.2	13.8	79.3	20.7	86.4	13.6	92.5	7.5
Denver, CO	56.0	44.0	85.1	14.9	89.4	10.6	88.2	11.8	92.7	7.3
Des Moines, IA	76.4	23.6	88.0	12.0	90.8	9.2	91.8	8.2	93.8	6.2
Detroit, MI	81.6	18.4	91.8	8.2	93.4	6.6	92.1	7.9	92.4	7.6
Durham, NC	51.3	48.7	86.2	13.8	86.0	14.0	85.2	14.8	87.8	12.2
El Paso, TX	87.0	13.0	91.9	8.1	92.8	7.2	94.1	5.9	95.7	4.3
Eugene, OR	52.8	47.2	85.1	14.9	88.6	11.4	89.0	11.0	93.6	6.4
Fargo, ND	46.4	53.6	89.8	10.2	91.9	8.1	92.1	7.9	94.3	5.7
Fort Collins, CO	48.1	51.9	87.7	12.3	89.2	10.8	92.4	7.6	94.5	5.5
Fort Wayne, IN	45.6	54.4	70.8	29.2	78.5	21.5	82.0	18.0	79.2	20.8
Fort Worth, TX	61.4	38.6	86.8	13.2	90.9	9.1	91.0	9.0	91.3	8.7
Gainesville, FL	61.4	38.6	70.4	29.6	82.4	17.6	88.7	11.3	92.3	7.7
Green Bay, WI	71.0	29.0	86.2	13.8	87.3	12.7	89.8	10.2	90.4	9.6
Greensboro, NC	56.8	43.2	89.0	11.0	88.9	11.1	89.3	10.7	88.6	11.4
Honolulu, HI	36.4	63.6	74.0	26.0	79.9	20.1	76.4	23.6	69.1	30.9
Houston, TX	65.2	34.8	87.6	12.4	91.1	8.9	91.5	8.5	91.7	8.3
Huntsville, AL	63.7	36.3	80.9	19.1	81.8	18.2	78.2	21.8	84.2	15.8
Indianapolis, IN	61.1	38.9	85.4	14.6	82.9	17.1	83.7	16.3	85.2	14.8
Jacksonville, FL	56.5	43.5	83.5	16.5	83.4	16.6	80.0	20.0	83.7	16.3
Kansas City, MO	61.2	38.8	86.8	13.2	85.4	14.6	87.0	13.0	83.4	16.6
Lafayette, LA	55.1	44.9	71.4	28.6	76.8	23.2	72.2	27.8	78.4	21.6
Las Vegas, NV	68.6	31.4	91.1	8.9	87.6	12.4	89.3	10.7	91.2	8.8
Lexington, KY	29.5	70.5	81.0	19.0	82.3	17.7	85.7	14.3	85.4	14.6
Lincoln, NE	53.4	46.6	79.0	21.0	82.6	17.4	84.2	15.8	90.3	9.7
Little Rock, AR	66.2	33.8	86.5	13.5	78.2	21.8	76.0	24.0	77.5	22.5
Los Angeles, CA	55.2	44.8	85.7	14.3	87.7	12.3	87.5	12.5	88.0	12.0
Louisville, KY	50.3	49.7	77.2	22.8	81.9	18.1	81.0	19.0	78.2	21.8
Madison, WI	47.1	52.9	87.9	12.1	88.1	11.9	89.4	10.6	89.8	10.2
Manchester, NH	51.8	48.2	85.9	14.1	88.1	11.9	92.7	7.3	92.2	7.8
McAllen, TX	81.6	18.4	90.0	10.0	94.4	5.6	96.7	3.3	98.3	1.7

Table continued on following page.

City	Preschool (%)		Kindergarten (%)		Grades 1 - 4 (%)		Grades 5 - 8 (%)		Grades 9 - 12 (%)	
	Public	Private	Public	Private	Public	Private	Public	Private	Public	Private
Memphis, TN	60.2	39.8	87.7	12.3	88.1	11.9	88.5	11.5	85.6	14.4
Miami, FL	61.1	38.9	80.7	19.3	85.9	14.1	86.9	13.1	91.6	8.4
Midland, TX	57.2	42.8	67.9	32.1	78.9	21.1	76.4	23.6	84.3	15.7
Milwaukee, WI	77.0	23.0	73.9	26.1	75.5	24.5	73.9	26.1	79.9	20.1
Minneapolis, MN	53.1	46.9	86.3	13.7	86.2	13.8	87.0	13.0	88.8	11.2
Nashville, TN	51.0	49.0	82.7	17.3	82.9	17.1	78.2	21.8	81.2	18.8
New Orleans, LA	42.8	57.2	76.0	24.0	75.5	24.5	80.0	20.0	78.6	21.4
New York, NY	67.6	32.4	78.2	21.8	80.9	19.1	80.6	19.4	80.3	19.7
Oklahoma City, OK	69.7	30.3	86.9	13.1	87.9	12.1	86.4	13.6	86.9	13.1
Omaha, NE	54.5	45.5	79.9	20.1	82.7	17.3	82.7	17.3	83.3	16.7
Orlando, FL	60.7	39.3	81.8	18.2	85.9	14.1	90.0	10.0	88.0	12.0
Philadelphia, PA	54.5	45.5	78.0	22.0	79.4	20.6	79.1	20.9	77.6	22.4
Phoenix, AZ	62.6	37.4	86.7	13.3	88.9	11.1	91.5	8.5	92.2	7.8
Pittsburgh, PA	53.9	46.1	71.0	29.0	75.1	24.9	79.8	20.2	79.1	20.9
Portland, OR	36.8	63.2	84.3	15.7	87.0	13.0	86.9	13.1	85.7	14.3
Providence, RI	58.9	41.1	80.8	19.2	89.3	10.7	86.2	13.8	90.1	9.9
Provo, UT	64.9	35.1	88.2	11.8	91.6	8.4	95.6	4.4	91.6	8.4
Raleigh, NC	33.6	66.4	86.9	13.1	85.2	14.8	87.2	12.8	86.8	13.2
Reno, NV	54.6	45.4	96.7	3.3	89.2	10.8	88.3	11.7	93.6	6.4
Richmond, VA	53.2	46.8	90.2	9.8	87.7	12.3	84.7	15.3	82.7	17.3
Rochester, MN	43.6	56.4	90.6	9.4	86.3	13.7	84.5	15.5	90.2	9.8
Sacramento, CA	56.9	43.1	92.4	7.6	91.3	8.7	92.3	7.7	89.5	10.5
Saint Louis, MO	56.5	43.5	85.1	14.9	83.3	16.7	82.7	17.3	84.0	16.0
Saint Paul, MN	64.7	35.3	82.1	17.9	89.2	10.8	87.3	12.7	90.7	9.3
Salem, OR	70.2	29.8	88.8	11.2	88.5	11.5	91.6	8.4	97.2	2.8
Salt Lake City, UT	52.1	47.9	81.8	18.2	85.6	14.4	90.6	9.4	93.7	6.3
San Antonio, TX	73.0	27.0	89.7	10.3	90.7	9.3	92.1	7.9	91.8	8.2
San Diego, CA	47.0	53.0	84.6	15.4	88.6	11.4	91.3	8.7	90.8	9.2
San Francisco, CA	25.0	75.0	67.5	32.5	69.1	30.9	68.5	31.5	72.8	27.2
San Jose, CA	43.5	56.5	83.1	16.9	86.1	13.9	87.4	12.6	87.1	12.9
Santa Rosa, CA	55.2	44.8	90.3	9.7	92.4	7.6	88.6	11.4	92.8	7.2
Savannah, GA	76.3	23.7	85.4	14.6	88.1	11.9	88.2	11.8	88.6	11.4
Seattle, WA	35.0	65.0	76.0	24.0	77.9	22.1	74.8	25.2	78.3	21.7
Sioux Falls, SD	59.5	40.5	86.0	14.0	85.9	14.1	86.2	13.8	86.7	13.3
Tampa, FL	46.6	53.4	86.5	13.5	86.6	13.4	81.5	18.5	83.5	16.5
Tucson, AZ	71.7	28.3	90.3	9.7	88.2	11.8	88.1	11.9	91.9	8.1
Tulsa, OK	65.1	34.9	83.2	16.8	82.9	17.1	82.2	17.8	82.6	17.4
Virginia Beach, VA	39.5	60.5	77.6	22.4	88.8	11.2	88.5	11.5	91.2	8.8
Washington, DC	74.8	25.2	90.5	9.5	85.6	14.4	83.0	17.0	79.9	20.1
Wichita, KS	61.8	38.2	82.0	18.0	84.6	15.4	84.4	15.6	86.3	13.7
Wilmington, NC	55.8	44.2	84.8	15.2	79.3	20.7	75.6	24.4	87.1	12.9
Winston-Salem, NC	60.4	39.6	88.7	11.3	88.2	11.8	90.5	9.5	90.4	9.6
U.S.	58.7	41.3	85.2	14.8	87.2	12.8	87.9	12.1	89.0	11.0

Note: Figures shown cover persons 3 years old and over
Source: U.S. Census Bureau, 2019-2023 American Community Survey 5-Year Estimates

School Enrollment by Grade and Control: Metro Area

Metro Area	Preschool (%)		Kindergarten (%)		Grades 1 - 4 (%)		Grades 5 - 8 (%)		Grades 9 - 12 (%)	
	Public	Private	Public	Private	Public	Private	Public	Private	Public	Private
Albuquerque, NM	60.4	39.6	84.3	15.7	86.3	13.7	88.4	11.6	90.3	9.7
Anchorage, AK	51.9	48.1	87.7	12.3	83.6	16.4	86.9	13.1	89.7	10.3
Ann Arbor, MI	53.0	47.0	89.6	10.4	85.0	15.0	84.6	15.4	91.8	8.2
Athens, GA	63.8	36.2	93.2	6.8	88.2	11.8	87.2	12.8	88.5	11.5
Atlanta, GA	56.1	43.9	84.1	15.9	88.3	11.7	87.2	12.8	88.5	11.5
Austin, TX	49.6	50.4	87.0	13.0	90.0	10.0	89.2	10.8	91.1	8.9
Baltimore, MD	47.0	53.0	82.9	17.1	84.6	15.4	84.0	16.0	84.2	15.8
Billings, MT	41.5	58.5	84.1	15.9	87.0	13.0	87.1	12.9	88.2	11.8
Boise City, ID	40.0	60.0	86.5	13.5	85.6	14.4	88.0	12.0	88.4	11.6
Boston, MA	45.6	54.4	87.8	12.2	90.3	9.7	89.1	10.9	85.9	14.1
Boulder, CO	48.1	51.9	87.6	12.4	88.7	11.3	91.5	8.5	93.0	7.0
Cape Coral, FL	61.4	38.6	86.9	13.1	88.2	11.8	88.7	11.3	90.3	9.7
Cedar Rapids, IA	74.7	25.3	87.6	12.4	88.4	11.6	88.3	11.7	89.7	10.3
Charleston, SC	47.5	52.5	82.7	17.3	86.5	13.5	87.9	12.1	87.7	12.3
Charlotte, NC	50.5	49.5	86.2	13.8	87.8	12.2	87.3	12.7	88.6	11.4
Chicago, IL	56.8	43.2	84.8	15.2	87.6	12.4	88.1	11.9	90.0	10.0
Cincinnati, OH	50.7	49.3	79.1	20.9	81.9	18.1	82.2	17.8	83.0	17.0
Clarksville, TN	62.8	37.2	85.3	14.7	86.8	13.2	86.0	14.0	87.6	12.4
Cleveland, OH	53.0	47.0	75.5	24.5	80.6	19.4	80.7	19.3	82.4	17.6
College Station, TX	61.4	38.6	87.5	12.5	90.5	9.5	87.7	12.3	90.5	9.5
Colorado Springs, CO	66.9	33.1	86.3	13.7	87.4	12.6	88.5	11.5	89.8	10.2
Columbia, MO	55.0	45.0	87.6	12.4	84.6	15.4	90.4	9.6	90.7	9.3
Columbia, SC	51.6	48.4	88.3	11.7	87.8	12.2	90.4	9.6	91.7	8.3
Columbus, OH	56.4	43.6	81.4	18.6	87.0	13.0	88.1	11.9	88.9	11.1
Dallas, TX	57.4	42.6	88.0	12.0	90.4	9.6	91.4	8.6	91.5	8.5
Davenport, IA	65.1	34.9	87.2	12.8	87.0	13.0	91.2	8.8	92.2	7.8
Denver, CO	58.5	41.5	86.4	13.6	89.3	10.7	89.9	10.1	91.6	8.4
Des Moines, IA	68.1	31.9	87.6	12.4	91.2	8.8	89.9	10.1	91.5	8.5
Detroit, MI	62.5	37.5	86.9	13.1	88.7	11.3	89.8	10.2	89.9	10.1
Durham, NC	43.5	56.5	80.2	19.8	85.4	14.6	85.0	15.0	89.7	10.3
El Paso, TX	87.0	13.0	94.1	5.9	93.1	6.9	94.4	5.6	96.2	3.8
Eugene, OR	54.2	45.8	84.1	15.9	87.0	13.0	89.6	10.4	91.4	8.6
Fargo, ND	65.0	35.0	90.0	10.0	89.1	10.9	90.7	9.3	91.7	8.3
Fort Collins, CO	52.8	47.2	85.7	14.3	85.4	14.6	86.7	13.3	88.2	11.8
Fort Wayne, IN	44.1	55.9	73.2	26.8	75.7	24.3	76.8	23.2	81.3	18.7
Fort Worth, TX	57.4	42.6	88.0	12.0	90.4	9.6	91.4	8.6	91.5	8.5
Gainesville, FL	53.9	46.1	72.0	28.0	76.7	23.3	78.1	21.9	86.5	13.5
Green Bay, WI	68.0	32.0	84.2	15.8	86.1	13.9	87.0	13.0	90.5	9.5
Greensboro, NC	56.8	43.2	86.7	13.3	85.9	14.1	85.7	14.3	87.9	12.1
Honolulu, HI	34.7	65.3	79.0	21.0	79.9	20.1	78.2	21.8	74.9	25.1
Houston, TX	57.2	42.8	88.1	11.9	90.9	9.1	92.0	8.0	91.7	8.3
Huntsville, AL	56.0	44.0	79.7	20.3	82.9	17.1	82.3	17.7	83.1	16.9
Indianapolis, IN	53.8	46.2	84.3	15.7	85.1	14.9	85.7	14.3	87.4	12.6
Jacksonville, FL	56.0	44.0	85.4	14.6	84.0	16.0	82.8	17.2	85.6	14.4
Kansas City, MO	60.8	39.2	86.2	13.8	87.9	12.1	88.5	11.5	88.5	11.5
Lafayette, LA	56.7	43.3	78.8	21.2	77.7	22.3	77.9	22.1	79.1	20.9
Las Vegas, NV	64.0	36.0	87.1	12.9	88.8	11.2	90.1	9.9	91.8	8.2
Lexington, KY	40.9	59.1	82.4	17.6	83.7	16.3	84.8	15.2	85.9	14.1
Lincoln, NE	54.3	45.7	79.6	20.4	81.9	18.1	84.4	15.6	90.5	9.5
Little Rock, AR	69.9	30.1	86.8	13.2	86.2	13.8	85.4	14.6	87.1	12.9
Los Angeles, CA	54.7	45.3	86.6	13.4	89.1	10.9	89.9	10.1	90.6	9.4
Louisville, KY	53.0	47.0	79.7	20.3	81.8	18.2	82.4	17.6	81.0	19.0
Madison, WI	64.6	35.4	89.5	10.5	88.4	11.6	90.8	9.2	93.5	6.5
Manchester, NH	45.6	54.4	81.4	18.6	85.2	14.8	87.5	12.5	89.8	10.2
McAllen, TX	93.3	6.7	96.4	3.6	97.7	2.3	98.1	1.9	98.7	1.3

Table continued on following page.

Metro Area	Preschool (%)		Kindergarten (%)		Grades 1 - 4 (%)		Grades 5 - 8 (%)		Grades 9 - 12 (%)	
	Public	Private	Public	Private	Public	Private	Public	Private	Public	Private
Memphis, TN	59.8	40.2	87.5	12.5	86.3	13.7	87.0	13.0	84.8	15.2
Miami, FL	50.2	49.8	80.4	19.6	84.2	15.8	85.0	15.0	85.7	14.3
Midland, TX	65.0	35.0	65.8	34.2	80.9	19.1	78.8	21.2	83.9	16.1
Milwaukee, WI	59.4	40.6	75.9	24.1	78.5	21.5	78.7	21.3	84.9	15.1
Minneapolis, MN	60.7	39.3	85.8	14.2	88.3	11.7	88.7	11.3	91.5	8.5
Nashville, TN	50.1	49.9	82.5	17.5	84.8	15.2	83.3	16.7	83.0	17.0
New Orleans, LA	50.8	49.2	76.7	23.3	76.5	23.5	78.6	21.4	75.1	24.9
New York, NY	58.7	41.3	80.9	19.1	83.9	16.1	84.6	15.4	83.7	16.3
Oklahoma City, OK	70.9	29.1	86.9	13.1	87.7	12.3	87.4	12.6	87.8	12.2
Omaha, NE	58.9	41.1	81.9	18.1	84.5	15.5	85.7	14.3	85.5	14.5
Orlando, FL	48.9	51.1	79.8	20.2	82.1	17.9	85.3	14.7	87.0	13.0
Philadelphia, PA	47.4	52.6	81.4	18.6	85.0	15.0	84.4	15.6	83.6	16.4
Phoenix, AZ	60.3	39.7	85.5	14.5	88.1	11.9	90.4	9.6	91.9	8.1
Pittsburgh, PA	52.6	47.4	81.9	18.1	87.4	12.6	89.1	10.9	89.6	10.4
Portland, OR	40.0	60.0	83.8	16.2	85.8	14.2	88.1	11.9	89.6	10.4
Providence, RI	57.9	42.1	85.5	14.5	89.4	10.6	88.9	11.1	88.7	11.3
Provo, UT	55.5	44.5	87.9	12.1	90.3	9.7	92.6	7.4	94.0	6.0
Raleigh, NC	33.6	66.4	82.6	17.4	85.2	14.8	85.7	14.3	87.6	12.4
Reno, NV	51.8	48.2	90.8	9.2	90.9	9.1	89.7	10.3	92.1	7.9
Richmond, VA	44.4	55.6	86.4	13.6	87.5	12.5	89.1	10.9	90.0	10.0
Rochester, MN	61.3	38.7	91.0	9.0	88.1	11.9	87.9	12.1	91.8	8.2
Sacramento, CA	55.0	45.0	87.3	12.7	89.8	10.2	90.5	9.5	90.7	9.3
Saint Louis, MO	53.9	46.1	82.1	17.9	82.1	17.9	83.2	16.8	84.7	15.3
Saint Paul, MN	60.7	39.3	85.8	14.2	88.3	11.7	88.7	11.3	91.5	8.5
Salem, OR	59.8	40.2	86.8	13.2	86.0	14.0	90.3	9.7	92.4	7.6
Salt Lake City, UT	57.4	42.6	84.7	15.3	89.9	10.1	93.4	6.6	93.9	6.1
San Antonio, TX	65.5	34.5	87.7	12.3	89.4	10.6	90.3	9.7	90.5	9.5
San Diego, CA	50.7	49.3	86.1	13.9	89.3	10.7	90.8	9.2	91.9	8.1
San Francisco, CA	38.9	61.1	81.4	18.6	84.7	15.3	83.8	16.2	85.8	14.2
San Jose, CA	36.2	63.8	80.1	19.9	84.7	15.3	85.9	14.1	86.5	13.5
Santa Rosa, CA	53.1	46.9	91.2	8.8	92.9	7.1	89.9	10.1	91.1	8.9
Savannah, GA	57.5	42.5	79.1	20.9	84.4	15.6	84.9	15.1	85.2	14.8
Seattle, WA	40.8	59.2	79.5	20.5	85.6	14.4	86.7	13.3	90.0	10.0
Sioux Falls, SD	64.5	35.5	86.8	13.2	86.8	13.2	87.8	12.2	87.7	12.3
Tampa, FL	54.3	45.7	82.4	17.6	84.7	15.3	84.3	15.7	86.4	13.6
Tucson, AZ	71.3	28.7	88.0	12.0	87.2	12.8	87.8	12.2	89.8	10.2
Tulsa, OK	67.2	32.8	84.6	15.4	84.2	15.8	85.3	14.7	85.5	14.5
Virginia Beach, VA	50.5	49.5	80.8	19.2	87.9	12.1	88.8	11.2	89.9	10.1
Washington, DC	45.5	54.5	82.8	17.2	86.8	13.2	87.5	12.5	88.2	11.8
Wichita, KS	63.2	36.8	80.5	19.5	85.1	14.9	86.3	13.7	87.5	12.5
Wilmington, NC	52.1	47.9	83.4	16.6	83.8	16.2	84.3	15.7	88.3	11.7
Winston-Salem, NC	48.5	51.5	85.5	14.5	87.3	12.7	89.0	11.0	86.7	13.3
U.S.	58.7	41.3	85.2	14.8	87.2	12.8	87.9	12.1	89.0	11.0

Note: Figures shown cover persons 3 years old and over; Figures cover the Metropolitan Statistical Area (MSA)
Source: U.S. Census Bureau, 2019-2023 American Community Survey 5-Year Estimates

Educational Attainment by Race: City

City	High School Graduate or Higher (%)					Bachelor's Degree or Higher (%)				
	Total	White	Black	Asian	Hisp.[1]	Total	White	Black	Asian	Hisp.[1]
Albuquerque, NM	90.9	94.6	94.0	88.3	84.4	38.7	45.2	38.8	51.0	25.4
Anchorage, AK	94.0	96.7	91.7	86.6	86.6	37.7	45.2	23.6	30.5	23.8
Ann Arbor, MI	97.6	98.6	92.7	97.2	92.8	77.7	79.7	44.8	85.2	75.5
Athens, GA	89.9	96.9	82.5	88.5	66.8	48.7	62.8	22.6	67.8	31.7
Atlanta, GA	93.0	98.5	87.9	97.7	86.1	58.4	81.2	34.6	86.7	50.5
Austin, TX	91.6	95.1	90.6	93.6	78.3	58.2	63.9	36.7	78.4	35.6
Baltimore, MD	87.2	92.9	85.7	92.2	70.0	35.4	62.2	20.0	73.3	31.3
Billings, MT	95.5	96.2	98.6	89.9	85.1	37.0	38.3	35.8	56.4	14.6
Boise City, ID	94.8	96.2	73.7	89.9	80.6	46.6	47.4	24.4	60.1	30.3
Boston, MA	88.9	96.4	86.4	80.9	72.8	54.1	72.5	26.7	57.4	26.6
Boulder, CO	96.9	98.3	95.0	95.1	78.4	76.8	79.1	43.7	79.9	48.6
Cape Coral, FL	93.2	94.9	87.7	90.2	87.3	25.7	26.8	21.3	50.2	18.9
Cedar Rapids, IA	94.1	95.5	81.1	88.4	90.0	32.9	33.6	15.5	55.7	25.0
Charleston, SC	95.9	98.3	86.7	92.1	87.9	57.7	65.3	22.9	67.6	39.8
Charlotte, NC	89.6	95.9	91.6	85.3	60.5	47.4	63.1	33.3	61.3	20.5
Chicago, IL	86.8	93.4	87.4	88.3	71.9	43.3	61.9	25.2	65.0	20.4
Cincinnati, OH	89.7	94.6	83.8	93.1	81.1	41.3	57.9	16.2	80.1	36.2
Clarksville, TN	94.2	95.8	95.2	84.5	84.8	30.6	33.8	27.3	27.8	19.9
Cleveland, OH	83.5	87.5	82.3	78.8	70.9	21.3	31.8	12.7	55.6	10.6
College Station, TX	94.6	97.4	88.7	95.6	83.0	57.1	60.8	24.5	79.1	40.4
Colorado Springs, CO	94.6	96.4	94.1	89.0	84.6	41.9	45.3	32.1	43.8	21.6
Columbia, MO	95.3	96.4	92.0	94.2	86.7	56.5	59.4	33.9	72.5	48.5
Columbia, SC	90.9	96.0	85.2	89.9	85.6	46.1	62.6	25.4	73.0	39.5
Columbus, OH	89.8	93.6	86.6	82.8	71.2	38.2	45.8	21.1	57.8	25.2
Dallas, TX	80.8	87.6	89.0	89.3	58.2	37.4	53.6	23.6	68.5	15.3
Davenport, IA	92.6	94.7	87.4	84.3	78.3	30.0	31.7	16.8	59.3	15.0
Denver, CO	91.4	96.4	91.5	87.1	72.5	55.6	66.7	31.4	58.1	23.3
Des Moines, IA	87.3	93.7	79.3	61.3	60.1	29.0	33.5	15.8	23.0	10.8
Detroit, MI	83.4	84.3	85.3	75.5	56.8	17.6	37.4	14.1	43.5	11.6
Durham, NC	91.4	96.1	91.7	92.8	59.7	55.7	70.7	39.4	76.8	22.1
El Paso, TX	81.9	87.0	94.8	88.4	78.7	27.5	31.5	30.8	52.7	23.9
Eugene, OR	94.8	95.7	98.0	92.9	86.2	44.2	44.8	37.2	59.1	33.3
Fargo, ND	95.3	96.6	82.3	87.0	95.2	43.2	44.3	20.1	69.9	31.7
Fort Collins, CO	97.6	98.4	87.7	95.1	91.1	59.9	62.0	34.6	76.2	37.0
Fort Wayne, IN	88.9	94.1	87.7	49.2	65.7	28.5	33.1	13.9	19.7	15.4
Fort Worth, TX	84.3	91.2	90.0	82.7	64.6	31.7	41.0	23.0	46.0	14.7
Gainesville, FL	94.3	96.5	87.4	96.9	94.7	51.7	57.0	28.8	77.5	61.4
Green Bay, WI	89.0	92.6	69.5	84.3	65.8	25.5	27.8	16.2	32.8	11.5
Greensboro, NC	90.1	95.2	89.5	75.7	70.2	39.9	52.3	28.0	46.5	19.4
Honolulu, HI	90.9	97.6	91.5	88.1	93.6	40.8	54.6	32.5	40.7	30.5
Houston, TX	80.3	88.5	89.9	86.6	60.7	36.0	50.8	27.4	61.7	16.7
Huntsville, AL	91.6	94.8	86.8	91.0	77.4	46.2	54.1	30.1	57.6	29.7
Indianapolis, IN	87.5	91.3	87.9	70.4	64.5	34.2	41.0	22.1	41.0	18.6
Jacksonville, FL	90.8	93.0	88.6	88.9	84.8	31.8	35.1	22.6	52.6	28.1
Kansas City, MO	91.8	94.9	89.8	89.9	73.9	37.8	47.4	17.5	49.5	20.7
Lafayette, LA	90.9	95.4	81.2	91.6	83.8	40.6	50.4	17.4	55.0	36.6
Las Vegas, NV	85.8	91.7	88.5	91.7	66.8	27.3	32.2	19.5	44.8	12.5
Lexington, KY	92.4	95.3	90.4	89.9	65.1	47.3	51.9	27.1	72.2	25.3
Lincoln, NE	93.0	95.2	86.6	81.2	70.7	41.0	42.7	25.0	43.3	21.1
Little Rock, AR	92.3	96.3	91.5	92.7	63.7	44.0	58.0	26.6	73.5	13.5
Los Angeles, CA	79.3	89.6	90.1	91.1	59.4	37.8	51.6	31.9	57.6	15.1
Louisville, KY	90.5	92.9	87.6	83.3	78.7	33.4	37.4	20.2	56.1	27.5
Madison, WI	95.7	97.7	91.9	92.5	78.5	59.2	62.9	25.6	70.4	37.4
Manchester, NH	88.7	91.3	75.7	81.2	68.7	33.5	35.4	22.8	35.6	13.5
McAllen, TX	79.9	85.7	99.5	89.7	77.2	32.0	35.4	31.6	64.7	28.6

Table continued on following page.

City	High School Graduate or Higher (%)					Bachelor's Degree or Higher (%)				
	Total	White	Black	Asian	Hisp.[1]	Total	White	Black	Asian	Hisp.[1]
Memphis, TN	87.4	93.9	87.8	86.8	52.0	28.2	49.9	17.9	60.0	17.8
Miami, FL	80.0	82.6	78.1	95.4	76.7	35.6	44.7	17.5	69.4	31.3
Midland, TX	86.5	91.9	90.5	70.2	74.6	33.7	40.3	20.1	39.1	22.1
Milwaukee, WI	85.5	92.8	86.0	74.3	64.6	26.6	41.0	13.7	32.7	12.0
Minneapolis, MN	91.1	97.2	74.9	86.3	71.6	54.5	65.6	19.1	62.7	31.0
Nashville, TN	90.2	93.9	89.5	83.4	61.8	46.9	56.0	29.8	55.1	20.5
New Orleans, LA	89.1	96.8	85.9	77.4	79.1	42.0	68.0	24.1	50.4	42.2
New York, NY	83.7	92.5	85.1	77.3	71.7	41.0	59.2	26.7	45.2	21.5
Oklahoma City, OK	87.8	91.4	90.7	81.6	61.7	34.0	38.4	26.1	48.0	12.8
Omaha, NE	90.5	95.1	86.9	71.7	61.9	40.3	45.7	18.6	50.2	15.0
Orlando, FL	91.9	95.6	84.1	93.4	90.9	42.2	53.5	21.7	59.3	33.9
Philadelphia, PA	87.4	93.5	88.1	74.3	72.6	34.6	51.0	20.4	42.0	19.5
Phoenix, AZ	84.4	91.2	89.2	89.2	66.9	32.3	38.9	27.3	62.6	13.6
Pittsburgh, PA	94.3	95.7	90.6	92.3	87.4	47.8	53.2	20.3	82.0	55.8
Portland, OR	93.3	96.2	88.6	81.7	80.0	53.5	58.1	29.8	47.3	35.7
Providence, RI	81.9	89.9	87.0	87.7	69.5	34.7	51.7	23.6	58.3	12.9
Provo, UT	92.5	95.3	99.6	84.9	75.2	45.0	49.0	29.9	52.7	20.8
Raleigh, NC	92.5	96.8	92.0	90.0	67.3	52.9	66.4	32.5	62.5	23.7
Reno, NV	89.3	94.9	91.5	90.5	65.3	35.7	39.9	26.6	49.2	15.2
Richmond, VA	89.3	96.6	85.0	90.3	61.4	44.1	70.1	16.1	64.9	25.2
Rochester, MN	94.5	97.2	73.9	86.1	78.6	50.1	51.6	25.7	61.6	34.9
Sacramento, CA	86.9	93.0	91.4	82.5	76.4	36.4	45.2	24.4	38.9	23.7
Saint Louis, MO	90.5	95.0	85.7	86.9	81.7	40.2	56.0	18.1	63.5	35.3
Saint Paul, MN	88.9	96.6	81.4	67.4	73.7	43.5	55.6	21.2	23.6	24.2
Salem, OR	88.7	93.5	94.1	86.4	63.7	31.4	35.1	27.7	46.3	12.8
Salt Lake City, UT	91.6	95.7	86.1	85.3	72.5	50.9	56.2	30.7	62.6	24.5
San Antonio, TX	84.3	88.4	91.0	85.7	78.0	28.7	33.7	25.0	56.5	19.4
San Diego, CA	90.2	95.2	90.0	90.2	76.2	49.9	57.6	31.3	57.3	25.4
San Francisco, CA	88.8	97.5	88.8	80.8	80.1	60.1	76.3	30.9	51.0	40.1
San Jose, CA	85.5	93.1	90.1	88.3	69.6	46.5	51.5	37.5	59.7	17.5
Santa Rosa, CA	85.5	94.7	85.7	83.6	63.0	34.8	42.5	21.8	45.8	14.6
Savannah, GA	89.9	95.3	86.3	81.6	86.9	32.0	47.8	17.9	46.9	32.4
Seattle, WA	95.7	98.4	89.9	91.2	87.8	67.5	72.6	33.8	69.8	49.3
Sioux Falls, SD	93.1	95.7	83.0	76.0	64.7	37.4	40.0	21.0	42.2	14.8
Tampa, FL	89.8	94.4	85.6	90.4	80.9	44.6	56.0	20.5	68.9	29.4
Tucson, AZ	87.3	91.8	87.3	88.4	76.7	30.2	35.6	17.5	51.9	17.3
Tulsa, OK	87.6	92.1	90.0	77.0	59.5	33.3	39.7	19.7	38.0	12.4
Virginia Beach, VA	94.7	96.4	92.7	89.4	89.9	40.4	44.2	27.9	46.6	32.5
Washington, DC	92.8	99.1	88.5	95.8	81.3	63.6	92.0	33.3	84.7	56.7
Wichita, KS	88.0	92.3	87.4	74.0	63.9	30.9	34.8	19.0	31.6	14.7
Wilmington, NC	93.5	96.4	84.9	87.8	77.5	45.8	51.7	23.0	61.8	30.2
Winston-Salem, NC	88.4	91.9	89.4	96.1	61.1	37.2	47.5	24.1	70.3	16.3
U.S.	89.4	92.9	88.1	88.0	72.5	35.0	37.7	24.7	57.0	19.9

Note: Figures shown cover persons 25 years old and over; (1) People of Hispanic origin can be of any race
Source: U.S. Census Bureau, 2019-2023 American Community Survey 5-Year Estimates

Educational Attainment by Race: Metro Area

Metro Area	High School Graduate or Higher (%)					Bachelor's Degree or Higher (%)				
	Total	White	Black	Asian	Hisp.[1]	Total	White	Black	Asian	Hisp.[1]
Albuquerque, NM	90.3	94.2	93.1	88.8	84.0	35.0	41.5	38.7	52.7	22.6
Anchorage, AK	94.1	96.2	91.7	86.6	87.7	34.0	38.9	23.5	29.7	23.9
Ann Arbor, MI	95.8	97.1	90.9	95.6	85.8	58.1	60.0	31.5	82.0	47.3
Athens, GA	89.8	94.2	82.4	85.0	66.0	43.5	49.5	21.4	64.9	30.8
Atlanta, GA	90.8	93.8	91.9	87.8	69.6	41.5	46.4	34.0	61.2	24.7
Austin, TX	91.6	94.9	93.3	93.8	78.2	49.9	54.2	36.5	76.1	29.0
Baltimore, MD	92.1	94.7	90.2	89.3	77.0	43.3	48.4	30.1	64.0	32.9
Billings, MT	95.2	95.8	99.0	87.5	84.4	33.5	34.3	31.1	47.3	15.7
Boise City, ID	92.5	94.9	80.7	90.9	72.9	36.6	38.2	24.7	55.8	19.1
Boston, MA	92.3	95.8	87.4	87.0	74.8	51.2	54.8	31.8	65.0	26.6
Boulder, CO	95.5	97.6	93.4	92.4	76.4	63.9	67.0	40.6	70.1	30.8
Cape Coral, FL	90.4	94.0	82.6	89.5	75.7	30.8	34.0	16.7	50.3	17.1
Cedar Rapids, IA	95.2	96.1	83.2	90.9	85.2	32.8	33.3	16.5	53.6	24.3
Charleston, SC	91.9	95.4	86.5	90.2	72.3	40.0	47.6	20.1	51.7	25.5
Charlotte, NC	90.4	93.4	90.6	88.0	67.0	39.0	42.6	30.0	61.9	21.4
Chicago, IL	89.7	94.4	89.4	91.3	71.8	40.9	47.4	25.8	67.0	18.6
Cincinnati, OH	92.3	93.5	87.9	88.6	76.7	36.9	38.1	22.8	63.4	31.1
Clarksville, TN	92.3	92.8	93.3	87.6	84.0	28.0	29.3	25.3	35.5	20.5
Cleveland, OH	91.7	93.6	87.0	87.8	78.0	33.4	36.9	18.3	63.6	19.0
College Station, TX	88.3	91.8	87.1	96.0	69.9	39.1	43.4	15.1	77.8	18.7
Colorado Springs, CO	95.1	96.6	95.2	90.1	86.4	41.0	43.8	32.5	44.9	23.2
Columbia, MO	94.0	94.6	91.5	92.8	87.6	47.5	48.9	28.5	71.0	38.4
Columbia, SC	91.1	93.5	88.9	91.0	75.3	35.0	39.2	27.3	64.1	22.7
Columbus, OH	92.1	94.2	87.4	86.3	75.0	39.4	41.8	23.9	62.6	27.7
Dallas, TX	87.3	92.0	92.2	90.0	66.3	38.5	42.8	31.6	65.4	17.8
Davenport, IA	92.4	94.5	83.5	82.5	77.4	29.4	30.4	14.2	61.6	16.8
Denver, CO	92.3	96.0	90.8	86.3	75.5	48.4	54.4	30.3	55.4	21.7
Des Moines, IA	93.5	96.3	82.0	73.9	69.3	39.1	40.8	20.1	44.7	17.4
Detroit, MI	91.2	92.9	88.4	89.5	76.9	34.1	36.5	19.4	66.4	26.5
Durham, NC	91.1	95.0	90.1	92.2	59.9	52.3	60.5	35.3	77.4	23.4
El Paso, TX	80.6	85.8	95.3	88.8	77.4	25.3	29.4	32.0	50.5	21.9
Eugene, OR	93.1	94.1	96.1	90.4	81.3	33.4	33.6	33.2	53.7	25.3
Fargo, ND	95.6	96.6	84.7	88.7	89.2	42.2	43.0	24.6	67.9	30.1
Fort Collins, CO	96.6	97.7	91.5	95.6	85.2	51.7	53.4	37.7	69.3	29.5
Fort Wayne, IN	90.7	93.8	88.5	59.3	68.5	29.7	32.0	15.8	29.2	16.9
Fort Worth, TX	87.3	92.0	92.2	90.0	66.3	38.5	42.8	31.6	65.4	17.8
Gainesville, FL	92.7	93.9	87.4	94.6	89.8	40.9	41.6	24.2	73.6	49.6
Green Bay, WI	93.3	95.2	74.2	85.9	69.6	29.9	30.8	18.3	44.5	15.5
Greensboro, NC	88.3	91.1	88.5	78.6	63.3	31.4	34.4	24.7	49.1	16.3
Honolulu, HI	92.9	97.2	95.8	90.6	94.5	37.7	51.2	32.8	39.2	29.2
Houston, TX	85.1	90.6	92.3	87.6	67.9	35.4	40.8	32.1	58.0	17.8
Huntsville, AL	91.5	93.3	88.5	91.9	77.4	42.4	45.2	33.2	63.5	30.7
Indianapolis, IN	91.1	93.5	88.2	81.4	70.5	37.8	40.4	24.9	54.4	24.0
Jacksonville, FL	92.1	93.8	88.5	89.6	87.1	35.1	37.9	23.6	52.4	30.2
Kansas City, MO	93.1	95.0	90.9	89.1	75.0	39.2	42.6	21.9	56.7	20.9
Lafayette, LA	87.0	90.1	79.6	72.7	76.8	27.0	30.1	15.1	36.6	27.1
Las Vegas, NV	86.8	91.8	90.6	90.6	69.6	27.3	31.1	21.2	42.9	12.7
Lexington, KY	91.9	93.9	90.6	89.7	65.7	41.1	43.4	25.4	67.8	23.0
Lincoln, NE	93.6	95.4	86.4	81.1	71.1	40.6	42.0	24.8	43.2	20.9
Little Rock, AR	92.1	93.9	91.4	89.9	68.2	32.9	35.4	25.8	55.9	17.4
Los Angeles, CA	82.2	90.4	91.1	89.2	65.7	37.4	46.4	31.8	55.5	16.2
Louisville, KY	91.3	92.7	87.7	86.4	77.4	32.1	33.7	20.6	60.2	25.4
Madison, WI	95.9	97.1	91.4	92.5	78.5	49.3	50.1	25.9	69.7	33.2
Manchester, NH	93.0	94.3	83.0	90.5	74.3	40.6	41.1	26.8	60.6	20.1
McAllen, TX	69.3	76.0	84.4	92.3	66.7	20.3	22.9	23.5	67.0	18.2

Table continued on following page.

Metro Area	High School Graduate or Higher (%)					Bachelor's Degree or Higher (%)				
	Total	White	Black	Asian	Hisp.[1]	Total	White	Black	Asian	Hisp.[1]
Memphis, TN	89.5	93.3	88.5	88.2	57.9	30.7	39.1	21.4	64.8	19.0
Miami, FL	86.9	90.6	84.2	88.6	81.7	35.6	42.4	22.4	56.3	31.2
Midland, TX	86.2	91.5	91.3	74.8	74.3	30.6	35.7	20.6	48.7	19.3
Milwaukee, WI	92.7	96.2	86.7	86.3	72.7	38.8	44.4	15.3	53.9	18.1
Minneapolis, MN	94.2	97.0	84.0	83.5	76.4	44.9	47.7	25.1	47.6	27.2
Nashville, TN	91.5	93.4	90.4	85.7	68.4	39.9	42.0	30.5	56.8	22.2
New Orleans, LA	87.5	92.2	85.3	80.0	74.8	33.0	41.2	22.5	47.7	25.0
New York, NY	87.6	93.7	86.9	84.4	74.1	43.5	52.7	28.4	57.0	22.8
Oklahoma City, OK	89.9	92.3	91.0	83.8	65.5	33.4	36.0	25.3	50.9	14.8
Omaha, NE	92.7	95.6	88.8	74.3	68.3	39.1	41.8	21.4	48.0	18.5
Orlando, FL	90.7	93.5	85.8	90.2	86.5	35.8	39.4	25.0	54.9	28.8
Philadelphia, PA	92.1	95.3	89.7	85.5	74.5	41.5	46.8	24.3	59.2	22.5
Phoenix, AZ	89.5	93.7	91.6	90.3	73.5	34.6	38.2	29.8	60.9	16.4
Pittsburgh, PA	94.9	95.4	91.7	87.5	86.9	37.4	37.8	21.5	69.8	39.9
Portland, OR	92.8	95.2	90.7	88.4	74.5	42.1	43.3	31.8	55.8	23.6
Providence, RI	88.4	90.8	85.6	88.6	72.1	35.0	37.5	25.4	56.3	16.8
Provo, UT	95.3	96.5	97.2	94.6	83.1	43.4	44.7	38.3	62.7	26.4
Raleigh, NC	92.9	96.0	92.2	93.3	69.1	50.2	55.5	33.9	76.2	22.7
Reno, NV	88.6	93.5	90.2	90.5	65.8	31.4	34.6	21.8	45.8	14.4
Richmond, VA	91.9	95.0	89.7	90.1	71.2	40.2	47.4	24.6	63.9	22.8
Rochester, MN	94.8	96.5	74.4	85.8	79.8	42.3	42.2	25.1	60.4	33.9
Sacramento, CA	90.1	94.4	91.4	85.1	78.1	36.3	39.2	26.0	45.0	22.0
Saint Louis, MO	93.3	94.7	88.8	90.9	82.6	37.6	40.1	22.0	68.6	31.0
Saint Paul, MN	94.2	97.0	84.0	83.5	76.4	44.9	47.7	25.1	47.6	27.2
Salem, OR	87.2	92.5	91.1	85.4	62.2	26.9	30.0	28.2	43.5	11.0
Salt Lake City, UT	91.8	95.2	84.3	86.9	74.6	37.8	40.9	25.4	52.0	18.6
San Antonio, TX	87.3	91.2	92.4	88.2	79.8	31.9	36.6	30.1	53.8	21.2
San Diego, CA	89.0	93.8	91.0	91.1	75.0	42.1	48.0	29.6	55.2	21.5
San Francisco, CA	89.5	96.2	91.4	88.4	73.3	52.4	61.6	32.3	59.9	25.1
San Jose, CA	89.1	94.7	92.0	91.9	72.1	54.8	57.5	42.1	69.5	20.2
Santa Rosa, CA	88.9	95.8	88.8	86.2	66.2	37.8	44.2	29.4	46.1	16.0
Savannah, GA	91.3	94.0	88.9	82.3	84.1	34.9	41.2	23.4	50.9	27.4
Seattle, WA	93.3	96.0	90.4	91.0	77.4	46.3	47.0	28.6	61.7	27.5
Sioux Falls, SD	93.7	95.6	83.4	76.1	66.5	35.7	37.4	20.1	40.3	16.0
Tampa, FL	90.9	93.1	89.2	86.4	82.3	34.0	35.4	26.6	54.2	25.9
Tucson, AZ	89.9	93.9	89.2	89.8	78.6	35.9	41.0	25.7	56.3	19.7
Tulsa, OK	90.1	92.7	90.7	77.9	66.0	29.8	32.6	21.1	33.6	15.1
Virginia Beach, VA	92.8	95.3	89.6	88.9	86.0	35.1	39.9	24.9	47.4	29.2
Washington, DC	91.5	96.2	92.8	91.8	70.7	53.8	64.4	39.1	67.2	29.3
Wichita, KS	90.3	93.5	87.6	75.1	67.1	31.5	34.2	19.0	32.5	16.4
Wilmington, NC	93.1	95.0	86.8	85.4	75.6	38.5	41.1	23.8	56.4	25.1
Winston-Salem, NC	89.2	91.0	90.0	88.5	63.8	29.6	31.4	24.6	54.1	14.7
U.S.	89.4	92.9	88.1	88.0	72.5	35.0	37.7	24.7	57.0	19.9

Note: Figures shown cover persons 25 years old and over; Figures cover the Metropolitan Statistical Area (MSA); (1) People of Hispanic origin can be of any race
Source: U.S. Census Bureau, 2019-2023 American Community Survey 5-Year Estimates

Cost of Living Index

Urban Area	Composite	Groceries	Housing	Utilities	Transp.	Health	Misc.
Albuquerque, NM	94.9	97.4	89.1	87.3	85.9	102.0	101.8
Anchorage, AK	122.8	126.5	133.1	112.4	113.6	147.1	114.1
Ann Arbor, MI	n/a	n/a	n/a	n/a	n/a	n/a	n/a
Athens, GA	98.9	100.4	97.3	99.4	95.0	96.7	100.8
Atlanta, GA	96.0	100.9	86.9	99.7	100.2	107.9	97.6
Austin, TX	97.3	96.6	104.1	98.6	94.9	98.6	92.2
Baltimore, MD	100.5	102.8	86.5	110.6	104.2	94.2	108.4
Billings, MT	99.8	103.5	95.3	82.7	120.0	114.8	98.9
Boise City, ID	102.1	103.7	101.0	77.8	109.9	98.2	106.6
Boston, MA	145.9	104.4	218.9	149.7	109.8	125.3	115.2
Boulder, CO	n/a	n/a	n/a	n/a	n/a	n/a	n/a
Cape Coral, FL	104.9	104.0	105.1	106.5	105.9	111.8	103.5
Cedar Rapids, IA	n/a	n/a	n/a	n/a	n/a	n/a	n/a
Charleston, SC	101.9	102.1	103.8	113.9	94.9	85.7	101.2
Charlotte, NC	98.9	101.1	84.8	101.3	94.4	99.6	110.0
Chicago, IL	115.1	103.9	140.1	96.7	107.3	107.9	107.0
Cincinnati, OH	96.0	100.7	87.3	99.6	96.2	94.8	100.4
Clarksville, TN	n/a	n/a	n/a	n/a	n/a	n/a	n/a
Cleveland, OH	91.4	99.8	81.2	85.5	96.7	92.2	96.1
College Station, TX	n/a	n/a	n/a	n/a	n/a	n/a	n/a
Colorado Springs, CO	101.9	101.9	110.2	75.7	95.1	95.5	104.0
Columbia, MO	90.0	96.2	79.7	96.8	84.8	98.8	94.3
Columbia, SC	89.2	99.1	69.2	117.6	80.6	75.6	98.3
Columbus, OH	95.3	100.6	96.5	104.2	87.5	82.3	93.6
Dallas, TX	101.7	98.9	95.1	115.6	91.2	104.5	107.4
Davenport, IA	90.1	97.4	76.8	83.2	105.1	97.3	94.6
Denver, CO	108.6	101.3	123.4	89.3	94.7	109.6	107.7
Des Moines, IA	85.8	99.6	66.1	80.8	93.2	87.2	94.9
Detroit, MI	103.3	101.0	106.0	100.6	103.7	107.0	102.0
Durham, NC	98.5	102.0	101.6	93.4	93.8	103.8	96.2
El Paso, TX	88.1	96.7	70.7	91.5	101.2	88.7	94.3
Eugene, OR	107.3	105.2	120.6	92.5	110.3	108.2	100.0
Fargo, ND	97.3	97.9	85.1	80.1	98.8	118.1	108.0
Fort Collins, CO	n/a	n/a	n/a	n/a	n/a	n/a	n/a
Fort Wayne, IN	90.3	99.0	77.5	91.0	100.4	97.4	93.1
Fort Worth, TX	96.0	99.3	85.8	116.7	94.7	105.7	97.0
Gainesville, FL	n/a	n/a	n/a	n/a	n/a	n/a	n/a
Green Bay, WI	90.5	97.9	80.9	82.0	102.8	95.1	93.4
Greensboro, NC	n/a	n/a	n/a	n/a	n/a	n/a	n/a
Honolulu, HI	186.8	130.4	310.0	197.6	133.6	120.8	130.4
Houston, TX	94.1	99.3	79.2	92.4	94.0	97.5	104.1
Huntsville, AL	90.8	100.2	72.3	88.7	96.5	92.5	100.7
Indianapolis, IN	88.8	98.0	76.9	88.4	98.0	86.9	92.5
Jacksonville, FL	92.9	104.0	87.1	89.7	87.2	85.2	96.0
Kansas City, MO	91.1	97.3	87.5	105.6	89.3	83.8	89.1
Lafayette, LA	87.2	97.1	64.5	84.1	97.9	80.7	100.5
Las Vegas, NV	98.5	103.7	104.6	113.8	115.0	85.2	85.1
Lexington, KY	91.9	100.5	77.2	84.4	97.3	97.6	99.7
Lincoln, NE	94.3	99.3	77.6	92.2	99.5	105.4	103.5
Little Rock, AR	93.4	97.3	77.6	84.2	94.5	84.6	107.8
Los Angeles, CA	149.4	109.3	232.5	107.2	136.1	101.1	118.9
Louisville, KY	94.1	99.1	80.1	83.2	96.7	114.9	102.4
Madison, WI	104.7	98.8	106.4	98.8	98.3	113.2	107.8
Manchester, NH	112.6	99.9	117.6	112.2	105.9	103.9	117.0
McAllen, TX	85.1	93.4	60.2	119.6	94.1	79.2	92.1
Memphis, TN	89.8	98.8	86.2	80.9	88.8	86.0	91.7

Table continued on following page.

Urban Area	Composite	Groceries	Housing	Utilities	Transp.	Health	Misc.
Miami, FL	120.9	110.8	157.4	104.9	100.6	98.1	107.4
Midland, TX	96.4	96.2	83.8	100.9	94.3	87.6	107.5
Milwaukee, WI	100.5	100.8	104.2	94.0	102.7	105.0	97.7
Minneapolis, MN	93.6	102.6	82.9	96.6	96.4	96.0	96.5
Nashville, TN	98.7	99.5	101.4	98.2	90.8	95.5	98.7
New Orleans, LA	112.4	99.2	148.7	71.6	95.6	102.6	104.0
New York, NY[2]	161.1	113.0	276.5	115.1	114.9	128.1	114.9
Oklahoma City, OK	82.2	94.9	60.1	96.8	91.3	103.9	86.0
Omaha, NE	91.9	99.1	82.5	84.2	94.4	94.0	97.5
Orlando, FL	96.4	104.7	91.7	103.7	97.4	91.9	95.2
Philadelphia, PA	103.2	104.1	99.2	105.5	105.3	96.2	106.0
Phoenix, AZ	106.3	102.8	115.6	106.6	105.4	91.6	102.2
Pittsburgh, PA	98.1	97.8	94.9	119.9	107.2	99.2	93.2
Portland, OR	116.6	107.2	146.0	86.6	127.4	110.5	101.9
Providence, RI	112.2	102.0	113.4	139.7	96.5	104.4	114.1
Provo, UT	102.5	96.7	111.3	93.2	107.4	89.9	100.5
Raleigh, NC	97.2	100.6	91.9	89.8	92.1	112.2	101.0
Reno, NV	104.0	102.9	110.9	93.4	123.5	88.5	98.6
Richmond, VA	94.2	99.9	84.6	96.2	95.3	91.1	99.2
Rochester, MN	n/a	n/a	n/a	n/a	n/a	n/a	n/a
Sacramento, CA	128.8	106.9	139.2	174.4	152.0	99.7	116.9
Saint Louis, MO	89.1	98.8	78.0	97.9	93.3	87.6	90.9
Saint Paul, MN	94.0	105.2	81.3	95.6	96.0	96.7	98.1
Salem, OR	n/a	n/a	n/a	n/a	n/a	n/a	n/a
Salt Lake City, UT	109.0	98.1	128.7	95.4	111.4	88.5	103.0
San Antonio, TX	91.2	94.5	79.0	81.8	94.3	111.3	98.5
San Diego, CA	145.3	111.1	212.1	139.4	140.9	102.2	113.9
San Francisco, CA	166.8	123.6	263.3	160.1	143.6	127.6	119.3
San Jose, CA	180.6	115.0	321.1	158.6	140.7	120.1	117.9
Santa Rosa, CA	n/a	n/a	n/a	n/a	n/a	n/a	n/a
Savannah, GA	93.8	102.5	78.1	99.5	102.7	113.7	96.4
Seattle, WA	145.1	110.3	212.2	101.4	128.4	128.5	122.4
Sioux Falls, SD	91.0	96.4	88.5	91.3	89.9	92.6	90.7
Tampa, FL	97.6	105.7	95.8	99.9	102.1	93.1	94.4
Tucson, AZ	n/a	n/a	n/a	n/a	n/a	n/a	n/a
Tulsa, OK	84.7	95.9	65.1	98.3	88.4	93.5	90.3
Virginia Beach, VA[3]	94.0	98.5	82.4	104.2	96.0	110.6	96.4
Washington, DC	141.9	105.9	222.4	102.4	107.9	117.0	113.2
Wichita, KS	88.8	94.9	65.9	98.2	97.5	94.3	99.6
Wilmington, NC	n/a	n/a	n/a	n/a	n/a	n/a	n/a
Winston-Salem, NC	93.4	97.0	77.5	101.7	92.1	105.8	101.5
U.S.	100.0	100.0	100.0	100.0	100.0	100.0	100.0

Note: The Cost of Living Index measures regional differences in the cost of consumer goods and services, excluding taxes and non-consumer expenditures, for professional and managerial households in the top income quintile. It is based on more than 50,000 prices covering almost 60 different items for which prices are collected three times a year by chambers of commerce, economic development organizations or university applied economic centers in each participating urban area. The numbers shown should be read as a percentage above or below the national average of 100. For example, a value of 115.4 in the groceries column indicates that grocery prices are 15.4% higher than the national average. Small differences in the index numbers should not be interpreted as significant. In cases where data is not available for the city, data for the metro area or for a neighboring city has been provided and noted as follows: (2) Brooklyn, NY; (3) Hampton Roads-SE Virginia
Source: The Council for Community and Economic Research, Cost of Living Index, 2024

Grocery Prices

Urban Area	T-Bone Steak ($/pound)	Frying Chicken ($/pound)	Whole Milk ($/half gal.)	Eggs ($/dozen)	Orange Juice ($/64 oz.)	Coffee ($/11.5 oz.)
Albuquerque, NM	14.86	1.51	4.61	3.01	4.27	5.45
Anchorage, AK	17.56	2.89	5.34	4.09	5.40	7.86
Ann Arbor, MI	n/a	n/a	n/a	n/a	n/a	n/a
Athens, GA	15.55	1.45	4.70	3.57	4.49	5.28
Atlanta, GA	15.52	1.44	4.67	3.38	4.47	5.59
Austin, TX	14.52	1.37	4.62	3.05	4.27	5.19
Baltimore, MD	15.52	1.44	4.64	3.35	4.34	5.56
Billings, MT	15.52	1.47	4.72	3.46	4.19	6.92
Boise City, ID	15.52	1.52	4.75	3.63	4.45	6.38
Boston, MA	15.52	1.51	4.76	3.03	4.54	5.39
Boulder, CO	n/a	n/a	n/a	n/a	n/a	n/a
Cape Coral, FL	15.51	1.46	4.69	3.46	4.51	5.45
Cedar Rapids, IA	n/a	n/a	n/a	n/a	n/a	n/a
Charleston, SC	15.51	1.64	4.54	3.41	4.43	5.46
Charlotte, NC	15.53	1.61	4.69	3.30	4.33	5.36
Chicago, IL	15.52	1.45	4.88	3.50	4.50	5.80
Cincinnati, OH	15.52	1.74	4.74	3.73	4.36	5.67
Clarksville, TN	n/a	n/a	n/a	n/a	n/a	n/a
Cleveland, OH	15.51	1.42	4.58	3.24	4.44	5.24
College Station, TX	n/a	n/a	n/a	n/a	n/a	n/a
Colorado Springs, CO	15.53	1.46	4.60	2.91	4.42	6.03
Columbia, MO	15.51	1.47	4.69	3.41	4.45	5.17
Columbia, SC	15.51	1.66	4.62	3.28	4.38	5.27
Columbus, OH	15.51	1.72	4.72	3.39	4.39	5.52
Dallas, TX	14.56	1.54	4.61	3.13	4.31	5.41
Davenport, IA	15.52	1.43	4.92	3.35	4.44	5.02
Denver, CO	15.52	1.45	4.62	2.98	4.42	6.16
Des Moines, IA	15.52	1.44	4.76	3.47	4.47	4.94
Detroit, MI	15.53	1.73	4.80	3.37	4.41	5.64
Durham, NC	15.53	1.48	4.61	3.25	4.39	5.40
El Paso, TX	14.86	1.41	4.63	2.97	4.27	5.42
Eugene, OR	15.53	1.92	4.92	3.47	4.49	6.40
Fargo, ND	15.51	1.46	4.85	3.12	4.28	5.46
Fort Collins, CO	n/a	n/a	n/a	n/a	n/a	n/a
Fort Wayne, IN	15.51	1.66	4.69	3.49	4.36	5.41
Fort Worth, TX	14.52	1.56	4.61	3.13	4.28	5.46
Gainesville, FL	n/a	n/a	n/a	n/a	n/a	n/a
Green Bay, WI	15.51	1.42	4.70	3.25	4.43	5.29
Greensboro, NC	n/a	n/a	n/a	n/a	n/a	n/a
Honolulu, HI	16.57	2.86	5.49	3.98	5.19	7.89
Houston, TX	14.53	1.62	4.64	3.18	4.33	5.40
Huntsville, AL	15.52	1.41	4.54	3.35	4.41	5.49
Indianapolis, IN	15.51	1.63	4.67	3.40	4.33	5.39
Jacksonville, FL	15.52	1.42	4.72	3.41	4.53	5.38
Kansas City, MO	15.52	1.45	4.70	3.17	4.38	5.06
Lafayette, LA	15.29	1.41	4.60	3.05	4.38	5.07
Las Vegas, NV	15.54	1.74	4.78	3.08	4.43	6.31
Lexington, KY	15.52	1.44	4.69	3.40	4.30	5.70
Lincoln, NE	15.51	1.44	4.68	3.13	4.43	5.17
Little Rock, AR	14.86	1.43	4.62	3.40	4.31	5.24
Los Angeles, CA	15.55	2.45	5.00	3.14	4.55	6.68
Louisville, KY	15.51	1.48	4.71	3.39	4.37	5.37
Madison, WI	15.51	1.43	4.77	3.34	4.44	5.60
Manchester, NH	15.51	1.42	4.71	2.98	4.42	5.31
McAllen, TX	14.52	1.28	4.54	2.96	4.22	5.08

Table continued on following page.

Urban Area	T-Bone Steak ($/pound)	Frying Chicken ($/pound)	Whole Milk ($/half gal.)	Eggs ($/dozen)	Orange Juice ($/64 oz.)	Coffee ($/11.5 oz.)
Memphis, TN	15.53	1.31	4.67	3.47	4.35	5.24
Miami, FL	15.52	1.45	4.80	3.77	4.78	5.91
Midland, TX	14.53	1.41	4.61	3.04	4.30	4.99
Milwaukee, WI	15.50	1.43	4.80	3.34	4.45	5.96
Minneapolis, MN	15.53	1.44	4.66	3.56	4.49	5.23
Nashville, TN	15.51	1.43	4.63	3.32	4.40	5.35
New Orleans, LA	15.51	1.36	4.66	3.19	4.38	4.94
New York, NY[2]	15.52	1.56	5.14	3.63	4.79	5.93
Oklahoma City, OK	15.34	1.46	4.55	2.97	4.28	5.16
Omaha, NE	15.51	1.44	4.87	3.22	4.43	5.50
Orlando, FL	15.52	1.45	4.63	3.47	4.53	5.53
Philadelphia, PA	15.46	1.52	4.70	3.48	4.41	5.43
Phoenix, AZ	15.53	1.77	4.76	2.95	4.40	6.24
Pittsburgh, PA	15.52	1.43	4.52	3.27	4.44	5.15
Portland, OR	15.52	1.89	4.93	3.57	4.49	6.85
Providence, RI	15.51	1.68	4.70	3.55	4.43	4.91
Provo, UT	15.52	1.54	4.57	2.91	4.17	5.79
Raleigh, NC	15.51	1.45	4.58	3.33	4.31	5.44
Reno, NV	15.53	2.26	4.66	2.91	4.36	5.88
Richmond, VA	15.51	1.43	4.65	3.38	4.37	5.55
Rochester, MN	n/a	n/a	n/a	n/a	n/a	n/a
Sacramento, CA	15.53	2.13	5.01	2.90	4.40	6.44
Saint Louis, MO	15.51	1.44	4.67	3.37	4.43	5.05
Saint Paul, MN	15.52	1.44	4.64	3.81	4.58	5.13
Salem, OR	n/a	n/a	n/a	n/a	n/a	n/a
Salt Lake City, UT	15.51	1.53	4.62	3.03	4.19	6.11
San Antonio, TX	14.53	1.33	4.57	2.98	4.25	5.05
San Diego, CA	15.56	2.40	5.07	3.17	4.63	6.78
San Francisco, CA	15.55	2.66	5.03	3.35	4.86	7.53
San Jose, CA	15.54	2.57	5.09	3.10	4.64	6.92
Santa Rosa, CA	n/a	n/a	n/a	n/a	n/a	n/a
Savannah, GA	15.52	1.43	4.72	3.53	4.53	5.62
Seattle, WA	15.51	1.98	4.94	3.87	4.58	7.06
Sioux Falls, SD	15.53	1.49	4.52	3.10	4.37	5.10
Tampa, FL	15.52	1.46	4.73	3.60	4.59	5.56
Tucson, AZ	n/a	n/a	n/a	n/a	n/a	n/a
Tulsa, OK	15.52	1.45	4.59	2.97	4.32	5.06
Virginia Beach, VA[3]	15.52	1.46	4.58	3.35	4.34	5.34
Washington, DC	15.51	1.42	4.62	3.47	4.44	5.77
Wichita, KS	15.50	1.43	4.66	3.16	4.30	5.36
Wilmington, NC	n/a	n/a	n/a	n/a	n/a	n/a
Winston-Salem, NC	15.51	1.46	4.60	3.19	4.30	5.15
Average[1]	15.42	1.55	4.69	3.25	4.41	5.46
Minimum[1]	14.50	1.16	4.43	2.75	4.00	4.85
Maximum[1]	17.56	2.89	5.49	4.78	5.54	7.89

*Note: **T-Bone Steak** (price per pound); **Frying Chicken** (price per pound, whole fryer); **Whole Milk** (half gallon carton); **Eggs** (price per dozen, Grade A, large); **Orange Juice** (64 oz. Tropicana or Florida Natural); **Coffee** (11.5 oz. can, vacuum-packed, Maxwell House, Hills Bros, or Folgers); (1) Average, minimum, and maximum values for all 276 areas in the Cost of Living Index report; n/a not available; In cases where data is not available for the city, data for the metro area or for a neighboring city has been provided and noted as follows: (2) Brooklyn, NY; (3) Hampton Roads-SE Virginia*
Source: The Council for Community and Economic Research, Cost of Living Index, 2024

Housing and Utility Costs

Urban Area	New Home Price ($)	Apartment Rent ($/month)	All Electric ($/month)	Part Electric ($/month)	Other Energy ($/month)	Telephone ($/month)
Albuquerque, NM	424,687	1,574	-	115.74	50.09	192.92
Anchorage, AK	758,772	1,670	-	108.68	138.69	193.41
Ann Arbor, MI	n/a	n/a	n/a	n/a	n/a	n/a
Athens, GA	483,427	1,622	-	113.87	91.54	192.87
Atlanta, GA	428,946	1,464	-	113.87	91.54	194.22
Austin, TX	500,842	1,849	-	137.02	59.06	203.47
Baltimore, MD	390,678	1,695	-	134.88	101.43	201.97
Billings, MT	517,409	1,317	-	94.77	60.66	185.25
Boise City, ID	514,076	1,611	-	83.70	59.41	179.42
Boston, MA	1,039,939	3,993	-	190.85	180.18	190.24
Boulder, CO	n/a	n/a	n/a	n/a	n/a	n/a
Cape Coral, FL	509,774	1,897	225.95	-	-	197.01
Cedar Rapids, IA	n/a	n/a	n/a	n/a	n/a	n/a
Charleston, SC	526,080	1,748	249.82	-	-	197.48
Charlotte, NC	398,825	1,562	213.43	-	-	189.47
Chicago, IL	566,384	3,240	-	113.94	70.31	212.43
Cincinnati, OH	443,467	1,416	-	116.95	90.88	189.55
Clarksville, TN	n/a	n/a	n/a	n/a	n/a	n/a
Cleveland, OH	391,639	1,431	-	83.27	78.55	189.85
College Station, TX	n/a	n/a	n/a	n/a	n/a	n/a
Colorado Springs, CO	557,240	1,828	-	86.01	42.49	192.15
Columbia, MO	451,668	1,041	-	114.12	78.36	199.61
Columbia, SC	328,383	1,205	-	119.24	143.41	195.98
Columbus, OH	482,718	1,613	-	146.60	76.69	189.10
Dallas, TX	477,656	1,572	-	171.06	80.72	203.47
Davenport, IA	387,652	1,218	-	85.51	62.12	200.43
Denver, CO	650,555	1,899	-	93.55	76.25	197.22
Des Moines, IA	359,756	846	-	84.52	63.10	188.12
Detroit, MI	568,077	1,560	-	134.21	78.36	187.38
Durham, NC	521,333	1,650	187.89	-	-	189.44
El Paso, TX	354,072	1,146	-	111.01	62.07	203.47
Eugene, OR	666,539	1,654	-	89.38	96.37	187.81
Fargo, ND	390,066	1,596	-	81.39	58.17	197.46
Fort Collins, CO	n/a	n/a	n/a	n/a	n/a	n/a
Fort Wayne, IN	364,871	1,370	-	109.31	68.72	192.42
Fort Worth, TX	422,585	1,470	-	170.29	80.72	210.13
Gainesville, FL	n/a	n/a	n/a	n/a	n/a	n/a
Green Bay, WI	447,400	1,055	-	90.06	61.14	188.34
Greensboro, NC	n/a	n/a	n/a	n/a	n/a	n/a
Honolulu, HI	1,681,170	4,424	529.02	-	-	187.39
Houston, TX	388,197	1,322	-	124.12	48.31	209.27
Huntsville, AL	361,221	1,123	172.74	-	-	189.28
Indianapolis, IN	360,369	1,336	-	99.46	70.12	192.42
Jacksonville, FL	391,862	1,714	170.55	-	-	197.76
Kansas City, MO	429,449	1,506	-	103.82	115.85	202.40
Lafayette, LA	306,872	1,150	-	96.15	60.82	190.09
Las Vegas, NV	554,723	1,576	-	160.52	94.44	188.64
Lexington, KY	380,651	1,239	-	82.51	72.69	194.48
Lincoln, NE	390,814	1,216	-	90.57	84.28	204.27
Little Rock, AR	407,536	1,155	-	76.85	69.20	208.40
Los Angeles, CA	1,311,286	2,988	-	163.45	65.93	194.86
Louisville, KY	388,161	1,369	-	82.51	72.69	188.14
Madison, WI	622,141	1,233	-	126.81	79.79	187.45
Manchester, NH	552,244	2,205	-	135.10	114.30	189.12
McAllen, TX	291,921	981	-	176.13	88.49	203.47

Table continued on following page.

Urban Area	New Home Price ($)	Apartment Rent ($/month)	All Electric ($/month)	Part Electric ($/month)	Other Energy ($/month)	Telephone ($/month)
Memphis, TN	404,407	1,598	-	105.22	38.46	195.12
Miami, FL	711,025	3,211	220.47	-	-	197.31
Midland, TX	400,707	1,483	-	150.59	53.85	202.34
Milwaukee, WI	541,477	1,627	-	123.28	67.66	187.62
Minneapolis, MN	405,152	1,419	-	98.70	98.25	191.53
Nashville, TN	519,432	1,670	-	105.42	77.00	223.33
New Orleans, LA	812,851	2,128	-	68.38	47.92	190.09
New York, NY[2]	1,411,780	3,995	-	157.71	92.60	203.07
Oklahoma City, OK	320,395	811	-	115.46	78.66	197.38
Omaha, NE	385,889	1,500	-	93.49	55.47	203.73
Orlando, FL	441,765	1,690	216.79	-	-	197.01
Philadelphia, PA	470,985	1,851	-	138.01	81.94	201.51
Phoenix, AZ	609,926	1,792	232.03	-	-	187.62
Pittsburgh, PA	478,461	1,602	-	137.23	130.44	200.01
Portland, OR	723,737	2,574	-	70.81	96.37	186.81
Providence, RI	474,141	2,453	-	171.99	161.54	198.12
Provo, UT	612,973	1,544	-	77.11	106.23	195.59
Raleigh, NC	466,683	1,514	-	107.05	69.13	189.30
Reno, NV	596,654	1,646	-	129.17	59.21	188.64
Richmond, VA	418,775	1,466	-	117.64	80.21	187.77
Rochester, MN	n/a	n/a	n/a	n/a	n/a	n/a
Sacramento, CA	718,604	2,241	-	397.28	53.75	191.51
Saint Louis, MO	427,558	1,128	-	100.98	92.58	203.68
Saint Paul, MN	404,109	1,358	-	92.16	101.15	192.06
Salem, OR	n/a	n/a	n/a	n/a	n/a	n/a
Salt Lake City, UT	717,422	1,758	-	96.56	93.13	196.83
San Antonio, TX	357,072	1,521	-	105.82	36.26	202.34
San Diego, CA	1,113,702	3,153	-	255.41	87.52	181.36
San Francisco, CA	1,383,739	3,749	-	264.12	131.73	205.06
San Jose, CA	1,860,932	3,311	-	267.58	131.25	192.30
Santa Rosa, CA	n/a	n/a	n/a	n/a	n/a	n/a
Savannah, GA	379,397	1,313	206.53	-	-	191.37
Seattle, WA	1,093,157	3,259	204.50	-	-	204.74
Sioux Falls, SD	509,371	977	-	103.68	71.55	198.68
Tampa, FL	455,535	1,796	203.80	-	-	197.76
Tucson, AZ	n/a	n/a	n/a	n/a	n/a	n/a
Tulsa, OK	339,822	935	-	118.37	80.52	197.22
Virginia Beach, VA[3]	389,841	1,484	-	120.02	103.90	187.93
Washington, DC	1,149,206	3,212	-	122.00	92.52	193.65
Wichita, KS	334,425	1,007	-	113.92	81.43	202.42
Wilmington, NC	n/a	n/a	n/a	n/a	n/a	n/a
Winston-Salem, NC	383,928	1,301	214.90	-	-	189.30
Average[1]	515,975	1,550	210.99	123.07	82.07	194.99
Minimum[1]	265,375	692	104.33	53.68	36.26	179.42
Maximum[1]	2,775,821	5,719	529.02	397.28	361.63	223.33

Note: **New Home Price** *(2,400 sf living area, 8,000 sf lot, in urban area with full utilities);* **Apartment Rent** *(950 sf 2 bedroom/1.5 or 2 bath, unfurnished, excluding all utilities except water);* **All Electric** *(average monthly cost for an all-electric home);* **Part Electric** *(average monthly cost for a part-electric home);* **Other Energy** *(average monthly cost for natural gas, fuel oil, coal, wood, and any other forms of energy except electricity);* **Telephone** *(price includes the base monthly rate plus taxes and fees for three lines of mobile phone service); (1) Average, minimum, and maximum values for all 276 areas in the Cost of Living Index report; n/a not available; In cases where data is not available for the city, data for the metro area or for a neighboring city has been provided and noted as follows: (2) Brooklyn, NY; (3) Hampton Roads-SE Virginia*
Source: *The Council for Community and Economic Research, Cost of Living Index, 2024*

Health Care, Transportation, and Other Costs

Urban Area	Doctor ($/visit)	Dentist ($/visit)	Optometrist ($/visit)	Gasoline ($/gallon)	Beauty Salon ($/visit)	Men's Shirt ($)
Albuquerque, NM	133.41	115.32	145.00	3.10	47.25	37.35
Anchorage, AK	243.83	173.17	265.00	3.68	50.00	45.44
Ann Arbor, MI	n/a	n/a	n/a	n/a	n/a	n/a
Athens, GA	123.75	128.33	97.63	3.12	56.40	40.51
Atlanta, GA	132.58	142.21	130.44	3.22	56.70	30.32
Austin, TX	109.05	135.58	126.98	2.98	67.39	27.11
Baltimore, MD	135.14	116.91	119.20	3.41	61.43	41.00
Billings, MT	215.23	110.57	164.07	3.33	38.78	36.85
Boise City, ID	169.88	102.77	145.10	3.61	52.55	48.06
Boston, MA	222.77	144.00	161.33	3.33	66.76	39.88
Boulder, CO	n/a	n/a	n/a	n/a	n/a	n/a
Cape Coral, FL	178.39	133.21	101.13	3.36	54.67	30.93
Cedar Rapids, IA	n/a	n/a	n/a	n/a	n/a	n/a
Charleston, SC	123.53	99.17	82.86	3.03	56.00	24.77
Charlotte, NC	157.61	120.57	92.08	3.12	79.44	57.64
Chicago, IL	179.67	126.00	113.83	3.55	62.23	34.52
Cincinnati, OH	158.21	98.92	97.57	3.18	39.43	41.70
Clarksville, TN	n/a	n/a	n/a	n/a	n/a	n/a
Cleveland, OH	117.00	111.33	110.47	3.21	40.20	39.79
College Station, TX	n/a	n/a	n/a	n/a	n/a	n/a
Colorado Springs, CO	134.99	106.17	132.00	3.04	50.14	30.58
Columbia, MO	182.67	95.67	138.50	3.10	45.42	37.14
Columbia, SC	150.00	58.67	67.33	3.12	38.83	34.56
Columbus, OH	115.70	94.35	93.20	3.19	49.51	36.47
Dallas, TX	138.26	133.49	135.65	3.07	72.78	43.45
Davenport, IA	167.17	105.92	108.62	3.41	39.87	34.38
Denver, CO	134.18	140.57	122.31	3.05	50.44	22.71
Des Moines, IA	119.38	101.96	128.70	3.15	42.46	37.61
Detroit, MI	183.09	126.33	95.64	3.42	60.83	52.14
Durham, NC	179.33	112.78	133.40	3.38	54.35	30.66
El Paso, TX	129.11	95.03	101.95	3.23	33.64	34.89
Eugene, OR	196.75	117.67	126.00	3.83	40.19	36.32
Fargo, ND	230.71	124.67	113.44	3.12	40.47	44.83
Fort Collins, CO	n/a	n/a	n/a	n/a	n/a	n/a
Fort Wayne, IN	137.75	106.33	122.67	3.32	33.28	39.34
Fort Worth, TX	138.71	136.11	137.89	3.03	52.39	37.44
Gainesville, FL	n/a	n/a	n/a	n/a	n/a	n/a
Green Bay, WI	167.58	112.11	84.28	3.14	30.42	26.22
Greensboro, NC	n/a	n/a	n/a	n/a	n/a	n/a
Honolulu, HI	201.94	127.00	258.67	4.58	75.33	58.48
Houston, TX	97.07	129.17	137.54	2.98	73.30	50.68
Huntsville, AL	121.00	115.28	99.56	3.04	58.56	30.30
Indianapolis, IN	112.66	105.53	77.80	3.35	39.07	43.61
Jacksonville, FL	106.53	98.40	97.76	3.34	79.67	30.27
Kansas City, MO	95.79	108.20	95.10	3.06	34.80	29.79
Lafayette, LA	95.33	95.87	120.20	3.01	40.73	44.86
Las Vegas, NV	110.44	99.25	100.78	4.13	48.86	25.05
Lexington, KY	144.23	113.73	92.42	3.19	60.23	44.97
Lincoln, NE	183.29	113.07	119.17	3.25	42.20	52.31
Little Rock, AR	133.00	83.67	105.53	2.95	52.55	47.99
Los Angeles, CA	130.00	133.17	127.53	4.85	94.00	38.64
Louisville, KY	152.10	159.00	107.05	3.21	43.89	48.00
Madison, WI	236.64	124.37	72.86	3.27	76.22	41.80
Manchester, NH	183.83	108.17	116.33	3.24	56.33	42.69
McAllen, TX	91.69	88.11	100.21	2.96	47.50	32.95

Table continued on following page.

Urban Area	Doctor ($/visit)	Dentist ($/visit)	Optometrist ($/visit)	Gasoline ($/gallon)	Beauty Salon ($/visit)	Men's Shirt ($)
Memphis, TN	112.80	97.80	83.95	3.00	46.92	27.44
Miami, FL	134.75	118.47	110.39	3.43	87.63	28.46
Midland, TX	97.50	108.17	132.67	3.13	69.08	43.45
Milwaukee, WI	174.22	122.03	86.17	3.30	44.20	32.41
Minneapolis, MN	170.09	100.86	120.48	3.16	40.96	41.19
Nashville, TN	122.71	110.37	114.45	3.08	48.65	32.66
New Orleans, LA	161.78	121.36	115.44	3.11	48.33	49.00
New York, NY[2]	192.84	171.93	152.60	3.43	68.80	44.04
Oklahoma City, OK	149.53	124.67	99.96	3.02	51.40	22.45
Omaha, NE	151.64	90.62	117.00	3.08	33.92	35.09
Orlando, FL	123.06	110.00	97.28	3.34	53.19	32.49
Philadelphia, PA	148.84	111.61	125.00	3.33	67.25	36.90
Phoenix, AZ	99.00	127.08	103.50	3.64	55.36	22.95
Pittsburgh, PA	96.56	128.63	105.71	3.67	44.32	28.77
Portland, OR	218.48	116.33	147.50	4.17	60.17	35.98
Providence, RI	168.33	117.58	111.08	3.28	50.22	31.37
Provo, UT	113.66	105.45	127.59	3.41	51.34	49.04
Raleigh, NC	146.67	153.61	109.33	3.23	55.17	32.17
Reno, NV	115.00	105.00	118.17	4.35	49.17	27.27
Richmond, VA	120.19	104.13	133.02	3.24	48.38	20.26
Rochester, MN	n/a	n/a	n/a	n/a	n/a	n/a
Sacramento, CA	151.58	121.82	173.55	5.28	71.49	36.48
Saint Louis, MO	92.32	115.88	95.55	3.38	41.97	28.19
Saint Paul, MN	169.08	101.40	118.46	3.16	41.44	42.25
Salem, OR	n/a	n/a	n/a	n/a	n/a	n/a
Salt Lake City, UT	129.02	100.40	125.47	3.38	56.68	44.66
San Antonio, TX	149.40	139.78	139.25	2.97	69.33	39.95
San Diego, CA	139.44	126.00	143.70	4.93	67.95	39.49
San Francisco, CA	183.65	160.37	168.34	5.07	86.22	48.81
San Jose, CA	212.00	131.83	166.92	5.00	65.28	32.93
Santa Rosa, CA	n/a	n/a	n/a	n/a	n/a	n/a
Savannah, GA	150.00	152.87	91.31	3.29	39.61	38.61
Seattle, WA	208.77	157.05	179.39	4.49	85.33	49.17
Sioux Falls, SD	116.42	116.32	140.94	3.04	40.11	30.74
Tampa, FL	126.57	112.70	118.00	3.36	48.00	27.91
Tucson, AZ	n/a	n/a	n/a	n/a	n/a	n/a
Tulsa, OK	109.57	109.83	111.11	2.95	35.40	29.28
Virginia Beach, VA[3]	144.92	148.93	69.03	3.20	42.70	32.71
Washington, DC	177.67	151.33	125.50	3.36	78.76	37.95
Wichita, KS	111.32	102.90	144.60	3.09	48.13	54.27
Wilmington, NC	n/a	n/a	n/a	n/a	n/a	n/a
Winston-Salem, NC	152.89	120.67	145.61	3.15	50.94	38.49
Average[1]	143.77	117.51	129.23	3.32	48.57	38.14
Minimum[1]	36.74	58.67	67.33	2.80	24.00	13.41
Maximum[1]	270.44	216.82	307.33	5.28	94.00	63.89

Note: **Doctor** *(general practitioners routine exam of an established patient);* **Dentist** *(adult teeth cleaning and periodic oral examination);* **Optometrist** *(full vision eye exam for established adult patient);* **Gasoline** *(one gallon regular unleaded, national brand, including all taxes, cash price at self-service pump if available);* **Beauty Salon** *(woman's shampoo, trim, and blow-dry);* **Men's Shirt** *(cotton/polyester dress shirt, pinpoint weave, long sleeves); (1) Average, minimum, and maximum values for all 276 areas in the Cost of Living Index report; n/a not available; In cases where data is not available for the city, data for the metro area or for a neighboring city has been provided and noted as follows: (2) Brooklyn, NY; (3) Hampton Roads-SE Virginia*
Source: The Council for Community and Economic Research, Cost of Living Index, 2024

Number of Medical Professionals

City	Area Covered	MDs[1]	DOs[1,2]	Dentists	Podiatrists	Chiropractors	Optometrists
Albuquerque, NM	Bernalillo County	503.5	30.6	87.4	9.4	24.9	17.7
Anchorage, AK	Anchorage Borough	384.5	55.4	134.9	5.9	65.7	31.5
Ann Arbor, MI	Washtenaw County	1,420.9	52.7	208.7	9.0	26.5	19.4
Athens, GA	Clarke County	392.7	17.7	50.0	3.8	21.5	16.2
Atlanta, GA	Fulton County	548.6	18.3	76.9	5.1	60.5	21.3
Austin, TX	Travis County	332.0	21.9	76.9	4.4	36.6	18.8
Baltimore, MD	Baltimore City	1,247.2	36.1	88.5	8.0	16.8	16.6
Billings, MT	Yellowstone County	379.2	40.0	101.3	9.4	38.6	26.9
Boise City, ID	Ada County	286.2	40.1	83.7	4.6	54.9	23.1
Boston, MA	Suffolk County	1,797.9	24.3	251.7	9.0	16.9	39.0
Boulder, CO	Boulder County	365.5	34.2	116.9	6.4	84.4	30.0
Cape Coral, FL	Lee County	198.8	29.9	56.1	7.9	28.8	13.3
Cedar Rapids, IA	Linn County	181.2	25.3	77.7	8.7	62.5	17.9
Charleston, SC	Charleston County	881.5	45.6	117.8	5.7	54.7	25.9
Charlotte, NC	Mecklenburg County	352.8	20.9	72.1	3.7	37.2	14.5
Chicago, IL	Cook County	472.9	34.3	100.5	12.9	30.1	22.5
Cincinnati, OH	Hamilton County	662.9	36.0	77.1	10.4	21.6	23.3
Clarksville, TN	Montgomery County	91.4	16.6	45.0	2.9	12.9	10.4
Cleveland, OH	Cuyahoga County	799.3	74.0	110.6	18.8	20.5	18.2
College Station, TX	Brazos County	254.5	20.2	58.0	3.3	19.6	18.0
Colorado Springs, CO	El Paso County	214.0	37.9	107.1	5.4	47.7	25.7
Columbia, MO	Boone County	864.2	95.9	78.6	5.8	41.2	28.0
Columbia, SC	Richland County	358.7	21.6	93.1	6.8	22.8	18.8
Columbus, OH	Franklin County	473.2	78.8	99.2	8.0	26.5	29.9
Dallas, TX	Dallas County	380.9	24.6	96.6	4.5	40.3	15.6
Davenport, IA	Scott County	256.4	56.3	85.5	5.2	190.5	16.6
Denver, CO	Denver County	610.0	36.3	84.8	6.8	40.6	17.3
Des Moines, IA	Polk County	221.1	118.9	80.8	12.3	63.7	21.2
Detroit, MI	Wayne County	348.3	61.0	80.1	9.8	19.1	12.4
Durham, NC	Durham County	1,206.3	21.9	77.2	4.2	21.1	13.7
El Paso, TX	El Paso County	231.2	22.1	49.5	4.7	9.2	10.8
Eugene, OR	Lane County	250.6	16.5	75.6	5.2	29.4	17.3
Fargo, ND	Cass County	401.6	26.5	78.4	5.1	75.9	33.6
Fort Collins, CO	Larimer County	251.9	39.3	85.2	6.5	57.4	21.3
Fort Wayne, IN	Allen County	272.1	33.5	72.7	5.6	23.8	26.6
Fort Worth, TX	Tarrant County	197.7	39.4	64.9	4.5	30.4	17.3
Gainesville, FL	Alachua County	1,059.4	68.3	193.4	5.6	26.9	19.2
Green Bay, WI	Brown County	265.5	25.6	80.7	3.3	50.5	19.9
Greensboro, NC	Guilford County	262.2	18.9	62.9	4.7	15.1	10.2
Honolulu, HI	Honolulu County	357.2	23.8	103.9	3.9	22.6	25.8
Houston, TX	Harris County	363.6	16.0	75.3	5.0	24.0	21.6
Huntsville, AL	Madison County	275.3	16.1	53.3	2.9	23.0	20.1
Indianapolis, IN	Marion County	475.0	31.6	95.4	6.9	17.5	22.1
Jacksonville, FL	Duval County	369.2	38.0	77.4	6.9	27.6	16.4
Kansas City, MO	Jackson County	343.6	110.1	94.5	7.1	49.3	20.2
Lafayette, LA	Lafayette Parish	383.7	17.3	71.3	4.0	33.6	14.4
Las Vegas, NV	Clark County	188.3	42.2	69.1	4.7	21.1	14.8
Lexington, KY	Fayette County	844.1	66.5	149.6	8.1	25.9	29.4
Lincoln, NE	Lancaster County	215.9	16.9	109.0	5.5	49.9	20.5
Little Rock, AR	Pulaski County	822.8	30.3	80.2	5.2	24.0	22.7
Los Angeles, CA	Los Angeles County	336.3	17.6	99.4	6.9	32.1	20.8
Louisville, KY	Jefferson County	506.3	25.2	107.8	8.5	28.2	17.9
Madison, WI	Dane County	669.0	28.0	77.3	5.2	45.9	21.9
Manchester, NH	Hillsborough County	235.1	26.7	85.2	6.6	26.9	22.5
McAllen, TX	Hidalgo County	145.8	4.7	31.4	1.6	8.0	7.2
Memphis, TN	Shelby County	429.3	17.8	78.8	4.0	15.5	33.0

Table continued on following page.

City	Area Covered	MDs[1]	DOs[1,2]	Dentists	Podiatrists	Chiropractors	Optometrists
Miami, FL	Miami-Dade County	415.2	27.2	81.5	10.0	20.1	16.3
Midland, TX	Midland County	154.1	6.4	60.4	2.3	14.1	11.9
Milwaukee, WI	Milwaukee County	431.6	36.6	92.8	7.1	22.0	12.1
Minneapolis, MN	Hennepin County	570.7	32.9	106.5	5.7	80.2	23.3
Nashville, TN	Davidson County	698.9	19.2	84.9	5.3	29.8	17.8
New Orleans, LA	Orleans Parish	1,005.0	33.8	86.5	4.9	10.2	8.8
New York, NY	New York City	545.5	24.3	90.9	13.8	16.8	19.8
Oklahoma City, OK	Oklahoma County	432.6	52.2	111.5	4.8	29.7	21.3
Omaha, NE	Douglas County	600.0	44.3	105.5	5.4	44.4	23.6
Orlando, FL	Orange County	349.3	28.9	54.1	4.1	29.8	14.1
Philadelphia, PA	Philadelphia County	663.2	66.9	86.4	16.3	15.6	20.8
Phoenix, AZ	Maricopa County	258.2	37.8	73.7	7.4	34.3	17.5
Pittsburgh, PA	Allegheny County	677.7	59.4	99.5	9.3	44.9	21.1
Portland, OR	Multnomah County	687.2	44.4	105.1	5.1	80.2	26.2
Providence, RI	Providence County	526.4	19.5	59.8	10.1	21.2	22.4
Provo, UT	Utah County	115.9	24.3	60.3	4.7	26.7	11.4
Raleigh, NC	Wake County	293.0	15.8	75.8	3.8	29.7	16.6
Reno, NV	Washoe County	310.2	25.2	72.1	4.4	30.7	23.7
Richmond, VA	Richmond City	822.6	63.6	155.7	13.5	7.4	15.7
Rochester, MN	Olmsted County	2,670.4	71.3	137.1	7.3	45.5	24.9
Sacramento, CA	Sacramento County	344.7	20.3	84.3	4.5	22.0	19.4
Saint Louis, MO	St. Louis City	1,491.0	56.9	71.0	4.3	23.4	21.7
Saint Paul, MN	Ramsey County	379.6	17.2	95.7	5.8	71.4	14.7
Salem, OR	Marion County	180.0	18.7	88.3	6.6	35.5	16.7
Salt Lake City, UT	Salt Lake County	422.6	23.4	83.1	6.6	29.7	15.1
San Antonio, TX	Bexar County	330.0	28.5	95.3	6.0	17.4	19.0
San Diego, CA	San Diego County	364.2	22.2	100.8	5.0	36.4	21.2
San Francisco, CA	San Francisco County	942.4	16.7	175.9	11.4	44.0	34.6
San Jose, CA	Santa Clara County	483.8	14.5	129.4	7.4	47.0	30.7
Santa Rosa, CA	Sonoma County	289.0	21.3	99.6	6.8	44.8	18.9
Savannah, GA	Chatham County	384.6	28.2	73.4	6.9	21.4	14.8
Seattle, WA	King County	521.6	19.0	118.3	6.4	48.4	24.3
Sioux Falls, SD	Minnehaha County	395.6	31.4	56.1	5.8	57.5	18.4
Tampa, FL	Hillsborough County	375.2	41.2	66.1	6.7	29.3	16.2
Tucson, AZ	Pima County	387.9	35.6	67.8	5.6	19.4	17.6
Tulsa, OK	Tulsa County	265.4	153.1	71.8	4.2	40.1	25.0
Virginia Beach, VA	Virginia Beach City	263.4	14.9	82.0	7.5	26.7	16.3
Washington, DC	District of Columbia	928.4	29.2	130.5	9.3	11.2	15.2
Wichita, KS	Sedgwick County	266.0	42.1	71.3	1.9	43.9	29.0
Wilmington, NC	New Hanover County	367.8	37.9	82.9	8.4	36.0	24.3
Winston-Salem, NC	Forsyth County	716.2	41.1	64.9	6.9	19.1	18.6
U.S.	U.S.	302.5	29.2	74.6	6.4	29.5	18.0

Note: All figures are the number of medical professionals per 100,000 population; Data as of 2023 unless noted; (1) Data as of 2022 and includes all active, non-federal physicians; (2) Doctor of Osteopathic Medicine
Source: U.S. Department of Health and Human Services, Health Resources and Services Administration, Bureau of Health Professions, Area Resource File (ARF) 2023-2024

Health Insurance Coverage: City

City	With Health Insurance	With Private Health Insurance	With Public Health Insurance	Without Health Insurance	Population Under Age 19 Without Health Insurance
Albuquerque, NM	91.7	60.1	45.1	8.3	5.0
Anchorage, AK	90.0	70.0	34.0	10.0	7.4
Ann Arbor, MI	97.2	86.7	20.9	2.8	2.1
Athens, GA	88.8	72.8	25.0	11.2	8.1
Atlanta, GA	89.5	70.4	27.2	10.5	6.2
Austin, TX	87.6	74.8	20.6	12.4	9.2
Baltimore, MD	94.2	58.5	46.8	5.8	3.8
Billings, MT	93.1	67.1	39.9	6.9	4.8
Boise City, ID	92.3	74.4	29.4	7.7	4.9
Boston, MA	97.0	69.9	35.8	3.0	1.9
Boulder, CO	96.5	83.8	21.0	3.5	1.0
Cape Coral, FL	88.4	65.5	38.4	11.6	10.1
Cedar Rapids, IA	95.5	71.1	36.8	4.5	1.6
Charleston, SC	93.6	79.0	27.0	6.4	2.0
Charlotte, NC	87.1	67.8	26.5	12.9	8.3
Chicago, IL	90.2	61.6	35.8	9.8	4.0
Cincinnati, OH	92.4	61.1	40.3	7.6	5.7
Clarksville, TN	90.7	72.1	34.3	9.3	4.3
Cleveland, OH	92.3	43.8	57.2	7.7	3.7
College Station, TX	91.9	83.0	16.5	8.1	4.7
Colorado Springs, CO	92.3	69.8	36.4	7.7	4.7
Columbia, MO	93.6	79.1	23.3	6.4	4.7
Columbia, SC	91.9	71.0	31.4	8.1	3.2
Columbus, OH	90.2	62.3	35.5	9.8	5.8
Dallas, TX	77.0	54.1	29.3	23.0	15.7
Davenport, IA	92.8	65.0	41.1	7.2	4.7
Denver, CO	91.2	68.3	30.8	8.8	5.3
Des Moines, IA	93.3	62.0	42.7	6.7	2.2
Detroit, MI	92.5	41.8	62.6	7.5	2.7
Durham, NC	88.4	70.6	27.4	11.6	8.6
El Paso, TX	79.0	53.1	34.9	21.0	11.9
Eugene, OR	94.5	68.2	39.0	5.5	2.3
Fargo, ND	93.9	79.5	26.0	6.1	4.5
Fort Collins, CO	94.4	78.3	25.0	5.6	4.8
Fort Wayne, IN	90.6	62.9	38.1	9.4	6.7
Fort Worth, TX	81.4	61.7	26.4	18.6	12.7
Gainesville, FL	91.8	76.6	23.8	8.2	5.0
Green Bay, WI	91.6	59.8	40.9	8.4	4.9
Greensboro, NC	90.9	65.5	35.7	9.1	4.1
Honolulu, HI	96.2	75.5	38.3	3.8	2.4
Houston, TX	76.0	52.1	30.3	24.0	16.0
Huntsville, AL	90.6	73.2	32.5	9.4	3.2
Indianapolis, IN	91.0	62.3	38.6	9.0	5.7
Jacksonville, FL	88.3	64.4	34.4	11.7	7.1
Kansas City, MO	88.7	68.3	29.8	11.3	7.4
Lafayette, LA	90.5	60.7	41.3	9.5	4.4
Las Vegas, NV	86.8	60.3	36.5	13.2	8.8
Lexington, KY	93.2	69.8	34.5	6.8	2.9
Lincoln, NE	93.3	76.3	28.6	6.7	3.9
Little Rock, AR	90.0	62.0	39.1	10.0	7.0
Los Angeles, CA	90.0	55.2	41.9	10.0	3.6
Louisville, KY	94.2	64.2	43.1	5.8	3.8
Madison, WI	95.7	81.9	24.1	4.3	2.9
Manchester, NH	91.2	66.6	35.0	8.8	4.9
McAllen, TX	74.2	48.4	32.3	25.8	14.9

Table continued on following page.

City	With Health Insurance	With Private Health Insurance	With Public Health Insurance	Without Health Insurance	Population Under Age 19 Without Health Insurance
Memphis, TN	85.2	55.1	41.3	14.8	8.6
Miami, FL	82.4	52.6	33.5	17.6	8.8
Midland, TX	85.2	72.0	21.3	14.8	11.7
Milwaukee, WI	90.9	52.2	46.7	9.1	3.6
Minneapolis, MN	94.1	69.5	32.8	5.9	2.8
Nashville, TN	87.4	69.0	29.0	12.6	9.0
New Orleans, LA	91.6	55.4	45.3	8.4	5.4
New York, NY	93.6	58.2	45.3	6.4	2.3
Oklahoma City, OK	86.0	63.0	34.4	14.0	7.6
Omaha, NE	90.3	69.2	31.0	9.7	6.9
Orlando, FL	86.1	64.6	27.6	13.9	8.0
Philadelphia, PA	92.8	58.8	45.9	7.2	4.5
Phoenix, AZ	85.5	58.6	34.6	14.5	9.8
Pittsburgh, PA	94.8	72.9	33.5	5.2	3.8
Portland, OR	94.5	71.5	33.1	5.5	2.1
Providence, RI	92.6	57.0	44.1	7.4	5.1
Provo, UT	90.6	78.6	17.5	9.4	9.8
Raleigh, NC	89.9	73.5	26.0	10.1	6.0
Reno, NV	89.5	67.9	31.5	10.5	7.0
Richmond, VA	90.2	63.3	36.9	9.8	7.2
Rochester, MN	95.7	79.7	30.5	4.3	3.7
Sacramento, CA	94.5	65.3	40.5	5.5	3.2
Saint Louis, MO	90.7	63.5	35.7	9.3	3.7
Saint Paul, MN	93.6	62.5	41.0	6.4	4.5
Salem, OR	92.6	63.9	41.9	7.4	1.9
Salt Lake City, UT	89.0	73.9	22.8	11.0	10.2
San Antonio, TX	82.5	58.4	33.8	17.5	9.8
San Diego, CA	93.7	71.9	31.7	6.3	3.6
San Francisco, CA	96.5	75.8	30.7	3.5	2.0
San Jose, CA	95.1	72.5	30.6	4.9	1.8
Santa Rosa, CA	93.6	67.8	39.1	6.4	3.9
Savannah, GA	86.2	59.3	36.7	13.8	5.7
Seattle, WA	95.6	80.5	23.5	4.4	1.8
Sioux Falls, SD	92.2	77.7	25.8	7.8	5.6
Tampa, FL	89.0	64.5	32.0	11.0	5.7
Tucson, AZ	89.0	57.0	42.7	11.0	7.4
Tulsa, OK	83.5	56.6	37.7	16.5	8.4
Virginia Beach, VA	93.5	78.0	30.8	6.5	3.8
Washington, DC	96.6	72.4	34.2	3.4	2.7
Wichita, KS	87.6	65.3	34.1	12.4	6.1
Wilmington, NC	88.4	69.5	32.5	11.6	8.0
Winston-Salem, NC	88.1	61.8	37.5	11.9	4.7
U.S.	91.4	67.3	36.3	8.6	5.4

Note: Figures are percentages that cover the civilian noninstitutionalized population
Source: U.S. Census Bureau, 2019-2023 American Community Survey 5-Year Estimates

Health Insurance Coverage: Metro Area

Metro Area	With Health Insurance	With Private Health Insurance	With Public Health Insurance	Without Health Insurance	Population Under Age 19 Without Health Insurance
Albuquerque, NM	91.9	59.2	47.2	8.1	5.0
Anchorage, AK	89.4	68.4	35.1	10.6	8.2
Ann Arbor, MI	96.7	81.5	28.7	3.3	2.0
Athens, GA	89.0	71.4	27.8	11.0	7.2
Atlanta, GA	87.8	69.1	28.2	12.2	7.2
Austin, TX	87.9	75.2	21.9	12.1	9.0
Baltimore, MD	95.1	74.5	34.4	4.9	3.6
Billings, MT	93.2	68.2	39.6	6.8	5.2
Boise City, ID	91.4	72.1	31.8	8.6	6.2
Boston, MA	97.2	76.4	33.5	2.8	1.6
Boulder, CO	95.6	79.6	26.6	4.4	2.0
Cape Coral, FL	87.5	62.0	43.6	12.5	9.7
Cedar Rapids, IA	96.3	74.8	35.1	3.7	1.4
Charleston, SC	90.3	71.9	32.2	9.7	6.8
Charlotte, NC	89.9	70.0	29.9	10.1	5.9
Chicago, IL	92.4	69.8	32.5	7.6	3.5
Cincinnati, OH	94.5	72.3	33.5	5.5	3.8
Clarksville, TN	90.7	69.7	36.3	9.3	6.7
Cleveland, OH	94.4	67.4	40.0	5.6	3.9
College Station, TX	88.1	73.2	24.7	11.9	7.6
Colorado Springs, CO	92.9	71.5	35.9	7.1	4.6
Columbia, MO	93.4	77.7	26.6	6.6	4.4
Columbia, SC	91.0	69.6	36.0	9.0	5.2
Columbus, OH	92.6	70.0	32.5	7.4	4.5
Dallas, TX	83.7	66.7	24.5	16.3	11.8
Davenport, IA	94.5	71.3	38.0	5.5	3.7
Denver, CO	92.2	72.2	29.4	7.8	5.0
Des Moines, IA	95.5	75.1	32.5	4.5	2.3
Detroit, MI	95.1	70.0	40.0	4.9	2.6
Durham, NC	90.2	72.6	29.5	9.8	6.1
El Paso, TX	78.1	52.1	34.3	21.9	12.9
Eugene, OR	94.1	63.9	44.5	5.9	2.9
Fargo, ND	94.8	80.6	25.8	5.2	4.2
Fort Collins, CO	94.3	74.9	31.0	5.7	3.8
Fort Wayne, IN	92.0	68.5	34.5	8.0	6.3
Fort Worth, TX	83.7	66.7	24.5	16.3	11.8
Gainesville, FL	90.9	71.2	30.8	9.1	5.2
Green Bay, WI	94.8	72.2	34.1	5.2	3.4
Greensboro, NC	90.2	64.1	37.2	9.8	4.2
Honolulu, HI	96.6	78.2	36.3	3.4	2.6
Houston, TX	81.3	61.4	27.1	18.7	12.6
Huntsville, AL	92.2	77.5	29.4	7.8	2.8
Indianapolis, IN	93.0	70.9	32.9	7.0	4.6
Jacksonville, FL	90.1	69.3	33.4	9.9	6.3
Kansas City, MO	91.1	74.1	27.9	8.9	5.6
Lafayette, LA	92.3	60.4	42.4	7.7	3.2
Las Vegas, NV	87.9	62.5	35.9	12.1	8.3
Lexington, KY	93.9	69.8	36.2	6.1	3.2
Lincoln, NE	93.7	77.6	28.1	6.3	3.8
Little Rock, AR	91.7	65.3	39.2	8.3	5.1
Los Angeles, CA	91.8	60.8	38.8	8.2	3.5
Louisville, KY	94.7	69.5	38.9	5.3	3.6
Madison, WI	96.3	82.6	26.5	3.7	2.8
Manchester, NH	94.0	77.1	29.3	6.0	4.0
McAllen, TX	70.3	37.7	37.5	29.7	15.7

Table continued on following page.

Metro Area	With Health Insurance	With Private Health Insurance	With Public Health Insurance	Without Health Insurance	Population Under Age 19 Without Health Insurance
Memphis, TN	88.9	64.1	36.1	11.1	6.4
Miami, FL	86.3	60.5	33.6	13.7	8.2
Midland, TX	84.7	70.7	21.7	15.3	12.1
Milwaukee, WI	94.6	70.6	35.5	5.4	2.8
Minneapolis, MN	95.7	77.3	30.9	4.3	2.7
Nashville, TN	90.6	72.8	28.6	9.4	5.8
New Orleans, LA	90.8	55.9	45.1	9.2	5.6
New York, NY	93.5	66.6	37.8	6.5	3.1
Oklahoma City, OK	87.7	66.8	33.5	12.3	7.3
Omaha, NE	92.9	74.5	29.2	7.1	4.7
Orlando, FL	88.7	66.6	31.4	11.3	6.3
Philadelphia, PA	94.7	72.5	35.5	5.3	3.4
Phoenix, AZ	89.3	66.2	34.1	10.7	8.6
Pittsburgh, PA	96.2	74.5	37.9	3.8	2.4
Portland, OR	94.2	72.3	34.0	5.8	3.2
Providence, RI	96.1	70.1	39.7	3.9	2.4
Provo, UT	92.3	82.1	17.4	7.7	6.0
Raleigh, NC	91.3	76.0	25.6	8.7	5.0
Reno, NV	90.4	69.0	32.8	9.6	6.8
Richmond, VA	93.2	73.3	33.5	6.8	5.0
Rochester, MN	95.6	79.5	31.1	4.4	4.0
Sacramento, CA	95.3	70.1	38.7	4.7	2.7
Saint Louis, MO	94.0	73.7	31.5	6.0	3.5
Saint Paul, MN	95.7	77.3	30.9	4.3	2.7
Salem, OR	92.0	63.0	42.6	8.0	3.3
Salt Lake City, UT	90.6	77.4	20.8	9.4	7.7
San Antonio, TX	85.0	64.6	31.8	15.0	9.1
San Diego, CA	93.2	69.6	34.3	6.8	3.8
San Francisco, CA	95.9	75.5	31.5	4.1	2.4
San Jose, CA	95.9	77.1	27.4	4.1	1.8
Santa Rosa, CA	94.6	71.3	38.3	5.4	3.2
Savannah, GA	88.0	67.8	32.8	12.0	6.6
Seattle, WA	94.4	75.5	29.6	5.6	2.7
Sioux Falls, SD	93.1	79.1	25.6	6.9	4.8
Tampa, FL	88.9	64.2	36.5	11.1	6.0
Tucson, AZ	91.1	62.8	42.8	8.9	7.0
Tulsa, OK	86.8	63.7	35.3	13.2	7.6
Virginia Beach, VA	93.3	73.2	35.8	6.7	4.0
Washington, DC	92.6	76.7	27.8	7.4	4.9
Wichita, KS	89.7	69.9	32.5	10.3	5.3
Wilmington, NC	90.4	71.3	38.0	9.6	6.8
Winston-Salem, NC	89.6	64.5	37.6	10.4	4.6
U.S.	91.4	67.3	36.3	8.6	5.4

Note: Figures are percentages that cover the civilian noninstitutionalized population; Figures cover the Metropolitan Statistical Area (MSA)
Source: U.S. Census Bureau, 2019-2023 American Community Survey 5-Year Estimates

Crime Rate: City

City	Total Crime	Violent Crime Rate				Property Crime Rate		
		Murder	Rape	Robbery	Aggrav. Assault	Burglary	Larceny -Theft	Motor Vehicle Theft
Albuquerque, NM	6,021.7	19.3	54.2	175.5	1,068.0	671.8	3,003.1	1,029.9
Anchorage, AK	3,953.3	7.7	150.2	161.7	742.0	334.0	2,132.4	425.2
Ann Arbor, MI	2,058.1	3.4	37.3	39.0	232.1	171.1	1,438.1	137.2
Athens, GA	2,950.7	3.9	60.2	61.7	305.6	238.4	2,063.4	217.6
Atlanta, GA	4,599.8	26.4	23.2	120.3	537.4	346.9	2,500.1	1,045.6
Austin, TX	3,804.7	6.7	50.3	93.3	348.8	468.0	2,125.2	712.4
Baltimore, MD	5,850.2	41.2	45.1	577.9	908.2	445.5	1,987.6	1,844.7
Billings, MT	4,487.3	7.4	83.2	123.6	674.0	346.1	2,723.2	529.8
Boise City, ID	1,512.1	2.1	67.9	21.9	177.7	131.7	971.9	138.8
Boston, MA	2,571.3	5.3	32.5	136.6	452.5	180.9	1,589.2	174.2
Boulder, CO	3,414.5	2.9	38.4	36.5	279.2	457.6	2,276.7	323.3
Cape Coral, FL	n/a	n/a	n/a	n/a	n/a	n/a	n/a	n/a
Cedar Rapids, IA	3,184.6	5.9	8.1	30.2	255.6	345.4	2,281.7	257.8
Charleston, SC	2,379.5	6.4	28.4	52.8	314.5	164.3	1,501.0	311.9
Charlotte, NC	4,562.0	9.4	25.4	128.4	563.0	430.0	2,578.2	827.7
Chicago, IL	4,038.7	19.0	47.3	412.3	128.1	280.1	2,145.0	1,006.8
Cincinnati, OH	4,956.6	22.0	71.4	208.4	426.2	617.2	2,416.3	1,195.2
Clarksville, TN	2,193.3	6.0	57.7	29.7	373.8	214.9	1,285.8	225.4
Cleveland, OH	6,515.8	38.8	119.5	448.1	1,096.8	894.3	2,475.2	1,443.0
College Station, TX	1,493.6	3.2	49.2	17.4	88.8	141.9	1,086.9	106.2
Colorado Springs, CO	4,386.7	4.9	104.2	76.4	506.5	521.6	2,354.6	818.4
Columbia, MO	2,897.3	7.7	59.4	33.2	285.5	307.1	1,859.5	344.9
Columbia, SC	4,223.4	7.8	45.2	107.4	596.5	455.8	2,537.2	473.5
Columbus, OH	3,089.1	10.5	115.3	117.5	141.8	412.2	1,553.0	738.9
Dallas, TX	4,701.5	18.5	36.8	157.8	458.4	470.3	2,126.6	1,433.1
Davenport, IA	4,501.0	9.0	102.1	91.1	488.4	688.6	2,601.3	520.5
Denver, CO	6,772.3	11.9	93.2	175.8	740.8	716.9	3,284.7	1,749.0
Des Moines, IA	4,056.1	4.3	69.2	90.6	542.8	451.2	2,271.3	626.7
Detroit, MI	6,785.7	40.6	109.3	225.5	1,676.7	756.9	2,485.8	1,490.8
Durham, NC	4,397.4	15.2	53.4	168.4	399.3	497.0	2,574.8	689.3
El Paso, TX	1,955.2	5.0	40.9	48.0	242.2	157.2	1,116.4	345.4
Eugene, OR	3,545.1	3.4	56.7	77.4	210.4	497.8	2,306.5	392.8
Fargo, ND	4,394.2	1.5	71.5	75.2	367.2	768.6	2,690.1	420.1
Fort Collins, CO	2,736.2	0.6	29.0	36.7	229.7	273.6	1,958.1	208.4
Fort Wayne, IN	2,623.8	9.6	43.7	64.9	153.1	251.0	1,800.3	301.0
Fort Worth, TX	3,135.9	8.7	69.1	71.2	340.8	391.4	1,763.5	491.2
Gainesville, FL	3,608.3	10.9	100.9	119.3	507.7	286.2	2,572.5	10.9
Green Bay, WI	1,915.3	5.7	66.3	31.3	283.4	215.1	1,029.2	284.3
Greensboro, NC	4,560.5	24.7	24.4	164.9	612.1	555.0	2,682.7	496.6
Honolulu, HI	2,128.6	0.6	28.0	51.7	105.8	193.1	1,377.3	372.0
Houston, TX	5,599.2	14.9	61.1	295.7	720.0	606.3	3,034.5	866.7
Huntsville, AL	834.6	2.7	15.1	17.4	94.8	101.9	521.4	81.4
Indianapolis, IN	4,653.4	18.9	55.9	174.2	782.0	615.8	2,229.9	776.8
Jacksonville, FL	n/a	n/a	n/a	n/a	n/a	n/a	n/a	n/a
Kansas City, MO	6,436.1	35.5	78.5	241.2	1,122.5	549.6	2,633.3	1,775.6
Lafayette, LA	5,421.0	23.1	24.7	98.1	672.4	1,017.6	3,291.8	293.3
Las Vegas, NV	3,551.8	8.0	49.8	77.6	334.6	524.7	1,681.3	875.9
Lexington, KY	3,004.7	4.4	56.6	76.9	115.9	337.8	2,022.9	390.3
Lincoln, NE	3,052.3	2.4	90.4	52.9	220.4	252.4	2,106.4	327.5
Little Rock, AR	7,228.6	30.5	122.2	223.2	1,425.2	925.7	4,003.7	498.1
Los Angeles, CA	3,666.8	8.6	51.4	230.1	530.0	406.4	1,764.3	676.0
Louisville, KY	4,385.4	22.9	32.7	148.2	561.8	498.8	2,104.4	1,016.8
Madison, WI	2,636.1	3.6	27.7	44.5	225.4	280.4	1,859.0	195.5
Manchester, NH	2,061.5	7.0	59.1	87.9	229.6	147.9	1,342.2	187.9

Table continued on following page.

City	Total Crime	Violent Crime Rate				Property Crime Rate		
		Murder	Rape	Robbery	Aggrav. Assault	Burglary	Larceny -Theft	Motor Vehicle Theft
McAllen, TX	2,092.9	4.8	35.7	24.0	79.6	111.2	1,774.4	63.2
Memphis, TN	11,214.8	57.0	73.4	451.1	2,030.5	1,110.9	4,942.0	2,549.9
Miami, FL	3,436.7	7.1	28.3	109.7	346.9	254.1	2,223.1	467.6
Midland, TX	2,321.6	5.2	63.6	33.3	328.3	274.3	1,354.5	262.5
Milwaukee, WI	4,136.0	31.0	74.3	284.4	1,048.0	418.1	1,278.7	1,001.6
Minneapolis, MN	6,384.2	17.0	86.7	339.8	688.1	605.7	2,806.3	1,840.7
Nashville, TN	5,533.6	14.5	59.1	163.4	892.0	401.7	3,232.8	770.2
New Orleans, LA	6,450.6	53.0	187.0	180.1	941.0	478.3	2,770.8	1,840.5
New York, NY	3,066.4	4.2	25.3	200.0	438.8	167.2	2,006.8	224.2
Oklahoma City, OK	3,571.8	9.0	68.9	88.0	471.6	566.1	1,965.4	402.7
Omaha, NE[1]	4,029.5	6.0	61.6	69.5	424.0	259.6	2,514.4	694.4
Orlando, FL[1]	4,864.3	10.3	72.7	137.1	615.7	449.9	3,173.7	404.9
Philadelphia, PA	6,039.7	26.0	46.6	336.1	574.4	363.9	3,161.8	1,530.9
Phoenix, AZ	3,268.6	11.5	65.6	168.8	538.9	342.6	1,577.4	563.9
Pittsburgh, PA	n/a	n/a	n/a	n/a	n/a	n/a	n/a	n/a
Portland, OR	6,575.8	11.8	51.1	193.1	459.2	792.8	3,756.6	1,311.2
Providence, RI	2,215.3	5.8	34.3	59.6	209.9	157.2	1,482.7	265.8
Provo, UT	1,531.8	0.0	60.3	16.0	98.5	110.0	1,149.5	97.6
Raleigh, NC	3,117.6	5.4	32.1	87.2	403.4	306.3	1,891.3	391.8
Reno, NV	3,234.8	6.8	102.2	111.6	375.1	381.9	1,838.8	418.3
Richmond, VA	4,078.2	26.9	29.5	97.1	204.1	287.3	2,899.2	534.3
Rochester, MN	1,754.4	0.8	36.1	22.9	102.4	182.7	1,283.2	126.2
Sacramento, CA	3,692.9	7.7	32.1	225.3	535.6	520.1	1,672.4	699.8
Saint Louis, MO	7,844.8	56.4	70.3	260.3	1,058.2	751.1	3,434.0	2,214.5
Saint Paul, MN	3,714.1	9.0	67.3	126.8	420.8	434.5	1,962.9	692.8
Salem, OR	3,650.5	5.0	15.1	98.7	328.7	384.2	2,312.7	506.0
Salt Lake City, UT	6,514.5	7.7	159.7	175.6	524.9	555.4	4,504.8	586.4
San Antonio, TX	6,089.1	10.9	97.8	120.5	465.0	546.5	3,568.2	1,280.2
San Diego, CA	2,229.6	2.9	21.5	87.4	306.1	201.5	1,118.7	491.6
San Francisco, CA	6,422.7	6.6	37.3	349.7	316.5	720.8	4,135.3	856.4
San Jose, CA[1]	3,178.2	3.7	93.4	132.1	298.2	405.9	1,568.7	676.1
Santa Rosa, CA	1,799.8	5.7	65.0	63.9	196.2	257.8	1,004.2	206.9
Savannah, GA	n/a	n/a	n/a	n/a	n/a	n/a	n/a	n/a
Seattle, WA	5,789.3	9.0	36.2	221.7	510.2	1,126.3	2,662.2	1,223.7
Sioux Falls, SD	2,864.1	0.5	16.9	32.4	385.4	287.6	1,635.4	505.9
Tampa, FL	2,115.0	10.2	42.4	65.4	341.8	194.1	1,272.2	188.9
Tucson, AZ	n/a	n/a	n/a	n/a	n/a	n/a	n/a	n/a
Tulsa, OK	4,850.8	8.8	101.5	100.0	702.2	878.8	2,486.1	573.5
Virginia Beach, VA	1,751.8	3.7	22.0	29.5	40.1	86.6	1,431.3	138.5
Washington, DC	5,205.1	38.9	38.4	558.0	412.1	245.1	2,905.0	1,007.6
Wichita, KS	5,864.8	9.9	87.8	104.7	930.0	548.2	3,662.4	521.9
Wilmington, NC	3,995.9	8.2	31.0	99.4	348.9	455.7	2,763.4	289.4
Winston-Salem, NC	3,897.6	16.7	34.9	97.2	737.7	629.4	1,994.6	387.1
U.S.	2,290.9	5.7	38.0	66.5	264.1	250.7	1,347.2	318.7

Note: Figures are crimes per 100,000 population in 2023 except where noted; (1) 2022 data; n/a not available.
Source: FBI, Table 8, Offenses Known to Law Enforcement, by State by City, 2022, 2023

Temperature & Precipitation: Yearly Averages and Extremes

City	Extreme Low (°F)	Average Low (°F)	Average Temp. (°F)	Average High (°F)	Extreme High (°F)	Average Precip. (in.)	Average Snow (in.)
Albuquerque, NM	-17	43	57	70	105	8.5	11
Anchorage, AK	-34	29	36	43	85	15.7	71
Ann Arbor, MI	-21	39	49	58	104	32.4	41
Athens, GA	-8	52	62	72	105	49.8	2
Atlanta, GA	-8	52	62	72	105	49.8	2
Austin, TX	-2	58	69	79	109	31.1	1
Baltimore, MD	-7	45	56	65	105	41.2	21
Billings, MT	-32	36	47	59	105	14.6	59
Boise City, ID	-25	39	51	63	111	11.8	22
Boston, MA	-12	44	52	59	102	42.9	41
Boulder, CO	-25	37	51	64	103	15.5	63
Cape Coral, FL	26	65	75	84	103	53.9	0
Cedar Rapids, IA	-34	36	47	57	105	34.4	33
Charleston, SC	6	55	66	76	104	52.1	1
Charlotte, NC	-5	50	61	71	104	42.8	6
Chicago, IL	-27	40	49	59	104	35.4	39
Cincinnati, OH	-25	44	54	64	103	40.9	23
Clarksville, TN	-17	49	60	70	107	47.4	11
Cleveland, OH	-19	41	50	59	104	37.1	55
College Station, TX	-2	58	69	79	109	31.1	1
Colorado Springs, CO	-24	36	49	62	99	17.0	48
Columbia, MO	-20	44	54	64	111	40.6	25
Columbia, SC	-1	51	64	75	107	48.3	2
Columbus, OH	-19	42	52	62	104	37.9	28
Dallas, TX	-2	56	67	77	112	33.9	3
Davenport, IA	-24	40	50	60	108	31.8	33
Denver, CO	-25	37	51	64	103	15.5	63
Des Moines, IA	-24	40	50	60	108	31.8	33
Detroit, MI	-21	39	49	58	104	32.4	41
Durham, NC	-9	48	60	71	105	42.0	8
El Paso, TX	-8	50	64	78	114	8.6	6
Eugene, OR	-12	42	53	63	108	47.3	7
Fargo, ND	-36	31	41	52	106	19.6	40
Fort Collins, CO	-25	37	51	64	103	15.5	63
Fort Wayne, IN	-22	40	50	60	106	35.9	33
Fort Worth, TX	-1	55	66	76	113	32.3	3
Gainesville, FL	10	58	69	79	102	50.9	Trace
Green Bay, WI	-31	34	44	54	99	28.3	46
Greensboro, NC	-8	47	58	69	103	42.5	10
Honolulu, HI	52	70	77	84	94	22.4	0
Houston, TX	7	58	69	79	107	46.9	Trace
Huntsville, AL	-11	50	61	71	104	56.8	4
Indianapolis, IN	-23	42	53	62	104	40.2	25
Jacksonville, FL	7	58	69	79	103	52.0	0
Kansas City, MO	-23	44	54	64	109	38.1	21
Lafayette, LA	8	57	68	78	103	58.5	Trace
Las Vegas, NV	8	53	67	80	116	4.0	1
Lexington, KY	-21	45	55	65	103	45.1	17
Lincoln, NE	-33	39	51	62	108	29.1	27
Little Rock, AR	-5	51	62	73	112	50.7	5
Los Angeles, CA	27	55	63	70	110	11.3	Trace
Louisville, KY	-20	46	57	67	105	43.9	17
Madison, WI	-37	35	46	57	104	31.1	42
Manchester, NH	-33	34	46	57	102	36.9	63
McAllen, TX	16	65	74	83	106	25.8	Trace

Table continued on following page.

City	Extreme Low (°F)	Average Low (°F)	Average Temp. (°F)	Average High (°F)	Extreme High (°F)	Average Precip. (in.)	Average Snow (in.)
Memphis, TN	0	52	65	77	107	54.8	1
Miami, FL	30	69	76	83	98	57.1	0
Midland, TX	-11	50	64	77	116	14.6	4
Milwaukee, WI	-26	38	47	55	103	32.0	49
Minneapolis, MN	-34	35	45	54	105	27.1	52
Nashville, TN	-17	49	60	70	107	47.4	11
New Orleans, LA	11	59	69	78	102	60.6	Trace
New York, NY	-2	47	55	62	104	47.0	23
Oklahoma City, OK	-8	49	60	71	110	32.8	10
Omaha, NE	-23	40	51	62	110	30.1	29
Orlando, FL	19	62	72	82	100	47.7	Trace
Philadelphia, PA	-7	45	55	64	104	41.4	22
Phoenix, AZ	17	59	72	86	122	7.3	Trace
Pittsburgh, PA	-18	41	51	60	103	37.1	43
Portland, OR	-3	45	54	62	107	37.5	7
Providence, RI	-13	42	51	60	104	45.3	35
Provo, UT	-22	40	52	64	107	15.6	63
Raleigh, NC	-9	48	60	71	105	42.0	8
Reno, NV	-16	33	50	67	105	7.2	24
Richmond, VA	-8	48	58	69	105	43.0	13
Rochester, MN	-40	34	44	54	102	29.4	47
Sacramento, CA	18	48	61	73	115	17.3	Trace
Saint Louis, MO	-18	46	56	66	115	36.8	20
Saint Paul, MN	-34	35	45	54	105	27.1	52
Salem, OR	-12	41	52	63	108	40.2	7
Salt Lake City, UT	-22	40	52	64	107	15.6	63
San Antonio, TX	0	58	69	80	108	29.6	1
San Diego, CA	29	57	64	71	111	9.5	Trace
San Francisco, CA	24	49	57	65	106	19.3	Trace
San Jose, CA	21	50	59	68	105	13.5	Trace
Santa Rosa, CA	23	42	57	71	109	29.0	n/a
Savannah, GA	3	56	67	77	105	50.3	Trace
Seattle, WA	0	44	52	59	99	38.4	13
Sioux Falls, SD	-36	35	46	57	110	24.6	38
Tampa, FL	18	63	73	82	99	46.7	Trace
Tucson, AZ	16	55	69	82	117	11.6	2
Tulsa, OK	-8	50	61	71	112	38.9	10
Virginia Beach, VA	-3	51	60	69	104	44.8	8
Washington, DC	-5	49	58	67	104	39.5	18
Wichita, KS	-21	45	57	68	113	29.3	17
Wilmington, NC	0	53	64	74	104	55.0	2
Winston-Salem, NC	-8	47	58	69	103	42.5	10

Source: National Climatic Data Center, International Station Meteorological Climate Summary, 9/96; NOAA

Weather Conditions

City	Temperature			Daytime Sky			Precipitation		
	10°F & below	32°F & below	90°F & above	Clear	Partly cloudy	Cloudy	0.01 inch or more precip.	1.0 inch or more snow/ice	Thunder-storms
Albuquerque, NM	4	114	65	140	161	64	60	9	38
Anchorage, AK	n/a	194	n/a	50	115	200	113	49	2
Ann Arbor, MI	n/a	136	12	74	134	157	135	38	32
Athens, GA	1	49	38	98	147	120	116	3	48
Atlanta, GA	1	49	38	98	147	120	116	3	48
Austin, TX	< 1	20	111	105	148	112	83	1	41
Baltimore, MD	6	97	31	91	143	131	113	13	27
Billings, MT	n/a	149	29	75	163	127	97	41	27
Boise City, ID	n/a	124	45	106	133	126	91	22	14
Boston, MA	n/a	97	12	88	127	150	253	48	18
Boulder, CO	24	155	33	99	177	89	90	38	39
Cape Coral, FL	n/a	n/a	115	93	220	52	110	0	92
Cedar Rapids, IA	n/a	156	16	89	132	144	109	28	42
Charleston, SC	< 1	33	53	89	162	114	114	1	59
Charlotte, NC	1	65	44	98	142	125	113	3	41
Chicago, IL	n/a	132	17	83	136	146	125	31	38
Cincinnati, OH	14	107	23	80	126	159	127	25	39
Clarksville, TN	5	76	51	98	135	132	119	8	54
Cleveland, OH	n/a	123	12	63	127	175	157	48	34
College Station, TX	< 1	20	111	105	148	112	83	1	41
Colorado Springs, CO	21	161	18	108	157	100	98	33	49
Columbia, MO	17	108	36	99	127	139	110	17	52
Columbia, SC	< 1	58	77	97	149	119	110	1	53
Columbus, OH	n/a	118	19	72	137	156	136	29	40
Dallas, TX	1	34	102	108	160	97	78	2	49
Davenport, IA	n/a	137	26	99	129	137	106	25	46
Denver, CO	24	155	33	99	177	89	90	38	39
Des Moines, IA	n/a	137	26	99	129	137	106	25	46
Detroit, MI	n/a	136	12	74	134	157	135	38	32
Durham, NC	n/a	n/a	39	98	143	124	110	3	42
El Paso, TX	1	59	106	147	164	54	49	3	35
Eugene, OR	n/a	n/a	15	75	115	175	136	4	3
Fargo, ND	n/a	180	15	81	145	139	100	38	31
Fort Collins, CO	24	155	33	99	177	89	90	38	39
Fort Wayne, IN	n/a	131	16	75	140	150	131	31	39
Fort Worth, TX	1	40	100	123	136	106	79	3	47
Gainesville, FL	n/a	n/a	77	88	196	81	119	0	78
Green Bay, WI	n/a	163	7	86	125	154	120	40	33
Greensboro, NC	3	85	32	94	143	128	113	5	43
Honolulu, HI	n/a	n/a	23	25	286	54	98	0	7
Houston, TX	n/a	n/a	96	83	168	114	101	1	62
Huntsville, AL	2	66	49	70	118	177	116	2	54
Indianapolis, IN	19	119	19	83	128	154	127	24	43
Jacksonville, FL	< 1	16	83	86	181	98	114	1	65
Kansas City, MO	22	110	39	112	134	119	103	17	51
Lafayette, LA	< 1	21	86	99	150	116	113	< 1	73
Las Vegas, NV	< 1	37	134	185	132	48	27	2	13
Lexington, KY	11	96	22	86	136	143	129	17	44
Lincoln, NE	n/a	145	40	108	135	122	94	19	46
Little Rock, AR	1	57	73	110	142	113	104	4	57
Los Angeles, CA	0	< 1	5	131	125	109	34	0	1
Louisville, KY	8	90	35	82	143	140	125	15	45
Madison, WI	n/a	161	14	88	119	158	118	38	40
Manchester, NH	n/a	171	12	87	131	147	125	32	19

Table continued on following page.

City	Temperature			Daytime Sky			Precipitation		
	10°F & below	32°F & below	90°F & above	Clear	Partly cloudy	Cloudy	0.01 inch or more precip.	1.0 inch or more snow/ice	Thunder-storms
McAllen, TX	n/a	n/a	116	86	180	99	72	0	27
Memphis, TN	1	53	86	101	152	112	104	2	59
Miami, FL	n/a	n/a	55	48	263	54	128	0	74
Midland, TX	1	62	102	144	138	83	52	3	38
Milwaukee, WI	n/a	141	10	90	118	157	126	38	35
Minneapolis, MN	n/a	156	16	93	125	147	113	41	37
Nashville, TN	5	76	51	98	135	132	119	8	54
New Orleans, LA	0	13	70	90	169	106	114	1	69
New York, NY	n/a	n/a	18	85	166	114	120	11	20
Oklahoma City, OK	5	79	70	124	131	110	80	8	50
Omaha, NE	n/a	139	35	100	142	123	97	20	46
Orlando, FL	n/a	n/a	90	76	208	81	115	0	80
Philadelphia, PA	5	94	23	81	146	138	117	14	27
Phoenix, AZ	0	10	167	186	125	54	37	< 1	23
Pittsburgh, PA	n/a	121	8	62	137	166	154	42	35
Portland, OR	n/a	37	11	67	116	182	152	4	7
Providence, RI	n/a	117	9	85	134	146	123	21	21
Provo, UT	n/a	128	56	94	152	119	92	38	38
Raleigh, NC	n/a	n/a	39	98	143	124	110	3	42
Reno, NV	14	178	50	143	139	83	50	17	14
Richmond, VA	3	79	41	90	147	128	115	7	43
Rochester, MN	n/a	165	9	87	126	152	114	40	41
Sacramento, CA	0	21	73	175	111	79	58	< 1	2
Saint Louis, MO	13	100	43	97	138	130	109	14	46
Saint Paul, MN	n/a	156	16	93	125	147	113	41	37
Salem, OR	n/a	66	16	78	118	169	146	6	5
Salt Lake City, UT	n/a	128	56	94	152	119	92	38	38
San Antonio, TX	n/a	n/a	112	97	153	115	81	1	36
San Diego, CA	0	< 1	4	115	126	124	40	0	5
San Francisco, CA	0	6	4	136	130	99	63	< 1	5
San Jose, CA	0	5	5	106	180	79	57	< 1	6
Santa Rosa, CA	n/a	43	30	n/a	365	n/a	n/a	n/a	2
Savannah, GA	< 1	29	70	97	155	113	111	< 1	63
Seattle, WA	n/a	38	3	57	121	187	157	8	8
Sioux Falls, SD	n/a	n/a	n/a	95	136	134	n/a	n/a	n/a
Tampa, FL	n/a	n/a	85	81	204	80	107	< 1	87
Tucson, AZ	0	18	140	177	119	69	54	2	42
Tulsa, OK	6	78	74	117	141	107	88	8	50
Virginia Beach, VA	< 1	53	33	89	149	127	115	5	38
Washington, DC	2	71	34	84	144	137	112	9	30
Wichita, KS	13	110	63	117	132	116	87	13	54
Wilmington, NC	< 1	42	46	96	150	119	115	1	47
Winston-Salem, NC	3	85	32	94	143	128	113	5	43

Note: Figures are average number of days per year
Source: National Climatic Data Center, International Station Meteorological Climate Summary, 9/96; NOAA

Air Quality Index

Metro Area (Days[1])	Percent of Days when Air Quality was...					AQI Statistics	
	Good	Moderate	Unhealthy for Sensitive Groups	Unhealthy	Very Unhealthy	Maximum	Median
Albuquerque, NM (365)	26.6	72.3	0.8	0.0	0.3	207	60
Anchorage, AK (365)	81.1	18.6	0.3	0.0	0.0	102	25
Ann Arbor, MI (365)	46.0	50.4	2.5	0.5	0.5	218	52
Athens, GA (365)	47.4	51.8	0.8	0.0	0.0	147	52
Atlanta, GA (365)	26.6	67.7	4.9	0.8	0.0	172	57
Austin, TX (365)	40.3	56.7	3.0	0.0	0.0	122	54
Baltimore, MD (365)	55.1	40.3	3.6	0.8	0.3	205	49
Billings, MT (357)	85.7	13.2	0.8	0.3	0.0	191	29
Boise City, ID (365)	49.3	49.9	0.8	0.0	0.0	120	51
Boston, MA (365)	52.1	46.0	1.9	0.0	0.0	136	50
Boulder, CO (365)	52.6	45.8	1.1	0.5	0.0	181	50
Cape Coral, FL (363)	94.5	5.2	0.3	0.0	0.0	101	35
Cedar Rapids, IA (365)	35.6	59.5	3.8	0.8	0.3	207	54
Charleston, SC (365)	57.8	41.6	0.5	0.0	0.0	105	47
Charlotte, NC (365)	39.7	58.1	2.2	0.0	0.0	150	53
Chicago, IL (365)	20.8	67.4	9.0	2.2	0.5	246	60
Cincinnati, OH (365)	25.2	68.2	5.2	1.4	0.0	197	57
Clarksville, TN (365)	56.2	42.5	1.4	0.0	0.0	117	47
Cleveland, OH (365)	31.5	64.1	3.0	1.1	0.3	285	57
College Station, TX (348)	67.0	33.0	0.0	0.0	0.0	79	39
Colorado Springs, CO (365)	65.8	33.7	0.3	0.3	0.0	154	47
Columbia, MO (244)	79.9	18.0	2.0	0.0	0.0	143	42
Columbia, SC (365)	54.5	44.4	1.1	0.0	0.0	123	48
Columbus, OH (365)	37.0	59.5	2.5	0.8	0.3	210	54
Dallas, TX (365)	20.5	64.9	12.1	2.5	0.0	177	60
Davenport, IA (365)	37.3	56.4	5.2	0.8	0.3	232	54
Denver, CO (365)	19.7	72.3	7.4	0.5	0.0	179	64
Des Moines, IA (365)	46.0	49.9	3.3	0.8	0.0	166	52
Detroit, MI (365)	18.6	74.0	6.3	0.8	0.3	226	61
Durham, NC (361)	69.5	29.4	1.1	0.0	0.0	121	44
El Paso, TX (365)	18.9	75.9	4.9	0.3	0.0	155	64
Eugene, OR (365)	52.1	43.6	2.5	1.6	0.3	211	49
Fargo, ND (358)	50.3	46.4	2.8	0.6	0.0	175	50
Fort Collins, CO (365)	47.9	50.7	1.1	0.3	0.0	156	51
Fort Wayne, IN (365)	45.2	52.1	1.9	0.5	0.3	223	52
Fort Worth, TX (365)	20.5	64.9	12.1	2.5	0.0	177	60
Gainesville, FL (365)	74.0	25.8	0.3	0.0	0.0	104	40
Green Bay, WI (365)	57.0	38.1	3.3	1.6	0.0	182	46
Greensboro, NC (365)	50.1	48.8	1.1	0.0	0.0	131	50
Honolulu, HI (365)	92.3	7.4	0.3	0.0	0.0	117	31
Houston, TX (365)	9.9	74.5	12.3	3.0	0.3	205	65
Huntsville, AL (364)	56.0	43.1	0.8	0.0	0.0	135	49
Indianapolis, IN (365)	21.9	71.5	5.5	0.5	0.5	259	60
Jacksonville, FL (365)	41.6	57.8	0.5	0.0	0.0	124	52
Kansas City, MO (365)	34.0	58.1	6.8	1.1	0.0	166	55
Lafayette, LA (365)	56.7	43.0	0.3	0.0	0.0	112	47
Las Vegas, NV (365)	29.0	63.8	6.8	0.3	0.0	197	61
Lexington, KY (365)	63.3	35.9	0.5	0.3	0.0	167	45
Lincoln, NE (283)	69.6	29.3	0.7	0.4	0.0	160	42
Little Rock, AR (365)	33.4	65.2	1.1	0.3	0.0	174	55
Los Angeles, CA (365)	11.2	64.9	14.2	8.8	0.8	210	67
Louisville, KY (365)	32.1	62.2	5.5	0.3	0.0	182	55
Madison, WI (365)	49.6	43.6	5.5	0.5	0.8	268	51
Manchester, NH (365)	83.6	15.1	1.4	0.0	0.0	119	39

Table continued on following page.

Metro Area (Days[1])	Percent of Days when Air Quality was...					AQI Statistics	
	Good	Moderate	Unhealthy for Sensitive Groups	Unhealthy	Very Unhealthy	Maximum	Median
McAllen, TX (357)	57.7	42.3	0.0	0.0	0.0	95	44
Memphis, TN (365)	28.5	67.4	4.1	0.0	0.0	140	55
Miami, FL (365)	37.3	61.6	0.3	0.8	0.0	170	53
Midland, TX (n/a)	n/a	n/a	n/a	n/a	n/a	n/a	n/a
Milwaukee, WI (365)	43.6	48.8	6.6	0.3	0.8	270	53
Minneapolis, MN (365)	36.7	55.1	6.6	1.6	0.0	190	55
Nashville, TN (365)	34.8	62.5	2.7	0.0	0.0	133	54
New Orleans, LA (365)	38.1	59.2	2.7	0.0	0.0	126	53
New York, NY (365)	29.3	64.1	4.7	1.6	0.3	278	56
Oklahoma City, OK (365)	35.1	60.8	4.1	0.0	0.0	143	54
Omaha, NE (365)	50.4	42.7	6.3	0.5	0.0	169	50
Orlando, FL (365)	71.0	28.2	0.8	0.0	0.0	115	44
Philadelphia, PA (365)	17.8	75.3	5.2	1.1	0.3	331	59
Phoenix, AZ (365)	8.5	67.9	20.3	2.7	0.3	709	78
Pittsburgh, PA (365)	26.8	66.6	5.5	0.5	0.5	237	58
Portland, OR (365)	60.0	38.4	1.1	0.5	0.0	153	43
Providence, RI (365)	54.8	42.2	3.0	0.0	0.0	140	48
Provo, UT (365)	55.1	44.7	0.3	0.0	0.0	104	48
Raleigh, NC (365)	50.4	48.2	1.4	0.0	0.0	130	50
Reno, NV (365)	52.3	47.7	0.0	0.0	0.0	97	50
Richmond, VA (365)	55.9	42.7	0.5	0.8	0.0	159	48
Rochester, MN (365)	51.8	44.1	3.8	0.3	0.0	167	49
Sacramento, CA (365)	35.3	60.8	3.8	0.0	0.0	143	58
Saint Louis, MO (365)	14.0	79.5	5.8	0.8	0.0	185	60
Saint Paul, MN (365)	36.7	55.1	6.6	1.6	0.0	190	55
Salem, OR (365)	73.4	25.5	1.1	0.0	0.0	128	38
Salt Lake City, UT (365)	40.5	55.1	4.1	0.3	0.0	154	54
San Antonio, TX (365)	41.6	55.1	2.7	0.3	0.0	309	53
San Diego, CA (365)	16.7	71.2	12.1	0.0	0.0	150	67
San Francisco, CA (365)	34.0	62.5	3.6	0.0	0.0	130	54
San Jose, CA (365)	61.6	37.3	1.1	0.0	0.0	134	45
Santa Rosa, CA (365)	88.5	11.0	0.5	0.0	0.0	117	33
Savannah, GA (352)	56.0	43.5	0.6	0.0	0.0	108	48
Seattle, WA (365)	51.0	47.1	1.1	0.8	0.0	195	50
Sioux Falls, SD (365)	64.4	28.2	6.3	1.1	0.0	181	44
Tampa, FL (365)	39.5	59.2	1.4	0.0	0.0	114	52
Tucson, AZ (365)	33.7	64.4	1.9	0.0	0.0	147	54
Tulsa, OK (365)	37.8	56.7	4.9	0.5	0.0	197	53
Virginia Beach, VA (365)	62.7	36.4	0.5	0.3	0.0	174	44
Washington, DC (365)	43.3	51.2	4.4	0.8	0.3	222	52
Wichita, KS (365)	44.7	54.0	1.1	0.3	0.0	157	52
Wilmington, NC (362)	65.5	34.3	0.3	0.0	0.0	142	44
Winston-Salem, NC (365)	40.3	57.8	1.6	0.3	0.0	154	53

Note: The Air Quality Index (AQI) is an index for reporting daily air quality. EPA calculates the AQI for five major air pollutants regulated by the Clean Air Act: ground-level ozone, particle pollution (also known as particulate matter), carbon monoxide, sulfur dioxide, and nitrogen dioxide. The AQI runs from 0 to 500. The higher the AQI value, the greater the level of air pollution and the greater the health concern. There are six AQI categories: "Good" The AQI is between 0 and 50. Air quality is considered satisfactory; "Moderate" The AQI is between 51 and 100. Air quality is acceptable; "Unhealthy for Sensitive Groups" When AQI values are between 101 and 150, members of sensitive groups may experience health effects; "Unhealthy" When AQI values are between 151 and 200 everyone may begin to experience health effects; "Very Unhealthy" AQI values between 201 and 300 trigger a health alert; "Hazardous" AQI values over 300 trigger health warnings of emergency conditions; Figures cover the Metropolitan Statistical Area (MSA); (1) Number of days with AQI data in 2023
Source: U.S. Environmental Protection Agency, Air Quality Index Report, 2023

Air Quality Index Pollutants

Metro Area (Days[1])	Percent of Days when AQI Pollutant was...					
	Carbon Monoxide	Nitrogen Dioxide	Ozone	Sulfur Dioxide[2]	Particulate Matter 2.5	Particulate Matter 10
Albuquerque, NM (365)	0.0	0.3	53.2	–	23.8	22.7
Anchorage, AK (365)	0.8	0.0	0.0	–	70.1	29.0
Ann Arbor, MI (365)	0.0	0.0	33.2	–	66.8	0.0
Athens, GA (365)	0.0	0.0	26.8	–	73.2	0.0
Atlanta, GA (365)	0.0	0.8	31.5	–	67.7	0.0
Austin, TX (365)	0.0	1.1	29.3	–	69.6	0.0
Baltimore, MD (365)	0.0	1.1	54.5	–	44.4	0.0
Billings, MT (357)	0.0	0.0	0.0	–	100.0	0.0
Boise City, ID (365)	0.0	0.3	44.9	–	54.0	0.8
Boston, MA (365)	0.0	0.5	36.7	–	62.7	0.0
Boulder, CO (365)	0.0	0.0	74.5	–	25.5	0.0
Cape Coral, FL (363)	0.0	0.0	100.0	–	0.0	0.0
Cedar Rapids, IA (365)	0.0	0.0	23.6	–	76.4	0.0
Charleston, SC (365)	0.0	0.0	24.4	–	75.1	0.5
Charlotte, NC (365)	0.0	0.0	45.8	–	54.2	0.0
Chicago, IL (365)	0.0	1.6	27.1	–	67.7	3.6
Cincinnati, OH (365)	0.0	0.5	25.5	–	72.1	1.9
Clarksville, TN (365)	0.0	0.0	23.3	–	76.7	0.0
Cleveland, OH (365)	0.5	0.0	27.1	–	71.2	1.1
College Station, TX (348)	0.0	0.0	0.0	–	100.0	0.0
Colorado Springs, CO (365)	0.0	0.0	91.5	–	8.5	0.0
Columbia, MO (244)	0.0	0.0	100.0	–	0.0	0.0
Columbia, SC (365)	0.0	0.3	32.9	–	66.8	0.0
Columbus, OH (365)	0.0	0.0	26.6	–	71.2	2.2
Dallas, TX (365)	0.0	0.5	40.5	–	58.4	0.5
Davenport, IA (365)	0.0	0.0	30.4	–	62.2	7.4
Denver, CO (365)	0.0	5.5	66.6	–	23.3	4.7
Des Moines, IA (365)	0.0	0.8	22.2	–	77.0	0.0
Detroit, MI (365)	0.0	0.5	11.5	–	87.9	0.0
Durham, NC (361)	0.0	0.0	45.2	–	52.4	2.5
El Paso, TX (365)	0.0	1.4	29.9	–	56.4	12.3
Eugene, OR (365)	0.0	0.0	21.4	–	78.6	0.0
Fargo, ND (358)	0.0	0.3	31.3	–	68.4	0.0
Fort Collins, CO (365)	0.0	0.0	83.3	–	16.7	0.0
Fort Wayne, IN (365)	0.0	0.0	38.9	–	61.1	0.0
Fort Worth, TX (365)	0.0	0.5	40.5	–	58.4	0.5
Gainesville, FL (365)	0.0	0.0	38.1	–	61.9	0.0
Green Bay, WI (365)	0.0	0.0	35.9	–	64.1	0.0
Greensboro, NC (365)	0.0	0.0	31.8	–	66.8	1.4
Honolulu, HI (365)	0.0	0.0	47.7	–	51.2	1.1
Houston, TX (365)	0.0	0.3	31.5	–	62.7	5.5
Huntsville, AL (364)	0.0	0.0	25.3	–	74.7	0.0
Indianapolis, IN (365)	0.0	0.0	19.2	–	80.8	0.0
Jacksonville, FL (365)	0.0	0.0	17.0	–	83.0	0.0
Kansas City, MO (365)	0.0	1.4	39.5	–	55.6	3.6
Lafayette, LA (365)	0.0	0.0	54.8	–	44.7	0.5
Las Vegas, NV (365)	0.0	0.3	67.7	–	27.7	4.4
Lexington, KY (365)	0.0	1.1	40.0	–	58.9	0.0
Lincoln, NE (283)	0.0	0.0	74.9	–	25.1	0.0
Little Rock, AR (365)	0.0	0.0	16.4	–	83.6	0.0
Los Angeles, CA (365)	0.0	1.4	41.1	–	55.6	1.9
Louisville, KY (365)	0.0	0.5	28.2	–	71.2	0.0
Madison, WI (365)	0.0	0.0	31.5	–	68.5	0.0
Manchester, NH (365)	0.8	0.0	80.3	–	18.9	0.0

Table continued on following page.

Metro Area (Days[1])	Percent of Days when AQI Pollutant was...					
	Carbon Monoxide	Nitrogen Dioxide	Ozone	Sulfur Dioxide[2]	Particulate Matter 2.5	Particulate Matter 10
McAllen, TX (357)	0.0	0.0	5.3	–	94.7	0.0
Memphis, TN (365)	0.0	0.0	34.2	–	65.8	0.0
Miami, FL (365)	0.0	3.6	13.7	–	82.7	0.0
Midland, TX (n/a)	n/a	n/a	n/a	–	n/a	n/a
Milwaukee, WI (365)	0.0	1.4	31.5	–	67.1	0.0
Minneapolis, MN (365)	0.3	0.8	33.4	–	61.1	4.4
Nashville, TN (365)	0.0	0.5	26.0	–	73.4	0.0
New Orleans, LA (365)	0.0	0.3	37.5	–	62.2	0.0
New York, NY (365)	0.0	4.1	27.7	–	68.2	0.0
Oklahoma City, OK (365)	0.0	2.2	42.7	–	54.2	0.8
Omaha, NE (365)	0.0	0.0	48.2	–	47.4	4.4
Orlando, FL (365)	0.0	0.5	55.1	–	44.4	0.0
Philadelphia, PA (365)	0.0	0.3	22.5	–	77.3	0.0
Phoenix, AZ (365)	0.0	0.0	41.9	–	24.1	34.0
Pittsburgh, PA (365)	0.0	0.0	19.7	–	80.3	0.0
Portland, OR (365)	0.0	1.1	42.7	–	56.2	0.0
Providence, RI (365)	0.0	0.3	41.9	–	57.8	0.0
Provo, UT (365)	0.0	0.3	63.3	–	36.2	0.3
Raleigh, NC (365)	0.0	0.3	32.1	–	67.7	0.0
Reno, NV (365)	0.0	1.1	67.9	–	30.7	0.3
Richmond, VA (365)	0.0	4.4	34.8	–	60.8	0.0
Rochester, MN (365)	0.0	0.0	32.6	–	67.4	0.0
Sacramento, CA (365)	0.0	0.0	60.5	–	39.5	0.0
Saint Louis, MO (365)	0.0	0.0	27.7	–	67.4	4.9
Saint Paul, MN (365)	0.3	0.8	33.4	–	61.1	4.4
Salem, OR (365)	0.0	0.0	35.6	–	64.4	0.0
Salt Lake City, UT (365)	0.0	5.5	60.0	–	32.3	2.2
San Antonio, TX (365)	0.0	0.3	37.5	–	62.2	0.0
San Diego, CA (365)	0.0	0.3	50.7	–	41.4	7.7
San Francisco, CA (365)	0.3	4.4	17.8	–	77.5	0.0
San Jose, CA (365)	0.0	0.0	57.5	–	41.9	0.5
Santa Rosa, CA (365)	0.3	0.0	64.9	–	34.5	0.3
Savannah, GA (352)	0.0	0.0	14.8	–	85.2	0.0
Seattle, WA (365)	0.0	0.8	32.9	–	66.3	0.0
Sioux Falls, SD (365)	0.0	1.6	69.6	–	26.3	2.5
Tampa, FL (365)	0.0	0.0	27.7	–	71.5	0.8
Tucson, AZ (365)	0.0	0.0	49.0	–	33.7	17.3
Tulsa, OK (365)	0.0	0.0	45.2	–	52.9	1.9
Virginia Beach, VA (365)	0.0	1.6	33.7	–	64.7	0.0
Washington, DC (365)	0.0	1.4	44.1	–	54.2	0.3
Wichita, KS (365)	0.0	0.5	45.2	–	51.2	3.0
Wilmington, NC (362)	0.0	0.0	25.1	–	74.9	0.0
Winston-Salem, NC (365)	0.0	0.0	27.7	–	72.3	0.0

Note: The Air Quality Index (AQI) is an index for reporting daily air quality. EPA calculates the AQI for five major air pollutants regulated by the Clean Air Act: ground-level ozone, particle pollution (also known as particulate matter), carbon monoxide, sulfur dioxide, and nitrogen dioxide. The AQI runs from 0 to 500. The higher the AQI value, the greater the level of air pollution and the greater the health concern; Figures cover the Metropolitan Statistical Area (MSA); (1) Number of days with AQI data in 2023; (2) Sulfur dioxide is no longer included in this table because SO_2 concentrations tend to be very localized and not necessarily representative of broad geographical areas like counties and CBSAs
Source: U.S. Environmental Protection Agency, Air Quality Index Report, 2023

Air Quality Trends: Ozone

Metro Area	1990	1995	2000	2005	2010	2015	2020	2021	2022	2023
Albuquerque, NM	0.072	0.070	0.072	0.073	0.066	0.066	0.071	0.071	0.071	0.067
Anchorage, AK	n/a	n/a	n/a	n/a	n/a	n/a	n/a	n/a	n/a	n/a
Ann Arbor, MI	0.025	0.034	0.035	0.023	0.034	0.064	0.067	0.063	0.066	0.072
Athens, GA	n/a	n/a	n/a	n/a	n/a	n/a	n/a	n/a	n/a	n/a
Atlanta, GA	0.088	0.089	0.089	0.077	0.067	0.069	0.059	0.064	0.063	0.072
Austin, TX	0.088	0.089	0.088	0.082	0.074	0.073	0.066	0.066	0.073	0.074
Baltimore, MD	0.100	0.103	0.088	0.089	0.084	0.073	0.064	0.071	0.066	0.073
Billings, MT	n/a	n/a	n/a	n/a	n/a	n/a	n/a	n/a	n/a	n/a
Boise City, ID	n/a	n/a	n/a	n/a	n/a	n/a	n/a	n/a	n/a	n/a
Boston, MA	0.078	0.085	0.067	0.075	0.066	0.065	0.053	0.059	0.066	0.060
Boulder, CO	n/a	n/a	n/a	n/a	n/a	n/a	n/a	n/a	n/a	n/a
Cape Coral, FL	0.069	0.066	0.073	0.071	0.065	0.058	0.061	0.055	0.058	0.064
Cedar Rapids, IA	n/a	n/a	n/a	n/a	n/a	n/a	n/a	n/a	n/a	n/a
Charleston, SC	0.059	0.075	0.076	0.077	0.068	0.054	0.053	0.059	0.059	0.056
Charlotte, NC	0.094	0.091	0.099	0.089	0.082	0.071	0.060	0.067	0.068	0.072
Chicago, IL	0.074	0.094	0.073	0.084	0.070	0.066	0.076	0.071	0.070	0.081
Cincinnati, OH	0.083	0.082	0.074	0.075	0.069	0.069	0.067	0.065	0.068	0.072
Clarksville, TN	n/a	n/a	n/a	n/a	n/a	n/a	n/a	n/a	n/a	n/a
Cleveland, OH	0.084	0.090	0.079	0.084	0.074	0.069	0.069	0.066	0.068	0.071
College Station, TX	n/a	n/a	n/a	n/a	n/a	n/a	n/a	n/a	n/a	n/a
Colorado Springs, CO	n/a	n/a	n/a	n/a	n/a	n/a	n/a	n/a	n/a	n/a
Columbia, MO	n/a	n/a	n/a	n/a	n/a	n/a	n/a	n/a	n/a	n/a
Columbia, SC	0.091	0.079	0.089	0.082	0.069	0.058	0.053	0.061	0.061	0.064
Columbus, OH	0.090	0.091	0.085	0.084	0.073	0.066	0.062	0.061	0.061	0.066
Dallas, TX	0.094	0.103	0.096	0.096	0.079	0.078	0.070	0.076	0.072	0.081
Davenport, IA	0.065	0.072	0.064	0.065	0.057	0.060	0.063	0.066	0.061	0.079
Denver, CO	0.076	0.070	0.069	0.077	0.069	0.072	0.081	0.082	0.074	0.073
Des Moines, IA	n/a	n/a	n/a	n/a	n/a	n/a	n/a	n/a	n/a	n/a
Detroit, MI	0.083	0.088	0.076	0.083	0.074	0.068	0.072	0.069	0.068	0.074
Durham, NC	0.078	0.080	0.082	0.079	0.074	0.061	0.051	0.063	0.058	0.066
El Paso, TX	0.080	0.078	0.082	0.074	0.072	0.071	0.076	0.071	0.071	0.071
Eugene, OR	0.068	0.062	0.056	0.068	0.058	0.070	0.054	0.061	0.058	0.060
Fargo, ND	n/a	n/a	n/a	n/a	n/a	n/a	n/a	n/a	n/a	n/a
Fort Collins, CO	0.066	0.072	0.074	0.075	0.072	0.070	0.070	0.077	0.070	0.067
Fort Wayne, IN	0.086	0.094	0.086	0.081	0.067	0.061	0.064	0.062	0.064	0.067
Fort Worth, TX	0.094	0.103	0.096	0.096	0.079	0.078	0.070	0.076	0.072	0.081
Gainesville, FL	n/a	n/a	n/a	n/a	n/a	n/a	n/a	n/a	n/a	n/a
Green Bay, WI	n/a	n/a	n/a	n/a	n/a	n/a	n/a	n/a	n/a	n/a
Greensboro, NC	0.097	0.089	0.089	0.082	0.076	0.064	0.057	0.066	0.063	0.067
Honolulu, HI	0.034	0.049	0.044	0.042	0.046	0.048	0.044	0.045	0.044	0.046
Houston, TX	0.119	0.114	0.102	0.087	0.079	0.083	0.067	0.072	0.068	0.079
Huntsville, AL	0.079	0.080	0.088	0.075	0.071	0.063	0.057	0.061	0.065	0.064
Indianapolis, IN	0.085	0.095	0.081	0.081	0.070	0.065	0.065	0.067	0.070	0.073
Jacksonville, FL	0.080	0.068	0.072	0.076	0.068	0.060	0.057	0.061	0.062	0.060
Kansas City, MO	0.075	0.095	0.087	0.082	0.067	0.063	0.064	0.067	0.066	0.074
Lafayette, LA	n/a	n/a	n/a	n/a	n/a	n/a	n/a	n/a	n/a	n/a
Las Vegas, NV	n/a	n/a	n/a	n/a	n/a	n/a	n/a	n/a	n/a	n/a
Lexington, KY	0.078	0.088	0.077	0.078	0.070	0.069	0.060	0.064	0.065	0.070
Lincoln, NE	0.057	0.060	0.057	0.056	0.050	0.061	0.054	0.059	0.055	0.068
Little Rock, AR	0.080	0.086	0.090	0.083	0.072	0.063	0.062	0.066	0.063	0.067
Los Angeles, CA	0.128	0.109	0.090	0.086	0.074	0.082	0.096	0.076	0.077	0.081
Louisville, KY	0.082	0.091	0.087	0.083	0.076	0.071	0.063	0.064	0.063	0.072
Madison, WI	0.077	0.084	0.072	0.079	0.062	0.064	0.070	0.066	0.062	0.082
Manchester, NH	0.085	0.088	0.070	0.082	0.067	0.061	0.055	0.061	0.058	0.065
McAllen, TX	n/a	n/a	n/a	n/a	n/a	n/a	n/a	n/a	n/a	n/a
Memphis, TN	0.088	0.095	0.092	0.086	0.076	0.065	0.063	0.067	0.071	0.071

Table continued on following page.

Metro Area	1990	1995	2000	2005	2010	2015	2020	2021	2022	2023
Miami, FL	0.068	0.072	0.075	0.065	0.064	0.061	0.058	0.057	0.063	0.061
Midland, TX	n/a	n/a	n/a	n/a	n/a	n/a	n/a	n/a	n/a	n/a
Milwaukee, WI	0.095	0.106	0.082	0.092	0.079	0.069	0.074	0.072	0.073	0.077
Minneapolis, MN	0.068	0.084	0.065	0.074	0.066	0.061	0.060	0.067	0.057	0.077
Nashville, TN	0.089	0.092	0.084	0.078	0.073	0.065	0.061	0.064	0.065	0.071
New Orleans, LA	0.082	0.088	0.091	0.079	0.074	0.067	0.061	0.060	0.061	0.068
New York, NY	0.101	0.105	0.089	0.090	0.080	0.074	0.064	0.069	0.067	0.071
Oklahoma City, OK	0.080	0.087	0.083	0.077	0.071	0.067	0.066	0.068	0.071	0.072
Omaha, NE	n/a	n/a	n/a	n/a	n/a	n/a	n/a	n/a	n/a	n/a
Orlando, FL	0.081	0.075	0.080	0.083	0.069	0.060	0.059	0.061	0.062	0.066
Philadelphia, PA	0.102	0.109	0.099	0.091	0.083	0.074	0.065	0.069	0.067	0.071
Phoenix, AZ	0.080	0.086	0.082	0.077	0.075	0.072	0.079	0.079	0.074	0.077
Pittsburgh, PA	0.080	0.100	0.084	0.083	0.077	0.070	0.066	0.066	0.064	0.067
Portland, OR	0.081	0.065	0.059	0.059	0.056	0.064	0.058	0.058	0.059	0.062
Providence, RI	0.106	0.107	0.087	0.090	0.072	0.070	0.065	0.067	0.060	0.066
Provo, UT	n/a	n/a	n/a	n/a	n/a	n/a	n/a	n/a	n/a	n/a
Raleigh, NC	0.093	0.081	0.087	0.082	0.071	0.065	0.054	0.062	0.064	0.064
Reno, NV	0.074	0.069	0.067	0.069	0.068	0.071	0.073	0.078	0.064	0.065
Richmond, VA	0.083	0.089	0.080	0.082	0.079	0.062	0.054	0.061	0.060	0.063
Rochester, MN	n/a	n/a	n/a	n/a	n/a	n/a	n/a	n/a	n/a	n/a
Sacramento, CA	0.087	0.092	0.085	0.084	0.072	0.073	0.072	0.072	0.067	0.069
Saint Louis, MO	0.077	0.084	0.074	0.078	0.069	0.067	0.066	0.067	0.070	0.077
Saint Paul, MN	0.068	0.084	0.065	0.074	0.066	0.061	0.060	0.067	0.057	0.077
Salem, OR	n/a	n/a	n/a	n/a	n/a	n/a	n/a	n/a	n/a	n/a
Salt Lake City, UT	n/a	n/a	n/a	n/a	n/a	n/a	n/a	n/a	n/a	n/a
San Antonio, TX	0.090	0.095	0.078	0.084	0.072	0.079	0.069	0.070	0.076	0.074
San Diego, CA	0.110	0.085	0.079	0.074	0.073	0.068	0.078	0.068	0.067	0.072
San Francisco, CA	0.062	0.077	0.060	0.060	0.063	0.064	0.062	0.064	0.057	0.053
San Jose, CA	0.078	0.084	0.065	0.063	0.072	0.067	0.066	0.067	0.062	0.057
Santa Rosa, CA	n/a	n/a	n/a	n/a	n/a	n/a	n/a	n/a	n/a	n/a
Savannah, GA	n/a	n/a	n/a	n/a	n/a	n/a	n/a	n/a	n/a	n/a
Seattle, WA	0.082	0.062	0.056	0.053	0.053	0.059	0.056	0.061	0.065	0.056
Sioux Falls, SD	n/a	n/a	n/a	n/a	n/a	n/a	n/a	n/a	n/a	n/a
Tampa, FL	0.080	0.075	0.081	0.075	0.067	0.062	0.063	0.060	0.061	0.066
Tucson, AZ	0.073	0.078	0.074	0.075	0.068	0.065	0.070	0.068	0.069	0.069
Tulsa, OK	0.086	0.091	0.081	0.072	0.069	0.061	0.061	0.063	0.070	0.072
Virginia Beach, VA	0.085	0.084	0.083	0.078	0.074	0.061	0.053	0.057	0.057	0.059
Washington, DC	0.075	0.083	0.073	0.069	0.069	0.067	0.057	0.066	0.061	0.069
Wichita, KS	0.077	0.069	0.080	0.074	0.075	0.064	0.059	0.061	0.072	0.066
Wilmington, NC	0.082	0.079	0.080	0.075	0.062	0.057	0.054	0.062	0.058	0.067
Winston-Salem, NC	0.084	0.086	0.089	0.080	0.078	0.065	0.058	0.062	0.057	0.066
U.S.	0.087	0.089	0.081	0.080	0.072	0.068	0.066	0.067	0.067	0.070

Note: Figures cover the Metropolitan Statistical Area (MSA); n/a not available. The values shown are the composite ozone concentration averages among trend sites based on the highest fourth daily maximum 8-hour concentration in parts per million. These trends are based on sites having an adequate record of monitoring data during the trend period. Data from exceptional events are included.
Source: U.S. Environmental Protection Agency, Air Quality Monitoring Information, "Air Quality Trends by City, 1990-2023"

Maximum Air Pollutant Concentrations: Particulate Matter, Ozone, CO and Lead

Metro Area	PM 10 (ug/m³)	PM 2.5 Wtd AM (ug/m³)	PM 2.5 24-Hr (ug/m³)	Ozone (ppm)	Carbon Monoxide (ppm)	Lead (ug/m³)
Albuquerque, NM	182	7.5	23	0.069	2	n/a
Anchorage, AK	130	4.2	18	n/a	2	n/a
Ann Arbor, MI	n/a	10.6	33	0.073	n/a	n/a
Athens, GA	n/a	9.3	26	0.068	n/a	n/a
Atlanta, GA	60	10.6	28	0.077	2	n/a
Austin, TX	53	10.4	25	0.074	2	n/a
Baltimore, MD	42	10.1	32	0.075	1	n/a
Billings, MT	n/a	6.7	29	n/a	n/a	n/a
Boise City, ID	84	n/a	n/a	0.066	1	n/a
Boston, MA	47	7.8	22	0.071	1	n/a
Boulder, CO	39	6.8	19	0.071	n/a	n/a
Cape Coral, FL	n/a	n/a	n/a	0.064	n/a	n/a
Cedar Rapids, IA	68	9.9	25	0.08	n/a	n/a
Charleston, SC	70	8.1	20	0.062	n/a	n/a
Charlotte, NC	51	10	26	0.073	2	n/a
Chicago, IL	137	11.2	31	0.086	1	0.1
Cincinnati, OH	111	12.2	44	0.077	1	n/a
Clarksville, TN	n/a	8.6	22	0.07	n/a	n/a
Cleveland, OH	147	12.8	40	0.075	5	0.04
College Station, TX	n/a	8	20	n/a	n/a	n/a
Colorado Springs, CO	32	5.4	13	0.069	1	n/a
Columbia, MO	n/a	n/a	n/a	0.072	n/a	n/a
Columbia, SC	44	8.2	22	0.069	1	n/a
Columbus, OH	97	10.9	36	0.069	1	0
Dallas, TX	70	10.7	23	0.084	2	0.07
Davenport, IA	109	10.4	28	0.08	1	n/a
Denver, CO	89	8.7	24	0.077	2	n/a
Des Moines, IA	56	10.2	31	0.077	n/a	n/a
Detroit, MI	161	14.7	46	0.079	2	0.03
Durham, NC	42	8	24	0.066	n/a	n/a
El Paso, TX	180	8.6	23	0.074	2	n/a
Eugene, OR	118	10.1	46	0.06	n/a	n/a
Fargo, ND	n/a	11.5	39	0.07	n/a	n/a
Fort Collins, CO	n/a	n/a	n/a	0.071	1	n/a
Fort Wayne, IN	n/a	10	33	0.075	n/a	n/a
Fort Worth, TX	70	10.7	23	0.084	2	0.07
Gainesville, FL	n/a	6.3	17	0.058	n/a	n/a
Green Bay, WI	n/a	9.5	38	0.075	n/a	n/a
Greensboro, NC	39	9.8	25	0.067	n/a	n/a
Honolulu, HI	46	4.1	10	0.046	0	n/a
Houston, TX	161	13.1	28	0.09	2	n/a
Huntsville, AL	61	8.6	21	0.067	n/a	n/a
Indianapolis, IN	147	13.7	44	0.077	2	n/a
Jacksonville, FL	55	7.9	20	0.062	1	n/a
Kansas City, MO	256	9.6	27	0.077	1	n/a
Lafayette, LA	48	8.2	15	0.068	n/a	n/a
Las Vegas, NV	209	8.2	27	0.074	2	n/a
Lexington, KY	28	8.3	27	0.07	n/a	n/a
Lincoln, NE	n/a	n/a	n/a	0.068	n/a	n/a
Little Rock, AR	39	10.8	23	0.07	1	n/a
Los Angeles, CA	124	11.1	28	0.103	3	0.02
Louisville, KY	96	10.7	32	0.075	2	n/a
Madison, WI	208	10.7	39	0.082	n/a	n/a
Manchester, NH	n/a	4.5	20	0.067	1	n/a
McAllen, TX	47	n/a	n/a	0.051	n/a	n/a

Table continued on following page.

Metro Area	PM 10 (ug/m³)	PM 2.5 Wtd AM (ug/m³)	PM 2.5 24-Hr (ug/m³)	Ozone (ppm)	Carbon Monoxide (ppm)	Lead (ug/m³)
Memphis, TN	67	10.6	27	0.074	1	n/a
Miami, FL	65	9.4	24	0.066	2	n/a
Midland, TX	n/a	n/a	n/a	n/a	n/a	n/a
Milwaukee, WI	209	11	39	0.08	1	n/a
Minneapolis, MN	118	10.6	41	0.079	4	0.46
Nashville, TN	57	10.2	25	0.076	2	n/a
New Orleans, LA	49	9.4	19	0.071	2	0.02
New York, NY	41	10.5	40	0.076	2	n/a
Oklahoma City, OK	89	9.2	21	0.074	1	n/a
Omaha, NE	79	9.7	33	0.082	1	0.06
Orlando, FL	54	6.8	16	0.069	1	n/a
Philadelphia, PA	174	13.3	37	0.074	1	0
Phoenix, AZ	387	9.8	32	0.083	2	n/a
Pittsburgh, PA	168	12	36	0.071	3	0
Portland, OR	27	6.5	25	0.068	1	n/a
Providence, RI	29	8.2	29	0.075	2	n/a
Provo, UT	76	6.8	21	0.066	1	n/a
Raleigh, NC	60	9.2	31	0.064	1	n/a
Reno, NV	63	7.2	18	0.067	2	n/a
Richmond, VA	65	8.7	28	0.067	1	n/a
Rochester, MN	n/a	9.6	33	0.074	n/a	n/a
Sacramento, CA	57	9.4	28	0.077	n/a	n/a
Saint Louis, MO	160	11.3	26	0.082	2	0.1
Saint Paul, MN	118	10.6	41	0.079	4	0.46
Salem, OR	n/a	n/a	n/a	0.064	n/a	n/a
Salt Lake City, UT	79	8.6	31	0.076	1	n/a
San Antonio, TX	50	9	26	0.076	1	n/a
San Diego, CA	142	12.5	24	0.08	1	0.02
San Francisco, CA	48	9.9	23	0.069	4	n/a
San Jose, CA	59	8.2	25	0.067	1	0.02
Santa Rosa, CA	48	5	17	0.046	1	n/a
Savannah, GA	n/a	8.8	24	0.061	n/a	n/a
Seattle, WA	17	8.5	29	0.068	1	n/a
Sioux Falls, SD	80	n/a	n/a	0.082	n/a	n/a
Tampa, FL	76	7.8	16	0.069	1	0.05
Tucson, AZ	201	7.8	16	0.07	1	n/a
Tulsa, OK	101	9.3	20	0.078	1	n/a
Virginia Beach, VA	62	8.1	28	0.066	1	n/a
Washington, DC	142	9.7	33	0.076	2	n/a
Wichita, KS	99	n/a	n/a	0.068	n/a	n/a
Wilmington, NC	45	6.8	19	0.067	n/a	n/a
Winston-Salem, NC	72	9.5	31	0.069	n/a	n/a
NAAQS[1]	150	15.0	35	0.075	9	0.15

Note: Data from exceptional events are included; Figures cover the Metropolitan Statistical Area (MSA); (1) National Ambient Air Quality Standards; ppm = parts per million; ug/m³ = micrograms per cubic meter; n/a not available
Concentrations: Particulate Matter 10 (coarse particulate)—highest second maximum 24-hour concentration; Particulate Matter 2.5 Wtd AM (fine particulate)—highest weighted annual mean concentration; Particulate Matter 2.5 24-Hour (fine particulate)—highest 98th percentile 24-hour concentration; Ozone—highest fourth daily maximum 8-hour concentration; Carbon Monoxide—highest second maximum non-overlapping 8-hour concentration; Lead—maximum running 3-month average
Source: U.S. Environmental Protection Agency, Air Quality Monitoring Information, "Air Quality Statistics by City, 2023"

Maximum Air Pollutant Concentrations: Nitrogen Dioxide and Sulfur Dioxide

Metro Area	Nitrogen Dioxide AM (ppb)	Nitrogen Dioxide 1-Hr (ppb)	Sulfur Dioxide AM (ppb)	Sulfur Dioxide 1-Hr (ppb)	Sulfur Dioxide 24-Hr (ppb)
Albuquerque, NM	8	43	n/a	n/a	n/a
Anchorage, AK	n/a	n/a	n/a	n/a	n/a
Ann Arbor, MI	n/a	n/a	n/a	n/a	n/a
Athens, GA	n/a	n/a	n/a	n/a	n/a
Atlanta, GA	15	48	n/a	5	n/a
Austin, TX	13	n/a	n/a	n/a	n/a
Baltimore, MD	15	45	n/a	4	n/a
Billings, MT	n/a	n/a	n/a	19	n/a
Boise City, ID	8	38	n/a	3	n/a
Boston, MA	11	45	n/a	5	n/a
Boulder, CO	n/a	n/a	n/a	n/a	n/a
Cape Coral, FL	n/a	n/a	n/a	n/a	n/a
Cedar Rapids, IA	n/a	n/a	n/a	10	n/a
Charleston, SC	7	n/a	n/a	6	n/a
Charlotte, NC	11	37	n/a	2	n/a
Chicago, IL	17	54	n/a	79	n/a
Cincinnati, OH	18	49	n/a	21	n/a
Clarksville, TN	n/a	n/a	n/a	n/a	n/a
Cleveland, OH	9	44	n/a	27	n/a
College Station, TX	n/a	n/a	n/a	29	n/a
Colorado Springs, CO	n/a	n/a	n/a	5	n/a
Columbia, MO	n/a	n/a	n/a	n/a	n/a
Columbia, SC	3	28	n/a	2	n/a
Columbus, OH	9	43	n/a	4	n/a
Dallas, TX	14	46	n/a	17	n/a
Davenport, IA	n/a	n/a	n/a	4	n/a
Denver, CO	24	65	n/a	6	n/a
Des Moines, IA	n/a	n/a	n/a	n/a	n/a
Detroit, MI	14	50	n/a	55	n/a
Durham, NC	n/a	n/a	n/a	3	n/a
El Paso, TX	15	57	n/a	6	n/a
Eugene, OR	n/a	n/a	n/a	n/a	n/a
Fargo, ND	4	n/a	n/a	3	n/a
Fort Collins, CO	n/a	n/a	n/a	n/a	n/a
Fort Wayne, IN	n/a	n/a	n/a	n/a	n/a
Fort Worth, TX	14	46	n/a	17	n/a
Gainesville, FL	n/a	n/a	n/a	n/a	n/a
Green Bay, WI	n/a	n/a	n/a	n/a	n/a
Greensboro, NC	n/a	n/a	n/a	4	n/a
Honolulu, HI	3	23	n/a	60	n/a
Houston, TX	18	60	n/a	13	n/a
Huntsville, AL	n/a	n/a	n/a	n/a	n/a
Indianapolis, IN	13	44	n/a	3	n/a
Jacksonville, FL	10	40	n/a	40	n/a
Kansas City, MO	11	45	n/a	6	n/a
Lafayette, LA	n/a	n/a	n/a	n/a	n/a
Las Vegas, NV	20	52	n/a	5	n/a
Lexington, KY	6	39	n/a	7	n/a
Lincoln, NE	n/a	n/a	n/a	n/a	n/a
Little Rock, AR	3	13	n/a	4	n/a
Los Angeles, CA	21	61	n/a	8	n/a
Louisville, KY	13	47	n/a	13	n/a
Madison, WI	n/a	n/a	n/a	n/a	n/a
Manchester, NH	n/a	n/a	n/a	1	n/a
McAllen, TX	n/a	n/a	n/a	n/a	n/a

Table continued on following page.

Metro Area	Nitrogen Dioxide AM (ppb)	Nitrogen Dioxide 1-Hr (ppb)	Sulfur Dioxide AM (ppb)	Sulfur Dioxide 1-Hr (ppb)	Sulfur Dioxide 24-Hr (ppb)
Memphis, TN	9	38	n/a	2	n/a
Miami, FL	15	53	n/a	2	n/a
Midland, TX	n/a	n/a	n/a	n/a	n/a
Milwaukee, WI	11	46	n/a	3	n/a
Minneapolis, MN	12	45	n/a	14	n/a
Nashville, TN	13	52	n/a	6	n/a
New Orleans, LA	8	39	n/a	52	n/a
New York, NY	19	60	n/a	5	n/a
Oklahoma City, OK	12	29	n/a	1	n/a
Omaha, NE	n/a	n/a	n/a	39	n/a
Orlando, FL	n/a	n/a	n/a	4	n/a
Philadelphia, PA	15	48	n/a	5	n/a
Phoenix, AZ	24	58	n/a	4	n/a
Pittsburgh, PA	9	38	n/a	65	n/a
Portland, OR	9	29	n/a	n/a	n/a
Providence, RI	13	35	n/a	3	n/a
Provo, UT	8	39	n/a	n/a	n/a
Raleigh, NC	9	36	n/a	2	n/a
Reno, NV	11	49	n/a	3	n/a
Richmond, VA	13	47	n/a	3	n/a
Rochester, MN	n/a	n/a	n/a	n/a	n/a
Sacramento, CA	9	33	n/a	2	n/a
Saint Louis, MO	10	43	n/a	38	n/a
Saint Paul, MN	12	45	n/a	14	n/a
Salem, OR	n/a	n/a	n/a	n/a	n/a
Salt Lake City, UT	16	57	n/a	5	n/a
San Antonio, TX	8	37	n/a	2	n/a
San Diego, CA	14	49	n/a	n/a	n/a
San Francisco, CA	11	102	n/a	18	n/a
San Jose, CA	13	44	n/a	2	n/a
Santa Rosa, CA	3	25	n/a	n/a	n/a
Savannah, GA	n/a	n/a	n/a	44	n/a
Seattle, WA	15	50	n/a	3	n/a
Sioux Falls, SD	5	40	n/a	1	n/a
Tampa, FL	9	36	n/a	48	n/a
Tucson, AZ	13	39	n/a	1	n/a
Tulsa, OK	6	33	n/a	3	n/a
Virginia Beach, VA	8	37	n/a	3	n/a
Washington, DC	16	47	n/a	3	n/a
Wichita, KS	6	23	n/a	2	n/a
Wilmington, NC	n/a	n/a	n/a	n/a	n/a
Winston-Salem, NC	7	40	n/a	2	n/a
NAAQS[1]	53	100	30	75	140

Note: Data from exceptional events are included; Figures cover the Metropolitan Statistical Area (MSA); (1) National Ambient Air Quality Standards; ppb = parts per billion; n/a not available
Concentrations: Nitrogen Dioxide AM—highest arithmetic mean concentration; Nitrogen Dioxide 1-Hr—highest 98th percentile 1-hour daily maximum concentration; Sulfur Dioxide AM—highest annual mean concentration; Sulfur Dioxide 1-Hr—highest 99th percentile 1-hour daily maximum concentration; Sulfur Dioxide 24-Hr—highest second maximum 24-hour concentration
Source: U.S. Environmental Protection Agency, Air Quality Monitoring Information, "Air Quality Statistics by City, 2023"

Appendix B: Metropolitan Area Definitions

Includes Metropolitan Statistical Areas (MSA) and Metropolitan Divisions (MD) referenced in this book.

Note: On July 21, 2023, the Office of Management and Budget (OMB) announced changes to metropolitan and micropolitan statistical area definitions. The current definitions are shown below.

Albuquerque, NM MSA
Bernalillo, Sandoval, Torrance, and Valencia Counties

Anchorage, AK MSA
Anchorage Municipality and Matanuska-Susitna Borough

Ann Arbor, MI MSA
Washtenaw County

Athens-Clarke County, GA MSA
Clarke, Madison, Oconee, and Oglethorpe Counties

Atlanta, GA

Atlanta-Sandy Springs-Roswell, GA MSA
Barrow, Bartow, Butts, Carroll, Cherokee, Clayton, Cobb, Coweta, Dawson, DeKalb, Douglas, Fayette, Forsyth, Fulton, Gwinnett, Haralson, Heard, Henry, Jasper, Lumpkin, Meriwether, Morgan, Newton, Paulding, Pickens, Pike, Rockdale, Spalding, and Walton Counties

Atlanta-Sandy Springs-Roswell, GA MD
Barrow, Butts, Carroll, Clayton, Coweta, Dawson, DeKalb, Douglas, Fayette, Forsyth, Fulton, Gwinnett, Heard, Henry, Jasper, Lumpkin, Meriwether, Morgan, Newton, Pickens, Pike, Rockdale, Spalding, and Walton Counties

Austin-Round Rock-San Marcos, TX MSA
Bastrop, Caldwell, Hays, Travis, and Williamson Counties

Baltimore-Columbia-Towson, MD MSA
Baltimore city; Anne Arundel, Baltimore, Carroll, Harford, Howard, and Queen Anne's Counties

Billings, MT MSA
Carbon, Stillwater, and Yellowstone Counties

Boise City, ID MSA
Previously Boise City-Nampa, ID MSA
Ada, Boise, Canyon, Gem, and Owyhee Counties

Boston, MA

Boston-Cambridge-Newton, MA-NH MSA
Essex, Middlesex, Norfolk, Plymouth, and Suffolk Counties, MA; Rockingham and Strafford Counties, NH

Boston, MA MD
Norfolk, Plymouth, and Suffolk Counties

Boulder, CO MSA
Boulder County

Cape Coral-Fort Myers, FL MSA
Lee County

Cedar Rapids, IA, MSA
Benton, Jones, and Linn Counties

Charleston-North Charleston, SC MSA
Berkeley, Charleston, and Dorchester Counties

Charlotte-Concord-Gastonia, NC-SC MSA
Anson, Cabarrus, Gaston, Iredell, Lincoln, Mecklenburg, Rowan, and Union Counties, NC; Chester, Lancaster, and York Counties, SC

Chicago, IL

Chicago-Naperville-Elgin, IL-IN MSA
Cook, DeKalb, DuPage, Grundy, Kane, Kendall, Lake, McHenry, and Will Counties, IL; Jasper, Lake, Newton, and Porter Counties, IN

Chicago-Naperville-Schaumburg, IL MD
Cook, DuPage, Grundy, McHenry, and Will Counties

Cincinnati, OH-KY-IN MSA
Brown, Butler, Clermont, Hamilton, and Warren Counties, OH; Boone, Bracken, Campbell, Gallatin, Grant, Kenton, and Pendleton County, KY; Dearborn, Franklin, and Ohio Counties, IN

Clarksville, TN-KY MSA
Montgomery and Stewart Counties, TN; Christian and Trigg Counties, KY

Cleveland, OH MSA
Ashtabula, Cuyahoga, Geauga, Lake, Lorain, and Medina Counties

College Station-Bryan, TX MSA
Brazos, Burleson, and Robertson Counties

Colorado Springs, CO MSA
El Paso and Teller Counties

Columbia, MO MSA
Boone, Cooper, and Howard Counties

Columbia, SC MSA
Calhoun, Fairfield, Kershaw, Lexington, Richland, and Saluda Counties

Columbus, OH MSA
Delaware, Fairfield, Franklin, Hocking, Licking, Madison, Morrow, Perry, Pickaway, and Union Counties

Dallas, TX

Dallas-Fort Worth-Arlington, TX MSA
Collin, Dallas, Denton, Ellis, Hunt, Johnson, Kaufman, Parker, Rockwall, Tarrant, and Wise Counties

Dallas-Plano-Irving, TX MD
Collin, Dallas, Denton, Ellis, Hunt, Kaufman, and Rockwall Counties

Davenport-Moline-Rock Island, IA-IL MSA
Scott County, IA; Henry, Mercer, and Rock Island Counties, IL

Denver-Aurora-Centennial, CO MSA
Adams, Arapahoe, Broomfield, Clear Creek, Denver, Douglas, Elbert, Gilpin, Jefferson, and Park Counties

Des Moines-West Des Moines, IA MSA
Dallas, Guthrie, Jasper, Madison, Polk, and Warren Counties

Detroit, MI

Detroit-Warren-Dearborn, MI MSA
Lapeer, Livingston, Macomb, Oakland, St. Clair, and Wayne Counties

Detroit-Dearborn-Livonia, MI MD
Wayne County

Durham-Chapel Hill, NC MSA
Chatham, Durham, Orange, and Person Counties

El Paso, TX MSA
El Paso and Hudspeth Counties

Eugene-Springfield, OR MSA
Lane County

Fargo, ND-MN MSA
Cass County, ND; Clay County, MN

Fort Collins-Loveland, CO MSA
Larimer County

Fort Wayne, IN MSA
Allen, Wells, and Whitley Counties

Fort Worth, TX

Dallas-Fort Worth-Arlington, TX MSA
Collin, Dallas, Denton, Ellis, Hunt, Johnson, Kaufman, Parker, Rockwall, Tarrant, and Wise Counties

Fort Worth-Arlington-Grapevine, TX MD
Johnson, Parker, Tarrant, and Wise Counties

Gainesville, FL MSA
Alachua, Gilchrist, and Levy Counties

Green Bay, WI MSA
Brown, Kewaunee, and Oconto Counties

Greensboro-High Point, NC MSA
Guilford, Randolph, and Rockingham Counties

Honolulu, HI
See Urban Honolulu, HI

Houston-Pasadena-The Woodlands, TX MSA
Austin, Brazoria, Chambers, Fort Bend, Galveston, Harris, Liberty, Montgomery, San Jacinto, and Waller Counties

Huntsville, AL MSA
Limestone and Madison Counties

Indianapolis-Carmel-Greenwood, IN MSA
Boone, Brown, Hamilton, Hancock, Hendricks, Johnson, Madison, Marion, Morgan, Shelby, and Tipton Counties

Jacksonville, FL MSA
Baker, Clay, Duval, Nassau, and St. Johns Counties

Kansas City, MO-KS MSA
Johnson, Leavenworth, Linn, Miami, and Wyandotte Counties, KS; Bates, Caldwell, Cass, Clay, Clinton, Jackson, Lafayette, Platte, and Ray Counties, MO

Lafayette, LA MSA
Acadia, Lafayette, St. Martin, and Vermilion Parishes

Las Vegas-Henderson-North Las Vegas, NV MSA
Clark County

Lexington-Fayette, KY MSA
Bourbon, Clark, Fayette, Jessamine, Scott, and Woodford Counties

Lincoln, NE MSA
Lancaster and Seward Counties

Little Rock-North Little Rock-Conway, AR MSA
Faulkner, Grant, Lonoke, Perry, Pulaski, and Saline Counties

Los Angeles, CA

Los Angeles-Long Beach-Anaheim, CA MSA
Los Angeles and Orange Counties

Los Angeles-Long Beach-Glendale, CA MD
Los Angeles County

Louisville/Jefferson County, KY-IN MSA
Clark, Floyd, Harrison, and Washington Counties, IN; Bullitt, Henry, Jefferson, Meade, Nelson, Oldham, Shelby, and Spencer Counties, KY

Madison, WI MSA
Columbia, Dane, Green, and Iowa Counties

Manchester-Nashua, NH MSA
Hillsborough County

McAllen-Edinburg-Mission, TX
Hidalgo County

Memphis, TN-AR-MS MSA
Fayette, Shelby and Tipton Counties, TN; Crittenden County, AR; Benton, DeSoto, Marshall, Tate and Tunica Counties, MS

Miami, FL

Miami-Fort Lauderdale-West Palm Beach, FL MSA
Broward, Miami-Dade, and Palm Beach Counties

Miami-Miami Beach-Kendall, FL MD
Miami-Dade County

Midland, TX MSA
Martin and Midland Counties

Milwaukee-Waukesha, WI MSA
Milwaukee, Ozaukee, Washington, and Waukesha Counties

Minneapolis-St. Paul-Bloomington, MN-WI MSA
Anoka, Carver, Chisago, Dakota, Hennepin, Isanti, Le Sueur, Mille Lacs, Ramsey, Scott, Sherburne, Washington, and Wright Counties, MN; Pierce and St. Croix Counties, WI

Nashville-Davidson–Murfreesboro–Franklin, TN MSA
Cannon, Cheatham, Davidson, Dickson, Hickman, Macon, Maury, Robertson, Rutherford, Smith, Sumner, Trousdale, Williamson, and Wilson Counties

New Orleans-Metairie, LA MSA
Jefferson, Orleans, Plaquemines, St. Bernard, St. Charles, St. James, and St. John the Baptist Parishes

New York, NY

New York-Newark-Jersey City, NY-NJ MSA
Bergen, Essex, Hudson, Hunterdon, Middlesex, Monmouth, Morris, Ocean, Passaic, Somerset, Sussex, and Union Counties, NJ; Bronx, Kings, Nassau, New York, Putnam, Queens, Richmond, Rockland, Suffolk, and Westchester Counties, NY

New York-Jersey City-White Plains, NY-NJ MD
Bergen, Hudson, and Passaic Counties, NJ; Bronx, Kings, New York, Putnam, Queens, Richmond, Rockland, and Westchester Counties, NY

Oklahoma City, OK MSA
Canadian, Cleveland, Grady, Lincoln, Logan, McClain, and Oklahoma Counties

Omaha, NE-IA MSA
Harrison, Mills, and Pottawattamie Counties, IA; Cass, Douglas, Sarpy, Saunders, and Washington Counties, NE

Orlando-Kissimmee-Sanford, FL MSA
Lake, Orange, Osceola, and Seminole Counties

Philadelphia, PA

Philadelphia-Camden-Wilmington, PA-NJ-DE-MD MSA
New Castle County, DE; Cecil County, MD; Burlington, Camden, Gloucester, and Salem Counties, NJ; Bucks, Chester, Delaware, Montgomery, and Philadelphia Counties, PA

Philadelphia, PA MD
Delaware and Philadelphia Counties

Phoenix-Mesa-Chandler, AZ MSA
Maricopa and Pinal Counties

Pittsburgh, PA MSA
Allegheny, Armstrong, Beaver, Butler, Fayette, Lawrence, Washington, and Westmoreland Counties

Portland-Vancouver-Hillsboro, OR-WA MSA
Clackamas, Columbia, Multnomah, Washington, and Yamhill Counties, OR; Clark and Skamania Counties, WA

Providence-Warwick, RI MSA
Bristol County, MA; Bristol, Kent, Newport, Providence, and Washington Counties, RI

Provo-Orem-Lehi, UT MSA
Juab and Utah Counties

Raleigh-Cary, NC MSA
Franklin, Johnston, and Wake Counties

Reno, NV MSA
Lyon, Storey, and Washoe Counties

Richmond, VA MSA
Amelia, Charles City, Chesterfield, Dinwiddie, Goochland, Hanover, Henrico, King and Queen, King William, New Kent, Powhatan, Prince George, and Sussex Counties; Colonial Heights, Hopewell, Petersburg, and Richmond Cities

Rochester, MN MSA
Dodge, Fillmore, Olmsted, and Wabasha Counties

Sacramento-Roseville-Folsom, CA MSA
El Dorado, Placer, Sacramento, and Yolo Counties

Saint Louis, MO-IL MSA
Bond, Calhoun, Clinton, Jersey, Macoupin, Madison, Monroe, and St. Clair Counties, IL; St. Louis city; Crawford (part–Sullivan city), Franklin, Jefferson, Lincoln, St. Charles, St. Louis, and Warren Counties, MO

Saint Paul, MN
See Minneapolis-St. Paul-Bloomington, MN-WI MSA

Salem, OR MSA
Marion and Polk Counties

Salt Lake City-Murray, UT MSA
Salt Lake and Tooele Counties

San Antonio-New Braunfels, TX MSA
Atascosa, Bandera, Bexar, Comal, Guadalupe, Kendall, Medina, and Wilson Counties

San Diego-Chula Vista-Carlsbad, CA MSA
San Diego County

San Francisco, CA

San Francisco-Oakland-Fremont, CA MSA
Alameda, Contra Costa, Marin, San Francisco, and San Mateo Counties

San Francisco-San Mateo-Redwood City, CA MD
San Francisco and San Mateo Counties

San Jose-Sunnyvale-Santa Clara, CA MSA
San Benito and Santa Clara Counties

Santa Rosa-Petaluma, CA MSA
Sonoma County

Savannah, GA MSA
Bryan, Chatham, and Effingham Counties

Seattle, WA

Seattle-Tacoma-Bellevue, WA MSA
King, Pierce, and Snohomish Counties

Seattle-Bellevue-Kent, WA MD
King County

Sioux Falls, SD-MN MSA
Lincoln, McCook, Minnehaha, and Turner Counties, SD; Rock County, MN

Tampa, FL

Tampa-St. Petersburg-Clearwater, FL MSA
Hernando, Hillsborough, Pasco, and Pinellas Counties

Tampa, FL MD
Hernando, Hillsborough, and Pasco Counties

Tucson, AZ MSA
Pima County

Tulsa, OK MSA
Creek, Okmulgee, Osage, Pawnee, Rogers, Tulsa, and Wagoner Counties

Urban Honolulu, HI MSA
Honolulu County

Virginia Beach-Chesapeake-Norfolk, VA-NC MSA
Camden, Currituck, and Gates Counties, NC; Chesapeake, Hampton, Newport News, Norfolk, Poquoson, Portsmouth, Suffolk, Virginia Beach and Williamsburg cities, VA; Gloucester, Isle of Wight, James City, Mathews, Surry, and York Counties, VA

Washington, DC

Washington-Arlington-Alexandria, DC-VA-MD-WV MSA
District of Columbia; Calvert, Charles, Frederick, Montgomery, and Prince George's Counties, MD; Alexandria, Fairfax, Falls Church, Fredericksburg, Manassas, and Manassas Park cities, VA; Arlington, Clarke, Culpepper, Fairfax, Fauquier, Loudoun, Prince William, Rappahannock, Spotsylvania, Stafford, and Warren Counties, VA; Jefferson County, WV

Washington, DC-MD MD
District of Columbia; Charles and Prince George's Counties, MD

Wichita, KS MSA
Butler, Harvey, Sedgwick, and Sumner Counties

Wilmington, NC MSA
Brunswick, New Hanover and Pender Counties

Winston-Salem, NC MSA
Davidson, Davie, Forsyth, Stokes, and Yadkin Counties

Appendix C: Government Type and Primary County

This appendix includes the government structure of each place included in this book. It also includes the county or county equivalent in which each place is located. If a place spans more than one county, the county in which the majority of the population resides is shown.

Albuquerque, NM
Government Type: City
County: Bernalillo

Anchorage, AK
Government Type: Municipality
Borough: Anchorage

Ann Arbor, MI
Government Type: City
County: Washtenaw

Athens, GA
Government Type: Consolidated
    city-county
County: Clarke

Atlanta, GA
Government Type: City
County: Fulton

Austin, TX
Government Type: City
County: Travis

Baltimore, MD
Government Type: Independent city

Baton Rouge, LA
Government Type: Consolidated city-parish
Parish: East Baton Rouge

Billings, MT
Government Type: City
County: Yellowstone

Boise City, ID
Government Type: City
County: Ada

Boston, MA
Government Type: City
County: Suffolk

Boulder, CO
Government Type: City
County: Boulder

Cape Coral, FL
Government Type: City
County: Lee

Cedar Rapids, IA
Government Type: City
County: Linn

Charleston, SC
Government Type: City
County: Charleston

Charlotte, NC
Government Type: City
County: Mecklenburg

Chicago, IL
Government Type: City
County: Cook

Cincinnati, OH
Government Type: City
County: Hamilton

Clarksville, TN
Government Type: City
County: Montgomery

Cleveland, OH
Government Type: City
County: Cuyahoga

College Station, TX
Government Type: City
County: Brazos

Colorado Springs, CO
Government Type: City
County: El Paso

Columbia, MO
Government Type: City
County: Boone

Columbia, SC
Government Type: City
County: Richland

Columbus, OH
Government Type: City
County: Franklin

Dallas, TX
Government Type: City
County: Dallas

Davenport, IA
Government Type: City
County: Scott

Denver, CO
Government Type: City
County: Denver

Des Moines, IA
Government Type: City
County: Polk

Detroit, MI
Government Type: City
County: Wayne

Durham, NC
Government Type: City
County: Durham

El Paso, TX
Government Type: City
County: El Paso

Eugene, OR
Government Type: City
County: Lane

Fargo, ND
Government Type: City
County: Cass

Fort Collins, CO
Government Type: City
County: Larimer

Fort Wayne, IN
Government Type: City
County: Allen

Fort Worth, TX
Government Type: City
County: Tarrant

Gainesville, FL
Government Type: City
County: Alachua

Green Bay, WI
Government Type: City
County: Brown

Greensboro, NC
Government Type: City
County: Guilford

Honolulu, HI
Government Type: Census Designated Place (CDP)
County: Honolulu

Houston, TX
Government Type: City
County: Harris

Huntsville, AL
Government Type: City
County: Madison

Indianapolis, IN
Government Type: City
County: Marion

Jacksonville, FL
Government Type: City
County: Duval

Kansas City, MO
Government Type: City
County: Jackson

Lafayette, LA
Government Type: City
Parish: Lafayette

Las Vegas, NV
Government Type: City
County: Clark

Lexington, KY
Government Type: Consolidated city-county
County: Fayette

Lincoln, NE
Government Type: City
County: Lancaster

Little Rock, AR
Government Type: City
County: Pulaski

Los Angeles, CA
Government Type: City
County: Los Angeles

Louisville, KY
Government Type: Consolidated city-county
County: Jefferson

Madison, WI
Government Type: City
County: Dane

Manchester, NH
Government Type: City
County: Hillsborough

McAllen, TX
Government Type: City
County: Hidalgo

Memphis, TN
Government Type: City
County: Shelby

Miami, FL
Government Type: City
County: Miami-Dade

Midland, TX
Government Type: City
County: Midland

Milwaukee, WI
Government Type: City
County: Milwaukee

Minneapolis, MN
Government Type: City
County: Hennepin

Nashville, TN
Government Type: Consolidated city-county
County: Davidson

New Orleans, LA
Government Type: City
Parish: Orleans

New York, NY
Government Type: City
Counties: Bronx; Kings; New York; Queens; Staten Island

Oklahoma City, OK
Government Type: City
County: Oklahoma

Omaha, NE
Government Type: City
County: Douglas

Orlando, FL
Government Type: City
County: Orange

Philadelphia, PA
Government Type: City
County: Philadelphia

Phoenix, AZ
Government Type: City
County: Maricopa

Pittsburgh, PA
Government Type: City
County: Allegheny

Portland, OR
Government Type: City
County: Multnomah

Providence, RI
Government Type: City
County: Providence

Provo, UT
Government Type: City
County: Utah

Raleigh, NC
Government Type: City
County: Wake

Reno, NV
Government Type: City
County: Washoe

Richmond, VA
Government Type: Independent city

Riverside, CA
Government Type: City
County: Riverside

Rochester, MN
Government Type: City
County: Olmsted

Rochester, NY
Government Type: City
County: Monroe

Sacramento, CA
Government Type: City
County: Sacramento

Saint Louis, MO
Government Type: Independent city

Saint Paul, MN
Government Type: City
County: Ramsey

Salem, OR
Government Type: City
County: Marion

Salt Lake City, UT
Government Type: City
County: Salt Lake

San Antonio, TX
Government Type: City
County: Bexar

San Diego, CA
Government Type: City
County: San Diego

San Francisco, CA
Government Type: City
County: San Francisco

San Jose, CA
Government Type: City
County: Santa Clara

Santa Rosa, CA
Government Type: City
County: Sonoma

Savannah, GA
Government Type: City
County: Chatham

Seattle, WA
Government Type: City
County: King

Sioux Falls, SD
Government Type: City
County: Minnehaha

Tampa, FL
Government Type: City
County: Hillsborough

Tucson, AZ
Government Type: City
County: Pima

Tulsa, OK
Government Type: City
County: Tulsa

Virginia Beach, VA
Government Type: Independent city

Washington, DC
Government Type: City
County: District of Columbia

Wichita, KS
Government Type: City
County: Sedgwick

Wilmington, NC
Government Type: City
County: New Hanover

Winston-Salem, NC
Government Type: City
County: Forsyth

Appendix D: Chambers of Commerce

Albuquerque, NM
Albuquerque Chamber of Commerce
P.O. Box 25100
Albuquerque, NM 87125
Phone: (505) 764-3700
Fax: (505) 764-3714
www.abqchamber.com

Albuquerque Economic Development Dept
851 University Blvd SE, Suite 203
Albuquerque, NM 87106
Phone: (505) 246-6200
Fax: (505) 246-6219
www.cabq.gov/econdev

Anchorage, AK
Anchorage Chamber of Commerce
1016 W Sixth Avenue, Suite 303
Anchorage, AK 99501
Phone: (907) 272-2401
Fax: (907) 272-4117
www.anchoragechamber.org

Anchorage Economic Development
Department
900 W 5th Avenue, Suite 300
Anchorage, AK 99501
Phone: (907) 258-3700
Fax: (907) 258-6646
aedcweb.com

Ann Arbor, MI
Ann Arbor Area Chamber of Commerce
115 West Huron, 3rd Floor
Ann Arbor, MI 48104
Phone: (734) 665-4433
Fax: (734) 665-4191
www.annarborchamber.org

Ann Arbor Economic Development
Department
201 S Division, Suite 430
Ann Arbor, MI 48104
Phone: (734) 761-9317
www.annarborspark.org

Athens, GA
Athens Area Chamber of Commerce
246 W Hancock Avenue
Athens, GA 30601
Phone: (706) 549-6800
Fax: (706) 549-5636
www.aacoc.org

Athens-Clarke County Economic
Development Department
246 W. Hancock Avenue
Athens, GA 30601
Phone: (706) 613-3233
Fax: (706) 613-3812
www.athensbusiness.org

Atlanta, GA
Metro Atlanta Chamber of Commerce
235 Andrew Young International Blvd NW
Atlanta, GA 30303
Phone: (404) 880-9000
Fax: (404) 586-8464
www.metroatlantachamber.com

Austin, TX
Greater Austin Chamber of Commerce
210 Barton Springs Road, Suite 400
Austin, TX 78704
Phone: (512) 478-9383
Fax: (512) 478-6389
www.austin-chamber.org

Baltimore, MD
Baltimore City Chamber of Commerce
P.O. Box 43121
Baltimore, MD 21236
443-860-2020
baltimorecitychamber.org

Baltimore County Chamber of Commerce
102 W. Pennsylvania Avenue, Suite 305
Towson, MD, 21204
Phone: (410) 825-6200
Fax: (410) 821-9901
www.baltcountychamber.com

Billings, MT
Billings Chamber of Commerce
815 S. 27th St
Billings, MT 59101
Phone: (406) 245-4111
Fax: (406) 245-7333
www.billingschamber.com

Boise City, ID
Boise Metro Chamber of Commerce
250 S. 5th Street, Suite 800
Boise City, ID 83701
Phone: (208) 472-5200
Fax: (208) 472-5201
www.boisechamber.org

Boston, MA
Greater Boston Chamber of Commerce
265 Franklin Street, 12th Floor
Boston, MA 02110
Phone: (617) 227-4500
Fax: (617) 227-7505
www.bostonchamber.com

Boulder, CO
Boulder Chamber of Commerce
2440 Pearl Street
Boulder, CO 80302
Phone: (303) 442-1044
Fax: (303) 938-8837
www.boulderchamber.com

Cape Coral, FL
Chamber of Commerce of Cape Coral
2051 Cape Coral Parkway East
Cape Coral, FL 33904
Phone: (239) 549-6900
www.capecoralchamber.com

Cedar Rapids, IA
Cedar Rapids Chamber of Commerce
424 First Avenue NE
Cedar Rapids, IA 52401
Phone: (319) 398-5317
Fax: (319) 398-5228
www.cedarrapids.org

Cedar Rapids Economic Development
50 Second Avenue Bridge, Sixth Floor
Cedar Rapids, IA 52401-1256
Phone: (319) 286-5041
Fax: (319) 286-5141
www.cedar-rapids.org

Charleston, SC
Charleston Metro Chamber of Commerce
P.O. Box 975
Charleston, SC 29402
Phone: (843) 577-2510
www.charlestonchamber.net

Charlotte, NC
Charlotte Chamber of Commerce
330 S Tryon Street
P.O. Box 32785
Charlotte, NC 28232
Phone: (704) 378-1300
Fax: (704) 374-1903
www.charlottechamber.com

Charlotte Regional Partnership
1001 Morehead Square Drive, Suite 200
Charlotte, NC 28203
Phone: (704) 347-8942
Fax: (704) 347-8981
www.charlotteusa.com

Chicago, IL
Chicagoland Chamber of Commerce
200 E Randolph Street, Suite 2200
Chicago, IL 60601-6436
Phone: (312) 494-6700
Fax: (312) 861-0660
www.chicagolandchamber.org

City of Chicago Department of Planning
and Development
City Hall, Room 1000
121 North La Salle Street
Chicago, IL 60602
Phone: (312) 744-4190
Fax: (312) 744-2271
www.cityofchicago.org/city/en/depts/dcd.html

Cincinnati, OH
Cincinnati USA Regional Chamber
3 East 4th Street, Suite 200
Cincinnati, Ohio 45202
Phone: (513) 579-3111
www.cincinnatichamber.com

Clarksville, TN
Clarksville Area Chamber of Commerce
25 Jefferson Street, Suite 300
Clarksville, TN 37040
Phone: (931) 647-2331
www.clarksvillechamber.com

Cleveland, OH
Greater Cleveland Partnership
1240 Huron Rd. E, Suite 300
Cleveland, OH 44115
Phone: (216) 621-3300
www.gcpartnership.com

College Station, TX
Bryan-College Station Chamber of
Commerce
4001 East 29th St, Suite 175
Bryan, TX 77802
Phone: (979) 260-5200
www.bcschamber.org

Colorado Springs, CO
Colorado Springs Chamber and EDC
102 South Tejon Street, Suite 430
Colorado Springs, CO 80903
Phone: (719) 471-8183
coloradospringschamberedc.com

Columbia, MO
Columbia Chamber of Commerce
300 South Providence Rd.
P.O. Box 1016
Columbia, MO 65205-1016
Phone: (573) 874-1132
Fax: (573) 443-3986
www.columbiamochamber.com

Columbia, SC
The Columbia Chamber
930 Richland Street
Columbia, SC 29201
Phone: (803) 733-1110
Fax: (803) 733-1113
www.columbiachamber.com

Columbus, OH
Greater Columbus Chamber
37 North High Street
Columbus, OH 43215
Phone: (614) 221-1321
Fax: (614) 221-1408
www.columbus.org

Dallas, TX
City of Dallas Economic Development
Department
1500 Marilla Street, 5C South
Dallas, TX 75201
Phone: (214) 670-1685
Fax: (214) 670-0158
www.dallas-edd.org

Greater Dallas Chamber of Commerce
700 North Pearl Street, Suite1200
Dallas, TX 75201
Phone: (214) 746-6600
Fax: (214) 746-6799
www.dallaschamber.org

Davenport, IA
Quad Cities Chamber
331 W. 3rd Street, Suite 100
Davenport, IA 52801
Phone: (563) 322-1706
quadcitieschamber.com

Denver, CO
Denver Metro Chamber of Commerce
1445 Market Street
Denver, CO 80202
Phone: (303) 534-8500
Fax: (303) 534-3200
www.denverchamber.org

Downtown Denver Partnership
511 16th Street, Suite 200
Denver, CO 80202
Phone: (303) 534-6161
Fax: (303) 534-2803
www.downtowndenver.com

Des Moines, IA
Des Moines Downtown Chamber
301 Grand Ave
Des Moines, IA 50309
Phone: (515) 309-3229
desmoinesdowntownchamber.com

Greater Des Moines Partnership
700 Locust Street, Suite 100
Des Moines, IA 50309
Phone: (515) 286-4950
Fax: (515) 286-4974
www.desmoinesmetro.com

Durham, NC
Durham Chamber of Commerce
P.O. Box 3829
Durham, NC 27702
Phone: (919) 682-2133
Fax: (919) 688-8351
www.durhamchamber.org

North Carolina Institute of Minority
Economic Development
114 W Parish Street
Durham, NC 27701
Phone: (919) 956-8889
Fax: (919) 688-7668
www.ncimed.com

El Paso, TX
City of El Paso Department of Economic
Development
2 Civic Center Plaza
El Paso, TX 79901
Phone: (915) 541-4000
Fax: (915) 541-1316
www.elpasotexas.gov

Greater El Paso Chamber of Commerce
10 Civic Center Plaza
El Paso, TX 79901
Phone: (915) 534-0500
Fax: (915) 534-0510
www.elpaso.org

Eugene, OR
Eugene Area Chamber of Commerce
1401 Williamette Street
Eugene, OR 97401
Phone: (541) 484-1314
Fax: (541) 484-4942
www.eugenechamber.com

Fargo, ND
Chamber of Commerce of Fargo Moorhead
202 First Avenue North
Fargo, ND 56560
Phone: (218) 233-1100
Fax: (218) 233-1200
www.fmchamber.com

Greater Fargo-Moorhead Economic
Development Corporation
51 Broadway, Suite 500
Fargo, ND 58102
Phone: (701) 364-1900
Fax: (701) 293-7819
www.gfmedc.com

Fort Collins, CO
Fort Collins Chamber of Commerce
225 South Meldrum
Fort Collins, CO 80521
Phone: (970) 482-3746
Fax: (970) 482-3774
fortcollinschamber.com

Fort Wayne, IN
City of Fort Wayne Economic Development
1 Main Street
Fort Wayne, IN 46802
Phone: (260) 427-1111
Fax: (260) 427-1375
www.cityoffortwayne.org

Greater Fort Wayne Chamber of Commerce
826 Ewing Street
Fort Wayne, IN 46802
Phone: (260) 424-1435
Fax: (260) 426-7232
www.fwchamber.org

Fort Worth, TX
Fort Worth Chamber of Commerce
777 Taylor Street, Suite 900
Fort Worth, TX 76102-4997
Phone: (817) 336-2491
Fax: (817) 877-4034
www.fortworthchamber.com

City of Fort Worth Economic Development
City Hall
900 Monroe Street, Suite 301
Fort Worth, TX 76102
Phone: (817) 392-6103
Fax: (817) 392-2431
www.fortworthgov.org

Gainesville, FL
Greater Gainesville Chamber
300 East University Avenue, Suite 100
Gainesville, FL 32601
Phone: (352) 334-7100
Fax: (352) 334-7141
www.gainesvillechamber.com

Green Bay, WI
Greater Green Bay Chamber
300 N. Broadway, Suite 3A
Green Bay, WI 54303
Phone: (920) 593-3400
www.greatergbc.org

Greensboro, NC
Greensboro Chamber of Commerce
111 W. February One Place
Greensboro, NC 27401
Phone: (336) 387-8301
greensboro.org

Honolulu, HI
The Chamber of Commerce of Hawaii
1132 Bishop Street, Suite 402
Honolulu, HI 96813
Phone: (808) 545-4300
Fax: (808) 545-4369
www.cochawaii.com

Houston, TX
Greater Houston Partnership
1200 Smith Street, Suite 700
Houston, TX 77002-4400
Phone: (713) 844-3600
Fax: (713) 844-0200
www.houston.org

Huntsville, AL
Chamber of Commerce of
Huntsville/Madison County
225 Church Street
Huntsville, AL 35801
Phone: (256) 535-2000
www.huntsvillealabamausa.com

Indianapolis, IN
Greater Indianapolis Chamber of Commerce
111 Monument Circle, Suite 1950
Indianapolis, IN 46204
Phone: (317) 464-2222
Fax: (317) 464-2217
www.indychamber.com

Jacksonville, FL
Jacksonville Chamber of Commerce
3 Independent Drive
Jacksonville, FL 32202
Phone: (904) 366-6600
Fax: (904) 632-0617
www.myjaxchamber.com

Kansas City, MO
Greater Kansas City Chamber of Commerce
2600 Commerce Tower
911 Main Street
Kansas City, MO 64105
Phone: (816) 221-2424
Fax: (816) 221-7440
www.kcchamber.com

Kansas City Area Development Council
2600 Commerce Tower
911 Main Street
Kansas City, MO 64105
Phone: (816) 221-2121
www.thinkkc.com

Lafayette, LA
Greater Lafayette Chamber of Commerce
804 East Saint Mary Blvd.
Lafayette, LA 70503
Phone: (337) 233-2705
Fax: (337) 234-8671
www.lafchamber.org

Las Vegas, NV
Las Vegas Chamber of Commerce
6671 Las Vegas Blvd South, Suite 300
Las Vegas, NV 89119
Phone: (702) 735-1616
Fax: (702) 735-0406
www.lvchamber.org

Las Vegas Office of Business Development
400 Stewart Avenue
City Hall
Las Vegas, NV 89101
Phone: (702) 229-6011
Fax: (702) 385-3128
www.lasvegasnevada.gov

Lexington, KY
Greater Lexington Chamber of Commerce
330 East Main Street, Suite 100
Lexington, KY 40507
Phone: (859) 254-4447
Fax: (859) 233-3304
www.commercelexington.com

Lexington Downtown Development
Authority
101 East Vine Street, Suite 500
Lexington, KY 40507
Phone: (859) 425-2296
Fax: (859) 425-2292
www.lexingtondda.com

Lincoln, NE
Lincoln Chamber of Commerce
1135 M Street, Suite 200
Lincoln, NE 68508
Phone: (402) 436-2350
www.lcoc.com

Little Rock, AR
Little Rock Regional Chamber
One Chamber Plaza
Little Rock, AR 72201
Phone: (501) 374-2001
Fax: (501) 374-6018
www.littlerockchamber.com

Los Angeles, CA
Los Angeles Area Chamber of Commerce
350 South Bixel Street
Los Angeles, CA 90017
Phone: (213) 580-7500
Fax: (213) 580-7511
www.lachamber.org

Los Angeles County Economic
Development Corporation
444 South Flower Street, 34th Floor
Los Angeles, CA 90071
Phone: (213) 622-4300
Fax: (213) 622-7100
www.laedc.org

Louisville, KY
The Greater Louisville Chamber of
Commerce
614 West Main Street, Suite 6000
Louisville, KY 40202
Phone: (502) 625-0000
Fax: (502) 625-0010
www.greaterlouisville.com

Madison, WI
Greater Madison Chamber of Commerce
615 East Washington Avenue
P.O. Box 71
Madison, WI 53701-0071
Phone: (608) 256-8348
Fax: (608) 256-0333
www.greatermadisonchamber.com

Manchester, NH
Greater Manchester Chamber of Commerce
889 Elm Street
Manchester, NH 03101
Phone: (603) 666-6600
Fax: (603) 626-0910
www.manchester-chamber.org

Manchester Economic Development Office
One City Hall Plaza
Manchester, NH 03101
Phone: (603) 624-6505
Fax: (603) 624-6308
www.yourmanchesternh.com

McAllen, TX
McAllen Chamber of Commerce
1200 Ash Avenue
McAllen, TX 78501
Phone: (956) 682-2871
Fax: (956) 687-2917
mcallenchamber.com

Memphis, TN
Greater Memphis Chamber
22 North Front Street, Suite 200
Memphis, TN 38103-2100
Phone: (901) 543-3500
memphischamber.com

Miami, FL
Greater Miami Chamber of Commerce
1601 Biscayne Boulevard
Miami, FL 33132-1260
Phone: (305) 350-7700
Fax: (305) 374-6902
www.miamichamber.com

The Beacon Council
80 Southwest 8th Street, Suite 2400
Miami, FL 33130
Phone: (305) 579-1300
Fax: (305) 375-0271
www.beaconcouncil.com

Midland, TX
Midland Chamber of Commerce
303 W. Wall Street, Suite 200
Midland, TX 79701
Phone: (432) 683-3381
www.midlandtxchamber.com

Milwaukee, WI
Greater Milwaukee Chamber of Commerce
6815 W. Capitol Drive, Suite 300
Milwaukee, WI 53216
Phone: (414) 465-2422
www.gmcofc.org

Minneapolis, MN
Minneapolis Regional Chamber
81 South Ninth Street, Suite 200
Minneapolis, MN 55402
Phone: (612) 370-9100
Fax: (612) 370-9195
www.minneapolischamber.org

Minneapolis Community Development
Agency
Crown Roller Mill
105 5th Avenue South, Suite 200
Minneapolis, MN 55401
Phone: (612) 673-5095
Fax: (612) 673-5100
www.ci.minneapolis.mn.us

Nashville, TN
Nashville Area Chamber of Commerce
211 Commerce Street, Suite 100
Nashville, TN 37201
Phone: (615) 743-3000
Fax: (615) 256-3074
www.nashvillechamber.com

TVA Economic Development
400 West Summit Hill Drive
Knoxville TN 37902
Phone: (865) 632-2101
www.tvaed.com

New Orleans, LA
New Orleans Chamber of Commerce
1515 Poydras Street, Suite 1010
New Orleans, LA 70112
Phone: (504) 799-4260
Fax: (504) 799-4259
www.neworleanschamber.org

New York, NY
New York City Economic Development
Corporation
110 William Street
New York, NY 10038
Phone: (212) 619-5000
www.nycedc.com

The Partnership for New York City
One Battery Park Plaza
5th Floor
New York, NY 10004
Phone: (212) 493-7400
Fax: (212) 344-3344
www.pfnyc.org

Oklahoma City, OK
Greater Oklahoma City Chamber of
Commerce
123 Park Avenue
Oklahoma City, OK 73102
Phone: (405) 297-8900
Fax: (405) 297-8916
www.okcchamber.com

Omaha, NE
Omaha Chamber of Commerce
1301 Harney Street
Omaha, NE 68102
Phone: (402) 346-5000
Fax: (402) 346-7050
www.omahachamber.org

Orlando, FL
Metro Orlando Economic Development
Commission of Mid-Florida
301 East Pine Street, Suite 900
Orlando, FL 32801
Phone: (407) 422-7159
Fax: (407) 425.6428
www.orlandoedc.com

Orlando Regional Chamber of Commerce
75 South Ivanhoe Boulevard
P.O. Box 1234
Orlando, FL 32802
Phone: (407) 425-1234
Fax: (407) 839-5020
www.orlando.org

Philadelphia, PA
Greater Philadelphia Chamber of
Commerce
200 South Broad Street, Suite 700
Philadelphia, PA 19102
Phone: (215) 545-1234
Fax: (215) 790-3600
www.greaterphilachamber.com

Phoenix, AZ
Greater Phoenix Chamber of Commerce
201 North Central Avenue, 27th Floor
Phoenix, AZ 85073
Phone: (602) 495-2195
Fax: (602) 495-8913
www.phoenixchamber.com

Greater Phoenix Economic Council
2 North Central Avenue, Suite 2500
Phoenix, AZ 85004
Phone: (602) 256-7700
Fax: (602) 256-7744
www.gpec.org

Pittsburgh, PA
Allegheny County Industrial Development
Authority
425 6th Avenue, Suite 800
Pittsburgh, PA 15219
Phone: (412) 350-1067
Fax: (412) 642-2217
www.alleghenycounty.us

Greater Pittsburgh Chamber of Commerce
425 6th Avenue, 12th Floor
Pittsburgh, PA 15219
Phone: (412) 392-4500
Fax: (412) 392-4520
www.alleghenyconference.org

Portland, OR
Portland Business Alliance
200 SW Market Street, Suite 1770
Portland, OR 97201
Phone: (503) 224-8684
Fax: (503) 323-9186
www.portlandalliance.com

Providence, RI
Greater Providence Chamber of Commerce
30 Exchange Terrace, Fourth Floor
Providence, RI 02903
Phone: (401) 521-5000
Fax: (401) 351-2090
www.provchamber.com

Rhode Island Economic Development
Corporation
Providence City Hall
25 Dorrance Street
Providence, RI 02903
Phone: (401) 421-7740
Fax: (401) 751-0203
www.providenceri.com

Provo, UT
Provo-Orem Chamber of Commerce
51 South University Avenue, Suite 215
Provo, UT 84601
Phone: (801) 851-2555
Fax: (801) 851-2557
www.thechamber.org

Raleigh, NC
Greater Raleigh Chamber of Commerce
800 South Salisbury Street
Raleigh, NC 27601-2978
Phone: (919) 664-7000
Fax: (919) 664-7099
www.raleighchamber.org

Reno, NV
Reno + Sparks Chamber of Commerce
449 S. Virginia Street, 2nd Floor
Reno, NV 89501
Phone: (775) 636-9550
www.thechambernv.org

Richmond, VA
Greater Richmond Chamber
600 East Main Street, Suite 700
Richmond, VA 23219
Phone: (804) 648-1234
www.grcc.com

Greater Richmond Partnership
901 East Byrd Street, Suite 801
Richmond, VA 23219-4070
Phone: (804) 643-3227
Fax: (804) 343-7167
www.grpva.com

Rochester, MN
Rochester Area Chamber of Commerce
220 South Broadway, Suite 100
Rochester, MN 55904
Phone: (507) 288-1122
www.rochestermnchamber.com

Sacramento, CA
Sacramento Metro Chamber
One Capitol Mall, Suite 700
Sacramento, CA 95814
Phone: (916) 552-6800
metrochamber.org

Saint Louis, MO
St. Louis Regional Chamber
One Metropolitan Square, Suite 1300
St. Louis, MO 63102
Phone: (314) 231-5555
www.stlregionalchamber.com

Saint Paul, OR
St. Paul Area Chamber
401 Robert Street N, Suite 150
St. Paul, MN 55101
Phone: (651) 223-5000
www.stpaulchamber.com

Salem, OR
Salem Area Chamber of Commerce
1110 Commercial Street NE
Salem, OR 97301
Phone: (503) 581-1466
www.salemchamber.org

Salt Lake City, UT
Salt Lake Chamber
175 E. University Blvd. (400 S), Suite 600
Salt Lake City, UT 84111
Phone: (801) 364-3631
www.slchamber.com

San Antonio, TX
The Greater San Antonio Chamber of
Commerce
602 E. Commerce Street
San Antonio, TX 78205
Phone: (210) 229-2100
Fax: (210) 229-1600
www.sachamber.org

San Antonio Economic Development
Department
P.O. Box 839966
San Antonio, TX 78283-3966
Phone: (210) 207-8080
Fax: (210) 207-8151
www.sanantonio.gov/edd

San Diego, CA
San Diego Economic Development Corp.
401 B Street, Suite 1100
San Diego, CA 92101
Phone: (619) 234-8484
Fax: (619) 234-1935
www.sandiegobusiness.org

San Diego Regional Chamber of Commerce
402 West Broadway, Suite 1000
San Diego, CA 92101-3585
Phone: (619) 544-1300
Fax: (619) 744-7481
www.sdchamber.org

San Francisco, CA
San Francisco Chamber of Commerce
235 Montgomery Street, 12th Floor
San Francisco, CA 94104
Phone: (415) 392-4520
Fax: (415) 392-0485
www.sfchamber.com

San Jose, CA
Office of Economic Development
60 South Market Street, Suite 470
San Jose, CA 95113
Phone: (408) 277-5880
Fax: (408) 277-3615
www.sba.gov

The Silicon Valley Organization
101 W Santa Clara Street
San Jose, CA 95113
Phone: (408) 291-5250
www.thesvo.com

Santa Rosa, CA
Santa Rosa Chamber of Commerce
1260 North Dutton Avenue, Suite 272
Santa Rosa, CA 95401
Phone: (707) 545-1414
www.santarosachamber.com

Savannah, GA
Savannah Chamber of Commerce
101 E. Bay Street
Savannah, GA 31402
Phone: (912) 644-6400
Fax: (912) 644-6499
www.savannahchamber.com

Seattle, WA
Greater Seattle Chamber of Commerce
1301 Fifth Avenue, Suite 2500
Seattle, WA 98101
Phone: (206) 389-7200
Fax: (206) 389-7288
www.seattlechamber.com

Sioux Falls, SD
Sioux Falls Area Chamber of Commerce
200 N. Phillips Avenue, Suite 102
Sioux Falls, SD 57104
Phone: (605) 336-1620
Fax: (605) 336-6499
www.siouxfallschamber.com

Tampa, FL
Greater Tampa Chamber of Commerce
P.O. Box 420
Tampa, FL 33601-0420
Phone: (813) 276-9401
Fax: (813) 229-7855
www.tampachamber.com

Tucson, AZ
Tucson Metro Chamber
212 E. Broadway Blvd
Tucson, AZ 85701
Phone: (520) 792-1212
tucsonchamber.org

Tulsa, OK
Tulsa Regional Chamber
One West Third Street, Suite 100
Tulsa, OK 74103
Phone: (918) 585-1201
www.tulsachamber.com

Virginia Beach, VA
Hampton Roads Chamber of Commerce
500 East Main Street, Suite 700
Virginia Beach, VA 23510
Phone: (757) 664-2531
www.hamptonroadschamber.com

Washington, DC
District of Columbia Chamber of Commerce
1213 K Street NW
Washington, DC 20005
Phone: (202) 347-7201
Fax: (202) 638-6762
www.dcchamber.org

District of Columbia Office of Planning and
Economic Development
J.A. Wilson Building
1350 Pennsylvania Ave NW, Suite 317
Washington, DC 20004
Phone: (202) 727-6365
Fax: (202) 727-6703
www.dcbiz.dc.gov

Wichita, KS
Wichita Regional Chamber of Commerce
350 W Douglas Avennue
Wichita, KS 67202
Phone: (316) 265-7771
www.wichitachamber.org

Wilmington, NC
Wilmington Chamber of Commerce
One Estell Lee Place
Wilmington, NC 28401
Phone: (910) 762-2611
www.wilmingtonchamber.org

Winston-Salem, NC
Winston-Salem Chamber of Commerce
411 West Fourth Street, Suite 211
Winston-Salem, NC 27101
Phone: (336) 728-9200
www.winstonsalem.com

Appendix E: State Departments of Labor

Alabama
Alabama Department of Labor
P.O. Box 303500
Montgomery, AL 36130-3500
Phone: (334) 242-3072
adol.alabama.gov

Alaska
Dept of Labor and Workforce Development
P.O. Box 11149
Juneau, AK 99822-2249
Phone: (907) 465-2700
www.labor.state.ak.us

Arizona
Industrial Commission or Arizona
800 West Washington Street
Phoenix, AZ 85007
Phone: (602) 542-4661
www.azica.gov

Arkansas
Department of Labor
10421 West Markham
Little Rock, AR 72205
Phone: (501) 682-4500
www.labor.ar.gov

California
Labor and Workforce Development
445 Golden Gate Ave., 10th Floor
San Francisco, CA 94102
Phone: (916) 263-1811
www.labor.ca.gov

Colorado
Dept of Labor and Employment
633 17th St., 2nd Floor
Denver, CO 80202-3660
Phone: (888) 390-7936
cdle.colorado.gov

Connecticut
Department of Labor
200 Folly Brook Blvd.
Wethersfield, CT 06109-1114
Phone: (860) 263-6000
www.ctdol.state.ct.us

Delaware
Department of Labor
4425 N. Market St., 4th Floor
Wilmington, DE 19802
Phone: (302) 451-3423
dol.delaware.gov

District of Columbia
Department of Employment Services
614 New York Ave., NE, Suite 300
Washington, DC 20002
Phone: (202) 671-1900
does.dc.gov

Florida
Florida Department of Economic Opportunity
The Caldwell Building
107 East Madison St. Suite 100
Tallahassee, FL 32399-4120
Phone: (800) 342-3450
www.floridajobs.org

Georgia
Department of Labor
Sussex Place, Room 600
148 Andrew Young Intl Blvd., NE
Atlanta, GA 30303
Phone: (404) 656-3011
dol.georgia.gov

Hawaii
Dept of Labor & Industrial Relations
830 Punchbowl Street
Honolulu, HI 96813
Phone: (808) 586-8842
labor.hawaii.gov

Idaho
Department of Labor
317 W. Main St.
Boise, ID 83735-0001
Phone: (208) 332-3579
www.labor.idaho.gov

Illinois
Department of Labor
160 N. LaSalle Street, 13th Floor
Suite C-1300
Chicago, IL 60601
Phone: (312) 793-2800
www.illinois.gov/idol

Indiana
Indiana Department of Labor
402 West Washington Street, Room W195
Indianapolis, IN 46204
Phone: (317) 232-2655
www.in.gov/dol

Iowa
Iowa Workforce Development
1000 East Grand Avenue
Des Moines, IA 50319-0209
Phone: (515) 242-5870
www.iowadivisionoflabor.gov

Kansas
Department of Labor
401 S.W. Topeka Blvd.
Topeka, KS 66603-3182
Phone: (785) 296-5000
www.dol.ks.gov

Kentucky
Department of Labor
1047 U.S. Hwy 127 South, Suite 4
Frankfort, KY 40601-4381
Phone: (502) 564-3070
www.labor.ky.gov

Louisiana
Louisiana Workforce Commission
1001 N. 23rd Street
Baton Rouge, LA 70804-9094
Phone: (225) 342-3111
www.laworks.net

Maine
Department of Labor
45 Commerce Street
Augusta, ME 04330
Phone: (207) 623-7900
www.state.me.us/labor

Maryland
Department of Labor, Licensing & Regulation
500 N. Calvert Street
Suite 401
Baltimore, MD 21202
Phone: (410) 767-2357
www.dllr.state.md.us

Massachusetts
Dept of Labor & Workforce Development
One Ashburton Place
Room 2112
Boston, MA 02108
Phone: (617) 626-7100
www.mass.gov/lwd

Michigan
Department of Licensing and Regulatory
Affairs
611 W. Ottawa
P.O. Box 30004
Lansing, MI 48909
Phone: (517) 373-1820
www.michigan.gov/lara

Minnesota
Dept of Labor and Industry
443 Lafayette Road North
Saint Paul, MN 55155
Phone: (651) 284-5070
www.doli.state.mn.us

Mississippi
Dept of Employment Security
P.O. Box 1699
Jackson, MS 39215-1699
Phone: (601) 321-6000
www.mdes.ms.gov

Missouri
Labor and Industrial Relations
P.O. Box 599
3315 W. Truman Boulevard
Jefferson City, MO 65102-0599
Phone: (573) 751-7500
labor.mo.gov

Montana
Dept of Labor and Industry
P.O. Box 1728
Helena, MT 59624-1728
Phone: (406) 444-9091
www.dli.mt.gov

Nebraska
Department of Labor
550 S 16th Street
Lincoln, NE 68508
Phone: (402) 471-9000
dol.nebraska.gov

Nevada
Dept of Business and Industry
3300 W. Sahara Ave, Suite 425
Las Vegas, NV 89102
Phone: (702) 486-2750
business.nv.gov

New Hampshire
Department of Labor
State Office Park South
95 Pleasant Street
Concord, NH 03301
Phone: (603) 271-3176
www.nh.gov/labor

New Jersey
Department of Labor & Workforce Devel.
John Fitch Plaza, 13th Floor, Suite D
Trenton, NJ 08625-0110
Phone: (609) 777-3200
lwd.dol.state.nj.us/labor

New Mexico
Department of Workforce Solutions
401 Broadway, NE
Albuquerque, NM 87103-1928
Phone: (505) 841-8450
www.dws.state.nm.us

New York
Department of Labor
State Office Bldg. # 12
W.A. Harriman Campus
Albany, NY 12240
Phone: (518) 457-9000
www.labor.ny.gov

North Carolina
Department of Labor
4 West Edenton Street
Raleigh, NC 27601-1092
Phone: (919) 733-7166
www.labor.nc.gov

North Dakota
North Dakota Department of Labor and
Human Rights
State Capitol Building
600 East Boulevard, Dept 406
Bismark, ND 58505-0340
Phone: (701) 328-2660
www.nd.gov/labor

Ohio
Department of Commerce
77 South High Street, 22nd Floor
Columbus, OH 43215
Phone: (614) 644-2239
www.com.state.oh.us

Oklahoma
Department of Labor
4001 N. Lincoln Blvd.
Oklahoma City, OK 73105-5212
Phone: (405) 528-1500
www.ok.gov/odol

Oregon
Bureau of Labor and Industries
800 NE Oregon St., #32
Portland, OR 97232
Phone: (971) 673-0761
www.oregon.gov/boli

Pennsylvania
Dept of Labor and Industry
1700 Labor and Industry Bldg
7th and Forster Streets
Harrisburg, PA 17120
Phone: (717) 787-5279
www.dli.pa.gov

Rhode Island
Department of Labor and Training
1511 Pontiac Avenue
Cranston, RI 02920
Phone: (401) 462-8000
www.dlt.state.ri.us

South Carolina
Dept of Labor, Licensing & Regulations
P.O. Box 11329
Columbia, SC 29211-1329
Phone: (803) 896-4300
www.llr.state.sc.us

South Dakota
Department of Labor & Regulation
700 Governors Drive
Pierre, SD 57501-2291
Phone: (605) 773-3682
dlr.sd.gov

Tennessee
Dept of Labor & Workforce Development
Andrew Johnson Tower
710 James Robertson Pkwy
Nashville, TN 37243-0655
Phone: (615) 741-6642
www.tn.gov/workforce

Texas
Texas Workforce Commission
101 East 15th St.
Austin, TX 78778
Phone: (512) 475-2670
www.twc.state.tx.us

Utah
Utah Labor Commission
160 East 300 South, 3rd Floor
Salt Lake City, UT 84114-6600
Phone: (801) 530-6800
laborcommission.utah.gov

Vermont
Department of Labor
5 Green Mountain Drive
P.O. Box 488
Montpelier, VT 05601-0488
Phone: (802) 828-4000
labor.vermont.gov

Virginia
Dept of Labor and Industry
Powers-Taylor Building
13 S. 13th Street
Richmond, VA 23219
Phone: (804) 371-2327
www.doli.virginia.gov

Washington
Dept of Labor and Industries
P.O. Box 44001
Olympia, WA 98504-4001
Phone: (360) 902-4200
www.lni.wa.gov

West Virginia
Division of Labor
749 B Building 6
Capitol Complex
Charleston, WV 25305
Phone: (304) 558-7890
labor.wv.gov

Wisconsin
Dept of Workforce Development
201 E. Washington Ave., #A400
P.O. Box 7946
Madison, WI 53707-7946
Phone: (608) 266-6861
dwd.wisconsin.gov

Wyoming
Department of Workforce Services
1510 East Pershing Blvd.
Cheyenne, WY 82002
Phone: (307) 777-7261
www.wyomingworkforce.org

Titles from Grey House

Visit www.GreyHouse.com for Product Information, Table of Contents, and Sample Pages.

Opinions Throughout History

Opinions Throughout History: Church & State
Opinions Throughout History: Conspiracy Theories
Opinions Throughout History: The Death Penalty
Opinions Throughout History: Diseases & Epidemics
Opinions Throughout History: Domestic Terrorism
Opinions Throughout History: Drug Use & Abuse
Opinions Throughout History: The Environment
Opinions Throughout History: Fame & Celebrity in America
Opinions Throughout History: Free Speech & Censorship
Opinions Throughout History: Gender: Roles & Rights
Opinions Throughout History: Globalization
Opinions Throughout History: Guns in America
Opinions Throughout History: Immigration
Opinions Throughout History: Law Enforcement in America
Opinions Throughout History: LGBTQ+ Rights
Opinions Throughout History: Mental Health
Opinions Throughout History: Nat'l Security vs. Civil & Privacy Rights
Opinions Throughout History: Presidential Authority
Opinions Throughout History: Refugees & Asylum Seekers
Opinions Throughout History: Robotics & Artificial Intelligence
Opinions Throughout History: Social Media Issues
Opinions Throughout History: Spies & Espionage
Opinions Throughout History: The Supreme Court
Opinions Throughout History: Truth & Lies in the Media
Opinions Throughout History: Voters' Rights
Opinions Throughout History: War & the Military
Opinions Throughout History: Workers Rights & Wages

General Reference

American Environmental Leaders
Constitutional Amendments
Encyclopedia of African-American Writing
Encyclopedia of Invasions & Conquests
Encyclopedia of Prisoners of War & Internment
Encyclopedia of the Continental Congresses
Encyclopedia of the United States Cabinet
Encyclopedia of War Journalism
The Environmental Debate
Environmental Sustainability: Skills & Strategies
Financial Literacy Starter Kit
From Suffrage to the Senate
The Gun Debate: Gun Rights & Gun Control in the U.S.
Historical Warrior Peoples & Modern Fighting Groups
Human Rights and the United States
Political Corruption in America
Privacy Rights in the Digital Age
The Religious Right and American Politics
Speakers of the House of Representatives, 1789-2021
US Land & Natural Resources Policy
The Value of a Dollar 1600-1865 Colonial to Civil War
The Value of a Dollar 1860-2024

This is Who We Were

This is Who We Were: Colonial America (1492-1775)
This is Who We Were: Civil War & Reconstruction
This is Who We Were: 1880-1899
This is Who We Were: In the 1900s
This is Who We Were: In the 1910s
This is Who We Were: In the 1920s
This is Who We Were: A Companion to the 1940 Census
This is Who We Were: In the 1940s (1940-1949)

This is Who We Were: In the 1950s
This is Who We Were: In the 1960s
This is Who We Were: In the 1970s
This is Who We Were: In the 1980s
This is Who We Were: In the 1990s
This is Who We Were: In the 2000s
This is Who We Were: In the 2010s

Working Americans

Working Americans—Vol. 1: The Working Class
Working Americans—Vol. 2: The Middle Class
Working Americans—Vol. 3: The Upper Class
Working Americans—Vol. 4: Children
Working Americans—Vol. 5: At War
Working Americans—Vol. 6: Working Women
Working Americans—Vol. 7: Social Movements
Working Americans—Vol. 8: Immigrants
Working Americans—Vol. 9: Revolutionary War to the Civil War
Working Americans—Vol. 10: Sports & Recreation
Working Americans—Vol. 11: Inventors & Entrepreneurs
Working Americans—Vol. 12: Our History through Music
Working Americans—Vol. 13: Education & Educators
Working Americans—Vol. 14: African Americans
Working Americans—Vol. 15: Politics & Politicians
Working Americans—Vol. 16: Farming & Ranching
Working Americans—Vol. 17: Teens in America
Working Americans—Vol. 18: Health Care Workers
Working Americans—Vol. 19: The Performing Arts

Grey House Health & Wellness Guides

Addiction Handbook & Resource Guide
Adolescent Mental Health Handbook & Resource Guide
Anxiety & Stress Handbook & Resource Guide
Attention Disorders Handbook & Resource Guide
The Autism Spectrum Handbook & Resource Guide
Autoimmune Disorders Handbook & Resource Guide
Breast Cancer Handbook & Resource Guide
Cardiovascular Disease Handbook & Resource Guide
Chronic Pain Handbook & Resource Guide
Dementia Handbook & Resource Guide
Depression Handbook & Resource Guide
Diabetes Handbook & Resource Guide
Nutrition, Obesity & Eating Disorders Handbook & Resource Guide

Consumer Health

Complete Mental Health Resource Guide
Complete Resource Guide for Pediatric Disorders
Complete Resource Guide for People with Chronic Illness
Complete Resource Guide for People with Disabilities
Older Americans Information Resource
Parenting: Styles & Strategies
Social Media & Your Mental Health
Teens: Growing Up, Skills & Strategies

Guide to Venture Capital & Private Equity Firms
Hudson's Washington News Media Contacts Guide
New York State Directory
Sports Market Place

Grey House Publishing | Salem Press | H.W. Wilson | 4919 Route 22, PO Box 56, Amenia NY 12501-0056

Grey House Imprints

Visit www.GreyHouse.com for Product Information, Table of Contents, and Sample Pages.

Grey House Titles, continued

Business Information

Business Information Resources
Complete Broadcasting Industry Guide: TV, Radio, Cable & Streaming
Directory of Mail Order Catalogs
Environmental Resource Handbook
Food & Beverage Market Place
Guide to Healthcare Group Purchasing Organizations
Guide to U.S. HMOs and PPOs

Education

Complete Learning Disabilities Resource Guide
Digital Literacy: Skills & Strategies

Statistics & Demographics

America's Top-Rated Cities
America's Top-Rated Smaller Cities
Profiles of California
Profiles of Florida
Profiles of Illinois
Profiles of Indiana
Profiles of Massachusetts
Profiles of Michigan
Profiles of New Jersey
Profiles of New York
Profiles of North Carolina & South Carolina
Profiles of Ohio
Profiles of Pennsylvania
Profiles of Texas
Profiles of Virginia
Profiles of Wisconsin

Canadian Resources

Associations Canada
Canadian Almanac & Directory
Canadian Environmental Resource Guide
Canadian Parliamentary Guide
Canadian Venture Capital & Private Equity Firms
Canadian Who's Who
Cannabis Canada
Careers & Employment Canada
Financial Post: Directory of Directors
Financial Services Canada
FP Bonds: Corporate
FP Bonds: Government
FP Equities: Preferreds & Derivatives
FP Survey: Industrials
FP Survey: Mines & Energy
FP Survey: Predecessor & Defunct
Health Guide Canada
Indigenous History & Culture in Canada
Libraries Canada
Major Canadian Cities: 50 Cities Compared, Ranked & Profiled

Books in Print Series

American Book Publishing Record® Annual
American Book Publishing Record® Monthly
Books In Print®
Books In Print® Supplement
Books Out Loud™
Bowker's Complete Video Directory™
Children's Books In Print®
El-Hi Textbooks & Serials In Print®
Forthcoming Books®
Law Books & Serials In Print™
Medical & Health Care Books In Print™
Publishers, Distributors & Wholesalers of the US™
Subject Guide to Books In Print®
Subject Guide to Children's Books In Print®

Weiss Financial Ratings

Financial Literacy Basics
Financial Literacy: How to Become an Investor
Financial Literacy: Planning for the Future
Weiss Ratings Consumer Guides
Weiss Ratings Guide to Banks
Weiss Ratings Guide to Credit Unions
Weiss Ratings Guide to Health Insurers
Weiss Ratings Guide to Life & Annuity Insurers
Weiss Ratings Guide to Property & Casualty Insurers
Weiss Ratings Investment Research Guide to Bond & Money Market
    Mutual Funds
Weiss Ratings Investment Research Guide to Exchange-Traded Funds
Weiss Ratings Investment Research Guide to Stock Mutual Funds
Weiss Ratings Investment Research Guide to Stocks

Grey House Publishing | *Salem Press* | *H.W. Wilson* | 4919 Route 22, PO Box 56, Amenia NY 12501-0056

Titles from Salem Press

Visit www.SalemPress.com for Product Information, Table of Contents, and Sample Pages.

LITERATURE
Critical Insights: Authors

Louisa May Alcott
Sherman Alexie
Dante Alighieri
Isabel Allende
Maya Angelou
Isaac Asimov
Margaret Atwood
Jane Austen
James Baldwin
Saul Bellow
Roberto Bolano
Ray Bradbury
The Brontë Sisters
Gwendolyn Brooks
Albert Camus
Raymond Carver
Willa Cather
Geoffrey Chaucer
John Cheever
Kate Chopin
Joseph Conrad
Charles Dickens
Emily Dickinson
Frederick Douglass
T. S. Eliot
George Eliot
Harlan Ellison
Ralph Waldo Emerson
Louise Erdrich
William Faulkner
F. Scott Fitzgerald
Gustave Flaubert
Horton Foote
Benjamin Franklin
Robert Frost
Neil Gaiman
Gabriel Garcia Marquez
Thomas Hardy
Nathaniel Hawthorne
Robert A. Heinlein
Lillian Hellman
Ernest Hemingway
Langston Hughes
Zora Neale Hurston
Henry James
Thomas Jefferson
James Joyce
Jamaica Kincaid
Stephen King
Martin Luther King, Jr.
Barbara Kingsolver
Abraham Lincoln
C.S. Lewis
Mario Vargas Llosa
Jack London
James McBride
Cormac McCarthy
Herman Melville
Arthur Miller
Toni Morrison
Alice Munro

Tim O'Brien
Flannery O'Connor
Eugene O'Neill
George Orwell
Sylvia Plath
Edgar Allan Poe
Philip Roth
Salman Rushdie
J.D. Salinger
Mary Shelley
John Steinbeck
Amy Tan
Leo Tolstoy
Mark Twain
John Updike
Kurt Vonnegut
Alice Walker
David Foster Wallace
H. G. Wells
Edith Wharton
Walt Whitman
Oscar Wilde
Tennessee Williams
Virginia Woolf
Richard Wright
Malcolm X

Critical Insights: Works

Absalom, Absalom!
Adventures of Huckleberry Finn
The Adventures of Tom Sawyer
Aeneid
All Quiet on the Western Front
All the Pretty Horses
Animal Farm
Anna Karenina
As You Like It
The Awakening
The Bell Jar
Beloved
Billy Budd, Sailor
The Bluest Eye
The Book Thief
Brave New World
The Canterbury Tales
Catch-22
The Catcher in the Rye
The Color Purple
Crime and Punishment
The Crucible
Death of a Salesman
The Diary of a Young Girl
Dracula
Fahrenheit 451
A Farewell to Arms
Frankenstein; or, The Modern Prometheus
The Grapes of Wrath
Great Expectations
The Great Gatsby
Hamlet
The Handmaid's Tale
Harry Potter Series
Heart of Darkness

The Hobbit
The House on Mango Street
How the Garcia Girls Lost Their Accents
The Hunger Games Trilogy
I Know Why the Caged Bird Sings
In Cold Blood
The Inferno
Invisible Man
Jane Eyre
The Joy Luck Club
Julius Caesar
King Lear
The Kite Runner
Life of Pi
Little Women
Lolita
Lord of the Flies
The Lord of the Rings
Macbeth
The Merchant of Venice
The Metamorphosis
Midnight's Children
A Midsummer Night's Dream
Moby-Dick
Mrs. Dalloway
Native Son
Nineteen Eighty-Four
The Odyssey
Of Mice and Men
The Old Man and the Sea
On the Road
One Flew Over the Cuckoo's Nest
One Hundred Years of Solitude
Othello
The Outsiders
Paradise Lost
The Pearl
The Plague
The Poetry of Baudelaire
The Poetry of Edgar Allan Poe
A Portrait of the Artist as a Young Man
Pride and Prejudice
A Raisin in the Sun
The Red Badge of Courage
Romeo and Juliet
The Scarlet Letter
Sense and Sensibility
Short Fiction of Flannery O'Connor
Slaughterhouse-Five
The Sound and the Fury
A Streetcar Named Desire
The Sun Also Rises
A Tale of Two Cities
The Tales of Edgar Allan Poe
Their Eyes Were Watching God
Things Fall Apart
To Kill a Mockingbird
Twelfth Night, or What You Will
Twelve Years a Slave
War and Peace
The Woman Warrior
Wuthering Heights

SALEM PRESS

Titles from Salem Press

SALEM PRESS

Visit www.SalemPress.com for Product Information, Table of Contents, and Sample Pages.

Critical Insights: Themes

The American Comic Book
American Creative Non-Fiction
The American Dream
American Multicultural Identity
American Road Literature
American Short Story
American Sports Fiction
The American Thriller
American Writers in Exile
Censored & Banned Literature
Civil Rights Literature, Past & Present
Coming of Age
Conspiracies
Contemporary Canadian Fiction
Contemporary Immigrant Short Fiction
Contemporary Latin American Fiction
Contemporary Speculative Fiction
Crime and Detective Fiction
Crisis of Faith
Cultural Encounters
Dystopia
Family
The Fantastic
Feminism Flash Fiction
Friendship
Gender, Sex and Sexuality
Going Into the Woods
Good & Evil
The Graphic Novel
Greed
Harlem Renaissance
The Hero's Quest
Historical Fiction
Holocaust Literature
The Immigrant Experience
Inequality
LGBTQ Literature
Literature in Times of Crisis
Literature of Protest
Love
Magical Realism
Midwestern Literature
Modern Japanese Literature
Nature & the Environment
Paranoia, Fear & Alienation
Patriotism
Political Fiction
Postcolonial Literature
Power & Corruption
Pulp Fiction of the '20s and '30s
Rebellion
Russia's Golden Age
Satire
The Slave Narrative
Social Justice and American Literature
Southern Gothic Literature
Southwestern Literature
The Supernatural
Survival
Technology & Humanity

Truth & Lies
Violence in Literature
Virginia Woolf & 20th Century Women Writers
War

Critical Insights: Film

Bonnie & Clyde
Casablanca
Alfred Hitchcock
Stanley Kubrick

Critical Approaches to Literature

Critical Approaches to Literature: Feminist
Critical Approaches to Literature: Moral
Critical Approaches to Literature: Multicultural
Critical Approaches to Literature: Psychological

Literary Classics

Recommended Reading: 600 Classics Reviewed

Novels into Film

Novels into Film: Adaptations & Interpretation
Novels into Film: Adaptations & Interpretation, Volume 2

Critical Surveys of Literature

Critical Survey of American Literature
Critical Survey of Drama
Critical Survey of Long Fiction
Critical Survey of Mystery and Detective Fiction
Critical Survey of Poetry
Critical Survey of Poetry: Contemporary Poets
Critical Survey of Science Fiction & Fantasy Literature
Critical Survey of Shakespeare's Film Adaptations
Critical Survey of Shakespeare's Plays
Critical Survey of Shakespeare's Sonnets
Critical Survey of Short Fiction
Critical Survey of World Literature
Critical Survey of Young Adult Literature

Critical Surveys of Graphic Novels

Heroes & Superheroes
History, Theme, and Technique
Independents & Underground Classics
Manga

Critical Surveys of Mythology & Folklore

Creation Myths
Deadly Battles & Warring Enemies
Gods & Goddesses
Heroes and Heroines
Legendary Creatures
Love, Sexuality, and Desire
World Mythology

Cyclopedia of Literary Characters & Places

Cyclopedia of Literary Characters
Cyclopedia of Literary Places

Grey House Publishing | Salem Press | H.W. Wilson | 4919 Route 22, PO Box 56, Amenia NY 12501-0056

SALEM PRESS

Titles from Salem Press

Visit www.SalemPress.com for Product Information, Table of Contents, and Sample Pages.

SALEM PRESS

Titles from Salem Press

Visit www.SalemPress.com for Product Information, Table of Contents, and Sample Pages.

Great Events from History

Great Events from History: American History, Exploration to the
  Colonial Era, 1492-1775
Great Events from History: American History, Forging a New Nation,
  1775-1850
Great Events from History: American History, War, Peace & Growth,
  1850-1918
Great Events from History: The Ancient World
Great Events from History: The Middle Ages
Great Events from History: The Renaissance & Early Modern Era
Great Events from History: The 17th Century
Great Events from History: The 18th Century
Great Events from History: The 19th Century
Great Events from History: The 20th Century, 1901-1940
Great Events from History: The 20th Century, 1941-1970
Great Events from History: The 20th Century, 1971-2000
Great Events from History: Modern Scandals
Great Events from History: African American History
Great Events from History: The 21st Century, 2000-2016
Great Events from History: LGBTQ Events
Great Events from History: Human Rights
Great Events from History: Women's History

Great Lives from History

Great Athletes
Great Athletes of the Twenty-First Century
Great Lives from History: The 17th Century
Great Lives from History: The 18th Century
Great Lives from History: The 19th Century
Great Lives from History: The 20th Century
Great Lives from History: The 21st Century, 2000-2017
Great Lives from History: African Americans
Great Lives from History: The Ancient World
Great Lives from History: American Heroes
Great Lives from History: American Women
Great Lives from History: Asian and Pacific Islander Americans
Great Lives from History: Autocrats & Dictators
Great Lives from History: The Incredibly Wealthy
Great Lives from History: Inventors & Inventions
Great Lives from History: Jewish Americans
Great Lives from History: Latinos
Great Lives from History: LGBTQ+
Great Lives from History: The Middle Ages
Great Lives from History: The Renaissance & Early Modern Era
Great Lives from History: Scientists and Science

History & Government

American First Ladies
American Presidents
The 50 States
The Ancient World: Extraordinary People in Extraordinary Societies
The Bill of Rights
The Criminal Justice System
U.S. Court Cases
The U.S. Supreme Court

SOCIAL SCIENCES

Civil Rights Movements: Past & Present
Countries, Peoples and Cultures
Countries: Their Wars & Conflicts: A World Survey
Education Today: Issues, Policies & Practices
Encyclopedia of American Immigration
Ethics: Questions & Morality of Human Actions
Issues in U.S. Immigration
Principles of Sociology: Group Relationships & Behavior
Principles of Sociology: Personal Relationships & Behavior
Principles of Sociology: Societal Issues & Behavior
Racial & Ethnic Relations in America
Weapons, Warfare & Military Technology
World Geography

HEALTH

Addictions, Substance Abuse & Alcoholism
Adolescent Health & Wellness
Aging
Cancer
Community & Family Health Issues
Integrative, Alternative & Complementary Medicine
Genetics and Inherited Conditions
Infectious Diseases and Conditions
Magill's Medical Guide
Men's Health
Nutrition
Parenting: Styles & Strategies
Psychology & Behavioral Health
Social Media & Your Mental Health
Teens: Growing Up, Skills & Strategies
Women's Health

Principles of Health

Principles of Health: Allergies & Immune Disorders
Principles of Health: Anxiety & Stress
Principles of Health: Depression
Principles of Health: Diabetes
Principles of Health: Hypertension
Principles of Health: Nursing
Principles of Health: Obesity
Principles of Health: Occupational Therapy & Physical Therapy
Principles of Health: Pain Management
Principles of Health: Prescription Drug Abuse
Principles of Health: Whole Body Wellness

BUSINESS

Principles of Business: Accounting
Principles of Business: Economics
Principles of Business: Entrepreneurship
Principles of Business: Finance
Principles of Business: Globalization
Principles of Business: Leadership
Principles of Business: Management
Principles of Business: Marketing

SALEM PRESS

Titles from Salem Press

SALEM PRESS

Visit www.SalemPress.com for Product Information, Table of Contents, and Sample Pages.

SCIENCE

Ancient Creatures
Applied Science
Applied Science: Engineering & Mathematics
Applied Science: Science & Medicine
Applied Science: Technology
Biomes and Ecosystems
Digital Literacy: Skills & Strategies
Earth Science: Earth Materials and Resources
Earth Science: Earth's Surface and History
Earth Science: Earth's Weather, Water and Atmosphere
Earth Science: Physics and Chemistry of the Earth
Encyclopedia of Climate Change
Encyclopedia of Energy
Encyclopedia of Environmental Issues
Encyclopedia of Global Resources
Encyclopedia of Mathematics and Society
Environmental Sustainability: Skills & Strategies
Forensic Science
Notable Natural Disasters
The Solar System
USA in Space

Principles of Science

Principles of Aeronautics
Principles of Anatomy
Principles of Archaeology
Principles of Architecture
Principles of Astronomy
Principles of Behavioral Science
Principles of Biology
Principles of Biotechnology
Principles of Botany
Principles of Chemistry
Principles of Climatology
Principles of Computer-aided Design
Principles of Computer Science
Principles of Cybersecurity
Principles of Digital Arts & Multimedia
Principles of Ecology
Principles of Energy
Principles of Environmental Engineering
Principles of Fire Science
Principles of Food Science
Principles of Forestry & Conservation
Principles of Geology
Principles of Graphic Design & Typography
Principles of Information Technology
Principles of Marine Science
Principles of Mass Communication
Principles of Mathematics
Principles of Mechanics
Principles of Microbiology
Principles of Modern Agriculture
Principles of Pharmacology
Principles of Physical Science
Principles of Physics
Principles of Probability & Statistics
Principles of Programming & Coding
Principles of Robotics & Artificial Intelligence
Principles of Scientific Research
Principles of Sports Medicine & Exercise Science
Principles of Sustainability

Principles of Zoology

CAREERS

Careers: Paths to Entrepreneurship
Careers in Archaeology & Museum Services
Careers in Artificial Intelligence
Careers in the Arts: Fine, Performing & Visual
Careers in the Automotive Industry
Careers in Biology
Careers in Biotechnology
Careers in Building Construction
Careers in Business
Careers in Chemistry
Careers in Communications & Media
Careers in Criminal Justice
Careers in Culinary Arts
Careers in Cybersecurity
Careers in Earth Science
Careers in Education & Training
Careers in Engineering
Careers in Environment & Conservation
Careers in Financial Services
Careers in Fish & Wildlife
Careers in Forensic Science
Careers in Gaming
Careers in Green Energy
Careers in Healthcare
Careers in Heavy Equipment Operation, Maintenance & Repair
Careers in Hospitality & Tourism
Careers in Human Services
Careers in Illustration & Animation
Careers in Information Technology
Careers in Intelligence & National Security
Careers in Law, Criminal Justice & Emergency Services
Careers in Mass Communication
Careers in the Music Industry
Careers in Manufacturing & Production
Careers in Medical Technology
Careers in Nursing
Careers in Physics
Careers in Protective Services
Careers in Psychology & Behavioral Health
Careers in Public Administration
Careers in Sales, Insurance & Real Estate
Careers in Science & Engineering
Careers in Social Media
Careers in Sports & Fitness
Careers in Sports Medicine & Training
Careers in Technical Services & Equipment Repair
Careers in Transportation
Careers in Travel & Adventure
Careers in Writing & Editing
Careers Outdoors
Careers Overseas
Careers Working with Infants & Children
Careers Working with Animals

Grey House Publishing | **Salem Press** | *H.W. Wilson* | 4919 Route 22, PO Box 56, Amenia NY 12501-0056

Titles from H.W. Wilson

Visit www.HWWilsonInPrint.com for Product Information, Table of Contents, and Sample Pages.

The Reference Shelf

Affordable Housing
Aging in America
Alternative Facts, Post-Truth and the Information War
The American Dream
Artificial Intelligence
Book Bans & Censorship
The Business of Food
Campaign Trends & Election Law
College Sports
Democracy Evolving
The Digital Age
Embracing New Paradigms in Education
Food Insecurity & Hunger in the United States
Future of U.S. Economic Relations: Mexico, Cuba, & Venezuela
Gene Editing & Genetic Engineering
Global Climate Change
Guns in America
Hacktivism
Hate Crimes
Health Conspiracies
Immigration & Border Control in the 21st Century
Income Inequality
Internet Abuses & Privacy Rights
Internet Law
Labor Unions
LGBTQ in the 21st Century
Marijuana Reform
Mental Health Awareness
Money in Politics
National Debate Topic 2020/2021: Criminal Justice Reform
National Debate Topic 2021/2022: Water Resources
National Debate Topic 2022/2023: Emerging Technologies & International Security
National Debate Topic 2023/2024: Economic Inequality
National Debate Topic 2024/2025: Intellectual Property Rights
National Debate Topic 2025/2026: The Arctic
New Developments in Artificial Intelligence
New Frontiers in Space
Policing in 2020
Pollution
Prescription Drug Abuse
Propaganda and Misinformation
Racial Tension in a Postracial Age
Reality Television
Renewable Energy
Representative American Speeches, Annual Editions
Reproductive Rights
Rethinking Work
Revisiting Gender
Russia & Ukraine
The South China Sea Conflict
Space Exploration
Sports in America
The Supreme Court
The Transformation of American Cities
The Two Koreas
UFOs
Vaccinations
Voting Rights
Whistleblowers

Core Collections

Children's Core Collection
Fiction Core Collection
Graphic Novels Core Collection
Middle & Junior High School Core
Public Library Core Collection: Nonfiction
Senior High Core Collection
Young Adult Fiction Core Collection

Current Biography

Current Biography Cumulative Index 1946-2025
Current Biography Magazine
Current Biography Yearbook

Readers' Guide to Periodical Literature

Abridged Readers' Guide to Periodical Literature
Readers' Guide to Periodical Literature

Indexes

Index to Legal Periodicals & Books
Short Story Index

Sears List

Sears List of Subject Headings
Sears List of Subject Headings, Online Database

History

American Game Changers: Invention, Innovation & Transformation
American Reformers
Speeches of the American Presidents

Facts About Series

Facts About the 20th Century
Facts About American Immigration
Facts About China
Facts About the Presidents
Facts About the World's Languages

Nobel Prize Winners

Nobel Prize Winners: 1901-1986
Nobel Prize Winners: 1987-1991
Nobel Prize Winners: 1992-1996
Nobel Prize Winners: 1997-2001
Nobel Prize Winners: 2002-2018

Famous First Facts

Famous First Facts
Famous First Facts About American Politics
Famous First Facts About Sports
Famous First Facts About the Environment
Famous First Facts: International Edition

American Book of Days

The American Book of Days
The International Book of Days

Grey House Publishing | **Salem Press** | **H.W. Wilson** | 4919 Route 22, PO Box 56, Amenia NY 12501-0056